The Structure of Language

PRENTICE-HALL INTERNATIONAL, INC., *London*
PRENTICE-HALL OF AUSTRALIA, PTY, LTD., *Sydney*
PRENTICE-HALL OF CANADA, LTD., *Toronto*
PRENTICE-HALL OF INDIA (PRIVATE) LTD., *New Delhi*
PRENTICE-HALL OF JAPAN, INC., *Tokyo*

The Structure of Language

Readings in
the Philosophy of Language

Jerry A. Fodor / Jerrold J. Katz

MASSACHUSETTS INSTITUTE OF TECHNOLOGY

Prentice-Hall, Inc.   Englewood Cliffs, New Jersey

Current printing (last digit):

13   12   11   10   9

LIBRARY OF CONGRESS CATALOG CARD NO.: 63-13288

PRINTED IN THE UNITED STATES OF AMERICA
85470-C

To our wives

Iris and Sylvia

The whale has a two-fold distinction among the fishes:
first, when seen from a distance,
it looms large among them
and, secondly, on close examination
it is found to be no fish at all.

—M. F. Meyer

Preface

Our primary incentive in compiling this anthology has been to bring to the attention of philosophers basic papers in the theory of language which suggest a new approach to philosophizing about language. We believe that current philosophizing has failed to provide either an adequate understanding of language or convincing answers to philosophical problems about language, and that a change in the way philosophers approach language is therefore necessary. We hope that the present collection of papers will help persuade philosophers that only an approach which integrates with empirical linguistics can succeed where current philosophy of language fails.

The introductory essay specifies the respects in which the approaches to language of the two dominant schools in current philosophy, Positivism and Ordinary Language Philosophy, have proved unsatisfactory, and thus the respects in which a new approach must be satisfactory if it is to offer an adequate understanding of language and convincing answers to philosophical questions. We show that the Positivist's approach to language, though it seeks a theory which is systematic in the way an account of language ought to be, is neither responsive to reasonable methodological controls nor attentive to empirical evidence about language in its theoretical constructions. We show that Ordinary Language Philosophy, though it correctly concentrates on the evidence from natural language and is sensitive to even quite subtle nuances of usage, is intrinsically incapable of providing an acceptable theory of language because of its characteristically unsystematic orientation. Where Positivism has given us a theory which fails to be a description of natural language, Ordinary Language Philosophy has given us particular descriptions which fail to be a theory. Thus, we show that a satisfactory approach must provide a systematic theory of the structure of a natural language within a framework for studying language which clearly articulates the empirical and methodological constraints upon linguistic description.

This anthology reflects our conviction that such an approach follows naturally from recent work in empirical linguistics. Its underlying conception is that basing the philosophical study of language upon the theoretical insights and concrete results of empirical linguistics is the only way to obtain a philosophy of language sharing the systematic orientation characteristic of Positivism and the attention to details of usage characteristic of Ordinary Language Philosophy but which, unlike both, determines its generalizations and theoretical constructions on the basis of an adequate methodology.

Thus, this anthology is primarily dedicated to presenting the recent work in linguistics which is most relevant to the development of a methodologically sound philosophy of language. "Linguistics" is here taken in its broadest sense to include papers in phonology, syntax, and semantics, and also papers in the psychology of language and in linguistic theory. Our selections have not been determined by a strict adherence to traditional academic distinctions between disciplines but rather by the principle that contributions should reveal a high degree of sophistication as to the nature, methods, and results of empirical inquiry into language and that they should wherever possible bear directly upon the questions about language with which philosophers are most concerned. Thus, though many of the papers in this collection are written by linguists, a sizable number are the contributions of philosophers interested in linguistics not only for its own sake but also for its philosophic implications.

A second incentive for the present anthology is to make readily available to researchers contributions to the study of language which have become relatively inaccessible or have not yet been published. Investigators in linguistics, psychology, and philosophy are frequently hampered by the unavailability of many basic papers in grammar, semantics, and linguistic theory. This has been due to a number of factors, among which is the extremely rapid development that these fields have undergone in recent years. This development has in some cases outstripped the capacity of journals to keep abreast of the newest contributions. Another factor is that many important papers have been written for research projects and have thus received only a very limited circulation in mimeographed form. Thus, nearly a third of the papers in this anthology have never before been published. Of those that have been published, most are now available only in back issues of the journals. Their inaccessibility is further increased by the fact that the revival of interest in the study of language, which has occurred in the last several years, has depleted the supply of reprints while increasing the demand for them. This anthology is, then, intended as a source book in which the research worker in language studies will find those papers that have contributed the new insights into the nature of language and the new conceptual frameworks for the theory of language which have emerged from recent investigations in linguistics and philosophy.

Finally, we have tried to compile an anthology which can serve by itself as a text for courses in the philosophy of language at the advanced undergraduate and graduate levels and which can serve, perhaps in conjunction with other material, as a text for courses in grammar, semantics, linguistic theory, and psycholinguistics. The desire that the anthology should be adequate as a text is reflected not only in the articles chosen, but also in the way the volume is constructed. We have arranged the material so that the information provided by papers in earlier sections supplies the background required to understand papers appearing in later sections, with the earliest papers themselves presupposing nothing more than a level of general sophistication which can reasonably be expected of the student who has reached advanced undergraduate or graduate status. Each section is preceded by an editor's introduction which presents background information and/or discusses the main problems treated in the section. The editors intend the present collection to fill the need for a text suitable for a course in the philosophy of language which deals with the most advanced and theoretically significant work in linguistics and philosophical analysis.

Our selection of material was guided more by our estimation of theoretical significance than by the desire to achieve representativeness. The latter played a role to the extent that representativeness is necessary if the volume is to serve as a text. But, in general, we have favored papers with a theoretical orientation, papers which contribute most directly to philosophical clarification, and papers which illuminate the empirical methodology of linguistic description, over papers which are merely typical of widely received views. In short, we have tried never to omit a paper which we regard as theoretically significant in the highest degree, although, at times, we included papers of lesser intrinsic significance to provide representativeness where needed.

Accordingly, we acknowledge that our collection cannot claim that certain popular viewpoints and positions in philosophy and linguistics have always received proportionately adequate representation. Perhaps the most salient example of this is the omission of conceptions of grammar that have dominated much of the modern taxonomic approach to linguistics and the correspondingly heavy emphasis on the transformational, generative approach to grammar. This exercise of editorial license reflects our estimation of the comparative scientific significance and importance of these approaches for philosophy.

However, it is by no means the case that omission of a paper necessarily indicates that in our estimation its significance is less than that of some of the papers anthologized. Some works of considerable importance to the philosophy of language are omitted simply because they are readily available in complete form, and excerpting is discouraged by the nature of the material. Two outstanding examples are the omission of papers by Wittgenstein and J. L. Austin. The major works of both these philosophers are now in print.

We have made every effort to assure that papers appear in complete, unexcerpted form and that authors have had the opportunity to make revisions in order to include their last-minute thoughts.

We wish to express our gratitude to those who have allowed us to use their work and to the editors and publishers who have kindly granted us permission to use material copyrighted by them. We also thank our friends and colleagues whose advice and encouragement have played a role in determining both the fact and the form of this volume.

J.A.F.

J.J.K.

Contents

I

INTRODUCTION*

I

This volume presents a new approach to traditional problems in the philosophy of language, one which attempts to solve them by using theories and methods drawn from empirical linguistics. To establish the need for a new approach we must show both that those currently accepted are inadequate and that no obvious modification of them is likely to prove satisfactory. In this introductory essay, we shall therefore examine the two dominant schools of thought in recent philosophy of language, ordinary-language philosophy and positivism. We shall argue both that they have failed to offer satisfactory solutions to traditional problems concerning language or to provide an understanding of the nature of language, and that any approach combining features of each to form a better philosophy of language than they have severally offered is precluded by the incompatibility of their basic claims.

If these arguments are sound, we will have established the need for a new approach. But, of course, on the basis of them alone, we cannot claim to have justified adopting the *particular* new approach that this volume presents. Our contention is that the cause of failure of the ordinary-language and positivist approaches is that theories and methods of linguistics are not made the basis for philosophizing about language. To establish this contention, and thus to justify our way of approaching the philosophy of language, we must let the papers anthologized in this volume speak for themselves.

II

The ordinary-language and positivist approaches present incompatible conceptions of the nature and study of language. Positivists contend that the structure of a natural language is illuminatingly like that of a logistic system and advocate that natural languages be studied through the construction of logistic systems. Ordinary-language philosophers deny that a logistic system can capture the richness and complexity of a natural language. Language, they contend, is an extremely complicated form of social behavior and should be studied through the detailed analysis of individual words and expressions. Thus, positivists tend to emphasize the need for

---

*This essay is an adapted version of the first half of J. J. Katz and J. A. Fodor, "What's Wrong with the Philosophy of Language?" *Inquiry*, Vol. 5 (Autumn 1962), pp. 197–237.

rational reconstruction or reformulation at precisely those points where ordinary-language philosophers are most inclined to insist upon the facts of usage.

This incompatibility has further ramifications. An artificial language or logistic system is fully determined by specifying its formation rules, its transformation rules, its meaning postulates, and its rules of reference (which provide designata for the system's expressions and truth conditions for its sentences). Thus, a theory of language modeled on a logistic system has deeply ingrained the view that a language functions primarily in the statement of truths. But it has been the recurrent theme of ordinary-language philosophy that one misconceives the nature of language when one treats one of its functions, such as asserting, as its essence, thereby failing to appreciate or attempt to explain its truly essential feature—the indefinitely large variety of uses to which it can be put.

The incompatibility between positivism and ordinary-language philosophy appears again at another level of analysis. Inherent in the very motivation for constructing artificial languages is the desire to eliminate ambiguity, vagueness, and imprecision of terms.[1] But the ordinary-language philosopher does not regard these features of language as per se undersirable. Rather, he thinks of them as performing an essential role in the use of language, viz., maintaining its expressive power and preserving communication by holding meanings relatively constant while our knowledge of the world changes. Waismann[2] has argued that "open texturedness" of terms allows us to assimilate new information into our current nomenclature, while this possibility would be precluded if we were to fix exact extensional boundaries. Other ordinary-language philosophers argue still more generally that an accurate description of the usage, meaning, or extension of an expression cannot suggest a sharp, formalizable distinction where there are, in fact, only blurred edges. It is pointed out, for example, that such a sentence as "the number of waves in the Atlantic Ocean is prime" is in no clear sense either true or false because the conventions needed to make the relevant determinations do not exist. Consider Wittgenstein's remark:

> How should we explain to someone what a game is? I imagine that we should describe *games* to him, and we might add: "This *and similar things* are called *games*." And do we know any more about it ourselves? Is it only other people whom we cannot tell exactly what a game is?—But this is not ignorance. We do not know the boundaries because none have been drawn. To repeat, we draw a boundary—for a special purpose. Does it take that to make the concept usable? Not at all! (Except for that special purpose.) No more than it took the definition: 1 pace = 75 cm to make the measure of length *one pace* usable.[3]

But not only is it false that terms and expressions in ordinary language are fully precise in respect of their use, meaning, or extension; it is unclear that any definite sense can be attached to the *general* requirement that they be made fully precise.

---

[1]Cf. N. Goodman, *The Structure of Appearance* (Cambridge, Mass.: Harvard University Press, 1951), pp. 5–6.

[2]Cf. F. Waismann, "Verifiability," in *Logic and Language*, first Series, ed. A. Flew (Oxford: Basil Blackwell, 1955).

[3]L. Wittgenstein, *Philosophical Investigations* (New York: The Macmillan Company, 1953), para. 69.

Thus, Wittgenstein concludes the above remark: "And if you want to say 'But still, before that it wasn't an exact measure,' then I reply 'very well, it was an inexact one—though you still owe me a definition of exactness.' "[4] But, clearly, we cannot pay this debt with a definition of "exactness" which requires of us that we always make every distinction it is possible to make. From this the ordinary-language philosopher concludes that, although in special circumstances we may be required to be especially precise, the requirement that we never be imprecise invites the questions: When do we stop? When have we been precise enough? According to the ordinary-language philosopher, in general, we usually need do no more than make the distinctions that exist in the language. To stop there is to stop at a natural point. But a definition of exactness which requires us to go further must provide a general method for deciding when enough distinctions have been drawn. By hypothesis, such a definition cannot tell us either to halt at the natural stopping point or to make every possible distinction. Yet, there is no motivation for stopping anywhere beyond the one and short of the other.

Disagreements between positivists and ordinary-language philosophers shade into differences of emphasis on various points. Thus, ordinary-language philosophers have by and large tended to occupy themselves with the *study of the use of words*, while positivists have been primarily concerned with *the analysis of sentences and their inference relations*. This difference does not simply represent a disagreement about research priorities. Rather, it reflects the ordinary-language philosopher's concern with the function of language in concrete interpersonal situations, as opposed to the positivist's interest in the structure of the *logical syntax* of the language of science. The conflict behind this difference is between the belief that language is best viewed as an articulate system with statable rules and the belief that talking about language is, at bottom, talking about an indefinitely large and various set of speech episodes.

Thus, the two schools differ in the linguistic units they choose for analysis. For the ordinary-language philosopher a theory of language is first and foremost a theory of words; the philosophy of language differs from lexicography in its techniques and methods but not in its goals. For the positivists, on the other hand, a theory of language is in the first instance a theory of sentences and sentence structures. We shall return to this point further on. Suffice it to note here that this disagreement involves the whole question of the status of the generative rules of language. It is thus directly concerned in any attempt to satisfy the traditional demands for a characterization of the linguistic skills of speakers and of the processes whereby a language is learned.

III

That there should be these fundamental incompatibilities between the two dominant viewpoints in the present philosophy of language might not justify taking a new approach to the philosophy of language were it the case that either revealed significant insights promising a systematic and comprehensive theory of language. We

---

[4]*Ibid.*

wish to argue, on the contrary, that both positivism and ordinary-language philosophy are mistaken in their basic assumptions about the nature of language and the techniques required to theorize about it successfully. As often happens in philosophy, what each school says about the shortcomings of its antagonist is substantially correct. Jointly, such criticisms show why *both* schools are wrong about the nature and study of language.

The ordinary-language philosopher correctly maintains against the positivist that a formalization is a revealing theory of a natural language only insofar as its structure reflects that of the language. What is needed is a theory based upon and representing the full structural complexity of a natural language, not one which reflects the relatively simple structure of some *arbitrarily* chosen artificial language.

That the choice of an artificial system on which to model one's theory of a language should *not* be arbitrary is crucial in two respects. In the first place, if the system is chosen arbitrarily, theories modeled on it cannot claim to be justified theories of a natural language. Artificial languages can differ widely in the types of structures they exhibit: they can be constructed to have any desired properties.[5] If no attention is paid to what sort of structure is manifested in *natural* language, there is no basis for a reasoned choice of an artificial language upon which to base a theory of syntax and semantics. If the choice is arbitrary, it follows that there are no effective constraints upon theory construction beyond the absurdly weak requirement that the theory be formal and consistent. But without empirical constraints on the content of a theory, all consistent formal theories are equally justified, regardless of how they picture a natural language.

In the second place, if an artificial system is chosen arbitrarily, it cannot be supposed to offer solutions to philosophically important problems. As we pointed out above, one can construct an artificial system with any desired properties. Thus, an artificial language can be constructed to contain *any* solution to a problem arising in connection with the linguistic or philosophical analysis of a natural language. There can then be as many artificial languages as there are different solutions to the problem under study. If we have chosen arbitrarily, there is no basis for asserting that any one of the artificial languages offers the *correct* solution.

Although it is true in principle that an artificial language can have any structure we care to give it, as a matter of fact, positivists have almost invariably built their

---

[5]Carnap writes: "Suppose that the author of a system wishes the predicates B and M to designate the properties *bachelor* and *married*, respectively. How does he know that these properties are incompatible and that therefore he has to lay down postulate P_1? This is not a matter of knowledge but of decision. His knowledge or belief that the English words *bachelor* and *married* are always or usually understood in such a way that they are incompatible may influence his decision if he has the intention to reflect in his system some of the meaning relations of English words. In this particular case, the influence would be relatively clear, but in other cases it would be much less so." Carnap goes on to say "Suppose he wishes the predicates Bl and R to correspond to the words *black* and *raven*. While the meaning of *black* is fairly clear, that of *raven* is rather vague in the everyday language. There is no point for him to make an elaborate study, based either on introspection or on statistical investigation of common usage, in order to find out whether *raven* always or mostly entails *black*. It is rather his task to make up his mind whether he wishes the predicates R and Bl of his system to be used in such a way that the first logically entails the second. If so, he has to add the postulate $(P_2) (x) (R_{(x)} \supset Bl_{(x)})$ to the system, otherwise not." R. Carnap, "Meaning Postulates," *Philosophical Studies*, 3 (1952), 65–73.

artificial languages on the model of *Principia Mathematica*. That this was an unfortunate choice is revealed by a comparison of the results of grammatical (especially transformational) analyses of English with the immensely simpler formation rules of such languages. Formally, the set of rules that characterize well-formedness in a logistic system of this type is a *context-free constituent structure grammar*. But the set of rules that characterize sentencehood in a natural language must at least be a *context-restricted constituent structure grammar*.[6] Moreover, if the grammatical description of natural languages is to be accomplished in the simplest and most revealing way, the grammatical rules must be transformational. (This point is argued at length in the papers by Chomsky anthologized here.) This means that the grammar of the familiar logistic systems is *essentially* weaker than the grammar of a natural language (such as English). But, such a formal comparison is anti climactic after one has directly compared the complexity of the syntactic structure of a natural language to that of a logistic system of the *Principia Mathematica* variety.

At this point, the positivist may argue as follows: "Our concern is to exhibit those features of a natural language which are reasonably systematic and coherent. True enough, we may leave much of the language undescribed, but this is only because much of the language is unsystematic, irregular, and explicable only as the product of historical accident." Notice, however, that the inability of a formal model to capture the full richness of a natural language may be construed as a measure *either* of the fortuitous character of the language *or* of the weakness of the model. It may of course be true that natural languages are incoherent and amorphous, but our failure to produce a systematic description does not *show* that this is so. It may show only that we have not looked deeply nor long enough and have thus missed the regularities that are, in fact, there. The supposed irregularity of the language may then be no more than a projection of our failure to describe it adequately. If the positivist insists that his description of the language is adequate, but that the language itself is unsystematic and irregular, then we reply that this is tantamount to the claim that his theory works except for its exceptions.

Notice two further points. It is no more than good methodology to assume that natural languages are highly systematic, even though this assumption may eventually prove false. For this is simply the supposition, customary throughout science, that the phenomena under study are governed by general laws. The effect of this assumption in the present case is to require that our formalizations be as exceptionless as possible. It is only by virtue of some such requirement that we can make reasoned and justified decisions between competitive formal characterizations of a language and can determine when a characterization of a feature of a natural language has fully represented the structure of that feature.

Second, the claim that a natural language is unsystematic and irregular seems extremely implausible when one recalls that children learn their native language and that such learning occurs in an amazingly short period of time. This achieve-

---

[6]For an explanation of these concepts, see N. Chomsky, "On the Notion 'Rule of Grammar,'" Sec. 2, which is reprinted in this volume. Footnote 8 of Chomsky's paper provides the references for a more detailed examination of the question of the generative capacity of various types of systems.

ment is explicable only on the assumption that what is learned is highly systematic and regular.

Still, it might be the case that an artificial system could provide an illuminating account of a natural language, even if it is greatly over-simplified. In other areas of science, theories are constructed as idealizations in order to reduce the complexity of the phenomena to manageable proportions and to describe their behavior in terms of simple laws. The physicist introduces the notion of an ideal gas and is thereby able to formulate Boyle's law without the complication involved in considering the fact that the product of pressure and volume actually varies somewhat with the temperature of a gas. Just in the sense in which ideal gases, rigid rods, and perfect vacuums are idealizations of physical states and objects, so it might be argued artificial languages are idealizations of natural languages. In fact, Carnap has argued in just this way.[7]

But, idealizations in science are not arbitrary. They are under strict empirical controls. A scientist who proposes an idealization is required to establish an isomorphism between it and the essential features of the phenomena. He can, of course, only do this indirectly: by showing that the idealization predicts accurately within a given margin of error, and by showing that the more actual conditions approximate to the ideal, the smaller this margin of error becomes. However, nothing corresponds to such empirical controls in the case of an artificial language regarded as an idealization of a natural language. There are no predictions about natural languages which follow from such idealizations in terms of which their adequacy may be determined. Suppose we have three artificial languages L_1, L_2, and L_3, each of which is regarded as an idealization of the natural language L. Suppose, further, that the sentence S in L is taken to be analytic in L_1, synthetic in L_2, and neither in L_3. How do we tell which of these languages is the best idealization of L? We must ask whether S is in fact analytic, synthetic, or neither, in L. But clearly we require a theory of the semantic structure of L to answer this question. Such a theory would have to explicate the notions *analytic in L, synthetic in L,* and so on. Since none of the artificial languages proposed by Carnap and his followers offer such explications[8] saying that these artificial languages are to be construed as idealizations of a natural language simply begs the question. So long as these idealizations employ concepts which are uninterpreted for natural languages, the claim that they illuminate in the way in which idealization does in other areas of science is false. Without the appropriate explications we have no way of determining how far an artificial language deviates from the facts of a natural language. Hence, unlike idealizations in other areas of science, these have no effective empirical controls.

Positivists distinguish two branches of semantics: theory of meaning and theory

---

[7] In *The Logical Syntax of Language*, Carnap says that the syntax of a natural language is "best represented and investigated by comparison with a constructed language which serves as a system of reference." He argues that a direct analysis of natural languages must fail just as a physical theory formulated in terms of actual entities must: the phenomena are too complex. He goes on to describe how the physicist idealizes and succeeds; Carnap recommends this way of studying natural languages to philosophers.

[8] Cf. W. V. Quine, "Two Dogmas of Empiricism," *From a Logical Point of View* (Cambridge, Mass.: Harvard University Press, 1953), pp. 20–46. (See especially Sec. 4.)

of reference. The former is primarily concerned with relations between linguistic entities and the latter with relations between linguistic entities and the world. Such notions as *analyticity, significance, synonymity,* and others are basic concepts of theory of meaning, while the basic concepts of theory of reference are *naming, reference, truth, extension,* and so on. In all the semantic theories thus far proposed, those of these concepts which are taken as primitives are also taken as so clear as to need no further analysis. This is perfectly legitimate if one is interested only in their formal relations within a logistic system. But from the point of view of application to natural languages, semantic theories in which such notions are unanalyzed primitives are empirically vacuous. It is abundantly evident that the questions we should like to have answered about natural languages include such questions as: When is a sentence significant? When are two expressions synonymous? When is an object referred to by an expression? However, no answer to these questions follows from the existence of a formal system in which relations of synonymity, reference, and so on are stipulated solely *for the expressions and sentences of that system.* What is required is a clarification of these concepts in their application to natural language. Formal semantics may then be appropriate as a means of systematizing our knowledge of a natural language. To proceed the other way around is to put the formal cart before the empirical horse.

Philosophers who have noticed the uninformativeness of positivist semantics have occasionally jumped to the conclusion that, if a system of formal semantics with unanalyzed primitives is not sufficient as a theory of natural language, what must be lacking are operational definitions of the primitive concepts based upon something like the field-linguist's techniques of elicitation.[9] However, this conclusion ignores the alternative of constructing a systematic theory of the semantic structure of a natural language. In fact, unless this alternative is exploited, the search for operational characterizations of semantic primitives cannot be expected to clarify these primitive concepts or to interpret them for natural languages.

Systems of formal semantics interconnect concepts in the theories of meaning and reference to their mutual illumination only if the primitive concepts are empirically interpreted. For example, given an operational characterization of synonymity, a system may explain analyticity in terms of the substituion of synonymous expressions in truths of logic and entailment in terms of the analyticity of the conditional. But beyond such interconnections these systems can afford no more clarification of their primitives than is provided by the results of behavioral tests for their application. Thus, the question whether two expressions are synonymous in a natural language might be answered by a behavioral test, but clearly a system of formal semantics contributes nothing to answering this question. If the concepts of a system of formal semantics are not otherwise empirically interpreted, then the tests themselves must provide the full account.

But now consider the problem of constructing such behavioral tests. First, there

---

[9]Outstanding examples of this approach are R. Carnap, "Meaning and Synonymy in Natural Languages," *Philosophical Studies,* **7** (1955), 33–47; and A. Naess, *Interpretation and Preciseness: A Contribution to the Theory of Communication.* Skrifter Norske Vid. Akademi, Oslo, II. Hist.-Filos. Klasse, No. 1 (1953).

is no reason to think that such notions as *significance, synonymity,* and the like can, in fact, be associated with any invariant property of the behavior of speakers. We could, as in the case of grammar, have a structural theory which accounts for the empirical data, without the central theoretical concepts each being directly related to a property of the behavior of speakers. For example, a test for grammaticality would assume there is a behavioral property that belongs to all grammatical sentences and *only* grammatical sentences. But this would be a generalization about the set of strings of words in the vocabulary of the language which would be false if the only property which grammatical strings had in common and no ungrammatical string shared was the abstract, nonbehavioral property of being countenanced as wellformed by a correct grammar. That such a situation obtains for the basic semantic concepts is suggested by recent philosophical controversies where no agreement can be found on even the simplest alleged cases of synonymity and analyticity.

Second, even if there should be a property in terms of which a reliable behavioral test for the application of a grammatical or semantic concept can be formulated, how shall we justify the claim to have found such a property? Let us take a concrete case. In *The Problem of Meaning in Linguistics,* Quine offers as the behavioral test for S being a grammatical sequence of phonemes that S has been or could be uttered by a speaker of the language without eliciting a bizarreness reaction. But this test fails in both directions. Anyone who attends to actual speech notices that almost all utterances are ungrammatical because of repetitions, false starts, arbitrary breaks, failures of agreement, interjections, and so on, yet most are not greeted by a bizarreness reaction. Conversely, almost any fully grammatical sentence could occur in a situation where it *would* produce a bizarreness reaction. Hence, the class of utterances that evoke bizarreness reactions is not co-extensive with the class of ungrammatical sequences of phonemes.

This criticism is supported by appealing to our pre-systematic intuitions about what are and what are not grammatical sentences. It could equally well have been supported by reference to a previously well-confirmed grammar, which would show that the set of strings characterized as grammatical is not co-extensive with the set of strings that produce bizarreness reactions. However, our intuitions are far less reliable in semantics than they are in grammar and there is no semantic theory comparable to present grammars. Thus, the claim to have a behavioral test for a *semantic* concept must, of necessity, rest upon weak and perhaps conflicting intuitions.

Some investigators faced with this situation have tried to compensate by introducing theoretical terms into their test questions. Thus, speakers are asked if two items are synonymous or if a sentence is analytic. But since they are not told how to interpret these terms, it is no wonder that the test results show only that the testee understands synonymity and analyticity no better than the tester.

The situation is, then, the following: If there is not invariant property of behavior associated with synonymity, analyticity, and the like, then the only alternative is to construct a theory of the semantic structure of the language. On the other hand, if there are such properties, the task of establishing them on the basis of intuitively clear cases seems at best an extremely difficult one which would be facilitated by constructing a semantic theory. Such a theory would then guide the search for such properties and justify the claim that what has been found is such a property. Hence, without exploiting the alternative of theory construction, it is unlikely that the primitives of formal semantics can be interpreted in a revealing way for natural languages.

We will now consider some features of the internal structure of systems of formal semantics in order to explore further the relation between such systems and natural languages. We will first consider theory of meaning and then turn to the theory of reference.

Let us assume that the systems of formal semantics we are examining are intended to describe the semantic structure of a natural language, English for the present case. We may ask how well the *type* of rules given in such systems is able to describe semantic relations of the type found in English. Systems of formal semantics contain separate stipulations for each case of a synonymous pair of expressions, e.g., "*occulist* is synonymous with *eyedoctor*," "*naked* is synonymous with *destitute of customary or natural covering*," "*Krebs citric acid cycle* is synonymous with *intracellular energy wheel*." Meaning relations weaker than synonymity are given by separate stipulations to the effect that certain sentences are analytic, e.g., "Everything that is red is colored." But what has *not* been noticed about this way of handling synonymity and weaker semantic relations is that it is, in principle, incapable of providing a fully adequate description. The difficulty is that in a natural language such as English there is no upper bound on the length of strings in pairs of synonymous expressions.[10] Similarly, there is no upper bound on the length of the expressions that are related by relations weaker than synonymy. This entails that no *listing* of pairs and sentences can explicate the semantic relations in the language. What is required is a recursive characterization of "analytic in L" and "synonymous in L," and this brings us again to the need for a theory of the semantic relations in a natural language.

It may be replied that artificial systems do employ recursive devices—such as those of propositional calculus—to specify an infinite set of analytic sentences. But this ignores the fact that, in the kind of case discussed above, recursiveness is not a feature solely of the rules for the logical words but also of the rules governing the construction of expressions out of nonlogical words.[11]

Let us turn now to the theory of reference in systems of formal semantics. In the first place, an argument parallel to the one above applies: only a proper subset of the reference relations can be given by recursive enumeration with the usual scheme, "X" *refers to* X, while there remain indefinitely many reference relations that cannot be so specified; in particular, all those cases in which a reference relation depends on the synonymity of two expressions. For every pair of distinct expressions in the language there is a pair of reference rules: "X_i" *refers to* X_i and "X_j" *refers to* X_j. But in all cases where "X_i" is synonymous with "X_j" so that (y) $(y \in X_i \equiv y \in X_j)$ is analytic, the theory omits two rules, viz. "X_i" *refers to* X_j and "X_j" *refers*

---

[10]For a discussion of the grammatical rules responsible for this feature of English, see R. Lees, "The Grammar of English Nominalizations," *International Journal of American Linguistics*, Vol. 26, No. 3 (July 1960).

[11]*Ibid.*

to X_i. Since the set of constructible synonymous expressions has no upper bound on the length of its members, indefinitely many reference relations which are attributable to semantic properties of the language remain unspecified by the system of formal semantics.

In the second place, the theory of reference employed in systems of formal semantics fails to give a satisfactory account of reference in the actual employment of language. What appears to underlie this failure is the fact that in systems of formal semantics a theory of reference is so formulated that none of the problems encountered in connection with the reference of expressions in a natural language are permitted to arise.

In general, such theories of reference take the following form: there are rules of designation which provide designata for individual constants and predicates in the vocabulary of the language, and rules of truth which constitute a recursive definition of "true in L" for the sentences of the language. Usually, first there is a rule determining a necessary and sufficient condition for the truth of each atomic sentence, and then a version of propositional logic and quantification theory is introduced to provide the rules for determining a necessary and sufficient condition for the truth of each compound sentence; for example, the familiar "*snow* designates snow," "*white* designates the property white," and the rule: a sentence consisting of a predicate applied to an individual constant is true if and only if the individual designated by the constant has the property designated by the predicate.

It is easy to see that such theories are incapable of dealing with the common problems of reference which arise in language. For instance, syntactic and semantic structures in natural language often determine whether a reference to something is involved or not. The sentence "I want to be the Pope" differs from the sentence "I want to meet the Pope" in that the Pope is referred to by the latter but not the former. Ambiguity provides another case in point. Consider, "I shot the man with a gun," which may refer to *the man* or to *the man with a gun.* Or "The dark green house is empty," which may refer to the house colored dark green or the green house with no lights on. Another problem of reference which requires more theoretical machinery than such theories contain is the problem of referential presuppositions discussed by Strawson and Nowell-Smith.[12] Still another is the problem of referential vagueness: Under what conditions is the referent of an expression definite? These problems, though they by no means exhaust the difficulties about reference, suffice to show that we know as little about reference and its complexities in natural language after consulting positivist theories of reference as we did before. Positivists construct their theories of reference explicitly to prohibit such problems arising, but avoiding a problem in this case is just a way of failing to solve it.

IV

The unsuitability of the positivist's view of natural language has led many philosophers to reject this approach and to turn instead to a careful study of the details of

---

[12]Cf. P. F. Strawson, "On Referring," in *Essays on Conceptual Analysis*, ed. A. Flew (London, 1955); P. H. Nowell-Smith, *Ethics* (Baltimore: Penguin Books, Inc. 1956).

a natural language. But the approach known as ordinary-language philosophy has been rightly criticized by the positivists as lacking in systematicity and theoretical orientation. One must agree with the positivist's charge against the ordinary-language philosopher that any account of a natural language which fails to provide a specification of its formal structure is *ipso facto* unsatisfactory. For it is upon this structure that the generative principles which determine the syntactic and semantic characteristics of a natural language depend. These principles determine how each and every sentence of the language is structured and how sentences and expressions are understood. It is his failure to appreciate the significance of the systematic character of the compositional features of languages which accounts for the ordinary-language philosopher's disregard of the study of sentences and sentential structure.

Ryle, for example, dismisses the study of sentences as a priori not within the scope of a philosophical analysis of language on the grounds that sentences do not have uses and that uses are what philosophers study. In a recent article, Ryle even claims that sentences are not part of language, but only of speech.[13] This is a rather curious move since the most characteristic feature of language is its ability to make available an infinity of sentences from which a speaker can choose appropriate and wholly novel ones to use when the need arises. That is to say, what qualifies one as a fluent speaker of a language is not the ability to imitate previously encountered utterances, but rather the ability to extrapolate from them and thus to freely produce and understand utterances never before encountered. This feature, however, must rely upon mechanisms which are recursive, and hence it cannot be reduced to any properties of the (necessarily finite) lexicon of the language. Furthermore, it is clear that since what we learn when we learn a language is precisely how to produce and understand new sentences, such learning must be explained as the assimilation of these recursive mechanisms.

The closest ordinary-language philosophy has come to providing a theory of language which might explain these phenomena is the so-called "use theory of meaning." What all variants of this theory have in common is the program of providing a careful characterization of the use of each philosophically interesting word in the language. It must be noticed, however, that even if such a program were successfully carried through for *every* word in the language, it would fail to explain how utterances are produced and understood. A solution to the problem of explicating the compositional mechanisms in language requires not only that we be able to characterize the meaning of the words of the language, but also that we be able to describe the function which determines the meaning of a sentence on the basis of the meanings of its components. But, without attention to the syntactic and semantic structures of the language, the problem of novel utterance cannot be solved, since the meaning of a sentence is partly determined by these structures.

A characterization of the use of a word is a description of the way it is employed by speakers. We may regard such a description as the dictionary entry for the word, thus using the notion *dictionary entry* here as a cover term for whatever type of

---

[13]Cf. G. Ryle, "Use, Usage, and Meaning," *Proceedings of the Aristotelian Society*, Supp. Vol. XXXV (1961). For Ryle's dismissal of the study of sentences, see "Ordinary Language," *The Philosophical Review*, Vol. LXII, No. 2 (April 1953).

characterization a use theory employs for describing uses. Thus, we may regard the ultimate aim of a use theory of meaning as that of writing a dictionary which provides the correct entry for each word in the language. But even to achieve this aim would be to fall far short of a semantic theory.

It is of course true that a good dictionary *intelligently applied by a fluent speaker of the language* enables him to characterize the meaning of every sentence of the language. But the skills the fluent speaker exercises in using a dictionary to understand sentences constitute an implicit theory of the syntactic and semantic structure of the language, and it is such a theory which ordinary-language philosophy fails to consider. What is needed is a reconstruction of these skills, for it is quite clear that they involve not only nonlexical facts about the language, but more significantly, the organizing principles of the language. Anyone who learns a foreign language discovers that to know a language is to know more than correct dictionary entries for its words. No matter how good a dictionary is, it can tell us nothing about these skills, since they are concerned with relating the meaning of a sentence to the meanings of the words appearing in it.

The failure of ordinary-language philosophy to consider this problem would be excusable were it easy to solve. But, in fact, it is exceedingly difficult. There are several reasons for this, of which we will mention only the most obvious here. At very best, a dictionary can enumerate the uses of a word and provide a small number of diagnostic sentences as examples of each use. In order to extrapolate beyond these few diagnostic sentences and determine the meaning of each of the infinitely many sentences of the language in which the word appears, we require at least the following: first, a complete grammar of the language, second, a characterization of the semantic import of grammatical forms, e.g., a way of distinguishing when adjective-noun constructions have the import of property attributions as in the expressions *blue vase* and *foolish virgin* and when they do not, as in the expressions *utter jerk* and *a certain smile*; third, in all cases where the dictionary provides more than one entry for a given word (and often it will provide many more than one) it will be necessary to have a procedure for deciding *which* entry characterizes an occurrence of the word in a given sentence. Simply consulting a good English dictionary on the word *play* will convince the reader of the need for such a procedure. The difficulty of satisfying these three pre-conditions is, then, a measure of the difficulty of the problem of relating the meanings of words to the meanings of sentences.

However, it is conceivable that the use theory of meaning in one or another of its variants might prove revealing at the lexical level even though it failed to explicate the compositional mechanisms of the language. To prove revealing at this level a theory must at least provide a basis for a unique assignment of semantic properties to lexical items. A theory is vacuous if it is unable to determine when two lexical items exhibit the same semantic property and when they do not.

This point has been appreciated in connection with theories of meaning based upon notions of *real essence* and *mental ideas*. Philosophers have correctly insisted that theories of meaning founded on either of these notions are wholly uninformative because there is no way to determine when the theory claims that two expressions express the same mental idea or denote the same real essence. But many philosophers have failed to appreciate the significance and scope of this requirement.

For by this requirement none of the variants of the use theory of meaning fares better than "real essence" or "mental idea" theories, since all such questions as the following are left wholly unanswered by any of the use theories of meaning so far proposed: Under what conditions do two words or expressions have the same use? When do the uses of a pair of words or expressions differ? How is the use of a word distinguished from misuses of that word? What determines when a word has more than one use? Thus, one is justified in concluding that there is no use *theory* of meaning. What we have instead is no more than a recommendation that questions about meaning are to be handled as questions about the use of words or expressions.

It may be replied by the use theorist that our requirement is to be satisfied by reference to rules of language: two expressions have the same use when their employment is governed by the same rules, and not otherwise. The program implicit in this reply seems appealing in that it appears to focus on the significance of structural regularities in the language, but the reply itself is unconvincing because we are left uninformed as to both the form and content of such rules. No one has ever adequately described what a rule of language *is*, although we are presented with a plethora of analogies for what a rule of language is *like*. Depending upon which ordinary-language analyst one reads, one is informed that a rule of language is like a recipe, or a rule of grammar, or a rule of logic, or a rule of a game, or a dance instruction, or perhaps a moral imperative. With such a variety already in vogue, one might as well compare a rule of language to a rule of thumb. Clearly, there is no basis for deciding which of these analogies is most profitably used to interpret the notion *rule of language*. Moreover, no analogy can explicate itself. In particular, even an illuminating analogy cannot itself say *why* it is illuminating. In the case of these putative analogies for rules of language, one would like to know what *precisely* are the features of rules of language which license the analogy. One would also like to know the respects in which rules of language are idiosyncratic; that is, the respects in which talking a language is neither like baking a cake, nor playing a game, nor dancing a dance. If someone says that the flow of electricity is like the flow of water, he succinctly summarizes a number of truths about electricity, but he also suggests a number of things which are false; for example, that puncturing a wire will cause the electricity to drip out. But we know this is false only because we know the laws of electricity. *What this shows is simply that we would know how to choose an analogy which is revealing and not misleading only if we knew exactly what a rule of language is.*

A variant of the use theory of meaning which says that sentences are classified by reference to the speech acts a speaker may perform by uttering the sentence under appropriate circumstances is open to the same sort of objections. The requirement discussed above demands, in the case of such a theory, that there be some general and systematic way of telling when two occurrences of a sentence instance the same speech act and when they are associated with distinct speech acts. It seems clear, however, that no examination of the syntactic and semantic characteristics of the utterance can per se determine the speech act with which the utterance is associated. The same utterance will be associated with a given speech act under certain environmental conditions but not under others. For example, if I utter "A traveling salesman was looking for a place to spend the night," then, depending upon the environmental conditions, I may be making an assertion, starting a joke, referring to a joke, giving an example, providing an explanation, quoting, informing, talking to myself, damaging my reputation, and so forth. But the environmental conditions that determine which, if any, of these acts I am performing can clearly not be discovered by merely examining the utterance. And since there is no way, and very likely could be no way, to systematize such conditions, the speech act theory does not satisfy the requirement that we be able to determine, given that certain conditions obtain, which speech acts are associated with an utterance occurring under those conditions.

Even in the case of the so-called *explicit performatives* (roughly, verbs *that can* appear in the context "I hereby . . .")[14], it is clear that an utterance of the appropriate sentence type does not invariably constitute a performance of the sort normally associated with the verb. The conditions under which an apparent performance "misfires" are themselves environmental. Hence, we are presented with the same problem encountered above. For example, if I utter the sentence "I hereby promise to marry her," I may be starting a joke, giving an example, quoting, talking to myself, reciting a randomly chosen sentence, making an honest woman of her, and so forth. Which of these I am doing, as well as or instead of promising, depends on contexual factors which the theory of explicit performatives, like the general theory of speech acts, does not systematize to any extent whatever.

The notion of use has proved an exceedingly difficult one in terms of which to frame a theory in part because of an undetected ambiguity. There *is* a sense in which it is true that the meaning of a word or expression is determined by its use. The actual use of a word or expression by speakers, i.e., the combinations into which the word or expression enters in sentences and the situations in which it is uttered, constitutes the data for any theory which hopes to answer questions about meaning. But to suppose that this fact lends support to what is usually called the use theory of meaning is to commit what we shall refer to as "the Use-Use Fallacy."

In the sense in which it is true that "meaning is dependent on use," all that this slogan claims is that semantic investigation must be responsible to empirical constraints framed in terms of the facts of linguistic behavior. However, the claim that questions of meaning should be *replaced* by questions about use has clearly never been intended in this sense, for then it would have been evident that the insistence upon the study of use does not amount to a theory of meaning, but only to a specification of the data relevant to such a theory. Once we are clear about the Use-Use-Fallacy, we see that there is no use *theory* of meaning.

Lacking a theory of meaning which would serve to theoretically characterize basic semantic concepts, to settle whether two uses of an expression are the same or different, to delineate deviations from the regularities in the language, and to provide some means for evaluating proposed solutions to philosophical problems arising in connection with the employment of language, the ordinary-language philosopher is increasingly forced to resort to his linguistic intuitions. It may be claimed that insofar as an analysis of language is relevant to solving philosophical problems all the information required is available by virtue of the fact that the

---

[14]J. Austin, "Other Minds," *Proceedings of the Aristotelian Society*, Supp. Vol. XX (1946).

investigator is a fluent speaker of the language.[15] In particular, the ordinary-language philosopher may claim that he is able to detect intuitively cases of linguistic oddity, and that what is relevant to the solution of a philosophical problem is precisely information about what it would be *odd* to say. Thus, it is held that what is required in the practice of philosophy is that we avoid using words in ways in which we would not ordinarily use them, but it is also held that we can generally tell by using our linguistic intuition when a word is used in an extraordinary way.

Granted that it is often intuitively clear when a given use is odd, it is equally clear that the mere knowledge *that* a use is odd is insufficient either for philosophical purposes or for a theory of language; it may be odd for any number of reasons, many of which are completely nonvicious. Consider the following utterances, all of which are odd for different reasons:

(1) I just swallowed my nose.
(2) I will show you fear in a handful of dust.
(3) This lovely red rose is a red rose.
(4) Physical objects do not exist.
(5) I have just been decapitated.
(6) Pain is the stimulation of C-fibers.

These utterances do not, of course, exhaust all the types of linguistic oddity, but even from this short list it seems clear that some of the things that can make an utterance odd are not such as to make that utterance philosophically objectionable. Hence, *if* a philosopher claims that an utterance is odd and *claims no more*, he has brought no effective criticism against an argument in which that utterance plays an essential role. Thus, accused of having used language oddly, the metaphysician who replies "So what?" replies correctly. What is needed is a theory which tells us what oddity is and indicates which kinds of oddity are philosophically objectionable and why.

But we do not wish to claim that an adequate theory of meaning will explicate oddity in such a way that every utterance which a theoretically unsophisticated speaker would call odd is so counted by the theory. Rather, it may be expected that it will reconstruct only those intuitions of oddity which are provoked by violations of semantic regularities of the language. Thus, for example, (1) and (3) would not be characterized as violations of the semantic regularities governing the language, since they elicit intuitions of oddity for reasons having nothing whatever to do with the structure of the language, i.e., (1) is odd because the fact it describes is so extremely unlikely and (3) is odd because it is too obviously true. For these reasons such cases are not philosophically objectionable.

Furthermore, there are cases when the oddity of an *utterance*, as opposed to an utterance *type*, depends upon features of its context. Thus, it would be odd to say "Goodbye!" on first arriving at a gathering or to say "Two tickets to Mars, please!," given our current state of technology. Similarly, where the context is a context of sentences in a discourse, its features may make an otherwise normal sentence appear

---

[15]Cavell, in fact, makes just this claim. Cf. "Must We Mean What We Say?" *Inquiry*, vol. 1, (1958). For our reply to him, see J. A. Fodor and J. J. Katz, "The Availability of What We Say?" *The Philosophical Review*, Vol. LXXII, No. 1 (January 1963).

odd. For example, imagine reading a book on calculus and in the middle of a discussion of the integration of rational functions coming across the sentence "Bring me a hot pastrami on rye bread!" This type of oddity differs from that exhibited by the previous examples, and it is conceivable that a special theory will be needed to deal with it. What these arguments show is that the claim that an utterance is odd is not, by itself, a revealing claim. Philosophical arguments based upon this claim thus often go astray. Witness the following case study:

> The last argument I shall consider on the subject of mind-body identity is a widely used linguistic argument. . . . Consider the sentence:
> (1) Pain *is identical with* stimulation of *C*-fibers. The sentence is deviant (so the argument runs, though not in this terminology): there is no statement that it could be used to make in a normal context. Therefore, if a philosopher advances it as a thesis he must be giving the words a new meaning, rather than expressing any sort of discovery. For example . . . one might begin to say "I have stimulated *C*-fibers" instead of "I have a pain." But then one would *merely* be giving the expression "has stimulated *C*-fibers" the new meaning "is in pain." The contention is that as long as the words keep their present meanings, (1) is unintelligible.
> I agree that the sentence (1) is a "deviant" sentence in present-day English. I do *not* agree that (1) can never become a normal, nondeviant sentence unless the words change their present meanings.
> The point, in a nutshell, is that what is deviant depends very much on context, including the state of our knowledge, and with the development of new scientific theories it is constantly occurring that sentences that did not previously "have a use," that were previously deviant, acquire a use—not because the words acquire *new* meanings, but because the old meanings, as fixed by the core of stock uses, *determine* a new use given the new context.[16]

What this example shows is that there can be agreement about the oddity of an utterance, but disagreement about the significance of its oddity. It is this latter sort of disagreement that we need to be able to resolve if the notion of oddity is to play an important role in philosophical polemics.

Furthermore, if it is true that the mere fact that we can tell intuitively when an utterance is odd is insufficient for philosophical purposes, it is equally true that it is inadequate for the purposes of a theory of language. This follows immediately if one accepts the claim that the goal of a theory of language must be at least to make explicit the generative principles that structure sentences. But even if one rejects this claim, the consequence of relying upon intuition alone to decide questions of oddity is that there is then no way to extrapolate one's decisions. Each decision must be handled by a new appeal to intuition, each sentence being treated as though it were unrelated to the rest of the language.[17] But then we have no theory whatever. All we have is overworked intuition. It is in this way that the ordinary-language

---

[16]H. Putnam, "Minds and Machines," in *Dimensions of Mind*, ed. Sidney Hook (New York: New York University Press, 1960), p. 166.

[17]The ordinary-language philosopher may complain that we have ignored the principle that similar cases are to be decided in a similar fashion. But if the ordinary-language philosopher invokes this principle he begs the question, since to specify what counts as relevant similarity is precisely to specify the generative rules that structure the sentences of the language.

philosopher's reliance upon linguistic intuition may have been responsible for his failure to develop an adequate theory of language.[18]

In effect, then, the major charge we have to bring against ordinary-language analysis is that it is a prioristic. Lacking a theory to characterize such key notions as *use*, *misuse*, *speech act*, and *rule of language*, a resort is made to the intuitions of the speaker (who, as often as not, is also the theorist). But one's intuitions—even one's intuitions about one's own speech habits—are by no means infallible. One can be wrong about "what one would say," since the utterances one has produced during one's lifetime constitute a corpus which is *itself* amenable to analysis in a manner differing in no essential respect from that of any other sample corpus drawn from the language. Just as the intuitions of speakers provide constraints upon a theory of a language, so a developed theory may correct and supplement the intuitions of speakers. On the other hand, if one has no theory, when questions of justification arise in connection with the adequacy of specific analyses of the use of expressions, the appeal to intuition, defended on a priori grounds, prevents an objective evaluation of the degree to which the analysis fits the verbal behavior of speakers.

It cannot be surprising, then, that the usual methods of ordinary-language analysis often yield solutions for philosophical problems which are as controversial as classical solutions. Uncontroversial solutions will be forthcoming to the extent that one can make explicit the empirical and theoretical requirements that a putative analysis must satisfy in order to be a revealing representation of the verbal habits of speakers. Unless it is decided what criteria an analysis must satisfy, our inability to decide between competitive solutions to philosophical problems simply reflects our inability to decide between competitive linguistic *analyses*.

---

[18]The rules of a linguistic theory are formulated to answer the question "What abilities have been acquired by someone who has learned a natural language?" To answer this question, linguists construct a theory that aims at matching the verbal behavior of fluent speakers and reconstructing the mechanisms that underlie linguistic communication.

One of the main dangers encountered in the construction of the rules of a linguistic theory is that they may be formulated so as to be workable only when an appeal to linguistic intuition is made. This means that in order for the rules to serve their intended purpose it is necessary that a fluent speaker exercise his linguistic abilities to guide their application. This, then, constitutes a vicious circularity: the rules are supposed to reconstruct the fluent speaker's abilities, yet they are unable to perform this function unless the speaker uses these abilities to apply them. As much of the abilities of the speaker as are required for the application of the rules, so much at least the rules themselves fail to reconstruct.

This, however, is not meant to imply that the appeal to linguistic intuition plays no role in theory construction in the study of language. The intuitions of fluent speakers determine the data for which a linguistic theory must account. For example, the fluent speaker intuitively recognizes the difference in structure between "Think of an example of such cases" and "Cases such of example an of think." Such intuitions establish sets of clear cases: of grammatically well-formed strings of words on the one hand, and of ungrammatical strings on the other. Clear cases, intuitively determined, provide the empirical constraints on the construction of a linguistic theory. The appeal to linguistic intuition is question begging when intuitions replace well-defined theoretical constructs in an articulated system of description, or when intuitions are permitted to determine the application of rules. Intuition in its proper role is indispensable to the study of language, but misused, it vitiates such a study.

V

The theory of language implicit in current work in linguistics deals with problems that have traditionally concerned philosophers of language, but it does so without falling victim either to the positivist's preconceptions about the structure of language and his lack of empirical controls or to the ordinary-language philosopher's illicit appeal to intuitive judgments and his unsystematic orientation. It thus provides a real alternative to theories of language found in the schools of positivism and ordinary-language philosophy, although it shares the concern with formalization characteristic of the former and the attention to details of usage characteristic of the latter.

Moreover, it provides the basis for a new conception of the nature of philosophy of language. Given a scientifically mature field of linguistics, the philosophy of language can be conceived of as a discipline concerned with the analysis of the concepts, theories, and methodology of linguistics. On this conception, the philosophy of language is the philosophy of linguistics, a discipline analogous in every respect to the philosophy of physics, the philosophy of mathematics, the philosophy of psychology, and the like.

It has perhaps been because of the lack of a viable alternative to positivist and ordinary-language philosophies of language that the shortcomings of both these approaches have not led to their abandonment. The conception of the philosophy of language just suggested provides such an alternative, insofar as linguistics offers a satisfactory theory of the grammatical and semantic structure of natural languages. To show that it does so is the burden of our anthology.

II

LINGUISTIC THEORY

Linguistic theory is a metatheory dealing with the properties of linguistic descriptions of natural languages. In particular, linguistic theory is concerned with whatever such descriptions have in common—with *universals* of linguistic description.

A feature of linguistic descriptions may be universal either because it represents a universal property of natural languages or because it is a consequence of the scientific aims and methodology of linguistics; hence, linguistic theory must treat questions about the content and form of individual linguistic descriptions. In practice, these questions range from the characterization of the formal properties of grammars to the enumeration of universal grammatical and semantic categories.

Three types of questions have been central to recent discussions in linguistic theory. Each of the papers in this section treats a facet of at least one of these questions. First, there is the question of the objectives of a linguistic description. To answer this question, a linguistic theory must provide a precise statement of what phenomena are to be accounted for by a theory in phonology, syntax, or semantics. Second, linguistic theory includes formal questions about linguistic descriptions and, in particular, questions about the types of rules linguistic descriptions employ. The problem here is to achieve a formal characterization of the structure of a linguistic description and a general account of the nature of explanation in each area of linguistics. Third, linguistic theory seeks to determine the methodological framework within which the construction of a linguistic description proceeds, where this framework may be taken to include a specification of the sorts of techniques the linguist may properly employ in arriving at his description. Since none of these questions can be answered independently of the others, the goal of linguistic theory is to provide a characterization of linguistic descriptions that offers a satisfactory solution for them all.

Among the problems in linguistic theory, some are *only* particularizations of classical problems in the philosophy of science. Thus, when we find linguists asking whether such constructs as phoneme, morpheme, noun phrase, and others correspond to any psychological reality or whether they are best considered mere classificatory conventions, we recognize a special case of the philosophical problem about the reality of the theoretical entities postulated in scientific theories. Again, when we find linguists asking whether explanations in linguistics can be causal, and, if not, what kind of explanations linguistics can provide, we recognize an instance of the philosophical problem about the nature of scientific explanation. Further problems in linguistic theory which are related in similar ways to problems in the philosophy of science center around the question of providing operational definitions for theoretical terms in linguistics and characterizing critera for choosing the simplest of the competing descriptions of a language.

Other problems in linguistic theory, although they are not particularizations of problems in the philosophy of science, depend for their solution upon solutions to problems in the philosophy of science. For example, it has become clear that the controversy over the generative approach to grammar cannot be resolved unless we solve such problems as the explanatory role of theories, the significance of methodological requirements, such as simplicity and precision, and so on.

1   The Problem of Meaning in Linguistics*

Willard V. Quine

I

Lexicography is concerned, or seems to be concerned, with identification of meanings, and the investigation of semantic change is concerned with change of meaning. Pending a satisfactory explanation of the notion of meaning, linguists in semantic fields are in the situation of not knowing what they are talking about. This is not an untenable situation. Ancient astronomers knew the movements of the planets remarkably well without knowing what sort of things the planets were. But it is a theoretically unsatisfactory situation, as the more theoretically minded among the linguists are painfully aware.

Confusion of meaning with reference has encouraged a tendency to take the notion of meaning for granted. It is felt that the meaning of the word *man* is as tangible as our neighbor and that the meaning of the phrase *Evening Star* is as clear as the star in the sky. And it is felt that to question or repudiate the notion of meaning is to suppose a world in which there is just language and nothing for language to refer to. Actually, we can acknowledge a worldful of objects and let our singular and general terms refer to those objects in their several ways to our hearts' content, without ever taking up the topic of meaning.

An object referred to, named by a singular term, or denoted by a general term can be anything under the sun. Meanings, however, purport to be entities of a special sort: the meaning of an expression is the idea expressed. There is considerable agreement among modern linguists that the idea of an idea, the idea of the mental counterpart of a linguistic form, is worse than worthless for linguistic

* W. Quine, *From a Logical Point of View* (2nd ed.; Cambridge, Mass.: Harvard University Press, 1961), pp. 47–64. Copyright 1953 and 1961 by The President and Fellows of Harvard College. Reprinted by permission.

science. I think the behaviorists are right in holding that talk of ideas is bad business even for psychology. The evil of the idea is that its use, like the appeal in Molière to a *virtus dormitiva*, engenders an illusion of having explained something. And the illusion is increased by the fact that things wind up in a vague enough state to insure a certain stability, or freedom from further progress.

Let us then look back to the lexicographer, supposed as he is to be concerned with meanings, and see what he is really trafficking in, if not in mental entities. The answer is not far to seek: the lexicographer, like any linguist, studies linguistic forms. He differs from the so-called formal linguist only in that he is concerned to correlate linguistic forms with one another in his own special way, namely, synonyms with synonyms. The characteristic feature of semantical parts of linguistics, notably lexicography, comes to be not that there is an appeal to meanings, but that there is a concern with synonymy.

What happens in this maneuver is that we fix on one important context of the baffling word *meaning*, namely the context *alike in meaning*, and resolve to treat this whole context in the spirit of a single word *synonymous*, thus not being tempted to seek meanings as intermediary entities. But, even supposing that the notion of synonymy can eventually be provided with a satisfactory criterion, still this maneuver only takes care of the one context of the word *meaning*—the context *alike in meaning*. Does the word also have other contexts that should concern linguists? Yes, there is certainly one more—the context *having meaning*. Here a parallel maneuver is in order: treat the context *having meaning* in the spirit of a single word, *significant*, and continue to turn our backs on the supposititious entities called meanings.

Significance is the trait with respect to which the subject matter of linguistics is studied by the grammarian. The grammarian catalogues short forms and works out the laws of their concatenation, and the end product of this is no more nor less than a specification of the class of all possible linguistic forms, simple and composite, of the language under investigation—the class of all significant sequences, if we accept a liberal standard of significance. The lexicographer, on the other hand, is concerned not with specifying the class of significant sequences for the given language, but rather with specifying the class of pairs of mutually synonymous sequences for the given language or, perhaps, pair of languages. The grammarian and the lexicographer are concerned with meaning to an equal degree, be it zero or otherwise; the grammarian wants to know what forms are significant, or *have* meaning, while the lexicographer wants to know what forms are synonymous, or *alike* in meaning. If it is urged that the grammarian's notion of significant sequences should not be viewed as resting on a prior notion of meaning, I applaud; and I say the lexicographer's notion of synonymy is entitled to the same compliment. What had been the problem of meaning boils down now to a pair of problems in which meaning is best not mentioned; one is the problem of making sense of the notion of significant sequence, and the other is the problem of making sense of the notion of synonymy. What I want to emphasize is that the lexicographer had no monopoly on the problem of meaning. The problem of significant sequence and the problem of synonymy are twin offspring of the problem of meaning.

II

Let us suppose that our grammarian is at work on a hitherto unstudied language and that his own contact with the language has been limited to his field work. As grammarian he is concerned to discover the bounds of the class K of significant sequences of the language. Synonymy correlations of members of K with English sequences and with one another are not his business; they are the business of the lexicographer.

There is presumably no upper limit to the lengths of members of K. Moreover, parts of significant sequences count as significant, down to the smallest adopted units of analysis; so such units, whatever they are, are the shortest members of K. Besides the length dimension, however, there is a dimension of thickness to consider. For, given two utterances of equal and arbitrary length and fairly similar acoustical make-up, we must know whether to count them as occurrences of two slightly different members of K or as two slightly different occurrences of one and the same member of K. The question of thickness is the question what acoustical differences to count as relevant and what ones to count merely as inconsequential idiosyncrasies of voice and accent.

The question of thickness is settled by cataloguing the *phonemes*—the single sounds, distinguished as coarsely as possible for purposes of the language. Two subtly differing sounds count as the same phoneme unless it is possible, by putting one for the other in some utterance, to change the meaning of the utterance.[1] Now the notion of phoneme, thus formulated, depends obviously and notoriously on the notion of sameness of meaning, or synonymy. Our grammarian, if he is to remain pure grammarian and eschew lexicography, must carry out his program of delimiting K without the help of a notion of phoneme so defined.

There seems indeed, at first glance, to be an easy way out: he can simply enumerate the phonemes needed for the particular language at hand and dispense with the general notion of phoneme defined in terms of synonymy. This expedient would be quite admissible as a mere technical aid to solving the grammarian's problem of specifying the membership of K if the problem of specifying the membership of K could itself be *posed* without prior appeal to the general notion of phoneme. But the fact is otherwise. The class K, which is the grammarian's empirical business to describe, is a class of sequences of phonemes, and each phoneme is a class of brief events. (It will be convenient to swallow this much Platonism for present purposes, though some logical maneuvers might serve to reduce it.) The grammarian's problem is in part objectively set for him thus: every speech event which he encounters in his field work counts as a sample of a member of K. But the delimiting of the several members of K, that is, the grouping of mutually resemblant acoustical histories into bundles of proper thickness to qualify as linguistic forms, needs also to have some objective significance if the task of the field grammarian is to be made sense of as an empirical and objective task at all. This need is fulfilled if the general notion of phoneme is at hand, as a general relative term: "x is a phoneme for language L," with variable x and L, or "x is a phoneme for speaker s," with variable

---

[1]Cf. Bloch and Trager, pp. 38–52, or Bloomfield, pp. 74–92.

x and *s*. Thereupon the grammarian's business, with respect to a language *L*, can be stated as the business of finding what sequences of phonemes of *L* are significant for *L*. Statement of the grammarian's purpose thus depends not only on *significant*, as we had been prepared to expect, but also on *phoneme*.

But we might still seek to free grammar of dependence on the notion of synonymy, by somehow freeing the notion of phoneme itself of such dependence. It has been conjectured, for example, by Bühler, that this might in principle be accomplished. Let the continuum of sounds be arranged in acoustical or physiological order in one or more dimensions, say two, and plotted against frequency of occurrence, so that we come out with a three-dimensional relief map in which altitude represents frequency of occurrence. Then it is suggested that the major humps correspond to the phonemes. There are abundant reasons to suspect that neither this oversimplified account nor anything remotely resembling it can possibly provide an adequate definition of the phoneme; and phonologists have not neglected to adduce such reasons. As a means of isolating other points of comparison between grammar and lexicography, however, let us make the unrealistic assumption that our grammarian has some such nonsemantical definition of phoneme. Then his remaining task is to devise a recursive description of a class *K* of forms which will comprise all and only those sequences of phonemes which are in fact significant.

The basic point of view is that the class *K* is objectively determinate before the grammatical research is begun; it is the class of the significant sequences, the sequences capable of occurring in the normal stream of speech (supposing for the moment that this terminology is itself significant). But the grammarian wants to reproduce this same class in other terms, formal terms; he wants to devise, in terms of elaborate conditions of phoneme succession alone, a necessary and sufficient condition for membership in *K*. He is an empirical scientist, and his result will be right or wrong according as he reproduces that objectively predetermined class *K* or some other.

Our grammarian's attempted recursive specification of *K* will follow the orthodox line, we may suppose, of listing *morphemes* and describing constructions. Morphemes, according to the books,[2] are the significant forms which are not resoluble into shorter significant forms. They comprise affixes, word stems, and whole words insofar as these are not analyzable into subsidiary morphemes. But we can spare our grammarian any general problem of defining morpheme by allowing him simply to list his so-called morphemes exhaustively. They become simply a convenient segmentation of heard phoneme sequences, chopped out as convenient building blocks for his purpose. He frames his constructions in the simplest way that will enable him to generate all members of *K* from his morphemes, and he cuts his morphemes to allow for the simplest constructions. Morphemes, like higher units such as might be called words or free forms, may thus be viewed simply as intermediate stages in a process which, over-all, is still describable as reproduction of *K* in terms of conditions of phoneme succession.

There is no denying that the grammarian's reproduction of *K*, as I have schematized it, is purely formal, that is, free of semantics. But the setting of the grammarian's

---

[2]Bloch and Trager, p. 54; Bloomfield, pp. 161–68.

problem is quite another matter, for it turns on a prior notion of significant sequence, or possible normal utterance. Without this notion, or something to somewhat the same effect, we cannot say what the grammarian is trying to do—what he is trying to match in his formal reproduction of *K*—nor wherein the rightness or wrongness of his results might consist. We are thus squarely confronted with one of the twin offspring of the problem of meaning, namely, the problem of defining the general notion of significant sequence.

III

It is not satisfactory to say that a significant sequence is simply any sequence of phonemes uttered by any of the *Naturkinder* of our grammarian's chosen valley. What are wanted as significant sequences include not just those uttered but also those which *could* be uttered without reactions suggesting bizarreness of idiom. The joker here is *could*; we cannot substitute *will*. The significant sequences, being subject to no length limit, are infinite in variety; whereas, from the dawn of the language under investigation to the time when it will have evolved to the point where our grammarian would disown it, only a finite sample of this infinite manifold will have been uttered.

The desired class *K* of significant sequences is the culmination of a series of four classes of increasing magnitude, *H, I, J,* and *K,* as follows. *H* is the class of observed sequences, excluding any which are ruled inappropriate in the sense of being nonlinguistic or belonging to alien dialects. *I* is the class of all such observed sequences and all that ever will happen to be professionally observed, excluding again those which are ruled inappropriate. *J* is the class of all sequences ever occurring, now or in the past or future, within or without professional observation—excluding, again, only those which are ruled inappropriate. *K,* finally, is the infinite class of all those sequences, with exclusion of the inappropriate ones as usual, which *could* be uttered without bizarreness reactions. *K* is the class which the grammarian wants to approximate in his formal reconstruction, and *K* is more inclusive even than *J,* let alone *H* and *I.* Now the class *H* is a matter of finished record; the class *I* is, or could be, a matter of growing record; the class *J* goes beyond any record, but still has a certain common-sense reality; but not even this can very confidently be said of *K,* because of the *could.*

I expect we must leave the *could* unreduced. It has some operational import, indeed, but only in a partial way. It does require our grammarian to bring into his formal reconstruction of *K* all of the actually observed cases, that is, all of *H.* Further, it commits him to the prediction that all cases to be observed in the future will conform, that is, all of *I* belongs in *K.* Further still, it commits him to the scientific hypothesis that all unobserved cases fall in this *K,* that is, all of *J.* Now what more does the *could* cover? What is the rationale behind that infinite additional membership of *K,* over and above the finite part *J*? This vast supplementary force of *could,* in the present instance and elsewhere, is perhaps a vestige of Indo-European myth, fossilized in the subjunctive mood.

What our grammarian does is evident enough. He frames his formal reconstruction of *K* along the grammatically simplest lines he can, compatibly with inclusion of *H*, plausibility of the predicted inclusion of *I*, plausibility of the hypothesis of inclusion of *J*, and plausibility, further, of the exclusion of all sequences which ever actually do bring bizarreness reactions. Our basis for saying what *could* be generally consists, I suggest, in what *is* plus *simplicity* of the laws whereby we describe and extrapolate what is. I see no more objective way of construing the *conditio irrealis*.

Concerning the notion of significant sequence, one of the two survivals of the notion of meaning, we have now observed the following. It is needed in setting the grammarian's task. But it is describable, without appeal to meanings as such, as denoting any sequence which could be uttered in the society under consideration without reactions suggesting bizarreness of idiom. This notion of a reaction suggesting bizarreness of idiom would want some refinement eventually. A considerable problem of refinement is involved also in the preliminary putting aside of so-called "nonlinguistic noises," as well as utterances in alien dialects. Also there is the general methodological problem, of a pretty philosophical kind, which is raised by the word *could*. This is a problem common to concept-building in most subjects (apart from logic and mathematics, where it happens to be well cleared up); I have outlined one attitude toward it.

We should also remind ourselves of the oversimplification that I made with regard to morphemes when I treated them merely as convenient phoneme sequences which our grammarian specifies by enumeration in the course of his formal reconstruction of the class of significant sequences from the phonemes. This is unrealistic because it requires our grammarian to exhaust the vocabulary instead of allowing him to leave certain open categories, comparable to our nouns and verbs, subject to enrichment *ad libitum*. If, on the other hand, we allow him some open morpheme categories, his reconstruction of the class *K* of significant sequences ceases to be a formal construction from phonemes; the most we can say for it is that it is a formal reconstruction from phonemes and his open morpheme categories. So the problem remains how he is going to characterize his open morpheme categories—since enumeration no longer serves. This gap must be watched for possible intrusion of an unanalyzed semantical element.

I do not want to take leave of the topic of significant sequence without mentioning one curious further problem which the notion raises. I shall speak now of English rather than a hypothetical heathen tongue. Any nonsensical and thoroughly un-English string of sounds can occur within a perfectly intelligible English sentence, even a true one, if, in effect, we quote the nonsense and say in the rest of our sentence that the quoted matter *is* nonsense or is not English or consists of four syllables or rimes with "Kalamazoo." If the whole inclusive sentence is to be called normal English speech, then the rubbish inside it has occurred in normal English speech, and we have thus lost the means of excluding any pronounceable sequence from the category of significant sequence. Thus we must either narrow our concept of normality to exclude, for present purposes, sentences which use quotation, or else we must narrow our concept of occurrence to exclude occurrence within quotation. In either event, we have the problem of identifying the spoken analogue of quotation marks and of doing so in general enough terms so that our concept of significant sequence will not be limited in advance to some one preconceived language such as English.

In any case, we have seen that the problem of significant sequence admits of considerable fragmentation; and this is one of the two aspects into which the problem of meaning seemed to resolve, namely, the aspect of the having of meaning. The fact that this aspect of the problem of meaning is in such halfway tolerable shape accounts, no doubt, for the tendency to think of grammar as a formal, nonsemantical part of linguistics. Let us turn now to the other and more forbidding aspect of the problem of meaning, that of likeness in meaning, or synonymy.

IV

A lexicographer may be concerned with synonymy between forms in one language and forms in another, or, as in compiling a domestic dictionary, he may be concerned with synonymy between forms in the same language. It is an open question how satisfactorily the two cases can be subsumed under a single general formulation of the synonymy concept, for it is an open question whether the synonymy concept can be satisfactorily clarified for either case. Let us first limit our attention to synonymy within a language.

So-called substitution criteria, or conditions of interchangeability, have in one form or another played central roles in modern grammar. For the synonymy problem of semantics such an approach seems more obvious still. However, the notion of the interchangeability of two linguistic forms makes sense only insofar as answers are provided to these two questions: (a) In just what sorts of contexual position, if not in all, are the two forms to be interchangeable? (b) The forms are to be interchangeable *salvo quo*? Supplanting one form by another in any context changes something, namely, form at least; and (b) asks what feature the interchange is to leave invariant. Alternative answers to (a) and (b) give alternative notions of interchangeability, some suited to defining grammatical correspondences and others, conceivably, to defining synonymy.

In another essay[3] we tried answering (b), for purposes of synonymy, with *veritate*. We found that something had still to be done about (a), in view, for example, of the difficulty presented by quotation. So we answered (a), lamely appealing to a prior conception of *word*. Then we found that interchangeability *salva veritate* was too weak a condition for synonymy if the language as a whole was *extensional* and that in other languages it was an unilluminating condition, involving something like a vicious circle.

It is not clear that the problem of synonymy discussed in those pages is the same as the lexicographer's problem. For in those pages we were concerned with *cognitive* synonymy, which abstracts from much that the lexicographer would want to preserve in his translations and paraphrases. Even the lexicographer is indeed ready to equate, as synonymous, many forms which differ perceptibly in imaginative associations and poetic value; but the optimum sense of synonymy for his purpose is probably narrower than synonymy in the supposed cognitive sense. However this

---

[3] "Two Dogmas of Empiricism," *Phil. Review*, LX (1951), 20–43.

may be, certainly the negative findings which were summed up in the preceding paragraph carry over; the lexicographer cannot answer (b) with *veritate*. The interchangeability which he seeks in synonymy must not merely be such as to assure that true statements remain true, and false ones false, when synonyms are substituted within them; it must assure further that statements go over into statements with which they as wholes are somehow synonymous.

This last observation does not recommend itself as a definition because of its circularity—forms are synonymous when their interchange leaves their contexts synonymous. But it has the virtue of hinting that substitution is not the main point and that what we need in the first place is some notion of synonymy for long segments of discourse. The hint is opportune; for, independently of the foregoing considerations, three reasons can be adduced for approaching the problem of synonymy from the point of view of long segments of discourse.

First, any interchangeability criterion for synonymy of short forms would obviously be limited to synonymy within a language; otherwise interchange would produce polyglot jumbles. *Inter*linguistic synonymy must be a relation, primarily, between segments of discourse which are long enough to bear consideration in abstraction from a containing context peculiar to one or the other particular language. I say "primarily" because interlinguistic synonymy might indeed be defined for the component forms afterward in some derivative way.

Second, a retreat to longer segments tends to overcome the difficulty of ambiguity or homonymy. Homonymy gets in the way of the law that if *a* is synonymous with *b* and *b* with *c*, then *a* is synonymous with *c*. For, if *b* has two meanings (to revert to the ordinary parlance of meanings), *a* may be synonymous with *b* in one sense of *b* and *b* with *c* in the other sense of *b*. This difficulty is sometimes dealt with by treating an ambiguous form as two forms, but this expedient has the drawback of making the concept of form depend on that of synonymy.

Third, there is the circumstance that in glossing a word we have so frequently to content ourselves with a lame partial synonym plus stage directions. Thus in glossing *addled* we say *spoiled* and add *said of an egg*. This widespread circumstance reflects the fact that synonymy in the small is no primary concern of the lexicographer; lame synonyms plus stage directions are quite satisfactory insofar as they expedite his primary business of explaining how to translate or paraphrase long speeches. We may continue to characterize the lexicographer's domain squarely as synonymy, but only by recognizing synonymy as primarily a relation of sufficiently long segments of discourse.

So we may view the lexicographer as interested, ultimately, only in cataloguing synonym pairs which are sequences of sufficient length to admit of synonymy in some primary sense. Naturally he cannot catalogue these true synonym pairs directly, in any exhaustive way, becuase they are altogether limitless in number and variety. His case is parallel to that of the grammarian, who for the same reason was unable to catalogue the significant sequences directly. The grammarian accomplished his end indirectly, by fixing on a class of atomic units capable of enumeration and then propounding rules for compounding them to get all significant sequences. Similarly, the lexicographer accomplishes his end indirectly—the end of specifying the infinitely numerous genuine pairs of long synonyms; and this he does by fixing on a class of short forms capable of enumeration and then explaining as systematically as he can how to construct genuine synonyms for all sufficiently long forms compounded of those short ones. These short forms are in effect the word entries in his glossary, and the explanations of how to construct genuine synonyms of all sufficiently long compounds are what appear as the glosses in his glossary, typically a mixture of quasi-synonyms and stage directions.

Thus the lexicographer's actual activity, his glossing of short forms by appeal to quasi-synonyms and stage directions, is not antithetical to his being concerned purely and simply with genuine synonymy on the part of forms sufficiently long to admit of genuine synonymy. Something like his actual activity is indeed the only possible way of cataloguing, in effect, the limitless class of pairs of genuinely synonymous longer forms.

I exploited just now a parallelism between the grammarian's indirect reconstruction of the limitless class of significant sequences and the lexicographer's indirect reconstruction of the limitless class of genuine synonym pairs. This parallelism bears further exploiting. It brings out that the lexicographer's reconstruction of the class of synonym pairs is just as formal in spirit as the grammarian's reconstruction of the class of significant sequences. The invidious use of the word *formal*, to favor grammar as against lexicography, is thus misleading. Both the lexicographer and the grammarian would simply list the membership of the respective classes in which they are interested, were it not for the vastness, the infinitude even, of the numbers involved. On the other hand, just as the grammarian needs, over and above his formal constructions, a prior notion of significant sequence for the setting of his problem, so the lexicographer needs a prior notion of synonymity for the setting of his. In the setting of their problems, the grammarian and the lexicographer draw equally on our heritage from the old notion of meaning.

It is clear from the foregoing reflections that the notion of synonymy needed in the statement of the lexicographer's problem is synonymy only as between sequences which are long enough to be pretty clean-cut about their synonymy connections. But in conclusion I want to stress what a baffling problem this remaining problem of synonymy, even relatively clean-cut and well-behaved synonymy, is.

V

Synonymy of two forms is supposed vaguely to consist in an approximate likeness in the situations which evoke the two forms and an approximate likeness in the effect of either form on the hearer. For simplicity let us forget this second requirement and concentrate on the first—the likeness of situations. What I have to say from here on will be so vague, at best, that this further inaccuracy will not much matter.

As everyone is quick to point out, no two situations are quite alike; situations in which even the same form is uttered are unlike in myriad ways. What matters rather is likeness in *relevant respects*. Now the problem of finding the relevant respects is, if we think of the matter in a sufficiently oversimplified way, a problem typical of empirical science. We observe a speaker of Kalaba, say—to adopt Pike's myth—and we look for correlations or so-called causal connections between the noises he makes and the other things that are observed to be happening. As in any empirical search for correlations or so-called causal connections, we guess at the relevance of one or another feature and then try by further observation, or even experiment, to confirm or refute our hypothesis. Actually, in lexicography this guessing at possible relevances is expedited by our natural familiarity with the basic lines of human interest. Finally, having found fair evidence for correlating a given Kalaba sound sequence with a given combination of circumstances, we conjecture synonymy of that sound sequence with another, in English, say, which is correlated with the same circumstances.

As I unnecessarily remarked, this account is oversimplified. Now I want to stress one serious respect in which it is oversimplified: the relevant features of the situation issuing in a given Kalaba utterance are in large part concealed in the person of the speaker, where they were implanted by his earlier environment. This concealment is partly good, for our purposes, and partly bad. It is good insofar as it isolates the subject's narrowly linguistic training. If we could assume that our Kalaba speaker and our English speaker, when observed in like external situations, differed only in how they say things and not in *what* they say, so to speak, then the methodology of synonymy determinations would be pretty smooth; the narrowly linguistic part of the causal complex, different for the two speakers, would be conveniently out of sight, while all the parts of the causal complex decisive of synonymy or heteronymy were open to observation. But of course the trouble is that not only the narrowly linguistic habits of vocabulary and syntax are imported by each speaker from his unknown past.

The difficulty here is not just that those subjective components of the situation are hard to ferret out. This difficulty, if it were all, would make for practical uncertainty and frequent error in lexicographical pronouncements, but it would be irrelevant to the problem of a theoretical definition of synonymy—irrelevant, that is, to the problem of coherently stating the lexicographer's purpose. Theoretically, the more important difficulty is that, as Cassirer and Whorf have stressed, there is in principle no separating language from the rest of the world, at least as conceived by the speaker. Basic differences in language are bound up, as likely as not, with differences in the way in which the speakers articulate the world itself into things and properties, time and space, elements, forces, spirits, and so on. It is not clear even in principle that it makes sense to think of words and syntax as varying from language to language while the content stays fixed; yet precisely this fiction is involved in speaking of synonymy, at least as between expressions of radically different languages.

What provides the lexicographer with an entering wedge is the fact that there are many basic features of men's ways of conceptualizing their environment, of breaking the world down into things common to all cultures. Every man is likely to see an apple or breadfruit or rabbit first and foremost as a unitary whole rather than as a congeries of smaller units or as a fragment of a larger environment, although from a sophisticated point of view all these attitudes are tenable. Every man will tend to segregate a mass of moving matter as a unit, separate from the static background, and to pay it particular attention. Again, there are conspicuous phenomena of weather which one man may be expected to endow with much the same conceptual boundaries as another and, similarly, some basic internal states such as hunger.

As long as we adhere to this presumably common fund of conceptualization, we can successfully proceed on the working assumption that our Kalaba speaker and our English speaker, observed in like external situations, differ only in how they say things and not in what they say.

The nature of this entering wedge into a strange lexicon encourages the misconception of meaning as reference, since words at this stage are construed, typically, by pointing to the object referred to. So it may not be amiss to remind ourselves that meaning is not reference even here. The reference might be the Evening Star, to return to Frege's example, and hence also the Morning Star, which is the same thing; but *Evening Star* might nevertheless be a good translation and *Morning Star* a bad one.

I have suggested that our lexicographer's obvious first moves in picking up some initial Kalaba vocabulary are at bottom a matter of exploiting the overlap of our cultures. From this nucleus he works outward, ever more fallibly and conjecturally, by a series of clues and hunches. Thus he begins with a fund of correlations of Kalaba sentences with English sentences at the level where our cultures meet. Most of these sentences classify conspicuously segregated objects. Then he breaks these Kalaba sentences down into short component elements and makes tentative English translations of these elements, compatible with his initial sentence translations. On this basis, he frames hypotheses as to the English translations of new combinations of those elements—combinations which as wholes have not been translated in the direct way. He tests his hypotheses as best he can by making further observations and keeping an eye out for conflicts. But, as the sentences undergoing translation get further and further from mere reports of common observations, the clarity of any possible conflict decreases; the lexicographer comes to depend increasingly on a projection of himself, with his Indo-European *Weltanschauung*, into the sandals of his Kalaba informant. He comes also to turn increasingly to that last refuge of all scientists, the appeal to internal simplicity of his growing system.

The finished lexicon is a case, evidently, of *ex pede Herculem*. But there is a difference. In projecting Hercules from the foot we risk error, but we may derive comfort from the fact that there is something to be wrong about. In the case of the lexicon, pending some definition of synonymy, we have no statement of the problem; we have nothing for the lexicographer to be right or wrong about.

Quite possibly the ultimately fruitful notion of synonymy will be one of degree: not the dyadic relation of a as synonymous with b, but the tetradic relation of a as more synonymous with b than c with d. But to classify the notion as a matter of degree is not to explain it; we shall still want a criterion or at least a definition for our tetradic relation. The big difficulty to be surmounted in devising a definition, whether of a dyadic relation of absolute synonymy or a tetradic relation of comparative synonymy, is the difficulty of making up our minds as to just what we are trying to do when we translate a Kalaba statement which is not a mere report on fairly directly observable features of the surrounding situation.

The other branch of the problem of meaning, namely the problem of defining significant sequence, led us into a contrary-to-fact conditional: a significant sequence is one that *could* be uttered without such and such adverse reactions. I urged that the operational content of this *could* is incomplete, leaving scope for free supplementary determinations of a grammatical theory in the light of simplicity considerations. But we are well schooled in acquiescing in contrary-to-fact conditionals. In the case of synonymy the tyranny of the developing system, the paucity of explicit objective controls, is more conspicuous.

2 Distributional Structure*

Zellig S. Harris

DOES LANGUAGE HAVE A DISTRIBUTIONAL STRUCTURE?

For the purposes of the present discussion, the term structure will be used in the following nonrigorous sense: a set of phonemes or a set of data is structured in respect to some feature, to the extent that we can form in terms of that feature some organized system of statements which describes the members of the set and their interrelations (at least up to some limit of complexity). In this sense, language can be structured in respect to various independent features. And whether it is structured (to more than a trivial extent) in respect to, say, regular historical change, social intercourse, meaning, or distribution—or to what extent it is structured in any of these respects—is a matter decidable by investigation. Here we will discuss how each language can be described in terms of a distributional structure, i.e., in terms of the occurrence of parts (ultimately sounds) relative to other parts and how this description is complete without intrusion of other features such as history or meaning. It goes without saying that other studies of language—historical, psychological, and so on—are also possible, both in relation to distributional structure and independently of it.

The distribution of an element will be understood as the sum of all its environments. An environment of an element A is an existing array of its co-occurrents, i.e., the other elements, each in a particular position, with which A occurs to yield an utterance. A's co-occurrents in a particular position are called its selection for that position.

1 Possibilities of structure for the distributional facts. To see that there can be a

---

*Z. Harris, "Distributional Structure," *Word*, **10**, No. 2–3 (August-December 1954), 146–62. Reprinted by permission.

distributional structure we note the following: first, the parts of a language do not occur arbitrarily relative to each other—each element occurs in certain positions relative to certain other elements. The perennial man in the street believes that when he speaks he freely puts together whatever elements have the meanings he intends; but he does so only by choosing members of those classes that regularly occur together and in the order in which these classes occur.

Second, the restricted distribution of classes persists for all their occurrences; the restrictions are not disregarded arbitrarily, e.g., for semantic needs. Some logicians, for example, have considered that an exact distributional description of natural languages is impossible because of their inherent vagueness. This is not quite the case. All elements in a language can be grouped into classes whose relative occurrence can be stated exactly. However, for the occurrence of a particular member of one class relative to a particular member of another class, it would be necessary to speak in terms of probability, based on the frequency of that occurrence in a sample.

Third, it is possible to state the occurrence of any element relative to any other element, to the degree of exactness indicated above, so that distributional statements can cover all the material of a language without requiring support from other types of information. At various times it has been thought that one could only state the normative rules of grammar (e.g., because colloquial departures from these were irregular) or the rules for a standard dialect, but not for *substandard* speech or slang; or that distributional statements had to be amplified by historical derivation (e.g., because the earlier form of the language was somehow more regular). However, in all dialects studied it has been possible to find elements having regularities of occurrence; and while historical derivation can be studied both independently and in relation to the distribution of elements,[1] it is always also possible to state the relative occurrence of elements without reference to their history (i.e., *descriptively*).

Fourth, the restrictions on relative occurrence of each element are described most simply by a network of interrelated statements, certain of them being put in terms of the results of certain others, rather than by a simple measurement of the total restriction on each element separately. Some engineers and mathematicians (as also phoneticians and experimental psychologists) who have become interested in language have sought a direct formulation of the total restrictions on occurrence for each element, say for each sound.[2] This would yield an expression for how the occurrences of each element depart from equiprobability and so would give a complete description of the occurrences of elements in the language. Now it is of course possible to enumerate the relative occurrences of a finite set of elements in finitely long utterances; but direct enumeration is of little interest because it yields no simple descrip-

---

[1] The investigation of historical regularity without direct regard to descriptive (synchronic) structure was the major achievement of the linguists of the late 1800's. There are incipient studies of historical-descriptive interrelations, as in H. M. Hoenigswald, "Sound Change and Linguistic Structure," *Language*, **22** (1946), 138–43; cf. A. G. Juillald, "A Bibliography of Diachronic Phonemics," *Word*, **9** (1953), 198–208. The independent study of descriptive structure was clarified largely by Ferdinand de Saussure's *Cours de linguistique générale*, the Prague Circle in its *Travaux du cercle linguistique de Prague*, Edward Sapir in various writings, and Leonard Bloomfield's *Language*.

[2] These approaches are discussed in M. Joos, "Description of Language Design," *Journal of the Acoustical Society of America*, **22** (1950), 702–8; and W. F. Twaddell, *ibid.*, **24** (1952), 607–11.

tion of the over-all occurrences of elements and because it does not order the restrictions in such a way that the larger restrictions get stated before the smaller ones. In contrast with this, it is possible to describe the occurrence of each element indirectly, by successive groupings into sets, in such a way that the total statements about the groupings of elements into sets and the relative occurrence of the sets are fewer and simpler than the total statements about the relative occurrence of each element directly.

We obtain then an ordered set of statements in terms of certain constructs—the sets at successive levels. Since the ordering of statements can be arranged so that the earlier ones will deal with the more inclusive sets, we can stop the process of setting up these statements at any convenient point and accept the unfinished list of statements as an approximation to the distributional facts—knowing that the subsequent statements will only make subsidiary corrections to the earlier statements. (This is not the case for the direct enumeration of restrictions, where the restrictions to be enumerated after a given point may be greater than those enumerated before.)

In view of this we may say that there is not only a body of facts about the relative occurrence of elements in a language, but also a structure of relative occurrence (i.e., of distribution). Hence the investigation of a language entails not only the empirical discovery of what are its irreducible elements and their relative occurrence, but also the mathematical search for a simple set of ordered statements that will express the empirical facts.[3] It may turn out that several systems of statements are equally adequate, for example, several phonemic solutions for a particular language (or only, say, for the long vowels of a language). It may also be that different systems are simpler under different conditions. For example, one system may be adequate in terms of successive segments of sound (with, at most, stress and tone abstracted), while another system may be simpler if we admit the analysis of the sounds into simultaneous components of varying lengths. Or, one system of stating distribution in respect to near neighbors (the usual environment for phonemic solutions) may be simple by itself, but if we are to imbed it in other statements about farther neighbors, we may find that when we choose a modified system, the statements covering the imbedding are simpler (i.e., a different phonemic solution may be more convenient for use in statements about morphemes). If the distributional structure is to be used as part of a description of speech, of linguistic behavior, then we will of course accept only such structures as retain a passably simple relation to the phonetic features. But for some other purpose, such as transmission or systemic analysis, phonetic complexity may be no serious objection. In any case, there is no harm in all this nonuniqueness,[4] since each system can be mapped onto the others so long as any special conditions are explicit and measurable.

Various questions are raised by the fact that there can be more than one (nontrivial) structural statement for a given language. Can we say whether a particular item of structural analysis contributes to the simplicity of the system? It may be possible to

---

[3]For a discussion of simplicity in this connection, see a forthcoming article by N. Chomsky, "Some Comments on Simplicity and the Form of Grammars."

[4]Y. R. Chao, "The Nonuniqueness of Phonemic Solutions of Phonetic Systems," *Bulletin of the Institute of History and Philology, Academia Sinica,* **4** (1934), 363–98. Cf. the two solutions of Annamese phonemes in M. B. Emeneau, *Studies in Vietnamese (Annamese) Grammar,* 9–22.

do this; for example, if a given analysis involves a particular classification of elements (say, verbs), we may try some variation on this classification (say, by subdivision into transitive and intransitive—distributionally defined) and see whether the resulting analysis is simpler or not. Can we say what is invariant under all the possible distributional structures for a given body of data? For example, for all the phonemic solutions in a given language, there remains constant the minimal network of phonemically distinct utterance-pairs in terms of which we can distinguish every phonemically distinct utterance.

The various structural systems considered here all have this in common—that they list items and their occurrences. There is at least one other type of structural statement which is essentially distributional but couched in different terms. This is the style which describes one linguistic form as being derived by some process (operation) from another. The item style says: Form A includes elements $e + f$, while form B includes elements $e + g$; and thus it describes all forms as combinations of elements. The process style says: Form A is derived from B by changing f into g; and thus it describes most forms as derived from certain base forms. The combinatorial or item style, which has a more algebraic form, is more parsimonious and representative for much of linguistic data. The process style, which is more similar to historical statements, is useful in certain situations, especially in compact morphophonemics.[5] Both styles are based solely on the relative occurrence of parts and are therefore distributional.

2 Reality of the structure. Some question has been raised as to the reality of this structure. Does it really exist, or is it just a mathematical creation of the investigator's? Skirting the philosophical difficulties of this problem, we should, in any case, realize that there are two quite different questions here. One: Does the structure really exist in the language? The answer is yes, as much as any scientific structure really obtains in the data which it describes—the scientific structure states a network of relations, and these relations really hold in the data investigated.[6]

Two: Does the structure really exist in the speakers? Here we are faced with a question of fact which is not directly or fully investigated in the process of determining the distributional structure. Clearly, certain behaviors of the speakers indicate perception along the lines of the distributional structure, for example, the fact that while people imitate nonlinguistic or foreign-language sounds, they *repeat* utterances of their own language[7] (i.e., they reproduce the utterance by substituting, for the sounds they heard, the particular corresponding variants which they habitually pronounce; hence, the heard sounds are perceived as members of correspondence

---

[5]This kind of formulation is best expressed in the work of Sapir and Newman; cf. reviews of D. Mandelbaum, ed., *Selected Writings of Edward Sapir, Language,* **27** (1951), 289–92; and of S. Newman, "Yokuts Language of California," *International Journal of American Linguistics,* **10** (1944), 196–211.

[6]An opposition has sometimes been claimed between real facts and mathematical manipulation of structure. This claim ignores the fact that science is (among other things) a process of indicating much data by few general statements and that mathematical methods are often useful in achieving this. Mathematical and other methods of arranging data are not a game but essential parts of the activity of science.

[7]As pointed out by K. Goldstein, *Language and Language Disturbances* (New York: Gruwe & Stratton, 1948).

sets). There are also evidences of perception of sounds in terms of their morpho-phonemic memberships.[8]

A reasonable expectation is that the distributional structure should exist in the speakers in the sense of reflecting their speaking habits.[9] Indeed, responses along the lines of distributional structure can be found in experimental psychology work.[10] However, speakers differ in the details of distributional perception. One speaker may associate the stem of *nation* with that of *native*, while another may not. Should the morpheme analysis be different for the two idiolects (individual dialects)? Even if we take the speaking habits to be some kind of social summation over the behaviors (and habits) of all the individuals, we may not find it possible to discover all these habits except by investigating the very speech events which we had hoped to corre-late with the (independently discovered) habits.

If, as Hockett proposes, we measure the habits by the new utterances which had not been used in the structural description, we have indeed a possible and sensible measure; and this applies both to real productivity (the use of elements in environ-ments in which they had not occurred before) and to arbitrarily unused data (utter-ances which may have occurred before, but which had not been used in deriving the distributional structure). However, even when our structure can predict new utter-ances, we do not know that it always reflects a previously existing neural association in the speakers (different from the associations which do not, at a given time, produce new utterances). For example, before the word *analyticity* came to be used (in modern logic), our data on English may have contained *analytic, synthetic, periodic, periodi-city, simplicity*, and the like. On this basis we would have made some statement about the distributional relation of *-ic* to *-ity*, and the new formation of *analyticity* may have conformed to this statement. But this means only that the pattern or the habit existed in the speakers at the time of the new formation, not necessarily before; the *habit*—the readiness to combine these elements productively—may have developed only when the need arose, by association of words that were partially similar as to composition and environment.

For the position of the speakers is after all similar to that of the linguist. They have heard (and used) a great many utterances among which they perceive partial similarities—parts which occur in various combinations with each other. They pro-duce new combinations of these along the lines of the ones they have heard. The formation of new utterances in the language is therefore based on the distributional relations—as changeably perceived by the speakers—among the parts of the pre-viously heard utterances.[11]

Concerning any habit, i.e., any predisposition to form new combinations along particular distributional lines rather than others, we know about its existence in the

---

[8]E.g., in E. Sapir, "La réalité psychologique des phonèmes," *Journal de Psychologie Normale et Pathologique*, **30** (1933), 247–65 (translated in D. Mandelbaum, ed., *Selected Writings of Edward Sapir*, 46–60).

[9]C. F. Hockett, review of "*Recherches Structurales*," *International Journal of American Linquis-tics*, **18** (1952), 98.

[10]As pointed out to the writer by A. W. Holt.

[11]This applies to the grammatical innovation involved in new formations; the selection of mor-phemes within a class is determined not only by these *grammatical* associations, but also semantic-ally. Cf. the first paragraph of Section 1 above.

speakers only if we have some outside evidence (such as association tests), or if new formations of the type in question have been formed by these speakers. The frequency of slips, new formations, and so on is enough to make us feel that the bulk of the major structural features are indeed reflected in speaking habits—habits which are presumably based, like the linguist's analysis, on the distributional facts. Aside from this, all we know about any particular language habit is the probability that new formations will be along certain distributional lines rather than others, and this is no more than testing the success of our distributional structure in predicting new data or formations. The particular distributional structure which best predicts new formations will be of greatest interest from many (not all) points of view; but this is not the same as saying that all of that structure exists in the speakers at any particular time prior to the new formations.[12]

DISTRIBUTION AND MEANING

3   Is there a parallel meaning structure? While the distinction between descriptive (synchronic) structure and historical change is by now well known, the distinction between distributional structure and meaning is not yet always clear. Meaning is not a unique property of language, but a general characteristic of human activity. It is true that language has a special relation to meaning, both in the sense of the classification of aspects of experience and in the sense of communication. But the relation is not simple. For example, we can compare the structures of languages with the structure of the physical world (e.g., the kind of phenomena that are expressed by differentiation and integration in calculus) or with what we know about the structure of human response (e.g., association, transference). In either case, it would be clear that the structure of one language or another does not conform in many respects to the structure of physical nature or of human response—that is, to the structure of objective experience from which we presumably draw our meanings. And if we consider the individual aspects of experience, the way a person's store of meanings grows and changes through the years while his language remains fairly constant or the way a person can have an idea or a feeling which he cannot readily express in the language available to him, we see that the structure of language does not necessarily conform to the structure of subjective experience, of the subjective world of meanings.[13]

---

[12]Here we have discussed whether the distributional structure exists in the speakers as a parallel system of habits of speaking and of productivity. This is quite different from the dubious suggestion made at various times that the categories of language determine the speakers' categories of perception, a suggestion which may be a bit of occupational imperialism for linguistics and which is not seriously testable as long as we have so little knowledge about people's categories of perception. Cf., for the suggestion, B. L. Whorf, "The Relation of Habitual Thought and Behavior to Language," A. I. Hallowell, L. Spier, S. Newman, eds., *Language, Culture and Personality*, pp. 75–93; and against it, E. H. Lennenberg, "Cognition in Ethnolinguistics," *Language*, **29** (1953), 463–71; L. S. Feuer, "Sociological Aspects of the Relation between Language and Philosophy," *Philosophy of Science*, **20** (1953), 85–100.

[13]In E. G. Schachtel's "On Memory and Childhood Amnesia," *Psychiatry*, **10** (1947), 1–26, it is suggested that the experiences of infancy are not recallable in later life because the selection of aspects of experience and the classification of experience embodied in language, which fixes experience for recall, differs from the way events and observations are experienced (and categorized) by the infant.

All this is not to say that there is not a great interconnection between language and meaning, in whatever sense it may be possible to use this word. But it is not a one-to-one relation between morphological structure and anything else. There is not even a one-to-one relation between the vocabulary and any independent classification of meaning; we cannot say that each morpheme or word has a single or central meaning or even that it has a continuous or coherent range of meanings. Accidents of sound change, homonymity, borrowing, forgotten metaphors, and the like can give diverse meanings to a number of phonemic occurrences which we have to consider as occurrences of the same morpheme. Aside from this, if we consider the suggestion of Kurt Goldstein[14] that there are two separate uses and meanings of language—the concrete (e.g., by certain brain-injured patients) and the abstract—it would follow that the same grammatical structure and much the same vocabulary can carry quite different types of speaking activity.

The correlation between language and meaning is much greater when we consider connected discourse. To the extent that formal (distributional) structure can be discovered in discourse, it correlates in some way with the substance of what is being said; this is especially evident in stylized scientific discourse (e.g., reports on experimental work) and above all in the formal discourses (proofs) of mathematics and logic. However, this is not the same thing as saying that the distributional structure of language (phonology, morphology, and at most a small amount of discourse structure) conforms in some one-to-one way with some independently discoverable structure of meaning. If one wishes to speak of language as existing in some sense on two planes—of form and of meaning—we can at least say that the structures of the two are not identical, though they will be found similar in various respects.

4 Are morphemes determined by meaning? Since there is no independently known structure of meanings which exactly parallels linguistic structure, we cannot mix distributional investigations with occasional assists from meaning whenever the going is hard. For example, if the morphemic composition of a word is not easily determined, we cannot decide the matter by seeing what are the component meanings of the word and assigning one morpheme to each. Do *persist, person* contain one morpheme each or two? In terms of meaning it would be difficult to decide, and the decision would not necessarily fit into any resulting structure. In terms of distribution we have *consist, resist, pertain, contain, retain*, and the like (related in phonemic composition and in sentence environment), but no such set for *person*; hence, we take *persist* as two morphemes, *person* as one.

Although rough indications of meaning are often used heuristically to guess at the morphemes of a word or utterance, the decision as to morphemic composition is always based on a check of what sections of that word or utterance are substitutable in a structured (patterned) way in that environment, as roughly indicated in the example above.

Where the meanings (in most cases, the translations) are not immediately suggestive, the analysis is laboriously distributional without any heuristic aids to test.

---

[14]*Human Nature in the Light of Psychopathology*, The William James Lectures for 1938–39, Chap. 3.

For example, in the Cherokee verb prefixes we find scores of forms,[15] e.g., /agwalə-nə́ʔəgi/ "I started," /sdəgadhénoha/ "I and another are searching for you," /sdəgad-hénohəgi/ "I searched for you two." These have obviously personal reference, but it is impossible to separate a small set of phonemic segments which will mean "I" or "I as subject," "I as object," and so on. It is nevertheless possible to discover the morphemes distributionally. First, we identify the words by their distributional relation to the rest of the sentence. We find that certain words with many different stems and a few different prefixes have certain types of environment in common. For example /zinəgali'a/ "I am cleaning" and /agiyoseha/ "I am hungry" occur in certain environments in which /uniyoseha/ "they are hungry" does not occur. We take a set of words each with different stems but which have the same environment in the sense referred to above. We will assume that the sameness in this feature of the environment correlates with some morphemic part that is the same in all these words (and is obviously not the stem).[16] This means that the different prefixes of these words contain alternants of the same morpheme; and we try to state a morphophonemic relation between /z/, /(a)g/, and so on, giving the environing conditions (in phonemic rather than morphemic terms if possible) in which each alternant occurs: we write the morpheme {z} and translate it "I." Another set, containing, e.g., /ozinəgali'a/ "I and others are cleaning," /ogiyoseha/ "I and others are hungry," would thus be analyzed (in the same manner, but with the aid of {z}) as containing two morphemes, {o} "others" and {z} "I." If we now turn to the set containing /osdinəgali'a/ "I and another are cleaning," /oginiyoseha/ "I and another are hungry," our morphophonemic knowledge about {z} enables us to separate out /d/, /n/, and so on, as alternants of some third morpheme {n}, with undetermined meaning. In /iginiyoseha/ "you and I are hungry" our known morphophonemics enables us to analyze the prefix as an alternant of {z} plus an alternant of this same {n}, where it seems to have the meaning "you." However, in /hinəgali'a/ "you (singular) are cleaning" we are unable to fit the /h/ into the morphophonemic regularities of {n}, and thus set up a new morpheme {h} "you"; and in /sdinəgali'a/ "you two are cleaning" we can satisfy the morphophonemic regularities by saying that there are two morphemes: the /s/ alternant of {h} plus the /d/ alternant of {n}.

In this way we can divide each prefix into a unique combination of morphophonemic alternants of the following morphemes: {z} "I," {h} "you (singular)," {a} "third person singular," {i} "plural" (always including "you," at least due to absence of {o}), {o} roughly "person(s) excluding you," {n} roughly "another person, you as first choice." These morphemes were obtained as solutions to the environmental regularities of the prefixed phonemes. The translations offered above are an attempt to assign a single meaning to each on the basis of the meanings of all those words in

---

[15]The following analysis can be fully understood only if one checks through the actual lists of Cherokee forms. The few forms cited here are taken from W. D. Reyburn, "Cherokee Verb Morphology II," *International Journal of American Linguistics*, **19** (1953), 259–73. For the analysis, see the charts and comments in Reyburn's work and in Z. S. Harris, "Cherokee Skeletal Grammar" and "Cherokee Grammatical Word Lists and Utterances" in the Franz Boas Collection of the American Philosophical Society Library.

[16]This assumption is based on the fact that each morpheme has a different distribution (Section 2.3), so that same feature of environment points to the same morpheme.

which it occurs. If we write the prefixes morphophonemically, then the meanings of some of the occurring combinations are: {*ozn*} (phonemically /*osd*/, etc.) "I and he," {*oz*} "I and they," {*zn*} "I and you (singular)" {*iz*} "I, you, and they," {*h*} "you (singular)," {*hn*} "you two," {*in*} "you (plural)." From this we can try to extract (as above) a single meaning contribution which {*n*} or {*o*} or {*i*} bring to each combination in which they are included. But it was not the isolation of these complicated central meanings (if that is always nontrivially possible) that led us to recognize {*n*}, etc., as morphemes. We do not even know that these central meanings exist for the speakers: the speakers may be subjectively using two homonymous {*n*} morphemes, or they may be using these prefix combinations as fixed whole entities with only a vague impression of the phonemic and morphophonemic regularities[17].

So far, we have not touched the great majority of verb forms, those which have objects together with the subjects. By using the morphophonemic relations established previously, we are able to extract the morphemes above from some of these new combinations, and small extensions of the morphophonemics reveal these morphemes in yet other combinations. Then we analyze the prefix in /gəiha/ "I am killing you" as {*z*} + {*n*}, and in /sgwúsədohda/ "you covered me" as {*h*} + {*z*}; and certain order statements about the two prefix components indicate the subject-object relation. The remaining phonemes of some of these prefixes can be grouped by rather simple morphophonemics into a few additional morphemes like {*g*} "animate object"; and so we finally obtain a morphemic analysis of all the prefixes. This analysis does not necessarily correlate with any meaning units we may have in mind about person and number. For example, it gives the same morphemes {*znn*} for the prefix in /sdəgadhénoha/ "I and another are searching for you (whether singular or dual but not plural)" and in /sdəgadhénohəgi/ "I searched for you two." Even if we find different phonemes with different meanings, e.g., /izə-gow'diha/ "I and he see you (plural)" and /izəy-olighi/ "I and they know you (singular)" the analysis may say that these are alternants of the same morphemic composition {*izn*}; in that case both meanings can be obtained for each form.

The methods indicated so sketchily above suggest how the morphemic composition of a word or utterance can be determined by the occurrence of each phoneme sequence relative to others: e.g., *per, con* relative to *sist, tain*; or /z/ /gi/, /o/, etc., relative to various features of environment which are common to /z/ and /gi/ as against /o/. The final decision as to morphemic analysis always depends on this relative occurrence of phoneme sequences, since the grammar then proceeds to state compactly the relative occurrence of the morphemes. That is, we set up as morphemes those phonemic sequences (or features) such that all utterances are compactly statable relative occurrences of them.

The chief difficulty with this is that it provides us only with a criterion that tells us whether a given phoneme sequence is a morpheme or not; more exactly, whether a particular segmentation of an utterance (once we propose it) divides it into morphemic segments. It does not provide us with a procedure which will directly yield a morphemic segmentation of an utterance. There is available, however, a procedure

---

[17]Since new formations of these combinations do not appear, we cannot apply the productivity tests of Section 3 to discover the speakers' morphemic recognition.

which yields most if not all of the morphemic segmentations of an utterance. In outline it is as follows: given any test utterance, associate many utterances whose first phoneme is the same as that of the test utterance, and note how many different phonemes follow the first in these utterances. Then consider utterances whose first two phonemes are the same as the first two of the test utterance, and note how many different phonemes follow the first two in these, and so on. If after the first n phonemes the number of different phonemes which follow the nth (in the associated utterances) is greater than the number after the first $n - 1$ phonemes or the first $n + 1$, then we place a tentative morpheme boundary after the nth. Various operations are needed to correct and check the correctness of each result; but together with the final test of patterned relative occurrence, this yields the morphemes of a language without any reference to meaning or informant response.

5 Meaning as a function of distribution. Distribution suffices to determine the phonemes and morphemes and to state a grammar in terms of them. However, both (a) in determining the elements and (b) in stating the relations between them, it turns out that the distributional structure does not give ideal coverage. It must either leave many details unsaid or else become extremely complicated. For example: (a) Morphemes are determined on the basis of a patterned independence (replaceability in utterances) in respect to other morphemes (or phoneme sequences); but not all morphemes have the same degree of independence—compare *hood* (*boyhood*) with *ness* (*bigness*). (b) The grammatical statements group morphemes into classes and then say that certain sequences of these classes occur; but not every member of the one class occurs (in any actual body of data) with every member of the other—not every adjective occurs with every noun. Finally, we may mention one other respect in which distribution fails to cover all the facts about speech occurrence. (c) We can state distributional regularities only within narrow domains—for phonology usually the immediately neighboring phonemes, for morphology usually the sentence or some part of the sentence.

At all these points where simple distributional regularities are no longer discoverable, people often revert to the position of our man in the street (Section 1) and say that here the only determinant is meaning: (a) *hood* has a meaning which ties it to certain few nouns; (b) with a given noun, e.g., *doctor*, there will be used those adjectives that make sense with it; (c) beyond the sentence there are no significant formal restrictions on what one says, and sentences are strung along purely according to meaning. Now meaning is of course a determinant in these and in other choices that we make when we speak. But as we make these choices we build a stock of utterances each of which is a particular combination of particular elements. And this stock of combinations of elements becomes a factor in the way later choices are made (in the sense indicated in the last two paragraphs of Section 2), for language is not merely a bag of words but a tool with particular properties which have been fashioned in the course of its use. The linguist's work is precisely to discover these properties, whether for descriptive analysis or for the synthesis of a quasi-linguistic system. As Leonard Bloomfield pointed out, it frequently happens that when we do not rest with the explanation that something is due to meaning, we discover that it has a formal regularity or "explanation." It may still be "due to meaning" in one sense, but it accords with a distributional regularity.

If we investigate in this light the areas where there are no simple distributional regularities, we will often find interesting distributional relations, relations which tell us something about the occurrence of elements and which correlate with some aspect of meaning. In certain important cases it will even prove possible to state certain aspects of meaning as functions of measurable distributional relations.

(a) There are different degrees of independence (Section 8). We find complete dependence in the various phonemes of one morpheme or in the various parts of a discontinuous morpheme (including grammatical agreement). In *hood* we have sufficient independence to make it a separate morpheme, but it is limited to very few predecessors. In *ness* there is more independence. The degree of independence of a morpheme is a distributional measure of the number of different morphemes with which it occurs and of the degree to which they are spread out over various classes or subclasses. The various members of a distributional class or subclass have some element of meaning in common, which is stronger the more distributional characteristics the class has. The major classes have the kind of common meanings that are associated, say, with the words *noun* or *adjective*.

(b) The fact that, for example, not every adjective occurs with every noun can be used as a measure of meaning difference. For it is not merely that different members of the one class have different selections of members of the other class with which they are actually found. More than that: if we consider words or morphemes *A* and *B* to be more different in meaning than *A* and *C*, then we will often find that the distributions of *A* and *B* are more different than the distributions of *A* and *C*. In other words, difference of meaning correlates with difference of distribution.

If we consider *oculist* and *eye doctor*[18] we find that, as our corpus of actually occurring utterances grows, these two occur in almost the same environments, except for such sentences as *An oculist is just an eye doctor under a fancier name*, or *I told him Burns was an oculist, but since he didn't know the professional titles, he didn't realize that he could go to him to have his eyes examined*. If we ask informants for any words that may occupy the same place as *oculist* in sentences like the above (i.e., have these same environments), we will not in general obtain *eye doctor*; but in almost any other sentence we would. In contrast, there are many sentence environments in which *oculist* occurs but *lawyer* does not; e.g., *I've had my eyes examined by the same oculist for twenty years*, or *Oculists often have their prescription blanks printed for them by opticians*. It is not a question of whether the above sentence with *lawyer* substituted is true or not; it might be true in some situation. It is rather a question of the relative frequency of such environments with *oculist* and with *lawyer* or of whether we will obtain *lawyer* here if we ask an informant to substitute any words he wishes for *oculist* (not asking what words have the same meaning). These and similar tests all measure the probability of particular environments occurring with particular elements, i.e., they measure the selections of each element.

It is impossible to obtain more than a rough approximation of the relatively common selection of a given word (with almost no indication of its rarer selection). But it

---

[18]This particular pair was suggested to me by Y. Bar-Hillel, who, however, considers that distributional correlates of meaning differences cannot be established.

is possible to measure how similar are the selection approximations of any two words (within various sets of data). If for two elements *A* and *B* we obtain almost the same list of particular environments (selection), except that the environment of *A* always contains some *X* which never occurs in the environment of *B*, we say that *A* and *B* are (complementary) alternants of each other, e.g., *knife* and *knive-*. If *A* and *B* have identical environments throughout (in terms of our data tests), we say that they are free variants, e.g., perhaps for /ekənamiks/ and /iykənamiks/ *economics*. If the environments of *A* are always different in some regular way from the environments of *B*, we state some relation between *A* and *B* depending on this regular type of difference, e.g., *ain't* and *am not* have frequent differences of a certain type in their environments (*ain't goin'* but *am not going*) which we would call dialectal. If *A* and *B* have almost identical environments except chiefly for sentences which contain both, we say they are synonyms: *oculist* and *eye doctor*. If *A* and *B* have some environments in common and some not (e.g., *oculist* and *lawyer*), we say that they have different meanings, the amount of meaning difference corresponding roughly to the amount of difference in their environments. (This latter amount would depend on the numerical relation of different to same environments, with more weight being given to differences of selectional subclasses.) If *A* and *B* never have the same environment, we say that they are members of two different grammatical classes (this aside from homonymity and from any stated position where both these classes can occur).

While much more has to be said in order to establish constructional methods for such a classification as above, these remarks may suffice to show how it is possible to use the detailed distributional facts about each morpheme. Though we cannot list all the co-occurrents (selection) of a particular morpheme or define its meaning fully on the basis of these, we can measure roughly the difference in selection between elements, say something about their difference in meaning, and also (above and Section 12) derive certain structural information.

(c) If we investigate the relative occurrence of any part of one sentence in respect to any part of the neighboring sentences in the same discourse, we will find that there are certain regularities (Section 10 end). The sequence of sentences is not entirely arbitrary; there are even certain elements (e.g., pronouns) whose occurrence (and meaning) is specifically related to the grammatically restricted occurrence of certain other morphemes in the neighboring sentences (Section 12, first paragraph). Such regularities (and meanings) will not extend from one discourse to another (except to another related in some relevant way to the first, successive lectures of a series). A consecutive (or seriate) discourse of one or more persons is thus the fullest environmental unit for distributional investigation.[19]

---

[19]It should be clear that only after we discover what kinds of distributional regularities there are among successive elements or sections in discourses can we attempt any organized semantic interpretation of the successions discovered. Various types of discourses have various types of succession (of sentences, clauses, or other intervals). In mathematics and the constructed "languages" of logic, certain conditions are imposed on what sentences can appear in succession in their connected discourses (proofs); each sentence (line in a proof) has to be a theorem or else derived from a preceding sentence in a particular way. This situation does not hold for natural languages, where the truth-value of logic is not kept constant through successive sentences and where the types of succession are more varied.

DISTRIBUTIONAL ANALYSIS

We now review briefly the basic analysis applicable to distributional facts.

6 Element. The first distributional fact is that it is possible to divide (to segment) any flow of speech into parts, in such a way that we can find some regularities in the occurrence of one part relative to others in the flow of speech. These parts are the discrete elements which have a certain distribution (set of relative locations) in the flow of speech; and each bit of speech is a particular combination of elements. The first operation is purely segmenting, arbitrary if need be. The first step of segmenting has to be independent of any particular distributional criterion, since we cannot speak of distributional relations until we have not only segments, but also a similarity grouping of them (Section 7). After the first segmenting of utterances, each segment is unique and has a unique environment (completely different from every other one); after the segments have been compared, and *similar* ones grouped together, we find that various of these similarity groupings have partially similar and partially different environments. Hence we can speak about the distributional relations of these similarity groupings.

If we wish to be able, in the later operations (Sections 8 and 9), to obtain elements (or classes of elements) whose distributions will have maximum regularity, we have to divide not only the time flow into successive portions, but also any single time segment (or succession of time segments) into simultaneous components (of one segment length, e.g., a tone, or longer, e.g., a pitch-stress contour). After we have set up the phonetically more obvious segmentations and simultaneities and have studied their distribution, we may find that more regular distributions can be obtained if we change our original segmentation of elements, even to ones that are phonetically less obvious and even if some of our adjusted elements become components which extend over various numbers of other elements.

7 Similarity. Another essential distributional fact is that some elements are similar to others in terms of certain tests, or are similar in the sense that if we group these similar elements into sets (*similarity groupings*), the distribution of all members of a set (in respect to other sets) will be the same as far as we can discover. This ultimately reduces to the similarity of sound segments under repetition or in the pair test, x_1 is similar to x_2, but not to y_1 if, when one native speaker repeats x_1z, x_2z, y_1z, . . ., a second speaker can guess correctly whether x_1z as against y_1z is being said, but not whether x_1z as against x_2z is being said. We call x_1 and x_2 free variants of each other (or members of a similarity grouping). Note that the pair test involves discrimination of sound but not of meaning.

8 Dependence (serial). To obtain a least set of elements sufficient for description we join any elements which are completely dependent: if A is a set of similar elements (a similarity grouping) and so is B, and (in a particular type of environment) only AB occurs (not necessarily contiguously), never A or B alone, then we set up AB as a single element (a single set of similar elements). Thereafter we don't have any two elements which are completely dependent upon each other in occurrence. But our elements have various degrees of dependence; for each element we can say that any utterance (or shorter domain) which contains it will also contain such and such other classes. For example, morpheme A may occur always close to (i.e., within a statable distance from) any one of a few or many B_1, B_2, ... If the sequence B_1A occurs in environments X, it may be that B_1 by itself also occurs in X (e.g., *kingdom* and *king*), or that B_1 does not (e.g., *kingly* and *king*).The B_1 with which A occurs may all have the same types of environment when they occur without A (e.g., all predecessors of *dom* are nouns), or some may have one type and some another (e.g., *ish* occurs with both nouns and adjectives). These are a few of the various degrees and types of occurrence-dependence which an element can have to the elements that occur in the same utterances as it does.

9 Substitutability (parallel). It will in general appear that various elements have identical types of occurrence-dependence. We group A and B into a substitution set whenever A and B each have the same (or partially same) environments X (X being, at first, elements and later, substitution sets of elements) within a statable domain of the flow of speech. This enables us to speak of the occurrence-dependence of a whole set of elements in respect to other such sets of elements. Some of the types of partial sameness of environment were listed in Section 5(b).

The elements of distributional structure are usually obtained by the operations of Section 6, Section 7, and the first paragraph of Section 8. The distributional relations are usually combinations of Sections 8 and 9. For example, *hood* occurs after few morphemes N_1, N_2, . . . of a certain substitution set (nouns), *ish* after many of them, *s* and its alternants after all or almost all of them. N_i + *hood* or N_i + *s* occur in the same large environments in which N_i occur alone. But N_i + *ish* occur in different environments than N_i alone; however *ish* also occurs after many members of another substitution set, A_1, A_2, . . . (adjectives), and both N_i + *ish* and A_i + *ish* occur in the larger environments of A_i alone.

10 Domains. All the statements about dependence and substitutability apply within some specified domain, the domain being determined either by nature (e.g., silence before and after an utterance) or by the types of environment within which there is regularity (e.g., the narrow restriction of *hood* is only to what precedes it and only to the first morpheme in that direction). It is often possible to state the co-occurrences of elements within a domain in such a way that that domain then becomes the element whose co-occurrences are regular within a larger domain, e.g., the occurrences of stems and suffixes within word-length and of words within phrases. Common types of domain are the word, phrase, and clause. In many cases the stretches of speech covered by certain long pitch and stress components (or fixed sequences of short pitch and stress components) are identical with the domains of distributional relations—word, sentence.

Although grammar has generally stopped with the sentence, it is possible to find distributional regularities in larger domains. There are certain sentence sequences in which the second can be described as a fixed modification of the first (e.g., with certain restrictions, in the case of questions and answers in English). There are certain types of distributional relation (e.g., between English active and passive, between *buy* and *sell*) which have particular kinds of regularity in (not necessarily immediately) neighboring sentences. For example, if one sentence contains noun A + active (transitive) verb B + noun C, and a neighboring sentence contains C + verb + A, there is a certain likelihood that the verb will be the passive of B; or if the neighboring sentence contains *C* + the passive of *B* + some noun, there is a certain likelihood that the second noun will be *A* or some noun which elsewhere in that discourse has similar individual environments (selection) to those of *A*. And if one sentence contains *A buys B from C*, and a neighboring sentence contains *C sells B to* + some noun, there is a good likelihood that the noun will be *A* or an environmentally similar noun (and given *C* + some verb + *B to A*, we may expect the verb to be *sell* or some environmentally similar one).[20]

Finally, if we take a whole connected discourse as environment, we find that there are certain substitution sets of morphemes which occur regularly (relative to the other sets) throughout the discourse or some portion of it;[21] these are not the major substitution sets of the language (e.g., nouns) or its grammatical subclasses, but new groupings which are often relevant only to that one discourse. And there are certain sequences of these sets which constitute the subdomains of the discourse, i.e., such that the sets are regular within these intervals and the intervals are regular within the discourse; these intervals are not necessarily sentences or clauses in the sense of grammatical structure. The regularities in a discourse are far weaker and less interrelated than those within a sentence; but they show that occurrence-dependence (and the environment relevant for distribution) can extend throughout a whole discourse.

11 Data. The distributional investigations sketched above are carried out by recording utterances (as stretches of changing sound) and comparing them for partial similarities. We do not ask a speaker whether his language contains certain elements or whether they have certain dependences or substitutabilities. Even though his "speaking habits" (Section 2) yield regular utterances, they are not sufficiently close to all the distributional details, nor is the speaker sufficiently aware of them. Hence we cannot directly investigate the rules of "the language" via some system of habits or some neurological machine that generates all the utterances of the language. We have to investigate some actual corpus of utterances and derive therefrom such regularities as would have generated these utterances—and would presumably generate other utterances of the language than the ones in our corpus. Statements about distribution are always made on the basis of a corpus of occurring utterances; one hopes that these statements will also apply to other utterances which may occur naturally. Thus when we say that the selectional difference in *oculist/lawyer* is greater than in *oculist/ eye doctor* (Section 5) or that the selection of nouns around the passive verb is the same as the selection around the active verb but with inverted order (Section

---

[20]Such relations as that of active to passive, or *buy* to *sell*, are essentially substitutability relations (Section 9), i.e., they show that certain elements have similar environments (e.g., partially inverted ones). The fact that they may appear in neighboring sentences is a serial relation (Section 8) which is a secondary characteristic of certain substitutabilities. Relations like that of active to passive are different from the essentially serial relations of successive intervals of a discourse, discussed at the end of Section 10.

[21]The fact that a discourse contains several or many occurrences of a given substitution class, often in parallel positions, brings out a rare relation in linguistics: the order of occurrence of various members of the same class. Something like this comes up in compound nouns or in successions of two or more adjectives (sometimes with preferred order). Usually, if two members of a class occur in one domain, their order is not regular (e.g., in most cases of *N and N*); but in compound nouns, for instance, certain members are frequent in the first *N* position and others in the second.

12) we mean that these relations will be approximated in any sufficiently large corpus (especially one built with the aid of eliciting) and that they will presumably apply to any sufficiently large additions to the corpus.

In much linguistic work we require for comparison various utterances which occur so infrequently that searching for them in an arbitrary corpus is prohibitively laborious. To get around this, we can use various techniques of eliciting, i.e., techniques which favor the appearance of utterances relevant to the feature we are investigating (without influencing the speaker in any manner that might bring out utterances which would not have sometimes occurred naturally). In particular, investigations of the selections of particular morphemes (Section 5, 12) can hardly be carried out without the aid of eliciting. Eliciting is a method of testing whether a certain utterance (which is relevant to our investigation) would occur naturally. In effect, we try to provide a speaker with an environment in which he could say that utterance—if he ever would naturally say it—without extracting it from him if he wouldn't. For example, if we are testing the active/passive relation we might offer a speaker noun A_1 + transitive verb B_1 and ask him to complete the sentence in many ways, obtaining a particular selection C_1, C_2 . . . after the verb. Then we can offer a speaker the passive verb B_1 + A_1 and ask him to begin the sentence in many ways, checking whether we get about the same selection C_1, C_2, . . . before the verb. We can repeat this for various A_i, and then for various B_i.

DISTRIBUTIONAL RELATIONS

The methods of Sections 6 to 11 yield first of all a representation of each utterance as a combination of elements. They also yield a set of statements about the utterances: what elements and regularities of combination suffice to represent the utterances. One can go beyond this and study the kinds of regularities and the kinds of relations among elements. As was pointed out at the end of Section 5(b), certain correlations may be discovered even in those distributional facts which are too individual to be directly useful.

12 As an example of the latter we may consider selectional similarity. For instance, it is impossible to list all the verbs that follow each particular noun or all the verbs that follow *who*. But it is possible to state the following relation between the verb selection of nouns and the verb selection of *who*. Under an eliciting test as in Section 11, we will get after *the pianist*—much the same verbs as we will get after *the pianist who*—and so for every noun. This means that the verb selection of *who* is the same as the verb selection of the noun preceding *who*. We have here a distributional characteristic that distinguishes such pronominal elements from ordinary nouns.

Or, we may consider the active/passive relation mentioned in Section 11. If we take a large number of sentences containing a transitive verb in English, e.g., *The kids broke that window last week*, we can elicit sentences consisting of the same verb but with the passive morpheme, the same nouns before and after it but in reverse order, and the same remainder of the sentence, e.g., *That window was broken by the kids last week*. Some of these sentences may be stylistically clumsy, so that they would not occur unless some special circumlocution were involved; but they are obtainable by otherwise valid eliciting techniques.[22] In contrast, if we seek such inversion without the passive, we will fail to elicit many sentences; we can get *The kids saw Mary last week* and *Mary saw the kids last week*, but to *The kids saw the movie* we will never— or hardly ever—get *The movie saw the kids* (even though this sentence is grammatical). Or, if we seek such selectional similarity (with or without inversion) for *broke/will break* or the like, we will find the same selection as to preceding and following nouns, but not always as to the rest of the sentence: *The kids broke that window* and *The kids will break that window*, but not *The kids will break that window last week* or *The kids broke that window if they don't watch out*. It thus appears that, using only distributional information about an ordinarily elicited corpus, we can find a relation between the active verb and the passive verb which is different from the relation between *-ed* and *will*.

13 The distributional regularities can themselves be a subject of study. One can consider recurrent types of dependence and substitutabilities that are found in a language (or in many languages) and find on one level such relations as *subject* and *object* (semantic names for distributional positions) and on a higher level of generality such relations as *constituent* and *head of a construction* (if *A* occurs in environment *X* and *AB* does too, but *B* does not, then *A* is the head of *AB*). One can consider the parts of a grammar which permit alternative distributional analyses and check their relation to language change and dialect or idiolect interrelations (since probably every linguistic structure has some points which are structurally in flux). One can investigate what are the structural characteristics of those parts of a language which are productive. Furthermore, one can survey what is similar and what is different in a great many language structures and how linguistic systems in general differ from such partially similar systems as mathematics and logistic "languages," sign languages, gestures, codes, and music.

---

[22]There will be a few exceptions where the passive is not obtainable. And if we try to elicit the active on the basis of the passive, we run into the difficulty of distinguishing between *by* of the passive (*The letter was finished by Carl*) and *by* as preposition (*The letter was finished by noon*).

3   Current Issues In Linguistic Theory*

Noam Chomsky

I. GOALS OF LINGUISTIC THEORY

1.1 In this paper,[1] I will restrict the term "linguistic theory" to systems of hypotheses concerning the general features of human language put forth in an attempt to account for a certain range of linguistic phenomena. I will not be concerned with systems of terminology or methods of investigation (analytic procedures).

The central fact to which any significant linguistic theory must address itself is this: a mature speaker can produce a new sentence of his language on the appropriate occasion, and other speakers can understand it immediately, though it is equally new to them. Most of our linguistic experience, both as speakers and hearers, is with new sentences; once we have mastered a language, the class of sentences with which we can operate fluently and without difficulty or hesitation is so vast that for all practical purposes (and, obviously, for all theoretical purposes), we can regard it as infinite. Normal mastery of a language involves not only the ability to understand immediately an indefinite number of entirely new sentences, but also the ability to identify deviant sentences and, on occasion, to impose an interpretation on them.[2]

---

*A revised and expanded version of a report presented to the session: *The logical basis of linguistic theory*, Ninth International Congress of Linguists (Cambridge, Mass.), 1962.

[1]This work was supported in part by the U.S. Army, the Air Force Office of Scientific Research, and the Office of Naval Research; and in part by the National Science Foundation (Grant G–13903).

The account of linguistic structure sketched below in part incorporates, and in part developed in response to many stimulating ideas of Zellig Harris and Roman Jakobson. Its present form is to a large extent a product of collaboration over many years with Morris Halle, to whom (along with Paul Postal and John Viertel) I am indebted for much helpful criticism of this paper. For references, see bibliography at the end of the paper.

[2]Cf. Chomsky (1955, chapter 4, 1961b), Ziff-(1961), Putnam (1961), Miller and Chomsky (1963). Apparently many linguists hold that if a context can be constructed in which an interpretation can be imposed on an utterance, then it follows that this utterance is not to be distinguished, for the purposes of study of grammar, from perfectly normal sentences. Thus, e.g., "colorless green ideas sleep furiously," "remorse felt John," "the dog looks barking," etc., are not to be distinguished, in this view, from "revolutionary new ideas appear infrequently," "John felt remorse," "the dog looks frightening," though the distinction can clearly be both stated and motivated on syntactic

It is evident that rote recall is a factor of minute importance in ordinary use of language, that "a minimum of the *sentences* which we utter is learnt by heart as such—that most of them, on the contrary, are composed on the spur of the moment," and that "one of the fundamental errors of the old science of language was to deal with all human utterances, as long as they remain constant to the common usage, as with something merely reproduced by memory" (Paul, 1886, 97.8). In this remark, it is only the reference to "the old science of language" that is subject to qualification. In fact, the realization that this "creative" aspect of language is its essential characteristic can be traced back at least to the seventeenth century. Thus we find the Cartesian view that man alone is more than mere automatism, and that it is the possession of true language that is the primary indicator of this (see Descartes, *Discourse on Method*, part V), developed by a follower along these lines (Cordemoy, 1668): "if the organs . . . had a certain settled order among them [i.e., if man were a "language-producing engine" such as, for example, an artificial speaking machine, rocks that produce an echo, or, to a confirmed Cartesian like Cordemoy, a parrot], they could never change it, so that when the first voice were heard, those that were wont to follow it would needs be heard also . . . whereas the words which I hear utter'd by Bodies, made like mine, have almost never the same sequel" (6) ". . . to speak, is not to repeat the same words, which have struck the ear, but to utter others to their purpose and suitable to them" (13). In any event, whatever the antiquity of this insight may be, it is clear that a theory of language that neglects this "creative" aspect of language is of only marginal interest.

On the basis of a limited experience with the data of speech, each normal human has developed for himself a thorough competence in his native language. This competence can be represented, to an as yet undetermined extent, as a system of rules that we can call the *grammar* of his language. To each phonetically possible utterance (cf. Section 4.2), the grammar assigns a certain *structural description* that specifies the linguistic elements of which it is constituted and their structural relations (or, in the case of structural ambiguity, several such structural descriptions). For some utterances, the structural description will indicate, in particular, that they are perfectly well-formed sentences. This set we can call the *language generated by the grammar*. To others, the grammar will assign structural descriptions that indicate the manner of their deviation from perfect well-formedness. Where the deviation is sufficiently limited, an interpretation can often be imposed by virtue of formal relations to sentences of the generated language.

The grammar, then, is a device that (in particular) specifies the infinite set of well-formed sentences and assigns to each of these one or more structural descriptions. Perhaps we should call such a device a *generative grammar* to distinguish it from descriptive statements that merely present the inventory of elements that appear in structural descriptions, and their contextual variants.

The generative grammar of a language should, ideally, contain a central *syntactic component* and two *interpretive components*, a *phonological component* and a

---

grounds. Thus grammar reduces to such matters as government, agreement, inflectional paradigms, and the like. This decision seems to me no more defensible than a decision to restrict the study of language structure to phonetic patterning.

semantic component. The syntactic component generates strings of minimal syntactically functioning elements (following Bolinger, 1948, let us call them *formatives*) and specifies the categories, functions and structural interrelations of the formatives and systems of formatives. The phonological component converts a string of formatives of specified syntactic structure into a phonetic representation. The semantic component, correspondingly, assigns a semantic interpretation to an abstract structure generated by the syntactic component. Thus each of the two interpretive components maps a syntactically generated structure onto a "concrete" interpretation, in one case phonetic, and in the other, semantic. The grammar as a whole can thus be regarded, ultimately, as a device for pairing phonetically represented signals with semantic interpretations, this pairing being mediated through a system of abstract structures generated by the syntactic component. Thus the syntactic component must provide for each sentence (actually, for each interpretation of each sentence) a semantically interpretable *deep structure* and a phonetically interpretable *surface structure*, and, in the event that these are distinct, a statement of the relation between these two structures. (For further discussion, see Katz and Postal, forthcoming.) Roughly speaking, it seems that this much structure is common to all theories of generative grammar, or is at least compatible with them. Beyond this loose and minimal specification, however, important differences emerge.

The generative grammar internalized by someone who has acquired a language defines what in Saussurian terms we may call *langue* (with a qualification to be specified below, in Section 1.2). In performing as a speaker or hearer, he puts this device to use. Thus as a hearer, his problem is to determine the structural description assigned by his grammar to a presented utterance (or, where the sentence is syntactically ambiguous, to determine the correct structural description for this particular token), and using the information in the structural description, to understand the utterance. Clearly the description of intrinsic competence provided by the grammar is not to be confused with an account of actual performance, as de Saussure emphasized with such lucidity (cf. also Sapir, 1921; Newman, 1941). Nor is it to be confused with an account of potential performance.[3] The actual use of language obviously involves a complex interplay of many factors of the most disparate sort, of which the grammatical processes constitute only one. It seems natural to suppose that the study of actual linguistic performance can be seriously pursued only to the extent that we have a good understanding of the generative grammars that are acquired by the learner and put to use by the speaker or hearer. The classical Saussurian assumption of the logical priority of the study of *langue* (and the generative grammars that describe it) seems quite inescapable.

In the background of the discussion below there will be two conflicting models of generative grammar. The first—which I will call the *taxonomic model*—is a direct outgrowth of modern structural linguistics. The second—which I will call the *trans-*

---

[3]The common characterization of language as a set of "verbal habits" or as a "complex of present dispositions to verbal behavior, in which speakers of the same language have perforce come to resemble one another" (Quine, 1960, 27) is totally inadequate. Knowledge of one's language is not reflected directly in linguistic habits and dispositions, and it is clear that speakers of the same language or dialect may differ enormously in dispositions to verbal response, depending on personality, beliefs, and countless other extra-linguistic factors.

formational model—is much closer to traditional grammar. It should be noted, however, that modern grammars are typically not conceived as generative grammars, but as descriptive statements about a given corpus (text). Hence the taxonomic model, as described below, is no more than an attempt to formulate a generative grammar which is in the spirit of modern procedural and descriptive approaches. The essential reliance on procedures of segmentation and classification, and on statements of syntagmatic and paradigmatic distribution, is widely shared, however (cf. de Saussure, Hjelmslev, Harris, among others); and these notions clearly suggest a generative grammar with the characteristics of the taxonomic model, as considered here.

The taxonomic model is simpler, more "concrete," and more "atomistic" than the transformational model. We can characterize it briefly in the following way. Each rule is of the form: element A has the member (variant, realization) X in the context Z-W. Let us call such a rule a *rewriting rule*. The syntactic component consists of an unordered set of rewriting rules, each of which states the membership of some phrase category or formative category in some context.[4] The structural description that it provides can be regarded as a labelled bracketing of the string of formatives, indicating the category of each substring which is a constituent. Let us call such a labelled bracketing, obtainable automatically from a single derivation, a *Phrasemarker* of this string of formatives. The phonological component consists of two distinct sets of rewriting rules. The first set (morphophonemic rules) states the phonemic constitution of morphophonemes or formatives with respect to stated contexts. The second set (phonetic rules) states the phonetic constitution of phonemes, with respect to stated contexts. Each of these sets is unordered.

The transformational model is far more complex and highly structured. The syntactic component is assumed to consist of two subcomponents. The first (constituent

---

[4]On the syntactic level, the taxonomic model is a generalization from Harris' morpheme-to-utterance statements, which constitute the nearest approach to an explicit generative grammar on this level. Furthermore, most modern work in syntax is actually more adequately formalized in terms of rewriting rules with null context (i.e., *context-free grammar*—in particular, this seems to be true of Pike's tagmemics, as of most work in IC analysis). Similarly, most, if not all of the work involving use of computers for analysis of sentence structure seems to fall within this narrower framework (cf. Gross, 1962). This is to say that both the sets of sentences generable and, much more importantly, even the systems of structural descriptions generable within the framework of IC analysis seem to be adequately represented by the mechanism of generation of strings and of structural descriptions (Phrase-markers) formalized within this theory (cf. Postal, 1964 in this connection). Though abstract study of such systems is recent, there is already a fairly substantial body of results. Cf. Chomsky (1963), Schützenberger and Chomsky (1963) for summaries of recent work. I do not think that the variations that have been proposed within this general framework have any bearing on the conclusions developed below, regarding the taxonomic model. From the point of view of linguistic adequacy, of course, the important question about a theory of grammar (e.g., the taxonomic model, or the theory of context-free grammar) is not so much the question of the sets of strings that are generable (the *weak generative capacity* of this theory), but rather that of the sets of structural descriptions that are generable within the framework of this theory (its *strong generative capacity*), and it is this that I will consider below. However, it is interesting to observe that several examples are now known of subparts of natural languages that are beyond the weak generative capacity of the theory of context-free grammar (cf. Postal, 1961, 1964; Miller and Chomsky, 1963). Though this is not the linguistically most significant deficiency of this theory, it is sufficient to show that in attempting to enrich the theory of grammar to overcome the inadequacies of such systems, we must not only go beyond them in strong generative capacity, but we must develop a theory that exceeds the theory of context-free grammar in weak generative capacity as well.

structure) subcomponent consists of an ordered set of rewriting rules that generate strings of formatives that we may call *C-terminal strings*. These constitute either a finite set, or a highly restricted infinite set. The second (transformational) subcomponent consists of a partially ordered set of complex operations called (*grammatical*) *transformations*, each of which maps a full Phrase-marker (or a pair, triple, etc., of Phrase-markers) of some terminal string (or a pair, triple, etc., of terminal strings) into a new *derived Phrase-marker* of a *T-terminal string*. Some of the rewriting and transformational rules may be obligatory, while others are optional. Application of all obligatory and perhaps some optional rules of the syntactic component, observing order, will give a T-terminal string with a derived Phrase-marker. The structural description of this string will be a set of Phrase-markers (one for each underlying C-terminal string, and, in addition, the derived Phrase-marker of the full string) and a representation of its "transformational history," what we may call a *Transformation-marker*. We will see below that all of this information plays a role in determining the interpretation of an utterance.[5] It is also essential to distinguish a lexicon, with rather different properties, but I will not go into this question here.

The phonological component of a transformational generative grammar consists of an ordered set of rewriting rules, an ordered set of transformational rules, and an ordered set of rewriting rules, in that order. The transformational rules, furthermore, apply in a cycle, first to the smallest constituents of a string, then to the next largest constituents, etc., until the maximal domain of phonological processes is reached. These are, technically, transformational rules since they involve the constituent structure of the utterance. This *transformational cycle* determines the phonetic form of syntactically complex units from the underlying (abstract) phonemic form of their components, using the manner of composition specified by the derived Phrase-marker.[6]

Notice that in the case of the transformational model, the symbols and structures that are manipulated, rewritten, and transformed as a sentence is generated may bear no very direct relation to any of its concrete subparts, whereas in the case of the taxonomic model each of the symbols that is rewritten in the generation of a sentence stands for a category to which some subpart of this sentence belongs (or category symbol by which it is represented). It is in this sense that the taxonomic model is both more concrete and more atomistic.

Investigation of the semantic component of a transformational grammar is quite recent. It has proceeded from the assumption, implicit in all studies of transformational grammar, that the grammatical functions and relations that play the primary role in determining the semantic interpretation of a sentence are those that are

---

[5]The most accessible summary of formal properties of grammatical transformations, from this point of view, is in Chomsky (1961a). For further details, see Chomsky (1955, chapters 8, 9). The most extensive study of English grammar within this framework is Lees (1960a). See the bibliography of the second printing (1962) of Chomsky (1957a) for references to much recent work. In addition, cf. Schachter (1961, 1962), Postal (1962).

[6]For examples of the operation of the transformational cycle in English, see Chomsky, Halle, Lukoff (1956), and improved statements in Miller and Chomsky (1963). For examples in Russian, see Halle (1961b). For examples in Latvian, see Halle and Zeps (forthcoming). The structure of the phonological component of a transformational grammar, with particular reference to English, is discussed in more detail in Halle and Chomsky (1960, forthcoming).

represented (in the manner described in section 4.1, below) in the underlying Phrase-markers generated by the constituent structure subcomponent, so that these Phrase-markers constitute the basic "content elements" underlying the interpretation of actual sentences (cf. Harris, 1957, pp. 290, 339–40; Chomsky, 1957, p. 92). For investigation of the semantic component, in which these vague suggestions are refined, sharpened, and considerably elaborated and developed, see Katz and Fodor (1963); Katz and Postal (forthcoming).

In terms of the characterization of a generative grammar given above (p. 51), we can distinguish between the taxonomic and transformational models in the following simple way. The syntactic component of a taxonomic grammar provides a single Phrase-marker for each utterance (in each interpretation) which serves both as deep structure and surface structure. That is, this single labelled bracketing of a formative sequence contains all information relevant to its semantic or phonetic interpretation. In a transformational grammar, the Phrase-markers of the underlying strings and the Transformation-marker constitute, jointly, the deep structure, and contain all information relevant to semantic interpretation; while the labelled bracketing that constitutes the final derived Phrase-marker of the T-terminal string is the surface structure which, presumably, contains all and only the information relevant to phonetic interpretation. Katz and Postal (forthcoming) have, furthermore, presented strong arguments for the view that singulary transformations make no contribution to semantic interpretation, so that the contribution of the Transformation-marker to the deep structure is minimal. In fact, recent and still unpublished work suggests that it can be entirely eliminated, but I will not pursue this matter further here. The important point is that according to this conception of grammatical structure, the categories and grammatical functions represented in the actual labelled bracketing of the temporally given string will, in general, not be those that determine the semantic interpretation of this string, though they will be directly related to its phonetic interpretation. It is in the system of underlying structures, that are mapped on to the actual given string by transformational rules, that the semantically significant categories and functions are represented.

1.2 Before continuing, it is instructive to consider these notions from the point of view of traditional grammar, as well as that of classical linguistic theory and of modern taxonomic linguistics.

It would not be inaccurate to regard the transformational model as a formalization of features implicit in traditional grammars, and to regard these grammars as inexplicit transformational generative grammars. The goal of a traditional grammar is to provide its user with the ability to understand an arbitrary sentence of the language, and to form and employ it properly on the appropriate occasion. Thus its goal is (at least) as far-reaching as that of a generative grammar, as just described. Furthermore, the rich descriptive apparatus of traditional grammar far exceeds the limits of the taxonomic model, though it is largely, and perhaps fully formalizable within the framework of the transformational model. However, it is important to bear in mind that even the most careful and complete traditional grammar relies in an essential way on the intuition and intelligence of the user, who is expected to draw the correct inferences from the many examples and hints (and explicit lists of irregularities) presented by the grammar. If the grammar is a good one, the user may succeed, but the deep-seated regularities of the language that he somehow discovers escape explicit formulation, and the nature of the abilities that enable him to perform this task remain a complete mystery. The vastness of these gaps can be appreciated only when one makes an attempt to construct explicit rules to account for the full range of structural information available to the mature user of a language.

Focusing on the notion of "creativity," one can distinguish two conflicting views regarding the essential nature of language in nineteenth-century linguistic theory. On the one hand, we have the Humboldtian view that "man muss die *Sprache* nicht sowohl wie ein todtes *Erzeugtes*, sondern weit mehr wie eine *Erzeugung* ansehen" (1836, Section 8, p. LV). The essence of each language is what Humboldt designates as its characteristic *Form* (not to be identified with "inner form"). The form of language is that constant and unvarying factor that underlies and gives life and significance to each particular new linguistic act. It is by having developed an internal representation of this form that each individual is capable of understanding the language and using it in a way that is intelligible to his fellow speakers. This characteristic form determines and inheres in each separate linguistic element. The role and significance of each individual element can be determined only by considering it in relation to underlying form, that is, in relation to the fixed generative rules that determine the manner of its formation. It is this underlying generative principle that the linguist must seek to represent in a descriptive grammar.

Compare, for example, such representative passages as these: „Das Verfahren der Sprache ist aber nicht bloss ein solches, wodurch eine einzelne Erscheinung zu Stande kommt; es muss derselben zugleich die Möglichkeit eröffnen, eine unbestimmbare Menge solcher Erscheinungen, und unter allen, ihr von dem Gedanken gestellten Bedingungen, hervorzubringen . . . [die Sprache] muss daher von endlichen Mitteln einen unendlichen Gebrauch machen" (Section 13, p. CXXII). „ . . . [die Form] . . . ist in ihrer Natur selbst eine Auffassung der einzelnen, im Gegensatze zu ihr als Stoff zu betrachtenden, *Sprachelemente* in *geistiger Einheit*. Denn in jeder Sprache liegt eine solche [Einheit], und durch diese zusammenfassende Einheit macht eine Nation die ihr von ihren Vorfahren überlieferte Sprache zu der ihrigen. Dieselbe Einheit muss sich also in der Darstellung wiederfinden; und nur wenn man von den zerstreuten Elementen bis zu dieser Einheit hinaufsteigt, erhält man wahrhaft einen Begriff von der Sprache selbst, da man, ohne ein solches Verfahren, offenbar Gefahr läuft, nicht einmal jene Elemente in ihrer wahren Eigentümlichkeit, und noch weniger in ihrem realen Zusammenhange zu verstehen" (Section 8, p. LXII). „Es versteht sich indess von selbst, dass in den Begriff der Form der Sprache keine Einzelheit als *isolirte* Thatsache, sondern immer nur insofern aufgenommen werden darf, als sich eine Methode der Sprachbildung an ihr entdecken lässt" (Section 8, p. LXII). „Die charakteristische Form der Sprachen hängt an jedem *einzelnen* ihrer kleinsten Elemente; jedes wird durch sie, wie unerklärlich es im Einzelnen sei, auf irgend eine Weise bestimmt. Dagegen ist es kaum möglich, Punkte aufzufinden, von denen sich behaupten liesse, dass sie an ihnen, einzeln genommen, entscheidend haftete" (Section 8, p. LIX). „Denn die Sprache ist ja nicht als ein daliegender, in seinem Ganzen übersehbarer, oder nach und nach mitteilbarer Stoff, sondern muss als ein sich ewig *erzeugender* angesehen werden, wo die Gesetze der Erzeugung bestimmt sind, aber der Umfang und gewissermassen auch die Art des Erzeugnisses gänzlich unbestimmt bleiben" (Section 9, p. LXXI). „Die Sprache besteht, neben den schon geformten Elementen, ganz vorzüglich auch aus Methoden, die Arbeit des Geistes, welcher sie die Bahn und die Form vorzeichnet, weiter fortzusetzen" (Section 9, p. LXXVII). „Das in dieser Arbeit des Geistes, den articulirten Laut zum Gedankenausdruck zu erheben, liegende Beständige und Gleichförmige, so vollständig, als möglich, in seinem Zusammenhange aufgefasst, und systematisch dargestellt, macht die *Form* der Sprache aus" (Section 8, p. LVIII).

In Humboldt's sense, *Form* extends beyond grammatical form (beyond "Redefügung" and "Wortbildung") to encompass also the substantive characterization of the sound system (Section 8, p. LX) and the principles of concept formation as embodied in the system of stems ("Grundwörter") (Section 8, p. LXI). "Überhaupt wird durch den Begriff Form nichts Factisches und Individuelles ausgeschlossen . . ." (Section 8, p. LXII).

From this conception of the nature of language, Humboldt derives his views concerning understanding of speech and acquisition of language. Speaking and understanding are, in his view, differing manifestations of the same underlying capacity, the same generative principle, mastery of which provides the speaker-hearer with the ability to use and understand all of the infinite range of linguistic items ("Mit dem *Verstehen* verhält es sich nicht anders. Es kann in der Seele nichts, als durch eigne Thätigkeit vorhanden sein, und Verstehen und Sprechen sind nur verschiedenartige Wirkungen der nämlichen Sprachkraft. Die gemeinsame Rede ist nie mit dem Übergeben eines Stoffes vergleichbar. In dem Verstehenden, wie im Sprechenden, muss derselbe aus der eigenen, innern Kraft entwickelt werden; und was der erstere empfängt, ist nur die harmonisch stimmende Anregung. Es ist daher dem Menschen auch schon natürlich, das eben Verstandene wieder gleich auszusprechen. Auf diese Weise liegt die Sprache in jedem Menschen in ihrem ganzen Umfange, was aber nichts Anderes bedeutet, als dass jeder ein . . . geregeltes Streben besitzt, die ganze Sprache, wie es äussere oder innere Veranlassung herbeiführt, nach und nach aus sich hervorzubringen und hervorgebracht zu verstehen"—Section 9, p. LXX). Furthermore, since language consists essentially of a "System von Regeln" as well as a "Vorrath von Wörtern" (cf. Section 9, p. LXXVIII), common to speaker and hearer, it follows that "Das *Sprechenlernen* der Kinder ist nicht ein Zumessen von Wörtern, Niederlegen im Gedächtnis, und Wiedernachlallen mit den Lippen, sondern ein Wachsen des Sprachvermögens durch Alter und Übung" (Section 9, p. LXXI). ". . . [Die Sprache] . . . lässt sich . . ., wenn es auch auf den ersten Anblick anders erscheint, nicht eigentlich lehren, sondern nur im Gemüthe wecken; man kann ihr nur den Faden hingeben, an dem sie sich von selbst entwickelt" (Section 6, p. L).

It is just this point of view concerning the essential nature of language that underlies and motivates recent work in generative grammar. Furthermore, the Humboldtian views concerning perception and acquisition have re-emerged, in many particulars, in the course of this work (cf., e.g., Chomsky, 1957a, 48; 1960; 1961a, Sections 1, 2; and the references of note 50, below). A generative grammar, in the sense sketched above, is an attempt to represent, in a precise manner, certain aspects of the *Form* of language, and a particular theory of generative grammar is an attempt to specify those aspects of form that are a common human possession—in Humboldtian terms, one might identify this latter with the underlying general form of all language ("Die Formen mehrerer Sprachen können in einer noch allgemeineren Form zusammenkommen, und die Formen aller thun dies in der That, insofern man überall bloss von dem Allgemeinsten ausgeht" ". . . dass man ebenso richtig sagen kann, dass das ganze Menschengeschlecht nur Eine Sprache, als dass jeder Mensch eine besondere besitzt"—Section 8, p. LXIII).There is one respect (to which we return directly below) in which this work diverges in principle from the Humboldtian frame-work; beyond this, the narrower limitations within which it has concretely developed (in particular, insofar as very little has been said, until quite recently, concerning semantic or conceptual structure) is a result not of any point of principle, but rather of the fact that there has been little to say about these further matters that could withstand serious analysis (cf. Section 2.3).

Humboldt's thoughts concerning the semantic aspect of linguistic form are, not surprisingly, rather obscure in certain respects. They are, however, original and sug-gestive and, in part, quite different from more recent and familiar views. I will only attempt a brief sketch, largely in paraphrase, of what seem to be their main outlines. For Humboldt, as for Frege and many others since, a word does not stand directly for a thing, but rather for a concept. There can, accordingly, be a multiplicity of ex-pressions for the same object, each representing a way in which this object has been conceived through the workings of the process of "Spracherzeugung," and Hum-boldt gives several Sanskrit examples, of the now familiar "morning star"–"evening star" type, to illustrate this (Section 11). The process of language-formation is, furthermore, constantly active. Thus, one cannot regard the lexicon of a language as a completed aggregate ("eine fertig daliegende Masse"), but rather only as "ein fortgehendes Erzeugnis und Wiedererzeugnis des wortbildenden Vermögens." (Section 13.) This is to say that the capacity of "Spracherzeugung" is constantly at work, not only in extending the system of concepts, but also in recreating it, in each perceptual act (thus memory limitations are overcome, since the system of con-cepts is not stored in full detail, but only in terms of its "generating principle"). In two respects, then, a system of concepts is not to be regarded as constituting a store of well-defined objects (as, apparently, it is for Saussure). In particular, even with the system fixed, Humboldt denies that understanding a linguistic expression is simply a matter of selecting the fully specified concept from a "store of concepts." It is rather that the received signs activate within the listener a corresponding link in his system of concepts ("dass sie gegenseitig in einander dasselbe Glied der Kette ihrer sinnlichen Vorstellungen und inneren Begriffserzeugungen berühren"—Section 20, CCXIII), causing a corresponding, but not identical concept to emerge. When a "key of the mental instrument" is touched, in this way, the whole system will resonate, and the emerging concept will stand in harmony with all that surrounds it to the most remote regions of its domain. Thus, a system of concepts is activated in the listener, and it is the place of a concept within this system (which may differ somewhat from speaker to speaker) that, in part, determines the way in which the hearer understands a linguistic expression. Finally, the concepts so formed are systematically interrelated in an "inner totality," with varying interconnections and structural relations (Section 20). This inner totality, formed by the use of language in thought, conception, and expression of feeling, functions as a conceptual world interposed through the constant activity of the mind between itself and the actual objects, and it is within this system that a word obtains its value ("Geltung"—cf. Saussure). Consequently, a language should not be regarded merely, or primarily, as a means of communication (Austauschungsmittel), and the instrumental use of language (its use for achieving concrete aims) is derivative and subsidiary. It is, for Humboldt, typical only of parasitic systems (e.g., "Sprachmischungen," as the lingua franca along the Mediterranean coast.)

For further discussion of Humboldtian general linguistics, see Viertel (forthcoming).

In sharp contrast to the Humboldtian conception, in the general linguistics of the nineteenth century, is the view that is perhaps expressed most clearly by Whitney (1872); namely, that "language in the concrete sense . . . [is] . . . the sum of words and phrases by which any man expresses his thought" (372); that study of speech is no more than study of a body of vocal signs; and that study of the origin and development of language is nothing more than study of origin and development of these signs. The problem of accounting for the acquisition of language, so conceived, disappears. ". . . the acquisition of language by children does not seem to us any mystery at all." It is not at all astonishing "that a child, after hearing a certain word used some scores or hundreds of times, comes to understand what it means, and then, a little later, to pronounce and use it . . .."

This narrowing of the scope of linguistics to the study of inventory of elements was occasioned not only by the dramatic successes of comparative linguistics, which operated within these limitations, but also by the unclarities and obscurities of formulation of Humboldt ("a man whom it is nowadays the fashion to praise highly, without understanding or even reading him"—Whitney, 1872, 333) and his successors. Furthermore, there were some serious confusions concerning the notion of "creativity." Thus it is significant that the comments of Paul's quoted above are from a chapter that deals with analogic change. He makes no distinction (just as Humboldt makes no clear distinction) between the kind of "creativity" that leaves the language entirely unchanged (as in the production—and understanding—of new sentences, an activity in which the adult is constantly engaged) and the kind that actually changes the set of grammatical rules (e.g., analogic change). But this is a fundamental distinction. In fact, the technical tools for dealing with "rule-governed creativity," as distinct from "rule-changing creativity," have only become readily available during the past few decades in the course of work in logic and foundations of mathematics. But in the light of these developments, it is possible to return to the questions to which Humboldt addressed himself, and to attempt to represent certain aspects of the underlying "Form of language," insofar as it encompasses "rule-governed creativity," by means of an explicit generative grammar.

Saussure, like Whitney (and possibly under his influence—cf. Godel, 1957, 32–3), regards *langue* as basically a store of signs with their grammatical properties, that is, a store of wordlike elements, fixed phrases, and, perhaps, certain limited phrase types (though it is possible that his rather obscure concept of "mécanisme de la langue" was intended to go beyond this—cf. Godel, 1957, 250). He was thus quite unable to come to grips with the recursive processes underlying sentence formation, and he appears to regard sentence formation as a matter of *parole* rather than *langue*, of free and voluntary creation rather than systematic rule (or perhaps, in some obscure way, as on the border between *langue* and *parole*). There is no place in his scheme for "rule-governed creativity" of the kind involved in the ordinary everyday use of language. At the same time, the influence of Humboldtian holism (but now restricted to inventories and paradigmatic sets, rather than to the full-scale generative processes that constitute *Form*) is apparent in the central role of the notions "terme" and "valeur" in the Saussurian system.

Modern linguistics is much under the influence of Saussure's conception of *langue* as an inventory of elements (Saussure, 1916, 154, and elsewhere, frequently) and his preoccupation with systems of elements rather than the systems of rules which were the focus of attention of traditional grammar and of the general linguistics of Humboldt. In general, modern descriptive statements pay little attention to the "creative" aspect of language; they do not face the problem of presenting the system of generative rules that assign structural descriptions to arbitrary utterances and thus embody the speaker's competence in and knowledge of his language. Furthermore, this narrowing of the range of interest, as compared with traditional grammar, apparently has the effect of making it impossible to select an inventory of elements correctly, since it seems that no inventory (not even that of phonemes) can be determined without reference to the principles by which sentences are constructed in the language (cf. Section 4.3-4). To the extent that this is true, "structural linguistics" will have suffered from a failure to appreciate the extent and depth of interconnections among various parts of a language system. By a rather arbitrary limitation of scope, modern linguistics may well have become engaged in an intensive study of mere artifacts. We return to this matter below.

In summary, a comparison of Humboldtian general linguistics with typical modern views reveals quite a number of basic differences. Thus Humboldt's belief that the instrumental function of language is derivative, and that it is the characteristic property only of parasitic special purpose systems, contrasts with the view of, for example, Bloomfield (1933, p. 22f.) and Wittgenstein (1958, p. 16–17) that this instrumental function is paradigmatic and basic, and that (for Wittgenstein) its study "is the study of primitive forms of language or primitive languages." Furthermore, Humboldt's conception of underlying form as a system of generative rules that defines the role of each element differentiates his approach strikingly from that of modern structural linguistics, with its emphasis on element and inventory. In the same vein, one may compare his account of how a rich system of generative principles is involved in understanding a particular utterance with the late view of Wittgenstein (1958, p. 42) that there is no necessity to suppose the whole "calculus of language" to be present to the mind as a permanent background for each act of language use. Correspondingly, Humboldt's account of perception in terms of a schematism involving a system of rules contrasts with the elementary data-processing approach characteristic of modern linguistic theory (cf. sections 4, 5, below). Finally, it is interesting to compare Humboldt's views on language-learning (which might, with certain reservations, be called "Platonistic"; cf., in this connection, Leibniz, *Discourse on metaphysics*, Section 26) with the typical modern notion expressed, for example, in Wittgenstein's claim (1958, p. 12–13, 27) that the meanings of words must not only be learned, but also taught (the only means being drill, explanation, or the supplying of rules that are used consciously and explicitly), or in the claim (cf., e.g., Quine, 1960, p. 9f.) that sentences are, typically, "learned" by some sort of process of stimulus-sentence conditioning or sentence-sentence association (with analogic extension of some elementary sort playing a marginal, and in principle dispensable role).

These rather random remarks and examples suggest that it might be instructive to delineate more precisely a "Humboldtian" and a "taxonomic-behaviorist" point of view concerning the nature of language, and to contrast the approaches to language use and acquisition to which these conflicting viewpoints give rise. I think it is historically accurate to regard the approach presented in this paper as basically Humboldtian in its assumption that serious investigation of language use and acquisition presupposes a study of underlying generative processes (for which, to be sure, actual performance will supply evidence), and that very little is to be expected of direct operational analysis of "mentalistic" terms or radical behaviorist reductionism of the sort that has been so dominant in modern speculation on language and cognition. Clarification and justification of this remark is an undertaking that goes well beyond the scope of this paper. I can do no more here than indicate certain points of contact between Humboldtian general linguistics, on the one hand, and recent work on generative grammar and its implications, on the other.

It is, incidentally, interesting to take note of a curious and rather extreme contemporary view to the effect that true linguistic science must *necessarily* be a kind of pre-Darwinian taxonomy concerned solely with the collection and classification of countless specimens, while any attempt to formulate underlying principles and to concentrate on the kinds of data that shed some light on these is taken to be some novel sort of "engineering."[7] Perhaps this notion, which seems to me to defy comment, is related to the equally strange and factually quite incorrect view (recently expressed, e.g., by Joos, 1961; Reichling, 1961; Mel'chuk, 1961; Juilland, 1961) that current work in generative grammar is in some way an outgrowth of attempts to use electronic computers for one or another purpose, whereas in fact it should be obvious that its roots are firmly in traditional linguistics.

1.3 The issues involved can be clarified by setting linguistic theory within the general framework of the study of human intellectual capacities and their specific character. Still remaining within the classical framework, as modified above, we can take as an objective for linguistic theory the precise specification of two kinds of abstract device, the first serving as a perceptual model and the second, as a model for acquisition of language.

utterance $------\blacktriangleright$ ⬚ A ⬚ $------\blacktriangleright$ structural description   (1a)

primary linguistic data $------\blacktriangleright$ ⬚ B ⬚ $------\blacktriangleright$ generative grammar   (1b)

The perceptual model A is a device that assigns a structural description D to a presented utterance U, utilizing in the process its internalized generative grammar G,

---

[7] See Bolinger (1960) for an elaboration of this point of view. See also the Introduction to Joos (1957).

where G generates a phonetic representation R of U with the structural description D. In Saussurian terms, U is a specimen of *parole* interpreted by the device A as a "performance" of the item R which has the structural description D and which belongs to the *langue* generated by G. The learning model B is a device which constructs a theory G (i.e., a generative grammar G of a certain *langue*) as its output, on the basis of primary linguistic data (e.g., specimens of *parole*), as input. To perform this task, it utilizes its given *faculté de langage*, its innate specification of certain heuristic procedures and certain built-in constraints on the character of the task to be performed. We can think of general linguistic theory as an attempt to specify the character of the device B. We can regard a particular grammar as, in part, an attempt to specify the information available in principle (i.e., apart from limitations of attention, memory, etc.) to A that makes it capable of understanding an arbitrary utterance, to the highly nontrivial extent that understanding is determined by the structural description provided by the generative grammar. In evaluating a particular generative grammar, we ask whether the information that it gives us about a language is correct, that is, whether it describes correctly the linguistic intuition of the speaker (Saussure's "conscience des sujets parlants," which to him, as to Sapir, provides the ultimate test of adequacy for a linguistic description). In evaluating a general theory of linguistic structure that is sufficiently explicit to offer an actual hypothesis about the character of B, we ask whether the generative grammars that it selects meet the empirical criterion of correspondence to the speaker's linguistic intuition, in the case of particular languages.

I will try to show that the taxonomic model (or any of its variants within modern study of language) is far too oversimplified to be able to account for the facts of linguistic structure and that the transformational model of generative grammar is much closer to the truth. To show that modern linguistics seriously underestimates the richness of structure of language and the generative processes that underlie it, it is necessary to sample the range of problems that cannot be attacked, or often even posed within the narrow limits that it sets. A variety of examples of this sort will be considered in the following sections. I will also try to show that these inadequacies and limitations may in part be traceable to an impoverished conception of the nature of human cognitive processes, and that a return to traditional concerns and view points, with the higher standards of explicitness that have emerged in modern linguistics, can perhaps provide new insights concerning perception and learning.

II. LEVELS OF SUCCESS FOR GRAMMATICAL DESCRIPTION

2.0 Within the framework outlined above, we can sketch various levels of success that might be attained by a grammatical description associated with a particular linguistic theory. The lowest level of success is achieved if the grammar presents the observed primary data correctly.[8] A second and higher level of success is achieved

---

[8]Innocuous as this comment may seem, it still requires qualification. What data is relevant is determined in part by the possibility for a systematic theory, and one might therefore hold that the

when the grammar gives a correct account of the linguistic intuition of the native speaker, and specifies the observed data (in particular) in terms of significant generalizations that express underlying regularities in the language. A third and still higher level of success is achieved when the associated linguistic theory provides a general basis for selecting a grammar that achieves the second level of success over other grammars consistent with the relevant observed data that do not achieve this level of success. In this case, we can say that the linguistic theory in question suggests an explanation for the linguistic intuition of the native speaker. It can be interpreted as asserting that data of the observed kind will enable a speaker whose intrinsic capacities are as represented in this general theory to construct for himself a grammar that characterizes exactly this linguistic intuition.

For later reference, let us refer to these roughly delimited levels of success as the levels of *observational adequacy, descriptive adequacy*, and *explanatory adequacy*, respectively. In terms of the notions of the preceding section, a grammar that aims for observational adequacy is concerned merely to give an account of the primary data (e.g., the corpus) that is the input to the learning device (1b); a grammar that aims for descriptive adequacy is concerned to give a correct account of the linguistic intuition of the native speaker; in other words, it is concerned with the output of the device (1b); and a linguistic theory that aims for explanatory adequacy is concerned with the internal structure of the device (1b); that is, it aims to provide a principled basis, independent of any particular language, for the selection of the descriptively adequate grammar of each language.

Modern linguistics has been largely concerned with observational adequacy. In particular, this is true of post-Bloomfieldian American linguistics (cf. below, Section 4.3–4), and apparently, of the London school of Firth, with its emphasis on the ad hoc character of linguistic description.[9] Traditional grammar, on the other hand, was explicitly concerned with the level of descriptive adequacy (and this interest persists, explicitly, in Sapir's work, as well as in current work in the traditional mold—cf. Sapir, 1933; Long, 1960). This difference between traditional and modern points of view is made particularly clear in modern critique of traditional grammars. Thus Nida, in his valuable study (1943) of English syntax within the immediate constituent framework, criticizes Jespersen sharply for his "serious distortion and complication of the formal and functional values" in assigning to "the doctor's arrival," but not "the doctor's house," a structural description that indicates that the Subject-Verb relation appears in the former but not in the latter phrase. But clearly Jespersen's account is correct on the level of descriptive adequacy, and the fact that the data-processing operations of modern linguistics fail to provide the correct information

---

lowest level of success is no easier to achieve than the others. As noted above, the fact that a certain noise was produced, even intentionally, by an English speaker does not guarantee that it is a well-formed specimen of his language. Under many circumstances it is quite appropriate to use deviant utterances. Furthermore, under normal conditions speech is subject to various, often violent distortions that may in themselves indicate nothing about the underlying linguistic patterns. The problem of determining what data is valuable and to the point is not an easy one. What is observed is often neither relevant nor significant, and what is relevant and significant is often very difficult to observe, in linguistics no less than in the freshman physics laboratory, or, for that matter, anywhere in science.

[9]Cf. Firth *et al.* (1957).

indicates only that they are based on an erroneous conception of linguistic structure, or that observational adequacy is being taken as the only relevant concern.[10] On the other hand, Jakobson's attempts to formulate universal phonological laws (cf. Section 4.2, below) might perhaps be regarded as indicating a concern for explanatory adequacy, on at least one level of grammar. It is clear that the question of explanatory adequacy can be seriously raised only when we are presented with an explicit theory of generative grammar that specifies the form of grammars and suggests a mechanism for selecting among them (i.e., an evaluation procedure for grammars of a specified form). The difference between observational and descriptive adequacy is related to the distinction drawn by Hockett (1958) between "surface grammar" and "deep grammar," and he is unquestionably correct in noting that modern linguistics is largely confined in scope to the former.

2.1 Levels of adequacy in phonology. A few linguistic examples may help to clarify the distinction between these various levels of adequacy. Consider first the case of so-called "accidental gaps" in the lexicon. Thus in English there is a word "pick" /pik/, but no /blik/ or /ftik/. The level of observational adequacy would be attained by a grammar that contained the rule: N → /pik/, but no lexical rule introducing /blik/ or /ftik/. To attain the level of descriptive adequacy, a grammar would have to provide, in addition, a general rule that sets up a specific barrier against /ftik/, but not against /blik/ (which would thus qualify as an accidental gap, a phonologically permissible nonsense syllable). This level would be achieved by a grammar that contained the generalization that in initial position before a true consonant (a segment which is consonantal and nonvocalic, in terms of Jakobson's distinctive features), a consonant is necessarily /s/. The level of explanatory adequacy would be attained by a linguistic theory that provides a principled reason for incorporating this generalization in a grammar of English, and for excluding the (factually correct) "rule" that in the context ♯ b − ik ♯ a liquid is necessarily /r/. Thus the theory might provide a general evaluation measure (simplicity measure) which would show how the former, but not the latter rule gives a more highly valued grammar. Such a theory would suggest an explanation for the linguistic intuition that /blik/, but not /ftik/, is a "possible" word, though neither has been heard. This is the intuition that would result from observation of actual utterances by a learner who constructs the most highly valued grammar of the appropriate form, as specified by this theory.[11]

---

[10]Nida also criticizes Jespersen, on essentially the same grounds, for describing "barking" in "the barking dogs" as an attributive of the same rank as "barks" in "the dog barks." Again Jespersen's decision seems to me unquestionably correct from the point of view of descriptive adequacy, though internally unmotivated (i.e., deficient from the point of view of explanatory adequacy).

[11]The theory of "morpheme structure rules" developed in Halle (1959a, 1959b) constitutes an attempt to reach the level of explanatory adequacy, in this case. Halle shows how consistent adherence to the principle of minimizing feature specifications in the phonological component provides a principled basis for the distinction between accidental and nonaccidental gaps. To my knowledge, this is the only attempt to provide a general basis for this distinction, though lists and charts that state much of the data that is to be explained have frequently appeared.

In his review of Halle (1959b), Ferguson (1962, 292) describes Halle's discovery of the role of morpheme structure rules as "a misfortune" not too different from certain defects of taxonomic grammars that Halle exposes (cf. Section 4.3, below). This is an extremely peculiar conclusion. No generalization is lost by distinguishing morpheme structure rules (which are obviously needed in a

Consider now the matter of predictable phonetic variants. Thus in my speech, the lexical item "telegraph" appears in many phonetic shapes, depending on context, in particular, the shapes (2i–iii) in the contexts ♯ – ♯, –ic, –y, respectively:

téligrǽf	(2i)
tèligrǽf	(2ii)
tilégrif.	(2iii)

Observational adequacy would be achieved by a grammar that merely states the facts, as I have just done, thus reproducing the observed data in a convenient arrangement. Such a grammar (called, technically, an *item-and arrangement grammar*) in effect treats the item "telegraph" as an exception, exactly as it treats "see"-"saw," "man"-"men," etc. Thus the grammar would be no more complex if the facts were, instead, that (2i) appears in the context –y, (2ii) in the context ♯ – ♯, and (2iii) in the context –ic, the rest of the language remaining fixed. Within this framework, there are no further questions to be raised, and there is nothing more to be said.

To achieve the level of descriptive adequacy, in this case, a grammar must treat the variants of "telegraph" as a special case of general rules applying as well to many other items. It must be able to account for the fact that the phonetic variation of "telegraph" is obviously not capricious, given the rest of English, as is the variation of "man." Not having heard the form "men," it is impossible for the linguist or learner to predict it. But this is not true in the case of (2).

The grammar would achieve the still higher level of explanatory adequacy, in this case, if the linguistic theory associated with it provides a framework for phonological rules and an evaluation measure meeting the following condition: the most highly valued set of rules of the appropriate form selected to generate a set of items from which the variants of "telegraph" are excluded would be the set of rules that in fact predict this contextual variation for "telegraph." In this case, the linguistic theory would provide a basis for explaining the facts presented in (2), in terms of other aspects of English and certain assumptions about the general character of grammars. It would make clear, in other words, the respect in which the actual contextual variation differs from the alternative mentioned in the paragraph following (2). The latter would lead to a less-highly valued grammar—it would not be predicted by the highest-valued grammar based on data that excludes (2). The theory of item-and-arrangement grammar obviously cannot meet this condition, and for this reason (which, clearly, generalizes to a host of similar examples) cannot be regarded seriously as a theory of grammar.[12] In such cases as this, neither the level of descriptive nor explanatory adequacy is easy to meet, and it is a fact worth considering that despite the exten-

---

full grammar, and which, as Halle shows, play a distinctive role in accounting for an otherwise unexplained area of linguistic fact) from other phonetic rules differing from them both in formal properties and in the phenomena that they describe. On the other hand, the deficiency of taxonomic grammars to which Ferguson alludes involves their inability to state certain generalizations, that is, their inability to achieve descriptive adequacy.

[12]See the references of the preceding footnote, and also Chomsky (1959, 1962), Miller and Chomsky (1963), for discussion of the problem of developing a phonological theory that meets this condition, for such cases.

sive investigations of English phonology in recent years, no attempt has even been made to meet them.

The point becomes even clearer when we consider phonetic variants that are syntactically conditioned. Thus English "tórrent" /tɔrent/ (cf. "torrential") has the reduced vowel [ɨ] in the second syllable, while the noun "tórment" /tɔrment/ retains the vowel [e]. The level of observational adequacy is attained by the preceding sentence. The level of descriptive adequacy would be achieved by a description that managed to relate these observations to the fact that there is a verb "tormént," but no verb "torrént" in English, by means of general rules about stress shifts in nouns derived from verbs ("pérmit," "permít," etc.), and about the role of stress in preventing vowel reduction. The level of explanatory adequacy requires a phonological theory that prescribes the general form of such syntactically determined phonetic processes, and that shows how the appropriate generalizations, in this case, would appear in the highest-valued grammar of the prescribed form, even if the items in question were not part of the observed data from which this grammar is constructed. Similarly, in the case of such familiar examples as "light house keeper" (with stress patterns 132, 213, 313), the level of descriptive adequacy requires, beyond a statement of these facts, a general account of the rules by which such stress patterns are assigned in syntactic constructions, and the level of explanatory adequacy will be achieved only when a general theory of such processes is forthcoming. It is examples of this sort that provide the motivation for the transformational cycle of the phonological component, since in these cases the phonetic shape of the full phrase is determined by that of its constituents.

2.2 Levels of adequacy in syntax. Consider next a few syntactic examples. Suppose that the sentences

$$\text{John is easy to please} \tag{3}$$
$$\text{John is eager to please} \tag{4}$$

are observed and accepted as well formed. A grammar that achieves only the level of observational adequacy would, again, merely note this fact in one way or another (e.g., by setting up appropriate lists). To achieve the level of descriptive adequacy, however, a grammar would have to assign structural descriptions indicating that *John* in (3) is the direct object of *please* (the words are grammatically related as in "This pleases John"),while in (4) it is the logical subject of *please* (as in "John pleases someone"). A theory of grammar that does not allow structural descriptions of this sort cannot achieve the level of descriptive adequacy. In cases of this sort, the taxonomic model of generative grammar discussed above (or any of its variants) cannot achieve the level of descriptive adequacy, since information of this kind cannot be represented in the Phrase-marker that it provides as the full structural description on the syntactic level. The transformational model does, however, make grammars available that can supply structural information of this sort, and therefore can, in this case at least, achieve the level of descriptive adequacy. In Section 4.1 we will return to the problem of assigning to (3) and (4) structural descriptions that provide the full range of syntactic information.

How might a transformational grammar achieve the level of explanatory adequacy in such a case as this? To achieve this level, the theory must provide for the selection of a descriptively adequate grammar, given such data as (3), (4), "John's eagerness (*easiness) to please . . .," "to please John is easy (*eager)," "John is an easy (*eager) fellow to please," "it pleases John," "John pleases everyone," "John is easy (eager) for us to please," "it is easy (*eager) to please John," "John is a person who (it) is easy to please," "this room is not easy to work in (to do decent work in)," "he is easy to do business with," "This knife is very difficult to cut (meat) with," "a hotel lobby is difficult (a difficult place) to meet people in," "he is not easy to get information from," "such flattery is easy to be fooled by," and many other similar and related structures.

The general theory, in other words, would have to make possible the formulation of the underlying generalizations that account for this arrangement of empirical data, and to distinguish these real generalizations from pseudo-simplifications that have no linguistic significance. In so doing, the theory would suggest an explanation for the linguistic intuition of native speakers as regards (3) and (4). This explanation would rest on the assumption that the concepts of grammatical structure and "significant generalization" made explicit in this theory constitute the set of tools used by the learner in constructing an internal representation of his language (i.e., a generative grammar), on the basis of presented linguistic data. There is fairly good reason to believe that in the case of (3), (4), the theory of transformational grammar can approach the level of explanatory adequacy by providing a partial explanation for the speaker's linguistic intuition.[13] That is, the grammar that assigns the correct structural descriptions contains generalizations that are not expressed in grammars that fail to provide the correct structural descriptions, and is thus higher-valued, in a sense which can apparently be made precise without much difficulty.

As a second syntactic example, consider the following arrangement of sentences and nonsentences: ("John found the book"-"John was a farmer"), ("the book was found by John"-*"a farmer was been by John"), ("did John find the book?"-*"did John be a farmer?"), (*"found John the book?"-"was John a farmer?"), ("John didn't find the book"-*"John didn't be a farmer"), (*"John foundn't the book"-"John wasn't a farmer"), ("John DID find the book"-*"John DID be a farmer"), ("Bill found the book and so did John"-*"Bill was a farmer and so did John"), (*"Bill found the book and so found John"-"Bill was a farmer and so was John"), etc. In short, as is well known, there are a variety of respects, of which these are a sample, in which "be" behaves quite differently from "find." Similarly, "be," but not "find," is an Auxiliary. Traditional grammars merely list these facts as anomalous, and make no attempt to relate them. It can easily be shown, however, that a transformational grammar with a constituent structure subcomponent containing the rules:

$$VP \rightarrow Aux + VP_1 \tag{5i}$$
$$Aux \rightarrow Aux_1 (Aux_2) \tag{5ii}$$
$$Aux_1 \rightarrow Tense (Modal) \tag{5iii}$$

---

[13]See Miller and Chomsky (1963). Cf. also Lees (1960b) for detailed discussion of a class of similar cases. For discussion of measures of evaluation that select grammars with significant generalizations over those that do not contain such generalizations, cf. Chomsky (1955, chapter 3; 1962a); Halle (1961a); Halle and Chomsky (forthcoming).

$$\text{Aux}_2 \rightarrow (\text{have} + \text{en}) (\text{be} + \text{ing}) \qquad \text{(5iv)}$$

$$\text{VP}_1 \rightarrow \begin{cases} \text{Verb} + \text{NP} \\ \text{be} + \text{Predicate} \end{cases} \qquad \text{(5v)}$$

(an analysis which has many independent motivations) will automatically provide for just this range of phenomena, thus reducing a mass of apparent idiosyncracies to underlying regularity (cf. Chomsky, 1955, chapters 7, 9; 1957a). In fact, a transformational grammar would have to be complicated considerably to generate the excluded sentences. Here again, then, it seems that the level of explanatory adequacy can be met by a transformational grammar and the theory associated with it.[14]

A similar problem is posed by certain English comparative constructions. We have such sentences as "John received a warmer welcome than Bill," "John is a kinder person than Bill," and "John knows a kinder person than Bill," where only the last is ambiguous ("than Bill is," "than Bill does"). Furthermore, although we can have such sentences as "Bill bought a bigger house than John did," "Mary has a bigger red balloon than John," we do not have "Bill bought the bigger house than John did," "Mary has a red bigger balloon than John," "Mary has a bigger redder balloon than John than Bill," etc. At the level of observational adequacy, a grammar might simply state a variety of facts of this kind. But we can in fact reach a higher level of adequacy in this case. Suppose that we have a transformational grammar of English constructed so as to generate in the most economical way the full range of adjectival constructions, excluding comparatives. It can be shown (cf. Smith, 1961) that a large variety of constructions involving comparatives will be generated automatically by the grammar, with the right arrangement of ambiguities, instances and apparent "exceptions," if we add to this grammar, at the appropriate point in the sequence of ordered rules, the generalized transformation that forms the simplest comparative constructions (namely, those of the form "John is taller than Bill (is)" from "John is tall," "Bill is tall"). Here, then, is an interesting case where it seems proper to say that the general theory of transformational grammar provides an explanation for a complex array of superficially quite disordered data.

The possibilities for attaining higher levels of adequacy, and the difficulties that attend this project, are well illustrated by the problem of formulating in a precise

---

[14]The well-known (and different) apparent anomalies of "have" are also largely accounted for by (5) and the rules for forming questions, negations, etc. Notice that from these facts one is led to the conclusion that "be," the modals and the auxiliary "have" are not Verbs, in contrast to the familiar treatment of these items as "defective verbs" (cf., e.g., Bloomfield, 1933, 223; or Austin, 1956, who discusses the fact that modals have no progressive or participal forms, and compares them in this respect to "know," etc.—actually, there is no more reason to comment on the lack of "to—," "—ing," or "—en" forms of modals than on the fact that nouns do not appear in these positions). Notice also that there is no optional rule of the grammar that allows one to select "be" (though there is an optional rule that allows one to select "be + Predicate"). In this respect, "be" is quite different from most lexical items. In general, it seems reasonable to regard an item as meaning-bearing just in case selection of it is subject to an optional rule (thus most lexical items are meaning-bearing, as are optional transformations and constructions given by rewriting rules, but not, e.g., phonemes). Where the grammar provides for an optional choice, it makes sense to search for the conditions under which it is appropriate to make this choice (this being one aspect of the study of meaning). Thus it would seem reasonable to inquire into the meaning of "Predication" (i.e., choice of "be + Predicate" in rule (5iii)), but not into the meaning of "be," which is no more subject to independent choice than are its particular variants or their individual phonemes.

way the rules for construction of relative clauses and interrogatives. These are related operations; a roughly adequate description would be the following. In each terminal string, zero or more Noun Phrases are assigned as a "prefix" the element *Wh*. To a string containing the Noun Phrase *Wh* + X we may now apply the transformation

$$Y - Wh + X - Z \Rightarrow Wh + X - Y - Z \tag{6}$$

Thus from the string underlying "John admires *Wh* + someone," we can form, by (6), the string underlying "*Wh* + someone John admires" (where Z, in this case, is null). The result of (6) is now subject to either the operation of Relativization, which embeds it in the Noun Phrase of a matrix sentence (giving, e.g., "he met someone *Wh* + someone John admires") or the operation of *Auxiliary Attraction* which brings the first part of the Auxiliary to the position following *Wh* + X (giving "*Wh* + someone does John admire"). Finally, the resulting string is subject to obligatory rules that replace *Wh* + X by "who . . .," "what . . .," etc. (giving "he met someone who John admires," "who does John admire").[15] Clearly Relativization can be applied only if the Noun of the phrase *Wh* + X is the same as that of the Noun Phrase in which it is embedded. If the string resulting from the operations just described still contains *Wh*-forms which do not introduce relative clauses (i.e., do not refer to a Noun which actually appears in the sentence in a designated position), then this string is an interrogative, and is to be answered by specification of the Noun Phrases that occupy the positions of these *Wh*-forms. Thus we may have such interrogatives as "who admires John?" (in which Auxiliary attraction has applied vacuously), "who(m) does John admire?," "who admires who(m)?," "he met someone who admires who(m)?," "he met someone who(m) who admires?," etc. Details aside, this much seems fairly clear and can be formalized without difficulty within the framework of transformational grammar.

When we investigate the matter more carefully, however, we find that certain additional conditions are necessary for descriptive adequacy. In particular, a closer analysis of American English shows that interrogatives which delete a Noun Phrase can be formed only from singular indefinite Noun Phrases (although relatives and nondeleting interrogatives are not subject to this restriction; thus, "the boys who are in the room," "which boys are in the room?," etc., are perfectly natural). We have such sentences as "you know a boy with (who has) a scar," "you know the boy with (who has) the scar," "who do you know with (who has) a scar?," "I know a boy who was expelled," "who do I know who was expelled?," "who is likely to come to the lecture tonight?," etc. (notice, incidentally, that though such questions

---

[15]More details are given in various places, for example, Chomsky (1957, 1962), Lees (1960). The formulation just outlined is suggested by remarks of E. S. Klima. Other sorts of questions can be described in essentially the same way, even yes-or-no questions (as is pointed out in Katz and Postal, forthcoming). It is hardly necessary to warn the reader of the informality of these descriptions. Notice in particular that throughout this discussion, where sentences are said to be "derived from other sentences by transformation," what should be understood is that the abstract forms (categorized terminal strings) underlying them are derived from abstract forms underlying these other sentences. Notice also that such rules as (6) should be regarded as constituting not a transformation, but rather a family of transformations, in the sense of Chomsky (1955, chapter 8), the kth member of which takes the kth analysis of a string that meets the structural condition and performs the specified operation.

are singular in form, they are neutral as to number in meaning—thus there is, in the last example, no implication that only one person is expected). On the other hand, such sentences as "you know a boy with (who has) the scar," "who do you know with (who has) the scar?," "who do I know who were expelled?," "who are likely to come to the lecture tonight?," etc., are unnatural and deviant. A still closer analysis shows that the distribution of natural and deviant interrogatives mirrors quite closely that of natural and deviant declaratives with singular indefinite *unspecified* Noun Phrases of the form "someone X," "something X," or their variants. Thus the sentences "he found something of yours," "what did he find of yours?," "he found someone else," "who else did he find?," and so on, are perfectly natural, whereas, in contrast, the parallel sentences "he found someone of yours," "who did he find of yours?," "he found a boy else," and so on, are either outright impossible or else highly unnatural. (Notice, however, that we can have "he found a friend of yours," etc., so that there is no simple explanation for this unnaturalness on semantic grounds.) Similarly, we have such phrases as "someone's book," "whose book"; but "something's cover," "what's cover" are both unnatural (though, once again, we find "its cover" alongside of "his book"). Notice also that the sentences "I found a place (in which, where) we can hide the gift," "I found something in which we can hide the gift" are quite natural, although "I found something where we can hide the gift" is not. Correspondingly, we have the interrogative "what did you find in which we can hide the gift?," but not "what did you find where we can hide the gift?" (the only natural interpretation for the latter is quite different, namely, as a paraphrase of "what did you find in the place in which we can hide the gift?"). Notice finally that a certain "semantic gap" in the usage of indefinites is mirrored in interrogatives. Thus "someone" is referentially restricted to humans, and, in many contexts, use of "something" is natural only with reference to inanimate objects, so that there is, in these contexts, no natural way to refer to an unspecified animal. And, in fact, the unnaturalness of such sentences as "I watched something eating its dinner," with reference to a cat, is carried over for the corresponding interrogatives "what is eating its dinner? (the cat or the dog?)," and so on.

Such examples indicate that for the formation of interrogatives, the transformation (6) must be limited to strings of the form $Y - Wh + some + (one, thing) + X - Z$ (where the element $Wh + some + (one, thing) + X$ is a Noun Phrase), although it is free from this restriction when used to form relative clauses. Equivalently, we may say that the Relativization transformation is obligatory in the case of a string $Wh + X$ which is formed by (6), unless $X = some (one, thing) \ldots$

With this improvement, we come much closer to descriptive adequacy. Still, the question remains whether it is possible to find a principled basis for the factually correct description, in this case. The problem of explanatory adequacy, once again, is that of formulating a general condition on the structure of a transformational grammar that will account for the difference, just noted, between the rules for forming relatives and the rules for forming interrogatives. A plausible solution to this problem is suggested by the observation that relatives and interrogatives differ in another respect as well; namely, in the case of Relativization, the element that is deleted in the embedded (constituent) string still appears in the matrix string, whereas in the case of interrogatives, the deleted element is not represented elsewhere in the sentence. The abstract forms (that is, the categorized terminal strings) underlying a sentence with a relative clause are therefore determinable, given the sentence. This would not be true of interrogatives if a restriction such as that of the preceding paragraph were not imposed. This observation suggests the following general condition on transformational grammar. Each major category has associated with it a "designated element" as a member. This designated element may actually be realized (e.g., "it" for abstract Nouns, "some (one, thing)"), or it may be an abstract "dummy element." It is this designated representative of the category that must appear in the underlying strings for those transformations that do not preserve, in the transform, a specification of the actual terminal representative of the category in question. In other words, a transformation can delete an element only if this element is the designated representative of a category, or if the structural condition that defines this transformation states that the deleted element is structurally identical to another element of the transformed string. A deleted element is, therefore, always recoverable.[16]

In conformity with this condition, the rules for forming interrogatives (but not relatives) must be limited in application to underlying strings containing $Wh + \sum$, where $\sum$ is one of these designated elements. It is clear, on other grounds, that the elements "some (one, thing)" are to be identified as designated representatives of the nominal categories. It follows, then, that interrogatives must reflect the distributional limitations of these designated elements. Hence the general condition on deletion operations just proposed can provide a partial explanation for the peculiar restrictions on the formation of interrogatives in English.

There are indications of a different sort that this condition is necessary for descriptive adequacy. In general, a sentence from which a phrase has been deleted by a grammatical operation is not interpreted as structurally ambiguous. Thus the sentences "his car was stolen" (with agent deletion), "John is eating" (with deletion of Object—for discussion of this class of verbs, see Lees, 1960a; Chomsky, 1962a), and so on, are surely not to be considered in the same light as "flying planes can be dangerous," "John doesn't know how good meat tastes," and other familiar examples of structural ambiguity. An elliptical sentence is not simply one that is subject to alternative interpretations. But if it is true that the interpretation of a sentence is determined by the structural descriptions of the strings that underlie it (as is supposed in the theory of transformational grammar), then the degree of ambiguity of a sentence should correlate with the number of different systems of structural description underlying it. In particular, if the condition that we have proposed is not met, the "elliptical sentences" given above should be multiply, in fact, infinitely ambiguous, since they should each have infinitely many sources. Thus "the car was stolen" could derive from "the car was stolen by the boy, . . . by the tall boy, . . . by the tallest of all the boys in the school," etc. In fact, the proposed condition establishes that each such sentence (similarly, "who did he see," etc.) is derived from a single source with an unspecified Noun Phrase instead of from infinitely many sources with different Noun Phrases, consistently with the manner in which these sentences are interpreted.

---

[16]This condition is, incidentally, particularly important for the study of the limits on generative capacity of transformational grammars. Cf. Matthews (1961).

In this case, then, it seems that we can formulate a well-motivated general condition that partially explains the facts stated in the descriptively adequate grammar. This condition predicts that such must be the linguistic intuition of anyone who constructs for himself a transformational grammar to deal with the linguistic data to which he has been exposed.

Further investigation of conditions on relatives and interrogatives raises interesting problems of a variety of different sorts. We have proposed that interrogatives are formed by rule (6) with X limited to Noun Phrases of the form "some (one, thing)" W. Thus from "I know someone who was expelled" (with W = "who was expelled"), we should derive "who who was expelled do you know"; from "he has something of yours" (with W = "of yours"), we should derive "what of yours does he have"; from "I know someone from Philadelphia" (with W = "from Philadelphia"), we should derive "who from Philadelphia do you know"; and so on. In these cases there are preferred alternatives, namely, "who do you know who was expelled," "what does he have of yours," "who do you know from Philadelphia." Considering these alternatives, we must either modify the rule (6) to allow it to apply only to the segment Determiner + Noun of a Noun Phrase of the form Determiner + Noun + Relative Clause, or we must conclude that the grammar contains a subsidiary rule (7), which applies after (6);

$$X - \text{relative} - Y \Rightarrow X - Y - \text{relative}, \qquad (7)$$

where X is an indefinite Noun Phrase (note that "from Philadelphia," "of yours," have the derived constituent structure of Relative Clause in the examples above, as does "who was expelled"). The choice between these alternatives is settled by the fact that rule (7) is necessary anyway, to account for such cases as "a man was here who comes from Philadelphia." It seems, then, that these examples do not necessitate a modification of the account of formation of relatives given above. What remains an interesting question, however, is the determination of the conditions under which (7) is optional, obligatory, or excluded, and the determination of its relation to the rule that deletes *who (what) + Tense + be* from relatives. Similarly, some rather subtle questions arise when we consider the problem of Relativization with (6) when X in (6) itself contains a relative clause.

Notice that although several Noun Phrases in a sentence may have *Wh* attached to them, the operation (6) must be limited to a single application to each underlying terminal string. Thus we can have "who saw what?," "you met the man who saw what?," "you read the book that who saw?," "you saw the book which was next to what?," etc., but not "who what saw?," "you saw the book which which was next to" (as a declarative), and so on, as could arise from multiple applications of this rule. These examples show that (6) cannot apply twice to a given string as a Relativization and cannot apply twice as an Interrogative transformation, but it is equally true that it cannot apply to a given string once as a Relativization and once as an Interrogative transformation. Thus if rule (6) has applied to form a string which is embedded as a relative clause, it cannot reapply to this embedded string, preposing one of its Noun Phrases to the full sentence. Thus we can have the interrogative "he saw the man read the book that was on what?," but not "what did he see the man read the book that was on"; and we can have "he wondered where John put what?," but not "what did he wonder where John put"; etc. Notice that although we can have such sentences as "who did he know who has something of yours" (from "who who has something (of yours) did he know," by rule (7)—similarly, "what did you see the man read that was on the table?," and so on), we cannot have "what did he know someone who has (of yours)." Thus we can prepose the first, but not the second of the indefinite Noun Phrases of "he knew someone who has something (of yours)," and this, too, is accounted for by the restriction of (6) to a single application to each terminal string.

Because of this constraint, sentences that appear superficially to be rather similar behave quite differently with respect to formation of questions and relatives. Thus consider the sentences (8):

Mary saw the boy walk towards the railroad station	(8i)
Mary saw the boy who was walking towards the railroad station	(8ii)
Mary saw the boy walking towards the railroad station	(8iii)

Sentences (8i) and (8ii) are unambiguous, but have different syntactic analyses. In the case of (8i), the phrase "walk towards the railroad station" is the Complement of the Verb (cf. Chomsky, 1955, 1962a), whereas in (8ii), the phrase "who was walking towards the railroad station" is a relative clause forming a single Noun Phrase with "the boy." But (8iii) is subject to either analysis, and is therefore ambiguous, as is obvious when we consider the corresponding passives: "the boy was seen walking towards the railroad station (by Mary)," "the boy walking towards the railroad station was seen (by Mary)." (Notice that there is a further ambiguity where "Mary" is taken as the subject of "walk", but this is irrelevant to the present discussion.) But consider the sentence "the railroad station that Mary saw the boy walking towards (towards which Mary saw the boy walking) is about to be demolished." Although this is formed from the structurally ambiguous sentence (8iii), it is quire unambiguous; its relative clause has only the interpretation that is parallel to (8i). Correspondingly, we find that only (8i), and not (8ii), is subject to Relativization of "railroad station." Exactly the same is true of interrogatives. Thus "what did Mary see the boy walking towards?" can have only the interpretation analogous to (8i), although the sentence that is its source can have either interpretation (more accurately, the categorized terminal string that is its unique source happens to be one of two terminal strings that underlie the ambiguous sentence "Mary saw the boy walking towards something.") This configuration of possible interpretations is again a consequence of the constraint just noted, which permits application of (6) to a Noun Phrase within a Verbal Complement, but not to one within a Relative clause.

The constraint that (6) may not reapply to a given string is thus necessary if the grammar is to achieve descriptive adequacy. Once again, to achieve the level of explanatory adequacy, we must find a principled basis, a general condition on the structure of any grammar, that will require that in the case of English the rule (6) must be so constrained. Various suggestions come to mind, but I am unable to formulate a general condition that seems to me satisfying.

Finally, it is clear that the first segment Y of the structural condition of rule (6) must be suitably restricted. Thus we cannot have such interrogatives as "what presumably did Bill see" from "presumably Bill saw something," and so on. This suggests that we restrict Y in (6) to the form NP + ... With this further condition, we also succeed in excluding such nonsentences as "what for me to understand would be difficult?," although the perfectly correct form "what would it be difficult for me to understand?" is still permitted. Thus this condition would account for a distinction between the occurrences of "for me to understand something" in the contexts— "would be difficult" and "it would be difficult"—, so far as applicability of (6) is concerned.[16a]

This discussion obviously does not exhaust the topic. For one thing, it by no means specifies the distributional peculiarities of relatives and interrogatives in full detail, and to the extent that this deficiency still remains, important questions of explanatory adequacy cannot even be raised. Furthermore, even where a partial explanatory account can be given, there are open questions that we have not dealt with. Thus in discussing designated members of categories we assumed that the representatives of the nominal categories were "someone," "something," and their variants, but the examples we gave to support this could equally well have been used to support the claim that the representatives are "everyone," "everything." In fact, in favor of the latter claim one might cite such examples as "whose reputations are at stake?" (suggested by P. Kiparsky), which have no source if "someone," "something" are taken as the unique designated elements. But if there are several alternative designated elements, the comments on "recoverability" must be slightly revised. In general, many aspects of relative and interrogative constructions remain to be accounted for, and it seems that the complex of problems relating to rule (6) should continue to provide a profitable testing ground for explanatory hypotheses concerning the form and applicability of grammatical rules.

Consider now one final example from the domain of syntax. Such sentences as

$$\text{I don't approve of his drinking (cooking driving, etc.).} \qquad (9)$$

are ambiguous (. . . the fact that he drinks, cooks, etc.; the manner in which he drinks, cooks, etc.).[17] An explanation for this is proposed in Chomsky (1955), and it can now be given a much better formulation as well as stronger support by several ingenious observations of Lees (1960a, 64f.) and Klima (personal communication). Among the many ways of converting declarative sentences into NP's in English (cf. Lees, 1960a), we have, in particular, two that can be described informally as follows:

$$\text{NP} - \text{Aux}_1 \,(\text{Aux}_2) \,\text{VP}_1 \Rightarrow \text{NP} + \text{Possessive} - \text{ing} \,(\text{Aux}_2) \,\text{VP}_1 \qquad (10)$$

$$\text{NP} - \text{Aux} - \text{Verb} - (\text{NP}) \Rightarrow \text{NP} + \text{Possessive} - \text{nom} + \text{Verb} - (\text{of} + \text{NP}). \quad (11)$$

The transformation (10) gives such noun phrases as "his refusing (having refused) to

---

[16a]Alternatively, one might attempt to account for this distinction by a condition that relies on the fact that in the illegitimate case the Noun Phrase to be preposed is continued within a Noun Phrase, while in the legitimate case, it is not. However, the condition that a Noun Phrase contained within a Noun Phrase is not subject to (6), though quite plausible and suggested by many examples, is apparently somewhat too strong, as we can see from such, to be sure, rather marginal examples as "who would you approve of my seeing?," "what are you uncertain about giving to John?," "what would you be surprised by his reading?," etc. There is certainly much more to be said about this matter.

[17]In the case of "cooking," there are, in fact, two more interpretations, since "cooking" is a Noun independently of the transformations (10), (11) below, and "cook" is one of those Verbs that undergo the transformation of $\text{NP}_1 - \text{V} - \text{NP}_2$ to $\text{NP}_2 - \text{V}$ [cf. Gleitman, 1960; Chomsky, 1962a] giving "NP cooks" (which is then subject to (10)) from, e.g., "they cook NP."

participate," "his rejecting the offer," "his (having been) destroying property," etc.; while (11) gives such examples as "his refusal to participate," "his rejection of the offer," "his destruction of property," etc. But the phrases constructed by (10), (11) must be inserted into other sentences in the NP position by a generalized transformation. And this insertion is carried out differently in the two cases. In the case of (10), the transform as a whole replaces the NP of the sentences into which it is inserted; thus the derived Phrase-marker of "his rejecting the offer surprised me"[18] will indicate simply that "his rejecting the offer" is an NP. In the case of (11), however, the element NP + Possessive replaces the Determiner of an NP of the form Determiner + Noun, while the element nom + VP$_1$ replaces the Noun of this NP.

Thus the derived Phrase-marker of "his rejection of the offer surprised me" will indicate that "his rejection of the offer" is an NP, that "his" is a Determiner, and that "rejection of the offer" is a Noun. There are several facts that motivate this decision. For one thing, note that in the case of the phrases formed by (11) (but not those formed by (10)), adjectives can be inserted. Thus we can have "his strange refusal to participate," "his unexpected rejection of the offer," "his wanton destruction of property," etc.; but not "his strange refusing to participate," "his unexpected rejecting the offer," "his wanton destroying property." But adjectives are introduced by transformation[19] in the position Determiner — Noun. Consequently, for the adjectivalization transformation to operate properly, this structure must be specified in the derived Phrase-marker of the NP formed by (11). Secondly, note that the position of the "NP + Possessive" construction in an NP formed by (11), but not (10), can be filled by "the" ("the refusal to participate," "the rejection of the offer," "the destruction of property"; but not "the refusing to participate," "the rejecting the offer," "the destroying property"). This indicates that paired with (11) is an otherwise identical operation that replaces the Noun of the matrix sentence by "nom + Verb (of NP)," leaving the Determiner "the" unaffected, and again shows that the paired transformation (11) replaces the Determiner (which is, in fact, "the") of the matrix sentence by the "NP + Possessive" construction, which thus takes on the structure Determiner by the general rule for substitution transformations (cf. references of note 18).

But now observe that although (9) is ambiguous, both (12) and (13) are quite unambiguous:

> I don't approve of his drinking the beer (driving a sports car)　(12)
> I don't approve of his excessive drinking (careless driving)　(13)

Furthermore, they have opposite interpretations. Thus (12) refers to the fact of his drinking the beer, driving a sports car, etc.; while (13) refers to the manner of his drinking (of the beer), of his driving, etc. The fact that adjectives can appear in (13) implies that in this case the phrases "his drinking," "his driving," etc., have the

---

[18]For discussion of how transformations impose derived phrase structure, see Chomsky (1955, 1961a), Matthews (1962), Postal (1962).

[19]In Chomsky (1955, 1962a) this is given as a separate adjectivalization transformation, but J. Applegate has pointed out that modifying adjectives must rather be introduced by a transformation of sentences with relative clauses, and this proposal has been adopted in Lees (1960), Smith (1961).

derived phrase structure Determiner-Noun, as in the case of "his rejection of the offer." They must thus be formed by the transformation (11). And observe, in fact, that there is no other nominalized form of these verbs (as "refusal" and "rejection" contrast with "refusing" and "rejecting"). Hence we conclude that there is an obligatory rule that assigns to the nominalizing morpheme *nom* introduced in (11) the shape /ing/ when it is affixed to "drink," "drive," etc., just as it assigns to *nom* the shape /æl/ when it is affixed to "refuse" and the shape /yɨn/ when it is affixed to "reject."

It follows that "drinking," "driving," etc., will be formed in two distinct ways, by (10) and by (11). Since these verbs are, furthermore, optionally intransitive, the full NP "his drinking," "his driving," etc., will also be generated in two ways, once by (10) (with the derived structure NP and the interpretation "fact that") and once by (11) (with the derived structure Determiner + Noun, as well as NP, and the interpretation "manner of"). Noting that adjectives cannot be inserted in (12) (giving, e.g., "I don't approve of his excessive drinking the beer"), we conclude that this is unambiguously derived by (10), consistent with its interpretation, in this case.

Notice that as the wh-question transformation was formulated, it does not yield "whose book (did you find)?", "which book (did you find)?", etc. To form these, it must be extended to apply also to underlying strings of the form X − Determiner + Noun − Y (note that possessive NP's are Determiners, replacing the definite article, in fact, by a transformation). Applying this observation to the present case, we see that this transformation will yield "whose excessive drinking surprised you?", etc., as it should, but that it will exclude "whose drinking the beer surprised you?", etc. (again, correctly), since the underlying NP in this case is not of the form Determiner + Noun. Similarly, "whose drinking surprised you?" will be derived from only one source (and it is, in fact, unambiguous), since only one of the potential sources is of the required form Determiner + Noun.

See Katz and Postal (forthcoming) for further discussion of the problems presented by such examples as (9). It seems clear that examples such as these are totally beyond the range of any version of the taxonomic model, as so far conceived. But again, it seems possible to achieve the levels of descriptive and even explanatory adequacy with a transformational grammar.

2.3 Levels of adequacy in semantics. I have given several examples of how a higher level of adequacy might be achieved by linguistic theory in the domains of phonology and syntax. It remains to consider the third major part of a synchronic description, namely, its semantic aspect. Here the problem is much more obscure. One might perhaps maintain that the condition of observational adequacy would be met by an account of situational regularities associated with actual discourse;[20] and that the condition of descriptive adequacy is in part achieved by a set of appropriately interrelated dictionary entries, an explicit portrayal of the structure of certain "semantic fields," a list of terms that enter into specific meaning-relations, e.g., synonymy, etc.

How might one hope to achieve a higher level of adequacy, in this case? It might plausibly be maintained that certain semantic features of a language can be partially explained in terms of underlying syntactic processes. As an example, consider the discussion of (9), above. Or consider the case of such adjectives as "interesting,"

---

[20]What are called "semantical regularities" by Ziff (1960a).

"astonishing," "intriguing," etc., which have the semantic property that they are "connected with a specific human 'reaction,' "[21] even where no explicit reference is made to the person who is interested, astonished, intrigued ("it was an intriguing plan," as distinct from "it was an elaborate plan," etc.). These adjectives have in common many important syntactic features that distinguish them from other Verb + ing forms (e.g., "the plan seems intriguing (*failing)," "a very intriguing (*failing) plan," etc.). Furthermore, they would be derived, in a transformational grammar, from sentences in which they appear as Verbs ("the plan intrigues one," etc.—cf. Chomsky, 1962a). But the class of verbs from which these adjectives derive are pure transitives with human objects.[22] Thus the structural description of the sentence "it was an intriguing plan," as provided by a transformational grammar, will contain the terminal string underlying "the plan intrigued one (i.e., unspecified human)" just as explicitly as it contains the past tense morpheme; and this fact might be suggested as the explanation for the cited semantic feature.

In general, as syntactic description becomes deeper, what appear to be semantic questions fall increasingly within its scope;[23] and it is not entirely obvious whether or where one can draw a natural bound between grammar and "logical grammar," in the sense of Wittgenstein and the Oxford philosophers. Nevertheless, it seems clear that explanatory adequacy for descriptive semantics requires, beyond this, the development of an independent semantic theory (analogous, perhaps, to the theory of universal phonetics as mentioned below) that deals with questions of a kind that can scarcely be coherently formulated today, in particular, with the question: what are the substantive and formal constraints on systems of concepts that are constructed by humans on the basis of presented data? Observe that the problem posed in Section 1 for general linguistics is a special case of this question, where the system of concepts that is acquired consists of the notions "well-formed sentence of L," "grammatical relation in L," "sound pattern of L," etc. Perhaps it is not too much to hope that this particular problem may serve as a useful paradigm case. We return to this speculation below in Section 5. In any event, it seems that formulation of a general semantic theory of some sort, independent of any particular language, is perhaps not an unreasonable task to undertake, and is a precondition for any far-reaching attempt to attain a level of explanatory adequacy in semantic description. We might observe, at this point, that many problems of universal semantics (as of universal phonetics) were raised and quite seriously studied in the seventeenth century (cf., for example, Wilkins, 1668), though rarely since.

----

[21]Cf. Nowell-Smith (1954, 85). Other adjectives may also be characterizable in this way for some different reason, but this is irrelevant to the correctness of the present observation.

[22]That is, "intrigue," "astonish," etc., do not undergo optional deletion of the object, as do "cook," "eat," etc.; and such sentences as "John amused the book" are clearly deviant. These observations are not refuted by the fact that deviant utterances with object deletion can be attested (cf., e.g., E. Wilson, *The American Earthquake*, Doubleday, 1958, 481: "The American Legion Posts, which dominate the later sections, startle, trouble and shock," where all three verbs belong to the category in question), just as the distinction between the classes of adjectives noted above is not obscured by instances such as "if the sea was not *very* raging. . . ." (B. Russell, *Inquiry into Meaning and Truth*, W. W. Norton & Co., 1940, 84). See note 2 and references there.

[23]For discussion see Harris (1954), Chomsky (1957a), Ziff (1960a), Katz and Fodor (1963), Katz and Postal (forthcoming).

2.4 Comprehensiveness of grammars. In the preceding discussion, three levels of adequacy have been loosely sketched that might be attained by a linguistic description in the areas of phonology, syntax, and semantics. Of these, only the levels of descriptive and explanatory adequacy (and, ultimately, only the latter) are of sufficient interest to justify further discussion. Notice, however, that these levels of success are discussed only for grammars that are paired with some linguistic theory. It is always possible to describe the linguistic intuition of the native speaker in a completely *ad hoc* way, in any particular case, if we drop the requirement that the grammar be constructed in accordance with some fixed model or if we allow the associated linguistic theory to be completely general and without content (e.g., if our linguistic theory merely states that a grammar is an arbitrary computer program). Presumably, this possibility needs no further discussion. It is important to bear in mind that a grammar that assigns correctly the mass of structural descriptions (remote as this is from present hopes) would still be of no particular linguistic interest unless it also were to provide some insight into those formal properties that distinguish a natural language from arbitrary, enumerable sets of structural descriptions. At best, such a grammar would help clarify the subject matter for linguistic theory, just as a fourteenth-century clock depicting the positions of the heavenly bodies merely posed, but did not even suggest an answer to the questions to which classical physics addressed itself.

In connection with the question of levels of success, we must also briefly consider the matter of coverage of data. Sapir's often quoted remark that "all grammars leak" is extremely misleading, insofar as it implies that there are grammars so comprehensive that the question of completeness of coverage can seriously be raised. But this is patently false. In the case of traditional (i.e., inexplicit generative) grammars, the gaps are not easy to locate because of the vagueness of the rules and the essential reliance on the linguistic intuition of the reader. One of the merits of an explicit generative grammar is that these gaps are immediately exposed. Anyone who is actively at work on a linguistic description can cite innumerable examples that fall beyond the range of rules as so far formulated, or that are incorrectly handled by these rules—it is, in fact, sufficient to open a book or to listen to a conversation at random to find countless examples of sentences and sentence types that are not adequately dealt with in traditional or modern grammars.

Comprehensiveness of coverage does not seem to me to be a serious or significant goal at the present stage of linguistic science. Gross coverage of data can be achieved in many ways, by grammars of very different forms. Consequently, we learn little about the nature of linguistic structure from study of grammars that merely accomplish this. Higher levels of adequacy, in the sense described above, have been achieved so far only in limited areas. But only by studying the properties of grammars that achieve higher levels of adequacy and by gradually increasing the scope of description without sacrificing depth of analysis can we hope to sharpen and extend our understanding of the nature of linguistic structure.

It is important to bear this in mind in considering the masses of linguistic data that lie beyond the scope of an explicit generative grammar, proposed for some fragment of a language. It is no criticism of such a grammar to point to data that is not encompassed by its rules, where this data has no demonstrated bearing on the correctness of alternative formulations of the grammar of this language or on alternative theories of language. Until incorporated in an explicit generative grammar, such examples simply stand as exceptions, no more relevant to the correctness of the already formulated rules than strong verbs and irregular plurals. Listing of innumerable examples is neither difficult nor very interesting; it is quite another matter to find rules that account for them, or a general theory of such rules.[24]

It is necessary to distinguish between exceptions to a grammar, and counter-examples to a proposed general theory of linguistic structure. Examples that lie beyond the scope of a grammar are quite innocuous unless they show the superiority of some alternative grammar. They do not show that the grammar as already formulated is incorrect. Examples that contradict the principles formulated in some general theory show that, to at least this extent, the theory is incorrect and needs revision. Such examples become important if they can be shown to have some bearing on alternative conceptions of linguistic structure.

III. ON OBJECTIVITY OF LINGUISTIC DATA

When we discuss the levels of descriptive and explanatory adequacy, questions immediately arise concerning the firmness of the data in terms of which success is to be judged (nor are difficulties lacking even on the level of observational adequacy—cf. note 8). For example, in the case of (3), (4) one might ask how we can establish that the two are sentences of different types, or that "John's eagerness to please . . ." is well formed, while "John's easiness to please . . ." is not, and so on. There is no very satisfying answer to this question; data of this sort are simply what constitute the subject matter for linguistic theory. We neglect such data at the cost of destroying the subject. It is not that these introspective judgments are sacrosanct and beyond any conceivable doubt. On the contrary, their correctness can be challenged and supported in many ways, some quite indirect. Consistency among speakers of similar backgrounds, and consistency for a particular speaker on different occasions is relevant information. The possibility of constructing a systematic and general theory

---

[24]These comments apply, it seems to me, to most of the examples presented by Bolinger (1960, 1961). These lists of examples could be extended indefinitely. In the form in which they are presented, they have, for the most part, no obvious bearing on the correctness of formulations of English grammar that have been proposed for certain fragments of the language, or of the theories that underlie them.

Bolinger does suggest (1961, 381) that his examples are in conflict with certain theories of generative grammar, and that they support an alternative view about the nature of language, about which he offers only the following hint: in a grammar of the sort he envisions, "constructions are not produced one from another or from a stock of abstract components, but filed side by side," and the speakers do not 'produce' constructions, but rather " 'reach for' them, from a preestablished inventory." It is difficult to comment on the proposal in this form, because of the vagueness of the notions "construction" and "filed." If by "construction" Bolinger means something like "sequence of word classes," then his proposal is ruled out at once. It is clear that the variety of normal sentences is so great that the number of word class sequences associated with them is far larger than the number of seconds in a lifetime. For quantitative estimates bearing on this question (which are furthermore highly conservative) see Miller, Galanter, Pribram (1960), Miller and Chomsky (1963). If he has in mind some more abstract principle by which constructions are "filed," it remains to be seen whether this proposal, when clearly formulated, will differ from current theories of generative grammar.

to account for these observations is also a factor to be considered in evaluating the probable correctness of particular observations (as in the case of any data—cf. note 8). Consequently the fact that a certain grammatical theory has had explanatory value in dealing with data from one language may be an important factor in determining the validity of data from some different language. Operational tests that consistently supported introspective judgment in clear cases would, were they available, also be relevant in determining the correctness of particular observations.

It is sometimes assumed that operational criteria have a special and privileged position, in this connection, but this is surely a mistake. For one thing, we can be fairly certain that there will be no operational criteria for any but the most elementary notions. Furthermore, operational tests, just as explanatory theories, must meet the condition of correspondence to introspective judgment, if they are to be at all to the point. Thus a test of degree of grammaticalness that failed to make a distinction between, e.g., "colorless green ideas sleep furiously" and "furiously sleep ideas green colorless" would, to this extent, prove itself to be an uninteresting test. When a criterion (operational or not) is proposed for some notion, we must first inquire whether the concept it delimits is at all close to the one in which we are interested.

It is surprising how frequently this point is overlooked. Thus many linguists have proposed that synonymy be measured somehow in terms of degree of distributional similarity (cf., e.g., Hoenigswald, 1960; Frei, 1961), and have then concluded that such pairs as "bachelor" and "unmarried man" are not synonymous, since one, but not the other, can occur in the context—*hood*, etc. But all that this observation shows is that the proposed criterion is entirely wrong, as, indeed, it clearly is.[25] However synonymy may ultimately be analyzed, it is a fact that a speaker of English need undertake no empirical investigation to determine whether some bachelors are married, as he must to determine whether some bachelors are red-haired; and such facts as this provide the basis for the conclusion that there is a meaning relation between "bachelor" and "unmarried man." A proposed characterization (such as the proposed distributional analysis) of these meaning relations which is inconsistent with these facts is, to that extent, shown to be wrong.

Similarly, consider Quine's proposed quasi-operational definition of a concept of "stimulus meaning" (1960). As this is defined, the stimulus meaning of a word varies widely with level of attention, set, gullibility, mood, visual acuity, cortical lesions, etc., while the meaning and reference of a term are independent of these

---

[25]A critical and still unanswered objection to any such approach has been given by Bar-Hillel (1954, 233). Frei also gives a "distributional" argument against the existence of homonyms (40), but again this is simply a proposal for terminological revision. He regards these terminological innovations as refuting the position (argued in Chomsky, 1957a) that there is no evidence for the claim that the notion of phonemic contrast can be defined in terms of sameness of meaning in a way which will provide a semantic basis for phonology. But in fact, he mistakes the question at issue, which was this: given a set of sentence tokens to which meaning is somehow assigned, can this information be used to determine which of these tokens contrast? Presumably, those who maintain that phonology can or must be based on meaning are claiming that the answer is affirmative. But if Frei is correct in assuming (41-2) that meaning can be assigned only to an element of *langue*, not to tokens (as, in fact, is also argued in Chomsky, 1957a, 98), then the claim under discussion is automatically shown to be vacuous.

factors. These, and the many further discrepancies,[26] suggest that the concept has little relevance to the study of meaning and reference; consequently, it is not at all clear why any serious consideration should be given to this particular operational test. Quine's concern with it appears to stem from his belief that it provides all of the objective information that can be obtained about any language (e.g., 39), and that all additional assumptions about a language are "arbitrary" and "unverifiable" (71–2, 80) since they are "undetermined by the speech dispositions" and might conceivably be "due to linguistic ingenuity or lucky coincidence" (Quine's thesis of "indeterminacy of translation," and, also, of grammar, since he regards grammar as somehow based on translation—cf. 68f.). But he offers no argument for the belief that this particular operational test, among the many that might be proposed, has some unique significance; and the thesis of indeterminacy seems to amount only to the assertion that a significant empirical assertion has logically conceivable alternatives, which is true but unexciting.[27]

In these and many other cases, what has not been shown is that the concept defined by the proposed operational criterion has some importance. In fact, at the present stage of the study of language, it seems rather obvious that the attempt to gain some insight into the range of data that we now have is likely to be far more fruitful than the attempt to make this data more firm, e.g., by tests for synonymy, grammaticalness, and the like. Operational criteria for these notions, were they available and correct, might soothe the scientific conscience; but how, in fact, would they advance our understanding of the nature of language, or of the use and acquisition of language?

IV. THE NATURE OF STRUCTURAL DESCRIPTIONS

A generative grammar contains a *syntactic component*, which generates strings of formatives and specifies their structural features and interrelations; a *phonological component*, which converts a string of formatives with a specified syntactic

---

[26]The stimulation X belongs to the (affirmative) stimulus meaning of the sentence Y if presentation of X prompts assent to Y (with various qualifications that are not relevant here). But in general, an object is correctly called a Y not just because of its appearance, but because of its function, or even its "history" (cf. comments by P. Foot, 1961, 47f.). The other notions defined in terms of "stimulus meaning" are likewise of dubious interest. Thus "stimulus analyticity," as defined, would seem to hold of many universally shared beliefs (e.g., "there have been some black dogs," or "the world is flat," at one period), and thus sheds little light on the important (but, as Quine has elsewhere demonstrated, quite obscure) notion of "connection of meaning."

[27]What seems open to question in this account is only the use of the words "arbitrary" and "unverifiable" to apply to empirical hypotheses that do not merely summarize evidence, that is, to all nontrivial assertions of science or common sense, to X's belief that Y is using "tomorrow" in the sense of X's "tomorrow" and not his "yesterday," etc. Furthermore, it seems that Quine's own discussions of indeterminacy of reference (e.g., 52f.; cf. also 78-9) should be unintelligible, on his own grounds, for his hypothesis that his readers do not understand his "rabbit" in the sense of "rabbit stage," etc., is "unverifiable" and "arbitrary," as he uses these terms.

Notice, in this connection, that though given a finite amount of evidence, it is trivially true that there are conflicting hypotheses compatible with it, it does not follow that there are certain conflicting hypotheses among which no decision can be made by any possible obtainable evidence. Given a decision to restrict evidence to "stimulus meaning," one no doubt could find irresolvable conflicts, but this would be an uninteresting consequence of an arbitrary decision.

structure into a phonetic representation; and a *semantic component*, which assigns a semantic interpretation to a string of formatives with a specified syntactic structure. After a brief discussion of structural descriptions on the syntactic level, we will turn to a more detailed account of alternative views as to the nature of phonological representation. For discussion of semantic interpretation of structures generated by the syntactic component, see Katz and Fodor (1963), Katz and Postal (forthcoming).

4.1   The syntactic component. A structural description on the syntactic level must indicate how a string of formatives is subdivided into constituents of varying scope (from formatives, at one extreme, to the full sentence, at the other) and what are the categories to which these substrings belong (Noun, Verb, Noun Phrase, Relative clause, etc.).[28] Such information can be presented as a labelled bracketing of a string of formatives or in some equivalent notation, e.g., a labelled tree such as (14) for the sentences (3), (4).

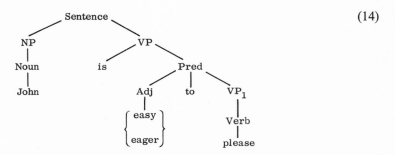

(14)

Such a representation is what we have called a *Phrase-marker*. In terms of such Phrase-markers, we can define grammatical relations, as certain subconfigurations. Thus the Subject-Predicate relation might be identified as the subconfiguration (Sentence; NP, VP), in which case it would hold between "John" and "is easy (eager) to please" in (14); and the Verb-Object relation could be defined as the configuration (VP$_1$; Verb, NP), in which case it would hold between "please" and "John" in "this may please John," with the obvious Phrase-marker; etc. Alternatively, these relations can be defined in terms of the heads of such configurations. For detailed proposals along these lines, see Chomsky (1955, chapter 6). It is the great merit of Pike's recent work in tagmemics to have focused attention on the importance of these notions, although his analysis of these relational notions is both redundant and (since it is a strictly categorial interpretation) not adequate—see Postal (1964, section vii).

Whatever exact decisions are made, it is evident, as observed in Section 2, above, that a great deal of relevant information is not representable in terms of a single Phrase-marker such as (14). Thus there is no way to indicate, in such a representation,

---

[28]The goal of traditional "universal grammar" was, in part, to give a substantive general account of these categories, thus fixing a universal "vocabulary" for the generative grammars of all languages. Presumably, such fixed universal category symbols would have to be defined in terms of formal properties of grammars and, perhaps, language-independent semantic properties of some sort. Whatever the feasibility of this enterprise may be, we will not consider it here, and will regard the category names for the time being as only conventional.

that when the adjective is "easy," the relation of "please" to "John" in (14) is that of Verb-Object, as in "this pleases John"; and that when the adjective is "eager," and is not followed by "for + NP," the relation of "John" to "please" in (14) is that of Subject-Verb, as in "John pleases us." Similarly, there is no way to indicate by a single labelled bracketing that in the sentence (15) the expressions "John," "please," and "gift" are related as they are in (16):

did John expect to be pleased by the gift?   (15)

The gift pleased John.   (16)

For reasons such as this, the taxonomic model of modern linguistics (cf. Section 1, above), which provides a single Phrase-marker of the type (14) as the structural description of a string, must be regarded as descriptively inadequate.

One might attempt to overcome this inadequacy by extending the definition of "grammatical relation" in the following way. Let us say that a grammatical relation holds of a certain pair (triple, etc.) of expressions (I) if they form part of a configuration of a Phrase-marker, as described above, or (II) if a "co-occurrence relation" of an appropriate sort[29] holds between the pair in question and a pair that has this grammatical relation in the sense of (I). Accordingly, we would say that in

---

[29]For a careful definition of one such notion, see Hiż (1961). This notion was introduced by Harris (1952a, 1952b) and studied in detail (Harris, 1957) as the basis for a theory of grammatical transformations. It is also mentioned in a similar connection by Bazell (1953), and is applied to Russian in Worth (1958). A grammatical transformation is defined, from this point of view, as a (symmetrical) relation holding between two sentence forms if corresponding positions in the two forms are filled by the same n-tuples of expressions. This relation is not part of generative grammar, as is the notion "grammatical transformation" of Section 1 and the references cited there, but is a structural relation holding of sentences and sentence forms described by a taxonomic, IC grammar (as in Harris, 1951a, chapter 16). The notions of "co-occurrence relation" and "generative transformation" are rather different in formal properties as well as in their role in actual syntactic description, and a great deal of confusion can result from failure to distinguish them. Thus it makes no sense to arrange co-occurrence relations "in sequence," but generative transformations can (and, in practice, must) be ordered and applied in sequence. The examples of Section 2 depend essentially on appropriate ordering and sequential application of transformational rules, and on appropriate choice of base versus derived forms (a distinction which is also not definable in terms of co-occurrence). Furthermore, co-occurrence is a relation defined on actual sentences, while generative transformations apply to abstract structures that often bear no close relation to actual sentences. Note also that in a generative transformational grammar, a direct, one-step transformational relation would hold between (16) and each of the sentences of (17); a somewhat more devious relation would hold between (16) and (15), which is derived by a sequence of transformations from a pair of strings, one of which underlies (16); and no relation at all would hold between (15)-(17i), or (17i)-(17ii), though all would be based on the terminal string underlying (16). From the point of view of co-occurrence, however, there is a "one-step" relation between both (16)-(17), and (17i)-(17ii), and no relation at all (because of "the gift brought happiness," etc.) between (15) and (16). Similarly, no co-occurrence relation would hold between (18iii) and (18ii) (because of "I met the boy"), though the latter is derived from the string underlying the former by a sequence of generative transformations. There are many other differences.

Harris' notion of transformation as a co-occurrence relation developed in the course of his work in the late 1940's on analysis of the structure of extended discourse. At the time, I was attempting to construct generative grammars for Modern Hebrew and English using Harris' morpheme-to-utterance procedures, with variables ranging over "long components," as a model for the syntactic component. There were serious difficulties in this, and the notion of grammatical transformation, when adapted and redesigned to enter the syntactic component of a generative grammar with ordered rules, seemed to overcome most of these.

did the gift please John?   (17i)

John was pleased by the gift.   (17ii)

where the grammatical relations are not expressible directly in terms of subconfigurations of the Phrase-marker, the Subject-Verb and Verb-Object relations hold
of the pairs "the gift" – "please" and "please" – "John," respectively, because any
triple of expressions that can replace "the gift," "please," and "John" in (17) can
also (with appropriate reordering) fill the positions of these expressions in (16),
where the grammatical relations are definable directly in terms of the Phrase-marker.

However, this approach seems to me to face insurmountable objections. Thus
although it may be true that a co-occurrence relation of the appropriate sort holds
between (16) and (17), it does not hold between (15) and (16), or (18i) and (16). Thus
"please" – "John" can be replaced by "bring" – "happiness" in (16), but not in (15)
or in (18i); but in all three cases these expressions are related as Verb-Object. And if
some modification is proposed to deal with this discrepancy, will it be able to distinguish the gramatically related "please" – "John" in (15) from the same pair,
grammatically unrelated, in "did John expect you to be pleased by the gift?" Or
consider the sentences (18ii-iv):

the gift pleased John but not Bill   (18i)

the book is what I want   (18ii)

I want the book   (18iii)

the clever boy saw the friendly man   (18iv)

In both (18ii) and (18iii), the Verb-Object relation holds of the pair "want" – "the
book"; but only in (18iii) can this pair be replaced by "met" – "the boy." In (18iv),
"clever" and "boy" are related as in "the boy is clever"; but in the latter, though not
in (18iv), the pair "plan" – "intriguing" can replace "boy" – "clever." Furthermore,
it seems that any pair that can replace "clever" – "boy" in (18iv) can replace "clever'
– "man" in the same sentence, though no grammatical relation at all holds of this
pair.

It is, of course, impossible to show that no possible modification of the notion of
co-occurrence could deal with such problems. However, for the present it seems
clear that any theory which, like the theory of phrase structure grammar, assigns a
single Phrase-marker such as (14) to an utterance is incapable of expressing deeper
structural relations and must therefore be ruled out by considerations of descriptive
adequacy.[30]

In the case of a transformational grammar, the syntactic description of a string of
formatives consists of a set of *underlying Phrase-markers* (one for each of the underlying simple strings from which the string is derived), a *derived Phrase-marker* such
as (14) that gives its superficial constituent structure, and a *Transformation-marker*
that expresses the manner of its derivation from underlying strings.[31] The deeper
structural information in the examples that we have discussed is provided by the

---

[30]Many other difficulties in the theory of phrase structure grammar are discussed in Chomsky
(1955, 1957a, 1961a); Postal (1961, 1963).

[31]For discussion of these matters, see the references of note 18. There are many open and difficult
questions here, but the general outlines of a satisfactory theory seem clear.

underlying Phrase-markers (for further details concerning the particular example (14), see Miller and Chomsky, 1963; see the references cited previously for the other cases). These examples are quite typical in this respect. In general, the grammatical relations that are expressed (in the manner indicated above) in the underlying Phrase-markers are those that constitute the deeper structure and determine the semantic interpretation of an utterance. The categorization expressed in the derived Phrase-marker plays a role in determining the form of the utterance (thus the "grammatical Subject" determines the number of the Verb Phrase, and the derived Phrase-marker determines the functioning of the phonological rules—cf. the references of note 6), but are irrelevant to its content. The primary motivation for the theory of transformational grammar lies in the fact that the significant grammatical functions and relations are expressed, in a natural way, only in underlying elementary Phrase-markers. For the present, the transformational model for generative grammar is unique in that it allows for the generation of structural information of a variety rich enough to account for facts of the kind discussed here and in Section 2, above—and, furthermore, to do so in many cases in a principled way, thus reaching the higher level of explanatory adequacy—though it is by no means without its problems.

4.2 The Phonological component. The phonological component of the grammar can be regarded as an input-output device which operates on a string of formatives, provided with a structural analysis by the syntactic component, and assigns to this string a representation as a string of phones. It is, in part, an open question to what extent structural information on the syntactic level is relevant to determining the phonetic form of a string of formatives. There is no doubt that information of the kind provided in the derived Phrase-marker is essential,[32] and there are scattered examples that suggest that deeper syntactic features may also play a role in determining the details of phonetic shape.

A rather classical view of the structure of the phonological component might be something like this. Formatives are of two types: grammatical and lexical (among the grammatical we count, as subtypes, class markers and junctural elements introduced by syntactic rules, e.g., word boundary). Each grammatical formative is represented by a single symbol. Each lexical formative is represented in a systematic orthography as a string of symbols, each of which is assigned to certain categories (Vowel, Consonant, Voiced, etc.). Each symbol can, in fact, be regarded as an abbreviation for the set of categories to which it belongs, and each lexical item can thus be represented by a *classificatory matrix* in which the columns stand for what we can call "segments" and the rows, for categories; the entry in the ith row and j^{th} column indicates whether the jth segment belongs to the ith category. These categories we may call (classificatory) distinctive features. Some squares of the matrix may be blank, where the feature in question can be supplied by a general rule (e.g., the entry for Rounding in the case of English Lax Front Vowels, which become, automatically, unrounded).

The rules of the phonological component are ordered, and apply in sequence to

---

[32]See the references of notes 6, 11, and 12 for details. All of these studies are based on the notion "transformational cycle" sketched in Section 1.

the string of formatives (utilizing, when this is relevant, the associated syntactic information) until ultimately a representation is reached in terms of a universal phonetic alphabet. The symbols of this alphabet are specified in terms of a set of phonetic features; hence the output of the phonological component can again be regarded as a matrix in which columns represent phones and rows, phonetic features of the universal system. The entry in the ith row and j^{th} column indicates whether the jth phone of the generated utterance possesses the ith feature, or the degree to which it possesses this feature (in the case of such features as stress). Classificatory distinctive features are by definition "binary"; phonetic features may or may not be. A representation in terms of phonetic features we can call a *phonetic matrix*, again regarding the symbols of the universal phonetic alphabet as mere conventional abbreviations for sets of feature specifications.

The universal phonetic alphabet is part of a universal phonetic theory. In addition to a fixed set of features, such a theory should contain general laws concerning possible combinations and contrasts. Steps toward such a theory are found in the work of the classical British phoneticians (Bell, Ellis, Sweet); in the "phonologie" of de Saussure's 1897 lectures;[33] and again in Jakobson's theory of distinctive features and phonetic universals (e.g., Jakobson, Fant and Halle, 1952). This theory constitutes a part of general linguistic theory, exactly as do the set of restrictions on the form of rules and the other constraints on the structure of a generative grammar. We will refer below to the requirement that a general linguistic theory must incorporate a universal phonetic theory, with a fixed alphabet, as the condition of *phonetic specifiability*. Note that a universal phonetic alphabet is the counterpart of a substantive theory of syntactic categories (see above, note 28) that assigns a fixed significance to the labels used in the syntactic component; but in the case of a phonetic alphabet, the construction of a concrete and substantive theory has, of course, been much more fully realized.

Let us assume that at a certain stage in the application of the rules of the phonological component, all grammatical formatives except junctures will have been eliminated and we have a representation in terms of classificatory matrices and junctures alone (with derived phrase structure indicated). At this point, for example, English "saw," which at the input stage is /sī/ + *past*, would be represented /sɔ̄/ (though English "heard," which at the input stage might be /hīr/ + *past*, might be represented /hīr‡d/, since the general rules that convert ī to e in many contexts, and that convert lax, noncompact vowels to [ɨ] before final /r/ (+ Consonant), would presumably not yet have applied). Similarly, at this stage, such a phrase as "telegraphic code" (at the phonetic level, perhaps [tʰeligræfikkʰlɔwd]) might still be represented /tele + græf + ik ‡ kōd/, or, more fully,

$$[_{NP}[_{Adj}[_N[_{Pre} \text{ tele }] \; [_{Stem} \text{ græf }] \,] \text{ ik}] \ddagger [_N \text{ kōd }] \,], \tag{19}$$

where the notation $[_A \text{ x }]$, with paired brackets, indicates that the bracketed string x

---

[33]Thus, for example, he claims that Nasalization is never distinctive for liquids in any language (1916, 74) and consequently need not be specified in the representation of, e.g., the nasalized /l/ of French "branlant." If this is true, then Nasalization need not be specified for liquids in the phonetic matrix for any language, just as Rounding need not be specified for Lax Front Vowels in the classificatory matrices of English.

is a string of the category A. This representation in terms of segments and junctures, with the derived constituent structure of the string still marked (since it plays a role in the determination of phonetic shape by subsequent phonological rules), we will call, tentatively, the level of *systematic phonemics*, implying by the word "systematic" that the choice of elements at this level is deeply determined by properties of both the syntactic and the phonological component. The representation in terms of the phones (and, possibly, phonetic junctures) that constitutes the output of the phonological component, we will call the level of *systematic phonetics*.

So far as I can see, there is no other significant level of representation that can be isolated in the phonological component. The input to the phonological component is, in effect, the lowest level of syntactic representation ("l'étage inférieur de la morphologie" of de Saussure, cf. Godel, 1957, 166) where segments are classified in terms of what will ultimately be phonetic characteristics ("caractères phoniques," *op. cit.*). The output of this component, as mentioned above, is essentially de Saussure's "phonologie," or the "narrow transcription" of the British phoneticians. The level of systematic phonemics is, essentially, the "phonological orthography" of Sapir (cf. Sapir, 1933), his "ideal sounds" and "true elements of the phonetic pattern" (cf. 1925, note 2); whereas systematic phonetics is his "phonetic orthography" (1933) or "objective phonemes" (1925). Similarly, systematic phonemics seems to be, in essence, the phonemics of Bloomfield's practice (1933) (in particular, when his "secondary phonemes" are not represented), though it is difficult to say whether it is in accord with his phonological theory, which is hardly a model of clarity.[34] Systematic phonemics would now generally be called "morphophonemics," in one of the several senses of this term. This terminological innovation is justified if there is a third, intermediate level of systematic representation, more closely related to sound and quite independent of syntactic structure, such as the system of representation now called "phonemic." However, as I will attempt to show below, the existence of an additional level is highly dubious, and for this reason I have preferred to keep the older term, modified by "systematic" to avoid confusion.

---

[34]It is instructive, in this connection, to recall the controversies aroused by Bloomfield's *Language*. In particular, Kent's review (1934) criticized it from the point of view of traditional (systematic) phonetics. Kent argues that "the difference between [s] and [š] is functional in English: shall we disregard it in citing Japanese, because it is not functional—even though we have the machinery for marking the distinction." In this vein, he criticizes Bloomfield's phonemicization of "secretary" [sekriterij] as /sekretejrij/ (which Bloomfield justifies, presumably, by reference to "secretarial" [sekritejrijil]), etc. In responding to the review, Bolling (1934) comments that to mark predictable phonetic variants, in particular, reduced variants of unstressed vowels, "would be like the meaningless underlining of a schoolgirl"; and he supports Bloomfield's phonemicizations by the argument that they mark only what is not predictable. It is interesting to note that the position that Bolling is attacking is, on many points, just the one that is adopted by the "neo-Bloomfieldian" linguists of the 1940's and 1950's, who characteristically criticize Bloomfield for failure to separate levels, and who return to a much "narrower" transcription. In particular, the marking of reduced variants of unstressed vowels is considered one of the major innovations in this development. We return to this issue directly.

The controversy between Kent and Bloomfield-Bolling concerns the choice between systematic phonetics and systematic phonemics. But it is clear that these are not alternatives, and that in fact both levels are significant in the description of a language. It was Bloomfield's summary rejection of phonetics as without scientific value or status, rather than his development of a higher level of representation, that should really have been at issue here.

In general, we can say, with Palmer (1958), that the place of the phonological component is "that of an ancillary technique; it provides a bridge between the grammatical statement and the direct observations that are reported in phonetics." For linguistic theory, the significant questions concerning the phonological component have to do with the choice of phonetic features (and, more generally, the universal phonetic theory), and with the conditions on the form and ordering of rules. The latter question, in particular, is of great importance, and phonological theory has suffered seriously from its neglect. As soon as the attempt to construct explicit rules to determine the phonetic shape of a string of formatives passes the most superficial and introductory stage, it becomes obvious that a fairly strict ordering must be imposed on phonological processes, if they are to be describable in full generality. Thus most of the examples in Sapir (1933) involve ordering, though he does not explicitly mention this fact. Bloomfield was much concerned with questions of ordering,[35] and his Menomini morphophonemics (1939) is the first modern example of a segment of a generative grammar with ordered rules. Bloomfield does not discuss the extent or depth of ordering in this grammar, and it is not easy to determine this from the examples that he gives. It apparently does not exceed five (cf. Bever, 1963). In the segment of the phonological component of Modern Hebrew presented in Chomsky (1951), a depth of ordering that reaches the range of twenty to thirty is demonstrated,[36] and this is surely an underestimate. Recent work (see note 32) gives strong support to the belief that ordering relations among phonological processes are quite strict; and, furthermore, it provides evidence that the ordering is not strictly linear, but is in part cyclic (see Section 1). Resolution of these questions seems to me the outstanding problem for contemporary phonology. Although several cases of ordering will be presented below, it is important to bear in mind that scattered examples cannot give an accurate indication of the extent or significance of ordering in a full grammar.

To make the discussion somewhat more concrete, consider the following simple example from English. We find such phonological regularities as the following

---

[35]Cf. Bloomfield (1933, 213). He regarded ordering of rules as an artifact—an invention of the linguist—as compared with order of constituents, which is "part of language." But this depreciation of the role of order of synchronic processes is just one aspect of the general antipathy to theory (the so-called "anti-mentalism") that Bloomfield developed and bequeathed to modern linguistics. This tendency fitted well with the operationalism, verificationism, and behaviorism that formed a dominant intellectual mood in the early 1930's. Harris showed (1951a, 237) that some of Bloomfield's examples of ordering can be handled by unordered rules that state the phonemic composition of a morphophoneme *in a strictly morphophonemic context*. But his method does not generalize to such examples as the one given directly below; and, furthermore, it is not clear whether the italicized condition on morphophonemic rules is compatible with the procedures by which they are established, since these procedures set up morphophonemes (similarly, phonemes) in terms of phonemic (respectively, phonetic) or mixed environments. There are important questions of principle here that have not been sufficiently clarified.

[36]That is, it is shown that a sequence of some twenty-five rules can be formed such that any interchange of adjacent rules will lead to a reformulation that increases complexity (and hence reduces generality). In the light of more recent work, the grammar presented there would have to be modified in many respects, but the conclusion concerning ordering, so it appears, would, if anything, be strengthened.

(where the notation $[s_1, s_2]$ is used for the "archiphoneme" consisting of the features common to s_1, s_2):[37]

$$\begin{Bmatrix}k\\t\end{Bmatrix} \to s \text{ in the context:} - + [i, y] \tag{20i}$$

$$[s, z] + [i, y] \to [š, ž] \text{ in the context:} - \text{Vowel} \tag{20ii}$$

Thus we have "opaque" – "opacity," "logic" – "logicism," "democrat" – "democracy," "pirate" – "piracy," in case (i); "race" – "racial," "express" – "expression," "erase" – "erasure," "enclose" – "enclosure," "revise" – "revision," in case (ii). Although various qualifications are needed, clearly rules such as these are needed in any grammar. But if these are regarded as purely classificatory, unordered rules to the effect that "morphophoneme" X has the "phoneme" Y as member (or realization, etc.) in the context Z–W, then they must be supplemented by the additional rule:

$$\begin{Bmatrix}k\\t\end{Bmatrix} + [i, y] \to š \text{ in the context:} - \text{Vowel}, \tag{21}$$

to account for "logician," "delicious" (cf. "delicacy"), "relate" – "relation," "ignite" – "ignition," etc. But clearly this rule is unnecessary if (20ii) can apply to the result of application of (20i), that is, if the rules are ordered as in (20).

The grammar containing just (20i), (20ii), in that order, will provide such derivations as:[38]

lajik + yɨn	prezident + i	prezident + i + æl
lajis + yɨn	prezidens + i	prezidens + i + æl (by (20i))
lajišin		prezidenš + æl (by (20ii))

(22)

The top line in (22) is the systematic phonemic representation, in each case, and the last line becomes the systematic phonetic by additional rules. But none of the intermediate stages has any systematic status at all, apparently. For each linguistic form, the number of intermediate representations will depend on the number of rules in the ordered sequence that apply to it, and this number will differ for different forms, indeed, for different subparts of the same sentence, phrase, or word.

Clearly a grammar that contains (21) as a rule is missing a generalization. In fact, consideration of additional examples shows immediately that several generalizations are being missed. Thus observe that alongside of (20) there is also the rule

$$z \to s \text{ in the context:} - + iv, \tag{23}$$

as in "abuse" – "abusive." But consider the forms "persuade" – "persuasive" – "persuasion," "corrode" – "corrosive" – "corrosion," etc. In a taxonomic grammar with no provision for applying rules in sequence, these regularities must be

---

[37]A natural evaluation measure ("simplicity" measure) for the phonological component (cf. Halle, 1961a) is the number of feature specifications it contains. In particular, then, the grammar is more highly valued (and more general) if rules are stated in terms of archiphonemes (and, furthermore, "generalized" archiphonemes such as C, V, etc.) rather than segments.

[38]As throughout, irrelevant details are omitted. In particular, for reasons beyond the scope of this discussion, the first vowel in "logic" should actually be not /a/ but /ɔ/ (cf. note 46), and /i/ should actually be the "archiphoneme" lax vowel.

accounted for by two entirely new rules, independent of (20), (21), (23), namely:

$$d \rightarrow s \text{ in the context:} - + \text{iv} \qquad (24\text{i})$$
$$d + [\text{i}, \text{y}] \rightarrow \check{\text{z}} \text{ in the context:} - \text{Vowel.} \qquad (24\text{ii})$$

If we allow rules to apply in sequence, the rules (24) are entirely superfluous. It is simply necessary to generalize (20i) to apply to [d, t] instead of simply /t/,[39] thus giving for "persuasive" the derivation (25) and for "persuasion" the derivation (26):

$$\text{perswēd} + \text{iv, perswēz} + \text{iv (by (20i)), perswēsiv (by (23))} \qquad (25)$$
$$\text{perswēd} + \text{yin, perswēz} + \text{yin (by (20i)), perswēžin (by (20ii)),} \qquad (26)$$

where again the first is the systematic phonemic and the last the systematic phonetic representation (details omitted).

Again, it is obvious that a grammar that accounts for this variety of phonetic facts by the rules (20) (suitably generalized) and (23), which are independently motivated, is much to be preferred, on grounds of descriptive adequacy, to one which contains in addition the rules (21), (24). The latter grammar is simply leaving significant generalizations unexpressed. But a descriptively adequate account in this case again requires that the rules be applied in the sequence given.

Finally, let us extend the analysis to include the forms (27), illustrating a point to which we will return below:

$$\text{decide [dīsa·yd]} \qquad (27\text{i})$$
$$\text{decided [dīsa·yDid]} - [\text{D}] = \text{alveolar flap} \qquad (27\text{ii})$$
$$\text{decisive [dīsaysiv]} \qquad (27\text{iii})$$
$$\text{delight [dīlayt]} \qquad (27\text{iv})$$
$$\text{delighted [dīlayDid].} \qquad (27\text{v})$$

To account for such facts as these, we must add to the phonological component containing the rules (20) and (23), the rules (28) and (29), where the order is now: (20i), (20ii), (23), (28), (29).

$$\text{a} \rightarrow \text{a· in the context:} - \text{(Glide) Voiced} \qquad (28)$$
$$[\text{t}, \text{d}] \rightarrow \text{D in the context: Stressed Vowel} - \text{Unstressed Vocalic.} \qquad (29)$$

Again, these can be generalized in familiar ways, and each is required, independently, by many other examples. With the rules so ordered we have such derivations as the following:

decide	*decided*	*decisive*	*delight*	*delighted*	*Rule*	(30)
dīsayd	dīsayd⧧d	dīsayd + iv	dīlayt	dīlayt⧧d		(a)
,,	,,	dīsayz + iv	,,	,,	(20i)	(b)
,,	,,	dīsays + iv	,,	,,	(23)	(c)
dīsa·yd	dīsa·yd⧧d	,,	,,	,,	(28)	(d)
,,	dīsa·ydid	,,	,,	dīlaytid		(e)
,,	dīsa·yDid	,,	,,	dīlayDid	(29)	(f)

---

[39]To this extent, this adjustment of (20i) simplifies the grammar (cf. note 37). Several qualifications are needed, however, which make the effect of the adjustment neutral, as regards complexity. Note that these rules should properly be stated strictly in terms of features. Thus, for example, rule (23) should assert, simply: [+ Continuant] → [− Voiced] in the context: — + iv.

Again details and well-known rules are omitted. Line (a) is the systematic phonemic and line (f) the systematic phonetic representation. At no other stage does the set of representations have any systematic character that I can detect. Perhaps (c) is what would be called "phonemic" by many structural linguists (though not, e.g., by Bloch). If so, it is to be observed that ordering of rules is also necessary to convert the "phonemic" representation to the phonetic one, in the optimal way, since clearly if (28) and (29) are not given in this order, the correct output will not be achieved. Thus the [D] of "delighted" is phonetically voiced, but is functionally Voiceless, for the application of rule (28)—thus it has the classificatory distinctive feature of Voicelessness and the phonetic feature of Voiced, in the framework proposed above.

As we enlarge the range of examples considered, the depth of required ordering increases (as does its complexity, when we introduce the transformational cycle). Investigation of this question has, so far, failed to reveal any systematic set of representation that might be taken as constituting a "level of representation" at any intermediate point in the operation of the phonological component, and therefore it seems necessary to conclude that systematic phonemics and systematic phonetics are the only two levels of representation that appear in structural descriptions provided by the phonological component. To fortify this conclusion, I would like to consider briefly the status of modern taxonomic phonemics, as seen from this point of view.

4.3 Taxonomic phonemics. Sound pattern has been taken as the primary object of study in modern, structural linguistics; it has, furthermore, been studied in relative or complete isolation from the syntactic setting within which phonological processes operate. In both of these respects, structural linguistics marks a departure from a more traditional point of view, which again emerges in recent work in generative grammar, as sketched above. Though modern phonologists have not achieved anything like unanimity, a body of doctrine has emerged to all or part of which a great many linguists would subscribe. Abstracting away from much variation, let us coin the term "taxonomic phonemics" to refer to this body of doctrine, thus emphasizing its striking reliance, in almost all versions, on procedures of segmentation and classification (identification of variants).[40]

Taxonomic phonemic theory constitutes the first attempt to formulate a linguistic theory with sufficient clarity and care so that questions of theoretical adequacy can seriously be raised. The development of taxonomic phonemics has led to standards of explicitness and precision that had rarely been attained in previous linguistic description, and to many new insights into sound structure. Furthermore, the period of its dominance has also been one of unparalleled extension of the range of linguistic investigation. For these reasons, the methodological and substantive assumptions that underlie this theory deserve careful and critical scrutiny. It seems to me, how-

---

[40]I naturally cannot hope to survey all contemporary points of view in the space of this paper, and I will concentrate on those that seem to me the clearest, referring to Troubetzkoy, Harris, Bloch, and Jakobson, among others. I will not consider glossematics (which, for reasons unclear to me, is often referred to as extremely rigorous and of high "operational preciseness"—cf., e.g., Haugen, 1951; Diderichsen, 1958), or the prosodic analysis of the London school, since I have been unable to find formulations of these positions that are explicit enough to show what evidence might count either for or against them, though the latter, in particular, seems to have certain relations to the point of view sketched above in Section 4.2.

ever, that they have not received the kind of critical appraisal that this position merits. In this discussion of taxonomic phonemics, I will attempt to show that several of the main methodological and substantive assumptions that have played a crucial role in taxonomic phonemics are invalid, and that, in several important respects, the theory of taxonomic phonemics, as it has emerged during the last thirty years, is less adequate than the phonemic theory that was implicit in the work of such pioneers of modern phonology as, for example, Edward Sapir.

Under discussion, then, are four potential levels of representation associated with the phonological component, namely, the levels of:

physical phonetics	(31i)
taxonomic phonetics	(31ii)
systematic phonetics	(31iii)
systematic phonemics	(31iv)

Physical phonetics is the study referred to by Troubetzkoy (1939) as "the science of the sounds of *parole*," a study with methods and goals entirely different from those of phonology (the "science of the sounds of *langue*"). It provides Bloomfield's "mechanical record of the gross acoustic features, such as is produced in the phonetics laboratory" (1933, 85); its status is not in question here, and no further attention will be given to it.

I will assume, for the purposes of this discussion, that the status of systematic phonemics ("morphophonemics," in one sense of the more usual modern phrase) is also not in question.

The status of systematic phonetics and the condition of phonetic specifiability (cf. p. 86, above), however, has been very much in question, and this level has, in fact, been explicitly rejected in many theoretical discussions. Thus for Bloomfield (*op. cit.*), the only kind of linguistic record that is "scientifically relevant," aside from that provided by physical phonetics, "is a record in terms of phonemes, ignoring all features that are not distinctive in the language." Phonetic transcription is dismissed as haphazard, limitless, accidental, and of no scientific value; and Bloomfield maintains that in phonology "we pay no heed to the acoustic nature of phonemes but merely accept them as distinct units and study their distribution" (p. 137). Troubetzkoy sometimes refers to phonemes as completely "abstract" units serving only a distinctive function. But elsewhere, he pays a great deal of attention to the systematization of the universal phonetic features that play a distinctive role in some language (structural phonetics—cf. 1939, 93f.). Bloomfield's apparent rejection of the level of structural phonetics reappears in an extreme form in Joos' (1957) summary of what he takes to be the characteristic view of American linguistics, namely, that "languages could differ from each other without limit and in unpredictable ways" (96), that "distinctive features are established *ad hoc* for each language or even dialect," and that "no universal theory of segments can be called upon to settle the moot points" (228). Similarly, Hjelmslev appears to deny the relevance of phonetic substance to phonological representation.

Nevertheless, it seems to me correct to regard modern taxonomic phonemics, of all varieties, as resting squarely on assumptions concerning a universal phonetic theory of the sort described above. Analysis of actual practice shows no exceptions to the reliance on phonetic universals. No procedure has been offered to show why, for example, initial [pʰ] should be identified with final [p] rather than final [t], in English, that does not rely essentially on the assumption that the familiar phonetic properties (Stop, Labial, etc.) are the "natural" ones. Harris might be interpreted as suggesting that a nonphonetic principle can replace reliance on absolute phonetic properties when he concludes (1951a, 66) that "simplicity of statement, as well as phonetic similarity, decide in favor of the p-pʰ grouping"; but this implication, if intended, is surely false. The correct analysis is simpler only if we utilize the familiar phonetic properties for phonetic specification. With freedom of choice of features, any arbitrary grouping may be made simpler. From innumerable examples of this sort, it seems that we must conclude that, despite disclaimers, all varieties of taxonomic phonemics rely essentially on the condition of phonetic specifiability. Furthermore, actual practice shows remarkable agreement as to which features constitute the universal phonetic system that is implicitly assumed.

It appears, then, that the status of systematic phonetics is also beyond dispute, though there is room for much discussion as to what is the actual character of the universal phonetic theory that underlies all descriptive practice. In any event, we can assume that each utterance of any language can be uniquely represented as a sequence of *phones*, each of which can be regarded as an abbreviation for a set of features (those that constitute the universal theory in question), in terms of which "phonetic similarity," "simplicity of statement," "pattern congruity," and so on, are defined.

Let us turn then to a more detailed investigation of taxonomic phonemics, taking this to be a theory that requires that phonological representations must, in addition to the condition of phonetic specifiability, meet conditions which, for the sake of this discussion, I will designate by the following terms:

linearity	(32i)
invariance	(32ii)
biuniqueness	(32iii)
local determinacy.	(32iv)

The linearity condition (32i) requires that each occurrence of a phoneme in the phonemic representation of an utterance be associated with a particular succession of (one or more) consecutive phones in its representing matrix, as its "member" or "realization"; and, furthermore, that if A precedes B in the phonemic representation, then the phone sequence associated with A precedes (is to the left of) that associated with B in the phonetic matrix. This condition follows from definitions of the phoneme as a class of phone sequences (as in post-Bloomfieldian American linguistics, typically)[41] or as a bundle of distinctive features (Bloomfield, Jakobson) or a minimal term in a phonological opposition (Prague circle).

---

[41]In the case of Bloch's very careful system of definitions (cf. Bloch, 1950, for a lucid sketch), the linearity condition is not necessarily met, but it is met, apparently, insofar as linear order is defined on phonemes at all. There are various unclarities here, despite the care of Bloch's presentation. Thus as the definitions stand, it is impossible for English [pʰ] to be a member of the phoneme /p/ (with [p]), since the defining qualities for /p/ are not coextensive with [pʰ] (or if a defining quality

The invariance condition (32ii) asserts that each phoneme P has associated with it a certain set $\varphi(P)$ of *defining features* (that is, $P = Q$ if and only if $\varphi(P) = \varphi(Q)$) and that wherever P occurs in a phonemic representation, there is an associated occurrence of $\varphi(P)$ in the corresponding phonetic representation. The invariance condition has no clear meaning unless the linearity condition is also met; I will assume, then, that it is inapplicable when linearity is violated. The invariance condition, in the form stated above, is required explicitly by Bloomfield, Troubetzkoy, Jakobson, and Bloch, for example, and appears to be implicit in many other conceptions. Where linearity and invariance are both met by a taxonomic phonemic representation, the string of phones is segmented into successive segments, each of which contains, along with redundant (determined) features, the defining features $\varphi(P)$ of some phoneme P, and the phonemic representation is just the sequence of these phonemes.

One can distinguish two versions of the invariance condition, depending on whether the features are taken to be *relative* (i.e., more or less along a certain phonetic dimension) or *absolute*. Jakobson explicitly accepts the relative version of the invariance condition, and Bloch, as I understand his account, seems to accept the absolute version. Under the absolute invariance condition, partial overlapping is excluded. If a certain occurrence of a phone P is assigned to a phoneme $\overline{P}$, then every other occurrence of P must be assigned to $\overline{P}$. Under the relative version of the invariance condition, certain cases of partial overlapping are permissible.

There are, however, some unresolved conceptual difficulties concerning the formulation of the relative invariance condition. Consider, e.g., a binary feature F such that a phone P in a certain context X–Y is assigned the feature $[+F]$ or $[-F]$ depending on its relation, in terms of the feature F, to some other phone Q in the context X–Y. But how is the context X–Y in question to be specified? If in terms of phones, then in general we can expect that the contrasting element Q will not appear in the context X–Y, but in a context X'–Y', where X' belongs to the same phoneme as X and Y' to the same phoneme as Y. If in terms of phonemes, then what happens when features that define X and Y are again relative to a context which, in this case, includes P and Q? For some discussion, see Chomsky (1957b).

Technically, the biuniqueness condition (32iii) asserts that each sequence of phones is represented by a unique sequence of phonemes, and that each sequence of phonemes represents a unique sequence of phones.[42] The biuniqueness condition is very widely maintained by modern phonologists, in particular, by those mentioned above.

---

need qualify only part of a phone, it would follow that, e.g., [sp] could be assigned to /p/ and to /s/). It is also unclear what is meant by the statement that the phonemes of a dialect must "accommodate all the phones." Thus English "solely" has a doubled [1], phonetically. By definition, this pair of successive segments constitutes a phone. Must this phone be a member of a phoneme, or can the phonemic representation have two /l/'s, given the requirement that the phonemes must accommodate the phones? Bloch's work illustrates an important point, namely, that as the explicitness of formulation of taxonomic phonemics increases, the difficulty of giving a consistent and descriptively adequate interpretation also increases. Thus as compared with the other phonemic theories under consideration here, Bloch's is quite explicit; but the difficulty of determining whether the conditions (32) are met is at least as great in the case of his phonological theory as in the case of the others.

[42]In this form, the condition is of course rarely met. What is intended, rather, is that each sequence of phonemes represents a sequence of phones that is unique up to free variation.

However, it is very difficult to formulate this condition in a manner that is actually in accord with their intentions. Consider, for example, Hockett's explicit discussion of it (1951). He considers a hypothetical language with no morphophonemic contrast between voiced and voiceless stops and with the rule:

$$\text{Stop} \rightarrow \text{Voiced, medially, in words.} \qquad (33)$$

Thus morphophonemic pat#atak becomes phonetic [patadak], while morphophonemic patat#ak becomes phonetic [padatak]. But, Hockett argues, if we hear [padatak] we do not know whether to transcribe /patat#ak/ or /pata#tak/. Consequently the morphophonemic representation fails the biuniqueness condition, and cannot be taken as the phonemic representation, which, in this case, must mark the distinction between voiced and voiceless consonants. This illustrative example, however, leaves many questions unanswered. Suppose, following Hockett, "that there is no word /pada/, or no word /tak/, or that, both of these words existing, they would not occur in this sequence." Or, suppose that there is a general rule to the effect that no word ends in a vowel. In any such case, "we can conclude that the proper representation would be *patat ak*" (/patat#ak/), and the morphophonemic representation would, technically, meet the biuniqueness condition and would thus qualify as phonemic, if we take this condition literally.

Hockett does not state whether he would accept this system as phonemic, in this case, but it is fairly clear from the context that he would not. In fact, a decision to accept it as phonemic would seem to be inconsistent with his principle of separation of levels, to which we return below, under any reasonable interpretation of this. It is fairly clear that linguists who accept the so-called biuniqueness condition would regard the situation just described as still being a violation of "biuniqueness" in the intended sense. That is, they do not mean by "biuniqueness" simply one-one correspondence, but rather a correspondence such that the unique phonemic representation corresponding to a given phonetic form can be determined by "purely phonetic" considerations, or perhaps, considerations involving only "neighboring sounds." This convention, which is rather difficult to state precisely, is what I have called the condition of local determinacy (32iv). Apparently it is this, rather than literal biuniqueness in the technical sense, that is required in taxonomic phonemics.

Notice that from the linearity and absolute invariance condition one can deduce a particularly strong form of the biuniqueness and local determinacy conditions, namely, as noted above, the condition that the phoneme corresponding to a particular phone can be determined independently of the context of this phone. That is, even partial overlapping is disallowed, and (32iv) is vacuous. Although, as noted above, the situation is still some what confused in the case of the relative invariance condition, it is clear that proponents of such positions (e.g., Jakobson, Harris) would disallow complete overlapping but not partial overlapping, since however they interpret the invariance condition, they do insist on some sort of "biuniqueness."

Although conditions (32i-iv) are (with a qualification to which I return below in Section 4.3) quite generally accepted, and though they do follow from familiar definitions of the phoneme, there are many examples showing that they are untenable. Consider first the linearity condition. Of the many examples that illustrate its incorrectness,[43] perhaps the simplest is one presented in a recent paper by Malécot (1960). He observes that Lax Vowel + Nasal is often realized as Nasalized Vowel before Unvoiced Stop, in English, so that, e.g., phonemic /kænt/ is phonetic [kãt], though phonemic /hænd/ is phonetic [hænd]. In the face of this evidence, no linguist would conclude that vowel nasalization is distinctive in English, and that "can't" – "cat" constitute a minimal pair, while "can't" – "canned" do not. Rather, in such a case, the linearity condition would be disregarded. Furthermore, there can be no doubt that this decision is correct. The phonetic representation can be derived from the phonemic, in this case, by the phonetic rules (34), ordered as given:

Vowel → Nasalized in the context: – Nasal Consonant   (34i)

Nasal → Ø in the context: Lax Vowel – Unvoiced Stop   (34ii)

Though perfectly general and straightforward, these rules happen to lead to a violation of the linearity condition.

A second and more extreme example of the violation of linearity is the case of the a-a· contrast, discussed above (p. 85, Section 4.2). The rules (28), (29), applied in this order, convert the systematic phonemic representations of row (I) of (35) first to row (II) and then to the systematic phonetic representation of row (III):

rayt⧧r	rayd⧧r	("writer," "rider," respectively)	35(I)
rayt⧧r	ra·yd⧧r	(by (28))	(II)
rayDɨr	ra·yDɨr	(by (29), etc.)	(III)

But here words which differ phonemically only in their fourth segments differ phonetically only in their second segments. Hence if phonemic representation is to play any significant role in linguistic description (if it is to be part of a grammar that achieves descriptive adequacy), the linearity condition must be rather grossly violated.

These violations of the linearity condition incidentally show, in yet another way,[44]

---

[43]For several, see Harris (1951a, chapters 7, 9).

[44]For further discussion, see Chomsky (1957a). Notice, for example, that such a pair as [r], [D] are in free variation and are assigned to the same phoneme in the context /θ-Vowel/ ("three,', "throw," etc.) in many English dialects, but replacement of one by the other in /bæ-l/ leads to a meaning difference ("battle," "barrel") (whereas, on the other hand, /t/ and /d/ can replace one another in the context /birn-/ ("burned," "burnt") with no change in meaning, though they would never be assigned to the same phoneme), so that the semantic criterion is falsified from right to left. And [ə], [r], though phonetically similar, clearly cannot be assigned to the same phoneme (cf. below) though they never contrast (with or without change of meaning), so that the criterion is falsified from left to right.

The history of the notion "contrast" in modern linguistics is very curious. Bloomfield (1926) took it as a primitive notion, and Harris provided a fairly effective operational test (1951a, 32f.), which is the only known device that can be used when the problem of determining contrast actually arises in practice. The only coherent attempt to define "contrast" has been Bloch's careful distributional definition. This has been frequently criticized, mainly on grounds of impracticality. Insofar as the criticism is valid, it shows only that "contrast" must be taken as a primitive notion. However, the criticism has almost universally been taken as showing that "contrast" must be defined in terms of "synonymy of utterance tokens" (e.g., Diderichsen, 1958), and in the background of the entire development has been the assumption that there is such a definition. Obviously, however, difficulties in one analysis do not show that another analysis is correct. And in fact there is no proposal for defining "contrast" in terms of "synonymy" that does not have obvious objections to it. In fact, the only definition I have been able to find or to construct that does not immediately fail

the incorrectness of the claim that phonology can (or, even more unaccountably, that it must) be based on synonymy, in its usual formulation to the effect that phonetically similar sounds are not assigned to the same phoneme if and only if replacement of one by the other in some context leads to a change of meaning (cf., e.g., Diderichsen, 1949). If what is meant by "context" is "phonetic context," then the criterion would give the result that V-Ṽ and a-a· constitute a phonological opposition (contrast) in English. If what is meant is "phonemic context," then obviously the question at issue is simply being begged. In general, it should be observed that "minimal pair" is not an elementary notion. It cannot be defined in phonetic terms, but only in terms of a completed phonemic analysis. Consequently, the "commutation test" is of only marginal interest if formulated, in the usual manner, as a procedure for phonemic analysis.

   Such violations of the linearity condition have not gone unnoticed by careful taxonomic phonologists, and it is instructive to consider the steps that have been taken to meet them. Troubetzkoy gives an example quite analogous to (34) both in the *Anleitung* and the *Grungdzüge* (1939, 46). He observes that the following phonological rules operate in Russian:

$$o \rightarrow \varrho \text{ in the context: } - 1 \qquad (36i)$$

$$1 \rightarrow \emptyset \text{ in the context: Vowel – Nasal Consonant} \qquad (36ii)$$

Thus phonemic /sólncă/ ("sun") is phonetic [sǫncə], and there is no necessity to set up /ǫ/ in contrast to /o/ as a new phoneme. Here the linearity condition is violated, as in (34); and, furthermore, the rules must be ordered as given. To account for such violations of linearity, Troubetzkoy proposes a general rule for phonemicization which we can state as follows:

> If the phone A is phonetically similar to the phone sequence BC, and A-BC are in free variation or complementary distribution, and BC is a realization of the phoneme sequence PQ, then A is to be regarded as a realization of PQ.   (37)

Thus [ǫ] is phonetically similar to and in complementary distribution with [ǫl], which is a realization of /ol/; thus [ǫ] is a realization of /ol/.[45] Similarly, nasalized vowels, in some English dialects, are in complementary distribution with Vowel + Nasal, and could thus be regarded as a realization of Vowel + Nasal, thus dealing with the violation of linearity caused by (34), in these dialects. Similarly, one might use the same argument to justify representing intervocalic and word final English [ŋ] as /ng/ (though to apply the argument in this case, complementary distribution

---

(Chomsky, 1957a, 95–6) not only requires (with Bloch) that each token appear in each possible context, but that it occur in each possible context with each "meaning," so that the "impracticality" of Bloch's proposal is compounded manyfold. Perhaps some semantic criterion for "contrast" exists. This we will not know, however, until proponents of this view take the same care in formulating their proposal as Bloch did in formulating his. Until such time, it can only be dismissed as a totally unsupported claim.

[45]Note that Troubetzkoy's rule must be modified, for adequacy, since as it stands it would require that [ǫl] be regarded as a realization of /ǫll/.

would have to be defined in terms of phonemically specified, rather than phonetically specified contexts).

However, the rule (37) seems to me not at all satisfying. It is entirely *ad hoc*, and it can only be taken as indicating that the definition of the phoneme as a minimal term of a phonological opposition is incorrect. More seriously, it cannot be applied in general, without absurdity. Thus, in English, the pairs [ṇ]-[ny], [yŭ]-[y] are phonetically similar and in complementary distribution, but it would be absurd, following the rule, to phonemicize [kitṇ] ("kitten") as /kitny/ or [yat] ("yacht") as /yŭat/. Even more serious for the taxonomic phonemicist is the fact that this rule can lead to a violation of biuniqueness. Thus consider the English [ă]-[a·] contrast ("write" – "ride"), discussed above. [ăy] appears only initially or after a consonant, and before an unvoiced consonant; [y] can never appear in this position. Since [y] and [ăy] are phonetically similar and [ăy] is a realization of /ay/, by Troubetzkoy's rule, [y] is a realization of /ay/. Aside from the absurdity, this leads to a violation of biuniqueness, in this case, since /y/ and /ay/ contrast ("ion" /ayan/ – "yon" /yan/). Hence aside from being *ad hoc*, this rule cannot be regarded as an extension of the notion "phoneme" to deal with the case of violation of linearity.

Troubetzkoy's informal comments and discussion of examples indicate that the rule, as he stated it, perhaps does not conform to his actual intentions. Suppose, in fact, that we were to restrict application of the rule (37) to the case in which B is a Lax Vowel and C a Liquid or Nasal. Then the violations of linearity in the Russian example (36) and the English example (34) (but not the example of English /ng/) would still be handled, while the counterexamples of the preceding paragraph would be ruled out. But now the entirely *ad hoc* character of the rule becomes even more clear, and surely with such a restrictive formulation as this no one would seriously regard it as constituting part of the definition of the fundamental concept "phoneme." Furthermore, it is still not difficult to construct counterexamples. Thus in many American dialects, [e] of "get" is in complementary distribution with [ɛr] of "berry," which is a realization of /er/; so that by the rule, even as amended, [e] must be regarded as a realization of /er/, and "get" must be phonemicized /gert/.

The rule (37) is a typical example of an *ad hoc* device invented to remedy an inadequacy of some general notion of "taxonomic phoneme," and this discussion of difficulties that it faces could be duplicated for other principles of this sort. These *ad hoc* revisions of a basically inadequate notion do not succeed in reaching the central issue. In such cases as those discussed above, it is clear that the acceptability of an analysis hinges on its effect on the grammar as a whole. Thus the rules (34i) and (34ii) are quite general and are independently motivated. A grammar that incorporates them is materially simpler then one that does not. But the rules: /yu/ → [y] before Vowels, or /er/ → [e] before Consonants, as in the absurd examples given above, obviously do not simplify the grammar of English. Similarly, Troubetzkoy's Russian example is well motivated by general systematic considerations; e.g., by the existence of such forms as /sólnešnij/, [sólnišnij], and by the fact that were (36) not incorporated in the grammar, then each occurrence of /o/ in the lexicon would have to be marked as distinct from /ǫ/, greatly complicating the grammar (cf. note 37). Similarly, the necessity of assigning English [ŋ] to /n/ (more accurately, to the archiphoneme Nasal) becomes obvious only when the full range of examples involving

Nasal + Stop in various syntactic positions comes under investigation. The fact that considerations of this sort are crucial suggests that any such "atomistic" rule as the one that Troubetzkoy suggests will fail.

General systematic considerations are, however, foreign to the point of view of taxonomic phonemics, and, in fact, they have often been criticized as circular (cf., e.g., Twaddell, 1935, 66). This criticism is correct, given the general "procedural" bias of modern phonology; but it shows only that the attempt to develop a taxonomic phonemics on the basis of analytic procedures of segmentation and classification, supplemented by such *ad hoc* rules as (37), is ill-conceived from the start.

The more extreme case of violation of linearity posed by "writer" – "rider" (which is beyond the range of (37) or any modification of it) is discussed by Harris (1951a, 70). He proposes that [ayD] be assigned to /ayt/ as a unit, and [a·yD] to /ayd/ as a unit, on general grounds of symmetry of distribution. But this is a rather vague notion, and it is not at all clear how it would fare once clarified. Furthermore, suppose that somehow a criterion of distributional symmetry can be formulated that has just the desired effect in this case. This result would still seem to be accidental and beside the point, since clearly in this case the critical factors are, once again, the generality and independent motivation of the rules (28), (29), and the relation of the forms in question to others; in particular, the relation of "writer" to "write" and "rider" to "ride," which would surely be expressed, on syntactic grounds, in the systematic phonemic representation. But these factors have nothing directly to do with distributional symmetry. They are, once again, of a general systematic character, and thus lie beyond the narrow scope of taxonomic phonemics. Finally, notice that Harris' proposal appears to involve an inconsistency with respect to the notion "distribution." Phonemes are to be defined in purely distributional terms. If the distribution is with respect to *phonetic* context, then the definition of "phoneme" is violated by his assignment of [a] and [a-] to /a/, since these phones contrast in the phonetic context [—y D]. If the distribution is with respect to *phonemic* context (an assumption difficult to reconcile with a procedural approach, as noted above), then the definition is violated by the assignment of [O] to /t/ or /d/, depending on the *phonetic* context in this case.

It seems to me, then, that the *ad hoc* devices for dealing with the violations of linearity are not defensible, and that the definition of a phoneme as "a bundle of [phonetic] distinctive features," "a class of phones in free variation or complementary distribution," or "a minimal term in a phonological opposition" can be maintained only if we are willing to tolerate such absurdities as the phonemic representations /kæt/, /rayDir/, /ra·yDir/ for "can't," "writer," "rider," and so on, in many other cases.

Consider now the invariance condition. Notice first that it fails in the case of violations of linearity such as those discussed above. However, it seems to me untenable even when linearity is preserved. Phonemic overlapping provides the clearest example of this. Thus consider an English dialect in which [D] is the allophone of /r/ in "throw" and of /t/ in "Betty" (where it contrasts with the /r/ of "berry" – cf. Bloch, 1941). Following the principle of invariance, we must assign [D] to /t/ in the context ♯ θ–, contrary not only to the speaker's intuition but also to the otherwise valid rules of consonant distribution. The situation is worse in dialects in which [D] and [r] are in free variation in this context and in intervocalic contrast, in which case no coherent solution is possible within the framework of (32), although the description of the facts is perfectly straightforward. The situation is still worse if we accept the absolute invariance condition, particularly if (as in Bloch, 1950) the features ("qualities") are defined in auditory terms. For it is known that in this case, not even the correct analysis of English stops is tenable, since /p/, /t/ and /k/ overlap (Schatz, 1953). For reasons such as these, then, it seems that the invariance condition cannot be accepted, however the condition of linearity is treated.

The biuniqueness condition is difficult to discuss because of the unclarity of formulation noted above. Nevertheless, certain consequences of accepting it are clear, and it seems to me that these are quite devastating, for anyone concerned with descriptive adequacy. Halle has pointed out that it is generally impossible to provide a level of representation meeting the biuniqueness condition without destroying the generality of rules, when the sound system has an asymmetry. Thus he gives the following, quite typical example from Russian (Halle, 1959b). In (38) the four forms in column I are given in systematic phonemic representation and in column III in systematic phonetic representation:

	I	II	III	
	d′at, l, i	d′at, l, i	d′at, l, i	(38)
	d′at, bi	d′ad, bi	d′ad, bi	
	ž′eč l, i	ž′eč l, i	ž′eč l, i	
	ž′eč bi	ž′eč bi	ž′eǰ bi	

The forms of column III are produced from those of column I by the general rule:

$$\text{Obstruent} \rightarrow \text{Voiced in the context}: - \text{Voiced Obstruent.} \qquad (39)$$

But the representations in column I fail the condition of biuniqueness as usually construed (in terms of local determinacy), and consequently would not be accepted as taxonomic phonemic. The representations in column II would be accepted as "phonemic" by taxonomic phonologists, because of the fact that t,-d, contrast, while č-ǰ do not. But if the grammar is to provide II as a level of representation, then it cannot incorporate the general rule (39), but must have in its place the two rules (40i) and (40ii), the first of which is taken as a rule relating "morphophonemic" to "phonemic" representation, and the second as relating "phonemic" to phonetic representation:

Obstruent → Voiced in the context: – Voiced Obstruent, except for c, č, x;   (40i)
c, č, x → Voiced in the context: – Voiced Obstruent.   (40ii)

It seems to me that the force of this example has not been sufficiently appreciated by taxonomic phonemicists. Where it has been noted at all, the discussion has not been adequate. Ferguson, in his review (1962) of Halle (1959b), discusses not the example given in the book under review (and reproduced above), but instead a Turkish example that had at first been proposed by Lees as analogous to Halle's, and then withdrawn by Lees as inappropriate (Lees, 1961, p. 63). Insofar as Ferguson's discussion carries over to the correct example that Halle gives, it amounts only to the observation that from the phonetic record alone it is possible to determine the underlying systematic phonemic (in his terms, morphophonemic) form in the case of c, č, x, but not in the case of the other obstruents. This is correct but irrelevant, since this information is provided just as explicitly in the grammar which incorporates only systematic phonemics and systematic phonetics as in the grammar which, in addition, adds an intermediate level of taxonomic phonemics. Thus the fact remains that in this case, the only effect of assuming that there is a taxonomic phonemic level is to make it impossible to state the generalization.

In the face of Halle's example, I do not see how one can fail to be uncomfortable in attributing to Russian a level of taxonomic phonemics. Furthermore, similar examples are not difficult to find in other languages. Bloch, in fact, gave a rather similar example in his discussion of phonemic overlapping (Bloch, 1941). In his dialect of English there are forms that might have the systematic phonemic representations of column I and the systematic phonetic representations of column III of (41):

	I	II	III	
"nod":	nad	na·d	na·d	
"knot":	nat	nat	nat	(41)
"bed":	bed	bed	be·d	
"bet":	bet	bet	bet	

Column I does not meet the biuniqueness condition because of such contrasts as "balm" – "bomb," "starry" – "sorry," "father" – "bother," and because of the fact that the vowel of "Pa'd (do it)" is that of "pod," phonetically. Column III can be derived from column I by the familiar rule of lengthening before voiced segments (of which (28) is a special case).[46] But Bloch is forced, by the biuniqueness condition, to accept II as the phonemic level of representation. Thus a full grammar of English, meeting this condition, would have to replace the general rule of vowel lengthening by two rules, the first of which applies only to /a/ and the second to all other vowels. The first would relate "morphophonemic" and "phonemic," and the second "phonemic" and phonetic representations. The situation is exactly analogous to the Russian example just given, and again we see that the effect of the biuniqueness condition is to complicate the grammar, that is, to prevent it from achieving descriptive adequacy.

The complicating effect of the biuniqueness condition has been commented on by several of its proponents. Thus Bloch remarks at once, in discussing the preceding example, that it leads to a loss of symmetry. Similarly, he remarks (1950, note 3) that the National Romanization which influenced his earlier, nonbiunique analysis

---

[46]This discussion is quite unaffected by the residual cases of a-a· contrast. For Bloch's dialect, "father," and "bother" have different vowels, quite independently of how we analyze the forms of (41). In fact, it is no accident that the short vowel in the a-a· pairs is generally spelled "o" while the long one is spelled "a." A good case can be made for the conclusion that the vowel phoneme of "nod," "knot," "bomb," etc., is actually /ɔ/, which in certain dialects goes to [a·] (merging with the variant of /a/), in others goes to [a] (giving the a-a· contrast), and in others remains [ɔ]. This assumption is required by many other considerations, e.g., to describe in the most general way the familiar ē → æ and ō → a alternations. Cf. Halle and Chomsky (forthcoming) for a detailed discussion. The issue is further complicated by dialects (cf. Sledd, 1959) in which liquids drop preconsonantly (giving long variants of short vowels in such words as "absolve" /æbsɔlv/—cf., "absolution"—etc.). This is just one of the many examples that show how wide a range of information is necessary to determine what is in fact a minimal pair.

of Japanese, though "neat and systematic," is not as close to a "phonemic notation" as the Hepburn Romanization, "unsystematic and cumbersome as it seems to be." Similarly, Hockett (1951) compares Bloch's "deceptively simple" nonbiunique analysis with his later "quite complicated . . . but obviously more accurate" taxonomic phonemic analysis. In fact, however, the "greater accuracy" of the latter seems to reside in nothing other than its observance of conditions (32i–iv). We return below to the question of why this is regarded as a sign of greater accuracy.

We have, as yet, said nothing about the principle of complementary distribution, which is the central concept of taxonomic phonemics as developed, for example, by Jones, Troubetzkoy, Harris, and Bloch. This principle is, basically, the principle of biuniqueness converted into a procedure. Regarded as an analytic procedure, its goal is to provide the minimally redundant representation meeting the conditions of biuniqueness and local determinacy. We will show, however, that it is in general incapable of providing the minimally redundant analysis meeting these conditions, and furthermore, that it may even lead to a nonbiunique analysis.

We can formulate the principle in this way (following Harris, 1951a, chapter 7): Given a set of representations in terms of phones, let us define the distribution $D(x)$ of the phone x as the set of (short-range) phonetic contexts in which x occurs. The relation of complementary distribution holds between phones x and y if $D(x)$ and $D(y)$ have no element in common. A *tentative phoneme* is a class of phones related pair-wise by the relation of complementary distribution. Some would require further that a defining phonetic property be associated with each tentative phoneme, marking each of its members and no other phone (the invariance condition).[47] A *tentative phonemic system* is a family of tentative phonemes meeting a condition of exhaustiveness. We find *the* phonemic system (or systems) by applying additional criteria of symmetry.

But consider the example of phonemic overlapping due to Bloch that was discussed above, namely, the case of a dialect with [D] as the realization of /r/ in "throw" and of /t/ in "Betty," where it contrasts with the [r] of "berry." The requirement of biuniqueness is preserved if we set up the phonemes /t/, with the allophone [D] in intervocalic, post-stress position, and /r/, with the allophone [D] after dental spirants. Given a phone in a phonetic context, we can now uniquely assign it to a phoneme; and given a phoneme in a phonemic context we can uniquely determine its phonetic realization (up to free variation). However, this solution, which is the only reasonable one (and the one Bloch accepted in his 1941 paper), is inconsistent with the principle of complementary distribution. In fact, the allophones [D] and [r] of /r/ are not in complementary distribution, since they both occur in the context [be-iy] ("Betty," "berry"). Hence complementary distribution is not a necessary condition for biuniqueness. Furthermore, the class of "tentative phonemic systems" as defined in the preceding paragraph will not include the optimal biunique system as a member, so that no supplementary criteria will suffice to select it from this class.

---

[47]This would be required by Troubetzkoy, Jakobson, and Bloch, but not by Harris (cf. 1951a, 72, note 28). He maintains that "any grouping of complementary segments may be called phonemic," and that further criteria have to do only with convenience, not with linguistic fact.

But now observe further that the class of tentative phonemic systems, as defined, will contain systems that fail the principle of biuniqueness. Thus, for example, [k] and [ă] are in complementary distribution in English (and, furthermore, share features shared by nothing else, e.g., in Jakobson's terms, the features Compact, Grave, Lax, Non-Flat). Hence they qualify as a tentative phoneme, and there is a tentative phonemic system in which they are identified as members of the same phoneme /K/. But in this phonemic system, "socked" [săkt] and "Scot" [skăt] will both be represented phonemically as /sKKt/. Similarly, [ə] and [r] are in complementary distribution (and share defining features) and thus qualify as a potential phoneme. But if they are identified as variants of /R/, we will have "prevail" /pRRvēl/, [prəveyl], "pervade" /pRRvēd/ [pərveyd], which is a violation of local determinacy, and of biuniqueness as generally construed. Consequently the principle of complementary distribution does not even provide a sufficient condition for biuniqueness. Since it provides neither a necessary nor a sufficient condition for biuniqueness, and, apparently, has no motivation except for its connection with biuniqueness, the principle of complementary distribution appears to be devoid of theoretical significance.

Related questions have been discussed by taxonomic phonemicists, but the general problem has apparently escaped attention. Troubetzkoy considers the example of English [r] and [ə], and gives a rule (1935, Rule IV; 1939, Rule IV) that would prevent them from being assigned to the same phoneme in case the sequence [ər] is in contrast with [ə]. This rule, as formulated, is not pertinent to the problem of preserving biuniqueness, and does not cover either of the examples of the preceding paragraph. It is, furthermore, entirely *ad hoc*, and thus simply serves to indicate a theoretical inadequacy of taxonomic phonemics.

Apparently only Harris has considered a special case of this problem explicitly. He points out (1951a, 62, note 10) that we might have phonetic representations [ṭray], [kray] for "try," "cry," where ṭ-k and ṛ-r are in complementary distribution. But if we were to set up a tentative phonemic system in the manner described above, we could have a phoneme /T/ with allophones [ṭ] before [ṛ] and [k] before [r], and a phoneme /R/ with allophones [ṛ], [r]. But now both "try" and "cry" would be represented /TRay/. To avoid this, Harris suggests that we first group [ṛ] and [r] into /r/, and then redefine distributions in terms of the newly specified contexts, in which [ṭ] and [k] now contrast before /r/. This procedure will avoid the difficulty in the particular case of "try," "cry," but not in the cases described above. Furthermore, the same procedure could just as well be used to group [ṭ] and [k] into /T/, thus keeping [ṛ] and [r] phonemically distinct (in further justification, we could point out that this regularizes distributions, since now /t/ occurs neither before /r/ or /l/, instead of, asymmetrically, only before /r/). Hence, as in the case of the procedures discussed above, it fails to distinguish permissible from impermissible applications. Finally, the procedure as stated is inconsistent with Harris' general requirement on the set of linguistic procedures (1951a, 7), namely, that operations must be "carried out for all the elements simultaneously" without any "arbitrary point of departure." In fact, this requirement was what made it possible for Harris to avoid Bloomfield's use of descriptive order (cf. note 35, above). But it is violated by the procedure just discussed.

4.4 Criteria for systematic phonemics. Systematic phonemics in the sense of

Sapir or of Section 4.2 does not observe the conditions (32) and is not based on such techniques as complementary distribution or, for that matter, on any analytic procedures of segmentation and classification.[48] Furthermore, construction of the set of ordered rules constituting the phonological component cannot be undertaken in isolation from the study of syntactic processes, just as study of the syntactic component cannot proceed without regard to the simplicity and generality of the rules that convert its output into a phonetic representation.

In analyzing a particular language, we must assume given a theory of generative grammar that specifies abstractly the form of grammars and a measure of evaluation for grammars. To fix the level of systematic phonemics for this language, we must attempt to construct the most highly valued grammar compatible with the primary data from this language (cf. Section 1). The level of systematic phonemics will consist of the set of representations that appear in derivations provided by this grammar at the point where grammatical morphemes other than junctures have been eliminated. It is certainly conceivable that there exist procedures of some sort that would facilitate the task of selecting this level of representation, but they are not, to my knowledge, available today. It is hardly likely that elementary taxonomic procedures of the kind that have been studied in modern structural linguistics can lead to the discovery of this level of representation. For the present, it seems that the most promising way to give a closer specification of this level of representation and the criteria that determine it is by refining the abstract conditions on the form of generative grammar, the measure of evaluation, and the universal features that define the phonetic matrices in terms of which the primary data is represented.

We observed in Section 4.2 that if a grammar is to achieve the level of descriptive adequacy, the rules of its phonological component must be ordered; and, in general, a derivation will contain many representations between the systematic phonemic and the systematic phonetic. We suggested that there is no set of intermediate representations that has any systematic significance. Whether or not this is true, we have now, in Section 4.3, accumulated evidence showing that if a level meeting the conditions associated with taxonomic phonemics is incorporated in a grammar, then many generalizations will not be expressible and descriptive adequacy cannot be achieved. It is important, then, to see whether there is some way of justifying the assumption that a level of taxonomic phonemics actually constitutes a part of linguistic structure.

4.5 The motivation for taxonomic phonemics. We are now concerned with the question: Why should it be assumed that a grammar must generate representations meeting the conditions (32), as part of the structural descriptions of utterances? What, in other words, is the justification for the theory of taxonomic phonemics, in any of its modern varieties?

Many linguists would perhaps take a position of the sort expressed by Twaddell (1935). In opposition to the "mentalistic" approach of Sapir (that is, the approach that is concerned with descriptive and explanatory adequacy), he proposes a method of phonemic analysis for which the following is "the only defense that may be offered": "this procedure . . . appears to be characterized by a minimum of the

---

[48]In the case of Sapir, it seems that the choice of examples in his important psychological reality paper (1933) was motivated by his rejection of these (at the time, still unformulated) conditions.

undemonstrable. With one coherent set of assumptions and conventions, which are indispensable to all scientific linguistic study, and one sound laboratory generalization, we may apply strictly mathematical methods and deduce a logically unimpeachable definition of some entity." (74). Thus the phoneme is "a mere terminological convenience" (68). There is no necessity for demonstrating "psychological reality" (i.e., descriptive adequacy), because "this demonstration would be a convenience rather than a necessity for linguistic study: it would represent a summary of the behavior of native speakers, a behavior which is already available for the student of language, though in less concentrated form" (58). The only legitimate activity for the linguist is "the study of phenomena and their correlations" (57—this value judgment Twaddell regards as a principle of "scientific methodology"); attempts to provide explanations on the basis of "mentalistic assumptions" are characterized as "fraud." Thus all that is asked of a linguistic notion or a linguistic description is that it meet the requirement of *consistency* and what we may call *convertibility* (namely, the account must be explicit enough to be convertible into some other, equally arbitrary framework) and, perhaps, in some sense, *simplicity* and *convenience*.

In part, Harris seems to take a similar position in his *Methods* (1951a, chapter 1). He describes his procedures as "merely ways of arranging the original data." The only general condition that they must meet is the biuniqueness condition, which is not justified on any external count, but simply is taken as defining the subject. The procedures must be "based on distribution, and be unambiguous, consistent, and subject to check." The criteria for selecting phonemes are stated only "to make explicit in each case what method [of data arrangement] is being followed" (63). Thus only consistency and convertibility (and convenience, for one or another purpose) is required of a linguistic theory or a grammatical description. But Harris also states (372–3) that "the work of analysis leads right up to the statements which enable anyone to synthesize or predict utterances in the language," that is, to a generative grammar. This constitutes a truth claim for the procedures, a claim which surely cannot be maintained if conflicting procedures meeting the conditions of consistency and convertibility are equally valid, and which would appear to be incompatible with Harris' earlier remark that the "over-all purpose . . . [of the procedures] . . . is to obtain a compact one-one representation of the stock of utterances in the corpus" (366). Furthermore, there are no known procedures which lead to this more ambitious, and far more significant goal. These conflicting remarks concerning what Hockett has called "metacriteria" (1955) illustrate a general ambivalence concerning goals that makes evaluation of modern taxonomic linguistics on its own terms rather difficult.

Insofar as consistency and convertibility are taken as the only valid metacriteria, linguistic theory is concerned only with the level of observational adequacy. This theory makes no claim to truth; no evidence conflicts with it, just as none can be offered in its support. The only criticism that is relevant is that taxonomic phonemics, as indicated above, seems more of an inconvenience than a convenience, if embedded within a full grammatical description. This point of view takes a theory to be, essentially, nothing more than a summary of data. In contrast, it has been repeatedly pointed out (most forcefully, by Karl Popper) that the prevailing attitude in the sciences is to regard data as of interest primarily insofar as it has bearing on the choice among alternative theories, and to search for data, however exotic, that will be crucial in this sense. In any event, there is surely no reason why the linguist must necessarily limit himself to "the study of phenomena and their correlations," avoiding any attempt to gain insight into such data by means of an explanatory theory of language, a theory which is, of course, "mentalistic," in that it deals with the character of mental activity rather than with its physical basis.

If one is unwilling to settle for just consistency and convertibility, what further justification can be offered for taxonomic phonemics? I have tried to show above that the internal linguistic evidence does not support taxonomic phonemics. Taxonomic phonemic representations do not contribute to the simplicity or generality of a grammar, but, in fact, have just the opposite effect. Therefore one must search for external evidence. In particular, it is important to ask whether reasonable requirements for a perceptual model ((la) of Section 1.3) or a learning or discovery model ((lb) of Section 1.3) have any bearing on the validity of taxonomic phonemics. Considerations of this sort may actually have been at the core of some theoretical and methodological studies.

One might try to justify the conditions (32) by arguing that speech perception involves two successive stages: the hearer first uses only local phonetic cues to identify the invariant criterial attributes that determine the successive taxonomic phonemes; and he then goes on to determine the deeper structure of the utterance (in particular, its systematic phonemic representation and its syntactic structure). This clearly seems to be the view of Jakobson (cf. Jakobson, Fant and Halle, 1952) and of Joos (1957, 92),[49] among others. However, there is no real basis for this account, and it is scarcely in accord with what little is known about complex perceptual processes, or, for that matter, about speech perception. Thus it is well known that intelligibility is preserved under gross phonetic distortion, which may be completely unnoticed when grammatical constraints are met; and brief exposure to an unfamiliar dialect is often sufficient to overcome unintelligibility or even an impression of strangeness (note that related dialects may differ greatly, sentence by sentence, in phonetic and taxonomic phonemic representations, though perhaps hardly at all on the level of systematic phonemics—cf. in this connection Halle, 1962; also Chomsky, 1959, for an analysis of some of the data presented by Sledd, 1955, 1958, from this point of view). Sapir is the only linguist to have presented careful observations of native perceptual responses relevant to this question, in his classic paper on psychological reality (1933), and his reports are directly counter to the taxonomic account of speech perception. Surely one would expect that in identifying an utterance, the hearer will bring to bear the full grammatical apparatus that determines the space of possibilities from which this utterance is drawn and the nature and interrelations of these objects. That is, one would naturally expect that, as in the case of other perceptual processes, the hearer's knowledge will provide a complex schema within which the actual signal is interpreted. To the extent that this is true, the "atomistic" view of the taxonomic phonologists will be in error. In any event, presently available

---

[49]To illustrate his point, Joos cites the example of someone who responded to "he has poise" with "what's a poy?" But this seems rather dubious support for his position, since the hearer in this case was puzzled by the apparent application of the unfamiliar lexical rule: N → poy, and had clearly assigned a full syntactic structure to the utterance. Thus this example does not support the independence of phonemic representation from syntactic structure in perception.

evidence does not support the taxonomic model given above as an adequate general account of speech perception.[50]

It remains to consider the status of taxonomic phonemics with respect to a model of acquisition of language. There is, in fact, an approach to the question on these grounds.

Suppose that we impose on the acquisition model the condition of *separation of levels*, which we can interpret as requiring that the level of systematic phonetic representation must be "rationalized" and converted to a level of taxonomic phonemic representation without reference to any morphological or syntactic information.[51] Observe that this condition is not to be confused with the conditions of biuniqueness and local determinacy. These (as all of the conditions (32)) pertain to the "perceptual model"; they assert that the phonemic correspondent to a given phonetic sequence must be determinable by operations involving only neighboring sounds, *once the phonemic system is fixed.* But the condition of separation of levels is not a formal condition on a phonemic system and on the rules that relate it to sound; it is a methodological condition on information relevant to determining the correct choice of a phonemic system. It thus pertains to an acquisition model such as (1b), rather than to a perceptual model such as (1a).

Nevertheless, there is a connection between the condition of separation of levels and the conditions of biuniqueness and local determinacy. If no higher-level information is relevant to determining what is the taxonomic phonemic system, it is natural to require that once the taxonomic phonemic system is fixed, on purely phonetic grounds, no higher-level information should be relevant to determining what is the sequence of taxonomic phonemes corresponding to a given sequence of phones. Consequently, an argument in support of the condition of separation of levels would, indirectly, provide a motivation for imposing the conditions of biuniqueness and local determinacy on the perceptual model as formal conditions on the notion "phoneme."

This is apparently the line of reasoning that has been followed insofar as justification for the conditions of biuniqueness and local determinacy has actually been offered. Thus, for example, Hockett gives only one argument in support of these conditions in the review cited above (Hockett, 1951), namely, that given these conditions "one knows definitely to what level each fact applies." Otherwise, we have a "hodge-podge arrangement." He is concerned here with the context of discovery, not perception, and is offering an argument in support of the condition of separation of levels rather than in support of the biuniqueness and local determinacy conditions directly. Similarly, in his important paper on phonemic overlapping (1941), Bloch

---

[50]For further discussion, see Halle and Stevens (1961), Miller and Chomsky (1963), and references there cited. For discussion in a similar vein on the syntactic level, see Matthews (1961).

[51]One or another form of this is implicit in all substantive discussions of linguistic procedures that I have been able to locate. Some linguists (e.g., Pike and Harris) would allow restricted use of certain higher-level information in phonology, where this can be obtained by "cyclic" or "spiral" procedures (cf. Pike, 1947, 1952; Harris, 1951a), but many American linguists insist on strict separation. Glossematicians also mention successive and intricately interwoven procedures of analysis and synthesis (Diderichsen, 1958). The kinds of procedures they have in mind also allow for some sort of interdependence of levels, but the reference to procedures is too vague for the extent of permitted interdependence to be determinable, in this case.

offers only one argument (an argument that Joos, in his comments, 1957, considers conclusive) to show why the biuniqueness condition must be maintained, namely, this: "Suppose that we are studying a new and unfamiliar dialect of English, and that we have succeeded in pairing the stressed and the unstressed vowels of such words as *at, them, could, will, so*, and the like; if we now hear a phrase like *oút of tówn*, with the unstressed vowel of the second word perceptually the same as those which we have already identified with various stressed alternants, how are we to treat this? We must defer the phonemic analysis until we chance to hear a stressed form of the same word, which may not occur at the dialect we are studying, or which, if it does occur, we may fail to recognize as 'the same word.'"

Both Bloch and Hockett are proposing that the condition of biuniqueness must be imposed on the notion "phoneme" because the model for acquisition must meet the condition of separation of levels. But it is important to observe that both of them are presenting an argument that is methodological rather than substantive. They do not suggest that an accurate model of the process of acquisition of language must incorporate the condition of separation of levels—that this is a fact about the design of language and about the intrinsic characteristics of an organism capable of learning a language under the empirically given conditions of time and access. They are considering rather the problems of gathering and organizing data, and thus their indirect argument for the conditions of biuniqueness and local determinacy at most shows that it would be convenient for the linguist if there were a level of representation meeting these conditions, but it does not bear on the question of the existence of this level as a part of linguistic structure.

Let us turn to the question of separation of levels as a substantive issue. As in the case of the conditions (32), two kinds of considerations are relevant: external considerations pertaining, in this case, to language acquisition rather than perception; and purely internal linguistic considerations. As to the former, Hockett has in fact suggested in various places (e.g., 1948) that the successive steps of the analyst should in some way parallel those of the language learner. But clearly the child does not master the phonology before proceeding to the syntax, and there is no possible justification for the principle of separation of levels from considerations of this sort.

It remains then to ask whether this condition can be justified (thus indirectly providing a justification for the biuniqueness and local determinacy conditions) on internal linguistic grounds, that is, by a demonstration that it contributes to the clarity, generality, or coherence of a full grammar. But it seems clear that this principle has rather the effect of detracting significantly from these qualities, and, in fact, that adherence to this principle makes it impossible to attain the levels of descriptive or explanatory adequacy. Consequently, the principle seems to be entirely superfluous, in either its stronger or weaker forms (see note 51).

The effects of strict application of a principle of separation of levels have often been discussed. The matter of word boundary that Hockett cites in his invented example discussed above illustrates the problems that arise when it is adopted. It has long been recognized that a phonemic system is quite unacceptable if no junctures are recognized. Consequently, linguists who adopt the principle of partial or complete separation of levels have attempted to devise analytic procedures that would make it possible to place junctures in appropriate places on the basis of phonetic evidence alone. These procedures make use of phonetic features that appear at utterance boundary to determine the position of junctures medially in utterances. Thus a juncture would be marked in "night rate" because it contains an utterance-final allophone of /t/ followed by an utterance-initial allophone of /r/. Apart from the counterexamples that have already been offered to this principle (and that remain unanswered—cf. e.g., Leopold, 1948; Harris, 1951a, 87; Chomsky, Halle, Lukoff, 1956, Section 2) it is clear that it cannot succeed because of examples of the following kind. In many dialects of English, /t/ has the allophone [D] in word final position after a weak stress and before a main stress—thus we have [ɨDédz] ("at Ed's"), [ɨDǽwr] ("at our"), [ðæDǽd] ("that ad"), contrasting with [iténd] ("attend") [itǽk] ("attack," "a tack") and with [idépt] ("adept"), [idǽpt] ("adapt"). But [D] occurs only medially, never finally. Thus any consideration involving utterance boundary will place junctures in exactly the wrong places. Alternatively, if no junctures are placed, [D] must be taken as a third alveolar stop, giving an equally unacceptable phonemic analysis. We must conclude, then, that there is no known method for assigning junctures in terms of phonetic evidence alone. Present methods do not distinguish permissible from impermissible applications, and, consequently, are useless as they stand. It seems unlikely that this difficulty can be remedied, and unless it is, the principle of separation of levels is entirely untenable.

As a second example, consider the much debated subject of English vocalic nuclei. According to a view that is widely held among American structuralists,[52] these are to be analyzed as short vowels plus one of the glides /y/, /w/ or /h/. On the purely phonetic grounds on which the question must be discussed by those who accept the principle of separation of levels, this is a very neat and well-motivated description. In particular, the post-vocalic /h/, representing a centering glide, can be used to account for such contrasts as "real" /rihl/, "really" /rihliy/ versus "reel" /riyl/, "Greeley" /griyliy/, etc.

If, however, we are concerned with selecting a phonemic system that will be compatible with a fully descriptively adequate grammar, this analysis becomes quite unacceptable. Thus observe that on the level of systematic phonemics, the words "real," "really" will be represented /riæl/, /riæl + li/ (because of "reality"), just as "total," "totally" are represented /tōtæl/, /tōtæl + li/ because of "totality," and "mobile" is represented /mōbil/ because of "mobility." Furthermore, the glide of "real," "really" is not to be distinguished on the level of systematic phonetics from that of "total," "totally," "mobile" (or, for that matter, "dialect," "betrayal," "refusal," "science," etc.), namely, [ɨ]. Hence in all of these cases the systematic phonetic representation can be derived from the systematic phonemic by the very general rule of English phonology that:

$$\text{Vowel} \rightarrow \text{ɨ when unstressed.}^{[53]} \tag{42}$$

---

[52]For an account of its background, see Gleason (1961, chapter 19). An important critique is presented in Sledd (1955).

[53]This rule is of course incorrect as stated (cf. "relaxation" [rɨlǽkséyšɨn], "condensation" [kàndɛnséyšin], etc.) if it is one of a set of unordered rules of a taxonomic grammar. But it is correct if it is embedded into a transformational cycle of the kind discussed above. Cf. references of note 6 for details.

If, however, we wish to provide the taxonomic phonemic representations /rihl/, /rihliy/, /towtil/, /towtiliy, /mowbil/, /dayilekt/, /biytreyil/, etc., as an intermediate stage of formal description, we must replace the general rule (42) by the three rules:

Vowels → i post-consonantally, when unstressed   (43i)

Vowels → h post-vocalically, when unstressed   (43ii)

h → i post-vocalically,   (43iii)

where the first two relate "morphophonemic" and "phonemic" representations, and the third relates "phonemic" and phonetic representations. Thus again we find that what may very well be the optimal taxonomic phonemic system is not incorporable into a descriptively adequate grammar. The failure to achieve descriptive adequacy, in this case, is traceable to the requirement of separation of levels in the underlying theory.

In his review of Halle (1959b), Ferguson (1962) criticizes Halle for his rejection of the biuniqueness and local determinacy conditions (condition (3a) in Halle's presentation), and offers a defense of these conditions. But he presents the issue incorrectly, and as a result neither his critique of Halle's position nor his arguments in support of biuniqueness and local determinacy are to the point. Since Ferguson's is the only recent discussion of this issue from the point of view of taxonomic phonemics, it is important to trace the argument with some care. Ferguson argues for what he calls "the autonomy of phonology," that is, the view that phonology is entirely independent of syntax and morphology, and that the biuniqueness and local determinacy conditions are thus reasonable. Halle's position—and the one that I have advocated here—is the direct contradictory of this, namely, the view that *some* phonetic processes depend on syntactic and morphological structure so that phonology as a whole cannot be studied, without distortion, in total independence of higher level structure. Let us call this the view that phonology is "nonautonomous." A third possible position we may call the assumption of "inseparability of phonology," that is, the view that *all* phonetic processes depend essentially on syntactic and morphological structure. This view has certainly never been advocated by anyone, and it is unnecessary to refute it. But it is the assumption of inseparability of phonology, not the assumption of nonautonomy of phonology, that Ferguson imputes to Halle, and against which he presents a series of arguments (to which we return directly). These arguments against the inseparability of phonology have no bearing on the question of autonomy of phonology. This failure to observe the distinction between inseparability of phonology and nonautonomy of phonology in fact vitiates Ferguson's argument entirely.

Specifically, Ferguson cites in favor of his position the undeniable fact that syntactic and morphological structure are not involved in certain sound changes and in certain aspects of language learning and dialectal variation. This observation is irrelevant to the issue of autonomy or nonautonomy of phonology (though it successfully demolishes the absurd thesis of inseparability of phonology). It is also apparent that morphology and syntax play an important role in specifying the range and character of certain sound changes (cf. much of Kuryłowicz' recent work, or e.g., Twaddell, 1935, p. 79), of certain aspects of phonological development in language learning, and of certain aspects of phonological dialectal variation. Consequently, to the extent that considerations of the sort that Ferguson adduces are relevant, they show nothing more than the untenability of the thesis of autonomy of phonology. It is true that in plotting isoglosses, "it is often quite clear that subareas of different phonological systems do not coincide well with subareas of grammatical systems and lexical inventories" (Ferguson, 290), just as it is clear that isoglosses drawn for vocalic systems often do not coincide with those drawn for consonantal systems. The argument from this to autonomy is equally apposite in both cases. Similarly, in the case of Ferguson's other examples.[54]

Finally, I should like to comment on Ferguson's assertion that Halle's theory (as also the theory of the present paper) does not provide machinery for describing phonetic data that is accounted for adequately by his autonomous phonology. He cites, e.g., the word *Audrey* with the cluster /dr/ as compared with *bedrock* with /d + r/ and *bedroom* with variation between /dr/ and /d + r/. In this case, a "nonautonomous" generative grammar would give rules stating that in *bedroom* the morpheme boundary sometimes does and sometimes does not become a phonetic juncture (depending on dialect or style, as the facts indicate). It would, on the other hand, make no such statement about *Audrey* (with no boundary) or *bedrock* (where the boundary always becomes phonetic juncture). I do not see what is the problem here, or how an autonomous phonology of type that Ferguson proposes would handle the situation any differently. Ferguson's example simply shows the absurdity of the claim that *every* morphemic boundary is a phonetic juncture, but surely no one has ever maintained this. What has been maintained is that syntactic and morphological considerations must be taken into account in determining when to handle phonetic facts by placement of junctures, and when to handle them by postulation of new phonemes, and Ferguson's remarks have no bearing on this question.

Summarizing, then, it seems that if we are concerned with descriptive and explanatory adequacy, only two levels of representation can be justified in structural descriptions provided by the phonological component, namely, the levels of systematic phonemics and systematic phonetics. The level of taxonomic phonemics is not incorporable into a descriptively adequate grammar. As noted in Section 4.2, this conclusion is close to the position of de Saussure and Sapir, and is close to Bloomfield's practice, though perhaps not his theory.

It is interesting to consider the kinds of criticism that have been offered by taxonomic linguists against de Saussure, Sapir, and Bloomfield. Wells (1947) criticizes de Saussure for not making use of the principle of complementary distribution with respect to a particular language in his "phonologie" (but only the analogous principle with respect to all languages). In his long review of Sapir's collected papers (1951b), Harris devotes very little attention to Sapir's fundamental theoretical papers on phonology (Sapir, 1925; 1933), and remarks only (293) that they confuse

---

[54]Ferguson's claim that a phonological theory that does not observe Halle's condition (3a) (biuniqueness and local determinancy) makes diachronic change incomprehensible is particularly astonishing. Would anyone really be willing to maintain that the phonology of, e.g., Sapir and Bloomfield, cannot accommodate sound changes that have been exhibited and explained by the post-Bloomfieldian linguists who have insisted on these conditions? His assertion that the principles of biuniqueness and local determinacy (note that it is just these that are at issue at this point in his discussion) underlie the achievements of the last century represents a curious interpretation of the history of linguistics.

phonology and morphophonemics. Similarly Joos comments (1957, 92) that "when we look back at Bloomfield's work, we are disturbed at this and that, but more than anything else, Bloomfield's confusion between phonemes and morphophonemes disturbs us." But it is important to observe that these and other critics have not actually demonstrated that the position of de Saussure, Sapir, or Bloomfield is in any way confused. The criticism relies on the assumption that systematic phonetics has no significant status (so that de Saussure's phonologie goes only "half way" towards Wells' taxonomic phonemics), and that taxonomic phonemics is a significant intermediate level of linguistic structure (so that Sapir and Bloomfield appear to be confusing morphophonemics and taxonomic phonemics in their systematic phonemics). Hence the criticism amounts only to the comment that de Saussure, Sapir, and Bloomfield have not developed the level of taxonomic phonemics, but only the levels of systematic phonetics and systematic phonemics. The criticism, then, is only as well founded as is the status of taxonomic phonemics.

There is, in fact, a real confusion in Bloomfield, and this has perhaps played a role in the development of taxonomic phonemics in American linguistics, at least. Bloomfield's assertion that only two kinds of representation are scientifically relevant on the level of sound has had a significant impact on later developments. One of Bloomfield's significant levels is physical phonetics. The other, if we follow his descriptive practice, is close to Sapir's systematic phonemics; or, if we follow his "bundle of distinctive features" theory (1933, 79), it is close to post-Bloomfieldian taxonomic phonemics. In any event, he explicitly denies any status to systematic (universal) phonetics. (Similarly, Troubetzkoy, despite his thorough-going reliance at every step on a universal phonetics, tends to disparage it in his theoretical remarks.) However, as we noted above, phonology of any sort is unthinkable without assumptions involving phonetic universals, and Bloomfield uses them constantly, as do all phonologists. Hence there are implicit assumptions concerning systematic phonetics in his descriptive and theoretical work. Furthermore, from the rejection of a level of systematic phonetic representation as the "lowest level" of representation to be provided in a grammar, post-Bloomfieldian linguists were forced to the conclusion that the phonemic level must be the lowest level of representation. Consequently, phonemic representation must be much closer to actual sound than in the case of the systematic phonemics of Sapir or of much of Bloomfield's practice. In particular, the conditions (32) become well motivated for this lowest level of representation, and the principle of complementary distribution is invoked to eliminate obvious redundancy (supplemented by various *ad hoc* and ineffective rules of the kind we have discussed above to take account of cases where the representations meeting (32) are too unintuitive).

In short, we find that there is a gradual return, in post-Bloomfieldian phonological theory, from the systematic phonemics of Sapir and (to a large extent) Bloomfield, to a much "narrower" system not too far removed from that of the phoneticians who were Bloomfield's critics (see note 34). It is in this sense that modern taxonomic phonemic representations are "more accurate," and it is for this reason that they are far more complex than the earlier systematic phonemic representations. In this way, the fundamental insights of the pioneers of modern phonology have largely been lost.

V. MODELS OF PERCEPTION AND ACQUISITION

A concern with perception and acquisition of language has played a significant role in determining the course of development of linguistic theory, as it should if this theory is ever to have broader scientific significance. But I have tried to show that the basic point of view regarding both perception and acquisition has been much too particularistic and concrete. It has failed totally to come to grips with the "creative" aspect of language use, that is, the ability to form and understand previously unheard sentences. It has, in general, failed to appreciate the degree of internal organization and the intricacy of the system of abstract structures that has been mastered by the learner, and that is brought to bear in understanding, or even identifying utterances. With regard to perceptual models, these limitations reveal themselves in such conditions as linearity, invariance, and biuniqueness; with regard to models of acquisition, in such methodological conditions as the principle of separation of levels, the attempt to define grammatical relations in terms of co-occurrence, and, in general, in the emphasis on elementary procedures of segmentation and classification that has dominated modern linguistic theory.[55]

These taxonomic models of acquisition are not far removed from the extremely limited paradigms of learning and concept formation, based exclusively on some notion of matching or similarity or possession of a common property from some fixed set of available properties, that are to be found in recent cognitive psychology. But it does not seem plausible that the kind of generative grammar that seems to be descriptively adequate might be acquired in a reasonably brief time (if at all) by an organism that brings to the learning task only a "quality space" and a "distance measure" along these dimensions. Evidence of the kind discussed above suggests that each natural language is a simple and highly systematic realization of a complex and intricate underlying model, with highly special and unique properties. To the extent that this observation can be substantiated, it suggests that the structure of the grammar internalized by the learner may be, to a presently quite unexpected degree, a reflection of the general character of his learning capacity rather than the particular course of his experience. It seems not unlikely that the organism brings, as its contribution to acquisition of a particular language, a highly restrictive characterization of a class of generative systems (potential theories) from which the grammar of its language is selected on the basis of the presented linguistic data. There is no a priori reason to expect that these potential theories are of the highly simple taxonomic variety with which modern linguistics has been preoccupied, and the linguistic evidence seems to show, in fact, that they are not.

In the case of perception of language, as noted above in Section 4.4, the step-by-step analytic models of taxonomic linguistics are not in the least convincing. The process of coming to understand a presented utterance can be quite naturally described, in part, as a process of constructing an internal representation (a "percept") of its full structural description. There is little reason to doubt that the full apparatus of the

---

[55]One might cite de Saussure as a source for this preoccupation with inventory and with taxonomic procedures. Cf. (1916, 154).

generative grammar that represents the hearer's linguistic competence is brought to bear immediately in carrying out this task. In particular, much of the perceived phonetic shape of an utterance (e.g., in English, the complex arrangements of reduced and unreduced vowels and stress contours) is a reflection of its syntactic structure. It would not be surprising to find that what the hearer (or the phonetician) perceives is an ideal pattern, not incompatible with the signal that actually reaches his ears, that is projected by the phonological component of his grammar from the syntactic description that he has assigned to this signal (cf. references of note 50).

In part, these questions belong to theoretical psychology. But purely linguistic research can play a fundamental role in adding substance to these speculations. A perceptual model that does not incorporate a descriptively adequate generative grammar cannot be taken very seriously. Similarly, the construction of a model of acquisition (whether a model of learning, or a linguistic procedure for discovery of grammars) cannot be seriously undertaken without a clear understanding of the nature of the descriptively adequate grammars that it must provide as output, on the basis of primary linguistic data (cf. Section 1.3). It presupposes, in other words, a general linguistic theory that achieves the level of explanatory adequacy. It is clear that we have descriptively adequate grammars, and underlying theories that reach the level of explanatory adequacy, only for a rather narrow range of linguistic phenomena in a small number of languages. It seems to me that present theories of transformational generative grammar provide a basis for extending and deepening our understanding of linguistic structure. In any event, whether or not this hope is ultimately justified, it seems clear that to pursue the goals of Section 1 in any serious way, it is necessary to go far beyond the restricted framework of modern taxonomic linguistics and the narrowly-conceived empiricism from which it springs.

BIBLIOGRAPHY

Austin, J., "Ifs and Cans," *Proceedings of the British Academy* (London), XLII (1956), 109–32.

Bar-Hillel, Y., "Logical Syntax and Semantice," *Language*, XXX (1954), 230–37.

Bazell, C. E., *Linguistic Form*. Istanbul: Istanbul Press, 1953.

Bever, T. G., "Theoretical Implications of Bloomfield's 'Menomini Morphophonemics,'" *Quarterly Progress Report No. 68*. Cambridge, Mass.: Research Lab. of Electronics, M.I.T. (1963), 197–203.

Bloch, B., "Phonemic Overlapping," *American Speech*, XVI (1941), 278–84. Reprinted in Joos (1957).

——, "Studies in Colloquial Japanese IV: Phonemics," *Language*, XXVI (1950), 86–125. Reprinted in Joos (1957).

Bloomfield, L., "A Set of Postulates for the Science of Language," *Language*, II (1926), 153–64. Reprinted in Joos (1957).

——, *Language*. New York: Holt, Rinehart & Winston, Inc., 1933.

——, "Menomini Morphophonemics," *Travaux du cercle linguistique de Prague*, VIII (1939), 105–115.

Bolinger, D. L., "On Defining the Morpheme," *Word*, IV (1948), 18–23.

——, "Linguistic Science and Linguistic Engineering," *Word*, XVI (1960), 374–91.

——, "Syntactic Blends and Other Matters," *Language*, XXXVII (1961), 366–81.

Bolling, G. M., "Comment on Kent's Review," *Language*, X (1934), 48–52.

Chomsky, N., "Morphophonemics of Modern Hebrew." Unpublished Master's thesis, Univ. of Penna., 1951. Mimeographed.

——, "The Logical Structure of Linguistic Theory." Unpublished manuscript, Cambridge, 1955. Mimeographed.

——, *Syntactic Structures*. The Hague: Mouton & Co., 1957a.

——, "Review of R. Jakobson and M. Halle, 'Fundamentals of Language,' " *International Journal of American Linguistics*, XXIII (1957b), 234–41.

——, "A Transformational Approach to Syntax," *Proceedings of the Third Texas Conference on Problems of Linguistic Analysis in English* (1958), ed. A. A. Hill (Texas, 1962a), 124–58.

——, "The Transformational Basis of Syntax," to appear in *Proceedings of the Fourth Texas Conference* (1959). Unpublished.

——, "On the Notion 'Rule of Grammar,' " *Structure of Language and Its Mathematical Aspects, Proceedings of the 12th Symposium in Applied Mathematics*, ed. R. Jakobson. Providence: American Mathematical Society, 1961a, 6–24.

——, "Some Methodological Remarks on Generative Grammar," *Word*, XVII (1961b), 219–39.

——, "Explanatory Models in Linguistics," *Logic, Methodology, and Philosophy of Science*, eds. E. Nagel, P. Suppes, and A. Tarski. Stanford: Stanford University Press, 1962b, 528–50.

——, "Formal Properties of Grammars," *Handbook of Mathematical Psychology*, Vol. II (1963), eds. P. Luce, R. Bush, E. Galanter. New York: John Wiley & Sons, Inc., 323-418.

Chomsky, N., M. Halle, and F. Lukoff, "On Accent and Juncture in English," in *For Roman Jakobson,* eds. M. Halle, H. Lunt, H. McLean. The Hague: Mouton & Co., 1956, 65–80.

de Cordemoy, G., *A Philosophicall Discourse Concerning Speech*. Translated from the first edition (1667), 1668.

Diderichsen, P., "Morpheme Categories in Modern Danish," in *Recherches Structurales, Travaux du Cercle Linguistiques de Copenhague*, Vol. V. Kulturforlag, Copenhague: Nordisk Sprog-Og, 1949, 134–53.

——, "The Importance of Distribution Versus Other Criteria in Linguistic Analysis," *Proceedings of the Eighth Congress of Linguists* (Oslo, 1958), 156–81.

Ferguson, C., "Review of Halle, '*The Sound Pattern of Russian*,' " *Language*, XXXVIII (1962), 284–97.

Firth, J. R., et al., *Studies in Linguistic Analysis*. Oxford, England: 1957.

Foot, P., "Goodness and Choice," *Proceedings of the Aristotelian Society, Supplementary Volume 35* (1961), 45–80.

Frei, H., "Désaccords," *Cahiers Ferdinand de Saussure*, XVIII (1961), 35–51.

Gleason, H. A., *Introduction to Descriptive Linguistics*, 2nd ed. New York: Holt, Rinehart & Winston, Inc., 1961.

Gleitman, L., Unpublished Master's thesis. Philadelphia: University of Pennsylvania, 1960.

Godel, R., *Les sources manuscrites du Cours de linguistique générale*. Geneva-Paris: Librairie E. Droz-Librairie Minard, 1957.

Gross, M., *On the Equivalence of Models of Language Used in the Fields of Mechanical Translation and Information Retrieval*. Cambridge, Mass.: M.I.T., 1962. Mimeographed.

Halle, M., "Questions of Linguistics," *Nuovo Cimento*, XIII (1959a), 494–517.
——, *The Sound Pattern of Russian*. The Hague: Mouton & Co., 1959b.
——, "On the Role of Simplicity in Linguistic Descriptions," *Structure of Language and Its Mathematical Aspects, Proceedings of the 12th Symposium in Applied Mathematics*, ed. R. Jakobson. Providence: American Mathematical Society, 1961a.
——, "Note on Cyclically Ordered Rules in the Russian Conjugation," *Quarterly Progress Report No. 63*. Cambridge, Mass.: M.I.T., Research Lab. of Electronics (1961b), 149–55.
——, Phonology in a Generative Grammar," *Word*, XVIII (1962), 54–72.

Halle, M. and N. Chomsky, "The Morphophonemics of English," *Quarterly Progress Report No. 58*. Cambridge, Mass.: M.I.T., Research Lab. of Electronics (1960), 275–81.
——, *The Sound Pattern of English* (forthcoming).

Halle, M. and K. Stevens, "Speech Recognition: A Model and A Program for Research," *IRE Transactions of Information Theory*, IT–8 (1962), 155–9.

Halle, M. and V. J. Zeps, *Latvian Morphology* (1962).

Harris, Z. S., *Methods in Structural Linguistics*. Chicago, 1951a.
——, "Review of Mandelbaum, (ed.), 'Selected Writings of Edward Sapir,'" *Language*, XXXVII (1951b), 288–332.
——, "Discourse Analysis," *Language*, XXVIII (1925b), 474–94.
——, "Distributional Structure," *Word*, X (1954), 146–62.
——, "Co-occurrence and Transformation in Linguistic Structure," *Language*, XXXIII (1957), 283–340.

Haugen, E., "Directions in Modern Linguistics," *Language*, XXVII (1951), 211–22. Reprinted in Joos (1957).

Hiż, H., "Congrammaticality, Batteries of Transformations and Grammatical Categories," in *Structure of Language and Its Mathematical Aspects, Proceedings of the 12th Symposium in Applied Mathematics*, ed., R. Jakobson. Providence: American Mathematical Society, 1961.

Hockett, C. F., "A Note on 'Structure,'" *International Journal of American Linguistics*, XIV (1948), 269–71.
——, "Review of Martinet, 'Phonology as Functional Phonetics,'" *Language*, XXVII (1951), 333–41.
——, "Two Models of Grammatical Description," *Word*, X (1954), 210–34.
——, *A Course in Modern Linguistics*. New York: The Macmillan Company, 1958.

Hoenigswald, H. M., *Language Change and Linguistic Reconstruction*. Chicago, 1960.

Humboldt, W. von, *Über die Verschiedenheit des menschlichen Sprachbaues* (Berlin, 1836). Facsimile edition (Bonn, 1960).

Jakobson, R., G. Fant, and M. Halle, *Preliminaries to Speech Analysis*. Cambridge, Mass., 1952.

Joos, M., ed., *Readings in Linguistics*. Washington, 1957.
——, "Linguistic Prospects in the United States," in *Trends in European and American Linguistics*, eds., Mohrmann, Sommerfelt, and Whatmough. Utrecht-Antwerp: Spectrum, 1961.

Juilland, A., *Structural Relations*. The Hague, 1961.

Katz, J. and J. Fodor, "The Structure of a Semantic Theory," *Language*, XXXIX (1963), 170–210.

Katz, J. and P. Postal, *An Integrated Theory of Linguistic Descriptions*. (Forthcoming, M.I.T. Press.)

Kent, R. G. "Review of Bloomfield, 'Language,'" *Language*, X (1934), 40–48.

Lees, R. B., *The Grammar of English Nominalizations*. Bloomington, 1960a.

——, A Multiply Ambiguous Adjectival Construction in English," *Language*, XXXVI (1960b), 207–21.

——, *Phonology of Modern Standard Turkish*. Bloomington, 1961.

Leopold, W. F., "German ch," *Language*, XXIV (1948), 179–80. Reprinted in Joos (1957).

Long, R. B., *The Sentence and Its Parts*. Chicago: University of Chicago Press, 1961.

Malécot, A., "Vowel Nasality as a Distinctive Feature in American English," *Language*, XXXVI (1960), 222–29.

Matthews, G. H., "Analysis by Synthesis of Sentences of Natural Languages," *First International Conference on Machine Translation*. Teddington, 1961.

——, Grammar of Hidatsa. Cambridge, Mass.: M.I.T., 1962. Mimeographed.

Mel'chuck, I. A., "Some Problems of Machine Translation Abroad," *Doklady na Konferentsii po Obrabotke Informatsii, Mashinnomu Perevodu i Avtomaticheskomu Chteniiju Teksta*. Akademiija Nauuk, SSSR, No. 6, Moscow, 1961, 1–44.

Miller, G. A. and N. Chomsky, "Introduction to the Formal Analysis of Natural Languages"; and "Finitary Models of Language Users," *Handbook of Mathematical Psychology*, Vol. II, eds. P. Luce, R. Bush, E. Galanter, 1962. 269–322; 419–492.

Miller, G. A., E. Galanter, and K. H. Pribram, *Plans and the Structure of Behavior*. New York: Holt, Rinehart & Winston, Inc., 1960.

Newman, S. S., "Behavior Patterns in Linguistic Structure: A Case Study," in *Language, Culture, and Personality*, eds. Spier, Hallowell, and Newman. Menasha, Wisconsin: Sapir Memorial Publication Fund, 1941.

Nida, E. A., *A Synopsis of English Syntax* (1943). Reprinted Norman, Oklahoma (1960).

Nowell-Smith, P., *Ethics*. London, Baltimore: Penguin Books, 1954.

Palmer, F. R., "Linguistic Hierarchy," *Lingua*, VII (1958), 225–41.

Paul, H., *Prinzipien der Sprachgeschichte*, 2nd ed. (1886). Translated into English, Longmans, Green & Co., London (1890).

Pike, K. L., "Grammatical Prerequisites to Phonemic Analysis," *Word*, III (1947), 155–72.

——, "More on Grammatical Prerequisites," *Word*, VIII (1952), 106–21.

Postal, P., "On the Limitations of Context-Free Phrase Structure Description," *Quarterly Progress Report No. 64*. Cambridge, Mass.: M.I.T., Research Laboratory of Electronics, 231–37.

——, *Some Syntactic Rules in Mohawk*, Ph.D. Dissertation, Yale University, 1962. Mimeographed.

——, *Constituent Structure: A Study of Contemporary Models of Syntactic Description*. Indiana University, Bloomington and Mouton and Co., The Hague, The Netherlands, 1964.

Putnam, H. "Some issues in the Theory of Grammar," in *Structure of Language and Its Mathematical Aspects, Proceedings of the 12th Symposium in Applied Mathematics*, ed. B. Jakobson. Providence: American Mathematical Society, 1961.

Quine, W. V., *Word and Object*. Cambridge, Mass.: M.I.T. Press, 1960.

Reichling, A., "Principles and Methods of Syntax: Cryptanalytical Formalism," *Lingua*, X (1961), 1–17.

Sapir, E., *Language*. New York: Harcourt, Brace & World, Inc., 1921.

——, "Sound Patterns in Language," *Language*, I (1925), 37–51. Reprinted in *Selected Writings of Edward Sapir*, ed. D. G. Mandelbaum, California, 1949.

——, "La réalité psychologique des phonèmes," *Journal de Psycholgie Normale et Pathologieque*, XXX (1933), 247–65. Reprinted in *Selected Writings of Edward Sapir*, California, 1949.

de Saussure, F., *Cours de linguistique générale*. Paris: C. Bally & A. Sechehaye, 1916. Page reference to the 4th edition, 1949.

Schacter, P., *A Contrastive Analysis of English and Pangasinan*. UCLA, 1961. Mimeographed.

——, *Rules for a Segment of Tagalog Grammar*. UCLA, 1962. Mimeographed.

Schatz, C. D., "The Role of Context in the Perception of Stops," *Language*, XXX (1954), 47–56.

Schützenberger, M. P. and N. Chomsky, "The Algebraic Theory of Context-Free Languages," in *Computer Programming and Formal Systems, Studies in Logic*, eds. P. Braffort and D. Hirschberg. North-Holland, Amsterdam, 118–61.

Sledd, J., "Review of G. L. Trager and H. L. Smith, 'Outline of English Structure,'" *Language*, XXXI (1955), 312–35.

——, "Some Question of English Phonology," *Language*, XXXIV (1958), 252–58.

——, *A Short Introduction to English Grammer*. Chicago: Scott, Foresman & Company, 1959.

Smith, C. S., "A Class of Complex Modifiers in English," *Language*, XXXVII (1961), 342–65.

Trubetzkoy, N. S., *Anleitung zu Phonologischen Beschreibungen*. Brno: Göttingen Vandechoeck & Ruprecht, 1935.

——, *Grundzüge der Phonologie*, 1939. Page references to the French translation by Cantineau (Paris, 1949).

Twaddell, W. F., *On Defining the Phoneme. Language Monograph No. 16*, 1935. Page references to reprinting in Joos (1957).

Viertel, J., *The Linguistic Theories of Humboldt*. In preparation.

Wells, R. S., "De Saussure's System of Linguistics," *Word*, III (1947), 1–31. Reprinted in Joos (1957).

Whitney, W. D., "Steinthal and the Psychological Theory of Language," *North American Review* (1872), 114. Reprinted in *Oriental and Linguistic Studies*. New York: Scribner, Armstrong & Co., 1874. First Series.

Wilkins, J. *An Essay towards a Real Character and a Philosophical Language*. London, 1668.

Wittgenstein, L., *The Blue and Brown Books*. New York: Harper & Row, Publishers, 1958.

Worth, D. S., "Transform Analysis of Russian Instrumental Construction," *Word*, XIV (1958), 247–90.

Ziff, P., *Semantic Analysis*. Ithaca, N.Y.: Cornell University Press, 1960a.

——, *On Understanding 'Understanding Utterances,'* " Philadelphia: University of Pennsylvania Press, 1960b. Mimeographed.

——, *About Grammaticalness*. Philadelphia: University of Pennsylvania Press, 1961. Mimeographed.

4   On the Notion "Rule of Grammar"*

Noam Chomsky

1 General desiderata for grammatical theory. The traditional aim of a grammar is to specify the class of properly formed sentences and to assign to each what we may call a *structural description* that is, an account of the units of which the sentence is composed, the manner of their combination, the formal relations of the sentence to other sentences, and so on. If we hope to go beyond traditional grammar in some significant way, it is essential to give a precise formulation of the notion *structural description of a sentence* and a precise account of the manner in which structural descriptions are assigned to sentences by *grammatical rules*. The rules contained in a traditional grammar are of widely diversified kinds, and there is no clear indication of what is to be the exact nature of a structural description. Modern linguistics has devoted a great deal of attention to clarifying the latter question, but has not considered with any seriousness the notion *grammatical rule*. Inattention to the process by which structural descriptions are generated and assigned to sentences leaves a serious gap in linguistic theory, however, and leaves open to serious doubt particular decisions about the inventory of elements in actual descriptive studies, since clearly such choices should not be independent of the complexity of the system of rules by which the structural description of each sentence is specified. In any event, it seems that a really insightful formulation of linguistic theory will have to begin by a determination of the kinds of permitted grammatical rules and an exact specification of their form and the manner in which they impose structural descriptions on each of an infinite set of grammatical sentences.

By a *grammar of the language L* I will mean a device of some sort (that is, a set of rules) that provides, at least, a complete specification of an infinite set of

*N. Chomsky, "On the Notion 'Rule of Grammar,' " *Proceedings of the Twelfth Symposium in Applied Mathematics*, **XII** (1961), 6–24. Reprinted by permission of the American Mathematical Society. This work was supported in part by the U.S. Army (Signal Corps), the U.S. Air Force (Office of Scientific Research, Air Research and Development Command), and the U.S. Navy (Office of Naval Research). It was also supported in part by the National Science Foundation. I am indebted to Morris Halle for several important suggestions.

grammatical sentences of L and their structural descriptions. In addition to making precise the notion *structural description*, the theory of grammar should meet requirements of the following kind. It should make available:

a class of possible grammars $G_1, G_2, \ldots,$ (1a)

a class of possible sentences $s_1, s_2, \ldots,$ (1b)

a function f such that $f(i, j)$ is the set of structural descriptions of the sentence s_i that are provided by the grammar $G_j,$ (1c)

a function $m(i)$ which evaluates $G_i,$ (1d)

a function g such that $g(i, n)$ is the description of a finite automaton that takes sentences of (1b) as input and gives structural descriptions assigned to these sentences by G_i (i.e., various, perhaps all members of $f(i, j)$) as output, where n is a parameter determining the capacity of the automaton.   (1e)

Equation (1a) is the requirement that the general theory of language must provide a schema and notation for grammatical description, a precise formulation of the notion *grammatical rule*.

Equation (1b) can be met by incorporating a fixed phonetic alphabet, for example, Jakobson's theory of distinctive features, as a part of linguistic theory.

Equation (1c) simply asserts that it must be possible to determine what a grammar states about particular sentences without exercise of intuition. The set $f(i, j)$ should contain more than one structural description only if the sentence s_i is ambiguous— that is, this is a reasonable empirical condition, one of many, on the grammar of a language.

Equation (1d) amounts to a demand for justification of grammars. That is, m may be a measure of complexity that leads to choice among alternative proposed grammars that are compatible with given data.[1] It is quite evident that if there is to be any hope of meeting Eqs. (1c–d) in any significant manner, the specification in Eqs. (1a–b) of tne available descriptive apparatus will have to be extremely narrow and limiting. To put it differently, only a fairly rigid and special set of assumptions about the nature of linguistic universals will make it possible to justify particular grammars in any general way.

Equation (1c) is a requirement of a different sort. A grammar, in the sense described above, is essentially a theory of the sentences of a language; it specifies this set (or generates it, to use a technical term which has become familiar in this connection)[2] and assigns to each generated sentence a structural description. It is not, however, a model of the speaker or hearer. It neither synthesizes particular sentences, as does the speaker, nor does it recognize the structure of presented sentences, as does the hearer.

---

[1]For discussion of the question of evaluation of grammars, see N. Chomsky, *Syntactic Structures* (The Hague: Mouton and Co., 1957), Chap. 6, and "A Transformational Approach to Syntax," *Proceedings of the Third Texas Conference on Problems of Linguistic Analysis in English, 1958,* (Texas, 1962), pp. 124–58; and M. Halle, "On the Role of Simplicity in Linguistic Descriptions," *Proceedings of the Twelfth Symposium in Applied Mathematics,* **XII** (1961).

[2]See, for example, E. Post, "Recursively Enumerable Sets of Positive Integers and Their Decision Problems," *Bull. Amer. Math. Soc.,* **50** (1944), 284–316.

It is quite neutral as between speaker and hearer in this respect. Equation (1c) would take us one step closer to a theory of the actual use of language. We can attempt to construct g in such a way that $g(i, n)$ will be a reasonable model for the production (or recognition) of sentences by the speaker (or hearer) who has internalized the grammar G_i and who has a memory capacity determined by the value of n. Notice that although the grammar G_i mastered by the user of a language is of course finite, it is not to be expected (and, in the case of natural languages, it is not in fact true) that a finite automaton can be constructed which will be able to accept (or generate) all and only the sentences generated by G_i, or which will be able to "understand" just these sentences (i.e., give the structural descriptions assigned to these sentences by G_i as outputs, when these sentences, but not others, are provided as inputs). This is no stranger than the fact that someone who has learned the rules of multiplication perfectly (perhaps without being able to state them) may be unable to calculate $3,872 \times 18,694$ in his head, although the rules that he has mastered uniquely determine the answer. We need only require of a reasonable procedure g that as n increases, the device $g(i, n)$ be capable of understanding, in the appropriate sense, more and more of the sentences generated by G_i (just as a reasonable model for the person who has learned arithmetic should have the property that as its memory aids and available time increase, more and more calculations should be correctly performed). It would be absurd to require of the grammars of Eq. (1a) that their output be the kinds of sets of strings, or sets of structural descriptions, that can be handled by strictly finite automata, just as it would be absurd to require (whether for the purposes of mathematical or psychological researches) that the rules of arithmetic be formulated so as to reflect precisely the ability of a human to perform calculations correctly in his head. Such a requirement would have neither theoretical nor practical motivation.

Among the rules of a grammar there are some that play a part in the generation of an infinite set of strings, each of which is an essentially orthographic representation of some grammatical sentence. These we will call *syntactic rules*; the final result of applying only these, we will call a *terminal string*. Other rules, called *morphophonemic*, convert a terminal string into the phonetic description of an utterance, that is, into one of the s_i's of Eq. (1b). The morphophonemic component of the grammar will not be discussed further here.[3]

Part of the structural description of a terminal string t will be a bracketing of t into phrases categorized into particular types. Call this element of the structural description a Phrase-marker (P-marker) of t. A P-marker can be represented as a labelled tree with the symbol S (standing for *sentence*) labelling the root, symbols of t labelling the endpoints, and phrase types (e.g., Noun Phrase (NP), Verb Phrase (VP), Noun (N)) as labels of other nodes. In studying syntactic theory, we assume as a known empirical condition, a partial specification of P-markers of many sentences in many languages, and we ask how a linguistic theory of the type shown in Eqs. (1a–c) can be constructed so that given a corpus, grammars chosen by the evaluation procedure m will provide P-markers that meet the given empirical conditions of adequacy.

---

[3] See Morris Halle, *Sound Pattern of Russian*, The Hague, 1959, for a detailed study of the structure of this component of a grammar.

2 Constituent structure grammars. A grammar is based on a certain vocabulary of symbols used for the representation of utterances and their parts, including, in particular, the a priori[4] phonetic alphabet provided by linguistic theory in accordance with the requirement of Eq. (1b). Suppose that a grammar contains, in addition, a designated *initial* symbol S and a designated *boundary* symbol $\sharp$. A particularly simple assumption about the form of grammars (Eq. (1a)) would be that each rule be an instruction of the form "rewrite φ as ψ" (symbolically, $\varphi \to \psi$), where φ and ψ are strings of symbols. Given such a grammar, we say that σ' *follows from* σ if $\sigma = \ldots$ $\varphi \ldots$ and $\sigma' = \ldots \psi \ldots$, (that is, if σ' results from substitution of ψ for a certain occurrence of φ in σ), where $\varphi \to \psi$ is a rule of the grammar. We say that a sequence of strings $\sigma_1, \ldots, \sigma_n$ is a φ-*derivation* if $\varphi = \sigma_1$ and for each i, σ_{i+1} follows from σ_i. A φ-derivation is *terminated* if its final line contains no substring χ such that $\chi \to \omega$ is a rule. In particular, we will be interested in terminated $\sharp S \sharp$-derivations, that is, terminated derivations that begin with the string $\sharp S \sharp$.[5]

Suppose that each syntactic rule $\varphi \to \psi$ meets the additional condition that there is a single symbol A and a non-null string ω such that $\varphi = \chi_1 A \chi_2$ and $\psi = \chi_1 \omega \chi_2$. This rule thus asserts that A can be rewritten ω (i.e., ω is of type A) when in the context $\chi_1 - \chi_2$, where χ_1 or χ_2 may, of course, be null. A set of rules meeting this condition[6] I will call a *constituent structure grammar*. If in each rule $\varphi \to \psi$, φ is a single symbol, the grammar (and each rule) will be called *context-free*; otherwise, *context-restricted*.[7] In the case of a constituent structure grammar, it is a simple matter to construct the procedure f required by Eq. (1c) that specifies the P-markers of the terminal strings. It is also not difficult to give a fairly reasonable specification of m of the condition of Eq. (1d).[8]

---

[4]From the standpoint of a particular grammar, that is.

[5]For a more careful account of such systems, and a study of some of their properties, see N. Chomsky, "On Certain Formal Properties of Grammars," *Information and Control*, Vol. 2 (1959).

[6]And, in fact, certain others which must be added to guarantee uniqueness of the associated P-marker. These do not affect anything discussed here. We need not require that the morphophonemic rules meet these conditions, since structural description on this level does not involve subdivision into further phrases.

[7]Immediate constituent analysis as developed within linguistics, particularly in the form given to this theory by Z. S. Harris, *Methods in Structural Linguistics*, (Chicago, Univ. of Chicago Press, 1951), Chap. 16, suggests a form of grammar similar to what is here called context-free constituent structure grammar. Another approach based on rather similar ideas originates in Leśniewski's theory of semantical categories and has been modified for linguistic purposes recently by Bar-Hillel, "A Quasi-arithmetical Notation for Syntactic Description," *Language*, Vol. 29 (1953), 47–58, Jan.-March, and Lambek, "The Mathematics of Sentence Structure," *Amer. Math., Monthly*, Vol. 65, March, 154–70 (1958) and "On the Calculus of Syntactic Types", this volume. The equivalence of context-free constituent structure grammars, categorial grammars in the sense of Y. Bar-Hillel and categorial grammars in the narrower sense of K. Ajdukiewicz, "Die Syntaktische Konnexität," *Studia Philosophica*, Vol. 1 (1935), is proven in Bar-Hillel,¹ Gaifman, and Shamir, "On Categorical and Phrase Structure Grammars," *Bull. Res. Council Israel* (where two theories that specify form of grammar are called equivalent if any language that can be represented by a grammar permitted by one theory can be represented by a grammar permitted by the other). Context-restricted constituent structure grammars have greater generative capacity (Chomsky, "On Certain Formal Properties of Grammars", Theorem 4, p. 147), and context-restricted rules are unavoidable, in practice, in grammatical description, whatever the theoretical possibilities may turn out eventually to be.

[8]See N. Chomsky, *Logical Structure of Linguistic Theory*, microfilm at Massachusetts Institute of Technology Libraries, (1955), Chap. 3.

For the remainder of this section we consider only context-free constituent structure grammars.

We say that φ *dominates* ψ $(\varphi \Rightarrow \psi)$ if there is a derivation $\sigma_1, \ldots, \sigma_n$ such that $\sigma_1 = \varphi$ and $\sigma_n = \psi$ (i.e., if ψ is a step of a φ-derivation). In terms of *self-dominance*, each nonterminal symbol A will be of one or more of four important types: (i) A is nonrecursive if for no non-null φ, ψ is it the case that $A \Rightarrow \varphi A \psi$; (ii) A is left-recursive if there is a non-null φ such that $A \Rightarrow A\varphi$; (iii) A is right-recursive if there is a non-null φ such that $A \Rightarrow \varphi A$; (iv) A is self-embedding if there are non-null φ, ψ such that $A \Rightarrow \varphi A \psi$. If a grammar contains left-recursive symbols, it will generate P-markers that branch indefinitely far to the left, as in Fig. 1(a); if it contains right-recursive symbols, it will generate configurations like that of Fig. 1(b); if it contains self-embedding symbols, it will generate such configurations as Fig. 1(c) and, in the interesting cases, will contain nested dependencies of arbitrary depth in the resulting terminal strings.

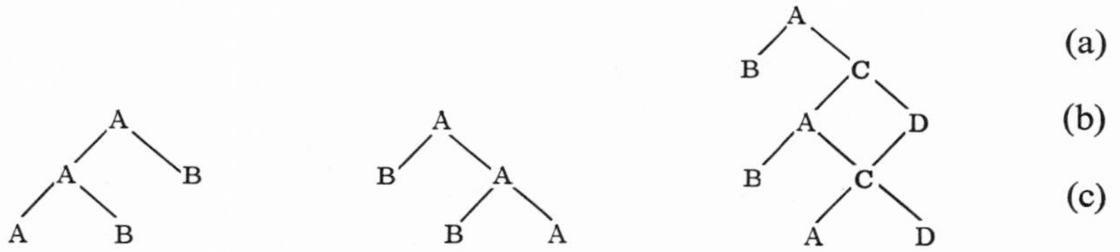

Figure 1

Nesting of dependencies is common in natural languages.[9] Consequently, if they

---

[9]For examples in English, which can easily be multiplied, see N. Chomsky, *Syntactic Structures*, Chap. 3. Both left- and right-recursive symbols have also been found in P-markers of every language so far studied from this point of view. In some (e.g., English), right-recursive structures are much more abundant; in others, the opposite appears to be the case (e.g., Japanese)—cf. B. Bloch, "Studies in Colloquial Japanese II: Syntax," *Language*, Vol. 22 (1946) in M. Joos (ed.), *Readings in Linguistics*. Sentence 24 of the analyzed text (p. 182 in *RiL*), for example, contains an embedded phrase with the following structure:

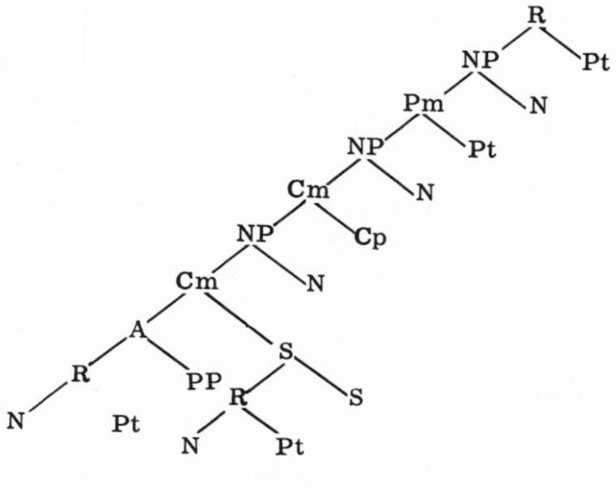

(I am indebted to Karl V. Teeter for this reference.) Although no language has yet been found to lack any of the types, (i–iv), it should be emphasized that study of questions of this sort has barely begun.

have constituent structure grammars at all, such grammars must contain many self-embedded symbols.

Suppose that Q is a P-marker. We say that $B = (a_1, \ldots, a_k)$ is a *branch* of Q, where each a_i is a node, if a_1 is the root and a_i is connected to a_{i+1}, for each $i < k$. Each node is labeled by some symbol. We say that $a_i \equiv a_j$ if the same symbol labels both a_i and a_j.

Suppose that B_1, B_2, and B_3 are three distinct branches of Q, where

$$B_1 = (a_1, \ldots, a_{j+k}), \tag{2a}$$
$$B_2 = (a_1, \ldots, a_j, b_1, \ldots, b_r), \tag{2b}$$
$$B_3 = (a_1, \ldots, a_j, c_1, \ldots, c_s) \ (j, k, r, s \geq 1), \tag{2c}$$
$$a_{j+k} \equiv a_j \not\equiv a_{j+i} \ (1 \leq i < k), \tag{2d}$$
$$b_r \text{ is to the left of } a_{j+k} \text{ and } c_s \text{ to the right of } a_{j+k} \text{ in } Q \tag{2e}$$

(in the obvious sense, which, to be made precise, requires labelling of lines as well as nodes in Q). In this case, we say that a_j is a *self-embedding node* in B_1. We now define the *degree* of Q as the largest integer n such that there is a branch $B = (a_1, \ldots, a_k)$ and a sequence of integers $(b_1, \ldots, b_n)$, $1 \leq b_i < b_{i+1} \leq k$ such that each a_{b_i} is self-embedding in B and for each i, j, $a_{b_i} \equiv a_{b_j}$.

In other words, the degree of a P-marker is the maximum number of times that some constituent is successively self-embedded—the maximal depth of self-embedding in this P-marker. In Fig. 1(c), for example, the degree would be 2.

In terms of these notions, we can turn to Eq. (1e), that is, the question how a constituent structure grammar is related in generative capacity to a finite automaton,[10]

---

[10]Or, finite N. Markov source in the sense of C. Shannon, *Mathematical Theory of Communication*, Urbana, University of Illinois Press, 1949. A finite automaton is a device with a finite number of states $S_0, \ldots, S_q$ and a finite vocabulary $a_0, \ldots, a_m$, and its behavior can be represented by a finite set of rules (i, j, k), where such a triple indicates that, when in state S_i, the device can switch to state S_k, emitting transition symbol a_j (equivalently, on reading the input symbol a_j). Where S_0 is a designated initial state, we can define a produced string as the sequence of transition symbols given as output (equivalently, the sequence of symbols accepted as input) when the device switches from S_0 to a first return to S_0. We can think of a_0 as the identity element in the output (input) alphabet. A set of sentences produced (accepted) by such a device is what C. S. Kleene has called a "regular event." Cf. C. S. Kleene "Representation of Events in Nerve Nets and Finite Automata," *Automata Studies*, (Princeton: Princeton University Press, 1956) for study of such devices from a point of view close to that adopted here; see also, N. Chomsky and G. A. Miller, "Finite State Languages," *Information and Control*, Vol. 1 (1958); M. Rabin and D. Scott, "Finite Automata and Their Decision Problems," *IBM J. Res. Develop.*, Vol. 3 (1959). Whether we regard such a device as producing or recognizing a sentence is inconsequential; it is merely a matter of how we decide to read the notation that defines it.

The assumption that sentences are produced or recognized by a device of this sort tells us almost nothing about the method of processing. For example, a finite automaton as a recognizing device may store a long (though bounded) sequence of symbols which it then processes from right to left, from center out, or whatever; it may process a string as it receives its symbols in left-to-right (temporal) order; it may do both, in some complex way. In the case of sentence recognition by humans, it is clear that storage of large units must often precede final processing— that is, it is easy to find examples of sentences, early parts of which cannot be interpreted until later parts are received.

In general, it is important to guard against the temptation to assume that the finite automaton (Markov source) model somehow implies left-to-right (temporal) processing of actual sentences, either in production or recognition. It is, of course, not surprising that an abstract system of such an unstructured type as that described above is so unilluminating (being compatible with so many specific alternatives) as a model for actual behavior.

that is, a device that presumably has the capacity of the speaker or hearer with fixed (in particular, without any) supplementary aids and that somehow produces or accepts sentences. It is easy to show that:

> A set of sentences cannot be represented by a finite automaton
> (i.e., is not a regular event) just in case all of its constituent   (3)
> structure grammars contain self-embedding symbols.[11]

We can also establish a closely related, but considerably more interesting result that can, slightly oversimplified,[12] be stated as follows:

> There is a mechanical procedure g such that where G_i is a
> constituent structure grammar,[12] $g(i, n)$ is the description of a
> finite automaton which, given a string s as input, will give as   (4)
> output all P-markers of degree $<n$ assigned to s by G_i.

To put the main point simply, Eq. (4) provides a program for a general purpose computer such that when the rules of a constituent structure grammar G are put in the memory and the size of memory is fixed, the device will "understand" any sentence generated by G that does not contain too much nesting of constituents of a single type. This device, is, furthermore, optimal. That is, it follows from Eq. (3) that the construction g cannot essentially be improved upon. If a grammar G generates P-markers of arbitrary degree, there will not, in general, exist a finite device that will accept (produce) just the sentences of the language specified by G. Therefore, the procedure g gives the best possible way of meeting the requirement of Eq. (1e), in the case of the linguistic theory that limits grammars to context-free constituent structure grammars[12] The automaton $g(i, n)$ fails only where success is in principle unattainable.

We may think of the automaton $g(i, n)$ as being, indifferently,[13] a model for the speaker or hearer who knows and uses the grammar G_i but has a finite memory that determines the permitted degree of self-embedding n. Of course, if the memory restriction is relaxed by allowing more time or computational aids, the bound n increases. Such a speaker or hearer, we would predict, should be unable to "process"

---

[11]For a simple proof of this, see N. Chomsky, "A Note on Phrase Structure Grammars," *Information and Control*, Vol. 2 (1959); an earlier proof, following from Eq. (4) is in "On Certain Formal Properties of Grammars," where the proof of Eq. (4) appears.

[12]The oversimplification is that in N. Chomsky, "On Certain . . . ," Eq. (4) is shown to hold only for a certain class K of constituent structure grammars limited (in order to simplify the proof of Eq. (4)) to those that have the lexicon (i.e., the rules that give terminal symbols) totally separated from grammatical rules and that permit only binary constituent breaks (with a few other restrictions)—thus, K is limited to grammars of the type that linguists usually consider as typical representatives of the results of immediate constituent analysis. However, it is also shown there that the class K is comprehensive enough to contain a grammar for each language for which there exists a context-free constituent structure grammar at all. Furthermore, it is quite easy to broaden the class K for which Eq. (4) holds to include grammars with rules of many other kinds, and it can probably be extended to include all context-free grammars. Equation (4), as stated here, involves a trivial modification of what is actually proven in Chomsky, "On Certain . . . ," (and, in fact, involves also a slight modification of the notion *finite automaton*, to provide for a specific sort of output). To the construction given there, a small number of rules would have to be added to permit $g(i, n)$ to actually draw the P-markers of the sentences that it "understands."

[13]See 10*n*. It should be re-emphasized that $g(i, n)$ as it stands is by no means a realistic model of the speaker or hearer who has mastered the grammar G_i, but at most, a first step towards such a model.

a sentence just in case it contains too much self-embedding, but should be able to understand or produce sentences with left- and right-recursive P-markers of great complexity or even with nesting of distinct constituents. This is the only prediction that follows from the assumption of finiteness of memory, and it seems to be fairly well borne out by the facts.[14]

Since there has been a good deal of confusion about the matters discussed above, I would like to re-emphasize some basic points. From the fact that memory is finite, the fact that a sentence is heard or spoken from *left-to-right* (i.e., through time), or the fact that the rules of a generative grammar (to be sharply distinguished from a model of the speaker or hearer) may be partially ordered, nothing whatsoever can be concluded about left- and right-branching in P-markers. All of these facts are perfectly compatible with left- or right-branching, extended arbitrarily far. Only self-embedding is incompatible with finiteness of memory.

Suppose, however, that we make the additional hypothesis (*A*) that the speaker produces the P-marker of a sentence *from top down* (that is, that he invariably selects grammatical constructions before he selects the words that he will use, etc.). From this it follows immediately that left-branching cannot be tolerated, beyond a certain limit.[15] By quite similar reasoning from the additional hypothesis (*B*) that the hearer produces a P-marker (i.e., constructs a structural description of a heard sentence) strictly *from bottom up*, it would follow that right-branching trees should not be tolerated beyond a certain point, though left-branching should offer no problem. Of these twin hypotheses, (*A*) seems to me to have neither any particular plausibility nor any empirical support, while (*B*) seems not totally implausible.[16] From (*B*) we

---

[14]Y. Yngve ("A Model and a Hypothesis for Language Structure," *Proceedings of the American Philosophical Society*, Vol. 104, no. 5, Oct. 1960, 444–66) has suggested that a grammar may contain devices that partially overcome the limitation on memory by allowing reformulation of sentences. This is an important observation. It appears that many of the singularly grammatical transformations of the type described are purely *stylistic* in the sense that they do not significantly change content and have only the effect of converting a string to an equivalent one with less self-embedding. Thus, there is a transformation which converts "that he left was unfortunate" (which embeds the sentence "he left") to "it was unfortunate that he left," which is right-branching rather than self-embedding; and there is a transformation that converts *the cover that the book that John has has* to *John's book's cover*, which is left-branching rather than self-embedding.

To complete the picture, however, we should note certain transformations that have, in general, the effect of *increasing* the complexity of the sentence that they reformulate, for example, the transformation that converts "I saw the old man" to "it was the old man whom I saw," "I gave the book to the old man" to "it was to the old man that I gave the book," etc.

It should also be noted that the concept of structural complexity that Yngve proposes differs from that stated above. In his formulation, left-branching and self-embedding contribute equally to what he calls *depth* (i.e., to structural complexity). That is, in his sense of *depth* there are P-markers of arbitrarily great depth that *can* be recognized (equivalently, produced) by a strictly finite automaton such as $g(i, n)$ of Eq. (4) (with n fixed).

[15]It is the assumption (*A*), rather than those stated in the preceding paragraph, that is the basis for the model proposed by Y. Yngve, *op. cit.*

[16]It is, however, by no means as obviously true as it may appear at first glance. There are, I believe, much more promising approaches to a theory of the listener. Cf., in particular, M. Halle and K. Stevens, "Analysis by Synthesis," forthcoming in *Information and Control*; M. Halle "Review of Sbornik po masinnomu perevodu," *Language*, Vol. 36 (1960); D. MacKay, "Mindlike Behavior in Artefacts," *British J. Philos. Sci.*, Vol. 2 (1951); J. Bruner, "Neural Mechanisms in Perception," in *The Brain and Human Behavior*, Solomon, Cobb, and Penfield (eds.), p. 122f.; and, more generally, the many discussions of the effect of set and expectancy in perception, which are quite relevant to these suggestions. The attempt to develop a reasonable account of the speaker

would predict that a hearer will tend to group left-branching units of a complex sentence (as, e.g., in *many more than half of the rather obviously much too easily solved problems*) as units quite readily, but that he would tend to treat right-branching units (as, e.g., *the book that was on the table that was near the door that was newly painted*) as successive and disjointed, rather than integrated segments, on first hearing.[17]

Whatever the facts may turn out to be when proper empirical study of this question is carried out, it is important to remember that neither (*A*) nor (*B*) is supported by the fact that unaided speakers (or hearers) cannot produce (or understand) sentences with too much self-embedding. This fact, and this alone, follows from the assumption of finiteness of memory (which no one, surely, has ever questioned). The automaton $g(i, n)$ guaranteed by (Eq. 4) essentially traces through the P-marker in a systematic manner, avoiding both the restriction against left- and right-branching, while preserving finiteness of memory. Similarly, other sorts of evidence that might be thought, on superficial examination, to support one or the other of (*A*) or (*B*), must also be regarded with caution. Thus, it has often been observed that there is a tendency to avoid a discontinuity when the intervening element is long or complex.[18] Thus, such a sentence as (a) "I called the man who read the book that was on the table that was near the door up" (with the discontinuous verb *call up*) is extremely awkward and would always be replaced by (b) "I called up the man . . . ." If, accepting the hypothesis (*A*), we measure *depth* in the manner suggested by Yngve, then the depth of (b) will be either the same as that of (a)[19] or less by one than that of (a).[20] In either case, however, the awkwardness of (a) can scarcely be attributed to depth, in this sense, since the depth of (a) is under any calculation less than that of such perfectly natural sentences as "quite a large majority of the students here are hard-working," and so on. Careful scrutiny of such cases seems to lead to the conclusion that the tendency to avoid discontinuities is independent of at least any simple consideration involving left-branching, self-embedding, or right-branching.

3 Transformational grammars. This discussion has so far been based on the assumption that the correct set of P-markers can be generated in a natural and

---

has, I believe, been hampered by the prevalent and utterly mistaken view that a generative grammar in itself provides or is related in some obvious way to a model for the speaker.

It seems to me very likely that attempts to construct a model for the speaker or hearer are quite premature at this point, since we can hardly claim to have an adequate characterization of the form of the grammars that provide the devices that are employed, in some way, in the production and understanding of speech.

[17]This seems not unlikely. Thus, in the right-branching case (as, e.g., in "the house that Jack built"), the reader would, I think, tend to place the intonation break before the *that*, in each clause, contrary to the immediate constituent analysis, a fact which may suggest that these right-branching structures are indeed more difficult to recognize.

[18]In some as yet undefined sense, cf., e.g., Chomsky, *Syntactic Structures, op. cit.*, p. 77n. The question is apparently not trivial. Thus, such a sentence as "I called the man you saw up" seems to me less natural than "I called almost all of the men from Boston up," and, in general, embedding of a short sentence (hence, self-embedding) seems less natural than embedding of a fairly long phrase. It is by no means obvious that grammatical or intonational considerations will be sufficient to account for relative naturalness in such cases.

[19]If the analysis of the construction, Article-Noun-Relative clause, is [Article (Noun-Relative Clause)].

[20]If the analysis accepted is (Article-Noun-Relative Clause) or [(Article-Noun) Relative Clause].

formally well-motivated way by a constituent structure grammar. There are strong reasons to believe that this is not the case, however. Immediate constituent analysis has been sharply and, I think, correctly criticized as, in general, imposing too much structure on sentences.[21] Consider, for example, such a sentence as:

Why has John always been such an easy fellow to please?   (5)

The whole is a sentence; the last several words constitute a noun phrase; the words can be assigned to categories. But, there is little motivation for assigning phrase structure beyond this. The same is true of the sentence, "I brought it in yesterday from the garage after dinner," and many others. In all such cases, immediate constituent analysis is not really to the point, and a constituent structure grammar would be most unrevealing. The extreme example of this difficulty is the case of true coordination, "the man was old, tired, tall, . . . , but friendly." The only correct P-marker would assign no internal structure at all within the sequence of coordinated items. But a constituent structure grammar can accommodate this possibility only with an infinite number of rules; that is, it must necessarily impose further structure, in quite an arbitrary way. Examples such as this are important as a reminder that, to achieve adequacy, a linguistic theory must provide grammars for every desired infinite set of P-markers, not only for every interesting infinite set of sentences (natural language). This requirement the theory of constituent structure cannot possibly meet.

The basic reason that the theory of grammar sketched above cannot be accepted, however, lies in its failure, in practice, to make possible the construction of simple and revealing grammars. An attempt to demonstrate this would go well beyond the bounds of this paper. I do not see, however, how this fact can be doubted by anyone who makes a serious attempt to apply in detail such a theory as this to a natural language.

A great many of the difficulties[22] that confront a constituent structure grammar seem to be overcome if we revise the schema for grammatical description (i.e., Eq. (1a)) in the following way. We limit the rewriting rules $\varphi \to \psi$ discussed above to a sequence of rules, used to generate a finite number of derivations of terminal strings, to each of which we associate, as before, a labeled tree representing constituent structure. In this way, we generate only those terminal strings that underlie the simplest sentences. These strings, however, embody all or most of the selectional restrictions on choice of elements. We now add to the grammar a set of operations of the type that have been called by Z. S. Harris[23] *grammatical transformations*. Each of

---

[21]See, e.g., J. Sledd, *A Short Introduction to English Grammar* (Chicago: Scott-Foresman, Inc., 1959.)

[22]For an indication of some of these, see Chomsky, *Logical Structure of Linguistic Theory, op. cit.*, Chaps. 7 and 8, and *Syntactic Structures, op. cit.*, Chap. 6.

[23]In his work on analysis of extended discourse ("Discourse Analysis," *Language*, Vol. 26 (1952), and "Discourse Analysis: a sample text," *ibid.*), Z. S. Harris brought to light the important fact that large areas of traditional grammar that had been quite overlooked in modern linguistics could be given a unified treatment in terms of some notion of grammatical transformation. In his "Co-occurrence and Transformation in Linguistic Structure," *Language*, Vol. 31 (1957), he developed a notion of grammatical transformation (with applications in English) as, essentially, a relation

these is a mapping of P-markers onto P-markers. The recursive property of the grammar is now attributed entirely to these transformations. I will now briefly describe how the schema for grammatical description can be extended to accommodate operations of the required kind and how these operations impose P-markers on the terminal strings formed by their application to already generated P-markers (i.e., how the function f of Eq. (1c), above, must be revised in accordance with this extension of the form of grammars.[24])

The motivation for adding transformational rules to a grammar is quite clear. There are certain sentences (in fact, simple declarative active sentences with no complex noun or verb phrases—or, to be more precise, the terminal strings underlying these) that can be generated by a constituent structure grammar in quite a natural way. There are others (e.g., passives, questions, sentences with discontinuous phrases and complex phrases that embed sentence transforms) that cannot be generated in an economic and natural way by a constituent structure grammar, but that are systematically related to sentences of simpler structure. Transformations that are constructed to express this relation can thus materially simplify the grammar when used to generate more complex sentences and their structural descriptions from already generated simpler ones.

The problem is to construct a general and abstract notion of grammatical transformation which will incorporate and facilitate the expression of just those formal relations between sentences that have a significant function in language.[25] It is clear,

---

holding between two sequences of morpheme classes which can be partially paired, class by class, so that the same choice of morphemes can occur in paired classes. D. Worth has applied this notion to the study of Russian inflection in his "Transform Analysis of Russian Instrumental Constructions," *Word*, Vol., 14 (1950). The approach that I will describe here bears little formal resemblance to this conception, although it was suggested by Harris' observation noted above. It is based on the account of grammatical transformations given in the references of 1*n* and 8*n*, and N. Chomsky's "Three Models for the Description of Language," I.R.E. *Transactions on Information Theory*, Vol. IT–2 (1956). For a study of large segments of English grammar in essentially these terms, going well beyond what is contained in the references just cited, see R. B. Lees, *A Grammar of English Nominalizations*, Baltimore: 1960 (supplement to *International Journal of American Linguistics*). This book also contains some material on Turkish and German. Further material on German is presented in J. R. Applegate, *Structure of the German Noun Phrase*, in preparation. This descriptive work on English has been extended in important ways in papers by R. B. Lees, forthcoming in *Language*; R. B. Lees and E. Klima, *Rules for English Pronominalization*, forthcoming; and Klima, *Negation*, forthcoming. Klima has presented material on Russian in his review of Galkina-Fedoruk's "Bezličnye predloženija v sovremennom Russkom jazyke," *Int. Jour. of Slavic Ling. and Poetics*, Vol. 5 (1961). Within essentially the same theoretical framework there is also a very detailed study of an American Indian language, G. H. Matthews, *A Grammar of Hidatsa*, forthscoming; cf., also, his "Ergative Relation in Hidatsa" *Quart. Prog. Rep. of Res. Lab. of Electronic-* (January, 1960) and (in preparation) grammars of several Philippine languages by R. Stockwell and several of his students.

[24]In fact, the notion *Structural Description of a Sentence "s"* must itself be extended to include along with the P-marker of *s* and of the strings underlying *s* transformationally, an object which we might call a *T*-marker that represents the transformational history of *s*. I will not go into this matter here, however.

[25]Just as in the case of P-markers, we must assume, for the purpose of constructing a significant concept, some advance knowledge of empirical conditions that the notion *grammatical transformation* must meet. Thus, we assume that a reasonable notion of grammatical transformation must lead to the conclusion that "John saw Bill" and "Bill was seen by John" are related quite differently than "John saw Bill" and "Bill saw John," and so on. I do not see what conceivable alternative there is to this approach, in the case of transformation or any other linguistic concept, nor does this seem to me to be in any way objectionable.

first of all, that application of a transformation to a string requires knowledge of the constituent structure of this string. Thus, the question transformation has the effect of preposing a certain element of the main verbal phrase of a declarative sentence. Applied to Eq. (6) it yields Eq. (7) but not Eq. (8):

The man who was here was old.	(6)
Was the man who was here old?	(7)
Was the man who here was old?	(8)

That is, we must know that the second, not the first occurrence of *was* is to be preposed, and this requires that the constituent structure be available. Similarly, we want the passive transformation to apply to "the man saw the boy" to produce "the boy was seen by the man," but not to "the man saw the boy leave" to form, say, "the boy leave was seen by the man." Thus, we must know what substrings of each sentence are Noun Phrase, Auxiliary, and Verb. A transformation cannot simply be an operation defined on terminal strings or morpheme class sequences with no further structure.

It would also defeat the ends of transformational analysis to regard transformations as higher level rewriting rules that apply to undeveloped phrase designations, that is, in the case of the passive, as a rule

$$\text{NP}_1 \text{ Auxiliary Verb NP}_2 \rightarrow \text{NP}_2 \text{ Auxiliary be Verb en by NP}_1 \qquad (9)$$

or something of this sort. Such a rule would be of the type discussed in Section 2, but would not meet the additional condition imposed on constituent structure rules (that is, the condition that only a single symbol be rewritten) that makes construction of the P-marker possible in the manner presupposed above.[26] A sufficient argument against this is that transformations, so formulated, would not provide a method for simplifying the grammar where selectional restrictions on choice of elements appear. Thus, among active sentences we find

the fact that the case was dismissed doesn't surprise me,	(11a)
Congress enacted a new law,	(11b)
the men consider John a dictator,[27]	(11c)
John felt remorse,	(11d)

---

[26]That is, a grammar would now be simply a set of rules $\varphi \rightarrow \psi$, where φ and ψ are strings of symbols. It would be, in other words, a system of a well-studied kind called technically a *semi-Thue system* [cf., e.g., M. Davis, "*Computability and Unsolvability,*" (New York: McGraw-Hill Book Co., Inc., 1958), Chap. 6]. Linguistic theory would, essentially, reduce to the assertion that a grammar is an arbitrary Turing machine, in this highly unstructured formulation. This is the most general (and consequently, least interesting) possible formulation of grammatical theory. The apparent gain in flexibility that results from thus dropping all constraints on the form of grammars is quite illusory, however, since it merely shifts the problem of specifying the formal features that make natural language distinctive, among arbitrary effectively specifiable (recursively enumerable) sets, from the characterization of Eq. (1a) (where this problem properly belongs) to the characterization of Eq. (1c–d). The revision of transformational theory criticized here is (if I understand him correctly) essentially that suggested implicitly by F. W. Householder, "*On Linguistic Primes,*" *Word*, Vol. 15 (1959), p. 233f., and *review of C. F. Hockett's "A Course in Modern Linguistics* (New York: The Macmillan Company, 1958) in *Language,* Vol. 35 (1959), pp. 506–7, 517.

and so on, but not the sequences formed by interchange of subject and object in such cases. In the corresponding passives the selectional relations are obviously preserved, appearing now in a different arrangement. If the passive transformation were to apply as a rewriting rule, at a stage of derivation preceding the application of the context-restricted rewriting rules that provide the selectional restrictions on the choice of subject, verb, object (as would be the case, e.g., if (10) were taken as the formulation of this rule), an entirely independent set of context-restricted rules would have to be given to determine the corresponding subject, verb, agent selection in the passive. One of the virtues of a transformational grammar is that it provides a means of avoiding this pointless duplication of selectional rules. But this advantage is lost if we apply the transformation before the selection of particular elements.[28] The same is true of most transformational rules.

It, therefore, seems to me evident that a transformational rule must apply to a full P-marker. Since transformational rules must re-apply to transforms, it follows that the result of applying a transformation must again be a P-marker, the *derived* P-marker of the terminal string resulting from the transformation. A grammatical transformation, then, is a mapping of P-markers into P-markers.

We can formulate such a notion of grammatical transformation in the following way. Suppose that Q is a P-marker of the terminal string t and that t can be subdivided into successive segments $t_1, \ldots, t_n$ in such a way that each t_i is traceable, in Q, to a node labelled A_i. We say, in such a case, that

$$t \text{ is } analyzable \text{ as } (t_1, \ldots, t_n; A_1, \ldots, A_n) \text{ with respect to } Q. \tag{11}$$

In the simplest case, a transformation T will be specified in part by a sequence of symbols $(A_1, \ldots, A_n)$ that defines its domain by the following rule:

$$\text{a string } t \text{ with P-marker } Q \text{ is in the domain of } T \text{ if } t \text{ is analyzable as } (t_1, \ldots, t_n; A_1, \ldots, A_n) \text{ with respect to } Q. \tag{12}$$

In this case, we will call $(t_1, \ldots, t_n)$ a *proper analysis* of t with respect to Q, T, and we will call $(A_1, \ldots, A_n)$ the *structure index* of T.

To complete the specification of the transformation T, we describe the effect that T has on the terms of the proper analysis of the string to which it applies. Thus, T may have the effect of deleting or permuting certain terms, of substituting one for another, of adding a constant string in a fixed place, and so on. Suppose that we associate with a transformation T an underlying *elementary transformation* T_{el} which is a formal operation of some sort on n terms, where the structure index of T is of length n. Let

$$T_{el}(i; t_1 \ldots, t_n) = \sigma_i \tag{13}$$

---

[27]More properly, we should have here the underlying terminal string "the men – consider a dictator – John," itself, of course, a transform of simpler strings.

[28]For each particular case, some *ad hoc* adjustment or principle can be employed to cope with the problem. But a general alternative to the transformational approach to this matter has not yet been suggested.

where $(t_1, \ldots, t_n)$ is the proper analysis of t with respect to Q, T, and T_{el} underlies T. Then the string resulting from application of the transformation T to the string t with P-marker Q is

$$T(t, Q) = \sigma_1 \ldots \sigma_n. \tag{14}$$

Obviously, we do not want any arbitrary mapping of the sort just described to qualify as a grammatical transformation. Thus, we would not want to permit in a grammar a transformation that associates such pairs as:

John saw the boy—I'll leave tomorrow, (15a)

John saw the man—why don't you try again, (15b)

John saw the girl—China is industrializing rapidly, (15c)

and so on,[29] but only such rules as express genuine structural relations between sentence forms, as, for example, active-passive, declarative-interrogative, declarative-nominalized sentence, and so on. We can avoid this by an additional and quite natural requirement on elementary transformations that can be formulated loosely as follows:

If T_{el} is an elementary transformation, then for all integers
i, n, and strings $x_1, \ldots, x_n, y_1, \ldots, y_n$, it must be the case
that $T_{el}(i; x_1, \ldots, x_n)$ is formed from $T_{el}(i; y_1, \ldots, y_n)$ by   (16)
replacing y_i in the latter by x_i, for each $i \leq n$.

In other words, the effect of an elementary transformation is independent of the particular choice of strings to which it applies.

This requirement has the effect of ruling out the possibility of applying transformations to strings of actually occurring words (or morphemes). Thus, no single elementary transformation meeting Eq. (16) can have the effect of replacing Eqs. (17a–b) by Eqs. (18a–b), respectively:

John will try (17a)

John tried (17b)

will John try (18a)

did John try (18b)

although this is clearly the effect of the simple question-transformation. The elementary transformation that we need in this case is that which converts $x_1 - x_2 - x_3$ to $x_2 - x_1 - x_3$, that is, the transformation T_{el} defined as follows, for arbitrary strings x_1, x_2, x_3:

$$T_{el}(1; x_1, x_2, x_3) = x_2; \; T_{el}(2; x_1, x_2, x_3) = x_1; \; T_{el}(3; x_1, x_2, x_3) = x_3. \tag{19}$$

---

[29]More correctly, the theory of transformations must be designed so that a relation of this sort could only be expressed by a sequence of transformations. Notice that a program such as Eqs. (1a–e) will collapse completely unless the choice of available transformations is strictly limited. The wider the class of permitted transformations, the more difficult it becomes to meet the requirement of Eq. (1d) in a significant way. Cf. 25*n*.

For a more adequate and precise formulation, see Chomsky, "Three Models for the Description of Language," *op. cit.*, p. 122.

But, if this is to yield Eq. 18(b), it will be necessary to apply it not to Eq. (17b) but rather to a hypothetical form

$$\text{John past try,} \tag{20}$$

parallel in structure to Eq. 17(a), that underlies Eq. (17b). In general, we cannot require that terminal strings be related in any very simple way to actual sentences. The obligatory mappings (transformational and morphophonemic) that specify the physical shape may reorder, add, or delete elements, and so on.[30]

The notion of transformation just described must be generalized in several directions, for empirical adequacy. First, we must allow transformations that apply to pairs of P-markers. Thus, the terminal string underlying the sentence in Eq. (21) is constructed transformationally from the already formed strings underlying Eqs. (22a–b) (with their respective P-markers):

$$\text{his owning property surprised me} \tag{21}$$
$$\text{it surprised me} \tag{22}$$
$$\text{he owns property}$$

We can provide for this possibility by allowing all strings

$$\sharp\, S\, \sharp\sharp\, S\, \sharp \ldots \sharp\, S\, \sharp \tag{23}$$

to head derivations in the underlying constituent structure grammar, instead of just $\sharp\, S\, \sharp$, as above (or in several equivalent and equally simple ways). We then allow such structure indices as

$$(\sharp,\ \text{NP},\ \text{V},\ \text{NP},\ \sharp,\ \sharp,\ \text{NP},\ \text{V},\ \text{NP},\ \sharp) \tag{24}$$

thus providing for Eq. (22) and similar cases (this necessitates a simple modification of Eq. (12) which I will not describe here).

We must also extend the manner in which the domain of a transformation and the proper analysis of the transformed string is specified. First, there is no need to require that the terms of a structure index be single symbols. Second, we can allow the specification of a transformation to be given by a finite set of structure indices. More generally, we can specify the domain of a transformation simply by a structural condition based on the predicate *analyzable* (cf. Eq. (11)). In terms of this notion, we can define identity of terminal strings and can allow for terms of the structure index to be unspecified. By this extension, which I will not describe here, we can provide an explicit and precise basis for the informal descriptions of transformations that have appeared in the linguistic literature.[31]

---

[30]Only on the level of words is the relation between sequence of elements in a representing string and actual time sequence in speech in general order-preserving. We cannot expect to meet this condition on the level of morphemes, phonemes, or any of the even more abstract syntactic levels.

It is important to note that in the case just discussed there are several quite independent reasons for setting up the same abstract underlying strings. Note also that the effect of the question transformation is to convert Eq. (17a) to Eq. (18a) and Eq. (20) to "past John try," which is converted to Eq. (18b) by an obligatory transformation of considerable, generality that introduces *do* as a bearer of an unaffixed affix.

[31]In particular, the transformational aspects of syntax described in the references cited in 1*n*, 8*n*, and 23*n*.

A grammatical transformation, then, is determined by a structural condition stated in terms of the predicate *analyzable* and an elementary transformation.[32] It was remarked previously, however, that a transformation must produce not merely strings, but derived P-markers. It remains, then, to show how constituent structure is assigned to the terminal string formed by a transformation. It seems that the best way to do this is by a set of rules that form part of general linguistic theory, rather than by an additional clause appended to the specification of each individual transformation. Precise statement of these rules would require an analysis of fundamental notions going well beyond the informal account sketched above, or for that matter, the more precise versions of it that have appeared previously. Nevertheless, certain features of a general solution to this problem seem fairly clear. We can, first of all, assign each transformation to one of a small number of classes, depending on the underlying elementary transformation on which it is based. For each such class we can state a general rule that assigns to the transform a derived Phrase-marker, the form of which depends, in a fixed way, on the Phrase-markers of the underlying terminal strings. A few examples will illustrate the kinds of principles that seem to be necessary.

Generalized transformations that produce a string from a pair of underlying strings (e.g., Eqs. (21–22)) appear to be the basic recursive devices in the grammar. That is, there is apparently a bound on the number of singulary transformations that can apply in sequence. Most generalized transformations are based on elementary transformations that substitute a transformed version of the second of the pair of underlying terminal strings[33] for some term of the proper analysis of the first of this pair.[34] In such a case, one general principle seems sufficient to determine the derived constituent structure of the transform. Suppose that the transformation replaces the symbol a of σ_1 (the matrix sentence) by σ_2 (the constituent sentence). The P-marker of the result is simply the former P-marker of σ_1 with a replaced by the P-marker of σ_2.[35]

It appears that all other generalized transformations are *attachment transformations* that take a term α of the proper analysis, with the term β of the structure index that most remotely dominates it (and all intermediate parts of the P-marker that are dominated by β and that dominate α), and attaches it (with, perhaps, a constant string) to some other term of the proper analysis. In this way, we form, for example,

---

[32]What we actually specify in this way is not merely *grammatical transformation* in extension (i.e. a class of pairs of P-markers), but *transformational rule*. That is, different such specifications may lead to the same transformation, in extension, in a particular language. In general, we are interested not so much in the extension of the notions *grammar* (i.e., a sequence $\sigma_1, \sigma_2, \ldots$ of elements of the class given in Eq. (1b)), *transformation*, and so on, but in the particular manner in which these devices are specified. The study of grammatical transformations, in extension, will become interesting only when it becomes possible to extend to transformational grammars studies of the kind carried out for constituent structure grammars in the references cited in 11*n*.

[33]In the terminology suggested by Lees, *A Grammar of English Nominalizations, op. cit.*, the *constituent string*. It is, for several reasons, convenient to analyze an operation such as Eqs. (21–22) into two transformations, one which converts Eq. (22b) into *his owning property* which is substituted, by the second transformation, for *it* of Eq. (22a). It is the second of these that we are discussing now.

[34]In Lees' terminology, the *matrix string*.

[35]The same notion can obviously be extended to singulary substitution transformations.

"John is old and sad" with the P-marker [Eq. (25)] from "John is old." "John is sad," by a transformation with the structure index (NP, is, *A*, ⧣⧣, NP, is, A).[36]

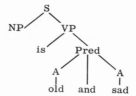

Figure 2

Many of the singular transformations are permutations of terms of the proper analysis. For example, one transformation converts Fig. 3(a) to Fig. 3(b):

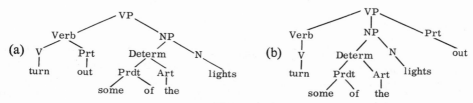

Figure 3

The general principle of derived constituent structure in this case is simply that the minimal change is made in the P-marker of the underlying string, consistent with the requirement that the resulting P-marker again be representable in tree form. The transformation that gives "turn some of the lights out" is based on an elementary transformation that permutes the second and third terms of a three-termed proper analysis; it has the structure index (V, Prt, NP). Figure 3(a–b) illustrates a characteristic effect of permutations, namely, that they tend to reduce the amount of structure associated with the terminal string to which they apply. Thus, while Fig. 3(a) represents the kind of purely binary structure regarded as paradigmatic in most linguistic theories, in Fig. 3(b) there is one less binary split and one new ternary division; and Prt is no longer dominated by Verb. Although binary divisions are characteristic of the simple structural descriptions generated by the constituent structure grammar, they are much more rarely found in P-markers associated with actual sentences. A transformational approach to syntactic description thus allows us to express the element of truth contained in the familiar theories of immediate constituent analysis, with their emphasis on binary splitting, without at the same time committing us to the arbitrary assignment of superfluous structure required by such theories. Furthermore, by continued use of attachment and permutation transformations, in the man-

---

[36]In addition, the structural condition associated with the transformation will specify that the first term of the proper analysis must be identical with the fourth. Clearly this is a special case of a much more general conjunction transformation (or family of transformations). I have oversimplified the description in several respects.

Again, we can extend this notion immediately to cover singularly attachment transformations.

ner illustrated above, we can generate classes of P-markers that cannot in principle be generated by constituent structure grammars (in particular, those associated with coordinate constructions) thus permitting us to overcome the intrinsic inadequacy of constituent structure grammars noted at the outset of this section.

Finally, certain singular transformation simply add constant strings at a designated place in the proper analysis, and others simply delete certain terms of the proper analysis. The former are treated just like attachment transformations. In the case of deletion, we delete nodes that dominate no terminal string and leave the P-marker otherwise unchanged. It is possible to restrict the application of deletion transformations in a rather severe way, apparently. In particular, it seems that it may be possible to place a limit both on the number of deletions that can apply in the derivation of a string and the length of the string that is deleted. The restrictions on applicability of deletion transformations play a fundamental role in determining what kinds of language (infinite set of strings) can be generated, in principle, by transformational grammars.

A transformational grammar, then, consists of a finite sequence of context-restricted rewriting rules $\varphi \to \psi$ and a finite number of transformations of the type just described, together with a statement of the restrictions on the order of application of these transformations. The result of a transformation is, in general, available for further transformation, so that an indefinite number of P-markers, of quite varied kinds, can be generated by repeated application of transformations. At each stage, a P-marker representable as a labeled tree is associated with the terminal string so far derived. Thus, we have sketched the outlines of a theory that meets the requirements of Eqs. (1a–c). There is a fairly substantial accumulation of evidence suggesting that it may be possible to meet empirical conditions of the kind mentioned at the end of Section 1 in widely different languages,[37] so that the search for a relatively straightforward technique of evaluation (Eq. (1d)) can be pressed with some hope for success. The question of requirement (Eq. (1c)), however, and, in fact, almost all questions concerning generative capacity of transformational grammars and realistic models for the speaker or hearer who uses such a grammar, remain completely open and, in fact, can scarcely be posed without further clarification of the concepts involved.

---

[37]See the reference cited in 23n.

5 Limitations of Phrase Structure Grammars*

Paul M. Postal

Linguistics is interested both in individual natural languages and in Language. This involves the grammarian in the two distinct but interrelated tasks of constructing grammars for particular languages and constructing a general theory of linguistic structure which will correctly characterize the universal grammatical features of all human languages.

An individual grammar must provide a description of the full set of sentences (well-formed strings, grammatical utterances) of the language under study, that is, it must provide an enumeration of all and only the well-formed strings and must automatically assign to each sentence a structural description showing the elements the sentence contains, their relations to each other, the relations of the sentence to other sentences, and so on. The structural description must provide an account of all the grammatical information about a sentence which is in principle available to the native speaker. Thus, for example, a grammar of English should inform us that (1) "John slept well today" and (2) "did John sleep well today" are sentences but that (3) "slept John well today" is not; that (2) is closely related to (1) in a sense in which it is not closely related to (4) "John ate well today," although (1) and (4) are closely related in another sense; that (5) "I don't like his driving" is structurally ambiguous in a sense in which (6) "I don't like fast driving" is not, since (5) may refer either to the fact of his driving or to the manner of his driving, and so on. A grammar has thus two tasks: it must enumerate each sentence and no nonsentence, and it must associate with each sentence a grammatical analysis which can provide

---

*This work was supported in part by the U.S. Army Signal Corps, the Air Force Office of Scientific Research, and the Office of Naval Research; and in part by the National Science Foundation. I am indebted to Noam Chomsky for extended discussion and criticism of the topics of this paper. Both he and Jerrold Katz read an earlier draft of this paper, and their comments are responsible for many improvements. Errors are my own.

the kind of structural information needed to explain examples of the types just illustrated, as well as many others. A grammar which generates sentences without providing them with structural descriptions is of no real linguistic interest. But, a grammar which cannot *in principle* generate just the correct set of sentences is not even a possible candidate for correctness. Naturally, these requirements are ideals to be met by grammars which claim completeness and adequacy.

Since the number of sentences of any language is infinite, it follows that a grammatical description cannot be a mere list of sentences and their associated structural descriptions, nor an inventory of the elements composing the latter. Rather, a grammar must instead be a finite mechanism capable of generating an infinite set of pairs of sentences and their structural descriptions. In other words, a grammar must be a set of explicit general rules, this set containing at least a proper subclass of rules which are recursive.

The fundamental questions for a general theory of linguistic structure are minimally to characterize precisely the possible kinds of linguistic rules, the possible kinds of structural descriptions, and the mechanical procedures which automatically, uniformly, and nonarbitrarily associate structural descriptions with generated sentences. Insofar as the study of particular languages is to bear on questions of the character of these universal grammatical features, this work must be directed toward determining exactly what sorts of rules can assign the kinds of structural descriptions needed to account for the rich store of structural information about sentences available to speakers of human languages. Such a program can only be successful if the student of individual languages brings to bear an explicit, precise conception of the form of grammatical rules and grammatical structural descriptions, a conception which includes a mechanical way of assigning a full grammatical analysis to each sentence.

A grammar may be conceived of as having two components, a syntax and a phonology. The former is concerned with the generation of infinite sets of strings of morphemes and their associated grammatical analyses. The latter deals with the way the objects enumerated in the syntax are related to their phonetic expressions in sound. We are concerned in the present paper only with syntax.

PHRASE STRUCTURE DESCRIPTION

Despite a wide variety of superficial differences, both of substance and terminology, there is, in the United States[1] and Europe, quite general agreement on the form of syntactic description. This view of sentence structure has been succinctly described:

> . . . the linguist . . . has assumed that the sentences of a language may each be analyzed into a linearly concatenated sequence of immediate constituents and that this bracketing or parsing operation may be performed at various levels of generality to yield a

---

[1] I have attempted to document this claim for American writings in P. M. Postal, *Constituent Structure*, Publication Thirty of the Indiana University Research Center in Anthropology, Folklore, and Linguistics (January 1964).

hierarchical branching diagram, such that any unit at any level is just a certain continuous string within some sentence or else a class of such strings drawn from different but grammatically equivalent sentences.[2]

Translating this conception of the structural descriptions of sentences into a characterization of the kind of general rules that can enumerate such descriptions, yields a picture of syntactic description something like the following: A grammar of a language, according to this prevailing view, consists of a finite, unordered list of ordered pairs of elements, where the left member of the pair is a single object called a *constituent, construction, tagmeme, phrase,* or *grammatical category,* and so on; and the right member of the pair is a finite string (minimally of length one) of constituents. Such pairs are to be interpreted as saying that the element on the left has as immediate constituents the string of elements on the right or that the element on the left may be expanded into the string on the right, and so on.[3] Thus, a typical pair might be (Noun Phrase: Article Noun). That is, a Noun Phrase may consist of an Article plus a Noun, in that order. There is no inherent limitation (other than finiteness) on the number of pairs which may contain the same left element. The full set of pairs containing identical left elements provides the full set of expansions for a single constituent. A full grammar is then a complete set of pairs for every constituent. The *highest* or *longest* constituent is *sentence.* The lowest order constituents are the morphemes which are introduced by pairs like (Noun: John), (Verb: eat), and so forth.

It is possible that, in some versions of the conception of grammar just sketched, some pairs would have associated with them certain (not necessarily continuous) strings of elements which would be the *environment* for an expansion. Such associated strings would restrict the possible expansions to certain contexts. For example, there might be pairs like (Verb: Verb Transitive in Nominal) which says that Verb may be expanded into Verb Transitive, but only when it occurs in a string followed by a Nominal.

Grammars of either of the two sorts just described, that is, either with or without pairs containing associated contexts, can generate an infinite set of sentences because of the possibility of embedding constituents in each other. Thus, there can be pairs of the form: (Prepositional Phrase: Preposition Noun Phrase), (Noun Phrase: Noun Prepositional Phrase). The structural description provided by such grammars is a single labeled hierarchical bracketing or labeled diagram such as:

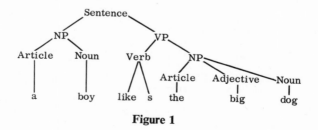

Figure 1

[2]R. B. Lees, review of N. Chomsky *Syntactic Structures* (The Hague: Mouton and Co., 1957) in *Language,* **33** (1957), 375–408.

[3]Other descriptions of the form of grammar involved in immediate constituent analysis are

Representations like Fig. 1 provide an account of constituency relations within the sentence, that is, they inform us, for any string of elements, whether it is a constituent and, if so, of what sort. Furthermore, they describe, for any constituent, what strings of elements are *its* constituents. These relations are, of course, expressed by the fact that some strings of elements are traceable to single nodes. A string of elements traceable to a node labeled *A* is said to *be an A* or to *be a member of* the construction *A* or a *member of the grammatical category A*, and so on. *A* may be said to have these elements as constituents or to *dominate* them.

Grammars embodying the ideas just discussed have been under development within modern linguistics for approximately thirty years. They have been applied to various portions of various languages by a large number of linguists of a wide variety of backgrounds.[4] The underlying theoretical ideas have been discussed in a wide group of publications.[5] Although there are many disagreements, the views just sketched can rightly be said to be the prevailing conception of syntactic description among modern linguists today. This is not to say that certain difficulties with this widespread model of syntax have not been noticed. Indeed, various authors have pointed out problems on several occasions. These have usually revolved around questions of discontinuities, agreement, free constituent order, and the degree of branching. However, because the requirement that a grammar be an explicit, structure-assigning set of rules was not accepted, the theoretical import of these difficulties was not sufficiently understood. They have, therefore, for the most part been met with ad hoc solutions or by-passed in one way or another. Recognition of the significance of difficulties with the phrase-structure model was also hindered by a tendency to restrict linguistic descriptions to rather small subparts of languages, often to that portion arbitrarily marked off by word boundaries and referred to as *morphology*. But, the chief aspect of modern linguistics which tended to obscure the inadequacies of the prevailing grammatical theory was the *methodological emphasis*

---

found in N. Chomsky, "A Transformational Approach to Syntax," in A. A. Hill (ed.), *Proceedings of the Third Texas Conference on Problems of Linguistic Analysis in English, 1958* (Austin, Texas: The University of Texas, 1962), pp. 124–58, reprinted in this volume; Z. S. Harris, *String Analysis of Sentence Structure* (The Hague: Mouton and Co. 1962), pp. 10–15; and Postal, *Constituent Structure, op. cit.*

[4]A few examples include B. Bloch, "Studies in Colloquial Japanese II: Syntax," *Language*, **22** (1946), 200–48; W. L. Chafe "Seneca Morphology: I–VIII," *International Journal of American Linguistics*, Vols. 26, 27 (1960–61); L. Newmark, *Structural Grammar of Albanian*, Publication Four of the Indiana University Research Center in Anthropology, Folklore, and Linguistics, (1961); E. A. Nida, *A Synopsis of English Syntax*, Second edition, Publication Number Four of the Summer Institute of Linguistics of the University of Oklahoma, Norman, Oklahoma (1960); V. B. Pickett, *The Grammatical Hierarchy of Isthmus Zapotec, Language*, Dissertation No. 56, Baltimore (1960); V. Waterhouse, *The Grammatical Structure of Oaxaca Chontal*, Publication Nineteen of the Indiana University Research Center in Anthropology, Folklore, and Linguistics (1962); and I. Y. Yen, *A Grammatical Analysis of Syau Jing*, Publication Sixteen of the Indiana University Research Center in Anthropology, Folklore, and Linguistics (1960).

[5]For example, B. Elson and V. B. Pickett, *Book Beginning Morphology-Syntax*, Summer Institute of Linguistics, Santa Ana, California (1961); Z. S. Harris, "From Morpheme to Utterance," *Language*, **22** (1946), 161–83, and *Methods in Structural Linguistics* (Chicago: The University of Chicago Press 1951); C. F. Hockett, "Two Models of Grammatical Description,"*Word*, **10** (1954), 210–31; S. M. Lamb, *Outline of Stratificational Grammar* (Berkeley, Calif.; University of California, 1961); and R. Wells, "Immediate Constituents," *Language*, **23** (1947), 81–117.

to be discussed later which turned attention away from criteria of adequacy and simplicity for grammatical descriptions and lead instead to a concentration on attempts to specify how the analysis of sentences might be discovered. It was, thus, not until 1956 that any real suggestion was made within the tradition of modern structural linguistics that the fundamental ideas involved in the phrase or immediate, constituent structure approach were inadequate as such.

It is, I think, important to note that this suggestion, first made in published form by N. Chomsky[6] but brought to the general attention of the linguistic public by Chomsky[7] and R. B. Lees,[8] was correlated with the fact that Chomsky was, as remarked by Lees[9], the first to really attempt to formalize and make precise the conceptions underlying immediate constituent analysis as a theory of syntax. That is, Chomsky was the first to ask how the ideas of phrase structure could be formulated so as to meet the condition that all sentences be enumerated and automatically provided with a correct grammatical analysis. Having provided a formalization which seemed to reconstruct the prevailing conception of syntax as described above,[10] Chomsky was for the first time in the position of being able to seriously inquire into the descriptive adequacy of the underlying theory.

It must be noted that, within the tradition of modern structural linguistics which developed the ideas of immediate constituent grammar,[11] little attention has been directed toward the task of precisely characterizing phrase structure as a generative theory. Rather, in line with the highly methodological and procedural orientation of modern linguistics, most effort has been directed toward the goal of formulating procedures of segmentation, classification, and substitution which could be used to discover the grammatical analyses of arbitrary sentences in arbitrary languages. This naturally led to the focusing of much attention on the notion of structural description,[12] but almost none on the finite devices or linguistic rules which the speaker must learn which can *assign* grammatical analyses to infinite sets of sentences. There was before Chomsky's work, thus, little interest in the goal of specifying exactly the character of the notions *linguistic rule*, *grammar*, and so forth. Concentration on the question of how linguistic descriptions or grammars might be discovered by explicit procedures thus had the curious result of inhibiting the attempt to specify exactly what a grammatical description was. There are dozens of articles in modern linguistics attempting to describe abstractly the nature of such elements as *phoneme*, *morpheme*, *word*, *constituent*, and other elements of structural descriptions. But for the most part one looks in vain prior to 1956 for works specifying the abstract charac-

---

[6]N. Chomsky, "Three Models for the Description of Language," *I.R.E. Transactions on Information Theory*, Vol. IT–2 (1956).

[7]N. Chomsky, *Syntactic Structures, op. cit.*

[8]Lees, review of Chomsky's *Syntactic Structures, op. cit.*

[9]*Ibid.*, pp. 385–86.

[10]I have argued (Postal, *Constituent Structure, op. cit.*) that Chomsky's formalization does, in fact, reconstruct the notions considered in such works as those mentioned in 5*n*.

[11]Building, of course, on much older and more traditional ideas involved in notions of parsing, parts of speech, and so on.

[12]With the corollary that this was almost always thought of in classificatory terms, that is, the structural description had to be composed of elements which were classifications of data or classifications of such classifications, and so forth.

ter of linguistic rules. Analogously, on the level of individual descriptions, the literature is full of descriptions of the inventories of elements found in the structural descriptions of sentences of particular languages. But again, prior to 1956, studies showing just what formal rules assign these structural descriptions to sentences are essentially nonexistent.

THE FORMALIZATION OF THE IDEAS OF PHRASE STRUCTURE

It was in the intellectual context just described that Chomsky, in 1956, showed that the ideas involved in phrase structure or immediate constituent description could be formalized in generative terms by considering that a phrase structure grammar consists of a finite set of rules of the form: $XAY \rightarrow XZY$, where the arrow is to be interpreted as the instruction 'is to be rewritten as' and:

Condition (1) X, Z, and Y are strings of symbols (X or Y or both possibly null) but A is a single symbol. (1a)

Condition (2) Z is not null. (1b)

Condition (3) A is not identical with Z. (1c)

Grammars of this type, called *phrase structure grammars*, are based on a finite vocabulary of elements, among which are a designated initial symbol S, standing for *sentence*, and a boundary symbol ♯. Such grammars automatically assign to generated sentences structural descriptions in the form of labeled bracketings like Fig. 1 by means of the notion *derivation*. A derivation is a finite sequence of strings of symbols beginning with ♯ S ♯, each successive line or string being formed by application of one and only one rule to one element in the preceding string. Finally, in running through the rules of some particular grammar a string will be reached which cannot be further changed by any of the rules because none of its elements appear on the left hand side of any rule. Such a string is called a *terminal string*, its symbols *terminal symbols*. Other symbols are *nonterminal*. In linguistic terms the terminal symbols are morphemes, the nonterminal symbols are higher order constituents, with S the highest.

A labeled branching diagram may then be uniformly associated with every set of equivalent derivations, equivalent derivations differing from each other only in the order in which symbols are rewritten. Thus, suppose there are rules of the form:

$R1$ $S \rightarrow A\ B$ (2a)

$R2$ $A \rightarrow C\ D$ (2b)

$R3$ $B \rightarrow E\ F\ G$ (2c)

Then there are two possible derivations of the one possible terminal string, namely:[13]

$S, AB, CDB, CDEFG$ (3a)

$S, AB, AEFG, CDEFG$ (3b)

---

[13]We omit the sentence boundary ♯.

A labeled branching diagram is then mechanically associated with a derivation by writing down the lines with the left-most string at the top and each successively right element successively lower. Then, starting at the top, elements are connected by line to their corresponding identities in the next lowest line or to the strings which have replaced them.[14] Thus, for derivations of Exs. (2a–b) we would have, respectively:

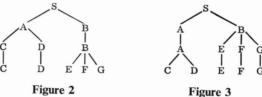

Figure 2   **Figure 3**

All but the highest identical elements in branches of the form are then erased. Both Fig. 2 and Fig. 3 thus reduce to:

Figure 4

It is now clearer in what sense *equivalent* derivations are equivalent, namely, in reducing to the same labeled tree, because corresponding elements have been re-written in identical ways. It is easy to see that, if more than one symbol is expanded by a single rule, or if the string into which the symbol is expanded is either null or identical to the original, or if each line of a derivation is not formed by only one rule application, it will not be possible to assign correct phrase structure descriptions in this way. No other precise method of assigning such structural descriptions to infinite sets of sentences has, however, ever been described. Thus, Conditions (1)–(3) and the limitations on derivations are all linguistically well motivated, the more so because they are pre-conditions for the uniform assignment of correct constituency relations to sentences by the only precise method known.

The conditions described above were the original set proposed by Chomsky and used as the basis of the phrase structure descriptions in his earlier work.[15] It was found, however,[16] that although necessary they are not sufficient. Within the above constraints it is possible to achieve permutations by means of rules like:

---

[14]This description must, of course, be made precise. In particular, the notion *corresponding* must be carefully analyzed. The actual formalization of the algorithm of tree construction from derivations is given in N. Chomsky, *The Logical Structure of Linguistic Theory*, mimeographed, Cambridge, Mass. (1955), Chap. 6.

[15]Chomsky, "Three Models for the Description of Language," *op. cit.* and *Syntactic Structures, op. cit.*

[16]N. Chomsky, "On Certain Formal Properties of Grammars," *Information and Control*, Vol. 2, No. 2 (1959).

$$R4 \ A \ B \ \rightarrow \ B \ B \tag{4a}$$
$$R5 \ B \ B \ \rightarrow \ B \ A \tag{4b}$$

When applied to a string AB these rules would derive the new string BA. But note that the associated tree would be of the form:

Figure 5

But this sort of description obliterates the asymmetry of the relation *is a* or its converse *dominate* which is a prerequisite of meaningful, phrase structure representations. For example, if English "will John come" is derived by the above method from representations underlying "John will come," the labeled bracketing will assert that *John* is a Modal like *will*, and that *will* is a Noun like *John*. Permutations thus result in absurd and unacceptable representations of constituent structure. But there is nothing in the characterization of phrase structure grammars by conditions (1)–(3) which predicts that such descriptions are any different from ordinary, intuitively correct analyses.

At least one further condition must thus be added to the characterization of phrase structure grammars in order to prevent permutations. Such a condition was stated by R. J. Parikh[17] and discussed by Chomsky.[18] A somewhat different condition is given by P. M. Postal.[19] We shall not state either of these or discuss them here since their exact character is irrelevant for our purposes. The important point is that the notion *phrase structure grammar* is subject to such a condition.

Condition (4) Permutations are excluded. (5)

THE ADEQUACY OF PHRASE STRUCTURE

In applying phrase structure grammars (in the precise sense) to natural languages, it soon became apparent that they were radically inadequate in a number of ways. These inadequacies were of two different sorts. First, the structural descriptions provided were not able, in an enormous number of cases, to provide an account of the kinds of structural information available to the native. These were not only cases of the kind (e.g., discontinuities) which had been noted by previous writers but also of many other types concerning ambiguities, relations among sentence types, relations between sentences and parts of sentences (as between nominalizations and full sentences), and so on. Second, when an effort was made to actually provide an

---

[17] R. J. Parikh, "Language Generating Devices," *Quarterly Progress Report No. 60,* (1960). Research Laboratory of Electronics, Massachusetts Institute of Technology.
[18] N. Chomsky, "Formal Properties of Grammars," in Eugene Halanter, R. Duncan Luce, R. R. Bush (eds.), *Handbook of Mathematical Psychology* (to appear).
[19] Postal, "Constituent Structure," *op. cit.*

enumeration of a wide variety of sentence types, the complexity involved in phrase structure description proved truly extraordinary; many simple and easily discovered regularities were excluded, many essentially identical parts of the grammar had to be repeated several times, and so forth. We do not have the space, nor is it necessary for our aim, to discuss or document in detail these inadequacies of phrase structure grammars.[20] Suffice it to say that consideration of these limitations on the part of phrase structure led Chomsky, building on insights of Z. S. Harris[21], to the formulation of a new conception of grammatical theory in which phrase structure rules were supplemented by new, more powerful devices called *transformations*. Within this new theory the notion of structural description is expanded to include for each sentence a whole *set* of labeled diagrams as well as a complex structure representing the transformations applied in a particular derivation. Following Chomsky, a group of linguists have attempted to show that not only are the major flaws of phrase structure overcome by transformational grammars, but that these provide in many ways a host of new insights into the structure of grammar.[22]

It must be admitted that the majority of linguists do not appear to have been convinced of the conclusions that (1) phrase structure grammars are inadequate; or (2) these inadequacies require a reformulation of grammatical theory in transformational terms as suggested by Chomsky. Many linguists appear to feel either that the inadequacies of phrase structure are not particularly damaging, or else, that whatever flaws can be shown can be eliminated by further elaboration and refinement of the underlying immediate constituent notions. They, therefore, reject the radical theoretical departure involved in a revision of linguistic theory to include transformational rules. This rejection naturally goes hand-in-hand with continued approval of the taxonomic approach of past work with its associated disinterest in the notion of grammatical rule.

GENERATIVE INADEQUACY OF CONTEXT-FREE PHRASE STRUCTURE GRAMMARS

In rejecting the theory of phrase structure as a model of human language, Chomsky was careful to point out that there was, at that time, no proof that phrase structure grammars could not enumerate the correct set of terminal strings. That is, there was

---

[20]For discussions of this, see Chomsky, *The Logical Structure of Linguistic Theory, op. cit.,* Chap. 7, *Syntactic Structures, op. cit.,* "A Transformational Approach to Syntax," *op. cit.,* and "On the Notion 'Rule of Grammar,' " *Proceedings of the Twelfth Symposium in Applied Mathematics,* **XII** (1961), 6–24, reprinted in this volume; Lees, review of Chomsky's *Syntactic Structures op. cit.,* "The Constituent Structure of Noun Phrases," *American Speech,* **XXXVI** (1961), 159–68, and "On Reformulating Transformational Grammars," *Vaprosy Jazykosznanija,* Vol. 10, No. 6 (1961); and Postal, "Some Syntactic Rules in Mohawk," Yale University Doctoral Dissertation 1962, "Mohawk Prefix Generation," To appear in *Proceedings of the IXth International Congress of Linguists,* Cambridge, Massachusetts, and *Constituent Structure, op. cit.*

[21]Z. S. Harris, "Co-occurrence and Transformation in Linguistic Structure," *Language,* Vol. 33, No. 3 (1957).

[22]For a bibliography of work on transformational grammar, see Chomsky, "On the Notion 'Rule of Grammar,' " *op. cit.* For descriptions of theory of transformational grammar, see papers by Chomsky in this volume.

no parallel to the demonstration[23] that the so-called "finite state," or "Markov process grammar," simply could not in principle enumerate the full set of English sentences. As Chomsky[24] put it:

> We have discussed two models for the structure of language—a communication theoretic model based on a conception of language as a Markov process and corresponding, in a sense, to the minimal linguistic theory; and a phrase structure model based on immediate constituent analysis. We have seen that the first is surely inadequate for the purposes of grammar and that the second is more powerful than the first and does not fail in the same way. Of course, there are languages (in our general sense) that cannot be described in terms of phrase structure . . ., but I do not know whether or not English is itself literally outside the range of such analysis.

That is, until recently the counter-evidence to the theory of phrase structure has been limited to demonstrations (completely sufficient for rejection) of inadequacy with respect to simplicity and assignment of structural descriptions. The major purpose of the present paper is to contribute to the demonstration that phrase structure grammars are an incorrect theory of human languages by showing that the counter-evidence to this theory can be extended to the domain of terminal string enumeration. In view of the fact that transformational grammar is the only theory known which circumvents the limitations of phrase structure, such evidence can be taken as indirect support for the claim that natural languages require transformational grammars.

In rules of the form $XAY \rightarrow XZY$, $X..Y$ represents the context for the expansion. Suppose, however, that it is insisted that in all cases rules contain no contexts. That is, suppose we add:

$$\text{Condition (5) If } XAY \rightarrow XZY, \text{ then } X \text{ and } Y \text{ are null.} \qquad (6)$$

Condition (5) requires that if a symbol A is expanded into a string Z then it is expanded into Z in every sequence in which it occurs. There is good reason to believe that much of contemporary syntactic theory actually reduces to this very weak version of phrase structure.[25] However, it is not in fact possible to enumerate natural languages with context-free phrase structure grammars. This claim can be proved by showing that Mohawk, one of the remaining Northern Iroquoian languages, is not a context-free phrase structure language, that is, by demonstrating that it is impossible to construct a finite set of context-free phrase structure rules which will enumerate all and only Mohawk sentences.

It has been proven by Chomsky[26] that the language consisting of all and only the strings $[XX]$ is not a context-free language, where X varies over an infinite set of strings in an alphabet of two or more symbols.[27] All of the sentences of such a language have a dependency structure like that shown in Fig. 6 in which, for all n, x_{n+i} must equal x_i for all i.

---

[23]Chomsky, "Three Models for the Description of Language," *op. cit.*

[24]Chomsky, *Syntactic Structures, op. cit.*, p. 34.

[25]This is argued in Postal, *Constituent Structure, op. cit.*

[26]Chomsky, "On Certain Formal Properties of Grammars," *op. cit.*

[27]Actually, the proof was given only for a special case but immediately carries over to the general type, however.

It can be demonstrated that Mohawk lies outside the bounds of context-free description by showing that it contains, as a subpart, an infinite set of sentences with the formal properties of the language [*XX*].

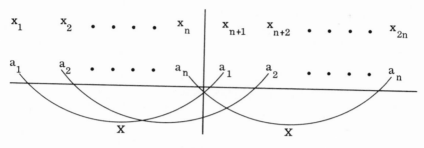

Figure 6

A simple Mohawk sentence may consist of a subject noun, a verb, and an object noun preceded by the particle *ne-* in that order.[28] A noun consists of a noun prefix, a noun stem, and a noun suffix which is often phonologically null. A verb consists minimally of a pronominal prefix, a base, and a suffix. Hence, there are sentences like:

> ka|ksa?a ka|nuhwe?|s ne- ka|nuhs|a?   the girl likes the house
> 1| 2 | 3 | 4 |5 | 6 | 7 |8

1. noun prefix
2. noun stem *child*
3. pronominal prefix
4. base—verb stem *to like*

5. suffix—serial aspect   (7)
6. noun prefix
7. noun stem *house*
8. noun suffix

It should be noted that the Base constituent of the verb in Ex. (7) is simply a single verb stem. However, the Base constituent may also consist of an incorporation-marker plus a verb stem. That is, one of the rules of Mohawk grammar is:

$$R6 \text{ Base} \rightarrow \text{(inc) Verb Stem} \tag{8}$$

And, there is an interesting process which incorporates the noun stem of the object of a sentence like Ex. (7) into the verb by substituting the noun stem for the incorporation-marker. In these cases the Base constituent then has the structure Noun Stem Verb Stem. Thus, there are sentences like:

$$\text{kaksa?a kanuhsnuhwe?s} \quad \text{the girl likes the house} \tag{9}$$

The crucial fact about incorporation from the present point of view is that, under certain conditions,[29] incorporation occurs in such a way that the external noun of the object is also present. One therefore finds sentences like:

$$\text{kaksa?a kanuhsnuhwe?s kik} \land \text{ kanuhsa?} \quad \text{the girl likes this house} \tag{10}$$

---

[28]For a more complete description of the relevant aspects of Mohawk sentence structure, see Postal, *Some Syntactic Rules in Mohawk, op. cit.*

[29]The condition is that a Modifier constituent precede the noun whose stem is to be doubled.

In such sentences there is a strict dependency of exactly the type shown in Fig. 6 between the incorporated noun stem and the noun stem of the external object noun. Thus, although there are such sentences as:

kaksa ?a kanuhwe ?s ne- ka ?sreht	the girl likes the car	(11)
kaksa ?a ka ?srehtnuhwe ?s	ditto	(12)
kaksa ?a ka ?srehtnuhwe ?s kik ∧ ka ?sreht	the girl likes this car	(13)

there are no sentences like:

*kaksa ?a kanuhsnuhwe ?s kik ∧ ka ?sreht	(14)
*kaksa ?a ka ?srehtnuhwe ?s kik ∧ kanuhsa ?	(15)

and so on.

There is then a subset of sentences in Mohawk which contain constituents whose dependency structure is representable by Fig. 6. Sentences can contain both incorporated noun stems and external noun objects only if the noun stem of the object is the same as the incorporated noun stem.[30] Hence, in order to show that Mohawk is not a context-free language, it is only necessary to show that the number of noun stems which can occur in such sentences is unlimited. This is in fact the case.

Almost any Base constituent can be nominalized by the addition of a nominalizing morpheme, [hsra/tsra], to derive an abstract neuter noun stem. Thus, from the verb base *nuhwe?* in Ex. 7, one can derive the noun stem *nuhwe?tsra* which occurs in the noun *kanuhwe?tsra?, the liking*. This nominalization can occur as well with Base constituents that contain incorporated noun stems. Hence, from the verb *ka?sreht-nuhwe?s* in Ex. 13 one can derive the noun stem *?srehtnuhwe?tsra* which occurs in the noun *ka?srehtnuhwe?tsra?, the liking of the car*. Now complex noun stems produced by this nominalization are themselves capable of being incorporated in verbs, hence capable of renominalization, of re-incorporation, and so on. Thus, the process of abstract noun stem formation is recursive, and there is no bound on the length of noun stems, and therefore no limit to the number of nouns.

This process of noun stem formation can be illustrated by showing the derivation of a rather long noun stem. The subject noun is omitted.

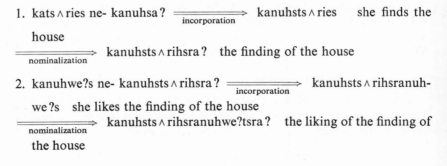

1. kats ∧ ries ne- kanuhsa ? $\xrightarrow[\text{incorporation}]{}$ kanuhsts ∧ ries   she finds the house

   $\xrightarrow[\text{nominalization}]{}$ kanuhsts ∧ rihsra ?   the finding of the house

2. kanuhwe?s ne- kanuhsts ∧ rihsra ? $\xrightarrow[\text{incorporation}]{}$ kanuhsts ∧ rihsranuh-we ?s   she likes the finding of the house

   $\xrightarrow[\text{nominalization}]{}$ kanuhsts ∧ rihsranuhwe?tsra ?   the liking of the finding of the house

---

[30]There are certain other cases where a verb contains an incorporated noun stem which does not match the following external noun stem. These are due to minor rules and do not effect the present discussion.

3. wao?taks ∧ ? ne- kanuhsts ∧ rihsranuhwe?tsra ? $\xrightarrow[\text{incorporation}]{}$ waonuhsts

∧ rihsranuhwe?tsraaks ∧ ?   the liking of the finding of the house is evil $\xrightarrow[\text{nominalization}]{}$ kanuhsts ∧ rihsranuhwe?tsraaks ∧ hsra ?   the evil of the liking of the finding of the house

4. kaharatats ne- kanuhsts ∧ rihsranuhwe?tsraaks ∧ hsra ? $\xrightarrow[\text{incorporation}]{}$

kanuhsts ∧ rihsranuhwe?tsraaks ∧ hsrakaratats   she praises the evil of the liking of the finding of the house $\xrightarrow[\text{nominalization}]{}$ kanuhsts ∧

rihsranuhwe?tsraaks ∧ hsrakaratattsra ?   the praising of the evil of the liking of the finding of the house

This last noun can occur perfectly well in a sentence with a verb containing an incorporated noun stem identical to its own:

> tkanuhsts ∧ rihsranuhwe?tsraaks ∧ hsrakaratattsrayeri ? kik ∧
> kanuhsts ∧ rihsranuhwe?tsraaks ∧ hsrakaratattsra?

We therefore see that the subset of sentences in Mohawk which requires an identity of constituents is, in fact, infinite and that the set of constituents which must be identical, namely, noun stems, is infinite. Further, the vocabulary is obviously greater than two. But since these are the crucial formal properties of the language [XX], it follows that:

Theorem: Mohawk cannot be enumerated by a context-free phrase structure grammar.

The result just reached has increased to a significant degree the minimal strength which is provably necessary for any general theory of linguistic structure. That is, by considering only the weakest of all possible requirements on grammars, that they enumerate the correct set of terminal strings, we have shown phrase structure systems which make no use of contexts to be too weak. This is thus an extension of the kind of result achieved by Chomsky[31] when he showed that the finite state conception of grammatical theory proposed by C. F. Hockett[32] and others was inadequate. The Markov process theory is equivalent to allowing rules of only the forms $A \to B\ c$, $A \to c$ (where A and B are single nonterminal symbols, and c is a single terminal symbol). The result reached here shows that it is not enough to extend grammatical theory to allow rules of the form $A \to B\ C$ (C a single nonterminal).[33]

It is extremely important to note that there is no known way of enumerating the construction which shows Mohawk beyond context-free description *even by using*

---

[31]Chomsky, "Three Models for the Description of Language," *op. cit.*

[32]C. F. Hockett, "A Manual of Phonology," *International Journal of American Linguistics*, Memoir 11, (Baltimore, 1955).

[33]Phrase structure grammars all of whose rules are of the form $A \to B\ C$, or $A \to a(B$ and C distinct nonterminals, a terminal) are called *normal* by Chomsky ("Formal Properties of Grammars," *op. cit.*, p. 78). In Chomsky's "On Certain Formal Properties of Grammars," where these were called *regular*, it is proved that any language which has a context-free grammar has a normal grammar. Thus, the restriction of trees to nodes with a maximum of two branches does not affect the set of terminal strings which can be generated. The generalization of this result to context-restricted grammars is probably true, but not yet proven.

context-restricted phrase structure rules. In fact, it is, I think, almost certainly true that such rules cannot enumerate the sentences of natural languages.[34] This is, however, not yet proven. Note that the lack of such a proof in no way supports the validity of such systems. There are sets of sentences in natural languages which, so far as we know at present, simply cannot be described in such terms regardless of the structural descriptions which are permitted.

It should perhaps be mentioned that Chomsky[35] was able to generate languages with the structure $[XX]$ by using context-restricted rules which make essential use of the power to permute and thus violate Condition (4). Even by using this device, which would reduce the phrase structure description of Mohawk sentences to absurdity, at least $6n^2$ rules are required to enumerate the construction, where n is the vocabulary involved in the equivalence. Furthermore, a minimum of six symbols must be mentioned in each rule. Since the relevant vocabulary in Mohawk is probably about a thousand, it follows that even this wholly unacceptable grammar requires on the order of six million rules mentioning thirty-six million grammatical symbols.

Although there is provably no context-free description of Mohawk noun stem doubling and no known context-restricted description of this construction, and although description involving permutations requires thirty-six million symbols while producing radically incorrect structural descriptions, infinite noun stem doubling can be described simply with two transformations which provide correct structural descriptions. First, the doubling of noun stems is accounted for by the transformation:[36]

$$X, \text{ inc, Verb Stem, (Suffix), (Modifier), Pre, Noun Stem, } Y$$
$$1 \quad 2 \qquad 3 \qquad\quad 4 \qquad\quad 5 \quad\; 6 \qquad 7 \qquad\; 8 \qquad (16)$$
$$1 \ldots 8 \Rightarrow 1, 7, 3, 4, 5, 6, 7, 8$$

This transformation substitutes a double of the Noun Stem constituent for the incorporation marker in the verb. The derivation of abstract noun stems from verb bases is described by the generalized transformation:

$$X, \text{ Noun Stem}_{\text{abstract}}, \; Y$$
$$1 \qquad\quad 2 \qquad\quad 3$$
$$U, \text{ Base, } W$$
$$4 \quad\; 5 \quad\;\; 6 \qquad\qquad\qquad (17)$$
$$1 \ldots 6 \Rightarrow 1, 5 + \text{hsra/tsra, } 3$$

---

[34]There is good reason to consider that this *inability* is a *sine qua non* for a system which correctly reconstructs or explicates the ideas of immediate constituent structure. It has long been recognized that discontinuities are exceptions to this conception of language. But the Mohawk noun-stem doubling construction is an instance of an *infinite* set of overlapping dependencies of exactly the type illustrated by discontinuities. Thus, if a system of rules can handle such dependencies, this is reason to believe that it fails to reconstruct the ideas involved in constituent structure, that is, the system is too rich. I do not think context-restricted rules are too rich in this sense. I think they cannot handle such dependencies and that they correctly reconstruct the richest possible conception of immediate constituent structure. The fact that natural languages contain instances of infinite, overlapping dependencies, should thus be taken as showing that the ideas involved in this type of analysis are too limited.

[35]Chomsky, "On Certain Formal Properties of Grammars," *op. cit.*

[36]This description of the incorporation transformation is a much simpler and more adequate version of that given in Postal, "Some Syntactic Rules in Mohawk." The analysis given there can be improved in a number of ways and will be in the published version.

The recursive properties of the construction are produced by allowing these two rules to be unordered and to apply repeatedly. Let me emphasize again that the transformational description is the only one known which is not extraordinarily complex and which provides anything like a reasonable structural description of the sentences involved.

It is at least logically possible, though quite unlikely, that other languages besides Mohawk can be enumerated by context-free phrase structure grammars. Note, however, that Y. Bar-Hillel and E. Shamir[37] have pointed out that constructions with *respectively* have the property [XX] and thus show English beyond context-free description if they are assumed grammatical. It must be admitted, however, that these constructions are somewhat peripheral.

It has recently been pointed out by Chomsky[38] that languages of the form [XY] are beyond context-free description, where X and Y vary over infinite sets of strings and where they are necessarily *not identical*. But English appears to possess a subpart with exactly this property, namely, comparatives. Thus, one may say:

> John is more successful as an artist than Bill is as a sculptor (18)
> John is more successful as an artist than Bill is (19)

but not:

> *John is more successful as an artist than Bill is as an artist (20)

Thus, the set of sentences with infinite, overlapping dependencies discovered in Mohawk is not an isolated curiosity but a special case of more common features of language.[39] We should thus expect to find similar constructions in all languages.

Regardless of how the case turns out for other languages, the demonstration for Mohawk is already sufficient to show that, even in terms of only the weakest formal requirements, general linguistic theory must allow richer devices than context-free phrase structure grammars. Furthermore, it appears that any adequate formalization of context-restricted grammars will not overcome the proven limitations of the theory of context-free grammars.

We are in a position to draw a methodological moral. Only by having available the formalization of the ideas of phrase structure was it possible to study these ideas precisely. Thus, the *application* of formal results reported above was directly dependent on this formalization. Similarly, as noted earlier, it was also the formulation of immediate constituent analysis in terms of a generative set of structure assigning rules which made especially perspicacious the flaws of phrase structure with respect to structural descriptions and simplicity. The present situation is then another of a long line of possible demonstrations within science of the principle that the possibility of confirming or disconfirming a theory is directly related to the precision with which it is formulated. Put differently, the requirements of preciseness and explicitness (formalization) for theories follow automatically from the desire to determine truth.

---

[37]Y. Bar-Hillel, and E. Shamir, "Finite-State Languages: Formal Representations and Adequacy Problems," *The Bulletin of the Research Council of Israel*, Vol. 8f, No. 3 (1960).

[38]Personal communication.

[39]Note that this feature is also found in English in constructions with *so*: "John read the book and so did Bill," "John read the book and so did Bill read the book," but hardly "*John read the book and so did Bill swim the channel."

III

GRAMMAR

To understand current work in grammar, it is essential to distinguish between what a grammar is *per se* and what it becomes when it is utilized for some special purpose. This distinction is, unfortunately, not always noticed and this has caused much misunderstanding about the aims and methods of grammar construction.

A grammar of a language can be used in teaching the language, in translating it, in establishing norms of usage, in constructing systems of information retrieval, and in numerous other ways as well. Nevertheless, a grammar is only incidentally a teaching aid, part of a translation scheme, a codification of proper usage, and the like. It becomes one of these when we apply it to some special task. But, just as grammars, like theories in the other empirical sciences, have a variety of practical applications, so they also share with other scientific theories a primary concern to describe and explain the world of our experience.

The grammar of a language is a theory of the sentences of that language. The construction of a grammar is undertaken with the aim of describing what well-formedness is in the language under study: what distinguishes the sentences of the language from sound sequences that fluent speakers do not accept as sentences. We expect that the description will reveal the principles of sentence construction characteristic of the language and will show how its sentences relate to one another. The basic job of a grammar is thus to provide a description of the structure of each sentence of the language. Such a description is adequate only when the structure assigned to a sentence reveals each grammatical feature speakers employ to understand the sentence.

As a description of the sentential structures of a language, a grammar is thus a scientific theory. Further support for this conception of what a grammar is comes from a survey of the characteristics grammars have in common with theories in sciences other than linguistics. First, a grammar is a system of statements employing theoretical concepts to formulate regularities in the phenomena under study; for example, the familiar notions *noun phrase, transitive verb, indirect object*, and so on, are employed to formulate generalizations about English sentences in precisely the same way as such notions as *pressure, charge, magnetic*, are employed to formulate physical laws.

Second, the rules of a grammar, thus being law-like statements, operate under the same sorts of empirical constraints as do law-like statements in other sciences.

Grammars that falsely characterize a feature of a language, e.g., grammars that imply consequences that are contravened by evidence obtained from fluent speakers, must be suitably revised. Thus, if a putative grammar of English implied that the definite article never appears immediately preceding a proper noun, that grammar would have to be revised to account for the fact that such strings as "The New York of the twenties was exciting," "The Paris that we once loved is no more," "The John of the Cross is in the Louvre," and so forth are indubitably sentences. This is to say that grammars, like other scientific theories, are open to empirical verification.

Third, the acceptance of putative grammatical rules is contingent upon their satisfying the usual methodological constraints found in science. Just as in physics, where the acceptance of a law is guided by considerations of simplicity, generality, fruitfulness, precision, and so on, so in grammar we prefer the simple rule to the complex one—the rule that reveals deep structure to the one that reveals only low-level structure or accidental regularities, and so on.

Fourth, the rules of a grammar make predictions. Only a very small, finite, proper subset of the infinite set of well-formed sentences of a language have been encountered by speakers. But, since a grammar gives a characterization of well-formedness that must be satisfied by *all* sentences of the language and by nothing that is not a sentence, it follows that in each of infinitely many cases of strings that speakers have not encountered the grammar predicts either that the string is grammatical or that it is not. Such predictions are in principle always testable against the intuitive judgments speakers make about grammaticality.

Finally, a grammar provides explanations of phenomena. The structural descriptions a grammar provides explain why such sentences as "He likes little boys and girls" are perceived as ambiguous, i.e. why such a sentence is read either with *little* as a modifer of both *boys* and *girls* or with *little* as a modifer of *boys* alone. Similarly, a grammar must explain why the string, "Who is John's partner" is understood to have a different syntactic structure in "I do not know who is John's partner" than it has in "They arrested the man who is John's partner."

6 Co-occurrence and Transformation in Linguistic Structure[*]

Zellig S. Harris

This paper defines a formal relation among sentences, by virtue of which one sentence structure may be called a transform of another sentence structure (e.g., the *active* and the *passive*, or in a different way *question* and *answer*). The relation is based on comparing the individual co-occurrences of morphemes. By investigating the individual co-occurrences (Sections 2 and 5 to 17), we can characterize the distribution of certain classes which may not be definable in ordinary linguistic terms (e.g., pronouns, Section 11). More important, we can then proceed to define transformation (Section 3), based on two structures having the same set of individual co-occurrences. This relation yields unique analyses of certain structures and distinctions which could not be analyzed in ordinary linguistic terms (Sections 15 to 24). It replaces a large part of the complexities of constituent analysis and sentence structure, at the cost of adding a level to grammatical analysis. It also has various analytic and practical applications (Section 37) and can enter into a more algebraic analysis of language structure (Sections 32, 34 and 36) than is natural for the usual classificatory linguistics. A list of English transformations is given in Sections 25 to 30. The main argument can be followed in Sections 1.1 (Co-occurrence defined), 2 (Constructional status), 3 (Transformation defined), 14 (Summary of constructions), 24 (Summary of sentence sequences), and 31 to 37 (The place of transformations in linguistic structure).[1]

---

[*]Z. S. Harris, "Co-occurrence and Transformation in Linguistic Structure," *Language*, **33**, No. 3 (July-September 1957), 283–340. Reprinted by permission of the Linguistic Society of America.
[1]The study of transformations arose out of the attempt to construct a method for analyzing language samples longer than a sentence; a preliminary list of English transformations is given in Z. Harris, "Discourse analysis," *Language*, **28** (1952), 18–23. Although the present paper was presented at the 1955 meeting of the Linguistic Society of America in Chicago, some of the details on English transformations have been added since that time, in connection with a project of the National Science Foundation.

THE METHOD OF ANALYSIS

1 Individual co-occurrence. The range of individual co-occurrence of a morpheme (or word) *i* is defined first of all as the environment of morphemes (or words) which occur in the same sentence with *i* (in some body of linguistic material). This is indeed the initial information available for morphological structure. Given utterances or sentences and given the morphemes, we can say that each morpheme *i* has the particular morphemes *j*, *k*, . . . as co-occurrents in the sentences in which *i* appears. Each morpheme has a unique set of co-occurrents (except for special morphemes such as some paradigmatic affixes which all occur with the same set of words and in the same sentences).

The individuality of morphemes in this respect makes it difficult to set up any compact description of a language. However, some morphemes have very similar (though not identical) sets of co-occurrents: thus, the set of co-occurrents for *cloth*—e.g., *The ( ) tore, The ( ) was torn, Get me a ( ) quick*—may have many morphemes in common with the set for *paper*, certainly many more than with the set for *diminish*. This suggests that morphemes can be grouped into classes in such a way that members of a class have rather similar sets of co-occurrents, and each class in turn occurs with specific other classes to make a sentence structure. In structural linguistics this classification is not set up on the basis of relative similarity of co-occurrents, but rather on the basis of a particular choice of diagnostic co-occurrents: *cloth* and *paper* both occur, say, in the environment *the ( ) is* (i.e. after *the* and before *is*), where *diminish* does not appear; we call this class *N*. And *diminish* and *grow* both occur, say, in *It will ( )*, where *paper* and *cloth* do not; we call this class *V*. The diagnostic environments (stretches of co-occurrents) are chosen in such a way that the resulting classes permit compact statements about oc-occurrence. For example, *cloth, paper, diminish, grow* all show some differences in their environments, so that no simple summary can be made. But in terms of the classes *N* and *V* we can say that every *N* occurs before some *V* in the environment *the ( ) V*, and every *V* occurs in the environment *the N ( )* for some *N*.

When we proceed to describe the structure of sentences (i.e. the choices of morphemes that occur in a sentence) in terms of these classes, we find that the work is of manageable proportions. In the sentences of any given language, only certain sequences of classes (set up as above for that language) will be found; and these sequences which constitute the sentences can be described as the products of a small number of elementary class sequences (constructions) which are combined in certain statable ways; for instance, the class sequence *TNPNV* (*The fear of war grew*) results from the elementary class sequences *TNV* and *NPN* by the substitution operation

From a time when this work was still at an early stage, Noam Chomsky has been carrying out partly related studies of transformations and their position in linguistic analysis; see his doctoral dissertation, "Transformational Analysis" (University of Pennsylvania, 1955), "Three Models for the Description of Language," *I.R.E. Transactions on Information Theory*, **IT-2**, No. 3 (1956), 113–24; and *Syntactic Structures* (The Hague, 1957), reviewed by R. B. Lees, *Language*, **33** (1957), 375–408. My many conversations with Chomsky have sharpened the work presented here, in addition to being a great pleasure in themselves.

$NPN = N$.[2] This compact description of sentence structure in terms of sequences of classes is obtained, however, at a cost: statements such as $NPN = N$ or "TNV is a sentence structure" do not mean that all members of NPN have been found in the same environments as all members of N or that all sequences of members of T, N, and V, in that order, have been found as sentences.

On the other hand, to describe a language in terms of the co-occurrences of the individual morphemes is virtually impossible: almost each morpheme has a unique set of co-occurrents; the set varies with individual speakers and with time (whereas the class combinations are relatively permanent); it is, in general, impossible to obtain a complete list of co-occurrents for any morpheme; and in many cases a speaker is uncertain whether or not he would include some given morpheme as a co-occurrent of some other one. Individual co-occurrence is thus not just the limiting case of morpheme classes, where the number of members per class is one. Classes are essentially different because they are defined by a diagnostic environment, chosen to yield a class-sequence structure.[3]

1.1 It follows that individual co-occurrence cannot be used, as indeed it has not been used, as the basic element of morphological construction. Even for discussions of individual co-occurrence itself, it is convenient to use the framework of classes and constructions. This leads now to an adjusted definition: for classes K, L in a construction c, the K-co-occurrence of a particular member L_i of L is the set of members of K which occur with L_i in c; for example, in the AN construction found in English grammar, the A-co-occurrence of *hopes* (as N) includes *slight* (*slight hopes of peace*) but probably not *green*. The K-co-occurrence of L_i is not necessarily the same in two different KL constructions: the N-co-occurrents of *man* (as N_i) in N_i *is a N*

---

[2]Notation: Morpheme and word classes: N (noun) and V (verb) as above; A (adjective) includes *large, old, extreme*, etc.; T (article) includes *the, a*; P (preposition) includes *of, from, to*, etc.; C (conjunction) includes *and, or, but*; D (adverb) includes *very, well, quickly*, etc. Classes of affixes (mostly suffixes, some prefixes): *na* indicates an affix such that $N + na$ (i.e. the sequence N *na*) yields an A word (a word substitutable for A morphemes): *papery, cloth-like*. Similarly *vn* after V yields an N word: *growth*; *nn* after N yields an N word: *growths, childhood*; and so on. And v (tense and verb "auxiliary" class, Section 10) includes *-ed will, can*, etc. S stands for sentence. The equivalence $A = B$ indicates that if sequence A occurs in a sentence, the substitution of B for A also yields a sentence. All these classes apply specifically to English; the analyses and transformations below have been set up for English data, although the principles are general and not limited to any particular langauge.

[3]It might be argued that individual co-occurrence is essentially different from morphological classification simply because it is a direct reflection of the speaker's combinations of meanings and is therefore not subject at all to investigation for distributional regularities. No doubt the speakers' meanings, or the knowledge and perceptions of the body of speakers, is a major factor in building up the co-occurrence set of each morpheme. But linguistic productivity, and other factors which are determined at least partly by structural and historical factors, also affect co-occurrence: different noun-making suffixes occur in *avoidance* and *evasion* for no semantic reason; *killing* occurs in *a ( ) sense of humor* but perhaps not in *a ( ) laugh*. Furthermore, it frequently happens that morphemes in one of their co-occurrences have idiomatic meanings which cannot reasonably be drawn from the meanings of the component morphemes in any other occurrences, so that one can hardly claim that the occurrence in question was based on the meaning of the morphemes. Nor can one easily predict what combinations will appear: *I saw them off* but not *I noticed them off*; *There's trouble ahead* and *There's trouble afoot*; *dressed chicken* but not *undressed chicken*. A seed catalog describes a marigold as *exceedingly double*, though one might not have expected a quantifier before a number word. The observed co-occurrences thus have to be taken as raw data for classification and comparison; they cannot be adequately derived from some nonlinguistic source such as "the desired combinations of meanings."

may include *organism, beast, development, searcher,* while the *N*-co-occurrents of *man* in $N_i's$ *N* may include *hopes, development, imagination,* and so on.

2 Constructional status. Although, as we have seen, individual co-occurrence cannot be used directly in discovering morphological relations, we do not have to disregard it (as we do in structural linguistics). In spite of the impossibility of obtaining complete or definite co-occurrence data, we can still consider various indirect questions (absolute or relative), such as whether a particular morpheme or class has some special property in its co-occurrence set or how the co-occurrence sets of two classes or class sequences compare. Such questions can fit into the class structure because each co-occurrence check would be within stated classes and constructions (by the adjusted definition); and the results can be then phrased as new statements, again about classes and constructions, as will be seen later. From the point of view of structural linguistics, this amounts to asking one of the few types of outside questions that are still relevant to it, for these are questions which are couched in terms of the raw data of structural morphology (the occurrence of morphemes in sentences) and which lead to additional information about interclass relations, yet which had not been asked in the original study of class environments.

Individual co-occurrences can be expressed in structural terms by saying that they are the values for which a structural formula is satisfied. That is, if we regard each statement about constructions ($NPN = N$ or $TNV = S$) as a formula which holds when particular morphemes (or sequences of them) occur in the positions indicated by their class marks, then we can say that the particular combinations of morphemes which co-occur in various instances of a construction are those which satisfy it (i.e. those for which the formula holds).[4]

We consider now the major applications of individual co-occurrence data within constructional morphology.

Given a construction (which is recognized by its place within larger constructions, up to a sentence), we can see some relations or different statuses among the participating classes by noting details of class occurrence for each class. For example, given by *AN* construction (*slight hopes*), we note that it is substitutable for *N* alone but not for *A* alone: both *slight hopes* and *hopes* occur in *their* ( ) *faded*. We can express the constructional equivalence $AN = N$ by defining in the place of these two a composite construction $(A)N$, with the parentheses indicating occasional omission; and in this new construction we can say that *N* is the *head*, meaning that it always is present when the construction occurs. Another kind of differential status for the classes in a construction is seen when one class has a correlation between its subclasses and some other element in or out of the construction (grammatical agreement); e.g., when nouns have each a particular gender suffix while the neighboring

---

[4]It can be readily seen that the statement "there is a statable set of *B*-co-occurrents for each A_i in the construction *A B'*" is equivalent to "the construction *A B* is satisfied (i.e., instances of it actually occur) for a statable set of A_i B_j pairs." For our present purposes, it will be sufficient to describe a construction thus: a construction is a sentence, or a class sequence, such that some construction is defined as a combination of that class sequence plus other class sequences. Thus, *T A N V* is a sentence construction; *T A N* (a member of the set of *N*-phrase constructions)' and *V* (a member of the set of *V*-phrase constructions) are each constructions, since *N*-phrase plus *V*-phrase defines a sentence. For all except certain transformational sentences we can replace the words above by these: a construction is a sentence or an immediate constituent of a construction.

adjective takes whichever gender suffix the noun has. (Again we might say that the noun is the *head*.)

To these considerations, the data about individual co-occurrence add a new factor. We note that in *TANV* (*The slight hopes faded*) each N_i has a specific set of *V*-co-occurrents which is hardly affected by the preceding *A*, while *A* does not (the *V*-co-occurrents of each A_i depend on the following *N*). Thus, *N* is that class in the *AN* construction which has fixed co-occurrence sets outside. Considerations of this type are available also in cases where the previously mentioned differentia of status are absent: in the construction *N v V* (noun plus tense, or auxiliary plus verb: *It faded, It grows, We may swim*) both *V* and *v* are always present, but each V_i has fixed *N*-co-occurrents (*hopes may grow*, but probably not *hopes may swim*), while each v_i occurs with any *N* that is in the co-occurrence set of its *V*, and with no other.

All these considerations together (the position, co-occurrence ranges, and other properties of classes or subconstructions within a construction) determine what we may call the constructional status or relation of each participating class or construction in a (larger) construction. We find various types of status in respect to individual co-occurrence: in *Vv* neither class has restricted co-occurrences (each v_i occurs with all *V*, and each V_i with all *v*), but in *VP* (*chalk up, tie up, tide over*) both have. In *AN* each class has fixed co-occurrences in the other, but only *N* has fixed co-occurrences in the neighboring *V*. The types of constructional status are useful in characterizing each construction and in analyzing various less obvious constructions (Sections 5 to 14).[5] Many of them serve to explicate intuitively known grammatical relations: in the *AN* type, one says that *A* modifies *N*. Finally, the types of constructional status themselves are partly determined by investigable conditions, such as the size of the participating classes.

Aside from the matter of constructional status there are certain subclasses of the major classes which are characterized only by peculiarities of their individual co-occurrence (Section 11).

3 Transformations defined. In addition to investigating the types of co-occurrence for various classes in a construction, as in Section 2, we can compare the co-occurrences in two different constructions which contain the same classes. In many such constructions, as in *N's N* and *N is a N* above, the co-occurrences are different. In some constructions the co-occurrences are about the same, and it is for these that transformations will be defined.

If two or more constructions (or sequences of constructions) which contain the same *n* classes (whatever else they may contain) occur with the same *n*-tuples of members of these classes in the same sentence environment, we say that the constructions are transforms of each other and that each may be derived from any other

---

[5] An example of indirect use of these considerations. Since the classes *A* and *N* in English contain in general different morphemes and words, the *A*-co-occurrence of N_i in AN_i and the *N*-co-occurrence of N_i in N_i *of N* will be different sets. But many *A* words contain *N* morphemes (having been formed by *N + na*: *wooden, glassy*); and for these *N na* N_i constructions (a subset of AN_i) we find that the *N*-co-occurrents are partially similar to the *N*-co-occurrents of N_i in N_i *of N* (*wooden table, table of wood, glassy surface, surface of glass*, but only *glassy stare*). This suggests that the status of N_i relative to ( ) *of N* is similar to the status of N_i relative to *N na* ( ), and hence relative to *A* ( ), since *N na* is just a subset of *A*. (Note that the difference of meaning between *glassy surface* and *surface of glass* is not relevant here.)

of them by a particular transformation. For example, the constructions $N\ V\ v\ N$ (a sentence) and $N's\ Ving\ N$ (a noun phrase) are satisfied by the same triples of N, V, and N (*he*, *meet*, *we*; *foreman*, *put up*, *list*; etc.); so that any choice of members which we find in the sentence we also find in the noun phrase and vice versa: *He met us, his meeting us . . .* ; *The foreman put the list up, the foreman's putting the list up . . . .* Where the class members are identical in the two or more constructions, we have a reversible transformation and may write; e.g., $N_1\ v\ V\ N_2 \leftrightarrow N_1's\ Ving\ N_2$ (and the set of triples for the first = the set for the second).[6]

In some cases all the *n*-tuples (the choices of one member each out of the *n* classes) which satisfy one construction (i.e., for which that construction actually occurs) also satisfy the other construction, but not vice versa. For example, every triple of N_1, V, and N_2 in the $N_1\ v\ V\ N_2$ *active* sentence (with some exceptions discussed below) can also be found, in reverse order, in the $N_2\ v\ be\ Ven\ by\ N_1$ *passive* sentence: *The kids broke the window, The window was broken by the kids*; *The detective will watch the staff, The staff will be watched by the detective.* However, some triples satisfy only the second sequence and not the first: *The wreck was seen by the seashore.* Such cases may be called one-directional or nonreversible transformations: $N_1\ v\ V\ N_2 \rightarrow N_2\ v\ be\ Ven\ by\ N_1$ (and the set of triples for the second includes the reversed set for the first). In some cases a transformation appears nonreversible because of some particular circumstance (such as the homonymity in the two *by*-constructions here) or because one construction is much less frequent (so that some word choices are not found in it), or the like. It may then be possible to formulate it as a reversible transformation with restricted conditions.

There are also cases in which many or most but not all of the *n*-tuples that satisfy one construction also satisfy another; such constructions are then not transforms of each other, but may have some kindred relation (Section 30). Finally, at the other extreme, if two constructions of the same classes have no *n*-tuples in common, so that any word choice which satisfies one fails to satisfy the other, we have yet another relation of linguistic interest.

Since transformations are based not on the absolute contents of a set of co-occurring *n*-tuples, but on the similarity between the set for different constructions, we do not even require a yes-or-no decision on whether any given *n*-tuple is in the set. We can accept graded decisions, and we do not even have to assert that any particular *n*-tuple never occurs. For example, the formulation might be that to the extent that any *n*-tuple satisfies $N_1\ v\ V\ N_2$, it also satisfies $N_1's\ Ving\ N_2$: *he*, *meet*, *we* certainly in both forms; *moon*, *eat*, *cheese* doubtfully or for particular environments in both forms; *soup*, *drink*, *abstraction* hardly at all in either form.

There may be differences in some respects between the sets satisfying two constructions, without precluding a transformational relation. For example, all or certain ones of the *n*-tuples may be less frequent or natural in one construction than in another. Differences of this kind need not restrict the transformation, if they can be indicated in an adequate manner.

As to the differences between the same-class constructions—for there must, of

---

[6]Same subscript means same member of the class: the second appearance of N_1 indicates the same morpheme as the first N_1.

course, be differences between them—these may consist of difference in order or in individual morphemes (affixes or words) or in added small or large classes. If it is impossible to specify which members of the added classes occur in each instance of the constructions, the statement of the transformation remains incomplete (Section 30).

One condition (mentioned above) which requires some discussion concerns the sentence environment in which the constructions are being compared. If the rest of the sentence, outside the constructions under consideration, is not taken into account, then, for example, *N Ved* and *N will V* would be transforms of each other; for the same pairs of *N, V* occur before *-ed* as with *will* (*The cliff crumbled, The cliff will crumble*). If, however, it is required that the rest of the sentence be identical, these are not transforms, for *-ed* and *will* differ in some of their more distant co-occurrents: *The cliff crumbled yesterday* but *The cliff will crumble tomorrow*. There are various reasons for excluding such pairs as *-ed* and *will*. One is that this yields transformations that can be usefully distinguished from the direct constructional operations, such as the combination of classes *Vv*, or the combining of *T* and *-s plural* with *N* (Section 36). Another reason is that the meaning difference in pairs like *-ed/will* seems much greater than that which is characteristic for transformations.[7]

The general requirement can be stated as follows: no domain (section of the sentence or the like) to which the two constructions are grammatically connected may admit co-occurring morphemes for one of the constructions which are not admitted for the other. Thus, the adverbial position at the end of the examples above is connectable both to *N Ved* and to *N will V* (both *N Ved D* and *N will V D* are grammatical sentence formulas); therefore, it would have to admit the same members in both cases, if these two are to be transforms. The effect of this requirement is to make the identity of co-occurrence stretch over the maximal grammatical domain, i.e., to preclude any inequality (restrictions) of co-occurrence that would narrow down what the grammar permits. In this sense the requirement safeguards the characteristic of transformations, which is to have no co-occurrence restrictions that are correlated with the difference between the two constructions (i.e., with zero as against *be . . . -en . . . by* plus reverse order in the active/passive or with *-ed* as against *will* in the present rejected case). Note that this formulation does not contravene the transformational standing of *N v V N* and *N's Ving N*, even though the sentence environment of the latter is lacking in the former. The latter, being a noun phrase, is always connected to the remaining constructions of its sentence (*We're uncertain about his meeting us*; *The foreman's putting the list up caused the wildcat*). But these additional sentence-parts cannot be connected to *N v V N* since that is a sentence in itself; hence, their absence here is due to grammatical conditions and not to any inequality of co-occurrence.

The consideration of meaning mentioned above is relevant because some major element of meaning seems to be held constant under transformation. There may be differences in meaning between two constructions that are transforms of each other, due to their external grammatical status: e.g., the fact that *N v V N* is a sentence while

---

[7]This requirement excludes, among others, the cases of small classes whose members have the same immediate neighbors but different co-occurrents elsewhere in the sentence, e.g., *and, or.*

N's Ving N is a noun phrase. There may be differences of emphasis or style, as between the active and the passive. And certain transforms have specific meaning differences associated with the specific morphemes they add, as between *assertion* and *question*. But aside from such differences, transforms seem to hold invariant what might be interpreted as the information content. This semantic relation is not merely because the same morphemes are involved. For example, *The man bit the dog* ($N_2 v V N_1$) contains the same morphemes as *The dog bit the man* ($N_1 v V N_2$), but it describes quite a different situation; and $N_2 v VN_1$ is not a transform of $N_1 v V N_2$, for many triples satisfy one but not the other (*The citizens destroyed the barracks* and *The bystander reported the accident* will hardly occur in reverse order). In contrast, *The man was bitten by the dog* ($N_2 v$ be V en by N_1) describes more or less the same situation as *The dog bit the man*, and is a transform of $N_1 v V N_2$, as seen above.

The determination and explication of this meaning relation is no simple matter and will be only touched upon in Section 37. But it points to one of the major utilities of transformational analysis.

4 Determining the evidence. To establish the transformations in any given language we need methods and, if possible, an organized procedure for seeking (Section 4.1) what constructions may contain identical co-occurrences; these methods should, if possible, be general, but additional ones may be based on special features of the language. And we need methods of checking (Sections 4.2 and 4.3) the co-occurrences in each construction, so as to see if they are indeed identical.

4.1 *Domains of transformation.* To find domains that may be transforms, we need to consider only constructions, since it appears that a given class has specifiable relations (restrictions) of individual co-occurrence only in respect to constructions, e.g., the relations appear between the head A class and nonhead class of a construction (N and A, respectively, in AN) or between the head of construction c and the head of construction k when $c + k$ in turn constitute a larger construction (N head of the noun phrase and V head of the verb phrase in the sentence $T A N + V v D$, *The new girl laughed loudly*). There are no co-occurrence relations between the A and the D here, these being two nonheads in the two constructions; but there is such a relation within the adjective phrase DA, where the A is the head (*partly new*). These domains may, however, be sequences of constructions, as when we wish to compare the sentence sequence $T N_1 V_2. T N_1 D V_3 T N$ with $T N_1$ who $V_2 D V_3 T N_4$ (*The king abdicated, ⧧ The king soon resumed the throne* vs. *The king who abdicated soon resumed the throne*).

The constructions must, of course, contain the same classes, the co-occurrences of whose members are to be checked; in the case of construction sequences some of the class members (indicated by class symbol with subscript) may occur twice, as the repeated N_1 in the last example above. The search for same-class constructions may become complicated, especially in languages where different class sequences can substitute for each other in the same constructions; for example, the position of A in the AN construction can be occupied also by N na (making it N na N, *childish laugh*), so that if we seek constructions containing two N we have not only N is N, $N P N$ (*Pines of Rome*), and the like, but also the *Nna N* case of the AN construction.

The conditions of search may be different according as the morphemes which are added in one or both constructions (added to the classes that are the same in both) are affixes or words, and according as they are uniquely specified morphemes, members of a small class, or members of a large class. For if the two constructions are expected to be transforms, the added material should not restrict which class members are going to occur; for example, in comparing $A_1ly\ A_2$ (*exceptionally large, undesirably noisy*) with $A_1\ A_2ness$ (*exceptional largeness, undesirable noisiness*) we might as well ask at the start if *-ness* occurs with all A (or with all of a specifiable subclass of A); for if it does not, then various values of A_2 will be lacking before *-ness* while present in the other construction; i.e., the other construction will be satisfied by some values which will not satisfy the *-ness* construction. Affixes are more likely, in many languages, to occur with only a restricted number of particular members of their neighboring class, so that constructions containing them often have other co-occurrences than same-class constructions which do not contain them. Among the affixes that do not restrict the members of their neighboring class are what are called paradigmatic affixes, such as tenses; however, such affixes often restrict word choices elsewhere in the sentence, as in the case of *-ed* and *will* above.

Given these considerations, there are various ways of collecting sets of tentative transforms. One can simply select sequences of morphemes and seek the same combinations in other constructions. One can go through the types of class construction in the language—affixings, compound words, word constructions, sentence sequences; eliminate those in which the added material introduces unique restrictions on the main classes; note which constructions contain the same classes (with changes of order or additions), or have subtypes with the same classes (like the $N\ na\ N$ subtype of $A\ N$); and chart each set of same-class constructions in some manner convenient for checking which of them have the same co-occurrences satisfying the same classes. One can make a preliminary test by choosing a wide semantic and morphological scatter of n-tuples satisfying one n-class construction and seeing if this arbitrary group also satisfies the other constructions of the same classes. Finally, one can go through some texts in the language and for each construction or sequence of them ask what other combination of the same major morphemes would be substitutable (acceptable to author or reader) in the same place in the text.

4.2 *Obtaining co-occurrence ranges.* To check whether the co-occurrences are identical in two n-class constructions (suspected of being transforms), we obtain a list of n-tuples which satisfy the first construction and ask whether each one also satisfies the second; and vice versa. Or, we hold constant $n - 1$ members of an n-tuple and ask for a list of members of the nth class satisfying the first construction and a list of members of that class satisfying the second. For example, to test $N_1\ v\ V\ N_2$ and $N_2\ v\ be\ Ven\ by\ N_1$, we begin, say, with *The cat drank* ( ) and ask for a list of words that would fill out the sentence, and then we offer ( ) *was drunk by the cat* and ask for a list of words that would fill out that sentence.

Such checking of individual co-occurrences is not practicable without an informant, i.e., a more or less native speaker of the language. It is impossible to survey everything that has been said or written in a language, even within a specified period. And if we wanted a sample that would serve for the language as a whole, we would need an impracticably large body of texts or other material. Work with an informant can be carried out under partly controlled conditions by various methods of eliciting, i.e., by presenting him with linguistic environments which favor the appearance of utterances relevant to our investigation, without influencing him in any way that might bring out utterances which would not sometimes occur naturally. Instead of wading through masses of speech and writing in search of the co-occurrents of *The cat drank*, we present this environment to a speaker and obtain a whole list. One has to guard, of course, against various factors which might bring out co-occurrents that would not occur outside the eliciting situation.

It is possible in various ways to control the validity of the elicited results for the language as a whole. Different informants may be asked for parallel lists, or one may be asked to fill one construction while a second fills the other. The validity of the lists as a sample of the co-occurrence range for the whole language may be checked by letting the sample grow: we may obtain a list of 50 items for *The child saw* ( ) and 50 for ( ) *was seen by the child*, and then an additional 50 each, and see if the two lists become more nearly identical as they grow, or—more relevantly—if the similarity increases faster with the growth of these lists than is the case when we build up two lists for *The child saw* ( ) and ( ) *saw the child*.

4.3 *Testing for identity of co-occurrence ranges.* In these applications, eliciting is like ordinary observation, i.e., hunting about for occurrences of our constructions, except that here the relevant data are concentrated. Questions of validation, statistical or other, are essentially the same as for ordinary observational data. However, eliciting can also be used to test whether a particular co-occurrent is acceptable, something which enables us to check whether the two sets of *n*-tuples satisfying two constructions are identical or only increasingly similar; observation and ordinary eliciting can only indicate similarity. In this test-eliciting we take the co-occurrents observed for one construction but not obtained for the other and ask the informant whether he would say them or has heard them. This is a very different type of experimental condition. It involves new and great sources of error, due to the suggestiveness of the material presented to the informant or due to his own response to the unusual linguistic situation. There are also uncertainties in the result: the informant may say that he is not sure or his response may reveal unsureness. And the results involve a new measure: degree or type of acceptability (natural, uncomfortable, nonceform); for example, if we are testing co-occurrents of ( )*ish*, an informant may be uncertain about *grandfatherish*, consider *deepish* uncomfortable, and *countryside-ish* a nonceform, and reject *uncle-ish* or *wise-ish* outright.

Since we cannot test all the co-occurrents of each construction in the other, we try to test a wide variety, checking to see if any relevant subclass satisfies one but not the other. Thus, we may test co-occurrents of widely different meanings or of different morphological structures: in comparing *A N* and *N is A*, we may test not only *A* but also *A aa* like *largeish*, *N na* like *childish*, and *V va* like *speaking*. We may test any co-occurrents which seem to be peculiar or metaphoric or productive to see if they also occur in the other construction. We may thus find the specific co-occurrents which are actually rejected (not merely have not been found) for one of the constructions; these co-occurrents become diagnostic for saying explicitly that the two constructions are not transforms.

4.4 *Summary.* We may say, then, that to determine transformations we need to find same-class constructions which seem relevant, collect and compare the co-occurrences in each, and test to see if differences between them are upheld. If one construction is less frequent (e.g., the passive as against the active), it is usually more convenient to begin with this and test to see if all its co-occurrents also satisfy the more frequent construction. It is of interest to note whether the relative frequency and the relative acceptability (from natural to nonce) of the co-occurrents are similar in both constructions and to see if we can list or characterize those co-occurrents which have not been found (or have been diagnostically rejected) in one construction as against the other.

The results can often be summarized in a chart of same co-occurrence, which organizes all the different constructions that exist for a given set of classes keeping constant the same co-occurrences where the set is satisfied in all the constructions by the same set of members.

CO-OCCURRENCE AS A STRUCTURAL PROPERTY

5 Just how much grammatical knowledge is needed before transformations can be investigated depends in part on how much work is put into discovering the transformations. It may be enough merely to identify the morphemes and to have a constructional analysis of the simpler sentence types (as in Section 34). For the present formulation, however, we will assume the whole of the usual structural grammar of the language, in order not to have to distinguish parts which are not needed.

6 Dependent elements in constructions. While some parts of grammar may not be needed, it is helpful if the parts which are used (e.g., the morpheme classes and the major constructions) have a very detailed analysis; for then the transformations are more apparent. This means a detailed investigation of how the occurrence of one morpheme or sequence (or stress or tone) in a sentence depends on the occurrence of some other in the same sentence or nearby, so that a change in one is accompanied by a change in the other. For example, if we offer an informant the utterance *The letter was returned ⧧ It must have been misaddressed* and ask him to substitute *The letters* for *The letter*, it is almost certain that he will also substitute *They* for *It*. If we get as many tense substitutions as we can in the sentence *The dog bit me as if he had been a man* we will probably find some tense combinations lacking, indicating some dependence between the two tense morphemes in this position. Some elements are completely dependent, as the *my* (or the *I*) in *I saw myself*.

In general, we can express certain dependent occurrences within a construction by a single discontinuous morpheme: Given *this book* but *these books*, and *The refugee became my friend* but *The refugees became my friends*, we can say that there is a discontinuous -*s* plural which occurs after both *A* and *N* of the *AN* construction and after both *N* of the *N is N* construction (and after just *N* when it occurs alone). This is preferable to saying that there are two occurrences of -*s*, but that each appears only if the other does. Similarly, given *I see* but *He sees*, and *You know* but *The child knows*, we can say that every *N* except *I* and *you* has another discontinuous -*s* (variant of present) which appears after the *NV* construction if there is no -*s* plural after the *N*.

In contrast, when we find dependent occurrence between two neighboring constructions, it may be more useful to say that a given element has occurred twice (i.e., that the two constructions have an element in common), than to say that a single element extends discontinuously over both constructions. One such case appears when a morpheme in one construction varies with a corresponding morpheme in the other: *I saw the doctor whom you by-passed* but *I saw the book which you by-passed*; similarly *The letter ... It ...* and *The letters ... They ...* above.[8] Here we can describe the dependence by saying that *-om, -ich, it* are positional alternants, of *doctor, book, letter*, respectively, in the positions illustrated. That is, in *I saw the N_i wh( ) you by-passed*, the ( )*om* and ( )*ich* are variant forms of certain N_i, and in the experimentally varied sequence *The N_i, was returned ( ) must have been misaddressed* the *it* is a variant form of the N_i.

Another type of dependence between two constructions appears when construction *c* (in the neighborhood of construction *k*) never contains a particular morpheme or class which is present in *k*. In such cases, if *c* is a unique construction in the grammar, whereas *c* plus the absent morpheme or class would be an otherwise known construction, we may say that the morpheme or class in question indeed occurs in *c* but in the form of a zero; that is, when the morpheme or class in question occurs in both *c* and *k*, its variant form in *c* is zero. We thus avoid having a unique construction in *c*. For example, in *The shelf is wider than the closet* we may obtain an additional *A* (with intonational change), as in *the shelf is wider than the closet is deep*, but the *A* will not be the same as the preceding one (*wide*). We can then say that, if there is no second *A*, a zero variant of the morpheme *wide* occurs at the end of the original sentence, so that although *wide* is the one *A* that seems not to occur there, we, so to speak, explain this by saying that *wide* is already present but in a zero form. Since *more than* and ( )*er than* occur in general between two whole sentence structures (*He knows more than I know, The shelf is wide* + ( )*er than* + *the closet is deep*), having just an *N* after ( )*er than* would be a unique construction for that position: *The shelf is wide* + ( )*er than* + *the closet*. This unique construction is avoided by saying that the morphemes *is wide* of the first sentence structure are present also in the second construction, so that the second is also a sentence structure. Note that this satisfies the meaning of the sentence, which indeed refers to the width of the closet.

This explanation is useful even when there is no dependence to be analyzed as a double occurrence. For example, in constructions like *I know whom you by-passed* or *Whom did you by-pass?* the *V, by-pass*, is never followed by an object *N*, though elsewhere it is. We can then say that *whom*—or, for other reasons, just the ( )*om*— is itself the object N_2 of *by-pass*, so that ( )*om you by-passed* becomes the well-known construction $N_1 v V N_2$ with the N_2 moved up. We avoid having unique constructions like *you by-passed* without object *N*.

These few examples will illustrate without further discussion the kind of detailed

---

[8]These are examples of two major types of environmental effect. In the first, the absent combinations (e.g., *book whom*) do not occur in ordinary use of the language. In the second, the absent combinations (e.g., *The letter was returned* #. *They must have been misaddressed*) can be found, but usually with different textual environment, often with different intonation, and, in any case not as the statistically checked experimental result of asking the informant to substitute *The letter* for *The letters*.

analysis which is entirely in terms of classes and constructions.[9] It will be found useful for what follows, in several respects. First, it helps specify the domain of a construction, or of what one might call a grammatical relation: *The one who knows doesn't tell* and *The ones who know don't tell* show that both *V* (*know, do*) carry the discontinuous *-s* of *The one*. Second, it shows the type of many obscure constructions, by eliminating some morphemes (as being discontinuous parts of others), discovering the presence of some (as alternant forms of others), and assigning some to known classes (by comparing their constructional status, e.g., for the *-om* object). For example, the sentence last cited seems to be a new complex construction N_1 *who* $V_2 V_3$, with both *V* connected to the same *N*; but analyzing *-o* as an alternant of the preceding *N* reveals two *N V* constructions, $N_1 V_2$ and *-o* (= N_1) V_3, without denying the fact that both *V* are related to *the one*. Third, the present kind of analysis separates out various relevant subclasses. For example, the plural morpheme extends over both *N* in *N was N, N seemed N*, etc., but not in *N saw N* (*The refugees saw my friend, The refugees saw my friends*). This puts *is, seem, become*, etc. into a special *V* subclass.

7 Considerations from co-occurrence. We now proceed to take into consideration, as a correction upon the class-construction grammar, any data of interest concerning the individual co-occurrences of members of each class.

Individual co-occurrence can be used even to identify a morpheme (or word) in cases where the phonemic composition does not suffice (i.e., in homonymity). For example, *flight* can be identified as *fly* plus a *vn* suffix and also as *flee* plus a *vn* suffix. Which of these it is in a given appearance depends on whether its co-occurrences in the sentence (or even beyond) conform to those of *fly* or to those of *flee*: in *rocket flight* we have the same co-occurrence as in *the rocket flies*; in *flight from danger* we have it as in *flee from danger*; and in *flight of the Polish crew to Denmark* we can match both *flew* and *fled* in *the Polish crew* ( ) *to Denmark*. Here indeed both identifications—and both meanings—are simultaneously operative. Somewhat analogously, we can consider the morphemic division of, say, *joker* and *hammer*: these are both *N, joke* and *ham* both exist as *V*, and *V* + er = *N*, so that one might ask if *hammer* is *ham* + *-er*. However, the co-occurrences of *joker* generally conform to those of *joke* (*He is a joker* and *He jokes* both occur before *even on serious subjects*, or *in the old slapstick style*, etc.), which is not in general the case for *hammer* and *ham*: *It is a hammer* but *He hams*; ( ) *for heavy construction* as against ( ) *instead of answering seriously*.[10]

The use of individual co-occurrence in investigating constructional status has been mentioned in Section 2. This can be used to check or carry further the constructional results of Section 6. For example, it follows from the methods of Section 6 that

---

[9]Further analyses will become possible in Section 7 when we add the consideration of individual co-occurrence, while the further step of setting up transformations (Section 15 ff.) is based on the added consideration of identical co-occurrences (Section 3).

[10]Two constructions of the same *n* classes may also be distinguished by their *n*-tuples, as two morphemes of the same phonemes are distinguished here. For example, if *PN* (*at this time,*) occurs in various sentence positions, we merely consider it the same construction but in different positions. If, however, the particular pairs of *P* and *N* are partly different in different positions (say at sentence beginning and medially), we define two separate *PN* constructions.

-om or *-ich* are alternant forms of their preceding N_i and are at the same time objects of the V_j following (i.e. have the same grammatical relation to the V_j as does N_k in the $N\ V_j\ N_k$ construction). This is supported by the fact that the N_i preceding *-om* $N\ V_j$ or *-ich* $N\ V_j$ is indeed one of the N_k co-occurrents of V_j: we can find both *doctor* and *book* in *He by-passed the* ( ).

Some constructions which have the same classes are nevertheless distinguishable by co-occurrence. For example, in such constructions as *The strain made him speak* the second V will always be one of the co-occurrents of the second N (in an NV sentence) but not necessarily of the first: *speaks* occurs after *He* but hardly after *The strain*. We can therefore say that N_2 is the subject of V_2 and that $N_1\ V_1\ N_2\ V_2$ contains an $N_2\ V_2$ sentence-construction.

The methods touched upon in Sections 6 and 7 will now be applied to obtain certain grammatical analyses in English which will be particularly useful in the subsequent statement of English transformations.

8 P N and D. Only the most relevant distinctions about these two constructions will be mentioned here. There are many subclasses of P and of D which differ in position relative to other classes and in type of co-occurrence with the members of these other classes. Among P, for example, *to* occurs before all V morphemes as well as before N; *of, at, from, into, for* have constructional relation only to their following N; *in, up, over,* etc., have constructional relation either to following N (*walk up the hill*) or to preceding V (*slice the meat up*). Among D, *very* occurs only before A or D, *quite* also before PN, *downward*, and so on, after V, *Aly* before *Aly, A,* or V, and after V, and often at the beginning of a sentence. Occasionally sequences $P\ P$ occupy the position of one P (*over to the side*).

Of the members of P which occur after V, particular $V\ P$ pairs co-occur (*think it over* but not *think it across*). The construction $P\ N$, in contrast, has very few restrictions on co-occurrence within it; but here the interest attaches rather to the co-occurrences of $P\ N$ as a unit with other parts of the sentence. $P\ N$ occurs directly after N with minor restrictions of co-occurrence: many but not all $N\ P\ N$ triples occur (*time of day, store near the corner*). Analogously after V: many but hardly all triples satisfy $V\ P\ N$ (*leave at night, pass in a rush*). Certain $P\ N$ occur in any of several sentence positions, initially or finally or between the N and the V, often separated by comma intonation; these seem to have no co-occurrence restriction to the N or to the V (*At this point he thought it over*). The $P\ N$ after N are similar in constructional status to A before N, and there is a partial similarity in the co-occurrence restrictions (where we can get the same classes in both, e.g., N_1 *na* N_2 and $N_2\ P\ N_1$ *wooden table* and *table of wood*; but not for *wooden smile, kind of wood*). The other $P\ N$, after V and in several sentence positions, are similar to D in constructional status and again partially in co-occurrence restrictions.

Some sequences require more detailed constructional analysis: $V\ P\ N$ may be $V\ P + N$ (*slice up the meat*, also *slice the meat up*) or $V + P\ N$ (*crawl up the bank*, but not *crawl the bank up*); similarly, for $V\ P\ P\ N$, etc. And in $V\ N_1\ P\ N_2$ the $N_1\ P\ N_2$ may be a unit as above, i.e., it may be one of the triples which satisfies $N_1\ P\ N_2$ in any position; the usual case then is a $V\ N_1$ pair plus an $N_1\ P\ N_2$ triple (*receive reports of unrest*). Or, $N_1\ P\ N_2$ may be a triple which hardly occurs except after this V (or certain V); then it may be a $V N_1$ pair plus a $V P N_2$ triple (*take the child to the laboratory*).[11]

Within $N P N$ there are several different types which are relevant to transformations. Certain N pairs which occur in $N_1 P N_2$ also occur in N_1, N_2 (i.e., with only comma intonation between them) or in N_1 *is* N_2; in these cases the sentence environment which occurs around $N_1 P N_2$ can often also be found around N_1 or N_2 alone: *I like the job of sorting*; *I like the job*; *I like sorting*; *The job is sorting*; *This job, sorting*, ... Similarly *They moved toward the goal of greater production*; *The goal is greater production*, etc. We might call these parallel $N P N$.[12]

By contrast, the great majority of $N_1 P N_2$ triples do not satisfy the other formulas above; and the sentence environments of these $N_1 P N_2$ will be found around N_1 alone but not in general around N_2: *This raised hopes for a settlement* and *This raised hopes*. N_1 has the same external co-occurrents as $N_1 P N_2$, but N_2 does not. In other respects, too, the N_1 is the head of the construction, e.g., only the N_1 participates in discontinuous morphemes that reach outside the construction: *A list of names is appended*; *Lists of names are appended*; *Hopes of peace are rising*. The $P N_2$ here has a constructional status (and co-occurrence pairing with N_1) somewhat similar to that of A; we may call it the $PN = A$ type.

In some $N_1 P N_2$ triples the head is N_2. That is, it is N_2 and not N_1 that occurs in the same sentence environments as the whole $N_1 P N_2$; and in many of these it is the N_2 rather than the N_1 that gets the discontinuous morpheme which extends to the next construction: *A number of boys were arguing*; *Lots of color brightens it*; *A part of the Moguls were illiterate*. Here it is the $N_1 P$ that is similar in status and co-occurrence to A, and the type may be called $N P = A$.

There are certain N_1 *of* N_2 (to be called reversible) which also occur in reverse order $N_2 P N_1$ (with P being *of* or some different P) in the same sentence environments. The N_1 here is usually one of a roughly statable subclass including *set, type, group, class*: *This type of bacteria grows readily*; *Bacteria of this type grow readily* (it is not claimed that the meanings are identical); *A clump of some villagers was milling about*; *Some villagers in a clump were milling about*. Reverse order in same environment (usually with change of P) also is found for some of the preceding types: *A great number of boys were arguing*; *Boys in great number were arguing*.[13]

For the $P N = A$ type of $N_1 P N_2$, and to a lesser extent for the other types, we can often find the same triples appearing in the construction N_1 *is* $P N_2$: *The hopes are for a settlement*; *This type is of bacteria*, *The bacteria are of this type*. However, certain triples cannot be obtained in the latter construction: *point of departure, time of day*. These are often the cases which seem more *idiomatic*; they may be called compound

---

[11]There are many special cases, homonymities, etc., which must be left for a later discussion.

[12]There is a minor special case of $N_1 P N_2$ in which the two N have both parallel and $P N = A$ characteristics, e.g., in *crushed against the wall of the building* or *heard the paddle of the canoe*. Internally, the $N P N$ is of the $P N = A$ type. But in relation to the preceding V, each N occurs in similar sentence environments as object N of that V. That is, N_1 and N_2 occur in same sentence environments after this V, even though they do not otherwise, and in respect to this they are parallel.

[13]The $P N = A$ type of $N_1 P_3 N_2$ also often occurs in reverse order, $N_2 P_4 N_1$, but with different sentence environment, usually different P, and with a change of headship: *The name of the lists is* "*Soldiers killed in battle*." Since the environment is not held constant, there is little interest in this unless some particular relations can be stated, e.g., between the P_3 and P_4 choices.

N P N, akin to compound words. A related close-knit sequence is the $P_1 N_2 P_3 N_4$ in which the $P_1 N_2 P_3$ occurs throughout in the same individual sentence environments as a single P: *He phoned in regard to a job*; *They won by dint of a fluke*. The $N_2 P_3 N_4$ members of this construction do not occur in N_2 *is* $P_3 N_4$, and some do not even occur together except after P_1. The analysis here is not $P_1 + N_2 P_3 N_4$, but $P_1 N_2 P_3$ (= compound P, compare the $P P$ compounds mentioned above) + N_4.

9 C. Members of the class C (*and, but, more than*, etc.) have in general the property that they occur between two instances of the same construction. Given an utterance containing C, it is in general possible to find a construction X immediately before C and a construction Y immediately after C, such that X and Y have the same status within the next larger construction; examples are *a pale but cheerful face*: two A within an N phrase; *the low wages and long hours in Detroit*: two $A N$ sequences within an N phrase; *The low wages and the long hours were the chief causes*: two N phrases within a sentence; *Either I go or you go*: two sentence structures within a sentence. This means that both X alone and Y alone can occur in the same structural environment as $X C Y$: *a pale face, a cheerful face*.[14] In some cases it seems as though we do not have identical constructions on both sides of C: *I'll take the first and you the second*; *We got there on time but not he*; *He came, and fast*; *He's bigger than you*. In Section 16, however, it will be seen that the shorter construction in each case contains zero forms of morphemes which are visible only in the longer construction and precisely enough zeros to make it the same construction.

It has been pointed out[15] that the positions in which C occurs can be used to test the immediate constituents of a structure, that is, the successive breakdown of a structure into the next largest constructions which are included within it. The two conjoined subconstructions have the same constituent status in the larger construction. For example, we have *He shingled and painted the roof*. The immediate constituents of *shingled the roof* are *shingled* and *the roof*; for *painted the roof* they are *painted* and *the roof*; and the two constituents *shingled* and *painted* are joined by C within their common next-larger construction ( ) *the roof*. But we do not have *He climbed to and painted the roof*. The immediate constituents of *climbed to the roof* are *climbed* and *to the roof*.

In addition to the equivalence in external status for both constructions, the two constructions around C are in general accepted more comfortably in English when their internal structure is similar: *bigger and better* rather than *big and better*. But this does not apply when junctures separate off C plus the second construction: *big, and better*, ...

Not only the class environments, but also the individual co-occurrences of X and of Y alone are often the same as for $X C Y$. This holds for certain members of C: *and*, many occurrences of *or*, etc. Even for *and* there are certain pairs of $X Y$ which

---

[14]Where X (or Y) in the given environment participates in a discontinuous morpheme extending to another construction, we find this participation on both X and Y of $X C Y$: *He reads*, *He reads and writes*. Certain C may be defined as participating in such an extending morpheme even where their X or Y alone would not: in N_i *and* N_j V, the V generally shows the plural morpheme even when $N_i V$ or $N_j V$ alone does not (*A man and woman are here* but *A man is here*).

[15]By Noam Chomsky.

do not occur singly in the same individual environments in which they occur together: *She and I don't see eye to eye*; *Sugar and water make syrup*; *It rocked to and fro.* These pairs, or certain properties of them as a subclass, can be investigated in order to distinguish them from all the others. There are great differences, both in this and other respects, among the various *C.*

10 v (auxiliaries). If we compare *He paints, He painted* with *He doesn't paint, He dóes paint, Did he paint?, Only then did he paint, I painted and so did he*, we see that in the presence of certain conditions (*not*, emphatic stress, question intonation, etc.) *V* + its suffix is replaced by *do* + that suffix + *V*; and that in a subset of these conditions (question, or after certain words) *do* + the suffix further changes places with the preceding *N*. If we consider that the main *V* here remains *paint*, it will not be easy to explain the occurrence of *do*. If we consider that the main *V* in the altered sentences is *do*, with *paint* as some secondary element (as it is, e.g., in *He learned to paint*) the grammar will be simpler. But it will turn out that the individual sentence environments in these altered sentences will be identical with those where *paint* is the *V*, even though in the altered sentences the *V* is now *do*. This is not the case in other sentences where *paint* is a secondary element: the individual sentence environments around *doesn't paint* are closely related to those around *paint*; but for, say, *learned to paint* we can find environments where *paint* might not occur, such as *He learned to paint from the impressionists.*

If now we compare *He will paint* with *He will not paint, He wíll paint, Will he paint?, Only then will he paint, I'll paint and so will he*, we see that under the same conditions the *V* + auxiliaries (*will, can*, etc.) do not change, except that in the subset of conditions mentioned above the auxiliary changes place with the preceding *N*. This and other considerations which will appear in Sections 10 and 11 suggest that the *-s, -ed* be considered affixes of *paint* even after they move in front of it and that the *do* which precedes them be considered not a morpheme at all but only a phonemic carrier for the suffixes when they do not have their *V* before them. (The suffixes occur only after a phonemic word, and interchange in position with *V* leaves them without a phonemic word.)

On this basis we can now analyze the forms which have neither suffix nor auxiliary: *They paint, They do not paint, They dó paint, Do they paint?, Only then do they paint, We paint and so do they.* We say that there is a zero suffix (variant of the *-s*) after the *V paint*, which moves in front of the *V* under the conditions indicated. Like the other suffixes, this zero is always attached to a preceding phonemic word, and here receives the carrier *do*.[16]

There are now two different interchanges of position (*inversions*). One is that the suffixes *-ed* and zero (with variant *-s*) of *V* appear in front of *V* under all the conditions of the type illustrated above; they then have the carrier *do*. The other is that both of these suffixes and also the auxiliaries *will, can*, etc. appear in front of the preceding (subject) *N* in the subset of conditions exemplified above. The first inversion

---

[16]This zero morpheme meets the requirements for a zero—of being determined by observable conditions (namely *I, you*, and plurals as subject); and it satisfies the meaning of *V* + zero, which is not just *V* in general but *V* in the present tense. The *-s*, third person singular, can now be considered an alternant of this zero, occurring with the remaining subjects.

simply brings the suffixes over to the auxiliary position, when certain elements (including the emphatic) come before the V.[17]

The class v has the following properties: (1) each occurs with each V; (2) V never occurs without some v or other, nor v without some V (apparent exceptions will be discussed in Sections 11.3 and 12); (3) each v may have some restrictions as to the separable D, PN in its sentence (e.g., -*ed* will hardly occur directly with *tomorrow*); (4) but aside from such restrictions, which apply to a given v equally for all V, the individual sentence environments of each V remain the same no matter what the v. Note that this is not the case for, say, *learned to paint, learned to talk*, where the sentence environments differ in various ways from those of *painted, talked*.

The first and third of these three properties also apply to the constructions in *He is painting, He has painted, He has been painting*. All constructions of this type can be described by saying that between the v and the V there occur, sometimes but not always, *have* ( )*en*, *be* ( )*ing*, or the first of these followed by the second; the empty parentheses mark the location of the following V word (including *have* and *be*). Then *He paints, He can paint* have v V; *is painting, may be painting* are $v + be$ ( )*ing* $+ V$; *has painted, had painted, will have painted* are $v + have$ ( )*en* $+ V$; *has been painting, could have been painting* are $v + have$ -*en* $+ be$ -*ing* $+ V$. These constructions may be viewed as expansions of v, constituting v-phrases of which the v proper is the head.[18]

11 Pro-morphemes. In class-structural terms the traditionally recognized category of pronoun cannot be defined. *I, he, this*, etc., are members of N by their class environments (e.g., all occur before V to make a sentence), but no adequate further distinction can be found for them. However, in terms of individual co-occurrence they are a distinct group. If we ask for the V-co-occurrents following *which* in *The bird which* ( ) or *I spotted the bird which* ( ), we will find, in both cases, a list including *sang, flew, fluttered, was shot*, etc. If we ask for the V-co-occurrents following *the bird* ( ) we will obtain a similar list (and can elicit an identical list). If we ask for the V-co-occurrents of *which* in *The wall which* ( ) or *I was watching the wall which* ( ), we will get *cracked, collapsed, was repainted*, etc., and this is also the list for *The wall* ( ). In general, the V-co-occurrents following *which* (those V whose subject is *which* by the methods of Section 6), in each sentence in which *which* appears, equal the V-

---

[17]For convenience, we will henceforth consider the -*ed* and zero (and -*s*) suffixes to be members of the auxiliary class v; this requires us to view *could, should*, etc. as independent members of v rather than as *can, shall*, etc. $+$ -*ed*. Alternatively we can regard the suffixes as a separate class, and *could* as *can* $+$ -*ed*, etc. But *should, would* often occur in environments where -*ed* does not otherwise occur (e.g. *I would, if he will too*). Furthermore, we would have to note that *can*, etc., occur with -*ed* (to make *could*) but not with -*s* (*He can*, but *He sees*). Note in the whole analysis the departure of structural considerations from historical antecedents.

[18]These are only combinations that constitute verb structures. To each of these can be added *be* -*en* just before the V, forming the passive of that construction; but this involves also a certain re-arrangement of the sentence environment (Section 26.1). A few other combinations occur, as in *He has had stolen from him two invaluable manuscripts*, which seems to contain $v + have$ -*en* $+ have$ -*en* $+ V$. But the constituent analysis here is not *he* (subject N) $+$ *has had stolen* (V) $+ PN +$ object N-phrase, for these cannot be rearranged like other N, V, PN, or replaced here by other N, V, PN. This sentence has to be analyzed as a transformation; even without that the *stolen* would be taken with *from him*, not with *has had*. Note the alternative form *He has had two invaluable manuscripts stolen from him*.

co-occurrents of the *N* immediately preceding the *which* in that sentence.[19] Now consider the fact that *which* may occur after any member of a particular (nonhuman) subclass of *N*. If we ask what is the total list of *V*-co-occurrents that follow *which* in all of its appearances (i.e., in any sentence whatever), we will see that it equals the total *V*-co-occurrents of all the members of its subclass. In one or another appearance of *which* we may find any *V*-co-occurrent of *bird*, or of *wall*, or of *book*, etc. Analogous properties will hold for other words traditionally called pronouns.

We can now generalize. There exist morphemes whose *X*-co-occurrents (for each class *X* in constructional relation to them), in each sentence, equal the *X*-co-occurrents of a morpheme (of class *Y*) occupying a stated position (or one of several stated positions), relative to them, in the same sentence (or sequence of sentences), and whose total *X*-co-occurrents in all the appearances of these morphemes equal the sum of the *X*-co-occurrents of all the members of the class *Y* (which occupies the stated position relative to them). Such morphemes will be called pro-morphemes of the class *Y*, or pro-*Y*. If the *Y* position with the same *X*-co-occurrents (roughly what is called the antecedent position) is uniquely determined, the pro-*Y* will be called bound. If it is not completely determined, the pro-*Y* may be called indeterminately bound; in this case we cannot tell definitely to which antecedent the pro-*Y* *refers*. The pro-*Y* can be viewed in each sentence as a positional (variant) form of its antecedent in that sentence, as was done for *-om* and *-ich* in Section 6.[20]

11.1 Pronouns. The morphemes *he, I,* and so on, which appear as pro-morphemes of the class *N* usually occur indeterminately bound, so that one cannot specify without investigation which preceding or following *N* has the same range of co-occurrents: *Mark came too late*; *Carl had taken his painting and gone off.* In many cases this pronoun is not bound at all, that is, it does not have the co-occurrence range of (and does not refer to) any *N* in its neighborhood, as in a story in which a character is never referred to except as *he*. Such pro-morphemes may be called free; they lack the pro-morpheme property of having antecedents, but possess the other property of having a co-occurrence range equal to the sum of co-occurrence ranges of a statable class (*N*). This is equivalent to saying that in each appearance of a pronoun, including a free pronoun, one can always find some noun of its subclass that could substitute for it, i.e., could be found in its position in that sentence.[21]

---

[19]The *N* being subject of the *V*. If *which* follows *N P N*, either of the *N* may be the one with similar co-occurrents: *I was watching the wall of books which ( ).*

[20]In English the antecedent is almost always in a different sentence structure from the pro-morpheme, though both sentence structures may be within the same sentence. (Sentence structure is used here to mean any sequence which is a transform of a sentence, such as *which had cracked* in *The wall which had cracked finally collapsed.*) An exception is pronoun + *self*, whose antecedent is almost always the subject: *Carl saw himself, Carl went by himself, Carl himself saw it.* This can perhaps be analyzed as not a pronoun but just a morpheme *self* (different from *the self*), with the subject having a discontinuous repetition (in pronoun form) before this *self*. However, pronoun + *'s* (which is a member of *A*) occurs freely in the same clause as its antecedent *N*: *He took his books.*

[21]The total co-occurrence range of a free *he* equals the total co-occurrence ranges of all bound *he*. A marginal case is such pronoun occurrences as unstressed *you're, we're, one's* in ( ) *only young once*, which can perhaps be replaced by all members of *N*, or perhaps only by a new subclass of *N* (*people, Jim*, etc.; whereas *one* can otherwise be substituted by any *N*). In contrast, the *it* of *It's raining* is not a pro-morpheme at all: almost no other morpheme can substitute for it here, so that this *it* is just a member of *N*.

One can study, for each structure that contains pro-morphemes, the degree and type of uncertainty in their boundedness (in the location of their antecedents), by such structural methods as their participation in discontinuous morphemes (*the man* will not be an antecedent for *they*), by the restriction of some pro-morphemes to particular subclasses (*the man* is not an antecedent for *she*), and by testing the co-occurrence ranges of the pro-morpheme and its putative antecedents.

Some pro-morphemes have statable antecedents only in very few structures. For example, *I* and *you* have *N, he,* or *she* as their antecedents, but only when in particular quote positions: *N said "I . . . ," . . . said to N " You . . . ;"* and they are replaced by *he* or *she* when the quote intonation is replaced by *that: N said that he . . . .* In addition, *I* and *you* replace each other in the question-answer sequence.

In some cases, a small set of pronouns covers (between them) the whole *N* class, each member of the set having only some subclass of *N* as its antecedent: *he* and *she* and *it*. Other pronouns range over the whole *N* or some subclass of it: *this, that, some, another, everyone,* etc.[22]

All these are (with some individual differences) pro-morphemes of the full *N*; phrase (including *N*-phrase *P N*-phrase = *N*-phrase: *The book of old songs . . . - it . . .*). This is a way of stating the fact that we do not find, for example, *the* or *old* before *it,* or *of songs* after *it.* These are therefore pro-*N*-phrases, and are members of the class *N*-phrase rather than of the class *N.* Hence *he, this,* etc. include *T* within them (i.e., they constitute a recurrence, or a variant form, of some neighboring *N*-phrase with its *the, a, some,* etc.), and this gives them an individuating semantic effect. That is, in *The man . . . he . . . ,* the pro-morpheme *he* indicates a recurrence not merely of the morpheme *man* but of the particular *man* individuated by its article *the.*

In addition, *one* occurs as a pro-*N* (except for mass nouns), not a pro-*N*-phrase: *He bought a large painting, but I'd prefer a small one; As to exams, the hardest ones are still to come.* There are also zero pro-*N,* whose antecedent is always in another sentence structure: *Her hair is lighter than her brother's* (where *hair* may be repeated in full, or by zero pro-*N*); *The people tried but soon gave up* (where *the people* recurs after *but* in the pro-*N*-phrase *they* or zero).[23]

11.2 The wh- pro-morphemes. If we consider *who,*[24] *which, what, where, when, why,* etc., we find that they can all be described as occurring in a specific position, namely, before a sentence structure S_2 which lacks some particular constituent. The methods of Section 6 show that the *wh-* word has precisely the status of this constituent.[25] Furthermore, since *wh-* is common to all these we extract it as a morpheme

---

[22]We also find *some* as a member of *T* (article class) in *some person.* Many words are members of more than one class.

[23]The *s* of *ours, yours,* etc., and the *n* of *mine* are also pro-*N*: *I'll take my book and you take yours.*

[24]The following analysis will show *who* to contain the morpheme *wh-* even though it lacks the phonemic /hw/.

[25]Various additional considerations show that these morphemes belong to the classes missing in the sentence structure that follows them. For example, *P* occurs in general only before *N,* but it also occurs before *whom, which, what (to whom, from which,* etc.). Throughout Section 11.2 *N* indicates *N*-phrase: the *wh-* words replace a full *N*-phrase and do not have *T* or *A* before them; and *V* will be used for *V*-phrase. Whenever *S* is written here directly after *wh-* it is understood that some part of this *S* is occupied by the post-*wh-* morpheme, e.g., *. . . who went* is *wh- S,* the *-o* being the subject *N; whom I saw* is *wh- S,* the *-om* being the object *N.*

which indicates this construction as a whole, while the residues of each *wh-* word are morphemes each with the specific constructional status of the section that is lacking in S_2. The *wh-* itself then precedes a complete S_2 (made complete by inclusion of the post-*wh-* element). In the thus completed S_2, *-o* is subject *N*-phrase, *-om* object *N*, *-ose* is *N's* (which is a member of *A*), *-ich* and *-at* are *N* or *A* (*A* if an *N* follows, as in *which books, what books*), *-ere, -en, -ither*, etc., are *P N*, and *-y* (of *why*) can be taken as *P N* or *C S* (subordinating conjunction plus sentence).

There are three main positions in which the whole *wh-* + S_2 occurs: with question intonation, as adjective-phrase after nouns, and as object or subject of another sentence. The list of post-*wh-* morphemes is slightly different after each of these.

wh- S?: *Who took the book?, Where did it go?, Where did it come from?, From where did it come?*. Here the post-*wh-* pro-morpheme is free, except that it will be shown in Section 18 to parallel (and to be pro-morphemically bound to) the corresponding *N*, *PN*, etc., in the accompanying assertion (*It went to the right.*). The *wh-* here may be viewed as a member of the class of sentence introducers or connectors.

In the other two positions, *wh-* + S_2 is imbedded within another sentence S_1.

N wh- S_2 (excluding *what, why*) occurring in any *N*-phrase position within S_1; the post-*wh-* morpheme filling any *N* (or, in the case of *-ere* etc., any *PN*) position within S_2; *The villagers who escaped reached home*; *He picked a flower which had dropped*; *I met the fellow whose papers I found*; *In the place which I mentioned*. *P* preceding *wh-* goes with the post-*wh-* morpheme in S_2: *From the place in which I stood* (*-ich* pro-*N* of *the place*); it parallels *wh-* + *PN*: *From the place where I stood* (*-ere* is *P* plus pro-*N* of *the place*). In each case the post-*wh-* pro-morpheme is bound to the immediately preceding *N* word as antecedent (or if *N P N* precedes, then to one of these *N*). Within its following S_2 the post-*wh-* morpheme can fill any *N* or *P N* position. Like other bound pro-*N*-phrases, the post-*wh-* pro-morpheme refers to the same individual as its antecedent. The *wh-*S_2 can be viewed as an *A*-phrase of the preceding *N* (like *The villagers escaping from the camp reached home*); and when it is separated off by comma intonation it has the co-occurrence characteristics of a descriptive *A* (*The villagers, who had escaped, . . .* ; see Section 23). The *wh-* in this construction can therefore be considered as a morpheme (i.e., a morpheme which is added to a sentence and yields an adjective), or as a conjunction *C* between the two sentence structures (*The villagers reached home* and *The villagers escaped, I met the man* and *I had found the man's papers*).[26]

wh- S_2 as subject or object: Here the post-*wh-* pro-morpheme is free, with no antecedent, and fills a place in its S_2. In *wh- S_2 V*, the *wh-* S_2 is subject of *V*: *What happened is history*; *Where I went is irrelevant*. In *N* + object-requiring *V* + *wh- S_2*, the whole *wh-* S_2 may seem (by co-occurrence comparisons) to be the object of the preceding *V*: *I saw who was there*. The *wh-* here may be viewed as an sn morpheme, making an *S* into a subject or object *N*-phrase. For the other cases, however, it is

---

[26]We find *that* in place of *who, whom, which*, and a zero morpheme in place of *whom, which*, when no *P* precedes these: *a flower that had dropped, the place I mentioned*. We regard *that* or zero as variants of *wh-*, with the *-o, -om, -ich* appearing after it in a zero variant. In the first S_1 *wh-* S_2 type below, *that* or a zero morpheme replaces the *wh-*, with the post-*wh-* morpheme appearing in full in S_2: *I know who came, I know that he came*. Justification for these analyses becomes apparent when all the constructions are compared.

simpler to say (as perhaps can also be said for the cases above) that S_2 is not the object or subject of S_1, but an independent sentence which shares a free pro-morpheme with S_1: *I found what you lost* being *I found N_i (-at) + You lost N_i (-at)*; the *wh-* is then a conjunction.[27] In *P wh- N* and *wh- P N*, the *N* is shared, but the *P* belongs to either or both of S_1 and S_2 depending on whether their *V* require *P*. *P* only in S_2: *I know with whom he sat*; *I know whom he sat with* (*I know -om + he sat with -om*); *I know where he sat* (*I know* + the pro-*N* part of *-ere*; + *he sat* + the *P* part of *-ere* + the pro-*N* part of *-ere*). *P* only in S_1: *I cooked with what(ever) we had* (*I cooked with -at + We had -at*); *I kept looking for what he had come with* (*I kept looking for -at + He had come with -at*); but in *wh- P N* (*-ere*, etc.) the *P* is hardly ever excluded from S_2. *P* in both: *I cooked with what he had cooked* (*I cooked with -at + He had cooked with -at*); *I stayed where we had lived previously* (*I stayed + -ere* as *P* plus pro-*N* + *We had lived previously + -ere* as *P* plus pro-*N*).[28]

11.3 Pro-V. If we compare *I'll go if you will* with *I'll go if you will go*, we see that *go* can have a zero variant in its second occurrence; this zero is analogous to, say, *-o* as second-occurrence variant of *the man* in *the man who* and satisfies the conditions for being called a pro-verb. In all cases like the short form above, the one *V (go)* is in the *V*-co-occurrence for both *N (I, you)* and is the antecedent of the bound zero pro-morpheme at the end. The auxiliary *v* may be different (*I'll go if you can't*) or the same, but in any case it occurs in full in the second part, so that the pro-morpheme covers only the *V* and not *v + V* (there is no *I'll go if you*). When we consider *I left when he did*, we understand (on the basis of Section 10) that this is the same construction: after the second *N* there is no *V (did)* but only the *-ed* tense (member of *v*) with a carrier *do*. The pro-*V* here is not *do* but zero, as in the other members of *v*. We find the tenses and other auxiliaries intermingled in *I left so that he would, I can go if they did*. We therefore analyze *I can* not as *N + V* but as *N + v +* zero pro-*V*, the antecedent *V* being usually present in the neighborhood. This accords with the absence after *can* and the like of the third-person *-s* which is found after all *V*.

The zero is actually a pro-morpheme of the *V*-phrase, including *V P* constructions, the object *N* and *V + P N (indirect object)*: *I'll go up if you will, He likes the nineteenth-century writers but I don't*. It is possible to have a pro-*V* with an object different from the antecedent; but in that case the auxiliary is included and we have a pro-*vV*: *I got the first copy and he the second*.[29]

---

[27]It is impossible to give here all the co-occurrence characteristics which justify these analyses, but as an example note that in sentences like *I found what you lost* the two verbs are always such as have some nouns (not merely pronouns) which are common to both their object ranges. We would hardly find, for example, *I bit what you extrapolated*.

[28]Among minor occurrences of *wh-* note these: *wh- S* constituting an independent subject *N*-phrase, primarily in *N is N* sentences and passives (*Who did it is a question, Who did it can no longer be discovered*); *wh-ever S* as independent *N*-phrase (*Whoever did it was a fool*); the construction *What a clean job!; while* as a *C*. Sentences like *I know where* may be analyzed as *I know where S* with the *S* present in a zero pro-morpheme; the antecedent *S* is usually present in the neighborhood.

[29]After constructions like *I am going, I have gone*, the second part is *but he isn't, but he hasn't*, not *but he doesn't*. The *is* and *has* operate like members of *v*. After *I will be going* the second part is *and so will you be* or *and so will you*, with the *be* repeated like a member of *v* or zeroed like a *V*. A similar situation occurs in *N is N* sentences: *He's a fool but she isn't, He'll be late but she won't be* or *but she won't*. And the case is similar for *V to V* and *V Ving* sequences: *I'll try to catch it if you will* or *if you try*.

In some constructions we can find, beside a full recurrence of the antecedent or a zero pro-*V*, also *do it, do that*, and *do so* as pro-*V*: *I'll buy some pictures* (or: *I'll go over*) *if you will* ( ) *too*. But after *so* as a separate morpheme, the pro-*V* is zero: *I went over and so did he* or *and so will he*. All these too are pro-*V*-phrase, and have the internal structure of a *V* + object. The original object can then recur as *PN* of the pro-*V*-phrase: *They repaid Tom*; *They did it to him but not to me*.

After *wh-* the pro-*V* is *-at . . . do*: *I don't know what he will do* or *What will* (or *did*) *he do?* (the antecedent in the following answer may be *He disappeared, He sold the books*, etc.).

These pro-*V* are usually bound, the antecedent appearing in another sentence structure within the same sentence or sometimes farther away in the neighborhood. Some of them also occur free: *Wait, I'll do it*; *He does it with a flourish*. All these contrast with *do* as a direct member of *V*: *This will do*; *When did you do the carvings?*; *I did them last summer*. (Note that the pro-*V do it* has no plural *do them*.)

Specific constructions have specific pro-*V*. For example, in *He'll manage better than I* we have full recurrence (*than I'll manage*), zero pro-*V* (*than I will*) and zero pro-*vV* (*than I*). In *Some spoke French and some German* we have full recurrence (*spoke German*) or zero pro-*vV*. In *I'll go rather than have you go* we find full recurrence and any pro-*V* except zero (*than have you do it*).

11.4 Pro-A, pro-S, pro-N-pair. A few morphemes satisfy the conditions for being pro-morphemes of *A*: *this, that*, and a number of words like *aforementioned, other*; also the second morphemes in *which, what*.

Of greater interest are the pro-*S*. In certain constructions and sentence sequences, *this, that, it, so*, zero, etc. operate as pro-*S* (or rather as pro-morphemes of *S* made into an *N*-phrase). The antecedent *S* (or nominalized *S*) is often immediately preceding. The pro-*S* can always be substituted by the antecedent, in nominalized form: *I'll go down there myself—that should do it* (*My going down there myself should do it*); *I don't like him—Why so?* (or *So I see*); *He said he didn't do it, and I believe it* (or *I believe he didn't do it*). And the *-y* of *why* may be considered a pro-*CS*: *Why would you choose it?—I would choose it because it's easy.*[30]

Among other pro-morphemes, we might note the cross-reference words. These occur as object of two *N* and a *V*, when otherwise the two *N* occur as subject and object of that *V*: *Men and women marry each other*, but *Men marry women* and *Women marry men*. The *each other* may then be viewed as a pro-morpheme of the *N* pair, distributing them in respect to the *V*.

12 Two-V constructions. Constructions including two *V* (*let go, want to have met, stop going*, etc.) are complicated in their details and cannot be completely structured without the aid of transformations. For our present purposes we will only note the main types and characteristics, omitting many details. Constructions with *to V*, *Ving* occurring alone (*The first problem is learning*; *To learn is not enough*) will be considered not here, but in Sections 25 to 30. In many of the constructions considered

---

[30]In *He came, and fast*, we satisfy the property of *C* of always occurring between identical constructions, by saying that a zero pro-*S* of *he came* occurs before *fast*. This is supported by the fact that the *D* word in the position of *fast* will always be in the *D*-co-occurrence of the verb of the preceding section (*came*).

here and in Section 13 only certain members of V occur, so that complicated over-lapping subclasses of V are determined by these forms, i.e., by whether they may be followed by V, *to V*, *Ving*, *V N N*, *N*, and so forth. In all cases the second V lacks the v (tenses or auxiliaries) although in some cases it may have the expansion of v, such as *be* ( )*ing*, *have* ( )*en*.

In all these cases both V are in the co-occurrence range of the preceding N. If we find, for example, *The dog came running*, *The clock stopped ticking*, *The boy tried to cough*, and *The clock began again, ticking loudly*, we can also find not only *The dog came*, *The clock stopped*, etc. but also *The dog ran*, *The clock ticked*, *The boy coughed*, etc. Both V are in the co-occurrence range of the first N in *N V N*, *Ving* (sometimes even without the comma): *The clock tolled the hour, ticking loudly*; but not for a sequence *N V N Ving* that never admits of a comma (*The stranger heard the clock ticking*), where the second V is not necessarily in the co-occurrence range of the first N. It follows from this that in constructions of the first types indicated above, there is a particular constructional relation between the first N and each of the V. This relation could be expressed by saying that N is the subject of each V, or perhaps by saying that the two V form a composite V-phrase whose subject is that N.

We consider first the constructional relations in the simplest case, where this prob-lem does not come up: *The phone call reminded me to be rushing off*, *He saw the car stalling on the tracks*, *He saw the car stall on the tracks*. Here the first N is (in general) in the subject range only of the first V, and the second N is so for the second V. At the same time, the second N is in the object range of the first $N V$. The first V is always a V that can be (or always is) followed by object N. Furthermore, when the second N happens to be the same person as the first, it is replaced by a pronoun + *self*, as is general for a same-person object: *I reminded myself to go*. When the second V happens to be the same as the first, it recurs in full, not in pro-V: *I remind you to remind him*. This is the only two-V form that has a regular passive: *The car was seen by him stalling* (or: *to stall*) *on the tracks*. We may call this the $N_1 V_1 N_2 + N_2 V_2$ type; the V_2 is, of course, a complete V-phrase, with or without an object N.

We next consider *I remember the dog barking there*, *His mates admired his speaking out*, *We let the water flow*, *I like children to behave*. Here the first N is subject of the first V but not of the second (the second V is not necessarily in the co-occurrence range of the subject N); the second N, however, is the subject of the second V. Furthermore, the first V is always one that can occur with object N; many of these first V (e.g., *like*) occur always with object N. So far, the relations are the same as in the preceding type. The difference, however, is that the second N is not necessarily one which is in the object range of the first $N V$; note *The scare made the girl scream*. Even where the second N is in the object range of the first $N V$, discourse analysis methods may show that it is not so in the given sentence, and this will in general fit our intuitive sense of the meaning: the person with opinions about behaving, above, probably does not like children. Since something in the sentence has to have the status of object to the first $N V$, we can say that if it is not the second N, then it is the whole second $N V$, writing the whole as $N_1 V_1 (N_2 V_2)$. While we cannot compare the co-occurrences of this whole class of $N_2 V_2$ pairs with objects elsewhere, we find many of them, when their structure is an N-phrase, occurring as object of the very same

$N_1 V_1$: *I like children's behavior, I remember the dog's bark* (or *barking*); the sequence *his speaking out* above can be analyzed as it stands as an *N*-phrase.[31]

A related construction is seen in *He avoided working, The longshoremen wanted to strike*. Here both *V* are in the range of the *N* as subject, and we might think of a two-*V* phrase. Since in the previous construction, however, we generally fail to find cases where the second *N* is identical with the first, we can say that the examples before us are simply those cases of the previous construction where the second *N* is the same as the first. That is to say, when the second *N* is identical with the first, even as to specific individual, it is (in general) represented by zero: *I wanted to write* is $N_1 V_1 (N_1 V_2)$ while *I wanted you to write* is $N_1 V_1 (N_2 V_2)$.[32]

We now consider the constructions where we find in the position of *to* also *in order to, so that,* and other sequences: *I need a ladder for you to paint the wall* (also, *in order for you to paint the wall*). Here not only the second *V* (as in the previous construction), but both *V* are complete *V*-phrases each with its object, if it is a *V* that, in general, occurs with objects. Hence, there is no problem of seeking some part of the second *N V* which may be object to the first. Each *N* is, by co-occurrence ranges, subject of the *V* after it. We can see this type therefore as two conjoined *N V*-structures, even though they are connected by words like *for* (which we might not expect as conjunctions) and even though the second verb has *to* instead of *v*. We may write it $N_1 V_1 C N_2 V_2$.

We further find *in order to* and the like substitutable for *to* even without a subject *N* for the second *V*: either because there is no second *N* at all (*I rose to speak*), or because the second *N* is object of the first *V* and is perhaps not in the subject range for the second *V*: *I need a ladder to fix that spot, I want a book to read*). Here, too, we note that the preceding construction, in general, lacked cases in which the second *N* is the same as the first, and we can say that, in general, when the second *N* denotes the same individual as the first, it takes a zero form. The second *V* then has as subject a zero recurrence of the first *N* and is indeed always in the co-occurrence range of the first *N*. This is $N_1 V_1 C N_1 V_2$.

There remain some sequences *V to V*, and *V Ving* which are not easily regarded as such $N_1 V_1 + N_1 V_2$ combinations. This is because we have these with a single N_1 but cannot obtain them naturally with N_2; hence, we cannot say that the zero is an *N* which happens to be the same as the first: *I'll go to sleep* (we can hardly match this with *I'll go for him to sleep* or the like), *We begin to observe* (no *We begin for someone to observe*), *He tried to stop, He tried stopping, I'll go on doing it*. These constructions contain a small subclass of *V* in their first position, and this subclass may be considered an auxiliary *V* which is added to many (though not necessarily all) *V* to make a larger *V*-phrase. The second *V* is the head of this *V*-phrase, since the rest of the sentence fits characteristically into the co-occurrence range of the second *V* rather than of the first. These auxiliary *V* + *to* or + *ing* are indeed somewhat similar to the *is* + *ing*, except that the latter occurs with all *V* and also that it precedes these auxiliary *V*.

---

[31]There are many subtypes. For example, there is no *The scare made the girl's scream*. Note the general similarities to the constructions of Section 13.

[32]Some first *V* have a *P* before the second *V*: *insist on going, insist on you going, succeed in taking, stop noticing, stop him from noticing, stop him noticing*.

13 *V N N* **constructions.** Two chief types of constructions seem to have two object *N* after the *V*. In one of these, e.g. *give the fellow a book, ask him a question,* the first *N* is always one which also appears in the *P N* range of that *V* (*give to the fellow, ask of him*); the second *N* may be one which is not in that range (*give tone to a book,* but hardly *ask P a question*).[33] Only a small number of *V*, the subclass *Vᵃ*, occur with such two object *N*.

A very different group is seen in *The oil magnates made Harding president, The committee named him an honorary member, We found the barn a shambles,* etc. The *V* here, in general different from *Vᵃ*, comprise a subclass *Vᵇ*. Neither *N* is necessarily in the *P N* range of the *V*. The distinguishing property is that the two *N* are always in each other's co-occurrence range (in the same order) for the construction $N_1 V^n N_2$ (where *Vⁿ* is a *V*-subclass including *be, become, seem, remain,* etc.). That is, we can find sentences *Harding is president, He became an honorary member, The barn remained a shambles.* Furthermore, the two *N* participate jointly in discontinuous morphemes which extend beyond a structure, such as *-s* plural: *He named them honorary members.*[34]

There are various constructions related to this one. Many members of *Vᵇ* occur also with *A* or *P N* in the position of the second object *N*: *They made him enthusiastic, We consider him too unserious, The staff found him in poor health.* Other *V*, outside *Vᵇ*, occur with *A* (and not *N*) in this second object position: *throw the door open.* Some members of *Vᵇ* and some other *V* occur with *as, to be,* between the two *N,* and the second *N* position may be occupied by *Ving* as well as by *A* or *P N*: *I see this as their only hope, We regard them as progressing satisfactorily, We consider him to be too unserious.*[35]

In the passive, there are two forms, both with the first *N* as passive subject: *He was named an honorary member by the committee* and *He was named by the committee an honorary member; He was found (to be) in poor health by the staff* and *He was found by the staff (to be) in poor health.* The first form is similar to the passive of *V P*-constructions (*N + V P + N*): *He took the project over, The project was taken over by him.* In both cases, the second member after the *V* (*an honorary member* and *over*) comes right after the *V* in the passive, when the first member, *he* and *the project,* appears as subject. However, in the *V N N* case there is the alternative form with the second member separated from the passive verb (*named by the committee an honorary member*), which does not exist for the *V P + N* case (there is no *was taken by him over*). The same two passive forms occur for *V N D*: *He shut the door quietly*

---

[33]It will be noted later that for each such construction $V N_1 N_2$ the same morphemes also occur in the construction $V N_2 P N_1$: *give a book to the fellow, ask a question of him.* But this is a transformational criterion, such as we are skirting here: the constructional status here is to be determined only by grammar and co-occurrence ranges. Some additional transformational properties characterize only this structure: the transformation of replacing the second *N* by its pro-*N* generally involves interchange of the two *N* (*give it to the fellow*) but not so for the first *N* (*give him a book*); there are two passive transformations, one of which shows the *P N* character of the first *N* (*A book was given to the fellow, The fellow was given a book*).

[34]Similarly, in *N Vⁿ N*: *They are honorary members.* The *shambles* above does not conflict since it is preceded by the singular *a* and is hence singular like its first *N barn.*

[35]This construction is thus seen to have some similarities to the $N_1 V_1 (N_2 V_2)$ of Section 12 (*We heard it flow,* etc.), although the V_1 there is not in the *Vᵇ* subclass. When transformations are considered, these two will be found to be special cases of the same transformation.

has *The door was shut quietly by him* and *The door was shut by him quietly*. The passive placing of second post-V members seems therefore to be a general property and does not imply that all similarly placed second members have the same constructional status. That is, we do not have to judge that *an honorary member* has a relation to *named* similar to that of *over* to *took*.[36]

14 Summary of constructions. A detailed analysis of the class constructions within each sentence type may make it possible to say that, of two sentence types A and B, A has the same construction as B except for the addition of some x: $A = B + x$. For example, *He didn't go* = *He went* + *not* (Section 10). When we add to this a consideration of the actual word choices (individual co-occurrences), we may be able to show that a single n-class construction is satisfied by several different sets of n-tuples, sets which occur elsewhere in different constructions. For example, $N P N$ is satisfied by one set of triples which also occur in reverse order ($N_2 P N_1$) and by another set in which the two N may each occur alone in the position of the $N P N$, and so on (Section 8). When we compare various partially similar constructions we may find that one of them can be considered a special case of another. For example, *who went* can be considered a special case of an $N V$ sentence (like *Carl went*) on the basis of considerations which make *-o* a special member of N (Sections 6 and 11). And when we compare the word choices in partially similar sentences (Section 7) or in neighboring sections of a sentence (Section 6), we may find that undecidable or unique constructions can be re-interpreted (by environmental considerations) as special cases of known constructions, as when *He knows more than I* is shown to be *He knows* + *more than* + *I know*. By so comparing sentences with similar or neighboring sentences, we prepare the ground for showing that all sentence structures are combinations or transformations of just a few simple sentence structures.

In particular, we note (Section 8) various subtypes of D and of P (including $P P$), to distinguish $V P + N$ from $V + P N$, and $V N + P N$ from $V + N P N$. Within $N_1 P N_2$ we distinguish the parallel type (where both N_1 and N_2 are substitutable for $N_1 P N_2$), the majority type $P N = A$ (where only N_1 is substitutable for $N_1 P N_2$), the type $N P = A$ (where N_2 is the head and substitutable for $N_1 P N_2$), the reversible type (where by the side of $N_1 P_i N_2$ there is also a substitutable $N_2 P_j N_1$), the compound type, and the $P N P = P$ type (which do not occur in N_1 *is* $P N_2$).

Concerning C (Section 9) we note that they occur between two instances of the same construction; i.e., given a construction Z containing C, it is possible to find a subconstruction X immediately before C and another subconstruction Y immediately after C, such that X and Y separately, and also XCY, have the same status within the next larger construction Z.

In Section 10, a class v was set up, including the tenses *-ed* and zero (without variant *-s*) and the auxiliaries *will, can*, etc. In the presence of *not*, emphatic stress, question intonation, etc., the suffix members of v (the tenses proper) move in front of their V to the position of the other v; they then appear with *do* as phonemic carrier. In the presence of question intonation and certain prefixed words, all v move in front of

---

[36]Furthermore, V has restricted co-occurrence relations to P (i.e., there are specific $V P$ pairs) in such forms as *He took the project over*, but V does not seem to have specific pairs with the second N of $V N N$. A different analysis of this and of forms like *threw the door open* is proposed by Noam Chomsky.

their subject N. There is also a v-phrase expansion: *have -en* and *be -ing* between the v and the following V.

Section 11 defined a set of subclasses called pro-morphemes. A small subclass of Y is called pro-Y if its X-co-occurrence range (for each constructionally related class X) equals the sum of X-co-occurrence ranges of all members of Y: e.g, the sum of V-co-occurrences of *he, she*, and *it* equals the sum of the V-co-occurrences of all N. A pro-Y is bound if, in each sentence in which it occurs, its X-co-occurrents, when in that environment, equal the X-co-occurrents of the particular Y which occupies a specified neighboring (antecedent) position in respect to the pro-Y: free (not bound) pro-N-phrases, *he, she, it, this*, etc., pro-N; *one*, zero (Section 11.1); pro-N (and -A) after *wh-* (Section 11.2) in the *wh-* question, in N *wh-* S_2 (bound to preceding N), and in *wh-* S_2 as subject or object of S_1 (free); pro-V-phrase, zero (bound); and free pro-V, *do it*, etc. (Section 11.3); pro-A and pro-S (*this*, etc.) and bound pro-N-pair (*each other*) (Section 11.4).

With the aid of the above, it is possible to analyze two-V constructions into several types (Section 12): N_1 V_1 N_2 + N_2 V_2 *The call reminded me to rush*; N_1 V_1 (N_2 V_2), the second sentence being object of the first, as in *The scare made the girl scream*; N_1 V_1 (N_1 V_2) as in *He avoided working* (the subject of V_2 being a zero recurrence of the subject of V_1); N_1 V_1 C N_2 V_2 as in *I want a ladder* (*in order*) *for you to paint the wall*; N_1 V_1 C N_1 V_2 as in *I want a book* (*in order*) *to read*; and V_1 to V_2 or V_1 V_2ing extended V-phrases (where no second subject could appear before *to* V_2 or V_2ing) as in *He tried to stop.*

In Section 13, V N N constructions are analyzed into V N_1 N_2 as variant of V N_2 P N_1, for certain V, as in *give him a book, give a book to him*; and N V (N_1 N_2) for other V, the N_1 N_2 being object of the V (and also occurring in N_1 *is* N_2 sentences), as in *The oil magnates made Harding president.*

From all this we can go on (Section 16) to show that in complicated sentences, in general, the two or more sections are separate simple sentence structures which have been combined in one of these relations or another.

TRANSFORMATIONS IN SENTENCE SEQUENCES

15 Certain sequences of two or more sentences have a special form for one of the sentences (usually the second): e.g., *Some groups have rebelled frequently ⧧ Some only rarely*, or *I've just been over there ⧧ Oh, you were there?* In addition, many sentences which have what might be called complex structures can be analyzed as containing a sequence of two or more sentences or sentence structures, some or all of which have special forms: *I met him coming back.* In all these cases the sections with special forms (*Oh, you were there?* or *him coming back*) can be shown to be transforms of ordinary independent sentences, in the sense of the definition of Section 3. These transforms can thus be viewed as variant forms of sentences. Some of these variant forms are positionally bound, occurring only in particular sentence sequences, e.g., *Some only rarely* or *him coming back*. Others also occur outside of the sentence sequences, e.g., *Oh, you were there?*

To obtain this result we first have to show that the sections in question occur in specifiable positions with respect to other sentences or sentence sections. Then we have to show that the sections in question are complete sentence structures, in the sense that they contain the same constructions as a sentence, with the same relations among these constructions. Finally, we have to show that they are transforms of independently occurring sentences, that is, that every *n*-tuple of morphemes that satisfies one of these special variant forms also satisfies an independent sentence.

The first task has been partly covered in Sections 5 to 13, where special sections were singled out from many sentence structures. These sections have various grammatical relations, of course, to the rest of the sentence in which they occur: in *I hear he returned* the *he returned* is the object of *I hear*; and in *The ticket which was lost is replaceable* the *which was lost* is an adjectival phrase of *ticket*. But that does not prevent these sections from having internal sentence structures on their own. In addition to these special sections within larger sentences, there is a host of particular sentence sequences, of which many will be listed below. In all of these, the special sentence form is often characterized by particular features: question intonation, contrastive stress, reduced main stress, special introductory words before the special (secondary) sentence (*and, though*, etc.) or before both sentences (*some . . . some . . .*, *some . . . others . . .*, etc.).

The second task, to show that the special sentence forms or sentence sections are complete sentence structures internally, is accomplished by methods of structural linguistics as in Section 6 and of individual co-occurrence as in Section 7. It is primarily a matter of filling out the special form by showing that it contains pro-morphemes or zero variants of elements which are present in the neighboring (primary) sentence or sentence section and that these can be filled out precisely up to the point of giving the secondary section the internal structure of a sentence. This will be sketched in Section 15.

Finally, the fact that these are indeed transforms will be discussed in Sections 25 to 30, where both these and the other transformations of English will be listed.

The result of Sections 15 to 24, then, will be to show that various types of sentence sequence and of complicated sentences are the product of one sentence with the transform of another sentence. There are certain transformations which, so to speak, change a sentence into a noun phrase or an adjectival phrase or a subordinate or coordinate clause. That is, given sentence S_2 such a transform of it $T S_2$ occurs next to another sentence S_1, with $T S_2$ filling one of these positions (*N*-phrase, etc.) within S_1. There is no correlation in English between the transformations and the positions they fill: several different transformations—$T_1 S_2, T_2 S_2$, etc.—may fill the same position within S_1 (e.g., there are several ways in which S_2 may be nominalized and appear as object of S_1); and the same transformation $T_1 S_2$ may fill different positions in S_1. Quite apart from its transformational form, there are restrictions of individual co-occurrence dictating which S_2 will fill which positions in S_1: not all $S_1 S_2$ combinations occur.

16 Pro-morphemes and zero-recurrence in sentence sequences. If we consider sentence sequences (or complicated sentence structures) in which one section contains pro-morphemes, we can often show that the pro-morpheme has the same co-occurrence relations as some particular antecedent morpheme or word or phrase present in the neighboring section (Sections 6 and 10). If we consider sections that are added to sentence structures (*but not I* after *He spoke there*) or imbedded within them (*committing myself* in *I avoided* [ ]), and if we compare certain of these sections with whole sentences, we find that there exist sentences which contain precisely the words of these sections plus words that are absent in these sections but are present in the neighboring one, e.g., *I did not speak* as compared with *not I*. Instead of merely noting the absence of such words from these sections, we can say that the whole sentences have certain positions filled which are empty in these sections. We put it this way because we can then proceed to say that these positions are actually not empty but are occupied by zero morphemes. We discover these zero morphemes by finding that the exigencies of grammatical description (in particular the methods of Sections 6 to 7) point to the effect, in these sections, of certain elements which are not visible in them but are present in neighboring sections; and instead of saying that the morphemes of the neighboring section reach over to affect the choice of morphemes in the other, we say that zero variants of those morphemes occur in this other section and operate within it—or, equivalently, that when this other section contains morphemes, identical with those of the neighboring section, these morphemes may have zero as a variant form in that position. This effect (on our section) which is correlatable with morphemes of the neighboring section, and which we thus attribute to the presence in our section of zero variants of those morphemes, is the restriction of co-occurrence range for the various elements of our section. For example, in *He spoke there but not* ( ), we may find various other *N*, not only *I*, but always such *N* as are in the subject range of *spoke*. Hence, we say that *spoke* recurs in *not I*, although in a zero variant form.

The result of this analysis, as we have seen, is to find in each such sentence sequence or complicated sentence structure, a sequence or a combination of two sentences, such that some morphemes recur in both sentences. These sequences then become merely a special case of all sentence sequences and combinations—the case when some morphemes happen to be identical in the two sentences.

We now look upon these structures as sentence combinations in which recurring morphemes have been replaced by pro-morphemes or zero variants. Whether the morpheme recurs in full or in pro-morpheme or zero form, depends upon the particular type of sentence combination, on the class of the morpheme, and on the position of the class in the sentence. Only sketchy indications can be given here of the mass of detail.

In some sentence combinations there are certain positions in which a recurring morpheme is always zero, for instance the *A* in *That one is wider than this one is* (though a different *A* is given in full: *That one is wider than this one is deep*). Similarly, the second subject *N* in *I avoided going*, the sentences being *I avoided* ( ) and *I went*; a different second subject appears in full (*I avoided Tom's haranguing*). In some sentence combinations there are positions in which a recurring morpheme appears either in full or as zero. In *He would buy books rather than records* (where *he would buy* is zeroed after *than*), we can also find *he would buy books rather than buy records* (where only *N* and *v* are zeroed). Similarly we have *Some people do ♯ Some people don't*, as well as *Some people do ♯ Some don't*. In some positions we find either full recurrence or pro-morphemes, but not zero, as for the second subject *N* in *The ideas kept changing as the ideas spread*, more comfortably . . . *as they spread*. In some positions the recurring morphemes may appear either in full, in pro-morpheme, or in zero forms, as is the case for most classes after *and*: *The man bought the books and the man sold the books, The man bought the books and he sold the books, The man bought the books and sold the books.* In some positions a recurring morpheme always appears as pro-morpheme, e.g., after *wh-*.

As to the effect on each class, some classes have no pro-morpheme, e.g., the auxiliary and tense class *v*. Some classes are hardly ever zeroed by themselves, e.g., *v* (perhaps in such forms as *Well, I might go and he stay*). The zeroing operates on constituents; thus, the *v V + N* (object) construction may recur in full (*I'll take a copy and he'll take a copy too*), or in pro-morpheme of the *V N* (*I'll take a copy and he'll do so too*), or in zero of *V N* but full recurrence of *v* (*I'll take a copy and he will too*), or in zero of the whole *v V N* (*I'll take a copy and he too*), or in pro-morpheme only of the *N* (*I'll take a copy and he'll take one too*); other possibilities do not appear. In two sentences connected by *and*, the recurring material around any constituent can be replaced by zero, provided the *and*, together with the remaining constituent, is joined to the corresponding constituent in the first sentence: *The cheap and dishonest electioneering continued* can be derived by such zeroings from *The cheap electioneering continued and the dishonest electioneering continued.*[37]

The position in which the recurring morpheme takes a variant form is specifiable, completely or partly, with respect to the particular sentence combination. In the case of bound pro-morphemes and zeros, the antecedent is usually completely specified. In the case of free pro-morphemes, the full morpheme will be replaced by a pro-morpheme in the second sentence or after a subordinating conjunction, but hardly otherwise: *Bill will do it if he can; If Bill can, he'll do it; If he can, Bill will do it*; but hardly *He will do it, if Bill can* (in the last case *He* is presumably the pronoun of some other antecedent).

17 Types of sentence combination. Establishing the antecedents of pro-morphemes and placing zero morphemes within sentence combinations can show that these sequences or complicated structures contain two or more sections, each of which has a sentence-like internal structure. It remains to investigate the different types of combination.

In some of these combinations what we may call the secondary section becomes a full sentence as soon as the pro-morphemes and zeros are replaced by the corresponding morphemes from the primary section. Examples are the sentence sequences question–answer and assertion–question (*The book disappeared ♯ What disappeared?*). Many irregular sentence structures appear only in a context: *I can't decide where to go ♯ Maybe to New York.* Here the second sentence is filled out to consist of the introducer *maybe* + zero variant of subject *I* + zero variant of verb *go* + *P N to New York* answering the pro-*P N where*. There are also matched introducers: *Some people will come ♯ Some won't* or *Others won't*, where the second sentence has zero for *people* and for *come*. Most conjunctions (*and, or, either . . . or, more than,* etc.) occur between two sentence structures that usually have a single sentence

---

[37]There may be small differences in meaning and large differences in style; this does not affect the fact (but only the interpretation) of the co-occurrence equivalences discussed above or the transformational equivalences discussed below.

intonation and are in many cases not recognizable as two sentences until the zeros are established. Yet another example is the *wh-* set (*The fellow whose pen you lost is back = the fellow is back + You lost the fellow's pen*).

In other combinations the second section can be shown indeed to have the constructional relations of a sentence among its parts, but the whole may not have the external form of a sentence. Zeros and pro-morphemes may not even be involved in it. Such are the *V* without *v* (but usually with *-ing* or *to*): *Being alone, he didn't go,* where zero subject *he* can be shown before *being*; *For John to win, he would have to try harder* or *To win, John would* . . . with zero *John* before *to win*; *him coming* in *I met him coming.* Such also are the nominalized sentences imbedded in others: *I resent his coming.* And such are the *A N* and *N P N* and other constructions that will be seen below to be extractable. In all these cases the sentence-like structures will be shown to be transforms of ordinary sentences; thus, *being alone* and *he being alone* are transforms of *He is alone.*

Aside from this question whether the filled-out section is a sentence or only a transform of a sentence, we may consider another distinction: whether the primary section is an independent sentence by itself or whether it requires the presence of the secondary. For example, the primary is self-sufficient before *C S* (conjunction + secondary *S*): *The car rounded the corner and stopped* is filled out to *The car rounded the corner + and the car stopped*; *I like him better than her* is filled out to *I like him + better than I like her.* It is also self-sufficient when the secondary is a *wh-* phrase separated by comma intonation, or a descriptive *A* or *P N*: *Snakes, which have no teeth, can't bite.* And in the $N V N_2 + N_2 V$ type of combination (Section 12): *I met him returning home = I met him + him* (or zero *he*) *returning home.* Various members of sentence sequences are also self-sufficient, e.g., an assertion or answer occurs independently of the question.

In contrast with this there are structures in which the primary section does not occur as a sentence by itself, without the secondary section either as a constituent of the primary or as a neighbor, sometimes specifically before it or after it. This may be because the structure of the primary is incomplete or because the individual co-occurrences would not appear without the secondary. Examples are certain matched introducers (e.g., *On the one hand* . . .) or the $N V N_2 + N_2 V$ type of combination when the shared N_2 is a pronoun (Section 11.2: *I saw who came = I saw who + who came* or *I saw N_1 + N_1 came*). In these cases the primary is not independent of the secondary (though for different reasons). Another example is in nominalized sentences which are subjects or objects of the primary: *I think* (*that*) *he can, He said 'It won't do,' I announced your coming, Bees buzzing around annoyed him* (where the primary is *N annoyed him*). Finally, the primary is not independent when the secondary is a *wh-* phrase without comma intonation, or a partitive *A* or *P N* (such as A_i, A_j in *some N_k are A_i.* ♯ *Some are A_j*), because the co-occurrences may then be different: one may find *Dogs which bark don't bite* or *A barking dog doesn't bite* even if one does not find *Dogs don't bite.*

Several additional distinctions characterize the various types of sentence combination; some of these will become apparent as they are surveyed. In the following pages the sentence combinations will be grouped by their major structural features rather than by the transformations that appear in them, since the latter will be summarized in Sections 25 to 30. These structural classifications are the question sequence, matched sentences, conjunctions, word-sharing, nominalized sentences, and the *wh-* forms.

18 The question sequence. We consider sequences of sentences in which the second has zero recurrences based on the first. A special case of this is the sequence of assertion and question (*John came here ‡ He did?* or *Did he?* or *Who came, did you say?*), or question and answer (*Who came? ‡ John* or *Did John come? ‡ Yes, he did*). In each pair, the composition of one sentence can be described in terms of its predecessor and is indeed seen to be a transform of it.

When the question is of the yes-no type, it contains a particular question element, the intonation, together with an optional interchange of v with subject N. The answer may contain the words *yes* or *no*. Aside from this, in the assertion-question and the question-answer pairs the second sentence repeats the first. The repetition may have zero recurrence for everything after the subject $N + v$ (*He'll come to you ‡ He will?* and *Will he come to you? ‡ He will.*), or for everything after $N v V N$ (*Did he take it yesterday? ‡ Yes, he took it.*); or it may have zeros for the whole $N v V N$ before any added material (*Will he get some today? ‡ Yes, today.*), or just for the $N v V$ while repeating the object N (*I'll take these two ‡ Just these two?*). Note that we cannot repeat the $N v V$ and zero the object N (we cannot very well answer *Yes, he'll get* or ask *Will you take?*). If the first sentence of the sequence is of the $N_1 V_1 (N_1 V_2)$ type (Section 12), the second V may be zeroed by itself: *I'd like to go ‡ You'd like to?*. The second sentence may thus repeat or zero the sections of its predecessor in any of the above ways: *Will he take these two today? ‡ Yes, he will*, or *Yes, he will take these two* or *Yes, these two* or *Yes, today*. In addition, the second sentence may have bound pro-morphemes in the manner that we have noticed for any secondary sentence: *Yes, he will take them* or *Yes, he will do so*. But in all cases the zeros and pro-morphemes are variants of their antecedent in the first sentence, so that the second sentence is a variant form of a full sentence. Sometimes some of the zeros are in the first sentence rather than the second. A notable characteristic of this sequence is that the altered forms occur equally in the question or in the assertion, depending only on which is the second.

When the question is of the *wh-* type, it contains *wh-* and its intonation, with a pro-morpheme following the *wh-*. This may be a pro-subject N (*-o, -at, -ich*), pro-object N (*-om, -at, -ich*), pro-A (*-ose; -at, -ich* before N), P + pro-N (*-en, -ere*, etc.), pro-V-phrase (*-at do*), etc. The part which is pro-morphemed in the question appears in full in the assertion, whatever the order of the two may be. Aside from this, the special forms are as above. The first sentence of the sequence, whether assertion or question, is generally complete. The second sentence contains the post-*wh-* pro-morpheme (if it is the question) or specific morphemes of the same constructional status (if it is the answer), and the remaining sections of the first sentence may be repeated, pro-morphemed, or zeroed just as in the yes-no question.[38]

---

[38]There is also a minor type of question-assertion sequence, as in *Did you go to Rome, or to Paris?*, *Did you, or she, do it?*. These have two like constituents joined by *or*, with a rising intonation on the first and a falling intonation at sentence-end. (It is distinct from the yes-no question *Did you or she do it?* with one rising intonation.) The assertion here is *I went to Rome* or *To Rome* (and *She*

Since each question contains the same words as its neighboring assertion (aside from interchanging *you* and *I*), we can say that it is obtained by a transformation (from that assertion) which takes place in the presence of the question elements. In the case of the *wh-* questions, there is the additional transformation of substituting the post-*wh-* pro-morpheme as a positional variant of the constructionally corresponding section of the assertion.

19 Matched sentences. There are in English, in addition to the question-assertion pairs, other sequences of matched sentences, namely sequences in which both sentences contain the same words in all but one or two positions. Those sequences are characterized by having contrastive stress or reduced stress on the second sentence (the last, if there are more than two); and by having the possibility of zero variants for the recurrent words in all but one of the sentences (usually in all but the first). Since all these characteristics may be found in other successions of sentences, one could say that the ones described above are merely those successive sentences which have various words in common. However, for transformational purposes it is convenient to consider these sentence sequences separately, because they are marked by certain introducers or adverbial phrases which thus become transformation indicators.

The more obvious type is the case of matched introducers, in which all sentences of the sequence have either the same or related introducing words: *Some people are cynical* ⧧ *Some are not* (also *Some people are not* or *Some are not cynical* or *Some are innocent*, etc.). Another pair of introducers is seen in *Some people are cynical* ⧧ *Others are not* etc. Since *some . . . some . . .* seems to occur with the same sentences as *some . . . others . . .* , it may itself be considered a transform of *some . . . others . . .* , quite apart from the relation between the two successive sentences in each case. There are many other matched introducers: *A few . . . a few . . .* , *a few . . . others . . .* , and, in general, pairs of partitive adjectives (e.g., *Reasoned decisions are sure to do some good here* ⧧ *Arbitrary ones are less so*). In all these cases the subject *N*, or the whole subject *N*-phrase, and the object *N*-phrase or the whole *V*-phrase, including the object, may have zero form in the second sentence (if the words are the same as in the first); after partitive *A* there is usually a pro-*N* (*ones*) for the subject, rather than a zero.

In another type of matched sentences we find all but one of the sentences (usually all but the first) containing special *D* or *P N* (or even appositional elements to the *N* and *V* sections), but otherwise repeating all or most of the words of the primary sentence: *The boys got home early* ⧧ *They really did* ⧧ *And so did we*, or *Tim gets up early* ⧧ *We all do*. Here the *V* may be zeroed, but not the subject *N* (except in particular circumstances).

The various sentences of a matched sequence are not transforms of each other, since there is generally some difference even between their expanded forms (aside from differences in the introducers), e.g., *The boys got home early, The boys really got*

---

or *She did* or *She did it*). The two or more constituents joined by *or* function like the post-*wh-*morpheme of that status (*to Rome*, or *to Paris* functions like *where*; the pro-morpheme equals a disjunction of members of its class). That is, the assertion always contains a constituent of that constructional status (e.g., *To Rome*, or perhaps *Neither*, *just to Marseilles*) and repetitions, pro-morphemes, or zeros of the rest of the question as above.

home early, We got home early. However, each reduced sentence is a transform of the complete sentences which we obtain by filling in its pro-morphemes and zeros: *They really did* is a transform of *The boys really got home early.* Each set of matched introducers constitutes a discontinuous morphemic element (*some ... some ...,* *a few ... others ...*) which provides the distinctive environment for the transformation.[39]

20 Conjunctions. A somewhat different type of sequence is that marked by conjunctions (*and, since,* etc.). Here we have two sentence structures joined by a morpheme of the conjunction class *C.* In the case of some members of *C* the two sentence structures always have a single sentence intonation extending over them: *He's taller than I am.* For many other members of *C* the two sentence structures sometimes have a single sentence intonation, sometimes separate intonations (often with comma intonation on the first, reduced or contrastive stress on the second): *I'll go there if I can* and *I'll go there, if I can.* Many members of *C* appear sometimes with matched introducers: *Some ... But others ....*

Another difference between conjunctions and matched introducers is that the two or more sentences joined by conjunctions may have no words in common, and yet the conjunctions or intonations may be the same as when they have. However, in those cases where the two sentences have the same words in corresponding positions, the occurrence of zeros and pro-morphemes is much the same as in matched sentences. The details as to which positions may be zeroed (or in some cases must be zeroed) differ for different members of *C* and also differ when the *C* occurs with comma intonation. For many *C* the subject *N* is never zeroed (but the *V* often is): so for *because, since, if, as if, as, unless, though, while* (*The sailors got the raise because they had organized for it; The children can see the trees next fall if they don't this fall.*)[40] For some *C* a large part of the primary sentence may be zeroed (or given in pro-morpheme or in full) in the secondary sentence; and for some *C* certain positions of the primary sentence are always zeroed in the secondary: *He is quick rather than careful.* For some *C,* if only one constituent in the secondary sentence contains different words from the primary, all the repeated words may be zeroed and the remaining constituent may be conjoined directly to its corresponding constituent in the primary. Thus, we have *He and I will come,* which we can derive from *He will come and I will come,* or *I can and will go* from *I can go and I will go.* In varying degrees this is the case for *and, or, either ... or ..., but, as well as, that is,* etc. The sections of the lead sentence that are zeroed after *and* and a few other *C* have been

---

[39]From this it follows, incidentally, that two matched sentences do not occur in identical environments even if their introducers seem to be identical: they really appear in two different positions in respect to their one discontinuous matching introducer: *people are cynical* occurs in position ( )$_1$ and *people are not cynical* occurs in position ( )$_2$ of the environment *Some* ( )$_1$ *Some* ( )$_2$.

[40]Some of these *C* occur also with a different transformation, in which the subject is zeroed and the *V* has -*ing* instead of a tense or auxiliary *v*: *The sailors got the raise while (still) organizing for it.* When the reconstructed secondary would be *N is N, N is A,* or *N is P N,* this transformation may treat *is* as a *V* or may drop the *is,* when the subject *N* is zeroed: *The sailors got the raise while being on duty or while on duty.* In this transformation the secondary sentence (*C + S*$_2$) often appears first: *While walking home, we found this stone.* In *Walking home, we found this stone* we can say there is a zero member of *C.* With zero and certain other *C,* the zeroed subject *N* is followed by *to V* in the place of *v V*: *To get there we must rush; They rushed so as to get there on time.*

indicated near the end of Section 16. A complete statement for all *C* involves a considerable body of detail.[41]

Most *C* occur before the second sentence; in the case of a few *C* the sentence with *C* may precede the other: *Since you won't, I'll go* or *Since you won't go, I will*. A few *C* are discontinuous, with one part occurring before each sentence: *Either you go or I will*, *If you go then I may too*. It is possible to distinguish certain subclasses of *C*, such as coordinating and subordinating, on the basis of the co-occurrence ranges within each sentence or of the relative positions of the sentences; e.g., whether each pair of sentences also occurs in reverse order for the same *C*.[42]

As in matched sentences, each reduced sentence is a transform of the complete sentence which we can reconstruct on the basis of the primary sentence, even though the reconstructed sentence has various sections which differ from the primary. Each different rule for zeroing is a different though related transformation, which takes place in the presence of the particular members of *C* for which that rule holds. The transformation of 41*n* is yet another, for particular *C*. The original long sentence is not merely the sum of the reconstructed sentences, but the sum of these with their conjunctions.[43]

21 Word sharing. In Section 20 we saw cases of two sections joined by a conjunction; in most cases one of these was clearly a sentence structure, while the other could be expanded into a sentence structure with the aid of the zero variants. Below we will see cases which are often quite similar, except that they are not so conveniently marked by a conjunction; they are complicated sentences which can be shown to contain transforms of two or more sentences. In Section 20 the two sentences are simply joined by a conjunction, and then often words are zeroed if they are the same as in the corresponding constructional position in the conjoined sentence. In the new type below, the sentences always have a word in common (otherwise they are not joinable), and they are joined by sharing their common word; that is, the word occurs only once, so that the two constructions which contain it overlap, or one is included in the other. The secondary sentence does not, in general, contain zero variants, except in that it does not repeat the word which it has in common with the primary sentence; but it contains various transformational changes.

A case rather similar to that of conjunctions (of the type in 41*n*) is *N V Ving* (*I was there working*), also *N V, Ving* (*I was there, working*), and *N V to V* (*I came to learn*), and *N V A* or *N V, A* (*We waited, breathless*; also with *N*-phrase or *P N* in place of *A*). Here the co-occurrence ranges show that the subject of the second *V* (or of *is A*) is the same as the subject of the first *V*. This can be analyzed as $N_1 V_1$ + zero

---

[41]Certain occurrences of *and* and *or* cannot be regarded as deriving in this way from two sentences; e.g. *Sugar and water make syrup* (compare *Sugar with water makes syrup*), *They argued back and forth*, *a black and white drawing*, *She and I disagreed*. It is generally possible to characterize these cases. Certain specific combinations of specific morphemes + *and* fall in this category, e.g., *between N and N* (*I lost it somewhere between Fifth and Sixth*). In the case of *N and N V each other* (*Electrons and positrons repel each other*) we do not directly expand the *N and N* because of the pro-*N*-pair *each other*.

[42]The distinctions have to be drawn carefully. Coordinating conjunctions do not necessarily have reversible order: *The goldfish ate too much and died*.

[43]*He is richer than you* is not *He is rich* + *you are rich* but *He is rich* + *-er than* + *you are rich*. Cf. Edward Sapir, "Grading: A Study in Semantics," *Philosophy of Science*, **11** (1944), 93–116.

conjunction $+ N_1 V_2$ (with the N_1 recurrence zeroed, and with the further transformation of replacing the second v by *to* or *ing*, or *be* $+ v$). Or, it can be analyzed as two sentences $N_1 V_1 + N_1 V_2$ (overlapping around the common N_1, and with the same further transformation as above).[44] A special case of this is the appositional sentence, e.g., *The stranger, a Frenchman, could not understand* from *The stranger could not understand* and *The stranger was a Frenchman*.

In the cases above the shared word is in the same constructional status in both sentences. When we have two sentences in which the shared word is not in the same constructional status, we can no longer apply the zeroings that occur with conjunctions; here the nonrepetition of the shared word can no longer be considered such a zero, but must be due to a new method of combining S.

We first consider cases like *I asked him to deny it, We finally found it lying in a corner, We saw it high above us*. In all these cases, the second N is both the object of the first V and the subject of the second V. These are then transforms of $N_1 V_1 N_2 + N_2 V_2$ (*We finally found it* + *It lay in a corner*, etc.). The transformations consist in the second sentence overlapping the first around the common word (i.e., not repeating the common word), as above; and in replacing the second v by *to* or *ing*, or dropping *be* $+ v$ (e.g., from *It was high above us*). We can usually find the same underlying sentences joined in a conjunction sequence, in the manner of Section 20; but then the transformations and the resultant are different (e.g., *We finally found it as it lay in a corner, I asked him if he would deny it*; note that the meaning is affected by the particular member of C).

When the common word is the object of both sentences, they overlap by having the second sentence in the passive transformation: *I bought a house built by him* from *I bought a house* + *He built a house*. Transforming the second sentence into the passive makes this object into a special case of the shared object-subject above, since *a house* is the subject of the passive.[45]

A different case arises in sentences like *The leaning tower collapsed, The plane-grounding order was issued at ten, They designed a circuit with a servo*, and in general wherever an N has subsidiary A or $P N$ phrases constructionally attached to it. In all the cases where the $A N$ pairs also satisfy N *is* A (*leaning tower*, and *the tower leans*) and where the $N P N$ triples also satisfy N *is* $P N$ (*the circuit is with a servo*), we can extract two sentences, e.g., *The tower collapsed* + *The tower leaned* or *The order was issued at ten* + *The order grounded planes*. Any sentence, then, which contains N_i in any position can combine by word-sharing (i.e., by sentence-overlapping)

---

[44]The first sentence may have an object, as in *I phoned him to learn what was going on*, transformed from $N_1 V_1 N_2$ and $N_1 V_2$. Superficially, this can be confused with the next case below ($N_1 V_1 N_2$ and $N_2 V_2$) until the various co-occurrence ranges are checked, as also the substitutability of C (*I phoned him in order to . . .*). When both N_1 and N_2 are in the subject range for V_2, the sentence is ambiguous, and both analyses (and both meanings) are possible. (Such homonymities appear wherever a single resultant structure is obtained from different transformations and underlying sentences.) Example: *We saw him up there* from *We saw him* + *We were up there* or from *We saw him* + *He was up there*.

[45]Another transformation for two sentences with the same object will be seen in Section 23. The shared words, like the zeros of the parallel sentences (Sections 18 to 20) and bound pro-morphemes in general, are not merely two independent occurrences of the same morpheme. Rather, the morpheme in question extends into the shared, zero, or pro-morphemed position in the next sentence. Hence, the meaning of the underlying sentences is not merely that I bought a house and that he built a house, but that the house that I bought and the one that he built are the same.

with the transform of any sentence which begins N_i *is* ( ); that is, it can so combine with any construction whose head is this N_i (e.g., *A* N_i, or N_i *P N*).[46]

22 Constructionally included sentences. Another type of sentence combination occurs when a transform of one sentence occupies a constructional position within another sentence: *They let the newcomer speak*, where *the newcomer speak* is object of *They let*, but neither *the newcomer* nor *speak* alone would occur as object. In the word-sharing combination the shared word fills a position in both sentences: in *I bought a house built by him*, we find *a house* both in the object range for *I bought* and also in the subject range for *built by him*. In such combinations it is not even necessary to find any grammatical relation between the two sentences, since each has its own complete structure; they simply overlap in sharing a word. In the present case, however, only the subsidiary sentence has a complete structure: *the newcomer speaks*, transformed by dropping the *v* into *the newcomer speak*. The primary sentence does not have a complete structure unless the subsidiary is taken as filling some status within it: *They let* does not otherwise occur without an object, and neither *the newcomer* nor *speak* but only their sum is in its object range.

In many cases of $N_1 V_1 N_2 V_2$, there is confusion or even homonymity between the analysis above as $N_1 V_1 (N_2 V_2)$, with $N_2 V_2$ as object, and the word-sharing analysis $N_1 V_1 N_2 + N_2 V_2$ (Section 21). This is so because N_2 may happen to be in the object range of V_1, yet in a particular sentence the object of V_1 may be the whole $N_2 V_2$ sentence. Whether a given $N_1 V_1 N_2 V_2$ belongs to one type or the other can be discovered by noting what other combining transformations are possible for the particular $N_1 V_1$ and $N_2 V_2$. For example, in *Everyone heard my brother denying the story* (in word-sharing analysis: $N_1 V_1 N_2 + N_2 V_2 N_3$), we find the same words also satisfying the transformation $N_1 V_1 N_2 C N_2 V_2 N_3$ (*Everyone heard my brother as he denied the story*), but in *Everyone awaited the reports announcing victory* ($N_1 V_1$ [$N_2 V_2 N_3$], in included-construction analysis) we find the same words also satisfying the transformation $N_1 V_1 N_2$ *that* $V_2 N_3$ (Section 23) *Everyone awaited the reports that announced victory*) and not the conjunction transformation. The distinction is also seen in the passive: *My brother was heard denying the story by everyone* or . . . *was heard by everyone denying the story*, but *The reports announcing victory were awaited by everyone*. In such cases, then, we can say that *brother* is separately the object of S_1 and the subject of S_2, while *reports announcing victory* as a whole is the object of S_1. Both analyses apply in the case of homonymity: for *The new pilot saw the paper lying there in the corner*, we have *The paper was seen by the new pilot, lying there in the corner* and *The paper was seen lying there in the corner by the new pilot* (both passives of $N_1 V_1 N_2 + N_2 V_2$, and both having the same meaning); but also *The paper lying there in the corner was seen by the new pilot* (passive of $N_1 V_1 (N_2 V_2)$, and with an appropriately different meaning).

When one sentence occupies a constructional position within another (without word-sharing), the position which it occupies is that of an N. There are many trans-

---

[46]This formulation overlooks the fact that certain sentences containing N_i may not co-occur with some particular N_i *is* ( ) sentences. The more exact statement therefore is: Any sentence S_1 which contains an N_i-phrase (provided the N-phrase is a transform of an N_i *is*[ ] sentence) can be analyzed as a shared-word combination of S_1 with N_i in place of the N_i-phrase $+$ the corresponding N_i *is* sentence.

formations that nominalize a sentence for such insertion, among them *N Ving* (as above), *N V* without the *v* (*the newcomer speak*), *if* or *whether* or *that* or zero plus *N v V* (*I wonder if he went, I insist that he went, I heard he went*), *that* or zero plus *N V* without the *v* (*I prefer that he go, I insist he leave*), *for N to V* (*For him to go is foolish*), *N's Ving* (*His leaving disturbs me*), etc. (Section 28).

The *N* position which is occupied by the transformed sentence may be the subject or object of the primary sentence, or virtually any other *N*, as in *P N* after *V* in *I count on his leaving, P N* after *N* in *The danger of his leaving is past.*

23 Sentences combined by *wh*-. The two types of sentences containing *wh*- (aside from questions, Section 11.2) can be analyzed as sentence sequences connected by *wh*-, with some *N, P N*, or *A* of the secondary sentence S_2 replaced by a pro-morpheme which stands immediately after the *wh*- at the beginning of S_2.

In the first type, the *wh*- (plus the subsidiary sentence S_2) occurs after any *N* of the primary sentence S_1; the following pro-morpheme has this *N* (or the first *N* of *N P N*) as its antecedent, though it may have any *N* or *P N* status in its own subsidiary sentence: *The fellow who passed, The fellow for whom I got it* or *The fellow who(m) I got it for, The place in which it was* and *The place where it was.* The whole *wh*- + S_2 thus occupies a constructional position within S_1, being an *A* phrase of one of its *N*. It is comparable to the word-sharing combinations (in particular to the last paragraph of Section 21) in that S_2 always has an *N* in common with S_1. But the transformational machinery is different, since the common word is not overlapped but repeated in pro-morpheme (something which permits the use here of more complex S_2). Other words in S_2 which are identical with words of the same status in S_1 may be zeros as in parallel sentences. When the *wh*- + S_2 is intonationally separated it has the properties of a descriptive *A*: *The report, for which I'd been waiting all day, finally arrived.* Otherwise, it can occur in matched sentences like a partitive adjective.

In this post-*N* type, a *wh*- word which is subject of its S_2 may have a variant *that* (*The fellow that passed*), and a *wh*- word which is object of S_2 (or part of *P N* with the *P* at the end of S_2) has variants *that* and zero (*The fellow I saw, The fellow that I got it for, The fellow I got it for*). These are subsidiary transformations of the *wh*- group.

The other main type has *wh*- + S_2 after the *V* or *V*-phrase of S_1. The *wh*- + S_2 occupies the position of subject, object, or *P N* of S_1, depending on the structure of S_1.[47] The pro-morpheme after *wh*- has its own status within S_2: -*o* is subject *N*, -*om* is object *N*, -*at* is *N*, -*ere* is *P N*; hence, we find *who saw, whom I saw, in what I found it, what I found it in, where I found it*, but not *where happened* (where -*ere* would have to be subject). In this type the pro-morpheme is free, and has no antecedent in S_1. There is thus no parallelism or word sharing here between S_1 and S_2, and the relation between them is the same as in the nominalized sentences of Section 22. It is also possible, however, to regard these as a special type of word-sharing combination if the pro-morpheme, rather than the whole *wh*- + S_2, is considered to be the object, subject, or *P N* of S_1 (according to the conditions of 48*n*), and at the same time to occupy whatever status it occupies within S_2. The transformational machinery in S_2 is, of course, the same by either analysis.

In the *wh*- positions of this post-*V* type we also find *wh*- words + *ever*: *Whatever*

---

[47]Cf. the end of Section 11.2.

I do seems to be wrong. However, *wh-* words + *ever*, and *wh-* words + certain special environments, occur in secondary sentences of the zero-*C* type mentioned in 41*n*: *Whatever you think, I'm going; I'm going no matter what you say.* We have here a *wh-* transform of S_2 with a zero-*C* combination of S_1 and S_2.

24 Summary of sentence sequences. We review all the cases where successive sentences are combined. In almost all such sequences one sentence (often the first) is not transformed and may be called the primary sentence. This can be determined for each type of combination.

There are several different co-occurrence relations between the *S*. Two or more sentences may each be completely independent of each other (except for transformational effects, to be mentioned later), as in some *S C S*. All but the primary sentence may be dependent in that some of their word co-occurrences do not appear in primaries, or in that S_1 and S_2 (with their particular word co-occurrences) do not occur in reverse order with the same connective (Section 17, some from Section 19, some *S C S*, first type in Section 23). Or, all the sentences may be dependent in that each contains elements that occur only in the neighborhood of the other, as in contrasting partitive adjectives. The question sentence may be considered completely dependent, since it is identical with the assertion, except for transformations and the introductory (or connective) question element.

There are also different constructional relations between the sentences in a sequence. Two or more sentences may be grammatically independent. Or, one sentence may occupy an unessential position in the other, e.g., constituting an *A*-phrase, or a *P N*, or an appositional *N*-phrase within the other (end of Section 21, first type in Section 23, and 41*n*). Or, one sentence may fill an essential position within the other, as its subject or object phrase (Section 22, end of Section 23).

There are various types of connectives between the sentences. In respect to intonation there may be mere succession of two sentence intonations (Section 17), or contrastive stress or reduced stress or comma intonation on the secondary sentences; or, the secondary sentence (in its transform) may simply be included in the intonation of the primary (e.g., *wh-* forms without comma). In respect to connecting morphemes there may be matched introducers, question markers, conjunctions between the sentences or before each one (and these *coordinating* if the two *S* are reversible within the same text, *subordinating* if not), *P* before a nominalized secondary sentence (41*n*), *wh-* of both types. Finally, the overlapping of Section 21 may be considered a type of connection, as also the positioning of S_2 in the subject or object or other position of S_1 (Section 22).

The types of transformation, mainly in secondary sentences, are as follows: pro-morphemes in all parallel sentences (Sections 17 to 20), and in a special way in Section 23; zeroing of parallel recurrent elements in parallel sentences (with different details for different connectives); inversion after the question element; and bringing the pro-morpheme constituent to the beginning of S_2 after *wh-*; dropping of *v* or *be* + *v* and in some cases adding *to* or *ing* to *V*; and many nominalizations of the secondary sentence. In Section 21 one can say that the shared word is zeroed in the secondary sentence.

In many cases the same S_1 S_2 sequence may occur with various connectives between them, or with various transformations on S_2, with the resultant meaning either virtually the same or different according to the connectives and the transformations in question.

THE TRANSFORMATIONS OF ENGLISH

25 The following list presents the major English transformations in bare outline. Each of these accords with the definition that the same *n*-tuples of class members satisfy the two or more constructions which are transforms of each other. A detailed discussion of each transformation cannot be given here; the reader can test them himself, although in some cases more complicated methods may be needed in order to characterize and isolate exceptions or special cases. This is not a complete list. Perhaps it is impossible to determine a complete list for any language; but this, if it is true, will not affect either the practical or the theoretical use of transformations. The transformations will be noted in three main groupings: those that occur in independent sentences ($S \leftrightarrow S$); those that occur in sequential sentences ($S_1 \leftrightarrow S_2$); and those that occur in sentences that occupy the position of an *N*-phrase ($S \leftrightarrow N$). Minor groupings will also be noted.

26 $S \leftrightarrow S$. The main types here are passive, introducers, alternative order, and various transformations of individual words.

26.1 $N_1 v V N_2 \rightarrow N_2 v$ *be Ven by* N_1 (passive): *The children were drinking milk, Milk was being drunk by the children.* Morphemically, *be -en* looks like one of the expanded members of *v*. But whereas every subject–verb pair that satisfies one member of *v* satisfies every other (*The children drink, The children were drinking*, etc.), they do not necessarily satisfy *be -en* (we would hardly find *Milk drank*). This *be -en* occurs after any member of *v*, including the expansions *be -ing, have -en*; the suffix part of all three occurs after the next verb morpheme in the sequence: *The children + ed + be -ing + drink + milk, Milk + ed + be -ing + be -en + drink + by + the children.* The *N* above represents any *N*-phrase. The *V* represents every *V* word, *V P* compounds (those in which the *P* may occur at sentence end: *They tore the paper up*), and certain other *V + P*: *The paper was torn up by them, His attempts were laughed at by everybody.*[48]

When N_2 is itself a transform of a sentence, we have two cases. If the transform has the internal structure of an *N*-phrase, it is treated as such: *The liberal weeklies opposed his sending the troops, His sending the troops was opposed by the liberal weeklies.* If the transformed secondary does not itself have an *N*-phrase structure (even though it occupies the position of an *N*-phrase in the primary sentence), or if it is a word-sharing combination rather than the object of the primary, then the passive of the primary sentence has either or both of the following two forms (Sections 12 and 22): $N_1 v V N_2 X \leftrightarrow N_2 v$ *be Ven X by* N_1 or $N_2 v$ *be Ven by* $N_1 X$ (X represents whatever follows N_2 in the transformed secondary active sentence).

---

[48]But other $V + P N$ do not have this transformation: there is no passive of *The flowers grew near the wall.* Nor does the passive occur with *N is N* sentences: *They became refugees, We are at peace.* In *N is N* sentences the long morphemes *-s* plural, and so on, extend over both *N*; the position of the second *N* can be occupied by any *N*-phrase, *P N*-phrase, or *A*-phrase (including *Ving*, or *Ven* from the passive); and a certain subclass of *V* including *become, remain*, and so forth, occurs in the position of *is*.

Thus, *The crowd trapped the secret police in their barracks, The secret police were trapped in their barracks by the crowd,* or *The secret police were trapped by the crowd in their barracks.*[49] Any additional material in the original sentence (introducers, D, P N) appears without change in the passive. The *by* of this transformation is homonymous with *by* as member of P;[50] and in some cases the whole transform of N_1 v V_2 N_3 is homonymous with the transform of N_4 v V_2 N_3 to which has been added *by* N_1 (as a P N): *They were seen by the front office* is a transform of *The front office saw them* but also a transform of N_4 *saw them by the front office*. The homonymy is made possible by the dropping of N_4 (Section 29). Because of this homonymy we cannot say that all N_2 v *be Ven by* $N_1 \leftrightarrow N_1$ v V N_2, so that the transformation appears one-directional.[51]

26.2 Introducers. There are a number of individual words or word sequences which occur before any sentence, so that we have a transformation $S \leftrightarrow$ Introducer $+ S$. Some of these sequences are members of the classes P N or D; others are N V or N V *that*. Examples: for V which do not occur with objects, N v $V \leftrightarrow$ *there* v V N (*A boy came, There came a boy*); and with certain exclusions, N_1 v V $N_2 \leftrightarrow$ *there* v V N_2 N_1 (*At this point there hit the embankment a shell from our own lines*). Another such transformation is $S \leftrightarrow$ *There* v *be* $+$ certain nominalizations of S (Section 28): *There was a barking of dogs, There was much chasing of cats by the dogs, There are the dogs chasing the cats, There will be people waiting there.*[52]

26.3 Certain similar introducers transform into an S any N (or A or P N) word or phrase (not merely one which is itself transformed from an S): *It* or *There* $+ v$ *be* (*It's a report, There will be a report*); this can be viewed as a grammatical element making N into S (an *ns* element by $2n$). Combining this with other transformations (by *wh-* or word-sharing combinations) yields various types of transformed sentences: N v $V \leftrightarrow$ *It's N that V* (*It's my brother that came*, also with *who* or *which* or zero in position of *that*); N v $V \leftrightarrow$ *There's N that v V*; N v $V + ($ $)$ *is A* $\leftrightarrow$ *It's A for*

---

[49]The V P mentioned above operates like the first X position. All these examples have shown the passive of a primary S_1 which includes a secondary S_2 in one of its N positions. The secondary S_2 could be transformed into a passive without affecting the primary: *Many thousands watched the daredevils race the cars, Many thousands watched the cars being raced by the daredevils.* Or, both primary and secondary can be transformed: *The cars being raced by the daredevils were watched by many thousands.* In the shared-word sequence (Section 21), the primary sentence can be transformed, but the secondary only if the results fits with the restrictions on word-sharing. In contrast, there is no passive of V *to* V constructions because these do not constitute a single sentence structure composed out of S_1 and S_2 but two parallel structures (Section 20): *I phoned to meet him.*

[50]The *by* which is a member of P has restrictions of co-occurrence; that is, it occurs between certain V_i and N_j and not between others. The *by* of the passive occurs between any V_i and N_j which satisfy N_j V_i.

[51]Among the many details omitted here are the characterizations of such exceptions which do not transform as *It caught fire*. There is a partial transformation with *-able* in the position of *-en*: *The milk is drinkable by the children.* But there are various restrictions on the occurrence of this *-able*, so that it can only be considered a quasi-transformation (Section 30). Note that there is a semantic addition in *-able* such as we do not have in the *-en* passive.

[52]There are many other introducers, with the constructional status of D, P N, or N V *that*, which occur with almost any sentence: *perhaps, certainly, in general, It is probable that*, etc. We could propose transformations, for example: $S \leftrightarrow$ *It is probable that S*; or N v V $D \leftrightarrow$ *How D N v V!* (*How quickly he came!*). Since there may be some S with which these do not occur, we have to consider them quasi-transformations (Section 30); note that they contribute more specific semantic additions than do the transformations.

N to V (*It's good for him to try*, via the nominalized first sentence occurring as subject of the second: *For him to try is good*); etc.

26.4 Alternative orders occur occasionally in several constructions, chiefly the following: $N_1 \, v \, V \, N_2 \leftrightarrow N_2 \, N_1 \, v \, V$ (*The public he always despised*); $N_1 \, v \, V \, N_2 \, X \leftrightarrow N_1 \, v \, V \, X \, N_2$ (*X* being the rest of the nominalized sentence whose subject is N_2, or being the *P* of *V P* compounds, or certain *D*), as in *He threw the door open, He threw open the door*. When of two sentences with the same subject one is made secondary by dropping the *v* or *v + be* (Section 28), the common subject may come before or after the remainder of the secondary: *N, X, V* $\leftrightarrow$ *X, N V* (*He, an inveterate libertarian, opposed the measure*). The two sentences here are *N is X* and *N V*.[53]

26.5 A few transformations can be set up in the environment of particular subclass or individual words. For a subclass V^g which includes *give* and *tell*, $V^g \, N_1 \, N_2 \leftrightarrow V^g \, N_2 \, to \, N_1$ (*give him this, give this to him*). As an individual example: $N_1 \, v \, be \, more$ *A* (or *Aer*) *than* $N_2 \leftrightarrow N_2 \, v \, be \, less \, A \, than \, N_1$ (*The sun is larger than the earth, The earth is less large than the sun*). But by no means can all logical or semantic opposites be transformationally paired in such a way. And even where this seems possible (for example between $N_1 \, v \, buy \, N_2 \, from \, N_3$ and $N_3 \, v \, sell \, N_2 \, to \, N_1$), there are usually so many special cases as to make these at best quasi-transformations (Section 30).

27 $S \leftrightarrow S_2$. There are quite a few transformations which change an independent sentence into a sequential one, these being the sentence combiners (or sequence markers) of Sections 17 to 20 and Section 23 with their attendant changes in the secondary sentence (including the order changes of 54*n*). This includes bound pro-morphemes in general (including *other*, many occurrences of *both*, etc.); the various distributions of zero recurrence for the various matched introducers, conjunctions, and other types of parallel sentences, including question; the specific matched introducers, question markers (with their *you/I* interchange), members of *C*, and *wh-*. All of these sentence-combiners have specific meanings, something which is not clearly the case for other transformations. We may consider these sentence combiners to be morphemic elements (which they generally are), and the attendant changes to be transformations. Many transformations are common to a variety of sentence-combiners, e.g., the zero recurrence. We may say then that the main transformations which are limited to S_2 position after various sentence combiners are these: bound pro-morphemes, zero recurrence, and certain order changes.

28 $S \leftrightarrow N$. The final large group contains transformations which nominalize a sentence, i.e., change to a form that can appear in one of the *N*-phrase positions of another sentence. Note that the transformations of Section 27 do not themselves carry any structural function, for example, to combine sentences or to make them into questions; this is done by the morphemic elements that appear in each case. Here we can say similarly that the various transformations do not themselves nominalize their sentences, but that this effect is due to the appearance of the sentences

---

[53]Certain dependent order changes may be mentioned here, though they can be regarded as part of the sentence-elements with which they occur. Most of these are limited to S_2 position (after particular combining elements). The order change $N \, v \rightarrow v \, N$ is usual with the question intonation, and always with the element *wh-?*; the inversion of tenses with *not* can be expressed by assuming *not* to occur before *v* and adding *not v → v not*; and the bringing of the pro-morphemed section to the beginning of the sentence occurs always after *wh-*.

in particular constructional positions within other sentences. The sentences then are
N-phrases by virtue of their position; but the transformations apply only when they
are in these positions.

Almost all these transformations involve dropping the *v* (and often the associated *be*, before *A*- and *N*-phrases); in most, the *v* is replaced by *to* or *-ing*. Particulars are given in the next thirteen subsections.

28.1 $N_1 v V (N_2) \leftrightarrow N_1$'s *Ving* ((*of*) N_2), and *Ving* ((*of*) N_2) *by* N_1 (parentheses
indicate occasional occurrence): *your reading* (*of*) *these things, reading* (*of*) *these
things by you.*[54] The result has an *N*-phrase structure, with *Ving* as head, (*of*) N_2 and
N_1's or *by* N_1 as modifiers (N_1 and N_2 being themselves whole *N*-phrases with their
own *T*, *A*); hence, *Ving* may have *-s* plural, and if it is subject of the primary sentence, this *-s* will extend to the *V* of the primary: *Your reading of these things is
incisive, Your readings of the play are incisive.*[55] *N is N* sentences (see 49*n*) occur only
in the first of these transformations, and without the *of*: *your being a writer, the
door's being open.*

28.2 $N v V \leftrightarrow Ving N$, the *N* being the head of the resulting *N*-phrase. Here the
whole *v*, including its expansion, is dropped, so that the *V* is a single word. The *N*
usually is also a single word; the *T* and most *A* that preceded *N* now precede the
whole sequence *Ving N*: *barking dogs*; *the dangerous barking dogs*. Although this
transformation differs from the preceding in various respects, homonymy between
them is possible in a particular case: when nothing precedes the *Ving*, and no *T*
precedes the N_2 above, and the N_1 above is dropped (Section 29), and, of course,
when the *N* happens to be in both the subject range and the object range of the *V*.
Thus, *The lobbyist visited some journalists* $\leftrightarrow$ *Visiting journalists* (, *he thought, might
help his plans*); *Journalists visited the new premier* $\leftrightarrow$ *Visiting journalists* (, *he thought,
might help his plans*). In those constructional situations in which homonymy is
possible the transformation is one-directional; for, given *Ving N*, we do not know
whether a pair *V*, *N* that satisfies it also satisfies *N v V* or also satisfies *v V N*. The
homonymy disappears if a long morpheme appears, because of the difference in
headship: *Visiting journalists was indeed helpful, Visiting journalists were indeed
helpful*. The present transformation holds for *V* without object *N*. For *V* with object
N it occurs often (as above), the object being then either dropped or prefixed to the
V: $\acute{N}_2$-*Ving* N_1 (often only a nonce form: *a journalist-visiting lobbyist*).

28.3 $N v V \leftrightarrow Ving of N$, with *Ving* as head: *the barking of dogs*. Here *V* is as
above, and homonymy is again possible with the transformation of Section 28.1,
when its subject N_1 is dropped: in *reading of plays*, *plays* is transformed from the
object (Section 28.1); in *barking of dogs*, *dogs* is transformed from the subject.

28.4 $N_1 v V (N_2) \leftrightarrow N_1 Ving (N_2)$. This does not have the internal structure of an
N-phrase; it occurs as object (after *V* or *P*), but not as subject of another sentence,

---

[54]Here and in the other transformations it is only the *v* proper (auxiliary or tense) that is dropped.
The expansions of *v* (*be -ing*, *have -en*) remain, and the *-ing* is added to the first of them (except that
the sequence *being Ving* is avoided): *He has read* → *His having read, He has been reading* → *His
having been reading.*

[55]After *-s* the parenthesized *of* always occurs. More restrictedly, as a quasi-transformation, we
have $\acute{N}_2$-*Ving* in the position of *Ving* (*of*) N_2: *your play-readings*. Another quasi-transformation is
N_1 *is a Ver of* N_2, $\acute{N}_1$ *is a* N_2-*Ver*, and (dropping the N_1) $\acute{N}_2$-*Ver*: *He is a play-reader*, etc.

the N_1 having an object affix when it is a pronoun (cf. Section 28.8): *They found the lobbyist* (or *him*) *visiting journalists.* It also occurs after *C*, in which case the N_1 is subject (and often zero, if the parallel primary sentence has the same subject): *They turned off, he going first*; *Taking the hint, he went away.* From sentences of the form *N is N* we have, for example, *They turned off, he being first.*

The next group replaces *v* by *to* rather than-*ing*.

28.5 $N_1 v V(N_2) \leftrightarrow for N_1 to V(N_2)$. This transformation occurs when its sentence is subject of another, or secondary to another; despite the *for*, it is an *N*-phrase, not a *P N*-phrase: *For him to visit journalists* (*is useless*); when the transformation is from the passive, for example, we have: *He praises paintings* → *Paintings are praised by him* → *For paintings to be praised by him* (*is most unusual*).

28.6 $N_1 v V(N_2) \leftrightarrow N_1 to V(N_2)$, with N_1 as head. This occurs when its sentence is subject or object of another sentence: *Actors to play the part* (*are plentiful*); (*We want*) *him to visit journalists.*

28.7 $N_1 v V N_2 \rightarrow N_2 to V$: *paintings to praise.* This transform of its sentence may be found in any *N* position of another sentence. The N_1 is often present nearby, often with some *P* preceding: (*Good*) *parts to play are rare for him.*

The remaining transformations contain neither *to* nor -*ing*.

28.8 $N_1 v V(N_2) \leftrightarrow N_1 V(N_2)$. This occurs when the sentence is object of certain *V* (*make, let, have, feel, see, hear*, etc.) in another sentence: *He took it* → (*I let*) *him take it.* The whole *v*, including expansions, is dropped. Some of these *V* of the primary sentence also occur with other transformations of the secondary: *I saw him take it, I saw him taking it.* This transformation also occurs, with other *V* of the primary sentence, after *that* or its zero variant: *I insist* (*that*) *he be there* (from the sentence *He is there*), *We demand* (*that*) *he stop it.* Here the N_1 does not have the object affix when it is a pronoun. As elsewhere, the object affix is determined not by the transformation but by the relation of the secondary sentence to the primary, i.e., by the combining element, which in one case is *that* and in the other is object position; *that* + S_2 can occur as subject of S_1 as well as object of S_1.

28.9 $N_1 v V(N_2) \leftrightarrow that N_1 v V(N_2)$, or with zero variant of *that*. This occurs as subject or object of other sentences, after particular *V* of the other sentence: *I believe* (*that*) *he went*; *I insist* (*that*) *he is there*; *That he took it is certain.* Although the same *V* of the primary sentence (*insist*) may appear with this transformation and with the preceding one, it appears in the two cases as member of different *V* subclasses, and the meaning is different.

28.10 $N_1 v V(N_2) \leftrightarrow "N_1 v V(N_2)."$ Any sentence may appear unchanged except for the intonation of quotation, after certain *V* (*said*, etc.) of the primary sentence, its status being object of that *V*.[56]

Aside from participating in many of the *v*-dropping transformations above, sentences of the form *N is N* (in the sense of 49*n*) have the following transformations.

28.11 $N_1 v be N_2 \leftrightarrow N_1 N_2$ as object of another sentence (after certain *V*): *They considered him a police agent*; also after some members of *C* (*as*, zero *C*), in which

---

[56]In a quoted-sentence object of N_1 *said to* N_2, *I* is a pronoun of N_1, *you* is a pronoun of N_2. The position of the quote marker can be occupied by *that* (or zero), in which case the special pronoun relations above do not hold, and certain changes occur in the *v*.

case N_1 does not have an object affix when it is a pronoun, and often is zeroed: *(As) a police agent, he was hunted down by the rebels.* The transform occurs in any N position of the primary sentence when N_2 is $P\ N$, or when N_2 is marked off by comma intonation; the relation of the secondary sentence to the primary is then of the word-sharing type. We see both cases in *The fellow from Paris, a small hamlet nearby, spoke up.*

28.12 N is $A \leftrightarrow A\ N$ in the word-sharing combination: *The storm is distant* → *The distant storm* (*rumbled*).

28.13 N_1 has $N_2 \leftrightarrow N_1$'s N_2; the result may appear (as a word-sharing combination) whenever N_2 appears.

29   Many-one transformations. Most of the preceding transformations are one-one in the sense that for each individual sentence there is one transform and conversely (except for cases of homonymity). The $N_1\ v\ V\ N_2 \to N_2\ to\ V$ (Section 28.7) is many-one, in that various sentences (with different subjects) have the same transform. All the *v*-dropping transformations may be considered many-one in this sense. Other many-one transformations follow.

29.1   Free pro-morphemes, e.g., $N_1\ v\ V \to He$ (or *She* or *It*) *v V*. These transformations are $S \to S$ and $I(S) \to I(S)$, where $I(S)$ indicates transformed S. For example, *The Hungarians rebelled* → *They rebelled*; *The rebels' setting up councils* (*led to a shadow government*) → *Their setting up councils* . . . If $I(S)$ is a nominalization, its pro-morpheme is a pro-S (really pro-nominalized-S), e.g., *This led to a shadow government.*

29.2   Dropping of *by N*, both in $S \leftrightarrow S$ and in $S \leftrightarrow N$ transformations; and the dropping of *N's* and *for N* in the $S \leftrightarrow N$ group. In all these cases the sections that are subject to dropping have the structural position of $P\ N$ and A, positions which are sometimes filled and sometimes not filled (i.e., which may structurally be considered droppable). As a result we have by the side of *Milk was being drunk by the children* also *Milk was being drunk*; by the side of *Your reading these things* also *Reading these things*; etc.

30   Quasi-transformations. There are many cases in which two constructions fall short, in one respect or another, of satisfying the conditions for a transformation. These cases may nevertheless be of interest for various purposes and may even be usable as transformations in restricted applications. Here only a brief indication will be given of the main types of quasi-transformations.[57]

One type of failure to meet the conditions is that in which the domain of transformation is smaller than a sentence. This is particularly of interest when the domain covers everything except separable D and $P\ N$ phrases (those that can be separated by comma intonation), for example $N_1\ v\ V\ (N_2) \leftrightarrow N_1\ v\ not\ V\ (N_2)$. In the transformations of Sections 26 to 29 it is understood, for the formulas given, that anything additional which occurs in the original sentence occurs also in the transform. Here this is no longer true. All central sentence constructions (subject phrase + verb phrase + N and $P\ N$ object phrases), with most of the separable D and $P\ N$ phrases, occur

---

[57]The case where the set of *n*-tuples that satisfy one construction is included in the set of *n*-tuples that satisfy another construction (rather than being identical with the other set) is a one-directional transformation (e.g., Section 26.1), but does not have to be regarded as a quasi-transformation.

also with *not*. But some separable *D* and *P N* phrases and other constructions do not occur so, or else are altered when *not* is added: *not* would hardly occur without further change in *How silent it all seemed!* or *She looked up at last.* This is the case with some separable *D* and *P N* and some introducers, which occur with every central construction but not with every (other) separable *D* or *P N*. Even *v* can be considered a quasi-transformation of this type: N_1 + present tense + $V(N_2) \leftrightarrow N_1 v V(N_2)$, or $N V(N_2) \leftrightarrow N v V(N_2)$; in the second formulation the starting point $N V$ is not a full sentence. We can go on from here to consider additions which have no restrictions of co-occurrence on the classes near them, but do have restrictions on the members of classes elsewhere in the sentence.

We have another failure to meet the conditions when the set of *n*-tuples that satisfies one construction is only partly similar to the set that satisfies the other construction, or almost but not quite identical with it. This is the case, for example, when the transformation holds for some not readily statable subclasses. Thus, for certain subclasses of N_1 and N_2 we have the relation N_1 *is* $N_2 \leftrightarrow N_2$ *is* N_1. It is also the case when the transformation holds for many but not all the members of a class, as in such individual quasi-transformations as $N v V \leftrightarrow N v$ *succeed in Ving*, or $N v$ $V \leftrightarrow N v$ *be able to V*, or for the examples of Section 26.5 and 52–53n. We have such incompleteness, for example, in the quasi-transformation $V Aly \rightarrow A Ver$ (*walk slowly, slow walker*), or in the various transformations that apply to various triples in the $N P N$ construction (for example, there are some subclasses for which $N_1 P_2 N_3 \rightarrow N_3 P_4 N_1$ holds: *groups of people, people in groups*). Other construction pairs which are partially satisfied are $N_1 P N_2$ and N_2 *na* N_1, or $V_1 P N_2$ and $V_1 N_2$ *na ly* (*a push with energy, an energetic push, he pushed with energy, he pushed energetically*).

Quasi-transformations of this incomplete type show certain relations between the constructions concerned. Furthermore, many of them are productive; that is, co-occurrences which are present in one of the two constructions but lacking in the other frequently appear in the second as new formations, thus making the co-occurrences in the two constructions more nearly similar. Constructions related by quasi-transformations may be a major avenue for productivity, as the extension of morphemes to co-occurrents or constructions in which they had not previously appeared.

A third failure to meet the conditions for a full transformation appears when a quasi-transformation specifies for one of its components a class rather than an individual morpheme. This may happen if we can say that for certain *N* subclasses, N_1 *of* $N_2 \rightarrow N_2 P N_1$; but the choice of *P* depends on the individual members of *N*. Or, if for given subclasses, $N_1 P N_2 \rightarrow N_2$ *na* N_1; but the choice of *na* depends on the particular co-occurrence of *na* with *N* (*wooden* but *national* etc.). Such relations are more useable if the class whose member remains to be specified is a small class. Even when the class is a large one, however, such a relation may be of interest, if some particular situation is afoot. For example, for many *V* we have $V_1 \rightarrow V_i V_1 vn$. That is, the V_1 appears in nominalized form preceded by a new V_i; the new V_i (and its choice depends on the V_1) does not have here any of its usual meanings, but contributes some aspectual meaning while verbalizing the $V_1 vn$: *give a push, take a look, take a step, do a dance, make an analysis*, etc. Here too the quasi-transformational relation seems to be productive.

Cases of this type can be formulated by saying, for example, that for each N-pair (out of a subclass of N-pairs) there exists a particular (choice of) *na*, such that $N_1 P N_2 \rightarrow N_2 na N_1$.

A fourth type of quasi-transformation appears when part of an addition to a construction has transformational or quasi-transformational status, while another part has not. Thus, *N v make* or *N v let* can be added as primary sentence to almost any other sentence (the secondary having the transformation of Section 28.8), but the choice of N depends in part on the individual words of the secondary.

Finally, some transformations may hold only if particular words are present in neighboring sentences. These are textually dependent transformations (Section 37).

THE PLACE OF TRANSFORMATIONS IN LINGUISTIC STRUCTURE

31 Elementary transformations. The difference between any two constructions which are satisfied by the same n-tuples of their word classes comprises a transformation. When we compare the constructional differences that are contributed by various transformations we may see that one such difference is the sum of two others; that is, the effect of one transformation can be obtained by successive application of the other two, perhaps in a particular order. For example, $N_1 v V N_2 \rightarrow N_2 v$ *be Ven* (*I saw him, He was seen*) is obtainable by the ordered succession of $N_1 v V N_2 \rightarrow N_2 v$ *be Ven by* N_1 (Section 26.1) and S *by* $N_1 \rightarrow S$ (dropping *by* N_1, or more generally dropping a separable $P N$, Section 29.2). Furthermore, comparison of various transformations may show that these can be combined out of certain elementary changes, even if these do not occur by themselves. Any transformation which is not obtainable by combining the effect of two or more other simpler transformations will be called an elementary transformation.

32 The algebra of transformations. The existence of elementary transformations makes it possible to regard all transformations as compoundings of one or more elementary ones. There are a great many transformational relations among constructions, e.g., $N_1 v V N_2 \rightarrow by$ wh + pro-morpheme v *be* N_1 *Ven ?* is a transformation (*The workers rejected the ultimatum, By whom was the ultimatum rejected?*). The list in Sections 25 to 30 is relatively short because it is in approximately elementary terms; the transformation just cited is not listed, but can be obtained from Section 26.1 plus the question transform of Section 27.

If we now consider a transform to be the effect of perhaps several elementary transformations, rather than always of just a single transformation, we have to see in what way the various elementary transformations can occur together. Here we have to bring into consideration the fact that transformations are restricted to particular structural environments. This is most obvious for the transformations of Sections 27 and 28, since, for example, zero recurrence appears only in secondary parallel sentences, and dropping of v without replacement by *to* or *-ing* occurs only after certain V (*make, let*, etc.). But it is also true for the other transformations, since, for example, the passive occurs only for sentences with $N v V N$ structure, hence not for *N is N.*[58] In view of this, we have to recognize that a given transformation does not apply to all sentences. And a given transformation T_1 operating on an appropriate sentence S_1 may leave the structure of S_1 altered in such a way that another transformation T_2, or for that matter T_1 again, cannot be applied to the altered $T_1 S_1$ even if it could have been applied to S_1 itself. For example, the passive T_p carries S_1 *The Hungarian workers staged a sit-down strike* into $T_p S_1$ *A sit-down strike was staged by the Hungarian workers*; but to the resultant $T_p S_1$ we can no longer apply T_p (to yield $T_p T_p S_1$), because the resultant has the structure $N v V P N$, which is not in general subject to T_p (see 49*n*).

It is sometimes possible to analyze the observed transformations into elementary ones in more than one way; and for each different analysis, the detailed algebra of how these elementary ones are compounded to yield the observed resultants will be correspondingly different.

The successive application of elementary transformations can be called their product. For example, the sentence *May there be mentioned now a certain secret?* can be derived from *N may mention now a certain secret* by the product of transformations $T_p T_d T_t T_q$ described in Sections 26.1, 29.2, 26.3, and 27 (question), respectively; along the way we have $T_p S$ (*A certain secret may be mentioned now by N*), $T_p T_d S$ (*A certain secret may be mentioned now*). $T_p T_d T_t S$ (*There may be mentioned now a certain secret*). Some products may not occur; or they may occur in one order but not in the other (e.g., T_d, dropping of *by N*, obviously occurs after but not before T_p). But this situation may be partly remedied by regarding certain transformations as positional variants of others.[59] Furthermore, all products may be said to occur, vacuously in some cases, if we say that wherever $T_i S$ does not observably occur (where S itself may be the resultant of various transformations), T_i will be said to occur with the identity value. That is, identity is treated as a positional variant of T_i for all positions where T_i does not otherwise occur. Under this view, $T_p T_p S$ for example occurs, but equals $T_p S$. This rather Herculean solution is, of course, of no interest except in cases where particular useful results can be obtained from it. Where products of particular transforms do occur in both orders, the result may or may not be the same; it usually is, e.g., $T_p T_q S_i = T_q T_p S_i$.

It is clear that we have here a set of transformations with a base set (the elementary transformations), with products of the base members yielding the various other members of the set. Multiplication in the product may be associative (in the mathematical sense), and it may be commutative, depending on the properties of the transformations in the particular language and in part on how the various elementary transformations are defined. We can now define an identity transformation as one which leaves an S unchanged. An inverse can then be defined for each transformation, as that which will undo the effect of the transformation in question: the inverse

---

[58]In general, a given structure may be subject to several transformations, e.g., $N v V N$, or the object N (or any N) position in a primary sentence. And a given transformation may occur in more than one structure, e.g., zero recurrence, or $N v$ inversion. It may be possible to characterize for a given language what types of transformations occur in what types of structures.

[59]If two transformations occur in complementary products, so that they do not both occur in the same position, we can call them positional variants of each other and say that they are the same transformation (but with the observed different values in the different positions).

$T_p{}^{-1}$ of T_p is $N_2\,v\,be\,Ven\,by\,N_1 \rightarrow N_1\,v\,V\,N_2$. The inverse $T_i{}^{-1}$, however, is of limited algebraic interest, because it usually occurs only after T_i, and will not combine with other T.

33 Addition (concatenation) of transformed sentences.   Many of the transformations appear only when their sentence occurs with another, in some secondary status to that other. Which particular sentences occur together is a matter of co-occurrence, like which members of two classes co-occur in a sentence. But how the sentences with their sequential transformations combine is of interest as showing an operation among transformed sentences, different from that of Section 32.

We have seen three general types of sentence-combining, each with its characteristic transformations: parallel sentences, overlapping sentences (by word-sharing), and sentences nominalized as subjects or objects of others. These can be combined and recombined, so long as the conditions for applying them are satisfied; but each combination requires a new sentence to co-occur with the others. As an example we take the rather involved sentence *For the refugees from Budapest to have made so much of my arranging their border-crossing seemed to me sadder than anything else they did.* Here *The refugees cross borders* (with pronoun *they*) is nominalized as object of *I arranged ( )*. This in turn is nominalized as object of *The refugees have made so much of ( )*. This overlaps *The refugees were from Budapest*; and it also is nominalized as subject of *( ) seemed sad to me*. The latter is conjoined by *-er than* with the zeroed parallel sentence *( ) seemed sad to me* whose subject (the only part of the parallel sentence not zeroed) is *anything else*, to which is added by sentence overlap the *wh-* transform of *they did anything else* (with zero variant of the *which* pronoun of *anything else*, and *they* pronoun of the correspondingly placed *the refugees*). Various sentences or combinations here, including the whole, could carry various nonsequential transformations of the type of Section 32, within the limits of their application. For example, the complete sentence could take the question transformation, aside from considerations of style (which could be lightened by using a different nominalization at the beginning).

34 The kernel.   It follows from Sections 32 and 33 that each sentence in the language can be expressed in terms of sequential and nonsequential transformations. Given any sentence, we can check it for all transformations; we will then find the sentence to consist of a sequence of one or more underlying sentences—those which have been transformed into the shapes that we see in our sentence—with various introductory or combining elements (as in Sections 15 to 24). We have thus a factorization of each sentence into transformations and elementary underlying sentences and combiners; the elementary sentences will be called sentences of the kernel of the grammar. Any two different sentences will have different factorizations, either the kernel sentences or the transformations being different; but one sentence may have two different factorizations, since two one-directional transformations (applied to partly different kernel sentences) may yield the same resultant sentence (homonymy).[60]

---

[60]The set of all sentences is closed with respect to transformations. If homonymous sentences can be suitably distinguished or marked, the set of all transformations (all the occurring products of the elementary transformations) yields a partition of the set of sentences. The set of transformations is thus a quotient set of the set of sentences. If we now map the set of sentences into the set of transform-

The kernel is the set of elementary sentences and combiners, such that all sentences of the language are obtained from one or more kernel sentences (with combiners) by means of one or more transformations. Each kernel sentence is of course, a particular construction of classes, with particular members of the classes co-occurring. If many different types of construction were exemplified by the various kernel sentences, the kernel would be of no great interest, especially not of any practical interest. But kernels generally contain very few constructions; and applying transformations to these few constructions suffices to yield all the many sentence constructions of the language. The kernel constructions of English seem to be only these:

$N v V$ (for V that occur without objects)
$N v V P N$ (for $P N$ that have restricted co-occurrence with particular V)
$N v V N$
N *is* N
N *is* A
N *is* $P N$
N *is* D

In addition there are a few minor constructions, such as
N *is between* N *and* N.
There are also some inert constructions which hardly enter into transformations (except quotation):
e.g., $N!$, *Yes*.[61]

Finally, there are the combiners and introducers of Sections 15 to 24 and the intonationally separable introducers and D and $P N$ phrases, all of which occur with any kernel sentence. The V in these formulas includes $V P$ compounds and $V D$; the A includes $D A$; the N includes compound N and special forms like unitary (compound) $N P N$, and carries various T and post-T words (quantifiers, etc.) as well as -*s* plural.[62]

Different decisions at various points in the analysis of transformations will yield a somewhat different set of kernel structures. The result, however, will not make a great deal of difference for the picture of the structure of the language, and even less for the structure of language in general.

Kernel sentences contain in general no parts that repeat elements elsewhere in the sentence or in other sentences near-by; such repetition has been eliminated by

---

ations (so that each sentence is associated with the particular product of transformations that is present in it), then those sentences which are carried into the identity transformation are the kernel of the set of sentences with respect to this mapping. These kernel sentences are precisely the underlying elementary sentences mentioned above.

[61]But $V!$ is an $N v V$ kernel sentence with zero variant of *you*, plus exclamatory intonation. Note that only sequential sentences, or sentences with internal evidence of zeros (as in the case of $V!$), are built up to full sentence structure. The traditional *Fire!* is left as it stands; we cannot know with what words to fill it out.

[62]Most cases of V *ing* will occur under V (either from *is -ing*, as an expansion of v, $+ V$; or else from various transforms of V). But some cases are members of A; these appear in co-occurrences which are not the same as those of the corresponding V. Example: *unyielding*, and *understanding* in *He has a very understanding manner*.

the setting up of independent elements (independent within a sentence) in structural linguistics and by the removal of dependences on other sentences in the course of transformational analysis.[63] The importance of this independence among kernel sentences is that the further grammar, the grammar of how kernel sentences are built up into the actual sentences of the language, does not have to specify very closely which kernel sentences are to be combined with which, except for the relatively loose restrictions of co-occurrence that hold among sentences. If two kernel sentences nevertheless have a special co-occurrence relation to each other, this must be stated in the grammar of constructions beyond the kernel—the grammar which contains the transformations and any other information that may be required to build all sentences.

In addition to exhibiting the minimal sentence constructions, the kernel sentences are thus also the domain of the major restrictions of co-occurrence in the language. The restrictions that determine which member of a class occurs with which member of its neighbor class are contained in the list of actual sentences that satisfy each of the kernel constructions. By the nature of transformations, they do not affect these co-occurrences. The word-co-occurrences in all sentences of the language are in general those of the kernel sentences, so that the only restrictions that remain outside the kernel are the much looser ones determining which sentences combine with which. In view of this, one may raise the question whether the kernel sentences may not be subdivided further into minimal domains of co-occurrence restriction, out of which the kernel sentences would then be built according to the grammar of kernel constructions (chiefly by means of a word-sharing combination of those minimal domains). In effect, this means extracting $N\ V$, $V\ N$ (object), $V\ P\ N$, $V\ D$, and $D\ A$ out of the structures which contain these (and the various compound words), and combining, say, $N_i\ V_j + V_j\ N_k$ to yield a sentence $N_i\ V_j\ N_k$.

35 Effect of transformations in the language structure. Transformations have some particular effects in the over-all structure of the language. They make possible an unbounded variety and length of sentences out of the stock of kernel sentences, thanks to the unbounded repeatability of various sequential transformations. They give an organized view of complex sentences (cf. Sections 5 to 24). As a result, they provide solutions for the structure of some constructions which are hardly solvable in the usual linguistic terms, for instance the structure of *flying planes* in *Flying planes is my hobby*; and can explain what are the differences in the two structures of a homonymous sentence (e.g., *They appointed a fascist chief of police*: both *A fascist is chief of police* transformed as subject of *They appointed ( )*, and *(The) chief of police is a fascist* transformed as word-sharing overlap in *They appointed a chief of police*).[64]

---

[63]The sentences of a kernel are therefore maximally independent of each other; one can say that they give the least possible information about each other. (In contrast, transforms obviously contain information about each other, as do sequential sentences.) Nevertheless, some kinds of dependences between sentences cannot be removed by the methods mentioned here and remain in the kernel. Such are for example dependences among loose and unspecifiable subclasses, e.g., the partitive adjectives of a particular noun: the occurrence of one of them in a kernel sentence tells us that a partly similar sentence with another partitive adjective of that noun also exists in the kernel.

[64]Both types of problems are discussed in detail and provided with a theoretical framework in N. Chomsky's dissertation, "Transformational Analysis."

Transformations can specify in general the differences and the similarities among sentences. Consider for example these four very similar sentences:

S_1 *Mary has a sad fate.*
S_2 *Mary's fate is sad.*
S_3 *Mary's fate is a sad one.*
S_4 *Mary's is a sad fate.*

These are transformed from some or all of three kernel sentences:

K_1 *Mary has a fate.*
K_2 *Fate is a fate.*
K_2 *Fate is sad.*

The following transformations are involved:

For S_1: K_3, overlap with K_1.
For S_2: K_1, *N has N* → *N's N*, overlap with K_3.
For S_3: K_1, *N has N* → *N's N*, overlap with K_2 (first *N*);
   K_2, pro-*N* of second *N*;
   K_3, overlap with K_2 (second *N*).
For S_4: K_1, *N has N* → *N's N*, overlap with K_2 (first *N*);
   K_2, zero recurrence of first *N*;
   K_3, overlap with K_2 (second *N*).

It is of interest to see that these sentences, which we would intuitively describe as semantically equivalent or almost equivalent, have the same kernel sentences—except that some of them lack K_2, which we would hardly expect to contribute a semantic change—and differ only in transformations.

Transformations often overcome structural restrictions of the kernel grammar. For example, the subject of a sentence is always present in English; but it can be dropped by transforming into the passive and then carrying out the drop transformation of Section 29.2[65] Or, a sentence *N v V*, without object or even *P N*, can be given the passive transformation by first applying a pro-*V*-phrase transformation (Section 29.1): *He stumbled unexpectedly, He did it unexpectedly, It was done by him unexpectedly.*

In many cases, transformations add flexibility in a direct way. They may change the grammatical status of a sentence into that of an *N*-phrase, thus making it possible to relate the sentence to an outside *N V* or *V N*, etc. They may bring out one part of the sentence for primary attention. And, of course, they yield stylistic variations.

36 Co-occurrence and transformation in structural theory. Important properties of linguistic structure are definable with respect to co-occurrence and transformations. Those constructional features of grammar which are well known from descriptive linguistics are in general limited to the kernel. In the kernel, the constructions are built up as concatenations of various included constructions, down to morpheme

---

[65]Such added flexibilities are often attained when a transformation gives the sentence the form of a different structure which has that flexibility, in this case the similarity between the passive and an *N V P N* sentence with omittable *P N*.

classes; various classes or sequences of classes (and their members) are substitutable for each other in particular positions of these constructions. Transformations cannot be viewed as a continuation of this constructional process. They are based on a new relation, which satisfies the conditions for being an equivalence relation and which does not occur in descriptive linguistics. All sentences which are described in constructional terms must have a specific constituent analysis, since the constructional analysis proceeds in terms of immediate constituents (component subconstructions). This is not necessary, however, for all sentences in transformational analysis. Some of the cruces in descriptive linguistics have been due to the search for a constituent analysis in sentence types where this does not exist because the sentences are transformationally derived from others. For this and other reasons a language cannot be fully described in purely constructional terms, without the transform relation.[66]

Some of the special operations on constructions which are set up in descriptive linguistics can be described in terms of transformations instead. For example, much of the expansion of constructions (e.g., $A N = N$, i.e., $A N$ is substitutable for N) is obtainable as a result of the sentence-overlapping transformations; this will be more general if the kernel constructions are subdivided into co-occurrence domains (Section 34, end). Transformations have partial similarity to certain elements and relations of descriptive linguistics. Most important of these is the similarity of transformations to variants, both free and positional. However, if A is to be a variant of B, A must be substitutable for B, or must have environments complementary to those of B, and the environments of A and B must be otherwise identical. These conditions cannot be explicitly met in the case of sentences because in descriptive linguistics environments are defined only up to sentence boundaries.

A major difference between the kernel and the rest of the language structure is that the individual co-occurrences among members of classes are in general contained within the kernel. The kinds of problems that are associated with this—for example the statistical determination of co-occurrents, the scaling of acceptance of co-occurrents, the differences among samples—all refer to the kernel. Between the kernel and the transformational structure it may be convenient to recognize a border area containing some of the types of quasi-transformations and productivity.

Finally, as has been mentioned, the kernel (including the list of combiners) is finite; all the unbounded possibilities of language are properties of the transformational operations. This is of interest because it is in general impossible to set up a reasonable grammar or description of a language that provides for its being finite. Although the sample of the language out of which the grammar is derived is of course finite, the grammar which is made to generate all the sentences of that sample will be found to generate also many other sentences, and unboundedly many sentences of unbounded length. If we were to insist on a finite language, we would have to include in our grammar several highly arbitrary and numerical conditions—saying, for example, that in a given position there are not more than three occurrences of *and* between N. Since a grammar therefore cannot help generating an unbounded language, it is desirable to have the features which yield this unboundedness separate from the rest of the grammar.

---

[66]This has been shown by Chomsky in the references given in 1*n*.

Our picture of a language, then, includes a finite number of actual kernel sentences, all cast in a small number of sentence structures built out of a few morpheme classes by means of a few constructional rules; a set of combining and introducing elements; and a set of elementary transformations, such that one or more transformations may be applied to any kernel sentence or any sequence of kernel sentences, and such that any properly transformed sentences may be added sequentially by means of the combiners.

The network of individual co-occurrence in language can provide more analysis of linguistic structure than is involved in transformations alone. The co-occurrences can provide us with a relation in language with respect to which we can discover a system of algebraic structures and algebraic relations in language. The central method here is to set up for each construction of two or more classes C_1, C_2, ... a correspondence which associates with each member of C_1 those members of C_2 that occur with it in that construction, and so on. The mappings differ for different constructions; several of them are many-valued, and the individual associations vary for different samples. It turns out, however, that permanent structures can be permanently characterized by particular types of mappings. The different structures so distinguished turn out to be significantly different in the economy of the language.

37 Applications. Transformations are applicable in various studies or utilizations of systems of a generally linguistic type. There are specific applications, for example, in linguistic typology—comparison of different types of language structure.[67]

The chief outside uses of transformations, however, depend upon their special meaning status. Meaning is a matter of evaluation and cannot be fitted directly into the type of science that is developed in structural linguistics or in transformation theory. Still, for various purposes it may be possible to set up some practical evaluation of meaning; and with respect to most of these evaluations, transformations will have a special status. That many sentences which are transforms of each other have more or less the same meaning, except for different external grammatical status (different grammatical relations to surrounding sentence elements), is an immediate impression. This is not surprising, since meaning correlates closely with range of occurrence, and transformations maintain the same occurrence range. When we have transformations which are associated with a meaning change, it is usually possible to attribute the meaning change to the special morphemes (combiners, introducers, subclasses of the primary V) in whose environment the transformation occurs. To what extent, and in what sense, transformations hold meaning constant is a matter for investigation; but enough is known to make transformations a possible tool for reducing the complexity of sentences under semantically controlled conditions.

It is possible to normalize any sequence of sentences by reducing each one to its kernels and their transformations. The text then becomes longer, but its component

---

[67]There are also possible applications in translation, for many languages are more similar in their kernel sentences than in their total structure (the transformations, and especially the details of the transformations, being more different). Translational equivalences can be established for the kernel combinations of words, and if necessary even for the elementary transformations as such. There is also some reason to think that the kernels may function differently in memory and thought from the transformations.

sentences are simpler, as is the kernel grammar according to which they are written. The kernel sentences are then available for comparison or arrangement, both within the discourse and as among discourses, in a way that the original sentences were not. Transformations can be checked by comparing the textual environments of a sentence and its transform, to see whether, say, a given $N \ V \ N$ triple which occurs in a given environment of other sentences will also occur in the same environment when it is transformed to the passive. Methods of this kind can be used to make various quasi-transformations acceptable as transformations in a given discourse, or to make one-directional transformations useable in both directions.

Transformations are much needed in discourse analysis; for though the method of discourse analysis is independent of them, the complexity of many sentences makes discourse analysis hardly applicable unless the text has first been normalized by transformations. For discourse analysis it is often not necessary to reduce sentences to their kernels, but only to transform those sentences and sections which contain the same words in such a way that they have the same structure, if this is possible.

7   A Transformational Approach to Syntax[*]

Noam Chomsky

I

The approach to syntax that I want to discuss here developed directly out of the attempts of Z. S. Harris to extend methods of linguistic analysis to the analysis of the structure of discourse.[1] This research brought to light a serious inadequacy of modern linguistic theory, namely, its inability to account for such systematic relations between sentences as the active-passive relation. There had been no attempt in modern linguistics to reconstruct more precisely this chapter of traditional grammar,[2] partly, perhaps, because it was thought that these relations were of a purely semantic character, hence outside the concern of formal, structural linguistics. This view was challenged by Harris, who has since devoted a good deal of research to showing that distributional methods of linguistic analysis[3] can be broadened and developed in such a way as to include, in a rather natural manner, the study of formal relations between sentences, and that this extension yields much additional insight into lin-

---

[*]N. Chomsky, "A Transformational Approach to Syntax," in A. A. Hill (ed.), *Proceedings of the Third Texas Conference on Problems of Linguistic Analysis in English, 1958* (Austin, Texas: The University of Texas, 1962), pp. 124–58. Reprinted by permission.

[1]Cf. Z. S. Harris, "Discourse Analysis" and "Discourse Analysis: a Sample Text," *Language*, **28** (1952), 18–23, 474–94.

[2]As for example, IC-analysis can be thought of as an attempt to make more rigorous the traditional notion of parsing. Transformational ideas are, of course, an important part of traditional grammar. E.g., O. Jespersen argues, on what we will reconstruct as transformational grounds, that "the doctor's arrival" is different in structure from "the man's house," despite superficial similarity, because of its relation to the sentence "the doctor arrives." This observation, which, I think, is entirely correct is criticized by E. A. Nida (*A Synopsis of English Syntax*, 1951, p. 143) as a "serious distortion and complication of the formal and functional values" (p. 10). Jespersen's remark that *barking* in "the barking dog" and *barks* in "the dog barks" are attributives of the same rank, again, I think, basically a correct observation (cf. Transformation 18a) is criticized on similar grounds.

[3]As exemplified, e.g., in his *Methods in Structural Linguistics* (Chicago: University of Chicago Press, 1951).

guistic structure.[4] The development of these ideas that I would like to report on briefly, however, follows a somewhat different course. It begins by questioning the adequacy of a certain view of the nature of linguistic theory that has dominated much recent work, and it attempts to reformulate the goals of linguistic theory in such a way that questions of a rather different nature are raised. And finally, it attempts to show that the concept of grammatical transformation, in something like Harris' sense, but with certain differences, is essential to answering these questions.

The central methodological concern in recent American linguistics has been the precise definition of such notions as Phoneme, Morpheme, and Immediate Constituent. Almost without exception,[5] phonemes have been thought of in relatively substantial terms as (in one formulation) certain classes of sounds, while morphemes are taken to be certain classes of sequences of phonemes, and constituents, certain classes of sequences of morphemes. The methodological problem for linguistic theory, then, has been to provide the general criteria for making these classifications, and the goal of the linguistic analysis of a particular language has been to isolate and list the particular classes, sequences, sequences of classes, etc., which are the phonemes, morphemes, constituents of these languages. A linguistic grammar of a particular language, in this view, is an inventory of elements, and linguistics is thought of as a classificatory science.

Furthermore, almost every approach to linguistic theory has attempted to formulate these definitions in such a way as to provide an essentially mechanical method that an investigator might use, in principle, to isolate the phonemes, morphemes and constituents in the analysis of a particular language. This interest in a discovery procedure for linguistic elements has motivated the insistence on strict separation of levels, bi-uniqueness of phonemic transcription (often with the additional and stronger requirement that if one occurrence of a physical event is assigned to a particular phoneme on one occasion, then every occurrence of that event must be assigned to the same phoneme — I will refer to this below as the strong form of the bi-uniqueness principle), phonemic identifiability of morphemes, and many other widely held doctrines.[6]

Neither the conception of a grammar as an inventory of elements nor the requirement that there be a discovery procedure for elements of the inventory is very easy to justify. A grammar of a language should at least be expected to offer a characterization of the set of objects that are sentences of this language, i.e., to enable its user to construct a list or enumeration of these utterances. It is not at all clear how an inventory of elements provides this information (just as it is not clear what the user of a traditional grammar brings to its paradigms and examples that enable him to produce new sentences and reject non-sentences). And as soon as we attempt to give a rigorous account of the process by which a grammar generates sentences, a variety of new

---

[4]For a recent and comprehensive report on this research, see Z. S. Harris, "Co-occurrence and Transformation in Linguistic Structure," *Language,* 33 (1957), pp. 283–340. Reprinted in this volume pp. 155–210.

[5]See however, Hockett, *Manual of Phonology,* pp. 14–5.

[6]I do not here raise the question whether ability to meet these requirements is a necessary condition for the existence of a discovery procedure. I think in fact it is not. I only mean to point out that these requirements are at least natural ones, if not necessary ones, for a linguistic theory whose immediate aim is to provide a discovery procedure for grammars.

considerations come to the fore. We find that some of the requirements that have been imposed on linguistic elements (e.g., the bi-uniqueness condition for phonemes) lead to extensive and unnecessary complication of the grammar, that certain others (e.g., the requirement of phonemic identifiability of morphemes) become entirely superfluous, while others (e.g., strict separation of levels) become almost unstatable. We find that there is strong reason to allow considerations of the form in which grammars are given and considerations of complexity of grammar to be basic factors in the selection of a set of phonemes, morphemes, etc., in analysis of a particular language. Consequently, we are led to abandon the attempt to define such terms as "phoneme," "morpheme" in general linguistic theory with no reference to the grammars in which these terms will appear. And introduction of systematic considerations of complexity of grammar into the definition of such basic notions as "phoneme" is quite incompatible with the requirement that there be a discovery procedure for linguistic elements, at least of the direct and straightforward kind usually contemplated. In other words, I think that the failure to offer a precise account of the notion "grammar" is not just a superficial defect in linguistic theory that can be remedied by adding one more definition. It seems to me that until this notion is clarified, no part of linguistic theory can achieve anything like a satisfactory development. I cannot hope to give a very convincing justification of this view in a review article of this nature,[7] but I will nevertheless try to indicate briefly, in the course of the discussion, why I think it is justified.

II

Suppose that we begin with the conception of grammar as a collection of inventories of elements,[8] certain classes of events called phonemes, classes of sequences of phonemes called morphemes, classes of sequences of morphemes called constituents, etc. Since there is no bound on the number of sentences in a language (we cannot point to the longest sentence of English), these lists must contain as *members* objects which themselves are analyzable into elements of the original list. We would like to state precisely how these lists can be used to formulate an indefinite number of sentences in the language. One of the *highest level* lists will say something about the *largest* constituents of a sentence—e.g., it may say that a sentence consists of an *NP* (noun phrase) and a *VP* (verb phrase). We can express this assertion in the notation:

$$\text{Sentence} \rightarrow NP + VP \text{ (where } \rightarrow \text{ means } rewrite\ as\text{)} \tag{1}$$

Another list may contain the information that the constituents of an *NP* may be *that* and another sentence ("that the man came—was unfortunate"), an article and

---

[7]For more elaborate presentation of this position, see my *Syntactic Structures*, chapter 6; Lees, "Review of *Syntactic Structures*," *Language*, 1957, pp. 378–82; Halle, *The Sound Pattern of Russian* (The Hague, 1959).

[8]Cf., e.g., Harris, *Methods*, Appendix to 20.3. This is one of the few attempts to formulate the properties of a grammar. A different sort of formulation has been suggested by Hockett (*Manual*, 021). We return to this below (10n), showing that it is a special case of a formalized version of Harris' formulation.

a noun (*the man*), *to* and a verb phrase ("to err is human"), and so on. We can express this information in the form:

$$NP \rightarrow \text{that} + Sentence \tag{2}$$
$$NP \rightarrow to + VP \tag{3}$$
$$NP \rightarrow T + N \text{ (Here } T \text{ means article)} \tag{4}$$

and so on. We can express similarly all other information about IC (Immediate Constituent) structure, at least insofar as constituents are continuous. This will give us a finite set of rules of the form $X \rightarrow Y$. Suppose we interpret each of these rules as the instruction "rewrite X as Y." We can now construct such derivations as the following:

$$\text{(5)}$$

1. *Sentence*
2. *NP   VP*   (formed by applying Eq. (1) to line 1)
3. *that Sentence VP*   (formed by applying Eq. (2) to line 2)
4. *that NP VP VP*   (formed by applying Eq. (1) to line 3)
5. *that T N VP VP*   (formed by applying Eq. (4) to line 4)

Continuing the derivation, applying rules of a similar nature, we might ultimately arrive at the sequence of morphemes that represents the sentence:

$$\text{that the man came was unfortunate} \tag{6}$$

Clearly we can associate with such a derivation a diagram in the form of a tree which will graphically describe what we can call the *phrase structure* of this utterance. In the case just outlined it might look something like this:

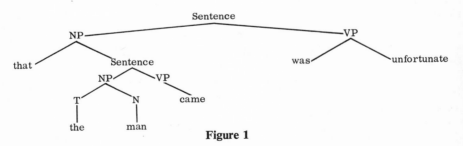

Figure 1

Given this diagram, uniquely constructible from the derivation,[9] we can determine mechanically whether a given sequence of morphemes in the final line of the derivation is a phrase (we ask, is it traceable back to a single node, as, e.g., *the man* is an *NP* since this is the label on the node to which it is traced, *was unfortunate* is a *VP*, and so on). It is evident that a finite number of rules of this type may enable us to generate an infinite number of derivations, because of the recursive character of such pairs of rules as in Eqs. (1) and (2). We can thus reformulate the grammar of lists so

---

[9] Actually the diagram may not be uniquely constructible unless certain additional conditions are placed on the rules $X \rightarrow Y$, but I will not go into this here. For a more precise formulation of the notions discussed here, see Chomsky, "Three Models for the Description of Language," *I.R.E. Transactions on Information Theory*, Vol. IT-2 (1956).

as to give a precise characterization of a certain class of sequences of morphemes (i.e., those for which there are derivations), and furthermore, we can extract mechanically from the derivation of a particular sentence a structural description of this sentence (a diagram such as (Fig. 1) interpreted in the manner given above).[10]

A grammar conceived as an inventory of elements must, of course, be supplemented by a list of *selectional rules* stating which members of co-occurring constructions can actually co-occur in a single sentence. Thus, the construction $V + Particle$ will be listed as a possible transitive verb, but further rules must be given to indicate which verb goes with which Particle. We can incorporate these restrictions in the grammar by allowing the term X in the rewriting rules $X \to Y$ to stand for a string of elements. A rule $ABC \to ADEFC$, for example, states in effect that B is rewritten DEF in the context $A - C$.[11] In converting the inventory to a grammar, then, we might have such rules as:

$$V_t \to V + Prt \tag{7a}$$
$$V \to look \tag{7b}$$
$$look + Prt \to look + up, \text{ i.e., } Prt \to up, \text{ but not } in, \text{ in the context } look\text{——} \tag{7c}$$

III

So far we have done nothing more than modify Harris' "Morpheme to Utterance" procedures (generalized to account for selection, in accordance with his intentions, in fact[12] showing how these ideas can provide us with a grammar which generates the sentences of the language in a uniform way, with a structural description automatically provided for each generated utterance. This modification, however, suggests a shift of interest that leads to some essential re-interpretation of the basic notions of constituent analysis. We now regard the goal of the linguistic analysis of a particular

---

[10]Consider now Hockett's theory of grammar (see 8*n*). This is an adaptation of Shannon's model of an information source. He discusses a device with a finite number of states $S_o, \ldots, S_q$, with transition between certain states permitted and morphemes produced with each transition. In our terms, such a device can be completely represented by a set of rules "$X \to Y$," where X is one of the symbols $S_o, \ldots, S_q$, and Y is of the form $A + B$, where B is again one of $S_o, \ldots, S_q$, and A is the morpheme emitted with transition from X to B. Hence, Hockett's model is a special case of what we have discussed. This restriction on the form of rules is essential, in the sense that it limits the set of languages that can be generated. It is, furthermore, too strong a restriction, since it can be shown that English, in particular, cannot be generated if it is met (cf. Chomsky, "Three Models for the Description of Language," *op. cit.*)

Hockett modifies this picture by assigning probabilities to the particular rules. However, this is an irrelevant complication. It seems clear that probabilistic considerations have nothing to do with grammar, e.g., surely it is not a matter of concern for the grammar of English that "New York" is more probable than "Nevada" in the context "I come from —." In general, the importance of probabilistic considerations seems to me to have been highly overrated in recent discussions of linguistic theory.

[11]It is essential that we require that only a single symbol be rewritten in converting X to Y. Otherwise, it will not be possible to reconstruct a tree such as Fig. 1 from the derivation. It is worth mentioning that the mathematical study of the various restrictions on grammars that have been mentioned gives rather interesting results and may eventually lead to important insight into linguistic structure.

[12]Harris, *Methods in Structural Linguistics*, Chap. 16, 77*n*.

language (on the IC-level) as the formulation of a set of rules of the form $X \rightarrow Y$, such that each sentence (and no nonsentence) has a derivation from *Sentence* in terms of these rules, and such that a structural description of the generated sentences (i.e., a tree such as in Fig. 1) is uniquely constructible from the derivation. We are not at the moment concerned with the question how the rules are discovered; we do not, for example, require that they be arrived at by some sort of substitution procedure, or by study of suprasegmental features, inflections, and so on[13]

Motivated now by the goal of constructing a grammar, instead of a rule of procedure for constructing an inventory of elements, we no longer have any reason to consider the symbols *NP*, *Sentence*, *VP*, and so forth, that appear in these rules to be names of certain classes, sequences, or sequences of classes, and so on, of concrete elements. They are simply elements in a system of representation which has been constructed so as to enable us to characterize effectively the set of English sentences in a linguistically meaningful way. We can thus avoid an enormous proliferation of classes and sequences. We must now, however, ask the question how the elements in this abstract system represent utterances, e.g., how the diagram (Fig. 1) is related to a specific physical event, or, let us say, to the phonetic representation of a physical event. We no longer require that the relation between the phonetic representation and the elements of the phrase structure representation be some elaboration of the relation of membership, as in the classificatory approach to linguistic description. The added flexibility obtained by dropping this rather *ad hoc* restriction[14] can be used to great advantage. This can be seen most clearly in the case of discontinuous elements, which have never been handled really successfully in the classificatory approach. To take one simple case, consider *NP*'s of the form *to + VP* (as in Eq. (3)). Notice first that this division gives the correct IC-analysis of these phrases. If we were, alternatively, to regard the main break in such phrases as *to keep the soldiers under control, to arrive at these results,*" (phrases which might occur in "—wasn't easy") as occurring between *keep* and *the, arrive* and *at* (or perhaps, *at* and *these*), we would be forced to give elaborate selectional rules for these *NP*'s to determine which IC's of the form *to + V* co-occur with which following objects, complements, and so on. These rules would be just a more complex version of certain selectional rules which must be given independently for the IC-analysis of the *VP*. This pointless elaboration of the grammatical description is avoided if these *NP*'s are analyzed as in Eq. (3), where the selectional relations are a matter internal to the *VP*, handled by the same rule that is used to develop ordinary *VP*'s.

---

[13]It should be emphasized that we are not simply dropping from consideration a condition that can easily be met. In fact, no known general formulation of such procedures leads to what every linguist would regard as the correct IC-analysis in the case of English, or, as far as I know, any other language. The word *general* is important here. It is, of course possible, in fact trivial, to find numerous purely formal procedures and criteria which will lead to any desired result in the analysis of a particular language. Cf. Lees, *op. cit.*, pp. 392–93. We shall return in Section X to the question how a particular formulation of the grammar is to be justified, if not by showing that it arises from the data by discovery procedures.

[14]From our point of view the restriction is *ad hoc* and arbitrary, but if the aim is a discovery procedure for linguistic elements, then simple substitution procedures are not unmotivated devices (cf. 6n). The deeper question is whether it is proper to allow the form of the theory of linguistic structure to be determined by our hope that there will be a simple discovery procedure for linguistic elements.

For exactly the same reasons, in such *NP*'s as *keeping the soldiers under control, arriving at these results*, the main IC-division should separate *ing* from the *VP*. In general, there is a very far-reaching (although not complete) parallel between *ing* and *to* in English. We can exploit this parallel, simplifying the grammar in consequence, by adding alongside of Eq. (3) the rule:

$$NP \rightarrow ing + VP \tag{8}$$

The *NP*'s *to keep the soldiers under control* and *keeping the soldiers under control* will now be represented on the phrase structure level by structural descriptions (i.e., trees such as in Fig. 1) terminating in the sequences:

$$\text{to keep the soldiers under control} \tag{9a}$$
$$\text{ing keep the soldiers under control} \tag{9b}$$

where in both cases, "keep . . . control" is traceable back to a node labeled *VP*. Equation (9a) is related to phonetic representation by a direct and simple (order-preserving) representation relation. Equation (9b) is related to phonetic representation less directly by a rule which asserts that:

$$\text{\textit{ing} followed by any } V \text{ represents the utterance consisting of this } V \atop \text{followed by \textit{ing} followed by word boundary} \tag{10}$$

We find that this rule is a special case of a more general regularity. Somewhere in the phrase-structure grammar there must be a specification of the set of elements that can appear in the context "the man—the book," i.e., the morpheme sequences *take, took, has taken, will take, is taking, may have been taking*, and so on. That is, there may be rules of the form

$$Verb \rightarrow \cdots \tag{11}$$

where . . . is a specification of these forms. If we insist on maintaining continuous constituents, having IC-analysis preserve word boundary or meeting the requirement that phrase structure representation be based on the membership relation and be determined by substitution procedures and the like, we will be compelled to give in place of . . . in Eq. (11) a rather elaborate list. There is, however, a much simpler characterization of . . . as a sequence of independently chosen elements. We give, in place of Eq. (11), the rules:

$$Verb \rightarrow Aux + V \tag{12a}$$
$$Aux \rightarrow C(M) \quad (have + en) \quad (be + ing) \tag{12b}$$
$$M \rightarrow can, will, may, shall, must \tag{12c}$$
$$C \rightarrow past, present \tag{12d}$$

where elements parenthesized may or may not be chosen in applying the instruction "rewrite X as Y." The sentence:

$$\text{John had been taking the book} \tag{13}$$

will now be represented by a tree terminating in the sequence of morphemes:

$$\textit{John past have en be ing take the book} \tag{14}$$

The relation of representation holding between Eq. (14) and the phonetic transcription of Eq. (13) will again be indirect and can be stated by the following rule:

> any sequence *affix* + *v* represents the sequence
> *v* + *affix* + *word boundary*, where *v* is any of *M, be, have,*   (15)
> or any *V*

Equation (10) is now eliminated as a special case of Eq. (15). The rule in Eq. (15) tells us that Eq. (14) represents the sequence of morphemes:

$$\textit{John have past} \ \sharp \ \textit{be en} \ \sharp \ \textit{take ing} \ \sharp \ \textit{the book} \tag{16}$$

($\sharp$ represents word boundary) which itself represents Eq. (13) by a direct representation relation.

The case for indirect representation, not based on the relation of membership, becomes even stronger when we consider such sentences as "did they see John" or "whom did they see." These are sentences that no linguist would ever consider as the starting point for application of techniques of IC-analysis—i.e., no one would ask how they can be subdivided into two or three parts, each of which has several constituents, going on to use this subdivision as the basis for analysis of other sentences, and so on. Yet there is nothing in the formulation of principles of procedure for IC-analysis that justifies excluding these sentences, or treating them somehow in terms of sentences already analyzed. To any speaker of English, it is evident that in the sentence "whom did they see," *they* is the subject, *did . . . see* is the past tense of *see*, and *whom* stands in place of the object. That is, this sentence is represented, in an extremely indirect way, by a tree terminating in the sequence:

$$\textit{they past see him,} \tag{17}$$

or something of this sort. Clearly any theory of language that makes it impossible in principle to discover this fact cannot be considered adequate. We will see below that the rules of representation that lead from Eq. (17) to such sentences as "did they see John" and "whom did they see" are, like Eq. (15), both reasonably simple and of considerable generality, although indirect and not based on membership, and hence apparently not compatible with the conception of grammar as an inventory. It is these rules that we will interpret as transformations.

We have seen that an inventory of constructions can be modified and converted into a grammar that generates utterances with structural descriptions, but that when we do this many of the conditions placed on elements of the inventory seem unmotivated and overly restrictive. In fact, it seems rather pointless to think of the grammar as derived from the inventory at all. We can avoid many complex and rather artificial problems altogether by reconstruing the goal of linguistic analysis as the construction of a grammar of a fixed form (in our case, with rules $X \rightarrow Y$, where only a single symbol of X is rewritten (cf. 11*n*) with rules of representation of a type that we have not yet specified) which enumerates all and only the sentences of the language. Instead of the grammar being essentially a list of the elements (and classes, sequences, and so on, of these) discovered by procedures of analysis, it is the grammar itself that is the primary end of linguistic analysis, and the constructions, phrases, and so forth, of the language under analysis are those provided by the structural descriptions (in our case, trees such as Fig. 1) that are the by-products of the generation of sentences by the grammar.

IV

Although this paper is primarily concerned with syntax, I think it is worth mentioning that we arrive at very similar conclusions when we consider *lower* levels of grammatical description. When we consider the rules of representation that relate (e.g., Eq. (16)) with a phonetic transcription, we find that these too can be given as rewriting rules of the form $X \rightarrow Y$.[15] For example, we can convert Eq. (16) to a phonetic transcription by such rules as:

$$
\begin{aligned}
have + past &\rightarrow h\mathit{æ}d \\
be \ \ \ + en &\rightarrow \ \ bin \\
take + ing &\rightarrow teyki\eta
\end{aligned}
\tag{18}
$$

Evidently, in such rules as Eqs. (12b–c) (and more generally, in all the phrase structure rules where specific morphemes are introduced, in particular, those phrase structure rules which correspond to the lexicon) it is absurd to represent the specific morphemes introduced in conventional orthography. We would, rather, enter these morphemes in some morphophonemic transcription which lends itself to generalizations and simplifications in the rules of Eq. (18), and so on. The question how to enter these morphemes into the grammar has been extensively studied by Morris Halle,[16] who has shown that many of the conditions conventionally placed on phonemic analysis are not only unmotivated, from this point of view, but lead to considerable and unnecessary complication of the grammar. Suppose, for example, that we have an *asymmetrical* phonemic system such as that of Russian, where /t/ has its voiced counterpart /d/, but /č/ does not have (phonemically) a voiced counterpart /y/, and where there is, furthermore, a rule requiring that consonant clusters be uniformly voiced or unvoiced. In the lexicon, we will have morphemes listed:

$$
\begin{aligned}
&d'at, \\
&\check{z}'e\check{c} \\
&l,i \\
&bi
\end{aligned}
\tag{19}
$$

and the syntactic rules will give derivations of lines which contain as subsequences:

$$
\begin{aligned}
&d'at, \ l,i \\
&d'at, \ bi \\
&\check{z}'e\check{c} \ l,i \\
&\check{z}'e\check{c} \ bi
\end{aligned}
\tag{20}
$$

---

[15]But note that we need not retain the restriction that only a single symbol be rewritten, since there is no linguistic meaning to trees on this level. There is also no recursiveness in the rules on this level.

[16]In *Sound Pattern of Russian.*

In place of the rules Eq. (18) we will have rules including the stipulation that:

obstruents become voiced in the context — + voiced obstruent   (21)

This rule will convert the representations of Eq. (20) into:

$$\begin{array}{l} \text{d'at, l,i} \\ \text{d'ad, bi} \\ \text{ž'eč l,i} \\ \text{ž'eǰ bi} \end{array} \qquad (22)$$

In the generation of utterances, the only representations that will appear are Eq. (20) at one level, and Eq. (22) at the next level, after application of Eq. (21). Utterances will never be represented in the *mixed* form:

$$\begin{array}{l} \text{d'at, li} \\ \text{d'ad, bi} \\ \text{ž'eč l,i} \\ \text{ž'eč bi} \end{array} \qquad (23)$$

In order to introduce a level or representation of the form (23) into the grammar, it would be necessary to arbitrarily split Eq. (21) into the two rules:

all obstruents except c, c, x become voiced in the context — + voiced obstruent (here and elsewhere + is to be read as a symbol for concatenation, not *open juncture.*)   (24a)

c, c, x become voiced in the context — + voiced obstruent   (24b)

Equation (24a) would now be considered a morphophonemic rule, converting Eq. (20) to Eq. (23), and Eq. (24b) a phonetic rule that converts Eq. (23) to Eq. (22). It is clear that this complication of the grammar is entirely pointless. But it is just this that is required by the widely accepted strong form of the biuniqueness principle (cf. Section I), since Eq. (23) would, in accordance with this principle, be regarded as the proper phonemic transcription of these utterances. This is a highly convincing example, I believe, of a phonemic parallel to the point made above with reference to syntax.[17] On the phonemic level, too, it seems that the view of a grammar as an inventory of elements can be profitably replaced by the conception of a grammar as a device of a specified form (on this level, the specification will be in terms of certain conditions on phonemic representation—see Halle's *Sound Pattern of Russian* for discussion) which characterizes the utterances of the language. Instead of viewing the phonological section of the grammar as an inventory of phonemes, constructed by procedures of analysis based on such rather arbitrary principles as biuniqueness we can construct the simplest possible grammar of the appropriate form and consider the phonemes of this language to be the elements that appear in the representation of utterances on the appropriate level in this grammar.

The familiar requirement of phonemic identifiability of morphemes is as pointless, in this framework, as the requirement of biuniqueness for phonemic descriptions.

---

[17]This situation is not peculiar to Russian.

In fact, just like the biuniqueness requirement, it serves only to introduce unmotivated (cf 6*n* and 14*n*) complication into the grammar. The question which part of the word /tuk/ is the past tense morpheme (i.e., is it the /u/, or a replacive {ey → u}, or a zero morpheme that determines a special allomorph of /teyk/, and so on) simply does not arise. In constructing representation rules of the form of Eq. (18) which determine, ultimately, the phonemic form of the sequences (such as Eq. (16)) generated by the phrase structure grammar, we will, of course, include such rules as:

$$teyk + past \;\rightarrow\; tuk$$
$$breyk + past \rightarrow browk \tag{25}$$
$$past \qquad\quad\; \rightarrow d$$

and somewhere further on in the grammar we will have phonetic rules such as:[18]

ɫ is introduced in the context: alveolar stop + — + alveolar stop + ♯   (26a)

voiced → voiceless in the context: voiceless + — + ♯   (26b)

These rules will provide the correct phonetic representation of the sequences of the form $V + past$ generated in the phrase structure grammar (notice that order is essential in both Eqs. 25 and 26). Our concern is only to present these rules of representation in the simplest and most general way, using the devices made available by our linguistic theory. The problem of *finding* the morpheme *past* in the phonetic representation has no clear meaning. It is much like the pseudo-problem of locating what we will call the transformation *Interrogative* in the phonetic representation of "whom did they see."

V

To return to the main theme of this paper, we see that a phrase structure grammar with rules of the form $XAY \rightarrow XZY$ (where A is a single symbol, and X, Y, Z are of arbitrary length, X, Y perhaps null) can convey much information concerning constituent structure, if we allow the representation relation that associates a structural IC-description such as Fig. 1 with a phonetic transcription to be an indirect one, not based on membership. We have also seen that in part, at least, we can also describe this representation relation by rewriting rules of the form $X \rightarrow Y$ (with no restrictions on X, Y), e.g., Eqs. (18), (25), and (26). Can we then regard a grammar as a set (perhaps partially ordered) of rules of the form $X \rightarrow Y$? I have argued elsewhere[19] that the cost of limiting the rules in this way is exorbitant. Although there apparently is a class of sentences in English that can be described appropriately in essentially this manner, if we attempt to extend the description to cover all sentences, we find inordinate complexity, inability to state many real generalizations and regularities or to account for many facts about English structure which are intuitively obvious to

---

[18]I do not attempt to give these here in the most general form. Clearly all these rules can be generalized.

[19]Cf. Chomsky, *Syntactic Structures*, Chap. 5; also Lees, *op. cit.*, pp. 385–88.

any native speaker.[20] A great many of these difficulties can be eliminated if we extend our concept of linguistic structure to include a new level of transformational analysis, corresponding to grammatical rules of an essentially different kind. A transformational rule will operate on a string of symbols *with* a particular structural description (a tree such as Fig. 1) and will convert it into a new string of symbols with a new structural description.[21] For example, one such transformation will convert any active sentence into a corresponding passive sentence. A transformational rule can be characterized by a description of the kind of *tree* to which it applies, and a description of the change (re-ordering, addition or deletion of elements, re-assignment of constituent boundaries, and so on) which it effects. Thus, the passive transformation applies to any sentence which is assigned, by its phrase structure derivation, the analysis of Eq. (27a), and it transforms the sentence analyzed in this way in the manner described in Eq. (27b):

$$NP, \; Aux, \; V, \; NP \tag{27a}$$

$$X_1 - X_2 - X_3 - X_4 \text{ is transformed to}$$
$$X_4 - X_2 - be + en + X_3 - by + X_1 \tag{27b}$$

$$John - past - see - Bill \tag{27c}$$

$$Bill - past - be + en + see - by + John \tag{27d}$$

For example, Eq. (27c) (which is analyzed in accordance with Eq. (27a)) will be converted by Eq. (27b) into Eq. (27d). Equation (27d) will then be converted by Eq. (15), Eq. (18), and so on into "Bill was seen by John." Equation (27c), had this transformation not been applied to it, would have been converted by Eq. (16), (19), and so on into "John saw Bill."

With transformational devices available, we can enormously simplify the grammar by limiting direct phrase structure generation to that small set of strings for which it operates smoothly, deriving all other sentences by transformation of strings so derived.

When we actually go about constructing a grammar for English, using both the phrase structure and transformational levels of description, we find that the rule of Eq. (15), which properly orders stems and affixes, is also best formulated in transformational terms.[22] Equations (15) and (27) are, however, transformations of

---

[20]Is it intrinsically impossible to describe English solely in terms of these devices, as it is demonstrably impossible in terms of the more limited type of rule discussed in 10*n*? This is an interesting theoretical question that is not easy to answer, because the mathematical structure of phrase structure grammar is not yet well understood and not easy to study. See Postal, "Limitations of Phrase Structure Grammars," this volume, pp. 137–151.

[21]Cf. Chomsky, "Three Models for the Description of Language," *op. cit.*, for a precise characterization of such transformations, but without specification of the structural description of the resulting string. In Chomsky's *Syntactic Structures*, a less formal version of this is presented with some hints as to "derived constituent structure" of the resulting string. The question of derived constituent structure is one of the many problems about transformations that have not been adequately treated. Cf. Lees, *op. cit.*, pp. 400–401. For a detailed, but by no means wholly satisfactory study of this, see my *Logical Structure of Linguistic Theory*, chapter VIII (1955, unpublished), see also my "On the Notion 'Rule of Grammar'," this volume, pp. 119–136; Matthews, *Hidatsa Syntax;* Postal, *Some Syntactic Rules in Mohawk* (Yale Univ. Dissertation, 1962), p. 140. We discuss this briefly in Section VIII.

[22]That the same is true of much, perhaps all, of inflectional and derivational morphology has been argued in Halle, *op. cit.*

very different kinds. Equation (27), as we have just seen, may or may not be applied in constructing a derivation—either way the result is a sentence. Such a rule will be called *optional*. Equation (15), however, is *obligatory*. If it is not applied, the result is not a sentence at all. We can now introduce the following terminology for grammars with both phrase structure and transformational levels. The last line of a phrase structure derivation (e.g., Eqs. (14) and (27c)) will be called a *terminal string*. A sentence of the language formed by applying to a terminal string only obligatory rules (i.e., obligatory transformations such as Eq. (15) and rules such as those of Eqs. (18), (25), and (26)) will be called a *kernel* sentence.[23] A sentence of the language formed by applying certain optional transformations, as well as all obligatory rules, of course, will be called a *derived sentence*.

VI

In constructing a grammar for a particular language, one of the decisions to be made concerning each class of sentence is whether to consider them to be kernel or derived sentences. I know of no general mechanical procedure for arriving at the answer to this question, just as I am unacquainted with any *general* (cf. 14*n*) mechanical procedure for arriving at a phonemic, morphological, or constituent analysis for the sentences of a language. To answer all of these questions, we must apparently do what any scientist does when faced with the task of constructing a theory to account for particular subject matter—namely, try various ways and choose the simplest that can be found. In studying English structure, I have found that in each case I have investigated, there are quite compelling reasons that lead one to assign particular sentences to the kernel or to derive them transformationally. Whether this will always be the case (i.e., whether there is a unique kernel for each language) is a matter for further empirical study of natural language and theoretical study of criteria of simplicity to permit a choice among proposed grammars (theories of these languages). I think that the question of uniqueness of phonemic, morphological, and constituent analysis has precisely the same status.

I have been discussing a grammar of a particular language here as analogous to a particular scientific theory, dealing with its subject matter (the set of sentences of this language) much as embryology or physics deals with its subject matter. I think that this view is justified. A grammar of L seeks to formulate laws (grammatical rules) in terms of theoretical constructs (particular transformations, phonemes, and so on) which govern the construction of sentences, i.e., which, in particular, correctly predict which physical events are and are not sentences acceptable to the native speaker, whether they have been observed or not. A difference between linguistics and embryology, however, is that the linguist will in general be concerned not only with the theory of English, for example, but also with the general theory of linguistic structure, with the formulation of the general properties of grammars. Just as a grammar of L can be regarded as, in part, a definition of the notion *sentence in L*, a general

---

[23]This term, like *grammatical transformation* itself, is Harris'. It is, like *transformation*, being used here in a sense somewhat different from his and in a different general framework.

theory of linguistic structure can be viewed as a partial definition of the notion *language*. These two interests (in the general theory, in particular grammars) cannot be developed in isolation from one another. Progress in each leads to deeper understanding of the other, and a real understanding of each is contingent on corresponding insight into the other. This paper has so far been primarily concerned with questions in the general theory of linguistic structure. We will now formulate briefly a small segment of English grammar, using the levels of analysis and corresponding grammatical devices described above.

VII

As a fragment of the phrase structure grammar for English we will consider the following sequences of rules:[24]

1. *Sentence* $\rightarrow NP + VP \ (Adv)$ $\hspace{4cm}$ (1–25, Eq. 28)

2. $VP \rightarrow Aux \left\{ \begin{array}{l} be \ \left\{ \begin{array}{l} Pred \\ Adv_1 \end{array} \right\} \\ VP_1 \end{array} \right\}$

3. $VP_1 \rightarrow V(\left\{ \begin{array}{l} NP \\ Pred \end{array} \right\})$

4. $V \rightarrow \left\{ \begin{array}{l} \left\{ \begin{array}{l} V_s \\ become \end{array} \right\} \text{in env.} - Pred \\ V_t \text{ in env.} - NP \\ V_i \text{ in env.} - \left\{ \begin{array}{l} \# \\ Adv \end{array} \right\} \end{array} \right\}$

5. $Adv \rightarrow \left\{ \begin{array}{l} \text{at 3 o'clock, in the morning, and so on} \\ \text{yesterday, every morning, and so on} \\ Adv_1 \end{array} \right\}$

---

[24]Obviously, this sketch is not intended to be definitive. It is just an example of what a part of English phrase structure grammar might look like. This grammar is to be used to generate sentences in the manner described in Chomsky's *Syntactic Structures*, Appendices 1, 2. That is, the rules are to be applied in the order given, each rule applied an arbitrary number of times before going on to the next—this comment applies significantly only to 9, in the present case. Parenthesized elements may be selected or not. Brackets enclose alternatives; that is, such an expression as $X \left\{ {Y \atop Z} \right\}$ stands for the pair of alternatives XY, XZ, and so on. To ensure that a terminal string results, it would be necessary to add a distinction between obligatory and optional rules. It will be clear that no attempt has been made here to present the rules in the technically simplest form. Most of this material is from Chomsky's *Logical Structure of Linguistic Theory* (1955, unpublished). For many improvements of this sketch, see Lees, *Grammar of English Nominalizations* (Bloomington, July, 1960); Chomsky, *Current Issues in Linguistic Theory* (this volume, pp. 50–118); Chomsky, *Some aspects of the theory of syntax* (forthcoming); and many papers and reports that have appeared since this paper was presented.

6. $Adv_1 \rightarrow \begin{cases} \text{in the house, at the theatre} \\ \text{there, away, home, and so on} \end{cases}$

7. $NP \rightarrow \begin{pmatrix} NP_{\text{sing}} \\ NP_{\text{pl}} \end{pmatrix}$

8. $Pred \rightarrow \begin{cases} NP_{\text{sing}} \text{ in env. } NP_{\text{sing}} + Aux \begin{cases} be \\ become \end{cases} - \\ NP_{\text{pl}} \text{ in env. } NP_{\text{pl}} + Aux \begin{cases} be \\ become \end{cases} - \\ Adj \end{cases}$

9. $Adj \rightarrow very + Adj$

10. $\begin{pmatrix} NP_{\text{sing}} \rightarrow T + N + \varphi \\ NP_{\text{pl}} \rightarrow T + N + S \end{pmatrix}$

11. $N \rightarrow \begin{cases} N_h \\ N_c \\ N_{ab} \text{ in env. } \begin{cases} \# \\ V_t \end{cases} T - \varphi \end{cases}$

12. $V_t \rightarrow V_T \begin{cases} Comp \\ Prt \end{cases}$

13. $V_t \rightarrow \begin{cases} V_{t1} & \text{in env. } N_h \ldots - \\ V_{t2} & \text{in env. } \qquad - \ldots N_h \\ \begin{cases} V_{t31} \\ V_{t32} \end{cases} & \text{in env. } N_h \ldots - \ldots N_c \end{cases}$

14. $V_T \rightarrow \begin{cases} V_{T_a}, V_{T_b}, V_{T_c}, V_{T_d}, V_{T_e}, V_{T_{e'}}, V_{T_f}, V_{T_{f'}}, V_{T_g}, V_{T_{g'}}, \\ \qquad \text{in env. } N_h \ldots - Comp \\ V_{T_x} \text{ in env. } - Prt \end{cases}$

15. $Prt \rightarrow out, in, up, away \ldots$
16. $T \rightarrow a, the$
17. $Aux \rightarrow C (M) (have + en) (be + ing)$
18. $C \rightarrow Present, Past$
19. $M \rightarrow can, may, will, shall, must$
20. $\begin{cases} N_h \rightarrow I, you, he, man, boy, \ldots \\ N_c \rightarrow it, table, book, \ldots \\ N_{ab} \rightarrow it, sincerity, justice, \ldots \end{cases}$
21. $V_i \rightarrow arrive, disappear, \ldots$

22. $V_s \rightarrow$ *feel, seem, . . .*
23. $V_{t_1} \rightarrow$ *admire, find, . . .*
    $V_{t_2} \rightarrow$ *terrify, astonish, . . .*
    $V_{t_{31}} \rightarrow$ *find, complete, . . .*
    $V_{t_{32}} \rightarrow$ *eat, smoke, . . .*
24. $V_{T_a} \rightarrow$ *consider, believe, . . .*
    $V_{T_b} \rightarrow$ *know, recognize, . . .*
    $V_{T_c} \rightarrow$ *elect, choose, . . .*
    $V_{T_d} \rightarrow$ *keep, put, . . .*
    $V_{T_e} \rightarrow$ *find, catch, . .*
    $V_{T_f} \rightarrow$ *imagine, prefer, . . .*
    $V_{T_g} \rightarrow$ *avoid, begin, . . .*
    $V_{T_{e'}} \rightarrow$ *persuade, force, . . .*
    $V_{T_{f'}} \rightarrow$ *want, expect, . . .*
    $V_{T_{g'}} \rightarrow$ *try, refuse, . . .*
    $V_{T_x} \rightarrow$ *take, bring, . . .*
25. $Adj \rightarrow$ *old, sad, . . .*

One derivation, for example, would reduce to the tree:

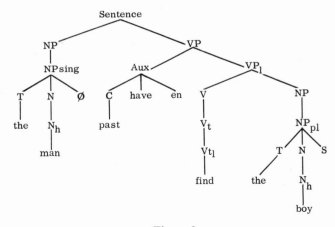

Figure 2

This represents the kernel sentence "the man had found the boys." Had rule 12 been applied, the segment, Fig. 3(a), of the tree might have been replaced by Fig. 3(b):

Figure 3(a) 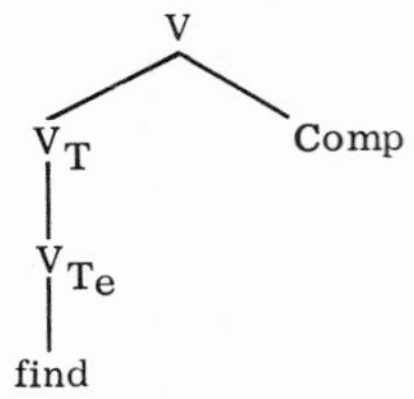   **Figure 3(b)**

With this change, the derivation (*Comp* means complement) would lead to the terminal string:

$$\text{the man } \varphi \text{ past have en find comp the boy } S \qquad (29)$$

which represents no kernel sentence but which, we will see, plays a part in representing, for example, "the man had found the boys playing in the yard."

The transformational level in English contains such operations as the following, described as in Eq. (27) (or *Syntactic Structures*, Appendix 2). The obligatory transformations are starred. In these rules the symbol $\rightarrow$ is used to mean *becomes by structural change*.

1. Passive: (1–16, Eq. 30)

   Structural Description: $(NP, Aux, V_t, NP, \left\{ \dfrac{Adv}{\underline{\hphantom{xx}}} \right\})$

   Structural Change: $X_1 - X_2 - X_3 - X_4 - X_5 \rightarrow$
   $$X_4 - X_2 - be + en + X_3 -$$
   $$by + X_1 - X_5$$

2. *Number:

   (a) SD: $(NP_{sing}, Present, X)$

   SC: $X_1 - X_2 - X_3 \rightarrow X_1 - S - X_3$

   (b) SD: $(NP_{pl}, Present, X$

   SC: $X_1 - X_2 - X_3 \rightarrow X_1 - \varphi - X_3$

3. Interrogative:

   SD: $\begin{cases} \text{(a) } NP, C, VP_1 \\ \text{(b) } NP, C + M, X \\ \text{(c) } NP, C + have, X \\ \text{(d) } NP, C + be, X \end{cases}$

   SC: $X_1 - X_2 - X_3 \rightarrow X_2 - X_1 - X_3$

4. Negation:

   SD: Same as 3.

   SC: $X_1 - X_2 - X_3 \rightarrow X_1 - X_2 + n\text{'}t - X_3$

5. Affirmation:

   Same as 4, except that A appears instead of *n't*.

6. Contraction:

   Same as 4, with *cntr* instead of *n't*, and $X_2 \neq C$ (The symbol $\neq$ means *does not equal*.)

7. Elliptic:

SD: Same as 3

SC: $X_1 - X_2 - X_3 \rightarrow X_1 - X_2$

8. So:

SD: Same as 3

SC: $X_1 - X_2 - X_3 \rightarrow so - X_2 - X_1$

9. *Object:

SD: $(X, V_t \text{ or } Prep, T + \begin{Bmatrix} he \\ I \end{Bmatrix}, Y)$

SC: $X_1 - X_2 - X_3 - X_4 \rightarrow$
$X_1 - X_2 - X_3 + m - X_4$

10. Separation:

(a) SD: (X, V_T, Prt, NP)

SC: $X_1 - X_2 - X_3 - X_4 \rightarrow$
$X_1 - X_2 - X_4 - X_3$
Obligatory if X_4 is a pronoun

(b) *SD: $(X, V_T, Comp, NP)$

SC: Same as (a)

11. Inversion:

SD: $(X, C + V_t, Y)$

SC: $X_1 - X_2 - X_3 \rightarrow$
$X_3 - X_2 - (easily, \ldots)$

12. *Auxiliary:

SD: (X, Af, v, Y)

SC: $X_1 - X_2 - X_3 - X_4 \rightarrow$
$X_1 - X_3 + X_2 - \# - X_4$
where *Af* is *en, ing, C, v* is *M, have, be, V*

13. *Word boundary:

$$SD: \quad (X, Y), \text{ where } X \neq v \text{ or } Y \neq Af$$

$$SC: \quad X_1 - X_2 \rightarrow X_1 - \sharp - X_2$$

14. *Do:

$$SD: \quad (X, \sharp, Af, Y)$$

$$SC: \quad X_1 - X_2 - X_3 - X_4 \rightarrow$$
$$X_1 - X_2 - do + X_3 - X_4$$

15. *Wh-:*

$$SD: \quad (X, T + \begin{Bmatrix} he \\ it \end{Bmatrix} (m) + \begin{Bmatrix} \varphi \\ S \end{Bmatrix}, Y)$$

$$SC: \quad X_1 - X_2 - X_3 \rightarrow wh\text{-} + X_2 - X_1 - X_3$$

16. Deletion:

$$SD: \quad (X, V_{t32}, Y)$$

$$SC: \quad \text{Same as 7}$$

In addition to the transformations listed above which convert sentences into sentences (except for 8 and 15), we must construct others which convert pairs of sentences into single sentences. For example, in such a sentence as:

$$\text{John's proving the theorem was a great surprise} \tag{31}$$

the grammatical subject is itself a transform of a terminal string. We can form this sentence by a transformation that operates on the pair of terminal strings:

$$\begin{Bmatrix} T - it - C + be + a + great + surprise \\ John - C - prove + the + theorem \end{Bmatrix} \tag{32}$$

converting the second into the string:

$$John + S - ing + prove + the + theorem \tag{33}$$

which is substituted for the *NP* subject of the first sentence of Eq. (32). All of the generalized transformations mentioned below operate on this paradigm. In each case, we will consider that the substituend takes the phrase structure of that which it replaces, e.g., Eq. (33) is an *NP* in Eq. (31). Thus, in general, further transformations can apply to strings formed by such operations.

We will describe these transformations in a uniform manner, giving the pair of analyses imposed on the strings to which the transformation applies, as in Eq. (32), stating what conditions hold on these strings, if any, and stating what transforms of the second sentence replace the components of the first. Thus, the transformation just discussed will be described in these steps:

$$SD: \begin{Bmatrix} T, \; it + \varphi, \; VP \\ NP, \; C, \; VP_1 \end{Bmatrix} \quad \left(= \begin{Bmatrix} X_1, X_2, X_3 \\ X_4, X_5, X_6 \end{Bmatrix} \right) \tag{34}$$

$SC:$ $X_4 + S$, or φ, replaces X_1; $ing + X_6$ replaces X_2

Among the generalized transformations in English are the following:

17. Nominalization: (17–20, Eq. 35)

    (a) $SD:$ Same as (34)

    (b) $SD:$ Same as (34)

            $SC:$ $to + X_6$ replaces X_2

    (c) $SD:$ Same as (34)

            $SC:$ $X_4 + S$, or φ, replaces X_1;

                  $nom + X_6$ replaces X_2

    (d) $SD:$ $\begin{Bmatrix} T, \; it + \varphi, \; VP \\ NP, \; C, \; V_i \end{Bmatrix}$

            $SC:$ $ing + X_6 + of + X_4$ replaces X_2

    (e) $SD:$ $\begin{Bmatrix} T, \; it + \varphi, \; VP \\ NP, \; Aux, \; V_t, \; Y \end{Bmatrix}$

            $SC:$ $X_4 + S$ may replace T;

                  $ing + X_6 + of + X_7$ replaces X_2

    (*f*) $SD:$ $\begin{Bmatrix} T, \; it + \varphi, \; VP \\ NP, \; C, \; be, \; Adj \end{Bmatrix}$

            $SC:$ $X_4 + S$ replaces X_1;

                  $nom + X_7$ replaces X_2

18. Nominalization:

    (a) $SD:$ $\begin{Bmatrix} X, \; N + \begin{Bmatrix} \varphi \\ S \end{Bmatrix} \; Y \\ T, \; N + \begin{Bmatrix} \varphi \\ S \end{Bmatrix}, \; Aux, \; V_i \end{Bmatrix}$

            Condition : $X_2 = X_5$

        $SC:$ $ing + X_7 + X_5$ replaces X_2

(b) SD: $X, N + \left\{ \begin{matrix} \varphi \\ S \end{matrix} \right\}, Y$

$T, N + \left\{ \begin{matrix} \varphi \\ S \end{matrix} \right\}, Aux + be, Adj$

Condition : $X_2 = X_5$

SC: $X_7 + X_5$ replaces X_2

19. Adjectivalization:

SD: $\left\{ \begin{matrix} NP, X, Adj \\ NP, Aux, V_{t_2}, NP \end{matrix} \right\}$

Condition : $X_1 = X_4$

SC: $ing + X_6$ replaces X_3

20. Complement:

(a) SD: $\left\{ \begin{matrix} X, V_T, Comp, NP \\ NP, Aux, be, Pred \end{matrix} \right\}$

Condition : X_2 is V_{T_a}

SC: X_5 replaces X_4; X_8 replaces X_3

(b) SD: Same

Condition : X_2 is V_{T_b}

SC: X_5 replaces X_4; $to + X_7 + X_8$ replaces X_3

(c) SD: Same

Condition : X_2 is V_{T_c}; X_8 is not Adj

SC: Same as (a)

(d) SD: $\left\{ \begin{matrix} X, V_T, Comp, NP \\ NP, Aux, be, Adv_1 \end{matrix} \right\}$

Condition: X_2 is V_{T_d}

SC: Same as (a)

(e) SD: $\left\{ \begin{matrix} X, V_T, Comp, NP \\ NP, Aux, VP_1 \end{matrix} \right\}$

Condition : X_2 is V_{T_e}

SC: X_5 replaces X_4; $ing + X_7$ replaces X_3

(e′) *SD*: Same as (e)

 Condition : X_2 is $V_{T_{e'}}$

 SC: Same as (e), with *to* in place of *ing*

(f) *SD*: Same as (e)

 Condition : X_2 is V_{T_f}

 SC: Same as (e)

(f′) *SD*: Same as (e)

 Condition : X_2 is $V_{T_{f'}}$

 SC: Same as (e′)

(g) *SD*: Same as (e)

 Condition: (1) X_2 is V_{T_g}

 (2) If X_1 is $T\begin{Bmatrix} I \\ you \end{Bmatrix} Y$, then

 $$X_1 = X_4$$

 If not, then X_4 is

 $$T + he + Z$$

 SC: Same as (e)

(g′) *SD*: Same as (e)

 Condition : (1) X_2 is $V_{T_{g'}}$

 (2) Same as 2 of (g)

 SC: Same as (e′)

The following transformations apply to a single sentence:

21. Pronoun: (21–23, Eq. 36)

 SD: $(X, \begin{Bmatrix} he \\ it \end{Bmatrix}, Y)$,

 where $X \neq Z + V_{T_{g,g'}} + T$

 SC: $X_1 - X_2 - X_3 \rightarrow X_1 - X_3$

22. *Deletion:

 SD: $(X, Aux + V_{T_{f,f',g,g'}} + Comp, Y)$

$$\text{where if } X_1 \text{ is } T \left\{ \begin{matrix} I \\ you \end{matrix} \right\} Z, \text{ then } X_3 = X_1$$

$$\text{if not, then } X_3 \text{ is } T + he + Z$$

$$SC: \quad X_1 - X_2 - X_3 \rightarrow X_1 - X_2$$

23. *Self:

$$SD: \quad \text{Same as } 22^*, \text{ but } X_2 = Aux + V_T + Comp$$

$$SC: \quad X_1 - X_2 - X_3 \rightarrow X_1 - X_2 - X_3 + self$$

VIII

I will now add a brief comment about several of these transformations to indicate how they operate on, e.g., such strings as those derived in Figs. 2 and 3. The number of each comment corresponds to the number of the transformation being discussed.

1. The passive converts the terminal strings of Fig. 1 into *the + boy + S — past + have + en + be + en — find — by + the + man + φ*, which by the succeeding obligatory transformations, represents "the boys had been found by the man." It converts Eq. (29) into *the + boy + S — past + have + en + be + en — find + comp — by + the + man + φ*. With a particular choice of complement, determined previous to application of the passive by transformation 20(e), this would represent, e.g., "the boys had been found playing in the yard by the man."

3. There are four cases in the structural description, for four different types of *Aux*. The four strings:

the man — present — watch the boy	(37a)
the man — present + will — watch the boy	(37b)
the man — present + have — en watch the boy	(37c)
the man — present + be — ing watch the boy	(37d)

are converted respectively into:

Present — the man — watch the boy	(38a)
Present will — the man — watch the boy	(38b)
Present have — the man — en watch the boy	(38c)
Present + be — the man — ing watch the boy	(38d)

which, respectively, represents the sentences:

does the man watch the boy (by application of 14*)	(39a)
will the man watch the boy	(39b)
has the man watched the boy	(39c)
is the man watching the boy.	(39d)

Notice that the string in Eq. (40) can be analyzed only as a case of (d). Consequently, its corresponding interrogative is Eq. (41):

the man Present be old	(40)
Present be the man old (is the man old *not* does the man be old)	(41)

Notice also that the string:

$$\text{\textit{the boy Present have a dollar}} \tag{42}$$

with its derivation, can be analyzed as a case of either (a) or (c). Consequently, the corresponding interrogative will be either Eq. (43a) (if analyzed as (a)) or Eq. (43b) (if analyzed as (c)):

Present — the boy have a dollar (does the boy have a
dollar, like Eq. (39a)) (43a)

Present have — the boy a dollar (has the boy a dollar).   (43b)

Have is the only *V* which has this possibility, just as it is the only one ambiguously analyzable by transformation 2.

Suppose further that the rule of the lexicon, e.g. Eq. (28 : 23) that introduces *have* is:

$$V_{t_x} \rightarrow \text{\textit{have (got)}} \tag{44}$$

where some later morphological rule, itself transformational, reads:

$$\sharp + \text{\textit{have}} + Af + \sharp + \text{\textit{got}} + \sharp \rightarrow \sharp + \text{\textit{have}} + Af + \sharp. \tag{45}$$

In this case, another alternative for the interrogative of Eq. (42) (with *got* chosen in Eq. (44)) will be:

Present + have — the boy — got a dollar (has the boy
got a dollar) (46)

4. Much as in the case of transformation 3, the negations of Eq. (37) will be, respectively:

the man doesn't watch the boy	(47a)
the man won't watch the boy	(47b)
the man hasn't watched the boy	(47c)
the man isn't watching the boy	(47d)

The negation of Eq. (40) will, correspondingly, be Eq. (48); and as negations of Eq. (42), we will have any of Eq. (49).

$$\text{the man isn't old} \tag{48}$$

the boy doesn't have a dollar	(49a)
the boy hasn't a dollar	(49b)
the boy hasn't got a dollar	(49c)

5. Corresponding to Eqs. (47–49), we have, respectively, Eqs. (50–52):

the man does + A watch the boy	(50a)
the man will + A watch the boy	(50b)
the man has + A watched the boy	(50c)
the man is + A watching the boy	(50d)

$$\text{\textit{the man is + A old}} \tag{51}$$

the boy does + A have a dollar	(52a)
the boy has + A a dollar	(52b)
the boy has + A got a dollar	(52c)

A morphophonemic rule will identify *A* a extra-heavy stress on the preceding morpheme. Notice that the rules do not permit *does* to occur in such positions as in Eq. (50a) without contrastive stress.

6. Corresponding to Eqs. (47–49), respectively, the contraction transformation gives Eqs. (53–55):

the man watches the boy	(53a)
the man will + cntr *watch the boy* (the man'll watch the boy)	(53b)
the man has + cntr *watched the boy* (the man's watched the boy)	(53c)
the man is + cntr *watching the boy* (the man's watching the boy)	(53d)
the man is + cntr *old* (the man's old)	(54)
the boy has a dollar	(55a)
the boy has + cntr *a dollar*	(55b)
the boy has + cntr *got a dollar* (the boy's got a dollar)	(55c)

In connection with *cntr* we add the transformational rule [Eq. (56)]* following transformation 13*.

$$SD: (NP, \sharp, X + cntr, Y) \text{ (where } Y = \text{got} \ldots \text{ if } X = \ldots \text{ have)}$$
$$SC: X_1 - X_2 - X_3 - X_4 \to X_1 + X_3 - X_4, \text{ where } X_3 \text{ is } X_3 \text{ minus its initial glides and vowels}$$
(56)

cntr is then treated as a *zero* morpheme. Equation (56) converts Eqs. (53–55) into the given parenthesized forms. These rules are designed for my speech, where "the boy has got a dollar" is impossible without contraction or emphasis of *has*.

7. This gives "the man does" ("who watches the boy"), "the man will" ("who will watch the boy"), "the man has" ("who has watched the boy"), "the man is" ("who is old"), "the boy does" ("who has a dollar"), "the boy has" ("who has (got) a dollar"), as, e.g., answers to the corresponding parenthesized forms. These correspond, respectively, to Eqs. (47–49).

8. This combines with conjunction to give such sentences as "John watches the boy and so does Bill," and so on. Again, there are, automatically, two forms for the main verb *have*, and an *anomalous* form for *be*.

All of the transformations 3–8 (this does not exhaust the list) are constructed on the same pattern. Notice that the actual behavior of *have, be, do*, usually treated as exceptional, follows here as an automatic consequence of the simplest rules set up for the *nonexceptional* cases and is thus shown to be really a case of higher level regularity.

9. This gives "I saw him" (instead of *he*). Notice that it automatically applies to the second *NP* of "I found him playing," "I saw him come," etc., in the pre-trans-

formed stage *I found + comp he, I saw + comp he*, etc., thus accounting for the fact that we have *him*, not *he*, in these sentences (*find + comp, see + comp* are V_t's).

10. Part (a) gives "I looked the word up" optionally from "I looked up the word," and "I looked it up" obligatorily from "I looked up it." Part (b) gives, e.g., "I found him playing" obligatorily from *I found + playing him* (*playing* is the *comp*, given by transformation 20e).

11. This gives, e.g., "the book reads easily" from *NP reads the book*.

15. Application of the *wh*-transformation is conditional on the interrogative transformation 3. It thus applies to forms like Eq. (38), but with pronouns as the relevant *NP*'s, to give Eq. (57) or Eq. (58), depending on whether subject or object is chosen as X_2. Further morphophonemic rules convert *wh + he* (*m*) into *who* (*m*), *wh + it* into *what*.

who watched the boy	(57a)
who will watch the boy	(57b)
who has watched the boy	(57c)
who was watching the boy	(57d)
whom did the man watch	(58a)
whom will the man watch	(58b)
whom has the man watched	(58c)
whom is the man watching	(58d)

From Eq. (41) this transformation will give only "who is old" (providing that a contextual phrase structure rule excludes pronouns from the context *the man is* —). From Eqs. (43) and (46), it yields only "who has a dollar" and "what has the boy" (which for my dialect, must be excluded), "what has the boy got." Notice that the correct word order, introduction of *do*, etc., in all these forms is provided automatically as a special case of already given rules, as a result of the fact that this transformation is preceded by transformation 3. If it is not preceded by transformation 3, this transformation gives simply relative clauses (which will then be handled by generalized transformations like those of Eq. (36)). Hence, it seems correct to say that Eqs. (57) and (58), etc., are classed as interrogatives because they are formed from interrogatives. (Cf. discussion of sentence type, Section IX.)

16. E.g., John eats food → John eats

17. These transformations give, respectively, such sentences as those of Eq. (59), where the second sentence (which is transformed into the *NP*) in each case is given in parentheses.

John's proving the theorem was a great surprise	(59a)
(John proves the theorem)	
To prove the theorem is difficult	(59b)
(John proves the theorem)	
John's refusal to come was a great surprise	(59c)
(John refuses to come)	
(*nom + refuse* → *refusal*, by morphophonemic rules)	
The growling of lions is frightening	(59d)
(lions growl)	

The proving of theorems is difficult (59e)
(*NP proves theorems*)
The country's safety is in danger (59f)
(the country is safe)

Notice that if a certain verb is in both V_i and V_t, then we will have ambiguous phrases of the form $ing + V + of + NP$. For example, application of Eq. (59d), where the nominalized sentence is "the hunters shoot," gives *the shooting of the hunters — is a scandal*, just as will application of Eq. (59c), where the nominalized sentence is "they shoot the hunters." Equations (59d–e) are not correspondingly ambiguous, since there are no kernel sentences "theorems prove," "they growl lions."

18. Part (a) gives Eq. (60), and part (b), Eq. (61).

growling lions are frightening (from lions are frightening, lions growl) (60)

the old man is sad (from the man is sad, the man is old) (61)

Notice that transformations 17a and 18a may lead to the same (hence ambiguous) sentence, if some verb is in both V_t and V_i. For example, from "planes are dangerous," "planes fly," 18a forms Eq. (62a); from "planes can be dangerous," "planes fly," 18a forms Eq. (62b); from "it is dangerous," "they fly planes," 17a forms Eq. (62c); from "it can be dangerous," "they fly planes," 17a forms Eq. (62b):

flying planes are dangerous (62a)
flying planes can be dangerous (62b)
flying planes is dangerous (62c)

The grammar thus *predicts* (correctly in this case) that Eq. (62b) will be ambiguous. Replacement of *flying planes* by *growling lions* and *proving theorems* gives, in each case, an unambiguous sentence, just as in the case of Eqs. (59d–e).

Notice that although 17a forms *growling lions, barking dogs*, from "lions growl," "dogs bark," it does not form *eating men, smoking men, drinking men*, etc., as plural *NP*'s with the stress pattern 2–1 (the fact that these may be compound nouns with stress pattern 1–3 is a different matter entirely) from "men eat," "men smoke," "men drink," etc., since these verbs are not V_i's, but V_t's, and the sentences "men eat," etc., are formed by transformation 16 from "men eat food," "men smoke pipes," "men drink beer," etc. With a few discrepancies, this seems to be the way this system operates in English. Notice, e.g., that though we cannot have *smoking men* (except, perhaps, in the sense, *men who are on fire*, in which case *smoke* is in fact a V_i), we do have *smoking embers* (from "embers smoke," where *smoke* is a V_i since we do not have "embers smoke pipes," etc.). I have not investigated this matter thoroughly, however, and qualifications may be needed.

19. This transformation introduces *interesting, terrifying*, etc.,into all adjectival contexts (when coupled with transformation 18b), e.g., into such contexts as *very—, seems—, —ly*, etc. Notice that the forms *growling, flying, barking*, etc. produced by 18a and appearing by virtue of this transformation, in the *adjectival* context *—N*,

are *not* introduced by any of the rules of the grammar into the contexts *very—*, *seems—*, *—ly.*[25]

20. In Part (a), *they — consider — comp — the assistant, the assistant — C — be — qualified*, which has the passive "the assistant is considered qualified by them" and the active declarative "they consider the assistant qualified," is formed by applying the obligatory transformation 10b*. The remaining transformations of 20 form, respectively such sentences as:

(b) we know the assistant to be qualified
(c) we elect him president
(d) we kept the car in the garage
(e) we found him playing the flute
(e′) we persuaded him to play the flute
(f) we imagined him playing the flute
(f′) we wanted him to play the flute
(g) we avoided us meeting him
(g′) we tried us to meet him

Application to (g), (g′) above of the obligatory transformation 22* (*before* application of 10b*) converts these into "we avoided meeting him," "we tried to meet him." Similarly, in the case of (f), (f′), if the object were *us* instead of *him*, as above, this same transformation would give "we imagined playing the flute," "we wanted to play the flute" (that is, just as the source of (f′) is the pair of terminal strings *we — past + want — comp — it, he — C — play + the + flute*, the source of "we wanted to play the flute" is the pair *we — past + want — comp — it, we — C — play + the + flute*). Correspondingly, application of the obligatory transformation 23* to (e), (e′) above, with the object *we* instead of *him*, would give "we found ourselves playing the flute," "we persuaded ourselves to play the flute." Application of the optional transformation 21 to *the man wanted — to play the flute—him* before application of 22* or 23* and 10b*, allows for such sentences as "the man wanted him to play the flute" alongside of "the man wanted to play the flute," that is, it allows for the dual referential function of third person pronouns.

Notice the symmetry of cases (e), (e′), (f′), (g), (g′). Transformation 12*, which inverts *ing* and the following *V*, allows us to exploit the far-reaching parallel between *to* and *ing*.

Notice also that the transformations of 20 lead to a good deal of ambiguity and to sentences of superficially similar structure, but with quite different sources in the grammar, as for example, in such sets as:

$$\text{the police — questioned — the man — behind closed doors}$$
$$(NP — Aux + V_t — NP — Adv) \tag{63a}$$

---

[25]The fact that such adjectives as *interesting, terrifying, astonishing* have a special semantic feature of suggesting a specific human reaction, has been pointed out by P. Nowell-Smith, *Ethics* (Baltimore: Penguin Books, Inc., 1954), pp. 84ff. We can perhaps explain this as a consequence of the fact that these words are in a real sense elliptical, with the human object in the underlying sentence from which they are formed, by transformation 19, deleted by the transformation.

the police — suspected — the man behind the bar
$(NP — Aux + V_t — NP)$ (63b)

the police — put — the man — behind bars
$(NP — Aux + V_t — NP — Comp)$ (63c)
they — found — the boy — studying in the library

$(NP — Aux + V_T — NP — Comp)$
$(NP — Aux + V_t — NP)$ (64a)

they — knew — the boy studying in the library   (64b)
$(NP — Aux + V_t — NP)$

they — kept — the car — in the garage
$(NP — Aux + V_T — NP — Comp)$ (65a)

they — kept — the car in the garage
$(NP — Aux + V_t — NP)$ (65b)

and many others. In all cases the proper analyses can be discovered by observing the behavior of these sentences under the passive transformation (Cf. Section X, comment 5.)

Quite generally, the transformations discussed above can be iterated to form more and more complex sentences. Thus, by successive applications of (e)–(g′) (with the required obligatory transformations) to the terminal strings *this event prompted comp it, I tried comp it, I visualized comp it, I forced comp it,* "he comes," we can form such sentences as "this event prompted me to try to visualize myself forcing him to come." We might then form the passive "I was prompted to try to visualize myself forcing him to come by this event," in exactly the manner discussed above. We could then go on to form interrogatives, or to nominalize it by 17a to (*my*) *being prompted to try to visualize myself forcing him to come* (*by this event*), inserting this as the subject of another sentence, to which further transformations could then be applied. In this way rules which are in themselves simple can be used to form a vast number of sentences of very great complexity, all of which, however, can be recognized as grammatical by the native speaker, despite their novelty.

To complete the transformational description, we must, just as in the phrase structure grammar, determine carefully the permitted order of transformations, along the lines roughly indicated above.

IX

Notice that we can extract a *structural description* from the process of transformational derivation of a sentence, just as we can from the phrase structure level. A sentence is represented on the transformational level by the sequence of operations by which it is derived from terminal strings, just as it is represented on the IC-level by trees such as those of Figs. 1–3, and on the phonemic level by a sequence of phonemes. The transformational representation of a sentence gives important clues as to how the sentence is understood, as we have seen in several examples discussed above. Thus, for example, dual representation on the transformational level correlates with ambiguity, just as it does on lower levels. The transformational level provides representations that correspond closely to the traditional (and to the native speaker, intuitively apparent) notion of sentence type. Kernel sentences are simple declaratives, transformation 3 gives interrogatives, transformations 3 plus 15 give the special class of *wh*-interrogatives,[26] 15 alone gives relative clauses, and so on. This explanatory power of transformational analysis, coupled with the very great simplification (e.g., elimination of apparent irregularities, simple recursive characterizations of complex sentences, etc.) that transformational devices introduce into the grammar, seems to me a very strong reason for developing linguistic theory in such a way as to permit transformational notions to play a central role in syntactic description.

I do not know whether grammatical transformations of this type will add sufficient flexibility to grammatical description to allow all the difficulties and inadequacies of phrase structure description to be overcome. It may be that still other devices and other forms of representation (other linguistic levels) of a quite different kind will be needed to provide a simple and revealing method for deriving all the grammatical sentences of natural languages. There seems to be little doubt, however, that transformational description greatly extends the power and effectiveness of grammars and that it will have to be incorporated in a complete linguistic theory.

Notice that the grammar sketched above is neither an item-and-arrangement nor item-process grammar, in the usual sense of these terms. Such rules as *Sentence → NP + VP* or *past → d* in the context *learn —*, are typical item-and-arrangement rules, while such rules as *take + past → tuk* are the paradigm for item-process rules. There is no essential difference (other than generality) between these rules in the above framework. This grammar is, furthermore, neither an *analytic* grammar (taking the point of view of the hearer or analyzing linguist) nor a *synthetic* grammar (taking the point of view of the speaker). It neither enables us to generate a particular sentence nor to analyze a particular sentence. It is merely a characterization and description, in the most neutral terms I can imagine, of the grammatical sentences of the language. The study of how to produce or analyze particular sentences (i.e., the study of actual human linguistic behavior) is an important one, which, I presume, will not go very far unless based on an adequate theory of grammar, but it is a further study, distinct from grammar in the sense in which the word has been used above.

X

Having given this fragmentary example of a transformational grammar, I would like to restate briefly some of the main points of the earlier theoretical discussion. The central notion to be defined in linguistic theory is, I believe, the notion *grammar of L* for an arbitrary natural language *L*. A grammar of *L* is a device which enumerates the sentences of *L* in such a way that a structural description can be mechanic-

---

[26]On other than transformational grounds (e.g., on grounds of word order or intonation), there seems to be little reason to classify such sentences as interrogatives at all, despite the fact, obvious to any speaker of the language, that they are a special class of interrogatives.

ally derived for each enumerated sentence. This structural description consists of various representations for the generated sentence, e.g., transformational, phrase structure, morphemic, phonemic, and perhaps others. The total set of representations of a particular type for all sentences of L constitutes a level of grammatical structure for L. The structural descriptions should, if the grammar is at all adequate, provide a basis for explaining how sentences are used and understood, in the manner touched on above.

The problem of finding even one grammar for any natural language is extremely difficult. Hence, the question how to choose among grammars is largely academic at the moment. Where the question does arise, however, as when we must decide whether to assign certain sentences to the kernel or to derive them by transformations, it seems to me that the decision must be based on a systematic measure of complexity of grammar.[27] For most of the cases for which our present rather primitive grammatical theories are at all adequate, the differences in complexity between the available alternatives are usually so gross that even relatively unsophisticated measures of complexity can often provide a clear and unique decision (e.g., consider the effect of assigning interrogatives to the kernel in the grammar described above and deriving declaratives from them by transformation). It is important, however, to devise precise and well-motivated measures. I will not go into the question here, except for the following brief comments.

1. The formal definition of *grammar* in general linguistic theory, that is, the careful specification of the form of grammars and the descriptive devices available for grammars, itself has a far-reaching effect in cutting down the number of possible

---

[27]I have stressed this repeatedly because it seems to me to be the major point on which I would like to take issue with a prevailing alternative view. A common view appears to be that to justify a grammatical description it is necessary and sufficient to exhibit some explicit procedure (preferably, purely formal) by which this description could have been mechanically constructed from the data. This view I find very strange. Why, first of all, should it be required that there be some relatively straightforward, completely general procedure for arriving at grammars from the data? (If the word *general* is dropped, the claim that discovery procedures can be provided reduces to a triviality —cf. 13*n*.) Why, furthermore, should exhibiting such a procedure be considered a justification of the result to which it leads? There are undoubtedly perfectly general and straightforward procedures for arriving at the most wild descriptions—e.g., we can define a *morpheme* in a perfectly general, straightforward, and formal way, with no mixing of levels, as any sequence of three phonemes. Clearly, it is necessary somehow to justify the procedure itself. It is surprising how often this point is overlooked in discussion of linguistic methodology. It is easy to find elaborate discussions of procedures for phonemic analysis, for instance, but there are few attempts to find some general and plausible principles from which it will follow that it is reasonable to set up phonemes on the basis of such principles as complementary distribution. (Where there is some reference to a guiding or motivating principle, it is generally some sort of principle of economy or simplicity, as in Harris, *Methods in Structural Linguistics, op. cit.* But I have tried to give examples to show that it is unlikely that the kind of discovery procedure usually considered can lead to what is clearly the simplest analysis in general.) This imbalance in methodological discussion may in part be motivated by the view (made explicit by Joos in *Readings in American Linguistics*, and taken there as a defining characteristic of a major tendency in American linguistics) that the search for explanations is a kind of infantile aberration that may affect philosophers or mystics, but not sober scientists whose only interest is "pure description," i.e., manipulation and arrangement of data. In opposition to this thesis, which can find little support in well-developed sciences, we find, among others, Jakobson, with his insistence on the relevance of investigations in many other fields to the formulation of linguistic theory, and Hockett, who has repeatedly pointed out the necessity for elucidating "meta-criteria" to determine the choice of a linguistic theory (cf., e.g., *Two Models Grammatical Description*).

alternatives. Thus, if we have decided to construct a grammar with a phrase structure and a transformational part, a great many possible descriptions are already eliminated. Hence, a part of the problem of choosing among grammars is absorbed by the theory of the form of grammar itself.

2. The major systematic feature always used, overtly or not, in choosing among alternative descriptions, is the degree of generalization achieved. We have a generalization when distinct statements about distinct linguistic elements can be replaced by the same or similar statements. It is therefore natural, and not difficult, to develop notational devices which will lead to a partial definition of complexity by converting considerations of complexity into considerations of length; that is, notations which allow grammatical statements to be coalesced to the extent that they are similar. In fact, the notational devices in the grammar presented above, if systematically used (which they were not) go a long way toward achieving this result. It is clear by cursory inspection that a great deal of further generalization is possible in this grammar.

3. A distinction was made above between obligatory and optional transformations. This distinction can actually be made much more general. On each level, we distinguish between optional and obligatory rules. The distinction between optional and obligatory is the natural extension to the whole of grammar of the phonemic-phonetic distinction on the phonological level. If we make this distinction systematically, we can view the grammar as being composed of two parts, an optional part which specifies the entire set of choices available to a speaker when producing a sentence (or to a listener when interpreting one), and an obligatory part which represents automatic machinery which need never be considered in producing or "understanding" a sentence. It is clear that the optional part is of primary interest and importance, especially if we intend to base a theory of the use and understanding of sentences on grammar. An obvious decision is to consider minimization of the optional part of the grammar to be the major factor in reducing complexity. I think that many of the traditional criteria of phonemic and morphological analysis, in the cases where these are in fact acceptable, can be shown to be interpretable as particular consequences of the decision to minimize the optional part of the grammar (the choices effectively available to the user of the language). If this is true, we can reduce the problem of justifying the separate and diverse criteria of analysis customarily used, to the problem of justifying this single decision, which seems a rather plausible one.

4. The problem of giving a general definition of simplicity of grammar is much like that of evaluating a physical constant. That is, we know in many cases what the results of grammatical description should be (e.g., we know which sentences are structurally ambiguous, and should, correspondingly, have dual representations on some level in a successful grammar), and we can attempt to define *simplicity* in general terms in such a way as to force us to choose the correct solution in particular cases.[28]

---

[28]There is no vicious circularity here. In the same way, we will try to define every other notion of general linguistic theory so that, in certain crucial and clear cases, we arrive at desired results, just as a scientist in any other field will try to construct his theories so that they predict correctly in particular cases. As long as the definitions given of *simplicity*, *phoneme*, etc., are quite general, this will not be reduced to a triviality. (Cf. 13*n*.)

5. In deciding between two alternative descriptions in a particular case there is in one sense only one criterion brought to bear, given a linguistic theory that specifies the form of grammar, namely, what is the effect of each alternative on the total complexity of grammar. It seems to me unlikely that any piecemeal, step-by-step, analytic procedure of any generality can be developed to lead directly to the simplest over-all solution in particular cases. We can often, however, bring out the particular considerations relevant to making a choice one way or another. Thus, in determining what phrase structure to assign to Eqs. (63–65), (67), (68) above, the behavior of these sentences under the passive transformation is of crucial importance. From Eq. (64a) ("they found the boy studying in the library"), we can form the passives "the boy was found studying in the library (by them)," "the boy studying in the library was found (by them)"; while in the case of Eq. (64b) ("they knew the boy was studying in the library"), we can form only "the boy studying in the library was known (by them)." Consequently, we analyze the first ambiguously, as $NP–Aux + V_T–NP–Comp$ or $NP–Aux–V_t–NP$, and the second only as $NP–Aux–V_t–NP$. The passive transformation thus offers a criterion for assigning constituent structure in these cases. That is, the whole grammar is simplified if these sentences are assigned phrase structure in such a way that an unmodified passive transformation will form from them just those sequences that are in fact English sentences. The question of how sentences behave under transformation is, I believe, one of the most effective considerations that can be brought to bear in determining their phrase structure. It is important to note, however, that this *criterion* for constituent analysis is just a special case of a general, systematic criterion of simplicity.

I think that the use of suprasegmental criteria in syntactic analysis can be viewed in much the same way. It is in many cases possible to predict rather intricate stress patterns from syntactic structure;[29] i.e., to show that stress can be omitted from the optional part of the grammar, with corresponding simplification of the grammar (see comment 3, above). Insofar as this is true, stress patterns can be used as a criterion for syntactic analysis, in much the same way as behavior under transformation. It would be pointless, however, to insist on this as a unique, or even over-riding criterion. It is best considered as a special case of a general simplicity criterion. In those cases where the whole grammar is simplified when intonational patterns are predictable only in some more indirect way,[30] the intonational criterion need not

---

[29]See Chomsky, Halle, Lukoff, "On Accent and Juncture in English," *For Roman Jakobson* (1957) for a demonstration of this for particular transformational constructions. It will be clear, in the light of the preceding discussion, why in that paper we proposed that the term *phonemic* is best withheld from the 4, 5, or 6 stress elements whose arrangement in syntactically (and phonetically) determined patterns was under discussion. If we reformulate the phonemic-phonetic distinction as a special case, on one particular level, of the general distinction between optional and obligatory, then these stress patterns, being part of the automatic, obligatory part of the grammar, will not be considered in the phonemics. I am now suggesting that the fundamental distinction in grammar is between optional and obligatory and that there is no point in maintaining strict separation of levels (whatever this means exactly—cf. Lees, *op. cit.*, pp. 381–82) within each of these segments of the grammar.

[30]As in the case of such ambiguous sentences as "flying planes can be dangerous," where the simplest (and obviously correct) description of the syntactic structure cannot be read off directly from intonational structure, since alternative analyses are required. Similarly, in many styles, such sentences as "the market collapsed," "I'll mark it 'elapsed'," "I'll mark it today," "I'll mark an exam," and so on, may have the same suprasegmental features associated with totally different syntactic structures.

be applied. In a sense, then, I think that those linguists who have insisted that a multiplicity of criteria must be brought to bear in each particular aspect of linguistic analysis, are correct, although in another (and more interesting) sense, there is only one criterion, over-all simplicity of the grammar, which may, in particular instances give rise to a variety of special considerations.

6. The goal of a grammar is to characterize all the utterances of the language. Where possible, it will use broad generalizations to do this. It will also list individual forms which do not fall under generalizations, i.e., exceptions. There are, in fact, exceptions to many of the transformational rules given above, perhaps all. These will have to be separately listed, unless some more general formulation can be found to account for them as well. The discovery of such exceptions is in itself of little interest or importance (although the discovery of an alternative formulation in which exceptions disappear would be highly important). We will no more give up the passive transformation, with the extensive simplification of the grammar to which it leads, because "Mary married John" has no passive, than would we give up the general rules of Eqs. (25–26) for the formation of regular past tenses, because they fail for *take, break,* etc.

It is to be taken for granted that in a system as vast and complex as an individual's entire speech behavior there will be all sorts of anomalies. The existence of exceptions need not affect our general policy of making the total description as simple as possible. It seems pointless to accept a principle of analysis which forces us to give up what simplifications of the grammar we can effect, because there are some recalcitrant cases. Yet certain, widely-held principles seem to do just this. Consider, for example, the strong ("once a phoneme, always a phoneme") form of the biuniqueness principle, mentioned above. A particular consequence of this principle is that no exceptions can be tolerated on the phonemic level. I have found several speakers for whom there is apparently only one case of an intervocalic, pre-stress, post-weak stress alveolar flap [D], namely, in *today*, where it contrasts with the /d/ of *to Denver, adept, to-do (a great to-do),* . . . and the /t/ of *attack, detest,*. . . .[31] If we accept the principle in question, we will have to mark the predictable post-stress [D] in *writer* ([rayDɨr]), *rider* ([ra:yDɨr]) as a phoneme /D/, with consequent complication of the morphophonemics. But now the two words *writer, rider* differ phonemically only in vowel length,[32] which must consequently be considered phonemic, so that the phonemic transcriptions are /rayDɨr/, /ra:yDɨr/. Using the biuniqueness principle again, we are forced to represent *write, ride, pot, pod,,* etc., phonemically as /rayt/, /ra:yd/, /pat/, /pa:d/, etc. Hence, we have the phonemes /t/, /D/, /d/, /a/, /a:/, and the phonemic transcriptions /rayDɨr/, /ra:Dɨr/, /rayt/, /ra:yd/, /pat/, /pa:d/. I do not know whether any phonemicist would be willing to follow these principles to their logical consequences. If, alternatively, our goal is, as described above, to construct the

---

[31]Though it is the regular variant of /t/ if a morpheme boundary follows in this case, e.g., in *at all, at Ellen's,* and so forth, in contrast with *attend, adept, a test,* and so forth. A linguist who insists that only phonological information is relevant to establishing junctures would, I presume, have to set up three phonemes /t/, /d/, /D/ independently of *today*.

[32]In my speech, where the difference in this case is between [əy] and [ay], this otherwise predictable distinction would now be forced to carry the distinctive burden, again adding pointlessly to the optional part of the grammar.

simplest grammar of the language, we can merely state this fact about *today* as a peculiar and unique phenomenon, leaving the rest of the phonemic description un-altered, with the transcriptions / raytɨr/, raydɨr/, /rayt/, /rayd/, /pat/, /pad/, where the phonetic form is predictable by very general and familiar phonetic rules of English, now supplemented by a low-level rule about *today*. The same is true in many other cases.

The one context in which raising of exceptions and counter-instances is to the point is in connection with some criterion proposed for isolation of certain elements or certain kinds of analysis. In this case, counter-instances show that the criterion is not a correct, or at least, not a fully correct one. But discovery of exceptions to grammatical generalizations is of no consequence in itself, except when it leads to an alternative, more comprehensive generalization.

In contrast with the view that the main methodological problem of linguistics is the elaboration of techniques for discovering and classifying linguistic elements and that grammars are inventories of these elements and classes, I have suggested that it can be profitable to conceive of a grammar of L as a theory of the sentences of L and to consider the methodological problem of linguistics to be the construction of a general theory of linguistic structure in which the properties of grammars, and of the structural descriptions and linguistic levels derived from them, are studied in an abstract way. An important part of this theory will be a procedure of evaluation that will permit choice between alternative proposed grammars for particular lan-guages. The question of how to arrive at a grammar of L, much like the problem of how to discover any scientific theory of a particular subject matter, is, in this view, not considered to be a concern of linguistics proper, at least in the present stage of its development, but to belong rather to the psychology of invention. If a general mechanical procedure for constructing grammars of the appropriate type from the raw data can be developed (and we are, I believe, very far from this), this will be a major achievement which will, for example, shed great light on the human ability to learn language. But a methodological requirement that the concepts of the theory of language be so chosen that simple and direct procedures of analysis can be used to determine their application in particular cases is no more justifiable in linguistics than in any other science, and it is likely to have the effect of distorting our concep-tion and understanding of linguistic structure.

8   Negation in English*

Edward S. Klima

It is not altogether unfitting for a study on negation to begin with a negative statement. At any rate, misinterpretation may be avoided if I specify at the outset what will *not* be the outcome of this particular investigation and what is *not* included in its formal descriptive apparatus. This is not to say that methods and objectives excluded here could not be the basis for interesting observations about negation and related linguistic phenomena; indeed, traditionally they have been just that.

In the first place, the approach adopted in this study will not consist of selecting words or constructions intuited to be similar (e.g., *not, never, nothing, nobody*), defining them as negative (perhaps in varying degrees), and describing their grammatical characteristics. For the purposes of grammatical description, there are important limitations inherent in such tactics; they leave unclear the question as to whether or not the groups selected and the relationships proposed are natural to the grammatical system as a whole; and, of course, the notion *natural to the grammatical system* is not explicated. In other words, the direct product of the analysis to be proposed in the present study will not consist of the formalization of categories from traditional (i.e., impressionistic, nonrigorous) grammar. Nor shall we operate with a refinement that provides the approach rejected above with a more explicit basis for classification in the form of a criterion whereby grammatical elements are classified, let's say, as negative if they result in sentences that are semantically equivalent to, or imply, otherwise identical sentences containing *not*. (By this criterion, for example, *im-* would be negative in "This is impossible" because it implies "This isn't possible.") This refinement, too, will be eschewed. To be valid in a strictly

*The material that appears here was first presented in a series of lectures at the Symposium on Transformational Analysis, University of Pennsylvania, November, 1959; and at the Symposium on Machine Translation, National Science Foundation, Washington, D.C., November, 1959. This work was supported in part by the National Science Foundation and in part by the U.S. Army Signal Corps, the Air Force Office of Scientific Research, and the Office of Naval Research.

grammatical analysis, even such a basis for classification, rigorous as it might be, would demand the unwarranted assumption that semantic categories are always matched by grammatical ones.

Furthermore, the analysis to be presented in this study will provide no way of knowing whether some arbitrary sentence or element thereof is negative. Take, for example, the words *never* and *not* in "John had never done it, and neither had Bill" and "John hadn't ever done it, and neither had Bill." These two words are grammatically similar with respect to *neither*, and sentences containing *never* or *not* are opposed to certain other sentences without these words (e.g., "John had already done it, and so had Bill") in that *so* occurs to the exclusion of *neither*; i.e., there is no sentence*[1] "He had already done it, and neither had she." The restriction in the occurrence of *neither*, as opposed to *so*, can be ascribed to a grammatical feature common to *never* and *not* in such sentences. Adopting conventional impressionistic terminology, we can label this feature *negative*. However, there is no way of *knowing* whether the same items *never* and *not* have the same grammatical features, labeled *negative*, in sentences that do not contain a *neither*- tag like ". . . , and neither had Bill" (e.g., in sentences like "John had never done it"). In short, no criterion will be offered according to which an arbitrary element of any sentence whatever can be classified as negative or not negative, independently of other sentences.

Finally—and very unfortunately—the analysis that shall be proposed offers in itself no interpretation of notions like *negative* that appear as designations of grammatical symbols. That is, as far as the formal grammatical analysis is concerned, labels like *negative* have no meaning above and beyond their grammatical function of specifying a structural position and some difference from other symbols.

I

1 Let's turn now to the positive side of the question. The point that I shall try to demonstrate in the present study is as follows: in the description of the *grammar* of English, there emerge, in a *natural* way, elements, categories, and intercategory relationships that correspond closely to certain traditional grammatical concepts couched generally in impressionistic terms and that will, I hope, aid in clarifying these concepts—concepts like *transitivity, subordination*, and, of particular relevance to this study, *sentence negation* as opposed to *word negation*, and so on. Particularly crucial here are the notions *grammar* and *in a natural way*.

2 By *grammar* will be understood *the rules for generating the sentences of the language*. The objective of these rules is to account for the *shape* of the sentences and to assign each a structure. By stressing shape, I mean to emphasize that the aspect of language of concern to grammar as the term is used here, consists of differences in the form of sentences (varying restrictions on the occurrence of elements with respect to one another), and not similarities and differences in the meaning of sentences. That "John had never done it, and neither had Bill" and "John hadn't ever done it, and neither had Bill" have the same meaning is thus not necessarily relevant

---

[1]For the use of symbols, see the Appendix entitled *Symbolism* at the end of this chapter.

grammatically. But, that certain structures in these and similar sentences contrast, as a class, with those in sentences like "John had already done it, and so had Bill" with respect to the *shape* of the permissible tags (i.e., ". . . , and neither had Bill," as opposed to ". . . , and so had Bill") is clearly within the domain of grammar.

3 Preference between alternative grammars of the same language will follow from some explicit criterion of excellence. The selection of the particular criterion to be employed depends on the extent to which the analysis resulting from the optimal grammar satisfying that criterion is *interesting and revealing*. The possibility is certainly not excluded that there may be several such criteria and, accordingly, several optimal grammars. In the following study, the criterion of excellence adopted will be that of shortness of rules as measured by counting the occurrence of symbols.

4 In speaking of grammatical elements, categories, and relationships emerging *in a natural way*, I mean to specify a nonarbitrariness that is a concomitant both of the objective of grammar rules and of the criterion of economy as adopted above; that is, that symbols representing grammatical categories are postulated only if the presence of such symbols accounts for some ultimate difference in the shape of sentences and if this difference cannot be accounted for more economically with some other combination of symbols (i.e., with another analysis) not including the symbol in question. Thus, all forms are considered the same until some formal reason to differentiate among them presents itself; and once in possession of a grammatically differentiated feature by necessity in one usage, a form will be assumed to have that feature everywhere else as well, pending the discovery of formal reasons to differentiate further. What cannot be *known* to be the same nonetheless can— and, in accordance with the principle of economy, must—be assumed the same until a difference is demonstrated.

5 In the present study, two factors outside the formal descriptive apparatus will ultimately affect the value of the analysis: success in discovering those patterns that reveal such peculiarities in occurrence as necessitate the recognition of special grammatical differences between forms; and astuteness in differentiating those peculiarities that are grammatical (e.g., the ungrammaticalness of *"this object are numerous") from those that are semantic (e.g., the contradictoriness of "The round object is square") and those that merely reflect the truth or falseness of statements of fact (e.g., the falseness of "The moon is square").

6 The analysis that follows is to be looked at as a particular segment of a complete grammatical analysis of English, such an analysis as is provided by a generative grammar.[2] The segment consists primarily of those of the grammar rules that are involved in constructions traditionally associated with negation, but parts of the grammar that involve other constructions are considered to the extent that they reveal grammatical peculiarities common also to negatives (constructions traditionally referred to as interrogative, restrictive, conditional, as well as to certain other subordinate constructions). The isolating of the particular grammar rules in question must be kept a completely neutral action, neither adding anything to the

---

[2]On generative grammars see Noam Chomsky, *Syntactic Structures* ('s Gravenhage, 1957); also R. B. Lees, "The Grammar of English Nominalizations," *International Journal of American Linguistics* XXVI (1960), Part II.

analysis nor even constituting a new grouping that is not already represented independently by a symbol in the grammar rules. Nothing is relevant except what occurs *in a natural way* (as discussed in Section 4) in the grammar as a whole. It is continuous and exclusive reference to the total system that prevents the analysis of a segment, isolated on a more or less notional basis and thus arbitrary (as far as the *grammar* is concerned), from being merely the more or less rigorous description of categories from traditional grammar. On the other hand, if the grammar itself contains distinctions analogous to those categories, then the existence of such analogs is at least one measure of how *interesting and revealing* (as in Section 3) the analysis is. The explanatory power represented by such analogs gives support to the particular choice of conventions employed in the formal system (conventions like the types of grammar rules permitted and the way of measuring the relative excellence of alternative grammars). Accordingly, we shall be interested in what is said, even quite impressionistically, about language, and especially in bits of insight into structural relationships between linguistic elements. In the scholarly work on English grammar of the past century, there is no lack of sophisticated expression of this sort of insight into the structure of the language. Certainly one way of evaluating the rules and conventions of a formal generative grammar (with respect, for example, to their psychological reality) is to compare the resultant analysis with carefully formulated observations made on the basis of just such sharpened linguistic insight.

II

7 Consider from this point of view the following sentences:

The students did *not* believe that it had happened.	(1a)
The students *never* believed that it had happened.	(1b)
The students *hardly* believed that it had happened.	(1c)
The students *rarely* believed that it had happened.	(1d)
None of the students believed that it had happened.	(1e)
Few students believed that it had happened.	(1f)
The students were *unable* to believe that it had happened.	(1g)
The students were *too* intelligent to believe that it had happened.	(1h)
The students *doubted* that it had happened.	(1i)

Scattered through various handbooks on English grammar are statements about sentences similar to these. While often differentiating the sentences in one way or another, in most cases the characterizations still contain some reference to a negative element. Kruisinga and Erades include *hardly* and *never* with *not* as "adverbs of modality expressing negation."[3] In sentences like those of Eq. (1f) *few*, according to Poutsma, is "distinctly negative,"[4] and according to Jespersen, ". . . may even in

---

[3]E. Kruisinga and P. A. Erades, *An English Grammar*, Vol. I (Groningen, 1953) 89.
[4]H. Poutsma, *A Grammar of Late Modern English* (Groningen, 1929), p. 1096.

many cases be considered negative rather than positive,"[5] while for a case like Eq. (1h), Jespersen writes, "negation is also implied in expressions with *too* ('she is too poor to give us anything she cannot . . .')"[6] Curme refers to *none* (Eq. (1e)) as the "negative form of *one*."[7] Words like *unable* (Eq. (1g)) are commonly analyzed as containing a negative prefix, and *doubt* (Eq. (1i)) is called, by Jespersen, "a verb of negative import."[8] As to their differentiation, in general only sentences containing *not* (Eq. (1a)) and *never* (Eq. (1b)) are considered instances of full sentence negation, while the others are characterized accordingly as they contain incomplete, special, or inherent negatives. To the extent that scholarly observations like these have not, in their sophistication, become dangerously adulterated with formal logic, Latin grammar, linguistic history, and the like, they can be regarded as reflecting just such insight into the structure of the language as has been shown to be valuable (as in Section 6). Let us put the question in the following form: granted the obvious grammatical differences between the italicized forms described as negative (the differences in the parts of speech represented: *rarely* in Eq. (1d), an adverb; *none* in Eq. (1e), a noun; *few* in Eq. (1f), an adjective; *doubt* in Eq. (1i), a verb) is there any reason to consider the intuited shared negativeness a single feature from a formal point of view? In other words, in the structural description of the sentences of the language as provided by the grammar rules that generate them, is it the case that a single symbol accounts for certain linguistic facts at the very places where negativeness is intuited? These are questions that will remain in the back of our minds during the ensuing investigation.

8 Some basic grammar rules for the generation of sentences. To get a general idea of the notion of generative grammar as rules for generating the grammatical sentences of a language, consider the following informal sketch. For the moment we shall examine only the general form of those parts of the grammar rules that pertain to simple sentences. The motivation for postulating these particular rules and their order will not be discussed in these illustrative examples.

8.1 *Constituent Structure*. Consider first the rules that account for the basic constituents of the sentence and their structures by the progressive ordered expansion (symbolized by a single arrow →) of single symbols into a string of other symbols until the ultimate lexical items are generated. We shall begin with an initial symbol *S*, to be referred to in the text as *S*(entence). The initial expansion of *S*(entence) may optionally include, aside from the Predicate and the Nominal functioning as subject, also the symbol wh. One of the functions of wh is to relate questions grammatically to the declaratives that those questions correspond to. Thus, "Will someone see something" and "Someone will see something" are related at the level of constituent structure by the absence versus the presence of constituent wh. The particular differences between declaratives and corresponding questions—for example, in word order—will be accounted for by rules given below in Section 8.2.

$$S \rightarrow \text{(wh) Nominal-Predicate} \qquad (2)$$

---

[5]Otto Jespersen, *The Philosophy of Grammar* (London, 1924), p. 324.

[6]Otto Jespersen, *Negation in English and Other Languages* (København, 1917), p. 37.

[7]Otto Jespersen, *A Modern English Grammar*, Part V, p. 455.

[8]George O. Curme, *A Grammar of the English Language*, Vol. III, "Syntax," Section 57.1.b. (Boston, 1931).

The Predicate will be further expanded into *Aux*(iliary)—representing the various helping verbs—adverbial constituents of Place and Time, and a *M*(ain) *V*(erb). The *M*(ain) *V*(erb) itself is expanded into a verb with or without an object Nominal (that is, transitive or intransitive, respectively).

$$\text{Predicate} \rightarrow Aux\text{-}MV(\text{Place}) (\text{Time}) \tag{3}$$

$$MV \rightarrow \begin{Bmatrix} \text{Verb(Nominal)} \\ \text{be-Predicative} \end{Bmatrix} \tag{4}$$

The *Aux*(iliary) of a sentence may consist of one or several helping verbs of which the perfect auxiliary (*have-PP*, the symbol *P*(ast) *P*(article) here representing the form assumed by the following verb when the perfect helping verb *have* precedes) must precede the progressive auxiliary (*be-PrP*, i.e,, *Pr*(esent)*P*(article))), and neither may precede a *M*(odal) auxiliary (*will* or *can*). The endings representing Tense appear on the initial verbal form of the Predicate, whether that initial verbal form is an auxiliary verb—and any of them may appear first—or the principal verb of the sentence when no auxiliary verbs occur. For this reason, Tense is assumed to precede the verbal constituents of the *Aux*(iliary) and every *Aux*(iliary) must contain at least Tense. The ultimate incorporation of Tense, *PP*, or *PrP*, into a following verbal form will be described by rules in Section 8.2.

$$Aux \rightarrow \text{Tense}(M) (have\text{-}PP) (be\text{-}PrP) \tag{5}$$

In *M*(odals), neither Tense form differentiates between singular and plural agreement with the subject Nominal (that is, "He can" is like "They can," "He could" is like "They could"). When Tense occurs in the *env*(ironment) of a *M*(odal), viz., before a *M*(odal), it is expanded as φ or *-ed*. Otherwise, Tense is expanded as Present or Past.

$$\text{Tense} \rightarrow \begin{Bmatrix} \varphi \\ \text{ed} \end{Bmatrix}, \text{ in } env. - M \tag{6}$$

$$\text{Tense} \rightarrow \begin{Bmatrix} \text{Present} \\ \text{Past} \end{Bmatrix} \tag{7}$$

$$M \rightarrow \begin{Bmatrix} \text{can} \\ \text{will} \end{Bmatrix} \tag{8}$$

The rules that expand the other symbols follow:

$$\text{Verb} \rightarrow V \tag{9}$$

$$V \rightarrow \begin{Bmatrix} \text{see} \\ \text{believe} \end{Bmatrix}, \text{ in } env. - \text{Nominal} \tag{10a}$$

$$V \rightarrow \text{happen} \tag{10b}$$

$$\text{Place} \rightarrow \text{there} \tag{11}$$

$$\text{Time} \rightarrow \text{then} \tag{12}$$

$$\text{Nominal} \rightarrow \begin{Bmatrix} \text{something-}Sg \\ \text{somebody-}Sg \\ \text{Noun}\begin{Bmatrix} Sg \\ Pl \end{Bmatrix} \end{Bmatrix} \qquad (13)$$

$$\text{Noun} \rightarrow \text{the writer} \qquad (14)$$

Accordingly, the constituent structure of the sentence "Someone will see something there" would be:

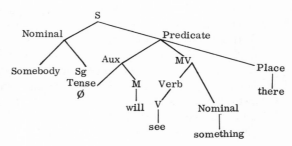

Figure 1

Strings of symbols such as this, with an unambiguous structure such as is represented by the diagram, are converted into sentences by the various re-arrangements, combinings, deletions, and additions described by transformational rules (symbolyzed by a double arrow ⇒). A convention will be adopted in this study whereby all rules describing constituent structure must precede the transformational rules in the grammar.

8.2 *Transformational Structure.* The Present tense, except in *M*(odals), agrees in number with the subject Nominal. That is, grammatically, the specification of the form of Present depends on whether the subject Nominal ultimately ends in *Sg* or *Pl*; e.g., "they see" but "he sees."

$$\text{I. verbal concord} \qquad (15)$$

$$Sg[\text{Present}]_{\text{Tense}} \Rightarrow Sg\,[S]_{\text{Tense}}$$
$$Pl[\text{Present}]_{\text{Tense}} \Rightarrow Pl[\varphi]_{\text{Tense}}$$

One of the grammatical differences between declarative sentences and questions is that certain constituents in the basic structure of the former occur as interrogative words in the latter, e.g., "Somebody will see something," but "What (replacing the object Nominal) will somebody see?" or "Who (replacing the subject Nominal) will see something?" In terms of the structure of the language, this can be described as the optional incorporation (symbolized by +) of certain constituents of the sentence into the wh which appears in Eq. (2); e.g., *what* represents wh + something and *who* represents wh + somebody.

II. incorporation into wh (optional)   (16)

wh-somebody-Predicate   ⇒ wh + somebody-Predicate
wh-Nominal-*Aux*-Verb-something ⇒ wh + something-Nominal-*Aux*-Verb

Another way that questions differ from corresponding declarative sentences is in their inverted word order, which will be described from the point of view of the constituent structure as a re-arrangement of certain constituents of the *Aux*(iliary). The re-arrangement occurs when the subject Nominal intervenes between wh, with or without incorporated constituents, and the Predicate. With respect to the relevance of the order of rules, note that the rule of *verbal concord* is most simply stated if it precedes the rule describing inversion, i.e., when all the subject Nominals are still in front of Tense.

III. wh-attraction

$$\underbrace{\text{wh} (+ \text{something})}_{1} \; \underbrace{[\text{somebody}]_{\text{Nominal}}}_{2} \; \underbrace{[\text{Tense-will-see-}X}_{3} \underbrace{]_{\text{Predicate}}}_{4} \Rightarrow \qquad (17)$$

$$\underbrace{\text{wh}(+ \text{something})}_{1} \; \underbrace{\text{Tense-will}}_{3} \; \underbrace{[\text{somebody}]_{\text{Nominal}}}_{2} \; \underbrace{\text{see-}X}_{4}$$

(where X contains an object Nominal if *something* is not attached to wh)

NOTE: a question without an interrogative word (i.e., where no constituents are incorporated into wh) also has inverted order (i.e., also undergoes wh-attraction, resulting, e.g., in the string, wh-Tense-*will* [somebody]$_{\text{Nominal}}$ see-something.)

In the direct yes-no question the constituent wh does not have a phonological form, i.e., a wh without incorporated constituents and which has not assumed the functions of a subordinate conjunction (e.g., *whether*) is deleted, i.e., *φ-will-somebody-see-something* and not *whether-will-somebody-see-something*.

IV. wh-deletion   (18)
wh-Nominal ⇒ φ-Nominal

Finally, the desinences of Tense appear suffixed to the first verbal element in the Predicate. The verbal constituents that follow the perfect auxiliary *have* and the progressive auxiliary *be* appear in appropriate participial form; i.e., the verbal affixes (Tense, *PP*, and *PrP*) are incorporated into the following verbal constituent:

V. Tense-attachment   (19)

$$\text{Tense} \begin{Bmatrix} M \\ \text{be} \\ \text{have} \\ V \end{Bmatrix} \Rightarrow \begin{Bmatrix} M \\ \text{be} \\ \text{have} \\ V \end{Bmatrix} + \text{Tense}$$

The rules for the incorporation of the *P*(ast)*P*(article) and the *Pr*(esent)*P*(article) are similar.

Other rules describe the special shape that words assume in certain functions; e.g., that the past tense of *see* is *saw*, i.e., *see* + Past ⇒ *saw*; see + *PP* ⇒ seen.

PRE-VERBAL ADVERBS I: THE NEGATIVE
PARTICLE *NOT*

9 Let us begin the investigation of negatives by considering certain distributional features of words like *never, always, so,* that occur within the Predicate before the *M*(ain) *V*(erb). For the purposes of exposition we shall refer to these words informally as *adverbs* without necessarily assuming that these words actually represent a symbol in the grammar. (Such terms when used in tentative rules will be written in bold-face miniscules.) The analysis will be in terms of provisional rules of grammar, provisional in that some will be improved, some rejected, in the course of the presentation.[9] Consider sentences like the following:

$$\text{The writers will} \begin{cases} \text{(a)} & \text{not, never, scarcely, hardly,} \\ & \text{rarely, seldom, barely, little} \\ \text{(b)} & \text{so, always, almost, usually,} \\ & \text{surely, sure, frequently,} \\ & \text{commonly, often, probably,} \\ & \text{fortunately, etc.} \end{cases} \text{believe the boy.} \qquad (20)$$

At this point the division into categories, (a) and (b), has no significance in the analysis. If the adverbs behaved everywhere in the sentence as they do here, then there would be no grammatical motivation for differentiating between them along the lines *negative* versus *positive*.[10] One of the possible locations of the adverb would be included in the following description of the sentence; *S*: Nominal-Tense-will-**adverb**-V- Nominal. The grammar might, but actually will not, include a rule of the general form **adverb** $\Rightarrow \begin{cases} \text{not} \\ \text{always} \end{cases}$.

10 Various differences in freedom of occurrence even within the simple sentence would, of course, require the recognition of grammatical distinctions among those constituents expanded from *adverb* (for example, not all occur initially). Included in these distinctions would be severe restrictions on the pre-verbal position of *not*. While sentences like those in Eq. (20) exist where *not* has the same location as the other adverbs, in the following sentences *not* is different:

$$\text{The writers} \begin{cases} \text{never, scarcely,} \\ \text{almost, always, etc.} \end{cases} \text{believed the boy.} \qquad (21)$$

---

[9]The constant re-examination of grammar rules already formulated, with a view to their possible improvement or possible rejection, is a characteristic of this study, and a natural consequence of the method of presentation used here. According to this method, grammar rules are postulated to account for certain *problem* sentences. Then the *problem* area is broadened by considering other sentences, and the existing rules are put to the test of the new sentences. A straight-forward presentation of the total grammar would of course be less cumbersome; however, the objective of the present study was not just to present the part of the generative grammar of English pertinent to negation, but also to show what makes certain grammatical phenomena a problem, and to show how some of these grammatical problems are solved. The less direct approach seemed better suited to the latter objectives.

[10]*Little* in the expression: "they little knew what to expect" also belongs to the category of negative **pre-**verbal adverbs.

The first of the following sentences is not grammatical; there are, however, sentences like the second:

*The writers *not* believed the boy. (22a)

The writers *did not* believe the boy. (22b)

11 The problem of *not* and the helping verb *do*. The syntax of *do* and *not* in such sentences as Eq. (22b) presents interesting problems. Certain facts which we will now examine suggest that *do* in sentences like this should be interpreted as a mere support for *not* (and for a few other elements). Such instances of *do* will be found to have their source in the Transformational Structure of the language; they will not be included in the dictionary. Pertinent to the status of *do* in these instances are the following considerations.

Do is unlike other *helping verbs*—as we shall refer, informally, to verbal forms that appear before the *M*(ain) *V*(erb) of the sentence. *Do* as a helping verb is similar to the *M*(odal) auxiliaries, for example, *will, can,* in not occurring in infinitive phrases (for example, *"They expected us to do leave him" like *"They expected us to can leave him"). But it is unlike the *M*(odals) in never occurring before the constituents of the *Aux*(iliary) expressing aspect, the perfect *have* or the progressive *be* (for example, "He may be leaving" but *"He does be leaving"). *Do* is also unlike the *M*(odals) in that it occurs in the imperative (for example, "Do come at five" but *"Must come at five"). On the other hand, *do* as a helping verb differs from the aspect auxiliaries *have* and *be* in that it never occurs with a preceding *M*(odal) (for example, *"He can do leave" but "He can be leaving"). If *do* were to be considered a lexical item on the same footing as any of these other helping verbs—an analysis that will be rejected for reasons given here and later—then its occurrence would exclude that of any other verbal member of the *Aux*(iliary), and the description of the constituent structure would contain such a rule as, $Aux \rightarrow \text{Tense} \begin{Bmatrix} (M) \text{ (have-}PP\text{) (be-}PrP\text{)} \\ \text{do} \end{Bmatrix}$. *Not* would then be described as occurring after the first helping verb—and only in sentences with a helping verb. "He will leave"—"He will not leave" would be considered paralleled by "He does leave"—"He does not leave"; that is, "He does not leave" would be "He does leave" plus an optional *not*. The sentence without a helping verb "He leaves" would then have no parallel with *not*.

And yet, in certain more complicated structures, the sequence *do*—*not* followed by the *M*(ain) *V*(erb) (for example, "He didn't leave her") functions specifically as the negative parallel to the *M*(ain) *V*(erb) alone (that is, "He left her"). Examples of such structures are found in the question type, "He will leave her, won't he?" "He has left her, hasn't he?" in which the tag, "..., won't he?", "..., hasn't he?" consists of a truncated question form of the *corresponding* negated source sentence. Included in this question type is the construction "He left her, didn't he?" To account for the latter, the particular pairing of the simple form and the form with *do-not* must be recognized in the grammar rules.

Do as a helping verb has very special distributional features, which must, of course, be accounted for in the grammar rules—and which should be accounted for with a minimum abuse of the principle of economy. A distributional asymmetry not already described which is very crucial in the analysis adopted below is the following.

While in the indicative, the "helping verb" *do* is excluded before all functions of *be*, it occurs with *be* in the imperative, obligatorily in negative imperatives, optionally in affirmative imperatives:

$$\text{*He does not be sitting there when I arrive.} \qquad (23a)$$
$$\text{Do not be sitting there when I arrive.} \qquad (23b)$$
$$\text{*He does be good.} \qquad (23c)$$
$$\text{Do be good.} \qquad (23d)$$

12 Grammar rules for the pre-verbal particles *not* and helping verb *do*. The rules accounting for the location of *not* and for the occurrences of *do* would have approximately the following form.

Aux(iliary) contains Tense and optionally one of the *M*(odal) verbs and/or the aspect auxiliaries; that is, *have* with *PP* and *be* with *PrP*, but not *do*. For example, in the sentence "He will have been sleeping for five hours," the *Aux*(iliary) has the form, Tense-*will-have-PP-be-PrP*. The particle *not*, or *so*, is placed after the element of the *Aux*(iliary) following Tense, if the sentence contains such an element, or after Tense-be, otherwise after Tense alone. We shall refer to this particular segmentation consisting of Tense $\begin{Bmatrix} M \\ \text{have} \\ \text{be} \end{Bmatrix}$ or Tense alone when the latter is followed directly by the principle verb (*V*) of the sentence as **aux^1**. Disregard for the moment the origin of *not* and *so*.

I. Pre-verbal Particle Placement

$$(a) \quad \left[\text{Tense-} \begin{Bmatrix} M \\ \text{have} \\ \text{be} \end{Bmatrix} \right]_{\text{aux}^1} \Rightarrow \text{Tense-} \begin{Bmatrix} M \\ \text{have} \\ \text{be} \end{Bmatrix} \begin{Bmatrix} \text{not} \\ \text{so} \end{Bmatrix} \qquad (24a)$$

$$(b) \quad [\text{Tense}]_{\text{aux}^1} \; V \Rightarrow \text{Tense} \begin{Bmatrix} \text{not} \\ \text{so} \end{Bmatrix} V \qquad (24b)$$

Tense, along with the other verbal affixes (*PrP* and *PP*), is incorporated into an immediately following verb form,

II. Tense-attachment

$$\text{Tense} \begin{Bmatrix} [\text{will}]_M \\ \text{have} \\ \text{be} \\ [\text{sleep}]_V \end{Bmatrix} \Rightarrow \begin{Bmatrix} \text{will} \\ \text{have} \\ \text{be} \\ \text{sleep} \end{Bmatrix} + \text{Tense} \qquad (25)$$

But note now, that if there is only one element of the *Aux*(iliary): Tense; then Eq. (24) produces the string, Tense-*not-V* (for example, *he*-Past-*not-sleep*), and here Eq. (25) does not apply, because Tense-attachment is blocked by *not*. Finally, any Tense left unattached to a verb form—whether because blocked by not or because of other re-arrangements—has *do* inserted before it as a support.

III. *Do*-support

$$\text{Tense} \Rightarrow do + \text{Tense} \qquad (26)$$

13 Resolution of problems involving *not* and helping verb *do*. The mere fact that an analysis shows asymmetry in the system does not invalidate that analysis, for certainly there is much asymmetry in language. For example, the copula *be* has no progressive; *must* and *need* (*not*) in the function of modal auxiliaries have no past tense form. On the other hand, demonstration that another analysis both resolves asymmetry and accounts for superficially unrelated features in other constructions does invalidate the weaker analysis. The treatment of the helping verb *do* as a transformationally introduced element accomplishes precisely this.

The three ordered transformational rules in Section 12 above account, in a simple way, for the various differences between *do* and those auxiliary verbs treated here as basic elements (*will*, progressive *be*, and so on), differences with an unsystematized appearance when they were enumerated in Section 11. With certain minor differences as to permissible environments, the rules for describing the particle *so* duplicate those of *not*. Their placement in the finite verb chain is the same and both occasion a supporting *do* in the same way.

The writers could so believe the boy.	(27a)
*The writers so believed the boy.	(27b)
The writers did so believe the boy.	(27c)

A seeming counter-argument to the transformational, nonbasic nature of *do* as a helping verb is provided by positive declaratives like "The writers did believe the boy," where *do* would seem not to be explained by the separation of Tense from the following verbal form, but in which *do* has emphatic stress. We can bring such instances of helping verb *do* under the general description presented in Eqs. (24–26) and at the same time maintain the parallelism between emphatic stress on *do* and emphatic stress on the second constituent of the *Aux*(iliary). For example, "The writers can [i.e., Tense-*can*] *stress* believe the boy," if emphasis is treated as a constituent (*Emph*) that has the same distributional characteristics as the particle *so* (see Eq. (24)) and that blocks attachment of Tense (Eq. (25)) in the same way as *so* does. *Emph* thus occasions *do*-support (Eq. (26)), but has no phonological shape.

Let's consider *Emph* a particle. The description of its location is, Tense $\begin{Bmatrix} M \\ be \\ have \end{Bmatrix}$ **particle**, or Tense-**particle**-*V*. The latter description holds when there are no auxiliary verbs in the sentence. The rule by which the constituent *Emph* attaches stress to the preceding word and then drops from the representation must follow *do*-support (Eq. (26)). The same three rules Eqs. (24–26) further justify themselves in explaining other instances of the helping verb *do* in sentences without the particles *not* and *so*. In certain interrogative sentences and sentences with an initial negative adverb, the Tense-marker—alone or with the second verbal constituent of the *Aux*(iliary), if there is one—is separated from the rest of the verb chain. In such sentences, the subject, rather than *not*, is the intervening constituent; again, when the Tense-marker is not immediately followed by a verb form to which Tense can be attached by Tense-attachment (Eq. (25)), *do* is inserted as a support in accordance with *do*-support (Eq. (26)).

$$\begin{Bmatrix} \text{Past-have} \\ \text{Past} \end{Bmatrix} \quad \text{the-writers} \begin{Bmatrix} \text{\textit{PP}-believe} \\ \text{believe} \end{Bmatrix} \quad \text{the-boy?}$$

$$\Rightarrow \begin{Bmatrix} \text{have} + \text{Past} \\ \text{Past} \end{Bmatrix} \quad \text{the-writers} \begin{Bmatrix} \text{believed} + \textit{PP} \\ \text{believe} \end{Bmatrix} \quad \text{the-boy?} \tag{28}$$

$$\Rightarrow \begin{Bmatrix} \text{have} + \text{Past} \\ \textit{do} + \text{Past} \end{Bmatrix} \quad \text{the writers} \begin{Bmatrix} \text{believe} + \textit{PP} \\ \text{believe} \end{Bmatrix} \quad \text{the-boy?}$$

"Had the writers believed the boy?"
"Did the writers believe the boy?"

$$\text{Nowhere} \begin{Bmatrix} \text{Past-have} \\ \text{Past} \end{Bmatrix} \quad \text{the-writers} \begin{Bmatrix} \text{\textit{PP}-believe} \\ \text{believe} \end{Bmatrix} \text{the-boy.} \tag{29}$$

$$\Rightarrow \text{Nowhere} \begin{Bmatrix} \text{had} \\ \text{did} \end{Bmatrix} \quad \text{the-writers} \begin{Bmatrix} \text{believed} \\ \text{believe} \end{Bmatrix} \text{the-boy.}$$

(by the same steps as Eq. (28))

The analysis of *do* as a transformationally introduced support for the *Tense*-marker when there is no other member of the *Aux*(iliary) accounts for the particular pairing, in tag-questions, of the simple positive declarative without helping verb and the negative tag with helping verb *do* ("The writers *believed* the boy, *didn't* they?"), for each is the regular result of a verb phrase in which the *Tense*-marker is the sole member of the *Aux*(iliary); that is, *The-writers-Past-believe-him, Past-n't-they*). The difference in the two forms is due to the fact that in the tag (Past-n't-they), Tense (i.e., Past) is not directly followed by a verb form to which it may be attached by Eq. (26) (that is, . . . , Past-*n't-they* ⇒ *do*-Past-*n't-they*).

The rules describing particle placement and the occurrence of the helping verb *do* also figure prominently in explaining the seemingly exceptional feature of the verbal chain in imperatives: the occurrence of *do* before *be* and *not be* in the imperative but not in the indicative. As will be seen, this difference turns out to be a regular consequence of a set of rules whose existence has independent justification in their role in accounting for other facts of the language. Consider an imperative like the following:

$$\text{Do not be sitting there then.} \tag{30}$$

I shall argue that (30) is derived transformationally from a source sentence of the following general form:

$$\text{You-Tense-will-not-be-sitting-there-then.} \tag{31}$$

The choice of elements that appear in the source but that do not appear in the imperative itself is not arbitrary. All such elements in some way account for the *shape* of permissible imperatives, following the principle stated in Section 2. Because of imperatives like:

$$\text{Protect yourself} \tag{32}$$

where the reflexive forms of *you* occur and no other reflexive pronouns, *you* singular or plural, is assumed to be the subject of the source sentence for every imperative.

The line of reasoning is this: on the one hand, the general rule in simple indicative sentences is that the reflexive pronoun (described here by the addition of *pro* and *reflex* to certain repeated Nominals) occurs as object when that object is identical to the subject; that is, Nominal$_1$-*Aux*-Verb-Nominal$_2$ $\Rightarrow$ Nominal$_1$-*Aux*-Verb-*pro*+Nominal+*reflex*, where Nominal$_1$ is the same as Nominal$_2$. On the other hand, although without a subject, imperative sentences may contain a reflexive as direct object, but that reflexive is limited to *yourself* or *yourselves*. Thus, with the assumption of a deleted subject *you*, the occurrence of and special restriction on reflexives in imperative sentences are described with rules that are necessary elsewhere in the grammar anyway. Although Eq. (30) contains no overt reflexes of the postulated subject Nominal *you*, that sentence and those like it will be assumed to be similar to Eq. (32) (which on the basis of reflexivization is assumed to have an underlying subject *you*). This assumption will be maintained until the need for differentiating them is shown, which is in accordance with the principle of Section 4. Because *not* (and *Emph*) occurs before *be* in imperatives, the existence (in the source) of not only Tense but also another constituent of the *Aux*(iliary) is postulated. This postulated auxiliary element ultimately has no phonological form in this position. In this way, preverbal particle placement (Eq. (24)) produces the correct order. That the constituent of the *Aux*(iliary) is analyzed specifically as *will* deleted results from the particular form of the tag *won't you* in imperatives like:

$$\text{Close the door, } won't \text{ you!} \tag{33}$$

Compare the syntax of this tag with the general formulation of such tags in other types of sentences:

$$\text{They } can \text{ close the door, } can't \text{ they?} \tag{34}$$

$$\text{They closed the door, didn't they?} \tag{35}$$

In indicatives, the tag repeats the Tense and, if there is one, the second member of the auxiliary chain, as well as the pronominalized subject Nominal. Included in the description of tags are the following ordered rules operative on a string like Eq. (31); the φ that appears as Tense results from the constituent structure rule (Eq. (6)) whereby Tense $\rightarrow \left\{ \begin{array}{c} \varphi \\ ed \end{array} \right\}$ preceding a M(odal). It is this Tense form with zero-ending proper to M(odals) (*He-run*+*s* but *He-can*+*φ-run*) that is carried over to the initial verbal form in imperatives, thus accounting for the difference in verb endings between "You *are* sitting there" but "*Be* sitting there."

$$\text{S:} \quad \text{you}[\varphi]_{\text{Tense}} \text{ will-not-be-ing-sit-there-then [after pre-} \atop \text{verbal particle placement, see Eq. (24)} \tag{36a}$$

$$\text{i.} \quad [\varphi]_{\text{Tense}} \text{ not-be-ing-sit-there-then [by some rule of } you \atop \text{and } will \text{ deletion]} \tag{36b}$$

$$\text{ii.} \quad [\varphi]_{\text{Tense}} \text{ not-be-sitt}+\text{ing-there-then [by Tense-attach-} \atop \text{ment, see Eq. (25)} \tag{36c}$$

$$\text{iii.} \quad do + \varphi \text{-not-be-sitt}+\text{ing-there-then [by } do\text{-support,} \atop \text{see Eq. (26)} \tag{36d}$$

The tag formation exemplified in Eq. (33) and a rule describing the occurrence of reflexives, in strings where they apply, would occur before the deletion of *you* and *will*.

14   Rules for the intra-*Aux*(iliary) positioning of *Adv*(erbs) and Particles. In describing the syntax of adverbial elements like *often* in the following sentences:

$$\text{Writers often accept such suggestions.} \tag{37a}$$

$$\text{Writers often have accepted such suggestions.} \tag{37b}$$

we shall extend the constituent structure rule that expands the *Aux*(iliary) so that it optionally includes an initial constituent *Adv*(erb) and replaces Eq. (5)):

$$Aux \rightarrow (Adv)\text{Tense}(M)(\text{have-}PP)(\text{be-}PrP) \tag{37c}$$

The constituent *Adv*(erb) will ultimately be represented by one or more adverbial elements (e.g., *often, really, sure*), whose previous derivational history will not be considered in this study; i.e., it is not claimed that all such adverbial elements as ultimately represent *Adv*(erb) result from the expansion of that symbol by rules of constituent structure. Some adverbial elements may have their origin in other constituents of the same sentence; e.g., in the constituent Time (see the constituent structure rule, Eq. (3)) in "Writers accept such suggestions now." We shall assume also that the pre-verbal particles (*not, so*) at some point in their derivational history likewise appear with representatives of the constituent *Adv*(erb). If there are several adverbial elements within the *Aux*, then each such element will itself have the status of an *Adv*(erb). In the following sentence, for example:

$$\text{Writers often don't really accept such suggestions.} \tag{38}$$

the *Aux* has the following form before the obligatory application of the rule of pre-verbal particle placement:[11]

$$Aux: \ [\text{often}]_{Adv} \ [\text{not}]_{PvP} \ \ [\text{really}]_{Adv} \ \ \text{Present} \tag{39}$$

The transformational rule of pre-verbal particle placement formulated in Eq. (24) is now extended to include any pre-verbal *Adv*(erb) that follows the particle:

$$\underbrace{\text{Nominal}(Adv)}_{1}\underbrace{\text{not}(Adv)}_{2} \underbrace{\textbf{aux}^1\text{-}}_{3}\underbrace{X}_{4} \Rightarrow \underbrace{\text{Nominal}(Adv)}_{1} \underbrace{\textbf{aux}^1\text{-}}_{3} \underbrace{\text{not}(Adv)}_{2} \underbrace{X}_{4} \tag{40}$$

Sentence (38) would include in its derivation the following:

$$\text{S: writers-often-not-really-Present-accept-suggestions} \tag{41a}$$

$$\begin{aligned}&\text{i.   writers-often-Present-not-really-accept-suggestions (by}\\&\text{pre-verbal particle placement, Eq. (40))}\end{aligned} \tag{41b}$$

$$\begin{aligned}&\text{ii.   writers-often-}do\text{-Present-not-really-accept suggestions}\\&\text{(by }do\text{-support, Eq. (26))}\end{aligned} \tag{41c}$$

---

[11]To account for the grammatically acceptable double negatives as in "he doesn't often really not understand," the sequence of *Adv*(erbs) and *PvP*'s must be extended to (not)(*Adv*(not))(*Adv*).

After the rule of pre-verbal particle placement, a rule of pre-verbal adverb placement optionally places remaining pre-verbal adverbial elements behind $\text{Tense} \begin{Bmatrix} M \\ be \\ have \end{Bmatrix}$, but not behind Tense alone. In this way the permitted segment differs from **aux**.[1]

$$\text{Nominal-}Adv\text{-Tense} \begin{Bmatrix} M \\ be \\ have \end{Bmatrix} X \Rightarrow \text{Nominal-Tense} \begin{Bmatrix} M \\ be \\ have \end{Bmatrix} Adv\text{-}X \qquad (42)$$

Thus, the sentence "Writers have often accepted such suggestions" differs from Eq. (37b) only in the optional application of Eq. (42).

PRE-VERBAL ADVERBS II: NEGATIVE PRE-VERBAL ADVERBS

15 *Either*-conjoining. While the basic elements of simple sentences do not necessitate the assumption of grammatical unity between the negative particle and the negative pre-verbal adverbs, the syntax of the following more complex sentences show that such unity is a grammatical fact:

$$\text{Publishers will} \begin{Bmatrix} \text{usually} \\ \text{always} \\ \text{not} \end{Bmatrix} \text{reject suggestions, and}$$

$$\text{writers will} \begin{Bmatrix} \text{not} \\ \text{scarcely} \\ \text{hardly} \\ \text{never} \\ \text{seldom} \\ \text{rarely} \end{Bmatrix} \text{accept them, either.} \qquad (43)$$

The description of sentences like those of Eq. (43), whose form is $S: S_b$-and-S_a-either, will be a special case of the simple conjoining of S(entences) as in:

Publishers will usually reject suggestions, and writers will never accept them. (44a)

Writers will never accept suggestions, and publishers will usually reject them. (44b)

In simple conjoining, one sentence (S_a), for example, "Writers will never accept suggestions," is appended to a base sentence (S_b), for example, "Publishers will usually reject suggestions," by means of *and*. From Eq. (44) it is clear that both source sentences qualify as base sentences; simple conjoining does not depend on the presence of pre-verbal adverbs or on their nature. *Either*-conjoining, on the other hand, occurs only when the sentence to be appended and enclosed in *and . . . either* contains *not* or one of the negative pre-verbal adverbs listed as category (a) in Eq. (20). Factors involving the predicates of the sentences to be conjoined—factors not necessarily grammatical in nature—enter into the incompatibility of other pairs of sentences from the point of view of *either*-conjoining; that is, there are certain re-strictions on the choice of predicates that could appear in the same position as *stay away* in "They stayed away, and we didn't return, either." At any rate, within the pre-verbal adverbs, the grammatical differentiation between negative pre-verbs and those that are not negative, must be recognized in order to account for the un-grammaticalness of sentences like the following, in which the source sentences are conjoined in the opposite order from Eq. (43).

$$\text{*Writers will never accept suggestions, and publishers}$$

$$\text{will} \begin{cases} \text{always} \\ \text{surely} \\ \text{usually} \\ \text{commonly} \end{cases} \text{reject them, either.} \tag{45}$$

Instead, sentences without a negative pre-verbal adverb like those incorrectly con-joined in Eq. (45), occur conjoined by means of *and . . . too*:

$$\text{Writers will never accept suggestions, and} \atop \text{publishers will always reject them, too.} \tag{46}$$

That the negative pre-verbal adverbs as a class are grammatically different from the other pre-verbal adverbs, and that the particle *not* is grammatically the same as the negative pre-verbal adverbs in this respect, is demonstrated by Eq. (43) as con-trasted to Eq. (45). As yet, however, there has been no discussion of how this shared differential feature should be represented in the grammar; for the time being, let *negative pre-verb* represent the negative particle *not* and the negative pre-verbal adverbs. The description of sentences characterized by *either*-conjoining would include a binary transformation that appends a sentence (S_a) with a *negative pre-verb* to a base sentence (S_b).

$$\text{*Either*-conjoining} \tag{47}$$

$$S_a: \quad \text{Nominal}_1\text{-}\textbf{negative pre-verb-}Aux\text{-}MV$$
$$S_b: \quad \text{Nominal}_2\text{-Predicate}$$
$$\Rightarrow \quad S_b\text{-and-}S_a\text{-}either$$

16   Negative appositive tag *not even*. In the following sentences, which are analyz-ed as a special case of conjoining, the *negative pre-verbs* again function together as a grammatical unit which must be distinguished in order to account for the shape of sentences. Thus, of the following two sets, there are sentences like the first (Eq. 48a)) but not like Eq. (48b):

$$\text{The writer will} \begin{cases} \text{not} \\ \text{never} \\ \text{seldom} \\ \text{rarely} \end{cases} \text{accept suggestions, not even reasonable ones.} \tag{48a}$$

$$\text{*The publisher} \begin{pmatrix} \begin{cases} \text{often} \\ \text{commonly} \\ \text{always} \end{cases} \end{pmatrix} \text{disregards suggestions, not even reasonable ones.} \tag{48b}$$

Without a "negative pre-verb," the only appositive tag that occurs is "The publisher disregards suggestions, even reasonable ones." Another type of basic sentence results in the following negative appositive tag:

$$\text{Writers will not accept anything, not even suggestions.} \qquad (49)$$

The analysis of a sentence like Eq. (49) will include a transformation operative on a pair of source sentences like the following:

$$
\begin{array}{l}
S_a: \quad \text{Writers-not-even-Tense-will-accept-suggestions.} \\
S_b: \quad \text{Writers-\textbf{negative pre-verb}-Tense-will-accept-anything.} \\
\Rightarrow \quad S_b,\text{-not-even-suggestions.}
\end{array} \qquad (50)
$$

The grammatical features characteristic of pairs of sentences which combine to form the negative appositive tag in Eq. (51) are: (a) in the base sentence (S_b), the presence of a negative pre-verb and of an unspecified constituent Y_1, unspecified in being absent (for example in Eq. (48a), "... accept-$[\varphi]_{Adj}$-suggestions ...") or in being represented by one of the indefinites, *anything*, as in Eq. (49); (b) in S_a, the presence of *not even* and the specification of the constituent Y_1, unspecified in S_b. The remaining parts of the sentences (represented by X and Z) are presumably the same.

$$
\begin{array}{l}
S_a: \quad \text{Nominal-not-even-}X\text{-}Y_1\text{-}Z \\[2mm]
S_b: \quad \text{Nominal-\textbf{negative pre-verb}-}X\left[\left[\begin{Bmatrix}\varphi \\ \text{indef}\end{Bmatrix}\right]Y_2\right]Z \\[2mm]
\Rightarrow \quad S_b,\ \text{not-even-}Y_1
\end{array} \qquad (51)
$$

The formulation that holds for the occurrence of the negative appositive tags based on the subject Nominal, is the same except for the order of elements.

$$\text{Writers will not believe him, not even good ones.} \qquad (52)$$

17 Tag-questions. Sentences like Eq. (53a) below (in which "..., will they?" will be referred to as the *tag*) are distinguished from those like Eq. (53b) and Eq. (53c) by the absence of *not* in the tag, and from those like Eq. (53d) by the absence of a particular intonation to which are associated incredulous or sarcastic overtones. Once again the grammatical relevance of the class of elements referred to here as *negative pre-verbs* asserts itself. For it is precisely the presence of one of the *negative pre-verbs*—whether adverb or particle—that distinguishes the simple sentences underlying the distinct set of tag-questions exemplified by Eq. (53a). If we permit ourselves to set aside examples like Eq. (53d) with its special intonation and emotive overtones, then sentences without a *negative pre-verb*, but with *not* in the tag, are paralleled by sentences with a *negative pre-verb* but without *not* in the tag.

$$\text{Writers will never accept suggestions, will they?} \qquad (53a)$$

$$\text{Publishers will reject suggestions, } \begin{Bmatrix}\text{will they not?} \\ \text{won't they?}\end{Bmatrix} \qquad (53b)$$

$$\text{Publishers will surely reject suggestions, } \begin{Bmatrix}\text{will they not?} \\ \text{won't they?}\end{Bmatrix} \qquad (53c)$$

$$\text{Writers will accept suggestions, will they!} \qquad (53d)$$

The tag in sentences like those above is composed of: (a) the interrogative marker wh-, which occurs in initial position in the original form of the sentence; (b) the pronominalized subject Nominal, and **aux¹** (the segment of the *Aux*(iliary) already encountered in Eq. (24), consisting of Tense and the next helping verb if there is one, or Tense-be; further constituents of the *Aux*(iliary) will be referred to as **aux²**). In the tag, *not* follows **aux¹** when the source sentence does not contain one of the negative pre-verbs; *not* may be contracted as in the tag variants of Eqs. (53b–c). Wh- motivates inversion. Note that by this analysis the source of the tag-question is the same as that of the simple yes-no question.

$$\text{I.   tag-question formation (optional)} \tag{54a}$$

$$\text{wh } [\text{Nominal-}X\text{-}\mathbf{aux^1}\ (\mathbf{aux^2})MV]_{seg_2} \Rightarrow seg_2\text{-wh-}pro + \text{Nominal-}\mathbf{aux^1}\ (not)$$

(where *not* is absent from the resulting tag if X in the source contains a negative pre-verb)

$$\text{II.   pre-verbal particle placement, as in 40} \tag{54b}$$

$$\text{III.   pre-verbal adverb placement, as in 42} \tag{54c}$$

$$\text{IV.   }neg\text{-contraction (optional): }\mathbf{aux^1}\text{-}not \Rightarrow \mathbf{aux^1} + not \tag{54d}$$

$$\text{V.   wh-attraction (obligatory)} \tag{54e}$$

$$\text{wh}(+ \begin{Bmatrix} \text{Nominal} \\ \text{Time} \\ \text{Place} \end{Bmatrix}) \underset{2}{\text{Nominal-}}\underset{3}{\mathbf{aux^1}(+\ not)} \Rightarrow$$

$$\text{wh}(+ \begin{Bmatrix} \text{Nominal} \\ \text{Time} \\ \text{Place} \end{Bmatrix}) \underset{3}{\mathbf{aux^1}\ (+\ not)}\underset{1}{\text{Nominal}}$$

(the same as at 17, but reformulated in terms of **aux¹** and *neg*-contraction)

Note that as a result of optional *neg*-contraction, the *not* in **aux¹** + *not* is interpreted as part of **aux¹** and is thus attracted to wh- along with **aux¹**; thus one result of wh-attraction is wh-**aux¹**+*not*-Nominal as in ". . . , won't they?" On the other hand, *not* in the sequence **aux¹**-*not*, without *neg*-contraction, is not attracted to wh-; thus an alternative result of wh-attraction is wh-**aux¹**-Nominal-*not* as in ". . . , will they not?" Later morphophonemic rules provide for forms like *won't*:

$$\text{verbal morphophonemics: will} + \varphi + \text{not} \Rightarrow \text{won't} \tag{55}$$

The derivation of a sentence like Eq. (53a) would include the following:

$$S: \text{ wh-writers}[\text{never}]_{\text{negative pre-verb}}\ [\varphi]_{\text{Tense}}\text{ will-accept-sug-gestions} \tag{56a}$$

i. Writers-never-φ-will-accept-suggestions,-wh-they-φ-   (56b)
will [by tag-question formation, Eq. (54a)]

ii. Writers-φ-will-never-accept-suggestions,-wh-they-φ-   (56c)
will [by pre-verbal adverb placement, Eq. (42)]

iii. Writers-φ-will-never-accept-suggestions,-wh-φ-will-   (56d)
they [by wh-attraction, Eq. (54e)]

iv. . . . , wh-will $+\ \varphi$-they [by Tense-attachment, Eq. (19)]   (56e)

v. . . . , will $+\ \varphi$-they [by deletion of wh-, Eq. (18)]   (56f)

A sentence like Eq. (53b) would have a derivation proper to sentences without a negative pre-verb.

S: wh-[publishers$[\varphi]_{\text{Tense}}$ will-reject-suggestions$]_{seg_1}$ (57a)

i. seg_1-wh-they-φ-will-not [by tag-question formation,   (57b)
Eq. (54a)]

ii. seg_1-wh-they-φ-will $+$ nt [by *neg*-contraction, Eq. (54d)]   (57c)

iii. seg_1-wh-φ-will $+$ will $+$ nt-they [by wh-attraction, Eq. (54e)]   (57d)

iv. seg_1-$[\varphi]_{\text{Tense}}$ will $+$ nt-they [by wh-deletion, Eq. (18)]   (57e)

18 *Neither*-tags. *Neither*-tags as in the following sentence:

Writers won't be accepting suggestions, and neither will publishers.   (58)

are a truncated and inverted form of the *either*-conjoining described in Section 15. Sentence (58) is derived from the following sentence (itself derived by either-conjoining by Eq. (47) in its most truncated form):

Writers won't be accepting suggestions,

$$\textit{and} \text{ publishers} \begin{cases} \text{won't be accepting them} \\ \text{won't be} \\ \text{won't} \end{cases}, \textit{either.} \qquad (59)$$

The transformation for *neither*-tags imposes an additional condition on the source sentences: the base sentence, rather than just the appended sentence as in *either*-conjoining, must contain a negative pre-verb; that is, *neither* appears at the front of the appended sentence followed by the subject Nominal and **aux**[1] in inverted order; the order is inverted because *neither* attracts **aux**[1] in the same way as the interrogative marker wh- does (see Eq. (54e)). The degree of truncation of the *neither*-tag will be determined by the deletions permissible in the appended *either*-clause, as exemplified in Eq. (59). In addition, *not* and the negative pre-verbal adverbs of the source of the appended sentences are absent from the *neither*-tag. Depending on the particular negative pre-verb in the base sentence, usage varies with respect to the freedom with which *neither*-tags may be appended to that base.

In the less differentiated idiolect, Idiolect *A*, all negative pre-verbs allow a *neither*-tag:

Writers will seldom accept suggestions, and neither will publishers.   (60)

Included in the derivation of sentences like Eq. (60) in Idiolect *A* would be the following (the general description of the transformations will be given at Eq. (65) after further consideration):

S: [Writers[φ]$_\text{Tense}$ will [seldom]$_\text{negative pre-verb}$ accept-suggestions]s_b and-publishers[φ]will-seldom-accept-them-*either*. [after *either*-conjoining, Eq. (47)]   (61a)

i. S_b-*and-neither*-publishers-φ-will. [by some form of *neither*-tag formation to be formulated in Eq. (65c)]   (61b)

ii. S_b-*and-neither*-φ-will-publishers. [by *neg*-attraction to be formulated at Eq. (65h)]   (61c)

A second idiolect, Idiolect *B*, is more highly differentiated with respect to negative pre-verbs, in that *neither*-tags occur with the pre-verbal constituents *not* and *never* but not with the other negative pre-verbs.

Writers will never accept suggestions, and neither will publishers.   (62)

Grammatically, this differentiation of *negative pre-verbs*, with respect to *neither*-tags in Idiolect *B*, could reflect either of the following situations: (a) that it is a simple grammatical fact, not further analyzable, that the particle *not* and the adverb *never*, which are syntactically no more similar than *not* and any other negative adverb, can each occur with a *neither*-tag; or (b) that the permissibility of *neither*-tags is a property of a grammatical element that occurs within the derivational structure of both *neither* and *not* (where a "grammatical element" must be *natural* to the grammatical system in the sense discussed in Section 4). In *situation* (a), the grammar would merely restate the superficial facts. This, of course, is all the grammar can rightly do for some constructional similarities. In *situation* (b), the grammar would be *explaining* the superficial facts. This is what makes a grammar more than a collection of diverse similarities and differences. It will be proposed that the similarity of *not* and *never* is an instance of *situation* (b). The grammatical element common to *not*, *neither*, and *never*, and as will be shown, involved in the derivation of many elements associated with negation, is *neg*, which when not combined with other constituents has the form *not*. The argument will include the following points: (a) that *neither* (in tags) results from the combination of the elements *neg* and *either* from an *either*-clause; (b) the condition for their combination in Idiolect *B* is the presence of *not* or *never* in the base sentence; (c) that truncation in the *either*-clause and in the *neither*-tag derived from the latter represents the deletion of major constituents identical to ones in the base sentences; (d) that the *neg* that combines to form *neither* in, for example, "Writers will never accept suggestions, and neither will publishers," is a constituent of the adverb *never* that occurs in the antecedent *either*-clause, ". . . and publishers will never accept them, either"; and finally, (e) that the form *never* results from the combination of the mobile constituent *neg* with the adverb *ever* and thus parallels the derivation of *neither*.

Thus, *in a very special sense*, *never* will be postulated equivalent to *not ever*, and the occurrence of the *neither*-tag, not only with the particle *not* but also with the adverb *never*, will be explained in terms of the inclusion of *not* in the latter. This characterization holds only *in a special sense* since the equivalence of *not ever* and *never* cannot be asserted in terms of the final shape of sentences; for *not ever* does not occur before the Tense-marker whereas *never* does (Eq. (63a) below) and *never* does not take the place of *ever* in sentences like Eq. (63b):

Writers never accept suggestions *vs* *Writers not ever accept
suggestions $\qquad$ (63a)

Writers don't ever accept suggestions *vs* *Writers do never
accept suggestions $\qquad$ (63b)

The special sense in which the equivalence holds is that of a more abstract description, in which *neg*, the constituent from which *not* is ultimately derived, does in fact combine with *ever*, ultimately yielding *never*. The transformational rule, referred to here as *neg*-incorporation (Eq. (64b)), is first in a group of ordered rules including the rule of pre-verbal particle placement and pre-verbal adverb placement discussed in Section 14. By *neg*—incorporation, *neg* loses its status as a pre-verbal particle (*PvP*) and is included in the constituent labeled *Adv*.

$$S: \quad \text{Nominal}[neg]_{PvP}[\text{ever}]_{Adv}\text{Tense} \begin{Bmatrix} M \\ \text{have} \\ \text{be} \end{Bmatrix} (\mathbf{aux^2})MV \qquad (64a)$$

   i.   *neg*-incorporation:

      a.   (optional): $neg[\text{ever}]_{Adv} \quad \Rightarrow [neg + \text{ever}]_{Adv}$ $\qquad$ (64b)

      b.   (obligatory): $[\text{ever}]_{Adv} \, neg \Rightarrow [neg + \text{ever}]_{Adv}$

   ii.   pre-verbal particle placement (obligatory), an elaboration of
      Eq. (24): $\qquad$ (64c)

$$[neg]_{PvP}(Adv)\mathbf{aux^1} \begin{Bmatrix} \mathbf{aux^2} \\ MV \end{Bmatrix} \Rightarrow \mathbf{aux^1}\text{-}neg(Adv) + \begin{Bmatrix} \mathbf{aux^2} \\ MV \end{Bmatrix}$$

Note now that *neg* + ever, as in Eq. (64b), is an *Adv*(erb) and not an instance of *neg*-ever; the latter sequence is a particle followed by an *Adv*(erb).

   iii.   Pre-verbal adverb placement (optional): $\qquad$ (64d)

$$Adv\text{-Tense}\begin{Bmatrix} M \\ \text{have} \\ \text{be} \end{Bmatrix}\text{-}X \Rightarrow \text{Tense}\begin{Bmatrix} M \\ \text{have} \\ \text{be} \end{Bmatrix}Adv + X$$

That is, the same as Eq. (42), but now *Adv*, after its replacement, is specified as belonging to the following constituent *X*, where *X* includes, among other things, *MV* and $\mathbf{aux^2}$.

   iv.   *neg*-contraction (optional):
      $\mathbf{aux^1}[neg]_{PvP}X \Rightarrow [\mathbf{aux^1} + neg]_{aux^1}\text{-}X$ (essentially as in
      Eq. (54d), but specifying that *neg* + *X*, e.g., *neg* + ever, $\qquad$ (64e)
      does not contract with a preceding verbal form).

The description of the *neither*-tag in Idiolect *B* utilizes the mechanism in Eq. (64). With the improvements made according to Eq. (64), only *neg* (with or without *ever*) rather than *negative pre-verb* need occur in the base and appended sentences.

The assignment of a new constituent structure to the relocated *Adv*(erbs) is particularly important for correctly predicting the truncated tags that occur as a result of deletions in the *either*-clause. The rules describing the *neither*-tag in Idiolect *B* (Eq. (65)) will begin after the sentences have undergone *either*-conjoining, described in Eq. (47).

$$S: \quad [\text{Nominal-}neg(Adv) \text{ Tense} \left(\begin{Bmatrix} M \\ \text{have} \\ \text{be} \end{Bmatrix}\right) (\mathbf{aux^2})MV]_{S_b} \, and[\text{Nominal-}$$

(65a)

$$neg(\text{ever})\text{-Tense} \left(\begin{Bmatrix} M \\ \text{have} \\ \text{be} \end{Bmatrix}\right) (\mathbf{aux^2})MV]_{S_a} \, either$$

I. Truncation (optional): All of the details of the various possible deletions will not be specified, but after the deletion of major identical constituents the following are among the forms that the *either*- clause may assume: $\qquad\qquad$ (65b)

$$\ldots and \text{ Nominal-}neg \begin{cases} \text{ever-}\mathbf{aux^1}\text{-}\mathbf{aux^2}, \, either \\ \text{ever-}\mathbf{aux^1} \, either \text{ [i.e.``}\ldots \text{and-Nom-} \\ \qquad\qquad\qquad \text{inal-never-does, } either.] \\ \mathbf{aux^1}, \, either \end{cases}$$

II. *neither*-tag formation (optional):

$$\ldots and\text{-Nominal-}neg \begin{cases} ever\text{-}\mathbf{aux^1}\text{-}\mathbf{aux^2}, \, either \\ \mathbf{aux^1}, \, either \end{cases}$$

(65c)

$$\ldots and \, neg + either\text{-Nominal} \begin{cases} ever\text{-}\mathbf{aux^1}\text{-}\mathbf{aux^2} \\ \mathbf{aux^1} \end{cases}$$

III. *neg*-incorporation(see(64b)), operative optionally in the base sentence S_b where *neg* may be incorporated into *ever*, but not operative in the appended tag structure since in the latter *neg* has already been associated with *either* $\qquad$ (65d)

IV. pre-verbal particle placement (see (64c)), with a following *Adv* included in $\mathbf{aux^2}$ or MV $\qquad\qquad$ (65e)

V. pre-verbal adverb placement (see the rule at (64d)) and note that after truncation (65b), pre-verbal adverb placement does not apply to certain deletion types. $\qquad$ (65f)

VI. *neg*-contraction (see the rule at (64e)) $\qquad\qquad$ (65g)

VII. *neg*-attraction (inversion): $\qquad\qquad\qquad\qquad\qquad\qquad$ (65h)
$$neg + either\text{-Nominal-}\mathbf{aux^1} \; X \Rightarrow neg + either\text{-}\mathbf{aux^1}\text{-Nominal-}X$$
$$\underbrace{}_{1} \underbrace{}_{2} \underbrace{}_{3} \underbrace{}_{4} \qquad \underbrace{}_{1} \underbrace{}_{3} \underbrace{}_{2} \underbrace{}_{4}$$

A sentence like "Writers will never accept suggestions, and neither will publishers" could have the following derivations after *either*-conjoining.

S: [Writers-*neg*-ever-Tense-will-accept-suggestions]s_b, *and* [pub-
     lishers-*neg*-ever-Tense-will-accept-them]s_a *either* (after *either*-   (66a)
     conjoining, Eq. (47)

i: S_b-*and*-publishers-*neg*-Tense-will-*either* (by truncation, Eq.
     (65b)   (66b)

ii: S_b-*and*-*neg* + *either*-publishers-Tense-will- (by *neither*-tag-
     formation, Eq. (65c))   (66c)

iii: [Writers-*neg* + ever-Tense-will-accept-suggestions]s_b *and*-S_a-
     either (by *neg*-incorporation, (64b), optionally applied to S_b)   (66d)

iv. S_b-*and*-publishers-Tense-will-*neg*-ever-accept-them-*either*
     (by pre-verbal particle placement, Eq. (64c))   (66e)

v: [Writers-Tense-will-*neg* + ever-accept-suggestions]s_b-*and*-
     publishers-Tense-will-*neg*-*either* (by pre-verbal adverb place-   (66f)
     ment Eq. (64d))

vi. S_b-*and*-*neg* + *either*-Tense-will-publishers (by *neg*-attraction,
     Eq. (65h))   (66g)

For Idiolect *A*, in the case of negative pre-verbs other than *not* and *never*, there is a lack of decisive linguistic facts. However, if the similarity, as pre-verbal adverb of, for example, *seldom* and *often*, is to be maintained, on the one hand, and the similarity, as pre-verbal particle of *not* and *so*, on the other hand, along with the over-all similarity between *not* and the negative pre-verbal adverbs, then the mechanism is already at hand for accounting for all these similarities in a nonarbitrary way: namely, by considering all the negative pre-verbal adverbs to be like *never*, in one respect (viz., instances of the constituent *Adv*(erb) that include *neg*), but unlike *never* in another respect (viz., without phonological reflexes of *neg*). Accordingly, the derivation of *seldom*, for example, would include the expansion of the constituent *Adv*(erb) to *seldom*, but only when following *neg*. In other words, the constituent structure rule would be preceded by another rule of *Adv*(erb) expansion restricted to an environment in which *neg* directly precedes.

$$neg\text{-}Adv \Rightarrow neg\text{-}seldom \qquad (67)$$

The transformational rule of *neg*-incorporation whereby optionally *neg*-ever $\Rightarrow$ *neg* + ever, that is, *never*, would also apply to *neg-seldom*, but obligatorily:

(*neg*-absorption by incomplete negatives:

$$neg[seldom]_{Adv} \Rightarrow [neg + seldom]_{Adv} \qquad (68)$$

By this analysis, all of the negative properties of the pre-verbal negative adverbs— as demonstrated by their participation with the negative particle in the constructions described by transformations of *either*-conjoining, negative appositive tag formation, and question tag-formation, but not *neither*-tag-formation—are accounted for by the presence of the pre-verbal particle *neg*, for at the point when these transformations apply, $[neg]_{PvP}[seldom]_{Adv}$ is not yet converted into $[neg + seldom]_{Adv}$. Sentences with negative pre-verbs other than *never* and *not* are correctly excluded from *neither*-tag formation (which also depends on the presence of the particle *neg*; (see Eq. (65)), because at that point in the set of ordered transformational rules, *neg* has already been incorporated obligatorily into the following negative pre-verbal adverb and has lost its status as a pre-verbal particle.

In Idiolect *A*, where all the negative adverbs occur with *neither*-tags, the *neg* in *neither* (i.e., *neg + either*) as in "Writers seldom accept suggestions and *neither* do publishers" has as its origin the *neg* that appears incorporated in *seldom* (that is, *neg + seldom*). We shall not go into further detail concerning the differences that Idiolect *A* manifests in connection with *neither*-tag formation.

<h2 style="text-align:center">SENTENCE NEGATION I</h2>

19 Definition. Let's define as instances of *sentence negation* those structures which permit the occurrence of the *either-clause* (Section 15), the negative appositive tag (Section 16), and the question tag without *not* (Section 17). We can differentiate further between strong and weak sentence negation depending on whether the structure permits or does not permit, respectively, the occurrence of the *neither*-tag (Section 18). By the analysis presented in Sections 15 to 18 all instances of sentence negation were characterized by the presence of the pre-verbal particle *neg* in the derivation; the differentiation into strong versus weak corresponds to how far down the derivation *neg* may retain its status as a pre-verbal particle, as opposed to being incorporated into another constituent. In the final shape of two of the words discussed, *never* and *neither*, the prefix *n-* (*n-ever*, *n-either*), can be attributed to the constituent *neg*.

20 Negative pre-verb versus pre-verbal adverb with negative prefix. Let's anticipate a full discussion of the words with so-called "negative" prefixes like the adverbs *unintentionally*, *unwisely*, or the predicate *be unwise* and compare them informally with the negative pre-verbs *never*, *seldom*, *rarely*, and so on, analyzed in Sections 15 to 18 as *neg + Adv*. One question that arises is this: do sentences like the following:

Writers will unintentionally reject suggestions.	(69a)
Writers unfortunately reject suggestions.	(69b)
Writers are unreceptive to suggestions.	(69c)

manifest any major syntactic differences from sentences like "Writers will never reject . . . ," "Writers hardly reject . . . ," "Writers are not wise to . . . ." The reason for the question is obvious: the adverb in Eq. (69a), for example, has the analysis *un-intentionally*, which is not unlike the analysis of *n-ever*; and the sequence, Tense-*be-un-wise* in Eq. (69c) is not entirely unlike the sequence, Tense-*be-neg-wise*; that is, ". . . *are not wise* . . . ." The answer is that the sentences in (69) do in fact differ from sentences with a negative pre-verb in exactly the sense discussed in Section 19; that is, the occurrence of *unintentionally*, *unfortunately*, or *unfaithful* does not result in structures that are instances of sentence negation. The following, for example, are not grammatical sentences.

*Publishers will unintentionally reject suggestions, and writers will unintentionally reject them, either.	(70a)

*Writers are unreceptive to suggestions, not even good ones. (70b)

And as a simple tag-question, without incredulous or sarcastic overtone, the following does not occur:

*Writers unfortunately reject suggestions, do they? (71)

SENTENCE NEGATION II

21 Special negatives: *not much, not many*. The description of Nominal will be extended to include the following constituent structure rule that optionally includes *Quant*(ifiers) in the expansion of the Nominal:

$$\text{Nominal} \rightarrow (Quant)\text{Noun} \begin{Bmatrix} Sg \\ Pl \end{Bmatrix} \qquad (72)$$

where among the words that ultimately have the structure of *Quant*(ifiers) are *much, many, some, a single*, and so on. So far, examination of sentence negation as defined in Section 19 had considered only the effect of pre-verbal adverbs and particles. Sentence negation, as manifested by the permissibility of the tag- and conjoined structures described in Sections 15 to 18, is found in sentences that contain the constituent *neg* as a part of the *Aux*(iliary). But consider now the following sentences in which *not*, one of the ultimate forms of *neg*, occurs rather before certain nominal quantifiers; all of the sentences are nonetheless instances of sentence negation, as defined in Section 19, in fact, of the strong variety, as is seen in example 73d below.

Not much rain fell, and not much snow fell either. (73a)
Not much rain fell, not even there. (73b)
Not much of the product was bought, was it? (73c)
Not much rain fell, and neither did much snow. (73d)

There are, however, certain peculiarities in the distribution of *not much* that relate also this occurrence of *not* to the pre-verbal particle *neg*; namely, although *not* occurs attached to the nominal quantifier *much* when the Nominal is subject, when the Nominal is object (or any other post-verbal complement), *not* occurs in the *Aux*(iliary) and has all the properties of any other occurrences of the pre-verbal particle *neg*. This is particularly clear in pairs of sentences consisting of an active and its corresponding passive:

Not much shrapnel hit the soldier. (74a)
The soldier was not hit by much shrapnel. (74b)
Not much food had been left by them. (74c)
They had not left much food. (74d)

When the subject of the active has *not much* (Eq. (74a)), then the *Aux*(iliary) of the corresponding passive has *not*, and the agent has *much* (Eq. (74b)). When the subject of the passive has *not much* (Eq. (74c)), then the *Aux*(iliary) of the corresponding active sentence has *not* and its object contains *much*. In general, it is the case that passive and corresponding active are related grammatically in the following way: the subject of the former is the object of the latter; the agent of the former, the subject of the latter; and the passive contains a passive auxiliary (*be* followed by the *P*(ast) *P*(articiple) of the following verb).

$$\text{passivization (optional)} \tag{75}$$

$$\text{Nominal}(neg)\textbf{aux}^1\text{-}X\text{-}V\text{-Nominal} \Rightarrow \text{Nominal} (neg)\textbf{aux}^1\text{-}X\text{-}be\text{-}PP\text{-}V\text{-}by\text{-Nominal}$$

$$\underbrace{}_{1}\ \underbrace{}_{2}\ _{3}\ _{4}\qquad\qquad _{4}\ \underbrace{}_{2}\ \underbrace{}_{3}\ _{1}$$

The difference in occurrence of the quantifier *not much* in active versus passive might, of course, simply indicate the incorrectness of the assumption that active and passive sentences correspond grammatically in the way described above. But if the ultimate position of *not* and the quantifier *much* is taken as basic, then other similarities are also lost from the system; for example, the general similarity in the internal structure of Nominals, whether in subject or in object function. Thus, with respect to the grammar as a whole, it would be advantageous to consider these differences, if it is at all possible, as reflecting positionally determined variation in the quantifier itself.

The quantifier *not much* will be analyzed as follows: *much*, when it occurs in subject position before **aux**^{1} in a sentence with the pre-verbal particle *neg*, attracts *neg*.

$$neg\text{-incorporation into Quantifiers:}$$

$$\left[Quant\text{-Noun-} \begin{Bmatrix} Sg \\ Pl \end{Bmatrix} \right]_{\text{Nominal}} neg\text{-Tense} \begin{Bmatrix} M \\ be \\ have \end{Bmatrix} X \Rightarrow \tag{76}$$

$$\left[neg + Quant\text{-Noun-} \begin{Bmatrix} Sg \\ Pl \end{Bmatrix} \right]_{\text{Nominal}} \text{Tense} \begin{Bmatrix} M \\ be \\ have \end{Bmatrix} X$$

The derivation of Eq. (74a) would include the following:

$$[much]_{Quant}\text{-shrapnel-}Sg\text{-}neg\text{-Past-hit-the-soldier} \tag{77a}$$

$$neg + [much]_{Quant}\text{-shrapnel-}Sg\text{-Past-hit-the-soldier [after rule 76]} \tag{77b}$$

When *much* occurs after the verb as in Eq. (74b) which is the passive of Eq. (74a), *neg* is left in the *Aux*(iliary).

    S: the-soldier-*neg*-Past-be-*PP*-hit-by[*much*]$_{Quant}$-shrapnel-*Sg* (after passivization, Eq. (75)) (78a)

    i. The-soldier-Past-be-*neg*-*PP*-by[*much*]$_{Quant}$-shrapnel-*Sg* (by pre-verbal particle placement, Eq. (64c)) (78b)

The transformational rule providing for the incorporation of the pre-verbal particle *neg* into a preceding nominal *Quant*(ifier) occurs after wh-attraction (inversion), since then even in the subject, the quantifier *much* does not occur preceded by *not* when Tense and contracted *neg* appear before the subject in questions:

$$\text{Didn't much shrapnel hit the soldier?} \tag{79}$$

Neither-tag formation, Eq. (65), which precedes wh-attraction, of course, also precedes *neg*-incorporation into *Quant*(ifiers):

$$\text{Not much shrapnel hit the soldier, and neither did much powder.} \tag{80}$$

In Eqs. (79–80), the rule of *neg*-incorporation does not apply because *neg* is situated in front of *much*.

The *Quant*(ifiers) *a, single, one, many, all, every, everyone,* share the same characteristics with respect to *neg*. The details vary considerably as to when and whether or not the incorporation of *neg* is obligatory.

22 Sentence negation by special negatives: *scarcely anybody, hardly anything, hardly any*. In sentences like the following, with an indefinite like *anybody* as subject:

$$\text{Scarcely anybody rejects suggestions.} \tag{81}$$

Scarcely, although determining the substantive *anybody*, is like a negative adverb on the one hand, in yielding an instance of weak sentence negation (that is, without the possibility of the *neither*-tag).

Scarcely anybody accepts suggestions, not even writers. (82a)

Most publishers will not accept suggestions, and
scarcely any writers will accept them, either. (82b)

On the other hand, *scarcely anybody* is like *not much* in the way its occurrence is determined by the position of the two elements; in subject Nominals with Tense following them, *scarcely* appears obligatorily preceding the indefinite. Active-passive forms are again instructive in demonstrating the mobility of the negative adverb.

$$\text{*Anybody scarcely hit anyone.} \tag{83a}$$
$$\text{Scarcely anybody hit anyone.} \tag{83b}$$
$$\text{*Anyone was hit by scarcely anybody.} \tag{83c}$$
$$\text{Scarcely anyone was hit by anybody.} \tag{83d}$$

A sentence like Eq. (83b) would have the following derivation:

$$[anybody]_{\text{Nominal}} \; neg + scarcely\text{-Tense-hit}[anyone]_{\text{Nominal}} \tag{84a}$$
$$[neg + scarcely\text{-}anybody]_{\text{Nominal}}\text{-Tense-hit-}anyone \tag{84b}$$

If the negative pre-verbal adverb and Tense precede the indefinite subject, then the latter (here, *anybody*), occurs free of the negative pre-verbal adverb:

$$\text{Scarcely ever does anybody hit anyone.} \tag{85}$$

Ever in Eq. (85) is itself an indefinite. Thus negative pre-verbal adverbs like *scarcely* occur obligatorily attached to the first indefinite in pre-Tense position.

23 Sentence negation by special negatives not preceded by *not* or a negative adverb: *nothing, nobody, no one, no, none, little, few, nowhere*. While *Quant*(ifiers) like *much*, or *everyone* occurring before the Tense-marker attract *not* (yielding *not much*, *not everyone*), *not* does not appear before the indefinites in the same way as the negative pre-verbal adverbs do; that is, there is "Scarcely anything happened" but not:

$$\text{*Not anything happened.} \tag{86}$$

At the same time, there are cases of sentence negation, of the strong type, that occur without the presence of even displaced negative pre-verbal adverbs or *not*.

Nobody rejects suggestions, not even writers.	(87a)
No one was pushed, and nobody was hit, either.	(87b)
No rain fell and neither did any snow.	(87c)

At first glance, the fact that the presence of nominal constituents like *nobody*, *no*, results in sentence negation, would seem to contradict our characterization of sentence negation as being associated with the pre-verbal particle *neg*. But the behavior of the constituent containing *nobody* in the following sentences shows clearly that *nobody* is similar in derivation to *not much* (that is, that it is another instance of the relocated pre-verbal particle *neg* in combination with another constituent). The syntactic pattern of *nobody* turns out to be similar to that of *scarcely anybody*:

No one has hit anybody.	(88a)
*Anybody has been hit by no one.	(88b)
Nobody has been hit by anyone.	(88c)
Nowhere has anybody been hit by anyone.	(88d)

where *anybody* or *anyone* may appear as object or agent in an active-passive pair but as subject in neither, except in Eq. (88d) when Tense precedes. That *nobody* is, in fact, to be derived from a sequence containing specifically *neg*, that is, *neg-anybody*, follows from active-passive sets like this:

Nobody gave much to anyone.	(89a)
No one was given much by anybody.	(89b)
Not much was given to anyone by anybody.	(89c)

Not in sentences like Eq. (89c), was shown in Section 21 to be derived from *neg*; it occurs in the Nominal when the latter occurs as subject before Tense. Equation (89a), which is the active corresponding to Eq. (89c), is without *not*; it does, however, have *nobody* which is a form that *anybody* (which appears in the passives, Eqs. (89b–c)) assumes as subject—under certain conditions. If it is assumed that those conditions include the presence in the sentence of *neg*, then the numerous superficial asymmetries in the sets of sentences above are resolved.

neg-incorporation into indefinites	(90)

$$any\text{-}X\text{-}neg\text{-}\text{Tense} \Rightarrow neg + any\text{-}X\text{-}\text{Tense}$$
[where *any* is the first indefinite in the sentence, and where *X* may include others]

The sequences $neg + any \begin{Bmatrix} thing \\ one \\ body \end{Bmatrix} \Rightarrow \begin{Bmatrix} nothing \\ no\ one \\ nobody \end{Bmatrix}$; that is, they are fused into a single

syntactic unit. With the *Quant*(ifiers) in Section 21 (for example, *neg-much*), on the other hand, the reflex of *neg* appears unfused as *not*. The outline presented in Eq.

(90) for an analysis of the negative indefinites can also be extended to solve certain superficial difficulties in the form of the *neither*-tag of sentences like:

No rain fell and neither did any snow.   (91)

The special problem has to do with differences between the subject Nominal in the tag of Eq. (91) and that of possible *either*-clauses. It will be recalled that the tag of sentences like the following:

Publishers don't accept suggestions and neither do writers.   (92)

was analyzed in Section 18 as derived from an *either*-clause with the same subject Nominal as ultimately appears in the *neither*-tag, and with a Predicate identical to that of the base sentences; that is, "*and* writers don't accept them *either*." By the same reasoning, however, the source of the tag in Eq. (91) would not be a grammatical sentence:

*. . . and any snow didn't fall either (that is, *and-*   (93)
any-snow-Past-*neg*-fall-*either*)

According to the analysis proposed in Eq. (90), the sequence yielding *any*-snow-Past-*neg*-fall would obligatorily have been converted into *neg* + *any*-snow-Past-fall, that is, "no rain fell." Only when *any* is no longer followed by *neg* in the *Aux*(iliary) does it retain its form as *any*, as in the case when *neg* is incorporated in preposed *either*; that is, . . . *and-neg* + *either*-any-rain-Past-fall. The latter via *neg*-attraction (inversion) as Eq. (65h) yields ". . . and neither did any snow fall." In such constructions *either* itself is like the indefinites in that when it occurs in front of *neg*, *neg* is ultimately incorporated into it. Hereafter, *either* will be considered an indefinite. As *neg* is always incorporated into the first in the series of indefinites, the preposed *either*, if it occurs, is always the constituent into which *neg* is incorporated and with which it fuses. Other indefinites in the clause are thus left unaffected. *Neither*-tag formation, as in Eq. (65), turns out to partake of two more general families of transformations: preposing (that is, of *either*), and *neg*-incorporation (that is, the incorporation of *neg* into indefinites). The derivation of Eq. (91) would include the following:

S: [any-rain[*neg*-Past]$_{Aux}$-fall]s_b-*and*-any-snow[*neg*-Past]$_{Aux}$-fall,   (94a)
     either [after *either*-conjoining, Eq. (47)]

   i. S_b-*and*-any-snow-*neg*-Past-*either* [by truncation, Eq. (65b)]   (94b)

  ii. S_b-*and*-*either*-any-snow-*neg*-Past [by preposing of *either*,   (94c)
     see (65f)]

  iii.   *neg* + any-rain-Past-fall-*and*-*neg* + *either*-any-snow-Past [by   (94d)
     neg-incorporation, Eq. (90)]

  iv. S_b-and-*neg* + *either*-Past-any-snow [by *neg*-attraction, (65h)]   (94e)

  v.   no-rain-Past-fall-*and*-*neither*-Past-any-snow [by *neg*-fusing   (94f)
     rules]

vi.   no-rain-fall + Past-*and-neither-do* + Past-any-snow [by
      Tense-attaching, Eq. (19), and *do*-support, Eq. (26)]   (94g)

The adverb *never* in sentences like "Writers never accept suggestions," already
described in Eq. (64b) as *neg* + ever, is just another instance of a negative indefinite.
The sequence *neg* + ever is derived from ever-*X-neg*-Tense (for example, from the
sequence Adverb-*neg*) in the same way as *nothing* is derived from *anything*. The same
condition holds as in other instances of the incorporation of *neg* into indefinites;
namely, that *neg* is incorporated to the first of the pre-verbal indefinites. This explains, for example, the alternation of *never* with *ever* in the active-passive pair:

> He never rejects anything.   (95a)
> Nothing ever is rejected by him.   (95b)

Equation (95a) includes in its derivation he-ever-*neg*-Tense-reject-anything. Equation (95b) includes anything-ever-*neg*-Tense-*be-PP*-reject-by-him. The first indefinite
attracts *neg*; that is, *ever* in Eq. (95a) and *anything* in Eq. (95b). *Ever* in the latter is
left unchanged. The negative indefinite adverbs *nowhere* and *no place* are described
in the same way. *Neg* is incorporated into and ultimately fused with *anywhere* and
any place. Provisionally, *little* and *few* will be analyzed as an optional fusing of
neg + *much,* and *neg* + *many,* respectively. In this way, the occurrence of *much*
and *many* in *neither*-tags like the following is brought into the system:

> Little rain fell, and neither did much snow.   (96a)
> Few writers accept suggestions, and neither do many
> publishers.   (96b)

THE CONVERSION OF *QUANT*(IFIERS) INTO INDEFINITES

24 The indefinite quantifier *any*. The *Quant*(ifiers) described in Sections 21 to
23 reveal certain significant pecularities in occurrence. *Any* in equations like (97a–
d) occurs when *neg* is present, but not in the corresponding affirmative.

> There wasn't any snow falling anywhere else.   (97a)
> *There was any snow falling anywhere else.   (97b)
> Not even then did any snow fall anywhere else.   (97c)
> *Even then any snow fell anywhere else.   (97d)

The occurrence of an indefinite (*anyone, anything, anywhere, any time,* and the like)
is not restricted to any one constituent in a sentence. Any number of indefinites may
occur in a given sentence—nor is the motivation of indefinites by *neg* restricted to
the clause in which *neg* occurs;

> They don't think that any rain fell anywhere else.   (98a)
> He hadn't realized that any time had elapsed.   (98b)

Examples like the last one are important in determining one aspect of the grammatical status of the indefinites, namely, (a) whether the indefinites that occur with

neg are basic sentence constituents whose occurrence is restricted to sentences that have *neg* as one of their basic elements, or (b) whether, in their occurrence with *neg*, the particular phonological forms that have been referred to as indefinites in this study (for example, the form *any* as a *Quant*(ifier) as contrasted to the forms *one*, *some*) are derivative in nature, reflecting merely the special shape assumed, in particular contexts, by basic constituents. (An example of derivativeness in this sense is *do* in its function as a support for Tense as in "Do not be sitting there then," the analysis of which is given in Eq. (36). Sentences like the following, which are related to Eq. (98), favor interpretation (b).

They think that rain fell somewhere else.	(99a)
*They think that any rain fell anywhere else.	(99b)
He had realized that some time had elapsed.	(99c)
*He had realized that any time had elapsed.	(99d)

The reason that interpretation (b) is favored involves the analysis of sentence-like structures of which the declarative *that*-clauses in Eq. (99) are examples. By "sentence-like structure" I mean a constituent of one sentence in which are repeated the relationships and restrictions included in the description of a simple independent sentence; for example, the fact that in Eq. (99c) only a small class of nouns like *time* can function as subject of verbs like *elapse*, repeats a fact pertinent to the description of the simpler sentence:

$$\text{Some time had elapsed.} \qquad (100)$$

If the description of the basic constituents—their relationship and restrictions— of simple sentences is provided (and this is approximately what is provided by the constituent structure, as in Section 8.1), then sentence-like structures (subordinate clauses, infinitive phrases, participial phrases) can be described as the result of certain operations that insert structures of one sentence, with varying addition, deletion and re-arrangement of elements, as constituents of another sentence. (This is provided by the rules that describe the transformational structure.) Let us elaborate the rules of constituent structure to include one such constituent whose elements mirror those of an independent sentence. Call this constituent *Comp*(lement). It will occur as one alternative in the expansion of the symbol Verb when no Nominal follows, that is:

$$\text{Verb} \rightarrow V\text{-}Comp \qquad (101)$$

The over-all internal structure of those sentence-like structures commonly called *declarative clauses* can be described as the embedding of a sentence (S_e) as a *Comp*-(lement) into a base sentence (S_b).

$$\text{declarative clause embedding} \qquad (102)$$

S_e: Some time had elapsed.
S_b: They think [so]$_{Comp}$
$\Rightarrow$ They think [that some time had elapsed]$_{Comp}$

However, the sentences of Eq. (98) present an apparent exception to this general characterization of clauses as embedded sentences, for the permissible declarative clauses in these sentences are not permissible independent sentences.

*Any rain fell anywhere else.	(103a)
*Any time had elapsed.	(103b)

The ungrammaticalness of Eq. (103) is attributable to the presence of the indefinite quantifiers *any* and *anywhere*. The permissibility of these indefinites in turn is determined not by the fact that they occur in a clause, for they are also inacceptable in Eqs. (98b) and (98d), but by the occurrence of the pre-verbal particle *neg* in the clause containing the indefinites as in Eq. (97a), or—and this is to be noted in particular—in a clause to which the clause containing the indefinites is subordinated as in Eq. (98). The constituent *neg*, even when motivating the occurrence of the indefinites in subordinate structures, has all the mobility described in Sections 21 and 23 (for example, it may combine with certain adverbs and *Quant*(ifiers) that occur in the same clause as *neg*).

Not a single writer thinks that any rain fell anywhere else.	(104a)
Never before had they realized that any time had elapsed.	(104b)
No one thinks any rain fell anywhere else.	(104c)

The relevance of these examples is that in them the clauses containing the indefinites are not directly subordinate to the constituents in which *neg* ultimately appears. In fact, the final effect of the pre-verbal particle *neg* may be buried in secondary elements. That is the situation in the adnominal modifier below, where the relationship of the elements of the modifier to subject Noun (*writers*) is not a basic feature of the sentence under discussion, but is derivative in the sense of having been taken over transformationally from a simpler sentence in which it is basic, for example, "They wrote some of the reports."

Even then the writers of none of the reports thought that any rain had fallen anywhere else.	(105)

Note, in addition, that in spite of the fact that the ultimate form of *neg* in a sentence like Eq. (105) is buried within derivative elements, the sentence is nonetheless an instance of sentence negation as defined in Section 19, since we have the following:

The writers of none of the reports thought so even then, and neither did the publishers of any of the brochures.	(106)

The derivation of sentences like Eqs. (105–106) with a special negative *none* will be consistent with that suggested for cases when the special negative is subject or quantifier to the subject Noun. This special negative will be analyzed as the result of the incorporation of the pre-verbal particle *neg* into an indefinite quantifier (for example, *anyone*, *any*). The incorporation is obligatory with the first indefinite quantifier before Tense, if there is one. Thus, the derivation of Eq. (105) and the base sentence of Eq. (106) includes the following:

The-writers-of[*any*]of-the-reports-*neg-aux-MV*	(107)

That an indefinite quantifier underlies also these instances of the special negative *none* is clear from the following alternative word order of the same sentence, where *neg* and Tense precede the indefinite (that is, "any of the reports"), and may result in an indefinite unfused with *neg*.

> *not* even then did the writers of *any* of the reports think so
> (that is, *neg*-even-then-Tense-the-writers-of-any-of-the-   (108)
> reports-think-so)

The restricted occurrence of the indefinite quantifiers will be interpreted in the following way: the presence of the pre-verbal particle *neg* provides a favorable environment for the occurrence of the indefinite quantifiers within the clause in which *neg* occurs, as well as in any clauses subordinate to the latter clause. Aside from *neg*, certain other constituents, to be discussed briefly in Section 41, similarly provide a favorable environment for the indefinites, for example, the characteristic marker of questions wh- ("They asked *whether any* rain had fallen anywhere else"), the restrictive *only* ("*only* then did *any* rain fall anywhere"). The structure of the indefinite quantifiers is like that of the *Quant*(ifiers) *some, a*, or $[\varphi]_{Quant}$ (that is, a zero-quantifier, a constituent without phonological shape). Simple *Quant*(ifiers) occur in "there was some snow on the ground" or "There was $[\varphi]_{Quant}$ snow on the ground," "That house has a roof," "He has $[\varphi]_{Quant}$ foresight." Parallel in structure are the following sentences with indefinite quantifiers: "There wasn't any snow on the ground," "That house doesn't have any roof," "He doesn't have any foresight." In all of the latter sentences, the occurrence of indefinite quantifiers depends on the presence of *neg* in the same clause, but this is not a necessary condition. In Eq. (98a) "They don't think that any rain fell anywhere else," the indefinite quantifier differs only in that its occurrence depends on a *neg* that lies outside the clause that contains the indefinite quantifiers.

This is not to say that all occurrences of *any, anyone, anywhere*, and other combined forms with *any-* are of the nature described above (for example, "Anyone can do that," "You may take any two apples"). Such occurrences of *any* will not be considered in this study; and no attempt will be made here to determine whether these too are instances of the indefinite quantifiers.[12] The grammar rules involved in accounting for the shape of the *Quant*(ifiers) in sentences like Eqs. (97) and (99) will include a constituent structure rule that includes various classes of *Quant*(ifiers) in the expansion of the constituent Nominal:

$$\text{Nominal} \rightarrow (Quant) \text{ Noun-Number}$$

$$Quant \;\; \rightarrow \begin{cases} Quant^1 \\ Quant^2 \\ Quant^3 \end{cases} \tag{109}$$

$$Quant^1 \;\; \rightarrow some, a, \varphi$$

---

[12]For a recent discussion of the status of words like *any, anybody, ever*, from the point of view of transformational grammar, see the controversy between Lees and Bolinger in R. B. Lees, "Review of D. Bolinger, 'Interrogative Structures in American English'," *Word* XVI (1960) and D. Bolinger, "Linguistic Science and Linguistic Engineering," *Word* XVI (1960); also the article by N. Chomsky, "Some Methodological Remarks on Generative Grammar," *Word* XVII (1961). Reprinted in part in this volume, pp. 384-389.

A transformational rule, which is ordered after declarative clause embedding (Eq. (102)), optionally incorporates the symbol *Indef*(inite) into the *Quant*(ifier) when the latter occurs in the same clauses as the pre-verbal particle *neg* or in a clause subordinate to the one containing *neg*. The rule is recursive, applying to any number of *Quant*(ifiers) in the sentence.

Indef-incorporation
(obligatory in certain environments)

$$S: \quad [neg]_{PvP} \, X\text{-}Quant \; \Rightarrow \; neg\text{-}X\text{-}Indef + Quant \tag{110a}$$
$$S: \quad \text{-}Quant\text{-}Y[neg]_{PvP} \; \Rightarrow \; Indef + Quant\text{-}Y\text{-}neg \tag{110b}$$

The derivation of a sentence like "That house doesn't have any roof" would include the following:

$$S: \quad \text{That-house-}neg\text{-Tense-have-}Quant^1\text{-roof} \tag{111a}$$

i. That-house-*neg*-Tense-have-*Indef* + *Quant*^{1}-roof [by *Indef*-
incorporation, Eq (110a) (111b)

ii. That-house-*do*-Tense-*neg*-have-*Indef*+ *Quant*^{1}-roof [by pre-
verbal particle placement, Eq. (24), and then *do* support, Eq. (111c)
(26)]

The rules outlined in Eq. (64c) that described special negatives like *no* and *nothing* as resulting from the incorporation of the pre-verbal particle *neg* into indefinite quanti-fiers occurring in the same clause as *neg* can now be given a more general analysis in terms of *Indef* + *Quant*; that is, *neg* is incorporated into a *Quant*(ifier) containing the symbol *Indef*. *Neg*-incorporation is obligatory for the first *Quant*(ifier) before Tense, if there is one (Eq. (112b)). Otherwise, the rule is optional (Eq. (112a)). Note that unlike *Indef*-incorporation, *neg*-incorporation still applies only within a given clause.

neg-incorporation
(a refinement of Eq. (90))

$$\text{(optional) } [neg]_{PvP} \, X[Indef + Y]_{Quant} \; \Rightarrow \; X\text{-}neg + [Indef + Y]_{Quant} \tag{112a}$$
$$\text{(obligatory) } [Indef + Y]_{Quant} \, Z[neg]_{PvP} \; \Rightarrow \; neg + [Indef + Y]_{Quant} \, Z \tag{112b}$$

Later rules provide for the conversion of the resultant chains of symbols into words:

$$Neg + Indef + Quant^1 \; \Rightarrow \; no \tag{113a}$$
$$Indef + Quant^1 \qquad \; \Rightarrow \; any \tag{113b}$$

25 The re-analysis of *ever* and *either* as indefinites. Earlier in this study, for example, Eq. (64), *ever* was treated as an adverb without further comment. In con-temporary English, the same peculiarities of occurrence characterize *ever* as do *any*; namely, *ever* occurs in negative, interrogative, and restrictive sentences whose corres-ponding simple, positive declaratives do not permit its occurrence. In addition, *ever* does not occur in simple, positive, declarative sentences in the way *any* does in "Any-one can do that." The expression *forever* must be treated separately. To account for the restrictions on *ever*, the same operations will be brought into play as in Sec-tion 24.

Consider now the constituent Time. It's original position is given in Eq. (3). Time, will be represented by, among other things, *sometimes* and *sometime*. Let us assume that Time can be relocated in pre-verbal position; that is, as a pre-verbal *Adv*(erb):

Pre-verbal Placement of Time (optional)

$$\text{Nominal-}Adv\text{-}Aux\text{-}MV\text{-Time} \Rightarrow \text{Nominal-}[Time]_{Adv}\text{-}Aux\text{-}MV \tag{114}$$

When Time occurs in a clause containing *neg* or in a clause subordinate to one containing *neg*, *Indef* may be incorporated into Time. The formulation is the same as in Eq. (110), but with Time replacing *Quant*. The inclusion of one symbol *Indef* in *a, a lot, many, somebody, sometime, once* would be an obvious refinement in the formulation, but this would entail complications that cannot be examined at this point. Finally, the form *ever* would result from the following rule: *Indef* + Time ⇒ *ever*. The derivation of:

$$\text{There won't ever be another party} \tag{115}$$

will include the following:

S: There-*neg*[*sometime*]$_{Time}$-Tense-will-be-another-party   (116a)

i.   There-*neg*-*Indef*+Time-Tense-will-be-another-party [by *Indef*-incorporation, Eq. (110)]   (116b)

ii.   There-Tense-will-*neg*-*Indef*+Time-be-another-party [by pre-verbal particle placement, Eq. (24)]   (116c)

iii.   There-will + φ + nt-ever-be-another-party [by Tense-attachment, Eq. (19), *neg*-contraction, Eq. (54d), and the development of *Indef* + Time]   (116d)

The word *never* results from the incorporation of *neg* in an *Indef* + Time in the same clause. As with the examples of *neg*-incorporation discussed in Section 23, the attachment is obligatory with the first occurrence of *Indef* + (which includes *Indef* + Time) preceding the pre-verbal particle *neg*; otherwise the attachment is optional. Consider the sentence:

$$\text{Never will there be another party.} \tag{117}$$

which is the same as Eq. (115), except that *Indef* + Time is initial. The derivation of Eq. (117) would include the following:

S: *Indef* + [*sometime*]$_{Time}$ there-*neg*-Tense-will-be-another-party [after *Indef*-incorporation, Eq. (110), and a rule for preposing Time]   (118a)

i.   *neg* + *Indef* + Time-there-Tense-will-be-another-party [by obligatory *neg*-incorporation, Eq. (112b)]   (118b)

ii.   *neg* + *Indef* + Time-Tense-will-there-be-another-party [by *neg*-attraction, Eq. (65h)]   (118c)

iii.   never-will + φ-there-be-another-party [after the development
of *neg* + *Indef* + Time into *never*, and Tense attachment,   (118d)
Eq. (19)]

The occurrence of *either* and *neither* in *either*-conjoining and in the *neither*-tag
will be accounted for by deriving *either*, also, by *Indef*-incorporation, with *too* as
the basic constituent; that is, Nominal-*neg-Aux-MV-too* ⇒ Nominal-*Aux-MV-
Indef* + *too*. The occurrence of initial *neither*, for example, in "No snow fell and
neither did any rain," is then a regular result of the occurrence of *Indef* in front of
neg, as is shown in the following derivation:

S: [Some]$_{Quant^1}$-snow-*neg*-Past-fall-and[some]$_{Quant^1}$-rain-*neg*-
Past-fall-*too* [after a rule of *too*-conjoining, see Section 15]   (119a)

   i.   *Indef* + *Quant*^{1}-snow-*neg*-Past-fall-and-*Indef-Quant*^{1}-rain-
neg-Past-fall-*Indef* + *too*   [by *Indef*-incorporation, Eq. (110)]   (119b)

   ii.   *Indef* + *Quant*^{1}-snow-*neg*-Past-fall-and-*Indef* + *too-Indef* + *Quant*^{1}
-Past-rain-*neg*-Past [by the preposing of *Indef* + *too*,   (119c)
and truncation Eq. (65b)]

   iii.   [*neg* + *Indef* + *Quant*^{1}-snow]$_{Nominal}$-Past-fall-and-*neg* + *Indef*
+ *too*-[*Indef* + *Quant*^{1}-rain]$_{Nominal}$Past [by *neg*-incorporation,   (119d)
Eq. (112)]

   iv.   [*neg* + *Indef* + *Quant*^{1}-snow]$_{Nominal}$-Past-fall-and-[*neg* + *Indef*
+ *too*]-Past [*Indef* + *Quant*^{1}-rain]$_{Nominal}$ [by *neg*-attraction,   (119e)
(65h)]

Finally, *Indef*-incorporation could be extended also to (adverbs of) Degree (for
example, *somewhat*) such that *Indef* + Degree ⇒ *at all*. This would account for the
permissibility of *at all* in the clause of Eq. (120a), but not in the corresponding simple
sentence below it.

I didn't realize that he admired her at all.   (120a)
*He admired her at all.   (120b)

Whereas there is no special combination of *neg* and the indefinite *at all*, the displacement of *not* in "He admired her not at all" will be analyzed as the optional
incorporation of the pre-verbal particle yielding *neg* + *Indef* + Degree. *Ever* and
at all can be thought of as replacing forms missing among the indefinites. That
is, there is no *anywhat*, *anytimes* corresponding to *somewhat* and *sometimes*,
the way *anywhere* correspond to *somewhere*, *anybody* to *somebody*, and so on. I
refer here simply to correspondence between forms. I am not speaking of correspondence in *syntactic* derivation; that is, I do not mean to say that sentences with
any and its combined forms are derived specifically from sentences with *some*.
Examples like "This house doesn't have any roof" indicate that this is not the case.
Rather, *some* is one of the several underlying forms from which *any* is derived syntactically.

There are other cases in which the *any*- and *no*-forms (the latter occurring by the
rule of *neg*-incorporation into *Indef*(inites) are also without a corresponding *some*-

form. The representative of *Quant* in these instances can be thought of as φ, or in some cases, perhaps, as *somewhat*.

> He isn't any smarter than she; he is no smarter than she;
> *he is some smarter than she; he is smarter than she. (121a)

> He doesn't like it any more than she does; he likes it no more than she does;
> *he likes it some more than she does; he likes (121b)
> it more than she does.

> He doesn't have any more than five books; he has no more than five books; *he has some more than five books; he (121c)
> has more than five books.

> He didn't get there any too soon; he got there none too soon; *he got there some too soon; he got there too soon. (121d)

In other instances the identity of the corresponding simple form is even more obscure:

> He doesn't live in New York any more; *he lives in New York some more. (122a)
> They aren't by any means finished; they are by no means finished; *they are by some means finished. (122b)

In certain dialects of English, however, *any more* occurs without the restrictions which motivate its treatment as a nonbasic element in standard literary English.[13] In the former dialects not only Eq. (122) occurs but also "He lives in New York any more." Consequently, *any more* would be treated as an adverbial expression with the same status as, for example, *these days* or *still*. The problem of its transformational derivation would then not arise in those dialects. In standard literary English, the word *anyway,* without a *syntactically* corresponding *someway,* is similarly nonderivative, for example, "He accepted anyway."

26 The conversion of quantifiers into indefinite quantifiers II: *not much* versus *a lot (of)*. The *Quant*(ifier) *much* has some of the same peculiarities as *any*. In sentences with a pre-verbal particle *neg*, (the question-marker wh- or restrictive *only*), which provides a favorable environment, *much* occurs:

> Not much rain fell. (123a)
> Not even then did much snow fall. (123b)
> Not much tobacco is being smoked this year. (123c)
> There isn't much tobacco being smoked this year. (123d)
> Writers don't accept suggestions much these days. (123e)
> Not many writers found that they liked it much. (123f)

---

[13]For a discussion of those dialects that use *any more* in affirmative sentences, see K. Malone, "*Any more* in the affirmative," *American Speech*, 7.460 (1931), and comments by D. W. Ferguson, *American Speech*, 7.231; C. W. Carter, Jr., *American Speech*, 7.235; J. H. Cox, *American Speech*, 7.236; and especially W. H. Eitner, "Affirmative *any more* in Present-day American speech," *Papers of the Michigan Academy of Science, Arts, and Letters*, 35:4.311–16 (1949), in section entitled "General Studies."

In corresponding positive sentences—provided that *much* is not preceded by *so* or *very*—*a lot* (*of*) or *a great deal* (*of*) generally occur instead of *much*.

A lot of rain fell.	(124a)
Even then a lot of snow fell.	(124b)
A lot of tobacco is being smoked this year.	(124c)
There is a lot of tobacco being smoked this year.	(124d)
Writers accept suggestions a lot these days.	(124e)
Many writers found that they liked it a lot.	(124f)

If we assume, however, as in Section 24, that *Indef* may be incorporated into the constituent *Quant*(ifier), also in the case of $Quant^2$ (where the latter represents *a lot* (*of*), *a great deal* (*of*), *many*), then *much* can be accounted for by the same mechanism as was used for *any* in Section 24; that is, in the favorable environment provided by *neg*, *Indef* is optionally added also to *Quant* when the latter is $Quant^2$.

$$[Quant^2]_{Quant} \Rightarrow Indef + Quant \text{ [under the same conditions as in Eq. (110)]} \tag{125a}$$

$$Indef + Quant^2\text{-Noun-Sg} \Rightarrow much\text{-Noun-Sg} \tag{125b}$$

If *Indef-Quant*² occurs before Tense and represents the first occurrence of an indefinite in the sentence, then the pre-verbal particle *neg* is obligatorily attracted to it, as was the case with other indefinites. Thus, the sentence (123a) includes the following in its derivation.

S: $[Quant^2]$-rain-*Sg*-*neg*-Tense-fall   (126a)

i.   *Indef* + $[Quant^2]_{Quant}$-rain-*Sg*-*neg*-Tense-fall [by optional *Indef*-incorporation, Eq. (110)]   (126b)

ii.   *neg* + $[Indef + Quant^2]$-rain-*Sg*-Tense-fall [by *neg*-incorporation, Eq. (90) (that is, Not[i.e., *neg*]much[i.e., *Indef* + $Quant^2$] rain fell)   (126c)

When the noun occurring with *Quant*(ifier) is plural, then the form assumed by the sequence *Indef* + $Quant^2$, *many*, is the same as one of the representatives of $Quant^2$. The difference in sense attributable to the presence of *Indef*, although the latter is phonologically zero, is clear in the following sentences:

Many smokers don't chew gum
(that is, $Quant^2$-smoker-*Pl*-*neg*-Tense-chew-gum [where   (127a)
optional *Indef*-incorporation, Eq. (110), is not applied])

Not many smokers chew gum
(that is, *neg*+*Indef*+$Quant^2$-smoker-*Pl*]$_{Nominal}$-Tense-chew-gum
[with the application of optional *Indef*-incorporation, Eq.   (127b)
(110), and subsequent *neg*-incorporation, Eq. (112)])

Example (127) is paralleled by "A lot of land isn't usable," that is, $[A\text{-lot-of}]_{Quant^2}$ -the-land-*Sg*-*neg*-Tense-be-usable, and "not much of the land is usable," that is, *neg*+*Indef*+$Quant^2$-the-land-*Sg*-Tense-be-usable.

SCOPE OF NEGATION I

27 *Neg* **in base sentence.** In Section 24, it was pointed out that the scope of *neg* with respect to the occurrence of the indefinites extended beyond the clause in which *neg* appears as pre-verbal particle and into subordinate clauses. However, while *neg* may be incorporated into even a secondary modifier, if *neg* and the modifier are in the same clause as in: "Even then the writers of none of the reports thought that any rain had fallen anywhere else," a *neg* in one clause cannot be incorporated into an *Indef* in another clause, even if the latter clause is subordinate to the former. Consider the following examples:

He didn't know that anything had happened. (128a)

He knew that nothing had happened. (128b)

The latter sentence will not be analyzed as resulting from the former by the incorporation of the pre-verbal particle *neg* from the main clause into *Indef*. Sentence (128b) has a different analysis, one in which the embedded sentence itself contains *neg*. The motivation for this differentiation is grammatical; it has to do with the desired economy in description discussed in Section 4. For example, if Eq. (128b) were derived from Eq. (128a), then a special statement would be needed to account for the permissibility of the *neither*-tag with Eq. (128a) but not with Eq. (128b), that is:

He didn't know that anything had happened and neither did she. (129a)

*He knew that nothing had happened and neither did she. (129b)

In infinitival and participial *Comp*(lements), on the other hand, not only may the occurrence of *Indef* be motivated by a *neg* occurring in the base sentence, but that *neg* may be incorporated into elements in the embedded *Comp*(lement). Note that at least in this respect infinitival and participial phrases are not simply reduced subordinate clauses.

I won't force you to marry anyone. (130a)

I will force you to marry no one. (130b)

I won't keep you living with anyone. (130c)

I will keep you living with no one. (130d)

That Eq. (130b), or at least one of the structures represented by that sequence of words, is a case of sentence negation, is seen from the presence of the *neither*-tag with that sentence as well as with Eq. (130a).

$$\left.\begin{matrix} \text{I won't force you to marry anyone} \\ \text{I will force you to marry no one} \end{matrix}\right\} \text{ and neither will he.} \qquad (131)$$

28 *Neg* **in embedded structures.** A pre-verbal particle *neg* that ultimately occurs in an embedded structure may also originate in the sentence that served as the source of the embedded structure. In that case, however, the scope of *neg* is restricted to the clause in which *neg* appears and to substructures subordinate to that clause. This restriction in the scope of a *neg* that has its origin in an embedded sentence, holds for the role *neg* plays in favoring the occurrence of indefinites as well as for the incorporation of *neg* into *Indef* (yielding, for example, *nothing*). A sentence like Eq. (130b) is thus structurally ambiguous. It is derived either from a structure underlying Eq. (130a), where the indefinite *anyone* is motivated by a *neg* occurring in the main clause, or from:

$$\text{I will force you not to marry anyone.} \tag{132}$$

The indefinite is motivated by the *neg* within the infinitival phrase and the elements of the infinitival phrase are derived from a source sentence with the following shape:

$$\text{You-}neg\text{-}\mathbf{aux}^1\text{-marry-Nominal} \tag{133}$$

In the same way, a sentence that is not itself an instance of sentence negation may nonetheless admit an *either*-clause or a negative appositive tag, by virtue of the inclusion of those elements in embedded structures in whose source such elements are regular.

> I will force you not to marry anyone, not even the man you love. (134a)

> Writers won't accept suggestions, and critics claim that publishers won't accept them now either. (134b)

However, since the source of:

> . . . , and critics claim that publishers won't accept them either (135)

is not itself an instance of sentence negation (that is, the base sentence "Critics claim [so]$_{Comp}$" does not have the pre-verbal particle *neg* in its derivation), the *neither*-tag is not admitted and *neither* (that is, *neg* + *either*) does not appear before the main clause (except with parenthetical *critics claim*, for example, ". . . and neither, critics claim, do publishers now").

The structure of certain *Comp*(lements) that are clausal in form was described in Eq. (101). With *decide* and *stop*, which belong to other classes of *V*(erbs) permissible without a following Nominal, the *Comp*(lements) are respectively infinitival and participial in form:

$$\text{I have decided to live with someone.} \tag{136a}$$
$$\text{I have stopped living with someone.} \tag{136b}$$

V(erbs) with a following Nominal (e.g., *force* and *keep* in Eqs. 130), i.e., certain transitive verbs, also occur with infinitival or participial *Comp*(lements). The class of *V*(erb) or *Adj*(ective) in the base sentence (S_b) determines the form of the *Comp*(lement)—i.e., the segmentation of the sentence to be embedded (S_e) and the particular elements added (*that*, *to*, *PrP*):

Comp-embedding

$$S_e: \quad \text{Nominal}(neg)\text{Tense}(M)(\text{have-}PP)(\text{be-}PrP)MV(\text{Place})(\text{Time}) \tag{137a}$$
$$\quad\quad\quad\quad\quad 1 \quad\quad 2 \quad\quad 3 \quad\quad\quad\quad\quad\quad\quad 4$$

$$S_b: \quad \ldots \begin{Bmatrix} V \\ Adj \end{Bmatrix} Comp \tag{137b}$$
$$\quad\quad\quad\quad\quad 5 \quad\quad 6$$

i.   ... $\left\{ \begin{array}{c} V \\ Adj \\ \scriptstyle 5 \end{array} \right\}$ $[that + S_e]_{Comp}$[declarative clause embedding]   (137c)

ii.   ... $\left\{ \begin{array}{c} V \\ Adj \\ \scriptstyle 5 \end{array} \right\}$ $[\underset{2}{(neg)to}\underbrace{(\text{have-}PP)(\text{be-}PrP)MV(\text{Place})(\text{Time})}_{4}]_{Comp}$ (137d)

[infinitival phrase embedding]

iii.   ... V $[\underset{5}{(neg)}\underset{2}{PrP}\underbrace{(\text{have-}PP)(\text{be-}PrP)MV(\text{Place})(\text{Time})}_{4}]_{Comp}$ (137e)

[participial phrase embedding]

In the case of infinitival and participial *Comp*(lements), a particular relationship holds between the subject Nominal of the sentence to be embedded and certain Nominals of the base sentence. If the *V*(erb) of the base sentence is accompanied by an object Nominal, then that object Nominal and the subject Nominal of the sentence to be embedded are the same, at least with certain *V*(erbs). Otherwise, the subject Nominals of the two source sentences are the same. In this study, further refinement in the analysis of the relationship between these Nominals will not be attempted.

Note that the incorporation of the *neg* of the base sentence into an *Indef* in a *Comp*(lement) can be considered blocked by *that* (which symbol will be considered the characteristic marker of subordinate clauses) but not by the characteristic markers of phrases (*to* and *PrP*).

CONSTITUENTS WHOSE OCCURRENCE IS FAVORED BY *NEG*

29   **Basic elements restricted in context versus derivative elements.** Certain constituents that occur in particular simple negative sentences do not occur in the corresponding positive sentences. One class of such constituents has been discussed in Section 24: the indefinite quantifiers *any* and *anything*. The indefinites have been described as derivative; that is, derived transformationally, in the environment of *neg*, from the basic constituent *Quant*(ifier). The argument presented for so treating them was that they appear in sentence-like structures (embedded clauses and phrases) whose source sentences do not themselves contain indefinite quantifiers.

Another class of expressions that occur in particular negative sentences but not in the corresponding positive ones will be considered *basic* elements, restricted, however, in certain occurrences, to sentences that include the pre-verbal particle *neg* among their other basic elements.[14] All such sentences are instances of sentence negation as defined in Section 19. Among the basic context-restricted constituents are (a) the *M*(odal) *need*:

Writers need not accept suggestions, not even good ones.   (138)

---

[14]For a long list of expressions favored by negation, see the article by E. Buyssens, "Negative contexts," *English Studies*, XL (1959).

(b) the verbal construction consisting of the *M*(odal) *can*, the *V*(erb) *help*, and a *Comp*(lement) consisting of the present participle:

> The writers can't help smiling at that, and neither can the   (139)
> publishers.

(c) the adverbials of Time consisting of *until* followed by a time expression:

> He did not get there until after the game, and neither did she.   (140)

It is important to note that it has not been claimed that *need* followed by the bare verb (that is, without *to*) must have a negative in the ultimate shape of the sentence, or that no affirmative sentences occur with *until then*, but only that in certain instances, these structures are permissible with *neg* but not without it.

30   The *M*(odal) *need*. The verb form *need* which occurs with *neg* followed by the bare verb as in Eq. (138), behaves like a typical *M*(odal) and thus contrasts with *need to*, which occurs with or without *neg* and behaves like other verbs with an infinitival *Comp*(lement): (a) unincorporated *neg* is ultimately located after the *M*(odal) *need* but before the *V*(erb) *need*. In the latter case *not* is preceded by supporting *do* when appropriate:

> Writers need not accept suggestions
> *versus*   (141)
> Writers do not need to accept suggestions

(b) the subject-verb agreement is the same for *M*(odal) *need* as for, for example, *must* (and neither occurs with Past as Tense-marker); that is, $[\varphi]_{\text{Tense}}[\textit{need}]_M$, as in the constituent structure rule of Eq. (6), the *V*(erb) *need*, on the other hand, has *-S-* as its third person present singular ending:

> He need not accept them *versus* He needs to accept them   (142a)

The *M*(odal) *need* does, however, differ from other *M*(odals) in not figuring in the tag of tag-questions, "he can't do it, can he?" In view of the fact that such tags depend on the existence of a positive-negative pair, this difference is not surprising. The constituent structure rule introducing *M*(odal) *need* occurs after the introduction of *neg* and alternates with the rule introducing the other *M*(odals).

> $M \rightarrow \textit{need}/\text{in } \textit{env.} \textit{ neg} \ldots (\textit{Adv})\text{Tense}—$ (142b)

$$M \rightarrow \begin{Bmatrix} \text{will} \\ \text{can} \\ \text{must} \\ \ldots \end{Bmatrix}$$ (142c)

The constituent structure rule for introducing *help* in the highly restricted context consisting of the pre-verbal particle *neg*, the *M*(odal) *can*, and the present participial *Comp*(lement), would be similar in form to the rule for *need*.

31   The Time adverbial *until then*. The special restrictions on the occurrence of this time expression deserve special consideration. Only with certain predicates does *until then* occur in negative sentences but not in the corresponding positive ones. Pairs like the following reveal that restriction:

That man didn't get there this time until five o'clock.	(143a)
*That man got there this time until five o'clock.	(143b)
That man slept until five o'clock.	(143c)
*A guest arrived this time until five o'clock.	(143d)
Guests arrived this time until five o'clock.	(143e)

The feature common to the various permissible uses of *until then* is the fact that they involve time span, which can be provided to the constituent occurring with *until then* in a variety of ways: (a) through the *V*(erb) itself (for example, *sleep* in Eq. (143c)), (b) through features of the Nominals involved (for example, the indefinite plurality of the subject Nominal in Eq. (143e), contrasted to Eq. (143d)), (c) and through negation as in Eq. (143a). The fact that the element *neg* provides a favorable environment for *until then*, in the same way as do certain classes of verbs and certain types of nominal specification, is not surprising if we give negation, in such cases, the by no means counter-intuitive interpretation of specifying the absence of what is predicated by the same sentence without *neg*. Simple absense would then also involve span of Time.

X

32 On the Interpretation of *not*. An important question arises with expressions like *M*(odal) *need not, cannot help doing something, not until then*. Should *not* be treated as part of the restricted constituent itself (that is, as an integral part of the *M*(odal), of the *V*(erb), and of the Time adverbial, respectively), or should it be treated as a special case of the pre-verbal particle *neg*. The latter interpretation is clearly appropriate for the special negatives *nobody, nothing, none*. The reasons include the fact that the alternation of the position of *neg* in the set of passives corresponding to "no one gave much to anybody even then" in Eq. (89) can best be explained by assuming the presence of the same mobile *neg* as occurs in the related "not even then did anybody give anyone anything." The same interpretation of *not* (that is, as derived from the pre-verbal particle *neg*) is appropriate for the context-restricted constituents such as *M*(odal) *need, until then*, and so on, in Sections 29 to 31. Included in the argument are the following reasons: (a) *until then*, even in those instances where *not* may not be missing, is treated as the same constituent as other instances of *until then*;

The nurse came in at five o'clock, until which time the patient had remained calm and hadn't even opened her eyes once.	(144)

(b) the constituent underlying the *not* that occurs with these context-restricted basic constituents enjoys the same mobility as other instances of the pre-verbal particle *neg* with respect to incorporation into the indefinites.

Nobody need mention that.	(145a)
No one got there this time until five o'clock.	(145b)
Not many writers can help smiling at that.	(145c)

Implicit in the analysis presented so far is the rejection of a basically different interpretation of negation. In the present study, negation—at least to the extent that sentence negation is involved—has been treated as (a) unitary (that is, attributable to the optional presence of a single constituent, the pre-verbal particle *neg*) and as (b) mobile (that is, the element to which negation is attributed may ultimately appear incorporated in and fused with other constituents). A different interpretation that is thus rejected would treat negation as: (a) *multiple* (that is, particular *negative* forms would be included among the basic representatives of most constituents at the constituent structure level, and any number of such basic negative constituents might occur in any given sentence), and as (b) *reductive* (that is, subsequent to permissible variation in word order, all negative constituents after the first one would be reduced to indefinite quantifiers). In accordance with the first characteristic of the rejected interpretation, the following string could occur in a derivation. "Nobody-never-will-give-no-one-nothing." The same string could optionally be re-arranged as "Never-nobody-will-give-nothing," and, with subsequent inversion, "Never-will-nobody-give-no–one-nothing." As a result of the reductive character of negation in this rejected interpretation, the latter two strings would ultimately yield "Nobody ever will give anyone anything" and "Never will anybody give anyone anything." The rejected analysis, however, would result in considerable complication in the description of those tags and conjoined elements which have been associated here with sentence negation, since any elements of the sentence, even elements in embedded structures, could, by their own right, result in sentence negation, except for elements in subordinate clauses. Thus, in one instance of sentence negation:

> The writers of none of the reports thought so even then,   (146)
> and neither did the publishers of any of the brochures.

the negative characteristics would be attributed directly to the element *none* in the embedded modifier (rather than indirectly by way of *any* and the basic but relocated *neg* as in Eq. (107)); the sentence would—incorrectly, I would maintain—be built up from some representation of the two sentences, "those writers thought so," which is not an instance of sentence negation, and "they wrote none of the reports." The rejected analysis would relate Eq. (146) to "the writers who had written none of the reports thought so," which is not an instance of sentence negation, and is, incidentally, quite different in sense from Eq. (146). In fact, Eq. (146) is much closer in sense to "The writers who had written the reports didn't think so," which similarity is reflected in the analysis proposed in this paper. A further objection to the rejected analysis is that it would necessitate the assumption of negatives in derivative structures like the clause "I didn't realize that any rain had fallen," if all indefinite quantifiers dependent on a negative are to be accounted for by the reduction of a negative—a demand that need not necessarily be made. Furthermore, the structural peculiarities of the set "I will force you not to marry anyone," "I won't force you to marry anyone," and ambiguous "I will force her to marry no one," discussed in Section 28, would go unresolved. Finally, a special provision would be required to permit the second *not* in "I couldn't force her not to marry anyone," to be left unreduced.

WORDS WITH *NEGATIVE AFFIXES*

33 Favorable environments for the indefinite quantifiers. In Section 20, it was seen that sentences containing constituents with the prefix *un-*, *in-*, *dis-*, or the suffix *-less*—however similar in meaning such sentences might be to sentences containing *not* or some other negative pre-verb (for example, *rarely*)—nonetheless were not instances of sentence negation ("He isn't happy and neither is she," but only "He is unhappy and so is she" and not *"He is unhappy and neither is she"). Moreover, whereas the presence of *neg* may motivate the occurrence of an indefinite quantifier in sentences like:

$$\text{They had not been happy about any of his actions} \qquad (147)$$

Sentences otherwise identical except for a negative prefix instead of the pre-verbal particle *neg* do not similarly provide a favorable environment for the indefinite quantifiers.

$$\text{*They had been unhappy about any of his actions.} \qquad (148)$$

Thus, with respect to those constituents of simple sentences examined so far, there is no reason to assume any especially close *grammatical* relationship between the negative pre-verb *not* and the so-called "negative" prefixes. If the language contained only those simple constructions, then the use of a single designation *negative* in describing both pre-verbal elements like *not* and prefixes like *un-* would have little motivation from the point of view of the grammar as characterized at Section 2. However, when sentence-like complementary structures (*that*-clauses, infinitive and participial phrases) are examined, it turns out that the presence of a constituent with a negative prefix, while not resulting in sentence negation, does in fact, have some of the same consequences with respect to the shape of a sentence as does the presence of *not*, *never*, *nobody*, or the other reflexes of the pre-verbal particle *neg*. Consider the following sentences:

a. He will be able to find some time for that.
b. He won't be able to find any time for that.
c. *He will be able to find any time for that.   (149)
d. He is unable to find any time for that.

a. It is conceivable that he could do more.
b. It isn't conceivable that he could do any more.
c. *It is conceivable that he could do any more.   (150)
d. It is inconceivable that he could do any more.

a. It is possible for him to do more.
b. It isn't possible for him to do any more.
c. *It is possible for him to do any more.   (151)
d. It is impossible for him to do any more.

a. It is likely that he will do more.
b. It isn't likely that he will do any more.
c. *It is likely that he will do any more.   (152)
d. It is unlikely that he will do any more.

a. He would be *wise* to do more.
b. He wouldn't be *wise* to do any more.
c. *He would be *wise* to do any more.   (153)
d. He would be *unwise* to do any more.

a. He liked doing *more* than necessary.
b. He didn't like doing *any more* than necessary.
c. *He liked doing *any more* than necessary.   (154)
d. He disliked doing *any more* than necessary.

a. It is *unusual* for rain to fall in January.
b. It isn't *usual* for any rain to fall in January.
c. *It is *usual* for any rain to fall in January.   (155)
d. It is *unusual* for any rain to fall in January.

In Eqs. 149–155, the *neg*(ative) aff(ix) (*un-*, *in-*, *dis-*) of sentence (d.) in each group, provides the necessary environment for the occurrence of indefinite quantifiers (*any*, and so on), whereas without the affix, only the simple quantifiers (*some*, φ, *a lot*, and so on) occur. In this respect, the affixes have the same effect as the pre-verbal particle *neg*, but the scope of the affix is restricted to sentence-like *Comp*(lements) subordinated to the constituents containing the affix, whereas the scope of pre-verbal particle *neg* extends over the whole sentence, including the constituents of *Comp*(lements). The rule for the formation of indefinites in complementary structures subordinated to a constituent with a negative affix (**neg-aff**) would have a form similar to the rule already formulated for *Indef*-incorporation.

> *Indef*-incorporation (optional) (same as Eq. (110), but   (156)
> extended to negative affixes)

$$\textbf{neg aff} \begin{Bmatrix} Adj \\ V \end{Bmatrix} [\ldots -Quant- \ldots]_{Comp} \Rightarrow$$

$$\textbf{neg aff} \begin{Bmatrix} Adj \\ V \end{Bmatrix} [\ldots Indef + Quant \ldots]_{Comp}$$

A sentence like Eq. (149d) would be the result of the addition of *Indef* to the constituent *Quant*(ifier) in a string with the following constituent analysis:

> S: He-Tense-will-be-[*un*]$_{Neg\text{-}aff}$[able]$_{Adj}$[to-find-$Quant^1$-
> time-for-that]$_{Comp}$ [after infinitival phrase embedding,   (157a)
> Eq. (137d)]

> i: He-Tense-will-be-*un*-able-to-find-*Indef* + $Quant^1$-time-
> for-that [after *Indef*-incorporation, Eq. (156)]   (157b)

34 Negative absorption: another feature common to *neg* and the negative affixes.
Negative absorption is a grammatical process postulated in order to account for certain special characteristics of sentences like the following:

> They don't think that writers can help smiling at that.   (158a)
> It's unlikely that he will get there until after the game.   (158b)
> I don't suppose that I need mention this again.   (158c)

The special characteristics are ones that appear to contradict certain general claims made here concerning sentences, namely: (a) that *Comp*(lements) reflect the relationships of the constituents in independent sentences, as discussed in Section 24 (but we certainly do not want to assume *"He will get there until after the game" to account for Eq. (158b)), and (b) that *until then, M*(odal) *need*, and the construction *cannot help doing something*, in certain independent simple sentences, occur with *neg* but not without it (see Section 29) (it is exactly this element *neg* that is missing from the complements in question). That is, sentence-like *Comp*(lements) to certain classes of *Adj*(ectives) and *V*(erbs)—the underlying source sentences of which *Comp*(lements) must contain *neg*—under certain conditions, themselves appear without *neg*. The conditions under which this is the case are relevant to the relationship between the negative affixes and the pre-verbal particle *neg*. This is seen in the following set of sentences:

It is likely that he won't get there this time until after the game. (159a)

*It is likely that he will get there this time until after the game. (159b)

It isn't likely that he will get there this time until after the game. (159c)

It is unlikely that he will get there this time until after the game. (159d)

The negative affix functions in the same way as the pre-verbal particle *neg* in providing the necessary environment for the occurrence, in a form without *neg*, of a clause whose corresponding independent source sentence cannot similarly occur without *neg*. This anomaly—from the point of view of the shape of the independent sentence—will be interpreted here as resulting from the absorption of the pre-verbal particle *neg* from the embedded sentence (that is, the subordinate clause) by the pre-verbal particle *neg* in the form of *n't* in Eq. (159c) or by the negative affix *un-* in the principle clause of Eq. (159d). Reasons for interpreting these facts as due to negative absorption will be given in the following section.

35 Inherent negatives. Consider again the constructions examined in Section 34: (a) **neg aff** $\begin{Bmatrix} V \\ Adj \end{Bmatrix}$ *Comp* and (b) $[neg]_{PvP}Aux \ldots Comp$. In both of these, the *Comp*(lement) lacks the pre-verbal particle *neg* that occurs in the corresponding independent sentence. On the basis of only these constructions, the absorption of the postulated pre-verbal particle *neg* from within the *Comp*(lement) could have another interpretation, namely, that the *neg* in the *Comp*(lement) of certain *V*(erbs) and *Adj*(ectives) is relocated either as a negative affix occurring with the latter constituent or as the pre-verbal particle *neg* in the main clause, provided that the latter does not already contain *neg*. Eq. (160a) could ultimately have the form of Eq. (160b), but it could also yield Eq. (160c) by the alternative interpretation under consideration, which lends itself more readily, in fact, to providing a grammatical explanation for the intuited similarity of Eqs. (160b–c).

They-Past-think[that-writers-*neg*-Tense-will-accept-suggestions]$_{Comp}$. (160a)

They thought that writers would not accept suggestions.   (160b)

They didn't think [that is, Past-*neg*-think] that writers
would accept suggestions.   (160c)

On the other hand, the same similarity is not felt between "It is possible for writers
not to accept suggestions" and "It is impossible for writers to accept suggestions."
A further reservation on the alternative interpretation of negative absorption under
consideration is provided by sentences like the following:

They doubt that I need ever consider the problem.   (161a)

He forbids her to have another child for several years.   (161b)

She's too weak to have another child until after the
operation.   (161c)

Doubt, forbid, and *too*—the constituents to which the *Comp*(lements) with missing
neg are subordinate—do not show any signs of *neg*. They suggest, rather, that
negative absorption should be interpreted as resulting not in the relocation of the
neg of the embedded sentence, but rather in its disappearance from the embedded
sentence when the base sentence contains: (a) certain classes of *Comp*(lement)
governors like *think* (but not *say*), *likely* (but not *fortunate*), and (b) a certain
favorable *negative* environment. That favorable negative environment consists of
the *negative* pre-verbal particle *neg*, a *neg*(ative) aff(ix), or an *inherently negative*
constituent like *doubt, forbid, too*. Since the inherent negatives behave like constituents with a negative affix, the former will be considered to include a **neg**(ative)
aff(ix), but without phonological shape. Thus, *unlikely* consists of the sequence
neg aff—*likely*, *impossible* of the sequence **neg aff**—*possible*, *dislike* of the sequence
neg aff—*like*. In these three instances a grammatically equivalent form exists without the affix. *Pointless* from [**neg aff**—*point*]$_{Adj}$ or *useless* from [**neg aff**—*use*]$_{Adj}$ are
not paralleled by corresponding unaffixed forms with the same function; that is,
there is no adjective *use*. These affixed forms do, however, have less direct parallels
in *of use* and *having some point*. The grammatical status of this parallelism will not
be investigated in this paper. Similarly, *doubt* from **neg aff**—*doubt* and *too* from
neg aff—*too* consist of constituents which do not occur without a negative affix.

Further support for the treatment of the *neg* of the base sentence as original and
not as representing the relocated *neg* of the *Comp*(lement), is that the phenomena
included above under negative absorption also occur when the *neg* in the base
sentence occurs in its various combined forms:

Scarcely anybody expected him to get there until after
five o'clock.   (162)

Nonetheless, the interpretation of negative absorption proposed in this study by
all means should be considered only tentative. It necessitates certain complications
which at least at this stage in the analysis of English syntax, are unprecedented; for
example, the sentence embedded as the *Comp*(lement) must contain the pre-verbal
particle *neg* if the base sentence into which it is embedded contains *neg*, or if the
constituent to which the *Comp*(lement) is subordinated contains a negative affix.
That is, there is a kind of *negative* agreement, whereby *Comp*(lements) subordinate

to constituents under negation may themselves contain any elements compatible with negation. This feature is expressed in the formalization by describing those *Comp*(lements) in terms of the shape of a source sentence that contains the pre-verbal particle *neg*. The *Comp*(lement) itself, however, need not contain *neg*, although it may, as is seen in the following sentences:

He is too intelligent not to recognize her talents. (163a)

He doubts that they won't accept any suggestions. (163b)

It isn't likely that there won't be any rain in January. (163c)

The fact that the *Comp*(lement) may, but need not, be under negation independently is expressed in the formalization by the possible second *neg* in the *Comp*(lement). This possible second *neg* has already been discussed in Section 14, Footnote 1. It is as if the negative element of the main clause has within its domain even the selection of basic elements within the complement while not precluding the presence within the latter of an independent pre-verbal particle *neg*. The formalization presented here comes very close to that interpretation—as close as it can and still preserve the convention adopted in Section 8—of requiring the specification of all basic elements and their structures (that is, the specification of constituent structure rules) before the re-arranging, combining, incorporating, and restructuring of those elements (that is, before the various operations described by the transformational rules).

$$neg\text{-absorption} \hspace{4cm} (164)$$

S_e: Nominal-*neg*-($X(neg)$) Tense(M) (have-PP) (be-PrP) MV(Place) (Time)

$\hspace{3cm}$ 1 $\hspace{1.2cm}$ 2 $\hspace{5cm}$ 3

S_b: Nominal $\left\{ \begin{array}{l} neg\text{-Tense}(M) \text{ (have-}PP) \left\{ \begin{array}{l} \text{(be-}PrP) \text{ think} \\ \text{be-likely} \end{array} \right\} \\ Aux \left\{ \begin{array}{l} neg\text{-doubt} \\ \text{be-}neg\text{-likely} \end{array} \right\} \end{array} \right\}$ $Comp$- Y

$\hspace{5.5cm}$ 4 $\hspace{4cm}$ 5 $\hspace{0.3cm}$ 6

$\Rightarrow$ *seg* 4 $\left[\text{THAT-Nominal } (neg) \right.$

$\hspace{3.5cm}$ 1 $\hspace{1.3cm}$ 2

$\hspace{1cm}$ ($X(neg)$)Tense (M) (have-PP) (be-PrP) MV (Place) (Time)$\left. \right]_{Comp}$ Y

$\hspace{5cm}$ 3 $\hspace{6cm}$ 6

THE CONSTITUENT: *neg*

36 The uniform treatment of *negative* features. To account for the similarities between the pre-verbal particle *neg* and its various combined forms (*nobody*, *nothing*) on the one hand, and the constituents negative inherently (*doubt*) or by affixation (like *unable*) on the other hand, it will be assumed that the same constituent (*neg*) is involved in both, that is, that *unable* is *neg* + *able*, *impossible*, *neg* + *possible*, and *doubt*, *neg* + *doubt*. The word *not* in sentences like "writers will not accept suggestions" is$[neg]_{PvP}$; that is, the same symbol but representing the constituent pre-verbal particle *neg* in the sentence in which it occurs. The fact that the structure of *neg* in the latter sentence is that of a pre-verbal particle, differentiates that occurrence of *neg* from those where *neg* has the structure of a negative affix. Similarly, the special negatives (*nobody* from *neg* + *Indef* + *Quant*, that is, for all practical purposes, *neg* + *anybody*, *never*; that is, *neg* + *ever*) differ from the negative affix words in that the *neg* that occurs in these special negatives is derived from a pre-verbal particle *neg in the same sentence*, (that is, *nobody*-Past-*give-much-to-anyone* is a form of the string *anybody*-[*neg*]$_{PvP}$-Past-*give-much-to-anyone*). The *neg* of words with a negative affix, on the other hand, are not so derived. The derivation of *neg* in affixes will be considered in Section 40. It is interesting to note that the nominal prefix *non-* unlike the negative affixes discussed does not permit the occurrence of elements associated with negation.

37 The constituent structure position of the pre-verbal particle *neg*. In Section 33 we examined certain similarities between constituents with a negative affix and constituents derived from an occurrence of *neg* with the structure of a pre-verbal particle in the sentence. Because of the similarities, among which negative absorption is particularly significant, it was proposed in Section 33 that the common *negativeness* of these markedly different types of constituents be ascribed to the presence of the same constituent, that is, *neg*. The differences in the scope of *neg* were found to depend on its constituent structure (that is, on whether it represents, or has represented in the same sentence, the pre-verbal particle) or whether it is part of the representation of certain major categories like Verb or Adjective. However, the grammatical relationship between the particular constituent structure of *neg* and its scope has not yet been formulated; that is, it has not yet been demonstrated that the *full scope* of the negative pre-verbal particle over the whole sentence and the *reduced scope* of the negative affixes over certain dependent sentence-like structures is one and the same phenomenon and that the differences in the two result naturally from the relationship of these two instances of *neg* to other constituents in the sentence. First, however, let us reconsider more closely the structural position of the pre-verbal particle *neg*.

As has been shown, the reflexes of the pre-verbal particle *neg* are located within certain major constituents of the *S*(entence): (a) within the *Aux*(iliary) in sentences like "Writers have *not* been accepting invitations," (b) as part of the subject Nominal in "*Not* much rain fell," and (c) as part of an adverb of Place in "They went *nowhere*," (d) within a prepositional modifier in "The writers of none of the reports thought so," (e) within an infinitival complement in "I will force you to marry no one." The fact that the reflexes of *neg* appear in such a variety of constituents leaves us without any reason, in the basic form of such sentences, to assign *neg* to any one of these constituents. The fact that the pre-verbal particle *neg*, regardless of whether it appears ultimately as part of a Noun or adverb of Place or *Aux*(iliary), and the like, motivates the occurrence of the indefinite quantifiers *any*, *anyone*, and so on, regardless of their constituency, is an argument against attributing the origin of *neg* (that is, its derivation at the level of constituent structure) to the expansion of any one such constituent like Nominal, adverb of Place, or *Aux*(iliary), in which its ultimately appears. Let us assume that *neg* appears, optionally, as part of the expansion of *S*(entence), along side of (a) the interrogative marker wh-, which is also optional, (b) the subject Nominal, and (c) the Predicate.

By this assumption, the constituent structure of *neg* is related to that of wh-. This relationship is not arbitrary. *Neg* is similar to wh- both in its constituent structure and in its relationship to the symbols with which it occurs. The effect of the pre-verbal particle *neg* in motivating the occurrence of the indefinites is matched by the similar effect of wh-, which similarly has as its scope the whole sentence. Moreover, *neg* shares with wh- not only the possibility of attachment with a great variety of constituents, but also the capacity of motivating inversion.

Who (wh + someone) will accept suggestions?
No one (*neg* + anyone) will accept suggestions. (165a)

When (wh + sometime) will he marry again?
Never (*neg* + ever) will he marry again. (165b)

We shall describe the scope of wh- and *neg* in terms of the concept "in construction with." This concept can be explicated most simply if we consider the constituent structure rules graphically, as in Fig. 1. Figure 2(b) represents the set of constituent structure rules given in Fig. 2(a).

$$w \rightarrow y\text{-}x^1\text{-}x^2$$
$$x^2 \rightarrow x^3\text{-}x^4$$
$$x^4 \rightarrow x^5\text{-}x^6$$

Figure 2 (a)   **Figure 2 (b)**

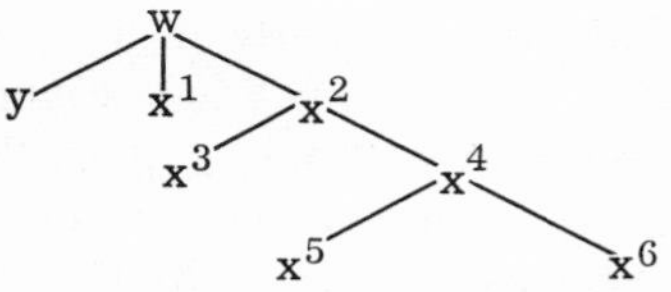

A constituent (for example, x^4 or x^5) is "in construction with" another constituent (in this case x^3) if the former is dominated by (that is, occurs somewhere lower down the branch of) the first branching node (that is, x^2) that dominates the latter (x^3). Similarly, y is "in construction with" x^1 as well as with x^2, since y is dominated by w (in fact, all three, y, x^1, and x^2, are "mutually in construction"). On the other hand, y is not "in construction with" x^3 since y is not dominated by x^2.

The rules and diagram of Fig. 2 are the same as the initial expansions in the description of the constituent structure of the *S*(entence).

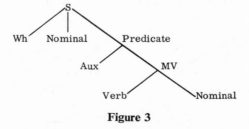

Figure 3

In Fig. 3, the subject Nominal and the Predicate, as well as all of the constituents into which the Predicate is expanded are "in construction with" wh-. Consider the constituent structure of a construction involving a negative affix "They are unable to accept any suggestions."

$$[they]_{Nominal}[Tense]_{Aux}be[\ [un]_{neg}[able]_{Adj}\ [to\ accept\ any\ suggestions]_{Comp}]_{Predicative} \tag{166}$$

The structure is the following:

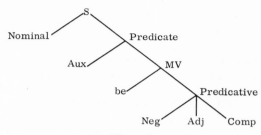

Figure 4

The *Comp*(lement) in Eq. (166), and everything dominated by it are "in construction with" *neg*. Similarly, in "they doubt that writers ever accept suggestions," where *neg*—Verb is *neg*—*doubt*, the *Comp*(lement) and all it contains (that is, [that writers ever accept suggestions]$_{Comp}$) are "in construction with" *neg*, whereas, for example, the subject Nominal *they* is not. The rule of *Indef*-incorporation (Eqs. (110) and (156)) can now be generalized to cover both the pre-verbal particle *neg* and the affix *neg* by restricting the application of the rule specifically to *Quant*(ifiers) "in construction with" *neg*.

The precise position of *neg* in the string consisting of the subject Nominal and the Predicate, is, however, not as clear as that of the interrogative marker wh-. The latter, as in Eq. (2), is described as occurring first in the string that results from one possible expansion of the *S*(entence), that is, $S \rightarrow$ wh-Nominal-Predicate. The reasons for selecting initial position as basic for wh- include the fact that in the final shape of sentences—and particularly in interrogative clauses (indirect questions)—wh- and its attachments do in fact occur initially. The original position of *neg* appears to be one of the following: (a) before the Predicate (that is, $S \rightarrow$ (wh-) Nominal(*neg*)Predicate, pre-Predicate position); or (b) before the whole declarative clause ($S \rightarrow$ (wh-)(*neg*)Nominal-Predicate: i.e., pre-Sentential position);

Figure 5 (a)   **Figure 5 (b)**

In both linear orders the same constituents are "in construction with" *neg*. Below I shall present grammatical facts that suggest the superiority of the second order over the first. But the first also accounts for certain facts. The assumption of pre-Predicate position of *neg* readily explains its position in infinitive phrases, for example, "For writers not to accept suggestions is reasonable." Also by permitting adverbs to cluster on either side of pre-Predicate *neg*, distinctions like the following are reflected in the grammar:

$$\text{writers don't often accept suggestions} \tag{167}$$

That is, *S*: writers-*neg*-often-Tense-accept-suggestions.

  i. writers-Tense-*neg*-often-accept-suggestions.
      [by pre-verbal particle placement, Eq. (24)]

  ii. writers-do-Tense-*neg*-often-accept-suggestions.
      [by *do*-support, Eq. (26)]

$$\text{writers often don't accept suggestions}$$

that is, *S*: writers-often-*neg*-Tense-accept-suggestions.   (168a)

  i. writers-often-Tense-*neg*-accept-suggestions.
      [by pre-verbal particle placement, Eq. (24)]   (168b)

  ii. writers-often-*do*-Tense-*neg*-accept-suggestions.
      [by *do*-support, (Eq. 26)]   (168c)

On the other hand, if the position of *neg* is assumed to be at the head of the sentence, after wh- if it occurs, then the pre-verbal particle parallels wh- and the negative affixes with respect to motivating the occurrence of indefinites.

$$\textit{Indef}\text{-incorporation [generalizing Eqs. (110) and (156)]} \tag{169}$$

$$\begin{Bmatrix} \text{wh-} \\ neg \end{Bmatrix} X\text{-}Quant\text{-}Y \Rightarrow \begin{Bmatrix} \text{wh-} \\ neg \end{Bmatrix} X\text{-}Indef + Quant\text{-}Y$$

For Eq. (169) to operate, the *Quant*(ifier) must be "in construction with" *neg* or wh-.

They sometimes inquire whether [that is, wh- in a subordinate clause] rain [that is, $[\varphi]_{Quant}$ rain] has fallen ⇒ They sometimes inquire whether any [that is, *Indef* + *Quant*] rain has fallen [where the interrogative clause and thus also the *Quant*(ifier) it dominates are in construction with wh-]   (170a)

We are unlikely to have rain [that is, $[\varphi]_{Quant}$rain] ⇒ We are unlikely to have any [that is, *Indef* + *Quant*] rain [where the infinitive *Comp*(lement) dominating it are "in construction with $[un]_{neg}$]   (170b)

We will not [that is, $[neg]_{PvP}$] have rain [that is, $[\varphi]_{Quant}$ rain] ⇒ We will not have any rain [where the object Nominal and the *Quant*(ifier) dominated by it are "in construction with" the pre-verbal particle *neg*].   (170c)

Moreover, front position of the pre-verbal particle *neg* would provide an explanation for the inverted word order that occurs with initial negatives along the same lines as inversion with wh-; that is, similar to wh-attraction (Eqs. (17) and (54e)).

Never have I seen so much rain.	(171a)
Nowhere do we see such things.	(171b)
Not in any other countries do you see such things.	(171c)
In no other countries do you see such things.	(171d)
Not even there did it rain.	(171e)

A pre-sentencial *neg*:

Figure 6

may have certain constituents of the *S*(entence) incorporated in it. Such a *neg* attracts to it the familiar segment of the *Aux*(iliary) that has been referred to as **aux**[1]. In certain structures (for example, Eq. (171d) versus Eq. (171e)) *neg* is fused with the incorporated constituent. It is significant that the occurrence of *neg* under consideration should have the particular structure that has been associated with sentence negation (that is, that of a pre-verbal particle, which, it is now being argued, has original pre-sentencial position) for instances of *neg* with other structures do not result in inversion.

Not long ago it rained.	(172a)
Not far away it was raining very hard.	(172b)
Not infrequently it rains very hard here.	(172c)
No more than three years ago, John was also doing it.	(172d)

When the pre-verbal particle *neg* does not have other constituents incorporated into it, then it assumes its position within the *Aux*(iliary). Accordingly, sentences 173a and 174a with inverted word order, where the subject Nominal and the Predicate are "in construction with" *neg*, are paralleled by the 'b' examples in which *neg* has the position in the *Aux*(iliary) already described by the rule of pre-verbal particle placement, Eq. (24). Sentences like those of Eq. (172), in which *neg* is not in construction with the subject Nominal and the Predicate, lack this parallel.

Not in any other countries do you see such things.	(173a)
You don't see such things in any other country.	(173b)

Not even there did it rain.	(174a)
It didn't rain even there (varying with "It didn't rain even there.")	(174b)

The same words (*not even two years ago* and *in not many years*) represent both structuring in the following pairs and are correspondingly ambiguous; but only with example (a) where *not* is a pre-verbal particle does inversion occur.

Not even two years ago was I there (that is, "I wasn't even there two years ago").	(175a)
Not even two years ago I was there,	(175b)

In not many years will Christmas fall on Sunday (varying
with "Not in many years will Christmas fall on Sunday";
that is, "Christmas will not fall on Sunday in many
years").   (176a)

In not many years, Christmas will fall on Sunday.   (176b)

Finally, the assumption of front position of *neg* accounts for its occurrence before
the subject Nominal when other constituents, particularly Tense, have been deleted.

The old people wanted to remain, but not the young
people.   (177a)

Suggestions, not corrections, are needed.   (177b)

Mary supports John, not John, Mary.   (177c)

Mary can come in, but not anybody else.   (177d)

If Mary is permitted to leave, then why not John   (177e)

If it is postulated that the pre-verbal particle *neg* originally has pre-sentential
position, then the various places where it ultimately occurs can be accounted for by
assuming that *neg* takes its position within the *Aux*(iliary) provided that it has not
been associated with a preposed element (that is, provided (a) that it does not have
the form *neg* + *X* as in "Not even then did it rain") and (b) that the string contains
Tense. To account for the occurrences of *neg* outside the *Aux*(iliary), I shall extend
the grammar by a *preliminary neg-placement* rule that precedes the rule already
formulated for correctly locating *neg* within the *Aux*(iliary) (that is, the rule of pre-
verbal particle placement, Eqs. (64c) and (24)).

preliminary *neg*-placement   (178)

$$neg\text{-Nominal-}[\text{Tense} \ldots]_{Aux} \Rightarrow \text{Nominal-}neg + [\text{Tense} \ldots]_{Aux}$$

After preliminary *neg*-placement but before the application of the rule for pre-
verbal particle placement, the position of *neg* (that is, *neg* + *Aux*) will account for
the phenomena that figured in the argument for original pre-predicate position of
neg; for example, the position of *neg* in infinitive phrases like " . . . for them *not* to
have accepted" versus "They have *not* accepted," mentioned in Section 37. The rule
for pre-verbal particle placement can be thought of as specifying the details of the
incorporation of *neg* into the string of verbal forms comprising the *Aux*(iliary);
that is, as interpreting *neg* + *Aux*. Further refinements of the grammar, that might
result from combining and reformulating these rules will not be considered in this
study. Included in the derivation of Eq. (171b) would be the following: "Nowhere
do we see such things."

S: *neg* + somewhere-we-Tense-see-such-things
[after the preposing of *somewhere*, the details of which
operation will not be examined here]   (179a)

i. *neg* + somewhere-Tense-we-see-such-things
[by *neg*-attraction, Eq. (65h)]   (179b)

ii. *neg* + somewhere-*do* + Tense-we-see-such-things
[by *do*-support, Eq. (26)]   (179c)

The sentence of Eq. (177c) would involve the following in its derivation:

$$S_a: \textit{neg}\text{-John-Tense-support-Mary}$$
$$S_b: \text{Mary-Tense-support-John} \qquad\qquad (180)$$
$$\Rightarrow S_b, \textit{neg}\text{-John-Mary}$$

[after the deletion of the repeated Tense-support from S_a, the result of which does not meet the requirements for the application of preliminary *neg*-placement, Eq. (178), since the appended sentence does not contain Tense]

In Eq. (177d), because of the deletion of the whole Predicate, including Tense, not only is the reflex of *neg* (i.e. *not*) left in original pre-sentencial position, but also the subject Nominal *anybody else* need not have *neg* incorporated into it, as would be the case if Tense were not deleted: "Mary can come in, but nobody else can" and not "Mary can come in, but anybody else can't."

The form of Eq. (177e) provides justification for assuming the particular position of *neg* with respect to wh- (i.e., wh-*neg*-Nominal-Predicate).

In contrast, the derivation of a full sentence, with *Aux*(iliary) intact, like "you don't see such things in any other country," given in Eq. (173b) above, would include:

$$S: \textit{neg}\text{-you-}[\text{Tense}]_{Aux}\text{-see-such-things-in-any-other-country} \qquad (181a)$$

i. You-*neg* + $[\text{Tense}]_{Aux}$-see-such-things-in-any-other-country [by preliminary *neg*-placement, Eq. (178)]   (181b)

ii. You-Tense-*neg*-see-such-things-in-any-other-country [by pre-verbal particle placement, Eq. (24)]   (181c)

iii. You-*do* + Tense + n't-see-such-things-in-any-other-country [by *neg*-contraction, Eq. (54d) and *do*-support, Eq. (26)]   (181d)

A seeming exception to the observations about the ultimate position of *not* is presented by

Not John but Mary supports the family.   (182)

Let us reconsider the rules presented so far and, briefly, their motivation. The *neg* of sentence negation was postulated as originally initial to account for sentences like "Mary supports John, not John, Mary," described in Eq. (180). The *neg* of sentence negation was assumed to be independent of other constituents in its origin to account for the great variety of positions that it may ultimately occupy in the sentence; having great mobility, it may be incorporated into certain, though not all constituents, and assumes its favourite position within the *Aux*(iliary), described by the rule of pre-verbal particle placement, (24), only when not so incorporated. The example above in Eq. (182) is exceptional if it is interpreted as representing the negated counterpart of "John . . . supports the family"; i.e., *neg*-John-X-Present-support-the-family, where X is interpreted as containing certain complementary material; namely, "but Mary." Exceptional in this sentence under such an interpretation is the fact that *neg*, although unable to be incorporated into John (since the latter is a proper noun) is nonetheless not drawn into the *Aux*(iliary). This interpretation suggests that at least this instance of negation is characterized by a *not* that originates grammatically as a partner to a particular noun, in this case John; i.e., that "not John" is one basic representation of the constituent Nominal. However, there is reason to assume that the analysis according to which Eq. (182) is an exception is incorrect, and that *John* (or *not John*) is not the subject of the sentence, but that the subject is Mary. By this preferred analysis, the sequence *not John but*, preceding the subject, results from one of the possible ways of conjoining the two sentences: "Mary supports the family" and "John does not support the family"; i.e., *neg*-John-Present-support-the-family, where a certain segment of the latter sentence (namely, *neg*-John) is appended to the former, and where an alternate conjoining results in "Mary, and/but not John, supports the family" and "Mary supports the family, and/but not John." Reason for considering as subject of Eq. (182) *Mary* rather than *not John* is the fact that in structurally related sentences like "Not the father but the grandparents support the family" the number of the verb (which is determined by the subject) is in this sentence determined by *the grandparents* (plural) and not by *the father* (singular). As a natural consequence of the preferred analysis, *not* in *Not John but Mary* remains in initial position not because it originates with the constituent *John* or because it is incorporated into the subject but because the *Aux*(iliary) in the sentence from which it is derived has been deleted. As further argument for the preferred analysis is the fact that in the formation of the negative appositive tag, *Mary* is treated as subject as is revealed by the form of the pronoun in the tag: "Not John but Mary supports the family, doesn't she?" The correctness of the preferred analysis in not treating (180) as an instance of sentence negation (since *not* does not originate in the base sentence) is also born out by the form of the tag.

SCOPE OF NEGATION: OCCURRENCE OF *NOT* WITHOUT SENTENCE NEGATION

38 *Not* in infinitive and gerund phrases and in subordinate clauses. The preceding paragraphs have led toward a structural characterization of sentence negation as resulting when *neg*, the subject Nominal, and the Predicate are "in construction with" one another and are directly dominated by *S*(entence): [(wh)*neg*-Nominal-Predicate]$_S$.

Consider again the structurally ambiguous sentences like "I would force her to marry no one." Take first the reading that is equivalent to "I wouldn't force her to marry anyone." We see that an original *neg* with a structure characteristic of sentence negation has sufficient mobility to attach itself optionally to an indefinite quantifier such as *anyone*, even in derivative complementary structures like infinitive and participial phrases. This displacement of *neg* does not prevent either sentence from being a case of sentence negation. Now take the reading equivalent to:

I would force her not to marry anyone. (183)

Although the ultimate words are the same, the second reading of the ambiguous sentence is not a case of sentence negation; the structure with which the sentence originates is not [*neg* [I]_{Nominal} [would-force-you-Comp]_{Predicate}]_S but rather I-would-force-you [*neg*-to-marry-anyone]_{Comp} from I-would [force-Comp]_{Verb} you.

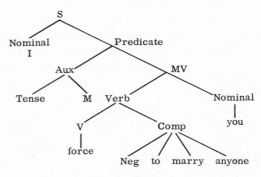

Figure 7

In sentences like Fig. 7, *neg* is a basic constituent of the sentence from which the infinitive *Comp*(lement) is derived:

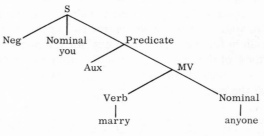

Figure 8

It is to be emphasized again that a *neg* that begins in pre-sentential position may ultimately end up embedded in nonclausal complementary structures. This mobility does not affect the status of *neg* in determining sentence negation as is clear in sentences like "The writers of *none* [that is, *neg* + *any*] of the reports thought so and *neither* did the publishers of any of the brochures," discussed in connection with Eq. (105). The origin of *neg* in the constituent structure of the sentence, and not its ultimate position, is crucial. In subordinate clauses, the situation is different. The occurrence of *not*, *no*, *nobody*, in subordinate clauses never entails sentence negation, as far as the main clause is concerned.

$$\text{He says that} \begin{cases} \text{there will } not \text{ be any rain} \\ \text{there will be no rain} \end{cases} \text{and } so \text{ does she.} \quad (184a)$$

He knows that no rain need fall and *so* does she. (184b)

In subordinate clauses, *neg* is always a constituent of the sentence from which the clause is derived. Note that according to the interpretation in Section 34, examples of negative absorption are regular cases of sentence negation, regular, in that the structure of a sentence like "They don't think that writers can help smiling at that," is described as $S \to neg$-Subject-Predicate. The rejected alternative interpretation of negative absorption whereby the *not* in "They don't think . . ." has its origin in the embedded sentence (that is, in the source of the subordinate clause) would be an exception to the general characterization of sentence negation and would thus necessitate a more complicated statement. It is assumed that the reason for the absence of sentence negation in Eq. (184) is that in the first two sentences *not* does not represent the pre-verbal particle *neg of the base sentence*; similarly, *no* in Eq. (184b) is not an incorporated and fused form of the $[neg]_{PvP}$ *from the base sentence*. However, there has been no reason to assume that the structure underlying *not* and *no* in embedded clauses and phrases is other than that of *neg*. There are positive reasons also to assume that, in the clause of Eq. (184a), the subject Nominal and the Predicate are "in construction with" the *neg* in question. The same is true of the infinitive phrase in Eq. (183). To this extent, the same structure is present in such clauses and phrases as is present in a source sentence of the form $[neg$-Nominal-Predicate$]_S$. The reason for this assumption is that the same sorts of phenomena characterize these embedded structures as do sentences: the mobility of *neg* and its combinability with the indefinites as in Eq. (184a), the occurrence of words restricted to special contexts like *need* in Eq. (184b), and features of sentence negation, included within the embedded structure, like *either* in:

$$\text{He knows that } no \text{ rain will fall and } no \text{ snow will, either.} \qquad (185)$$

The point here is that the sentence in Eq. (185) itself is not a case of sentence negation but the source sentence of the embedded clause is, and thus *either* may occur.

39 Other occurrences of *not* without sentence negation. With respect to sentence negation, the status of the following occurrences of *not* is not so clear as is the case of negative words in an embedded structure derived from a source sentence, itself an instance of sentence negation.

He found something interesting there not long ago,
{*and neither did she.
{ and so did she. } (186a)

He had spoken with someone else *not* many hours earlier, (186b)
hadn't he.

There was some rain not long ago, {*not even in the desert.
{ even in the desert. } (186c)

There will be rain somewhere else in *no* time, *won't* there. (186d)

He married a *not* unattractive girl, and you did too. (186e)

Writers not infrequently reject suggestions,
{*and neither do publishers.
{ and so do publishers. } (186f)

He is content with not 200 a year, and so is she. (186g)

Not a few authors criticized him severely, didn't they? (186h)

The sentences of Eq. (186) are clearly not instances of sentence negation. A further indication of this is that in sentences that are the same except for the preposing of *not* and the Time adverbial, initial *not* does not motivate inversion (that is, *neg*-attraction, Eq. (65h)).

Not many hours earlier he had spoken with someone else.	(187a)
Not long ago there was rain falling.	(187b)

These contrast with sentences in which initial *not*, or any other reflex of the pre-verbal particle *neg* (postulated here to have original pre-sentencial position) entails inversion:

Not even then was there rain falling.	(188a)
At *no* [that is, *neg* + *any*] time was there rain falling.	(188b)

Finally, in sentences like those of Eq. (187), *not* does not permit the occurrence of indefinite quantifiers, differing thus from the *not* that represents *neg* as a pre-verbal particle (Eq. (188)). In this way, Eq. (189a) below contrasts with Eqs. (189b–d).

Not even then was there any [that is, *Indef* + *Quant*] rain falling.	(189a)
*Not long ago there was any rain falling.	(189b)
At no time will there be any rain even there.	(189c)
*In no time there will be any rain anywhere else.	(189d)

Occurrences of *not* without sentence negation, as in Eq. (186c, d) also lack the alternation between *not* and the special negatives like *no* and *nowhere*, in pairs of sentences that differ otherwise only in word order. This alternation was found to depend on the mobility of the *neg* of sentence negation and the possibility of pre-posing certain constituents that contain an indefinite (the occurrence of which is itself motivated by *neg*). Take, for example, the variation possible in Eg. (190) but not in Eg. (191):

There *won't* be any rain at any time even there.	(190a)
There will be no rain at any time even there.	(190b)
At no time will there be any rain even there.	(190c)
In no time there will be rain even there.	(191a)
*There won't be rain even there in any time.	(191b)

Certain cases of *not* without sentence negation are also unusual with respect to the regular variation between *not much* and *little*, *not many* and *few*, in that instead of *little*, the form is *a little*; instead of *few*, *a few*:

Not much rain fell last year—Little rain fell last year [with sentence negation]	(192a)
Not much later he left—A little later he left [without sentence negation]	(192b)
Not many writers accept suggestions—Few writers accept suggestions [with sentence negation]	(192c)
Not many years ago I was there—A few years ago I was there [without sentence negation]	(192d)

Finally, when the *not* of sentence negation and the *not* of constituent negation appear in otherwise identical sentences, there is a clear case of ambiguity.

Not even two years ago could you enter without paying.	(193a)
Not even two years ago you could enter without paying.	(193b)

These facts raise the following question: To what shall we attribute the differences between the *not* of sentence negation and those occurrences of *not* without sentence negation, examined in this section? The latter occurrences of *not* will be referred to as the *not* of constituent negation. The difference cannot be explained in any obvious way by assuming that in its final location in the sentence the *not* of constituent negation is always more completely integrated into another constituent, for the *not* in Eq. (194a), as an instance of sentence negation, is not included to any lesser extent in the prepositional phrase than is the *not* of Eq. (194b).

In not many years will Christmas fall on Sunday.	(194a)
In not many years Christmas will fall on Sunday.	(194b)

Note also that the ultimate pre-verbal position of *not* does not necessarily imply sentence negation, for Eq. (186f) is only a case of constituent negation.

Let us assume that sentences like Eq. (186a), in which *not* figures in the expression *not long ago*, do not have the structure *neg*-Nominal-Predicate and that *not* thus does not represent pre-sentencial *neg*. By this assumption, the various phenomena that otherwise characterize sentences with special negatives and $[not]_{PvP}$ that are derived from pre-sentencial *neg* words are accounted for. Note also that the special features of the *not* of constituent negation contribute to the argument against considering the *not* of sentence negation (for example, *not much* in Eq. (192a), in fact any reflex of the *neg* of sentence negation) to have its origin in the various constituents in which it ultimately appears; for if such were the analysis, the *not* of constituent negation and the *not* of sentence negation would have the same structure. A further question that arises, however, is whether or not there are grammatical reasons to associate the *not* of constituent negation (for example, *not long ago*) with the symbol *neg*; that is, whether or not grammatical facts depend on the assumption that *not* in *not long ago* includes *neg* in its derivation. The following sentences are relevant to the question:

It wasn't long ago that he found something interesting there.	(195a)
He had spoken with someone else, which hadn't been many hours earlier.	(195b)
He married a woman $\left\{ \begin{array}{l} \text{, and she wasn't unattractive.} \\ \text{who wasn't unattractive.} \end{array} \right\}$	(195c)
The rejecting of suggestions by writers isn't infrequent.	(195d)

The sentences above are significant in that expressions containing the *not* of constituent negation that occur in Eq. (186) also occur above with *not* as a regular preverbal particle originating presumably in pre-sentencial position. Thus, the feature that differentiates Eq. (195a) from "He found something there not long ago" is not the nature of *long ago* when it occurs in a sentence containing *not* (and note that the two syntactically different occurrences are felt to have the same meaning, unlike

Eq. (193a) versus Eq. (193b). The difference between the two occurrences is due solely to the basically different original structural position of *not* and *long ago* in the two sentences.

Leaving to Section 40 further consideration of the nature of the correspondence between sentence negation in Eq. (195) and constituent negation in Eq. (186), let us tentatively describe the *not long ago* of constituent negation by the following extension of the constituent structure expansion of Time:

$$\text{Time} \rightarrow (neg) \text{ long} \begin{cases} \text{ago} \\ \text{after} \\ \text{before} \end{cases} \tag{196}$$

"He found something interesting there not long ago" will have the following structure, similar to that of words with a negative affix:

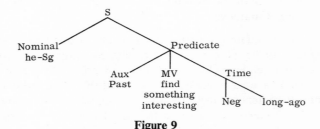

Figure 9

The postulated similarity between the *not* of constituent negation and the negative affixes can be used in stating the distribution of these negatives with adverbal and adjectival expressions: (a) that the *neg* of constituent negation does not occur at all with certain adjectival expressions [for example, *an ungood book*, or *a not good book*]; (b) that when it occurs with certain constituents (*neg-clear*), it appears as an affix (*unclear*); (c) that when it occurs with another class of constituents, it appears as *not* (for example, *long ago*, and also the class including *clear* when that latter already occurs with *neg*; that is, *neg-long-ago* appears as *not long ago*, *neg-neg-clear* as *not unclear*).

CONSIDERATIONS PERTINENT TO THE GRAMMATICAL DERIVATION OF THE *NEG* CONSTITUENT NEGATION.

40 The negative affixes. In the preceding sections, ample evidence has been given that a sentence with constituent negation, e.g., "She is *unhappy*" is not an alternate form of a sentence with sentence negation, e.g., "She "*isn't happy*" in the way that "He *won't ever* come back" is another form of "He will *never* come back" and "Has*n't anybody* called?" is another form of "Has *nobody* called?" Implicit in the description given so far is an analysis of constituent negation that treats the symbol *neg* as part of certain constituents (an optional part with words like *unhappy* and an obligatory part with words like *doubt*). According to this analysis, the grammar would contain constituent structure rules like the following: Predicative →

(*neg*) *Adj*. This analysis amounts to saying that while the negative elements in sentence negation and constituent negation are the same, the *relationships* between the negative element and the sentence in which it occurs in constituent negation, on the one hand, and in sentence negation, on the other, are grammatically independent of one another.

There are certain constructions involving constituent negation, however, which suggest that in some cases a closer relationship may exist between the structure of sentence negation and that of constituent negation. Consider the following sentences:

They are solving this problem.	(197a)
This problem is being solved.	(197b)
This problem is solved.	(197c)
This problem is as yet unsolved.	(197d)

They are accounting for these facts.	(198a)
These facts are being accounted for.	(198b)
These facts are accounted for.	(198c)
These facts are still unaccounted for.	(198d)

The problem is this: regardless of the inner structure of the (c) examples above (which in one reading is that of Nominal-*Aux-be*-Predicative as in "the problem is already difficult") the constituents *solved* and *accounted for* of the (c) examples are not simple *Adj*(ectives) but are derivative elements. Their origin is in the verbs *solve* and *account for*. The relationship between the transitive verbs and the past participles is syntactic and not just morphological. By this I mean that the possible objects of the transitive verbs in the (a) examples are the same as the possible subjects in the (c) examples; i.e., the relationship is the same as between the (a) examples and the corresponding unambiguous passives in the (b) examples (described by the rule of passivization, Eq. (75)). A transformation will be assumed that inserts the passive past participle (*PP*) into the constituent Predicative, when the object Nominal of the active sentence is the same as the subject Nominal of the base sentence.

$$
\begin{aligned}
&S_e\text{: They-Tense-solve-the-problem} \\
&S_b\text{: The problem-Tense-be-Predicative} \\
\hline
&\Rightarrow \text{The problem-Tense-be-}[PP\text{-solve}]_{\text{Predicative}}
\end{aligned}
\qquad (199)
$$

Accordingly, the form that is embedded as the Predicative is the past participle of *solve* and *account for*. This formulation, however, does not account for the (d) examples, in that while the verbal part (minus negative prefix) of the negatived *P*(assive) *P*(article) bears the same relationship to the subject in Eq. (198d) as exists in regular passive/active pairs, a corresponding active verb with a negative prefix does not exist; i.e., there is no *"They *un*solved this problem"—*"They *un*accounted for these facts." It was noted that the structure of the (c) examples may be different in one reading from that of passive sentences. In the (d) examples this structural difference is clear, for, while the passive sentences permit the progressive, "This problem is being solved," the (d) examples do not (*"This problem is being unsolved"). This restriction is characteristic of representatives of Predicative; i.e., of *Adj*(ectives) and Place (adverbs). (Thus the absence of *"The box is being green" and *"The box is being on the table.") The simple past participle in one of its structures and the negative passive participle will be considered as derivative representatives of the Predicative; Eq. (197d) would have the structure:

$$\text{the-problem-Tense-be } [neg\text{-}PP\text{-solve}]_{\text{Predicative}} \qquad (200)$$

where the Predicative is from an active sentence in which *problem* is the object of the verb *solve*. Whether *neg* in Eq. (200) has its origin in the active sentence from which the passive past particle is derived or whether it is a basic part of the expansion of the Predicative as in Predicative → *neg-Adj*, with the derivative *PP-solve* embedded in the place of *Adj*, is a question that must await further investigation.

It was mentioned above that the negative passive participles are not paralleled by corresponding verbs with the prefix *un-*. This is not contradicted by the fact that aside from "The table is uncovered" there is an active "They uncover the table," for there is also a progressive "The table is being uncovered"; all of which lends support to the grammatical basis of the traditional distinction between negative *un* and privative *un*, and specifically to the assumption that *uncovered* as the passive participle to *uncover* does not contain *neg*. This assumption becomes all the more satisfying when the ambiguity of "The table remained uncovered" is considered.

Now we shall consider, in an informal way, a possible analysis of one instance of the *not* of constituent negation. Let us assume that "He is marrying a not unattractive woman" is somehow related to the two sentences "He is marrying a woman" and "That woman isn't unattractive" where *not* in the source sentence resulting in the attribute represents the pre-verbal particle *neg* in its position after preliminary *neg* Placement (Eq. (178)), i.e., *neg-that woman*-Tense-*be* [*unattractive*)$_{\text{Predicative}}$, ⇒ *that-woman-neg* + [Tense]$_{Aux}$*be* [*unattractive*]$_{\text{Predicative}}$. As the attribute is embedded, *be* and its tense-marker are regularly removed leaving *neg-neg-attractive*. One of the important details would be excluding from this attributivization the (a) examples (below) but not the (b) examples.

*a not good example: that example isn't good	(201a)
a not very good example: that example isn't very good	(201b)
*a not attractive woman: that woman isn't attractive	(202a)
a not unattractive woman: that woman isn't unattractive	(202b)
*a not clear formulation: that formulation isn't clear	(203a)
a not clearly formulated question: that question isn't clearly formulated.	(203b)

In order that *not* may be included in the pre-nominal attribute, the *Adj*(ective) or *P*(ast) *P*(articiple) must itself be preceded by a modifier. It is significant that the negative prefix *un* is treated here in the same way as adverbs are treated.

The occurrence and the behavior of the *neg* of constituent negation in pre-nominal attributive position in similar but not identical to the occurrence of the pre-verbal particle *neg* and its reflexes in relative clauses and in certain other embedded post-nominal modifiers that can be regarded as reduced relative clauses.

$$\begin{array}{l}\text{A woman not attractive enough to qualify—} \\ \text{A woman who isn't attractive enough to qualify}\end{array} \qquad (204)$$

$$\begin{array}{l}\text{The letters not copied in that way—} \\ \text{The letters that haven't been copied in that way}\end{array} \qquad (205)$$

It was observed in Section 28 that a *neg* that has its origin in the source of an embedded structure does not include the base sentence in its scope, that is, the base sentence that includes the embedded structure does not have the characteristics of sentence negation:

$$\begin{array}{l}\text{*The letters not copied in that way were legible and neither} \\ \text{were the numbers.}\end{array} \qquad (206)$$

The appropriate restriction in the scope of the *neg* of constituent negation is provided for if pre-nominal attributive modifiers are derived from relative clauses whose source sentence contains a pre-verbal particle *neg*.

XV

41 Constituents Similar to the Negatives: Interrogatives, Restrictives, Conditionals, Adversatives. It was observed in Section 37 that *wh* and *neg* share various syntactic characteristics. To some extent these characteristics are also shared by the restrictive *only*: (a) certain, but not necessarily the same constituents, may be incorporated into all three; for example *only then, not even then*, (and with fusion) *nowhere* (from *neg* + anywhere), *what* (from *wh* + *something* or perhaps from *wh* + anything); all three motivate inversion when the subject Nominal intervenes, that is, has not itself been incorporated into *wh*, *neg*, or *only*. Thus there is inversion in "only then do they see it," "What do they see?", "Not even then do they see it"; but with subject Nominal incorporated into *only*, no inversion, "only the writers see it." As these examples indicate, at certain points in the derivation of sentences, *only* may occur in pre-sentential position; i.e., S: *only* + *X*-Nominal-Predicate. (c) furthermore, as in the case of *neg* and *wh*, indefinites may occur in constituents in construction with pre-sentential restrictive *only*. This includes constituents in subordinate clauses and other sentence-like structures. Thus while the indefinites in *"Young writers ever accept suggestions with any sincerity" are not permissible, they are in the following:

$$\begin{array}{l}\text{Only young writers ever accept suggestions with any} \\ \text{sincerity.}\end{array} \qquad (207a)$$

$$\text{Only his sister expects him to write any more novels.} \qquad (207b)$$

$$\begin{array}{l}\varphi \text{ [}wh\text{ without incorporations] do young writers ever} \\ \text{accept suggestions with any sincerity?}\end{array} \qquad (207c)$$

$$\begin{array}{l}\text{Who [}wh + \text{somebody] expects him to write any more} \\ \text{novels?}\end{array} \qquad (207d)$$

$$\begin{array}{l}\text{Nobody [}neg + \text{anybody] ever accepts suggestions with} \\ \text{any sincerity.}\end{array} \qquad (207e)$$

$$\text{Nobody expects him to write any more novels.} \qquad (207f)$$

The details of the syntax of the restrictive *only* will not be elaborated in this study. Note, however, as one difference from *neg*, that the occurrence of *only* in *Aux*(iliary) is not sufficient motivation for the occurrence of the indefinites: "His sister will not expect him to write any more novels," but not *"His sister will only expect him to write any more novels."

The question now arises as to the grammatical nature of the similarities between *neg*, *wh*, and *only*. In the analysis of the diverse elements involved in negation: *not*, *n't* (the contracted form), *no* (as in *nobody*), *in-* (as in *incapable*), *un-* (as in *unlikely*), *dis-* (as in *dislike*), *-less* (as in *useless*); *seldom*, *doubt*, or *without* (all three negative, but without phonological reflex of negation), the varying similarities in syntactic behavior were ascribed to a common underlying syntactic symbol *neg*. The differences in behavior were attributed to differences in the various rules optionally or obligatorily applicable to the particular syntactic structures containing *neg*. Without distorting the facts too much, one could describe all these negatives as going back (in the synchronic sense, of course) to an original *not*, provided that one understands this in the context of a complex structure of ordered rules. However, the same sort of explicit relationship with *neg* cannot convincingly be assumed for interrogative *wh* and restrictive *only*. The reason is not difference in sense, but rather the fact that those phenomena most characteristic of sentence negation as described in Section 19 are absent in the case of *wh* and *only*, even when the latter are pre-sentencial in position. The ways in which *neg*, *wh*, and *only* are similar beg for some formal expression within the grammar that does not necessitate the assumption of some total morpheme shared by them and occurring in their structure. What is needed here is some formal device whereby, above and beyond the syntactic symbols that figure in the derivation of morphemes, individual morphemes can be described as similar to others in certain respects and different in others. Consider, for example, the Nouns *Mary* and *Bill* and grammatical aspects of these words that are pertinent in describing various types of pronoun formation. That both are proper nouns enters into the exclusion of *restrictive* relative clauses with these words as antecedents (i.e., *"John that lives here left"); that both contain another grammatically differentiating feature characterized semantically as *human* accounts for the form of the relative pronoun *who* rather than *what*; furthermore, that another grammatical feature, *feminine*, characterizes *Mary* but not *John* is relevant to the anaphoric pronoun in the tag of "Mary left, didn't she?" To incorporate these observations into the grammatical system, let us assume that morphemes can be further analyzed into bundles of grammatico-semantic features ($[X]^{GSF}$). Thus, the ultimate lexical items carry along with them not only a string of phonemes but also a bundle of such features.[15]

It will be recalled that in the discussion of inherent negatives in Section 35, *doubt*, *too*, and *without* were assumed to contain the syntactic symbol *neg*. With these words, however, *neg* was assumed to have no phonological form; i.e., *neg* + *doubt*

---

[15] A discussion of another area where peculiarities in the *shape* of possible grammatical sentences can be analyzed as the result of grammatico-semantic features in the structure of individual morphemes will be found in my paper "Structure at the lexical level," *Proceedings of the 1961 International Conference on Machine Translation of Language and Applied Linguistic Analysis*, 1 (London, 1962), 97–108.

had the form *doubt*, and the *V*(erb) *doubt* did not occur without the symbol *neg*+. The motivation for this was to give *doubt*, which behaved syntactically in the same way as, for example, *dislike* (*neg* + *like*), the same structure as *dislike*. With the notion of a morpheme as a bundle of grammatico-semantic features, the arbitrariness involved in representing all grammatical characteristics of words in terms of syntactic symbols exclusively is removed. We can consider the notation *neg*+ in inherent negatives like *neg* + *doubt* to represent part of the grammatico-semantic specification of the one-morpheme lexical item *doubt*. The use of the same symbol (+) for the result of the incorporation of one constituent into another and for the notion of grammatico-semantic feature is intentional, for it is assumed here that the two are not basically different.

As for the grammatical similarities of *neg*, *wh*, and *only*, these will now be described as resulting from the presence of a common grammatico-semantic feature to be referred to as *Affect*(ive). Any *Quant*(ifier) in construction with a constituent that contains the feature *Affect*(ive) may ultimately appear as an indefinite. Note, however, that only *neg* permits the occurrence of *either*, described at (119) as resulting from the incorporation of *Indef* into *too*. This restriction is, of course, an argument against considering *either* to be similar to *any*.

A further consequence of the presence of the feature *Affect*(ive) is that in pre-sentential position, morphemes containing that feature motivate inversion, as is seen in the examples in (207). Thus the individual rules of inversion described by *neg*-attraction (Eq. (65h)) and *wh*-attraction (Eq. (54e)) are generalized and extended to pre-sentential *only* by a rule of *Affect*-attraction.

I. *Indef*-incorporation (generalizing Eq. (169),
$$[Affect]^{GSF} X\text{-}Quant\text{-}Y \Rightarrow Affect\text{-}X\text{-}Indef + Quant\text{-}Y \tag{208a}$$
Condition: *Quant* is in construction with the constituent containing *Affect*

II. *Affect*-attraction (generalizing Eqs. (54e) and (65h),
$$[Affect]^{GSF} Nominal\text{-}\mathbf{aux^1}\text{-}\mathbf{aux^2} = Affect\text{-}\mathbf{aux^1}\text{-}Nominal\text{-}\mathbf{aux^2} \tag{208b}$$

where the constituent containing the feature *Affect* may have other constituents incorporated into it.

This rule would not account for inversion with *so* (for example, "So far had they gone that they could see the mountains"), since *so* does not permit the occurrence of indefinite quantifiers like *ever* and *any*. Interrogative clauses will be analyzed as questions embedded in other sentences. The occurrence of indefinite quantifiers in such clauses is thus accounted for in the same way as in questions:

He wondered whether [i.e., wh + Subord(inator)] young writers ever accept suggestions with any sincerity. (209)

When wh-, with or without incorporated elements, assumes the function of a conjunction (symbolized in Eq. (209) by the association of *wh* with the symbol Subord), inversion is blocked; thus "I wonder what they will accept" and "What they will accept is unknown" but "What will they accept?" In this way, subordinate wh is like the *neg* of constituent negation in "not long ago he lived in New York" which contrasts with "not even then did he live in New York." Certain other conjunctions also contain $[Affect]^{\text{GSF}}$: *if, before* (but not *after*), *lest* (but not *unless*), *than*. Consider now the permissibility of the indefinite quantifiers in the following (a) examples but not in the (b) examples:

$$\text{I am } \textit{surprised} \text{ that he } \textit{ever} \text{ speaks to her.} \tag{210a}$$

$$\text{I am } \textit{sure} \text{ that he } \begin{Bmatrix} *ever \\ sometimes \end{Bmatrix} \text{ speaks to her} \tag{210b}$$

$$\text{He was } \textit{ashamed} \text{ to take } \textit{any} \text{ more money.} \tag{211a}$$

$$\text{He was } \textit{glad} \text{ to take } \textit{some} \text{ more money.} \tag{211b}$$

$$\text{He was } \textit{stupid} \text{ to become any heavier.} \tag{212a}$$

$$\text{He was } \textit{smart} \text{ to become } \begin{Bmatrix} *any \\ \varphi \\ somewhat \end{Bmatrix} \text{ heavier.} \tag{212b}$$

$$\text{He was } \textit{reluctant} \text{ to see } \textit{any} \text{ more patients.} \tag{213a}$$

$$\text{He was } \textit{anxious} \text{ to see } \textit{some} \text{ more patients.} \tag{213b}$$

$$\text{He was } \textit{against} \text{ doing } \textit{anything} \text{ like that.} \tag{214a}$$

$$\text{He was } \textit{in favor} \text{ of doing } \textit{something} \text{ like that.} \tag{214b}$$

The indefinites similarly occur in the *Comp*(lements) to the following constructions: *it is absurd to, he is afraid to, annoyed that, to dare one to, to defy one to, it is difficult to, to forget to, to refuse to, to deny that, to dissuade from, amazed that, warn against, hate to.* We shall refer to all of these words (i.e., *absurd, ashamed,* and so on, when they occur in these constructions) as *Advers(atives)*.

As was the case with *neg, wh,* and *only,* here too we shall assume that the feature *Affect* is contained by words like *stupid* (but not *smart*), *ashamed* (but not *glad*) *surprised* (but not *sure*) and so on in the (a) examples (but not the (b) examples in Eqs. (210-214)). We shall assume further that the presence of $[Affect]^{\text{GSF}}$ accounts for the occurrence of the indefinites in complementary clauses and phrases "in construction with" the words containing the feature in question. The particular pairing in Eqs. (210-214) has, of course, not been demonstrated to be a grammatical fact. What has been indicated is that *stupid, ashamed, surprised, reluctant,* and so on, cluster at one pole with respect to certain grammatical phenomena and that *smart, glad, sure,* and *anxious* cluster at the other pole. Once the antinymous pairs are granted, however, the members are no longer just simple opposites but differ in a particular way. For among the words containing the feature Affect are words with a negative affix, and in words like *unlikely*, $[Affect]^{\text{GSF}}$ is attributable directly to the negative prefix. In this sense, *unlikely* and *likely* are also antinymous pairs grammatically, and *stupid* (contrasted with *smart*) has at least one of the grammatical features that the negative prefix *un-* lends to *likely* in the *Affect*(ive) word *unlikely*. The permissibility of the indefinites with the *Affect*(ive) member of such antinymous pairs as in Eqs. (210-214) is, of course, itself not sufficient reason to consider words like *surprised* and *stupid* to be inherent negatives, any more than it is reason to consider them interrogatives or restrictives. It will be found, however, that certain adversatives like *difficult* (*to*), *afraid* (*to*), *fail* (*to*),[16] but not adversatives like *surprising* (*that*), or *stupid* (*to*), come very close to functioning like negatives in constructions with *much less* exemplified in Eq. (215) below.

> He could not [*neg* of sentence negation] read the text, much less translate it. (215a)

> It's $\begin{Bmatrix}\text{impossible [negative affix]}\\ \text{*possible}\end{Bmatrix}$ to read it, much less translate it. (215b)

> He's $\begin{Bmatrix}\text{unwilling [negative prefix]}\\ \text{*willing}\end{Bmatrix}$ to rent the house, much less buy it. (215c)

> I $\begin{Bmatrix}\text{doubt [inherent negative]}\\ \text{*think}\end{Bmatrix}$ that he can read the text, much less translate it. (215d)

> $\begin{Bmatrix}\text{Nobody [sentence negation by special negative]}\\ \text{*everybody}\end{Bmatrix}$ would rent it, much less buy it. (215e)

> I'm $\begin{Bmatrix}\text{afraid [adversative]}\\ \text{ashamed [adversative]}\\ \text{*proud}\end{Bmatrix}$ to talk about it, much less write about it. (215f)

> He $\begin{Bmatrix}\text{failed [adversative]}\\ \text{refused [adversative]}\\ \text{*agreed}\end{Bmatrix}$ to read it correctly much less translate it. (215g)

> It's $\begin{Bmatrix}\text{difficult [adversative]}\\ \text{hard [adversative]}\\ \text{*easy}\end{Bmatrix}$ to travel with him, much less room with him. (215h)

The decision as to whether or not the adversatives in Eq. (215) are to be considered inherent negatives of the type characterized by constituent negation (syntactically paralleling, for example, *unwise* must await the discovery of other decisive grammatical facts.

CONCLUSION

The general observations about negation to be drawn from this study are not startling. Native speakers of English are most probably aware of them instinctively. It is not surprising that what turns out in this study to be a negative or like a negative

---

[16]Jespersen writes about the pair *fail* : *succeed*: "There seem to be some words with inherent negative meaning though positive in form: compare pairs like absent: present, fail: succeed. But though we naturally look upon the former in each of these pairs as the negative (*fail* = *not succeed*), nothing hinders us from logically inverting the order (*succeed* = *not fail*). These words, therefore, cannot properly be classed with such formally negative words as *unhappy*, etc." Otto Jespersen, *Negation in English and Other Languages* (København, 1917), p. 42. The fact that *fail*, but not *succeed*, motivates the occurrence of indefinites in a complementary infinitival clause and also permits the construction with *much less* in Eq. (215g) argues against Jespersen.

is what speakers of English have always felt to be one. Everyone knows, for example, that *never* and *not ever* are the same. There is no question in anyone's mind that of the pair *fail* = *succeed*, the first is negative. All speakers of English will admit to the similarity of "to be unhappy" and "not to be happy." Nor will they deny that if such similarity also applies to the capacity of items to occur with the same words around them, then "to be unhappy" and "not to be happy" also differ in certain respects, on the basis of the absence of a pair "she isn't happy, *and neither is he*" = *"she is unhappy, *and neither is he.*"

This study of negation has not tried to establish previously unrecognized categories, but rather to elucidate already existing ones. It was assumed that elucidation would be provided by the answers to questions like: what is the formal aspect of negation? If certain items are formally similar as negative, what are the grammatical consequences of this fact? And the problem has been approached in a special way, by asking: what answers to these questions emerge in writing a generative grammar of the English language?

The principle grammatical notions developed in this study concern the scope of negation (i.e., the structures over which the negative element has its effect) and the structural position of the negative element in the sentence. The scope of negation varies according to the origin of the negative element in the sentence (over the whole, over subordinate complementary structures alone, or only over the word containing the negative element). A single independent negative element, whose simplest reflex is *not*, is found to account for sentence negation; its scope is the whole sentence, but because that element is mobile and capable of fusing with other elements (for example in *nobody*), its ultimate position and form have great latitude. When the negative element originates in other constituents (as for example in the extreme case of *doubt*), the scope of negation is restricted to structures subordinate to those constituents. However, granted the differences due to varying scope, it was found that the phenomena connected with negation could be described grammatically on the basis of a single negative element.

APPENDIX

Constituent Structure

The linguistic facts discussed in the preceding study ultimately suggest the following constituent structure rules. Included among these are representative lexical structure rules with the right side of the arrow boxed in. The box is divided by a semicolon into two sections, the first containing some of the necessary grammatico-semantic features (*GSF*) of the item and the second containing its phonological description, abbreviated here by the given morpheme written between slashes (*/shrapnel/*). The material in a box along with the appropriate environmental restrictions represents more or less a dictionary entry.

1. S → (wh)(neg)(Adv(neg))(Adv)Nominal-Predicate

2. Predicate → Aux-MV(Place)(Time)

3. MV → $\begin{Bmatrix} \text{Verb(Nominal)} \\ \text{V-Predicative} \end{Bmatrix}$

4. Place → | Place, Indet, . . . ; /somewhere/ |

5. Time → | Time, . . . ; /now/ |

6. Nominal → $\left\{ \begin{array}{l} \text{Pronoun-Sg} \\ \text{(Quant)Noun-No} \end{array} \right\}$

7. Pronoun → $\left[\begin{array}{l} \boxed{\text{Pronoun, Indet, Human, . . . ; /somebody/}} \\ \boxed{\text{Pronoun, Indet, Inan, . . . ; /something/}} \\ \quad . . . \end{array} \right]$

8. Noun → $\left[\begin{array}{l} \boxed{\text{Noun, Human, Proper, Masc, . . . ; /John/}} \\ \boxed{\text{Noun, Inan, Mass, . . . ; /shrapnel/}} \\ \quad . . . \end{array} \right]$

9. Verb → (neg)V(Comp)

10. V → $\left[\begin{array}{l} \boxed{\text{V, } \phi\text{-neg aff, } \textit{that}\text{-Comp, weak conj, . . . ; /doubt/}}, \text{ in } \textit{env},\\ \begin{bmatrix} \text{Noun} \\ \text{Human} \end{bmatrix}^{\text{GSF}} \text{No-Aux-neg\_\_\_\_Comp . . .} \\ \boxed{\text{V, } \textit{dis}\text{-neg aff, } \textit{ing}\text{-Comp, weak conj, . . . ; /like/}}, \text{ in } \textit{env},\\ \begin{bmatrix} \text{Noun} \\ \text{Human} \end{bmatrix}^{\text{GSF}} \text{No-Aux(neg)\_\_\_\_Comp . . .} \\ \boxed{\text{V, irreg conj, . . . ; /be/}}, \text{ in } \textit{env.}\text{\_\_\_\_Predicative} \\ \quad . . . \end{array} \right]$

11. Predicative → (neg)Adj(Comp)

12. Adj → $\left[\begin{array}{l} \boxed{\text{Adj, } \textit{un}\text{-neg aff, } \textit{to}\text{-Comp, . . . ; /able/}}, \text{ in } \textit{env.}\text{\_\_\_\_Comp} \\ \boxed{\text{Adj, Advers, Affect, to-Comp, . . . /reluctant/}}, \text{ in } \textit{env.} \\ \begin{bmatrix} \text{Noun} \\ \text{Human} \end{bmatrix}^{\text{GSF}} \text{No-Aux-be-Comp} \\ \quad . . . \end{array} \right]$

13. No → $\left\{ \begin{array}{l} \text{Sg} \\ \text{Pl} \end{array} \right\}$

14. Quant → $\left[\begin{array}{l} \text{Quant}^1, \text{ in } \textit{env.}\text{\_\_\_\_} [\text{Mass}]^{\text{GSF}} \\ \text{Quant}^2, \text{ in } \textit{env.}\text{\_\_\_\_} \left\{ \begin{array}{l} [\text{Mass}]^{\text{GSF}} \\ [\text{Noun}]^{\text{GSF}} \text{ Pl} \end{array} \right\} \\ \text{Quant}^3, \text{ otherwise} \end{array} \right]$

15. Quant¹ → | Quant¹, Indet, . . . ; /some/ |
| Quant¹, Indet, . . . ; / ϕ / |

16. Quant² → | Quant², Indet, . . . ; /many/ |, in *env.*____[Noun]^{GSF} Pl

17. Quant³ → | Quant³, . . . ; /each/ |

18. Aux → Tense(M)(have-PP)(be-PrP)

19. Tense → $\left[\begin{array}{l} \left\{ \begin{array}{l} \Phi \\ \text{ed} \end{array} \right\}, \text{ in the } \textit{env.}\text{\_\_\_\_M} \\ \left\{ \begin{array}{l} \text{Present} \\ \text{Past} \end{array} \right\}, \text{ otherwise} \end{array} \right]$

20. $M \rightarrow \left\{ \begin{array}{l} \boxed{M, V, \ldots ; /\text{need}/}, \text{ in } \textit{env. } \text{neg}(\text{Adv})(\text{Adv}), \ldots \left\{ \begin{array}{l} \text{Sg} \\ \text{Pl} \end{array} \right\} \phi\_\_\_ \\ \boxed{M, V, \ldots , /\text{will}/} \\ \boxed{M, V, \ldots ; /\text{can}/} \\ \ldots \end{array} \right\}$

21. $\text{Adv} \rightarrow \left\{ \begin{array}{l} \boxed{\text{Adv, Freq}, \ldots ; /\text{seldom}/}, \text{ in } \textit{env. } \text{neg}\_\_\_ \\ (\text{neg}) \ \boxed{\text{Adv, } \textit{un}\text{-neg aff}, \ldots ; /\text{fortunately}/} \end{array} \right\}$

22. $\text{neg} \rightarrow \boxed{\text{neg, Affect}; /\text{—}/}$, with the form *not* when not associated with other morphemes

23. $\text{wh} \rightarrow \boxed{\text{wh, Affect}; /\text{—}/}$

Sketch of the Main Rules Discussed

The following structural descriptions give the results of the application of representative constituent structure rules that figure in the transformations sketched below.

(1) A negative interrogative sentence with a transitive verb and quantifiers in both subject and object

S: wh-neg[Quant-Noun-No]$_{\text{Nominal}}$
$\left[[\textbf{aux}^1\textbf{-aux}^2]_{\text{Aux}} \ [[\text{V}]_{\text{Verb}}[\text{Quant-Noun-No}]_{\text{Nominal}}]_{\text{MV}} \right]_{\text{Predicate}}$

(2) A simple declarative sentence with predicate adjective and complement

S: Nominal $\left[\text{Aux } [\text{be } [\text{Adj-Comp}]_{\text{Predicative}}]_{\text{MV}} \right]_{\text{Predicate}}$

(3) A simple declarative sentence whose Verb contains a complement

S: Nominal $\left[\text{Aux } [[\text{V-Comp}]_{\text{Verb}}]_{\text{MV}} \right]_{\text{Predicate}}$

(4) Incomplete negation with *seldom*

S: neg-seldom-Nominal-Predicate

(5) A negative sentence that includes an Adv(erb) in its negation, but which is itself further specified by an adverb. (The original structural position of the various types of adverbs has not been definitively ascertained.)

S:Adv-neg-Nominal-[Adv-Aux-MV]$_{\text{Predicate}}$, or S:Adv-neg-Adv-Nominal-Predicate

Transformational Structure

In the transformations below, all of them apply first in terms of neg, and then the pertinent ones (Indef-incorporation, incorporation into wh-, Affect-attraction) apply proceeding from wh. The order of the rules is relevant.

I. Passivization (optional). A sentence with a regular transitive verb may occur with the object of that verb as subject and the subject of the active sentence as agent.

(wh)(neg) X-Nominal-Aux[Verb-Nominal-Y]$_{\text{Predicate}} \Rightarrow$ 1, 5, 3-be-PP, 4, by-2

           1   2   3   4   5   6

II. Comp-embedding (obligatory). Certain verbs and adjectives take as their complements whole sentences with various additions and deformations. Among such embedded structures are clauses, and infinitival phrases.

$$\left.\underbrace{\mathrm{S_e}\left[X\genfrac{\{}{\}}{0pt}{}{V}{Adj}\right.}_{1}\underbrace{Comp}_{2}\right]_{\mathrm{S_b}}\;\right| \;\Rightarrow\; 1,[\mathrm{S_e}]_2$$

III. *too*-conjoining (optional). One declarative sentence can be appended to another by the addition of *and . . . too*. (The first step in *either*-conjoining.)

$$\left.\begin{array}{c}\mathrm{S_a}\\\mathrm{S_b}\end{array}\right| \;\Rightarrow\; \mathrm{S_b}\text{-and-}\mathrm{S_a}\text{-too}$$

IV. Indef-incorporation. Indet(erminate) constituents (*too, sometime, somewhere, once, a* as well as *Quant*(ifiers) like *many, some*) that occur in construction with Affect(ive) constituents (*wh, neg, reluctant*) may, or in certain contexts must, become indefinites.

$$\underbrace{X[Affect]^{GSF}}_{1}\;\underbrace{Y\;[Indet]^{GSF}}_{2}\;\underbrace{Z}_{3} = 1, \text{Indef} + 2, 3$$

V. Negative appositive tag (optional). A negative sentence (even with the incomplete negatives *seldom, rarely*) may have appended to it the tag *not even "constituent,"* composed of a more specified constituent of an otherwise identical negative sentence.

$$\left.\begin{array}{c}[\text{neg-}X[\text{constituent}^1]_YZ]_{\mathrm{S_a}}\\ [\text{neg-}X[\text{constituent}^2]_YZ]_{\mathrm{S_b}}\end{array}\right| \Rightarrow \mathrm{S_b}\text{-not-even-constituent}^1$$

VI. Tag-question formation (optional). The string underlying a simple yes-no question can have its initial interrogative marker postposed and included in a tag that carries *neg* if the source string is without *neg*. If the source contains *neg*, then the tag is without it.

$$\underbrace{\text{wh-}}_{1}\underbrace{\text{Nominal-}}_{2}\underbrace{\text{aux}^1}_{3}\underbrace{\text{-X}}_{4} \Rightarrow 2,3,4,1,\text{neg,Pro} + 2,3$$

$$\underbrace{\text{wh-}}_{1}\underbrace{neg\text{-}}_{2}\underbrace{\text{Nominal-}}_{3}\underbrace{\text{aux}^1}_{4}\underbrace{\text{-X}}_{5} \Rightarrow 2,3,4,5,1,\text{Pro} + 3,4$$

VII. *neg*-absorption by incomplete negatives (obligatory). To a certain point, sentences with incomplete negatives (*seldom, rarely*) function as if they contained the *not* characterized by sentence negation; past that point (i.e., after the absorption of neg by, e.g., *seldom*) the similarity between complete negation and incomplete negation ends (may precede VI).

$$\underbrace{\text{neg-}}_{1}\underbrace{X\text{-}}_{2}\underbrace{\text{seldom}}_{3} \Rightarrow 2,\text{neg} + 3$$

VIII. *neg*-absorption by neg. The neg connected with certain constituents (e.g., that inherent to *doubt*) may absorb a neg from a subordinate embedded structure.

$$\underbrace{X\text{-neg-}Y}_{1}\;\underbrace{[\text{neg-}}_{2}\underbrace{Z\text{-Nominal-Predicate}]_{\mathrm{Comp}}}_{3} \Rightarrow 1,3$$

IX. Truncation. In certain types of conjoining and tag-formation, identical elements with a certain structure may be deleted.

X. Preposing rules (optional). Certain constituents, including adverbs, indefinite quantifiers (*ever, anywhere,* the *either* of *either*-conjoining) may occur in front of the subject Nominal, with close association with *neg* (neg + constituent) in some cases.

$$\underbrace{\text{(neg)}}_{1}\underbrace{\text{Nominal-}}_{2}\underbrace{\text{X-}}_{3}\underbrace{\text{constituent-Y}}_{4} \Rightarrow 1,3,2,4$$

XI. Preliminary *neg*-placement (obligatory). Provided that Tense has not already been deleted by some form of truncation, the neg of sentence negation is moved from pre-sentential position to a position directly before the Aux(iliary), where it remains in the case of infinitival and participial phrases.

$$\text{(wh)neg-Nominal-Aux-X} \Rightarrow 1,3,2,4$$
$$\qquad 1 \qquad 2 \qquad 3 \qquad 4$$

XII. neg-incorporation into indefinites. If there are any indefinites before the neg of sentence negation (located at this point in front of the Aux(iliary)), then neg is obligatorily incorporated into the first of these in the sentence; otherwise neg is optionally incorporated into a following indefinite occurring in the same clause (sentence-conjoining *either* is not considered to be in the clause preceding it) (This generalizes neg-incorporation into quantifiers, neg-incorporation into *ever*, and the pertinent part of *neither*-tag formation.)[17]

$$\text{(a) obligatory: Indef-X (Indef) Y-neg-Z} \Rightarrow \text{neg} + 1,2,4$$
$$\qquad\qquad\qquad 1 \qquad 2 \qquad 3\ 4$$

$$\text{(b) optional: X-neg-Y-Indef} \Rightarrow 1,3,\text{neg} + 4$$
$$\qquad\qquad 1\ 2\ 3\ 4$$

XIII. Pre-verbal particle placement (obligatory). In a sentence with a finite verb, *so* and sentence-negation neg (when the latter has not been incorporated into or absorbed by other constituents) are situated inside the Auxiliary, after the first helping verb after Tense, if there is one.

$$\text{neg(Adv)}\mathbf{aux^1} \Rightarrow 2,1$$
$$\qquad 1 \qquad 2$$

XIV. Pre-verbal adverb placement (optional). Adverbs not preceded by neg optionally occur inside the Auxiliary only if there is a helping verb.

$$\text{Adv-X-}\mathbf{aux^1}\text{(neg(Adv))} \Rightarrow 2,1,3$$
$$\quad 1 \quad 2 \qquad 3$$

XV. neg-contraction (optional). An unincorporated neg following a verb or verbal affix may be incorporated into the latter.

$$\mathbf{aux^1}\text{-neg} \Rightarrow 1 + \text{neg}$$
$$\quad 1 \quad 2$$

XVI. Verbal concord (obligatory). In the Present tense of non-modal verbs, the subject Nominal determines the form of the Tense morpheme.

XVII. Incorporation into wh (optional). Certain constituents may be incorporated into the interrogative marker wh.

$$\text{wh-X-constituent-Y} \Rightarrow 1 + \text{constituent}, 2, 4$$
$$\quad 1\ 2 \qquad 3 \qquad 4$$

---

[17]Both *Indef*-incorporation and *neg*-incorporation can be interpreted as the addition of *Indef* and *neg* to the GSF specification of the basic morpheme or as the replacement of the feature *Indet* by the feature *Indef*, such that whereas the reading /a/ or /ϕ/ is given by the dictionary for an entry with the features $\begin{bmatrix} \text{Quant}^1 \\ \text{Indet} \end{bmatrix}^{\text{GSF}}$ a rule states that the reading is /any/ if Indef is found in the GSF specification. Similarly, incorporation into *wh* can be interpreted as adding to the GSF specification of *wh* the features of some other morpheme in the sentence.

XVIII. Affect-attraction (obligatory). When constituents like *wh* and *neg*, which contain the feature Affect(ive), occur in their original pre-sentential position, there is inverted word order.

$$\left\{\begin{matrix}[\text{Affect}]^{GSF}_{wh}(+X)\\ [\text{Affect}]^{GSF}_{neg}+X\end{matrix}\right\}\underbrace{\text{Nominal-}\textbf{aux}^1\text{-Y}}_{} \Rightarrow 1,3,2,4$$

$$\underbrace{}_{1}\quad\underbrace{}_{2}\ \underbrace{}_{3}\ \underbrace{}_{4}$$

XIX. Tense attachment (obligatory). The verbal affixes are incorporated into an immediately following verb.

$$\text{e.g., }\underbrace{\text{Past-}}_{1}\underbrace{\text{V}}_{2} \Rightarrow 2 + \text{Past}$$

XX. *Do*-support (obligatory). If due to inversion or to pre-verbal particle placement, a verbal affix has had no immediately following verb into which to be incorporated, then it is supplied with the verb *do*.

$$\text{e.g., }\underbrace{\text{X-}}_{1}\underbrace{\text{Past-}}_{2}\underbrace{\text{Y}}_{3} \Rightarrow 1, \text{do} + \text{past}, 3$$

XXI. wh-deletion (obligatory). The question marker *wh*, when not in grammatical association with another constituent, is deleted.

$$\underbrace{\text{wh-}}_{1}\underbrace{\text{X}}_{2} \Rightarrow 2$$

Symbolism

(1) An asterisk * indicates the non-existence of a structure or sentence.

(2) - indicates simple concatenation; X-Y reads the symbol X followed by the symbol Y.

(3) → describes rules of constituent structure; X → Y-Z is read X is rewritten as, or expanded to, Y-Z.

(4) ( ) indicates the optional presence of a constituent and simple concatenation is implied; i.e., - is not necessary between the contents of ( ) and the symbol on either side.

(5) { } indicate a selection of one, and simple concatenation is implied. Thus in accordance with the symbolism described in (4) and (5), $X(\left\{\begin{matrix}Y\\Z\end{matrix}\right\})$ reads X alone or followed by either Y or Z.

(6) [ ] indicates structure; $[X]_Y$ reads an X that is dominated by (in having been expanded from, or in replacing symbols expanded from) Y, and simple concatenation is implied.

(7) + indicates the association of two symbols, with one incorporated into the other; $[X + Y]_Y$ specifies that X is incorporated into Y. At the present state of syntactic research, it is sometimes unknown which of two associated constituents dominates the other, in other instances specification of the dominating constituent may not be relevant to the problem at hand; in such cases + will occur alone.

(8) X → Y-Z/in env—W represents contextual restrictions in the expansion of a symbol; it is read X, when in the environment of a following W, is rewritten as Y-Z.

(9) ⇒ describes transformational rules; $[X-Y]_A \Rightarrow [Y-W-X]_B$ reads any sequence X-Y that is an A is convertible into the sequence Y-W-X, which sequence is a B.

(10) φ indicates a constituent without phonological shape.

(11) S_b, S_a, S_e are respectively base sentence, appended sentence, and embedded sentence in transformations which associate two sentences or more.

(12) X:Y-Z is read any structure X that consists of X followed by Y, where X and Y can represent terminal symbols or constituents that dominate terminal symbols. These symbols need not represent the same level of derivation; e.g., S: John-Predicate reads any S(entence) in which the Predicate is preceded by John; i.e., in effect, all simple sentences, with initial

subject, that have John as subject Nominal. Note that in the derivation of sentences, by the time the subject Nominal has been expanded to John, the constituent Predicate will itself already have been expanded into certain of those constituents that it dominates.

(13) X-Y-Z indicates the segmentation of a string of constituents into one consisting of

    1 2

X and the other of Y-Z.

(14) seg 1,2, etc. is another way of referring to segmentation as in (13), e.g., $[Y-Z]_{seg}$ 1,2.

(15) Roman numerals indicate the relative order of transformational rules.

(16) Boldface miniscules as in **aux** represent syntactic entities which do not have their origin either in the constituent structure rules or in the transformational rules, or which function merely as tentative elements for the purpose of facilitating the presentation of particular problems.

(17) X^1, X^2, represent different occurrences of the symbol X when reference to them requires this differentation.

(18) X, Y, and Z are used in the various rules as cover symbols for whatever may occur in the positions occupied by those symbols.

(19) Small Roman numerals (i, ii) refer to successive strings in the derivation of sentences, as the relevant transformations apply in their appropriate order.

Transformations Discussed

Numbers before the semi-colon refer to the statement of rules. Those after the semicolon cite major places where those rules are referred to.

Affect-attraction (208b)
Comp-embedding (137); (157a), p. 293
declarative clause embedding (102)
do-support (26); (36d), (41c), (94g), (167), (168c), (179c), (181d)
either-conjoining (47); (61a), (65a), (66a), (94a), (111c)
incorporation into *wh* (16)
Indef-incorporation (110), (156), (169), (125), (156), (208a); (111b), (116b), (118a), (119b), (126b), (127)
negative appositive tag (51)
neg-absorption (164)
neg-attraction (65h); (61c), (66g), (94e), (118c), (119e), (126c), (179b)
neg-contraction (54d), (64e); (57c), (65g), (116d), (181d)
neg-fusing rules (94f), (113a)
neg-incorporation by incomplete negatives (64b); (65d), (66b)
neg-incorporation into Indef(inites) (90), (112); (94d), (118b), (119d), (126b), (127), (157b)
neg-incorporation into Quant(ifiers) (76)
neg-incorporation into *seldom* (68)
neither-tag formation (65c); (61b), (66f)
passivization (75); p. 403, p. 309
preliminary neg-placement (178); (180), (181b)
pre-posing of *either* (94c); (119c)
pre-posing of *not* p. 306
pre-posing of *somewhere* (179a)
pre-posing of Time (118); p. 306
pre-verbal adverb placement (42), (64d); (54c), (56b), (65f), (66f)
pre-verbal particle placement (24), (40), (64c); (36a), (41b), (54b), (65e), (66e), (111c), (116c), (167a), (168b)
pre-verbal placement of Time (114)

tag-question formation (54a); (56b), (57b)
Tense-attachment (19), (25); (36c), (56e), (94g), (116d), (118d)
too-conjoining p. 338, line 8
truncation (65b); (66b), (94b), (119c)
verbal concord (15)
verbal morphophonemics (55)
wh-attraction (17), (54e); (56d), (57d), p. 299
wh-deletion (18); (56f), (57e), (207b)
will-deletion (36b)
you-deletion (36b)

9   On the Bases of Phonology*

Morris Halle

I

Our central concern in this section is the framework to be used for characterizing speech in a linguistic description. It is required of such a framework that it not only make it possible to represent the observed data with a sufficient degree of accuracy, but also that this representation lead to reasonable, fruitful, insightful, and simple descriptions of the relevant facts. As an illustration consider the following example.

It is an easily observed fact that speakers of English can produce plural forms of nouns regardless of whether or not they have ever heard the noun before. This bit of linguistic behavior is usually described by saying that in forming the regular plural [ɪ z] is added if the noun ends in [s z š ž č ǯ] (e.g., *busses, causes, bushes, garages, beaches, badges*); [s] is added if the noun ends in [p t k θ f] (e.g., *caps, cats, cakes, fourths, cuffs*); and [z] is added in all other cases.

Underlying this rule is the assumption that the speech signal is a linear sequence of discrete entities variously termed phonemes, sounds, segments, allophones, and so on. It is this assumption which makes it possible to give the concise account quoted above. Without making use of the phoneme these facts can be expressed only with the greatest laboriousness as one can easily convince oneself by trying to give the rule in terms of syllables, words, or such clear acoustical properties as periodicity, formant behavior, noise spectrum, and the like.

The layman may regard as somewhat paradoxical our terming as an assumption the proposition that speech is a linear sequence of sounds. It does not seem to be widely known that when one examines an actual utterance in its purely physical manifestation as an acoustical event, one does not find in it obvious markers which would allow one to segment the signal into entities standing in a one-to-one

---

*This is a revised version of M. Halle, "Questions of Linguistics," published in the supplement to *Il Nuovo Cimento* **13**, Series X (1958), 494–517.

relationship with the phonemes that, the linguist would say, compose the utterance.[1]

The inability of instrumental phoneticians to propose a workable segmentation procedure has, however, not resulted in a wholesale abandonment of the phoneme concept. Only a few easily frightened souls have been ready to do without the phoneme. The majority has apparently felt that absence of a simple segmentation procedure does not warrant abandoning the discrete picture of speech. The most important justification that could perhaps be offered for this stand is that almost every insight gained by modern linguistics from Grimm's Law to Jakobson's distinctive features depend crucially on the assumption that speech is a sequence of discrete entities. In view of this fact many linguists have been willing to postulate the existence of discrete entities in speech even while accepting as true the assertion of instrumental phoneticians that there are no procedures for isolating these entities. There are numerous precedents in science for such a position. For instance, Helmholtz postulated that electric current is a flow of discrete particles without having isolated or even having much hope of isolating one of these particles. The status of the phoneme in linguistics is, therefore, analogous to that of electrons in physics, and since we do not regard the latter as fictional, there is little reason for applying this term to phonemes. They are every bit as real as any other theoretical entity in science. It now appears, moreover, that the insurmountable difficulties encountered in the attempt to state a procedure for segmenting the speech signal are no bar to constructing a device which will transform (continuous) speech into sequences of discrete entities.[2]

In addition to viewing utterances as composed of phonemes, the phonemes themselves shall be regarded here as simultaneous actualizations of a set of attributes. This view can be traced back almost to the very beginnings of abstract concern with language since rudimentary schemes for classifying speech sounds are implicit already in the earliest alphabets. This is hardly surprising, for it is all but self-evident that speech sounds form various intersecting classes. Thus, for instance, the final sounds in the words *ram, ran, rang* share the property of nasality; i.e., the property of being produced with a lowered velum, which allows air to flow through the nose. In a similar fashion, the sound [m] shares with the sounds [p] and [b] the property of being produced with a closure at the lips, or, as phoneticians would say, of having a bilabial *point of articulation*.

The proposed frameworks differ, of course, from one another, and up to the present, phoneticians have not agreed on any single framework that is to be used in all linguistic descriptions. In the present study I shall utilize the *distinctive feature framework* that is due primarily to R. Jakobson. Since the distinctive features have

----

[1] For discussion of some of the evidence, see P. Ladefoged's contribution to the Teddington Symposium, *The Mechanization of Thought Processes*, National Physical Laboratories, Symposium #10 (London 1959). Analogous observations have been made also with regard to other physiological, motor aspects of speech; cf. the report by Menzerath on his x-ray moving pictures of speech at the Fourth International Congress of Linguists (Copenhagen, 1938).

[2] For a discussion of these procedures see D. MacKay "Mindlike Behaviours of Artefacts," *Brit. J. for the Phil. of Sci.*, **2**, (1959) 105–21, and M. Halle and K. N. Stevens, "Speech Recognition: A Model and a Program for Research," pp. 604-612 in this volume.

been described in detail elsewhere, I shall present here only the articulatory correlates of the most important features and comment briefly on some of them.[3]

ARTICULATORY CORRELATES OF THE DISTINCTIVE
FEATURES (PARTIAL LIST)

In the description below four degrees of narrowing in the vocal tract will be distinguished.

The most extreme degree of narrowing, termed *contact*, is present when two opposite parts of the vocal tract touch. Stop consonants such as [p] [d] or [k] are articulated with *contact* at different points in the vocal tract.

A less extreme degree of narrowing, termed *occlusion*, is one capable of producing turbulence. *Occlusions* are characteristically involved in the production of fricatives such as [v] [s] or [š].

The next degree of narrowing, termed *obstruction*, is exemplified in the articulation of glides such as [w] or [j].

The fourth degree of narrowing, termed *constriction*, is that manifest in the articulation of diffuse ("high") vowels such as [i] or [u].

VOCALIC—NONVOCALIC: vocalic sounds are produced with a periodic excitation and with an open oral cavity, i.e., one in which the most extreme degree of narrowing is a *constriction;* nonvocalic sounds are produced with an oral cavity narrowed at least to the degree of an *obstruction* or with an excitation that is not periodic.

CONSONANTAL—NONCONSONANTAL: consonantal sounds are produced with *occlusion* or *contact* in the central path through the oral cavity; nonconsonantal sounds are produced with lesser degrees of narrowing in the central path of the oral cavity.

GRAVE—NONGRAVE: grave sounds are articulated with a primary narrowing located at the periphery of the oral cavity (i.e., at the lips or in the velar or pharyngeal region); nongrave sounds are articulated with a primary narrowing located in the central (i.e., dental-alveolar-palatal) region of the oral cavity.

FLAT—NONFLAT: flat sounds are produced with a secondary narrowing at the periphery of the oral cavity; nonflat sounds are produced without such a narrowing.[4]

---

[3]The fact that in the following list, reference is made only to the articulatory properties of speech and nothing is said about the acoustical properties, is not to be taken as an indication that the latter are somehow less important. The only reason for concentrating here exclusively on the former is that these are more readily observed without instruments. If reference were to be made to the acoustical properties of speech it would be necessary to report on experimental findings of fair complexity which would expand this paper beyond its allowed limits. For a fuller discussion, see R. Jakobson, C. G. M. Fant, M. Halle, *Preliminaries to Speech Analysis* Cambridge, Mass.; M.I.T. Press, 1963.

[4]Sounds produced with a single narrowing which is located at the periphery of the oral cavity may be classed either as flat or nonflat; they are, of course, grave. Sounds articulated with two narrowings, of which one is central and the other peripheral, are acute and flat; whereas sounds articulated with two narrowings both of which are peripheral are grave and flat.

DIFFUSE—NONDIFFUSE: diffuse sounds are produced with a narrowing which in degree equals or exceeds that of a *constriction* and is located in the front part of the vocal tract; nondiffuse sounds are articulated with narrowings which are either of a lesser degree or are located in the back part of the vocal tract. The dividing line between *front* and *back* is further retracted for vowels than for other sounds: for the vowels, *front* includes almost the entire oral cavity, while for other sounds, the dividing line between *front* and *back* runs between the alveolar and palatal regions.

COMPACT—NONCOMPACT: this feature is restricted to vowels. Compact vowels are produced with a forward flanged oral cavity which contains no *constrictions* or narrowings of higher degree; noncompact vowels are produced with an oral cavity that is not forward flanged.

STRIDENT—NONSTRIDENT: this feature is restricted to consonantal sounds. Strident sounds are produced by directing the air stream at right angles across a sharp edged obstacle or parallel over a rough surface, thereby producing considerable noisiness which is the major acoustical correlate of stridency. Nonstrident sounds are produced with configurations in which one or several of the factors mentioned are missing.

VOICED—VOICELESS: voiced sounds are produced by vibrating the vocal cords; voiceless sounds are produced without vocal vibration.

NASAL—NONNASAL: nasal sounds are produced by lowering the velum, thereby allowing air to pass through the nasal pharynx and nose; nonnasal sounds are produced with a raised velum which effectively shuts off the nasal pharynx and nose from the rest of the vocal tract.

CONTINUANT—INTERRUPTED: continuant sounds are produced with a vocal tract in which the passage from the glottis to the lips contains no narrowing in excess of an *occlusion*; interrupted sounds are produced with a vocal tract in which the passage from the glottis to the lips is effectively closed by *contact*.

The first two features on the above list produce a quadripartite division of the sounds of speech into (1) vowels, which are vocalic and nonconsonantal; (2) liquids, [r], [l], which are vocalic and consonantal; (3) consonants, which are nonvocalic and consonantal; and (4) glides, [h], [w], [j], which are nonvocalic and nonconsonantal. This division differs from the traditional one—into vowels and nonvowels (consonants).

A further difference between most standard systems and the distinctive feature system lies in the treatment of two major classes of segments, the vowels and the consonants. In most standard systems these two classes are described in terms of features which are totally different: consonants are described in terms of "points of articulation," whereas vowels are described in terms of the so-called "vowel triangle." In the distinctive feature system, on the other hand, these two classes are handled by the same features, *diffuse–nondiffuse*, and *grave-acute*.[5]

---

[5]Over 2000 years ago, Hindu phoneticians had the idea of treating vowels and consonants together. Their solution differs from the one proposed here in that it classified vowels as well as consonants in terms of their points of articulation.

The manner in which individual speech sounds are characterized in terms of distinctive features is illustrated in Table 1. As can be seen there, [s] is characterized as nonvocalic, consonantal, nongrave, diffuse, strident, nonnasal, continuant, voiceless; or [m] is characterized as nonvocalic, consonantal, grave, diffuse, nonstrident, nasal, noncontinuant, voiced. The alphabetic symbols [s] and [m], by which we conventionally designate these sounds are, therefore, nothing but abbreviations standing for the feature complexes just mentioned. It is as feature complexes, rather than as indivisible entities, that speech sounds will be regarded hereinafter.

Table 1

DISTINCTIVE FEATURE REPRESENTATION OF THE CONSONANTS OF ENGLISH

	p	b	m	f	v	k	g	t	d	θ	ð	n	s	z	č	ž	š	ž
VOCALIC	−	−	−	−	−	−	−	−	−	−	−	−	−	−	−	−	−	−
CONSONANTAL	+	+	+	+	+	+	+	+	+	+	+	+	+	+	+	+	+	+
GRAVE	+	+	+	+	+	+	−	−	−	−	−	−	−	−	−	−	−	−
DIFFUSE	+	+	+	+	+	−	−	+	+	+	+	+	+	+	−	−	−	−
STRIDENT	−	−	−	+	+	−	−	−	−	−	−	−	+	+	+	+	+	+
NASAL	−	−	+	−	−	−	−	−	−	−	−	+	−	−	−	−	−	−
CONTINUANT	−	−	−	+	+	−	−	−	−	+	+	−	+	+	−	−	+	+
VOICED	−	+	+	−	+	−	+	−	+	−	+	+	−	+	−	+	−	+

It is obvious that we can use the features to refer conveniently to classes of speech sounds. Thus, for instance, all sounds represented in Table 1 belong to the class of consonants, and as such they share the features *nonvocalic* and *consonantal*. We note moreover that the consonants [s z č ž š ž] are the only ones that share the features *nongrave* and *strident*; or [p b f v m] alone share the features *grave* and *diffuse*. On the other hand, [m] and [s] share no features which would distinguish them from all other consonants. If we wanted to designate the class containing the sounds [m] and [s] in distinctive feature terminology, we should have to give a long, cumbersome list of features. We shall say that a set of speech sounds forms a *natural class* if fewer features are required to designate the class than to designate any individual sound in the class. Hence, the first three sets of sounds cited above form natural classes, whereas the set containing [m] and [s] is not a natural class.

Jakobson has shown that in describing the most varied linguistic facts we commonly encounter sets of sounds which form natural classes in the distinctive feature framework and that only rarely does one meet sets of sounds which require long, cumbersome lists of distinctive features for their characterization. As a case in point consider again the formation of English noun plurals. As was noted above, [ɪ z] is added if and only if the noun ends in [s z š ž č ž]. But as we have already seen it is precisely this class of consonants that is exhaustively characterized by the features *nongrave* and *strident*. Similarly, the nouns to which the suffix [s] is added end in consonants all of which are characterized by the feature *unvoiced*. These coincidences are important, for the distinctive features were evidently not postulated with the express purpose of affording a convenient description of the rules for forming the English plural.

The total number of different distinctive features is quite small; there seem to be about fifteen. These 15 attributes are sufficient to characterize all segments in all languages. Since we cannot have knowledge of all languages—e.g., of languages which will be spoken in the future—the preceding assertion must be understood as a statement about the nature of human language in general. It asserts in effect that human languages are phonetically much alike, that they do *not* "differ from one another without limit and in unpredictable ways." Like all generalizations this statement can be falsified by valid counter-examples. It can, however, not be proven true with the same conclusiveness. The best that can be done is to show that the available evidence makes it very likely that the statement is true. Most important in this connection is the fact that all investigations in which large numbers of languages have been examined—from E. Siever's *Grundzüge der Phonetik* (1876) to Trubetzkoy's *Grundzüge der Phonologie* (1939)—have operated with an extremely restricted set of attributes. If this can be done with about a hundred languages from all parts of the globe, there appears good reason to believe that a not greatly enlarged catalogue of attributes will be capable of handling the remaining languages as well.

If it is true that a small set of attributes suffices to describe the phonetic properties of all languages of the world, then it would appear quite likely that these attributes are connected with something fairly basic in man's constitution, something which is quite independent of his cultural background. Psychologists might, therefore, find it rewarding to investigate the phonetic attributes, for it is not inconceivable that these attributes will prove to be productive parameters for describing man's responses to auditory stimuli in general. It must, however, be noted that for purposes of linguistics, the lack of psychological work in this area is not fatal. For the linguist it suffices if the attributes selected yield reasonable, elegant, and insightful descriptions of all relevant linguistic data. And this in fact they accomplish.

II

It has been noted that in linguistic descriptions utterances are represented as sequences of discrete segments, which themselves are characterized by means of distinctive features. Although in many instances there is a one-to-one relationship between the segments and specific stretches of the acoustical signal, there are many instances where this relationship is anything but simple. The part of linguistics that is concerned with the relationship between segment (phoneme) and sound is called *phonology*.

A complete description of a language must include a list of all existing morphemes of the languages, for without such a list the grammar would fail to distinguish a normal English sentence such as "it was summer," from the jabberwocky "'twas brillig." Our purpose in preparing a scientific description of a language is, however, not achieved if we give only an inventory of all existing morphemes; we must also describe the structural principles that underlie all existing forms. Just as syntax must be more than an inventory of all observed sentences of a language, so phonology must be more than a list of its morphemes.

In order to generate a specific sentence it is obviously necessary to supply the grammar with instructions for selecting from the list of morphemes the particular morphemes appearing in the sentence. Instead of using an arbitrary numerical code which tells us nothing about the phonetic structure of the morphemes, it is possible—and also more consonant with the aims of a linguistic description—to utilize for this purpose the distinctive feature representation of the morphemes directly. In other words, instead of instructing the grammar to select item (#7354), we instruct the grammar to select the morpheme which in its first segment has the features *nonvocalic, consonantal, diffuse, grave, voiced*, and so on; in its second segment, the features *vocalic, nonconsonantal, diffuse, acute*, and the like; in its third segment, the features *vocalic, consonantal*, and so forth. Instructions of this type need not contain information about all features but only about features or feature combinations which serve to distinguish one morpheme from another. This is a very important fact since in every language only certain features or feature combinations can serve to distinguish morphemes from one another. We call these features and feature combinations *phonemic*, and we say that in the input instructions only phonemic features or feature combinations must occur.[6]

Languages differ also in the way they handle nonphonemic features or feature combinations. For some of the nonphonemic features there are definite rules; for others the decision is left up to the speaker who can do as he likes. For example, the feature of aspiration is nonphonemic in English; its occurrence is subject to the following conditions:

All segments other than the voiceless stops [k], [p], [t] are unaspirated.

The voiceless stops are never aspirated after [s].

Except after [s], voiceless stops are always aspirated before an accented vowel.

In all other positions, aspiration of voiceless stops is optional.

A complete grammar must obviously contain a statement of such facts, for they are of crucial importance to one who would speak the language correctly.

In addition to features which, like *aspiration* in English, are never phonemic, there are features in every language that *are* phonemic, but only in those segments where they occur in conjunction with certain other features; for example, the feature of voicing in English is phonemic only in the nonnasal consonants—all other segments except [h] are normally voiced, while [h] is voiceless.

So far we have dealt only with features which are nonphonemic regardless of neighboring segments. There are also cases where features are nonphonemic because they occur in the vicinity of certain other segments. As an example we might take the segment sequences at the beginning of English words. It will be recalled here that the features *vocalic–nonvocalic* and *consonantal–nonconsonantal* distinguish four classes of segments: vowels, symbolized here by *V*, that are vocalic and nonconsonantal; consonants, symbolized by *C*, that are nonvocalic and consonantal; liquids [r], [l], symbolized by *L*, that are vocalic and consonantal; the glide [h],

---

[6]The requirement to represent morphemes in the dictionary by phonemic features only is a direct consequence of the simplicity criterion discussed on pp. 335ff in this volume.

symbolized by *H*, that is nonvocalic and non-consonantal.[7] We shall be concerned solely with restrictions on these four classes; all further restrictions within the classes are disregarded here.

English morphemes can begin only with *V, CV, LV, HV, CCV, CLV*, and *CCLV*: *odd, do, rue, who, stew, clew, screw.* A number of sequences are not admitted initially, —e.g. *LCV, LLV*. These constraints are reflected in the following three rules which are part of the grammar of English:

RULE 1: If a morpheme begins with a consonant followed by a nonvocalic segment, the latter is also consonantal

RULE 2: If a morpheme begins with a sequence of two consonants, the third segment in the sequence is vocalic

RULE 3: If between the beginning of a morpheme and a liquid or a glide no vowel intervenes, the segment following the liquid or the glide is a vowel

These rules enable us to specify uniquely a number of features in certain segment sequences:

vocalic	−	−		
consonantal	+		+	

is converted by rules 1, 2, and 3

into

vocalic	−	−	+	+
consonantal	+	+	+	−

which stands for a sequence *CCLV*, e.g., *straw.*

The above rules must be applied in the given order. If no order is imposed, they will have to be given in a much more complex form. An interesting illustration of the effects of ordering on the complexity of the rules is provided by the Finnish vowel system, which shall now be examined. Finnish has eight vowel sounds which can be characterized by means of the following distinctive feature matrix.

	[æ]	[a]	[e]	[ö]	[o]	[i]	[ü]	[u]
flat	−	−	−	+	+	−	+	+
compact	+	+	−	−	−	−	−	−
diffuse	−	−	−	−	−	+	+	+
grave	−	+	−	−	+	−	−	+

This matrix is clearly redundant, since it utilizes four binary features to

---

[7] We consider the semivowels [j] as in *you* and [w] as in *woo*, to be positional variants of the lax vowels [i], [u], respectively; cf. N. Chomsky and M. Halle, *The Sound Pattern of English* (to appear).

characterize eight entities. The redundant features have been omitted in the table below.

	[æ]	[a]	[e]	[ö]	[o]	[i]	[ü]	[u]
flat	−	−	−	+	+	−	+	+
compact	+	+	−			−		
diffuse			−	−	−	+	+	+
grave	−	+		−	+		−	+

The omitted nonphonemic features are supplied by the following rules:

RULE 4: Flat vowels are noncompact.

RULE 5: Compact vowels are nondiffuse.

RULE 6: Noncompact nonflat vowels are nongrave.

The treatment just proposed has an interesting further consequence. In Finnish there is a restriction on what vowels can occur in a given word (vowel harmony). The Finnish word can contain a selection either from the set [i e ü ö æ] or from the set [i e u o a]. If [e i] are temporarily set aside, one could propose that Finnish is subject to

RULE 7: In a word all vowels are either grave or nongrave, depending on the nature of the root morpheme.

If [e i] are included, Rule 7 leads to incorrect results, since in words with *grave* root morphemes, [e] and [i] would be turned by Rule 7 into grave vowels, whereas in fact they remain nongrave. This incorrect result is immediately avoided if we let Rule 6 apply after, rather than before Rule 7, for Rule 6 makes all nonflat non-compact vowels nongrave and Rule 7 does not affect either flatness or compactness of any vowel.

III

In the preceding, the distinctive features have been utilized for two separate purposes. On the one hand, they have been used to characterize different aspects of vocal tract behavior, such as the location of the different narrowings in the vocal tract, the presence or absence of vocal cord vibration, lowering or raising of velum, and so forth. On the other hand, the features have functioned as abstract markers for the designation of individual morphemes. It is necessary at this point to give an account of how this dual function of the features is built into the theory.

As already noted the rules that constitute the phonological component of a grammar relate a matrix consisting of abstract markers—the phonemic representation—to a matrix where each marker represents a particular aspect of vocal tract behavior. The latter matrix is our counterpart of the conventional phonetic transcription. In the phonemic representation the different features are allowed to assume only two values, plus or minus. In this representation, however, no phonetic content is associated directly with the features which function here as abstract differential markers.

The rules of the phonological component modify—at times quite radically—the matrices of the phonological representation: the rules supply values to non-phonemic features, they change the values of certain features, and they assign a phonetic interpretation to the individual rows of the matrix. The phonetic interpretation assigned to the rows of the matrix is uniform for all languages; i.e., some row in the matrix will be associated with the feature VOCALIC-NONVOCALIC, another with the feature CONSONANTAL-NONCONSONANTAL, and so on. This fact explains our practice of designating the rows in the phonemic matrices which represent abstract differential markers, by names of the different phonetic features. When we designate a given row in the phonemic matrix by the name of a particular phonetic feature, we imply that the grammar will ultimately associate this row with the phonetic feature in question.

The statement that the assignment of phonetic interpretations to phonemic matrices is uniform for all languages reflects the fact that the articulatory apparatus of man is the same everywhere, that men everywhere are capable of controlling the same few aspects of their vocal tract behavior. The phonetic features represent, therefore, the capacities of man to produce speech sounds and constitute, in this sense, the universal phonetic framework of language. Since not all phonetic features are binary, the phonological component will include rules replacing some of the pluses and minuses in the matrices by integers representing the different degrees of intensity which the feature in question manifests in the utterance. Thus, for instance, the fact that the English [ʌ] as in *pup* is less grave ("back") than English [u] as in *poop* will be embodied in a phonological rule replacing the plus for the feature gravity by a higher integer in the vowel in *poop* than in the vowel in *pup*.

In the light of the above, the extensive discussion concerning the claim that the distinctive features are binary appears to have been due primarily to an identification of abstract phonemic markers with the phonetic features with which they are associated by the rules of the grammar. Once a distinction is made between abstract phonemic markers and phonetic features, there is little ground for disagreement, for the fact that there are many more than two phonetically distinct degrees of gravity does not invalidate the claim that in the abstract phonemic representation of morphemes there are only binary features.

10   Phonology in Generative Grammar[*]

Morris Halle

A generative grammar is formally a collection of statements, rules, or axioms which describe, define, or generate all well-formed utterances in a language and only those. The theory of generative grammars consists of a set of abstract conditions which determine the form of the statements admitted in such grammars and which govern the choice among alternative descriptions of a given body of data.[1]

In the part of the grammar that is of interest here, all statements are of the form:

$$A \rightarrow B \text{ in the environment } X\underline{\quad}Y \atop Z \tag{1}$$

where A, B, X, Y, Z are symbols of a particular alphabet or zero, and "$\rightarrow$" can be read "is to be rewritten as." The statements are, moreover, subject to a special notational convention which allows us to coalesce partly identical statements by factoring the parts that are identical. For instance, (1) and:

$$C \rightarrow D \text{ in the environment } X\underline{\quad}Y \atop Z \tag{2}$$

can be coalesced into:

$$\begin{Bmatrix} A \rightarrow B \\ C \rightarrow D \end{Bmatrix} \text{ in the environment } X\underline{\quad}Y \atop Z \tag{3}$$

* M. Halle, "Phonology in Generative Grammar," *Word*, **18** (1962), 54–72. Reprinted by permission. This work was supported in part by the U.S. Army (Signal Corps), the U.S. Navy (Office of Naval Research), and the U.S. Air Force (Office of Scientific Research, Air Research and Development Command), and in part by the National Science Foundation. I want also to express my gratitude to the Center for Advanced Study in the Behavorial Sciences, Stanford, California, and to the J. S. Guggenheim Foundation for providing me with a year that could be fully devoted to study, of which the present essay is one tangible result. Thanks are due also to various colleagues and friends who have been kind enough to comment on details of an earlier published version of this paper.

[1]For more detailed discussions of generative grammars, see N. Chomsky, *Syntactic Structures* (The Hague, 1957); M. Halle, *The Sound Pattern of Russian* (The Hague, 1959); R. B. Lees, *A*

The theory of generative grammar postulates, moreover, a mechanical procedure by means of which preferred descriptions are chosen from among several alternatives. The basis of this choice, which in accordance with common usage is termed *simplicity*, must be some formal feature of the set of statements. In many obvious cases, simplicity can be equated with brevity. Thus, a short formula, like that embodied in Verner's Law, for example, is normally regarded as simpler and hence preferred over a list of all forms implied by the formula. It would seem, therefore, natural to attempt to extend this notion of simplicity to all cases. In order to accomplish this, it is necessary to define a formal measure of length of descriptions which would appropriately mirror all considerations that enter into simplicity judgments. For example, in all cases where independent grounds exist for preferring one of several alternative descriptions, the preferred description must also be judged shorter than the rest by the proposed measure of length.

The measure of length that apparently possesses the desired properties is the number of alphabetic symbols (capital letters in (1–3) or the symbols by which these are replaced in later examples) appearing in the description. Given two alternative descriptions of a particular body of data, the description containing fewer such symbols will be regarded as simpler and will, therefore, be preferred over the other.

In the rest of this paper, I shall outline in detail some consequences of these abstract conditions on the form of phonological descriptions and exhibit the manner in which, by mechanical application of the proposed simplicity measure, certain formulations are chosen from among several alternatives. The plausibility and intrinsic appeal of the descriptions so selected will provide the primary justification not only for the proposed simplicity criterion, but also for the theory of generative grammar, of which the criterion is an integral part.

I

It has been noted above that the symbols appearing in the statement of a generative grammar belong to a restricted alphabet. In phonology, the majority of statements deal exclusively with segments or segment sequences. In order to simplify the discussion, I shall consider here only statements of this type and exclude from consideration statements involving junctures, morpheme class-markers, and so on. In the present discussion, the capital letters will, therefore, represent phonological segments, classes of segments, or sequences of these.

There are basically two ways in which phonological segments have been treated in linguistic descriptions. In some descriptions they are represented as further indivisible entities; in others, as complexes of properties. In order to choose between these two manners of representation, I propose to compare them in situations where the preferred solution is self-evident. The statement:

/a/ is replaced by /æ/ if followed by /i/   (4)

is evidently simpler than the statement:

/a/ is replaced by /æ/ if followed by /i/ and preceded by /i/   (5)

Grammar of English Nominalizations (Bloomington, Indiana, 1960); N. Chomsky and M. Halle, *The Sound Pattern of English* (in preparation).

Translating into the standard form of (1) and regarding phonological segments as indivisible entities, we obtain:

$$/a/ \rightarrow /æ/ \text{ in the } env.\underline{\hspace{1cm}}/i/ \tag{6a}$$

$$/a/ \rightarrow /æ/ \text{ in the } env. /i/\underline{\hspace{1cm}}/i/ \tag{6b}$$

Alternatively, if we regard phonological segments as complexes of properties,[2] we obtain:

$$[+\text{grave}] \rightarrow [-\text{grave}] \text{ in } env. \begin{bmatrix} \underline{\hspace{2cm}} \\ +\text{vocalic} \\ -\text{consonantal} \\ -\text{diffuse} \\ +\text{compact} \\ -\text{flat} \end{bmatrix} \begin{bmatrix} +\text{vocalic} \\ -\text{consonantal} \\ +\text{diffuse} \\ -\text{compact} \\ -\text{flat} \\ -\text{grave} \end{bmatrix} \tag{7a}$$

$$[+\text{grave}] \rightarrow [-\text{grave}] \text{ in } env. \begin{bmatrix} +\text{vocalic} \\ -\text{consonantal} \\ +\text{diffuse} \\ -\text{compact} \\ -\text{flat} \\ -\text{grave} \end{bmatrix} \begin{bmatrix} \underline{\hspace{2cm}} \\ +\text{vocalic} \\ -\text{consonantal} \\ -\text{diffuse} \\ +\text{compact} \\ -\text{flat} \end{bmatrix} \begin{bmatrix} +\text{vocalic} \\ -\text{consonantal} \\ +\text{diffuse} \\ -\text{compact} \\ -\text{flat} \\ -\text{grave} \end{bmatrix} \tag{7b}$$

Either reformulation of (4) is to be preferred by the proposed simplicity criterion over the corresponding reformulation of (5), since the equivalents of (4) utilize three (respectively 13) symbols versus four (respectively, 19) symbols utilized in the equivalents of (5).

Consider, however, the following pair of statements for a language possessing the three front vowels /æ/, /e/, /i/:

$$/a/ \text{ is replaced by } /æ/, \text{ if followed by } /i/ \tag{8a}$$

$$/a/ \text{ is replaced by } /æ/, \text{ if followed by any front vowel} \tag{8b}$$

Here (8b) is the more general rule and is, therefore, to be preferred over (8a). Translating the two statements into the standard form and viewing phonemes as indivisible entities, we obtain:

$$/a/ \rightarrow /æ/ \text{ in the } env.\underline{\hspace{1cm}}/i/ \tag{9a}$$

$$/a/ \rightarrow /æ/ \text{ in the } env.\underline{\hspace{1cm}} \begin{Bmatrix} /i/ \\ /e/ \\ /æ/ \end{Bmatrix} \tag{9b}$$

Regarding phonemes as complexes of features, we obtain:

$$[+\text{grave}] \rightarrow [-\text{grave}] \text{ in the } env. \begin{bmatrix} \underline{\hspace{2cm}} \\ +\text{vocalic} \\ -\text{consonantal} \\ -\text{diffuse} \\ +\text{compact} \\ -\text{flat} \end{bmatrix} \begin{bmatrix} +\text{vocalic} \\ -\text{consonantal} \\ +\text{diffuse} \\ -\text{compact} \\ -\text{flat} \\ -\text{grave} \end{bmatrix} \tag{10a}$$

---

[2] I shall use here the Jakobsonian distinctive features as the properties in terms of which segments are to be characterized. The choice of a different phonetic framework, however, would not affect the outcome of the present comparison. In view of the decision to operate with the distinctive feature framework, all references below to segments as "/s/" or as "labial stops" are to be understood as unofficial circumlocutions introduced only to facilitate the exposition, but lacking all systematic import. For a brief discussion of the distinctive features, see pp. 326–327 of this volume.

$$[+ \text{grave}] \rightarrow [- \text{grave}] \text{ in the } env. \begin{bmatrix} \overline{} \\ +\text{vocalic} \\ -\text{consonantal} \\ -\text{diffuse} \\ +\text{compact} \\ -\text{flat} \end{bmatrix} \begin{bmatrix} +\text{vocalic} \\ -\text{consonantal} \\ -\text{grave} \end{bmatrix} \qquad (10b)$$

The alternative reformulations of (8) are not consistent with each other: (9a) utilizes fewer symbols than (9b), whereas (10a) utilizes more symbols than (10b). Since we know on independent grounds that (10b) is more general than (10a) and must, therefore, be preferred over the latter, the results obtained in the reformulations (9) are also inconsistent with the results obtained in (6), where the preferred statement required fewer symbols. It follows, therefore, that if we wish to operate with the simplicity criterion that has been proposed here, we must regard phonological segments as complexes of properties.

Finally, compare (10b) with the following:

$$\text{/a/ is replaced by /æ/ if followed by /i/, /p/, or /z/} \qquad (11)$$

Translated into standard form with phonemes regarded as indivisible entities, (11) would read:

$$\text{/a/} \rightarrow \text{/æ/ in the } env. \begin{Bmatrix} \text{/i/} \\ \text{/p/} \\ \text{/z/} \end{Bmatrix} \qquad (12)$$

Since (12) utilizes exactly the same number of symbols as (9b), it will be judged by the proposed simplicity criterion as of the same complexity as (9b). There can, however, be little doubt that linguists would regard (9b) as simpler than (11), on the grounds that the environment in the former is constituted by a *natural class* of phonemes (cf. pp. 328 of this volume), while in the latter the environment is made up of an odd, unsystematic collection of phonemes. The proposed simplicity criterion thus yields a counter-intuitive result if it is applied to statements in which phonemes are regarded as indivisible entities.

It can readily be seen that if (11) is translated into the standard form utilizing distinctive features instead of phonemes, it will require considerably more symbols than (10b), for we shall have to specify /i/, /p/, /z/ by their whole complement of features, whereas in (10b) we are able to take advantage of the fact that the set /i/, /e/, /æ/ constitutes a natural class and can, therefore, be unambiguously specified by fewer features than any of its members. We observe that the intuitively correct result is yielded by the proposed simplicity criterion in conjunction with a representation of phonemes as bundles of distinctive features, whereas the above counter-intuitive result is obtained if phonemes are regarded as indivisible entities. The failure of the simplicity criterion in the latter case is due to the fact that the notion of *natural class* has no obvious meaning if phonemes are regarded as indivisible entities.

It is, of course, conceivable that a simplicity criterion may be formulated that yields the proper results even when segments are represented as indivisible entities. The burden of proof, however, is clearly on those who reject the view that segments are complexes of distinctive features. Rather than explore here alternative simplicity criteria, I shall attempt to justify the proposed view of phonological segments by examining some of its consequences. These consequences will incidentally provide ample justification for the decision to operate with the Jakobsonian distinctive feature framework rather than with one of the other phonetic frameworks (IPA or Jespersen's antalphabetic notation, and so on).

II

Significant simplifications can be achieved by imposing an order on the application of the rules. Consider in this connection the rules which constitute the essence of the Sanskrit vowel sandhi. In Whitney's *Grammar*, where order of application is not a factor, the vowel sandhi is described by means of the following four rules:

(1) Two similar simple vowels, short or long, coalesce and form the corresponding long vowel . . . (Section 126)

(2) An *a*-vowel combines with a following *i*-vowel to *e*; with a *u*-vowel, to *o* . . . (Section 127)

(3) The *i*-vowels, the *u*-vowels and the *r* before a dissimilar vowel or a diphthong, are each converted into its own corresponding semi-vowel, *y* or *v* or *r* . . . (Section 129).

(4) Of a diphthong, the final *i*- or *u*-element is changed into its corresponding semi-vowel, *y* or *v*, before any vowel or diphthong: thus *e* (really *ai* . . .) becomes *ay*, and *o* (that is *au* . . .) becomes *ay* . . . (Section 131).

If the first three rules are applied in the order (1), (3), (2), two important economies can be effected. First, in rule (3), the qualification "before a dissimilar vowel or a diphthong" can be simplified to "before a vowel," for at the point where rule (3) applies, only sequences of dissimilar vowels remain, since rule (1) replaces all sequences of identical vowel by single long vowels. Moreover, rule (4) can be dispensed with altogether. Since rule (3) converts /i/ and /u/ in position before vowel into /y/ and /v/, respectively, no sequences of /ai/ and /au/ in position before vowel will ever be turned into /e/ or /o/, respectively, by the subsequent application of rule (2). Inasmuch as rule (2) is the only source of /e/ and /o/ in the language, there is now no need for rule (4), whose sole function is to convert /e/ and /o/ into /ay/ and /av/ in those cases where by the proposed ordering of the rules, /e/ and /o/ could not have arisen. Thus, the forms quoted by Whitney as requiring rule (4) are handled properly without it: /naia/ and /bʰaua/ are turned by rule (3) into /naya/ and /bʰava/ to which rule (2) does not apply. The same stems without the suffix /a/, on the other hand, are not subject to rule (3) and are, therefore, affected by (the later) rule (2), which converts /nai/ into /ne/ and /bʰau/ into /bʰo/.

In sum, rule (4) is superfluous as long as the proposed ordering of the rules is maintained. Should we choose to allow random access to the rules or impose a different order on the rules, we should have to pay for it by admitting rule (4). Our simplicity criterion leaves us no alternative but to choose the former solution.

III

A complete description of a language must evidently include a list of all actually occurring morphemes, i.e. the dictionary of the language. Being part of the description, the dictionary is also subject to the notational conventions and simplicity criterion that have been outlined above. The items in the dictionary will, therefore, be given in the form of sequences of distinctive feature complexes. For instance, in place of an entry /dɔg/, our dictionary might contain the entry

$$
\begin{bmatrix}
-\text{vocalic} \\
+\text{consonantal} \\
-\text{strident} \\
-\text{compact} \\
-\text{grave} \\
-\text{continuant} \\
-\text{nasal} \\
-\text{tense} \\
+\text{diffuse} \\
-\text{flat} \\
+\text{voiced}
\end{bmatrix}
\begin{bmatrix}
+\text{vocalic} \\
-\text{consonantal} \\
-\text{strident} \\
+\text{compact} \\
+\text{grave} \\
+\text{continuant} \\
-\text{nasal} \\
+\text{tense} \\
-\text{diffuse} \\
+\text{flat} \\
+\text{voiced}
\end{bmatrix}
\begin{bmatrix}
-\text{vocalic} \\
+\text{consonantal} \\
-\text{strident} \\
-\text{compact} \\
+\text{grave} \\
-\text{continuant} \\
-\text{nasal} \\
-\text{tense} \\
-\text{diffuse} \\
-\text{flat} \\
+\text{voiced}
\end{bmatrix}
\qquad (13)
$$

This representation contains an excessive number of features. As can be seen in (14), English vowels—i.e., segments that are $\begin{bmatrix} +\text{vocalic} \\ -\text{consonantal} \end{bmatrix}$—are all non-nasal, nonstrident, voiced, and continuant. Moreover, compact (low) vowels are

	u	o	ɔ	a	i	e	æ
vocalic	+	+	+	+	+	+	+
consonantal	−	−	−	−	−	−	−
nasal	−	−	−	−	−	−	−
continuant	+	+	+	+	+	+	+
strident	−	−	−	−	−	−	−
flat	+	+	+	−	−	−	−
compact	−	−	+	+	−	−	+
diffuse	+	−	−	−	+	−	−
grave	+	+	+	+	−	−	−
voiced	+	+	+	+	+	+	+

(14)

The distinctive feature composition of vowels in certain dialects of modern English. The feature of tenseness has not been specified since the system contains seven tense and seven nontense vowels.

always nondiffuse (nonhigh); while all flat (rounded) vowels are always grave (back). Nonflat (unrounded) vowels, on the other hand, are invariably nongrave (front) only if they are also noncompact (nonlow). This suggests that the redundant features be omitted in all dictionary entries in which the respective vowels figure and be introduced by a special rule:[3]

$$\left\{\begin{array}{ll} \text{a.} & [+\text{compact}] \to [-\text{diffuse}] \\ \text{b.} & [X] \to \begin{bmatrix} -\text{nasal} \\ -\text{strident} \\ +\text{continuant} \\ +\text{voiced} \end{bmatrix} \\ \text{c.} & [+\text{flat}] \qquad \to [+\text{grave}] \\ \text{d.} & \begin{bmatrix} -\text{flat} \\ -\text{compact} \end{bmatrix} \to [-\text{grave}] \end{array}\right\} \text{ in the } env. \begin{bmatrix} +\text{vocalic} \\ -\text{consonantal} \end{bmatrix} \qquad (15)$$

where $[X]$ represents an arbitrary feature complex. Given (15), the vowel in (13) can be represented by the feature complex:

$$\begin{bmatrix} +\text{vocalic} \\ -\text{consonantal} \\ +\text{compact} \\ +\text{flat} \\ +\text{tense} \end{bmatrix} \qquad (16)$$

i.e., by five instead of eleven features.

The simplicity criterion clearly demands that this procedure be followed in the representation of every dictionary entry, for it allows us to shorten the dictionary, which is an integral part of a grammar, by many hundreds of features at the slight additional cost represented by the thirteen features utilized in (15). In general, we must omit features in all dictionary representations, whenever these can be introduced by a rule that is less costly than the saving it effects.

IV

Among the redundancies that must be eliminated are those where the appearance of a given feature in a segment is contextually determined. Thus, it is generally true that if an English word begins with a sequence of two consonants, the first is invariably /s/: /st/, /sp/, /sk/, /sm/, /sn/ are the only two-consonant—i.e. $\begin{bmatrix} -\text{vocalic} \\ +\text{consonantal} \end{bmatrix}$

---

[3]In order to shorten the formulaic representations of the rules and to make them more perspicuous, the convention has been adopted that an expression of the form:

$$[+A] \to [-B] \text{ in } env. [+C] [\text{---}] [-D]$$

is equivalent to the rewrite rule:

$$\alpha \to - \text{ in } env. [+C] \begin{bmatrix} \text{---}B \\ +A \end{bmatrix} [-D]$$

where $A\ B\ C\ D$ stand for particular features and α represents an arbitrary coefficient; i.e., either "+" or "−", and the dash before B indicates the position where the minus is to be inserted.

—sequences admitted in word initial position. This suggests immediately that in the dictionary representation of all items beginning with two consonants, we omit in the first consonant all but the features $\begin{bmatrix} -\text{vocalic} \\ +\text{consonantal} \end{bmatrix}$; i.e., all features that differentiate that consonant from all other consonants of the language. The omitted features are then introduced by the following rule:

$$\begin{bmatrix} -\text{vocalic} \\ +\text{consonantal} \end{bmatrix} \rightarrow \begin{bmatrix} +\text{strident} \\ -\text{compact} \\ -\text{grave} \\ +\text{tense} \\ +\text{continuant} \end{bmatrix} \text{ in env. } \#\begin{bmatrix} \rule{1cm}{0.4pt} \end{bmatrix}\begin{bmatrix} -\text{vocalic} \\ +\text{consonantal} \end{bmatrix} \qquad (17)$$

As a result of (17) the description is shortened by five features for every dictionary item beginning with two consonants. Thus, a very great saving is realized in the dictionary at the cost of the nine features mentioned in (17).[4] This saving has the additional effect of ruling out forms such as /vnig/, /tsaym/, and /gnayt/.

Consider now such sequences as /bik/, /θōd/, or /nis/. Like the aforementioned /tsaym/, /gnayt/, and /vnig/, none are actual English words. If, however, we attempted to exclude them by means of a rule like (17), we should discover that the cost of the rule—i.e., the number of features mentioned in the rule—would exceed that of the saving that might be effected in the dictionary. For instance, since *big, bin, bid, bit, bib, biff* are all English words, the rule that excludes /bik/ would have to read:

$$\begin{bmatrix} -\text{vocalic} \\ +\text{consonantal} \\ -\text{compact} \\ -\text{strident} \end{bmatrix} \rightarrow [-\text{tense}] \text{ in env. } \begin{bmatrix} -\text{vocalic} \\ +\text{consonantal} \\ -\text{strident} \\ +\text{grave} \\ -\text{compact} \\ -\text{nasal} \\ -\text{tense} \end{bmatrix}\begin{bmatrix} +\text{vocalic} \\ -\text{consonantal} \\ +\text{diffuse} \\ -\text{compact} \\ -\text{tense} \\ -\text{grave} \end{bmatrix} [\rule{1cm}{0.4pt}] \qquad (18)$$

And at the cost of the 18 features mentioned in (18), we could effect a saving of one feature in the dictionary. The simplicity criterion, therefore, does not allow us to include (18) in a description of English.

The presence of (17) and the absence of (18) in a description of English mirrors the English speaker's intuition about his language. The presence of (17) corresponds to the fact that speakers of English will regard /vnig/, /tsaym/, and /gnayt/ as not only meaningless, but also as totally unEnglish; impossible by the rules of their language. The absence of (18) and a host of similar rules corresponds to the fact that English speakers will accept the equally meaningless /bik/, /θōd/, and /nis/ as possible English words, perhaps as words found in an unabridged dictionary rather than in the vocabulary of the average speaker.

In attempting to satisfy the simplicity criterion, we are, thus, forced to incorporate

---

[4]We may note that the idea of representing segments in a given form by less than their normal complement of features is essentially identical with the "archiphoneme" concept that was first proposed by Jakobson in *Travaux du Cercle Linguistique de Prague* II (1928) and was used for a time by the Prague School. Since the Prague School did not operate consistently with features but rather regarded the phoneme as the ultimate phonological entity, great difficulties were soon experienced with this concept, which ultimately led to its official abandonment.

into every complete generative grammar a characterization of the distinction between admissible and inadmissible segment sequences. This fact effectively cuts the
ground out from under the recent suggestion that generative grammars be supplemented with special phonological grammars,[5] since the sole purpose of these
special grammars is to characterize the distinction between admissible and inadmissible segment sequences.

V

In the study of dialects, it has been common in recent years to focus primary
attention on the facts of the utterance and to concern oneself primarily with such
questions as the mutual intelligibility of two dialects, the similarities and differences
of cognate utterances, of their phoneme repertories, distributional constraints, and
so on. Instead of following this procedure, we propose to focus here on the grammars
of the dialects, i.e., on the ordered set of statements that describe the data, rather
than on the data directly.

That the two approaches are distinct in quite fundamental ways can be seen if
we examine the manner in which "Pig Latin," a "secret" language popular among
schoolchildren in the United States, would be described from these two points of
view. If we compared utterances in Pig Latin with their cognates in General American, we should be struck by the extreme differences between them:

General American	Pig Latin
/str'īt/	/'ītstrē/
/str'īts/	/'ītstrē/
/k'æt/	/'ætkē/
/k'æts/	/'ætskē/
/r'ōz	/'ōzrē/
/r'ōzɨz/	/'ōzɨzrē/

We observe that the distribution of phonemes in Pig Latin differs radically from
that in General American, for in the former all words end in the vowel /ē/, and very
unusual consonant clusters abound. We note also that infixation rather than pre-
fixation and suffixation is the major morphological device. In view of this, we are
hardly surprised to find that Pig Latin is incomprehensible to the uninitiated speaker
of General American. Since these are precisely the observations we would expect to
make if we compared the utterances in two totally unrelated languages, we are led to
conclude that Pig Latin and General American are unrelated, or, at best, only remotely related tongues; a conclusion which is patently false.

The picture would be radically different if instead of "hugging the phonetic ground
closely" we were to compare the grammars of General American and Pig Latin.
From this point of view, the difference between the two is that Pig Latin contains a
morphophonemic rule that is absent in the more standard dialects:

Shift initial consonant cluster to end of word and add /ē/   (19)

---

[5]Cf. F. Householder, "On Linguistic Primes," *Word*, **15** (1959), 231–39; and H. Contreras and
S. Saporta, "The Validation of a Phonological Grammar," *Lingua*, **9** (1960), 1–15.

Since (19) is the only difference between the grammars of Pig Latin and General American, we conclude that Pig Latin is a *ciphered* form of General American, a somewhat special dialect of the latter, a conclusion which is obviously right. But this result follows only if instead of concentrating on the utterances, we shift primary attention to the grammars that underlie the utterances.[6]

VI

Since grammars consist of ordered sets of statements, differences among grammars are due to one or both of the following: (a) different grammars may contain different rules; (b) different grammars may have differently ordered rules. The case of Pig Latin exemplifies difference (a). An interesting example of difference (b) was discussed by M. Joos in a paper entitled "A Phonological Dilemma in Canadian English."[7] In certain Canadian dialects "the diphthongs /aj/ and /aw/ . . . each have two varieties. One . . . begins with a lower-mid vowel sound; it is used before any fortis consonant with zero juncture . . . *white, knife, shout, house.* The other is used in all other contexts: . . . *high, find, knives*; *how, found, houses.* Note the difference in singular and plural of irregular nouns, including *wife*: *wives.*" To account for this difference, Joos suggests the rule:

"/a/ is a lower-mid vowel . . . in diphthongs followed by fortis consonants" (20)

Moreover, like many other American dialects, these dialects contain the rule that:

in intervocalic position /t/ is voiced and lenis /d/ (21)

Joos notes that the speakers of these dialects "divide into two groups according to their pronunciation of words like *typewriter*. Group *A* says [tɐɪprɛɪdɚ] while Group *B* says [tɐɪpraɪdɚ]. . . . Group *A* distinguishes *writer* from *rider*, *clouting* from *clouding* by the choice of the diphthong alone. . . . Group *B* has shifted the articulation of all vowels alike before the new /d/ from earlier /t/ . . . from *write* to *writer* there is both the phonemic alternation from /t/ to /d/, and the phonetic alternation from [ɐɪ] to [aɪ]."

The dilemma referred to in the title of Joos' paper is, therefore, a lawful consequence of the fact that in the grammar of Group *A*, Rule (20) precedes Rule (21), while in the grammar of Group *B*, the reverse order obtains. Hence, in the speech of

---

[6]Secret languages like Pig Latin are extremely common. J. Applegate in "Phonological Rules of a Subdialect of English," *Word*, **17** (1961), 186–93 has described a "secret language" spontaneously created by some children in Cambridge, Mass. The difference between the grammar of this "language" and standard English consisted of the two ordered rules: (1) in a word containing several identical stop consonants, all but the first of these is replaced by a glottal stop; and (2) all continuants are replaced by the cognate stops. As a result of these two rules, we find in the language of the children the following deviations from standard English:

/baʔiy/	Bobby	/dǝd/	does
/diʔ/	did	/takt/	talks
/dayʔ/	died	/teykt/	takes
/peyʔr/	paper		
/keyʔ/	cake		

[7]*Language*, **18** (1942), 141–44.

Group *A* /taɪpraɪtɚ/ is converted by Rule (20) into [tɐɪprɐɪtɚ] which then is turned by Rule (21) into [tɐɪprɐɪdɚ]. In the speech of Group *B*, on the other hand, /taɪpraɪtɚ/ is first turned by Rule (21) into [taɪpraɪdɚ] and then by Rule (20) into [tɐɪpraɪdɚ].[8]

Since ordered rules are all but unknown in present day synchronic descriptions, the impression has spread that the imposition of order on statements in a synchronic description is always due to an oversight, to an unjustifiable confusion of synchronic and diachronic.[9] I must therefore stress that, in the preceding examples, order is determined by the simplicity criterion alone and that no historical considerations have entered in establishing it.

VII

A complete scientific description of a language must pursue one aim above all: to make precise and explicit the ability of a native speaker to produce utterances in that language. We can, therefore, enquire how the acquisition of this ability is viewed within the framework of a generative grammar. It has been suggested by Chomsky that language acquisition by a child may best be pictured as a process of constructing the simplest (optimal) grammar capable of generating the set of utterances, of which the utterances heard by the child are a representative sample.[10] The ability to master a language like a native, which children possess to an extraordinary degree, is almost completely lacking in the adult. I propose to explain this as being due to deterioration or loss in the adult of the ability to construct optimal (simplest) grammars on the basis of a restricted corpus of examples. The language of the adult—and hence also the grammar that he has internalized—need not, however, remain static: it can and does, in fact, change. I conjecture that changes in later life are restricted to the addition of a few rules in the grammar and that the elimination of rules and hence a wholesale restructuring of his grammar is beyond the capabilities of the average adult.

The addition of rules may—although it need not invariably—result in a grammar

---

[8]Joos notes that in the speech of Group *A*, the observed phenomenon is restricted to certain classes of words. This restriction does not affect the point illustrated here, viz., that data of the kind described by Joos can best be accounted for by postulating different orders of rules in grammars of different dialects.

[9]Thus, for example, Hockett confesses to being unable to conceive of ordered statements in terms other than historical: ". . . if it is said that the English past tense form *baked* is "formed" from *bake* by a "process" of "suffixation," then no matter what disclaimer of historicity is made, it is impossible not to conclude that some kind of priority is being assigned to *bake* as against *baked* or the suffix. And if this priority is not historical, what is it?" ("Two Models of Linguistic Description," *Word* 10 [1954], 233). Synchronic ordering was used by both Bloomfield and Sapir and to a certain extent also by younger linguists (Joos, *op. cit.*, Voegelin, Swadesh) who later abandoned it, however.

[10]This view of language learning was once almost a commonplace among linguists. I have found clear statements to this effect in the writings of linguists as diverse as Humboldt, Hermann Paul, and Meillet. Cf. for example, the following comment made by Meillet in 1929: ". . . chaque enfant doit acquérir par lui-même la capacité de comprendre le parler des gens de son groupe social et de l'employer. La langue ne lui est pas livrée en bloc, tout d'une pièce. Il n'entend jamais autre chose que des phrases particulières, et ce n'est qu'en comparant ces phrases entre elles qu'il arrive à saisir le sens des paroles qu'il entend et à parler à son tour. Pour chaque individu, le langage est ainsi une recréation totale faite sous l'influence du milieu qui l'entoure." *Linguistique historique et linguistique générale*, II (Paris 1952), 74.

that is not optimal (the simplest) for the set of utterances that it generates. As an example, consider the consequences of expanding (15) by the addition of subpart (e):

$$
\left.
\begin{array}{lll}
\text{a.} & [+\text{compact}] \rightarrow [-\text{diffuse}] \\
\text{b.} & [X] \rightarrow \begin{bmatrix} -\text{nasal} \\ -\text{strident} \\ +\text{continuant} \\ +\text{voiced} \end{bmatrix} \\
\text{c.} & [+\text{flat}] \rightarrow [+\text{grave}] \\
\text{d.} & \begin{bmatrix} -\text{flat} \\ -\text{compact} \end{bmatrix} \rightarrow [-\text{grave}] \\
\text{e.} & \begin{bmatrix} -\text{flat} \\ +\text{compact} \end{bmatrix} \rightarrow [+\text{grave}]
\end{array}
\right\}
\text{ in the env. } \begin{bmatrix} +\text{vocalic} \\ -\text{consonantal} \end{bmatrix} \quad (22)
$$

As can be readily seen from (14), the addition of subpart (e) amounts to a coalescence of /a/ → /æ/. The distribution of gravity in vowels is, therefore, completely determined, and (22) must be replaced by the following, simpler rule (16 vowels 11 features):

$$
\left.
\begin{array}{lll}
\text{a.} & [+\text{compact}] \rightarrow [-\text{diffuse}] \\
\text{b.} & [X] \rightarrow \begin{bmatrix} -\text{nasal} \\ -\text{strident} \\ +\text{continuant} \\ -\text{grave} \\ +\text{voiced} \end{bmatrix} \\
\text{c.} & [+\text{flat}] \rightarrow [+\text{grave}]
\end{array}
\right\}
\text{ in the env. } \begin{bmatrix} +\text{vocalic} \\ -\text{consonantal} \end{bmatrix} \quad (23)
$$

Observe that (22e), which was the cause of the whole upheaval, does not even figure in (23), which nevertheless generates precisely the same set of utterances as (22).[11]

Since every child constructs his own optimal grammar by induction from the utterances to which he has been exposed, it is not necessary that the child and his parents have identical grammars, for, as we have just seen, a given set of utterances can be generated by more than one grammar. In the case where (22e) was added to the grammar, I should therefore postulate that the adult, who of necessity is maximally conservative, would have a grammar containing (22), whereas his children would have grammars with the simpler rule (23). It is clear that such discontinuities in the grammars of successive generations must exercise a profound influence on the further evolution of the language.[12]

---

[11]For a discussion of further consequences of the addition of rules such as Eq. (22e), see Sections X to XII.

[12]The significance of discontinuities in the transmission of language from generation to generation was discussed over fifty years ago by A. Meillet: "Il faut tenir compte tout d'abord du caractère essentiellement discontinu de la transmission du langage: l'enfant qui apprend à parler ne reçoit pas la langue toute faite: il doit la recréer tout entière à son usage d'après ce qu'il entend autour de lui. . . . Cette discontinuité de la transmission du langage ne suffirait à elle seule à rien expliquer, mais, sans elle, toutes les causes du changement auraient sans doute été impuissantes à transformer le sens des mots aussi radicalement qu'il l'a été dans un grand nombre de cas: d'une manière générale d'ailleurs, la discontinuité de la transmission est la condition première qui détermine la possibilité et les modalités de tous les changements linguistiques." *Linguistique historique et linguistique générale*, I (Paris, 1948), p. 236. I am indebted to E. S. Klima for drawing my attention to the quoted passage.

VIII

Linguistic change is normally subject to the constraint that it must not result in the destruction of mutual intelligibility between the innovators—i.e., the carriers of the change—and the rest of the speech community. Except in such special cases as "secret languages" like Pig Latin or different varieties of thieves' argot, all changes must preserve comprehensibility for the rest of the speech community. This restriction clearly affects the content of the rules to be added; e.g., a rule such as (19) has little chance of survival under normal conditions, for it renders the utterances incomprehensible to the rest of the community. It is equally obvious that the number of rules to be added must also be restricted, for very serious effects on intelligibility can result from the simultaneous addition of even two or three otherwise innocuous rules.

It may be somewhat less obvious that the requirement to preserve intelligibility also restricts the place in the order where rules may be added. All other things being equal, a rule will affect intelligibility less if it is added at a lower point in the order than if it is added higher up. I am unable at present to characterize the place in the order where rules may be added with a minimum impairment of intelligibility. Such additions, however, seem characteristically to occur at points where there are natural breaks in the grammar.[13]

Because of the intelligibility constraint the type of change most likely to survive is the one involving the addition of a single, simple rule at the end of certain natural subdivisions of the grammar. It can readily be seen that in cases where the addition of such a rule does not affect the over-all simplicity of the grammar, the order of rules established by purely synchronic considerations—i.e., simplicity—will mirror properly the relative chronology of the rules. This fact was noted by Bloomfield in his important "Menomini Morphophonemics":

> The process of description leads us to set up each morphological element in a theoretical *basic* form and then to state the deviations from this basic form which appear when the element is combined with other elements. If one starts with the basic forms and applies our statements . . . in the order in which we give them, one will arrive finally at the forms of words as they are actually spoken. Our basic forms are not ancient forms, say of the Proto-Algonquian parent language, and our statements of internal sandhi are not historical but descriptive and appear in a purely descriptive order. However, our basic forms do bear some resemblance to those which would be set up for a description of Proto-Algonquian, some of our statements of alternation . . . resemble those which would appear in a description of Proto-Algonquian, and the rest . . ., as to content and order, approximate the historical development from Proto-Algonquian to present-day Menomini.[14]

---

[13]E.g. before the first morphophonemic rule involving immediate constituent structure of the utterance (i.e., at the end of the morpheme structure (MS) rules); at the end of the cyclical rules which eliminate the immediate constituent structure of the utterance from the representation; before the phonological rules that eliminate boundary markers (junctures) from the representation.

[14]*Travaux du Cercle linguistique de Prague* **VIII** (1939) 105–15. This study is unaccountably omitted in C. F. Hockett's "Implications of Bloomfield's Algonquian Studies," *Language*, **24** (1949), 117–31. Cf. also Bloomfield's comments on "descriptive order" in his *Language* (New York; Holt, Rinehart & Winston, Inc., 1933), pp. 213, 222.

IX

It has been proposed here that the primary mechanism of phonological change is the addition of rules to the grammar with special (although not exclusive) preference for the addition of single rules at the ends of different subdivisions of the grammar. If we now assume that rules are added always singly and always at a given spot in the grammar, then it follows that the synchronic order of the rules will reflect the relative chronology of their appearance in the language. Moreover, under this condition the proposed simplicity criterion can be used as a tool for inferring the history of the language, for it allows us to reconstruct various stages of a language even in the absence of external evidence such as is provided by written records or by borrowings in or from other languages. It seems to me that such an assumption is made in many studies in historical phonology. In fact, I should like to argue that the reconstruction of the evolution of the Indo-European language family, which is perhaps the most impressive achievement of nineteenth-century linguistics, was possible only by making use of the proposed simplicity criterion to establish an order among the descriptive statements: this order was then taken to reflect their relative chronology.

My point can perhaps be illustrated most graphically by a discussion of the so-called "Laws" of Grimm and of Verner, which, with good reason, are considered among the cornerstones of Indo-European reconstruction. The "Laws" describe stages in the evolution of the Germanic languages from the Indo-European proto-language, stages, which it should be noted, are not attested by any external evidence.

The Indo-European proto-language is supposed to have had a single strident continuant consonant s, which was voiceless; and a fairly complex system of non-strident noncontinuants (stops), of which for present purposes we need to consider only one series, namely the voiceless one consisting of p, t, k, k^w. The part of Grimm's Law that is of interest here can be formulated as follows:

> in certain environments C_G, the precise nature of which need not concern us here, voiceless, nonstrident non-continuants are replaced by their cognate continuants (24)

i.e., $p \to f, t \to \theta, k \to x, k^w \to x^w$. At a later time Germanic is supposed to have been subjected to Verner's Law, which can be formulated as follows:

> in certain environments C_V, all voiceless continuants are replaced by their voiced cognates (25)

i.e., $f \to v, \theta \to \eth, \chi \to \gamma, x^w \to \gamma^w$, and, n.b., $s \to z$.

If we choose to believe with the majority that Verner's Law was later than Grimm's Law (or at least the part of Grimm's Law that was cited here), then we must also assume that at the stage Verner's Law came into the language the language possessed voiceless continuants from two sources: the s which descended unchanged from Indo-European and the voiceless, nonstrident continuants produced by Grimm's Law. The fact that Verner's Law applies without distinction to voiceless continuants from both sources is always cited as the crucial evidence in favor of regarding Verner's Law later than Grimm's Law. This evidence, however, carries weight only if we accept a criterion of simplicity much like the one that was stated above, for the facts can also be accounted for fully by a set of unordered rules:

in the environment where both C_G and C_V are satisfied, voiceless, nonstrident, noncontinuants are replaced by their cognate, voiced continuants   (26a)

in the environment where C_G but not C_V is satisfied, voiceless nonstrident, noncontinuants are replaced by their cognate (voiceless) continuants   (26b)

in the environment C_V, $s \rightarrow z$ (26c)

By the proposed simplicity criterion we must reject the unordered rules, for they are evidently more complex than the ordered alternative. Since there is no external evidence that the language in fact passed through a stage at which it was subject only to Grimm's Law and was not subject to Verner's Law, the acceptance of the traditional chronology of these "laws" is based wholly on considerations of simplicity.

X

It was noted in Section VIII that as a result of the requirement that linguistic change not disrupt mutual intelligibility between the innovators and the rest of the speech community, the new rules are ordinarily added at the end of the grammar or of one of its major subdivisions. The addition of rules at other places, is not, however, completely excluded. In such instances the order of rules in the synchronic description will not properly mirror their relative chronology. This situation is well illustrated by the Middle English dialects in which both tense (long) /æ/ and /ā/ became /ē/ simultaneously with tense (long) /ɔ/ becoming /ō/.[15] The tense vowel system of these dialects was originally like that in (14) and was also subject to the phonetic rules given in (15). The change in question can be accounted for very elegantly if we assume that (15) was modified as shown in (27) by the addition of subpart (e*) before subpart (c) rather than after subpart (d); i.e., at a place other than the end of the grammar:

$$
\left\{
\begin{array}{lll}
\text{a.} & [+\text{compact}] & \rightarrow [-\text{diffuse}] \\
\text{b.} & [X] & \rightarrow \begin{bmatrix} -\text{nasal} \\ -\text{strident} \\ +\text{continuant} \\ +\text{voiced} \end{bmatrix} \\
\text{e*.} & [X] & \rightarrow [-\text{compact}] \\
\text{c.} & [+\text{flat}] & \rightarrow [+\text{grave}] \\
\text{d.} & \begin{bmatrix} -\text{flat} \\ -\text{compact} \end{bmatrix} & \rightarrow [-\text{grave}]
\end{array}
\right\} \text{ in the } env. \begin{bmatrix} \overline{+\text{vocalic}} \\ -\text{consonantal} \\ +\text{tense} \end{bmatrix} \quad (27)
$$

---

[15]Some scholars believe that the change /ā/ → /ē/ was later by 50 years than the changes /æ/ → /ē/ and /ɔ/ → /ō/. If they are right, my example is a hypothetical, rather than an actually attested instance. This does not affect its validity, however, since the example does not violate any known **constraints** on the structure or on the evolution of language.

Part (e*) of (27) converts the three compact nondiffuse (low) vowels to their non-compact (mid) cognates; i.e., /æ/ → /ē/, /ā/ → /γ/, and /ɔ/ → /ō/. Since the resulting vowels are still subject to (27c), /γ/ is immediately fronted to /ē/. Thus, the falling together of /ā/ and /æ/ in /ē/ does not require us to assume a separate fronting of /ā/ → /æ/, provided that we allow rules to be added to places other than the end of the grammar or the end of its major subdivisions.

XI

In discussing (22) the effects of the addition of subpart (e) in Section VII, it was observed that the addition of rules may result in a grammar which is not the simplest for the set of utterances it generates and that the identical set of utterances may be generated by a simpler grammar. Since the addition of subpart (e) to — (22) eliminates also the phonetic contrast between the phonemes /a/ and /æ/ in all utterances of the dialect, the question naturally arises whether such a suppression of a phonetic contrast necessarily leads also to simplifications in the dictionary. In other words, since /æ/ and /a/ are not in contrast phonetically, must this contrast also be eliminated from the dictionary representation of lexical items? One's first reaction is to answer this question in the affirmative, for it seems pointless to use different feature complexes to represent segment-types that are never distinguished phonetically. And yet there are cases where this would not be so, where simplicity considerations force us to maintain distinct representations of segment-types that never contrast phonetically.

In certain Russian dialects, nondiffuse (nonhigh) vowels preceded by sharp (soft) consonants in pretonic position are actualized as /i/ or as /a/ depending on the vowel under the accent. Of interest here are those among the dialects which possess the so-called "seven vowel system," a system that is substantially identical with that presented in (14).[16] In some of these dialects, the distribution of the pretonic vowel is governed by the rule:

> after sharp consonants, nondiffuse vowels in pretonic posi-
> tion are pronounced /i/ if the accented vowel is compact   (28)
> (/ɔ a æ/), otherwise they are pronounced /a/

In these dialects, which are subject to what is technically known as "dissimilative jakan'e of the Obojansk type," we find, therefore, that /s,ɔl'o/ *village* (nom. sg.) is pronounced [s,al'o], whereas /s,ɔl'ɔm/ *village* (instr. sg.) is pronounced [s,il'ɔm]. In

---

[16] The phoneme that derives historically from /o/ under rising tone is represented in (14) as /o/ and the reflex of the so-called "jat'" is represented in (14) as /e/. Other reflexes of Old Russian /o/ and /e/ and of the strong *jers* are represented in (14) by /ɔ/ and /æ/, respectively. I regard therefore the distinction between the two types of /o/ and of /e/, as one of noncompact *versus* compact, rather than as one of tense *versus* lax, as is done in most dialectological studies. I hope to justify this departure from tradition in a study now in preparation, in which, incidentally, I shall also try to show that the "dissimilative jakan'e of the Žizdra type" is a special case of (28). See now my "Akan'e: the treatment of nondiffuse unstressed vowels in Southern Russian dialects," (in press).

some of these dialects, the distinction between compact /ɔ/ and /æ/ and noncompact /o/ and /e/ is lost, yet the vowels in pretonic position are treated as before; e.g., [s,il'ɔm] but [s,al'ɔ]. In such dialects, therefore, phonetically identical segments —[ɔ]— produce distinct results in the distribution of the pretonic vowel. If the distinction between these etymologically distinct yet phonetically identical vowels were to be eliminated from the representation of morphemes, the statement of the distribution of the pretonic vowel (28) would become hopelessly complex.[17] Considerations of simplicity would dictate that the distinction between the respective segment-types be maintained and that their phonetic coalescence be accounted for by adding to the end of the grammar the rule:

$$[-\text{compact}] \rightarrow [+\text{compact}] \text{ in the environment } \begin{bmatrix} +\text{vocalic} \\ -\text{consonantal} \\ -\text{diffuse} \end{bmatrix} \quad (29)$$

XII

The two possibilities discussed in Sections X and XI—that of adding rules to the grammar at places other than the end and that of maintaining a phonemic distinction in the dictionary even when the distinction is not directly present in any utterance— suggest that phonemes that have fallen together at one stage in the evolution of a language may at a later stage emerge again as completely distinct entities. The point being made here is that it is not only that phoneme types that have merged at one stage may re-appear at a later stage, but that the re-emerging phonemes correspond precisely to their historical antecedents which had previously coalesced. The latter development has usually been regarded as impossible on theoretical grounds, yet if our theory is correct such developments are anything but impossible.

As an hypothetical example, consider a language containing the seven vowel system shown in (14) which is subject to the phonetic rule (23) causing all reflexes of

---

[17]These phenomena have recently been discussed by K. F. Zaxarova "Arxaičeskie tipy dissimiljati-vnogo jakan'ja v govorax Belgorodskoj i Voronežskoj oblastej," *Materialy i issledovanija po russkoj dialektologii* (Moscow, 1959), with the significant comment that *"jakan'e* of the Obojansk type can continue to exist in dialects in which the system of stressed vowels corresponding to [this type of *jakan'e*—M. H.] is being or has already been lost." (p. 21).

Cases where distinct morphophonemic processes take place in what from a phonetic point of view are indistinguishable contexts are by no means rare. An intricate example is discussed by N. Chomsky and me in our forthcoming *Sound Pattern of English*. We show that, in order to account for the different stress patterns of such pairs as *hyperbola* and *avocado*, for the difference in vowel length in such pairs as *balm* and *bomb*, and for a few other phenomena, it is necessary to maintain a distinction between lax /ɔ/ and tense /ā/ even in General American where these two segment types are phonetically never distinct.

A third example is provided by those Northern Russian dialects in which the affricate /c/ has become /s/. The distinction between affricate and continuant must, however, be marked in the dictionary in order to account for the fact that in position before /e/, the /s/ which is the reflex of the affricate /c/ is not sharped, whereas the reflex of the continuant is sharped; e.g. (prep. sg), /l,is'e/ *fox* and /l,ic'e/ *face* are implemented phonetically as [l,is,'ɛ] and [l,is'ɛ], respectively. Cf. V. G. Orlova, *Istorija affrikat v russkom jazyke* (Moscow, 1959), especially pp. 164–166.

/a/ to merge into /æ/. Suppose that (23) were to be modified as shown in (30) by the addition of subpart (d*) before subpart (b) rather than after subpart (c):

$$
\left\{
\begin{array}{ll}
\text{a.} & [+\text{compact}] \rightarrow [-\text{diffuse}] \\
\text{b.} & [X] \rightarrow \begin{bmatrix} -\text{nasal} \\ -\text{strident} \\ +\text{voiced} \\ +\text{continuant} \\ -\text{grave} \end{bmatrix} \\
\text{d*.} & \begin{bmatrix} -\text{flat} \\ +\text{compact} \\ -\text{grave} \end{bmatrix} \rightarrow [-\text{compact}] \\
\text{c.} & [+\text{flat}] \rightarrow [+\text{grave}]
\end{array}
\right\}
\text{ in the } env.\ \begin{bmatrix} \overline{+\text{vocalic}} \\ -\text{consonantal} \end{bmatrix} \quad (30)
$$

Observe that before the addition of subpart (d*) the original seven vowels are phonetically actualized as follows:

$$
\begin{array}{ccccccc}
i & e & æ & a & ɔ & o & u \\
| & | & \vee & & | & | & | \\
i & e & æ & & ɔ & o & u
\end{array}
\qquad (31)
$$

As a result of adding (d*), which coalesces /æ/ → /e/, the original seven vowels are implemented as follows:

$$
\begin{array}{ccccccc}
i & e & æ & a & ɔ & o & u \\
| & | & / & / & | & | & | \\
i & e & & æ & ɔ & o & u
\end{array}
\qquad (32)
$$

Observe that the changes cannot be explained if it is assumed that because (23) eliminates the phonetic distinction between /æ/ and /a/, this distinction is also lost in the representation of all morphemes, so that the phonemic system corresponding to (23) is that given in the lower row of (31). No difficulties are experienced in accounting for the change if we postulate that, for reasons of the kind discussed in Section XI, /a/ and /æ/ remained distinct entities even though every /a/ was actualized phonetically as /æ/. Subpart (d*), which was introduced at a later point in time, could then affect the original seven vowels as shown in (32).[18]

The example just reviewed suggests a possible solution to some of the traditional puzzles of historical linguistics. Thus, for example, it is well known that in Elizabethan English, the reflexes of Middle English long /ǣ/ rime with the reflexes of Middle English long /ā/, both of which are assumed to have become /ē/; e.g., *beat* rimes with *late* rather than with *feet*. In the late seventeenth century, a radical change is found; reflexes of /ǣ/ now rime with those of /ē/ rather than with those of /ā/. To account for this, we assume that Middle English had a tense vowel system like that

---

[18]We are not taking into consideration here the fact that after the addition of subpart (d*), simplicity considerations may lead us to postulate a six vowel system like that in the lower row of Eq. (32) and to revise radically Rule (30). This would not affect the grammar of the carriers of the change, but only that of their children. Since it is the change itself that is of interest here, rather than its consequences for the speech of the next generation, the simplifications in the grammar of the later generations are of no relevance.

in (14) and, moreover, that in the Early Modern English period, this tense vowel system was subject to (23), now appropriately modified to affect tense vowels only, which caused /ā/ → /æ/ [cf. (31)]. We then postulate that the Great Vowel Shift operated on this system, thereby yielding the following reflexes of the original seven vowels:

$$
\begin{array}{ccccccc}
i & e & æ & a & ɔ & o & u \\
| & | & | & / & | & | & | \\
aj & & i & e & & o & u & aw \\
\end{array}
\tag{33}
$$

which are the long vowels of Shakespeare and his contemporaries. Assume further that the various morphophonemic processes of English, in particular the shortening of long vowels which played such a major role in derivational morphology, required the maintenance of the original seven vowel system in spite of the rather radical transformations effected by the phonetic rules which now include not only (23) but also the analogue of the Great Vowel Shift. The changes in the late seventeenth century can then be accounted for by postulating the addition of (d*) to (23); i.e., the replacement of (23) by (30). Operating on the original seven vowel system of (14), (30) followed by the Vowel Shift rule yields the following correspondences:

$$
\begin{array}{ccccccc}
i & e & æ & a & ɔ & o & u \\
| & | & / & / & | & | & | \\
aj & & i & & e & o & u & aw \\
\end{array}
\tag{34}
$$

which are the reflexes of the Middle English long vowels in the language of today.[19]

---

[19]The comments on the history of English are meant to be merely suggestive. A detailed study of this topic is being planned by my colleague S. J. Keyser.

IV

EXTENSIONS OF GRAMMAR

A grammar describes syntactic structure *within* the boundaries of single sentences. (In particular, it describes constituent structure and transformational relations.) But grammar says nothing about the relations *between* sentences in a stretch of intelligible discourse. Thus, one natural way grammatical analysis might be extended is by developing a theory which represents whatever structural relations between sentences obtain by virtue of the fact that the sentences form a connected discourse (as opposed to a random assortment of sentences). This program of extending grammatical analysis beyond sentence boundaries in order to describe how the sentences of a coherent discourse interconnect and interrelate to carry the information that the discourse conveys was first suggested by Zellig Harris in "Discourse Analysis."

The study of structural relations between sentences in a discourse, if it should prove fruitful, obviously has serious consequences for such areas as information retrieval, mechanical translation, and stylistics. But it also has important implications for philosophy. Harris has himself suggested that discourse analysis may enable us to determine the conditions under which a pair of terms are synonymous in a given discourse. Such a notion of local synonymity would do many of the things that have traditionally been required of the concept of synonymity. In particular, it would yield a well-defined notion of analytic sentence, though only relative to given discourses.

Moreover, a theory of discourse analysis would enable us to explain how speakers resolve grammatical ambiguities in a sentence when such resolution turns on features of the sentence's context in a discourse. For example, consider the stretch of discourse ". . . . The man tried to stop cursing. But he was unable to restrain himself and was eventually arrested for profanity." In isolation, the sentence "the man tried to stop cursing." is grammatically ambiguous. But, embedded in the above context, it is only read in one way. A system of discourse analysis should explicate the mechanism of such contextual disambiguation and show how to justify the claim that a certain sentence is to be read in such-and-such a way in such-and-such a discourse.

Finally, discourse analysis may afford a more complete theory of cognitive significance than any so far proposed. The theories of cognitive significance proposed to date are, without exception, constructed to deal with only single sentences in isolation from context. Hence, they fail to cover cases of nonsignificance of discourses where each sentence of the discourse is meaningful but where the sentences are incoherently arranged. Presumably, a theory of discourse analysis would set forth the conditions under which such failures of significance occur.

Another way grammatical analysis may be extended is by adding to the grammar a theory which describes the structure of semi-grammatical strings of words. That such a theory is properly a part of linguistics follows from two considerations: first, that linguistics seeks to describe whatever the speaker knows about the structure of his language, enabling him to use and understand it; and second, that speakers can use and understand strings of words which, although they are not fully grammatical, are not fully ungrammatical either. A theory which accounts for this ability would seek to explain the respects in which semi-grammatical strings diverge from the norm of full grammaticality and the respects in which they do not. For example, the semi sentence *John frightens sincerity* may be characterized as grammatical in one respect—it is an instance of the grammatical structure Noun + Verb + Object—and ungrammatical in another—it violates the grammatical restriction that the verb *frightens* takes animate objects.

Like the extension of grammatical analysis to discourse analysis, the extension to semi sentences promises important consequences for philosophy. The most direct consequence is for the construction of a criterion of cognitive significance. Marhenke, was, as far as we are aware, the first philosopher to notice this.

> . . . Though every sentence is a string of words, not every string of words is a sentence, for a sentence may be either grammatical or ungrammatical, and some strings of words are neither. A sentence is ungrammatical if it resembles, in a certain degree, a correctly constituted sentence. How great a departure from the grammatical norm is permissible before a string of words ceases to be an ungrammatical sentence we do not need to decide: we may suppose that any string of words is an acceptable sentence if a grammarian finds it possible to restore it to grammatical correctness. Now, although compliance with the rules of grammar is not a necessary condition of significance, the transformability of an ungrammatical sentence into one that is grammatically sound is a necessary condition of significance. A string of words that fails to satisfy this condition is not a sentence and hence meaningless.*

The present section presents Harris' original paper on discourse analysis and three papers on the topic of semi-grammaticality which represent different approaches to the problem of describing the native speaker's ability to use and understand sentences that are not fully grammatical.

---

*P. Marhenke, "The Criterion of Significance," in *Semantics and the Philosophy of Language*, ed. L. Linsky (Urbana, Ill.: University of Illinois Press, 1952), p. 141.

11   Discourse Analysis*

Zellig S. Harris

This paper presents a method for the analysis of connected speech (or writing).[1] The method is formal, depending only on the occurrence of morphemes as distinguishable elements; it does not depend upon the analyst's knowledge of the particular meaning of each morpheme. By the same token, the method does not give us any new information about the individual morphemic meanings that are being communicated in the discourse under investigation. But the fact that such new information is not obtained does not mean that we can discover nothing about the discourse but how the grammar of the language is exemplified within it. For even though we use formal procedures akin to those of descriptive linguistics, we can obtain new information about the particular text we are studying, information that goes beyond descriptive linguistics.

This additional information results from one basic fact: the analysis of the occurrence of elements in the text is applied only in respect to that text alone—that is, in respect to the other elements in the same text and not in respect to anything else in the language. As a result of this, we discover the particular interrelations of the morphemes of the text as they occur in that one text; and in so doing we discover something of the structure of the text, of what is being done in it. We may not know just WHAT a text is saying, but we can discover HOW it is saying—what are the patterns of recurrence of its chief morphemes.

Definite patterns may be discovered for particular texts, or for particular persons, styles, or subject-matters. In some cases, formal conclusions can be drawn from

---

*Z. S. Harris, "Discourse Analysis," *Language*, **28** (1952), 1–30. Reprinted by permission.

[1]It is a pleasure to acknowledge here the cooperation of three men who have collaborated with me in developing the method and in analyzing various texts: Fred Lukoff, Noam Chomsky, and A. F. Brown. Earlier investigations in the direction of this method have been presented by Lukoff, "Preliminary analysis of the linguistic structure of extended discourse," University of Pennsylvania Library (1948). A detailed analysis of a sample text has appeared in Z. Harris, "Discourse Analysis: A Sample Text," *Language*, **28**, No. 4 (1952), 474.

the particular pattern of morpheme distribution in a text. And often it is possible to show consistent differences of structure between the discourses of different persons or in different styles or about different subject matters.

PRELIMINARIES

1 The problem. One can approach discourse analysis from two types of problem, which turn out to be related. The first is the problem of continuing descriptive linguistics beyond the limits of a single sentence at a time. The other is the question of correlating "culture" and language (i.e., nonlinguistic and linguistic behavior).

The first problem arises because descriptive linguistics generally stops at sentence boundaries. This is not due to any prior decision. The techniques of linguistics were constructed to study any stretch of speech, of whatever length. But in every language it turns out that almost all the results lie within a relatively short stretch, which we may call a sentence. That is, when we can state a restriction on the occurrence of element A in respect to the occurrence of element B, it will almost always be the case that A and B are regarded as occurring within the same sentence. Of English adjectives, for instance, we can say that they occur before a noun or after certain verbs (in the same sentence): *the dark clouds, the future seems bright*; only rarely can we state restrictions across sentence boundaries, e.g., that if the main verb of one sentence has a given tense-suffix, the main verb of the next sentence will have a particular other tense-suffix. We cannot say that if one sentence has the form NV, the next sentence will have the form N. We can only say that most sentences are NV, some are N, and so on; and that these structures occur in various sequences.

In this way descriptive linguistics, which sets out to describe the occurrence of elements in any stretch of speech, ends up by describing it primarily in respect to other elements of the same sentence. This limitation has not seemed too serious, because it has not precluded the writing of adequate grammars: the grammar states the sentence structure; the speaker makes up a particular sentence in keeping with this structure and supplies the particular sequence of sentences.

The other problem, that of the connection between behavior (or social situation) and language, has always been considered beyond the scope of linguistics proper. Descriptive linguistics has not dealt with the meanings of morphemes; and though one might try to get around that by speaking not of meanings, but of the social and interpersonal situation in which speech occurs, descriptive linguistics has had no equipment for taking the social situation into account: it has only been able to state the occurrence of one linguistic element in respect to the occurrence of others. Culture-and-language studies have therefore been carried on without benefit of the recent distributional investigations of linguistics. For example, they list the meanings expressed in the language by surveying the vocabulary stock; or, they draw conclusions from the fact that in a particular language a particular set of meanings is expressed by the same morpheme; or, they discuss the nuances of meaning and usage of one word in comparison with others (e.g., in stylistics). Culture-and-language studies have also noted such points as that phrases are to be taken in their total meaning rather than as the sum of the meanings of their component morphemes, e.g., that *How are you* is a greeting rather than a question about health—an example that illustrates the correlation of speech with social situation. Similarly, personality characteristics in speech have been studied by correlating an individual's recurrent speech features with recurrent features of his behavior and feeling.[2]

2 Distribution within discourse. Distributional or combinatorial analysis within one discourse at a time turns out to be relevant to both of these problems.

On the one hand, it carries us past the sentence limitation of descriptive linguistics. Although we cannot state the distribution of sentences (or, in general, any inter-sentence relation) when we are given an arbitrary conglomeration of sentences in a language, we can get quite definite results about certain relations across sentence boundaries when we consider just the sentences of a particular connected discourse —that is, the sentences spoken or written in succession by one or more persons in a single situation. This restriction to connected discourse does not detract from the usefulness of the analysis, since all language occurrences are internally connected. Language does not occur in stray words or sentences, but in connected discourse— from a one-word utterance to a ten-volume work, from a monolog to a Union Square argument. Arbitrary conglomerations of sentences are indeed of no interest except as a check on grammatical description; and it is not surprising that we cannot find interdependence among the sentences of such an aggregate. The successive sentences of a connected discourse, however, offer fertile soil for the methods of descriptive linguistics, since these methods study the relative distribution of elements within a connected stretch of speech.

On the other hand, distributional analysis within one discourse at a time yields information about certain correlations of language with other behavior. The reason is that each connected discourse occurs within a particular situation—whether of a person speaking or of a conversation or of someone sitting down occasionally over a period of months to write a particular kind of book in a particular literary or scientific tradition. To be sure, this concurrence between situation and discourse does not mean that discourses occurring in similar situations must necessarily have certain formal characteristics in common, while discourses occurring in different situations must have certain formal differences. The concurrence between situation and discourse only makes it understandable, or possible, that such formal correlations should exist.

It remains to be shown as a matter of empirical fact that such formal correlations do indeed exist, that the discourses of a particular person, social group, style, or subject matter exhibit not only particular meanings (in their selection of morphemes) but also characteristic formal features. The particular selection of morphemes cannot be considered here. But the formal features of the discourses can be studied by distributional methods within the text; and the fact of their correlation with a particular type of situation gives a meaning-status to the occurrence of these formal features.

---

[2]Correlations between personality and language are here taken to be not merely related to correlations between culture and language, but actually a special case of these. The reason for this view is that most individual textual characteristics (as distinguished from phonetic characteristics) correlate with those personality features which arise out of the individual's experience with socially conditioned interpersonal situations.

3 Conjunction with grammar. The method presented here is thus seen to grow out of an application of the distributional methods of linguistics to one discourse at a time. It can be applied directly to a text, without using any linguistic knowledge about the text except the morpheme boundaries. This is possible because distributional analysis is an elementary method and involves merely the statement of the relative occurrence of elements, in this case *morphemes.* To establish the method for its own sake, or for possible application to nonlinguistic material, no prior knowledge should be used except the boundaries of the elements.

However, when we are interested not in the method alone but in its results, when we want to use the method in order to find out all that we can about a particular text, then it is useful to combine this method with descriptive linguistics. To this end we would use only those statements of the grammar of the language which are true for any sentence of a given form. For example, given any English sentence of the form N_1VN_2 (e.g., *The boss fired Jim*), we can get a sentence with the noun phrases in the reverse order N_2—N_1 (*Jim — the boss*) by changing the suffixes around the verb,[3] *Jim was fired by the boss.* The justification for using such grammatical information in the analysis of a text is that since it is applicable to any N_1VN_2 sentence in English it must also be applicable to any N_1VN_2 sentence in the particular text before us, provided only that this is written in English. The desirability of using such information is that in many cases it makes possible further applications of the discourse-analysis method.

How this happens will appear in Section 7.3; but it should be said here that such use of grammatical information does not replace work that could be done by the discourse-analysis method, nor does it alter the independence of that method. It merely transforms certain sentences of the text into grammatically equivalent sentences (as N_1VN_2 above was transformed into $N_2V^*N_1$), in such a way that the application of the discourse-analysis method becomes more convenient, or that it becomes possible in particular sections of the text where it was not possible to apply it before. And it will be seen that the decision where and how to apply these grammatical transformations need not be arbitrary but can be determined by the structure of the text itself.

The applicability of the discourse-analysis method in particular texts can be further increased if we not only use the ordinary results of grammar but also extend descriptive linguistics to deal with the special distributions of individual morphemes. There are cases, as will be seen in Section 7.3, when we would like to use information not about all the morphemes of some class (like the transformability of V into V^*) but about a particular member of the class, about a restriction of occurrence which is true for that one morpheme but not for the others of its class. Such information is not in general available today; but it can be obtained by methods which are basically those of descriptive linguistics.

Finally, the applicability of discourse analysis in particular texts can sometimes be increased if we draw our information not only from the grammar of the language

---

[3]When the verb is transformed to suit such an inversion of subject (N_1 above) and object (N_2), we may call the new verb form the conjugate of the original form and write it V^*. Then an active verb has a passive verb as its conjugate, and a passive verb has an active verb as its conjugate.

but also from a descriptive analysis of the body of speech or writing of which our text is a part. This larger body of material may be looked upon as the dialect within which the text was spoken or written, and we can say as before that any distributional statement which is true for all sentences of a given form in that dialect will also hold for any sentence of that form in the text under consideration.

THE METHOD

4 The nature of the method. We have raised two problems: that of the distributional relations among sentences and that of the correlation between language and social situation. We have proposed that information relevant to both of these problems can be obtained by a formal analysis of one stretch of discourse at a time. What KIND of analysis would be applicable here? To decide this, we consider what is permitted by the material.

Since the material is simply a string of linguistic forms arranged in successive sentences, any formal analysis is limited to locating linguistic elements within these sentences—that is, to stating the occurrence of elements. We cannot set up any method for investigating the nature or composition of these elements, or their correlations with nonlinguistic features, unless we bring in new information from outside.

Furthermore, there are no particular elements, say *but* or *I* or *communism*, which have a prior importance, such as would cause us to be interested in the mere fact of their presence or absence in our text. Any analysis which aimed to find out whether certain particular words, selected by the investigator, occur in the text or not, would be an investigation of the CONTENT of the text and would be ultimately based on the MEANINGS of the words selected. If we do not depend upon meaning in our investigation, then the only morphemes or classes which we can deal with separately are those which have grammatically stated peculiarities of distribution.

Since, then, we are not in general interested in any particular element selected in advance, our interest in those elements that do occur cannot be merely in the tautologic statement THAT they occur, but in the empirical statement of HOW they occur: which ones occur next to which others, or in the same environment as which others, and so on—that is, in the relative occurrence of these elements with respect to each other. In this sense, our method is comparable to that which is used, in the case of a whole language, in compiling a grammar (which states the distributional relations among elements), rather than in compiling a dictionary (which lists all the elements that are found in the language, no matter where).

Finally, since our material is a closed string of sentences, our statement about the distribution of each element can only be valid within the limits of this succession of sentences, whether it be a paragraph or a book. We will see in Section 7.3 that we can sometimes use information about the distribution of an element outside our material; but this can be only an external aid, brought in after the distribution of the element within the discourse has been completely stated.

5 General statement of the method. It follows from all this that our method will have to provide statements of the occurrence of elements and, in particular, of the relative occurrence of all the elements of a discourse within the limits of that one discourse.

5.1 *Elements in Identical Environments.* We could satisfy this requirement by setting up detailed statements of the distribution of each element within the discourse, just as in descriptive linguistics we could set up individual statements summarizing all the environments (i.e., the distribution) of each element in various sentences of the language. However, such individual statements are unmanageably large for a whole language and are unwieldy even for a single text. In both cases, moreover, the individual statements are an inconvenient basis for inspection and comparison and for the deriving of general statements. Therefore, in discourse analysis as in descriptive linguistics, we collect those elements which have like distributions into one class and thereafter speak of the distribution of the class as a whole rather than of each element individually.

When two elements have identical distributions, this operation of collecting presents no problem. In descriptive linguistics, however, the opportunity rarely occurs, since few words have identical distributions throughout a language.[4] It may occur more frequently in a repetitive text, where two words may be always used in identical parallel sentences—e.g., in stylistically balanced myths, in proverbs, in sloganeering speeches, and in "dry" but meticulous scientific reports.

5.2 *Elements in Equivalent Environments.* In the much more frequent case where two elements occur in environments which are almost but not quite identical, we may be able to collect them into one distributional class by setting up a chain of equivalences connecting the two almost identical environments.[5] This is done in descriptive linguistics when we say that the class of adjectives A occurs before the class of nouns N, even though a particular A (say, *voluntary*) may never occur before a particular N (say, *subjugation*). It is done in discourse analysis when we say that two stretches which have the same environment in one place are equivalent even in some other place where their environment is not the same.

Suppose our text contains the following four sentences: *The trees turn here about the middle of autumn*; *The trees turn here about the end of October*; *The first frost comes after the middle of autumn*; *We start heating after the end of October*. Then we may say that *the middle of autumn* and *the end of October* are equivalent because they occur in the same environment (*The trees turn here about—*), and that this equivalence is carried over into the latter two sentences. On that basis, we may say further that *The first frost comes* and *We start heating* occur in equivalent environments. (The additional word *after* is identical in the two environments.) Such chains, which carry over the equivalence of two stretches from one pair of sentences where their environment is indeed identical to another pair of sentences where it is not, must of course be constructed with adequate safeguards, lest everything be made equivalent to everything else and the analysis collapse. This problem appears also in setting up classes in descriptive linguistics; the kind of safeguards necessary in discourse analysis will be discussed in Section 6.1.

More generally, if we find the sequences AM and AN in our text, we say that M is equivalent to N or that M and N occur in the identical environment A, or that M

---

[4] Two personal names may have identical distributions. Thus, for every sentence containing *Bill* we may find an otherwise identical sentence containing *Jim* instead.

[5] I owe a clarification of the use of such chains to the unpublished work of Noam Chomsky.

and N both appear as the environment of the identical element (or sequence of elements) A; and we write $M = N$. Then if we find the sequence BM and CN (or MB and NC) in our text, we say that B is (secondarily) equivalent to C, since they occur in the two environments M and N which have been found to be equivalent; and we write $B = C$. If we further find BK and CL, we would write $K = L$ by virtue of their having occurred in the secondarily equivalent environments B and C; and so on. As an example, let us continue our text fragment with the following sentence: *We always have a lot of trouble when we start heating but you've got to be prepared when the first frost comes.* Then we would say that *We always have a lot of trouble* is equivalent (for this text) to *but you've got to be prepared.*

Saying that $B = C$ does not mean that they are IN GENERAL equal to each other, or that they MEAN the same thing. The equal sign is used only because the relation between B and C satisfies the technical requirements of the relation which is generally marked by that sign. All we mean when we write $B = C$ is that this relation is a step in a chain of equivalences: on the one hand, B and C are found in equivalent environments (M and N); and on the other, any two environments in which B and C are found will be considered equivalent (K and L).

It is not relevant to ask, "Is it TRUE that $B = C$?" or "Have we the RIGHT to say that $K = L$ merely because $B = C$ and because BK and CL occur?" All that is proposed here is a method of analysis; the only relevant questions are whether the method is usable and whether it leads to valid and interesting results. Whether the method is usable can be judged on the basis of its operations, without regard to its results, as yet unseen. Whether these results are of interest will be considered in Sections 8 to 10, where we will see that the chains of equivalence reveal a structure for each text. There is no question whether we have the "right" to put $K = L$, because all we indicate by $K = L$ is that BK and CL occur and that $B = C$. The justification will depend on the fact that when we put all the equivalences together we will obtain some information about the structure of the text.

5.3 *Equivalence Classes.* After discovering which sequences occur in equivalent environments, we can group all of them together into one equivalence class. In our formulaic statement we have $A = B$ (both occur before M), and $A = C$ (both before N), and $B = C$, so that we consider A, B, C all members of one equivalence class. Similarly, M, N, K, L are members of another single equivalence class. In our example, *The trees turn here in* (T_1) and *The first frost comes after* (T_2) and *We start heating after* (T_3) are all members of one equivalence class T, while *the middle of autumn* (E_1) and *the end of October* (E_2) are members of another equivalence class E. There is yet a third class E' consisting of *We always have a lot of trouble when* and *but you've got to be prepared when*. E' is obviously related to E, since both occur with the last two members of T. But E occurs AFTER T, whereas E' occurs BEFORE T.

In terms of these classes, the five sentences of our text fragment can be written as six formulas (since the last sentence was a double one): TE, TE, TE, TE, $E'T$, $E'T$. It is clear that we cannot make one class out of E and E'; but we can say that when the order of E and T is reversed (when E is *reflected* in T), we get E' instead of E. If we change the members of E' to the form they would have if they came after T instead of before, then those changed members of E' become regular members of E. For example, we might say *We start heating at the cost of a lot of trouble always, but the first frost comes in a way you've got to be prepared for.* This sentence has the form *TE TE.* The new phrase *at the cost of a lot of trouble always* is a member of *E* by virtue of its occurrence after *T*; we can mark it E_3. Of course, we must show that it is equivalent to *We always have a lot of trouble,* except for the reversed position in respect to *T*; to show this, we need techniques which will be discussed in Section 7.3. Similarly, we must show that the new *E* phrase *but . . . in a way you've got to be prepared for* (E_4) is the *T* reflection of the *E'* phrase *but you've got to be prepared when.* If we can show these two reflection-equivalences, we can replace the two *E'* phrases by the changed phrases which we get when we put them in the *E* position. As a result we have two more members of *E*, and no peculiar *E'* class.

In such ways we can set up equivalence classes (like *E*) of all sequences which have equivalent environments, i.e., the same equivalence classes on the same side (before or after), within the text. The elements (or sequences of elements) which are included in the same equivalence class may be called equivalent to, or substituents of, each other. We will see later (Section 10) that in some respects (especially in extensions of the text) they may be considered substitutable or interchangeable for each other. In that case the equivalence class may also be called a substitution class.

Note especially that the operation of grouping nonidentical forms into the same equivalence class does not depend upon disregarding small differences in meaning among them, but upon finding them in equivalent environments. This means either finding them in identical environments (*the middle of autumn* and *the end of October* both occur in the environment *The trees turn here in* —) or else finding them in environments which are at the ends of a safeguarded chain of equivalences (*The first frost comes* and *We start heating* occur in the equivalent environments *after the middle of autumn* and *after the end of October*). The method is thus fundamentally that of descriptive linguistics and not of semantics.

5.4 *Sentence Order.* At this point we come to an operation not used in descriptive linguistics: representing the order of successive occurrences of members of a class. In descriptive linguistics order comes into consideration only as the relative position of various sections of a sequence, as when the order of article and noun is described by saying that the first precedes the second along the line of a noun phrase. In discourse analysis we have this kind of order as among the sections of a sentence, e.g., the different orders of *E* and *E'* in respect to *T*.

The order of successive sentences, or of some particular word class in various sentences (say, the relation of successive subjects), is not generally relevant to descriptive linguistics, because its distributional statements are normally valid within only one sentence at a time. Here, however, where we are dealing with a whole discourse at once, this problem is a real one. If we were considering each sentence separately and relating it to others only for purposes of structural comparison, we could say (as in descriptive linguistics) that each sentence in our text fragment consists of *TE*. But since we are speaking of the text as a whole, we cannot say that it consists merely of *TE* six times over. The particular members of *E* and of *T* are different in the various sentences; and these differences may be (for all we know) peculiar to this text, or to a group of similar texts.

Our text fragment can be structurally represented by a double array, the horizontal axis indicating the material that occurs within a single sentence or subsentence, and the vertical axis (here broken into two parts) indicating the successive sentences:

$$T_1 E_1 \qquad T_3 E_2$$
$$T_1 E_2 \qquad T_3 E_3$$
$$T_2 E_1 \qquad T_2 E_4$$

In this double array, the various symbols in one horizontal row represent the various sections of a single sentence or subsentence of the text, in the order in which they occur in the sentence (except insofar as the order has been altered by explicit transformations in the course of reducing to symbols, as in the change from E' to E). The vertical columns indicate the various members of an equivalence class, in the order of the successive sentences in which they occur.

The reason the order of symbols in a row may differ from the order of elements in a sentence is that our linguistic knowledge of sentence structure enables us to deal with the elements separately from their order. We do this when we disregard in our symbols any order that is automatic and that would re-appear as soon as our symbols are translated back into language, as when *but* . . . is included in E_4 even though it is necessarily separated from E_4 in the actual sentence (since *but* generally occurs at the beginning of a sentence structure, no matter which section of the sentence it may be related to). We also perform this separation of elements from their order when we replace some nonautomatic order which has morphemic value by the morphemes which are grammatically equivalent to it; for example, when we replace $N_1 V N_2$ by $N_2 V^* N_1$ (replacing *The boss fired Jim* by *Jim was fired by the boss*); or when, in our text fragment, E' before T is replaced by E after T.

In contrast with this cavalier treatment of horizontal order, we cannot alter anything about the order within a vertical column. Here we have no prior linguistic knowledge to tell us which orderings of sentences (if any) are automatic and therefore not to be represented, or which orderings can be replaced by different but equivalent orderings. A closer study of sentence sequences in the language may some day give us such information in the future; for instance, to take a very simple case, it might show that sentence sequences of the form *P because Q* are equivalent to sequences of the form *Q so P*, or that *P and Q* is interchangeable with *Q and P* (whereas *P but Q* may not be similarly interchangeable with *Q but P*).[6] Furthermore, a closer study of a particular text, or of texts of a particular type, may show that certain whole sequences of sentences are equivalent or interchangeable; and with this information we may be able to simplify the vertical axis of the double array, for example, by finding periodically repeated vertical patterns. Pending such specific information, however, the vertical axis is an exact reproduction of the order of the sentences or sub sentences in the text.

5.5 *Summary.* We can now survey the whole method as follows. We call elements (sections of the text—morphemes or morpheme sequences) equivalent to each other if they occur in the environment of (other) identical or equivalent elements.

---

[6]Mathematics, and to a greater extent logic, have already set up particular sentence orders which are equivalent to each other. This equivalence can be rediscovered linguistically by finding that the distribution of each sequence is equivalent to that of the others. Our interest here, however, is to discover other equivalences than those which we already know to have been explicitly built into a system.

Each set of mutually equivalent elements is called an equivalence class. Each successive sentence of the text is then represented as a sequence of equivalence classes, namely those to which its various sections belong. We thus obtain for the whole text a double array, the horizontal axis representing the equivalence classes contained in one sentence and the vertical axis representing successive sentences. This is a tabular arrangement not of sentence structures (subjects, verbs, and the like), but of the patterned occurrence of the equivalence classes through the text.

If the different sentences contain completely different classes, the tabular arrangement is of no interest; but this is generally not the case. In almost every text there are passages in which particular equivalence classes recur, in successive sentences, in some characteristic pattern. The tabular arrangement makes it possible to inspect this pattern; and we can derive from it various kinds of information about the text, certain structural analyses of the text, and certain critiques of the text. For the equivalence classes, which are set up distributionally, the tabular arrangement shows the distribution. For the text as a whole, the tabular arrangement shows certain features of structure.

6 Procedure. We will now illustrate the procedure in detail by applying it to a specific text, of a type as common today as any other that reaches print.[7]

Millions Can't Be Wrong!

Millions of consumer bottles of X– have been sold since its introduction a few years ago. And four out of five people in a nationwide survey say they prefer X– to any hair tonic they've used. Four out of five people in a nationwide survey can't be wrong. You too and your whole family will prefer X– to any hair tonic you've used! Every year we sell more bottles of X– to satisfied customers. You too will be satisfied!

6.1 *Determining the Equivalence Classes.* The first step in discourse analysis is to decide which elements are to be taken as equivalent to each other, i.e., placed in the same column of the tabular arrangement. This is not always automatic—simply a matter of finding which elements have identical environments; for (1) there may be several ways of breaking a sentence down into equivalent parts, and (2) we must decide which way to look for the less obvious equivalence chains.

The simplest starting point is to consider the more frequently repeated words of the text. Almost every text has particular words which occur a great many times;[8] and these will often be key words of that text. The various occurrences of such a

---

[7]This is the actual text of an advertisement, found on a card which had presumably been attached to a bottle of hair tonic. A considerable number of advertisements have been analyzed, because they offer repetitive and transparent material which is relatively easy to handle at this stage of our experience with discourse analysis. Many other kinds of texts have been analyzed as well—sections of textbooks, conversations, essays, and so on; and a collection of these will be published soon.

[8]This will be true, though to a lesser extent, even in the writing of those who obey the school admonition to use synonyms instead of repeating a word. In such cases the synonyms will often be found in the same environments as the original not-to-be-repeated word. In contrast, when a writer has used a different word because he intends the particular difference in meaning expressed by it, the synonym will often occur in correspondingly different environments from the original word.

word can certainly be put into one column, i.e., one equivalence class. And the neighboring words can be put into another single equivalence class because they occur in identical environments. In our text no key words are apparent; but we can start with the identical, and hence of course equivalent, repeated sequence *can't be wrong*. Then *Millions* is equivalent (for this text) to *Four out of five people in a nationwide survey*, since both occur before that sequence.

This first step might of course also be performed for such repeated words as *of*. But if we were to collect all the environments of the word *of*, we could not use the resulting equivalence class to build up a chain of further equivalences, because nothing else would be found in their environment. Whereas the class containing *millions* and *four out of five* . . . , which we obtain from repetitions of *can't be wrong*, will be found, in later paragraphs, to tie up with other sections of this text.

From this utilization of repetitions we go on to construct chains of equivalence—that is, we ask what other environments occur for *Millions* and for *Four out of five* . . . . For *Millions* we have one other environment, namely *of consumer bottles*, etc. It will turn out in our further work (Section 9) that this environment clashes with the environments of *Four out of five* . . . . Therefore, we will tentatively set aside the sequence *of consumer bottles*, etc. As for *Four out of five people in a nationwide survey*, we find it in one other environment: before *say they prefer X– to any hair tonic they've used*.

We proceed along this equivalence chain by looking for some other environment in which *say they prefer X–* . . . occurs. There is one such occurrence, but it differs by having *you* where the first occurrence has *they*. At first it seems that this difference makes it impossible for us to consider the two sequences equivalent, since our method provides for no approximation technique, no measurement of more and less difference, such as might permit us to say that these two sequences are similar enough to be considered equivalent. Indeed, since we do not operate with the meanings of the morphemes, the replacing of *they* by *you* might constitute a great difference (as it would if the whole text dealt with the distinction between *you* and *they*). As they stand, therefore, these two sequences would be left unrelated by our method; at most that method could separate out the identical and the different portions. It so happens, however, that a little consideration shows these two sequences to be contextually identical—that is, identical in respect to their relevant environment or context. This will be seen in Section 7.1.

In constructing chains of equivalence the first safeguard is adherence to the formal requirements of the method. If we never make any approximations, never overlook some "small" difference in environment, we will be certain that any two members of one equivalence class have at least one environment in common. If we wish to put two elements into one class even though no environment of one is identical with some environment of the other, it will have to be at the cost of some explicit assumption, added to the method, which equates the two environments or nullifies their difference.

The final factor in our decision to include or not to include two elements in one equivalence class is the way the resulting class will function in the analysis of the text, i.e., the kind of double array we get by using that class. This factor must play a part, since there are often various possible chains of equivalence that equally satisfy our method. The criterion is not some external consideration like getting the longest possible chain, but rather the intrinsic consideration of finding some patterned distribution of these classes, i.e., finding some structural fact about the text in terms of these classes. In other words, we try to set up such classes as will have an interesting distribution in our particular text. This may seem a rather circular safeguard for constructing equivalence chains. But it simply means that whenever we have to decide whether to carry an equivalence chain one step further, we exercise the foresight of considering how the new interval will fit into our analyzed text as it appears when represented in terms of the new class. This kind of consideration occurs in descriptive linguistics when we have to decide, for example, how far to subdivide a phonemic sequence into morphemes.[9]

One might ask what right we have to put two words into one equivalence class merely because they both occur in the same environment. The answer is that the equivalence class indicates no more than the distributional work which its members do in the text. If the two words occur only in identical or equivalent environments in this text, then in this text there is no difference in their distribution (aside from their order in the column, which is preserved). We are not denying any difference in meaning, or in distribution outside this text.

So far we have recognized two equivalence classes. One, which we will mark *P*, at present includes:

Millions
Four out of five people in a nationwide survey

The other, which we will mark *W*, at present includes

can't be wrong
say they prefer X– to any hair tonic they've used.

6.2 *Segmentation.* Once we have a rough idea of what equivalence classes we wish to try out in our text, we segment the text into successive intervals in such a way as to get, in each interval, like occurrences of the same equivalence classes. If our classes so far are *P* and *W*, and if we have a few *PW* successions, we try to segment into intervals each containing precisely one *P* and one *W*. For example, the title of the advertisement is represented by *PW*. The first sentence after the title seems to contain a *P* (the word *Millions*), but the rest of the sentence neither equals nor contains *W*; hence the sentence is as yet unanalyzed, and even its *P* is in doubt.

Assignment of an element to a particular class is always relative to the assignment of its environment. The elements are not defined except in relation to their environment. For all we know, *Millions* in this sentence might not even be the same word as *Millions* in the title. In descriptive linguistics two phonemically identical segments are the same morpheme only if they occur in the same morpheme class: *sun* and *son* would presumably have to be considered the "same" morpheme, no less than *table* (of wood) and *table* (of statistical data). If they occur in different morpheme classes,

---

[9]Cf. Harris, *Methods in Structural Linguistics*, p. 160 (Chicago, 1951). It goes without saying that this vague use of foresight is a preliminary formulation. Detailed investigations will show what may be expected from different kinds of equivalence chains and will thus make possible a more precise formulation of safeguards.

e.g., *sea* and *see*, they certainly are not the same morpheme; and if we want to keep in view the connection between (*a*) *table* and (*to*) *table*, we have to speak of classed and unclassed morphemes and say that the unclassed morpheme *table* appears both in the *N* class and in the *V* class. Similarly, if *Millions* occurs twice we try to consider it a repeated "same" morpheme (hence in the same class), and so consider its two environments equivalent. But we may find later that a better text-analysis is obtained by not considering those two environments equivalent (because the first environment is equivalent to one sequence *A* in the text, while the second is equivalent to a different sequence *B* which is not equivalent to *A*). In that case we may have to consider the two occurrences of *Millions* as belonging to two different classes. In Section 9, we will find this to be the case here.

To return to our segmentation. The second sentence in our text is *PW*, and the third is *PW*. Hence we try to segment our text into successive stretches each of which will contain just *PW* and no more. These stretches will then be the successive rows of our double array. They will often be whole sentences, but not necessarily: they may also be the separate sections of a compound sentence, each of which has its own sentence structure (as in the two *E'T* of Section 5.3). But they may also be any other stretches taken out of the sentence. For example, if we found in our advertisement the sentence *Millions of people—four out of five—can't be wrong when they say they prefer X–*, which as it stands seems to consist of *PPWW*, we would try to reduce it to two *PW* intervals. Such less obvious segmentations require care, since we want not only the *P* and the *W* occurrences to be the same in each interval, but also the relation between *P* and *W* to be the same. When each whole sentence in a string is reduced to *PW*, the relation between *P* and *W* in each interval is the same; from descriptive linguistics we know it is the relation of subject to predicate. We do not need to use this specific information in tabulating our text as a succession of *PW*, but we do assume that whatever the relation between *P* and *W* in one interval, it is the same in all the other intervals. Otherwise we would be wrong in saying, when we see such a double array as the successive *TE* of Section 5.4, that the successive intervals are identical in terms of *T* and *E*. Techniques for checking the sameness of the relation between the equivalence classes in each row will be discussed in Sections 7.2 and 7.3.

6.3 *Sets of Like Segments*. The attempt to divide a text into intervals containing the same equivalence classes (in the same relation to each other) will not generally succeed throughout a whole text. There may be individual sentences here and there which simply do not contain these classes. These may turn out to be introductory sentences or offshoots of some other set of equivalence classes. And there may be successive sections of the text, each of which contains its own equivalence classes different from those of other sections. These may be paragraph-like or chapter-like subtexts within the main text.

In the course of seeking intervals which contain the same classes, our procedures will discover the limits of this sameness, i.e., the points at which we get text-intervals containing different classes. In the general case, then, a text will be reduced not to a single set of identical rows (each row, like *TE*, representing an interval with the same equivalence classes), but to a succession of sets of identical rows, with occasional individually different rows occurring at one point or another.

Having obtained this result, we compare the various sets and individual rows to see what similarities and differences exist among them in the arrangement of their classes, whether the specific classes are different or not. We try to discover patterns in the occurrence of such similarities among the successive sets and individually different rows. For example, let a text come out to be *AB TE TE TE A'B' EP EP AB KD LM LM K'D' MS MS MS FBV MS*. Then, using [*TE*] to indicate a set of *TE* intervals, and temporarily disregarding the *FBV*, we can represent the text by *AB*[*TE*] *A'B'* [*EP*] *AB KD* [*LM*] *K'D'* [*MS*]. We note, further, that *AB* [*TE*] *A'B'* [*EP*] and *KD* [*LM*] *K'D'* [*MS*] are structurally identical: both have the form *w* [*xy*] *w'* [*yz*]. This form is a particular relation of *w*, *x*, *y*, and *z*. Our text consists of two occurrences of this structure, with the *w* of the first occurrence (that is, the *AB*) appearing again between the two structures (or before the second structure), and with a unique *FBV* before the end of the last structure.

7 Accessory techniques. The main procedure, as described in the foregoing section, must be refined and supplemented by a number of accessory techniques.

7.1 *Independent Occurrence*. The distribution of equivalence classes (their pattern of occurrence), and the segmentation of intervals containing them, depend on what we recognize as an occurrence of an element. At first sight, this would seem to be trivial: in the stretch *say they prefer X– to any hair tonic they've used* we obviously find *say* once, *they* twice, and so on. Closer consideration, however, will show that not all occurrences of elements are independent: there are some elements which occur, in a given environment, only when some other element is present. This situation is known from descriptive linguistics; for example, the *-s* of *he walks* is taken not as an independent element but as an automatic concomitant of *he*, by comparison with *I walk, you walk*;[10] and in forms like *both he and I* the *and* always occurs if *both* is present, so that *both . . . and* can be taken as one element rather than two. In the same way, if in a particular text we find identical (repeated) or different elements, of which one occurs only if the other is present, we conclude that these occurrences are not independent of each other and mark their joint occurrence as a single element in the representation of the text.

For *they prefer X– to any hair tonic they've used*, our only comparison is *you too and your whole family will prefer X– to any hair tonic you've used*. In each case, the stretch before *prefer* contains the same word that we find before *'ve*. We can therefore say that the word before *'ve* is not independent; rather, the choice of one or the other member of the set *they/you* depends on which word of that set occurs before *prefer*. Writing *Q* as a sign to repeat that member of the set *they/you* which occurs in the stretch before *prefer*, we obtain:

> *they prefer X– to any hair tonic Q've used*
> *You . . . will prefer X– to any hair tonic Q've used*

It now appears that by reducing these stretches to their independent elements, the latter sections have become identical. On this basis, the beginning sections of these two sentences are found to have identical environments, and hence to be equivalent.

---

[10]The *-s* is also a part of all singular nouns (*The child walk-s*, etc.). Or else, *walks, goes*, and the like can be taken as alternants of *walk, go*, etc., after *he* and singular nouns.

Since the first of these beginning sections was included in our class *P*, we can now include the section *You too . . . in P* as well.[11]

This is only one kind of dependent occurrence. There are many others which have to be investigated; and the resulting information is of use both to discourse analysis and to a more detailed descriptive linguistics.

One major example is that of the pronouns. If the advertisement had read *You . . . will prefer it* instead of *you . . . will prefer X–*, we would at first regard *it* as a new element, to be placed in a new equivalence class. However, the occurrence of *it* is dependent on the occurrence of *X–*: if the preceding *X–* had contained the plural morpheme (*X–s*), the pronoun in this sentence would have been *them*. Other words of the *it* group, say *he* or *you*, will not occur here as long as *X–* occurs in the preceding sentence; but they could occur if certain other words were used in place of *X–*. The same is true of words like *this/these, who/which*, which also depend on particular words occurring somewhere else in the passage. Without using any information about the meaning of these pronouns, or about their "referring" to preceding nouns, we can conclude from their distribution in the text that they are not independent elements: they contain a (discontinuous) portion of the occurrence of the morpheme with which they correlate.

Another type of dependent occurrence is found in such expressions of cross reference as *each other* and *together*, which carry out in language some of the functions filled in mathematical expressions by variables—but in the vaguer and more complex way that is characteristic of language. The sentence *Foster and Lorch saw each other at the same moment* is normal; but if we drop the words *and Lorch*, every native speaker of English will immediately replace *each other* by something else. To put it differently: we will not find any sentence that contains *each other* but does not contain either the expression *and Z* or a plural morpheme in the relevant noun. Furthermore, although we will find the sentence *Electrons and positrons attract each other*, we will not find—at least in a physics textbook—the same sentence with the words *and positrons* omitted, unless there are also other changes such as *repel* in place of *attract*.

It may be noted that dependent elements are especially prone to be assigned to different equivalence classes in their various occurrences, since each occurrence of them is assigned to the class of whatever element correlates with that particular occurrence. If the text contained *You will prefer X–, You will prefer it, The survey showed, It showed*, the first occurrence of *it* would be assigned to the class of *X–*, the second *it* to the class of *survey*.

In all such cases the special relations of dependent occurrence among particular elements can be eliminated by considering the dependent element to be simply a portion of that element with which it correlates (upon which its occurrence depends). It should be clear that when we speak of dependence, the term is only required to

---

[11]Before this can be done, some further operations must be carried out to reduce *Four out of five . . . say they prefer . . .* to two *PW* sequences: *Four . . . say . . .* and *They prefer . . .*, with the sentence *You . . . will prefer . . .* as a third *PW* sequence. Otherwise, the words *say they* would be left hanging, since the *P* section (equivalent to *Millions*) is only *Four out of five people in a nation*wide *survey*, and the corrected *W* section (identical with the *W* of *You . . . will prefer . . .*) is only *prefer X– to any hair tonic Q've used*. See Section 9.

apply within a particular text. The dependence of pronouns or cross-reference words upon some neighboring noun may hold in every text in which these words occur; but the dependence between the two occurrences of *they* or of *you* in our text is peculiar to this text. Elsewhere we may find the sentence *they prefer X– to any hair tonic you've used*; but in this particular text such a sentence does not occur. It is for that reason that in this text we can tell what the second pronoun must be by looking at the first one.

7.2 *Subdivisions of Sentences.* The recognition of dependent elements affects our decision concerning the number of intervals into which a particular sentence is to be subdivided.

Where an element has dependent portions spread over a domain, we generally have to consider the whole domain as entering into one interval with that element. For example, in *they prefer X– to any hair tonic they've used* we have established that the two occurrences of *they* are interdependent in this text. Hence, we can analyze this section into *they* (occurring over both positions) plus . . . *prefer X– to any hair tonic . . . 've used*; and similarly for the sentence with *you* (also over both positions). This is a more general treatment than that of Section 7.1, which gave favored status to the first occurrence of *they* and of *you* by considering the second occurrence to be dependent on the first, and which made the identity of the two sentences in their latter portions depend on their both containing the same kind of dependence (Q). The present treatment eliminates dependence by viewing the single *they* or *you* as occurring over two positions and makes the second parts of the sentences identical without qualification. The effect of this new treatment is that since the two-position *they* stretches over almost the whole length of the second part, the whole of that second part has to be kept in the same interval as *they*. The consolidation of the two occurrences of *they* thus precludes our setting up two intervals here; otherwise we might have set up two intervals: *they prefer* . . . , and either *they've used* or *Q've used*.

On the other hand, there are cases where recognition of dependence leads us to distinguish more intervals than we might otherwise. Take the sentence *Casals, who is self-exiled from Spain, stopped performing after the fascist victory.* If we investigate the text in which this is imbedded we will find that the *who* is dependent upon *Casals*, much as the second *they* above is dependent upon the first: the text includes *And the same Casals who* . . . , but later *The records which* . . . . We may therefore say that the *who* "contains" *Casals*, i.e., either continues it or repeats it. But which does it do? If *who* continues *Casals*, we have one interval, the first section (C) being *Casals who*, while the second section (S) is *is self-exiled . . . stopped* . . . . If *who* repeats *Casals* instead of continuing it, we have two intervals, one imbedded in the other: the first consists of *Casals* (again C) plus *stopped performing* (marked S_1), the second of *who* (taken as an equivalent of *Casals*) plus *is self-exiled* (S_2). We would be led to the second choice only if we could show in terms of the text that *is self-exiled . . .* and *stopped performing . . .* are two separate elements (not just two portions of one long element)—for example, if we found in the text two additional sentences: *The press failed to say why he stopped performing, etc. But he has stated publicly why he is self-exiled, etc.* In either case *who* contains *Casals*. But if the original sentence is *Casals who S*, we analyze it as *CS*, whereas if (on the basis of the later sentences) we view the original sentence as *Casals who* S_2S_1, we analyze it as CCS_2S_1, and divide it into two intervals CS_2 and CS_1, with the result that S_2 and S_1 are equivalent since they both occur after *C*. The only difference between taking a dependent element as a continuation and taking it as a repetition is in the number of intervals—one or two—into which we then analyze the total.

We have seen here that when a sentence contains an element *A* which is dependent upon *B*, we have the choice of taking the whole sentence as one interval, with *A* simply a continuation of *B*, or as two intervals—one containing *B* and the other containing *A* in the same class as *B*. The latter choice will generally be taken if the rest of the sentence can be divided into two comparable sections, one to go with *A* and the other with *B*.

Choices of this type can arise even where there are no dependent forms. For example, in our second text we have the further sentence *The self-exiled Casals is waiting across the Pyrenees for the fall of Franco*. We wish to put *self-exiled* in the same class as *is self-exiled* . . . , since the same morphemes are involved (provided we can show from the text itself that *self-exiled* is equivalent to *self-exiled from Spain*). This gives us the peculiar sentence structure S_2CS_3, as compared with the previous *CS* sentences. Now if by good fortune the text also contained the sentence *Casals is waiting across the Pyrenees for the fall of Franco* (which is too much to ask in the way of repetition), we would be in position to make the following analysis. We have as sentences of the text CS_1, *C is* S_2, S_2CS_3, CS_3. The sequences S_1 and S_2 and S_3 are all members of one equivalence class *S*, since they all occur after *C*. Our problem lies with the maverick S_2CS_3. Let us now say that any sentence X_1AX_2 can be "transformed" into *A is* X_1: AX_2.[12] This means that if X_1AX_2 occurs in the text, then *A is* X_1: AX_2 also occurs in the text. In that case we will consider X_1AX_2 equivalent to *A is* X_1: AX_2; as a new structure our maverick has disappeared. We replace S_2CS_3 by the transformationally equivalent *C is* S_2 and CS_3, both of which occur elsewhere in the same text.

We may proceed on this basis even to transformations which are not already justified by the text, provided they do not conflict with the text. Thus, we find in the text the sentences *The memorable concerts were recorded in Prades* . . . *The concerts were recorded first on tape*. We can represent this as MNR_1: NR_2 (the equivalence of R_1 and R_2 being shown, let us suppose, elsewhere in the text), and we would transform the first sentence into *N is M*: NR_1. This does not mean that we claim that our transformation *N is M* (*The concerts were memorable*) actually occurs in the text, or that there is no stylistic or other difference between saying *The memorable concerts were recorded in Prades* and saying *The concerts were memorable: The concerts* (or *They*) *were recorded in Prades*. All that our transformation means is that MNR_1 is taken as equivalent to *N is M*: NR_1 because S_2CS_3 is actually found as an equivalent of *C is* S_2: CS_3, in the sense that both occur in the modified text.

On the one hand, we have eliminated from our tabular arrangement the peculiar interval structure MNR_1 or S_2CS_3—peculiar because the other intervals all have the

---

[12] In such formulas as *A is* X_1: AX_2, the italic colon indicates the end of a sentence or interval. (It is used instead of a period because that might be mistaken for the period at the end of a sentence in the author's exposition.)

form *NR* or *CS*. On the other hand, we have discovered that *M* (or rather *is M*) is a member of the *R* class. But our most important result is that a sentence may be represented as two intervals even when it does not contain two sets of the requisite equivalence classes. This happens when we can show that a single class in the sentence relates independently to two other classes or elements elsewhere. That class is then repeated, once in each interval; and each interval will indicate separately its relation to one of the other classes.[13]

These difficulties in dividing a sentence into intervals arise from questions about the manner in which the equivalence classes relate to each other. In a sentence, the various morphemes or sequences do not merely occur together; they usually have a specific relation to each other which can be expressed by one or more morphemes of order: *You wrote Paul* and *Paul wrote you* differ only in their morphemic order. If we find several *CS* intervals in our text, that means that *C* has a particular relation to *S*—that of occurring with it and before it. Since we are operating without meaning, we do not know what this relation is, but we are careful to represent the same morphemic order in the sentence by the same class order in the interval. Now when we find S_2CS_3, we do not know how this order relates to the order *CS*, and we can make no comparison of the two sentences. It is therefore desirable to re-arrange the unknown S_2CS_3 so that it will contain the same classes in the same order as other intervals—and of course, we must show that the re-arrangement is equivalent, for this text, to the original. In most cases this can be done only if we break the unknown sentence, by means of such transformations as have been discussed above, into two or more intervals, in such a way that the smaller intervals have a form which occurs in this text.

In this way we get a great number of structurally similar intervals even in a text whose sentences are very different from each other.

7.3 *Grammatical Transformations.* Up to this point we have seen how the structure of a text can be investigated without using any information from outside the text itself. The straightforward procedure is to set up equivalence classes and to discover patterned (i.e., similar or partly similar) combinations of these classes in successive intervals of the text. Often, however, we get many small classes and dissimilar intervals, because the sentences are so different from each other; when this happens, we find that by comparing the sentences of the text we can sometimes show that one section of one sentence is equivalent (for this text) to a different section of another sentence, and therefore contains the same classes. The extent to which we can do this depends upon the amount of repetition in the text.

We raise now the question of advancing further in the same direction by using information from outside the text. The information will be of the same kind as we have sought inside the text, namely whether one section of a sentence is equivalent to another (in the sense that *MNR* is equivalent to *N is M: NR*). It will go back to the same basic operation, that of comparing different sentences. And it will serve the

---

[13]The case which we have been considering here is the important one of the sequence adjective + noun + verb, in which the noun relates independently to the adjective and to the verb. The adjective can be represented as a predicate of the noun in the same way as the verb. This will be discussed in Section 7.3.

same end: to show that two otherwise different sentences contain the same combination of equivalence classes, even though they may contain different combinations of morphemes. What is new is only that we base our equivalence not on a comparison of two sentences in the text, but on a comparison of a sentence in the text with sentences outside the text.

This may seem to be a major departure. One may ask how we know that any equivalence discovered in this way is applicable to our text. The justification was given in Section 3 above: if we can show that two sequences are equivalent in any English sentences in which they occur, then they are equivalent in any text written in English. If in any English sentence containing XAY, the XAY is equivalent to A is $X: AY$, then if we find S_2CS_3 in our English text we can say that it is equivalent to C is $S_2: CS_3$.

But what is *equivalence*? Two ELEMENTS are equivalent if they occur in the same environment within the sentence. Two SENTENCES in a text are equivalent simply if they both occur in the text (unless we discover structural details fine enough to show that two sentences are equivalent only if they occur in similar structural positions in the text). Similarly, two sentences in a language are equivalent if they both occur in the language. In particular, we will say that sentences of the form A are equivalent to sentences of the form B, if for each sentence A we can find a sentence B containing the same morphemes except for differences due to the difference in form between A and B. For example, N_1VN_2 is equivalent to N_2 is V-en by N_1 because for any sentence like *Casals plays the cello* we can find a sentence *The cello is played by Casals*.

We do not claim that two equivalent sentences necessarily mean exactly the same thing or that they are stylistically indifferent. But we do claim that not all sentences are equivalent in this sense: the relation of equivalence is not useless, as it would be if it were true for all sentences. For example, N_1VN_2 is not equivalent to N_1 is V-en by N_2, because the latter form will be found only for certain N_1 and N_2 forms (*I saw you* and *I was seen by you*) but not for all forms (we will not find *Casals is played by the cello*).[14] We claim further that the application of this grammatical equivalence from outside the text will enable us to discover additional similar intervals in our text, beyond what we could get merely from comparing the text sentences with each other. Thus, we can show that in various environments *who, he,* etc., are grammatically equivalent to the preceding noun, and that N_1 who V_1V_2 is equivalent to $N_1V_2: N_1V_1$. Then, in *Casals, who is self-exiled . . . stopped performing . . .* , we have two intervals $CS_1: C$ is S_2. We would have this result (without having to worry whether *Casals who* is one continued occurrence of C or two repeated occurrences) even if there were no other occurrences of *who* within the text, i.e., when no analysis could be made of *who* on internal textual grounds. The usefulness of grammatical equivalence is especially great if, for example, we have a number of intervals all containing *Casals*, besides many others interlarded among the first but containing *he,* and if we can find no common textual environments to show that

---

[14]True, one might claim that this last sentence is still *grammatical*. But present-day grammar does not distinguish among the various members of a morpheme class. Hence, to require that sentence B must contain the same morphemes as sentence A is to go beyond grammar in the ordinary sense.

Casals and *he* are equivalent. As soon as we accept this equivalence grammatically, we can show that all the environments of *Casals* are equivalent to those of *he*; and this in turn can make other equivalences discoverable textually.

Grammatical equivalence can be investigated more systematically if we introduce a technique of experimental variation. Given a sentence in form A and a desired form B, we try to alter A by only the formal difference that exists between it and B, and see what happens then to our A. Given *The memorable concerts were recorded . . . ,* suppose that we want to make this MNR sentence comparable in form to previous intervals beginning with N. To this end, we seek a variation of the sentence beginning *The concerts.* We may do this by putting an informant into a genuine social speech situation (not a linguistic discussion about speech) in which he would utter a sentence beginning *The concerts* and containing the words *memorable* and *recorded.*[15] Or, we may do it by the tedious job of observation, hunting for a sentence that begins with *The concerts* and contains *memorable* and *recorded.* By either method, we might get *The concerts were memorable and were recorded,* or something of the sort,[16] whence we learn that when M (or any adjective) is shifted to the other side of N (its following noun) one inserts *is*; MN is equivalent to N *is* M. In this way we discover that when MNR is shifted to a form beginning with N, an *is* appears between N and the following M.

This technique of varying the grammatical form of a sentence while keeping its morphemes constant cannot be used within a text; for there all we can do is to inspect the available material. But it can be used in the language outside the text, where we have the right, as speakers, to create any social situation which might favor another speaker's uttering one rather than another of the many sentences at his disposal. It is especially useful in a language like English, where so many morphemes occur in various grammatical classes.

The preceding paragraph indicates the basic safeguard in applying grammatical equivalence to extend our textual equivalence classes. We do not merely ask, What sentence forms are equivalent to MNR? There may be many. We ask instead, Since N . . . is a common form in this text, and since we find also MNR, can we replace this by an equivalent sentence of the form N . . . ? The direction of change is not arbitrary, but comes entirely from the text. As before, it is a matter of dividing our sentences into the most similar intervals possible. All we ask is whether there is a grammatical equivalence which would connect MNR with the form N . . . ; the answer is yes, provided an *is* appears in the form. This in turn yields *is* M as equivalent to R. As elsewhere in linguistics, the method does not collapse all sentences into any arbitrary form we choose; it simply enables us to describe the rarer forms of the text (MNR) in terms of the common ones (N . . .).

---

[15]To give a crude example, one can read the text sentence *The memorable concerts were recorded* in company with an informant, and then stop and say to him, in an expectant and hesitant way, "That is to say, the concerts—," waiting for him to supply the continuation.

[16]We may find a great many sentences beginning with *The concerts* and containing the other two words, e.g., *The concerts were not memorable but were nevertheless recorded.* These sentences will contain various words in addition to those of the original sentence; but the only new word which will occur in ALL sentences of the desired form NMR (or rather in a subclass of the NMR sentences) will be a form of the verb *to be*. Hence, this is the only new word that is essential when changing to that form.

For analysis purely within the text, all we need to know are the morpheme boundaries. To utilize grammatical equivalences we need to know also the morpheme class to which each morpheme in our text belongs, since grammatical statements concern classes rather than individual morphemes. The grammatical statement in this instance is that adjective + noun is equivalent to noun + *is* + adjective; to apply it to our sequence MN, we must know that the M is an adjective and the N a noun.

It has been found empirically that a relatively small number of grammatical equivalences are called upon, time after time, in reducing the sentences of a text to similar intervals. Hence, even a nonlinguist can get considerable information about the text by using (in addition to the internal textual method) a prepared list of major grammatical equivalences for the language. Some frequently used equivalences are given here, without any evidence for their validity, and with only a very rough indication of the sentence-environments in which they hold:[17]

(1) If we find XCY, then $X = Y$ (X is equivalent to Y). The C is a conjunction like *and, but, or*, or else, under special circumstances, a phrase like *as well as, rather than, A-er than*. The X and Y must be in the same grammatical class. Thus, in *I phoned him but he was out*, X and Y are each NV; in *I saw it but went on*, the Y is only the verb phrase *went on*, and hence the X can include only the verb phrase *saw it* (not the whole sequence *I saw it*). It follows that $N_1V_1CN_2V_2$ is equivalent to two intervals $N_1V_1: N_2V_2$, and $NV_1CV_2 = NV_1: NV_2$.

(2) The sequence N_1 *is* N_2 indicates that $N_1 = N_2$. The class of *is* includes *remains* and other verbs.

(3) $\hat{N}_1\hat{N}_2$, with a primary stress on each N, indicates that $N_1 = N_2$; e.g. *The pressure P increases* is equivalent to *The pressure increases* and *P increases*.

(4) NV (*that*) $NV = NV: NV$; e.g., *I telegraphed that we'll arrive tomorrow* is equivalent to *I telegraphed: We'll arrive tomorrow*.

(5) $N_1VN_2 = N_2V^*N_1$, where V and V^* are respectively active and passive, or passive and active.

(6) $N_1PN_2 = N_2P^*N_1$; e.g. (*They seek*) *the goal of certainty* is equivalent to some such form as (*They seek*) *certainty as a goal*. The change in prepositions when two nouns are reversed is far greater than the corresponding change in verbs. In verbs the change is effected simply by adding or subtracting the passive morpheme and the word *by*; in prepositions it is effected by replacing one form by an entirely different form. The pairs of equivalent prepositions are not fixed: between certain nouns, the substitute for *of* may be *as*; between others, it may be *with*. Nevertheless, it is possible to find structures in which the nouns of the sequence N_1PN_2 are reversed.

(7) $N_1PN_2 = A_2N_1$, i.e., the morpheme of the second noun occurs in an adjectival form before the prior noun, as in *medical training* for *training in medicine*.

(8) Pronouns like *he*, and certain words with initial *wh-* and *th-*, repeat a preceding noun. Which noun they repeat (when there are several nouns preceding) depends on the details of the grammatical environment; usually it is the immediately preceding noun or the last noun that occurs in a comparable grammatical environment.

---

[17] A for adjective, N for noun, V for verb, P for preposition. Subscripts indicate particular morphemes, regardless of their class.

Thus, *who = the man* in *The man who phoned left no name* (N *who* $V_1V_2 = NV_2$: NV_1); *who = my roommate* in *The man spoke to my roommate, who told him to call again* ($N_1V_1N_2$ *who* $V_2 = N_1V_1N_2$: N_2V_2). There are many variant ways of determining which noun is repeated by a pronoun and which verb belongs with each noun. In *the man who phoned*, no subject can be inserted before *phoned*, hence *who* must be taken as subject. In *The man I phoned was out*, we reduce first to *I phoned: The man was out*; then, since no object can be inserted after *phoned* in the original sentence, we set *the man* as the object[18] of *phoned* and obtain the equivalent *I phoned the man: The man was out* ($N_1N_2V_1V_2 = N_2V_1N_1$: N_1V_2).

(9) NV_1, V_2-*ing* $= NV_1$: NV_2; e.g., *They escaped, saving nothing* is equivalent to *They escaped: They saved nothing.*

(10) $N_1CN_2VX = N_1VN_2$: N_2VN_1. Here X represents a class of cross-reference expressions like *each other*; e.g., *The Giants and the Dodgers each beat the other twice* is equivalent to *The D beat the G twice: The G beat the D twice.* The equivalence differs somewhat for different groups of X forms.

(11) $ANV = N$ *is* A: NV, as in the example *the self-exiled Casals* . . . in Section 7.2. So also $NVAN_1 = NVN_1$ *who is* $A = NVN_1$: N_1 *is* A; e.g., *They read the interdicted books = They read the books which were interdicted = They read the books: The books were interdicted.*

(12) $N_1VN_2PN_3 = N_1VN_2$: N_1VPN_3. That is, a double object can be replaced by two separate objects in two intervals which repeat the subject and verb; e.g., *I bought it: I bought for you* for *I bought it for you.*

These grammatical equivalences preserve the morphemes and the grammatical relations among them, though in a changed grammatical form. We cannot get $N_1VN_2 = N_2VN_1$, because that would change the subject-object relation to the verb; but $N_2V^*N_1$ is obtainable as an equivalent of N_1VN_2 because the verb too is changed here, in a way that preserves its grammatical relation to the now reversed nouns. Preservation of the grammatical relations is essential, because such relations are always to be found among the morphemes in a sentence. That is to say, there are restrictions of substitutability and order and intonation among the various morphemes (or morpheme classes) in a sentence; and when we move from one sentence to an equivalent sentence, we want, upon moving back to the original sentence, to get back the same restrictions—since the original, like all sentences, is defined by the restrictions among its parts. Therefore, when we break up a sentence into various intervals for a tabular arrangement, we do not want two combinations of the same equivalence classes (say our first and second *TE* combinations above) to represent different grammatical relations. Accordingly, when we transform a sentence containing certain equivalence classes, we are careful to preserve the original grammatical relations among them.

Sometimes, however, we find sections of a sentence which contain none of our equivalence classes; that is (in the simplest case), they contain no material which recurs elsewhere in the text. The grammatical relation of unique sections to the

---

[18]The only way to express the exclusion of an object here purely in terms of occurrence of elements is to say that the object already occurs. This cannot be *I*, since that is the subject of *phoned*; hence it must be the other N, *the man*.

rest of the sentence must be preserved in our tabular arrangement no less than the relation of recurrent sections; but here we escape the problem of preserving their relation while changing their relative position, since we have no reason to change their position at all: it is only our equivalence classes that we wish to re-arrange. All we want of this nonrecurrent material is to know its relation to our equivalence classes and to indicate this relation in our analysis. We may not be able to learn this from a study of our text alone; but we can learn it by bringing in grammatical information or experimental variation. For an example we return to the sequences *Casals, who is self-exiled from Spain . . .* and *the self-exiled Casals . . . .* If the latter is S_2C, the former is C, C is S_2 *from Spain*. Since *from Spain* does not recur, we want only to know where to keep it when we arrange our equivalence classes, i.e., what its relation is to these classes. From the grammar we know that in sentences in the form *NV APN* the smallest unit of which *PN* is an immediate constituent is *APN* and that this *APN* is replaceable by *A* alone.[19] Therefore, if the *A* happens to be a member of one of our equivalence classes while the *PN* is not, we associate the *PN* with the *A* in its equivalence column by writing *APN* instead of *A* as the member of the class.

More generally, material that does not belong to any equivalence class, but is grammatically tied to a member of some class, is included with that member to form with it an expanded member of the class in question. Thus, *self-exiled from Spain* is now in the same class as *self-exiled*. The justification for this is that since the material does not occur again in this text (or occurs again only in the same grammatical relation to the same equivalence class), its only effect, when the text is represented in terms of particular equivalence classes, is precisely its relation to the particular member to which it is grammatically tied.

An interesting special case arises when two members of the same equivalence class constitute jointly the next larger grammatical unit of their sentence (i.e., are the immediate constituents of that unit), for example when the two are an adjective and a following noun, where $AN = N$. In such a case we may consider that the two together constitute just one member of their class and fit together into a single interval. If we took them as two occurrences of their class, we would have to put each occurrence into a separate interval.

Grammatical information is especially useful in the recognition of sentence connectives. These morphemes are easily identified from formal grammar, quite independently of their meaning, but may not be identifiable as such on purely textual evidence. Their importance lies in the fact that many sentences of a text may contain the same classes except for some unassigned words, often at the beginning, which are grammatically connecters or introducers of sentences; they stand outside the specific classes which comprise the sentence or interval. In our tabular arrangement these elements can be assigned, by their grammatical position, to a special front column. We can go beyond this and assign to this front column any material which is not assignable to any of the equivalence columns. Sometimes such connecting material is not immediately obvious; note that many sentences of the form NV *that* N_1V_1 can be analyzed as consisting of the equivalence classes N_1V_1 with the NV *that* relegated to the front column. Consider, for example, *We are proud that these concerts*

---

[19]Semantically one would say that the *PN* "modifies" the *A*.

were recorded by our engineers. Here the known members of equivalence classes are *concerts* and *recorded.* The preceding words do not recur in the text and are not grammatically tied to any particular class member. Quite the contrary, they can be grammatically replaced by introductory adverbs like *indeed,* even though in a purely grammatical sense they are the major subject and predicate of the sentence.

In addition to making use of the grammatical relations of whole grammatical classes, we can use information about the relation of particular morphemes or grammatical subclasses to grammatical classes. For instance, it is possible to establish that intransitive verbs (in some languages) form a subclass which never occurs with an object and which is equivalent to a transitive verb plus an object. In a given text, this may enable us to put a transitive verb with its object in the same column as a comparably placed intransitive verb.

Finally, there are a great many detailed equivalences which apply to particular morphemes. This information is not provided by descriptive linguistics, which deals generally with whole morpheme classes. But it can be obtained by linguistic methods, since it deals with matched occurrences and special restrictions, though in most cases it is necessary to study the restrictions over more than one sentence at a time. Suppose, for example, that we find the words *buy* and *sell* in a text. Their environments in that text may not be sufficiently similar to place them in the same equivalence class, even though it might promote the analysis of the text if we could do so. But if we investigate a good number of other short texts in which the two words occur, we will find that the two often appear in matched environments and that in certain respects they are distributional inverses of each other; that is, we will find many sequences like N_1 *buys from* N_2: N_2 *sells to* N_1 (*I bought it from him at the best price I could get, but he still sold it to me at a profit*). If the environments of *buy* and *sell* in our text are similar to the matched environments of the other short texts, we may be able, by comparison with these wider results, to put the two into one equivalence class in our text after all, or even to analyze one as the inverse of the other.

In this way we can put more words into one textual class than would otherwise be possible, and we can make use of what would seem to be special semantic connections between words (as between *buy* and *sell,* or even between a transitive verb and the presence of an object) without departing from a purely formal study of occurrences. The reason is that differences in meaning correlate highly with differences in linguistic distribution; and if we have two related words whose distributional similarities cannot be shown within the confines of our text, we will often be able to show them in a larger selection of texts, even of very short ones.

The kind of outside information which has been indicated here has been only sketched in scattered examples, both because the field is vast and because a great deal remains to be done. Further work in this direction will not only be useful to discourse analysis but will also have interest as an extension of descriptive linguistics.

RESULTS

8 The double array. As a product of discourse analysis we obtain a succession of intervals, each containing certain equivalence classes. For a tabular arrangement we write each interval under the preceding one, with the successive members of each class forming a column, as in Section 5.4 above. The very brief text of Section 7.2 is arranged as follows:[20]

$$C \ S_1$$
$$C \ S_2 \quad (S_2 \text{ after } C \text{ is } is \ S_2)$$
$$C \ S_2 \quad (= S_2C \text{ without the } is)$$
$$C \ S_3$$
$$N \ R_0 \quad (= MN; \ R_0 = is \ M)$$
$$N \ R_1$$
$$N \ R_2$$

The horizontal rows show the equivalence classes present in each interval, arranged according to their order (or other relation) within the interval. The vertical columns indicate the particular members of each class which appear in the successive intervals. Material which is a member of no equivalence class, but is grammatically tied to a particular member of some class, is included with that member in its column; thus *in Spain* is included in the first S_2. Material which is a member of no equivalence class, and is not grammatically tied to a particular member of some class, is placed in a front column (not illustrated here), which will be found to include morphemes that relate the sentences or intervals to each other or mark some change in several classes of a single interval. The tabular arrangement thus represents the original one-dimensional text in a two-dimensional array, where each element has two coordinates: one horizontal, in respect to the other elements of its interval; and one vertical, in respect to the other members of its class.

This double array can be viewed as representing the whole text, since every morpheme of the text is assigned to one class or another in the array and since the array preserves the relations among the morphemes. Even when a large number of textual and grammatical transformations have been carried out, the classes and their members are defined at each step in such a way that the text can always be reproduced from the array plus the full definition of the classes in it. The individual intervals in the array may not be "idiomatic"—that is, they may not naturally occur in speech. But the preservation of idiom is not one of the requirements of our method. All we ask is that the succession of intervals should be textually and grammatically equivalent to the original text. Although the array may suggest a critique or a possible improvement of the text, it is not meant to be used instead of the original.

The double array can also be viewed as indicating the purely distributional relations among the equivalence classes which figure in it. From this viewpoint we can operate upon the tabular arrangement and investigate its properties. We can develop ways of simplifying the array, for example by drawing out common elements or by grouping together larger sets of equivalent sequences than we used in the formation

---

[20]The array given here represents the following sentences, taken from a review of some recent phonograph records: *Casals, who is self-exiled from Spain, stopped performing after the fascist victory. . . . The self-exiled Casals is waiting across the Pyrenees for the fall of Franco. . . . The memorable concerts were recorded in Prades. . . . The concerts were recorded first on tape.* (The other sentences analyzed in Section 7.2 were composed by me for comparison with these.) The sentences do not represent a continuous portion of the text. This fact limits very materially the relevance of the double array; but that does not concern us here, since the array is intended only as an example of how such arrangements are set up.

of the array. We can learn how to accommodate various special cases, such as a mobile class which appears in close relation now with one class now with another or which appears a different number of times in various intervals. We can try to regularize or "normalize" the array by matching all the intervals, so as to establish a single "normal" interval with which all the actual intervals can be compared: for instance, given an interval from which one of the classes is absent, we can try to transform it into one that includes all the classes, preserving equivalence during the transformation. We can attempt to formulate a general statement covering the changes in successive members of a class as we go down a column, in an effort to "explain" or "predict" the particular form taken by the classes of each interval— that is, to derive the successive intervals from the normal form.

All such operations with the array have the effect of isolating the most general independent elements in terms of which we can describe the text (ultimately the horizontal and vertical axes) and of bringing out their relations to each other in the text. In this sense, all such operations are but further refinements of our initial procedures.

9 Findings. Various conclusions can be drawn about a particular text or type of text by studying the properties of its double array, either directly or in its most simplified forms. Many of these conclusions may well have been obtainable intuitively without such formal analysis; but intuition does not yield results that are either explicit or rigorous. In some respects, moreover, the complexity and size of the material make it impossible for us to draw all the relevant conclusions without painstaking formal analysis. The sample texts used in the present paper have been necessarily too short and too simple to show what kind of conclusions the analysis yields about a particular text or style—that must be left for a future presentation of a longer sample text, though the details of method and the range of conclusions obtainable by means of it could be shown only through the analysis of a great many discourses. To give some slight idea of these conclusions, we will complete here the analysis of our first text (Section 6).

The analysis was left at the following point: *P* has as members *Millions, Four out of five people in a nationwide survey, You too will, (and) your whole family will.* *W* has as members *can't be wrong, prefer X– to any hair tonic . . 've used.* Four of the sentences (including the title) are represented by five *PW* intervals.

At this point it is difficult to proceed without recourse to grammatical equivalence (see 10*n*). In *four out of five . . . say they prefer . . .* we have *P* and *W* but with *say they* intervening. If our text happened to contain *they* and *four out of five . . .* in equivalent environments, we could analyze this sentence directly. In the absence of this, we appeal to the grammatical equivalence of *they* with the preceding, comparably situated noun: *four out of five . . .* as subject of *say*, parallel to *they* as subject of *prefer*. We therefore put *they* into the same class *P* as *four out of five*. Then the sentence becomes *P say PW*, which is analyzed as two intervals *P say: PW*, on the basis of the formula *NV (that) NV = NV: NV*; and on this basis *say* is a member of *W*, since it occurs after *P* to make a whole interval.

We now turn to the last sentence, *You too will be satisfied.* The first part is a known *P*; hence *be satisfied* is included in *W*. This gives us a start for working on the preceding sentence, *Every year we sell more bottles of X– to satisfied consumers.* Now

X– to satisfied consumers is grammatically *X– to AN*, which is equivalent to *X– to N: N is A*. In this way we obtain an interval *consumers are satisfied*; and since the second part of this is *W*, we place *consumers* in *P*. The rest of the sentence contains new classes: Since *bottles* occurs elsewhere in the text, we regard it as representing a possible equivalence class and mark it *B*; with this occurrence of *B* we associate the word *more*, which does not occur elsewhere and which is grammatically tied to *bottles*. Since *sell* occurs elsewhere in *sold* ($=$ *sell* $+$ part of the passive morpheme), we mark it *S*; and we associate with it *every year*, which is grammatically tied to it. (*Every year* is similar in only one morpheme to *since . . . years ago* in the first sentence; rather than try to get these phrases into new equivalence classes, we note that each is tied to the member of *S* that occurs near it, and we associate each phrase with its member of *S*.) There remains *we*, which is not grammatically part of either the *B*-phrase or the *S*-phrase; even though it seems not to occur again, we place it tentatively in a new class *I*. (We will see below that a zero form of *I* may be said to occur in the first sentence.) Thus, we get *ISB to P*. This in turn can be somewhat simplified, since it is grammatically equivalent to *ISB: IS to P*.

Finally there is the first sentence, *Millions of consumer bottles of X– have been sold since its introduction a few years ago*. If we start with *Millions* as a known *P*, we obtain an unanalyzable remainder beginning with *of*. Instead, we match *bottles of X– have been sold* with *we sell bottles of X–*. The first has the form $N_1 V$; the second is $N_2 V N_1$. Grammatically, *have been sold* is *sell* $+$ past $+$ passive; hence, if we take *sell* as *V*, then *been sold* is V^*. Grammatically also, V $+$ passive $+$ *by N* is equivalent to V $+$ passive alone (*is sold by us* $=$ *is sold*). Hence, the lack of any *by us* after *sold* does not prevent our matching the two clauses. To *we sell bottles* as $N_2 V N_1$ we match *bottles have been sold* as $N_1 V^* = N_1 V^* N_2$; we can even say that the passive morpheme, with or without the following "agent" (*by* $+$ *N*) is equivalent to the subject of the active verb (i.e., the verb without the passive morpheme). If *we sell bottles of X–* is *ISB*, then *bottles of X– have been sold* is the equivalent BS^*I with zero *I*. The section *since . . . years ago* we associate with the preceding S^*, as also the past tense morpheme, since neither of these figures elsewhere in our equivalence classes. *Millions* and *consumer* are both members of *P*,[21] but there is no way of making use of this fact. Grammatically, *consumer bottles* is $N_1 N_2 = N_2$, and *millions of* N_2 is $N_3 P N_2 = N_2$, so that the whole sequence is grammatically tied to *bottles* (as *more* was tied to *bottles* above), leaving the sentence as BS^*I. This means that there are two occurrences of *P* words which are lost by being included in an occurrence of *B*. There is no other distributional relation that this *Millions* and this *consumer* have to any other class occurrence in the text (except their analogy to *more*); hence there is no way of including them in the double array. The same morphemes indeed occur elsewhere as *P*, but in different relations to other classes.

This points up the confusing relation of the title to the first sentence. If we start with the title, we come upon *Millions* in the first sentence and assign it to *P*, on the basis of the title, only to find that there is no class *P* in the final analysis of the sen-

---

[21]We have *consumers* in *P*; and since the singular-plural distinction does not figure in our classes, we can associate the dropping of the *-s* with the occurrence of *consumers* in the first sentence. By dropping the *-s* from the *P*-element *consumers* we get a *P*-form *consumer* for the sentence.

tence. (The millions who can't be wrong turn out to be bottles.[22]) If we begin with the body of the advertisement, we have a class *P* (*four out of five*; *you*) which relates to *W*, and a class *B* (*bottles, millions of . . . bottles*) which relates to *S*; and if we then proceed to the title, we find there the *W* preceded not by any known *P* word or by a new word which we can assign to *P*, but by a word which has elsewhere been associated with a member of *B*. (The bottles show up as people.) This is the formal finding which parallels what one might have said as a semantic critique—namely, that the text of the advertisement (millions of bottles sold; many people can't be wrong in preferring *X–*) fails to support the title (millions can't be wrong).

The double array for the advertisement is not interesting in itself:

PW	*Millions of People Can't be Wrong!*
*BS*I* (the *B* containing pseudo-*P*)	*Millions of consumer bottles . . . have been sold . . .*
CPW	*And four out of five people . . . say*
PW	*they prefer X– . . .*
PW	*Four out of five people . . . can't be wrong.*
PW	*you too will prefer X– . . .*
PW	*your whole family will prefer X– . . .*
*BS*I*(=ISB)	*Every year we sell more bottles of X–*
*S*I* to *P*	*we sell to consumers*
PW	*consumers are satisfied*
PW	*You too will be satisfied!*

10 Interpretations. The formal findings of this kind of analysis do more than state the distribution of classes or the structure of intervals or even the distribution of interval types. They can also reveal peculiarities within the structure, relative to the rest of the structure. They can show in what respects certain structures are similar or dissimilar to others. They can lead to a great many statements about the text.

All this, however, is still distinct from an INTERPRETATION of the findings, which must take the meanings of the morphemes into consideration and ask what the author was about when he produced the text. Such interpretation is obviously quite separate from the formal findings, although it may follow closely in the directions which the formal findings indicate.

Even the formal findings can lead to results of broader interest than that of the text alone. The investigation of various types of textual structure can show correlations with the person or the situation of its origin, entirely without reference to the meanings of the morphemes. It can also show what are the inherent or the removable weaknesses (from some given point of view) of a particular type of structure. It can find the same kinds of structure present in different texts and may even show how a particular type of structure can serve new texts or nonlinguistic material.

Finally, such investigation performs the important task of indicating what additional intervals can be joined to the text without changing its structure. It is often

---

[22]Since *millions of consumers* would be a natural English phrase (P_1 *of* $P_2 = P_2$), the effect of using the almost identical sequence *millions of consumer* in front of *bottles* is to give a preliminary impression that the sentence is talking about *P*; but when one reaches the word *bottles* one sees that the subject of the sentence is *B*, with the *P* words only adjectival to *B*.

possible to show that if, to the various combinations of classes that are found in the existing intervals of the text, we add intervals with certain new combinations of classes, the description of the textual structure becomes simpler and exceptions are removed (provided we leave intact any intrinsic exceptions, such as boundary conditions). The adding of such intervals may regularize the text from the point of view of discourse analysis. If for example our text contains $AB: AC: ZB$, we may say that Z is secondarily equivalent to A, since both occur before B, but only A before C. If there are no textually intrinsic exceptions governing this restriction on Z, we can on this basis add the interval ZC to the text. In this extended text the equivalence $A = Z$ is now a matter of complete substitutability in an identical range of environments, rather than just the secondary result of a chain of equivalences. The addition of such intervals has a very different standing from the addition of arbitrary intervals to the text. If we want to know what is implied but not explicitly stated in a given text or if we want to see what more can be derived from a given text than the author has already included, this search for adjoinable intervals becomes important.

SUMMARY

Discourse analysis performs the following operations upon any single connected text. It collects those elements (or sequences of elements) which have identical or equivalent environments of other elements within a sentence and considers these to be equivalent to each other (i.e., members of the same equivalence class). Material which does not belong to any equivalence class is associated with the class member to which it is grammatically most closely tied. The sentences of the text are divided into intervals, each a succession of equivalence classes, in such a way that each resulting interval is maximally similar in its class composition to other intervals of the text. The succession of intervals is then investigated for the distribution of classes which it exhibits, in particular for the patterning of class occurrence.

The operations make no use of any knowledge concerning the meaning of the morphemes or the intent or conditions of the author. They require only a knowledge of morpheme boundaries, including sentence junctures and other morphemic intonations (or punctuation). Application of these operations can be furthered by making use of grammatical equivalences (or individual morpheme occurrence relations) from the language as a whole, or from the linguistic body of which the given text is a part. In that case it is necessary to know the grammatical class of the various morphemes of the text.

Discourse analysis yields considerable information about the structure of a text or a type of text, and about the role that each element plays in such a structure. Descriptive linguistics, on the other hand, tells only the role that each element plays in the structure of its sentence. Discourse analysis tells, in addition, how a discourse can be constructed to meet various specifications, just as descriptive linguistics builds up sophistication about the ways in which linguistic systems can be constructed to meet various specifications. It also yields information about stretches of speech longer than one sentence; thus it turns out that while there are relations among successive sentences, these are not visible in sentence structure (in terms of what is subject and what is predicate, or the like), but in the pattern of occurrence of equivalence classes through successive sentences.

12   Degrees of Grammaticalness*

Noam Chomsky

Since the point has been widely misunderstood, I would like to emphasize that I am using the terms "grammatical" and "degree of grammaticalness" in a technical sense (which is, however, not unrelated to the ordinary one). In particular, when a sentence is referred to as semi-grammatical or as deviating from some grammatical regularity, there is no implication that this sentence is being "censored"[1] or ruled out or that its use is being forbidden. Nor, so far as I can see, are there any "onto-logical" considerations involved[2] except insofar as these are reflected in grammatical categories and subcategories. Use of a sentence that is in some way semi-grammatical is no more to be censured than use of a transform that is remote from the kernel. In both cases, what we are attempting to do is to develop a more refined analysis of sentence structure that will be able to support more sophisticated study of the use and interpretation of utterances. There are circumstances in which the use of gram-matically deviant sentences is very much in place. Consider, e.g., such phrases as Dylan Thomas' "a grief ago,"[3] or Veblen's ironic "perform leisure." In such cases, and innumerable others, a striking effect is achieved precisely by means of a departure from a grammatical regularity.

Given a grammatically deviant utterance, we attempt to impose an interpretation on it, exploiting whatever features of grammatical structure it preserves and what-ever analogies we can construct with perfectly well-formed utterances. We do not, in this way, impose an interpretation on a perfectly grammatical utterance (it is

---

*N. Chomsky, "Some Methodological Remarks on Generative Grammar," *Word*, 17 (1961), 219–39. Reprinted by permission.
[1]R. Jakobson, "Boas' View of Grammatical Meaning," *American Anthropologist*, Vol. LXI (1959), 144.
[2]N. Chomsky, "The Logical Structure of Linguistic Theory" (MIT Library, Cambridge, Mass., 1955), p. 377; Jakobson, *op. cit.*, p. 144.
[3]One of the examples analyzed in Ziff's interesting study of the problem of deviation from grammaticalness, "On Understanding 'Understanding Utterances,'" (mimeographed, 1960).

precisely for this reason that a well-chosen deviant utterance may be richer and more effective). Linguists, when presented with examples of semi-grammatical, deviant utterances, often respond by contriving possible interpretations in constructed contexts, concluding that the examples do not illustrate departure from grammatical regularities. This line of argument completely misses the point. It blurs an important distinction between a class of utterances that need no analogic or imposed interpretation and others that can receive an interpretation by virtue of their relations to properly selected members of this class. Thus, e.g., when Jakobson observes that "golf plays John" can be a perfectly perspicuous utterance,[4] he is quite correct. But when he concludes that it is therefore as fully in accord with the grammatical rules of English as "John plays golf," he is insisting on much too narrow an interpretation of the notion "grammatical rule"—an interpretation that makes it impossible to mark the fundamental distinction between the two phrases. The former is a perspicuous utterance precisely because of the series of steps that we must take in interpreting it—a series of steps that is initiated by the recognition that this phrase deviates from a certain grammatical rule of English, in this case, a selectional rule that determines the grammatical categories of the subject and object of the verb *play*. No such steps are necessary in the case of the nondeviant (and uninteresting) "John plays golf."

I am not, of course, suggesting that every difficult, interesting, or figurative expression is semi-grammatical (or conversely). The important question, as always, is to what extent significant aspects of the use and understanding of utterances can be illuminated by refining and generalizing the notions of grammar. In the cases just mentioned, and many others, I think that they can. If this is true, it would be arbitrary and pointless to insist that the theory of grammatical structure be restricted to the study of such relatively superficial matters as agreement, inflectionally marked categories, and so on.[5]

In short, it seems to me no more justifiable to ignore the distinctions of subcategory that give the series "John plays golf," "golf plays John," "John plays and," than to ignore the rather similar distinctions between seeing a man in the flesh, in an abstract painting, and in an inkblot. The fact that we can impose an

---

[4]Jakobson, *op. cit.*, p. 144.

[5]Notice that if we do, arbitrarily, limit the study of grammar in this way, we cannot even account for the difference between:

> colorless green ideas sleep furiously
> furiously sleep ideas green color

one the one hand, and

> harmless seem dogs young friendly (-less—s—ly)
> friendly young dogs seem harmless (-ly—s—less)

on the other, since this difference can be expressed only in terms of categories that are established in terms of syntactic considerations that go well beyond inflection. But if we distinguish between the first two "sentences" above by rules involving such syntactic categories as Adjective, Noun, etc., we can just as well distinguish "John plays golf" from "golf plays John" by rules involving such syntactic subcategories as Animate Noun, etc. These are simply a refinement of familiar categories. I do not see any fundamental difference between them. No general procedure has ever been offered for isolating such categories as Noun, Adjective, etc., that would not equally well apply to such subcategories as are necessary to make finer distinctions.

interpretation in the second case and sometimes even the third, using whatever cues are present, does not obliterate the distinction between these three strata.

Examples such as these provide a motive for the study of degrees of grammaticalness. Thus, in addition to such types of data as:

phonetic transcriptions	(1a)
judgments of conformity of utterance tokens	(1b)
judgments of well-formedness	(1c)
ambiguity that can be traced to structural origins	(1d)
judgments of sameness of difference of sentence type	(1e)
judgments concerning the propriety of particular classifications or segmentations	(1f)

we can try to account for the observation that such phrases as (2a) are not as extreme in their violation of grammatical rules as (2b), though they do not conform to the rules of the language as strictly as (2c):

> a grief ago; perform leisure; golf plays John; colorless green ideas sleep furiously; misery loves company; John frightens sincerity; what did you do to the book, understand it? (2a)

> a the ago; perform compel; golf plays aggressive; furiously sleep ideas green colorless; abundant loves company; John sincerity frightens; what did you do to the book, justice it? (2b)

> a year ago; perform the task; John plays golf; revolutionary new ideas appear infrequently; John loves company; sincerity frightens John; what did you do to the book, bite it? (2c)

Here too, we can find innumerable relatively clear cases, and we can attempt to express these distinctions in a generative grammar (and, more importantly, we can try to find some basis for them through the study of generative grammar).

The question then arises: by what mechanism can a grammar assign to an arbitrary phone sequence a structural description that indicates its degree of grammaticalness, the degree of its deviation from grammatical regularities, and the manner of its deviation.

Suppose that we have a grammar that generates an infinite set of utterances with structural descriptions. Let us call the units in terms of which these utterances are represented by the neutral term *formatives* (following a suggestion of Bolinger's). Suppose, in addition, that we have an m-level hierarchy of categories of formatives with the following structure. On level one we have a single category denoted C_1^1, the category of all formatives. On level two, we have categories labeled $C_1^2, \ldots, C_{n_2}^2$. On level three, we have categories $C_1^3, \ldots, C_{n_3}^3$, where $n_3 > n_2$, and so on, until we reach the mth level with categories $C_1^m, \ldots, C_{n_m}^m$ ($1 < n_2 < \ldots < n_m$). On each level, the categories are exhaustive in the sense that each formative belongs to at least one, perhaps more (in the case of grammatical homonymy). We might also require that each level be a refinement of the preceding one, i.e., a classification into subcategories of the categories of the preceding level.

Let us assume, furthermore, that the mth level categories are the smallest categories that appear in the rules of the generative grammar. That is, the members of C_1^m are mutually substitutable in the set of generated utterances. Many of them may contain just a single formative.

For concreteness, think of the formatives as English words.[6] Suppose we have a three-level hierarchy. Then C_1^1 is the class of all words. Let $C_1^2 = $ Nouns, $C_2^2 = $ Verbs, $C_3^2 = $ Adjectives, $C_4^2 = $ everything else. Let $C_1^3, \ldots, C_j^3$ be subcategories of Verbs (pure transitives, those with inanimate objects, etc.); subcategories of Nouns, and so on. Every sequence of words can now be represented by the sequence of first-level, second-level, third-level categories to which these words belong. Thus, "misery loves company" is represented $C_1^1 C_1^1 C_1^1$ on level one, $C_1^2 C_2^2 C_1^2$ (i.e., *NVN*) on level two, $N_{abstr} V_k N_{abstr}$ on level three (where these are the appropriate C_i^3's). One of the selectional rules of the generative grammars (i.e., in the transformational model of [*SS*], one of the context-restricted constituent structure rules) will specify that V_k occurs only with animate subjects. Thus "misery loves company" will not be generated by the grammar, although "John loves company" will. However, "misery loves company" has a level two representation in common with a generated utterance, namely, *NVN*. We therefore call it semi-grammatical, on level two. "Abundant loves company," on the other hand, has only a level one representation in common with a generated utterance and is therefore labeled completely ungrammatical.

Without going into details, it is obvious how, in a similar way, a degree of grammaticalness can be assigned to any sequence of formatives when the generative grammar is supplemented by a hierarchy of categories. The degree of grammaticalness is a measure of the remoteness of an utterance from the generated set of perfectly well-formed sentences, and the common representing category sequence will indicate in what respects the utterance in question is deviant.[7] The more narrowly the mth level categories circumscribe the generated language (i.e., the more detailed the specification of selectional restrictions) the more elaborate will be the stratification of utterances into degrees of grammaticalness. No utterances are "lost" as we refine a grammatical description by noting more detailed restrictions on occurrence in natural sentences. By adding a refinement to the hierarchy of categories, we simply subdivide the same utterances into more degrees of grammaticalness, thus increasing the power of the grammar to mark distinctions among utterances.[8]

---

[6]This is merely an illustrative example.

[7]We can represent only one "dimension" of deviation from grammaticalness in this way. There are others. In obvious ways, we could give a more refined stratification of utterances by considering their parts, but I will not go into this.

[8]What is the natural point where continued refinement of the category hierarchy should come to an end? This is not obvious. As the grammatical rules become more detailed, we may find that grammar is converging with what has been called logical grammar. That is, we seem to be studying small overlapping categories of formatives, where each category can be characterized by what we can now (given the grammar) recognize as a semantic feature of some sort. If this turns out to be true in some interesting sense when the problem is studied more seriously, so much the better. This will show that the study of principles of sentence formation does lead to increasingly deeper insights into the use and understanding of utterances, as it is continually refined.

Thus, a generative grammar supplemented with a hierarchy of categories can assign a degree of grammaticalness to each sequence of formatives. If we could show how a hierarchy of categories can be derived from a generative grammar, then the latter alone would assign degree of grammaticalness. There are, in fact, several ways in which this might be possible.

Notice, first, that a transformational grammar will have such symbols as Noun, Adjective, . . . (in addition to much narrower subcategories) at intermediate levels of representation, even if it is designed to generate only a narrow class of highly grammatical sentences, since these larger categories will simplify the descriptions of the domains of transformational rules. Thus, we can expect to find a hierarchy of categories embedded within the constituent structure rules of the transformational grammar. This might be the appropriate hierarchy, or a step towards its construction.[9]

We might approach the question of projecting a hierarchy of categories from a set of utterances in a different way, by defining "optimal k-category analysis," for arbitrary k. Suppose, for simplicity, that we have a corpus of sentences all of the same length. Let $C_1, \ldots, C_k$ be (perhaps overlapping) categories that give an exhaustive classification of the formatives appearing in the corpus. Each sentence is now represented by at least one category sequence. Each such category sequence, in turn, is the representation of many sequences of formatives, in particular, of many that may not be in the original corpus. Thus, a choice of k categories extends the corpus to a set of sentences that are not distinguishable, in terms of these categories, from sentences of the corpus. It is natural to define the optimal k-category analysis as that which extends the corpus the least, i.e., which best reflects substitutability relations within the corpus. Given, for each k, the optimal k-category analysis, we might select the optimal k-category analysis as a level of the hierarchy if it offers a considerable improvement over the optimal k-1-category analysis, but is not much worse than the optimal $k + 1$-category analysis (this could be made precise, in various ways). It is easy to see that there are circumstances under which the optimal k-category analysis might contain overlapping classes (homonyms).[10] It is also easy to drop the restriction that all sentences be of the same length and that

---

[9]This possibility was suggested by some remarks of R. B. Lees.

[10]In general, it is to be expected that overlapping of categories will lead to an extension of the set of generated sentences, since categories will now be larger. Therefore, in general an analysis with disjoint categories will be preferred, by the evaluation procedure suggested above, over an analysis with an equal number of overlapping categories. Suppose, however, that the overlap includes true homonyms—suppose, e.g., that the categories N and V are allowed to overlap in such elements as /riyd/ (*read, reed*), etc. We now have two ways of representing the sentences *read the book* (namely, *VTN* or *NTN*), *the reed looks tall* (*TNVA* or *TVVA*), and so on, instead of just one (e.g., *VTN* and *TVVA*, if /riyd/ is assigned to V). We can select, in each case, the representation which is required, on independent grounds, by other sentences, i.e., *VTN* and *TNVA*, in this example. In this way we can reduce the number of generated sentences by allowing categories to overlap. Overlapping of categories will be permitted, then, when the gain that can be achieved in this way more than compensates for the loss resulting from the fact that categories are larger. We might inquire then whether homonyms can be defined as elements that are in the overlaps in the optimal set of categories on some level. Some evidence in favor of this assumption is presented in "The Logical Structure of Linguistic Theory."

the corpus be finite. Such suggestions as these, when made precise,[11] offer an alternative way in which the generative grammar itself may impose degrees of grammaticalness on utterances that are not directly generated, through the intermediary of the category hierarchy projected from the set of generated sentences.

This suggestion is schematic and no doubt very much oversimplified. Nevertheless, such an approach as this to the problem of defining syntactic categories has many suggestive features and offers some important advantages over the alternatives (e.g., substitution procedures)[12] that have been described in the literature (cf. "The Logical Structure of Linguistic Theory" for a detailed discussion—in particular, it allows for the possibility of setting up a hierarchy of categories and subcategories and for a principled and general solution to the problem of recognizing homonyms). I mention it here to indicate one way in which the further investigation of deviation from grammaticalness might be systematically pursued.

---

[11]This approach to degrees of grammaticalness was described in more detail in "The Logical Structure of Linguistic Theory." It was presented, with some supporting empirical evidence, in a Linguistic Institute lecture in Chicago in 1954, and again in the discussions of the IVth Texas conference, 1959.

[12]It is often proposed that categories be defined in terms of particular sets of inflectional morphemes, but unless some general method is given for selecting the relevant sets (none has ever been proposed, to my knowledge), such definitions are completely *ad hoc* and simply avoid the problem of discovering the basis for categorization.

13 On Understanding "Understanding Utterances"*

Paul Ziff

1 Of course understanding an utterance is something complicated. I would not claim to understand exactly what is involved. But I want to suggest and explore at least one aspect of a certain way of understanding understanding utterances, a way having at least the virtue of leading us with ease along an edge of conjecture from perplexity to doubt. In this way we shall know what we do not know.

2 Certain utterances can be understood without attending to the particular linguistic environment, i.e., the particular discourse, in which they occur or without attending to the context of utterance.

I say to you here and now; "hippopotami are graceful." Probably you have never before heard anyone say this. Even so, you can and most likely do understand it. But if you do, it cannot be on the basis of the discourse in which the utterance has just occurred or on the basis of the context of utterance.

Even though not all utterances can be understood without attending to the particular discourse in which they occur or without attending to the context of utterance, there are nonetheless an indeterminate number of utterances that can be so understood. I propose to consider and examine closely at least part of what is involved in understanding such utterances before attending to the complications that arise in attending to the discourse and the context of utterance.

3 If I attribute an understanding of an utterance to you, what is it that I am attributing?

I shall suppose that the semantic analysis of an utterance consists in associating with it some set of conditions, that the semantic analysis of a morphological element

---

*I have here profited from various discussions with L. Gleitman, Z. Harris, H. Herzberger, and H. Hiż.

having meaning in the language consists in associating with it some set of conditions; I shall suppose this without further discussion here.[1]

Given such suppositions, it then seems reasonable to suppose that part of what is involved in understanding an utterance is understanding what conditions are relevantly associated with the utterance. Of course, this can only be part of what is involved in understanding an utterance, but it is all that I shall be concerned with here.

4 Someone says, "hippopotami are graceful," and we understand what is said. In some cases we understand what is said without attending to the discourse the utterance has occurred in or without attending to the context of utterance. How do we do it?

It seems reasonable to suppose that part of what is involved is that such an utterance is understood on the basis of its syntactic structure and morphemic constitution. Assuming that part of what is involved in understanding an utterance is understanding what conditions are relevantly associated with the utterance, this means that we take a certain set of conditions to be associated with such an utterance on the basis of its syntactic structure and morphemic constitution.

5 But if this is so, then understanding an utterance must somehow involve an apprehension of the specific syntactic structure of the utterance as well as an identification of its morphemic constitution.

I propose to say nothing here about morphological matters and hence nothing about the problems that arise in the identification of the morphemic constitution of an utterance. Instead, I shall be concerned with certain problems that arise in the apprehension of the syntactic structure of an ordered sequence of morphemes constituting an utterance.

6 The utterances of a natural language constitute an indeterminate set. Each member of the set has a syntactic structure. But although many utterances have the same structure, there are indeterminately many utterances of different structures.

Thus, "The cat that ate the rat is here" differs in structure from "The cat that ate the rat that ate the cat is here" which in turn differs in structure from "The cat that ate the rat that ate the cat that ate the rat is here" and so on.

7 If one understands an utterance, then one has somehow apprehended the syntactic structure of that utterance. Since one can understand an indeterminate number of structurally distinct utterances this means that one can somehow apprehend an indeterminate number of distinct syntactic structures of an indeterminate number of utterances.

For this to be possible it is essential that the structure of the language be essentially projective in character. The apprehension of an indeterminate number of distinct syntactic structures of an indeterminate number of utterances must involve some sort of projection from some determinate finite basis. The utterances of the language must have a certain order and must be interrelated in certain ways. Apprehending the syntactic structure of an utterance is essentially a matter of locating that utterance in the structure of the language.

---

[1]See P. Ziff, *Semantic Analysis* (Ithaca, N.Y.: Cornell University Press, 1960). Although these suppositions are ultimately of considerable importance in the analysis I shall present, they are of little importance within the confines of the present discussion. Anyone who objects to them may ignore them so far as the present discussion is concerned.

8 For theoretic purposes, the utterances of a natural language may be thought of as constituting an infinite set. Generally speaking, syntactic theory is in part concerned with the projection of an infinite set from some finite set on the basis of various procedures. But however this may be done, the projected infinite set will, at best, be an infinitely large, proper subset of the infinite set of utterances of the language.

(An analogy may be helpful here: The well-formed formulas of a logistic system, of some familiar type, constitute an infinite set. Theorems of the system will constitute an infinitely large subset of the set of well-formed formulas. This infinitely large subset may be a projection from some finite set of axioms on the basis of certain procedures. But in the normal case the projected infinite set will at best be a proper subset of the infinite set of well-formed formulas: in the normal case, not every well-formed formula will be a theorem.)

9 Generally speaking, if one is concerned with semantic analysis it is useful to consider and, as it were, to operate with a proper subset of the set of what are traditionally classed grammatical utterances, viz., the set of syntactically non-deviant utterances. For example, "he stepped on a green thought" may be classed as a grammatical utterance but, even so, it is syntactically deviant: one can readily discern a syntactic regularity in English which the utterance in question deviates from; the deviation is owing to the co-occurrence of *green* and *thought* in the given linguistic environment.

Syntactically deviant utterances of English thus include both those utterances exemplifying problems of co-occurrence as well as those utterances traditionally classed as ungrammatical.

The syntactically nondeviant utterances of a language are those utterances included in the finite set constituting the simplest and most adequate basis for projection as well as those utterances included in the projected infinite set. In consequence, the grammatical utterances of a language are primarily those utterances that accord simply with the dominant syntactic regularities to be found in the language.

(In terms of the preceding analogy, nondeviant utterances are analogous to theorems and not simply to well-formed formulas of a logistic system. That one can also think of the well-formed formulas of a logistic system as the analogues of nondeviant utterances in a natural language is here irrelevant: one analogy need not preclude another. And there is an important dis-analogy here: for unlike theorems and nontheorems of a logistic system, no sharp line divides nondeviant from deviant utterances.)

10 To class an utterance of the language as syntactically deviant is not to claim that it is devoid of syntactic structure. If an utterance were devoid of syntactic structure it could not reasonably be classed as an utterance of any language whatever. Neither is it to claim that it is devoid of any syntactic structure peculiar to the language in question, for if that were the case the utterance could not reasonably be classed as an utterance of that language.

A syntactically deviant utterance of English is both an utterance of English and a deviant utterance in virtue of its structure. The utterance is an utterance of English in that its structure is that of an English utterance. But in so far as the utterance is syntactically deviant, its structure must differ from that of a nondeviant English utterance. Consider the utterances "Man shoots woman" and "The men grief the women." Some of us can understand these utterances. That means that some of us can somehow apprehend the syntactic structures of these utterances. But these utterances are syntactically deviant, indeed ungrammatical in a traditional sense. And that means that the distinction between the nondeviant and the deviant cannot be a distinction between utterances having and utterances lacking structure: it can only be a distinction between types of structure.

11 Understanding an utterance involves an apprehension of the syntactic structure of the utterance, and apprehending the syntactic structure of an utterance is a matter of locating the utterance in the structure of the language.

Since the syntactically nondeviant utterances occupy a different position in the structure of the language from the syntactically deviant utterances, there is necessarily a difference between what is involved in understanding a syntactically nondeviant utterance and what is involved in understanding a syntactically deviant utterance—if one is to understand how it is that we do understand deviant utterances, it is essential to realize this.

12 Apprehending the syntactic structure of a nondeviant utterance is a matter of grasping the simplest relation between the utterance and the set of nondeviant utterances.

Since the utterance in question is itself a nondeviant utterance and hence included in the set of nondeviant utterances, the simplicity of the relation between the utterance and the set of nondeviant utterances is essentially a matter of the internal simplicity of the set of nondeviant utterances. And since the set of nondeviant utterances is an infinite set projected from some finite basis, the simplicity of the set is a matter of the simplicity of the finite basis and of the procedures of projection.

13 Apprehending the syntactic structure of a syntactically deviant utterance is also a matter of grasping the simplest relation between the utterance and the set of nondeviant utterances. But since the utterance in question is not itself a nondeviant utterance, the simplicity of the relation between the utterance and the set of nondeviant utterances is not a matter of the internal simplicity of the set of nondeviant utterances. A deviant utterance has that structure that constitutes the terminus of the simplest route from the regular grammar to the utterance in question.

14 The concept of the simplest route from the regular grammar is I believe essential to the understanding of understanding deviant utterances. But to explicate precisely what such a concept involves and to illustrate its fruitfulness it is necessary to consider, if only briefly, the structure of the set of nondeviant utterances.

The structure of a set of nondeviant utterances is described by a grammar of the language. A grammar is a syntactic system of elements corresponding in certain specifiable ways to elements of the language in question. The syntactic system (not described but only) suggested here will be that developed by N. Chomsky.[2]

15 Syntactically nondeviant utterances are both those utterances, called *kernels*, included in the finite set constituting the simplest basis for projection as well as those utterances, called *transforms*, that are included in the projected infinite set.

---

[2] See his *Syntactic Structures* ('s Gravenhage: Mouton and Co., 1957).

The class of kernels is some finite class of structured n-tuples of morphological elements of the language. More particularly, the kernels of a language are those utterances of the language having the simplest structure and providing the most adequate basis for projection. Thus, presumably utterances like "The house is red," "The cat is on the mat," "The man eats the cake," and so on would be kernels of English.

16 A particular kernel structure may be defined by a set of rules in a syntactic system, a grammar. The rules of the grammar correspond (more or less) to the dominant regularities to be found in the language.

For example, the structure of "The man eats the cake" or of "The woman eats the pie" can be defined by the following set of rules (where $\rightarrow$ is read "can be rewritten as" and where S is the class of sentences, NP is the class of noun phrases, VP is the class of verb phrases, T the class of definite articles, V the class of verbs, and N the class of nouns):

$$S \rightarrow NP_1\text{-}VP$$
$$NP_i \rightarrow T\text{-}N_i \tag{1}$$
$$VP \rightarrow V\text{-}NP_2$$

and the utterance "The man eats the cake" may then be derived by adding the following rules:

$$T \rightarrow \text{the}$$
$$N_1 \rightarrow \text{man, woman}$$
$$N_2 \rightarrow \text{cake, pie} \tag{2}$$
$$V \rightarrow \text{eats}$$

(These rules are offered here merely by way of example, not as actual rules of English grammar.)

17 The class of transforms is an infinite class of structured n-tuples of morphological elements of the language. The structure of a transform may be thought of as the result of a complex operation over structures of one or more kernels.

The structure of a particular transform may be defined by a set of rules in the grammar. For example, the structure of "The cake was eaten by the man" can be defined in the grammar by adding to the previous set of rules the optional rules:

$$NP_1\text{-}V\text{-}NP_2 \rightarrow NP_2\text{-be-}V\text{-en-by-}NP_1$$
$$\text{be-eats-en-by} \rightarrow \text{is eaten by} \tag{3}$$

(Of course, in an actual grammar one would not introduce an isolated and limited rule like (3). Instead, one would formulate more general morphophonemic rules and rules pertaining to tenses of which the effect of (3) would be a consequence.) The structure of the transform "The cake is eaten" can then be defined by adding the further optional rule:

$$NP_2\text{-be-}V\text{-en-by-}NP_1 \rightarrow NP_2\text{-be-}V\text{-en} \tag{4}$$

18 Whether or not an adequate grammar of English will contain rules such as those of (1–4), or rules like them, depends primarily on two factors: first, on whether such a grammar enables us to derive a set of sentences conforming to our intuitive notions of what constitutes the set of grammatical utterances; secondly, on the simplicity of the syntactic system. For example, instead of (3) one could adopt the rule:

$$T\text{-}N_1\text{-}V\text{-}T\text{-}N_2 \rightarrow T\text{-}N_2\text{-be-}V\text{-en-by-}T\text{-}N_1 \qquad (5)$$

and instead of (4) one could adopt the rule (where Φ indicates deletion):

$$by\text{-}NP \rightarrow \Phi \qquad (6)$$

Whether (3) or (5) or (4) or (6) should be adopted can be decided on the grounds of the adequacy and the simplicity of the resultant syntactic system.

19 Consider such utterances as "House the is red," "I saw man kiss woman," "The men the women kiss," "The men grief the women," "Over there is a green thought," and "He expressed a green thought." Intuitively speaking, one is inclined to say different things about these different utterances, while at the same time saying that all are deviant. "House the is red" sounds simply like a mistake, or possibly a childish way of talking; but "I saw man kiss woman" sounds like something a foreigner would say; "The men the women kiss" resembles poetry, while "The men grief the women" has the air of a semi-clever remark. One is inclined to say that *thought* in "Over there is a green thought" has a nonliteral use, whereas not *thought* but *green* has a nonliteral use in "He expressed a green thought."

All such intuitions can be explicated in terms of the concept of the simplest route from the regular grammar.

20 Consider the utterance "He expressed a green thought": it might seem as though the utterance were deviant owing simply to the combination of *green* and *thought*. That this is not the basic reason is indicated by the fact that the class of elements that can occur without syntactic deviation in the environment "he expressed a green . . ." is null, e.g., "He expressed a green tree" is also deviant. Hence, the deviance of "He expressed a green thought" cannot be attributed to *thought*. It can only be attributed to *green*. Let E_i be the class of elements that can occur without syntactic deviation in the environment "He expressed a . . . thought": then we can relate the utterance to the regular grammar by invoking the rule $E_i \rightarrow green$.

On the other hand, the utterance "Over there is a green thought" is deviant owing to the occurrence of *thought*. Let E_j (where $i \neq j$) be the class of elements that can occur in the environment "over there is a green . . .": then by invoking the rule $E_j \rightarrow thought$ we can relate the utterance to the regular grammar.

Since the deviance of "That is a green thought" can be attributed either to *green* or to *thought*, apart from a particular discourse or context of utterance, the utterance is ambiguous; one could be referring either to a *green* thing or to a certain *thought*.

21 The utterance "The men the women kiss" sounds poetic; it is also ambiguous, for one can easily hear it as equivalent to "The men kiss the women" or to "The women kiss the men." That it is deviant is owing to the fact that it has the form $NP_i\text{-}NP_j\text{-}V$: presumably no such structure can be derived as the structure of a single sentence in the regular grammar. Thus "The men the women kiss" should not be confused with the nominalized utterance in "The men the women kiss are here," for this utterance is related to the kernels "The men are here" and "The women kiss the men."

One could relate the utterance "The men the women kiss" to the regular grammar by invoking either the rule $NP_i\text{-}V\text{-}NP_j \to NP_i\text{-}NP_j\text{-}V$ or the rule $NP_i\text{-}V\text{-}NP_j \to NP_j\text{-}NP_i\text{-}V$. Insofar as either route from the regular grammar is equally simple, the utterance must be structurally ambiguous. Note that if one were concerned with the utterance "The man the cake ate," only the rule $NP_i\text{-}V\text{-}NP_j \to NP_i\text{-}NP_j\text{-}V$ would do; if one were instead to invoke the rule $NP_i\text{-}V\text{-}NP_j \to NP_j\text{-}NP_i\text{-}V$, one could derive "The man the cake ate" only if "The cake ate the man" were a non-deviant utterance—presumably no such utterance can be derived in our regular grammar.

That the utterance "The men the women kiss" has a poetic sound is simply owing to the fact that inversions corresponding to the invoked rules occur primarily in poetic discourses. In such discourses such structures serve a useful purpose, for they are productive of ambiguities.

22 The utterances "The men grief the women," "I saw man kiss woman," and "House the is red" offer no difficulties here. The first requires the rule $E_K \to grief$, where E_K is the class of elements that enter into the transformation "The men caused the women E_K" $\to$ "the men E_K the women," e.g., "The men caused the women trouble" transforms to "The men trouble the women." The second calls for a rule having the effect of $Ar \to \Phi$, where Ar is the class of articles. Utterances that are deviant owing to the deletion of articles are frequently encountered in news reports and in the speech of foreigners. Notice that an utterance like "I saw men kiss women" may simply be the plural counterpart of the ungrammatical "I saw man kiss woman," in which case it too is deviant—and in such a case one *can* almost hear the accent of a foreigner. The third, "House the is red," sounds simply like a mistake, owing to the fact that it obviously calls for the rule $T\text{-}N \to N\text{-}T$, and such a rule would (generally) be utterly pointless.

23 Various problems are posed by this method of analysis. But the most obvious and pressing are these: how does one find a route from the regular grammar to the utterance; and what determines which of alternative routes is the simplest?

24 How one finds a route from the regular grammar to the utterance is primarily a matter of identifying the source of the utterance's deviance. Having done that it is no great problem to invent and invoke the rule to suit the purpose. But identifying the source of deviance can be an exceedingly subtle and difficult task. The problem can, however, be divided.

There are (at least) two prominent types of deviation that can be distinguished. Certain utterances deviate in regular ways, others in irregular ways.

What I am suggesting is that the utterances of a language can be divided into at least four relatively distinct syntactic classes (distinct perhaps as red, blue, green, and yellow are distinct): the class of kernels, the class of transforms, the class of (what I shall call) *variants*, and the class of (what I shall call) *inventions*.

25 Variants are utterances that deviate from the syntactic regularities of the language in some regular way. Thus, they are variations on standard themes. Whether a deviant utterance is a variant is indicated by the type of rule that must be invoked to relate it to the regular grammar in the simplest possible way. With respect to variants the simplest type of rules involve either inversion or deletion or addition. Thus, "The man the cake ate" is an instance of inversion; "Man eats woman in lifeboat" is an instance of deletion; "The a man a that a I a saw a is a here a" is an instance of addition.

26 Inventions are utterances that deviate from the syntactic regularities of the language in irregular ways. Thus, they are not variations but, as it were, genuine inventions. Whether a deviant utterance is an invention is also indicated by the type of rule that must be invoked to relate it in the simplest possible way to the regular grammar. With respect to inventions the simplest type of rules involve either the extension of word classes or the contraction of word classes. Thus, "The men grief the women" is an instance of invention calling for the extension of a word class. Contraction, however, is a more complicated matter.

27 Cases involving the contraction of word classes warrant special mention here for they occur only when there is some sort of semantic difficulty; thus, they are not strictly syntactic in character though they have a syntactic effect.

Consider the utterance "Even though my heart is in my chest and I am in the lowlands, my heart is in the highlands"; unless we distinguish between the two occurrences of *heart* or among the three occurrences of *in* we have a self-contradictory utterance. The simplest way to resolve the difficulty is to assume that a contraction of a word is involved.

Let E_o be the class of elements to which the environment "my . . . is in the highlands" is open. We then invoke the rule to the effect that *heart* is a member of E_o on the prior supposition that it is not; this may be written as:

$$(E_o \rightarrow \text{heart}) \mid E_o \rightarrow \text{heart} \qquad (7)$$

where the expression to the left of the vertical line indicates that the rule expressed by the expression to the right of the vertical line is invoked on the supposition expressed by the expression to the left of the vertical line. The effect of the supposition is to make deviant the utterance "Even though my heart is in my chest and I am in the lowlands, my heart is in the highlands." Then by invoking the rule, we relate the utterance to the regular grammar. If this procedure seems unduly artificial, it should be noted that the supposition was dictated by a desire to avoid a semantic difficulty, whereas the rule was invoked merely to relate the utterance to the regular grammar.

Another type of word class contraction is exemplified by "Josef is a boy, but George is a child": again, the simplest way to avoid a semantic difficulty is to assume that a contraction of a word class is involved. Let E_c be the class of elements to which the environment "George is a . . ." is open. We then invoke the rule to the effect that *child* is a member of E_c on the prior supposition that *boy* is not:

$$-(E_c \rightarrow \text{boy}) \mid E_c \rightarrow \text{child} \qquad (8)$$

Still another type of word class contraction is exemplified by "a dog is a dog, but a cat is a cat." Generally speaking, word-class contraction always involves a prior supposition that a certain class is closed to a certain element and the invocation of a rule to the effect that a certain class, perhaps another class, is open to a certain element, perhaps another element.[3]

---

[3]I am inclined to suppose that word-class contraction is intimately related to so-called "appreciative" and "depreciative pregnancies" in the use of words. See W. Empson, *The Structure of Complex Words*.

28 I should like to suggest that there are five basic types of routes from the regular grammar to a syntactically deviant utterance. In consequence, there are five types of rules that may be invoked; (where capital letters are variables for word classes and lower case letters are variables for words) these five types of rules may be rendered schematically as follows:

$$\cdots A \cdots B \cdots \rightarrow \cdots B \cdots A \cdots \qquad \text{(9a)}$$
$$\cdots A \cdots B \cdots \rightarrow \cdots A \cdots \qquad \text{(9b)}$$
$$\cdots A \cdots \rightarrow \cdots A \cdots B \cdots \qquad \text{(9c)}$$
$$A \rightarrow a \qquad \text{(9d)}$$
$$(A \rightarrow a) \mid B \rightarrow b \qquad \text{(9e)}$$

The first is the rule of inversion, the second of deletion, the third of addition, the fourth of word-class extension, and the fifth of word-class contraction.

(It should be noted that rules of the form $a \rightarrow b$, e.g., *the* $\rightarrow$ *house*, have been excluded from consideration here. For example, an utterance like "I put the door out and closed the cat" is perhaps best dealt with by invoking the pair of rules *door* $\rightarrow$ *cat* and *cat* $\rightarrow$ *door*. But this is a matter of morpheme identification. Intuitively speaking, one draws a line between, e.g., "house the is red," a case of inversion, and "I put the door out and closed the cat," a case of morpheme identification. How the line is drawn is a complex matter that I cannot discuss at this point.)

I am inclined to suppose that these five basic types of rules constitute the simplest type of routes from the regular grammar to syntactically deviant utterance types.

29 Answering one question always seems to give rise to another: what reason is there to suppose that the simplest routes are the five indicated? That I feel inclined to say so proves nothing—that you agree with me, if you do, still proves nothing.

The five types of rules indicated do not of course exhaust the list of possible rules. For example, one could formulate a mad rule like $ABCDEFG \rightarrow CBAEGDF$. Given such a rule, one could then directly relate an utterance like "saw man the the it window in" to the regular grammar.[4] Indeed, it would be a variant of "The man saw it in the window." So by designating the five indicated types of rules as the simplest routes, an infinite number of others have been excluded. But with what justification?

Here I am inclined to say that the five types of rules indicated somehow reflect the basic structure of the language, for they seem to follow what, at present, seems to be the general pattern of transformations. Thus, inversion occurs in the passive and in interrogative transformations, addition in conjunctive transformations, deletion in all sorts of transformations, while word class extension is a feature of nominalizing transformations.

30 However, even if I am right in claiming that these five types of rules con-

---

[4]Note that on the simplest analysis "Saw man the the it window in" would be a semi grammatical utterance, for it could be a transform by deletion, thus, according to the rules $NP_i\text{-}V\text{-}NP_j \rightarrow NP_j$, $NP \rightarrow N\text{-}N\text{-}N\text{-}N\text{-}N\text{-}N\text{-}N$, it would have the form "*Saw, man, the, the, it, window, in.*" As such, the utterance might occur as a response to "What are the words?" or "What did you say?" and so forth. Further note that this interpretation would be consistent with the natural intonation contour of such an utterance, viz., a contour indicative of a list.

stitute the simplest types of routes back to the regular grammar, so far I have at best characterized, as it were, the logical space of operations. There is still the problem of deciding in a given case which of alternative routes is the simplest; e.g., one could relate the utterance "The men grief the women" to the regular grammar by invoking either the rule $E_k \rightarrow grief$, where E_k is the class of elements that enter into the transformation "The men cause the women E_k" $\rightarrow$ "The men E_k the women," or the rule $E_m \rightarrow grief$, where E_m is the class of elements that can occur without deviation in the environment "The men . . . the women," or the rule $V \rightarrow grief$, where V is the class of verbs. No doubt the simplicity of a route must depend on the strength of the rule, the character of the classes involved, and so forth. But I can say nothing helpful about these matters here.

Finally, I have so far said nothing about the significance of syntactically non-deviant utterances. If we relate a deviant utterance to the regular grammar by invoking certain rules, how do the rules serve to determine the significance of the utterance? To answer this question we must first consider how the structure of a nondeviant utterance serves to determine the significance of the utterance. That is a long and difficult story.

14   Semi-sentences*

Jerrold J. Katz

I

As everyone knows, speakers can understand not only well-formed utterances of their language (sentences) but they can also understand utterances that are not well-formed. Such ungrammatical strings, *semi-sentences* as we shall call them,[1] are frequently heard in every-day conversation and are, in certain circumstances, the best way of communicating exactly what one wishes, e.g., "It happened a grief ago" or "I have overconfidence in you." Since they, as well as fully grammatical strings, are understood by speakers, a theory that explains how speakers are capable of understanding them is necessary to continue the account of the speaker's linguistic knowledge begun by the grammar. A theory of semi-sentences, a theory that characterizes the set of ungrammatical strings that the speaker's knowledge of linguistic structure enables him to understand and explains why the members of this set are comprehensible, is, therefore, to be regarded as an integral part of the description of a language, not as a bonus it is nice but not necessary to have.

II

Recent investigations concerning the form of a grammar best suited to describing a natural language show that a grammar is a formal system whose rules permit the derivation of every grammatical string in the language while, at the same time, insuring that no ungrammatical string can be derived in the system.[2] Thus, such a

*This work was supported in part by the U.S. Army Signal Corps, the Air Force Office of Scientific Research, and the Office of Naval Research; in part by the National Science Foundation (Grant G–16526); and in part by the National Institutes of Health (Grant MH–04737–02).

[1]Chomsky refers to such strings as "semi-grammatical." My usage derives from his, but I do not wish to commit myself at the outset to viewing the problem as one having to do only with *grammatical* ill-formedness. As will become evident in the final section of the present paper, I think semantic ill-formedness is also part of the problem.

[2]This conception of grammar is due to Chomsky. Cf. his book *Syntactic Structures* ('s Gravenhage, 1957).

grammar *generates* a list of strings of elements in the vocabulary of the language which, if extended sufficiently, contains any sentence but which—no matter how far it is extended—never contains a string that is not a sentence. Since the knowledge of grammar a speaker possesses is knowledge of the grammatical structure of sentences, not a knowledge of individual sentences per se, a generative grammar must generate the sentences of a language in a way that reveals their grammatical structure. This a generative grammar does with rules constructed in such a way that the derivation of a sentence is the basis for assigning it a structural description specifying the elements out of which it is constructed and their constructional relations.

The generative form of a grammar determines some of the empirical constraints upon the structural descriptions that the grammar produces for sentences. Since the assignment of structural properties to substrings of sentences is the mechanism of sentence generation,[3] the strings that a grammar generates provide the basis for an empirical check on its structural description. If some grammatical sentences are not derivable, some grammatical structures of the language are not represented by the grammar; and if some ungrammatical strings are derivable, some ungrammatical structures are countenanced as legitimate forms in the language. In the former case, the rules of grammar would be incomplete, while in the latter they would include some that are incorrect.

Given all this, however, we are faced with the consequence that a grammar of a language cannot describe the grammatical structure of semi-sentences, even though it is the aim of grammar construction to discover what a speaker knows about grammatical structure that enables him to understand utterances in his language. For, given that the structure description of a string is provided by its derivation, structural descriptions are assigned only to strings that are generated, that is, only to sentences (the empirical constraints being what they are). Yet, as remarked above, it is clear that speakers can understand semi-sentences, strings that are partly grammatical and partly ungrammatical. So it is also clear that, in some sense, speakers know their *structure*, such as it is, too. This, then, raises the question: can a generative grammar only explicate the speaker's knowledge of the structure of fully well-formed strings? Can such grammar say nothing about the structure of partly structured and partly unstructured strings?

There is good reason why this question should not be answered affirmatively. A semi-sentence is, after all, partly grammatical. Hence, the knowledge that enables a speaker to understand sentences—his knowledge of the rules of the grammar—must be identically the knowledge that enables him to understand semi-sentences, for semi-sentences are understood in terms of their well-formed parts. Moreover, the knowledge a speaker uses to recognize the respects in which a semi-sentence is ungrammatical is also his knowledge of grammaticality: knowledge of the grammatical rules is here employed to discover instances of their violation. Let us consider an example which will illustrate these points. The semi-sentence "Scientists truth the universe" is partly grammatical, and the knowledge that enables a speaker to understand this semi-sentence in terms of its grammatical parts must be identically the knowledge of grammar that helps him understand "Scientists study the

---

[3]E.g. the generation of the sentence "The man hit the ball" is accomplished by such property assignments as characterizing *The man* as a noun phrase.

universe," "Scientists discover facts about the universe," and so on. On the other hand, the speaker knows that the semi-sentence "Scientists truth the universe" is ungrammatical because the word *truth* cannot appear in the context "Scientists . . . the universe." This knowledge is identically the knowledge that only verbals can enter this context and that *truth* is not a verbal.

But if the preceding question is answered in the negative, we seem to be faced with a paradoxical conclusion. Though the knowledge a speaker requires to understand well-formed sentences and the knowledge he requires to understand semi-sentences is one and the same, and though a generative grammar can represent all the grammatical knowledge a speaker has and can account for how he is able to understand sentences, yet such a grammar cannot account for how a speaker is able to understand semi-sentences.

The appearance of paradox is immediately dispelled, however, once we realize that these facts do not conflict as they first seem to. The task a speaker performs when he understands a semi-sentence involves, in addition to his use of grammatical knowledge, the use of knowledge of another kind. The conclusion to be drawn here is simply that a generative grammar does not provide an answer to the question of what relations between well-formed parts of a string and ill-formed parts of that string allow the string to be understood by speakers and what relations do not. A grammar tells us what is and what is not grammatical, but it does not say what combinations of what is and what is not grammatical are comprehensible to the speakers of the language.

Thus, we need a theory of semi-sentences: a theory whose basic aim is to describe the ways grammatical parts and ungrammatical parts can combine to produce sentence-like strings which speakers understand, even though they are not strictly, or even "not so strictly," well-formed.

III

A semi-sentence, such as "Scientists truth the universe," can be regarded as instancing a degree of deviation from the norm of full grammaticality. Different semi-sentences differ in the extent of their deviation from full grammaticality (and in their manner also), but nothing is a semi-sentence that goes too far. That is to say, there is a point after which comprehensibility is lost. The situation for a theory of semi-sentences is, then, this: such a theory must distinguish between semi-sentences, strings that deviate from full well-formedness but not to the point of incomprehensibility, and nonsense strings, just "word salad," strings that depart from grammaticality so far that they are thereby rendered incomprehensible.[4] We thus require that:

R1: A theory of semi-sentences partitions the set of ungrammatical strings into two exclusive and jointly exhaustive proper subsets: the set *SS* of semi-sentences and the set *NS* of nonsense strings.

---

[4]At this point, we may raise the question of how one can be sure that the case under analysis is a semi-sentence. Of course, there is no way to forecast *a priori* what tests will be relevant, but, in general, one can be sure if one can obtain a consensus from fluent speakers indicating that the string is understood by each of them in the same way, if one can ascertain that the string can be paraphrased in the language (since nonsense strings cannot), and so on and the string is ungrammatical.

Further, however, such a theory must offer some account of how speakers utilize the grammatical structure and the ungrammatical features of semi-sentences to understand them. Thus, we require also that:

R2: A theory of semi-sentences explicate the speaker's knowledge of the patterns of deviation from grammaticality that preserve intelligibility.

A semi-sentence such as "A scientist truth universe" or "Many scientist truthing universe" may be regarded as instancing a somewhat greater degree of deviation from full grammaticality than does the semi-sentence "Scientists truth the universe." And nothing we would want to call a semi-sentence deviates as far as "Truth a scientists universe the." Thus, a theory of semi-sentences may go further than satisfying Requirements 1 and 2 by establishing an ordering among the members of *SS* which ranks each semi-sentence in terms of its degree of departure from complete well-formedness. Of course, a theory that does this in addition to satisfying Requirement 1 and Requirement 2 might be considered preferable to one that does not, but we cannot require of a theory of semi-sentences that it so rank them, over and above satisfying these requirements. A theory satisfying Requirements 1 and 2 explicates the principles underlying the speaker's understanding of semi-sentences. It explicates the notion *semi-sentence of L*, whereas a theory that only ranks strings in terms of their degree of departure from full grammaticality at best gives only approximate estimates of the membership of the set of semi-sentences of a language.

IV

Chomsky offered the first and most penetrating theory of semi-sentences.[5] The main idea behind his proposal is that speakers are able to understand a semi-sentence because they know how to assign it a degree of grammaticalness which marks its manner and extent of deviation from full well-formedness. His theory, which seeks to explain how speakers assign degree of grammaticalness, consists of a system of levels of grammaticalness within which each string constructable from the vocabulary of the language can be represented at all and only those levels on which it is grammatical. Chomsky's theory would satisfy Requirement 1 if and only if the strings representable on levels l thru k are all and only the grammatical strings, the strings representable on levels $k + l$ thru $k + n$ are all and only the semi-sentences, and the strings representable on levels $k + n + l$ thru m are all and only the nonsense strings (where $k \geq l$, $k + n \geq k + l$, and m is the number of levels in the system).

Chomsky's full account also contains a general procedure for constructing such a system for a language given only a grammar of that language. But we shall not consider this procedure here. Our reason is that our examination of Chomsky's theory of semi-sentences will reveal it to fail Requirement 1 and thus to be inadequate as a theory of semi-sentences. Clearly, no general procedure for projecting a certain type

---

[5]N. Chomsky, *The Logical Structure of Linguistic Theory*, M.I.T. Library; "Some Methodological Remarks on Generative Grammar," (the present volume under the title "Degrees of Grammaticalness") *Word*, **17** (1961) 219–39; and N. Chomsky, and G. A. Miller, "Introduction to the Formal Analysis of Natural Languages" *Handbook of Mathematical Psychology*, Luce, Bush, and Galanter (editors), (New York: John Wiley & Son, Inc., 1963).

of system of levels of grammaticalness from a grammar is called for if such a theory is known to be inadequate as a theory of semi-sentences.[6]

Chomsky's theory is as follows:

Suppose we have a grammar G that generates a fairly narrow (though of course infinite) set $L(G)$ of well-formed sentences. How could we assign to each string not generated by the grammar a measure of its deviation in at least one of the many dimensions in which deviation can occur? We might proceed by first selecting some unit—for concreteness, let us choose *word units* and, for convenience, let us not bother to distinguish in general between different *inflectional forms* (e.g., between *find, found, finds*). Next, set up a hierarchy $\mathscr{C}$ of classes of these units, where $\mathscr{C} = \mathscr{C}_1, \ldots, \mathscr{C}_N$, and for each $i \leq N$:

$$\mathscr{C}_i = \{C_1^i, \ldots, C_{a_i}^i\}, \qquad \text{where} \quad a_1 > a_2 > \ldots > a_N = 1; \tag{22}$$

$$C_j^i \text{ is nonnull; and}$$

$$C_j^i \subset C_k^i \text{ if, and only if, } j = k$$

$\mathscr{C}_1$ is the most highly differentiated class of categories; $\mathscr{C}_N$ contains but a single category. Other conditions might be imposed (e.g., that $\mathscr{C}_i$ be a refinement of $\mathscr{C}_{i+j}$), but (22) will suffice for the present discussion.

$\mathscr{C}_i$ will be called the *categorization of order i*; its members will be called *categories of order i*. A sequence $C_{b_1}^i, \ldots, C_{b_q}^i$ of categories of order i is called a *sentence-form* of order i; it is said to generate the string of words $w_1 \ldots w_q$ if, for each $j \leq q$, $w_j \in C_{b_j}^i$. Thus, the set of all word strings generated by a sentence-form is the Cartesian product of the sequence of categories.

We have described $\mathscr{C}$ and G independently; let us now relate them. We say that a set Σ of sentence-forms of order i *covers* G if each string of $L(G)$ is generated by some member of Σ. We say that a sentence-form is *grammatical* with respect to G if one of the strings that the sentence-form generates is in $L(G)$—*fully grammatical*, with respect to G, if each of the strings that it generates is in $L(G)$. We say that $\mathscr{C}$ is *compatible* with G if for each sentence w of $L(G)$ there is a sentence-form of order one that generates w and that is fully grammatical with respect to G. Thus, if $\mathscr{C}$ is compatible with G, there is a set of fully grammatical sentence-forms of order one that covers G. We might also require, for compatibility, that $\mathscr{C}_1$ be the smallest set of word classes that meets this condition. Note that in this case the categories of $\mathscr{C}_1$ need not be pairwise disjoint. For example, *know* will be in C_i^1 and *no* in C_j^1, where $i \neq j$, although they are phonetically the same. If two words are mutually substitutable throughout $L(G)$, they will be in the same category C_j^1, if $\mathscr{C}_1$ is compatible with G; but the converse is not necessarily true.

We will say that a string w is *i-grammatical* (has degree of grammaticalness i) with respect to G, $\mathscr{C}$, if i is the least number such that w is generated by a grammatical sentence-form of order i. Thus, the strings of the highest degree of grammaticalness are those of order 1, the order with the largest number of categories. All strings are grammatical of order N or less since $\mathscr{C}_N$ contains only one category.

---

[6]In conversation, Chomsky has pointed out to me that he intends his procedure for projecting a hierarchy of categories from a grammar to be construed as part of the explanation of how the ability to comprehend deviant strings is acquired by speakers. If a procedure such as the one he has sketched is a component in a language-learning device, then that device acquires the ability to comprehend deviant strings (in the sense of the hierarchy of categories) automatically when it learns the grammar of a language. This view raises many interesting questions but, unfortunately, they go beyond the bounds of the present discussion.

These ideas can be clarified by an example. Suppose that G is a grammar of English and that $\mathscr{C}$ is a system of categories compatible with it and having a structure something like this:

$$\mathscr{C}_1 : \quad \begin{aligned} N_{\text{hum}} &= \{\text{boy, man,} \ldots\} \\ N_{\text{ab}} &= \{\text{virtue, sincerity,} \ldots\} \\ N_{\text{comp}} &= \{\text{idea, belief,} \ldots\} \\ N_{\text{mass}} &= \{\text{bread, beef,} \ldots\} \\ N_{\text{comm}} &= \{\text{book, chair,} \ldots\} \\ V_1 &= \{\text{admire, dislike,} \ldots\} \\ V_2 &= \{\text{annoy, frighten,} \ldots\} \\ V_3 &= \{\text{hit, find,} \ldots\} \\ V_4 &= \{\text{sleep, reminisce,} \ldots\} \end{aligned} \qquad (23)$$

and so on

$$\mathscr{C}_2 : \quad \begin{aligned} \text{Noun} &= N_{\text{hum}} \cup N_{\text{ab}} \cup \ldots \\ \text{Verb} &= V_1 \cup V_2 \cup \ldots \end{aligned}$$

and so on

$$\mathscr{C}_3 : \quad \text{Word}$$

This extremely primitive hierarchy $\mathscr{C}$ of categories would enable us to express some of the grammatical diversity of possible strings of words. Let us assume that G would generate "*the boy cut the beef,*" "*the boy reminisced,*" "*sincerity frightens me,*" "*the boy admires sincerity,*" "*the idea that sincerity might frighten you astonishes me,*" "*the boy found a piece of bread,*" "*the boy found the chair,*" "*the boy who annoyed me slept here,*" and so on. It would not, however, generate such strings as "*the beef cut sincerity,*" "*sincerity reminisced,*" "*the boy frightens sincerity,*" "*sincerity admires the boy,*" "*the sincerity that the idea might frighten you astonishes me,*" "*the boy found a piece of book,*" "*the boy annoyed the chair,*" "*the chair who annoyed me found here,*" and so on. Strings of the former type would be one-grammatical (as are all strings generated by G); strings of the latter type would be two-grammatical; all strings would be three-grammatical, with respect to this primitive categorization.

Many of the two-grammatical strings might find a natural use in actual communication, of course. Some of them, in fact, (e.g., "misery loves company") might be more common than many one-grammatical strings (infinitely many of which have zero probability and consist of parts which have zero probability, effectively).

A speaker of English can impose an interpretation on many of these strings by considering their analogies and resemblances to those generated by the grammar he has mastered, much as he can impose an interpretation on an abstract drawing. One-grammatical strings, in general, like representational drawings, need have no interpretation *imposed* on them to be understood. With a hierarchy such as $\mathscr{C}$ we could account for the fact that speakers of English know that, for example, "colorless green ideas sleep furiously," is surely to be distinguished, with respect to well-formedness, from "revolutionary new ideas appear infrequently," on the one hand, and from "furiously sleep ideas green colorless" or "harmless seem dogs young friendly" (which both have the same frame of grammatical morphemes), on the other; and so on, in indefinitely many similar cases.[7]

This theory is such that no line can be drawn between a pair of levels such that all and only sentences and semi-sentences are representable on some level on one side of this line and all and only nonsense strings are representable on some level on the other side of this line. Thus, such a theory does not decide which ungrammatical

---

[7] N. Chomsky and G. A. Miller, *op. cit.*

strings belong to *SS* and which belong to *NS*. Hence, Chomsky's theory fails to satisfy Requirement 1. To establish this we must show:

> For any pair of levels *i* and *j* (neither *i* nor *j* = 1 and *i* < *j*), there are indefinitely many pairs of strings [*X, Y*] such that *X* is *i*-grammatical and *Y* is *j*-grammatical (thus *X* has a higher degree of grammaticalness than *Y* but neither is grammatical) and such that it is the case both that *X* is in *NS* and *Y* is in *SS*.

One could also show that the following is true:

> There are levels such that each has pairs of strings [*X, Y*] representable on it but *X* is in *NS* and *Y* is in *SS*.[8]

We shall not try to show this, however, because the argument is, in substance, the same as for the previous one.

Let us begin by considering the example Chomsky gives of his theory: The string "The chair who annoyed me found here" is 2-grammatical in Chomsky's example of an *N*-level hierarchy of categories, whereas the string "Here found me annoyed who chair the" is 3-grammatical. This supports the interpretation of Chomsky's theory as a theory of semi-sentences: the 2-grammatical string is understandable (the string means "the chair annoyed me, and someone found the chair here") while the 3-grammatical one is not. But this interpretation breaks down. For *X* we may take "The sincerity that the idea frightens you astonishes me" or "The beef cut sincerity." Such strings are 2-grammatical, i.e., they have the proper word-category relations but not the proper word-subcategory relations, but are quite incomprehensible to speakers of English. For *Y* we may take such strings as "If there is any truth in what he says, it would be to insist foolish" or "She is pretty, charming, plays tennis with the finest people, sweet, and happy." Each of these strings is prevented from being 2-grammatical because it contains an ill-formed word category (or phrase category) relation; but, though 3-grammatical, each is, nevertheless, easily comprehensible to English speakers.

To show that Chomsky's type of theory is not adequate we must show that, for any other example of this type of theory, we can construct indefinitely many counter-examples of this kind, i.e., pairs in which the string ranked more grammatical is not comprehensible and the string ranked less grammatical is comprehensible. To show why there always are such counter-examples we may argue as follows: A string *S* fails to receive a representation at a level *i* (and at all levels *i*-1, *i*-2, . . . , 1) if there is a single restriction holding between a pair of categories at level *i* which *S* violates. Thus, a string *S* can violate a restriction which prevents it from reaching *i*-grammaticalness, while another string *S'* contains no violations of restrictions at level *i* and so receives a higher degree of grammaticalness than *S*, even though, otherwise, *S* contains less structural distortion than *S'* and is, consequently, intelligible to speakers whereas *S'* is not. Another way to put this point is to say that, although *S* fails to receive a representation at *i* (failing at a level requiring only one improper relation among an *n*-tuple of formatives belonging to categories at that level) and although *S'* may be representable at *i*, *S* may be so little ungrammatical with respect to the

---

[8]E.g., the strings "the beef cut sincerity" and "the boy found a piece of book" that Chomsky uses as examples in the quoted piece on page 405 above.

relations at levels *i*-1, *i*-2, . . . , 1 (even though *S* is not representable on these levels) while *S'* is highly ungrammatical with respect to the relations at these levels that *S* has, over-all, sufficient structure to enable it to be understood while *S'* does not. Thus, for any particular realization of Chomsky's conception of a category-hierarchy, there will be *S* and *S'* pairs, and their existence shows that Requirement 1 is unsatisfied.

V

Another proposal for a theory of semi-sentences comes from Ziff.[9] Ziff seeks to explain how semi-sentences are understood on analogy to the way Chomsky explains how fully grammatical strings are understood. Understanding the structure of a grammatical sentence requires grasping the simplest relation between that sentence and the set of grammatical sentences;[10] by analogy, then, understanding a semi-sentence requires grasping the simplest relation between that sentence and the set of sentences.[11] The uniqueness of Ziff's proposal lies in his suggestion regarding how we should construe the notion *simplest relation to the set of sentences*. He suggests that we interpret this notion as that of the simplest route from the grammar to the semi-sentence—to be formalized as the simplest rule for deriving the semi-sentence from a grammatical sentence.

Paradigmatic of Ziff's conception of how to relate semi-sentences to the set of grammatical sentences with rules that constitute the simplest route back is his treatment of the semi-sentence "He expressed a green thought." This case is accounted for by the rule $E_i \rightarrow green$, where E_i represents the class of elements that can occur without syntactic deviation in the environment "he expressed a . . . thought.[12] Such a rule Ziff calls a "word-class extension rule," and beside these he cites four other types: word-class contraction rules, inversion rules, deletion rules, and addition rules.[13] Generally, differences between these rules are not significant for our discussion; when they are, we indicate this. Otherwise we shall take the above case as paradigmatic.

Because of an ambiguity in Ziff's presentation, there are two ways to interpret the rules that Ziff proposes as an explication of the notion *simplest route back to the grammatical sentences*. But both fail to satisfy Requirement 1.

On the first of these interpretations, however, no set of rules of the kind Ziff suggests can even constitute a theory. On this interpretation, the sentence environment in terms of which we give the definition of the grammatical class that figures in a rule *R*, e.g., the class E_i in the example above, characterizes the domain of the rule *R*. Thus, the rule $E_i \rightarrow w_j$, which takes the well-formed string of words (or morphemes) $X + w_i + Y$ (where *X* and *Y* represent strings of words (or morphemes) and *X* or *Y* but not both may be null) into the ill-formed string $X + w_j + Y$ is an instruction to substitute its right hand symbol for its left only in the environment

[9]Ziff, P. "On Understanding 'Understanding Utterances' " in this volume.

[10]As Chomsky usually puts it: the rules of a grammar are the simplest set of rules that represent the structural relations between the members of the set of sentences.

[11]This, of course, is also what Chomsky is saying when he requires that we select the simplest procedure for projecting a hierarchy of categories from a grammar. Cf. 7*n* of this paper.

[12]Ziff, *op. cit.*, Sect. 20.

[13]Ziff, *ibid.*, Sect., 28.

$X \ldots Y$. Since the set of semi-sentences is infinite, a theory of semi-sentences must consist of a set of rules that formally represents this infinite set without representing any member of the infinite set of nonsense strings. This is simply a consequence of Requirement 1. But rules of the kind we are now considering require that we have a separate rule for each semi-sentence we wish to account for. That this is the case follows from the fact that the symbol to the left of the arrow designates a class of elements that is defined in terms of the environment that results from replacing an element in the sentence $X + w_i + Y$ by a substitution symbol and the fact that the symbol to the right of the arrow designates that element which, when substituted for the substitution symbol, turns the environment into the semi-sentence $X + w_j + Y$. For there is, then, a one-one correspondence between rules and semi-sentences such that when a semi-sentence is different from another, its image under this correspondence is different. Therefore, for rules of this kind to do the job, Requirement 1 requires there would have to be infinitely many of them (there must be as many rules as semi-sentences according to the previous one-one correspondence). But, since any theory has to contain only a finite number of rules (we cannot write down more), Ziff's proposal, on the present interpretation, cannot be a theory, since, in principle, any set of rules of the kind he suggests will always omit infinitely many rules that are needed and thus will always leave infinitely many semi-sentences unaccounted for.

Hence, we are left with the second of the two interpretations of Ziff's proposal. According to this more plausible one, the environment referred to in the definition of the symbol on the left-hand side of the arrow in one of Ziff's rules (e.g., the environment "He expressed a . . . thought" referred to in the definition of the symbol "E_i" in the rule "$E_i \rightarrow green$") is considered a diagnostic environment, i.e., an abstract representation of a set of specific sentential environments. Formulating Ziff's rules in the equivalent notation "$X + w_i + Y \rightarrow X + w_j + Y$," the present interpretation relaxes the restriction that w_j, X, and Y represent strings of words (or morphemes) and allows them to represent strings of syntactic markers or strings of words (or morphemes) and syntactic markers, as well. Thus, rules of Ziff's variety are now free of any restriction which limits their application in such a way that a different rule is required for each different semi-sentence that is to be accounted for. But on this interpretation Ziff's proposal also fails Requirement 1.

The basic idea underlying Ziff's theory is that understanding a semi-sentence involves grasping the simplest relation between it and the set of sentences. Presumably, then, what distinguishes semi-sentences from nonsense strings, strings that speakers cannot understand, is that the relation to the set of sentences is too complex in the case of the latter. Ziff nowhere says this, but it seems necessary for without it the theory does not coherently develop its basic idea. However, presuming this, Ziff's rules are such that any member of *NS* can be related to the grammatical sentences by a rule that is no more complex than those Ziff cites (in fact, they are the simplest that can be written in the form that Ziff prescribes). For example, the nonsense string "The saw cut his sincerity" can be related to "The saw cut his finger" by the rule $E_k \rightarrow sincerity$, where E_k represents the class of elements that can occur without syntactic deviation in the environment "The saw cut his . . . ." Thus, any nonsense string is in the set that Ziff's rules characterize, since the rules necessary to put them there are, like the above rule, as simple as any that are needed to put semi-sentences there.

This sort of point can be pushed further to show how inadequate Ziff's proposal actually is. The symbol S will be needed for the left side of certain of Ziff's rules because "... is a sentence," "I know that ...," and so on are important diagnostic environments. But, this being so, Ziff requires only one rule: $S \rightarrow$ any ungrammatical string.[14] In fact, since simplicity is determined in terms of number of rules as well as in terms of number of symbols per rule, this rule, which allows every element in NS to count as a member of SS, is the simplest theory of the kind Ziff advocates and hence, according to his account, the most preferable.

Even without presuming that the reason that semi-sentences are comprehensible while nonsense strings are not is that the former involves a simple relation to the grammatical sentences while the latter involves one too complex to be graspable by speakers, we can show that Ziff's proposal fails Requirement 1. The difference between the present interpretation of Ziff's rules and the former one is that now the application of these rules is regarded as free of restriction to a single sentential context. Hence, such a rule can be applied in the course of a derivation whenever there is an nth line that contains the left-hand symbol of the rule. But, since this is the case, there will be indefinitely many derivations whose terminal line is a nonsense string. For example, in Section 20 of his paper Ziff gives the rules:

(1) $E_i \rightarrow$ *green*,   where E_i is the set of all and only the elements which when substituted in the environment "He expressed a ... thought" yield a syntactically regular sentence.

(2) $E_j \rightarrow$ *thought*, where E_j is the set of all and only the elements which when substituted in the environment "Over there is a green ..." yield a syntactically regular sentence.

With (1) and (2) we can obtain, *inter alia*, "It is green for convicts to break thoughts" from the derivation for "it is reasonable for convicts to break rocks"; "His green in solving the problem is green" from the derivation for "His difficulty in solving the problem is comprehensible"; and so on. Use of the other four types of rules, the inversion, deletion, addition, and word-class contraction rules, only makes it far easier to obtain members of NS. For example, by Ziff's inversion rule,[15] from "He thinks it is green for convicts to break thoughts" we can obtain "He it is green for convicts to break thoughts thinks." Using Ziff's addition rule,[16] we can get "He a it a is green for a convicts a to break a thoughts a thinks." Thus, Ziff's proposal fails to satisfy Requirement 1 in indefinitely many cases. There is no conception of what systematic features distinguishes the semi-sentences from the nonsense strings.

VI

Since previous proposals for a theory of semi-sentences have proven inadequate, in the following sections of this paper, we shall try to formulate an adequate conception of the form of a theory that satisfies both Requirements 1 and 2.

---

[14]This device was suggested to me by Jerry A. Fodor.

[15]Ziff, *op. cit.*, Sect. 21.

[16]Ziff, *ibid.*, Sect. 25.

The construction of a theory of the semi-sentences of a natural language, like the construction of a grammar,[17] must proceed as an explication. What is assumed is an ability on the part of speakers that must be reconstructed in the form of a system of rules whose results match the verbal performance of speakers. Namely, the ability to understand indefinitely many semi-sentences never prevously encountered.[18] The pattern of explication is parallel to the explication of "sentence of *L.*" We have the notion *semi-sentence of L* and we have clear cases of both grammatical sentences and nonsense strings. We have to find the most conceptually economical set of rules that handles the clear cases correctly. Of course, not all cases will be clear ones, but, then, there are other conditions of adequacy that can be imposed upon the explicatum. The rules must be as simple in form and as general as possible. They should suggest insights into the nature of language. Even the requirement that such a theory decide upon the semi-sentencehood of strings in extremely unclear cases is a condition of adequacy. Such a theory should, just as does a generative grammar in the case of grammaticality, carry us beyond our clear-cut intuitions and clarify cases about which our intuitions are unclear or even nonexistent.

VII

How far can a string depart from grammaticality and still avoid being a nonsense string? We cannot say that a semi-sentence is a string that departs from grammaticality to some degree but not to the point where no structure remains because some nonsense strings exhibit a great deal of structure. A string such as "The of is likes man the" is clearly in *NS* and clearly contains no structure that any string of English words does not have also. But a string such as "The of is likes the man," though certainly in *NS* too, does contain some grammatical structure over and above what makes it simply a string of English words: the expression *likes the man* in this string is a verb phrase and *the man* is a noun phrase. Thus, we shall say rather that a semi-sentence is a string that has not deviated from grammaticality so far that it no longer has sufficient structure to be understood. Strings in *NS* may exhibit structure, but they do not exhibit the right sort to be comprehensible to speakers.

Thus, we have:

> A string is a semi-sentence of the language *L* if and only if it is not generated by an optimal grammar of *L* and has sufficient structure to be understood by the speakers of *L.*

The first conjunct of the definiens expresses a condition that is necessary for membership in *SS*, but the second, which provides us with our sufficient condition, unlike the first, is not formal, i.e., there are no procedures of formal manipulation that suffice to determine when this condition is fulfilled. Therefore, we may regard the task of framing a theory of semi-sentences as just the task of transforming this nonformal condition into an equivalent one that is formal. The question, then, is what

---

[17] Cf. N. Chomsky, *Syntactic Structures*, Ch. 2.

[18] Cf. J. Katz and J. Fodor, "The Structure of a Semantic Theory," Sect. 4, reprinted in this volume, for the type of argument that underlies this point.

formal condition determines when a string has sufficient structure to be comprehensible. To answer it, we must be able to explain just how a speaker uses the structure in a semi-sentence in order to find out what it means.

VIII

The present paper offers the following explanation: a speaker knows (in the sense in which he knows the rules of the grammar of his language) a system of rules that enables him to associate a non-null set of grammatical sentences with each semi-sentence. This association is performed on the basis of the structure that the semi-sentence has. And the speaker's understanding of the semi-sentence is nothing other than his understanding of the sentences in the set with which the semi-sentence is associated. The system of rules transfers the meaning(s) from an associated set of sentences to the semi-sentence by virtue of establishing the association. Thus, we could say that the speaker interprets the semi-sentence as if it were actually those sentences associated with it by the rules. Thus, let us call the set of sentences that have their meaning(s) transferred to a semi-sentence its *comprehension set* and let us call the rules which accomplish this transference *transfer rules*.

An extremely important consequence for the study of semi-sentences follows from this explanation. It would be natural to think that a semi-sentence whose comprehension set contains more than one sentence is ambiguous, the degree of its ambiguity being a direct function of the number of sentences in its comprehension set. But, strictly speaking, this is false. A semi-sentence such as "Man bit dog" has a comprehension set that contains at least "The man bit the dog," "A man bit a dog," "The man bit some dog," "Some man bit a dog," and so on. Nonetheless, this semi-sentence is not ambiguous. What is involved here is clearly that the sentences in the comprehension set are paraphrases of one another. Thus, we see that a consequence of our explanation is that a theory of semi-sentences cannot be solely a syntactic theory but must contain a semantic component, one that is rich enough to provide some means of deciding when two sentences are paraphrases of each other. Then we can say that a semi-sentence is ambiguous n ways if and only if its comprehension set contains n sentences none of which is a paraphrase of any other sentence in the set, and no more than n such sentences.

A convenient way to formally mark the distinction between *SS* and *NS* that is required by Requirement 1 is to build our rules so that semi-sentences are always associated with a comprehension set containing a finite number of (paraphrase-independent) sentences, whereas nonsense strings are always associated with a comprehension set containing no members or a comprehension set containing an infinite number of sentences. Either way we would explain why nonsense strings cannot be understood by speakers while semi-sentences can.

For us, then, the notion *sufficient structure to be understood* is analyzed as *structure that suffices to permit a semi-sentence to be associated with a finite number of sentences, each of which is a possible reading of the semi-sentence.* This is another step, but since the condition is not formal, it is not the final step.

The final step is a theory of semi-sentences which reconstructs the speaker's ability to understand semi-sentences in terms of a system of transfer rules that formally represents the set of semi-sentences by establishing a one-many mapping of elements in SS onto elements in $G(L)$ such that the image of a semi-sentence $*S$ in the set $G(L)$ is just those sentences $S_1, S_2, \ldots, S_n$ such that a speaker's understanding of $S_i (1 \leq i \leq n)$ is a possible way of understanding $*S$. Such a theory would afford a reduction of the problem of how speakers understand semi-sentences to the problem of how they understand the well-formed sentences of their language.

IX

The significant question at this stage of research is, then, what is the abstract form of a system of transfer rules. The answer this paper offers should not be regarded as final. It is one of perhaps a large number of proposals within the framework of which work on the highly complicated problem of semi-sentences can fruitfully begin.

A system of transfer rules may be regarded as containing *at most* a rule for each rule of the grammar (the same transfer rule may relate to more than one rule of the grammar). Each transfer rule tells how the rule(s) of the grammar to which it corresponds can be violated without leading to derivations whose terminal lines are strings in NS. A theory of semi-sentences thus generates semi-sentences (without generating any nonsense strings) when the transfer rules are used to construct their "semi-derivations." The comprehension set for a semi-sentence must be constructable from its semi-derivation in a mechanical way.

Phrase-structure semi-derivations begin with the symbol SS instead of S and consist of a finite number of lines each of which is derivable from the preceding line by an application of either a transfer rule (corresponding to one of the phrase-structure rules of the grammar) or a phrase-structure rule of the grammar. Similarly, a transformational semi-derivation begins with one or more phrase-structure semi-derivations, together with perhaps one or more phrase-structure derivations, and consists of a finite number of lines each of which is derivable from the preceding line by an application of either a transfer rule (corresponding to one of the transformations of the grammar) or a transformation of the grammar. Each semi-derivation contains at least one application of both a transfer rule and a rule of the grammar—each application of a transfer rule being indicated in, for example, the manner in which we indicate the introduction of a premise in a proof in a system of natural deduction. Thus, a semi-sentence has a derivation which marks both its grammatical structure and the respects in which it is ungrammatical. Moreover, subject to the considerations in Section XI of the present paper, given the semi-derivation of a semi-sentence, we can determine which sentences are in its comprehension set by a mechanical procedure: include all and only those sentences whose grammatical derivation is identical to the semi-derivation except for containing a legitimate application of the grammatical rule R wherever the semi-derivation contains an application of the transfer rule R' which corresponds to R.

A phrase-structure rule such as the one that develops the symbol N into N_{am} when N is the object of a verb such as *terrify, astonish, surprise, frighten,* and the like may have corresponding to it a transfer rule that relaxes this restriction, permitting N to become N_{inam}. Thus, the rule would, *inter alia*, lead to such semi-sentences as "The spooky forest frightens the potato," "The kind man surprised and astonished the table," and so forth, the fairytale cases as I call them. In some cases, we may require a phrase-structure transfer rule that develops a marker into one less than the markers it normally goes into. A case of this kind might be the one that removes articles to produce such semi-sentences as "Man bit dog." However, it would appear that the highest level phrase-structure rules, e.g., $S \rightarrow NP + VP(Adv)$, $VP \rightarrow Aux + MV$, and so on are not violated at all, or if they are, this happens only under very special circumstances.

What we need is some way of distinguishing between those phrase-structure rules which develop phrases, those which develop word classes, and those which develop word classes or word subclasses into word subclasses that cross-classify words. Then we can try to find an analysis of the differences that result when different types of rules are violated. It seems that a theory of the kind Chomsky has suggested is adapted to handling deviations from grammaticality that arise in the area of cross-classification of words.

A transformation is characterized by a structural analysis of the string or strings to which it applies (together with a condition) and a formally stated structural change that the rule effects on strings satisfying its structural analysis (and condition). Thus, the passive transformation, as ordinarily stated, is:

Structural Analysis: $\underset{1}{NP} + \underset{2}{Aux} + \underset{3}{V_t} + \underset{4}{NP}$

Structural Change: $4 + 2 + be + en + 3 + by + 1$

A transfer rule corresponding to a transformation would also be characterized by a structural analysis and a structural change. An example of a putative transfer rule corresponding to this transformation is:

Structural Analysis: $\underset{1}{NP} + \underset{2}{Aux} + \underset{3}{V} + \underset{4}{NP}$

Structural Change: $4 + 2 + (be + en) + 3 + by + 1$

where parentheses indicate an optional element. This transfer rule enables us to produce such semi-sentences as: "Ten dollars (was) cost by the book," "The ball hit by the man," "The woman was resembled by the child," and the like. The semi-sentence "Ten dollars was cost by the book" thus contains the sentence "The book costs ten dollars" in its comprehension set, and "The ball hit by the man" has a comprehension set containing the sentence "The ball was hit by the man" and "The man hit the ball.[19]

Transfer rules such as those above are of the lowest order of generality and, as such, are the least preferable. We prefer transfer rules where each rule relates to a very large number of transformations or phrase-structure rules, whichever the case

---

[19]This is a good case of a semi-sentence not being ambiguous because the sentences in its comprehension set are paraphrases of each other.

may be, and tells us how to relax the restrictions on those rules.[20] We wish to avoid as far as possible having transfer rules which, like the rule for the semi-passive given above, is defined for only one rule of the grammar. But this presupposes a classification of phrase-structure rules and transformations such that, in terms of it, we can formulate transfer rules for classes of grammatical rules. Each transfer rule will then be an instruction to the effect that a certain class of rules can be permissibly violated in such-and-such a way under so-and-so conditions. For example, we may have a transfer rule that says that any phrase-structure rule which develops word-class markers or word-subclass markers into word-subclass markers and which is context restricted may be used without its customary context restriction; or one that says that no phrase-structure rule that develops phrases can be violated.

Clearly, however, such transfer rules by themselves are not sufficient to prevent a theory of semi-sentences from also generating nonsense strings. Thus, a system of transfer rules will have to include some that restrict the number and kind of further violations in a derivation in terms of the number and kind of violations that have already occurred. These "traffic rules" complete the definition of the notion *semi-derivation* by restricting the application of transfer rules to prevent the compounding of ill-formedness to the point where all intelligibility is lost. An example of a putative traffic rule is:

> No transfer rule R' corresponding to the rule of the grammar R can take the last line of an unterminated derivation, L_n, into the line L_{n+1} if L_n is of the form XEY and R' applies to XEY partly because E satisfies the marker M in the structural analysis of R', and it is the case both that E resulted from a previous application of a transfer rule (and could not have been obtained by applying a rule of the grammar) and that the structural analysis of R and R' differ with respect to M.

Such a rule is clearly not adequate by itself but it serves to convey some idea of what such traffic rules might be like.

In Section 23 of his paper, Ziff takes the string "The a man a that a I a saw a is a here a" as a semi-sentence and claims that it should be accounted for by what he calls an addition rule. It is true that this string is ungrammatical. It is also true that speakers of English will understand the string (it will mean what "The man that I saw is here" means to them). Nevertheless, I think it is a mistake to take such strings to be semi-sentences and *ipso facto* to try to construct one's theory to account for them. The reason for thinking this is that what one does in order to understand such strings is quite different from what one does in order to understand genuine semi-sentences. In the latter case, one recognizes a systematic distortion of structure and a certain undistorted structure and uses both to relate the semi-sentence to its image in $G(L)$. But, in the former case, one perceives the *sentence* as a perceptual figure against a background; in the case of Ziff's example, "The man that I saw is here" is perceived against . . . *a* . . . *a* . . . *a* . . . *a* . . . *a* . . . *a*. Whereas in the case of understanding a semi-sentence a speaker utilizes his knowledge of the structure of the language to find a meaning for something that is not well-formed, here the

---

[20]My co-worker, Mr. Paul Postal, points out that, since the transfer rules of a theory of semi-sentences constitutes an account of the speaker's ability to understand semi-sentences, the fewer and more general the transfer rules that are required, the less complex the ability attributed to the speaker and the more plausible the attribution.

speaker utilizes his perceptual skill to find something that is well-formed! He perceives a certain relation between certain elements in the stimulus material, and this makes it possible to group them together, thus throwing the remaining elements into a group and thereby setting them apart to reveal a sentence.

Of course, the relation which must be grasped to throw the irrelevant elements into the background must be simple enough, otherwise the speaker will not stand much of a chance of making the necessary figure-ground distinction, and the string will simply be a jumble of words to him.[21] But, even the simplest relations of this kind can prove too difficult for some speakers, while others find it easy to fathom quite complicated ones. This variation in performance with intelligence (or whatever it is) contrasts with the performance of speakers with respect to some purely linguistic skill, where no significant individual differences are found. Semi-sentences are comprehensible to each speaker according only to his linguistic abilities. Since a necessary condition for something to be part of the subject matter of a linguistic theory is that each speaker be able to perform in that regard much as every other does,[22] we can conclude that such cases as the above are not part of the subject matter to be accounted for by a theory of semi-sentences in linguistics.

Further support for this conclusion comes from the observation that such strings, strictly speaking, have no constituent structure. This makes it impossible to regard them as on a par with strings having sufficient structure to use as a basis for understanding them. Thus, we shall classify strings of this kind as nonsense strings.

Doing this, however, means that we admit that some nonsense strings can be understood. But there is nothing damaging in this admission because we do not have to say that these nonsense strings are understood by virtue of the speaker's knowledge of the structure of his language and the patterns of deviation from structural normality that preserve intelligibility. We can say simply that understanding such strings is like seeing a hidden configuration as a result of perceptual reorganization or insightfully grasping the idea underlying a number series. The speaker's performance depends not on his knowledge of the language's mechanisms of preserving intelligibility under structural change but, rather, on his pattern recognition skills.[23]

The moral is simply that we should never abandon a transfer rule simply because some strings that speakers understand do not accord with the rule. Strings that a speaker can understand owing to ingenuity in grouping elements or past experience with noise factors in speech cannot count as counter-examples to an otherwise satisfactory rule. Nor, on the other hand, can such strings count by themselves as the substantiating evidence for accepting a putative transfer rule.

---

[21]The relation can range from the simplest to the subtlest numerical function. And, of course, relations that are not merely numerical functions are possible, e.g., "Find nation the nationalize hidden national sentence nationally."

[22]Cf. Katz and Fodor, *op. cit*, Sect. 7.

[23]Much, perhaps most, actual speech consists of ungrammatical but intelligible strings that are nonetheless not fruitfully taken as semi-sentences. There are false starts, repetitions, breath-catching and thought-catching interjections, and so forth. Every speaker has heard many instances of each variety and has, on this basis, acquired the skill of filtering out such noise or otherwise keeping such intrusions from interfering with his perception of the sentence he is hearing.

XI

An optimal grammar together with an optimal theory of syntactic deviation are not enough to provide a theory of semi-sentences that will satisfy Requirements 1 and 2 not only because, as we have seen, we require a decision procedure for paraphrase but, more significantly, because, in the first place, understanding sentences and semi-sentences involves grasping their semantic structure, and, in the second place, there are strings that are semantically ill-formed but comprehensible. Hence, explaining how deviation from well-formed structural patterns occurs and how intelligibility is preserved is explaining something about the semantic structure of the language also.

One way to look at the semantic component in a theory of semi-sentences is to use the above conception of the nature of a syntactic theory of semi-sentences to obtain a picture of the form of the semantic component of a theory of semi-sentences. Let us suppose we have a semantic theory of the kind described in "The Structure of a Semantic Theory."[24] Then, we shall construct transfer rules so that there is one which applies to each projection rule of the semantic theory. Such "semantic" transfer rules, like their syntactical counter-parts, show how a violation of a rule can be made without leading to the production of a string in *NS*. As in the case of "syntactic" transfer rules, traffic rules will be required to prevent compounding of violations that produce nonsense strings.

But this way of looking at the semantic component may be oversimplified because it neglects the interaction of syntactic and semantic components. There are different strings that have the same syntactic structure and the same distortion of syntactic structure, though one is comprehensible and the other not, owing to some semantic difference between them. If this is the case quite generally, then the construction of transfer rules of both semantic and syntactic types will have to be carried out jointly in order to obtain comprehension sets whose members have just the desired meaning, the one accorded to the semi-sentence by the speakers of the language. But this problem must remain for further investigations.

---

[24]Katz and Fodor, *op. cit.*

V

SEMANTICS

Unlike such relatively mature areas of linguistics as phonology and syntax, semantics exists not as a field of scientific investigation but rather as a heterogeneous collection of proposals for the creation of such a field. There are various reasons for this unhappy state of affairs. For one, the area of semantics, both in philosophy and linguistics, has been a repository for problems about language which theorists wish to avoid and for problems whose answers theorists need to presuppose to carry out work in progress. For another, in semantics it has proved difficult to agree on which problems are central and which are peripheral. Again, the problems that clearly are central to the development of semantics are exceedingly difficult and recalcitrant to systematic exploration. Thus, the only way one can present an accurate picture of semantics, as one currently finds it, is to exhibit some of its heterogeneity.

The papers in this section are intended to do this. But they are also intended to reflect the major systematic conceptions of the nature and goals of semantics that have dominated recent work, and to present the main theoretical problems encountered by philosophers and linguists who have been exploring semantics. In addition, the papers in this section represent a wide variety of current issues and deal with some of the philosophical implications of semantical problems and the solutions proposed for them. The failure to include any semantic studies from ordinary language philosophy not only reflects the difficulty of obtaining permission to reprint some of the most important studies written from this viewpoint and the accessibility (in inexpensive form) of many others* but is also due to the fact that this book emphasizes a highly theoretical concern with language while such studies deal primarily with quite detailed facts about English.

---

*For example, V. Chappell (ed.), *Ordinary Language* (Englewood Cliffs, N.J.: Prentice-Hall, Inc., 1964).

15   Foundations of Logic and Mathematics*

Rudolf Carnap

LOGICAL ANALYSIS OF LANGUAGE: SEMANTICS AND SYNTAX

1 Theoretical Procedures in Science. The activities of a scientist are in part practical: he arranges experiments and makes observations. Another part of his work is theoretical: he formulates the results of his observations in sentences, compares the results with those of other observers, tries to explain them by a theory, endeavors to confirm a theory proposed by himself or somebody else, makes predictions with the help of a theory, etc. In these theoretical activities, deduction plays an important part; this includes calculation, which is a special form of deduction applied to numerical expressions. Let us consider, as an example, some theoretical activities of an astronomer. He describes his observations concerning a certain planet in a report, O_1. Further, he takes into consideration a theory T concerning the movements of planets. (Strictly speaking, T would have to include, for the application to be discussed, laws of some other branches of physics, e.g., concerning the astronomical instruments used, refraction of light in the atmosphere, etc.) From O_1 and T, the astronomer deduces a prediction, P; he calculates the apparent position of the planet for the next night. At that time he will make a new observation and formulate it in a report O_2. Then he will compare the prediction P with O_2 and thereby find it either confirmed or not. If T was a new theory and the purpose of the procedure described was to test T, then the astronomer will take the confirmation of P by O_2 as a partial confirmation for T; he will apply the same procedure again and again and thereby obtain either an increasing degree of confirmation for T or else a disconfirmation. The same deduction of P from O_1 and T is made in the case where T is already

---

*R. Carnap, "Foundations of Logic and Mathematics," *International Encyclopedia of Unified Science* Vol. I, pp. 143–71. Reprinted by permission.

scientifically acknowledged on the basis of previous evidence, and the present purpose is to obtain a prediction of what will happen tomorrow. There is a third situation in which a deduction of this kind may be made. Suppose we have made both the observations described in O_1 and in O_2; we are surprised by the results of the observation described in O_2 and therefore want an explanation for it. This explanation is given by the theory T; more precisely, by deducing P from O_1 and T and then showing that O_2 is in accordance with P ("what we have observed is exactly what we had to expect").

These simple examples show that the chief theoretical procedures in science—namely, testing a theory, giving an explanation for a known fact, and predicting an unknown fact—involve as an essential component deduction and calculation; in other words, the application of logic and mathematics. It is one of the chief tasks of this essay to make clear the role of logic and mathematics as applied in empirical science. We shall see that they furnish instruments for deduction, that is, for the transformation of formulations of factual, contingent knowledge. However, logic and mathematics not only supply rules for transformation of factual sentences, but they themselves contain sentences of a different, nonfactual kind. Therefore, we shall have to deal with the question of the nature of logical and mathematical theorems. It will become clear that they do not possess any factual content. If we call them true, then another kind of truth is meant, one not dependent upon facts. A theorem of mathematics is not tested like a theorem of physics, by deriving more and more predictions with its help and then comparing them with the results of observations. But what else is the basis of their validity? We shall try to answer these questions by examining how theorems of logic and mathematics are used in the context of empirical science.

The material on which the scientist works in his theoretical activities consists of reports of observations, scientific laws and theories, and predictions; that is, formulations in language which describe certain features of facts. Therefore, an analysis of theoretical procedures in science must concern itself with language and its applications. In Sections 2 to 10, we shall outline an analysis of language and explain the chief factors involved. Three points of view will be distinguished, and accordingly three disciplines applying them, called pragmatics, semantics, and syntax. These will be illustrated by the analysis of a simple, fictitious language. . . .

2 Analysis of Language. A language, as, e.g., English, is a system of activities or, rather, of habits, i.e., dispositions to certain activities, serving mainly for the purposes of communication and of co-ordination of activities among the members of a group. The elements of the language are signs, e.g., sounds or written marks, produced by members of the group in order to be perceived by other members and to influence their behavior. Since our final interest in this essay concerns the language of science, we shall restrict ourselves to the theoretical side of language, i.e., to the use of language for making assertions. Thus, among the different kinds of sentences, e.g., commands, questions, exclamations, declarations, etc., we shall deal with declarative sentences only. For the sake of brevity we shall call them here simply *sentences*.

This restriction to declarative sentences does not involve, in the investigation of processes accompanying the use of language, a restriction to theoretical thinking.

Declarative sentences, e.g., "this apple is sour," are connected not only with the theoretical side of behavior but also with emotional, volitional, and other factors. If we wish to investigate a language as a human activity, we must take into consideration all these factors connected with speaking activities. But the sentences, and the signs (e.g., words) occurring in them, are sometimes involved in still another relation. A sign or expression may concern or designate or describe something, or, rather, he who uses the expression may intend to refer to something by it, e.g., to an object or a property or a state of affairs; this we call the *designatum* of the expression. (For the moment, no exact definition for *designatum* is intended; this word is merely to serve as a convenient, common term for different cases—objects, properties, etc.— whose fundamental differences in other respects are not hereby denied.) Thus, three components have to be distinguished in a situation where language is used. We see these in the following example: (1) the action, state, and environment of a man who speaks or hears, say, the German word *blau*; (2) the word *blau* as an element of the German language (meant here as a specified acoustic [or visual] design which is the common property of the many sounds produced at different times, which may be called the tokens of that design); (3) a certain property of things, viz., the color blue, to which this man—and German-speaking people in general—intends to refer (one usually says, "the man means the color by the word," or "the word means the color for these people," or " . . . within this language").

The complete theory of language has to study all three components.[1] We shall call *pragmatics* the field of all those investigations which take into consideration the first component, whether it be alone or in combination with the other components. Other inquiries are made in abstraction from the speaker and deal only with the expressions of the language and their relation to their designata. The field of these studies is called *semantics*. Finally, one may abstract even from the designata and restrict the investigation to formal properties—in a sense soon to be explained—of the expressions and relations among them. This field is called *logical syntax*. The distinction between the three fields will become more clear in our subsequent discussions.

3 Pragmatics of Language *B*. In order to make clear the nature of the three fields and the differences between them, we shall analyze an example of a language. We choose a fictitious language *B*, very poor and very simple in its structure, in order to get simple systems of semantical and syntactical rules.

Whenever an investigation is made about a language, we call this language the *object-language* of the investigation, and the language in which the results of the investigation are formulated the *metalanguage*. Sometimes object-language and metalanguage are the same, e.g., when we speak in English about English. The theory concerning the object-language which is formulated in the metalanguage is sometimes called metatheory. Its three branches are the pragmatics, the semantics, and

---

[1]That an investigation of language has to take into consideration all the three factors mentioned was in recent times made clear and emphasized especially by C. S. Peirce, by Ogden and Richards, and by C. Morris "Foundations of the Theory of Signs," *Encyclopedia of Unified Science*, Vol. I, No. 2 (Chicago: University of Chicago Press, 1955), pp. 78–137. Morris made it the basis for the three fields into which he divides semiotic (i.e., the general theory of signs), namely, pragmatics, semantics, and syntactics. Our division is in agreement with his in its chief features. For general questions concerning language and its use compare also L. Bloomfield, "Linguistic Aspects of Science," *Encyclopedia of Unified Science*, Vol. I, No. 4, pp. 216–277.

the syntax of the language in question. In what follows, B is our object-language, English our metalanguage.

Suppose we find a group of people speaking a language B which we do not understand; nor do they understand ours. After some observation, we discover which words the people use, in which forms of sentences they use them, what these words and sentences are about, on what occasions they are used, what activities are connected with them, etc. Thus, we may have obtained the following results, numbered here for later reference."

PRAGM. 1: Whenever the people utter a sentence of the form "*. . . ist kalt,*" where ". . . " is the name of a thing, they intend to assert that the thing in question is cold.

PRAGM. 2*a*: A certain lake in that country, which has no name in English, is usually called *titisee*. When using this name, the people often think of plenty of fish and good meals.

PRAGM. 2*b*: On certain holidays the lake is called *rumber*; when using this name, the people often think—even during good weather—of the dangers of storm on the lake.

PRAGM. 3: The word *nicht* is used in sentences of the form "nicht . . .," where ". . ." is a sentence. If the sentence ". . ." serves to express the assertion that such and such is the case, the whole sentence "nicht . . ." is acknowledged as a correct assertion if such and such is not the case.

In this way we slowly learn the designata and mode of use of all the words and expressions, especially the sentences; we find out both the cause and the effect of their utterance. We may study the preferences of different social groups, age groups, or geographical groups in the choice of expressions. We investigate the role of the language in various social relations, etc.

The pragmatics of language B consists of all these and similar investigations. Pragmatical observations are the basis of all linguistic research. We see that pragmatics is an empirical discipline dealing with a special kind of human behavior and making use of the results of different branches of science (principally social science, but also physics, biology, and psychology).

4 Semantical Systems. We now proceed to restrict our attention to a special aspect of the facts concerning the language B which we have found by observations of the speaking activities within the group who speak that language. We study the relations between the expressions of B and their designata. On the basis of those facts we are going to lay down a system of rules establishing those relations. We call them *semantical rules*. These rules are not unambiguously determined by the facts. Suppose we have found that the word *mond* of B was used in 98 per cent of the cases for the moon and in 2 per cent for a certain lantern. Now it is a matter of our decision whether we construct the rules in such a way that both the moon and the lantern are designata of *mond* or only the moon. If we choose the first, the use of *mond* in those 2 per cent of cases was right—with respect to our rules; if we choose the second, it was wrong. The facts do not determine whether the use of a certain expression is right or wrong but only how often it occurs and how often it leads to the effect intended, and the like. A question of right or wrong must always refer to a system of rules. Strictly speaking, the rules which we shall lay down are not rules of the factually given language *B*; they rather constitute a language system corresponding to *B* which we will call the *semantical system B-S*. The language *B* belongs to the world of facts; it has many properties, some of which we have found, while others are unknown to us. The language system *B-S*, on the other hand, is something constructed by us; it has all and only those properties which we establish by the rules. Nevertheless, we construct *B-S* not arbitrarily but with regard to the facts about *B*. Then we may make the empirical statement that the language *B* is to a certain degree in accordance with the system *B-S*. The previously mentioned pragmatical facts are the basis—in the sense explained—of some of the rules to be given later (PRAGM. 1 for *SD* 2*a* and *SL* 1, PRAGM. 2*a,b* for *SD* 1*a*, PRAGM. 3 for *SL* 2).

We call the elements of a semantical system *signs*; they may be words or special symbols like *0*, +. A sequence consisting of one or several signs is called an *expression*. As signs of the system *B-S*, we take the words which we have found by our observations to be words of *B* or, rather, only those words which we decide to accept as "correct." We divide the signs of *B-S*—and, in an analogous way, those of any other semantical system—into two classes: *descriptive* and *logical* signs. As descriptive signs we take those which designate things or properties of things (in a more comprehensive system we should classify here also the relations among things, functions of things, etc.). The other signs are taken as logical signs: they serve chiefly for connecting descriptive signs in the construction of sentences but do not themselves designate things, properties of things, etc. Logical signs are, e.g., those corresponding to English words like *is, are, not, and, or, if, any, some, every, all*. These unprecise explanations will suffice here. Our later discussions will show some of the differentiae of the two classes of signs.[2]

5 Rules of the Semantical System *B-S*. In order to show how semantical rules are to be formulated and how they serve to determine truth conditions and thereby give an interpretation of the sentences, we are going to construct the semantical rules for the system *B-S*. As preliminary steps for this construction we make a classification of the signs and lay down rules of formation. Each class is defined by an enumeration of the signs belonging to it. The signs of *B-S* are divided into descriptive and logical signs. The descriptive signs of *B-S* are divided into names and predicates. Names are the words *titisee, rumber, mond*, etc. (here a complete list of the names has to be given). Predicates are the words *kalt, blau, rot*, etc. The logical signs are divided into logical constants (*ist, nicht, wenn, so, fuer, jedes*) and variables (*x, y*, etc.). For the general description of forms of expressions we shall use blanks like "...," "---," etc. They are not themselves signs of *B-S* but have to be replaced by expressions of *B-S*. If nothing else is said, a blank stands for any expression of *B-S*. A blank with a subscript *n, p, s*, or *v* (e.g., "...$_n$") stands for a name, a predicate, a sentence, or a variable, respectively. If the same blank occurs several times within a rule or a statement, it stands at all places for the same expression.

---

[2]Semantics as an exact discipline is quite new; we owe it to the very fertile school of contemporary Polish logicians. After some of this group, especially Lesniewski and Ajdukiewicz, had discussed semantical questions, Tarski, in his treatise on truth, made the first comprehensive systematic investigation in this field, giving rise to very important results.

The rules for formation determine how sentences may be constructed out of the various kinds of signs.

RULES OF FORMATION: An expression of *B-S* is called a *sentence* (in the semantical sense) or a *proposition* of *B-S*, if and only if it has one of the following forms, *F*1–4: *F*1, "...$_n$ ist - - -$_p$," (e.g., "*mond ist blau*"); *F*2, "*nicht* ...$_s$" (e.g., "*nicht mond ist blau*"); *F*3, "*wenn* ...$_s$, *so* - - -$_s$" (e.g., "*wenn titisee ist rot, so mond ist kalt*"); *F*4, "*fuer jedes* .. $_v$, - .. -," where "- .. -" stands for an expression which is formed out of a sentence not containing a variable by replacing one or several names by the variable "...$_v$" (e.g., "*fuer jedes x, x ist blau*"; "*fuer jedes y, wenn y ist blau, so y ist kalt*"). The partial sentence in a sentence of the form *F*2 and the two partial sentences in a sentence of the form *F*3 (indicated above by blanks) are called *components* of the whole sentence. In order to indicate the components of a sentence in case they are themselves compound, commas and square brackets are used when necessary.

RULES *B-SD*. *Designata of descriptive signs:*

SD 1. The *names* designate things, and especially
   (*a*) each of the thing-names *titisee* and *rumber* designates the lake at such and such a longitude and latitude;
   (*b*) *mond* designates the moon;
   Etc. [Here is to be given a complete list of rules for all the names of *B-S*.]

SD 2. The *predicates* designate properties of things, and especially
   (*a*) *kalt* designates the property of being cold;
   (*b*) *blau* designates the property of being blue;
   (*c*) *rot* designates the property of being red;
   Etc. [for all predicates].

RULES *B-SL*. *Truth conditions* for the sentences of *B-S*. These rules involve the *logical signs*. We call them the *L*-semantical rules of *B-S*:

SL 1. *ist*, form *F*1. A sentence of the form "...$_n$ ist - - -$_p$" is true if and only if the thing designated by "...$_n$" has the property designated by "- - -$_p$."

SL 2. *nicht*, form *F*2. A sentence of the form "*nicht* ...$_s$" is true if and only if the sentence "...$_s$" is not true.

SL 3. *wenn* and *so*, form *F*3. A sentence of the form "*wenn* ...$_s$, *so* - - -$_s$" is true if and only if "...$_s$" is not true or "- - -$_s$" is true.

SL 4. *fuer jedes*, form *F*4. A sentence of the form "*fuer jedes* .. $_v$, - .. -," where "- .. -" is an expression formed out of a sentence by replacing one or several names by the variable "...$_v$," is true if and only if all sentences of the following kind are true: namely, those sentences constructed out of the expression "- .. -" by replacing the variable "...$_v$" at all places where it occurs within that expression by a name, the same for all places; here names of any things may be taken, even of those for which there is no name in the list of names in *B-S*. (Example: the sentence "*fuer jedes x, x ist blau*" is true if and only if every sentence of the form "...$_n$ ist blau" is true; hence, according to *SL* 1, if and only if everything is *blue*.)

The rule *SL* 1, in combination with *SD*, provides direct truth conditions for the sentences of the simplest form; direct, since the rule does not refer to the truth of other sentences. *SL* 2–4 provide indirect truth conditions for the compound sentences by referring to other sentences and finally back to sentences of the simplest form. Hence, the rules *B-SD* and *SL* together give a general definition of "*true in B-S*" though not in explicit form. (It would be possible, although in a rather complicated form, to formulate an explicit definition of "true in *B-S*" on the basis of the rules given.) A sentence of *B-S* which is not true in *B-S* is called *false* in *B-S*.

If a sentence of *B-S* is given, one can easily construct, with the help of the given rules, a direct *truth-criterion* for it, i.e., a necessary and sufficient condition for its truth, in such a way that in the formulation of this condition no reference is made to the truth of other sentences. Since to know the truth conditions of a sentence is to know what is asserted by it, the given semantical rules determine for every sentence of *B-S* what it asserts—in usual terms, its "meaning"—or, in other words, how it is to be translated into English.

> EXAMPLES: (1) The sentence "*mond ist blau*" is true if and only if the moon is blue. (2) The sentence "*fuer jedes x, wenn x ist blau, so x ist kalt*" is true if and only if every thing—not only those having a name in *B-S*—either is not blue or is cold; in other words, if all blue things are cold. Hence, this sentence asserts that all blue things are cold; it is to be translated into the English sentence "all blue things are cold."

Therefore, we shall say that we *understand* a language system or a sign or an expression or a sentence in a language system, if we know the semantical rules of the system. We shall also say that the semantical rules give an *interpretation* of the language system.[3]

6 Some Terms of Semantics. We shall define some more terms which belong to the metalanguage and, moreover, to the semantical part of the metalanguage (as is seen from the fact that the definitions refer to the semantical rules). Any semantical term is relative to a semantical system and must, in strict formulation, be accompanied by a reference to that system. In practice the reference may often be omitted without ambiguity (thus we say, e.g., simply "synonymous" instead of "synonymous in *B-S*").

Two expressions are said to be semantically synonymous, or briefly, *synonymous*, with each other in a semantical system *S* if they have the same designatum by virtue of the rules of *S*. Hence, according to *SD* 1a, the signs *titisee* and *rumber* are semantically synonymous with one another in *B-S*. They are, however, not what we might call pragmatically synonymous in *B*, as is shown by PRAGM. 2a,b. Since the transition from pragmatics to semantics is an abstraction, some properties drop out of consideration and hence some distinctions disappear. Because of the semantical synonymity of the names mentioned, the sentences "*titisee ist kalt*" and "*rumber ist kalt*" are also semantically synonymous. These two sentences have the same truth conditions, although different pragmatical conditions of application. Suppose that the lake is

---

[3]We have formulated the semantical rules of the descriptive signs by stating their designata, for the logical signs by stating truth conditions for the sentences constructed with their help. We may mention here two other ways of formulating them which are often used in the practice of linguistics and logic. The first consists in giving *translations* for the signs and, if necessary, for the complex expressions and sentences, as it is done in a dictionary. The second way consists in stating *designata* throughout, not only for the descriptive signs as in *SD*, but also for expressions containing the logical signs, corresponding to *SL*. Example (corresponding to *SL* 1): A sentence of the form " . . .$_n$ *ist* - - -$_p$" designates (the state of affairs) that the thing designated by " . . .$_n$" has the property designated by " - - -$_p$."

cold and hence the sentence *"titisee ist kalt"* is true. Then the sentence *"rumber ist kalt"* is also true, even if sinfully spoken on a working day. If this happened by mistake, people would tell the speaker that he is right in his belief but that he ought to formulate it—i.e., the same belief—in another way.

We shall apply the semantical terms to be defined not only to sentences but also to classes of sentences. In what follows we shall use S_1, S_2, etc., for sentences; C_1, C_2, etc., for classes of sentences; T_1, T_2, etc., stand both for sentences and for classes of sentences. (These S and C with subscripts have nothing to do with the same letters without subscripts, which we use for semantical systems and calculi, e.g., *B-S* and *B-C*.) We understand the assertion of a class of sentences C_1 as a simultaneous assertion of all the sentences belonging to C_1; therefore, we make the following definition: a *class* of sentences C_1 is called *true* if all sentences of C_1 are true; false, if at least one of them is false. T_1 and T_2 (i.e., two sentences, or two classes of sentences, or one sentences and one class) are called *equivalent* with each other, if either both are true or both are false. T_2 is called an *implicate* of T_1, if T_1 is false or T_2 is true. T_1 is said to *exclude* T_2 if not both are true.

7 L-Semantical Terms. Let us compare the following two sentences: "Australia is large" (S_1) and "Australia is large, or Australia is not large" (S_2). We see that they have a quite different character; let us try to give an exact account of their difference. We learn S_1 in geography but S_2 in logic. In order to find out for each of these sentences whether it is true or false, we must, of course, first understand the language to which it belongs. Then, for S_1 we have to know, in addition, some facts about the thing whose name occurs in it, i.e., *Australia*. Such is not the case for S_2. Whether Australia is large or small does not matter here; just by understanding S_2 we become aware that it must be right. If we agree to use the same term *true*[4] in both cases, we may express their difference by saying that S_1 is factually (or empirically) true while S_2 is logically true. These unprecise explanations can easily be transformed into precise definitions by replacing the former reference to understanding by a reference to semantical rules. We call a sentence of a semantical system S (logically true or) *L-true* if it is true in such a way that the semantical rules of S suffice for establishing its truth. We call a sentence (logically false or) *L-false* if it is false in such a way that the semantical rules suffice for finding that it is false. The two terms just defined and all other terms defined on their basis we call *L-semantical terms*. If a sentence is either *L*-true or *L*-false, it is called *L-determinate*, otherwise (*L*-indeterminate or) *factual*. (The terms *L-true*, *L-false*, and *factual* correspond to the terms *analytic*, *contradictory*, and *synthetic*, as they are used in traditional terminology, usually without exact definitions.) If a factual sentence is true, it is called (factually true or) *F-true*; if it is false, (factually false or) *F-false*. Every sentence which contains only logical signs is *L*-determinate. This is one of the chief characteristics distinguishing logical

---

[4]*Terminological remark:* The use of the word *true* in everyday language and in philosophy is restricted by some to factual sentences, while some others use it in a wider sense, including analytic sentences. We adopted here the wider use; it is more customary in modern logic (e.g., *truth function, truth-value-table*), and it turns out to be much more convenient. Otherwise, we should always have to say in the semantical rules and in most of the semantical theorems *true or analytic* instead of *true*. Semantical rules stating truth-conditions in the sense of *F-true* would become very complicated and indeed indefinite.

from descriptive signs. (Example: "For every object x and every property F, if x is an F then x is an F" is *L*-true. There are no sentences of this kind in the system *B-S*.)[5]

Classification of sentences of a semantical system:

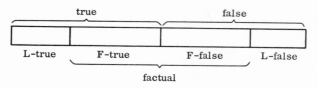

Figure 1

The definitions given can easily be transferred to classes of sentences. C_1 is called *L*-true if it is possible to find out that C_1 is true with the help of the semantical rules alone, hence if all sentences of C_1 are *L*-true. C_1 is called *L*-false if it is possible to find out with the help of the semantical rules that C_1 is false, i.e., that at least one sentence of C_1 is false (in this case, however, all sentences of C_1 may be factual). If C_1 is either *L*-true or *L*-false, it is called *L*-determinate, otherwise factual.

If the semantical rules suffice to show that T_2 is an implicate of T_1, we call T_2 an *L-implicate* of T_1. This relation of *L*-implication is one of the fundamental concepts in logical analysis of language. The criterion for it can also be formulated in this way: the semantical rules exclude the possibility of T_1 being true and T_2 false; or in this way: according to the semantical rules, if T_1 is true, T_2 must be true. This last formulation of the criterion shows that *L*-implication, as defined here, is essentially the same as what is usually called logical consequence or deducibility or strict implication or entailment, although the form of the definitions of these terms may be different. Our definition is a semantical one as it refers to the semantical rules. Later we shall discuss the possibility of defining a corresponding syntactical term.

EXAMPLES: (1) "*mond ist rot*" (S_1); "*wenn mond ist rot, so titisee ist kalt*" (S_2); "*titisee ist kalt*" (S_3). We shall see that S_3 is an *L*-implicate of the class C_1 consisting of S_1 and S_2. According to the definition of *implicate* (Section 6), if S_3 is true, S_3 is an implicate of C_1. The same holds if S_1 is false because C_1 is then also false. The only remaining case is that S_1 is true and S_3 is false. In this case, according to rule *SL* 3

---

[5]Examples of sentences in *B-S*: (1) We found earlier (Section 5) that the sentence "*mond its blau*" (S_1) is true in *B-S* if and only if the moon is blue. Hence, in order to find out whether S_1 is true or false, not only must we know the rules of *B-S* but we have to make observations of the moon. Hence S_1 is not *L*-determinate but *factual*. (2) Let us analyze the sentence "*wenn mond ist blau, so mond is blau*" (S_2). According to rule *SL* 3, a *wenn-so* sentence is true if its first component is not true or its second component is true. Now, if S_1 is true the second component of S_2 is true, and hence S_2 is true; and if S_1 is not true, then the first component of S_2 is not true, and hence S_2 is again true. Thus S_2 is true in any case, independently of the facts concerning the moon; it is true merely in virtue of rule *SL* 3. Therefore S_2 is *L*-true. (3) The sentence "*nicht, wenn mond ist blau, so mond ist blau*" (S_3) has S_2 as its component; and we found S_2 to be true on the basis of *SL* 3. Therefore, according to *SL* 2, S_3 is not true but false. And, moreover, it is false not because some fact happens to be the case but merely by virtue of the rules *SL* 3 and 2. Hence, S_3 is *L*-false.

(Section 5), S_2 is false and, hence, C_1 is false too, and S_3 is an implicate of C_1. Thus, we have found, without examining the facts described by the sentences, and merely by referring to the semantical rules, that S_3 is an implicate of C_1. Therefore, S_3 is an L-implicate of C_1. (2) *"fuer jedes x, x ist blau"* (S_4); *"mond ist blau"* (S_5). We shall see that S_5 is an L-implicate of S_4. If S_5 is true, S_5 is an implicate of S_4. And if S_5 is not true, then according to *SL* 4 (Section 5), S_4 is not true, and, hence, S_5 is again an implicate of S_4. We found this result by merely referring to a semantical rule. Therefore, S_5 is an L-implicate of S_4.

T_1 and T_2 are said to be *L-equivalent* if the semantical rules suffice to establish their equivalence, in other words, if T_1 and T_2 are L-implicates of each other. L-equivalent sentences have the same truth conditions; therefore, they say the same thing, although the formulations may be quite different.

> EXAMPLE: *"mond ist kalt"* (S_1); *"nicht, mond ist kalt"* (S_2); *"nicht, nicht, mond ist kalt"* (S_3). These sentences are factual; the semantical rules do not suffice for finding out their truth or falsity. But they suffice for showing that S_1 and S_3 are equivalent. If S_1 is true, S_2 is, according to *SL* 2 (Section 5), false, and hence S_3 true. Therefore, in this case, S_1 and S_3 are equivalent. And, if S_1 is false, then S_2 is true and S_3 is false; hence, S_1 and S_3 are again equivalent. Thus, on the basis of the semantical rules, S_1 and S_3 cannot be other than equivalent. Therefore they are L-equivalent.

If S_1 is an L-true sentence, then the truth of S_1 can be established without any regard to the facts, e.g., to the properties of the things whose names occur in S_1. Therefore, S_1 does not convey any information about facts; this is sometimes formulated by saying that an L-true sentence has no factual content. Suppose S_2 to be an L-implicate of the class of sentences C_1. Then S_2 is an implicate of C_1, and hence, if the sentences of C_1 are true, S_2 is also true; and, moreover, this relation between C_1 and S_2 can be found to hold without taking into account any facts. Therefore, S_2 does not furnish any new information concerning facts that were not already given by C_1. This is sometimes expressed by saying that logical deduction does not increase the factual content of the premises. The two characteristics just explained of L-truth and L-implication (which have been especially emphasized by Wittgenstein) are very important for a clear understanding of the relation between logic and empirical knowledge.

8 Logical Syntax. We distinguished three factors in the functioning of language: the activities of the speaking and listening persons, the designata, and the expressions of the language. We abstracted from the first factor and thereby came from pragmatics to semantics. Now we shall abstract from the second factor also and thus proceed from semantics to syntax. We shall take into consideration only the expressions, leaving aside the objects, properties, states of affairs, or whatever may be designated by the expressions. The relation of designation will be disregarded entirely. As this relation is the basis of the whole semantical system, it might seem as if nothing would be left. But we shall soon see that this is not the case.

A definition of a term in the metalanguage is called *formal* if it refers only to the expressions of the object-language (or, more exactly, to the kinds of signs and the order in which they occur in the expressions) but not to any extra-linguistic objects and especially not to the designata of the descriptive signs of the object-language.

A term defined by a formal definition is also called formal, as are questions, proofs, investigations, etc., in which only formal terms occur. We call the formal theory of an object-language, formulated in the metalanguage, the *syntax* of the object-language (or the logical syntax, whenever it seems necessary to distinguish this theory from that part of linguistics which is known as syntax but which usually is not restricted to formal terms). A formal definition, term, analysis, etc., is then also called syntactical.

The definitions of all semantical terms refer directly or indirectly to designata. But some of these terms—e.g., *true, L-true, L-implicate*—are attributed not to designata but only to expressions; they designate properties of, or relations between, expressions. Now our question is whether it is possible to define within syntax, i.e., in a formal way, terms which correspond more or less to those semantical terms, i.e., whose extensions coincide partly or completely with theirs. The development of syntax—chiefly in modern symbolic logic—has led to an affirmative answer to that question. Especially is the possibility of defining in a formal way terms which completely correspond to *L-true* and *L-implicate* of fundamental importance. This shows that logical deduction can be completely formalized.

A *syntactical system* or *calculus* (sometimes also called a formal deductive system or a formal system) is a system of formal rules which determine certain formal properties and relations of sentences, especially for the purpose of formal deduction. The simplest procedure for the construction of a calculus consists in laying down some sentences as primitive sentences (sometimes called *postulates* or *axioms*) and some rules of inference. The primitive sentences and rules of inference are used for two purposes, for the construction of proofs and of derivations. We shall call the sentences to which the proofs lead *C-true* sentences (they are often called provable or proved sentences or theorems of the calculus). A derivation leads from any not necessarily *C*-true sentences, called the premisses, to a sentence, called the conclusion. We shall call the conclusion a *C-implicate* of the class of premisses (it is sometimes called derivable or derived or [formally] deducible or deduced from the premisses or a [formal] consequence of the premisses). A calculus may (but usually does not) also contain rules which determine certain sentences as *C-false*. If the rules of a calculus determine some sentence as both *C*-true and *C*-false, the calculus is called *inconsistent*; otherwise *consistent*. (If, as is usually done, no rules for *C-false* are given, the calculus cannot be inconsistent.) In order to explain this procedure, we shall construct the calculus *B-C* as an example.[6]

9 The Calculus *B-C*. While the sentences of a semantical system are interpreted, assert something, and therefore are either true or false, within a calculus the sentences

---

[6]Logical syntax has chiefly grown out of two roots, one being formal logic, founded by Aristotle, the other the axiomatic method, initiated by Euclid. The general idea of operations with calculi goes back to Leibniz; since the middle of the last century it has been developed in the systems of symbolic logic into a comprehensive discipline. Among the founders of symbolic logic, or logistic, Boole (1854) is especially to be mentioned. More comprehensive systems (including the higher functional calculus) were created by Schroeder (1890), Frege (1893), Peano (1895), and Whitehead and Russell (1910). Frege was the first to formulate explicitly and to fulfil strictly the requirement of formality, i.e., of a formulation of rules of logic without any reference to designata. Hilbert considerably developed the axiomatic method, in its application both to geometry and to classical mathematics.

are looked at from a purely formal point of view. In order to emphasize this dis-tinction, we sometimes call sentences as elements of a semantical system *propositions* and as elements of a calculus *formulas*.

We constructed earlier a semantical system *B-S* on the basis of the language *B*, but not, as we have seen, uniquely determined by *B*. Analogously, we shall now construct a calculus *B-C* on the basis of *B*. As preliminary steps for the construction of the syntactical rules proper, which we shall then call rules of transformation, we have to make a *classification* of the signs of *B-C* and to lay down *syntactical rules of formation Fc*1–4. But they correspond exactly to the classification and the rules of forma-tion *F*1–4 of *B-S* (Section 5); these rules were already formal. Therefore we shall not write them down again.

> CALCULUS *B-C*. *Rules of Transformation*:
> *PS*. A sentence of *B-C* is called a *primitive sentence* of *B-C*, if it has one of the following forms, *PS* 1–4:
> *PS* 1. *wenn . . ., so [wenn nicht . . ., so - - -]*;
> *PS* 2. *wenn [wenn nicht . . ., so . . .], so . . .*;
> *PS* 3. *wenn [wenn . . ., so - - -], so [wenn [wenn - - -, so . - . -], so [wenn . . ., so . - . -]]*;
> *PS* 4. *wenn [fuer jedes . ., - . . -], so - . - . -*; here " . ." is a variable, "- . - . -" is a sentence which does not contain *fuer jedes* but contains a name" . - ." one or several times, and "- . . -" is an expression constructed out of "- . - . -" by replacing " . - ." at one or several (not necessarily all) places by the variable " . . ." (Examples: (1) "*wenn [fuer jedes x, x ist rot], so mond ist rot*"; (2) see sentence (3) in the first example of a derivation, at the end of this section.)
> *R*.   *Rules of Inference:* The relation of direct derivability holds if and only if one of the following conditions is fulfilled:
> *R* 1. *Rule of Implication:* From "*wenn . . ., so - - -*" and " . . .," " - - -" is directly derivable in *B-C*.
> *R* 2. *Rule of Synonymity:* The words *titisee* and *rumber* may be exchanged at any place (i.e., if S_2 is constructed out of S_1 by replacing one of those words at one place by the other one, then S_2 is directly derivable from S_1 in *B-C*).

A *proof* in *B-C* is a sequence of sentences of *B-C* such that each of them is either a primitive sentence or directly derivable from one or two sentences preceding it in the sequence. A sentence S_1 of *B-C* is called *provable* in *B-C* if it is the last sentence of a proof in *B-C*. A sentence of *B-C* is called *C·true* in *B-C* if and only if it is prov-able in *B-C*; a sentence " . . ." is called *C-false* in *B-C* if and only if "*nicht . . .*" is provable in *B-C*. (For *B-C*, provability and *C*-truth coincide, and likewise deriv-ability and *C*-implication; for other calculi, this is in general not the case.

A *derivation* in *B-C* with a class C_1 of premises is a sequence of sentences of *B-C* such that each of them is either a sentence of C_1 or a primitive sentence or directly derivable from one or two sentences preceding it in the sequence. The last sentence of a derivation is called its *conclusion*. S_2 is called *derivable* from C_1 and also a *C-implicate* of C_1 if it is the conclusion of a derivation with the class of premises C_1

Both the rules of formation and the rules of transformation of *B-C* do not in any way refer to designata; they are strictly formal. Nevertheless, they have been chosen with regard to *B-S* in such a way that the extension of the terms *C-true*, *C-false*, and *C-implicate* in *B-C* coincides with that of *L-true*, *L-false*, and *L-implicate*, respec-tively, in *B-S*. There are an infinite number of other possible choices of primitive sentences and rules of inference which would lead to the same result. This result gives the practical justification for our choice of the rules of *B-C*. A calculus in itself needs no justification.[7]

CALCULUS AND INTERPRETATION

10 Calculus and Semantical System. We shall investigate the relations which may hold between a calculus and a semantical system. Sometimes we shall use as

---

[7]The calculus *B-C* corresponds to a restricted form of the so-called "lower functional calculus," as constructed by Hilbert and Bernays. *PS* 1–3 and R 1 correspond to the so-called "sentential calculus." That the lower functional calculus is complete, i.e., that it exhausts the extension of *L*-truth and *L*-implication, has been shown by Gödel.

Example of a proof in B-C. If in the following sequence the blank " . . ." is always replaced by the same sentence, e.g., "*titisee ist blau*," the sequence fulfils the conditions—as shown by the remarks on the left side—and therefore is a proof. Hence, any sentence of the form "*wenn . . . , so . . .*" is provable and *C*-true in *B-C*, e.g., "*wenn titisee ist blau, so titisee ist blau.*"

PS 1	*wenn . . . , so [wenn nicht . . . , so . . .]*	(1)
PS 2	*wenn [wenn nicht . . . , so . . .], so . . .*	(2)
PS 3	*wenn [wenn . . . , so [wenn nicht . . . , so . . .]].* *so [wenn [wenn [wenn nicht . . . , so . . .], so . . .], so [wenn . . . , so . . .]]*	(3)

(here, "*wenn nicht . . . , so . . .*" has been taken for "- - -," and " . . ." for " .-.-")

(1) (3) *R* 1	*wenn [wenn [wenn nicht . . , so . . .], so . . .], so [wenn . . . , so . . .]*	(4)
(2) (4) *R* 1	*wenn . . . , so . . .*	(5)

First example of a derivation in B-C:

Premisses	*titisee ist blau*	(1)
	fuer jedes x, [wenn x ist blau, so x ist kalt]	(2)
PS 4	*wenn [fuer jedes x, [wenn x ist blau, so x ist kalt]], so [wenn titisee ist blau, so titisee ist kalt]*	(3)
(2) (3) *R* 1	*wenn titisee ist blau, so titisee ist kalt*	(4)
(1) (4) *R* 1	*Conclusion: titisee ist kalt*	(5)

If we interpret these sentences as in *B-S*, (1) says that a certain object is blue, (2) says that all blue things are cold (see example (2) at the end of Section 5), (5) says that that object is cold. Here, however, the conclusion is derived from the premisses in a formal way, i.e., without making use of an interpretation.

Second example of a derivation in B-C:

Premisses	*wenn mond ist blau, so mond ist kalt*	(1)
	nicht mond ist kalt	(2)
Provable:	*wenn [wenn mond ist blau, so mond ist kalt], so [wenn nicht mond ist kalt, so nicht mond ist blau]*	(3)
(1) (3) *R* 1	*wenn nicht mond ist kalt, so nicht mond ist blau*	(4)
(2) (4) *R* 1	*Conclusion: nicht mond ist blau*	(5)

(3) is a provable sentence. To save space, we do not give its proof here. Suppose that the proof of (3) has been constructed earlier, then the example shows how its result can be used in a derivation. According to the definitions previously given for *proof* and *derivation*, any proof may also occur as a part of a derivation. If this happens, we can abbreviate the derivation; we write in the derivation not all the sentences of the proof, whose last sentence we intend to use, but only this one sentence, as we have done in the example given with sentence (3). In this way a sentence which has been proved once can be used in derivations again and again.

examples the calculus *B-C* and the semantical system *B-S* as discussed before. Suppose a calculus is given—it may be designated by *Z-C* or briefly *C*—and a semantical system—designated by *Z-S* or *S*. We call *S* an *interpretation* of *C* if the rules of *S* determine truth criteria for all sentences of *C*; in other words, if to every formula of *C* there is a corresponding proposition of *S*; the converse is not required.

Suppose *S* fulfils the following condition: for any T_1, T_2, T_3, and T_4, if T_2 is a *C*-implicate of T_1 in *C*, T_2 is an implicate of T_1 in *S*; if T_3 is *C*-true in *C*, it is true in *S*; if T_4 is *C*-false in *C*, it is false in *S*. If an interpretation *S* of *C* fulfils the condition stated, we call it a *true interpretation* of *C*; otherwise a *false interpretation*. If the semantical rules suffice to show that *S* is a true interpretation of *C*, then we call *S* an *L-true interpretation* of *C*. In this case *C*-implication becomes *L*-implication; every *C*-true sentence becomes *L*-true, and every *C*-false sentence becomes *L*-false. If, on the other hand, these semantical rules suffice to show that *S* is a false interpretation, we call *S* an *L-false interpretation*. If *S* is an interpretation but neither an *L*-true nor an *L*-false interpretation of *C*, we call *S* a *factual interpretation* of *C*. In this case, in order to find out whether the interpretation is true, we have to find out whether some factual sentences are true; for this task we have to carry out empirical investigations about facts. An interpretation *S* of *C* is called a *logical interpretation* if all sentences of *C* become logical sentences of *S* (i.e., sentences containing logical signs only), otherwise a *descriptive interpretation*. A logical interpretation is always *L*-determinate. Applying these definitions to the system of our former example: *B-S* is a true and, moreover, *L*-true, and descriptive interpretation of *B-C*.

The class of the sentences which are *C*-true in *C* is, interpreted by *S*, a class of assertions; we call it the *theory correlated* to *C* by *S*. If the interpretation is true, *L*-true or logical, respectively, the correlated theory is likewise true, *L*-true or logical, respectively; the converse does not hold generally.

Previously we had a semantical system *B-S* and then constructed a calculus *B-C* "in accordance with" *B-S*. What was meant by this can now be formulated: we intended to construct *B-C* in such a way that *B-S* is a true interpretation of *B-C*. It is easy to see that for any given semantical system *S* it is possible to construct a calculus *C* of that kind. All we have to do is to select partial domains, as small as we wish, of the extensions of *implicate in S*, *true in S*, and *false in S* (usually the null class), and then lay down formal definitions of *C-implicate*, *C-true*, and possibly *C-false*, in such a way that their extensions correspond to these partial domains. On the other hand, it is an important problem whether it is possible to construct for a given system *S* a calculus *C* such that *C* is not only in accordance with *S*, in the sense explained, but that the extensions of *C-implicate*, *C-true*, and (if defined at all) *C-false* coincide with those of *L-implicate*, *L-true*, and possibly *L-false*, respectively. If this is the case, we call *C* an *L-exhaustive calculus* with respect to *S*. Thus, *B-C* is *L*-exhaustive with respect to *B-S*. (We do not define a term for the case that the extensions of *C-implicate*, *C-true*, and *C-false*, coincide with those of *implicate*, *true*, and *false* because that would be impossible for any somewhat richer language system, e.g., for any language system of a branch of science.)[8]

---

[8]In order to answer the question of the possibility of an *L*-exhaustive calculus, we have to distinguish two fundamentally different kinds of rules of transformation, which we call finite and transfinite rules. By *finite rules* we understand those of the customary kind: primitive sentences

11 On the Construction of a Language System. We found earlier that the pragmatical description of a language gives some suggestions for the construction of a corresponding semantical system without, however, determining it. Therefore, there is a certain amount of freedom for the selection and formulation of the semantical rules. Again, if a semantical system S is given and a calculus C is to be constructed in accordance with S, we are bound in some respects and free in others. The rules of formation of C are given by S. And in the construction of the rules of transformation we are restricted by the condition that C must be such that S is a true interpretation of C, as discussed before. But this still leaves some range of choice. We may, for instance, decide that the class of C-true sentences is to be only a proper subclass of the class of L-true sentences, or that it is to coincide with that class (as we did in constructing B-C), or that it is to go beyond that class and comprehend some factual sentences, e.g., some physical laws. When the extensions of C-*true* and C-*implicate* are decided, there is still some possibility of choice in the construction of the rules, e.g., primitive sentences and rules of inference, leading to those extensions. This choice, however, is not of essential importance, as it concerns more the form of presentation than the result.

If we are concerned with a historically given language, the pragmatical description comes first, and then we may go by abstraction to semantics and (either from semantics or immediately from pragmatics) to syntax. The situation is quite different if we wish to construct a language (or rather a language system, because we lay down rules), perhaps with the intention of practical application, as for making communications or formulating a scientific theory. Here we are not bound by a previous use

---

and rules of inference each of which refers to a finite number of premises (in most cases one or two). Almost all rules used by logicians up to the present time are finite. Finite rules are applied in the construction of proofs and derivations of the usual kind, which are finite sequences of sentences, as we have seen in the examples in B-C. A rule of transformation is called *transfinite* if it refers to an infinite number of premises. Because of this number being infinite, a transfinite rule cannot be used within a proof or derivation; a procedure of deduction of an entirely new kind is necessary. We call a calculus *finite* if all its rules of transformation are finite, otherwise *transfinite*. It may be remarked that some logicians reject transfinite rules.

We shall make the following terminological distinction: the terms C-*implicate* and C-*true* are applied generally with respect both to finite and to transfinite calculi. On the other hand, we shall restrict the corresponding terms *derivable* and *provable* to finite calculi. Thus, we call T_2 a C-implicate of T_1 in C, if it is possible to obtain T_2 from the premises T_1 by a procedure of deduction of any kind in C; and we call T_3 C-true if it is possible to obtain T_3 by a procedure of deduction without premises. If C is a finite calculus—as, e.g., B-C—the deduction takes the form of a finite sequence of sentences, either a derivation or a proof. In this case T_2 is called, moreover, derivable from T_1, and T_3 is called, moreover, provable.

Now we come back to the problem whether it is possible to construct for a given semantical system S and L-exhaustive calculus C. The answer can now be formulated (but not proved here). The answer depends upon the degree of complexity of S; more precisely, it depends upon whether there are in S a sentence S_2 and an infinite class of sentences C_1 such that S_2 is an L-implicate of C_1 but not an L-implicate of any finite subclass of C_1. (Example: S contains a name for every object of an infinite domain: a_1, a_2, a_3, etc. P is a descriptive predicate. C_1 is the [infinite] class of all sentences of the form "... is a P" where "..." is one of the object names. S_2 is the sentence "for every x, x is a P." If this is not the case, then there is a finite L-exhaustive calculus C. If, however, it is the case, an L-exhaustive calculus C can be constructed if and only if transfinite rules are admitted. For, because C_1 is infinite, S_2 cannot be derivable from C_1. If we decide in a given case to admit transfinite rules, we have to accept the complications and methodological difficulties connected with them. It was first shown by Gödel that a calculus of the ordinary kind (in our terminology, a finite calculus) cannot be constructed for the whole of arithmetic.

of language, but are free to construct in accordance with our wishes and purposes. The construction of a language system Z may consist in laying down two kinds of rules, the semantical rules (Z-S or briefly S) and the syntactical rules (calculus Z-C or C). As a common basis for both, according to our former discussion, we have to make a classification of the signs which we intend to use and lay down rules of formation Z-F. Z-S consists of two parts, rules for the descriptive signs (Z-SD or SD) and rules for the logical signs (Z-SL or SL).

In constructing the system Z, we can proceed in two different ways—different as to the order of S and C. Here the order is not unessential, for, if we have chosen some rules arbitrarily, we are no longer free in the choice of others.

The first method consists in first constructing S and then constructing C. We start with a classification of the kinds of signs which we want, and rules F determining the forms of sentences which we intend to use. Then we lay down the rules SD; we choose objects, properties, etc., for which we wish to have direct designations, and then signs to designate these objects, properties, etc. Next we construct the rules SL; we choose signs to be used as logical signs and state for each of them the conditions of the truth of the sentences constructed with its help. (As mentioned before, we may also proceed by indicating the translations of the sentences containing logical signs, or giving their designata.) After this we proceed to syntax and construct the calculus C, e.g., by stating primitive sentences and rules of inference. It has been explained already that, if S is given or constructed, we are limited in constructing C in some essential respects, because C must be such that S is a true interpretation of C: but we are free in other respects.

The *second method* for constructing Z is first to construct C and then S. We begin again with a classification of signs and a system F of syntactical rules of formation, defining "sentence in C" in a formal way. Then we set up the system C of syntactical rules of transformation, in other words, a formal definition of "C-*true*" and "C-*implicate*." Since so far nothing has been determined concerning the single signs, we may choose these definitions, i.e., the rules of formation and of transformation, in any way we wish. With respect to a calculus to be constructed there is only a question of expedience or fitness to purposes chosen, but not of correctness.

Then we add to the uninterpreted calculus C an interpretation S. Its function is to determine truth conditions for the sentences of C and thereby to change them from formulas to propositions. We proceed in the following way. It is already determined by the rules F which expressions are formulas in C. Now we have to stipulate that each of them is also a proposition in S. By the syntactical classification of the signs it is not yet completely settled which signs are logical and which descriptive. In many cases there is still a considerable amount of freedom of choice in this respect. After having stated which signs are to be logical and which descriptive, we construct the rules SL for the logical signs. Here our choice is restricted to some extent by the requirement that the interpretation must be true.

Finally we establish the rules SD for the descriptive signs. Here we have to take into account the classification of signs. We choose the designata for each kind of signs and then for each sign of that kind. We may begin with individual names. First we choose a field of objects with which we wish to deal in the language to be constructed, e.g., the persons of a certain group, the towns of a certain country, the colors, geometrical structures, or whatever else. Then we determine for each individual name, as its designatum, one object of the class chosen. Then, for each predicate, we choose a possible property of those objects, etc. In this way, a designatum for every descriptive sign is chosen. If we decide to make S an L-true interpretation of C, we have a great amount of freedom for the choice of the rules SD. Otherwise, we find some essential restrictions. If some of the C-true formulas are to become factual propositions, they must be factually true. Therefore, in this case, on the basis of our factual knowledge about the objects which we have chosen as subject matter of Z, we have to take care that the interpretations for the descriptive names, predicates, etc., i.e., their designata, are chosen in such a way that those factual C-true sentences are actually true.

12 Is Logic a Matter of Convention? There has been much controversial discussion on the question whether or not logic is conventional. Are the rules on which logical deduction is based to be chosen at will and, hence, to be judged only with respect to convenience but not to correctness? Or is there a distinction between objectively right and objectively wrong systems so that in constructing a system of rules we are free only in relatively minor respects (as, e.g., the way of formulation) but bound in all essential respects? Obviously, the question discussed refers to the rules of an interpreted language, applicable for purposes of communication; nobody doubts that the rules of a pure calculus, without regard to any interpretation, can be chosen arbitrarily. On the basis of our former discussions we are in a position to answer the question. We found the possibility—which we called the second method— of constructing a language system in such a way that first a calculus C is established and then an interpretation is given by adding a semantical system S. Here we are free in choosing the rules of C. To be sure, the choice is not irrelevant; it depends upon C whether the interpretation can yield a rich language or only a poor one.

We may find that a calculus we have chosen yields a language which is too poor or which in some other respect seems unsuitable for the purpose we have in mind. But there is no question of a calculus being right or wrong, true or false. A true interpretation is possible for any given consistent calculus (and hence for any calculus of the usual kind, not containing rules for C-*false*), however the rules may be chosen.

On the other hand, those who deny the conventional character of logic, i.e., the possibility of a free choice of the logical rules of deduction, are equally right in what they mean if not in what they say. They are right under a certain condition, which presumably is tacitly assumed. The condition is that the "meanings" of the logical signs are given before the rules of deduction are formulated. They would, for instance, insist that the rule $R\,1$ of B-C ("from '*wenn* . . . , *so* - - -' and '. . . ,' '- - -' is directly derivable" [Section 9]) is necessary; that it would be wrong to change it arbitrarily, e.g., into $R\,1^*$: "from '*wenn* . . . , *so* - - -' and '*nicht* . . . ,' ' - - -' is directly derivable." What they presumably mean is that the rule $R\,1^*$ is incorrect on the basis of the presupposed "meaning" of the signs *wenn*, *so*, and *nicht*. Thus, they have in mind the procedure which we called the first method (Section 11): we begin by establishing the semantical rules SL or assume them as given—obviously this is meant by saying that the"meaning" is given—and then we ask what rules of deduction, i.e., syntactical rules of transformation, would be in accordance with the presupposed semantical rules. In this order of procedure, we are, as we have seen, indeed bound in the choice of the rules in all essential respects. Thus, we come to a reconciliation of the opposing views. And it seems to me that an agreement should easily be attainable in the other direction as well. The anti-conventionalists would certainly not deny that the rule *R* 1* can also be chosen and can lead to correct results, provided we interpret the logical signs in a different way (in the example given, we could interpret "*wenn* . . . , *so* - - -," e.g., as ". . . or - - -").

The result of our discussion is the following: logic or the rules of deduction (in our terminology, the syntactical rules of transformation) can be chosen arbitrarily and hence are conventional if they are taken as the basis of the construction of the language system and if the interpretation of the system is later superimposed. On the other hand, a system of logic is not a matter of choice, but either right or wrong, if an interpretation of the logical signs is given in advance. But even here, conventions are of fundamental importance; for the basis on which logic is constructed, namely, the interpretation of the logical signs (e.g., by a determination of truth conditions) can be freely chosen.

It is important to be aware of the conventional components in the construction of a language system. This view leads to an unprejudiced investigation of the various forms of new logical systems which differ more or less from the customary form (e.g., the intuitionist logic constructed by Brouwer and Heyting, the systems of logic of modalities as constructed by Lewis and others, the systems of plurivalued logic as constructed by Lukasiewicz and Tarski, etc.), and it encourages the construction of further new forms. The task is not to decide which of the different systems is "the right logic" but to examine their formal properties and the possibilities for their interpretation and application in science. It might be that a system deviating from the ordinary form will turn out to be useful as a basis for the language of science.

16   The Need for Abstract Entities in Semantic Analysis*

Alonzo Church

We distinguish between a *logistic system* and a *formalized language* on the basis that the former is an abstractly formulated calculus for which no interpretation is fixed, and thus has a syntax but no semantics; but the latter is a logistic system together with an assignment of meanings to its expressions.

As primitive basis of a logistic system it suffices to give, in familiar fashion: (1) the list of primitive symbols or *vocabulary* of the system (together usually with a classification of the primitive symbols into categories, which will be used in stating the formation rules and rules of inference); (2) the *formation rules*, determining which finite sequences of primitive symbols are to be *well-formed* expressions, determining certain categories of well-formed expressions—among which we shall assume that at least the category of *sentence* is included—, and determining (in case *variables* are included among the primitive symbols) which occurrences of variables in a well-formed expression are *free* occurrences and which are *bound* occurrences;[1] (3) the transformation rules or *rules of inference*, by which, from the *assertion* of certain sentences (the *premisses*, finite in number), a certain sentence (the *conclusion*) may be *inferred*; (4) certain asserted sentences, the *axioms*.

In order to obtain a formalized language it is necessary to add, to these *syntactical rules* of the logistic system, *semantical rules* assigning meanings (in some sense) to the well-formed expressions of the system.[2] The character of the semantical rules will

---

*A. Church "The Need for Abstract Entities in Semantic Analysis, "*Contributions to the Analysis and Synthesis of Knowledge*, Proceedings of the American Academy of Arts and Sciences, **80**, No. 1 (July 1951), 100–112. Reprinted by permission.

[1]For convenience of the present brief exposition we make the simplifying assumption that sentences are without free variables and that only sentences are asserted.

[2]The possibility that the meaningful expressions may be a proper subclass of the well-formed expressions must not ultimately be excluded. But again for the present sketch it will be convenient to treat the two classes as identical—the simplest and most usual case. Compare, however, 13*n*.

depend on the theory of meaning adopted, and this in turn must be justified by the purpose which it is to serve.

Let us take it as our purpose to provide an abstract theory of the actual use of language for human communication—not a factual or historical report of what has been observed to take place, but a norm to which we may regard every-day linguistic behavior as an imprecise approximation, in the same way that, e.g., elementary (applied) geometry is a norm to which we may regard as imprecise approximations the practical activity of the land-surveyor in laying out a plot of ground or of the construction foreman in seeing that building plans are followed. We must demand of such a theory that it have a place for all observably informative kinds of communication—including such notoriously troublesome cases as belief statements, modal statements, conditions contrary to fact—or at least that it provide a (theoretically) workable substitute for them. And solutions must be available for puzzles about meaning which may arise, such as the so-called "paradox of analysis."

There exists more than one theory of meaning showing some promise of fulfilling these requirements, at least so far as the formulation and development have presently been carried. But the theory of Frege seems to recommend itself above others for its relative simplicity, naturalness, and explanatory power—or, as I would advocate, Frege's theory as modified by elimination of his somewhat problematical notion of a function (and in particular of a *Begriff*) as *ungesättigt*, and by some other changes which bring it closer to present logistic practice without loss of such essentials as the distinction of sense and denotation.

This modified Fregean theory may be roughly characterized by the tendency to minimize the category of *syncategorematic* notations—i.e., notations to which no meaning at all is ascribed in isolation but which may combine with one or more meaningful expressions to form a meaningful expression[3]—and to reduce the categories of meaningful expressions to two, (proper) *names* and *forms*, for each of which two kinds of meaning are distinguished in a parallel way.

A name, or a *constant* (as we shall also say, imitating mathematical terminology), has first its *denotation*, or that of which it is a name.[4] And each name has also a *sense*—which is perhaps more properly to be called its meaning, since it is held that complete understanding of a language involves the ability to recognize the sense of any name in the language, but does not demand any knowledge beyond this of the denotations of names. (Declarative) *sentences*, in particular, are taken as a kind of names, the denotation being the *truth-value* of the sentence, *truth* or *falsehood*, and the sense being the *proposition* which the sentence expresses.

A name is said to *denote* its denotation and to *express* its sense, and the sense is said to be *a concept of* the denotation. The abstract entities which serve as senses of

---

[3]Such notations can be reduced to at most two, namely the notation (consisting, say, of juxtaposition between parentheses) which is used in application of a singulary function to its argument and the abstraction operator λ. By the methods of the Schönfinkel-Curry combinatory logic it may even be possible further to eliminate the abstraction operator, and along with it the use of variables altogether. But this final reduction is not contemplated here—nor even necessarily the simpler reduction to two syncategorematic notations.

[4]The complicating possibility is here ignored of *denotationless names*, or names which have a sense but no denotation. For though it may be held that these do occur in the natural languages, it is possible, as Frege showed, to construct a formalized language in such a way as to avoid them.

names let us call *concepts*—although this use of the word *concept* has no analogue in the writings of Frege and must be carefully distinguished from Frege's use of *Begriff*. Thus, anything which is or is capable of being the sense of some name in some language, actual or possible, is a concept.[5] The terms *individual concept, function concept*, and the like are then to mean a concept which is a concept of an individual, of a function, etc. A *class concept* may be identified with a *property*, and a *truth-value concept* (as already indicated) with a proposition.

Names are to be meaningful expressions without free variables, and expressions which are analogous to names except that they contain free variables, we call *forms* (a rather wide extension of the ordinary mathematical usage, here adopted for lack of a better term).[6] Each variable has a *range*, which is the class of admissible *values* of the variable.[7] And analogous to the denotation of a name, a form has a *value* for every system of admissible values of its free variables.[8]

The assignment of a value to a variable, though it is not a syntactical operation, corresponds in a certain way to the syntactical operation of substituting a constant for the variable. The denotation of the substituted constant represents the value of the variable.[9] And the sense of the substituted constant may be taken as representing a *sense-value* of the variable. Thus, every variable has, besides its range, also a *sense-range*, which is the class of admissible sense-values of the variable. And analogous to the sense of a name, a form has a *sense-value* for every system of admissible sense-values of its free variables.[10]

The following principles are assumed.[11] (i) Every concept is a concept of at most

------

[5]This is meant only as a preliminary rough description. In logical order, the notion of a concept must be postulated and that of a possible language defined by means of it.

[6]Frege's term in German is *Marke*—the form or *Marke* must of course not be confused with its associated abstract entity, the *function*. The function differs from the form in that it is not a linguistic entity and belongs to no particular language. Indeed the same function may be associated with different forms; and if there is more than one free variable, the same form may have several associated functions. But in some languages it is possible from the form to construct a name (or names) of the associated function (or functions) by means of an abstraction operator.

[7]The idea of allowing variables of different ranges is not Fregean, except in the case of functions in Frege's sense (i.e., as *ungesättigt*), the different categories of which appear as ranges for different variables. The introduction of *Gegenstandsbuchstaben* with restricted ranges is one of the modifications here advocated in Frege's theory.

[8]Exceptions to this are familiar in common mathematical notation. E.g., the form x/y has no value for the system of values 0,0 of x, y. However, the semantics of a language is much simplified if a value is assigned to a form for every system of values of the free variables which are admissible in the sense that each value belongs to the range of the corresponding variable. And for purposes of the present exposition we assume that this has been done. (Compare 4n.)

[9]Even if the language contains no constant denoting the value in question, it is possible to consider an extension of the language obtained by adjoining such a constant.

[10]The notion of a sense-value of a form is not introduced by Frege, at least not explicitly, but it can be argued that it is necessarily implicit in his theory. For Frege's question, "How can a = b, if true, ever differ in meaning from a = a?" can be asked as well for forms a and b as for constants and leads to the distinction of value and sense-value of a form just as it does to the distinction of denotation and sense of a constant. Even in a language like that of *Principia Mathematica*, having no forms other than propositional forms, a parallel argument can be used to show that from the equivalence of two propositional forms A and B the identity in meaning of A and B in all respects is not to be inferred. For otherwise how could $A \equiv B$ if true, (i.e., true for all values of the variables) ever differ in meaning from A $\equiv$ A.

[11]For purposes of the preliminary sketch, the metalanguage is left unformalized, and such questions are ignored as whether the metalanguage shall conform to the theory of types or to

one thing. (ii) Every constant has a unique concept as its sense. (iii) Every variable has a nonempty class of concepts as its sense-range. (iv) For any assignment of sense-values, one to each of the free variables of a given form, if each sense-value is admissible in the sense that it belongs to the sense-range of the corresponding variable, the form has a unique concept as its sense-value. (v) The denotation of a constant is that of which its sense is a concept. (vi) The range of a variable is the class of those things of which the members of the sense-range are concepts. (vii) If S, s_1, s_2, $\ldots$, s_m are concepts of A, a_1 a_2, $\ldots$, a_m, respectively, and if S is the sense-value of a form F for the system of sense-values s_1, s_2, $\ldots$, s_m of its free variables x_1, x_2, $\ldots$, x_m, then the value of F for the system of values a_1, a_2, $\ldots$ a_m of x_1, x_2, $\ldots$, x_m is A. (viii) If C' is obtained from a constant C by replacing a particular occurrence of a constant c by a constant c' that has the same sense as c, then C' is a constant having the same sense as C.[12] (ix) If C' is obtained from a constant C by replacing a particular occurrence of a constant c by a constant c' that has the same denotation as c, then C' is a constant having the same denotation as C.[13] (x) If C' is obtained from a constant C by replacing a particular occurrence of a form f by a form f' that has the same free variables as f, and if, for every admissible system of sense-values of their free variables, f and f' have the same sense-value, then C' is a constant having the same sense as C.[12] (xi) If C' is obtained from a constant C by replacing a particular

---

some alternative such as transfinite type theory or axiomatic set theory. Because of the extreme generality which is attempted in laying down these principles, it is clear that there may be some difficulty in rendering them precise (in their full attempted generality) by restatement in a formalized metalanguage. But it should be possible to state the semantical rules of a particular object language so as to conform, so that the principles are clarified to this extent by illustration.

It is not meant that the list of principles is necessarily complete or in final form, but rather a tentative list is here proposed for study and possible amendment. Moreover it is not meant that it may not be possible to formulate a language not conforming to the principles, but only that a satisfactory general theory may result by making conformity to these principles a part of the definition of a formalized language (compare 12n).

[12]In the case of some logistic systems which have been proposed (e.g., by D. Hilbert and P. Bernays), if semantical rules are to be added, in conformity with the theory here described and with the informally intended interpretation of the system, it is found to be impossible to satisfy (viii), (x), and (xiv), because of restriction imposed on the bound variables which may appear in a constant or form used in a particular context. But it would seem that modifications in the logistic system necessary to remove the restriction may reasonably be considered nonessential and that in this sense (viii), (x), (xiv) may still be maintained.

In regard to all of the principles it should be understood that nonessential modifications in existing logistic systems may be required to make them conform. In particular the principles have been formulated in a way which does not contemplate the distinction in typographical style between free and bound variables that appears in systems of Frege and of Hilbert-Bernays.

In (x) and (xi), the condition that f' have the same free variables as f can in many cases be weakened to the condition that every free variable of f' occur also as a free variable of f.

[13]Possibly (ix) and (xi) should be weakened to require only that if C' is well-formed, then it is a constant having the same denotation as C. Since there is in general no syntactical criterion by which to ascertain whether two constants c and c' have the same denotation, or whether two forms have always the same values, there is the possibility that the stronger forms of (ix) and (xi) might lead to difficulty in some cases. However, (ix) as here stated has the effect of preserving fully the rule of substitutivity of equality—where the equality sign is so interpreted that $[c_1 = c_2]$ is a sentence denoting truth if and only if c_1 and c_2 are constants having the same denotation—and if in some formalized languages, (ix) and (xi) should prove to be inconsistent with the requirement that every well-formed expression be meaningful (2n.), it may be preferable to abandon the latter. Indeed the preservation of the rule of substitutivity of equality may be regarded as an important advantage of a Fregean theory of meaning over some of the alternatives that suggest themselves.

occurrence of a form f by a form f' that has the same free variables as f, and if, for every system of values of their free variables which are admissible in the sense that each value belongs to the range of the corresponding variable, f and f' have the same value, then C' is a constant having the same denotation as C.[13] (xii) If x_1, x_2, $\ldots$, x_m are all the distinct variables occurring (necessarily as bound variables) in a constant C, if y_1, y_2, $\ldots$, y_m are distinct variables having the same sense-ranges as x_1, x_2, $\ldots$, x_m, respectively, and if C' is obtained from C by substituting y_1, y_2, $\ldots$, y_m throughout for x_1, x_2, $\ldots$, x_m, respectively, then C' is a constant having the same sense as C. (xiii) If x_1, x_2, $\ldots$, x_m are the distinct variables occurring in a constant C, if y_1, y_2, $\ldots$, y_m are distinct variables having the same ranges as x_1, x_2, $\ldots$, x_m, respectively, and if C' is obtained from C by substituting y_1, y_2, $\ldots$, y_m throughout for x_1, x_2, $\ldots$, x_m, respectively, then C' is a constant having the same denotation as C. (xiv) The result of substituting constants for all the free variables of a form is a constant, if the sense of each substituted constant belongs to the sense-range of the corresponding variable.[12] (xv) The sense of a constant C thus obtained by substituting constants c_1, c_2, $\ldots$, c_m for the free variables x_1, x_2, $\ldots$, x_m of a form F is the same as the sense-value of F when the senses of c_1, c_2, $\ldots$, c_m are assigned as the sense-values of x_1, x_2, $\ldots$, x_m.

To these must still be added principles which are similar to (vii)–(xv), except that substitution is made in forms instead of constants, or that forms and variables as well as constants are substituted for the free variables of a form. Instead of stating these here, it may be sufficient to remark that they follow if arbitrary extensions of the language are allowed by adjoining (as primitive symbols) constants which have as their senses any concepts that belong to sense-ranges of variables in the language, if the foregoing principles are assumed to hold also for such extensions of the language, and if there is assumed further: (xvi) Let an expression F contain the variables x_1, x_2, $\ldots$, x_m; and suppose that in every extension of the language of the kind just described and for every substitution of constants c_1, c_2, $\ldots$, c_m for the variables x_1, x_2, $\ldots$, x_m, respectively, if the sense of each constant belongs to the sense-range of the corresponding variable, F becomes a constant; then F is a form having x_1, x_2, $\ldots$, x_m as its free variables.

To those who find forbidding the array of abstract entities and principles concerning them which is here proposed, I would say that the problems which give rise to the proposal are difficult and a simpler theory is not known to be possible.[14]

---

[14]At the present stage it cannot be said with assurance that a modification of Frege's theory will ultimately prove to be the best or the simplest. Alternative theories demanding study are: the theory of Russell, which relies on the elimination of names by contextual definition to an extent sufficient to render the distinction of sense and denotation unnecessary; the modification of Russell's theory, briefly suggested by A. Smullyan (*The Journal of Symbolic Logic*, **13** (1948), 31–37), according to which descriptive phrases are to be considered as actually contained in the logistic system rather than being (in the phrase of Whitehead and Russell) "mere typographical conveniences," but are to differ from names in that they retain their need for scope indicators; and finally, the theory of Carnap's *Meaning and Necessity*.

Although the Russell theory has an element of simplicity in avoiding the distinction of two kinds of meaning, it leads to complications of its own of a different sort, in connection with the matter of scope of descriptions. The same should be said of Smullyan's proposed modification of the theory. And the distinctions of scope become especially important in modal statements, where they cannot be eliminated by the convention of always taking the minimum scope, as Smullyan has shown (*op. cit*).

To those who object to the introduction of abstract entities at all I would say that I believe that there are more important criteria by which a theory should be judged. The extreme demand for a simple prohibition of abstract entities under all circumstances perhaps arises from a desire to maintain the connection between theory and observation. But the preference of (say) *seeing* over *understanding* as a method of observation seems to me capricious. For just as an opaque body may be seen, so a concept may be understood or grasped. And the parallel between the two cases is indeed rather close. In both cases the observation is not direct but through intermediaries—light, lens of eye or optical instrument, and retina in the case of the visible body, linguistic expressions in the case of the concept. And in both cases there are or may be tenable theories according to which the entity in question, opaque body or concept, is not assumed, but only those things which would otherwise be called its effects.

The variety of entities (whether abstract or concrete) which a theory assumes is indeed one among other criteria by which it may be judged. If multiplication of entities is found beyond the needs of the workability, simplicity, and generality of the theory, then the razor shall be applied.[15] The theory of meaning here outlined I

Moreover, in its present form it would seem that the Russell theory requires some supplementation. For example, "I am thinking of Pegasus," "Ponce de Leon searched for the fountain of youth," "Barbara Villiers was less chaste than Diana" cannot be analyzed as "(Ec) [x is a Pegasus $\equiv_\psi x = c$] [I am thinking of c]," "(Ec) [x is a fountain of youth $\equiv_\psi x = c$] [Ponce de Leon searched for c]," "(Ec) [x is a Diana $\equiv x = c$] [Barbara Villiers was less chaste than c]" respectively—if only because of the (probable or possible) difference of truth-value between the given statements and their proposed analyses. On a Fregean theory of meaning the given statements might be analyzed as being about the individual concepts of Pegasus, of the fountain of youth, and of Diana rather than about some certain winged horse, some certain fountain, and some certain goddess. For the Russell theory it might be suggested to analyze them as being about the property of being a Pegasus, the property of being a fountain of youth, and the property of being a Diana. This analysis in terms of properties would also be possible on a Fregean theory, although perhaps slightly less natural. On a theory of the Russell type the difficulty arises that names of properties seem to be required, and on pain of re-admitting Frege's puzzle about equality (which leads to the distinction of sense and denotation in connection with names of any kind), such names of properties either must be analyzed away by contextual definition—it is not clear how—or must be so severely restricted that two names of the same property cannot occur unless trivially synonymous.

[15]Here a warning is necessary against spurious economies, since not every subtraction from the entities which a theory assumes is a reduction in the variety of entites.

For example, in the simple theory of types it is well known that the individuals may be dispensed with if classes and relations of all types are retained; or one may abandon also classes and relations of the lowest type, retaining only those cf higher type. In fact, any finite number of levels at the bottom of the hierarchy of types may be deleted. But this is no reduction in the variety of entities, because the truncated hierarchy of types, by appropriate deletions of entities in each type, can be made isomorphic to the original hierarchy—and indeed the continued adequacy of the truncated hierarchy to the original purposes depends on this isomorphism.

Similarly, the idea may suggest itself to admit the distinction of sense and denotation at the nth level and above in the hierarchy of types, but below the nth level to deny this distinction and to adopt instead Russell's device of contextual elimination of names. The entities assumed would thus include only the usual extensional entities below the nth level, but at the nth level and above they would include also concepts, concepts of concepts, and so on. However, this is no reduction in the variety of entities assumed, as compared to the theory which assumes at all levels in the hierarchy of types not only the extensional entities but also concepts of them, concepts of concepts of them, and so on. For the entities assumed by the former theory are reduced again to

hold exempt from such treatment no more than any other, but I do advocate its study.

Let us return now to our initial question as to the character of the semantical rules which are to be added to the syntactical rules of a logistic system in order to define a particular formalized language.

On the foregoing theory of meaning the semantical rules must include at least the following: (5) *rules of sense*, by which a sense is determined for each well-formed expression without free variables (all such expressions thus becoming names). (6) *rules of sense-range*, assigning to each variable a sense-range; (7) *rules of sense-value*, by which a sense-value is determined for every well-formed expression containing free variables and every admissible system of sense-values of its free variables (all such expressions thus becoming forms).

In the case of both syntactical and semantical rules there is a distinction to be drawn between *primitive* and *derived* rules, the primitive rules being those which are stated in giving the primitive basis of the formalized language, and the derived rules being rules of similar kind which follow as consequences of the primitive rules. Thus, besides primitive rules of inference there are also derived rules of inference, besides primitive rules of sense also derived rules of sense, and so on. (But instead of "derived axioms" it is usual to say *theorems*.)

A statement of the denotation of a name, the range of a variable, or the value of a form does not necessarily belong to the semantics of a language. For example, that "the number of planets" denotes the number nine is a fact as much of astronomy as it is of the semantics of the English language and can be described only as belonging to a discipline broad enough to include both semantics and astronomy. On the other hand, a statement that "the number of planets" denotes the number of planets is a purely semantical statement about the English language. And indeed it would seem that a statement of this kind may be considered as purely semantical only if it is a consequence of the rules of sense, sense-range, and sense-value, together with the syntactical rules and the general principles of meaning (i)–(xvi).

Thus, as derived semantical rules rather than primitive, there will be also: (8) *rules of denotation*, by which a denotation is determined for each name; (9) *rules of range*, assigning to each variable a range; (10) *rules of value*, by which a value is determined for every admissible system of values of its free variables.

By stating (8), (9), and (10) as primitive rules, without (5), (6), and (7), there results what may be called the *extensional part* of the semantics of a language. The remaining *intensional part* of the semantic does not follow from the extensional part. For the sense of a name is not uniquely determined by its denotation, and thus a particular rule of denotation does not of itself have as a consequence the corresponding rule of sense.

---

isomorphism with those assumed by the latter, if all entities below the nth level are deleted and appropriate deletions are made in every type at the nth level and above.

Someone may object that the notion of isomorphism which is introduced here is irrelevant and insist that any subtraction from the entities assumed by a theory must be considered a simplification. But to such an objector I would reply that his proposal leads (in the cases just named, and others) to perpetual oscillation between two theories T_1 and T_2, T_1 being reduced to T_2 and T_2 to T_1 by successive "simplifications" *ad infinitum*.

On the other hand, because the metalinguistic phrase which is used in the rule of denotation must itself have a sense, there is a certain sense (though not that of logical consequence) in which the rule of denotation, by being given as a primitive rule of denotation, uniquely indicates the corresponding rule of sense. Since the like is true of the rules of range and rules of value, it is permissible to say that we have fixed an *interpretation* of a given logistic system, and thus a formalized language, if we have stated only the extensional part of the semantics.[16]

Although all the foregoing account has been concerned with the case of a formalized language, I would go on to say that in my opinion there is no difference in principle between this case and that of one of the natural languages. In particular, it must not be thought that a formalized language depends for its meaning or its justification (in any sense in which a natural language does not) upon some prior natural language, say English, through some system of translation of its sentences into English—or, more plausibly, through the statement of its syntactical and semantical rules in English. For speaking in principle, and leaving all questions of practicality aside, the logician must declare it a mere historical accident that you and I learned from birth to speak English rather than a language with less irregular, and logically simpler, syntactical rules, similar to those of one of the familiar logistic systems in use today—or that we learned in school the content of conventional English grammars and dictionaries rather than a more precise statement of a system of syntactical and semantical rules of the kind which has been described in this present sketch. The difference of a formalized language from a natural language lies not in any matter of principle, but in the degree of completeness that has been attained in the laying down of explicit syntactical and semantical rules and the extent to which vaguenesses and uncertainties have been removed from them.

For this reason the English language itself may be used as a convenient though makeshift illustration of a language for which syntactical and semantical rules are to be given. Of course, only a few illustrative examples of such rules can be given in brief space. And even for this it is necessary to avoid carefully the use of examples involving English constructions that raise special difficulties or show too great logical irregularities, and to evade the manifold equivocacy of English words by selecting and giving attention to just one meaning of each word mentioned. It must also not be asked whether the rules given as examples are among the "true" rules of the English language or are "really" a part of what is implied in an understanding of English; for the laying down of rules for a natural language, because of the need to fill gaps and to decide doubtful points, is as much a process of legislation as of reporting.

With these understandings, and with no attempt made to distinguish between primitive and derived rules, following are some examples of syntactical and semantical rules of English according to the program which has been outlined.[17]

(1) VOCABULARY: *equals five four if is nine number of planet planets plus round the then the world*—besides the bare list of primitive symbols (words) there must be

---

[16]As is done in the forthcoming revised edition of my *Introduction to Mathematical Logic, Part I*.

[17]For convenience, English is used also as the metalanguage, although this gives a false appearance of triviality or obviousness to some of the semantical rules. Since the purpose is only illustrative, the danger of semantical antinomies is ignored.

statements regarding their classification into categories and systematic relations among them, e.g., that *planet* is a common noun,[18] that *planets* is the plural of *planet*,[19] that *the world* is a proper noun, that *round* is an adjective.

(2) FORMATION RULES: if *A* is the plural of a common noun, then the ∩ *number* ∩ *of* ∩ *A* is a singular term. A proper noun standing alone is a singular term. If *A* and *B* are singular terms, then *A* ∩ *equals* ∩ *B* is a sentence. If *A* is a singular term and *B* is an adjective, then *A* ∩ *is* ∩ *B* is a sentence.[20] If *A* and *B* are sentences, then *if* ∩ *A* ∩ *then* ∩ *B* is a sentence. (Here singular terms and sentences are to be understood as categories of well-formed expressions; a more complete list of formation rules would no doubt introduce many more such.)

(3) RULES OF INFERENCE: where *A* and *B* are sentences, from *if* ∩ *A* ∩ *then* ∩ *B* and *A* to infer *B*. Where *A* and *B* are singular terms and *C* is an adjective, from *A* ∩ *equals* ∩ *B* and *B* ∩ *is* ∩ *C* to infer *A* ∩ *is* ∩ *C*.

(4) AXIOMS-THEOREMS: "if the world is round, then the world is round"; "four plus five equals nine."

(5) RULES OF SENSE: *round* expresses the property of roundness; *the world* expresses the (individual) concept of the world. "the world is round" expresses the proposition that the world is round.

(6) RULES OF DENOTATION: *round* denotes the class of round things; *the world* denotes the world; "the world is round" denotes the truth-value thereof that the world is round.[21]

On a Fregean theory of meaning, rules of truth in Tarski's form—e.g., " 'the world is round' is true if and only if the world is round"—follow from the rules of denotation for sentences. For that a sentence is true is taken to be the same as that it denotes truth.

---

[18]For present illustrative purposes the question may be avoided whether common nouns in English, in the singular, shall be considered to be variables (e.g., *planet* or *a planet* as a variable having planets as its range), or to be class names (e.g., *planet* as a proper name of the class of planets), or to have *no status at all in a logical grammar* (see Quine's *Methods of Logic*, p. 207), or perhaps to vary from one of these uses to another according to context.

[19]Or, possibly *planet* and *s* could be regarded as two primitive symbols, by making a minor change in existing English so that all common nouns form the plural by adding *s*.

[20]If any one finds unacceptable the conclusion that therefore "the number of planets is round" is a sentence, he may try to alter the rules to suit, perhaps by distinguishing different types of terms. This is an example of a doubtful point, on the decision of which there may well be differences of opinion. The advocate of a set-theoretic language may decide one way and the advocate of type theory another, but it is hard to say that either decision is the *true* decision for the English language as it is.

[21]But, of course, it would be wrong to include as a rule of denotation: "the world is round" denotes truth. For this depends on a fact of geography extraneous to semantics (namely, that the world *is* round).

17   Speaking of Objects*

Willard V. Quine

I

We are prone to talk and think of objects. Physical objects are the obvious illustration when the illustrative mood is on us, but there are also all the abstract objects, or so there purport to be: the states and qualities, numbers, attributes, classes. We persist in breaking reality down somehow into a multiplicity of identifiable and discriminable objects, to be referred to by singular and general terms. We talk so inveterately of objects that to say we do so seems almost to say nothing at all; for how else is there to talk?

It is hard to say how else there is to talk, not because our objectifying pattern is an invariable trait of human nature, but because we are bound to adapt any alien pattern to our own in the very process of understanding or translating the alien sentences.

Imagine a newly discovered tribe whose language is without known affinities. The linguist has to learn the language directly by observing what the natives say under observed circumstances, encountered or contrived. He makes a first crude beginning by compiling native terms for environing objects; but here already he is really imposing his own patterns. Let me explain what I mean. I will grant that the linguist may establish inductively, beyond reasonable doubt, that a certain heathen expression is one to which natives can be prompted to assent by the presence of a rabbit, or reasonable *facsimile*, and not otherwise. The linguist is then warranted in according the native expression the cautious translation "There's a rabbit," "There we have a rabbit," "Lo! a rabbit," "Lo! rabbithood again," insofar as the differences among these English sentences are counted irrelevant. This much translation can be objective, however exotic the tribe. It recognizes the native expression as in effect a rabbit-heralding sentence. But the linguist's bold further step, in which he imposes his own

---

*W. V. Quine, "Speaking of Objects," *Proceedings and Addresses of the American Philosophical Association*, 1957–58 (Yellow Springs, Ohio: Antioch Press, 1958), pp. 5–22. Reprinted by permission.

object-positing pattern without special warrant, is taken when he equates the native expression or any part of it with the *term* "rabbit."

It is easy to show that such appeal to an object category is unwarranted even though we cannot easily, in English, herald rabbits without objectification. For we can argue from indifference. Given that a native sentence says that a so-and-so is present, and given that the sentence is true when and only when a rabbit is present, it by no means follows that the so-and-so are rabbits. They might be all the various temporal segments of rabbits. They might be all the integral or undetached parts of rabbits. In order to decide among these alternatives we need to be able to ask more than whether a so-and-so is present. We need to be able to ask whether this is the same so-and-so as that and whether one so-and-so is present or two. We need something like the apparatus of identity and quantification; hence far more than we are in a position to avail ourselves of in a language in which our high point as of even date is rabbit-announcing.

And the case is yet worse: we do not even have evidence for taking the native expression as of the form "A so-and-so is present"; it could as well be construed with an abstract singular term, as meaning that rabbithood is locally manifested. Better just Rabbiteth, like Raineth.

But if our linguist is going to be as cagey as all this, he will never translate more than these simple-minded announcements of observable current events. A cagey linguist is a caged linguist. What we want from the linguist as a serviceable finished product, after all, is no mere list of sentence-to-sentence equivalences, like the airline throwaways of useful Spanish phrases. We want a manual of instructions for custom-building a native sentence to roughly the purpose of any newly composed English sentence, within reason, and vice versa. The linguist has to resolve the potential infinity of native sentences into a manageably limited list of grammatical constructions and constituent linguistic forms, and then show how the business of each can be approximated in English; and vice versa. Sometimes perhaps he will translate a word or construction not directly but contextually, by systematic instructions for translating its containing sentences; but still he must make do with a limited lot of contextual definitions. Now once he has carried out this necessary job of lexicography, forwards and backwards, he has read our ontological point of view into the native language. He has decided what expressions to treat as referring to objects, and, within limits, what sorts of objects to treat them as referring to. He has had to decide, however arbitrarily, how to accommodate English idioms of identity and quantification in native translation.

The word "arbitrary" needs stressing, not because those decisions are wholly arbitrary, but because they are so much more so than one tends to suppose. For, what evidence does the linguist have? He started with what we may call native observation sentences, such as the rabbit announcement. These he can say how to translate into English, provided we impute no relevance to the differences between "Here a rabbit," "Here rabbithood," and the like. Also he can record further native sentences and settle whether various persons are prepared to affirm or deny them, though he find no rabbit movements or other currently observable events to tie them to. Among these untranslated sentences he may get an occasional hint of logical connections, by finding say that just the persons who are prepared to affirm *A* are prepared to affirm *B* and deny *C*. Thereafter his data leave off and his creativity sets in.

What he does in his creativity is attribute special and distinctive functions to component words, or conspicuously recurrent fragments, of the recorded sentences. The only ways one can appraise these attributions are as follows. One can see whether they add up to representing the rabbit sentence and the like as conforming to their previously detected truth conditions. One can see also how well they fit the available data on other sentences: sentences for which no truth conditions are known, but only the varying readiness of natives to affirm or deny them. Beyond this we can judge the attributions only on their simplicity and naturalness—to *us*.

Certainly the linguist will try out his theory on the natives, springing new sentences authorized by his theory, to see if they turn out right. This is a permuting of the time order: one frames the theory before all possible data are in and then lets it guide one in the eliciting of additional data likeliest to matter. This is good scientific method, but it opens up no new kind of data. English general and singular terms, identity, quantification, and the whole bag of ontological tricks may be correlated with elements of the native language in any of various mutually incompatible ways, each compatible with all possible linguistic data, and none preferable to another save as favored by a rationalization of the *native* language that is simple and natural to *us*.

It makes no real difference that the linguist will turn bilingual and come to think as the natives do—whatever that means. For the arbitrariness of reading our objections into the heathen speech reflects not so much the inscrutability of the heathen mind, as that there is nothing to scrute. Even we who grew up together and learned English at the same knee, or adjacent ones, talk alike for no other reason than that society coached us alike in a pattern of verbal response to externally observable cues. We have been beaten into an outward conformity to an outward standard; and thus it is that when I correlate your sentences with mine by the simple rule of phonetic correspondence, I find that the public circumstances of your affirmations and denials agree pretty well with those of my own. If I conclude that you share my sort of conceptual scheme, I am not adding a supplementary conjecture so much as spurning fathomable distinctions; for, what further criterion of sameness of conceptual scheme can be imagined? The case of a Frenchman, moreover, is the same except that I correlate his sentences with mine not by phonetic correspondence but according to a traditionally evolved dictionary.[1] The case of the linguist and his newly discovered heathen, finally, differs simply in that the linguist has to grope for a general sentence-to-sentence correlation that will make the public circumstances of the heathen's affirmations and denials match up tolerably with the circumstances of the linguist's own. If the linguist fails in this, or has a hard time of it, or succeeds only by dint of an ugly and complex mass of correlations, then he is entitled to say—in the only sense in which one *can* say it—that his heathens have a very different attitude toward reality from ours; and even so he cannot coherently suggest what their attitude is. Nor, in principle, is the natural bilingual any better off.

When we compare theories, doctrines, points of view, cultures, on the score of what sorts of objects there are said to be, we are comparing them in a respect which

---

[1]See Richard von Mises, *Positivism* (Cambridge, Mass.: Harvard University Press, 1951) pp. 46 ff.

itself makes sense only provincially. It makes sense only as far afield as our efforts to translate our domestic idioms of identity and quantification bring encouragement in the way of simple and natural-looking correspondences. If we attend to business we are unlikely to find a very alien culture with a predilection for a very outlandish universe of discourse, just because the outlandishness of it would detract from our sense of patness of our dictionary of translation. There is a notion that our provincial ways of positing objects and conceiving nature may be best appreciated for what they are by standing off and seeing them against a cosmopolitan background of alien cultures; but the notion comes to nothing, for there is no $\pi o\tilde{v}$ $\sigma\tau\hat{\omega}$.[2]

II

Yet, for all the difficulty of transcending our object-directed pattern of thought, we can examine it well enough from inside. Let us turn our attention from the heathen, who seemed to have a term for "rabbit," to our own child at home who seems to have just acquired his first few terms in our own language: "mama," "water," perhaps "red." To begin with, the case of the child resembles that of the heathen. For though we may fully satisfy ourselves that the child has learned the trick of using the utterances "mama" and "water" strictly in the appropriate presences, or as means of inducing the appropriate presences, still we have no right to construe these utterances in the child's mouth as terms, at first, for things or substances.

We in our maturity have come to look upon the child's mother as an integral body who, in an irregular closed orbit, revisits the child from time to time; and to look upon red in a radically different way, viz., as scattered about. Water, for us, is rather like red, but not quite; things can be red, but only stuff is water. But the mother, red, and water are for the infant all of a type: each is just a history of sporadic encounter, a scattered portion of what goes on. His first learning of the three words is uniformly a matter of learning how much of what goes on about him counts as the mother, or as red, or as water. It is not for the child to say in the first case. "Hello! mama again," in the second case "Hello! another red thing," and in the third case "Hello! more water." They are all on a par: Hello! more mama, more red, more water. Even this last formula, which treats all three terms on the model of our provincial adult bulk term "water," is imperfect; for it unwarrantedly imputes an objectification of matter, even if only as stuff and not as bits.

Progressively, however, the child is seen to evolve a pattern of verbal behavior that finally comes to copy ours too closely for there to be any sense in questioning the general sameness of conceptual scheme. For perspective on our objectifying apparatus we may consider what steps of development makes the difference between the "mama"-babbling infant who cannot be said to be using terms for objects, and the older child who can.

---

[2] For a fuller development of the foregoing theme see my "Meaning and Translation" in Reuben Brower, ed., *On Translation* (Cambridge, Mass.: Harvard University Press, 1959). For criticisms that have benefitted the above section of the present essay and ensuring portions I am grateful to Burton Dreben.

It is only when the child has got on to the full and proper use of *individuative* terms like "apple" that he can properly be said to have taken to using terms as terms, and speaking of objects. Words like "apple," and not words like "mama" or "water" or "red," are the terms whose ontological involvement runs deep. To learn "apple" it is not sufficient to learn how much of what goes on counts as apple; we must learn how much counts as *an* apple, and how much as another. Such terms possess built-in modes of individuation.

Individuative terms are commonly made to double as bulk terms. Thus, we may say "There is some apple in the salad," not meaning "some apple or other"; just as we may say "Mary had a little lamb" in either of two senses. Now we have appreciated that the child can learn the terms "mama," "red," and "water" quite well before he ever has mastered the ins and outs of our adult conceptual scheme of mobile enduring physical objects, identical from time to time and place to place; and in principle he might do the same for "apple," as a bulk term for uncut apple stuff. But he can never fully master "apple" in its individuative use, except as he gets on with the scheme of enduring and recurrent physical objects. He may come somewhat to grips with the individuative use of "apple" before quite mastering the comprehensive physical outlook, but his usage will be marred by misidentifications of distinct apples over time, or misdiscriminations of identical ones.

He has really got on to the individuative use, one is tempted to suppose, once he responds with the plural "apples" to a heap of apples. But not so. He may at that point have learned "apples" as another bulk term, applicable to just so much apple as is taken up in apple heaps. "Apples," for him, would be subordinated to "apple" as is "warm water" to "water," and "bright red" to "red."

The child might proceed to acquire "block" and "blocks," "ball" and "balls," as bulk terms in the same fashion. By the force of analogy among such pairs he might even come to apply the plural "-s" with seeming appropriateness to new words, and to drop it with seeming appropriateness from words first learned only with it. We might well not detect, for a while, his misconception: that "-s" just turns bulk terms into more specialized bulk terms connoting clumpiness.

A plausible variant misconception is this: "apple" bulkwise might cover just the apple stuff that is spaced off in lone apples, while "apples" still figures as last suggested. Then apples and apple would be mutually exclusive rather than subordinate the one to the other. This variant misconception could likewise be projected systematically to "block" and "blocks," "ball" and "balls," and long escape exposure.

How can we ever tell, then, whether the child has really got the trick of individuation? Only by engaging him in sophisticated discourse of "that apple," "not that apple," "an apple," "same apple," "another apple," "these apples." It is only at this level that a palpable difference emerges between genuinely individuative use and the counterfeits lately imagined.

Doubtless the child gets the swing of these peculiar adjectives "same," "another," "an," "that," "not that," contextually: first he becomes attuned to various longer phrases or sentences that contain them, and then gradually he develops appropriate habits in relation to the component words as common parts and residues of those longer forms. His tentative aquisition of the plural "-s," lately speculated on, is itself a first primitive step of the kind. The contextual learning of these various particles goes on simultaneously, we may suppose, so that they are gradually adjusted to one another and a coherent pattern of usage is evolved matching that of one's elders. This is a major step in acquiring the conceptual scheme that we all know so well. For it is on achieving this step, and only then, that there can be any general talk of objects as such. Only at this stage does it begin to make sense to wonder whether the apple now in one's hand is the apple noticed yesterday.

Until individuation emerges, the child can scarcely be said to have general *or* singular terms, there being no express talk of objects. The pre-individuative term "mama," and likewise "water" and "red" (for children who happen to learn "water" and "red" before mastering individuation), hark back to a primitive phase to which the distinction between singular and general is irrelevant. Once the child has pulled through the individuative crisis, though, he is prepared to re-assess prior terms. "Mama," in particular, gets set up retroactively as the name of a broad and recurrent but withal individual object, and thus as a singular term *par excellence*. Occasions eliciting "mama" being just as discontinuous as those eliciting "water," the two terms had been on a par; but with the advent of individuation the mother becomes integrated into a cohesive spatiotemporal convexity, while water remains scattered even in space-time. The two terms thus part company.

The mastery of individuation seems scarcely to affect people's attitude toward "water." For "water," "sugar," and the like the category of bulk terms remains, a survival of the pre-individuative phase, ill fitting the dichotomy into general and singular. But the philosophical mind sees its way to pressing this archaic category into the dichotomy. The bulk term "water" after the copula can usually be smoothly reconstrued as a general term true of each portion of water, while in other positions it is usually more simply construed as a singular term naming that spatio-temporally diffuse object which is the totality of the world's water.

III

I have urged that we could know the necessary and sufficient stimulatory conditions of every possible act of utterance, in a foreign language, and still not know how to determine what objects the speakers of that language believe in. Now if objective reference is so inaccessible to observation, who is to say on empirical grounds that belief in objects of one or another description is right or wrong? How can there ever be empirical evidence against existential statements?

The answer is something like this. Grant that a knowledge of the appropriate stimulatory conditions of a sentence does not settle how to construe the sentence in terms of existence of objects. Still, it does tend to settle what is to count as empirical evidence for or against the truth of the sentence. If we then go on to assign the sentence some import in point of existence of objects, by arbitrary projection in the case of the heathen language or as a matter of course in the case of our own, thereupon what has already been counting as empirical evidence for or against the truth of the sentence comes to count as empirical evidence for or against the existence of the objects.

The opportunity for error in existential statements increases with one's mastery of the verbal apparatus of objective reference. In one's earliest phase of word-learning, terms like "mama" and "water" were learned which may be viewed retrospectively as names each of an observed spatiotemporal object. Each such term was learned by a process of reinforcement and extinction, whereby the spatiotemporal range of application of the term was gradually perfected. The object named is assuredly an observed one, in the sense that the reinforced stimuli proceeded pretty directly from it. Granted, this talk of name and object belongs to a later phase of language learning, even as does the talk of stimulation.

The second phase, marked by the advent of individuative terms, is where a proper notion of object emerges. Here we get general terms, each true of each of many objects. But the objects still are observable spatiotemporal objects. For these individuative terms, e.g., "apple," are learned still by the old method of reinforcement and extinction; they differ from their predecessors only in the added feature of internal individuation.

Demonstrative singular terms like "this apple" usher in a third phase, characterized by the fact that a singular term seriously used can now, through error, fail to name: the thing pointed to can turn out to be the mere façade of an apple, or maybe a tomato. But even at this stage anything that we do succeed in naming is still an observable spatiotemporal object.

A fourth phase comes with the joining of one general term to another in attributive position. Now for the first time we can get general terms which are not true of anything; thus "blue apple," "square ball." But when there are things at all of which the thus formed general terms are true, they are still nothing new; they are just some among the same old observables whereof the component terms are true.

It is a fifth phase that brings a new mode of understanding, giving access to new sorts of objects. When we form compounds by applying relative terms to singular terms, we get such compounds as "smaller than that speck." Whereas the nonexistence of observable blue apples is tantamount to the nonexistence of blue apples, the nonexistence of observable objects smaller than that speck is not taken as tantamount to the nonexistence of objects smaller than that speck. The notable feature of this fifth phase is not that it enables us to form meaningful singular terms devoid of reference, for that was already achieved on occasion with "this apple"; nor that it enables us to form meaningful general terms true of nothing, for that was already achieved with "blue apple"; but that it enables us, for the first time, to form terms whose references can be admitted to be forever unobservable without yet being repudiated, like blue apples, as nonexistent.

Such applying of relative terms to singular terms is the simplest method of forming terms that purport to name unobservables, but there are also more flexible devices to much the same effect: the relative clause and description.

And there comes yet a sixth phase, when we break through to posits more drastically new still than the objects smaller than the smallest visible speck. For the objects smaller than the speck differ from observable objects only in a matter of degree, whereas the sixth phase ushers in abstract entities. This phase is marked by the advent of abstract singular terms like "redness," "roundness," "mankind," purported names of qualities, attributes, classes. Let us speculate on the mechanism of this new move.

One wedge is the bulk term. Such terms can be learned at the very first phase, we saw, on a par with "mama." We saw them diverge from "mama" at the second phase, simply on the score that the woman comes then to be appreciated as an integrated spatiotemporal thing while the world's water or red stuff ordinarily does not. For the child, thus, who is not on to the sophisticated idea of the scattered single object, the bulk term already has an air of generality about it, comparable to the individuative "apple"; and still it is much like the singular "mama" in form and function, having even been learned or learnable at the first phase on a par with "mama." So the bulk term already has rather the hybrid air of the abstract singular term. "Water" might, from the very advent of individuation, even be said to name a shared *attribute* of the sundry puddles and glassfuls rather than a scattered portion of the world *composed* of those puddles and glassfuls; for the child of course adopts neither position.

Moreover, there is a tricky point about color words that especially encourages the transition to abstract reference. "Red" can be learned as a bulk term, like "water," but in particular it applies to apples whose insides are white. Before mastering the conceptual scheme of individuation and enduring physical object, the child sees the uncut red apple, like tomato juice, simply as so much red exposure in the passing show, and, having no sense of physical identity, he sees the subsequently exposed white interior of the apple as irrelevant. When eventually he does master the conceptual scheme of individuation and enduring physical object, then, he has to come to terms with a preacquired use of "red" that has suddenly gone double: there is red stuff (tomato juice) and there are red things (apples) that are mostly white stuff. "Red" both remains a bulk term of the ancient vintage of "water" and "mama," and becomes a concrete general term like "round" or "apple." Since the child will still not clearly conceive of "red" as suddenly two words, we have him somehow infusing singularity into the concrete general; and such is the recipe, however, unappetizing, for the abstract singular. The analogy then spreads to other general terms, that were in no such special predicament as "red," until they all deliver abstract singulars.

Another force for abstract terms, or for the positing of abstract objects, lies in abbreviated cross-reference. E.g., after an elaborate remark regarding President Eisenhower, someone says: "The same holds for Churchill." Or, by way of supporting some botanical identification, one says: "Both plants have the following attribute in common"—and proceeds with a double-purpose description. In such cases a laborious repetition is conveniently circumvented. Now the cross-reference in such cases is just to a form of words. But we have a stubborn tendency to reify the unrepeated matter by positing an attribute, instead of just talking of words.

There is indeed an archaic precedent for confusing sign and object; the earliest conditioning of the infant's babbling is ambiguous on the point. For suppose a baby rewarded for happening to babble something like "mama" or "water" just as the mother or water is looming. The stimuli which are thus reinforced are bound to be two: there is not only the looming of the object, there is equally the word itself, heard by the child from his own lips. Confusion of sign and object is original sin, coeval with the word.

We have seen how the child might slip into the community's ontology of attributes by easy stages, from bulk terms onward. We have also seen how talk of attributes will continue to be encouraged, in the child and the community, by a certain convenience of cross-reference coupled with a confusion of sign and object. We have in these reflections some materials for speculation regarding the early beginnings of an ontology of attributes in the childhood of the race. There is room, as well, for alternative or supplementary conjectures; e.g., that the attributes are vestiges of the minor deities of some creed outworn.[3] In a general way such speculation is epistemologically relevant, as suggesting how organisms maturing and evolving in the physical environment we know might conceivably end up discoursing of abstract objects as we do. But the disreputability of origins is of itself no argument against preserving and prizing the abstract ontology. This conceptual scheme may well be, however accidental, a happy accident; just as the theory of electrons would be none the worse for having first occurred to its originator in the course of some absurd dream. At any rate the ontology of abstract objects is part of the ship which, in Neurath's figure, we are rebuilding at sea.[4] We may revise the scheme, but only in favor of some clearer or simpler and no less adequate over-all account of what goes on in the world.

IV

By finding out roughly which nonverbal stimulations tend to prompt assent to a given existential statement, we settle, to some degree, what is to count as empirical evidence for or against the existence of the objects in question. This I urged at the beginning of Section III. Statements, however, existential and otherwise, vary in the directness with which they are conditioned to nonverbal stimulation. Commonly a stimulation will trigger our verdict on a statement only because the statement is a strand in the verbal network of some elaborate theory, other strands of which are more directly conditioned to that stimulation. Most of our statements respond thus to reverberations across the fabric of intralinguistic associations, even when also directly conditioned to extralinguistic stimuli to some degree. Highly theoretical statements are statements whose connection with extralinguistic stimulation consists pretty exclusively in the reverberations across the fabric. Statements of the existence of various sorts of subvisible particles tend to be theoretical, in this sense; and, even more so, statements of the existence of certain abstract objects. Commonly such statements are scarcely to be judged otherwise than by coherence, or by considerations of over-all simplicity of a theory whose ultimate contacts with experience are remote as can be from the statements in question. Yet, remarkably enough, there are abstract existence statements that do succumb to such considerations. We have had the wit to posit an ontology massive enough to crumble of its own weight.

For there are the paradoxes of classes. These paradoxes are usually stated for classes because classes are a relatively simple kind of abstract object to talk about, and also because classes, being more innocent on the face of them than attributes, are more fun to discredit. In any event, as is both well known and obvious, the paradoxes of classes go through *pari passu* for attributes, and again for relations.

---

[3]Thus, Ernst Cassirer, *Language and Myth* (New York: Harper & Row, Publishers, 1946), pp. 95 ff.

[4]Otto Neurath, "Protokollsätze," *Erkenntnis*, Vol. 3 (1932).

The moral to draw from the paradoxes is not necessarily nominalism, but certainly that we must tighten our ontological belts a few holes. The law of attributes that was implicit in our language habits or that fitted in with them most easily was that *every* statement that mentions a thing attributes an attribute to it; and this cultural heritage, however venerable, must go. Some judicious *ad hoc* excisions are required at least.

Systematic considerations can press not only for repudiating certain objects, and so declaring certain *terms* irreferential; they can also press for declaring certain *occurrences* of terms irreferential, while other occurrences continue to refer. This point is essentially Frege's,[5] and an example is provided by the sentence "Tom believes that Tully wrote the *Ars Magna*." If we assert this on the strength of Tom's confusion of Tully with Lully, and in full appreciation of Tom's appreciation that Cicero did not write the *Ars Magna*, then we are not giving the term "Tully" purely referential occurrence in our sentence "Tom believes that Tully wrote the *Ars Magna*"; our sentence is not squarely about Tully. If it were, it would have to be true of Cicero, who *is* Tully.

It was only after somehow deciding what heathen locutions to construe as identity and the like that our linguist could begin to say which heathen words serve as terms and what objects they refer to. It was only after getting the knack of identity and kindred devices that our own child could reasonably be said to be talking in terms and to be talking of objects. And it is to the demands of identity still, specifically the substitutivity of identity, that the adult speaker of our language remains answerable as long as he may be said to be using terms to refer.

We are free so to use the verb "believes" as to allow ensuing terms full referential status after all. To do so is to deny "Tom believes that Tully wrote the *Ars Magna*" in the light of Tom's knowledge of Cicero and despite his confusion of names. The fact is that we can and do use "believes" both ways: one way when we say that Tom believes Tully wrote *Ars Magna*, and the other way when we deny this, or when, resorting to quantification, we say just that there is *someone* whom Tom believes to have done thus and so. Parallel remarks are suited also to others of the *propositional attitudes*, as Russell calls them: thus doubting, wishing, striving, along with believing.

Man in a state of nature is not aware of the doubleness of these usages of his, nor of the strings attached to each; just as he is not aware of the paradoxical consequences of a naïve ontology of classes or attributes. Now yet another ontological weakness that we are likewise unaware of until, philosophically minded, we start looking to coherence considerations, has to do with the individuation of attributes.

The positing of attributes is accompanied by no clue as to the circumstances under which attributes may be said to be the same or different. This is perverse, considering that the very use of terms and the very positing of objects are unrecognizable to begin with except as keyed in with idioms of sameness and difference. What happens is that at first we learn general patterns of term-talk and thing-talk with help of the necessary adjuncts of identity; afterward we project these well-learned grammatical

---

[5]See Frege, "On Sense and Reference," translated in Geach and Black, eds., *Philosophical Writings of Gottlob Frege* (Oxford: Basil Blackwell, 1952); and in (Feigl and Sellars, eds.), *Readings in Philosophical Analysis* (New York: Appleton Century Crofts, Inc, 1949). See also my *From a Logical Point of View*, (Cambridge, Mass.: Harvard University Press, 1953), Essay 8.

forms to attributes, without settling identity for them. We understand the forms as referential just because they are grammatically analogous to ones that we learned earlier, for physical objects, with full dependence on the identity aspect.

The lack of a proper identity concept for attributes is a lack that philosophers feel impelled to supply; for, what sense is there in saying that there are attributes when there is no sense in saying when there is one attribute and when two? Carnap and others have proposed this principle for identifying attributes: two sentences about x attribute the *same* attribute to x if and only if the two sentences are not merely alike in truth value for each choice of x, but necessarily and analytically so, by sameness of meaning.[6]

However, this formulation depends on a questionable notion, that of sameness of meaning. For let us not slip back into the fantasy of a gallery of ideas and labels. Let us remember rather our field lexicographer's predicament: how arbitrary his projection of analogies from known languages. Can an empiricist speak seriously of sameness of meaning of two conditions upon an object x, one stated in the heathen language and one in ours, when even the singling out of an object x as object at all for the heathen language is so hopelessly arbitrary?

We could skip the heathen language and try talking of sameness of meaning just within our own language. This would degrade the ontology of attributes; identity of attributes would be predicated on frankly provincial traits of English usage, ill fitting the objectivity of true objects. Nor let it be said in extenuation that all talk of objects, physical ones included, is in a way provincial too; for the way is different. Our physics is provincial only in that there is no universal basis for translating it into remote languages; it would still never condone defining physical identity in terms of verbal behavior. If we rest the identity of attributes on an admittedly local relation of English synonymy, then we count attributes secondary to language in a way that physical objects are not.

Shall we just let attributes be thus secondary to language in a way that physical objects are not? But our troubles do not end here; for the fact is that I see no hope of making reasonable sense of sameness of meaning even for English. The difficulty is one that I have enlarged on elsewhere.[7] English expressions are supposed to mean the same if, vaguely speaking, you can use one for the other in any situation and any English context without *relevant* difference of effect; and the essential difficulty comes in delimiting the required sense of relevant.

V

There is no denying the access of power that accrues to our conceptual scheme through the positing of abstract objects. Most of what is gained by positing attributes, however, is gained equally by positing classes. Classes are on a par with attributes on the score of abstractness or universality, and they serve the purposes of

---

[6]Rudolf Carnap, *Meaning and Necessity* (Chicago: Univ. of Chicago Press, 1947), p. 23.

[7]Two Dogmas of Empiricism," *Philosophical Review*, **60** (1951), 20–43 reprinted in my *From a Logical Point of View*. See further my "Carnap and Logical Truth," *Synthese* 12 (1960), pp. 350–374.

attributes so far as mathematics and certainly most of science are concerned; and they enjoy, unlike attributes, a crystal-clear identity concept. No wonder that in mathematics the murky intensionality of attributes tends to give way to the limpid extensionality of classes; and likewise in other sciences, roughly in proportion to the rigor and austerity of their systematization.

For attributes one might still claim this advantage over classes: they help in systematizing what we may call the *attributary attitudes*—hunting, wanting, fearing, lacking, and the like. Consider hunting, for example. Lion-hunting is not, like lion-catching, a transaction between men and individual lions, for it requires no lions. We analyze lion-catching, rabbit-catching, etc. as having a catching relation in common and varying only in the individuals caught; but what of lion-hunting, rabbit-hunting, etc.? If any common relation is to be recognized here, the varying objects of the relation must evidently be taken not as individuals but as kinds. Yet not kinds in the sense of classes, for then unicorn-hunting would cease to differ from griffin-hunting. Kinds rather in the sense of attributes.

Some further supposed abstract objects that are like attributes, with respect to the identity problem, are the *propositions*—in the sense of entities that somehow correspond to sentences as attributes correspond to predicates. Now if attributes clamor for recognition as objects of the attributary attitudes, so do propositions as objects of the propositional attitudes: believing, wishing, and the rest.[8]

Overwhelmed by the problem of identity of attributes and of propositions, however, one may choose to make a clean sweep of the lot and undertake to manage the attributary and propositional attitudes somehow without them. Philosophers who take this austere line will perhaps resort to actual linguistic forms, sentences, instead of propositions, as objects of the propositional attitudes; and to actual linguistic forms, predicates, instead of attributes, as objects of the attributary attitudes.

Against such resort to linguistic forms one hears the following objection, due to Church and Langford.[9] If what are believed are mere sentences, then "Edwin believes the English sentence *S*" goes correctly into German as "Edwin glaubt den englischen Satz *S*," with *S* unchanged. But it also goes correctly into German as "Edwin glaubt" followed by a German translation of *S* in indirect discourse. These two German reports, one quoting the English sentence and the other using German indirect discourse, must then be equivalent. But they are not, it is argued, since a German ignorant of English cannot equate them. Now I am not altogether satisfied with this argument. It rests on the notion of linguistic equivalence, or sameness of meaning; and this has seemed dubious as a tool of philosophical analysis. There is, however, another objection to taking linguistic forms as objects of the attributary and propositional attitudes; viz., simply that that course is discouragingly artificial. With this objection I sympathize.

Perhaps, after all, we should be more receptive to the first and least premeditated of the alternatives. We might keep attributes and propositions after all, but just not try to cope with the problem of their individuation. We might deliberately acquiesce

[8] See my "Quantifiers and propositional attitudes," *Journal of Philosophy*, **53** (1956), 177–87.

[9] Alonzo Church, "On Carnap's Analysis of Statements of Assertion and Belief," *Analysis*, **10** (1950), 97–99, reprinted in Margaret Macdonald, ed., *Philosophy and Analysis* (Oxford and New York: Basil Blackwell and Philosophical Library, 1954).

in the old unregenerate positing of attributes and propositions without hint of a standard of identity. The precept "no entity without identity" might simply be relaxed. Certainly the positing of first objects makes no sense except as keyed to identity; but those patterns of thing talk, once firmly inculcated, have in fact enabled us to talk of attributes and propositions in partial grammatical analogy, without an accompanying standard of identity for them. Why not just accept them thus, as twilight half-entities to which the identity concept is not to apply?[10] If the disreputability of their origins is undeniable, still bastardy, to the enlightened mind, is no disgrace. This liberal line accords with the Oxford philosophy of ordinary language.

What might properly count against countenancing such half-entities, inaccessible to identity, is a certain disruption of logic. For, if we are to tolerate the half-entities without abdication of philosophical responsibility, we must adjust the logic of our conceptual scheme to receive them and then weigh any resulting complexity against the benefits of the half-entities in connection with propositional and attributary attitudes and elsewhere.

But I am not sure that even philosophical responsibility requires settling for one all-purpose system.[11] Propositional and attributary attitudes belong to daily discourse of hopes, fears, and purposes; causal science gets on well without them. The fact that science has shunned them and fared so well could perhaps encourage a philosopher of sanguine temper to try to include that erstwhile dim domain within an overhauled universal system, science worthy throughout. But a reasonable if less ambitious alternative would be to keep a relatively simple and austere conceptual scheme, free of half-entities, for official scientific business and then accommodate the half-entities in a second-grade system.

In any event the idea of accommodating half-entities without identity illustrates how the individuative, object-oriented conceptual scheme so natural to us could conceivably begin to evolve away.

It seemed in our reflections on the child that the category of bulk terms was a survival of a pre-individuative phase. We were thinking ontogenetically, but the phylogenetic parallel is plausible too: we may have in the bulk term a relic, half vestigial and half adapted, of a pre-individuative phase in the evolution of our conceptual scheme. And some day, correspondingly, something of our present individuative talk may in turn end up, half vestigial and half adapted, within a new and as yet unimagined pattern beyond individuation.

Transition to some such radically new pattern could occur either through a conscious philosophical enterprise or by slow and unreasoned development along lines of least resistance. A combination of both factors is likeliest; and anyway the two differ mainly in degree of deliberateness. Our patterns of thought or language have been evolving, under pressure of inherent inadequacies and changing needs, since the dawn of language; and, whether we help guide it or not, we may confidently look forward to more of the same.

---

[10]Frege did so in *Grundgesetze der Arithmetik*, where he was at pains not to subject *Begriffe* to identity. See also Geach, "Class and Concept," *Philosophical Review*, **64** (1955), 561–770.

[11]See J. B. Conant, *Modern Science and Modern Man* (New York: Columbia University, 1952), pp. 98 ff.

Translation of our remote past or future discourse into the terms we now know could be about as tenuous and arbitrary a projection as translation of the heathen language was seen to be. Conversely, even to speak of that remote medium as radically different from ours is, as remarked in the case of the heathen language, to say no more than that the translations do not come smoothly. We have, to be sure, a mode of access to future stages of our own evolution that is denied us in the case of the heathen language: we can sit and evolve. But even those historical gradations, if somehow traced down the ages and used as clues to translation between widely separated evolutionary stages, would still be gradations only, and in no sense clues to fixed ideas beneath the flux of language. For the obstacle to correlating conceptual schemes is not that there is anything ineffable about language or culture, near or remote. The whole truth about the most outlandish linguistic behavior is just as accessible to us, in our current Western conceptual scheme, as are other chapters of zoology. The obstacle is only that any one intercultural correlation of words and phrases, and hence of theories, will be just one among various empirically admissible correlations, whether it is suggested by historical gradations or by unaided analogy; there is nothing for such a correlation to be uniquely right or wrong about. In saying this I philosophize from the vantage point only of our own provincial conceptual scheme and scientific epoch, true; but I know no better.

18   Meaning and Translation*

Willard V. Quine

I. STIMULUS MEANING

Empirical meaning is what remains when, given discourse together with all its stimulatory conditions, we peel away the verbiage. It is what the sentences of one language and their firm translations in a completely alien language have in common. So, if we would isolate empirical meaning, a likely position to project ourselves into is that of the linguist who is out to penetrate and translate a hitherto unknown language. Given are the native's unconstrued utterances and the observable circumstances of their occurrence. Wanted are the meanings; or wanted are English translations, for a good way to give a meaning is to say something in the home language that has it.

Translation between languages as close as Frisian and English is aided by resemblance of cognate word forms. Translation between unrelated languages, e.g., Hungarian and English, may be aided by traditional equations that have evolved in step with a shared culture. For light on the nature of meaning we must think rather of *radical* translation, i.e., translation of the language of a hitherto untouched people. Here it is, if anywhere, that austerely empirical meaning detaches itself from the words that have it.

The utterances first and most surely translated in such a case are perforce reports of observations conspicuously shared by the linguist and his informant. A rabbit

*W. V. Quine, "Meaning and Translation," in R. A. Brower, ed., *On Translation* (Cambridge, Mass.: Harvard University Press, 1959). Copyright 1959 by the President and Fellows of Harvard College. Reprinted by permission.

This essay was an adaptation of part of a work then in progress, *Word and Object*, Cambridge, Mass.: M.I.T. Press, 1960. In the spring of 1957 I presented most of this essay as a lecture at the University of Pennsylvania, Columbia University, and Princeton University; and members of those audiences have helped me with their discussion. I used parts also at the fourth Colloque Philosophique de Royaumont, April 1958, in an address that since appeared as "Le myth de la signification" in the proceedings of the colloquium, *La Philosophie Analytique*, Paris: Editions de Minuit, 1962.

scurries by, the native says "Gavagai," and our jungle linguist notes down the sentence "Rabbit" (or "Lo, a rabbit") as tentative translation. He will thus at first refrain from putting words into his informant's mouth, if only for lack of words to put. When he can, though, the linguist is going to have to supply native sentences for his informant's approval, despite some risk of slanting the data by suggestion. Otherwise he can do little with native terms that have references in common. For, suppose the native language includes sentences S_1, S_2, and S_3, really translatable respectively as "Animal," "White," and "Rabbit." Stimulus situations always differ, whether relevantly or not; and, just because volunteered responses come singly, the classes of situations under which the native happens to have volunteered S_1, S_2, and S_3, are of course mutually exclusive, despite the hidden actual meanings of the words. How then is the linguist to perceive that the native would have been willing to assent to S_1 in all the situations where he happened to volunteer S_3, and in some but perhaps not all of the situations where he happened to volunteer S_2? Only by taking the initiative and querying combinations of native sentences and stimulus situations so as to narrow down his guesses to his eventual satisfaction.

Therefore, picture the linguist asking "Gavagai?" in each of various stimulatory situations, and noting each time whether the native is prompted to assent or dissent or neither. Several assumptions are implicit here as to a linguist's power of intuition. For one thing, he must be able to recognize an informant's assent and dissent independently of any particular language. Moreover, he must be able ordinarily to guess what stimulation his subject is heeding—not nerve by nerve, but in terms at least of rough and ready reference to the environment. Moreover, he must be able to guess whether that stimulation actually prompts the native's assent to or dissent from the accompanying question; he must be able to rule out the chance that the native assents to or dissents from the questioned sentence irrelevantly as a truth or falsehood on its own merits, without regard to the scurrying rabbit which happens to be the conspicuous circumstance of the moment.

The linguist does certainly succeed in these basic tasks of recognition in sufficiently numerous cases, and so can we all, however unconscious we be of our cues and method. The Turks' gestures of assent and dissent are nearly the reverse of ours, but facial expression shows through and sets us right pretty soon. As for what a man is noticing, this of course is commonly discernible from his orientation together with our familiarity with human interests. The third and last point of recognition is harder, but one easily imagines accomplishing it in typical cases: judging, without ulterior knowledge of the language, whether the subject's assent to or dissent from one's sudden question was prompted by the thing that had been under scrutiny at the time. One clue is got by pointing while asking; then, if the object is irrelevant, the answer may be accompanied by a look of puzzlement. Another clue to irrelevance can be that the question, asked without pointing, causes the native abruptly to shift his attention and look abstracted. But enough of conjectural mechanisms; the patent fact is that one does, by whatever unanalyzed intuitions, tend to pick up these minimum attitudinal data without special linguistic aid.

The imagined routine of proposing sentences in situations is suited only to sentences of a special sort: those which, like "Gavagai," "Red," "That hurts," "This one's face is dirty," etc., command assent only afresh in the light of currently observable circumstances. It is a question of *occasion sentences* as against *standing sentences*. Such are the sentences with which our jungle linguist must begin, and the ones for which we may appropriately try to develop a first crude concept of meaning.

The distinction between *occasion* sentences and standing sentences is itself definable in terms of the notion of prompted assent and dissent which we are supposing available. A sentence is an occasion sentence for a man if he can sometimes be got to assent to or dissent from it, but can never be got to unless the asking is accompanied by a prompting stimulation.

Not that there is no such prompted assent and dissent for standing sentences. A readily imaginable visual stimulation will prompt a geographically instructed subject, once, to assent to the standing sentence "There are brick houses on Elm Street." Stimulation implemented by an interferometer once prompted Michelson and Morley to dissent from the standing sentence "There is ether drift." But these standing sentences contrast with occasion sentences in that the subject may repeat his old assent or dissent unprompted by current stimulation, when we ask him again on later occasions; whereas an occasion sentence commands assent or dissent only as prompted all over again by current stimulation.

Let us define the *affirmative stimulus meaning* of an occasion sentence S, for a given speaker, as the class of all the stimulations that would prompt him to assent to S. We may define the *negative* stimulus meaning of S similarly in terms of dissent. Finally, we may define the *stimulus meaning* of S, simply so-called, as the ordered pair of the affirmative and negative stimulus meanings of S. We could distinguish degrees of doubtfulness of assent and dissent, say, by reaction time, and elaborate our definition of stimulus meaning in easily imagined ways to include this information; but for the sake of fluent exposition let us forbear.

The several stimulations, which we assemble in classes to form stimulus meanings, must themselves be taken for present purposes not as dated particular events but as repeatable event forms. We are to say not that two stimulations have occurred that were just alike, but that the same stimulation has *recurred*. To see the necessity of this attitude consider again the positive stimulus meaning of an occasion sentence S. It is the class Σ of all those stimulations that *would* prompt assent to S. If the stimulations were taken as events rather than event forms, then Σ would have to be a class of events which largely did not and will not happen, but which would prompt assent to S if they were to happen. Whenever Σ contained one realized or unrealized particular event σ, it would have to contain all other unrealized duplicates of σ; and how many are there of *these*? Certainly it is hopeless nonsense to talk thus of unrealized particulars and try to assemble them into classes. Unrealized entities have to be construed as universals, simply because there are no places and dates by which to distinguish between those that are in other respects alike.

It is not necessary for present purposes to decide exactly when to count two events of surface irritation as recurrences of the same stimulation, and when to count them as occurrences of different stimulations. In practice, certainly the linguist need never care about nerve-for-nerve duplications of stimulating events. It remains, as always, sufficient merely to know, e.g., that the subject got a good glimpse of a rabbit. This is sufficient because of one's reasonable expectation of invariance of behavior under any such circumstances.

The affirmative and negative stimulus meanings of a sentence are mutually exclusive. We have supposed the linguist capable of recognizing assent and dissent, and we mean these to be so construed that no one can be said to assent to and dissent from the same occasion sentence on the same occasion. Granted, our subject might be prompted once by a given stimulation σ to assent to S, and later, by a recurrence of σ, to dissent from S; but then we would simply conclude that his meaning for S had changed. We would then reckon σ to his affirmative stimulus meaning of S as of the one date and to his negative stimulus meaning of S as of the other date. At any one given time his positive stimulus meaning of S comprises just the stimulations that *would* prompt him then to assent to S, and correspondingly for the negative stimulus meaning; and we may be sure that these two classes of stimulations are mutually exclusive.

Yet the affirmative and negative stimulus meaning do not determine each other; for the negative stimulus meaning of S does not ordinarily comprise all the stimulations that would not prompt assent to S. In general, therefore, the matching of whole stimulus meanings can be a better basis for translation than the matching merely of affirmative stimulus meanings.

What now of that strong conditional, the "would prompt" in our definition of stimulus meaning? The device is used so unquestioningly in solid old branches of science that to object to its use in a study as shaky as the present one would be a glaring case of misplaced aspiration, a compliment no more deserved than intended. What the strong conditional defines is a disposition, in this case a disposition to assent to or dissent from S when variously prompted. The disposition may be presumed to be some subtle structural condition, like an allergy and like solubility; like an allergy, more particularly, in not being understood. Whatever the ontological status of dispositions, or the philosophical status of talk of dispositions, we are familiar enough in a general way with how one sets about guessing, from judicious tests and samples and observed uniformities, whether there is a disposition of a specified sort.

II. THE INSCRUTABILITY OF TERMS

Impressed with the interdependence of sentences, one may well wonder whether meanings even of whole sentences (let alone shorter expressions) can reasonably be talked of at all, except relative to the other sentences of an inclusive theory. Such relativity would be awkward, since, conversely, the individual component sentences offer the only way into the theory. Now the notion of stimulus meaning partially resolves the predicament. It isolates a sort of net empirical import of each of various single sentences without regard to the containing theory, even though without loss of what the sentence owes to that containing theory. It is a device, as far as it goes, for exploring the fabric of interlocking sentences, a sentence at a time. Some such device is indispensable in broaching an alien culture, and relevant also to an analysis of our own knowledge of the world.

We have started our consideration of meaning with sentences, even if sentences of a special sort and meaning in a strained sense. For words, when not learned as sentences, are learned only derivatively by abstraction from their roles in learned sentences. Still there are, prior to any such abstraction, the one-word sentences; and, as luck would have it, they are (in English) sentences of precisely the special sort already under investigation—occasion sentences like "White" and "Rabbit." Insofar then as the concept of stimulus meaning may be said to constitute in some strained sense a meaning concept for occasion sentences, it would in particular constitute a meaning concept for general terms like "White" and "Rabbit." Let us examine the concept of stimulus meaning for a while in this latter, conveniently limited, domain of application.

To affirm sameness of stimulus meaning on the part of a term for two speakers, or on the part of two terms for one or two speakers, is to affirm a certain sameness of applicability: the stimulations that prompt assent coincide, and likewise those that prompt dissent. Now is this merely to say that the term or terms have the same *extension*, i.e., are true of the same objects, for the speaker or speakers in question? In the case of "Rabbit" and "Gavagai" it may seem so. Actually, in the general case, more is involved. Thus, to adapt an example of Carnap's, imagine a general heathen term for horses and unicorns. Since there are no unicorns, the extension of that inclusive heathen term is that simply of "horses." Yet we would like somehow to say that the term, unlike "horse," *would* be true also of unicorns, if there were any. Now our concept of stimulus meaning actually helps to make sense of that wanted further determination with respect to nonexistents. For stimulus meaning is in theory a question of direct surface irritations, not horses and unicorns. Each stimulation that would be occasioned by observing a unicorn is an assortment of nerve-hits, no less real and in principle no less specifiable than those occasioned by observing a horse. Such a stimulation can even be actualized, by papier-mâché trickery. In practice also we can do without deception, using descriptions and hypothetical questions, if we know enough of the language; such devices are indirect ways of guessing at stimulus meaning, even though external to the definition.

For terms like "Horse," "Unicorn," "White," and "Rabbit"—general terms for observable external objects—our concept of stimulus meaning thus seems to provide a moderately strong translation relation that goes beyond mere sameness of extension. But this is not so; the relation falls far short of sameness of extension on other counts. For, consider "Gavagai" again. Who knows but what the objects to which this term applies are not rabbits after all, but mere stages, or brief temporal segments, of rabbits? For in either event the stimulus situations that prompt assent to "Gavagai" would be the same as for "Rabbit." Or perhaps the objects to which "Gavagai" applies are all and sundry undetached parts of rabbits; again the stimulus meaning would register no difference. When from the sameness of stimulus meanings of "Gavagai" and "Rabbit" the linguist leaps to the conclusion that a gavagai is a whole enduring rabbit, he is just taking for granted that the native is enough like us to have a brief general term for rabbits and no brief general term for rabbit stages or parts.

Commonly we can translate something (e.g., "for the sake of") into a given language though nothing in that language corresponds to certain of the component syllables (e.g., to "the" and to "sake"). Just so the occasion sentence "Gavagai" is translatable as saying that a rabbit is there, though no part of "Gavagai" nor anything at all in the native language quite correspond to the term "rabbit." Synonymy of "Gavagai" and "Rabbit" as sentences turns on considerations of prompted assent, which transcend all cultural boundaries; not so synonymy of them as terms. We are right to write "Rabbit," instead of "rabbit," as a signal that we are considering it in relation to what is synonymous with it as a sentence and not in relation to what is synonymous with it as a term.

Does it seem that the imagined indecision between rabbits, stages of rabbits, and integral parts of rabbits should be resoluble by a little supplementary pointing and questioning? Consider, then, how. Point to a rabbit and you have pointed to a stage of a rabbit and to an integral part of a rabbit. Point to an integral part of a rabbit and you have pointed to a rabbit and to a stage of a rabbit. Correspondingly, for the third alternative. Nothing not distinguished in stimulus meaning itself will be distinguished by pointing, unless the pointing is accompanied by questions of identity and diversity: "Is this the same gavagai as that? Do we have here one gavagai or two?" Such questioning requires of the linguist a command of the native language far beyond anything that we have as yet seen how to account for. More, it presupposes that the native conceptual scheme is, like ours, one that breaks reality down somehow into a multiplicity of identifiable and discriminable physical things, be they rabbits or stages or parts. For the native attitude might, after all, be very unlike ours. The term "gavagai" might be the proper name of a recurring universal rabbit-hood; and *still* the occasion sentence "Gavagai" would have the same stimulus meaning as under the other alternatives above suggested. For that matter, the native point of view might be so alien that from it there would be just no semblance of sense in speaking of objects at all, not even of abstract ones like rabbithood. Native channels might be wholly unlike Western talk of this and that, same and different, one and two. Failing some such familiar apparatus, surely the native cannot significantly be said to posit objects. Stuff conceivably, but not things, concrete *or* abstract. And yet, even in the face of this alien ontological attitude, the occasion sentence "Gavagai" could still have the same stimulus meaning as "(Lo, a) rabbit." Occasion sentences and stimulus meanings are general coin, whereas terms, conceived as variously applying to objects in some sense, are a provincial appurtenance of our object-positing kind of culture.

Can we even imagine any basic alternative to our object-positing pattern? Perhaps not, for we would have to imagine it in translation, and translation imposes our pattern. Perhaps the very notion of such radical contrast of cultures is meaningless, except in this purely privative sense: persistent failure to find smooth and convincing native analogues of our own familiar accessories of objective reference, such as the articles, the identity predicate, the plural ending. Only by such failure can we be said to perceive that the native language represents matters in ways not open to our own.

III. OBSERVATION SENTENCES

In sections one and two we came to appreciate sameness of stimulus meaning as an, in some ways, serviceable synonymy relation when limiting to occasion sentences. But even when thus limited, stimulus meaning falls short of the requirement implicit in ordinary, uncritical talk of meaning. The trouble is that an informant's prompted assent to or dissent from an occasion sentence may depend only partly on the present prompting stimulation and all too largely on his hidden collateral information. In distinguishing between occasion sentences and standing sentences (Section 1), and deferring the latter, we have excluded all cases where the informant's assent or dissent might depend wholly on collateral information, but we have not excluded cases where his assent or dissent depends mainly on collateral information and ever so little on the present prompting stimulation. Thus, the native's assent to "Gavagai" on the occasion of nothing better than an ill-glimpsed movement in the grass can have been due mainly to earlier observation, in the linguist's absence, of rabbit enterprises near the spot. And there are occasion sentences the prompted assent to which will *always* depend so largely on collateral information that their stimulus meanings cannot be treated as their "meanings" by any stretch of the imagination. An example is "Bachelor"; one's assent to it is prompted genuinely enough by the sight of a face, yet it draws mainly on stored information and not at all on the prompting stimulation except as needed for recognizing the bachelor friend concerned. The trouble with "Bachelor" is that its meaning transcends the looks of the prompting faces and concerns matters that can be known only through other channels. Evidently then we must try to single out a subclass of the occasion sentences which will qualify as *observation sentences*, recognizing that what I have called stimulus meaning constitutes a reasonable notion of meaning for such sentences at most. Occasion sentences have been defined (Section 1) as sentences to which there is assent or dissent but only subject to prompting; and what we now ask of observation sentences, more particularly, is that the assent or dissent be prompted always without help of information beyond the prompting stimulation itself.

It is remarkable how sure we are that each assent to "Bachelor," or a native equivalent, would draw on data from the two sources—present stimulation and collateral information. We are not lacking in elaborate if unsystematic insights into the ways of using "Bachelor" or other specific words of our own language. Yet, it does not behoove us to be smug about this easy sort of talk of meanings and reasons, for all its productivity; for, with the slightest encouragement, it can involve us in the most hopelessly confused beliefs and meaningless controversies.

Suppose it said that a particular class Σ comprises just those stimulations each of which suffices to prompt assent to an occasion sentence S outright, without benefit of collateral information. Suppose it said that the stimulations comprised in a further class Σ', likewise sufficient to prompt assent to S, owe their efficacy rather to certain widely disseminated, collateral information, C. Now couldn't we just as well have said, instead, that on acquiring C, men have found it convenient implicitly to change the very *meaning* of S, so that the members of Σ' now suffice outright like members of Σ? I suggest that we may say either; even historical clairvoyance would reveal no distinction, though it reveal all stages in the acquisition of C, since meaning can evolve *pari passu*. The distinction is illusory. What we objectively have is just an evolving adjustment to nature, reflected in an evolving set of dispositions to be prompted by stimulations to assent to or dissent from occasion sentences. These dispositions may be conceded to be impure in the sense of including worldly knowledge, but they contain it in a solution which there is no precipitating.

Observation sentences were to be occasion sentences, the assent or dissent to which is prompted always without help of collateral information. The notion of help of collateral information is now seen to be shaky. Actually the notion of observation sentence is less so, because of a stabilizing statistical effect which I can suggest if for a moment I go on speaking uncritically in terms of the shaky notion of collateral information. Now some of the collateral information relevant to an occasion sentence *S* may be widely disseminated, some not. Even that which is widely disseminated may in part be shared by one large group of persons and in part by another, so that few if any persons know it all. Meaning, on the other hand, is social. Even the man who is oddest about a word is likely to have a few companions in deviation.

At any rate the effect is strikingly seen by comparing "Rabbit" with "Bachelor." The stimulus meaning of "Bachelor" will be the same for no two speakers short of Siamese twins. The stimulus meaning of "Rabbit" will be much alike for most speakers; exceptions like the movement in the grass are rare. A working concept that would seem to serve pretty much the purpose of the notion of observation sentence is then simply this: *occasion sentence possessing intersubjective stimulus meaning.*

In order then that an occasion sentence be an observation sentence, is it sufficient that there be *two* people for whom it has the same stimulus meaning? No, as witness those Siamese twins. Must it have the same stimulus meaning for all persons in the linguistic community (however *that* might be defined)? Surely not. Must it have *exactly* the same stimulus meaning for even two? Perhaps not, considering again that movement in the grass. But these questions aim at refinements that would simply be misleading if undertaken. We are concerned here with rough trends of behavior. What matters for the notion of observation sentence here intended is that for significantly many speakers the stimulus meanings deviate significantly little.

In one respect, actually the intersubjective variability of the stimulus meaning of sentences like "Bachelor" has been understated. Not only will the stimulus meaning of "Bachelor" for one person differ from that of "Bachelor" for the next person; it will differ from that of any other likely sentence for the next person, in the same language or any other.

The linguist is not free to survey a native stimulus meaning *in extenso* and then to devise *ad hoc* a great complex English sentence whose stimulus meaning, for him, matches the native one by sheer exhaustion of cases. He has rather to extrapolate any native stimulus meaning from samples, guessing at the informant's mentality. If the sentence is as nonobservational as "Bachelor," he simply will not find likely lines of extrapolation. Translation by stimulus meaning will then deliver no wrong result, but simply nothing. This is interesting because what led us to try to define observation sentences was our reflection that they were the subclass of occasion sentences that seemed reasonably translatable by identity of stimulus meaning. Now we see that the limitation of this method of translation to this class of sentences is self-enforcing. When an occasion sentence is of the wrong kind, the informant's stimulus meaning for it will simply not be one that the linguist will feel he can plausibly equate with his own stimulus meaning for any English sentence.

The notion of stimulus meaning was one that required no multiplicity of informants. There is in principle the stimulus meaning of the sentence for the given speaker at the given time of his life (though in guessing at it the linguist may be helped by varying both the time and the speaker). The definition of observation sentence took wider points of reference: it expressly required comparison of various speakers of the same language. Finally, the reflection in the foregoing paragraph reassures us that such widening of horizons can actually be done without. Translation of occasion sentences by stimulus meaning will limit itself to observation sentences without our ever having actually to bring the criterion of observation sentence to bear.

The phrase "observation sentence" suggests, for epistemologists or methodologists of science, datum sentences of science. On this score, our version is by no means amiss. For our observation sentences as defined are just the occasion sentences on which there is pretty sure to be firm agreement on the part of well-placed observers. Thus, they are just the sentences to which a scientist will finally recur when called upon to marshal his data and repeat his observations and experiments for doubting colleagues.

IV. INTRASUBJECTIVE SYNONYMY OF OCCASION SENTENCES

Stimulus meaning remains defined all this while for occasion sentences generally, without regard to observationality. But it bears less resemblance to what might reasonably be called meaning when applied to nonobservation sentences like "Bachelor." Translation of "Soltero" as "Bachelor" manifestly cannot be predicated on identity of stimulus meanings between persons; nor can synonymy of "Bachelor" and "Unmarried man."

Curiously enough, though, the stimulus meanings of "Bachelor" and "Unmarried man" are, despite all this, identical for any one speaker. An individual will at any one time be prompted by the same stimulations to assent to "Bachelor" and to "Unmarried man"; and similarly for dissent. What we find is that, though the concept of stimulus meaning is so very remote from "true meaning" when applied to the inobservational occasion sentences "Bachelor" and "Unmarried man," still synonymy is definable as sameness of stimulus meaning just as faithfully for these sentences as for the choicest observation sentences—as long as we stick to one speaker. For each speaker, "Bachelor" and "Unmarried man" are synonymous in a defined sense (viz., alike in stimulus meaning) without having the same meaning in any acceptably defined sense of "meaning" (for stimulus meaning is, in the case of "Bachelor," nothing of the kind). Very well; let us welcome the synonymy and let the meaning go.

The one-speaker restriction presents no obstacle to saying that "Bachelor" and "Unmarried man" are synonymous for the whole community, in the sense of being synonymous for each member. A practical extension even to the two-language case is not far to seek if a bilingual speaker is at hand. "Bachelor" and "Soltero" will be synonymous for him by the intra-individual criterion, viz., sameness of stimulus meaning. Taking him as a sample, we may treat "Bachelor" and "Soltero" as synonymous for the translation purposes of the two whole linguistic communities that he represents. Whether he is a good enough sample would be checked by observing the fluency of his communication in both communities, by comparing other bilinguals, or by observing how well the translations work.

But such use of bilinguals is unavailable to the jungle linguist broaching an untouched culture. For radical translation the only concept thus far at our disposal is sameness of stimulus meaning, and this only for observation sentences.

The kinship and difference between intrasubjective synonymy and radical translation require careful notice. Intrasubjective synonymy, like translation, is quite capable of holding good for a whole community. It is intrasubjective in that the synonyms are joined for each subject by sameness of stimulus meaning for him; but it may still be community-wide in that the synonyms in question are joined by sameness of stimulus meaning for every single subject in the whole community. Obviously, intrasubjective synonymy is in principle just as objective, just as discoverable by the outside linguist, as is translation. Our linguist may even find native sentences intrasubjectively synonymous without finding English translations—without, in short, understanding them; for he can find that they have the same stimulus meaning, for the subject, even though there may be no English sentence whose stimulus meaning for himself promises to be the same. Thus, to turn the tables: a Martian could find that "Bachelor" and "Unmarried man" were synonyms without discovering when to assent to either one.

"Bachelor" and "Yes" are two occasion sentences which we may instructively compare. Neither of them is an observation sentence, nor, therefore, translatable by identity of stimulus meaning. The heathen equivalent ("Tak," say) of "Yes" would fare poorly indeed under translation by stimulus meaning. The stimulations which—accompanying the linguist's question "Tak?"—would prompt assent to this queer sentence, even on the part of all natives without exception, are ones which (because exclusively verbal in turn, and couched in the heathen tongue) would never have prompted an unspoiled Anglo-Saxon to assent to "Yes" or anything like it. "Tak" is just what the linguist is fishing for by way of assent to whatever heathen occasion sentence he may be investigating, but it is a poor one, under these methods, to investigate. Indeed we may expect "Tak," or "Yes," like "Bachelor," to have the same stimulus meaning for no two speakers even of the same language; for "Yes" can have the same stimulus meaning only for speakers who agree on every single thing that can be blurted in a specious present. At the same time, sameness of stimulus meaning does define intrasubjective synonymy, not only between "Bachelor" and "Unmarried man" but equally between "Yes" and "Uh huh" or "Quite."

Note that the reservations of Section 2 regarding coextensiveness of terms still hold. Though the Martian find that "Bachelor" and "Unmarried man" are synonymous occasion sentences, still in so doing he will not establish that "bachelor" and "unmarried man" are coextensive general terms. Either term to the exclusion of the other might, so far as he knows, apply not to men but to their stages or parts or even to an abstract attribute; compare Section 2.

Talking of occasion sentences as sentences and not as terms, however, we see that we can do more for synonymy within a language than for radical translation. It appears that sameness of stimulus meaning will serve as a standard of intrasubjective synonymy of occasion sentences without their having to be observation sentences.

Actually, we do need this limitation: we should stick to short and simple sentences. Otherwise subjects' mere incapacity to digest long questions can, under our definitions, issue in difference of stimulus meanings between long and short sentences which we should prefer to find synonymous. A stimulation may prompt assent to the short sentence and not to the long one just because of the opacity of the long one; yet we should then like to say not that the subject has shown the meaning of the long sentence to be different, but merely that he has failed to penetrate it.

Certainly the sentences will not have to be kept so short but what some will contain others. One thinks of such containment as happening with help of conjunctions, in the grammarians' sense: "or," "and," "but," "if," "then," "that," etc., governing the contained sentence as clause of the containing sentence. But it can also happen farther down. Very simple sentences may contain substantives and adjectives ("red," "tile," "bachelor," etc.) which qualify also as occasion sentences in their own right, subject to our synonymy concept. So our synonymy concept already applies on an equal footing to sentences some of which recur as parts of others. Some extension of synonymy to longer occasion sentences, containing others as parts, is then possible by the following sort of construction.

Think of $R(S)$ first as an occasion sentence which, though moderately short, still contains an occasion sentence S as part. If now we leave the contained sentence blank, the partially empty result may graphically be referred to as $R(. . .)$ and called (following Peirce) a *rheme*. A rheme $R(. . .)$ will be called *regular* if it fulfills this condition: for each S and S', if S and S' are synonymous and $R(S)$ and $R(S')$ are idiomatically acceptable occasion sentences short enough for our synonymy concept, then $R(S)$ and $R(S')$ are synonymous. This concept of regularity makes reasonable sense thus far only for short rhemes, since $R(S)$ and $R(S')$ must, for suitably short S and S', be short enough to come under our existing synonymy concept. However, the concept of regularity now invites extension, in this very natural way: where the rhemes $R_1(. . .)$ and $R_2(. . .)$ are both regular, let us speak of the longer rheme $R_1(R_2(. . .))$ as regular too. In this way we may speak of regularity of longer and longer rhemes without end. Thereupon, we can extend the synonymy concept to various long occasion sentences, as follows. Where $R(. . .)$ is any regular rheme and S and S' are short occasion sentences that are synonymous in the existing, unextended sense and $R(S)$ and $R(S')$ are idiomatically acceptable combinations at all, we may by extension call $R(S)$ and $R(S')$ synonymous in turn—even though they be too long for synonymy as first defined. There is no limit now to length, since the regular rheme $R(. . .)$ may be as long as we please.

V. TRUTH FUNCTIONS

In Sections 2 and 3 we accounted for radical translation only of observation sentences, by identification of stimulus meanings. Now there is also a decidedly different domain that lends itself directly to radical translation: that of *truth functions* such as negation, logical conjunction, and alternation. For, suppose as before that assent and dissent are generally recognizable. The sentences put to the native for assent or dissent may now be occasion sentences and standing sentences indifferently. Those that are occasion sentences will of course have to be accompanied by a prompting stimulation, if assent or dissent is to be elicited; the standing sentences, on the other hand, can be put without props. Now by reference to assent and dissent we can state *semantic criteria* for truth functions; i.e., criteria for determining whether a given native idiom is to be construed as expressing the truth function in question. The semantic criterion of negation is that it turns any short sentence to which one will assent into a sentence from which one will dissent, and vice versa. That of conjunction is that it produces compounds to which (so long as the component sentences are short) one is prepared to assent always and only when one is prepared to assent to each component. That of alternation is similar but with the verb "assent" changed twice to "dissent."

The point about short components is merely, as in Section 4, that when they are long, the subject may get mixed up. Identification of a native idiom as negation, or conjunction, or alternation, is not to be ruled out in view of a subject's deviation from our semantic criteria when the deviation is due merely to confusion. Note well that no limit is imposed on the lengths of the component sentences to which negation, conjunction, or alternation may be applied; it is just that the test cases for first spotting such constructions in a strange language are cases with short components.

When we find a native construction to fulfill one or another of these three semantic criteria, we can ask no more toward an understanding of it. Incidentally we can then translate the idiom into English as "not," "and," or "or" as the case may be, but only subject to sundry, humdrum provisos; for it is well known that these three English words do not represent negation, conjunction, and alternation exactly and unambiguously.

Any construction for compounding sentences from other sentences is counted in logic as expressing a truth-function if it fulfills this condition: the compound has a unique "truth value" (truth or falsity) for each assignment of truth values to the components. Semantic criteria can obviously be stated for all truth-functions along the lines already followed for negation, conjunction, and alternation.

One hears talk of prelogical peoples, said deliberately to accept certain simple self-contradictions as true. Doubtless overstating Levy-Bruhl's intentions, let us imagine someone to claim that these natives accept as true a certain sentence of the form "*p* ka bu *p*" where "ka" means "and" and "bu" means "not." Now this claim is absurd on the face of it, if translation of "ka" as "and" and "bu" as "not" follows our semantic criteria. And, not to be dogmatic, what criteria will you have? Conversely, to claim on the basis of a better dictionary that the natives *do* share our logic would be to impose our logic and beg the question, if there were really a meaningful question here to beg. But I do urge the better dictionary.

The same point can be illustrated within English, by the question of alternative logics. Is he who propounds heterodox logical laws really contradicting our logic, or is he just putting some familiar old vocables ("and," "or," "not," "all," etc.) to new and irrelevant uses? It makes no sense to say, unless from the point of view of some criteria or other for translating logical particles. Given the above criteria, the answer is clear.

We hear from time to time that the scientist in his famous freedom to resystematize science or fashion new calculi is bound at least to respect the law of contradiction. Now what are we to make of this? We do flee contradiction, for we are after truth. But what of a revision so fundamental as to count contradictions as true? Well, to begin with, it would have to be arranged carefully if all utility is not to be lost. Classical logical laws enable us from any one contradiction to deduce all statements indiscriminately; and such universal affirmation would leave science useless for lack of distinctions. So the revision which counts contradictions as true will have to be accompanied by a revision of other logical laws. Now all this can be done; but, once it is done, how can we say it is what it purported to be? This heroically novel logic falls under the considerations of the preceding paragraph, to be reconstrued perhaps simply as old logic in bad notation.

We *can* meaningfully contemplate changing a law of logic, be it the law of excluded middle or even the law of contradiction. But this is so only because while contemplating the change we continue to translate *identically*: "and" as "and," "or" as "or," etc. Afterward, a more devious mode of translation will perhaps be hit upon which will annul the change of law; or perhaps, on the contrary, the change of law will be found to have produced an essentially stronger system, demonstrably not translatable into the old in any way at all. But even in the latter event any actual conflict between the old and the new logic proves illusory, for it comes only of translating identically.

At any rate we have settled a people's logical laws completely, so far as the truth-functional part of logic goes, once we have fixed our translations by the above semantic criteria. In particular, the class of the *tautologies* is fixed: the truth-functional compounds that are true by truth-functional structure alone. There is a familiar tabular routine for determining, for sentences in which the truth-functions are however immoderately iterated and superimposed, just what assignments of truth-values to the ultimate component sentences will make the whole compound true; and the tautologies are the compounds that come out true under all assignments.

It is a commonplace of epistemology (and therefore occasionally contested) that just two very opposite spheres of knowledge enjoy irreducible certainty. One is the knowledge of what is directly present to sense experience, and the other is knowledge of logical truth. It is striking that these, roughly, are the two domains where we have made fairly direct behavioral sense of radical translation. One domain where radical translation seemed straightforward was that of the observation sentences. The other is that of the truth-functions; hence also in a sense the tautologies, these being the truths to which only the truth-functions matter.

But the truth-functions and tautologies are only the simplest of the logical functions and logical truths. Can we perhaps do better? The logical functions that most naturally next suggest themselves are the *categoricals*, traditionally designated *A*, *E*, *I*, and *O*, and commonly construed in English by the construction "all are" ("All rabbits are timid"), "none are," "some are," "some are not." A semantic criterion for *A* perhaps suggests itself as follows: the compound commands assent (from a given speaker) if and only if the positive stimulus meaning (for him) of the first component is a subclass of the positive stimulus meaning of the second component. How to vary this for *E*, *I*, and *O* is obvious enough, except that the whole idea is wrong in view of Section 2. Thus, take *A*. If "hippoid" is a general term intended to apply to all horses and unicorns, then all hippoids are horses (there being no unicorns), but still the positive stimulus meaning of "Hippoid" has stimulus patterns in it, of the sort suited to "Unicorn," that are not in the positive stimulus meaning of "Horse." On this score the suggested semantic criterion is at odds with "All S and P" in that it goes beyond extension. And it has a yet more serious failing of the opposite kind; for, whereas rabbit stages are not rabbits, we saw in Section 2 that in point of stimulus meaning there is no distinction.

The difficulty is fundamental. The categoricals depend for their truth on the objects, however external and however inferential, of which the component terms are true; and what those objects are is not uniquely determined by stimulus meanings. Indeed, the categoricals, like plural endings and identity, make sense at all only relative to an object-positing kind of conceptual scheme; whereas, as stressed in Section 2, stimulus meanings can be just the same for persons imbued with such a scheme and for persons as alien to it as you please. Of what we think of as logic, the truth-functional part is the only part the recognition of which, in a foreign language, we seem to be able to pin down to behavioral criteria.

VI. ANALYTICAL HYPOTHESES

How then does our linguist push radical translation beyond the bounds of mere observation sentences and truth functions? In broad outline as follows. He segments heard utterances into conveniently short recurrent parts, and thus compiles a list of native "words." Various of these he hypothetically equates to English words and phrases, in such a way as to reproduce the already established translations of whole observation sentences. Such conjectural equatings of parts may be called *analytical hypotheses* of translation. He will need analytical hypotheses of translation not only for native words but also for native constructions, or ways of assembling words, since the native language would not be assumed to follow English word order. Taken together these analytical hypotheses of translation constitute a jungle-to-English grammar and dictionary, which the linguist then proceeds to apply even to sentences for the translation of which no independent evidence is available.

The analytical hypotheses of translation do not depend for their evidence exclusively upon those prior translations of observation sentences. They can also be tested partly by their conformity to intrasubjective synonymies of occasion sentences, as of Section 4. For example, if the analytical hypotheses direct us to translate native sentences S_1 and S_2 respectively, as "Here is a bachelor" and "Here is an unmarried man," then we shall hope to find also that for each native the stimulus meaning of S_1 is the same as that of S_2.

The analytical hypotheses of translation can be partially tested in the light of the thence derived translations not only of occasion sentences but, sometimes, of standing sentences. Standing sentences differ from occasion sentences only in that assent to them and dissent from them may occur unprompted (cf. Section 1), not in that they occur only unprompted. The concept of prompted assent is reasonably applicable to the standing sentence "Some rabbits are black" once, for a given speaker, if we manage to spring the specimen on him before he knows there are black ones. A given speaker's assent to some standing sentences can even be prompted repeatedly; thus, his assent can genuinely be prompted anew each year to "The crocuses are out," and anew each day to "The *Times* has come." Standing sentences thus grade off toward occasion sentences, though there still remains a boundary, as defined midway in Section 1. So the linguist can further appraise his analytical hypotheses of translation by seeing how the thence derivable translations of standing sentences compare with the originals on the score of prompted assent and dissent.

Some slight further testing of the analytical hypotheses of translation is afforded by standing sentences even apart from prompted assent and dissent. If, for instance, the analytical hypotheses point to some rather platitudinous English standing sentence as translation of a native sentence *S*, then the linguist will feel reassured if he finds that *S* likewise commands general and unprompted assent.

The analytical hypotheses of translation would not in practice be held to equational form. There is no need to insist that the native word be equated outright to any one English word or phrase. One may specify certain contexts in which the word is to be translated one way and others in which the word is to be translated in another way. One may overlay the equational form with supplementary semantical instructions *ad libitum*. "Spoiled (*said of an egg*)" is as good a lexicographical definition as "addled," despite the intrusion of stage directions. Translation instructions having to do with grammatical inflections—to take an extreme case—may be depended on to present equations of words and equations of constructions in inextricable combination with much that is not equational. For the purpose is not translation of single words nor translation of single constructions, but translation of coherent discourse. The hypotheses the linguist arrives at, the instructions that he frames, are contributory hypotheses or instructions concerning translation of coherent discourse, and they may be presented in any form, equational or otherwise, that proves clear and convenient.

Nevertheless there is reason to draw particular attention to the simple form of analytical hypothesis which does directly equate a native word or construction to a hypothetical English equivalent. For hypotheses need thinking up, and the typical case of thinking up is the case where the English-bred linguist apprehends a parallelism of function between some component fragment of a translated whole native sentence *S* and some component word of the English translation of *S*. Only in some such way can we account for anyone's ever thinking to translate a native locution radically into English as a plural ending, or as the identity predicate " = ," or as a categorical copula, or as any other part of our domestic apparatus of objective reference; for, as stressed in earlier pages, no scrutiny of stimulus meanings or other behavioral manifestations can even settle whether the native shares our object-positing sort of conceptual scheme at all. It is only by such outright projection of his own linguistic habits that the linguist can find general terms in the native language at all, or, having found them, match them with his own. Stimulus meanings never suffice to determine even what words are terms, if any, much less what terms are co-extensive.

The linguist who is serious enough about the jungle language to undertake its definitive dictionary and grammar will not, indeed, proceed quite as we have imagined. He will steep himself in the language, disdainful of English parallels, to the point of speaking it like a native. His learning of it even from the beginning can have been as free of all thought of other languages as you please; it can have been virtually an accelerated counterpart of infantile learning. When at length he does turn his hand to translation, and to producing a jungle-to-English dictionary and grammar, he can do so as a bilingual. His own two personalities thereupon assume the roles which in previous pages were divided between the linguist and his informant. He equates "Gavagai" with "Rabbit" by appreciating a sameness of stimulus meaning of the two sentences for himself. Indeed he can even use sameness of stimulus meaning to translate nonobservational occasion sentences of the type of "Bachelor"; here the intrasubjective situation proves its advantage (cf. Section 4). When he brings off other more recondite translations, he surely does so by essentially the method of analytical hypotheses, but with the difference that he projects these hypotheses from his prior separate masteries of the two languages, rather than using them in mastering the jungle language. Now though it is such bilingual translation that does most justice to the jungle language, reflection upon it reveals least about the nature of meaning; for the bilingual translator works by an intrasubjective communing of a split personality, and we make operational sense of his method only as we externalize it. So let us think still in terms of our more primitive schematism of the jungle-to-English project, which counts the native informant in as a live collaborator rather than letting the linguist first ingest him.

VII. A HANDFUL OF MEANING

The linguist's finished jungle-to-English manual is to be appraised as a manual of sentence-to-sentence translation. Whatever be the details of its expository devices of word translation and syntactical paradigm, its net accomplishment is an infinite *semantic correlation* of sentences: the implicit specification of an English sentence for every one of the infinitely many possible jungle sentences. The English sentence for a given jungle one need not be unique, but it is to be unique to within any acceptable standard of intrasubjective synonymy among English sentences; and conversely. Though the thinking up and setting forth of such a semantic correlation of sentences depend on analyses into component words, the supporting evidence remains entirely at the level of sentences. It consists in sundry conformities on the score of stimulus meaning, intrasubjective synonymies, and other points of prompted and unprompted assent and dissent, as noted in Section 6.

Whereas the semantic correlation exhausts the native sentences, its supporting evidence determines no such widespread translation. Countless alternative over-all semantic correlations, therefore, are equally compatible with that evidence. If the linguist arrives at his one over-all correlation among many without feeling that his choice was excessively arbitrary, this is because he himself is limited in the correlations that he can manage. For he is not, in his finitude, free to assign English sentences to the infinitude of jungle ones in just any way whatever that will fit his supporting evidence; he has to assign them in some way that is manageably systematic with respect to a manageably limited set of repeatable speech segments. The word-by-word approach is indispensable to the linguist in specifying his semantic correlation and even in thinking it up.

Not only does the linguist's working segmentation limit the possibilities of any eventual semantic correlation. It even contributes to defining, for him, the ends of translation. For he will put a premium on structural parallels: on correspondence between the parts of the native sentence, as he segments it, and the parts of the English translation. Other things being equal, the more literal translation is seen as more literally a translation.[1] Technically a tendency to literal translation is assured anyway, since the very purpose of segmentation is to make long translations constructible from short correspondences; but then one goes farther and makes of this tendency an objective—and an objective that even varies in detail with the practical segmentation adopted.

It is by his analytical hypotheses that our jungle linguist implicitly states (and indeed arrives at) the grand synthetic hypothesis which is his over-all semantic correlation of sentences. His supporting evidence, such as it is, for the semantic correlation is his supporting evidence also for his analytical hypotheses. Chronologically, the analytical hypotheses come before all that evidence is in; then such of the evidence as ensues is experienced as pragmatic corroboration of a working dictionary. But in any event the translation of a vast range of native sentences, though covered by the semantic correlation, can never be corroborated or supported at all except cantilever fashion: it is simply what comes out of the analytical hypotheses when they are applied beyond the zone that supports them. That those unverifiable translations proceed without mishap must not be taken as pragmatic evidence of good lexicography, for mishap is impossible.

We must then recognize that the analytical hypotheses of translation and the grand synthetic one that they add up to are only in an incomplete sense hypotheses. Contrast the case of translation of "Gavagai" as "Lo, a rabbit" by sameness of stimulus meaning. This is a genuine hypothesis from sample observations, though possibly wrong. "Gavagai" and "Lo, a rabbit" have stimulus meanings for the two speakers, and these are the same or different, whether we guess right or not. On the other hand, no sense is made of sameness of meaning of the words that are equated in the typical analytical hypothesis. The point is not that we cannot be sure whether the analytical hypotheses is right, but that there is not even, as there was in the case of "Gavagai," an objective matter to be right or wrong about.

Complete radical translation does go on, and analytical hypotheses are indispensable. Nor are they capricious; on the contrary, we have just been seeing, in outline, how they are supported. May we not then say that in those very ways of thinking up and supporting the analytical hypotheses a sense *is* after all given to sameness of meaning of the expressions which those hypotheses equate? No. We could claim this only if no two conflicting sets of analytical hypotheses were capable of being supported equally strongly by all theoretically accessible evidence (including simplicity considerations).

This indefinability of synonymy by reference to the methodology of analytical hypotheses is formally the same as the indefinability of truth by reference to scientific method. Also, the consequences are parallel. Just as we may meaningfully speak of the truth of a sentence only within the terms of some theory or conceptual scheme, so on the whole we may meaningfully speak of interlinguistic synonymy of words and

---

[1]Hence also Carnap's concept of structural synonymy. See his *Meaning and Necessity* (Chicago, 1947), section 14–16.

phrases only within the terms of some particular system of analytical hypotheses.

The method of analytical hypotheses is a way of catapulting oneself into the native language by the momentum of the home language. It is a way of grafting exotic shoots on to the old familiar bush until only the exotic meets the eye. Native sentences not neutrally meaningful are thereby tentatively translated into home sentences on the basis, in effect, of seeming analogy of roles within the languages. These relations of analogy cannot themselves be looked upon as the meanings, for they are not unique. And anyway the analogies weaken as we move out toward the theoretical sentences, farthest from observation. Thus, who would undertake to translate "Neutrinos lack mass" into the jungle language? If anyone does, we may expect him to coin new native words or distort the usage of old ones. We may expect him to plead in extenuation that the natives lack the requisite concepts; also that they know too little physics. And he is right, but another way of describing the matter is as follows. Analytical hypotheses at best are devices whereby, indirectly, we bring out analogies between sentences that have yielded to translation and sentences that have not, and so extend the working limits of translation; and "Neutrinos lack mass" is way out where the effects of such analytical hypotheses as we manage to devise are too fuzzy to do much good.

Containment in the Low German continuum facilitated translation of Frisian into English (Section 1), and containment in a continuum of cultural evolution facilitated translation of Hungarian into English. These continuities, by facilitating translation, encourage an illusion of subject matter: an illusion that our so readily intertranslatable sentences are diverse, verbal embodiments of some intercultural proposition or meaning, when they are better seen as the merest variants of one and the same intracultural verbalism. Only the discontinuity of radical translation tries our meanings: really sets them over against their verbal embodiments, or more typically, finds nothing there.

Observation sentences peel nicely; their meanings, stimulus meanings, emerge absolute and free of all residual verbal taint. Theoretical sentences such as "Neutrinos lack mass," or the law of entropy, or the constancy of the speed of light, are at the other extreme. For such sentences no hint of the stimulatory conditions of assent or dissent can be dreamed of that does not include verbal stimulation from within the language. Sentences of this extreme latter sort, and other sentences likewise that lie intermediate between the two extremes, lack linguistically neutral meaning.

It would be trivial to say that we cannot know the meaning of a foreign sentence except as we are prepared to offer a translation in our own language. I am saying more: that it is only relative to an, in large part, arbitrary manual of translation that most foreign sentences may be said to share the meaning of English sentences, and then only in a very parochial sense of meaning, viz., use-in-English. Stimulus meanings of observation sentences aside, most talk of meaning requires tacit reference to a home language in much the same way that talk of truth involves tacit reference to one's own system of the world, the best that one can muster at the time.

There being (apart from stimulus meanings) so little in the way of neutral meanings relevant to radical translation, there is no telling how much of one's success with analytical hypotheses is due to real kinship of outlook on the part of the natives and ourselves, and how much of it is due to linguistic ingenuity or lucky coincidence. I am not sure that it even makes sense to ask. We may alternately wonder at the inscrutability of the native mind and wonder at how very much like us the native is, where in the one case we have merely muffed the best translation, and in the other case we have done a more thorough job of reading our own provincial modes into the native's speech.

Usener, Cassirer, Sapir, and latterly B. L. Whorf have stressed that deep differences of language carry with them ultimate differences in the way one thinks, or looks upon the world. I should prefer not to put the matter in such a way as to suggest that certain philosophical propositions are affirmed in the one culture and denied in the other. What is really involved is difficulty or indeterminacy of correlation. It is just that there is less basis of comparison—less sense in saying what is good translation and what is bad—the farther we get away from sentences with visibly direct conditioning to nonverbal stimuli and the farther we get off home ground.

19 The Structure
of a Semantic Theory*

Jerrold J. Katz and Jerry A. Fodor

This paper does not attempt to present a semantic theory of a natural language, but rather to characterize the abstract form of such a theory. A semantic theory of a natural language is part of a linguistic description of that language. Our problem, on the other hand, is part of the general theory of language, fully on a par with the problem of characterizing the structure of grammars of natural languages. A characterization of the abstract form of a semantic theory is a metatheory which answers such questions as: What is the domain of a semantic theory? What are the descriptive and explanatory goals of a semantic theory? What mechanisms are employed in pursuit of these goals? What are the empirical and methodological constraints upon a semantic theory?

Conceivably, differences between languages may preclude a uniform solution to the problem of finding an abstract characterization of the form of semantic theories. But this too is part of the problem. We want to know both what can be prescribed about semantic theories independent of differences between languages, or given certain truths about all languages, and what aspects of semantic theories vary with what aspects of particular natural languages. In the present paper, we approach the problem of abstractly characterizing the form of semantic theories by describing the structure of a semantic theory of English. There can be little doubt but that the results achieved will apply directly to semantic theories of languages closely related to English. The present investigation will also provide results that can be applied to semantic theories of languages unrelated to English and suggestions about how to proceed with the construction of such theories. But the question of the extent of their applicability to semantic theories of more distant languages will be left for subsequent investigation.

*This work was supported in part by the U.S. Army Signal Corps, the Air Force Office of Scientific Research, and the Office of Naval Research; and in part by the National Science Foundation. Reprinted by permission from *Language*, Vol. 39 (April-June 1963), pp. 170-210.

We may put our problem this way: What form should a semantic theory of a natural language take to accommodate in the most revealing way the facts about the semantic structure of that language supplied by descriptive research? This question is of primary importance at the present stage of the development of semantics because semantics suffers not from a dearth of facts about meanings and meaning relations in natural languages, but, rather, from the lack of an adequate theory to organize, systematize, and generalize those facts. Facts about the semantics of natural languages have been contributed in abundance by many diverse fields including philosophy, linguistics, philology, psychology, and so on. Indeed, a compendium of such facts is readily available in any good dictionary. At present, however, the superabundance of facts obscures a clear view of their interrelations and of the principles providing their underlying structure.

This is not meant to deny that investigators in these fields have proposed semantic theories. But, in general, such theories have been either too loosely formulated or too weak in explanatory and descriptive power to account adequately for the available semantic facts. Moreover, taken together, these theories form a heterogeneous and disconnected assortment. Philosophical inquiry into the meaning and use of words has neither drawn upon nor contributed to semantic investigation in psychology and linguistics. Correspondingly, accounts of meaning proposed by linguists and psychologists cannot in any obvious way be connected with theories current in philosophy or with one another. In each case, the character of the theory and its constructs is so radically idiosyncratic, so peculiar to the realm of discourse from which it comes, that it is practically impossible to determine its relevance to theories and constructs from other realms of discourse. This becomes apparent from even the most cursory comparison of the work of such semantic theorists as Bloomfield, Carnap, Harris, Osgood, Quine, Russell, Skinner, Tarski, Wittgenstein, and Ziff. In the writings of these theorists, one finds explications of meaning based upon everything from patterns of retinal stimulation, to stimuli controlling verbal behavior, to affective factors in the response to words, to intensions, to sentential truth conditions, to conditions for nondeviant utterances, to distribution, to rules of use. As Chomsky has insightfully observed:

> Part of the difficulty with the theory of meaning is that "meaning" tends to be used as a catch-all term to include every aspect of language that we know very little about. Insofar as this is correct, we can expect various aspects of this theory to be claimed by other approaches to language in the course of their development[1].

Such broad disagreement, extending not only to questions about the nature of meaning but even to questions about the kinds of considerations relevant to the construction of a semantic theory is attributable to the failure of investigators to deal seriously with metatheoretic questions about the abstract form of semantic theories. A characterization of the form of a semantic theory can be expected to accomplish the following. It defines the domain of a semantic theory by telling us what phenomena a semantic theory seeks to describe and explain and what kinds of facts about them are theoretically relevant in semantic investigation. Also, characterizing the

---

[1] N. Chomsky, *Syntactic Structures* (2nd ed.: L. Mouton & Co.: 's Gravenhage, 1962), p. 103, 10 *n*.

form of a semantic theory clarifies the goals of semantic description. Vaguely formulated goals can then be refined, and this can lead in turn to the discovery that certain putative goals are unacceptable, that others are interrelated, and that some take priority. Without such a clarification, competing theories of meaning are not even so much as comparable. With such clarification, the goals of semantic theory can be aligned with those of other areas of linguistics to afford an over-all picture of what an adequate description of a natural language describes. Further, by characterizing the form of semantic generalizations and of the manner in which they can systematically interrelate, a metatheory shows how semantic theories can effect a reduction of the superabundance of facts to manageable proportions by representing them in a system consisting of a small number of compact, interrelated generalizations. Finally, the metatheory determines the empirical and methodological constraints upon a semantic theory. Thus, it enables investigators to evaluate competing semantic theories by assessing the degree to which they satisfy such constraints. Inadequate conceptions of meaning can then be pushed to the point where their inadequacy becomes fully apparent.

THE PROJECTION PROBLEM

A full synchronic description of a natural language is a grammatical and semantic characterization of that language (where the term *grammatical* is construed broadly to include, besides syntax, phonology, phonemics, and morphology). Hence, a semantic theory must be constructed to have whatever properties are demanded by its role in linguistic description. Since, however, the goals of such description are reasonably well understood and since, in comparison to semantics, the nature of grammar has been clearly articulated, we may expect that, by studying the contribution semantics will be required to make to a synchronic description of a language, we can clarify the subject, the form of generalizations, the goals, and the empirical and methodological constraints of a semantic theory. Our first step toward determining the contribution a semantic theory is required to make toward a linguistic description of a natural language will be to delineate the contribution a grammar makes. Our aim is, in this way, to factor out the contribution of a semantic theory.

A fluent speaker's mastery of his language exhibits itself in his ability to produce and understand the sentences of his language, *including indefinitely many that are wholly novel to him* (i.e., his ability to produce and understand *any* sentence of his language[2]). The emphasis upon novel sentences is important. The most characteristic feature of language is its ability to make available an infinity of sentences from which the speaker can select appropriate and novel ones to use as the need arises. That is to say, what qualifies one as a fluent speaker is not the ability to imitate previously heard sentences but rather the ability to produce and understand sentences

---

[2]There are exceptions, such as sentences with technical words that the speaker does not know, sentences too long for the speaker to scan in his lifetime, and so on. But these exceptions are of no systematic importance. Analogously, a person's mastery of an algorithm for propositional calculus can be said to exhibit itself in his ability to mechanically decide whether *any* well-formed formula of propositional calculus is a tautology, even though some well-formed formulae are too long for human processing and so forth.

never before encountered. The striking fact about the use of language is the absence of repetition—almost every sentence uttered is uttered for the first time. This can be substantiated by checking texts for the number of times a sentence is repeated. It is exceedingly unlikely that even a single repetition of a sentence of reasonable length will be encountered.

A synchronic description of a natural language seeks to determine what a fluent speaker knows about the structure of his language that enables him to use and understand its sentences. Since a fluent speaker is able to use and understand any sentence drawn from the *infinite* set of sentences of his language, and since, at any time, he has only encountered a *finite* set of sentences, it follows that the speaker's knowledge of his language takes the form of rules which project the finite set of sentences he has fortuitously encountered to the infinite set of sentences of the language. A description of the language which adequately represents the speaker's linguistic knowledge must, accordingly, state these rules. The problem of formulating these rules we shall refer to as the *projection problem*.

This problem requires for its solution rules which project the infinite set of sentences in a way which mirrors the way speakers understand novel sentences. In encountering a novel sentence, the speaker is not encountering novel elements but only a novel combination of familiar elements. Since the set of sentences is infinite and each sentence is a different concatenation of morphemes, the fact that a speaker can understand any sentence must mean that the way he understands sentences he has never previously encountered is compositional: on the basis of his knowledge of the grammatical properties and the meanings of the morphemes of the language, the rules the speaker knows enable him to determine the meaning of a novel sentence in terms of the manner in which the parts of the sentence are composed to form the whole. Correspondingly, then, we can expect that a system of rules which solves the projection problem must reflect the compositional character of the speaker's linguistic skill.

A solution to the projection problem is certainly something less than a full theory of speech. In particular, it does not provide a theory of speech production (or recognition). The difference between a description of a language and a theory of speech production is the difference between asking for a characterization of the rules of language a speaker knows and asking for an account of how he actually applies such rules in speaking. Some things that are left out by the first theory but not by the second are: considerations of the psychological parameters of speech production (e.g., limitations of immediate memory, level of motivation, and so on); developmental accounts of the way the child becomes a fluent speaker (by conditioning? by the exploitation of innate mechanisms? by some combination of innate endowment and learning?). Although such problems about speech production lie outside the scope of a theory of a language, a theory of a language is essential to a theory of speech production. It is first necessary to know what is acquired and used before it is sensible to ask how it is acquired and used.

These considerations show that what is asked for when we ask for a description of a natural language is a solution to the projection problem for that language. If we are to discover the goals of semantics by subtracting from the goals of a description of a language whatever the grammar contributes to the solution of the projection problem, we must consider the contribution of grammar.

LINGUISTIC DESCRIPTION MINUS GRAMMAR
EQUALS SEMANTICS

The significance of transformational grammars for our present purposes is that they provide a solution for the grammatical aspect of the projection problem. (That is to say, transformational grammars answer the question: what does the speaker know about the phonological and syntactic structure of his language which enables him to use and understand any of its sentences, including those he has never previously heard?) They do so by providing rules which generate the sentences of the speaker's language. In particular, these rules generate infinitely many strings of morphemes which, although they are sentences of the language, have never been uttered by speakers. Moreover, a transformational grammar generates the sentences a speaker is, in principle, capable of understanding in such a way that their derivations provide their structural descriptions. Such descriptions specify: the elements out of which a sentence is constructed, the grammatical relations between these elements and between the higher constituents of the sentence, the relations between the sentence and other sentences of the language, and the ways the sentence is ambiguous together with an explanation of why it is ambiguous in these ways. Since it is this information about a novel sentence which the speaker knows and which enables him to understand its syntactic structure if and when he encounters the sentence, an adequate transformational grammar of a language *partially* solves the projection problem for the language.

A semantic theory of a language completes the solution of the projection problem for the language. Thus, semantics takes over the explanation of the speaker's ability to produce and understand infinitely many new sentences at the point where grammar leaves off. Since we wish to determine, when we have subtracted the problems in the description of a language properly belonging to grammar, what problems belong to semantics, we must begin by gaining some grasp of how much of the projection problem is left unsolved by an optimal grammar.

One way to appreciate how much of understanding sentences is left unexplained by grammar is to compare the grammatical characterizations of sentences to what we know about their semantic characterizations. If we do this, we notice that the grammar provides identical structural descriptions for sentences that are different in meaning and different structural descriptions for sentences that are identical in meaning. The former will be the case for all morphemically distinct substitution instances of a given sentential type. For example, "The dog bit the man" and 'The cat bit the woman." The latter will be the case for all instances of sentential synonymy. For example, "The dog bit the man" and "The man was bitten by the dog."[3]

This indicates some of the types of problems that even an optimal grammar cannot deal with. In general, it is obvious that in no sense of meaning does the structural description the grammar assigns to a sentence specify either the meaning of the

---

[3]Moreover, sentences that are given the same structural description can differ in that one may be semantically ambiguous or anomalous without the other being so. Compare, for example, "The bill is large," "The paint is silent," and "The street is wide," all of which receive the same structural description from the grammar.

sentence or the meaning of its parts. Such considerations must now be made precise in order that we may apply our formula, *linguistic description minus grammar equals semantics*, to determine a lower bound on the domain of a semantic theory. Later in this section we will fix an upper bound by determining what problems lie outside the concerns of a complete linguistic description.

Grammars seek to describe the structure of a sentence *in isolation from its possible settings in linguistic discourse (written or verbal) or in nonlinguistic contexts (social or physical)*. The justification which permits the grammarian to study sentences in abstraction from the settings in which they have occurred or might occur is simply that the fluent speaker is able to construct and recognize syntactically well-formed sentences without recourse to information about settings, and this ability is what a grammar undertakes to reconstruct. Every facet of the fluent speaker's linguistic ability which a grammar reconstructs can be exercised independently of information about settings: this is true not only of the ability to produce and recognize sentences but also of the ability to determine syntactic relations between sentence types, to implicitly analyze the syntactic structure of sentences, and to detect grammatical ambiguities. Since, then, the knowledge a fluent speaker has of his language enables him to determine the grammatical structure of any sentence without reference to information about setting, grammar correspondingly forms an independent theory of this independent knowledge.

We may generalize to arrive at a sufficient condition for determining when an ability of speakers is the proper subject matter of a synchronic theory in linguistics. The generalization is this: *If speakers can employ an ability in apprehending the structure of any sentence in the infinite set of sentences of a language without reference to information about settings and without significant variation from speaker to speaker, then that ability is properly the subject matter of a synchronic theory in linguistics.*

The first question in determining the subject matter of a semantic theory is: can we find an ability which satisfies the antecedent of the above generalization, which is beyond the range of grammatical description and which is semantic in some reasonable sense? If we can, then that ability falls within the domain of a semantic theory.

In order to find such an ability, let us consider a communication situation so constructed that no information about setting can contribute to a speaker's understanding of a sentence encountered in that situation. Any extragrammatical ability a speaker can employ to understand the meaning of a sentence in such a situation will *ipso facto* be considered to require semantic explanation. The type of communication situation we shall consider is the following: a number of English speakers receive an anonymous letter containing only the English sentence S. We are interested in the difference between this type of situation and one in which the same anonymous letter is received by persons who do not speak English but are equipped with a completely adequate grammar of English. To investigate what the first group can do by way of comprehending the meaning of S that the second group cannot is to factor out the contribution of grammar to the understanding of sentences. We will only investigate aspects of linguistic ability which are invariant from individual to individual within each group. We thus assure that the abilities under investigation are a function not of idiosyncrasies of a speaker's personal history but only of his knowledge of his language.

Suppose S is the sentence "The bill is large." Speakers of English will agree that this sentence is ambiguous, i.e., that it has at least two readings: according to one, it means that some document demanding a sum of money to dispense a debt exceeds in size most such documents, and according to another, it means that the beak of a certain bird exceeds in bulk those of most similar birds. However, the fact that this sentence is ambiguous between these readings cannot be attributed to its syntactic structure since, syntactically, its structure on both readings is:

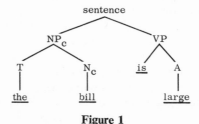

Figure 1

That is, the group who *do not* speak English but *are* equipped with a grammar can say no more about "The bill is large" than what is represented in Fig. 1. Thus, this sentence, which is marked as unambiguous by the grammar, will be understood as ambiguous by a fluent speaker. From this difference between the performances of the two groups, it follows that one facet of the speaker's ability that a semantic theory will have to reconstruct is that he can detect nonsyntactic ambiguities and characterize the content of each reading of a sentence.

Now suppose S is the sentence "The bill is large but need not be paid." Speakers of English will understand this sentence only on readings in which *bill* means an order to pay a sum of money to dispense a debt. This shows that a speaker can disambiguate parts of a sentence in terms of other parts and thereby determine the number of readings of a sentence. Thus, another facet of the speaker's semantic ability is that of determining the number of readings a sentence has by exploiting semantic relations in the sentence to eliminate potential ambiguities.

Now let S be the sentence "He painted the walls with silent paint." English speakers will at once recognize that this sentence is anomalous in some way. For example, they will distinguish it from such sentences as "He painted the walls with red paint" and "He painted the walls with silent rollers" by applying to it such epithets as *odd*, *peculiar*, *bizarre*, and the like. Although it is clear that the speaker does not have the explicit conceptual machinery to correctly characterize the difference between these sentences, his consistent use of such rough labels shows that he is aware of some sort of linguistic anomaly. But the group who do not speak English and are equipped only with a grammar will regard all these sentences as fully regular since there is no grammatical basis for distinguishing between them. Hence, another facet of the semantic ability of the speaker is that of detecting semantic anomalies. Correspondingly, a semantic theory will be needed to mark the distinction between semantically anomalous sentences and semantically regular sentences, insofar as this distinction is *not* coextensive with the distinction the grammar makes between ungrammatical and grammatical strings of morphemes.

Finally, whatever sentence the anonymous letter contains, as a rule, speakers of English can easily decide what sentences are paraphrases of it and what are not in the sense that they can answer such questions as: what does the letter say? does the letter say such-and-such? how can what the letter says be rephrased? This facet of the speaker's ability cannot be referred to his mastery of grammar either, for the group who are equipped with a grammar but who do not speak English will be unable to tell whether or not a sentence is a paraphrase of *S*. The reasons are simply that there need be no definite grammatical relation between a sentence and its paraphrases; e.g., "Two chairs are in the room" and "There are at least two things in the room and each is a chair;" and that where a definite grammatical relation obtains between a pair of sentences, neither need be a paraphrase of the other, e.g., "The ball was hit by the man" and "The ball was hit," "The man hit the ball," and "The man did not hit the ball."[4] Thus, still another facet of the speaker's semantic ability which must fall within the domain of a semantic theory is his paraphrasing skill.

We can now tentatively characterize the lower bound on the domain of a semantic theory since we have found an ability of speakers which cannot be accounted for by grammar, which is semantic in a reasonable sense and which enables speakers to apprehend the semantic structure of an infinite number of sentences without information about setting and independent of individual differences between speakers. We thus take the goals of a semantic theory to include at least the explication of each facet of this ability and of the interrelations between them.

The speaker's exercise of this ability, which henceforth we shall refer to as *the ability to interpret sentences*, provides empirical data for the construction of a semantic theory, just as the construction of a grammar draws upon empirical data supplied by the exercise of the speaker's ability to distinguish well-formed sentences from ungrammatical strings, to recognize syntactic ambiguity, and to appreciate relations between sentence types. A semantic theory describes and explains the interpretative ability of speakers: by accounting for their performance in determining the number and content of the readings of a sentence; by detecting semantic anomalies; by deciding upon paraphrase relations between sentences; and by marking every other semantic property or relation that plays a role in this ability.

Having now fixed a lower bound on the domain of a semantic theory, our next step must be to fix an upper bound, thus uniquely determining the set of problems forming the domain of a semantic theory of a natural language.

Previous conceptions of semantics have usually defined the goals of a semantic description of a natural language in such a way that to achieve them a semantic theory would have to account for the manner in which settings determine how an utterance is understood. We shall now show that to set the goals of a semantic theory this high is to set them too high. Once we have shown that a semantic theory cannot be expected to account for the way settings determine how an utterance is understood, we will have fixed an upper bound on the domain of semantic theories.

---

[4] Cf. N. Chomsky, *op. cit.*, Appendix II for the transformations which relate these sentences.

That is, we will have shown that a semantic theory is a theory of the speaker's ability to interpret the sentences of his language.

The abstract form of a theory of how settings control the understanding of utterances of sentences is as follows. Such a theory is a function F whose arguments are a sentence S, a grammatical description of S, GS, a semantic interpretation of S, IS (where IS is the set of possible readings of S), and an abstract characterization of a setting, C. $F(S, GS, IS, C)$ is:

(1) The particular reading in IS speakers of the language give S in settings of the type C, or

(2) An n-tuple ($n \geqslant 2$) of the readings from IS that speakers of the language give S if S is ambiguous n-ways in settings of type C, or

(3) The null element if speakers of the language give S none of the readings in IS when S occurs in settings of type C.

The value of $F(S, GS, IS, C)$ is (1) just in case C fully disambiguates S, i.e., C determines a unique reading from the one or more in IS; it is (2) just in case C fails to fully disambiguate S; it is (3) just in case an occurrence of S in C is token-odd.[5]

An example of each of these cases will clarify this abstract formulation by showing how a theory of this form would explicate the speaker's ability to choose the reading(s) a setting determines for a sentence occurring in it. As an example of case (1), consider the sentence "The shooting of the hunters was terrible." This sentence is ambiguous between the reading r_1 on which it means that it was terrible that the hunters were shot and the reading r_2 on which it means that the marksmanship of the hunters was very bad. This ambiguity will be represented in IS. The theory F must decide which of these readings the sentence bears in settings which disambiguate it, and it must decide in which settings the sentence remains ambiguous. If, then, an utterance of the sentence occurs as an answer to the question "How good was the marksmanship of the hunters?" i.e., if C represents a situation in which the marksmanship of the hunters is clearly at issue, then, *ceteris paribus*, the value of F would have to be r_2.[6] Now consider case (2). An ambiguous sentence such as "He follows Marx" occurring in a setting in which it is clear that the speaker is remarking about intellectual history cannot bear the reading "he dogs the footsteps of Groucho." However, this setting leaves the sentence ambiguous between the readings "he is a disciple of Karl's" and "he postdates Karl." Thus, F will have to have these latter two readings as its value for this sentence and setting as arguments. Finally, let us consider case (3). Suppose the sentence "This is the happiest night of my life" is uttered during the middle of the day. Since this sentence is uttered in a setting lacking conditions which utterances of this sentence presuppose, the occurrence is a case of token-oddity. Thus, for this sentence-occurrence F must give the null element as its value, i.e., none of the readings this sentence has in IS are selected by C.

This, then, is the abstract form of a theory about the effect of setting upon the way speakers understand sentences. Any particular theory is complete just to the extent that it solves the problems incorporated in this abstract formulation. A complete

---

[5]Semantic type oddity is precluded by the assumption that IS contains at least one reading.

[6]In the case where a sentence has exactly one reading in IS, i.e., is unambiguous, that reading must be assigned to the sentence in each and every normal setting by the theory.

theory of this kind is more powerful in principle than a theory of the semantic interpretation of sentences in isolation. But a theory of settings must contain a theory of semantic interpretation as a proper part because the readings that a speaker attributes to a sentence in a setting are a selection from among those that sentence has in isolation. It is clear that, *in general*, a sentence cannot have readings in a setting which it does not have in isolation. Of course, there are cases in which a sentence may have a reading for some speakers in some settings which it does not have in isolation for all speakers. But these cases are essentially idiomatic in the sense that meaning is determined either by special stipulation (passwords, nonce-senses, and so on) or by special rules (some codes, and the like) or by special information about the intentions of the speaker. If a theory of the selective effect of setting were required to deal with such cases, no such theory would be possible because any sentence may be made to mean anything you like simply by constructing the setting to include the appropriate stipulation.[7] Since, then, the readings that a speaker gives a sentence in setting are a selection from those the sentence has in isolation, a theory of semantic interpretation is logically prior to a theory of the selective effect of setting.

The abstract formulation given above may be realized in the form of a theory of either of two kinds, depending on how the notion of setting is construed. One kind of theory of setting selection construes the setting of an utterance to be the non-linguistic context in which the utterance occurs, i.e., the full socio-physical environment of the utterance. The other kind takes the setting of an utterance to be the linguistic context in which the utterance occurs, i.e., the written or spoken discourse of which the utterance is a part. We shall consider, in turn, the possibility of constructing a theory of each of these types.

The first kind of theory of setting selection seeks to account for the way in which aspects of the socio-physical world control the understanding of sentences. Differing varieties of this kind of theory may be obtained by varying the aspects of the socio-physical environment of which the rules of the theory are permitted to take account and by varying the spatio-temporal parameters of the environment. But clearly a necessary condition that any variety of this kind of theory must satisfy is that its construction of setting is so defined that it is able to represent all the nonlinguistic information required by speakers to understand sentences. Insofar as a theory fails to satisfy this condition, that theory is incomplete since there is some information which determines the way speakers understand a sentence but which the theory fails to represent as part of the setting of that sentence. If a theory fails to represent information which speakers actually utilize in understanding sentences, the theory fails to fully explain the mechanism by which such information contributes to the process of understanding.

However, a complete theory of this kind is not possible in principle because to satisfy the above necessary condition, it would be required that the theory represent

---

[7] Take the following example. Let m be a one-to-one mapping of the set of English sentences onto itself such that the image of each sentence is a sentence which differs in meaning from it. Then the sentence "The sentence S which immediately follows this sentence is to be understood as $m(S)$," is a setting such that the meaning of a sentence occurring in it is not one of the meanings of that sentence in isolation.

all the knowledge speakers have about the world. That this is so can be seen from even a few examples which show how nonlinguistic information of any kind may be involved in the understanding of a sentence. Consider (1) "Our store sells alligator shoes" and (2) "Our store sells horse shoes." In normal settings (e.g., as signs in a store window, as newspaper advertisements), occurrences of (1) will be taken on the reading "our store sells shoes made from alligator skins" while (2) will be taken on the reading "our store sells shoes for horses." Notice, however, that (1) is open to the reading "our store sells shoes for alligators" and (2) is open to the reading "our store sells shoes made from the skin of horses." From this it follows that for a theory of setting selection to choose the correct reading for (1) it must represent the fact that, to date, alligators do not wear shoes, although shoes for people are sometimes made from alligator skin. Conversely, if the theory is to choose the correct reading for (2), it must represent the fact that horses wear shoes, although shoes for people are not made from the skin of horses. Other examples illustrate much the same point. Compare the three sentences: "Should we take junior back to the zoo?" "Should we take the lion back to the zoo?" "Should we take the bus back to the zoo?" Information which figures in the choice of the correct readings for these sentences includes the fact that lions, but not children and busses, are often kept in cages. Three further cases of the same sort are: "Can I put the wallpaper on?" and "Can I put the coat on?" "Joe jumped higher than the Empire State Building" and "Joe jumped higher than you;" "Black cats are unlucky" and "People who break mirrors are unlucky."[8]

For practically any item of information about the world, the reader will find it a relatively easy matter to construct an ambiguous sentence whose resolution in context requires the representation of that item.[9] Since a complete theory of setting selection must represent as part of the setting of an utterance any and every feature of the world which speakers need to determine the preferred reading of that utterance and since, as we have just seen, practically any item of information about the world is essential to some disambiguations, two conclusions follow. First, such a theory cannot in principle distinguish between the speaker's knowledge of his language and his knowledge of the world because, according to such a theory, part of the characterization of a *linguistic* ability is a representation of virtually all knowledge about the world speakers share. Second, since there is no serious possibility of systematizing all the knowledge of the world that speakers share and since a theory of the kind we have been discussing requires such a systematization, it is *ipso facto* not a serious model for semantics. However, none of these considerations is intended to rule out the possibility that, by placing relatively strong limitations on the information about the world that a theory can represent in the characterization of a setting, a *limited* theory of selection by socio-physical setting can be

---

[8]The authors wish to express their gratitude to Mr. David Bellugi for referring them to *My Little Golden Book of Jokes* from which the above examples are drawn.

[9]The authors have convinced themselves of the truth of this claim by making it the basis of a party game. The game consists in one person supplying a fact, however obscure, and the others trying to construct a sentence which that fact disambiguates. Although this game is not remarkably amusing, it is surprisingly convincing.

constructed. What these considerations do show is that a *complete* theory of this kind is not a possibility.

The second kind of realization of the abstract formulation of a theory of setting selection is one in which the setting of an occurrence of a sentence is construed as the written or spoken discourse of which the occurrence is a part. Such a theory has a strong and a weak version. The strong version requires that the theory interpret a discourse in the same way a fluent speaker would (i.e., mark the ambiguities the speaker marks, resolve the ambiguities the speaker resolves, detect the anomalous strings the speaker detects, recognize paraphrase relations the speaker recognizes, and do so both within and across sentence boundaries). Since, however, in so interpreting a discourse, a speaker may need to bring to bear virtually any information about the world that he and other speakers share, the argument given against a complete theory of selection by socio-physical setting applies equally against the strong version of a theory of selection by discourse. Thus, we need only consider the weak version.

The weak version of such a theory requires only that the theory interpret discourses just insofar as the interpretation is determined by grammatical and semantic relations which obtain within and among the sentences of the discourse; i.e., it interprets discourses as would a fluent speaker afflicted with amnesia for non-linguistic facts but not with aphasia. Thus, such a theory seeks to disambiguate sentences and sequences of sentences in terms of grammatical and semantic relations between them and the sentences which form their setting in a discourse, to determine when an occurrence of a sentence or a sequence of sentences is rendered anomalous by the sentences which form its setting in a discourse, and to recognize paraphrase relations between pairs of sentences and pairs of sequences of sentences in a discourse.[10]

But it is not at all clear that the weak version of theory of discourse-setting selection has greater explanatory power in these respects than a theory of semantic interpretation, since except for a few types of cases, discourse can be treated as a single sentence in isolation by regarding sentence boundaries as sentential connectives.[11] As a matter of fact, this is the natural treatment. In the great majority of cases, the sentence break in discourse is simply *and*-conjunction. (In others, it is *but, for, or,*

---

[10]For examples of studies toward a theory of this kind, Cf. Z. S. Harris, "Discourse Analysis," *Language*, **26** (1952), 1–30; and H. Herzberger, "Contextual Analysis," (doctoral dissertation, Princeton University, 1957).

[11]To illustrate this, let us consider the two-sentence discourse: "I shot the man with a gun," "If the man had had a gun too, he would have shot me first." The first sentence of this discourse is ambiguous in isolation, but not in this setting. But the problem of explaining this disambiguation is the same as the problem of explaining why the single sentence "I shot the man with a gun, but if the man had had a gun too, he would have shot me first," does not have an ambiguous first clause. Likewise, consider the discourse, "I heard the noise," "The noise was completely inaudible," and its single sentence equivalent, "I heard the noise, and the noise was completely inaudible." In showing why the single sentence is anomalous, a theory of semantic interpretation exhibits precisely those semantic relations in which the anomaly of the discourse resides. This technique of replacing discourses or stretches in discourses with single compound sentences, by using sentential connectives in place of sentence boundaries, clearly has a very extensive application in reducing problems of setting selection to problems of semantic interpretation of sentences in isolation. Thus, given a theory of semantic interpretation, it is unclear how much is left for a theory of setting selection to explain.

and so on.)[12] Hence, for every discourse, there is a single sentence which consists of the sequence of *n*-sentences that comprises the discourse connected by the appropriate sentential connectives and which exhibits the same semantic relations exhibited in the discourse. But since the single sentence is, *ex hypothesi*, described by a theory of semantic interpretation, in every case in which a discourse can be treated as a single sentence, a theory of semantic interpretation is as descriptively powerful as a theory of setting selection.

We opened the discussion of theories of setting selection in order to fix an upper bound on the domain of a semantic theory of a natural language. The result of the discussion is that, where such a theory is not reducible to a theory of semantic interpretation, it cannot be completed without systematizing all the knowledge about the world that speakers share and keeping such a systematization up-to-date as speakers come to share more knowledge. We remarked that a limited theory of how sociophysical setting determines how an utterance is understood is possible, but we pointed out that even then such a theory would blur the distinction between the speaker's knowledge of his language (his linguistic ability) and the speaker's knowledge of the world (his beliefs about matters of fact). Therefore, since it is unlikely that anything stronger than a theory of semantic interpretation is possible and since such a theory is an essential part of a linguistic description, it is eminently reasonable to fix the upper bound of a semantic theory of a natural language at the point where the requirements upon a theory of semantic interpretation are satisfied.

THE COMPONENTS OF A SEMANTIC THEORY

In the previous sections we have characterized the domain of a semantic investigation and circumscribed the descriptive and explanatory goals of a semantic theory of a natural language. Now we must determine what mechanisms a semantic theory employs in reconstructing the speaker's ability to interpret sentences in isolation. We have seen that this ability is systematic in that it enables the speaker to understand sentences he has never heard before and to produce novel sentences that other speakers understand in the way he understands them. To account for this ability, a semantic theory must be so formulated that its output matches the interpretive performance of a fluent speaker. In this section, we describe the form of semantic theories.

It is widely acknowledged and certainly true that one component of a semantic

---

[12]Sometimes a discourse cannot be directly converted into a compound sentence in this way. For example, the discourse "How are you feeling today?" "I am fine, thanks" does not convert to "*How are you feeling today and I am fine, thanks" because the compound sentence is ungrammatical. But the fact that sentences of different types cannot be run together in the obvious way may not pose a serious problem because it is not at all clear that less obvious conversions will not lead to a satisfactory treatment of such cases within a theory of semantic interpretation. For example, we may convert the discourse just cited into the single sentence, "*X* asked, 'How are you feeling today?' and *Y* replied, 'I am fine, thanks.' " If such conversions can be carried out generally, then any problem about disambiguation, detection of anomaly, and so on that can be raised and/or solved in a theory of setting selection can be raised and/or solved by reference to an analogon in the theory of semantic interpretation. But even if such conversions cannot be carried out generally, the most interesting and central cases will still be within the range of a theory of semantic interpretation.

theory of a natural language is a dictionary of that language. The rationale for including a dictionary as a component of a semantic theory is based on two limitations of a grammatical description. First, a grammar cannot account for the fact that some sentences which differ *only* morphemically are interpreted as different in meaning (e.g., "The tiger bit me" and "The mouse bit me"), while other sentences which differ only morphemically are interpreted as identical in meaning (e.g., "The oculist examined me" and "The eyedoctor examined me"). Second, a grammar cannot account for the fact that some sentences of radically different syntactic structure are synonymous (e.g., "Two chairs are in the room" and "There are at least two things in the room, and each is a chair"), while other syntactically different sentences are not. In each case, the interpretation of the sentences is determined in part by the meanings of their morphemes and by semantic relations among the morphemes. The rationale for including a dictionary as a component of a semantic theory is precisely to provide a representation of the semantic characteristics of morphemes necessary to account for the facts about sentences and their interrelations that the grammar leaves unexplained.

What has always been unclear about a semantic theory is what component(s) it contains besides a dictionary and how the components of a semantic theory relate to one another and to the grammar. We can find this out by asking in what respects a dictionary and grammar alone are not sufficient to match the fluent speaker's interpretations of sentences.

Let us imagine a fluent speaker of English presented with the infinite list of sentences and their structural descriptions generated by a grammar of English. Given an accurate dictionary of English, *which he applies by using his linguistic ability*, the fluent speaker can semantically interpret any sentence on the list under any of its grammatical derivations. He can determine the number and content of the readings of a sentence, tell whether or not a sentence is semantically anomalous, and decide which sentences on the list are paraphrases. Now contrast the fluent speaker's performance with the performance of a machine which *mechanically*[13] applies an English dictionary to a sentence on the list by associating with each morpheme of the sentence its dictionary entry. It is clear that the dictionary usually supplies more senses for a lexical item than it bears in almost any of its occurrences in sentences. But the machine will not be able to select the sense(s) the morpheme actually bears in a given sentential context, except insofar as the selection is already determined by the grammatical markers assigned to the morpheme in the derivation of the sentence. For example, the machine will be able to choose the correct sense of *seal* in "Seal the letter" insofar as the choice is determined by the fact that in this sentence *seal* is marked as a verb, and the correct sense of *seal* in "The seal is on the letter insofar as the choice is determined by the fact that in this sentence *seal* is marked as a noun. But the machine will not be able to distinguish the correct sense of *seal* in "One of

---

[13]The qualification *mechanically* is important: it precludes the employment of linguistic skills not represented by the grammar or the dictionary. It is precisely the possession of such skills which distinguishes the fluent speaker from the nonspeaker equipped with a grammar and a dictionary. Hence, the degree to which the nonspeaker is permitted access to such skills is the degree to which we obscure what must be accounted for. Conversely, by prohibiting their employment, as we do by the qualification *mechanically*, we bring into clear relief just the skills that a semantic theory of a natural language must account for.

the oil seals in my car is leaking" from such incorrect senses as *a device bearing a design so made that it can impart an impression* or *an impression made by such a device* or *the material upon which the impression is made* or *an ornamental or commemorative stamp* and so forth, since all of these senses can apply to nominal occurrences of *seal*. What the machine is failing to do is to take account of or utilize the semantic relations between morphemes in a sentence. Thus, the machine cannot determine the correct number and content of readings of a sentence; nor can it distinguish semantically anomalous sentences from semantically regular ones. Since the machine will associate a dictionary entry with each morpheme in a sentence, it does not distinguish cases in which the sense of a morpheme or string of morphemes in a sentence precludes other morphemes in the sentence bearing *any* of the senses that the dictionary supplies for them. (E.g., the machine cannot distinguish "The wall is covered with silent paint" from "The wall is covered with fresh paint.") Finally, the machine cannot tell which sentences on the list are paraphrases of each other in any case except the one in which the sentences are of exactly the same syntactic structure and corresponding words in each sentence are either identical or synonymous.

The comparison between a fluent speaker and this machine reveals the respects in which a grammar and dictionary by themselves do not suffice to interpret sentences the way a speaker of the language does. What the fluent speaker has at his disposal which the machine does not are rules for applying the information in the dictionary which take account of semantic relations between morphemes and of the interaction between meaning and syntactic structure in determining the correct semantic interpretation for any of the infinitely many sentences the grammar generates. Thus, a semantic theory of a natural language must have such rules as one of its components if it is to match the speaker's interpretations of sentences.

We thus arrive at the following conception of a semantic theory. The basic fact that a semantic theory must explain is that a fluent speaker can determine the meaning of a sentence in terms of the meanings of its constituent lexical items. To explain this fact, a semantic theory must contain two components: a dictionary of the lexical items of the language and a system of rules (which we shall call *projection rules*) which operates on full grammatical descriptions of sentences and on dictionary entries to produce semantic interpretations for every sentence of the language. Such a theory would explain how the speaker applies dictionary information to sentences and would thus solve the projection problem for semantics by reconstructing the speaker's ability to interpret any of the infinitely many sentences of his language. The central problem for such a theory is that a dictionary usually supplies more senses for a lexical item than it bears in an occurrence in a given sentence, for a dictionary entry is a characterization of *every* sense a lexical item can bear in any sentence. Thus, the effect of the projection rules must be to select the appropriate sense of each lexical item in a sentence in order to provide the correct readings for each distinct grammatical structure of that sentence. The semantic interpretations assigned by the projection rules operating on grammatical and dictionary information must account in the following ways for the speaker's ability to understand sentences: they must mark each semantic ambiguity a speaker can detect; they must explain the source of the speaker's intuitions of anomaly when a sentence evokes them; they must suitably relate sentences speakers know to be paraphrases of each other.[14]

Pictured in this way, a semantic theory interprets the syntactic structure a grammatical description of a language reveals. This conception thus gives content to the notion that a semantic theory of a natural language is analogous to a model which interprets a formal system. Further, it explicates the exact sense of the doctrine that the meaning of a sentence is a function of the meanings of the parts of the sentence. The system of projection rules is just this function.

THE STRUCTURE AND EVALUATION OF DICTIONARY ENTRIES

We have seen that the two components of a semantic theory of a natural language are a dictionary and a set of projection rules. In the present section, we shall describe the form that a dictionary entry must take in a semantic theory, and we shall discuss how, in an empirical study of the semantics of a natural language, we can evaluate the adequacy of proposed dictionary entries for the lexical items of that language. The next section will describe the form of the projection rules.

From the viewpoint of a semantic theory, a dictionary entry consists of two parts: a grammatical portion which provides the parts-of-speech classification for the lexical item, and a semantic portion which represents each of the distinct senses the lexical item has in its occurrences as a given part of speech. (This leaves out much of what is conventionally found in a dictionary entry, e.g., pronunciation, etymology, chronology, and so forth. However, such information is not relevant to a synchronic semantic description of a language.) Thus, for example, the word *play* receives an entry which has grammatical and semantic components as follows:

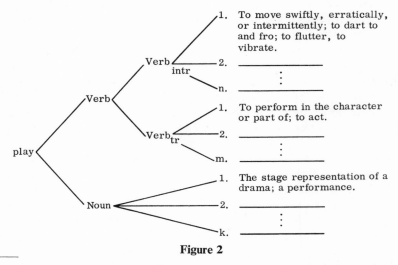

1. To move swiftly, erratically, or intermittently; to dart to and fro; to flutter, to vibrate.

1. To perform in the character or part of; to act.

1. The stage representation of a drama; a performance.

Figure 2

As pictured in Fig. 2, the grammatical portion classifies the syntactic roles the lexical item can play in sentences, while the semantic portion supplies one *sense* of the lexical item as the terminal element of each complete, distinct, descending path through the tree which represents the entry. The sense terminating each path can in turn be analyzed into two parts: a *sense-characterization* (which appears mandatorily) and a sequence of one or more synonyms (which appear optionally).

The central concept to be studied in this section is that of a sense-characterization of a lexical item. We can justify our concern with sense-characterizations to the exclusion of synonyms on the grounds that the concept *synonymity* can be reconstructed in terms of the concept *sense-characterization* but not vice versa. Therefore, the information about synonyms which a dictionary must provide can be given solely in terms of sense-characterizations but not vice versa. In particular, two lexical items have *n*-synonymous senses if and only if they have *n*-paths in common, and two lexical items are fully synonymous if and only if they have identical entries, i.e., every path of one is a path of the other. The explicit inclusion of synonyms in a dictionary entry, which is the common practice of conventional dictionaries, is a redundancy introduced to save the user the effort of discovering the synonyms of a lexical item by comparing its sense-characterizations with those of every other item in the dictionary. In short, the practice of listing the synonyms of an item is simply a technique of cross-reference. This follows from the fact that it must be a condition upon the adequacy of a dictionary that items which are synonymous in *n* of their senses have *n*-paths in common.

Dictionaries[15] give substantially the following entry for the word *bachelor*:

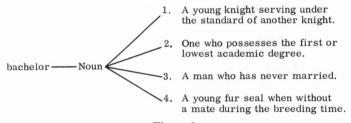

1. A young knight serving under the standard of another knight.
2. One who possesses the first or lowest academic degree.
3. A man who has never married.
4. A young fur seal when without a mate during the breeding time.

Figure 3

However, for reasons which will presently be made clear, the presentation of dictionary entries in the form exemplified in Figs. 2 and 3 is not adequate for a

---

speaker learns item by item, in a more or less rote fashion, and is something that he is constantly learning more of. Knowledge of the rules for applying the dictionary, on the other hand, is gained early and *in toto* and is exercised whenever a speaker uses his language. Correspondingly, the utilization of what is learned in learning a dictionary consists in recalling relatively independent bits of information. In the case of the rules, what is involved is the exercise of a faculty for coding and decoding linguistic information. The rules organize whatever systematic, nongrammatical information the speaker has about his language and are thus, in the strongest sense, essential to a knowledge of the language. To know a natural language, one *must* know these rules, but one need not know more than a small fraction of its vocabulary.

[15]Our sources for dictionary information throughout this paper have been *The Shorter Oxford English Dictionary* and *Webster's New Collegiate Dictionary*.

semantic theory. Instead, a semantic theory requires entries in a form exemplified in Fig. 4:

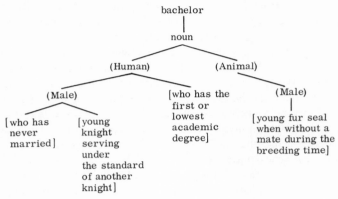

Figure 4

The unenclosed elements in Fig. 4 are *grammatical markers*, the elements enclosed in parentheses are what we shall call *semantic markers*; and the expressions enclosed in brackets are what we shall call *distinguishers*. We have already commented upon the function of grammatical markers. The semantic markers and distinguishers are used as the means by which we can decompose the meaning of a lexical item (on one sense) into its atomic concepts, thus enabling us to exhibit the semantic structure *in* a dictionary entry and the semantic relations *between* dictionary entries. That is, the semantic relations among the various senses of a lexical item and among the various senses of different lexical items are represented by formal relations between markers and distinguishers.

It is clear that any lexical information that a conventional dictionary entry can represent can also be represented by an entry in the normal form shown in Fig. 4. It is equally clear that any semantic relations that can be reconstructed from the former type of entry can also be reconstructed from the latter. For instance, distinct senses continue to be represented as distinct paths, synonymous senses of a lexical item continue to be represented in terms of identity of paths, and so on. However, there are semantic relations which can be reconstructed from entries in our normal form but not from entries in the conventional dictionary form. One such relation is that of *sex-antonymy*. This relation holds between the members of such pairs of words as *bachelor* and *spinster*, *man* and *woman*, *aunt* and *uncle*, *bride* and *groom*, *brother* and *sister*, *cow* and *bull*. What formally characterizes a sex-antonymous pair of words is that the members have identical paths except that where one has the semantic marker (*Male*) the other has the semantic marker (*Female*). Since there are indefinitely many important semantic relations which cannot be formally reconstructed from entries in the conventional dictionary form, this way of writing dictionary entries has a serious theoretical disadvantage. But this disadvantage is not the primary reason for introducing our normal form. The primary reason is that a formalization of the conventional dictionary entry is required in order to permit a formal statement of the projection rules. We will go into this in more detail later.

Semantic markers are the elements in terms of which semantic relations are expressed in a theory. Here there is a strong analogy to grammatical markers, since a grammatical marker (such as Noun, Verb, Adjective) is an element in terms of which syntactic relations are expressed. Thus, the semantic markers assigned to a lexical item in a dictionary entry are intended to reflect whatever systematic semantic relations hold between that item and the rest of the vocabulary of the language. On the other hand, the distinguishers assigned to a lexical item are intended to reflect what is idiosyncratic about the meaning of that item.[16] Generally speaking, a change in the system of semantic markers has extensive ramifications throughout the entire semantic theory, i.e., such a change radically alters the semantic relations which the theory claims obtain between indefinitely many words in the language. But a change in a distinguisher merely alters the relation between the item whose distinguisher has been changed and items which were its synonyms. For example, if the distinction between the markers (*Male*) and (*Female*) were obliterated in a semantic theory of English, not only would every pair of sex-antonymous words be represented as synonymous but the indefinitely many other semantic relations involving this distinction would also be incorrectly represented by the theory. In contrast, eliminating the distinguisher [*young fur seal when without a mate during the breeding time*] would merely prevent a theory from representing one sense of *bachelor* and whatever synonymity relations obtained between that sense of *bachelor* and certain senses of other words.

Branching under a semantic marker is sometimes singular but, very often, it is dyadic (or greater).[17] Since every path in a dictionary entry represents a distinct sense of a lexical item, a lexical item whose dictionary entry contains polyadic branching has more than one sense, i.e., is ambiguous. From the viewpoint of the semantic interpretation of sentences, polyadic branching represents the possibility of sentential semantic ambiguity in any sentence in which the ambiguous lexical item appears. For a necessary condition on the semantic ambiguity of a sentence is that it contain an ambiguous lexical item. But, clearly, this condition is not also sufficient since not all sentences containing ambiguous lexical items are themselves ambiguous. Consider the sentence "The stuff is light enough to carry." The dictionary entry for the word *light* exhibits branching into the semantic markers (*Color*) and (*Weight*). Such branching is required to account for the ambiguity of such sentences as "The stuff is light," "He wears a light suit in the summer," and so on. Since, however, "The stuff is light enough to carry is unambiguous, it follows that the expression *enough to carry* somehow selects one of the paths in the dictionary entry for *light* and excludes the other(s). Hence, the semantic interpretation of "The stuff is light enough to carry" must explain why the occurrence of *light* in this sentence is understood according to the sense in which *light* is a weight adjective.

In short, if a semantic theory is to predict correctly the number of ways speakers

---

[16]This does not preclude the possibility that certain semantic relations among lexical items may be expressed in terms of interrelations between their distinguishers. Cases of such relations are those between color names.

[17]Of course, in the entries for some lexical items, there will be paths in which the lowest semantic marker dominates nothing, i.e., paths that do not terminate in distinguishers.

will take a sentence to be ambiguous and the precise content of each term of each ambiguity, then it must be able to determine every case in which a sentence containing ambiguous lexical items is itself ambiguous and every case in which selection resolves such ambiguities. But this, in turn, amounts to accepting the condition that a dictionary must be so constructed that every case of lexical ambiguity is represented by polyadic branching and that every case of selection can be represented as the exclusion (by some sentential material) of one or more branches. Semantic anomaly can then be construed as the limiting case of selection: the case where there is a lexical item in a sentence *all* of whose paths are excluded by selections due to other material in the sentence.

Given the principle that semantic relations are expressed in terms of semantic markers alone, we can see that the primary motivation for representing lexical information by semantic markers will be to permit a theory to express those semantic relations which determine selection and thereby to arrive at the correct set of readings for each sentence. That selection must be represented in terms of semantic markers follows from the fact that selection is a semantic relation between parts of a sentence together with the principle that all semantic relations are expressed by semantic markers. Thus, the markers in each entry in the dictionary must be sufficient to permit a reconstruction of the operation of the mechanisms of selection in each sentence in which the lexical item receiving that entry appears.

Another consequence of expressing semantic relations solely in terms of semantic markers is that distinguishers, when they appear in a path in a dictionary entry, must appear as terminal elements; i.e., there must be no branching under a distinguisher. If branching under a distinguisher were allowed, then the theory would posit at least one semantic relation which its dictionary fails to represent by semantic markers, viz., the one between the senses of the lexical item differentiated by that branching.

The distinction between markers and distinguishers is meant to coincide with the distinction between that part of the meaning of a lexical item which is systematic for the language and that part of the meaning of the item which is not. In order to describe the systematicity in the meaning of a lexical item, it is necessary to have theoretical constructs whose formal interrelations compactly represent this systematicity. The semantic markers *are* such theoretical constructs. The distinguishers, on the other hand, do not enter into theoretical relations within a semantic theory. The part of the meaning of a lexical item that a dictionary represents by a distinguisher is thus the part of which a semantic theory offers no general account.

We must now consider the basis on which to decide to represent some lexical information by semantic markers and other lexical information by distinguishers. We thus not only clarify the basis for such decisions, but clarify further the nature of markers and distinguishers.

In the last analysis, the decision to represent a piece of lexical information by semantic markers or by distinguishers can only be justified by showing that it leads to correct interpretations for sentences. What, therefore, must be explained is how such decisions effect the assignment of semantic interpretations and, conversely, how the requirement that a theory assign semantic interpretations correctly effects decisions about the way in which a piece of lexical information is represented.

A particular semantic theory of a natural language can *represent* only those sentential semantic ambiguities resulting from the occurrence of a lexical item for which the dictionary of the theory provides an entry which contains two or more paths. That is, the degree of semantic ambiguity a semantic interpretation assigns to a sentence is a function of the degree of branching within the entries for the lexical items appearing in the sentence, branching into markers, distinguishers, or a combination of both counting equally in determining degree of ambiguity. However, a particular semantic theory of a natural language can *resolve* only those sentential semantic ambiguities which result from the occurrence of lexical material associated with dictionary entries containing two or more paths that differ by at least one semantic marker. This limitation on a semantic theory's power to resolve ambiguities is a direct consequence of the fact that selection can operate only upon semantic markers. Hence, decisions to represent a piece of lexical information by markers or distinguishers determine in part what semantic ambiguities will be only marked in the semantic interpretation of sentences and what will be both marked and resolved.

The decision to represent a piece of lexical information by a marker or a distinguisher is controlled by two kinds of considerations. Since we wish to construct a semantic theory in such a way that its output matches the performance of a fluent speaker, we want the theory to represent in its semantic interpretations just those semantic ambiguities that the fluent speaker can mark and to resolve just those ambiguities that he can resolve. This will mean that in theory construction what lexical information is represented by markers and what is represented by distinguishers will be controlled by our evidence about the disambiguations a fluent speaker can make. Let us take as an example the case of the word *bachelor*. If the dictionary entry is as given in Fig. 4, every sentence in which *bachelor* appears will be represented as ambiguous between the senses given by the paths: *bachelor* → Noun → (*Human*) → (*Male*) → [*who has never married*]; and *bachelor* → Noun → (*Human*) → (*Male*) → [*young knight serving under the standard of another knight*]. Since this ambiguity of *bachelor* is represented only by a difference of distinguishers, there is no way that a theory whose dictionary contains this entry can resolve it. But though this is an absolute limitation on such a theory, it is not an absolute limitation on the construction of semantic theories in general. If we notice that fluent speakers do not take such sentences as "The old bachelor finally died" to be ambiguous, then we can construct our semantic theory to accommodate this simply by taking the lexical information that a bachelor in the second sense is necessarily young to be marker information rather than distinguisher information. This is done by adding the marker (*Young*) to the marker system and rewriting the dictionary entry for *bachelor* accordingly. (See Figure 5)

The second kind of consideration which controls what lexical information is included in the system of semantic markers is the desire for systematic economy. The addition of new semantic markers, as in the case above, is made in order to increase the precision and scope of a semantic theory, but in so doing it also increases the complexity of the theory's conceptual apparatus. Since allowing more complexity often coincides with greater precision and scope, the decision as to what lexical information to include in the marker system of a semantic theory should be made on the basis of a strategy which seeks to maximize systematic economy: the greatest possible conceptual economy with the greatest possible explanatory and descriptive power. If such decisions are optimally made, there should eventually come a point when increasing the complexity of a semantic theory by adding new markers no longer yields enough of an advantage in precision or scope to warrant the increase. At this point, the system of semantic markers should reflect exactly the systematic features of the semantic structure of the language.

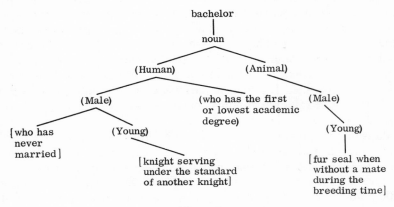

Figure 5

Thus far we have reconstructed four types of information which conventional dictionaries provide about a lexical item: its part of speech classification, its number of senses, its systematic semantic features, and its idiosyncratic features. There is one further type of information which conventional dictionaries give that is relevant to synchronic semantic description: information about the relation between features of certain combinations into which a lexical item may enter and the sense the item bears in those combinations. For example, consider *The Shorter Oxford English Dictionary* entry for the word *honest*: "...3. of persons: of good moral character, virtuous, upright,... of women: chaste, 'virtuous',...". The "of persons" and "of women" are intended to indicate that the senses that follow them apply only under the conditions that they specify. That is, these specifications indicate that if the nominal head which *honest* modifies refers to a person without specification of sex, then *honest* has the meaning "of good moral character, virtuous, or upright," and if the nominal head refers to a woman, then *honest* means *either* "of good moral character, virtuous, or upright" *or* "chaste." Our reconstruction of this type of dictionary information must follow conventional dictionary procedure as far as it goes, but should go further in that the reconstruction should provide *all* the information necessary to determine selection and exclusion. Where the conventional dictionary, by using such devices as "of ...," tells us what a word means in certain combinations, our reconstruction must do this systematically and also provide a basis for determining what combinations are semantically acceptable and what are not.

For our reconstruction, we shall use left and right angles enclosing a Boolean function of syntactic or semantic markers. Such configurations of symbols will be affixed to the terminal element of a path (either the distinguisher or the last semantic marker if there is no distinguisher) and will be construed, relative to the projection rules, as providing a necessary and sufficient condition for a semantically acceptable combination. Thus, for example, the angle-material terminally affixed to the path of a modifier determines the applicability of *that* path of the modifier to a sense of a nominal head. In particular, a path in the dictionary entry for *honest* will be: *honest* → (*Adjective*) → (*Evaluative*) → (*Moral*) → [*innocent of illicit sexual intercourse*] [(*Human*) and (*Female*)]. This is to be construed as saying that an adjectival occurrence of *honest* receives the interpretation, (*Evaluative*) → (*Moral*) → [*innocent of illicit sexual intercourse*], just in case the head it modifies has a path containing both the semantic markers (*Human*) and (*Female*). How in actual practice a semantic theory utilizes angle-material to determine selection/exclusion relations to obtain semantic interpretations of sentences can only be made clear by the statement of the projection rules.

This concludes the characterization of our normal form for dictionary entries. A dictionary is, then, a list (ordered or not) of the lexical items of the language, each item being associated with an entry in our normal form. The question of whether the lexical items are to be words, morphemes, or some other unit, we do not attempt to decide here. However, certain considerations are relevant to this decision. The most important consideration is that we choose the unit that will enable us to describe the largest amount of the compositional structure of the language. As a rule, the meaning of a word is a compositional function of the meanings of its parts, and we would like to be able to capture this compositionality. An approach which directs us to choose as lexical items those syntactic units in terms of which we can reconstruct a maximum of compositional structure has, moreover, simplicity in its favor. Wherever we can use composition, dictionary entries are avoided. Thus, instead of having an entry for each verb which takes the prefix *de* and a separate entry for *de* plus that verb, we must choose our lexical units so that the dictionary need only contain an entry for *de* and an entry for the unprefixed form of each verb. This economy can be achieved because *de* + verb combinations are compositional wherever the verb is semantically marked as (*Process*) → (*Reversible Process*).

It will be noticed that the dictionary is so formulated that all semantic properties and relations which are represented in entries are *formally* represented. This is required so that, given a formal statement of the projection rules (i.e., the application of the rules being defined solely in terms of the shapes of the symbols to which they apply and the operations the rules effect in producing their output being mechanical), the question of what semantic interpretation is assigned to a given sentence can be answered by formal computations without the aid of linguistic intuitions or insights. The need to have a formal semantic theory derives from the necessity of avoiding vacuity; for a semantic theory is vacuous to the extent that the speaker's intuitions or insights about semantic relations are essentially relied on in order that the rules of the theory apply correctly. Thus, it is uninformative to be told that an English sentence exhibits a semantic relation *R* just in case it satisfies the condition *C* if the condition *C* is so formulated that we cannot know *C* to be satisfied without essentially relying on a speaker's intuitive knowledge of semantic relations such as

R. A formal theory is *ipso facto* not vacuous in this respect since no knowledge about semantic relations in any language is required to determine the correct application of its rules.[18]

Now we turn to the question of how the adequacy of dictionary entries can be evaluated. It is often assumed that a semantic theory must yield a feasible mechanical procedure which enables the linguist to actually construct a dictionary from information about the verbal behavior of speakers. Every proposal for such a procedure has, however, proven egregiously unsuccessful, and we believe this to be in the nature of the case. Likewise, we think that those theorists who have insisted upon a mechanical procedure for deciding whether or not a putative dictionary entry is optimal have set their aims too high; we regard the practical impossibility of such a decision procedure as also in the nature of the case. We shall not argue directly for these claims. We make them primarily to warn the reader against construing the conception of a semantic theory proposed in this paper as either a mechanical discovery procedure or a mechanical decision procedure for dictionary entries.

However, this paper can be understood as proposing a conception of semantic theory which, *inter alia*, provides a procedure for determining which of two proposed dictionary entries is the best for a given language, but this evaluation procedure differs considerably from that usually envisioned by semantic theorists. On our conception, a dictionary is only one component of a semantic theory which has as its other component a set of projection rules for semantically interpreting sentences on the basis of the dictionary. Only the theory as a whole can be subjected to empirical test. This means that if a semantic theory gives incorrect interpretations for sentences, one must then decide whether to revise some dictionary entries, some projection rules, or some of each. Thus, questions of evaluation are to be raised primarily about entire semantic theories. Nonetheless, there is a derivative sense in which such questions can be raised about particular dictionary entries, viz., given projection rules and other dictionary entries that are sufficiently well established, which of the two candidate entries yields the best interpretations for sentences? This conception of evaluating dictionary entries differs from the usual one in that it makes such evaluations a matter of the degree to which the entry helps achieve the purpose of a dictionary within a theory of semantic interpretation. Semantic theorists usually conceive of such evaluation as effected by criteria which select the

---

[18]However, in order to utilize a semantic theory to enable a nonspeaker to understand sentences in the language it describes, the nonspeaker must understand the theory in the full sense in which this includes understanding the intended interpretation of the constructs of the theory and of their theoretical relations. But it is not necessary to understand the theory in that sense in order to derive the semantic interpretations the theory provides for sentences. This is guaranteed by the requirement that the theory be formal. The situation may be illuminated by an analogy to machine translation. Suppose we have a formal translation function which takes each sentence in a *source* language into its image in a *target* language. Given such a function, we can automatically associate the sentences of the two languages, and we can do so without appeal to linguistic intuitions about either language. But in order to use the function to *understand* the sentences of the target language, one must understand their images in the home language. Precisely the same situation obtains in the case of a semantic theory: the theory automatically associates an interpretation with each sentence, but this enables us to understand a sentence only insofar as we understand the theory which provides the interpretation.

preferable of two entries *simply* on the basis of facts about the verbal behavior of speakers, thus overlooking the fact that it is the interpretation of sentences, not the construction of dictionaries, that is the objective of a semantic theory. Because they have overlooked this fact, their criteria for evaluating dictionary entries are invariably too weak in that these criteria fail to utilize systematic constraints on the semantic interpretation of sentences (matching the fluent speaker's ability to determine the number of readings of sentences, the content of the readings, and their paraphrase relations) in choosing a preferable dictionary entry.

The controls on a semantic theory of a natural language are, therefore, nothing more than the usual empirical and methodological constraints imposed upon any scientific theory: the requirement that a semantic theory match the fluent speaker's ability to interpret sentences is the particular form that the general methodological requirement that a scientific theory accord with the facts takes in the case of semantics. If certain consequences of a semantic theory conflict with the facts about the performance of fluent speakers, various revisions in the dictionary component, in the projection rule component, and in both must be tried out and compared to determine which solution best accommodates the available linguistic evidence.

THE PROJECTION RULE COMPONENT

We have seen that a grammar is a device which enumerates an infinite list of strings of morphemes, including every string that is a sentence and no string that is not, and assigns each sentence a structural description, i.e., grammatical markers specifying the elements out of which a string is constructed, their arrangement, and the syntactic relations holding between them. A sentence and its structural description provide the input to a semantic theory. A semantic theory has as its output a semantic interpretation of each sentence given it as input. We may picture the situation as in Fig. 6.

Fig. 6 shows the input to a semantic theory to be a sentence S together with a structural description consisting of the n-derivations of S, $d_1, d_2, \ldots, d_n$, one for each of the n-ways that S is grammatically ambiguous. The output of the semantic theory is shown as k_1 readings for d_1, k_2 readings for d_2, \ldots, k_m readings for d_n, each reading corresponding to a term of a semantic (nongrammatical) ambiguity of S on some derivation. The schema $\rho_i(d_j)$ represents the ith reading of d_j (which the semantic theory supplies).

We can now characterize the notion *semantic interpretation of the sentence S* as the conjunction ψd_1 & ψd_2 & \ldots & ψd_n of the semantic interpretations of the n-derivations of S plus any statements about S that follow from conventions (1) to (8). The semantic interpretation of S *on the derivation d_j* is the output of the dictionary and projection rule components for S on d_j together with the statements about S on d_j that can be made on the basis of the conventions:

(1) If $k_1 + k_2 + \cdots + k_m = 1$, then S is unambiguous.
(2) If $k_1 + k_2 + \cdots + k_m > 1$, then S is $k_1 + k_2 + \cdots + k_m$ ways ambiguous.
(3) If $k_1 + k_2 + \cdots + k_m = 0$, then S is anomalous.
(4) If the set of readings assigned to the derivation d_j, $\rho_1(d_j)$, $\rho_2(d_j)$, \ldots, $\rho_{k_j}(d_j)$, has exactly one member, then S is unambiguous on d_j.

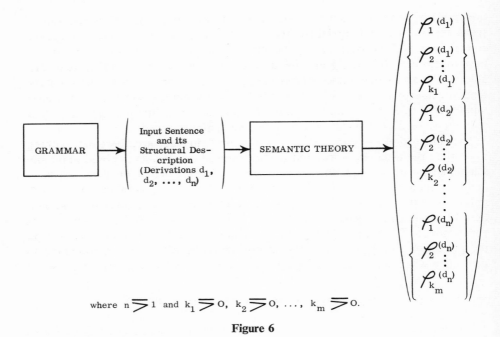

where $n \gtrless 1$ and $k_1 \gtrless 0$, $k_2 \gtrless 0$, ..., $k_m \gtrless 0$.

Figure 6

(5) If the set of readings assigned to the derivation d_j has more than one member, then S is k_i ways semantically ambiguous on d_j.

(6) If the set of readings assigned to d_j is null, then S is semantically anomalous on d_j.

(7) If S and another sentence P have at least one reading in common, then S and P are paraphrases on that reading.

(8) If S and P have all readings in common, then S and P are full paraphrases.

We can schematize the relation between the dictionary component and the projection rule component:

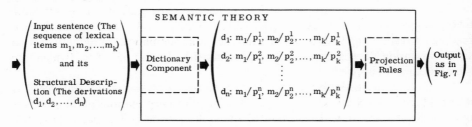

Figure 7

The input to the dictionary component consists of a sentence S represented by a sequence of lexical items, $m_1, m_2, \ldots, m_k$, and the set of derivations of S. The symbol, P_j^i, stands for a finite, non-null set of paths drawn from the dictionary entry for the lexical item m_j in S and such that any path in the dictionary entry for m_j is in the set just in case the path contains grammatical markers which assign m_j the syntactic role it has on the derivation d_i. The symbol, /, represents the association between a lexical item and a subset of the set of paths in its dictionary entry. The association is effected by the instruction (I) which, together with the dictionary, comprises the dictionary component:

(I) For each pair d_i and m_j, the path p in the entry for m_j is assigned to the set P_j^i if, and only if, p has as its initial subpath the sequence of grammatical markers $g_1, g_2, \ldots, g_r$ and the derivation d_i contains the path $g_1 \rightarrow g_2 \rightarrow \cdots \rightarrow g_r \rightarrow m_j$.

The instruction (I) chooses as relevant to the semantic interpretation of a sentence on a given derivation only those paths from the dictionary entries for each of the lexical items in the sentence which are compatible with the lower-level syntactic structure of the sentence on that derivation. The output of the dictionary component is thus a mapping of a finite, non-null set of paths onto each m_j for each d_i. This output, as Fig. 7 shows, is, in turn, the input to the projection rules.

We can now give a general picture of the operations whereby the projection rule component converts its input into a semantic interpretation. Each sentence the grammar makes available for semantic interpretation has associated with it n-derivations marking the n-ways in which it is structurally ambiguous. Each derivation marks constituent structure in a way that can be represented by a tree diagram. We shall employ such tree diagrams in the following pages, *but it is to be understood that projection rules can take account of information about the transformational history of a sentence which is not represented in a tree diagram.*

Figure 8 gives the derived constituent structure of the sentence "the man hits the

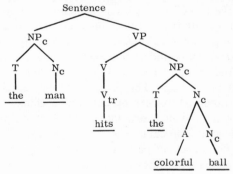

Figure 8

colorful ball."[19] The dictionary component associates sets of paths with such a tree

---

[19]It can be argued on grammatical grounds that the phrase *the colorful ball* should be represented simply as:

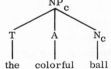

i.e., without the internal syntactic structure it is given in Fig. 8. This representation would not include the information (which will be required by the projection rules) that *colorful* is a modifier of the head *ball*. But the need for this sort of information does not commit us to the assumption that all branching in derived constituent structure trees is binary. For such information can be obtained by examining the transformational history of the sentence. This is a typical case of the way a projection rule can utilize information taken from the transformational history of the sentences to which it is applied.

in the manner specified by instruction (I). Thus, after the application of instruction (I), we have:

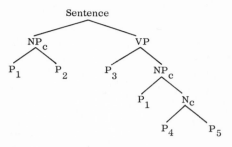

Figure 9

The marking of the lexical items *the, man, hits, the, colorful,* and *ball* as, respectively, Article, Noun concrete, Verb transitive, Article, Adjective, and Noun concrete, which at first glance may seem to have been lost in the application of instruction (I), is actually represented as the common initial subpath of every p in each P_j^i, e.g., P_3 is the set of paths all of whose members begin $hits \rightarrow V \rightarrow V_{tr}$.

The general way in which the projection rule component works is by proceeding from the bottom to the top of a constituent structure tree and effecting a series of amalgamations, starting with the output of instruction (I) and amalgamating sets of paths dominated by a grammatical marker, thus assigning a set of readings to the concatenation of lexical items under that marker by associating the result of the amalgamation with the marker until the highest marker *Sentence* is reached and associated with a set of readings. The projection rules amalgamate sets of paths dominated by a grammatical marker by combining elements from each of them to form a new set of paths which provides a set of readings for the sequence of lexical items under the grammatical marker. Amalgamation is an operation of joining elements from different sets of paths under a given grammatical marker just in case these elements satisfy the appropriate selection restrictions represented by material in angles.

Let us now give an example of how a semantic theory of English might interpret a sentence and, in this way, exhibit some of the projection rules for English.[20] As our example, we choose the sentence "the man hits the colorful ball" under the derivation given in Fig. 8.

The projection rule component receives this sentence and its derivation as input after instruction (I) has operated. (See Fig. 9.) The first step for the projection rule component is to amalgamate each set of paths under each of the grammatical markers which immediately dominates *only* sets of paths and to associate with the dominating marker the amalgam so obtained. Thus, in the case of Fig. 9, the first step is to amalgamate either P_4 and P_5 or P_1 and P_2, the order being immaterial.

---

[20]It should be made perfectly clear that the rules we shall give are not intended as contribution to a semantic theory of English but only as examples of the type of rules such a theory would employ.

Let us first take the amalgamation of P_4 and P_5. The paths comprising the set P_4 are:

$$P_4$$

(1) *Colorful* → Adjective → (*Color*) → [*Abounding in contrast or variety of bright colors*] ⟨(*Physical Object*) v (*Social Activity*)⟩

(2) *Colorful* → Adjective → (*Evaluative*) → [*Having distinctive character, vividness, or picturesqueness*] ⟨(*Aesthetic Object*) v (*Social Activity*)⟩

The paths comprising the set P_5 are:

$$P_5$$

(1) *Ball* → Noun concrete → (*Social Activity*) → (*Large*) → (*Assembly*) → [*For the purpose of social dancing*]

(2) *Ball* → Noun concrete → (*Physical Object*) → [*Having globular shape*]

(3) *Ball* → Noun concrete → (*Physical Oject*) → [*Solid missile for projection by engine of war*]

$P_4 1$ is the sense of *colorful* in "The gift came in a colorful wrapper"; $P_4 2$ is the sense of *colorful* in "No novel is less colorful than Middlemarch, excepting Silas Marner"; $P_5 1$ is the sense of *ball* in "The queen danced at the French ambassador's ball"; $P_5 2$ is the sense of *ball* in "Tennis is played with a ball"; $P_5 3$ is the sense of *ball* in "The balls whistle free o'er the bright blue sea." It will be noticed that the sense of *ball* in "He plays ball better than Babe Ruth" is not represented by a path in P_5, although such a path is to be found in the dictionary entry for *ball*. This is because *ball*, when it means the game, is not a concrete noun and so instruction (I) eliminates the path which represents that sense.

The amalgamation of P_4 and P_5 is accomplished by the following projection rule:

(R_1)   Given two paths of the form

(1)   Lexical String$_1$ → syntactic markers of head → (a_1) → (a_2) → $\cdots$ → (a_n) → [1] ⟨set of strings of markers Ω_1⟩

(2)   Lexical String$_2$ → syntactic markers of modifier → (b_1) → (b_2) → $\cdots$ → (b_m) → [2] ⟨set of strings of markers Ω_2⟩

such that there is a substring σ of the string of syntactic or semantic head markers and $\sigma \in \Omega_2$. There is an amalgam of the form

Lexical String$_2$ + Lexical String$_1$ → dominating node marker → (a_1) → (a_2) → $\cdots$ → (a_n) → (b_1) → (b_2) → $\cdots$ → (b_m) → [[2] [1]] ⟨Ω_1⟩,

where any b_i is null when $(\exists a_i) (b_i = a_i)$ and [[2] [1]] is [1] when [2] = [1].[21]

The amalgam of P_4 and P_5 is the set of derived paths P_6:

$$P_6$$

(1) *Colorful* + *ball* → Noun concrete → (*Social Activity*) → (*Large*) → (*Assembly*) → (*Color*) → [[*Abounding in contrast or variety of bright colors*] [*For the purpose of social dancing*]]

(2) *Colorful* + *ball* → Noun concrete → (*Physical Object*) → (*Color*) → [[*Abounding in contrast or variety of bright colors*] [*Having globular shape*]]

---

[21]The reason why Ω_1 appears in the output of (R_1) is that some heads are, in turn, modifiers of other heads (e.g., adjectives are heads for adverbs and also modifiers for nouns in such cases as (*light* [*red*] *ball*). In these cases, the conditions in Ω_1 will be required for selection.

(3)   *Colorful + ball* → Noun concrete → (*Physical Object*) → (*Color*) → [[*Abounding in contrast or variety of bright colors*] [*Solid missile for projection by engine of war*]]

(4)   *Colorful + Ball* → Noun concrete → (*Social Activity*) → (*Large*) → (*Assembly*) → (*Evaluative*) → [[*Having distinctive character, vividness, or picturesqueness*] [*For the purpose of social dancing*]]

There were six possible amalgamations from the combination of P_4 and P_5, but only four derived paths because, of the possible combinations of $P_4 2$ with elements of P_5, only the combination $P_4 2$ and $P_5 1$ satisfies the selection restriction ⟨(*Aesthetic Object* v (*Social Activity*))⟩. Thus, (R_1) predicts the semantic anomaly of *colorful + ball* on the reading where *colorful* has the sense represented by $P_4 2$ and *ball* has either the sense represented by $P_5 2$ or the sense represented by $P_5 3$. Another example of how (R_1) contributes to the formalization of the distinction between what is semantically acceptable and what is semantically anomalous is the following: The expression *spinster insecticide* would be regarded as anomalous by speakers of English, and this can be predicted on the basis of (R_1) and the dictionary entries for *spinster* and *insecticide*. The relevant path for *spinster* is: *spinster* → Adjective → (*Human*) → (*Adult*) → (*Female*) → [*Who has never married*] ⟨(*Human*)⟩. On the basis of these paths, (R_1) assigns no reading to the expression *spinster insecticide*, (i.e. (R_1) predicts that *spinster insecticide* is semantically anomalous) because the path for *insecticide* does not contain the semantic marker (*Human*) which is necessary to satisfy the selection restriction associated with *spinster*.

The projection rule (R_1) introduces the semantic markers in the path of the modifier just below the string of semantic markers in the path of the head, eliminating from the path of the modifier semantic material already present in the path of the head and associating the distinguishers with one another. The operation of (R_1) corresponds closely to our intuitive notions of the nature of attribution. Attribution is the process of creating a new semantic unit compounded from a modifier and a head, whose semantic properties are those of the head, *except that the meaning of the compound is made more determinate than that of the head by the information the compound obtains from the modifier.* As Lees comments:

> We cannot get along with a single common noun to refer to a familiar common object, but must have at every moment modifiers with which to construct new more complex names to use for all the specific instances of that object which we encounter and talk about. Thus, we cannot, without extensive ambiguity, refer on every occasion to our favorite beverage by means of the single word *coffee*; instead we name its individual instances with such phrases as "my coffee," "that cold cup of coffee you left there," "some fresh coffee on the shelf," " a new brand of coffee," "pretty tasteless coffee," "Turkish coffee," and so on. There is no known limitation on the number of distinct objects for which we must at some time or other have distinctive names, and clearly no dictionary is large enough to contain them all, for a great many of the names which we employ have never before been uttered. Like full sentences themselves, there is no longest name, and there must consequently be an infinity of new names available for us to use when and if the need arises.[22]

---

[22]R. B. Lees, "The Grammar of English Nominalizations," *International Journal of American Liguistics*, **26**, No. 3 (July 1960), xvii-iii.

Although Lees is commenting on the grammar of nominal compounds, what he says applies equally well to their semantics and to the semantics of other modifier-head constructions. It is only because there is a systematic way of understanding the meaning of such constructions in terms of the meanings of their parts that the infinite stock of strings produced by the grammatical mechanism for creating new modifier-head constructions can be employed by speakers to refer to familiar objects.

As we have just mentioned, the meaning of a compound is more determinate than the meaning of its head in respect of the information the compound obtains from its modifier(s). Let us consider an example. The word *aunt* is indeterminate as to age (i.e., neither the sentence "My aunt is an infant" nor "My aunt is aged" has any special semantic properties), but *spinster*, as we have observed above, contains the semantic marker (*Adult*) in its path. This marker is carried over to the compound when (R_1) operates to produce an interpretation for *spinster aunt*. Thus, *spinster aunt* is made more determinate (with respect to age) than is *aunt*. This shows up in a comparison between the sentences "My spinster aunt is an infant" and "My spinster aunt is aged," the former of which is contradictory while the latter is not.

The limiting case, where the addition to the compound of semantic material from the modifier is zero, is of considerable theoretical significance. The compound *unmarried bachelor* is a case in point. The erasure clause in (R_1), i.e., "any b_i is null when $(\exists a_i)$ $(b_i = a_i)$ and $[[2][1]]$ is $[1]$ when $[2] = [1]$," tells us to delete from the path of the modifier any semantic material already represented in the path of the head. Thus, in forming the compound *unmarried bachelor* all the semantic information in the path of the modifier *unmarried* will be deleted so that the derived path for *unmarried bachelor* will contain no more than the semantic material which comes from the path for *bachelor*. The failure of the modifier to add semantic information would appear to account for the intuition that such expressions as *unmarried bachelor* are redundant and that, correspondingly, such statements as "Bachelors are unmarried" are *empty, tautological, vacuous, uninformative*. Thus, we have a new explanation of the analyticity of a classical type of analytic truth.[23] Moreover, this feature of the projection rules provides another empirical constraint on a semantic theory: if the theory characterizes an expression or sentence as redundant in the above sense, then the theory is confirmed if speakers take the expression or sentence in the appropriate way and is disconfirmed if they do not.

The next step in the semantic interpretation of "The man hits the colorful ball" is the amalgamation of P_1 and P_2. The entry for *the* in standard dictionaries is exceedingly complex primarily because the information required to make the correct selections among the various senses of *the* for its sentential occurrences is extremely complicated. Thus, we shall have to simplify and not try to represent all the information actually needed in the dictionary entry for *the*.

P_1 contains only the path: *the* → Noun phrase concrete → Definite Article → [*Some contextually definite*]. Other paths in the dictionary entry for *the*, viz., those corresponding to the generic senses of the definite article, are not assigned to P_1 by instruction (I) because only the above path contains the sequence of grammatical

---

[23]Cf. J. J. Katz, "Analyticity and Contradiction in Natural Language" in the present volume.

markers as its initial subpath which dominates *the* in the derivation in Fig. 8.[24]
P_2 contains only the path: *man* → Noun concrete → Noun masculine → (*Physical Object*) → (*Human*) → (*Adult*) → (*Male*). Other paths in the dictionary entry for *man*, viz., the path corresponding to the sense of *man* in "Man is occasionally rational" and the path corresponding to the sense of *man* in "Every man on board ship was saved except an elderly couple," do not appear in P_2, the former because in that sense *man* is not a concrete noun and the latter because in that sense *man* is not a masculine noun. The rule which amalgamates P_1 and P_2 is:

(R_2)   Given two paths of the form

(1) Lexical String₁ → syntactic markers of noun → semantic markers of head → [1]

(2) Lexical String₂ → syntactic markers of article → semantic markers of article → [2] ⟨set of strings of markers Ω⟩

such that there is a substring σ of the string of syntactic or semantic nominal markers and $\sigma \in \Omega$. There is an amalgam of the form

Lexical String₂ + Lexical String₁ → dominating node marker → semantic markers of article → [2] → semantic markers of noun → [1].

The application of (R_2) to P_1 and P_2 produces the derived path: *the* + *man* → Noun phrase concrete → [*Some contextually definite*] → (*Physical Object*) → (*Human*) → (*Adult*) → (*Male*). This path is the only member of the set P_7 shown in Fig. 10.

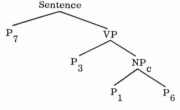

Figure 10

The amalgamation of P_1 and P_6 works in exactly the same way and yields P_8:

$$P_8$$

(1)   *The* + *colorful* + *ball* → Noun phrase concrete → [*Some contextually definite*] → (*Social Activity*) → (*Large*) → (*Assembly*) → (*Color*) → [[*Abounding in contrast or variety of bright colors*] [*For the purpose of social dancing*]]

(2)   *The* + *colorful* + *ball* → Noun phrase concrete → [*Some contextually definite*] → (*Physical Object*) → (*Color*) → [[*Abounding in contrast or variety of bright colors*] [*Having globular shape*]]

(3)   *The* + *colorful* + *ball* → Noun phrase concrete → [*Some contextually definite*] → (*Physical Object*) → (*Color*) → [[*Abounding in contrast or variety of bright colors*] [*Solid missile for projection by engine of war*]]

---

[24]In taking NP_c as part of the sequence of grammatical markers in the dictionary entry for *the*, we are not claiming that *the* is a concrete noun phrase, but only that it occurs as an element of a concrete noun phrase and that, when it does, it has the sense in P_1. This constitutes an extension of the notion of a "part of speech classification," but a natural and necessary one.

(4) *The + colorful + ball* → Noun phrase concrete → [*Some contextually definite*] → (*Social activity*) → (*Large*) → (*Assembly*) → (*Evaluative*) → [[*Having distinctive character, vividness, or picturesqueness*] [*For the purpose of social dancing*]]

This leaves us with only the part of the constituent structure tree shown in Fig. 11 still to be interpreted.

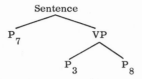

Figure 11

P_3 is as follows:

$$P_3$$

(1) *hits* → Verb → Verb transitive → (*Action*) → (*Instancy*) → (*Intensity*) → [*Collides with an impact*] ⟨SUBJECT: (*Higher Animal*) v (*Improper Part*) v (*Physical Object*), OBJECT: (*Physical Object*)⟩[25]

(2) *hits* → Verb → Verb transitive → (*Action*) → (*Instancy*) → (*Intensity*) → [*Strikes with a blow or missile*] ⟨SUBJECT: (*Human*) v (*Higher Animal*), OBJECT: (*Physical Object*), INSTRUMENTAL: (*Physical Object*)⟩

$P_3 1$ is the sense of *hits* in "The rock hits the ground with a thud." $P_3 2$ is the sense of *hits* in "The man hits the ground with a rock." It will be noticed that the representation of verbs includes between angles selection restrictions upon the subject and objects of the verb. This information is represented by markers of the form "SUBJECT: α," "OBJECT: β," and "INSTRUMENTAL: γ," where α, β, and γ, respectively, represent conditions on the paths associated with the subject, object and instrumental.

A few comments on this dictionary entry for *hits* as a transitive verb are necessary. We claim no more than rough accuracy for the above characterization. Our interest here, as throughout the present paper, is with prescribing the abstract form of a semantic theory rather than with actually writing one. Thus, the above characterization is intended primarily to illustrate how the results of a linguistic analysis are to be formally presented in order that the projection rules can utilize them. But we have tried to make our examples account for the fundamental semantic features. In the present case, the failure to mark an achievement sense of *hits* is not an oversight. We choose not to mark a special sense of *hits* in which it is an achievement verb because the behavior of *hits* diverges in significant ways from that of such paradigmatic achievement verbs as *sees* and *hears*. Thus, unlike "He hit the ball intentionally," "He saw the picture intentionally" is anomalous (except where it

---

[25]Here some explanation is called for. *Instancy* is assigned to those verbs representing durationless events. Any sentence whose main verb is marked *Instancy* which is of the form "*Subject + Verb + ed + Object + for + numerical quantifier + measure of time*" will be understood to mean that the object was verbed more than once. Compare "He hit the ball for three hours" with "He studied the book for three hours." Next, *Intensity* is assigned to those verbs taking such adverbs as *hard*, *soft*, *gently*. Finally, the marker *Improper Part* is assigned to lexical items that represent wholes which the language contrasts with their parts.

means that he went to see the picture intentionally), and "He heard the music intentionally" is anomalous (except where it means that he didn't *just* overhear the music). This is perhaps related to the fact that one can intentionally miss the ball, although one cannot in the relevant sense intentionally fail to hear the music. If, however, it should turn out that *hits* must be given a special, achievement sense, such a sense can be represented within the formalism of the present paper in a straightforward manner.

The projection rule which amalgamates P_3 and P_8 is:

(R_3)   Given two paths of the form

(1) Lexical String$_1$ → syntactic markers of main verb → semantic markers → [1] ⟨sets of strings of markers α, β⟩

(2) Lexical String$_2$ → syntactic markers of object of main verb → Remainder of object path

such that there is a substring σ of the string of syntactic or semantic markers of the object and $\sigma \in \beta$. There is an amalgam of the form

Lexical String$_1$ + Lexical String$_2$ → dominating node marker → semantic markers of main verb → [1] → String analyzed *Remainder of object path* ⟨set of strings of markers α⟩

The application of (R_3) to P_3 and P_8 yields P_9.

Figure 12

P_9 contains the following paths:

P_9

(1) *hits + the + colorful + ball* → *VP* → *(Action)* → *(Instancy)* → *(Intensity)* → *[Collides with an impact]* → *[Some contextually definite]* → *(Physical Object)* → *(Color)* → *[[Abounding in contrast or variety of bright colors] [Having globular shape]]* ⟨SUBJECT: *(Higher Animal)* v *(Improper Part)* v *(Physical Object)*⟩

(2) *hits + the + colorful + ball* → *VP* → *(Action)* → *(Instancy)* → *(Intensity)* → *[Collides with an impact]* → *[Some contextually definite]* → *(Physical Object)* → *(Color)* → *[[Abounding in contrast or variety of bright colors] [Solid missile for projection by engine of war]]* ⟨SUBJECT: *(Higher Animal)* v *(Improper Part)* v *(Physical Object)*⟩

(3) *hits + the + colorful + ball* → *VP* → *(Action)* → *(Instancy)* → *(Intensity)* → *[Strikes with a blow or missile]* → *[Some contextually definite]* → *(Physical Object)* → *(Color)* → *[[Abounding in contrast or variety of bright colors] [Having globular shape]]* ⟨SUBJECT: *(Human)* v *(Higher Animal)*⟩

(4) *hits + the + colorful + ball* → *VP* → *(Action)* → *(Instancy)* → *(Intensity)* → *[Strikes with a blow or missile]* → *[Some contextually definite]* → *(Physical Object)* → *(Color)* → *[[Abounding in contrast or variety of bright colors] [Solid missile for projection by engine of war]* ⟨SUBJECT: *(Human)* v *(Higher Animal)*⟩

Finally, the projection rule which operates on P_7 and P_9 to assign a set of readings to *Sentence* is:

(R_4)   Given two paths of the form

   (1)   Lexical String$_1$ $\rightarrow$ syntactic markers of verb phrase $\rightarrow$ Remainder of verb phrase path

   (2)   Lexical String$_2$ $\rightarrow$ syntactic markers of subject $\rightarrow$ Remainder of subject path

such that there is a substring σ of the string of syntactic or semantic markers of the subject and $\sigma \in \alpha$. There is an amalgam of the form

Lexical String$_2$ + Lexical String$_1$ $\rightarrow$ dominating node marker $\rightarrow$ String analyzed *Remainder of subject path* $\rightarrow$ String analyzed *Remainder of verb phrase path* deleting substring $\langle \alpha \rangle$

The application of (R_4) to P_7 and P_9 yields the set P_{10}:

$$P_{10}$$

(1)   *The + man + hits + the + colorful + ball $\rightarrow$ Sentence $\rightarrow$ [Some contextually definite] $\rightarrow$ (Physical Object) $\rightarrow$ (Human) $\rightarrow$ (Adult) $\rightarrow$ (Male) $\rightarrow$ (Action) $\rightarrow$ (Instancy) $\rightarrow$ (Intensity) $\rightarrow$ [Collides with an impact] $\rightarrow$ [Some contextually definite] $\rightarrow$ (Physical Object) $\rightarrow$ (Color) $\rightarrow$ [[Abounding in contrast or variety of bright colors] [Having globular shape]]*

(2)   *The + man + hits + the + colorful + ball $\rightarrow$ Sentence $\rightarrow$ [Some contextually definite] $\rightarrow$ (Physical Object) $\rightarrow$ (Human) $\rightarrow$ (Adult) $\rightarrow$ (Male) $\rightarrow$ (Action) $\rightarrow$ (Instancy) $\rightarrow$ (Intensity) $\rightarrow$ [Collides with an impact] $\rightarrow$ [Some contextually definite] $\rightarrow$ (Physical Object) $\rightarrow$ (Color) $\rightarrow$ [[Abounding in contrast or variety of bright colors] [Solid missile for projection by engine of war]]*

(3)   *The + man + hits + the + colorful + ball $\rightarrow$ Sentence $\rightarrow$ [Some contextually definite] $\rightarrow$ (Physical Object) $\rightarrow$ (Human) $\rightarrow$ (Adult) $\rightarrow$ (Male) $\rightarrow$ (Action) $\rightarrow$ (Instancy) $\rightarrow$ (Intensity) $\rightarrow$ [Strikes with a blow or missile] $\rightarrow$ [Some contextually definite] $\rightarrow$ (Physical Object) $\rightarrow$ (Color) $\rightarrow$ [[Abounding in contrast or variety of bright colors] [Having globular shape]]*

(4)   *The + man + hits + the + colorful + ball $\rightarrow$ Sentence $\rightarrow$ [Some contextually definite] $\rightarrow$ (Physical Object) $\rightarrow$ (Human) $\rightarrow$ (Adult) $\rightarrow$ (Male) $\rightarrow$ (Action) $\rightarrow$ (Instancy) $\rightarrow$ (Intensity) $\rightarrow$ [Strikes with a blow or missile] $\rightarrow$ [Some contextually definite] $\rightarrow$ (Physical Object) $\rightarrow$ (Color) $\rightarrow$ [[Abounding in contrast or variety of bright colors] [Solid missile for projection by engine of war]]*

Therefore, a semantic theory of English containing rules and entries as given above characterizes the sentence "The man hits the colorful ball" as having the following semantic interpretation: the sentence is not semantically anomalous; it is four ways semantically ambiguous on the derivation in Fig. 8; each term corresponds to a reading in P_{10}; it is a paraphrase of any sentence which has one of the readings in P_{10}; and it is a full paraphrase of any sentence that has the set of readings P_{10} assigned to it. The semantic theory interprets the constituent structure tree in Fig. 8 in the way shown in Fig. 13, thus displaying which of the possible combinations of paths at a given node yielded derived paths for that node and which possible combinations were blocked. (See Figure 13.)

This completes our example of how a semantic theory of English might interpret a sentence generated by the grammar. Before we conclude our discussion of projection rules, we must consider the question of whether the projection rule component will contain types of projection rules different from the type employed above.

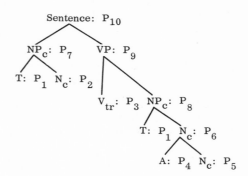

Figure 13

What is characteristic of rules (R_1) to (R_4) is that each rule operates on a part of a partially semantically interpreted constituent structure characterization, amalgamates paths from two sets of paths that are dominated by a particular node, and assigns to that node the set of amalgams as readings for the lexical string that the node dominates. Let us call such rules "type 1 projection rules." These rules must assign semantic interpretations to some of the sentences generated by the grammar, but they need not be the means by which EVERY sentence receives a semantic interpretation. We can conceive of another type of projection rule ("type 2 projection rules") in the following way. We restrict the application of type 1 projection rules to some formally determined proper subset of the set of sentences. Then we introduce type 2 projection rules to provide a semantic interpretation for every sentence that does not receive a semantic interpretation on the basis of type 1 projection rules. Since those sentences that the grammar produces without the aid of optional transformations, i.e., the kernel sentences, will be semantically interpreted by type 1 projection rules, the type 2 projection rules will assign semantic interpretations to sentences that are constructed with the use of optional transformations. Suppose S has been constructed from a certain set of source sentences by the optional transformation T. A type 2 rule is a rule which operates on the semantic interpretations of these source sentences and on either the derived constituent structure characterization of S or on the transformation T in order to produce a semantic interpretation of S. Type 2 projection rules should assign semantic interpretations in such a way as to reconstruct the manner in which the meaning of a sentence that is constructed by such a transformation T is a function of the meanings of each of the sentences used by T in S's construction.

The basic theoretical question that remains open here is just what proper subset of the set of sentences is semantically interpreted using type 1 projection rules only. One striking fact about transformations is that a great many of them (perhaps all) produce sentences that are identical in meaning to the sentence(s) out of which the transform was built.[26] In such cases, the semantic interpretation of the transformationally constructed sentence must be identical to the semantic interpretation(s) of the source sentence(s) at least with respect to the readings assigned at the sentence level. For example, sentences that are related to each other by the passive transformation, e.g., "The man eats cake" and "Cake is eaten by the man," have the same meaning, except perhaps in instances where quantifiers are involved.[27] For another example, sentence conjunctions, e.g., "The man ate the cake and candy" which comes from "The man ate the cake" and "The man ate the candy." Or, again, stylistic variants such as "There is something about it that puzzles me," "There is about it something that puzzles me," and "There is something that puzzles me about it." It would be theoretically most satisfying if we could take the position that transformations never change meaning. But such a generalization runs up against such cases as the question transformation, the imperative transformation, the negation transformation, and others. Such troublesome cases might be troublesome only because of an inadequacy in the way we are now formulating these transformations or these cases might represent a real departure from the otherwise uniform generalization that meaning is invariant under grammatical transformations. Until we can determine whether any transformations change meaning, and if some do, which do and which do not, we shall not know what sentences should be semantically interpreted with type 2 projection rules and how to formulate such rules.

Nevertheless, we can decide the cases that are clear. The set of sentences that will be semantically interpreted using type 1 projection rules include the sentences produced without the aid of optical transformations. Suppose we permit NO type 2 projection rule for any transformation that we know preserves meaning, and instead we introduce the convention that any sentences related by such a transformation *T* belongs to an equivalence class, all of whose members receive the same semantic interpretation. Then the facts that there will always be a kernel sentence in such an equivalence class and that every kernel sentence has a semantic interpretation on the basis of type 1 projection rules means that every nonkernel sentence in such an equivalence class automatically receives the semantic interpretation of its kernel co-member, which makes them all paraphrases as desired.

This treatment is by far the best method of marking paraphrase relations (and other semantic properties) among stylistic variants which result from the operation of a permutation transformation. This method avoids having a special type 2 rule in each such case: such special type 2 rules have no function except to state the empty fact that these transformations do not affect meaning. This method also avoids the use of type 1 rules on a sentence that is produced by a permutation transformation. This is very highly desirable because, since such transformations produce sentences with derived constituent structure characterizations having far less labeled bracketing than is found in the constituent structure characterization

---

[26]For the background of this point, cf. J. A. Fodor, "Projection and Paraphrase in Semantics," *Analysis*, **21.4** (March 1961), 73–77; and J. J. Katz, "A Reply to 'Projection and Paraphrase in Semantics,' " *Analysis*, **22.2** (Dec. 1961), 36–41.

[27]In these instances, too—if it is true that both active and passive have the same meaning because both are ambiguous.

of the source sentence, it is generally the case that what labeled bracketing survives is too little to permit type 1 rules to be able to semantically interpret the derived sentence.

This treatment has the same merits in the cases of transformations that permute in such a way as to produce discontinuous elements in the transform and also in the cases of transformations that delete material. Thus, with this treatment we can most simply account for the paraphrase relations between (and other semantic properties of) such pairs as: "John looked up the rule" and "John looked the rule up"; and "Harry plays chess as well as Bill plays chess" and "Harry plays chess as well as Bill."

The possibility of type 2 projection rules presents two options for the construction of the projection rule component of a semantic theory. Either the projection rule component will consist of type 1 rules alone, or it will contain both type 1 and type 2 rules. The question whether type 2 rules will be required, and if so, to what extent, is a question to which no answer is possible here. Many considerations enter into answering it, including both methodological considerations such as conceptual economy, descriptive and explanatory power, and so on, and particular considerations concerning the structure of individual languages such as the degree to which transformational relations between sentences are independent of semantic relations between them.[28]

METATHEORY

In the present section, we shall discuss the theoretical perspective from which we have been treating the problem of characterizing the abstract form of a semantic theory. That is, we shall discuss the nature of semantic metatheory. We shall also consider some of the consequence of adopting an explicit metatheory in semantics.

There are two motivations for constructing an explicit metatheory for an area in linguistics, and thus for constructing an explicit metatheory for semantics.[29] First, the same scientific curiosity which makes us inquire into the semantic structure of individual languages *a fortiori* makes us interested in what is common in the semantic structure of families of language or of all languages. Thus, a metatheory for semantics must be a theory which represents semantic universals. Second, there must be *well-established* criteria for choosing among different semantic theories for the same language, where each theory is, as far as we can tell, compatible with the available evidence from fluent native speakers. But if a set of such criteria is to be well established, it must itself be shown to give desirable results with a wide variety of different languages, i.e., it must consistently choose, from language to language, the best semantic theory. Thus, a semantic theory must provide criteria for evaluating individual semantic theories and establish the adequacy of such criteria. We can incorporate both these motivations if we construct a metatheory which contains an

---

[28]A more general and comprehensive discussion of this problem is to be found in J. J. Katz and P. Postal, *An Integrated Theory of Linguistic Descriptions*, M.I.T. Press, 1964.

[29]The conception of a metatheory for semantics is adapted from Chomsky's conception of a metatheory for grammar, which he refers to as "linguistic theory." Cf. Chomsky, *op. cit.*, and *The Logical Structure of Linguistic Theory*, microfilmed, M.I.T.

enumeration of the semantic markers from which the theoretical vocabulary of each particular semantic theory is drawn and a specification of the form of the rules for a semantic theory of a natural language. For the enumeration and the specification provide both a representation of semantic universals and a basis on which to evaluate particular semantic theories (e.g., we may adopt the rule that the preferable theory is the one which is rated highest by a metric which compares rules in the specified form and chooses the one requiring the smallest number of markers from the enumeration given in the metatheory).

The semantic markers which we have utilized in our discussions of dictionary entries and projection rules are, of course, only examples. But if we imagine them functioning in a putative semantic theory of English, then the claim for them would have to be that they are drawn from the enumeration of markers provided by the methatheory, just as the claim for the projection rules would have to be that they are each instances of a form specified by the metatheory. Thus, a semantic marker is simply a theoretical construct which receives its interpretation in the semantic metatheory and is on a par with such scientific constructs as atom, gene, valence, and noun phrase. A marker such as (*Human*) or (*Color*) is, then, not an English word, but a construct represented by one.

A metatheory for semantics must, further, exhibit the relations between semantics and other areas of linguistics. We have discussed the relation between grammatical and semantic rules at some length. We must now consider the relation between grammatical and semantic markers.

Much confusion has been generated in the study of language by the search for a line between grammar and semantics. This is because what has been sought when students of language have tried to draw such a line is a criterion to determine when a concept expressing something about the structure of a language is syntactical and when it is semantical. But the trouble has always been that every criterion proposed seems to be invalidated by examples of concepts which can, with apparently equal justice, be regarded as either syntactical or semantical. That is, there appears to be an overlap between the sets of syntactic and semantic markers. For example, such markers as *Male, Female, Human, Animal, Animate, Concrete, Abstract*, and so on, appear to fall in this overlap. But the confusion engendered in the search for a line between grammar and semantics is unwarranted because the overlap exists in name only.

This becomes clear once one ceases to search for a criterion to decide which markers are properly syntactic or semantic, and instead asks whether the line between grammatical and semantic markers can be drawn in terms of the theoretical functions they perform.[30] For example, in the grammar the distinction between abstract and concrete nouns is drawn in order to construct adequate rules for generating sentences containing nominalizations. According to Lees:

> . . .there are certain restrictions on subject/predicate-nominal combinations based on abstractness (as well as perhaps on other lower-order nominal categories). There is a small class of (abstract) nouns which may appear on copula sentences opposite both

---

[30]It is not at all clear even that the request for such a criterion is a reasonable one. Would one ask for an analogous criterion to distinguish the concepts of physics and the concepts of chemistry?

nominalizations and concrete nominals: "the problem is that he went there," "the problem is his going there," "the problem is his tonsils," and the like for such nouns N_a as *problem, trouble, thing, reason, cause, question*, and so on. Nominalizations occur opposite only these latter nouns, while concrete nominals N_e occur opposite either other concretes or one of these latter abstract nouns N_a: "that he came home is the trouble," but not "*that he came home is that she left," or again: "his stomach is the cause," "his stomach is an organ," but not: "*his stomach is his having gone there."[31]

The distinction between mass and count nouns is, analogously, drawn in order to handle the syntactic relations between nouns and their articles and quantifiers, e.g., the mass noun *blood* in the singular takes *the* and *some* but not numerical quantifiers: "The blood was found" but not "*One blood was found." Likewise, the distinction between animate nouns and inanimate nouns and between masculine nouns and feminine nouns has to do (among other things) with pronoun agreement. For example, "The girl gave her own dress away," but not "*The girl gave his own dress away" or "*The girl gave its own dress away."

On the other hand, semantic markers are introduced to specify something about the meaning of lexical items. Thus, where it appears that a marker is common to both grammar and semantics, what is in fact the case is that there are two distinct markers having the same or similar names. This is most clear from the fact that it is often *not* the case that a lexical item receiving a certain grammatical marker also receives the corresponding semantic marker. For if we always assign a semantic marker when the corresponding grammatical marker is assigned, then in many cases lexical items will be given the wrong sense characterizations. For instance, grammatically the words *ship, England, fortune*, and *fate* are marked feminine, but clearly they cannot receive the semantic marker (*Female*) if sentences are to receive the correct semantic interpretations. Again, such words as *pain, ache, twinge* must be marked as concrete nouns, but they cannot be marked as (*Physical Object*) if we are to account for such anomalies as "The pain weighs three pounds." Conversely, if we always assigned a grammatical marker whenever the corresponding semantic marker is assigned, then either the grammar will fail to generate some grammatical sentences or it will generate some ungrammatical strings, or it will fail to assign structure properly. For instance, semantically the nouns *child, baby*, and *infant* must be marked (*Human*) to obtain correct sense characterizations and correct semantic interpretations. But if they are marked as human nouns, the grammar will fail to generate such sentences as "The baby lost its rattle."

Thus, grammatical and semantic markers have different theoretical import. Grammatical markers have the function of marking the formal differences upon which the distinction between well-formed and ill-formed strings of morphemes rests, whereas semantic markers have the function of giving each well-formed string the conceptual content that permits them to be represented in terms of the message they communicate to speakers in normal situations. They are concerned with different kinds of selection and they express different aspects of the structure of a language. We can, therefore, justifiably regard semantic markers as theoretical constructs distinct from the markers employed in grammatical description.

---

[31]R. B. Lees, *op. cit.*, p. 14.

20 Analyticity and Contradiction in Natural Language*

Jerrold J. Katz

The primary significance of this paper lies in its solution to the problem of distinguishing analytic and synthetic truths raised by W. V. Quine in his "Two Dogmas of Empiricism."[1] This solution is based on the conviction that Quine's skepticism can be overcome within the framework of a conception of the nature of a semantic theory of a natural language while, in the absence of such a framework, techniques such as those R. Carnap[2] and other empiricists have proposed cannot hope to surmount Quine's fastidious skepticism. Accordingly, this paper first presents a conception of the nature of a semantic theory to serve as a framework and then proceeds within this framework to draw the analytic-synthetic distinction by introducing definitions of the terms *analytic sentence, synthetic sentence,* and *contradictory sentence* which beg no questions of empirical justification and which formally specify the set of analytic sentences, the set of synthetic sentences, and the set of contradictory sentences.

THE NATURE OF A SEMANTIC THEORY

A semantic theory of a natural language[3] has as its goal the construction of a system of rules which represents what a fluent speaker knows[4] about the semantic structure

---

*This work was supported in part by the U.S. Army, the Air Force Office of Scientific Research, and the Office of Naval Research; in part by the National Science Foundation (Grant G-16526); and in part by the National Institute of Health (Grant MH-04737-02).

[1] W. V. Quine, "Two Dogmas of Empiricism," in *From a Logical Point of View* (Cambridge, Mass.: Harvard University Press, 1953), pp. 20–46.

[2] R. Carnap, "Meaning and Synonymy in Natural Language," *Philosophical Studies*, **VI**, No. 3, (April 1955), 33–47.

[3] J. J. Katz, and J. A. Fodor, "The Structure of a Semantic Theory," *Language*, **40** (1963), reprinted in this volume. 1 shall henceforth use the initials "SST" to refer to this paper.

[4] Here I anticipate such an objection as the following: "How can you say a fluent speaker *knows*

of his language that permits him to understand its sentences. The idea behind this conception of a semantic theory is that such knowledge takes the form of recursive rules that enable the speaker to compose, albeit implicitly, the meaning of any sentence of his language out of the familiar meanings of its elementary components.

This idea has the following two-part rationale. First, the most impressive fact about linguistic competence is that a fluent speaker can understand a sentence even though he has never previously encountered it. In principle,[5] he can understand any of the infinitely many sentences of his language. But since, at any time in his life, the speaker can have encountered only a finite subset of the infinite set of sentences of his language, we can conclude that his knowledge of the semantic structure takes the form of recursive rules which fix a meaning for each of the infinitely many sentences. Second, since a speaker's ability to understand sentences also depends on his knowing the meanings of their elementary components, the lexical items in the vocabulary of the language, we can conclude that the meaning the rules fix for a sentence must be a compositional function of the antecedently known meanings of the lexical items appearing in it. Hence, a semantic theory must contain rules that represent the speaker's knowledge of the semantic structure of his language. Such rules must explicate the compositional function which determines how he utilizes the meanings of the lexical items in a sentence to understand what that sentence means.

A semantic theory consists of two components. First, a dictionary which provides a meaning for each lexical item of the language. Second, a finite set of "projection rules." These use information supplied by the dictionary for the lexical items in a sentence and information about the sentence's syntactic structure supplied by the grammar of the language in order to assign the sentence a semantic interpretation.

Since information about a sentence's syntactic structure is needed to assign it a semantic interpretation, it is convenient to let the output of a grammar be the input to a semantic theory. In this way, each sentence considered by a semantic theory is represented as a concatenation of morphemes whose constituent structure is given in the form of a hierarchical categorization of the syntactical parts of the concatena-

---

something if he cannot say what it is you claim he knows?" I do not think anything hangs on my *having* the word *know*. I intend to convey the idea that the fluent speaker has acquired the means necessary for performing a task whose character compels us to admit that its performance results from the application of rules. Among the reasons which compel us to make this admission is that cited by Miller, Pribram, and Galanter, viz., that the task of understanding any twenty word sentence is one a fluent speaker can perform, yet the number of twenty word sentences is 10^{30} while the number of seconds in a century is only 3.15 times 10^9—G. A. Miller, K. Pribram, and E. Galanter, *Plans and the Structure of Behavior* (New York: Holt, Rinehart & Winston, Inc. 1960), pp. 146–47.

[5]I say "in principle" because in practice limitations of perception, memory, mortality, and so on, prevent the speaker from applying his knowledge of the rules of the language to provide himself with the meaning of certain sentences. This situation is exactly analogous to the case of a person's knowledge of the rules of arithmetic computation. Knowing how to perform any computation, knowing the rules of arithmetic computation, is not sufficient to enable someone to actually perform any (specific) computation; for, again, limitations of perception, memory, mortality, and the like stand in the way.

tion.[6] The sentence "The boys like candy" is represented by the concatenation of morphemes *the + boy + s + like + candy* which is hierarchically categorized as follows: the whole string is categorized as a sentence at the highest level of the hierarchy; *the + boy + s* is categorized as a noun phrase, and *like + candy* is categorized as a verb phrase at the next level of the hierarchy; *the* is categorized as an article; *boy + s* is categorized as a noun, *like* as a verb, and *candy* as a noun; and so forth on the next and lower levels of the hierarchy. We can represent such a categorization in the form of a labeled tree diagram in which the notion *the sequence of morphemes m belongs to the category c* is formalized by the notion *m is traceable back to a node labeled c*.[7] We call such a representation a *constituent structure characterization* of a sentence. The constituent structure characterization of "The boys like candy" is roughly:[8]

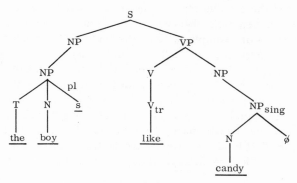

Figure 1

The input to a semantic theory are sentences represented as terminal elements within their constituent structure characterizations, together with any further grammatical information that an optimal grammar supplies about them.[9]

A semantic theory takes, one after another, the discrete outputs of the grammar and operates on them. This operation reconstructs the manner in which a speaker employs the syntactic structure of a sentence to determine its meaning as a function of the meanings of its lexical items. The result of this operation is a semantic interpretation of the sentence. Hence, we must first consider just what a semantic interpretation ought to tell us about a sentence.

---

[6]Such information will be needed to provide the difference upon which rests the distinction in meaning between sentences composed of exactly the same morphemes, e.g., "Gourmets do approve of people eating," "Gourmets do approve of eating people," "Do gourmets approve of people eating?" and so on.

[7]N. Chomsky, *Syntactic Structures*, Second Printing (Mouton and Co., 's Gravenhage, 1962), Chapter 4. In general, we shall follow Chomsky's conception of syntax.

[8]I will use the notational abbreviations: *S* for a sentence, *NP* for a noun phrase, *VP* for a verb phrase, *N* for a noun, *V* for a verb, *T* for an article, *A* for an adjective, *C* for a co-ordinating conjunction, and the subscript symbols *sing*, *pl*, and *tr* for the syntactic properties of nominal singularness, nominal pluralness, and verbal transitivity, respectively.

[9]In particular, an optimal grammar will include a specification of the transformational history for each sentence. Cf. N. Chomsky, *op. cit.*

The semantic interpretations produced by a semantic theory constitute the theory's description of the semantic structure of a language. Since a speaker's knowledge of semantic structure manifests itself in his verbal performance, the fundamental question about this performance is "what manifests the speaker's knowledge of the semantic structure of his language?" Some of the ways in which the speaker manifests his knowledge are as follows: he differentiates semantically acceptable from semantically anomalous sentences; he recognizes ambiguities stemming from semantic relations; he detects semantic relations between expressions and sentences of different syntactic type and morpheme constitution; and so forth. Hence, semantic interpretations must formally mark as semantically acceptable and anomalous those sentences that the speaker differentiates as acceptable and anomalous, mark as semantically ambiguous those sentences that the speaker regards as such, mark as semantically related in such-and-such a fashion just those expressions and just those sentences that the speaker detects as so related, and so forth. Otherwise, the semantic theory cannot claim to represent the speaker's semantic knowledge. For example, a semantic theory of English would have to produce a semantic interpretation for "The bank is the scene of the crime" that marks it as semantically ambiguous, semantic interpretations for the sentences "He paints with silent paint" and "Two pints of the academic liquid!"[10] that mark them as semantically anomalous, semantic interpretations for "he paints silently" and "Two pints of the muddy liquid!" that mark them as semantically acceptable, and semantic interpretations which mark the sentences "Eye doctors eye blonds," "Oculists eye blonds," "Blonds are eyed by eye doctors," and so on, as paraphrases of each other but mark "Eye doctors eye what gentlemen prefer" as *not* a paraphrase of any of these sentences.

Now, to finish describing the form of a semantic theory of a natural language, we need only characterize the notions *dictionary entry*, *semantic interpretation*, and *projection rule*.

Within a semantic theory, the dictionary entries provide the basis from which the projection rules of the theory derive the semantic interpretations they assign sentences. The notion *dictionary entry* must be such that in it we have a normal form for the dictionary entries in a semantic theory. This normal form must enable us to represent lexical information in a formal manner. Also, it must be sufficient in conceptual machinery to provide a representation of everything which the projection rules require to assign correct semantic interpretations.

In the majority of cases,[11] a dictionary entry consists of a finite number of sequences of symbols, each sequence consisting of an initial subsequence of syntactic markers, followed by a subsequence of "semantic markers," then, optionally, one "distinguisher," and finally a "selection restriction." Dictionary entries can be represented in the form of tree diagrams, such as in Fig. 2, where each sequence in the entry for

---

[10] For the first of these two examples, I am indebted to Professor Uriel Weinreich, and for the second to Professor George A. Miller.

[11] In the small minority of cases, dictionary entries consist of instructions, e.g., the rules for *not* that are given in the third section of this paper. For a further discussion of the type of entry found in the vast majority of cases see Sect. 6 of SST.

a lexical item appears as a distinct path rooted at that lexical item.[12] Semantic markers are represented enclosed within parentheses, the distinguishers are represented enclosed within brackets, and the selection restrictions are represented within angles. Each complete path, each sequence, represents a distinct sense of the lexical item in whose entry it appears. Thus, in Fig. 2 the lexical item *bachelor* is represented as having four distinct senses.

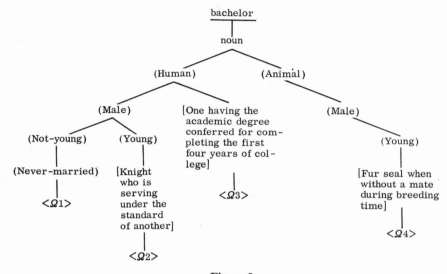

Figure 2

Semantic markers are the formal elements a semantic theory employs to express semantic relations of a general nature. For example, the appearance of the semantic marker (Male) in the dictionary entries for senses of *bachelor, uncle, man, lion, priest, father*, etc., but not in the dictionary entries for senses of *spinster, stone, adult, philosopher, virtue, pea*, etc., represents the fact that the former items have a common semantic component in their meanings which the latter items lack, and, thus, the fact that these former items are semantically similar in a way that the latter ones are not. In contrast, distinguishers are the formal elements employed to represent what is idiosyncratic about the meaning of a lexical item. A distinguisher serves to distinguish a lexical item from those that are closest to it in meaning. Thus, a semantic marker found in the path of a certain lexical item will also be found in the paths of many other lexical items throughout the dictionary, whereas a distinguisher found in the path of a certain lexical item will not be found anywhere else in the dictionary.

---

[12]Two comments on Fig 2. First, the word *bachelor*, although a noun, can select and exclude other nouns in various types of constructions, e.g., in noun-noun cases as "He is my bachelor friend," or in noun-in-apposition cases such as "Mr. Smith, the neighborhood bachelor, is here." Thus, we must represent *bachelor* having a selection restriction for each sense; thus, the terminal elements for each path in Fig. 2 is a selection restriction enclosed in angles. Second, the particular selections restrictions are omitted because their inclusion would only complicate matters unnecessarily at this point.

This difference can be more fully appreciated if one compares the consequences of eliminating a semantic marker from a dictionary with the consequences of eliminating a distinguisher. In the former case, indefinitely many semantic relations between the expressions of the language which were marked by the eliminated semantic marker would no longer be marked, whereas in the latter case, only the distinction in sense which was marked by the eliminated distinguisher would no longer be marked.[13] Therefore, semantic markers and distinguishers represent the semantic properties from which the meaning of a lexical item is constructed. They may be regarded as expressing the most elementary components of the semantic content of lexical items, i.e., those components down into which the whole meaning of lexical items can be analyzed.

A lexical item is ambiguous if, and only if, its entry contains at least two distinct paths. Ambiguity at the lexical level is the source of semantic ambiguity at the sentence level. Thus, a necessary, although not sufficient, condition for a syntactically unambiguous sentence to be semantically ambiguous is that it contains an ambiguous lexical item. For example, the source of the semantic ambiguity of "He likes to wear a light suit in the summer" is the lexical ambiguity of the word *light*. Since an adequate dictionary entry for a lexical item must mark every one of its ambiguities, the dictionary entry for *light* must represent this lexical item as branching into one path containing the semantic marker *Color* but not *Weight* and another containing the semantic marker *Weight* but not *Color*.

However, an ambiguous lexical item in a syntactically unambiguous sentence is not sufficient for that sentence to be semantically ambiguous. For example, the sentence "The stuff is light enough to carry," although it contains the ambiguous word *light*, is not understood in the sense in which *light enough to carry* means light enough in color to be carried. Thus, when there is an ambiguous lexical item in a semantically unambiguous sentence, the grammatical relations and the meanings of the other constituents can prevent this item from bearing more than one of its senses. The selection of some senses and exclusion of others occurs as a result of the other constituents of the sentence. Such selection is of fundamental importance because, together with lexical ambiguity, it partly determines whether a sentence is anomalous, whether a sentence is semantically unambiguous, whether two sentences are paraphrases of each other, and other semantic properties of sentences that a semantic theory marks.

Thus, a path for a lexical item must contain a selection restriction that determines the combinations into which the item can enter and the sense(s) it bears in those combinations. The formal representation of selection restrictions can be regarded as a device for indicating such information as *The Shorter Oxford English Dictionary's* qualification that the word *honest* when applied to persons means "of good moral character, virtuous, upright" and applied to women is ambiguous between this sense and the sense of *chaste*. We shall use left and right angles enclosing a Boolean function of syntactic or semantic markers to formally represent such selection restrictions. Such configurations of symbols will be affixed as the terminal

---

[13]For a further examination of the distinction between the notions *semantic marker* and *distinguisher* see Sect. 6 of SST.

element of a path and will be construed as providing a necessary and sufficient condition for a semantically acceptable combination of that path with another. Thus, for example, the selection restriction affixed to the path of a modifier determines the applicability of that path of the modifier to a sense of a head. Instances of modifier-head relations are: adjective-noun modification, adverb-verb modification, adverb-adjective modification. In particular, a path in the dictionary entry for *honest* will be: *honest* → adjective → (*Evaluative*) → (*Moral*) → [*Innocent of illicit sexual intercourse*] <(*Human*) and (*Female*)>. This is to be construed as saying that an adjectival occurrence of *honest* receives the interpretation, (*Evaluative*) → (*Moral*) → [*Innocent of illicit sexual intercourse*], just in case the head it modifies has a path containing both the semantic marker (*Human*) and the path semantic marker (*Female*).

In sum, a path contains syntactic markers that determine the syntactic classification of a lexical item, semantic markers that represent the semantic properties that the item has in common with many other lexical items, (optionally) a distinguisher that represents its idiosyncratic features, and finally a selection restriction.

The next notion to explain is *projection rule*. Let us suppose that an English grammar provides a semantic theory with the input sentence "The boys like candy" together with the constituent structure characterization as given in Fig. 1. The first step the theory performs in assigning a semantic interpretation to this sentence is to correlate each of its lexical items, i.e., *the, boy, s, like,* and *candy,* with all, and only, the paths from their dictionary entries that are compatible with the syntactic categorization the lexical items are given in the constituent structure characterization.

The correlation works as follows: if a path from the dictionary entry for the lexical item m_j contains syntactic markers which attribute to m_j the same syntactic categorization that it has in the constituent structure characterization d_i, then this path is assigned to the set of paths P_j^i which is correlated with the occurrence m_j in d_i. Thus, the lexical item m_1 is associated with the set of paths P_1^i, m_2 is associated with P_2^i, and so on.[14] Referring to Fig. 1, the result of this step may be pictured as converting the diagram into one in which *the* is associated with the set of paths P_1^i, *boy* is associated with P_2^i, *s* is associated with P_3^i, *like* is associated with P_4^i, and *candy* is associated with P_5^i (although no other change is made). Thus, for example, P_5^i contains paths representing each of the senses that *candy* has as a noun but none of the paths representing its senses as a verb (e.g. "The fruits candy easily"). This rule which associates senses with the occurrences of lexical items in constituent structure characterizations is the first projection rule.

There are type one projection rules and type two projection rules. Type one projection rules utilize the information about the meanings of the lexical items contained in the paths belonging to the sets of paths assigned in the above manner in order to provide a characterization of the meaning of every constituent of a sentence, including the whole sentence. For example, in "The boys like candy," besides the characterizations of the meaning of *the, boy, s, like,* and *candy* obtained from their dictionary entries, type one projection rules must provide characterizations of the

---

[14]For a full discussion of this step see the treatment of rule (I) in SST, Sect. 7.

meaning of *The boys, like candy*, and "The boys like candy." This type one projection rules do by combining the characterizations of the meaning of lower constituents to form a characterization of the meaning of the higher constituents. Thus, type one projection rules effect a series of amalgamations of paths, proceeding from the bottom to the top of a constituent structure characterization, by embedding paths into each other to form a new path, the amalgam. The amalgam is assigned to the set of paths associated with the node (i.e., the point at which an *n*-ary branching occurs) that immediately dominates the sets of paths from which the paths amalgamated were drawn. The amalgam provides one of the meanings for the sequence of lexical items that the node dominates. In this manner, a set of alternative meanings given in the form of derived paths is provided for every sequence of lexical items dominated by a syntactic marker in the constituent structure characterization, until the highest syntactic marker *S* is reached and associated with a set of derived paths giving the meanings for the whole sentence.

Amalgamation is the operation of forming a composite path made up of one path from each of the *n*-different sets of paths dominated by a syntactic marker. This composite path is then a member of the set of paths associated with the node that that syntactic marker labels. The joining of a pair of paths occurs just in case one of the paths satisfies the selection restrictions in the other. If the syntactic marker dominates just the sets of paths $P_1^i, P_2^i, \ldots, P_n^i$ and P_1^i contains k_1 paths, P_2^i contains k_2 paths, $\ldots$, P_n^i contains k_m paths, then the set of paths that is associated with the dominating marker contains at most $(k_1 \cdot k_2 \cdot \ldots \cdot k_m)$ members and possibly zero members if selection restrictions prevent every possible amalgamation from forming. Each path which is in the set assigned to the dominating node marker is called *a reading for the lexical string that this marker dominates in the constituent structure characterization d_i.* The number of readings that is thus allotted to a string of lexical items determines its degree of semantic ambiguity. A string with no readings is anomalous, a string with exactly one reading is unambiguous, and a string with two or more readings is semantically ambiguous two or more ways.

An example of a projection rule of type one is:

(*R*1)   Given two paths associated with nodes branching from the same node labeled *SM*, one of the form

Lexical String$_1$ → syntactic markers of head → (a_1) → (a_2) → $\cdots$ → (a_n) → [1] $\langle \Omega 1 \rangle$

and the other of the form

Lexical String$_2$ → syntactic markers of the modifier of the head → (b_1) → (b_2) → $\cdots$ → (b_m) → [2] $\langle \Omega 2 \rangle$

such that the string of syntactic or semantic markers of the head has a substring σ which satisfies $\langle \Omega 2 \rangle$, then there is an amalgam of the form

Lexical String$_2$ + Lexical String$_1$ → dominating node marker *SM* → (a_1) → (a_2) → $\cdots$ → (a_n) → (b_1) → (b_2) → $\cdots$ → (b_m) → [[2] [1]] $\langle \Omega_1 \rangle$,

where any b_i is null just in case there is an a_j such that $b_i = a_j$, and [[2] [1]] is simply [1] just in case [2] = [1]. This amalgam is assigned to the set of paths associated with the node labeled *SM* that dominates Lexical String$_2$ + Lexical String$_1$.[15]

---

[15]This erasure clause is included to avoid pointlessly duplicating semantic markers and distinguishers in the path for a compound expression. Thus, for example, it makes no sense to

(*R*1) explicates the process of attribution, i.e., the process of creating a new semantic unit compounded from a modifier and head whose semantic properties are those of the head, except that the meaning of the compound is more determinate than the head's by virtue of the semantic information contributed by the modifier. The modifier-head relations which must be known for (*R*1) to apply will be specified by the grammar of the language. An example of an amalgamation produced by (*R*1) is the joining of the path, *colorful* → adjective → (*color*) → [*Abounding in contrast or variety of bright colors*] <(*Physical object*) v (*Social activity*)>, and the path, *ball* → noun → (*Physical object*) → [*Of globular shape*], to produce the new compound path, *colorful* + *ball* → noun → (*Physical object*) → (*color*) → [[*Abounding in contrast or variety of bright colors*] [*Of globular shape*]]. An example of an amalgamation that is prevented by a selection restriction is that of the path, *colorful* → adjective → (*Evaluative*) → [*Of distinctive character, vividness, or picturesqueness*] <(*Aesthetic Object*) v (*Social Activity*)>, with the path for *ball* just given above. This possible amalgamation is precluded because the selection restriction in the path of the modifier requires that this path be joined only with paths of heads that contain either the semantic marker (*Aesthetic object*) or the semantic marker (*Social activity*) whereas this path of *ball* contains neither one of these semantic markers.

Other type one projection rules are formulated in a similar manner, utilizing other grammatical relations to produce similar types of amalgamations. Type two rules work differently and are best explained after we explain the concept of a semantic interpretation of a sentence.

A semantic theory receives more than one constituent structure characterization for a sentence if that sentence is syntactically ambiguous. Figures 3 and 4 show the two constituent structure characterizations for the syntactically ambiguous sentence "I like little boys and girls."

Let $d_1, d_2, \ldots, d_n$ be the constituent structure characterizations that the grammar provides for the *n*-ways syntactically ambiguous sentence *S*. We will define the "semantic interpretation of *S*" to be (1) the conjunction ψd_1 & ψd_2 & $\ldots$ & ψd_n of the semantic interpretations of the *n*-constituent structure characterizations of *S*, and (2) the statements about *S* that follow from the definition schema:

(*D*) *S* is *fully X* if and only if *S* is *X* on every d_i

The semantic interpretation ψd_i of the constituent structure characterization d_i of *S* is (1) the constituent structure characterization d_i, each node of which is associated with its full set of readings, (i.e., every reading that can belong to the set on the basis of the dictionary entries and the projection rules does belong to it), and (2) the statements about *S* that follow from (1) together with the definitions:

(*D*1) *S* is *semantically anomalous on d_i* if, and only if, the set of paths associated with the node labeled *S* in d_i contains no members.

(*D*2) *S* is *semantically unambiguous on d_i* if, and only if, the set of paths associated with the node labeled *S* in d_i contains exactly one member.

---

include the semantic markers (*Human*) and (*Female*) twice in the path associated with the compound *spinster aunt* because both of the constituent paths contain occurrences of both. The second occurrence of (*Human*) or (*Female*) would provide no semantic information whatever.

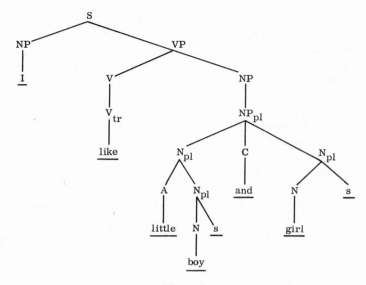

Figure 3

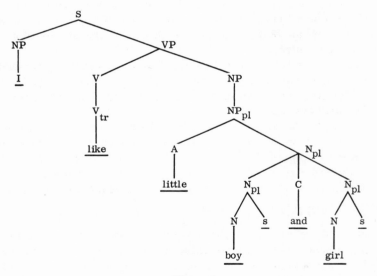

Figure 4

(D3) S is *n-ways semantically ambiguous on* d_i if, and only if, the set of paths associated with the node labeled S in d_i contains exactly *n*-members ($n \geqslant 2$).

(D4) S_1 and S_2 are *paraphrases on a reading with respect to their characterizations* d_i *and* d_j if, and only if, the set of paths associated with the node labeled S in d_i and the set of paths associated with the node labeled S in d_j have a reading in common.

(D5) S_1 and S_2 are *full paraphrases with respect to their characterizations* d_i *and* d_j if, and only if, the set of paths associated with the node labeled S in d_i and the set of paths associated with the node labeled S in d_j have exactly the same membership.

as well as other definitions for other semantic properties of sentences and corresponding definitions for constituents of sentences, e.g., (D1.1). *NP is semantically anomalous on* d_i *if, and only if, the set of paths associated with the node labeled NP in* d_i *contains no members.*

Since these definitions are self-explanatory, we can now return to our account of the projection rules and explain the concept of a type two projection rule.

A grammar employs two types of syntactic rules to achieve its aim of assigning the correct constituent structure characterization to each sentence of the language.[16] The first type are rules which rewrite single symbols on the basis of information which comes from the linear context of the symbol. Such rules construct constituent structure characterizations such as those in Figs. 1, 3, and 4 in somewhat the following manner: the first rule rewrites the initial symbol *S* (standing for "*sentence*") as *NP* + *VP* (which categorizes a noun-phrase + verb-phrase sequence as a sentence), then a rule can be used to rewrite *NP* as either NP_{sing} or NP_{pl}, then other rules can be used to rewrite *VP* as either *V* + *NP* or V_{intr} or *be* + *Pred*, still other rules to rewrite VP_{sing} as *T* + *N*, *T* as *the*, *N* as *boy* (or *man, coat, mouse*, etc.) and so forth.[17]

It has been shown that a grammar can assign constituent structure characterizations correctly only if some of its rules use information about the derivational history of sentences.[18] Thus, in addition to the previous type of rules, grammars contain "transformational rules." Such rules operate on entire constituent structure characterizations, or any of their parts, and map labeled trees onto labeled trees. In this way, simpler sentences are transformed into more complex ones, and the transformed sentences are assigned a constituent structure characterization.

Type two projection rules are intended to explicate the manner in which transformational rules preserve or change meaning. Linguists have observed that, in general, the sentence resulting from the application of a transformational rule to a set of source sentences is related in meaning to these source sentences in a definite, systematic way.[19] The employment of type two rules is intended to reveal the facts of language that underly this observation.

Type two projection rules produce a semantic interpretation ψd_i for the constituent structure characterization d_i constructed by the operation of the transformation *T* out of the set of constituent structure characterizations $d_1, d_2, \ldots, d_n$. Such projection rules operate on a set of semantic interpretations $\psi d_1, \psi d_2, \ldots, \psi d_n$. and the transformation *T* to produce the semantic interpretation ψd_i. They assign semantic

---

[16]Although this is not the only aim of a grammar. Cf. N. Chomsky, "On the Notion 'Rule of Grammar,' " *Proceedings of the Twelfth Symposium in Applied Mathematics, The Structure of Language and its Mathematical Aspects*, ed. by Roman Jakobson, American Mathematical Society, (1961), pp. 6–24.

[17]Cf. N. Chomsky, "A Transformational Approach to Syntax," *Third Texas Conference on Problems in the Analysis of English*, ed. by A. A. Hill, forthcoming.

[18]Cf. Chomsky's *Syntactic Structures*, "On the Notion 'Rule of Grammar,' " and *The Logical Structure of Linguistic Theory*, (1955), microfilm at M.I.T. Library. Also, cf. P. Postal, "Limitations of Phrase-Structure Grammars."

[19]This point has been discussed outside the context of the conception of a semantic theory adopted in the present paper in two recent articles: J. A. Fodor, "Projection and Paraphrase in Semantics," *Analysis*, **21.4** (March 1961), 73–77; and J. J. Katz, "A Reply to 'Projection and Paraphrase in Semantics,' " *Analysis*, **22.2** (December 1961), 36–41.

interpretations in such a way as to reconstruct the manner in which the meaning of the sentence that was constructed by T is a function of the meanings of each of the sentences that were used by T in its construction.

THE SOLUTION TO QUINE'S PROBLEM

The present paper is an essay in semantic metatheory.[20] A metatheory of semantic theories is needed to inform the field linguist of what types of facts to look for and what is the most revealing form to arrange them in. Given that he has acquired the relevant linguistic facts and has suitably arranged them, definitions such as (D), $(D1)$, $(D2)$, $(D3)$, $(D4)$, and $(D5)$ are the basis on which the field linguist can make illuminating statements about the sentences of the language he is studying. However, these definitions are not by themselves enough to enable the field linguist to say everything he should say about the semantic properties of sentences. On the basis of $(D1)$ to $(D5)$, the linguist can say what formal relations determine whether a sentence is acceptable or anomalous, what relations determine whether a sentence is unambiguous or ambiguous, and what relations determine whether a sentence is a paraphrase of another or not. But the linguist requires a notion of semantic interpretation that, by virtue of further definitions, will enable him to tell also when a sentence is analytic, contradictory, or synthetic, when two sentences are inconsistent with each other, and so on. Accordingly, the present paper extends the concept of a semantic interpretation by adding definitions of the notions *analytic sentence*, *contradictory sentence*, *synthetic sentence*, *inconsistent sentences*, among others. Thus, this paper not only offers a reply to Quine's challenge to the empiricists to show that the analytic-synthetic distinction is more than mere dogma but continues the metatheoretic study into the nature of a semantic theory begun in previous publications.[21]

In SST, the basic idea behind the present paper's treatment of the concept of an analytic sentence was expressed as follows:

> The limiting case [of modification], where the addition to the compound of semantic material from the modifier is zero, is of considerable theoretical interest. The compound *unmarried bachelor* is a case in point. The erasure clause in $(R1)$, i.e., "any b_i is null when there is an a_j such that $b_i = a_j$, and $[[2] [1]] = [1]$ just in case $[2] = [1]$," tells us to delete from the path of the modifier any semantic material already represented in the path of the head. Thus, in forming the compound *unmarried bachelor* all the semantic information in the path of the modifier *unmarried* will be deleted so that the derived path for *unmarried bachelor* will contain no more than the semantic material which comes from the path for *bachelor*. The failure of the modifier to add semantic information would appear to account for the intuition that such expressions as *unmarried bachelor* are redundant and that, correspondingly, such statements as "bachelors are unmarried" are "empty," "tautological," "vacuous," "uninformative." Thus, we have a new explanation of the analyticity of a classical type of analytic truth.[22]

---

[20]A full discussion of the nature of a semantic metatheory will be found in SST, Sect. 8.
[21]Cf. SST and J. J. Katz and P. Postal, *An Integrated Theory of Linguistic Descriptions*, M.I.T. Press, 1964.
[22]SST, Sect. 7.

The explanation of analyticity suggested in this passage, although it is developed only for sentences of the $NP + is + A$ type, can be extended to explain the analyticity of all copula sentences. The analyticity of noncopula sentences will be taken up after we conclude our whole discussion of the copula type.

To obtain a general, formal definition of *analytic sentence* for present tense copula sentences, we will require some auxiliary notions. We will use the symbol p_1 for a path from the set of paths associated with the node labeled NP that is immediately dominated by the node labeled S (i.e., the node that dominates the string of lexical items that is the subject of the sentence). We will use the symbol p_2 for a path from the set of paths associated with the node labeled VP that is immediately dominated by the node labeled S (i.e., the node that dominates the string of lexical items that consists of the verb *is* followed by its nominal or adjectival predicate). That is, p_1 and p_2 are paths that are amalgamated to produce a reading, which we shall represent by $r_{1,2}$, for the sentence as a whole. We will use the term *semantic element* to refer either to a semantic marker or to a distinguisher.

Given these auxiliary notions, we add to $(D1)$ to $(D5)$ the definition:

> $(D6)$ The copula sentence S is *analytic on the reading* $r_{1,2}$ if, and only if, every semantic element e_i in p_2 is also in p_1 and for any complex semantic element $\{e_1 \cup e_2 \cup \ldots \cup e_n\}$ in the path p_2, there is a semantic element e_j such that $1 \leqslant j \leqslant n$ and e_j is in the path p_1.[23]

$(D6)$ formalizes the idea that analyticity is the predicative vacuity that results from the failure of the path associated with the predicate to contribute semantic elements to the path associated with the subject when these paths are amalgamated to produce a reading for the sentence.

Checking $(D6)$ for its applicability to analytic sentences of each of the copula types, the $NP + is + A$ cases and the $NP + is + NP$ cases, we find that both types come under $(D6)$ as is indicated by the examples: "Bachelors are unmarried," "The happy child is happy," "The man who is cheerful is cheerful," and so on and "The pediatrician who loves her is a doctor who loves her," "The man who stole the cake is the man by whom the cake was stolen," "Stones are physical objects," "Spinsters are adult women who have never married," and so on. In each of these examples, the sentence is analytic because every semantic element in the path from the set of paths associated with the verb phrase is also found in the path from the set associated with the noun-phrase subject.

The concept of "analytic sentence" just characterized is that of "analytic on a reading," but there is another concept of sentential analyticity, *viz.*

> $(D6')$ S is *fully analytic on* d_i if, and only if, the set of readings assigned to the node labeled S in d_i is non-null and, for every reading $r_{1,2}$ in this set, S is analytic on $r_{1,2}$

Sentences that are merely analytic on a reading are as plentiful as natural numbers (e.g., the sentences usually encountered in philosophical discussions of analyticity, "Bachelors are unmarried," "Vixens are foxes.") On the other hand, sentences that

---

[23]The notation $\{e_1 \cup e_2 \cup \ldots \cup e_n\}$ will be explained below in connection with the discussion of the rules for *not*. In $(D7)$ and $(D8)$ we will take S to be a variable for copula sentences.

are fully analytic are not found in natural language, except in areas where a highly technical nomenclature is in use. Some philosophers claim that, for example, "Bachelors are unmarried" is not analytic because *bachelor* can refer to married men or women who possess a bachelor's degree. Other philosophers regard such criticism as beside the point. Disagreement of this kind can be resolved using the above distinction.

In terms of (*D*6), analyticity is the counterpart, on the sentence level, of the relations of synonymy and meaning inclusion, found on the level of lexical items and expressions.[24] Intuitively, this is a desirable feature since it brings out the formal structure underlying the often made observation that analyticity is somehow connected with these relations. The question arises whether we can so construct our definition of "contradictory sentence" that it reconstructs contradictoriness as the counterpart, on the sentence level, of the relation of antonymy on the level of lexical items and expressions. It will become quite clear that an adequate definition of "contradictory sentence" must be constructed in such a way that this relationship between contradictoriness and antonymy is a feature of its definiens.

There are many special antonymy relations between words and expressions. One example, is the relation of "sex-antonymy."[25] A pair of lexical items is *sex-antonymous* just in case they have identical paths except that where one has the semantic marker (*Male*) the other has the semantic marker (*Female*). Some instances are: *woman and man; bride and groom; aunt and uncle; cow and bull.* The majority of antonymous lexical items are not sets of pairs but sets of *n*-tuples. For example, there are the species-antonymous lexical items, one example of a species-antonymous *n*-tuple being: *child, cub, puppy, kitten, cygnet,* and so on. Then, there are the age-antonymous *n*-tuples: *infant, child, adolescent,* and *adult; puppy and dog; cub and lion; cub and bear; cygnet and swan;* and so on. Moreover, there are *n*-tuples of lexical items that are distinguisher-wise antonymous, e.g., the *n*-tuple of simple color adjectives (*blue, yellow, green, red, orange*). These form an antonymous *n*-tuple because the path associated with each is identical except for the distinguisher which differentiates that color adjective from the others.

The definition of "sex-antonymy" cannot restrict the set of sex-antonymous pairs to a membership consisting only of lexical items. By definition, this set includes infinitely many cases of pairs of constructible expressions. For example, *the happy man* and *the happy woman; my mother's friend's father's aunt* and *my mother's friend's father's uncle; the cow that the farmer's son raised* and *the bull that the farmer's son raised;* and so on *ad infinitum.*[26] Moreover, the situation is the same for every other type of antonymy. Since every set of antonymous *n*-tuples contains infinitely many members, we will have to construct a definition of each type of

---

[24]We can say that a pair of lexical items are *synonymous on a sense* if, and only if, their dictionary entries have one path in common, and we can say a pair of lexical items are *fully synonymous* if, and only if, their dictionary entries are exactly the same. Two expressions are *synonymous on a pair of readings* if, and only if, they have a reading in common, and expressions are *fully synonymous* if, and only if, they have every reading in common.

[25]SST, Sect. 6.

[26]For the rules of grammar that explain why this set is infinite cf. R. B. Lees, "The Grammar of English Nominalizations," *International Journal of American Linguistics,* **26**, No. 3 (July 1960).

antonymy and a definition of the general notion *antonymous n-tuple* that formally represents the relevant infinite set.

The most natural way to construct such definitions is the following. Let us suppose that the semantic markers and the distinguishers of a semantic theory are grouped into antonymous *n*-tuples. This will mean that the antonymous *n*-tuples of semantic elements are so represented by the notation of the theory that the membership of any *n*-tuple can be uniquely determined from the symbols that represent the semantic elements. Then, we can define the general notion of antonymy as follows:

(1) Two lexical items or constructible expressions m_i and m_j are *antonymous on their paths* p_{m_i} *and* p_{m_j} if and only if p_{m_i} and p_{m_j} contain different semantic elements from the same antonymous *n*-tuple of semantic elements.

(2) $m_1, m_2, \ldots, m_n$ are *an X-antonymous n-tuple of constructible expressions* if, and only if, the paths $p_{m_1}, p_{m_2}, \ldots, p_{m_n}$ associated with them respectively each contains a different semantic element from the *X*-antonymous *n*-tuple of semantic elements.

We can now define the notion *contradictory sentence:*

(D7) *S* is *contradictory on the reading* $r_{1,2}$ *of* d_i if, and only if, p_1 and p_2 contain different semantic elements from the same antonymous *n*-tuple of semantic elements.

Thus, what is asserted about a sentence when its semantic interpretation marks it as contradictory is that the amalgamation that provides a reading for the sentence combines antonymous elements. Examples of contradictory sentences are: "A bride is a groom," "My round table is square," "Red is green," "Those who play badly are those who play well," "The loser of the game we are playing is the winner of the game we are playing," and so on.

Synthetic sentence can now be defined in terms of (*D6*) and (*D7*):

(D8) *S* is *synthetic on the reading* $r_{1,2}$ *of* d_i if, and only if,
S is neither analytic on $r_{1,2}$ nor contradictory

Examples of synthetic sentences are: "That woman is a spinster," "The loser of the game we are playing is a bachelor," "The groom is reluctant," "Red is the color of my house."[27]

In order for definitions (*D6*) to (*D8*) to apply generally, certain other concepts need to be explicated. One such explication is the rules for determining the semantic effect of sentential negation.

The negation of a sentence can be formed in a number of ways. We can put the word *not* after the verb *be*, as in "The table is not an antique." We can put expressions such as "It is not the case that" in front of full sentences, as in the sentence. "It is not the case that the table is an antique." We can prefix the sentence by *that* and add *is false* to the end, as in "That it is so is false."[28] We shall consider only the type of negativ-

---

[27]Thus, set of synthetic sentences in English includes "There are no more integers than even integers" and other semi-sophisticated mathematical truths, as well as the sophisticated ones. We shall draw the moral at the very end of this paper.

[28]The use of a negative prefix does not convert a sentence into its negation. Thus, the sentence "John is unlucky" is not the negation of "John is lucky," whereas the sentence "John is not lucky" is the negation of "John is lucky." To appreciate this, one must observe that the sentences "John

ization in which the negation of a sentence is formed by adding *not*. Negations formed in other ways, by virtue of being actual sentence negations, are synonymous with the negations of the same sentences that are formed by adding *not*. Thus, restricting consideration to negations formed by adding *not* does not impose a limitation on our treatment because, by (*D*4) and (*D*5) which require that synonymous sentences receive the same readings at the sentence level, whatever semantic properties a semantic interpretation assigns to the negation of a sentence formed in this way will also be assigned to the negation of that sentence which is formed in another manner. Moreover, we shall make the reasonable assumption that the scope of a negative in a sentence is determined by the grammatical analysis of the sentence.[29] Then, we can formally characterize a range of application for the *not*-rules by allowing them to operate on any path in the set of paths that provides the readings for the constituent in the scope of *not*. This constituent will be the main verb phrase of the sentence so that the *not*-rules operate on p_2's. For example, in the case of the sentence "The table is not an antique," the *not*-rules apply to any path that provides a reading for the constituent *an antique*. What we have to determine now is the effect of the operation of the *not*-rules on the paths which fall in their range of application.

Preliminary to stating the *not*-rules, let us define an operator which we shall call the *antonymy operator* and symbolize by $A/$:

(3) If the semantic elements $e_1, e_2, \ldots, e_n$ are an antonymous *n*-tuple, then
    (a) $A/e_i (1 \leqslant i \leqslant n) = \{e_1 \cup e_2 \cup \ldots \cup e_{i-1} \cup e_{i+1} \cup \ldots \cup e_n\}$ (b) $A/A/e_i = e_i$

We will call a function of semantic elements a "complex semantic element" and will treat complex semantic elements exactly like semantic elements for the purpose of amalgamation.

Suppose we hear the English sentence "That adult is not a spinster." As fluent speakers, we know that this sentence says that the person referred to by its subject is not a spinster, but we do not know from this sentence alone whether this is because that person is male or because that person is married or both. On the other hand, we do know that that person's being human has nothing whatsoever to do with the fact that he or she is not a spinster. These considerations suggest the first of our *not*-rules.

(*NR*) Let $e_1, e_2, \ldots, e_k$ be all the semantic elements in a path in the range of *not* such that no $e_i (1 \leqslant i \leqslant k)$ occurs in p_1 and no A/e_i occurs in p_1. Then $e_1, e_2, \ldots, e_k$ are replaced by the complex semantic element $\{A/e_1 \cup A/e_2 \cup \ldots \cup A/e_k\}$.

Each set in the union of sets $\{A/e_1 \cup A/e_2 \cup \ldots \cup A/e_k\}$ is a union of semantic elements, i.e., each $A/e_i (1 \leqslant i \leqslant k)$ is, according to (3) above, the union of all the members

---

is unlucky" and "John is not lucky" are not synonymous. The former means that John has bad things happening to him regularly by chance, while the latter means that John has very few good things happening to him by chance. Thus, "John is not unlucky" means that John does not have bad things happening to him regularly, not that he has any good thing happening to him. On the other hand, "John is not not lucky" means that he has good things happening to him regularly.

[29]The question of whether a negative somewhere in a sentence makes that sentence the negation of the sentence without that negative is a matter for the grammar to decide. Cf. E. Klima "Negation," in the present volume.

of the antonymous n-tuple to which e_i belongs except e_i itself; e.g., if e_i belongs to an antonymous pair, then A/e_i is simply the semantic marker or distinguisher that is antonymous with e_i.

Using (NR) to obtain a reading for the sentence "That adult is not a spinster," we achieve, with respect to what factors are and what are not in the meaning of this sentence, a result which is fully in accord with our linguistic intuition as speakers of English. The amalgamation of a path for *that adult* and a path for *is not a spinster* which is required to provide a reading for the whole sentence is preceded by an operation of (N/R) which replaces the semantic markers (*Female*) and (*Unmarried*) in the path for *a spinster* by the complex semantic marker $\{A/(Female)\ A/(Unmarried)\}$, i.e., $\{(Male)\cup(Married)\}$. Thus, when the path for *is not a spinster* is amalgamated with the path for *that adult* by ($R1$)[30] the complex marker from the path of *a spinster*, $\{(Male)\cup(Married)\}$, will become an element of the reading for the whole sentence. This, then, is to say formally what we agreed on above, namely, that adult is either a male or married or both. We also agreed that the person's being human has nothing to do with he or she not being a *spinster*. Formally, the semantic marker (*Human*) which is in the path for *a spinster* already appears in the path for *that adult*, and therefore (NR) leaves it intact. But ($R1$)'s erasure clause deletes it so that it does not enter the path for *that adult*. Finally, ($D8$) enables us to mark "That adult is not a spinster" as a synthetic sentence.

We now introduce the two further *not*-rules, (NR') and (NR''), which complete our account of the operation of negation.

> (NR') (1) For all those e_i in a path in the range of *not* such that there is a semantic element antonymous to e_i in p_1, e_i is replaced by A/e_i.
>
> (2) If (NR) did not apply and if (NR') (1) does not apply, then any e_i in a path in the range of *not* that also occurs in p_1 is replaced by A/e_i.
>
> (NR'') If (NR') applies to a path, then any semantic element in that path that does not also occur in p_1 and that has not entered that path by the application of (NR') that permits this application of (NR'') is nullified.

With these rules, we can show that, in accordance with the dicta of logic, a semantic theory built on the model given in the previous section and supplemented with the definitions from the present section will mark the negation of a contradictory sentence as analytic and will mark the negation of an analytic sentence as contradictory. Now we want to explain why there is such a relation between contradictory and analytic sentences, and in so doing explain also the workings of (NR') and (NR'').

First, let us show that the negation of a contradictory sentence will be marked analytic. Assume we are given a sentence that is contradictory in the sense of ($D7$). When the conversion of this contradictory sentence into its negation brings *not* in, there will then be semantic elements $e_1, e_2, \ldots, e_n$ ($n \geqslant 1$) in the path which will be in the range of *not* such that each element has an antonymous element in the path p_1. For example, if the contradictory sentence were "A bride is a groom," then $n = 1$, $e_1 = (Male)$, and e_1's antonymous element in $p_1 = (Female)$. The negation of the

---

[30]By ($R1$) because this is a modifier-head relation.

contradictory sentence has *not* located so that its range includes any path assigned as a reading to the verb phrase in the contradictory sentence. Thus, if p_3 is a path in the range of *not*, then by (NR') (1), each semantic element e_i $(1 \leqslant i \leqslant n)$ in p_3 will be replaced by A/e_i prior to the amalgamation of p_1 and p_2. Hence, in the amalgamation of p_1 and p_2, any semantic elements in p_2 that have an antonym in p_1 will be converted into their antonym so that the erasure clause of the projection rule amalgamating p_1 and p_2 deletes them as a duplication. For example, in the sentence "A bride is not a groom," the semantic marker (*Male*) is replaced by $A/(Male)$, i.e., (*Female*), so that in the amalgamation of the path for *is not a groom* and the path for *a bride* the former path does not contribute $A/(Male)$ because the presence of (*Female*) in the latter path causes it to be deleted prior to amalgamation. Such deletion will also be the fate of any semantic elements in p_2 that are in p_1 as well; e.g., the semantic marker (*Human*) in the path assigned as a reading to *is a groom* will not be added to a path for *a bride* when such a path is amalgamated with a path for *is not a groom* because (*Human*) appears in the path for *a bride*. If there are any semantic elements in p_3 such that neither they nor their antonym is in p_1 (as there are not in "A bride is a groom" but are in "A bride is a reluctant groom"), then, by (NR''), each is nullified. Consequently, in the amalgamation of p_1 and p_2, p_2 will be vacuous, and so by $(D6)$, the sentence will be analytic. Therefore, we conclude that the negation of a contradictory sentence is analytic.

Next we must show that the negation of an analytic sentence is contradictory. Assume we are given a sentence that is analytic in the sense of $(D6)$. It follows, that there are semantic elements $e_1, e_2, \ldots, e_n$ $(n \geqslant 1)$ in the path p_2 for this analytic sentence such that each e_i $(1 \leqslant i \leqslant n)$ is also in p_1. Thus, in the negation of the sentence, (NR') (2) replaces e_1 by A/e_1, e_2 by A/e_2, ..., and e_n by A/e_n. Consequently, p_1 and p_2 will each contain a different semantic element from the same n-tuple of antonymous semantic elements, and the negation of the analytic sentence will be contradictory by $(D7)$. For example, suppose we began with the analytic sentence "That spinster is a female who never married." Then, $n = 2$ and $e_1 = (Female)$ and $e_2 = (never\text{-}married)$. Then, (NR') (2) converts (*Female*) into $A/(Female)$, i.e., (*Male*), and (*never-married*) into $A/(never\text{-}married)$, i.e., (*at least once married*). But since *that spinster* is assigned a path containing both (*never-married*) and (*Female*), the sentence "that spinster is not a female who never married" is contradictory by virtue of the fact that its semantic interpretation now satisfies $(D7)$.

The negation of a synthetic sentence comes out, as it should, to be synthetic. By $(D8)$, a synthetic sentence will have a path p_2 which contains semantic elements $e_1, e_2, \ldots, e_n$ $(n \geqslant 1)$ that do not also occur in p_1. Moreover, by $(D8)$, $A/e_1, A/e_2, \ldots, A/e_n$ do not occur in p_1 either. The *not*-rules only replace e_1 by A/e_1, e_2 by A/e_2, ..., e_n by A/e_n in the path p_2 of the negation of the synthetic sentence. Since *ex hypothesi* $A/e_1, A/e_2, \ldots, A/e_n$ are not in p_1, the negation of a synthetic sentence does not satisfy $(D6)$. Since *ex hypothesi* $e_1, e_2, \ldots, e_n$ are not in p_1, it does not satisfy $(D7)$ either. Since the negation of a synthetic sentence is neither analytic nor contradictory, by $(D8)$, it is synthetic. For example, the paths p_2 for the sentences "That adult is not a spinster," "The apple is not red," and so on will add new semantic information that is consistent with what is in the corresponding paths p_1 when the p_1 and p_2 amalgamation takes place, and so each of these sentences will be marked synthetic.

The motivation for (NR'') deserves further comment. Consider the sentence "An uncle is a spinster." This sentence is contradictory because the path for *An uncle* and the path for *is a spinster* contain different semantic markers from the same *n*-tuple of antonymous semantic elements; i.e., the former contains (*Male*) and the latter (*Female*). Thus, we require that the negation of this sentence be analytic. But, without (NR''), the negation of "An uncle is a spinster" would not be analytic, since there is a semantic element, viz., (*Unmarried*), in the path p_2 which is not in p_1. Hence, the need for (NR'') stems from the need to cancel such semantic elements in order that we maintain the consequence that the negation of any contradictory sentence is analytic and that we preserve the generality of (*D6*).

Before concluding this section, let us briefly look at some further consequences of our definitions. The definitions together with the *not*-rules provide a formal means of sharply distinguishing contradictory and analytic sentences, on the one hand, from anomalous sentences, on the other. The practice of regarding contradictory and analytic sentences as *odd* and *ipso facto* grouping them together with semantically anomalous sentences is not harmful when it is made fully clear that the term *odd* refers to sentence-uses in specific situations and means only that in those situations that use is somehow inappropriate. In this sense, synthetic sentences can be *odd*, e.g., "I just swallowed my nose," and anomalous sentences can, in some situations, i.e., giving an example, telling a joke, be *non-odd*.[31] However, often this sense of *odd* is not distinguished from the sense in which it means "violates the semantic restrictions necessary to meet the standard of semantic well-formedness," i.e., semantically anomalous. This is unfortunate because it has led some philosophers to believe that analytic, contradictory, and anomalous sentences are all odd, pure and simple, and this classifies together such dissimilar cases as "An uncle is a spinster" and "A bachelor is unmarried," on the one hand, and "the paint is silent" and "Two pints of the academic liquid," on the other. With the conceptual apparatus of selection restrictions on amalgamation (formulated in terms of functions of semantic elements enclosed within angles) and (*D1*) as the basis for marking anomaly and with (*D6*) and (*D7*) and the *not*-rules as the basis for marking analyticity and contradiction, we obtain the intuitively desirable result that semantic interpretations mark semantically anomalous sentences differently from the way they mark contradictory and analytic sentences. That is, sentences that are anomalous receive no reading at the sentence level while sentences that are either contradictory or analytic receive a reading having properties which enable them to be appropriately marked.

Another matter worth noticing is the following. Consider a sequence of sentences such as "The flower is red," "The flower is not red," "the flower is not not red," and so on.[32] The third sentence in this sequence is grammatically constructed from the

---

[31]Cf. J. J. Katz and J. A. Fodor, "What's Wrong with the Philosophy of Language?" *Inquiry*, **5** (1962), 215–18.

[32]The reader may object that at some point there are too many occurrences of the word *not* in the succeeding sentences for them to be acceptable English. This is perhaps so. But if there is such a point, then none of the sentences beyond it will be grammatical, and consequently none will be generated by the grammar and provided as input to the semantic theory. Thus, the semantic theory will interpret only those sentences in such sequences that are grammatical, since a semantic theory operates only on sentences it receives from the grammar. Hence, the projection rules are stated generally in order not to decide at what point sentences in such a sequence stop and ungrammatical strings begin.

second by the negation-transformation,[33] the fourth is so constructed from the third, the fifth from the fourth, and so on. We may thus regard the third sentence as having the syntactic bracketing (*The flower*) (*is not*(*not* (*red*))). Employing (*NR*) for the operation of the *not* whose range is the path that is associated with just the word *red*, we replace this path's distinguisher e_i by A/e_i. Again applying (*NR*), but this time for the *not* whose range is the path that is associated with the expression *not red*, i.e., the path resulting from the former operation of (*NR*), we replace the semantic element A/e_i by $A/A/e_i$, which is simply e_i by (3). Thus, the reading assigned to the third sentence is the same as that assigned to the first. But this means that from the *not*-rules follows a version of the law of double negation: $X + not + not + Y = X + Y$.[34]

Furthermore, given the fact that the subject of both every odd numbered sentence in the above sequence of sentences and every even numbered sentence in this sequence is the same, it follows that every odd numbered sentence is synonymous with every other odd numbered sentence and that every even numbered sentence is synonymous with every other even numbered sentence. This is the intuitively correct result. Moreover, if we lay down the definition

> (*D9*) S_1 and S_2 are *inconsistent on a pair of readings* if the reading of one is the same as a reading of the negation of the other, i.e., if one sentence is synonymous with (or a paraphrase of) the other's negation

we can show that in the sequence of sentences we are considering (and, of course, in other similar sequences) the odd numbered sentences are inconsistent with the even numbered sentences, since every sentence in this sequence is inconsistent with its immediate successor.

Finally, a matter that needs to be mentioned for the sake of a complete treatment of contradiction, viz., the case of contradictory sentences that involve a conjunction of two incompatible predications, e.g., "The line is straight and not straight," "The creature is a cub and a pup," "The team has won the game and lost it," and so on. Although at first glance such cases appear to be outside the scope of (*D7*), this is not so. Nevertheless, showing that they can be marked as contradictory on the basis of (*D7*) requires a more complicated discussion than we can afford here.[35] Instead, then, let us simply show that such cases can be marked as contradictory within a semantic theory of our type. If we look at the grammatical structure of these cases, we notice that they are constructed from two source sentences by using the conjunction-transformation; i.e., given two sentences of the form $S_1 = X - Y_1 - Z$ and $S_2 = X - Y_2 - Z$, where Y_1 and Y_2 are constituents of the same type in their respective sentences S_1 and S_2, we may construct a new sentence $S_3 = X - Y_1 + and +$

---

[33]Cf. E. Klima, *op. cit.*

[34]This result should be taken into account in the controversy over the status of the law of double negation in the foundations of mathematics, specifically at the point at which some philosophers deny there is justification for double negation in the meaning of the word *not* in English. It can be argued on the basis of the material in the text that double negation has as strong support in the semantic structure of English as there is for simplication in the meaning of *and* in English.

[35]To show how this can be done involves using type two projection rules in such a way that one of the two conjoined sentence fragments has the path associated with it amalgamated with a path associated with the subject before the other's.

$Y_2 - Z$.[36] Thus, the first of our examples is constructed from the two source sentences "The line is straight" and, "The line is not straight" ($X = $ *the line is*, $Y_1 = $ *straight*, $Y_2 = $ *not straight*, and $Z = $ null element). Moreover, we notice that the two source sentences are inconsistent in the sense of ($D9$). Hence, we can mark the sentence "The line is straight and not straight" and other cases of incompatible predication as contradictory by the rule that the conjunction of two inconsistent copula sentences is contradictory.[37]

This concludes our treatment of analyticity and contradiction in copula sentences, but the problem of analyticity and contradiction in natural language is by no means now solved. Although philosophers have raised and discussed this problem almost exclusively in terms of copula sentences, any complete treatment of analyticity and contradiction must also provide a basis for marking these properties in noncopula sentences, i.e., sentences in which the verb is transitive or intransitive. That a complete treatment of the problem must cover sentences of these types follows from the fact that the grammar makes analytic, synthetic, and contradictory sentences of each of these types available for semantic interpretation.

Analytic Sentences

(1) The man who runs every race runs every race.
(2) The owner of the team owns the team.
(3) The person who lent Sam the book lent the book to Sam.
(4) What costs lots of money costs lots of money.
(5) The sweating man sweats sometimes.
(6) The child who often sleeps sleeps often.

Contradictory Sentences

(1) The loser of the game we like best wins the game we like best.
(2) Those who play badly play well.
(3) The owner of the team does not own the team.
(4) The sweating man never sweats.
(5) Persons who do not lend books lend books.
(6) The child who sleeps often seldom sleeps.

These examples cannot be handled by the straightforward maneuver of changing the category of the variable S in ($D6$) to ($D8$) so that it ranges over sentences of any type, instead of just copula sentences. This is because such a change would lead to false predictions. For example, because of the antonymous words *old* and *young*, the sentence "Old men like young girls" will have a semantic element in the path associated with its noun-phrase subject that is antonymous with one in the path associated with its verb phrase, and thus, according to ($D7$), a semantic theory of English will predict that this sentence is contradictory when, in fact, it is synthetic. A more sophisticated treatment is necessary.

From the viewpoint of grammar, each of the above examples of analytic and

---

[36] N. Chomsky, *Syntactic Structures*, *op. cit.*

[37] Also, we can mark the sentence "The line is straight or not straight" and other cases of exhaustive alternation as analytic by the rule that the disjunction of n-copula sentences is analytic if, and only if, each sentence introduces a different semantic element from the same antonymous n-tuple of semantic elements and every semantic element from this n-tuple is introduced by some embedded sentence.

contradictory noncopula sentences are constructed from two source sentences by the operation of a transformation that embeds one into the other. For example, the last of the sentences listed as analytic is constructed by the relative clause transformation by embedding the sentence "The child often sleeps" in the form of the fragment *who often sleeps* into the matrix sentence "The child sleeps often" just after the shared noun phrase.[38] Likewise, the last of the sentences listed as contradictory is constructed by this transformation, but in this case the embedded sentence is "The child sleeps often" and the matrix sentence is "The child seldom sleeps." Moreover, from these examples we see that the embedded sentence and the matrix sentence for an analytic sentence are synonymous or else the reading of the embedded sentence contains no semantic elements not in the reading for the matrix sentence, i.e., the embedded sentence is redundant, e.g., "The child often sleeps" and "The child sleeps often," and that the embedded sentence and the matrix sentence for a contradictory sentence are inconsistent, e.g., "The child sleeps often" and "The child seldom sleeps." But, furthermore, the embedded sentence and the matrix sentence for a synthetic, transformationally compound sentence are neither synonymous nor inconsistent, e.g., "The old men like young girls" has as its embedded sentence "The men are old" and as its matrix "The men like young girls." Thus, in order to mark noncopula sentences as analytic, synthetic, and contradictory, we shall add the definitions:

> (*D*10) A transformationally compound sentence S is *analytic on a reading* if the matrix sentence and the sentence embedded into the matrix to construct S are paraphrases on a reading or if the embedded sentence is redundant.
>
> (*D*11) A transformationally compound sentence S is *contradictory on a reading* if the matrix sentence and the sentence embedded into the matrix to form S are inconsistent on a pair of readings.
>
> (*D*12) A transformationally compound sentence S is *synthetic on a reading* if the sentence S is neither analytic nor contradictory.[39]

We may now propose an explication of entailment—the relation that holds between the antecedent and the consequent of a conditional when the latter follows from the former by virtue of a meaning relation between them. The customary explicandum is the notion that a sentence is entailed by another if, and only if, the conditional that has the latter as its antecedent and the former as its consequent is analytic. However, the absence of an adequate theory of analyticity in natural language has frustrated all attempts to replace this explicandum by a satisfactory explicatum: with no formal means for identifying conditionals which are analytic, there can be no formal means of deciding whether one sentence entails another or not. But, since the present paper gives a theory of analyticity in natural language, we may look for an extension of this theory which covers conditional sentences and in this way provides a satisfactory explicatum for entailment.

---

[38]Cf. C. S. Smith, "A Class of Complex Modifiers in English," *Language*, 37 (1961), 342–65.

[39]There are many points about the implementation of these definitions for which this is neither the time nor the place, but it should be pointed out that both the matrix sentence and the sentence embedded in it must be of maximum size when the question of their synonymy or inconsistency comes up. Cf. N. Chomsky, "The Logical Basis of Linguistic Theory," *Proceedings of the Ninth International Congress of Linguists*, M.I.T. (1962), pp. 520–24; also in the present volume.

The first step in providing such an explicatum is to set forth the definition:

(D13) The sentence S_1 entails the sentence S_2 if, and only if, the conditional "If S_1, then S_2" is analytic.

The second and final step is to set forth a definition (D14) of the term *analytic* which appears in (D13). The sentence S to which (D14) will apply must be of the form:

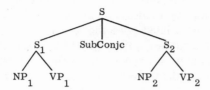

Figure 5

where S_1 is the antecedent of S (NP_1 being S_1's subject and VP_1 being S_1's main verb phrase), $SubConj_c$ is a conditional subordinating conjunction, e.g., $If \ldots$, $then \ldots$, $\ldots implies \ldots$, and so on, and S_2 is the consequent of S (NP_2 being S_2's subject and VP_2 being S_2's main verb phrase).

(D14) A sentence S (having the form depicted in Fig. 5) is *analytic on the reading* $r_{1,2}$ if, and only if,
    (a) it is the case that the reading r_1 for the whole sentence S_1 and the reading r_2 for the whole sentence S_2 which are amalgamated to form $r_{1,2}$ are, respectively, formed from the amalgamation of $r(NP_1)$ and $r(VP_1)$, where $r(NP_1)$ is the reading for NP_1 and $r(VP_1)$ is the reading for VP_1, and the amalgamation of $r(NP_2)$ and $r(VP_2)$, where $r(NP_2)$ is the reading of NP_2 and $r(VP_2)$ is the reading for VP_2 and
    (b) it is the case that the relation between $r(NP_1)$ and $r(NP_2)$ and the relation between $r(VP_1)$ and $r(VP_2)$ is exactly that which (D6) specifies for p_1 and p_2, i.e., all semantic elements in $r(NP_2)$ are in $r(NP_1)$ and all semantic elements in $r(VP_2)$ are in $r(VP_1)$.

The following examples illustrate the type of sentences whose analyticity is adequate grounds for asserting the entailment of their consequent by their antecedent. We may use them to help explain (D14).
    (1) If that person is a bachelor, then that person is male.
    (2) If a spinster is foolish, then a woman is foolish.
    (3) If a spinster is an aunt, then a woman is someone's relative.
The need to mark (1) as analytic shows that the relation between $r(VP_1)$ and $r(VP_2)$ must be that which (D6) requires of p_1 and p_2. While the need to mark (2) as analytic shows that the relation between $r(NP_1)$ and $r(NP_2)$ must be that which (D6) requires of p_1 and p_2—(3) is simply a mixed case.

Quine's complaint concerning previous attempts to draw the analytic-synthetic distinction has been that they are either circular because they assume notions that ought to be analyzed or empty because they offer no analysis whatever. Quine has demanded that the criterion we use for distinguishing between analytic and synthetic sentences avoid two traditional stumbling blocks. The criterion must not be circular: it must not require a knowledge of the sentence's analyticity nor a knowledge of other semantic properties in analyticity's tight little circle. The criterion must not be a mere stipulation: it must provide an effective means of empirically justifying the attribution of analytic status to a sentence.

We now have such a criterion, but, it is crucial to note, we have it only because we have a metatheory which characterizes the nature of a semantic theory. The metatheory tells us that a sentence S is analytic, synthetic, or contradictory depending on whether the semantic elements in p_1 and p_2 of S satisfy $(D6)$, $(D7)$, or $(D8)$.[40] A particular semantic theory of a natural language tells us, in turn, what semantic elements are in the path associated with the lexical items in S and hence what semantic elements are in the paths p_1 and p_2 of S. That the paths p_1 and p_2 of S have just the semantic elements that they need to have for S to satisfy $(D6)$ is, therefore, a matter of the correctness of the theory's dictionary entries for the lexical items in S and the correctness of the theory's projection rules that are employed to semantically interpret the constituent structure characterization of S. Both are needed to provide the derived paths p_1 and p_2. But their correctness, as Quine requires, is a matter that can be entirely settled independently of settling the particular question of S's analyticity. For the question of their correctness is a question about the adequacy of the semantic theory for marking the semantic ambiguity, anomaly, paraphrase relations, analyticity, and so on in the case of infinitely many sentences other than S, namely, those that contain some of the lexical items that are in S or those that are semantically interpreted by using some of the same projection rules that are used to obtain the derived paths p_1 and p_2 of S. Independently of an examination of S, the semantic theory can be empirically tested by comparing the claims that it makes about the semantic properties of sentences in a sample drawn from this infinite set with the linguistic intuitions of speakers. If the semantic interpretations of the theory assert that certain sentences are semantically ambiguous n-ways and they indeed are, that other sentences are anomalous and they are, that certain pairs are paraphrases and they are, and so on, then the theory is confirmed; otherwise disconfirmed. That a highly confirmed semantic theory predicts the analyticity of S is the only empirical justification that the claim that S is analytic can have, or needs. Finally, since a semantic theory's prediction that a particular sentence is analytic derives from a definition whose definiens refers solely to formal features of a semantically interpreted constituent structure characterization, there is no circularity in the way a semantic theory of the sort we have described here handles the classification and explanation of analytic sentences. For we not only provide a recursive specification of the analytic sentences of a language but we also explain what formal structure it is claimed that a sentence has when a semantic theory predicts that the sentence is analytic.

The notion *analytic sentence* that we have explicated does not cover all the cases usually described as necessary truths. Thus, our explication explains why some

---

[40]And if S is transformationally compound, depending on whether the semantic interpretations of the matrix sentence and the sentence embedded into the matrix sentence to form S satisfy $(D10)$, $(D11)$, or $(D12)$. The argument in the case of $(D10)$, $(D11)$, and $(D12)$ will be parallel; thus, it will be omitted.

necessary truths, viz., the analytic ones, are necessary, but it leaves open the question why those necessary truths that are not predicatively vacuous are necessary. Thus, the conception of analyticity and contradiction in natural language developed in this paper draws the analytic-synthetic distinction at essentially the point where Kant sought to draw it. Empiricists are thus returned from the fire of dogmatism to the frying pan of unanalyzed, synthetic necessary truths.

VI

PSYCHOLOGICAL IMPLICATIONS

There are two ways in which information from linguistics is relevant to investigations in psychology. The first has frequently been pursued by behavioral scientists. It consists of using information from linguistics in the formulation of statements which express the way a speaker's perception, production, or assimilation of linguistic material are controlled by features of his history and stimulus situation. Most experiments in what is usually called *psycholinguistics* seek empirical confirmation or disconfirmation for such statements. This way of utilizing material from linguistics attempts to answer such questions as: What sorts of conditions are required for language learning? What features of the speaker's environment determine the utterances he produces? What characteristics of a speaker's history influence his production and understanding of utterances? What physical features of an utterance are essential in coding the message it conveys?

The second way in which linguistics is relevant to investigations in psychology is less obvious and has been less often pursued. It does not seek primarily to formulate statements expressing the stimulus parameters controlling the speaker's verbal performance. Rather, it regards the speaker as a "device" with the innate capacity to assimilate the systematic structure in natural languages when exposed to the appropriate environments. Linguistics, in describing a language, describes the linguistic structure the speaker of the language has assimilated. Psychologists pursuing this way seek to provide a model of a device for assimilating structures such as those linguistics describes.

More generally, given a characterization of the structure of a natural language, it can be considered a condition of adequacy upon any theory of human learning that it be able to account for the assimilation of systems with this structure. Similarly, given a characterization of the skills employed in using a language, we may consider it a condition of adequacy upon any theory of perception or behavior that it be able to account for the employment of skills as complex as verbal skills. Thus, for example, no theory of learning which is unable to explain how grammars with transformational components are learned can be an adequate account of human learning; no theory of behavior which is unable to explain the freedom of many verbal productions from the control of local stimulation can be an adequate account of human behavior.

Each of the papers in this section concerns this second sort of psychological investigation of language. In each case, the argument proceeds by confronting one or another model of human behavior or learning or perception with facts or theories about the structure of language or linguistic skills and by evaluating the adequacy of the model in terms of its ability to accommodate them. One of the papers in this section presents negative results for the model it examines. Chomsky's paper shows that verbal behavior cannot be accounted for by Skinner's form of functional analysis. On the other hand, two of the papers present positive results supporting psychological models. Lenneberg's paper shows how certain features of natural language and certain psychological facts together support the contention that significant types of linguistic structure are innate. Halle and Stevens argue from characteristics of the phonology of natural languages to the adequacy of their model of speech recognition.

21   A Review of B. F. Skinner's *Verbal Behavior**

Noam Chomsky

I

A great many linguists and philosophers concerned with language have expressed the hope that their studies might ultimately be embedded in a framework provided by behaviorist psychology, and that refractory areas of investigation, particularly those in which meaning is involved, will in this way be opened up to fruitful exploration. Since this volume is the first large-scale attempt to incorporate the major aspects of linguistic behavior within a behaviorist framework, it merits and will undoubtedly receive careful attention. Skinner is noted for his contributions to the study of animal behavior. The book under review is the product of study of linguistic behavior extending over more than twenty years. Earlier versions of it have been fairly widely circulated, and there are quite a few references in the psychological literature to its major ideas.

The problem to which this book is addressed is that of giving a "functional analysis" of verbal behavior. By functional analysis, Skinner means identification of the variables that control this behavior and specification of how they interact to determine a particular verbal response. Furthermore, the controlling variables are to be described completely in terms of such notions as *stimulus, reinforcement, deprivation*, which have been given a reasonably clear meaning in animal experimentation. In other words, the goal of the book is to provide a way to predict and control verbal behavior by observing and manipulating the physical environment of the speaker.

Skinner feels that recent advances in the laboratory study of animal behavior permit us to approach this problem with a certain optimism, since "the basic pro-

---

*N. Chomsky, "A Review of B. F. Skinner's *Verbal Behavior*" (New York: Appleton-Century-Crofts, Inc., 1957) in *Language*, **35**, No. 1 (1959), 26–58. Reprinted by permission.

cesses and relations which give verbal behavior its special characteristics are now fairly well understood . . . the results [of this experimental work] have been surprisingly free of species restrictions. Recent work has shown that the methods can be extended to human behavior without serious modification (3).[1]

It is important to see clearly just what it is in Skinner's program and claims that makes them appear so bold and remarkable. It is not primarily the fact that he has set functional analysis as his problem, or that he limits himself to study of *observables*, i.e., input-output relations. What is so surprising is the particular limitations he has imposed on the way in which the observables of behavior are to be studied, and, above all, the particularly simple nature of the *function* which, he claims, describes the causation of behavior. One would naturally expect that prediction of the behavior of a complex organism (or machine) would require, in addition to information about external stimulation, knowledge of the internal structure of the organism, the ways in which it processes input information and organizes its own behavior. These characteristics of the organism are in general a complicated product of inborn structure, the genetically determined course of maturation, and past experience. Insofar as independent neurophysiological evidence is not available, it is obvious that inferences concerning the structure of the organism are based on observation of behavior and outside events. Nevertheless, one's estimate of the relative importance of external factors and internal structure in the determination of behavior will have an important effect on the direction of research on linguistic (or any other) behavior, and on the kinds of analogies from animal behavior studies that will be considered relevant or suggestive.

Putting it differently, anyone who sets himself the problem of analyzing the causation of behavior will (in the absence of independent neurophysiological evidence) concern himself with the only data available, namely the record of inputs to the organism and the organism's present response, and will try to describe the function specifying the response in terms of the history of inputs. This is nothing more than the definition of his problem. There are no possible grounds for argument here, if one accepts the problem as legitimate, though Skinner has often advanced and

---

[1]Skinner's confidence in recent achievements in the study of animal behavior and their applicability to complex human behavior does not appear to be widely shared. In many recent publications of confirmed behaviorists there is a prevailing note of skepticism with regard to the scope of these achievements. For representative comments, see the contributions to *Modern Learning Theory* (by W. K. Estes *et al.*; New York: Appleton-Century-Crofts, Inc., 1954); B. R. Bugelski, *Psychology of Learning* (New York: Holt, Rinehart & Winston, Inc., 1956); S. Koch, in *Nebraska Symposium on Motivation*, **58** (Lincoln, 1956); W. S. Verplanck, "Learned and Innate Behavior," *Psych. Rev.*, **52**, (1955), 139. Perhaps the strongest view is that of H. Harlow, who has asserted ("Mice, Monkeys, Men, and Motives," *Psych. Rev.*, **60**, [1953] 23–32) that "a strong case can be made for the proposition that the importance of the psychological problems studied during the last 15 years has decreased as a negatively accelerated function approaching an asymptote of complete indifference." N. Tinbergen, a leading representative of a different approach to animal-behavior studies (comparative ethology), concludes a discussion of *functional analysis* with the comment that "we may now draw the conclusion that the causation of behavior is immensely more complex than was assumed in the generalizations of the past. A number of internal and external factors act upon complex central nervous structures. Second, it will be obvious that the facts at our disposal are very fragmentary indeed"—*The Study of Instinct* (Toronto: Oxford Univ. Press, 1951), p. 74.

defended this definition of a problem as if it were a thesis which other investigators reject. The differences that arise between those who affirm and those who deny the importance of the specific "contribution of the organism" to learning and performance concern the particular character and complexity of this function, and the kinds of observations and research necessary for arriving at a precise specification of it. If the contribution of the organism is complex, the only hope of predicting behavior even in a gross way. will be through a very indirect program of research that begins by studying the detailed character of the behavior itself and the particular capacities of the organism involved.

Skinner's thesis is that external factors consisting of present stimulation and the history of reinforcement (in particular, the frequency, arrangement, and withholding of reinforcing stimuli) are of overwhelming importance, and that the general principles revealed in laboratory studies of these phenomena provide the basis for understanding the complexities of verbal behavior. He confidently and repeatedly voices his claim to have demonstrated that the contribution of the speaker is quite trivial and elementary, and that precise prediction of verbal behavior involves only specification of the few external factors that he has isolated experimentally with lower organisms.

Careful study of this book (and of the research on which it draws) reveals, however, that these astonishing claims are far from justified. It indicates, furthermore, that the insights that have been achieved in the laboratories of the reinforcement theorist, though quite genuine, can be applied to complex human behavior only in the most gross and superficial way, and that speculative attempts to discuss linguistic behavior in these terms alone omit from consideration factors of fundamental importance that are, no doubt, amenable to scientific study, although their specific character cannot at present be precisely formulated. Since Skinner's work is the most extensive attempt to accommodate human behavior involving higher mental faculties within a strict behaviorist schema of the type that has attracted many linguists and philosophers, as well as psychologists, a detailed documentation is of independent interest. The magnitude of the failure of this attempt to account for verbal behavior serves as a kind of measure of the importance of the factors omitted from consideration, and an indication of how little is really known about this remarkably complex phenomenon.

The force of Skinner's argument lies in the enormous wealth and range of examples for which he proposes a functional analysis. The only way to evaluate the success of his program and the correctness of his basic assumptions about verbal behavior is to review these examples in detail and to determine the precise character of the concepts in terms of which the functional analysis is presented. Section 2 of this review describes the experimental context with respect to which these concepts are originally defined. Sections 3 and 4 deal with the basic concepts—*stimulus*, *response*, and *reinforcement*—Sections 6 to 10 with the new descriptive machinery developed specifically for the description of verbal behavior. In Section 5 we consider the status of the fundamental claim, drawn from the laboratory, which serves as the basis for the analogic guesses about human behavior that have been proposed by many psychologists. The final section (Section 11) will consider some ways in which further linguistic work may play a part in clarifying some of these problems.

II

Although this book makes no direct reference to experimental work, it can be understood only in terms of the general framework that Skinner has developed for the description of behavior. Skinner divides the responses of the animal into two main categories. *Respondents* are purely reflex responses elicited by particular stimuli. *Operants* are emitted responses, for which no obvious stimulus can be discovered. Skinner has been concerned primarily with operant behavior. The experimental arrangement that he introduced consists basically of a box with a bar attached to one wall in such a way that when the bar is pressed, a food pellet is dropped into a tray (and the bar press is recorded). A rat placed in the box will soon press the bar, releasing a pellet into the tray. This state of affairs, resulting from the bar press, increases the *strength* of the bar-pressing operant. The food pellet is called a *reinforcer*; the event, *a reinforcing event*. The strength of an operant is defined by Skinner in terms of the rate of response during extinction (i.e., after the last reinforcement and before return to the pre-conditioning rate).

Suppose that release of the pellet is conditional on the flashing of a light. Then the rat will come to press the bar only when the light flashes. This is called *stimulus discrimination*. The response is called a *discriminated operant* and the light is called the *occasion* for its emission: this is to be distinguished from elicitation of a response by a stimulus in the case of the respondent.[2] Suppose that the apparatus is so arranged that bar-pressing of only a certain character (e.g., duration) will release the pellet. The rat will then come to press the bar in the required way. This process is called *response differentiation*. By successive slight changes in the conditions under which the response will be reinforced, it is possible to shape the response of a rat or a pigeon in very surprising ways in a very short time, so that rather complex behavior can be produced by a process of successive approximation.

A stimulus can become reinforcing by repeated association with an already reinforcing stimulus. Such a stimulus is called a *secondary reinforcer*. Like many contemporary behaviorists, Skinner considers money, approval, and the like to be secondary reinforcers which have become reinforcing because of their association with food, etc.[3] Secondary reinforcers can be *generalized* by associating them with a variety of different primary reinforcers.

---

[2] In *Behavior of Organisms* (New York: Appleton-Century-Crofts, Inc., 1938), Skinner remarks that "although a conditioned operant is the result of the correlation of the response with a particular reinforcement, a relation between it and a discriminative stimulus acting prior to the response is the almost universal rule" (178–79). Even emitted behavior is held to be produced by some sort of "originating force" (51) which, in the case of operant behavior is not under experimental control. The distinction between eliciting stimuli, discriminated stimuli, and "originating forces" has never been adequately clarified and becomes even more confusing when private internal events are considered to be discriminated stimuli (see below).

[3] In a famous experiment, chimpanzees were taught to perform complex tasks to receive tokens which had become secondary reinforcers because of association with food. The idea that money, approval, prestige, etc. actually acquire their motivating effects on human behavior according to this paradigm is unproved, and not particularly plausible. Many psychologists within the behaviorist movement are quite skeptical about this (cf. 23*n*). As in the case of most aspects of human behavior, the evidence about secondary reinforcement is so fragmentary, conflicting, and complex that almost any view can find some support.

Another variable that can affect the rate of the bar-pressing operant is drive, which Skinner defines operationally in terms of hours of deprivation. His major scientific book, *Behavior of Organisms,* is a study of the effects of food-deprivation and conditioning on the strength of the bar-pressing response of healthy mature rats. Probably Skinner's most original contribution to animal behavior studies has been his investigation of the effects of intermittent reinforcement, arranged in various different ways, presented in *Behavior of Organisms* and extended (with pecking of pigeons as the operant under investigation) in the recent *Schedules of Reinforcement* by Ferster and Skinner (1957). It is apparently these studies that Skinner has in mind when he refers to the recent advances in the study of animal behavior.[4]

The notions *stimulus, response, reinforcement* are relatively well defined with respect to the bar-pressing experiments and others similarly restricted. Before we can extend them to real-life behavior, however, certain difficulties must be faced. We must decide, first of all, whether any physical event to which the organism is capable of reacting is to be called a stimulus on a given occasion, or only one to which the organism in fact reacts; and correspondingly, we must decide whether any part of behavior is to be called a response, or only one connected with stimuli in lawful ways. Questions of this sort pose something of a dilemma for the experimental psychologist. If he accepts the broad definitions, characterizing any physical event impinging on the organism as a stimulus and any part of the organism's behavior as a response, he must conclude that behavior has not been demonstrated to be lawful. In the present state of our knowledge, we must attribute an overwhelming influence on actual behavior to ill-defined factors of attention, set, volition, and caprice. If we accept the narrower definitions, then behavior is lawful by definition (if it consists of responses); but this fact is of limited significance, since most of what the animal does will simply not be considered behavior. Hence, the psychologist either must admit that behavior is not lawful (or that he cannot at present show that it is—not at all a damaging admission for a developing science), or must restrict his attention to those highly limited areas in which it is lawful (e.g., with adequate controls, bar-pressing in rats; lawfulness of the observed behavior provides, for Skinner, an implicit definition of a good experiment).

Skinner does not consistently adopt either course. He utilizes the experimental

---

[4]Skinner's remark quoted above about the generality of his basic results must be understood in the light of the experimental limitations he has imposed. If it were true in any deep sense that the basic processes in language are well understood and free of species restriction, it would be extremely odd that language is limited to man. With the exception of a few scattered observations (cf. his article, "A Case History in Scientific Method," *The American Psychologist,* **11** [1956] 221–33), Skinner is apparently basing this claim on the fact that qualitatively similar results are obtained with bar pressing of rats and pecking of pigeons under special conditions of deprivation and various schedules of reinforcement. One immediately questions how much can be based on these facts, which are in part at least an artifact traceable to experimental design and the definition of *stimulus* and *response* in terms of *smooth dynamic curves* (see below). The dangers inherent in any attempt to *extrapolate* to complex behavior from the study of such simple responses as bar pressing should be obvious and have often been commented on (cf., e.g., Harlow, *op. cit.*). The generality of even the simplest results is open to serious question. Cf. in this connection M. E. Bitterman, J. Wodinsky, and D. K. Candland, "Some Comparative Psychology," *Am. Jour. of Psych.,* **71** (1958), 94–110, where it is shown that there are important qualitative differences in solution of comparable elementary problems by rats and fish.

results as evidence for the scientific character of his system of behavior, and analogic guesses (formulated in terms of a metaphoric extension of the technical vocabulary of the laboratory) as evidence for its scope. This creates the illusion of a rigorous scientific theory with a very broad scope, although in fact the terms used in the description of real-life and of laboratory behavior may be mere homonyms, with at most a vague similarity of meaning. To substantiate this evaluation, a critical account of his book must show that with a literal reading (where the terms of the descriptive system have something like the technical meanings given in Skinner's definitions) the book covers almost no aspect of linguistic behavior, and that with a metaphoric reading, it is no more scientific than the traditional approaches to this subject matter, and rarely as clear and careful.[5]

III

Consider first Skinner's use of the notions *stimulus* and *response*. In *Behavior of Organisms* (9) he commits himself to the narrow definitions for these terms. A part of the environment and a part of behavior are called *stimulus* (eliciting, discriminated, or reinforcing) and *response*, respectively, only if they are lawfully related; that is, if the *dynamic laws* relating them show smooth and reproducible curves. Evidently, stimuli and responses, so defined, have not been shown to figure very widely in ordinary human behavior.[6] We can, in the face of presently available evidence, continue to maintain the lawfulness of the relation between stimulus and response only by depriving them of their objective character. A typical example of *stimulus control* for Skinner would be the response to a piece of music with the utterance *Mozart* or to a painting with the response *Dutch*. These responses are asserted to be "under the control of extremely subtle properties" of the physical object or event (108). Suppose instead of saying *Dutch* we had said *Clashes with the wallpaper, I thought you liked abstract work, Never saw it before, Tilted, Hanging too low, Beautiful, Hideous, Remember our camping trip last summer?*, or whatever else might come into our minds when looking at a picture (in Skinnerian translation, whatever other responses exist in sufficient strength). Skinner could only say that each of these responses is under

---

[5]An analogous argument, in connection with a different aspect of Skinner's thinking, is given by M. Scriven in "*A Study of Radical Behaviorism*," *Univ. of Minn. Studies in Philosophy of Science*, I. Cf. Verplanck's contribution to *Modern Learning Theory*, *op. cit.* pp. 283–88, for more general discussion of the difficulties in formulating an adequate definition of *stimulus* and *response*. He concludes, quite correctly, that in Skinner's sense of the word, stimuli are not objectively identifiable independently of the resulting behavior, nor are they manipulable. Verplanck presents a clear discussion of many other aspects of Skinner's system, commenting on the untestability of many of the so-called "laws of behavior" and the limited scope of many of the others, and the arbitrary and obscure character of Skinner's notion of *lawful relation*; and, at the same time, noting the importance of the experimental data that Skinner has accumulated.

[6]In *Behavior of Organisms*, Skinner apparently was willing to accept this consequence. He insists (41–42) that the terms of casual description in the popular vocabulary are not validly descriptive until the defining properties of stimulus and response are specified, the correlation is demonstrated experimentally, and the dynamic changes in it are shown to be lawful. Thus, in describing a child as hiding from a dog, "it will not be enough to dignify the popular vocabulary by appealing to essential properties of *dogness* or *hidingness* and to suppose them intuitively known." But this is exactly what Skinner does in the book under review, as we will see directly.

the control of some other stimulus property of the physical object. If we look at a red chair and say *red*, the response is under the control of the stimulus *redness*; if we say *chair*, it is under the control of the collection of properties (for Skinner, the object) *chairness* (110), and similarly for any other response. This device is as simple as it is empty. Since properties are free for the asking (we have as many of them as we have nonsynonymous descriptive expressions in our language, whatever this means exactly), we can account for a wide class of responses in terms of Skinnerian functional analysis by identifying the *controlling stimuli*. But the word *stimulus* has lost all objectivity in this usage. Stimuli are no longer part of the outside physical world; they are driven back into the organism. We identify the stimulus when we hear the response. It is clear from such examples, which abound, that the talk of *stimulus control* simply disguises a complete retreat to mentalistic psychology. We cannot predict verbal behavior in terms of the stimuli in the speaker's environment, since we do not know what the current stimuli are until he responds. Furthermore, since we cannot control the property of a physical object to which an individual will respond, except in highly artificial cases, Skinner's claim that his system, as opposed to the traditional one, permits the practical control of verbal behavior[7] is quite false.

Other examples of *stimulus control* merely add to the general mystification. Thus, a proper noun is held to be a response "under the control of a specific person or thing" (as controlling stimulus, 113). I have often used the words *Eisenhower* and *Moscow*, which I presume are proper nouns if anything is, but have never been *stimulated* by the corresponding objects. How can this fact be made compatible with this definition? Suppose that I use the name of a friend who is not present. Is this an instance of a proper noun under the control of the friend as stimulus? Elsewhere it is asserted that a stimulus controls a response in the sense that presence of the stimulus increases the probability of the response. But it is obviously untrue that the probability that a speaker will produce a full name is increased when its bearer faces the speaker. Furthermore, how can one's own name be a proper noun in this sense?

---

[7]253f. and elsewhere, repeatedly. As an example of how well we can control behavior using the notions developed in this book, Skinner shows here how he would go about evoking the response *pencil*. The most effective way, he suggests, is to say to the subject, "Please say *pencil*" (our chances would, presumably, be even further improved by use of "aversive stimulation," e.g., holding a gun to his head). We can also "make sure that no pencil or writing instrument is available, then hand our subject a pad of paper appropriate to pencil sketching, and offer him a handsome reward for a recognizable picture of a cat." It would also be useful to have voices saying *pencil* or *pen and* .. in the background; signs reading *pencil* or *pen and* .. ; or to place a "large and unusual pencil in an unusual place clearly in sight." "Under such circumstances, it is highly probable that our subject will say *pencil*." "The available techniques are all illustrated in this sample." These contributions of behavior theory to the practical control of human behavior are amply illustrated elsewhere in the book, as when Skinner shows (113–14) how we can evoke the response *red* (the device suggested is to hold a red object before the subject and say, "Tell me what color this is").

In fairness, it must be mentioned that there are certain nontrivial applications of *operant conditioning* to the control of human behavior. A wide variety of experiments have shown that the number of plural nouns (for example) produced by a subject will increase if the experimenter says "right" or "good" when one is produced (similarly, positive attitudes on a certain issue, stories with particular content, etc.; cf. L. Krasner, "Studies of the Conditioning of Verbal Behavior," *Psych. Bull.*, **55** [1958], for a survey of several dozen experiments of this kind, mostly with positive results). It is of some interest that the subject is usually unaware of the process. Just what insight this gives into normal verbal behavior is not obvious. Nevertheless, it is an example of positive and not totally expected results using the Skinnerian paradigm.

A multitude of similar questions arise immediately. It appears that the word *control* here is merely a misleading paraphrase for the traditional *denote* or *refer*. The assertion (115) that so far as the speaker is concerned, the relation of reference is "simply the probability that the speaker will emit a response of a given form in the presence of a stimulus having specified properties" is surely incorrect if we take the words *presence*, *stimulus*, and *probability* in their literal sense. That they are not intended to be taken literally is indicated by many examples, as when a response is said to be "controlled" by a situation or state of affairs as "stimulus." Thus, the expression *a needle in a haystack* "may be controlled as a unit by a particular type of situation" (116); the words in a single part of speech, e.g., all adjectives, are under the control of a single set of subtle properties of stimuli (121); "the sentence *The boy runs a store* is under the control of an extremely complex stimulus situation" (335); "*He is not at all well* may function as a standard response under the control of a state of affairs which might also control *He is ailing*" (325); when an envoy observes events in a foreign country and reports upon his return, his report is under "remote stimulus control" (416); the statement *This is war* may be a response to a "confusing international situation" (441); the suffix *-ed* is controlled by that "subtle property of stimuli which we speak of as action-in-the-past" (121) just as the *-s* in *The boy runs* is under the control of such specific features of the situation as its "currency" (332). No characterization of the notion *stimulus control* that is remotely related to the bar-pressing experiment (or that preserves the faintest objectivity) can be made to cover a set of examples like these, in which, for example, the *controlling stimulus* need not even impinge on the responding organism.

Consider now Skinner's use of the notion *response*. The problem of identifying units in verbal behavior has of course been a primary concern of linguists, and it seems very likely that experimental psychologists should be able to provide much-needed assistance in clearing up the many remaining difficulties in systematic identification. Skinner recognizes (20) the fundamental character of the problem of identification of a unit of verbal behavior, but is satisfied with an answer so vague and subjective that it does not really contribute to its solution. The unit of verbal behavior—the verbal operant—is defined as a class of responses of identifiable form functionally related to one or more controlling variables. No method is suggested for determining in a particular instance what are the controlling variables, how many such units have occurred, or where their boundaries are in the total response. Nor is any attempt made to specify how much or what kind of similarity in form or *control* is required for two physical events to be considered instances of the same operant. In short, no answers are suggested for the most elementary questions that must be asked of anyone proposing a method for description of behavior. Skinner is content with what he calls an *extrapolation* of the concept of operant developed in the laboratory to the verbal field. In the typical Skinnerian experiment, the problem of identifying the unit of behavior is not too crucial. It is defined, by fiat, as a recorded peck or bar-press, and systematic variations in the rate of this operant and its resistance to extinction are studied as a function of deprivation and scheduling of reinforcement (pellets). The operant is thus defined with respect to a particular experimental procedure. This is perfectly reasonable and has led to many interesting results. It is, however, completely meaningless to speak of extrapolating this concept of operant to ordinary verbal behavior. Such "extrapolation" leaves us with no way of justifying one or another decision about the units in the "verbal repertoire."

Skinner specifies "response strength" as the basic datum, the basic dependent variable in his functional analysis. In the bar-pressing experiment, response strength is defined in terms of rate of emission during extinction. Skinner has argued[8] that this is "the only datum that varies significantly and in the expected direction under conditions which are relevant to the 'learning process.' " In the book under review, response strength is defined as "probability of emission" (22). This definition provides a comforting impression of objectivity, which, however, is quickly dispelled when we look into the matter more closely. The term *probability* has some rather obscure meaning for Skinner in this book.[9] We are told, on the one hand, that "our evidence for the contribution of each variable [to response strength] is based on observation of frequencies alone" (28). At the same time, it appears that frequency is a very misleading measure of strength, since, for example, the frequency of a response may be "primarily attributable to the frequency of occurrence of controlling variables" (27). It is not clear how the frequency of a response can be attributable to anything BUT the frequency of occurrence of its controlling variables if we accept Skinner's view that the behavior occurring in a given situation is "fully determined" by the relevant controlling variables (175, 228). Furthermore, although the evidence for the contribution of each variable to response strength is based on observation of frequencies alone, it turns out that "we base the notion of strength upon several kinds of evidence" (22), in particular (22–28): emission of the response (particularly in unusual circumstances), energy level (stress), pitch level, speed and delay of emission, size of letters etc. in writing, immediate repetition, and—a final factor, relevant but misleading—over-all frequency.

Of course, Skinner recognizes that these measures do not co-vary, because (among other reasons) pitch, stress, quantity, and reduplication may have internal linguistic functions.[10] However, he does not hold these conflicts to be very important, since the proposed factors indicative of strength are "fully understood by everyone" in the culture (27). For example, "if we are shown a prized work of art and exclaim *Beautiful!*, the speed and energy of the response will not be lost on the owner." It does not appear totally obvious that in this case the way to impress the owner is to shriek *Beautiful* in a loud, high-pitched voice, repeatedly, and with no delay (high

---

[8]"Are Theories of Learning Necessary?", *Psych. Rev.*, **57** (1950), 193–216.

[9]And elsewhere. In his paper "Are Theories of Learning Necessary?" Skinner considers the problem how to extend his analysis of behavior to experimental situations in which it is impossible to observe frequencies, rate of response being the only valid datum. His answer is that "the notion of probability is usually extrapolated to cases in which a frequency analysis cannot be carried out. In the field of behavior we arrange a situation in which frequencies are available as data, but we use the notion of probability in analyzing or formulating instances of even types of behavior which are not susceptible to this analysis" (199). There are, of course, conceptions of probability not based directly on frequency, but I do not see how any of these apply to the cases that Skinner has in mind. I see no way of interpreting the quoted passage other than as signifying an intention to use the word *probability* in describing behavior quite independently of whether the notion of probability is at all relevant.

[10]Fortunately, "In English this presents no great difficulty" since, for example, "relative pitch levels ... are not ... important" (25). No reference is made to the numerous studies of the function of relative pitch levels and other intonational features in English.

response strength). It may be equally effective to look at the picture silently (long delay) and then to murmur *Beautiful* in a soft, low-pitched voice (by definition, very low response strength).

It is not unfair, I believe, to conclude from Skinner's discussion of response strength, the *basic datum* in functional analysis, that his *extrapolation* of the notion of probability can best be interpreted as, in effect, nothing more than a decision to use the word *probability*, with its favorable connotations of objectivity, as a cover term to paraphrase such low-status words as *interest, intention, belief*, and the like. This interpretation is fully justified by the way in which Skinner uses the terms *probability* and *strength*. To cite just one example, Skinner defines the process of confirming an assertion in science as one of "generating additional variables to increase its probability" (425), and more generally, its strength (425–29). If we take this suggestion quite literally, the degree of confirmation of a scientific assertion can be measured as a simple function of the loudness, pitch, and frequency with which it is proclaimed, and a general procedure for increasing its degree of confirmation would be, for instance, to train machine guns on large crowds of people who have been instructed to shout it. A better indication of what Skinner probably has in mind here is given by his description of how the theory of evolution, as an example, is confirmed. This "single set of verbal responses . . . is made more plausible—is strengthened—by several types of construction based upon verbal responses in geology, paleontology, genetics, and so on" (427). We are no doubt to interpret the terms *strength* and *probability* in this context as paraphrases of more familiar locutions such as "justified belief" or "warranted assertability," or something of the sort. Similar latitude of interpretation is presumably expected when we read that "frequency of effective action accounts in turn for what we may call the listener's 'belief' " (88) or that "our belief in what someone tells us is similarly a function of, or identical with, our tendency to act upon the verbal stimuli which he provides" (160).[11]

I think it is evident, then, that Skinner's use of the terms *stimulus, control, response*, and *strength* justify the general conclusion stated in the last paragraph of Section 2. The way in which these terms are brought to bear on the actual data indicates that we must interpret them as mere paraphrases for the popular vocabulary commonly used to describe behavior and as having no particular connection with the homonymous expressions used in the description of laboratory experiments. Naturally, this terminological revision adds no objectivity to the familiar *mentalistic* mode of description.

IV

The other fundamental notion borrowed from the description of bar-pressing experiments is *reinforcement*. It raises problems which are similar, and even more serious. In *Behavior of Organisms*, "the operation of reinforcement is defined as the

---

[11]The vagueness of the word *tendency*, as opposed to *frequency*, saves the latter quotation from the obvious incorrectness of the former. Nevertheless, a good deal of stretching is necessary. If *tendency* has anything like its ordinary meaning, the remark is clearly false. One may believe strongly the assertion that Jupiter has four moons, that many of Sophocles' plays have been irretrievably lost, that the earth will burn to a crisp in ten million years, and so on, without experiencing the slightest tendency to act upon these verbal stimuli. We may, of course, turn Skinner's assertion into a very unilluminating truth by defining "tendency to act" to include tendencies to answer questions in certain ways, under motivation to say what one believes is true.

presentation of a certain kind of stimulus in a temporal relation with either a stimulus or response. A reinforcing stimulus is defined as such by its power to produce the resulting change [in strength]. There is no circularity about this: some stimuli are found to produce the change, others not, and they are classified as reinforcing and nonreinforcing accordingly" (62). This is a perfectly appropriate definition[12] for the study of schedules of reinforcement. It is perfectly useless, however, in the discussion of real-life behavior, unless we can somehow characterize the stimuli which are reinforcing (and the situations and conditions under which they are reinforcing). Consider first of all the status of the basic principle that Skinner calls the "law of conditioning" (law of effect). It reads: "if the occurrence of an operant is followed by presence of a reinforcing stimulus, the strength is increased" (*Behavior of Organisms*, 21). As *reinforcement* was defined, this law becomes a tautology.[13] For Skinner, learning is just change in response strength.[14] Although the statement that presence of reinforcement is a sufficient condition for learning and maintenance of behavior is vacuous, the claim that it is a necessary condition may have some content, depending on how the class of reinforcers (and appropriate situations) is characterized. Skinner does make it very clear that in his view reinforcement is a necessary condition for language learning and for the continued availability of linguistic responses in the adult.[15] However, the looseness of the term *reinforcement* as Skinner uses it in the book under review makes it entirely pointless to inquire into the truth or falsity of this claim. Examining the instances of what Skinner calls *reinforcement*, we find that not even the requirement that a reinforcer be an identifiable stimulus is taken seriously. In fact, the term is used in such a way that the assertion that reinforcement is necessary for learning and continued availability of behavior is likewise empty.

To show this, we consider some examples of *reinforcement*. First of all, we find a heavy appeal to automatic self-reinforcement. Thus, "a man talks to himself . . . because of the reinforcement he receives" (163); "the child is reinforced automatically when he duplicates the sounds of airplanes, streetcars . . ." (164); "the young child alone in the nursery may automatically reinforce his own exploratory verbal behavior when he produces sounds which he has heard in the speech of others" (58); "the speaker who is also an accomplished listener 'knows when he has correctly echoed a response' and is reinforced thereby" (68); thinking is "behaving which automatically affects the behaver and is reinforcing because it does so" (438; cutting one's finger should thus be reinforcing, and an example of thinking); "the verbal fantasy,

---

[12]One should add, however, that it is in general not the stimulus as such that is reinforcing, but the stimulus in a particular situational context. Depending on experimental arrangement, a particular physical event or object may be reinforcing, punishing, or unnoticed. Because Skinner limits himself to a particular, very simple experimental arrangement, it is not necessary for him to add this qualification, which would not be at all easy to formulate precisely. But it is of course necessary if he expects to extend his descriptive system to behavior in general.

[13]This has been frequently noted.

[14]See, for example, "Are Theories of Learning Necessary?", *op. cit.*, p. 199. Elsewhere, he suggests that the term *learning* be restricted to complex situations, but these are not characterized.

[15]"A child acquires verbal behavior when relatively unpatterned vocalizations, selectively reinforced, gradually assume forms which produce appropriate consequences in a given verbal community" (31). "Differential reinforcement shapes up all verbal forms, and when a prior stimulus enters into the contingency, reinforcement is responsible for its resulting control. . . . The availability of behavior, its probability or strength, depends on whether reinforcements *continue* in effect and according to what schedules" (203–4); elsewhere, frequently.

whether overt or covert, is automatically reinforcing to the speaker as listener. Just as the musician plays or composes what he is reinforced by hearing, or as the artist paints what reinforces him visually, so the speaker engaged in verbal fantasy says what he is reinforced by hearing or writes what he is reinforced by reading" (439); similarly, care in problem solving, and rationalization, are automatically self-reinforcing (442–43). We can also reinforce someone by emitting verbal behavior as such (since this rules out a class of aversive stimulations, 167), by not emitting verbal behavior (keeping silent and paying attention, 199), or by acting appropriately on some future occasion (152: "the strength of [the speaker's] behavior is determined mainly by the behavior which the listener will exhibit with respect to a given state of affairs"; this Skinner considers the general case of "communication" or "letting the listener know"). In most such cases, of course, the speaker is not present at the time when the reinforcement takes place, as when "the artist . . . is reinforced by the effects his works have upon . . . others" (224), or when the writer is reinforced by the fact that his "verbal behavior may reach over centuries or to thousands of listeners or readers at the same time. The writer may not be reinforced often or immediately, but his net reinforcement may be great" (206; this accounts for the great "strength" of his behavior). An individual may also find it reinforcing to injure someone by criticism or by bringing bad news, or to publish an experimental result which upsets the theory of a rival (154), to describe circumstances which would be reinforcing if they were to occur (165), to avoid repetition (222), to "hear" his own name though in fact it was not mentioned or to hear nonexistent words in his child's babbling (259), to clarify or otherwise intensify the effect of a stimulus which serves an important discriminative function (416), and so on.

From this sample, it can be seen that the notion of reinforcement has totally lost whatever objective meaning it may ever have had. Running through these examples, we see that a person can be reinforced though he emits no response at all, and that the reinforcing *stimulus* need not impinge on the *reinforced person* or need not even exist (it is sufficient that it be imagined or hoped for). When we read that a person plays what music he likes (165), says what he likes (165), thinks what he likes (438-39), reads what books he likes (163), etc., BECAUSE he finds it reinforcing to do so, or that we write books or inform others of facts BECAUSE we are reinforced by what we hope will be the ultimate behavior of reader or listener, we can only conclude that the term *reinforcement* has a purely ritual function. The phrase "*X* is reinforced by *Y* (stimulus, state of affairs, event, etc.)" is being used as a cover term for "*X* wants *Y*," "*X* likes *Y*," "*X* wishes that *Y* were the case," etc. Invoking the term *reinforcement* has no explanatory force, and any idea that this paraphrase introduces any new clarity or objectivity into the description of wishing, liking, etc., is a serious delusion. The only effect is to obscure the important differences among the notions being paraphrased. Once we recognize the latitude with which the term *reinforcement* is being used, many rather startling comments lose their initial effect—for instance, that the behavior of the creative artist is "controlled entirely by the contingencies of reinforcement" (150). What has been hoped for from the psychologist is some indication how the casual and informal description of everyday behavior in the popular vocabulary can be explained or clarified in terms of the notions developed in careful experiment and observation, or perhaps replaced in terms of a better scheme. A mere terminological revision, in which a term borrowed from the laboratory is used with the full vagueness of the ordinary vocabulary, is of no conceivable interest.

It seems that Skinner's claim that all verbal behavior is acquired and maintained in "strength" through reinforcement is quite empty, because his notion of reinforcement has no clear content, functioning only as a cover term for any factor, detectable or not, related to acquisition or maintenance of verbal behavior.[16] Skinner's use of the term *conditioning* suffers from a similar difficulty. Pavlovian and operant conditioning are processes about which psychologists have developed real understanding. Instruction of human beings is not. The claim that instruction and imparting of information are simply matters of conditioning (357–66) is pointless. The claim is true, if we extend the term *conditioning* to cover these processes, but we know no more about them after having revised this term in such a way as to deprive it of its relatively clear and objective character. It is, as far as we know, quite false, if we use *conditioning* in its literal sense. Similarly, when we say that "it is the function of predication to facilitate the transfer of response from one term to another or from one object to another" (361), we have said nothing of any significance. In what sense is this true of the predication *Whales are mammals*? Or, to take Skinner's example, what point is there in saying that the effect of *The telephone is out of order* on the listener is to bring behavior formerly controlled by the stimulus *out of order* under control of the stimulus *telephone* (or the telephone itself) by a process of simple conditioning (362)? What laws of conditioning hold in this case? Furthermore, what behavior is *controlled* by the stimulus *out of order*, in the abstract? Depending on the object of which this is predicated, the present state of motivation of the listener, etc., the behavior may vary from rage to pleasure, from fixing the object to throwing it out, from simply not using it to trying to use it in the normal way (e.g., to see if it is really out of order), and so on. To speak of "conditioning" or "bringing previously available behavior under control of a new stimulus" in such a case is just a kind of play-acting at science (cf. also 43*n*).

V

The claim that careful arrangement of contingencies of reinforcement by the verbal community is a necessary condition for language-learning has appeared, in one form or another, in many places.[17] Since it is based not on actual observation, but on analogies to laboratory study of lower organisms, it is important to determine the status of the underlying assertion within experimental psychology proper. The most common characterization of reinforcement (one which Skinner explicitly re-

---

[16]Talk of schedules of reinforcement here is entirely pointless. How are we to decide, for example, according to what schedules covert reinforcement is *arranged*, as in thinking or verbal fantasy, or what the scheduling is of such factors as silence, speech, and appropriate future reactions to communicated information?

[17]See, for example, N. E. Miller and J. Dollard, *Social Learning and Imitation* (New York, 1941), pp. 82–83, for a discussion of the "meticulous training" that they seem to consider necessary for a child to learn the meanings of words and syntactic patterns. The same notion is implicit in O. H. Mowrer's speculative account of how language might be acquired, in *Learning Theory and Personality Dynamics*, (New York: The Ronald Press, Inc., 1950), Chap. 23. Actually, the view appears to be quite general.

jects, incidentally) is in terms of drive reduction. This characterization can be given substance by defining drives in some way independently of what in fact is learned. If a drive is postulated on the basis of the fact that learning takes place, the claim that reinforcement is necessary for learning will again become as empty as it is in the Skinnerian framework. There is an extensive literature on the question of whether there can be learning without drive reduction (latent learning). The "classical" experiment of Blodgett indicated that rats who had explored a maze without reward showed a marked drop in number of errors (as compared to a control group which had not explored the maze) upon introduction of a food reward, indicating that the rat had learned the structure of the maze without reduction of the hunger drive. Drive-reduction theorists countered with an exploratory drive which was reduced during the pre-reward learning, and claimed that a slight decrement in errors could be noted before food reward. A wide variety of experiments, with somewhat conflicting results, have been carried out with a similar design.[18] Few investigators still doubt the existence of the phenomenon. E. R. Hilgard, in his general review of learning theory,[19] concludes that "there is no longer any doubt but that, under appropriate circumstances, latent learning is demonstrable."

More recent work has shown that novelty and variety of stimulus are sufficient to arouse curiosity in the rat and to motivate it to explore (visually), and in fact, to learn (since on a presentation of two stimuli, one novel, one repeated, the rat will attend to the novel one),[20] that rats will learn to choose the arm of a single-choice maze that leads to a complex maze, running through this being their only "reward";[21] that monkeys can learn object discriminations and maintain their performance at a high level of efficiency with visual exploration (looking out of a window for 30 seconds) as the only reward;[22] and, perhaps most strikingly of all, that monkeys and apes will solve rather complex manipulation problems that are simply placed in their cages, and will solve discrimination problems with only exploration and manipulation as incentives.[23] In these cases, solving the problem is apparently its own "re-

---

[18]For a general review and analysis of this literature, see D. L. Thistlethwaite, "A Critical Review of Latent Learning and Related Experiments," *Psych. Bull.*, **48** (1951), 97–129. K. Mac-Corquodale and P. E. Meehl, in their contribution to *Modern Learning Theory op. cit.*, carry out a serious and considered attempt to handle the latent learning material from the standpoint of drive-reduction theory, with (as they point out) not entirely satisfactory results. W. H. Thorpe reviews the literature from the standpoint of the ethologist, adding also material on homing and topographical orientation (*Learning and Instinct in Animals* [Cambridge, 1956]).

[19]*Theories of Learning*, 214 (1956).

[20]O. E. Berlyne, "Novelty and Curiosity as Determinants of Exploratory Behavior," *Brit. Jour. of Psych.*, **41** (1950), 68–80; *id.*, "Perceptual Curiosity in the Rat," *Jour. of Comp. Physiol. Psych.*, **48** (1955), 238–46; W. R. Thompson and L. M. Solomon, "Spontaneous Pattern Discrimination in the Rat," *ibid.*, **47** (1954), 104–7.

[21]K. C. Montgomery, "The Role of the Exploratory Drive in Learning," *ibid.* pp. 60–63. Many other papers in the same journal are designed to show that exploratory behavior is a relatively independent primary "drive" aroused by novel external stimulation.

[22]R. A. Butler, "Discrimination Learning by Rhesus Monkeys to Visual-Exploration Motivation," *ibid.*, **46** (1953), 95–98. Later experiments showed that this "drive" is highly persistent, as opposed to derived drives which rapidly extinguish.

[23]H. F. Harlow, M. K. Harlow, and D. R. Meyer, "Learning Motivated by a Manipulation Drive," *Jour. Exp. Psych.*, **40** (1950), 228–34, and later investigations initiated by Harlow. Harlow has been particularly insistent on maintaining the inadequacy of physiologically based drives and homeostatic need states for explaining the persistence of motivation and rapidity of learning in primates. He points out, in many papers, that curiosity, play, exploration, and manipulation are,

ward." Results of this kind can be handled by reinforcement theorists only if they are willing to set up curiosity, exploration, and manipulation drives, or to speculate somehow about acquired drives[24] for which there is no evidence outside of the fact that learning takes place in these cases.

There is a variety of other kinds of evidence that has been offered to challenge the view that drive reduction is necessary for learning. Results on sensory-sensory conditioning have been interpreted as demonstrating learning without drive reduction.[25] Olds has reported reinforcement by direct stimulation of the brain, from which he concludes that reward need not satisfy a physiological need or withdraw a drive stimulus.[26] The phenomenon of imprinting, long observed by zoologists, is of particular interest in this connection. Some of the most complex patterns of behavior of birds, in particular, are directed towards objects and animals of the type to which they have been exposed at certain critical early periods of life.[27] Imprinting is the most striking evidence for the innate disposition of the animal to learn in a certain direction and to react appropriately to patterns and objects of certain restricted types, often only long after the original learning has taken place. It is, consequently, unrewarded learning, though the resulting patterns of behavior may be refined through reinforcement. Acquisition of the typical songs of song birds is, in some cases, a type of imprinting. Thorpe reports studies that show "that some characteristics of the normal song have been learned in the earliest youth, before the bird

---

for primates, often more potent drives than hunger and the like, and that they show none of the characteristics of acquired drives. Hebb also presents behavioral and supporting neurological evidence in support of the view that in higher animals there is a positive attraction in work, risk, puzzle, intellectual activity, mild fear and frustration, and so on. ("Drives and the CNS," *Psych. Rev.*, **62** [1955], 243–54.) He concludes that "we need not work out tortuous and improbable ways to explain why men work for money, why children learn without pain, why people dislike doing nothing."

In a brief note ("Early Recognition of the Manipulative Drive in Monkeys," *British Journal of Animal Behaviour*, 3 [1955], 71–72), W. Dennis calls attention to the fact that early investigators (G. J. Romanes, 1882; E. L. Thorndike, 1901), whose "perception was relatively unaffected by learning theory, did note the intrinsically motivated behavior of monkeys," although, he asserts, no similar observations on monkeys have been made until Harlow's experiments. He quotes Romanes (*Animal Intelligence* [1882]) as saying that "much the most striking feature in the psychology of this animal, and the one which is least like anything met with in other animals, was the tireless spirit of investigation " Analogous developments, in which genuine discoveries have blinded systematic investigators to the important insights of earlier work, are easily found within recent structural linguistics as well.

[24]Thus, J. S. Brown, in commenting on a paper of Harlow's in *Current Theory and Research in Motivation* (Lincoln: Univ. of Nebraska Press, 1953), argues that "in probably every instance [of the experiments cited by Harlow] an ingenious drive-reduction theorist could find some fragment of fear, insecurity, frustration, or whatever, that he could insist was reduced and hence was reinforcing" (53). The same sort of thing could be said for the ingenious phlogiston or ether theorist.

[25]Cf. H. G. Birch and M. E. Bitterman, "Reinforcement and Learning: The process of Sensory Integration," *Psych. Rev.*, **56** (1949), 292–308.

[26]See, for example, his paper "A Physiological Study of Reward" in D. C. McClelland, ed., *Studies in Motivation* (New York: Appleton-Century-Crafts, Inc., 1955), pp. 134–43.

[27]See Thorpe, *op. cit.*, particularly pp. 115–18 and 337–76, for an excellent discussion of this phenomenon, which has been brought to prominence particularly by the work of K. Lorenz (cf. "Der Kumpan in der Umwelt des Vogels," parts of which are reprinted in English translation in C. M. Schiller, ed., *Instinctive Behavior* [New York: International Universities Press, 1957], pp. 83–128).

itself is able to produce any kind of full song."[28] The phenomenon of imprinting has recently been investigated under laboratory conditions and controls with positive results.[29]

Phenomena of this general type are certainly familiar from everyday experience. We recognize people and places to which we have given no particular attention. We can look up something in a book and learn it perfectly well with no other motive than to confute reinforcement theory, or out of boredom, or idle curiosity. Everyone engaged in research must have had the experience of working with feverish and prolonged intensity to write a paper which no one else will read or to solve a problem which no one else thinks important and which will bring no conceivable reward— which may only confirm a general opinion that the researcher is wasting his time on irrelevancies. The fact that rats and monkeys do likewise is interesting and important to show in careful experiment. In fact, studies of behavior of the type mentioned above have an independent and positive significance that far outweighs their incidental importance in bringing into question the claim that learning is impossible without drive reduction. It is not at all unlikely that insights arising from animal-behavior studies with this broadened scope may have the kind of relevance to such complex activities as verbal behavior that reinforcement theory has, so far, failed to exhibit. In any event, in the light of presently available evidence, it is difficult to see how anyone can be willing to claim that reinforcement is necessary for learning, if reinforcement is taken seriously as something identifiable independently of the resulting change in behavior.

Similarly, it seems quite beyond question that children acquire a good deal of their verbal and nonverbal behavior by casual observation and imitation of adults and other children.[30] It is simply not true that children can learn language only through "meticulous care" on the part of adults who shape their verbal repertoire through careful differential reinforcement, though it may be that such care is often the custom in academic families. It is a common observation that a young child of immigrant

---

[28]*Op. cit.*, p. 372.

[29]See, e.g., J. Jaynes, "Imprinting: Interaction of Learned and Innate Behavior," *Jour. of Comp. Physiol. Psych.*, **49** (1956), 201–6, where the conclusion is reached that "the experiments prove that without any observable reward, young birds of this species follow a moving stimulus object and very rapidly come to prefer that object to others."

[30]Of course, it is perfectly possible to incorporate this fact within the Skinnerian framework. If, for example, a child watches an adult using a comb and then, with no instruction, tries to comb his own hair, we can explain this act by saying that he performs it because he finds it reinforcing to do so, or because of the reinforcement provided by behaving like a person who is "reinforcing" (cf. 164). Similarly, an automatic explanation is available for any other behavior. It seems strange at first that Skinner pays so little attention to the literature on latent learning and related topics, considering the tremendous reliance that he places on the notion of reinforcement; I have seen no reference to it in his writings. Similarly, F. S. Keller and W. N. Schoenfeld, in what appears to be the only text written under predominantly Skinnerian influence, *Principles of Psychology* (New York: Appleton-Century-Crofts, Inc., 1950), dismiss the latent-learning literature in one sentence as "beside the point," serving only "to obscure, rather than clarify, a fundamental principle" (*the law of effect*, 41). However, this neglect is perfectly appropriate in Skinner's case. To the drive-reductionist, or anyone else for whom the notion *reinforcement* has some substantive meaning, these experiments and observations are important (and often embarrassing). But in the Skinnerian sense of the word, neither these results nor any conceivable others can cast any doubt on the claim that reinforcement is essential for the acquisition and maintenance of behavior. Behavior certainly has some concomitant circumstances, and whatever they are, we can call them *reinforcement*.

parents may learn a second language in the streets, from other children, with amazing rapidity, and that his speech may be completely fluent and correct to the last allophone, while the subtleties that become second nature to the child may elude his parents despite high motivation and continued practice. A child may pick up a large part of his vocabulary and "feel" for sentence structure from television, from reading, from listening to adults, etc. Even a very young child who has not yet acquired a minimal repertoire from which to form new utterances may imitate a word quite well on an early try, with no attempt on the part of his parents to teach it to him. It is also perfectly obvious that, at a later stage, a child will be able to construct and understand utterances which are quite new, and are, at the same time, acceptable sentences in his language. Every time an adult reads a newspaper, he undoubtedly comes upon countless new sentences which are not at all similar, in a simple, physical sense, to any that he has heard before, and which he will recognize as sentences and understand; he will also be able to detect slight distortions or misprints. Talk of "stimulus generalization" in such a case simply perpetuates the mystery under a new title. These abilities indicate that there must be fundamental processes at work quite independently of "feedback" from the environment. I have been able to find no support whatsoever for the doctrine of Skinner and others that slow and careful shaping of verbal behavior through differential reinforcement is an absolute necessity. If reinforcement theory really requires the assumption that there be such meticulous care, it seems best to regard this simply as a *reductio ad absurdum* argument against this approach. It is also not easy to find any basis (or, for that matter, to attach very much content) to the claim that reinforcing contingencies set up by the verbal community are the single factor responsible for maintaining the strength of verbal behavior. The sources of the "strength" of this behavior are almost a total mystery at present. Reinforcement undoubtedly plays a significant role, but so do a variety of motivational factors about which nothing serious is known in the case of human beings.

As far as acquisition of language is concerned, it seems clear that reinforcement, casual observation, and natural inquisitiveness (coupled with a strong tendency to imitate) are important factors, as is the remarkable capacity of the child to generalize, hypothesize, and "process information" in a variety of very special and apparently highly complex ways which we cannot yet describe or begin to understand, and which may be largely innate, or may develop through some sort of learning or through maturation of the nervous system. The manner in which such factors operate and interact in language acquisition is completely unknown. It is clear that what is necessary in such a case is research, not dogmatic and perfectly arbitrary claims, based on analogies to that small part of the experimental literature in which one happens to be interested.

The pointlessness of these claims becomes clear when we consider the well-known difficulties in determining to what extent inborn structure, maturation, and learning are responsible for the particular form of a skilled or complex performance.[31] To

---

[31]Tinbergen, *op.cit.*, Chap. VI, reviews some aspects of this problem, discussing the primary role of maturation in the development of many complex motor patterns (e.g., flying, swimming) in lower organisms, and the effect of an "innate disposition to learn" in certain specific ways and

take just one example,[32] the gaping response of a nestling thrush is at first released by jarring of the nest, and, at a later stage, by a moving object of specific size, shape, and position relative to the nestling. At this later stage the response is directed toward the part of the stimulus object corresponding to the parent's head, and characterized by a complex configuration of stimuli that can be precisely described. Knowing just this, it would be possible to construct a speculative, learning-theoretic account of how this sequence of behavior patterns might have developed through a process of differential reinforcement, and it would no doubt be possible to train rats to do something similar. However, there appears to be good evidence that these responses to fairly complex "sign stimuli" are genetically determined and mature without learning. Clearly, the possibility cannot be discounted. Consider now the comparable case of a child imitating new words. At an early stage we may find rather gross correspondences. At a later stage, we find that repetition is of course far from exact (i.e., it is not mimicry, a fact which itself is interesting), but that it reproduces the highly complex configuration of sound features that constitute the phonological structure of the language in question. Again, we can propose a speculative account of how this result might have been obtained through elaborate arrangement of reinforcing contingencies. Here too, however, it is possible that ability to select out of the complex auditory input those features that are phonologically relevant may develop largely independently of reinforcement, through genetically determined maturation. To the extent that this is true, an account of the development and causation of behavior that fails to consider the structure of the organism will provide no understanding of the real processes involved.

It is often argued that experience, rather than innate capacity to handle information in certain specific ways, must be the factor of overwhelming dominance in determining the specific character of language acquisition, since a child speaks the language of the group in which he lives. But this is a superficial argument. As long as we are speculating, we may consider the possibility that the brain has evolved to the point where, given an input of observed Chinese sentences, it produces (by an *induction* of apparently fantastic complexity and suddenness) the *rules* of Chinese grammar, and given an input of observed English sentences, it produces (by, perhaps, exactly the same process of induction) the rules of English grammar; or that given an observed application of a term to certain instances, it automatically predicts the extension to a class of complexly related instances. If clearly recognized as such, this speculation is neither unreasonable nor fantastic; nor, for that matter, is it beyond the bounds of possible study. There is of course no known neural structure capable of performing this task in the specific ways that observation of the resulting behavior might lead us to postulate; but for that matter, the structures capable of

---

at certain specific times. Cf. also P. Schiller, "Innate Motor Action as a Basis for Learning," in C. H. Schiller, ed., *Instinctive Behavior* (New York: International Universities Press, 1957), pp. 265–88, for a discussion of the role of maturing motor patterns in apparently insightful behavior in the chimpanzee.

Lenneberg (*The Capacity for Language Acquisition*, this volume) presents a very interesting discussion of the part that biological structure may play in the acquisition of language, and the dangers in neglecting this possibility.

[32]From among many cited by Tinbergen, *op. cit.*, p. 85.

accounting for even the simplest kinds of learning have similarly defied detection.[33]

Summarizing this brief discussion, it seems that there is neither empirical evidence nor any known argument to support any *specific* claim about the relative importance of "feedback" from the environment and the "independent contribution of the organism" in the process of language acquisition.

VI

We now turn to the system that Skinner develops specifically for the description of verbal behavior. Since this system is based on the notions *stimulus, response,* and *reinforcement,* we can conclude from the preceding sections that it will be vague and arbitrary. For reasons noted in Section 1, however, I think it is important to see in detail how far from the mark any analysis phrased solely in these terms must be and how completely this system fails to account for the facts of verbal behavior.

Consider first the term *verbal behavior* itself. This is defined as "behavior reinforced through the mediation of other persons" (2). The definition is clearly much too broad. It would include as *verbal behavior,* for example, a rat pressing the bar in a Skinner-box, a child brushing his teeth, a boxer retreating before an opponent, and a mechanic repairing an automobile. Exactly how much of ordinary linguistic behavior is *verbal* in this sense, however, is something of a question: perhaps, as I have pointed out above, a fairly small fraction of it, if any substantive meaning is assigned to the term *reinforced.* This definition is subsequently refined by the additional provision that the mediating response of the reinforcing person (the *listener*) must itself "have been conditioned *precisely in order to reinforce* the behavior of the speaker" (225, italics his). This still covers the examples given above, if we can assume that the *reinforcing* behavior of the psychologist, the parent, the opposing boxer, and the paying customer are the result of appropriate training, which is perhaps not unreasonable. A significant part of the fragment of linguistic behavior covered by the earlier definition will no doubt be excluded by the refinement, however. Suppose, for example, that while crossing the street I hear someone shout *Watch out for the car* and jump out of the way. It can hardly be proposed that my jumping (the mediating, reinforcing response in Skinner's usage) was conditioned (that is, I was trained to jump) precisely in order to reinforce the behavior of the speaker; and similarly, for a wide class of cases. Skinner's assertion that with this refined definition "we narrow our subject to what is traditionally recognized as the verbal field"(225) appears to be grossly in error.

VII

Verbal operants are classified by Skinner in terms of their "functional" relation to discriminated stimulus, reinforcement, and other verbal responses. A *mand* is defined

---

[33]Cf. K. S. Lashley, "In Search of the Engram," *Symposium of the Society for Experimental Biology,* 4 (1950), 454–82. R. Sperry, "On the Neural Basis of the Conditioned Response," *British Journal of Animal Behavior,* 3 (1955), 41–44, argues that to account for the experimental results of Lashley and others, and for other facts that he cites, it is necessary to assume that high-level cerebral activity of the type of insight, expectancy, and so on is involved even in simple conditioning. He states that "we still lack today a satisfactory picture of the underlying neural mechanism" of the conditioned response.

as "a verbal operant in which the response is reinforced by a characteristic consequence and is therefore under the functional control of relevant conditions of deprivation or aversive stimulation" (35). This is meant to include questions, commands,
etc. Each of the terms in this definition raises a host of problems. A mand such as
Pass the salt is a class of responses. We cannot tell by observing the form of a response
whether it belongs to this class (Skinner is very clear about this), but only by identifying the controlling variables. This is generally impossible. Deprivation is defined
in the bar-pressing experiment in terms of length of time that the animal has not been
fed or permitted to drink. In the present context, however, it is quite a mysterious
notion. No attempt is made here to describe a method for determining "relevant conditions of deprivation" independently of the "controlled" response. It is of no help
at all to be told (32) that it can be characterized in terms of the operations of the
experimenter. If we define deprivation in terms of elapsed time, then at any moment
a person is in countless states of deprivation.[34] It appears that we must decide that the
relevant condition of deprivation was (say) salt-deprivation, on the basis of the fact
that the speaker asked for salt (the reinforcing community which "sets up" the mand
is in a similar predicament). In this case, the assertion that a mand is under the control of relevant deprivation is empty, and we are (contrary to Skinner's intention)
identifying the response as a mand completely in terms of form. The word *relevant*
in the definition above conceals some rather serious complications.

In the case of the mand *Pass the salt*, the word *deprivation* is not out of place,
though it appears to be of little use for functional analysis. Suppose however that
the speaker says *Give me the book*, *Take me for a ride*, or *Let me fix it*. What kinds of
deprivation can be associated with these mands? How do we determine or measure
the relevant deprivation? I think we must conclude in this case, as before, either that
the notion *deprivation* is relevant at most to a minute fragment of verbal behavior,
or else that the statement "*X* is under *Y*-deprivation" is just an odd paraphrase for
"*X* wants *Y*," bearing a misleading and unjustifiable connotation of objectivity.

The notion *aversive control* is just as confused. This is intended to cover threats,
beating, and the like (33). The manner in which aversive stimulation functions is
simply described. If a speaker has had a history of appropriate reinforcement
(e.g., if a certain response was followed by "cessation of the threat of such injury—
of events which have previously been followed by such injury and which are therefore
conditioned aversive stimuli"), then he will tend to give the proper response when the
threat which had previously been followed by the injury is presented. It would
appear to follow from this description that a speaker will not respond properly
to the mand *Your money or your life* (38) unless he has a past history of being killed.
But even if the difficulties in describing the mechanism of aversive control are somehow removed by a more careful analysis, it will be of little use for identifying operants for reasons similar to those mentioned in the case of deprivation.

It seems, then, that in Skinner's terms there is in most cases no way to decide
whether a given response is an instance of a particular mand. Hence it is meaning-

---

[34]Furthermore, the motivation of the speaker does not, except in the simplest cases, correspond
in intensity to the duration of deprivation. An obvious counter-example is what Hebb has called
the "salted-nut phenomenon" (*Organization of Behavior* [New York, 1949], p. 199). The difficulty is
of course even more serious when we consider *deprivations* not related to physiological drives.

less, within the terms of his system, to speak of the *characteristic* consequences of a mand, as in the definition above. Furthermore, even if we extend the system so that mands can somehow be identified, we will have to face the obvious fact that most of us are not fortunate enough to have our requests, commands, advice, and so on characteristically reinforced (they may nevertheless exist in considerable *strength*). These responses could therefore not be considered mands by Skinner. In fact, Skinner sets up a category of "magical mands" (48–49) to cover the case of "mands which cannot be accounted for by showing that they have ever had the effect specified or any similar effect upon similar occasions" (the word *ever* in this statement should be replaced by *characteristically*). In these pseudo-mands, "the speaker simply describes the reinforcement appropriate to a given state of deprivation or aversive stimulation." In other words, given the meaning that we have been led to assign to *reinforcement* and *deprivation*, the speaker asks for what he wants. The remark that "a speaker appears to create new mands on the analogy of old ones" is also not very helpful.

Skinner's claim that his new descriptive system is superior to the traditional one "because its terms can be defined with respect to experimental operations" (45) is, we see once again, an illusion. The statement "*X* wants *Y*" is not clarified by pointing out a relation between rate of bar-pressing and hours of food-deprivation; replacing "*X* wants *Y*" by "*X* is deprived of *Y*" adds no new objectivity to the description of behavior. His further claim for the superiority of the new analysis of mands is that it provides an objective basis for the traditional classification into requests, commands, etc. (38–41). The traditional classification is in terms of the intention of the speaker. But intention, Skinner holds, can be reduced to contingencies of reinforcement, and, correspondingly, we can explain the traditional classification in terms of the reinforcing behavior of the listener. Thus, a question is a mand which "specifies verbal action, and the behavior of the listener permits us to classify it as a request, a command, or a prayer" (39). It is a request if "the listener is independently motivated to reinforce the speaker"; a command if "the listener's behavior is ... reinforced by reducing a threat"; a prayer if the mand "promotes reinforcement by generating an emotional disposition." The mand is advice if the listener is positively reinforced by the consequences of mediating the reinforcement of the speaker; it is a warning if "by carrying out the behavior specified by the speaker, the listener escapes from aversive stimulation"; and so on. All this is obviously wrong if Skinner is using the words *request, command*, etc., in anything like the sense of the corresponding English words. The word *question* does not cover commands. *Please pass the salt* is a request (but not a question), whether or not the listener happens to be motivated to fulfill it; not everyone to whom a request is addressed is favorably disposed. A response does not cease to be a command if it is not followed; nor does a question become a command if the speaker answers it because of an implied or imagined threat. Not all advice is good advice, and a response does not cease to be advice if it is not followed. Similarly, a warning may be misguided; heeding it may cause aversive stimulation, and ignoring it might be positively reinforcing. In short, the entire classification is beside the point. A moment's thought is sufficient to demonstrate the impossibility of distinguishing between requests, commands, advice, etc., on the basis of the behavior or disposition of the particular listener. Nor can we do this on the basis of the typical behavior of all listeners. Some advice is never taken, is always bad, etc., and similarly, with other kinds of mands. Skinner's evident satisfaction with this analysis of the traditional classification is extremely puzzling.

VIII

Mands are operants with no specified relation to a prior stimulus. A *tact*, on the other hand, is defined as "a verbal operant in which a response of given form is evoked (or at least strengthened) by a particular object or event or property of an object or event" (81). The examples quoted in the discussion of stimulus control (Section 3) are all tacts. The obscurity of the notion *stimulus control* makes the concept of the tact rather mystical. Since, however, the tact is "the most important of verbal operants," it is important to investigate the development of this concept in more detail.

We first ask why the verbal community "sets up" tacts in the child—that is, how the parent is reinforced by setting up the tact. The basic explanation for this behavior of the parent (85–86) is the reinforcement he obtains by the fact that his contact with the environment is extended; to use Skinner's example, the child may later be able to call him to the telephone. (It is difficult to see, then, how first children acquire tacts, since the parent does not have the appropriate history of reinforcement.) Reasoning in the same way, we may conclude that the parent induces the child to walk so that he can make some money delivering newspapers. Similarly, the parent sets up an "echoic repertoire" (e.g., a phonemic system) in the child because this makes it easier to teach him new vocabulary, and extending the child's vocabulary is ultimately useful to the parent. "In all these cases we explain the behavior of the reinforcing listener by pointing to an improvement in the possibility of controlling the speaker whom he reinforces" (56). Perhaps this provides the explanation for the behavior of the parent in inducing the child to walk: the parent is reinforced by the improvement in his control of the child when the child's mobility increases. Underlying these modes of explanation is a curious view that it is somehow more scientific to attribute to a parent a desire to control the child or enhance his own possibilities for action than a desire to see the child develop and extend his capacities. Needless to say, no evidence is offered to support this contention.

Consider now the problem of explaining the response of the listener to a tact. Suppose, for example, that *B* hears *A* say *fox* and reacts appropriately—looks around, runs away, aims his rifle, etc. How can we explain *B*'s behavior? Skinner rightly rejects analyses of this offered by J. B. Watson and Bertrand Russell. His own equally inadequate analysis proceeds as follows (87–88). We assume (1) "that in the history of [*B*] the stimulus *fox* has been an occasion upon which looking around has been followed by seeing a fox" and (2) "that the listener has some current 'interest in seeing foxes'—that behavior which depends upon a seen fox for its execution is strong, and that the stimulus supplied by a fox is therefore reinforcing." *B* carries out the appropriate behavior, then, because "the heard stimulus *fox* is the occasion upon which turning and looking about is frequently followed by the reinforcement of seeing a fox," i.e., his behavior is a discriminated operant. This explanation is unconvincing. *B* may never have seen a fox and may have no current interest in seeing one, and yet may react appropriately to the stimulus *fox*.[35] Since exactly the same behavior may take place when neither of the assumptions is fulfilled, some other mechanism must be operative here.

Skinner remarks several times that his analysis of the tact in terms of stimulus control is an improvement over the traditional formulations in terms of reference and meaning. This is simply not true. His analysis is fundamentally the same as the traditional one, though much less carefully phrased. In particular, it differs only by indiscriminate paraphrase of such notions as *denotation* (reference) and *connotation* (meaning), which have been kept clearly apart in traditional formulations, in terms of the vague concept *stimulus control*. In one traditional formulation a descriptive term is said to denote a set of entities and to connote or designate a certain property or condition that an entity must possess or fulfil if the term is to apply to it.[36] Thus, the term *vertebrate* refers to (*denotes, is true of*) vertebrates and connotes the property *having a spine* or something of the sort. This connoted defining property is called the meaning of the term. Two terms may have the same reference but different meanings. Thus, it is apparently true that the creatures with hearts are all and only the vertebrates. If so, then the term *creature with a heart* refers to vertebrates and designates the property *having a heart*. This is presumably a different property (a different general condition) from having a spine; hence the terms *vertebrate* and *creature with a heart* are said to have different meanings. This analysis is not incorrect (for at least one sense of meaning), but its many limitations have frequently been pointed out.[37]

---

[35]Just as he may have the appropriate reaction, both emotional and behavioral, to such utterances as *the volcano is erupting* or *there's a homicidal maniac in the next room* without any previous pairing of the verbal and the physical stimulus. Skinner's discussion of Pavlovian conditioning in language (154) is similarly unconvincing.

[36]J. S. Mill, *A System of Logic* (1843). R. Carnap gives a recent reformulation in "Meaning and Synonymy in Natural Languages," *Phil. Studies*, **6** (1955), 33–47, defining the meaning (intension) of a predicate *Q* for a speaker *X* as "the general condition which an object *y* must fulfil in order for *X* to be willing to ascribe the predicate *Q* to *y*." The connotation of an expression is often said to constitute its "cognitive meaning" as opposed to its "emotive meaning," which is, essentially, the emotional reaction to the expression.

Whether or not this is the best way to approach meaning, it is clear that denotation, cognitive meaning, and emotive meaning are quite different things. The differences are often obscured in empirical studies of meaning, with much consequent confusion. Thus, Osgood has set himself the task of accounting for the fact that a stimulus comes to be a sign for another stimulus (a buzzer becomes a sign for food, a word for a thing, etc.). This is clearly (for linguistic signs) a problem of denotation. The method that he actually develops for quantifying and measuring meaning (cf. C. E. Osgood, G. Suci, P. Tannenbaum, *The Measurement of Meaning* [Urbana: Univ. of Illinois Press, 1957]) applies, however, only to emotive meaning. Suppose, for example, that *A* hates both Hitler and science intensely, and considers both highly potent and "active," while *B*, agreeing with *A* about Hitler, likes science very much, although he considers it rather ineffective and not too important. Then, *A* may assign to "Hitler" and "science" the same position on the semantic differential, while *B* will assign "Hitler" the same position as *A* did, but "science" a totally different position. Yet, *A* does not think that "Hitler" and "science" are synonymous or that they have the same reference, and *A* and *B* may agree precisely on the cognitive meaning of "science." Clearly, it is the attitude toward the things (the emotive meaning of the words) that is being measured here. There is a gradual shift in Osgood's account from denotation to cognitive meaning to emotive meaning. The confusion is caused, no doubt, by the fact that the term *meaning* is used in all three senses (and others). [See J. Carroll's review of the book by Osgood, Suci, and Tannenbaum in *Language*, **35**, No. 1 (1959).]

[37]Most clearly by Quine. See *From a Logical Point of View* (Cambridge, 1953), especially Chaps. 2, 3, and 7.

The major problem is that there is no good way to decide whether two descriptive terms designate the same property.[38] As we have just seen, it is not sufficient that they refer to the same objects. *Vertebrate* and *creature with a spine* would be said to designate the same property (distinct from that designated by *creature with a heart*). If we ask why this is so, the only answer appears to be that the terms are synonymous. The notion *property* thus seems somehow language-bound, and appeal to "defining properties" sheds little light on questions of meaning and synonymy.

Skinner accepts the traditional account *in toto*, as can be seen from his definition of a tact as a response under control of a property (stimulus) of some physical object or event. We have found that the notion *control* has no real substance and is perhaps best understood as a paraphrase of *denote* or *connote* or, ambiguously, both. The only consequence of adopting the new term *stimulus control* is that the important differences between reference and meaning are obscured. It provides no new objectivity. The stimulus controlling the response is determined by the response itself; there is no independent and objective method of identification (see Section 3). Consequently, when Skinner defines *synonymy* as the case in which "the same stimulus leads to quite different responses" (118), we can have no objection. The responses *chair* and *red* made alternatively to the same object are not synonymous, because the stimuli are called different. The responses *vertebrate* and *creature with a spine* would be considered synonymous because they are controlled by the same property of the object under investigation; in more traditional and no less scientific terms, they evoke the same concept. Similarly, when metaphorical extension is explained as due to "the control exercised by properties of the stimulus which, though present at reinforcement, do not enter into the contingency respected by the verbal community" (92; traditionally, accidental properties), no objection can be raised which has not already been levelled against the traditional account. Just as we could "explain" the response *Mozart* to a piece of music in terms of subtle properties of the controlling stimuli, we can, with equal facility, explain the appearance of the response *sun* when no sun is present, as in *Juliet is [like] the sun.* "We do so by noting that Juliet and the sun have common properties, at least in their effect on the speaker" (93). Since any two objects have indefinitely many properties in common, we can be certain that we will never be at a loss to explain a response of the form *A is like B*, for arbitrary *A* and *B*. It is clear, however, that Skinner's recurrent claim that his formulation is simpler and more scientific than the traditional account has no basis in fact.

Tacts under the control of private stimuli (Bloomfield's "displaced speech") form a large and important class (130–46), including not only such responses as *familiar* and *beautiful*, but also verbal responses referring to past, potential, or future events or behavior. For example, the response *There was an elephant at the zoo* "must be understood as a response to current stimuli, including events within the speaker himself" (143).[39] If we now ask ourselves what proportion of the tacts in actual life

---

[38] A method for characterizing synonymy in terms of reference is suggested by Goodman, "On Likeness of Meaning," *Analysis*, **10** (1949), 1–7. Difficulties are discussed by Goodman, "On Some Differences about Meaning," *ibid.*, **13** (1953) 90–96. Carnap, *op. cit.*, presents a very similar idea (Section 6), but somewhat misleadingly phrased, since he does not bring out the fact that only extensional (referential) notions are being used.

[39] In general, the examples discussed here are badly handled, and the success of the proposed analyses is overstated. In each case, it is easy to see that the proposed analysis, which usually has

are responses to (descriptions of) actual current outside stimulation, we can see just how large a role must be attributed to private stimuli. A minute amount of verbal behavior, outside the nursery, consists of such remarks as *This is red* and *There is a man*. The fact that *functional analysis* must make such a heavy appeal to obscure internal stimuli is again a measure of its actual advance over traditional formulations.

IX

Responses under the control of prior verbal stimuli are considered under a different heading from the tact. An *echoic operant* is a response which "generates a sound pattern similar to that of the stimulus" (55). It covers only cases of immediate imitation.[40] No attempt is made to define the sense in which a child's echoic response is "similar" to the stimulus spoken in the father's bass voice; it seems, though there are no clear statements about this, that Skinner would not accept the account of the phonologist in this respect, but nothing else is offered. The development of an echoic repertoire is attributed completely to differential reinforcement. Since the speaker will do no more, according to Skinner, than what is demanded of him by the verbal community, the degree of accuracy insisted on by this community will determine the elements of the repertoire, whatever these may be (not necessarily phonemes). "In a verbal community which does not insist on a precise correspondence, an echoic repertoire may remain slack and will be less successfully applied to novel patterns." There is no discussion of such familiar phenomena as the accuracy with which a child will pick up a second language or a local dialect in the course of playing with

---

an air of objectivity, is not equivalent to the analyzed expression. To take just one example, the response *I am looking for my glasses* is certainly not equivalent to the proposed paraphrases: "When I have behaved in this way in the past, I have found my glasses and have then stopped behaving in this way," or "Circumstances have arisen in which I am inclined to emit any behavior which in the past has led to the discovery of my glasses; such behavior includes the behavior of looking in which I am now engaged." One may look for one's glasses for the first time; or one may emit the same behavior in looking for one's glasses as in looking for one's watch, in which case *I am looking for my glasses* and *I am looking for my watch* are equivalent, under the Skinnerian paraphrase. The difficult questions of purposiveness cannot be handled in this superficial manner.

[40]Skinner takes great pains, however, to deny the existence in human beings (or parrots) of any innate faculty or tendency to imitate. His only argument is that no one would suggest an innate tendency to read, yet reading and echoic behavior have similar "dynamic properties." This similarity, however, simply indicates the grossness of his descriptive categories.

In the case of parrots, Skinner claims that they have no instinctive capacity to imitate, but only to be reinforced by successful imitation (59). Given Skinner's use of the word *reinforcement*, it is difficult to perceive any distinction here, since exactly the same thing could be said of any other instinctive behavior. For example, where another scientist would say that a certain bird instinctively builds a nest in a certain way, we could say in Skinner's terminology (equivalently) that the bird is instinctively reinforced by building the nest in this way. One is therefore inclined to dismiss this claim as another ritual introduction of the word *reinforce*. Though there may, under some suitable clarification, be some truth in it, it is difficult to see how many of the cases reported by competent observers can be handled if *reinforcement* is given some substantive meaning. Cf. Thorpe, *op. cit.* p. 353f.; K. Lorenz, *King Solomon's Ring* (New York, 1952), pp. 85–88; even Mowrer, who tries to show how imitation might develop through secondary reinforcement, cites a case, *op. cit.*, p. 694, which he apparently believes, but where this could hardly be true. In young children, it seems most implausible to explain imitation in terms of secondary reinforcement.

other children, which seem sharply in conflict with these assertions. No anthropological evidence is cited to support the claim that an effective phonemic system does not develop (this is the substance of the quoted remark) in communities that do not insist on precise correspondence.

A verbal response to a written stimulus (reading) is called *textual behavior*.

Other verbal responses to verbal stimuli are called *intraverbal operants*. Paradigm instances are the response *four* to the stimulus *two plus two* or the response *Paris* to the stimulus *capital of France*. Simple conditioning may be sufficient to account for the response *four* to *two plus two*,[41] but the notion of intraverbal response loses all meaning when we find it extended to cover most of the facts of history and many of the facts of science (72, 129); all word association and "flight of ideas" (73–76); all translations and paraphrase (77); reports of things seen, heard, or remembered (315); and, in general, large segments of scientific, mathematical, and literary discourse. Obviously, the kind of explanation that might be proposed for a student's ability to respond with *Paris* to *capital of France*, after suitable practice, can hardly be seriously offered to account for his ability to make a judicious guess in answering the questions (to him new): *What is the seat of the French government?*, . . . *the source of the literary dialect?*, . . . *the chief target of the German blitzkrieg?*, etc., or his ability to prove a new theorem, translate a new passage, or paraphrase a remark for the first time or in a new way.

The process of "getting someone to see a point," to see something your way, or to understand a complex state of affairs (e.g., a difficult political situation or a mathematical proof) is, for Skinner, simply a matter of increasing the strength of the listener's already available behavior.[42] Since "the process is often exemplified by relatively intellectual scientific or philosophical discourse," Skinner considers it "all the more surprising that it may be reduced to echoic, textual, or intraverbal supplementation" (269). Again, it is only the vagueness and latitude with which the notions *strength* and *intraverbal response* are used that save this from absurdity. If we use these terms in their literal sense, it is clear that understanding a statement cannot be equated to shouting it frequently in a high-pitched voice (high response strength), and a clever and convincing argument cannot be accounted for on the basis of a history of pairings of verbal responses.[43]

---

[41]Although even this possibility is limited. If we were to take these paradigm instances seriously, it should follow that a child who knows how to count from one to 100 could learn an arbitrary 10 × 10 matrix with these numbers as entries as readily as the multiplication table.

[42]Similarly, "the universality of a literary work refers to the number of potential readers inclined to say the same thing" (275; i.e., the most "universal" work is a dictionary of clichés and greetings); a speaker is "stimulating" if he says what we are about to say ourselves (272); etc.

[43]Similarly, consider Skinner's contention (362–65) that communication of knowledge or facts is just the process of making a new response available to the speaker. Here the analogy to animal experiments is particularly weak. When we train a rat to carry out some peculiar act, it makes sense to consider this a matter of adding a response to his repertoire. In the case of human communication, however, it is very difficult to attach any meaning to this terminology. If *A* imparts to *B* the information (new to *B*) that the railroads face collapse, in what sense can the response *The railroads face collapse* be said to be now, but not previously, available to *B*? Surely *B* could have said it before (not knowing whether it was true), and known that it was a sentence (as opposed to *Collapse face railroads the*). Nor is there any reason to assume that the response has increased in strength, whatever this means exactly (e.g., *B* may have no interest in the fact, or he may want it suppressed). It is not clear how we can characterize this notion of "making a response available" without reducing Skinner's account of "imparting knowledge" to a triviality.

X

A final class of operants, called *autoclitics*, includes those that are involved in assertion, negation, quantification, qualification of responses, construction of sentences, and the "highly complex manipulations of verbal thinking." All these acts are to be explained "in terms of behavior which is evoked by or acts upon other behavior of the speaker" (313). Autoclitics are, then, responses to already given responses, or rather, as we find in reading through this section, they are responses to covert or incipient or potential verbal behavior. Among the autoclitics are listed such expressions as *I recall, I imagine, for example, assume, let X equal . . .*, the terms of negation, the *is* of predication and assertion, *all, some, if, then*, and, in general, all morphemes other than nouns, verbs, and adjectives, as well as grammatical processes of ordering and arrangement. Hardly a remark in this section can be accepted without serious qualification. To take just one example, consider Skinner's account of the autoclitic *all* in *All swans are white* (329). Obviously we cannot assume that this is a tact to all swans as stimulus. It is suggested, therefore, that we take *all* to be an autoclitic modifying the whole sentence *Swans are white*. *All* can then be taken as equivalent to *always*, or *always it is possible to say*. Notice, however, that the modified sentence *Swans are white* is just as general as *All swans are white*. Furthermore, the proposed translation of *all* is incorrect if taken literally. It is just as possible to say *Swans are green* as to say *Swans are white*. It is not always possible to say either (e.g., while you are saying something else or sleeping). Probably what Skinner means is that the sentence can be paraphrased "*X is white* is true, for each swan X." But this paraphrase cannot be given within his system, which has no place for *true*.

Skinner's account of grammar and syntax as autoclitic processes (Chap. 13) differs from a familiar traditional account mainly in the use of the pseudo-scientific terms *control* or *evoke* in place of the traditional *refer*. Thus, in *The boy runs*, the final *s* of *runs* is a tact under control of such "subtle properties of a situation" as "the nature of running as an *activity* rather than an object or property of an object."[44] (Presumably, then, in *The attempt fails, The difficulty remains, His anxiety increases*, etc., we must also say that the *s* indicates that the object described as the attempt is carrying out the activity of failing, etc.) In *the boy's gun*, however, the *s* denotes possession (as, presumably, in *the boy's arrival, . . . story, . . . age*, etc.) and is under the control of this "relational aspect of the situation" (336). The "relational autoclitic of order" (whatever it may mean to call the order of a set of responses a response to them) in *The boy runs the store* is under the control of an "extremely complex stimulus situation," namely, that the boy is running the store (335). *And* in *the hat and the shoe* is under the control of the property "pair." *Through* in *the dog went through the hedge* is under the control of the "relation between the going dog and the hedge" (342). In general, nouns are evoked by objects, verbs by actions, and so on.

Skinner considers a sentence to be a set of key responses (nouns, verbs, adjectives) on a skeletal frame (346). If we are concerned with the fact that Sam rented a leaky

---

[44](332). On the next page, however, the *s* in the same example indicates that "the object described as *the boy* possesses the property of running." The difficulty of even maintaining consistency with a conceptual scheme like this is easy to appreciate.

boat, the raw responses to the situation are *rent, boat, leak*, and *Sam*. Autoclitics (including order) which qualify these responses, express relations between them, and the like, are then added by a process called *composition* and the result is a grammatical sentence, one of many alternatives among which selection is rather arbitrary. The idea that sentences consist of lexical items placed in a grammatical frame is of course a traditional one, within both philosophy and linguistics. Skinner adds to it only the very implausible speculation that in the internal process of composition, the nouns, verbs, and adjectives are chosen first and then are arranged, qualified, etc., by autoclitic responses to these internal activities.[45]

This view of sentence structure, whether phrased in terms of autoclitics, syncategorematic expressions, or grammatical and lexical morphemes, is inadequate. *Sheep provide wool* has no (physical) frame at all, but no other arrangement of these words is an English sentence. The sequences *furiously sleep ideas green colorless* and *friendly young dogs seem harmless* have the same frames, but only one is a sentence of English (similarly, only one of the sequences formed by reading these from back to front). *Struggling artists can be a nuisance* has the same frame as *marking papers can be a nuisance*, but is quite different in sentence structure, as can be seen by replacing *can be* by *is* or *are* in both cases. There are many other similar and equally simple examples. It is evident that more is involved in sentence structure than insertion of lexical items in grammatical frames; no approach to language that fails to take these deeper processes into account can possibly achieve much success in accounting for actual linguistic behavior.

XI

The preceding discussion covers all the major notions that Skinner introduces in his descriptive system. My purpose in discussing the concepts one by one was to show that in each case, if we take his terms in their literal meaning, the description covers almost no aspect of verbal behavior, and if we take them metaphorically, the description offers no improvement over various traditional formulations. The terms borrowed from experimental psychology simply lose their objective meaning with this extension, and take over the full vagueness of ordinary language. Since Skinner limits himself to such a small set of terms for paraphrase, many important distinctions are obscured. I think that this analysis supports the view expressed in Section 1, that elimination of the independent contribution of the speaker and learner (a result which Skinner considers of great importance, cf. 311–12) can be achieved only at the cost of eliminating all significance from the descriptive system, which then operates at a level so gross and crude that no answers are sug-

---

[45]One might just as well argue that exactly the opposite is true. The study of hesitation pauses has shown that these tend to occur before the large categories—noun, verb, adjective; this finding is usually described by the statement that the pauses occur where there is maximum uncertainty or information. Insofar as hesitation indicates on-going composition (if it does at all), it would appear that the "key responses" are chosen only after the "grammatical frame." Cf. C. E. Osgood, unpublished paper; F. Goldman-Eisler, "Speech Analysis and Mental Processes," *Language and Speech*, **1** (1958), 67.

gested to the most elementary questions.[46] The questions to which Skinner has addressed his speculations are hopelessly premature. It is futile to inquire into the causation of verbal behavior until much more is known about the specific character of this behavior; and there is little point in speculating about the process of acquisition without much better understanding of what is acquired.

Anyone who seriously approaches the study of linguistic behavior, whether linguist, psychologist, or philosopher, must quickly become aware of the enormous difficulty of stating a problem which will define the area of his investigations, and which will not be either completely trivial or hopelessly beyond the range of present-day understanding and technique. In selecting functional analysis as his problem, Skinner has set himself a task of the latter type. In an extremely interesting and insightful paper,[47] K. S. Lashley has implicitly delimited a class of problems which can be approached in a fruitful way by the linguist and psychologist, and which are clearly preliminary to those with which Skinner is concerned. Lashley recognizes, as anyone must who seriously considers the data, that the composition and production of an utterance is not simply a matter of stringing together a sequence of responses under the control of outside stimulation and intraverbal association, and that the syntactic organization of an utterance is not something directly represented in any simple way in the physical structure of the utterance itself. A variety of observations lead him to conclude that syntactic structure is "a generalized pattern imposed on the specific acts as they occur" (512), and that "a consideration of the structure of the sentence and other motor sequences will show . . . that there are, behind the overtly expressed sequences, a multiplicity of integrative processes which can only be inferred from the final results of their activity" (509). He also comments on the great difficulty of determining the "selective mechanisms" used in the actual construction of a particular utterance (522).

Although present-day linguistics cannot provide a precise account of these integrative processes, imposed patterns, and selective mechanisms, it can at least set itself

---

[46]E.g., what are in fact the actual units of verbal behavior? Under what conditions will a physical event capture the attention (be a stimulus) or be a reinforcer? How do we decide what stimuli are in "control" in a specific case? When are stimuli "similar"? And so on. (It is not interesting to be told, e.g., that we say *Stop* to an automobile or billiard ball because they are sufficiently similar to reinforcing people [46].)

The use of unanalyzed notions like *similar* and *generalization* is particularly disturbing, since it indicates an apparent lack of interest in every significant aspect of the learning or the use of language in new situations. No one has ever doubted that in some sense, language is learned by generalization, or that novel utterances and situations are in some way similar to familiar ones. The only matter of serious interest is the specific "similarity." Skinner has, apparently, no interest in this. Keller and Schoenfeld, *op. cit.*, proceed to incorporate these notions (which they identify) into their Skinnerian "modern objective psychology" by defining two stimuli to be similar when "we make the same sort of *response* to them" (124; but when are responses of the "same sort"?). They do not seem to notice that this definition converts their "principle of generalization" (116), under any reasonable interpretation of this, into a tautology. It is obvious that such a definition will not be of much help in the study of language learning or construction of new responses in appropriate situations.

[47]"The Problem of Serial Order in Behavior," in L. A. Jeffress, ed., *Hixon Symposium on Cerebral Mechanisms in Behavior* (New York: John Wiley & Sons Inc., 1951).

Reprinted in F. A. Beach, D. O. Hebb, C. T. Morgan, H. W. Nissen, eds., *The Neuropsychology of Lashley* (New York: McGraw-Hill Book Company, 1960). Page references are to the latter.

the problem of characterizing these completely. It is reasonable to regard the grammar of a language L ideally as a mechanism that provides an enumeration of the sentences of L in something like the way in which a deductive theory gives an enumeration of a set of theorems. (*Grammar*, in this sense of the word, includes phonology.) Furthermore, the theory of language can be regarded as a study of the formal properties of such grammars, and, with a precise enough formulation, this general theory can provide a uniform method for determining, from the process of generation of a given sentence, a structural description which can give a good deal of insight into how this sentence is used and understood. In short, it should be possible to derive from a properly formulated grammar a statement of the integrative processes and generalized patterns imposed on the specific acts that constitute an utterance. The rules of a grammar of the appropriate form can be subdivided into the two types, optional and obligatory; only the latter must be applied in generating an utterance. The optional rules of the grammar can be viewed, then, as the selective mechanisms involved in the production of a particular utterance. The problem of specifying these integrative processes and selective mechanisms is nontrivial and not beyond the range of possible investigation. The results of such a study might, as Lashley suggests, be of independent interest for psychology and neurology (and conversely). Although such a study, even if successful, would by no means answer the major problems involved in the investigation of meaning and the causation of behavior, it surely will not be unrelated to these. It is at least possible, furthermore, that such a notion as *semantic generalization*, to which such heavy appeal is made in all approaches to language in use, conceals complexities and specific structure of inference not far different from those that can be studied and exhibited in the case of syntax, and that consequently the general character of the results of syntactic investigations may be a corrective to oversimplified approaches to the theory of meaning.

The behavior of the speaker, listener, and learner of language constitutes, of course, the actual data for any study of language. The construction of a grammar which enumerates sentences in such a way that a meaningful structural description can be determined for each sentence does not in itself provide an account of this actual behavior. It merely characterizes abstractly the ability of one who has mastered the language to distinguish sentences from nonsentences, to understand new sentences (in part), to note certain ambiguities, etc. These are very remarkable abilities. We constantly read and hear new sequences of words, recognize them as sentences, and understand them. It is easy to show that the new events that we accept and understand as sentences are not related to those with which we are familiar by any simple notion of formal (or semantic or statistical) similarity or identity of grammatical frame. Talk of generalization in this case is entirely pointless and empty. It appears that we recognize a new item as a sentence not because it matches some familiar item in any simple way, but because it is generated by the grammar that each individual has somehow and in some form internalized. And we understand a new sentence, in part, because we are somehow capable of determining the process by which this sentence is derived in this grammar.

Suppose that we manage to construct grammars having the properties outlined above. We can then attempt to describe and study the achievement of the speaker, listener, and learner. The speaker and the listener, we must assume, have already acquired the capacities characterized abstractly by the grammar. The speaker's task is to select a particular compatible set of optional rules. If we know, from grammatical study, what choices are available to him and what conditions of compatibility the choices must meet, we can proceed meaningfully to investigate the factors that lead him to make one or another choice. The listener (or reader) must determine, from an exhibited utterance, what optional rules were chosen in the construction of the utterance. It must be admitted that the ability of a human being to do this far surpasses our present understanding. The child who learns a language has in some sense constructed the grammar for himself on the basis of his observation of sentences and nonsentences (i.e., corrections by the verbal community). Study of the actual observed ability of a speaker to distinguish sentences from nonsentences, detect ambiguities, etc., apparently forces us to the conclusion that this grammar is of an extremely complex and abstract character, and that the young child has succeeded in carrying out what from the formal point of view, at least, seems to be a remarkable type of theory construction. Furthermore, this task is accomplished in an astonishingly short time, to a large extent independently of intelligence, and in a comparable way by all children. Any theory of learning must cope with these facts.

It is not easy to accept the view that a child is capable of constructing an extremely complex mechanism for generating a set of sentences, some of which he has heard, or that an adult can instantaneously determine whether (and if so, how) a particular item is generated by this mechanism, which has many of the properties of an abstract deductive theory. Yet this appears to be a fair description of the performance of the speaker, listener, and learner. If this is correct, we can predict that a direct attempt to account for the actual behavior of speaker, listener, and learner, not based on a prior understanding of the structure of grammars, will achieve very limited success. The grammar must be regarded as a component in the behavior of the speaker and listener which can only be inferred, as Lashley has put it, from the resulting physical acts. The fact that all normal children acquire essentially comparable grammars of great complexity with remarkable rapidity suggests that human beings are somehow specially designed to do this, with data-handling or "hypothesis-formulating" ability of unknown character and complexity.[48] The study of linguistic structure may ultimately lead to some significant insights into this matter. At the moment the

---

[48]There is nothing essentially mysterious about this. Complex innate behavior patterns and innate "tendencies to learn in specific ways" have been carefully studied in lower organisms. Many psychologists have been inclined to believe that such biological structure will not have an important effect on acquisition of complex behavior in higher organisms, but I have not been able to find any serious justification for this attitude. Some recent studies have stressed the necessity for carefully analyzing the strategies available to the organism, regarded as a complex "information-processing system" (cf. J. S. Bruner, J. J. Goodnow, and G. A. Austin, *A Study of Thinking* [New York, 1956]; A. Newell, J. C. Shaw, and H. A. Simon, "Elements of a Theory of Human Problem Solving," *Psych. Rev.*, **65**, [1958], 151–66), if anything significant is to be said about the character of human learning. These may be largely innate, or developed by early learning processes about which very little is yet known. (But see Harlow,"The Formation of Learning Sets,"*Psych. Rev.*, **56** (1949), 51–65, and many later papers, where striking shifts in the character of learning are shown as a result of early training; also D. O. Hebb, *Organization of Behavior*, 109 ff.). They are undoubtedly quite complex. Cf. Lenneberg, *op. cit.*, and R. B. Lees, review of N. Chomsky's *Syntactic Structures* in *Language*, 33 (1957), 406f, for discussion of the topics mentioned in this section.

question cannot be seriously posed, but in principle it may be possible to study the problem of determining what the built-in structure of an information-processing (hypothesis-forming) system must be to enable it to arrive at the grammar of a language from the available data in the available time. At any rate, just as the attempt to eliminate the contribution of the speaker leads to a "mentalistic" descriptive system that succeeds only in blurring important traditional distinctions, a refusal to study the contribution of the child to language learning permits only a superficial account of language acquisition, with a vast and unanalyzed contribution attributed to a step called *generalization* which in fact includes just about everything of interest in this process. If the study of language is limited in these ways, it seems inevitable that major aspects of verbal behavior will remain a mystery.

22   The Capacity for Language Acquisition*

Eric H. Lenneberg

There is a tendency among social scientists to regard language as a wholly learned and cultural phenomenon, an ingeniously devised instrument, purposefully introduced to subserve social functions, the artificial shaping of an amorphous, general capacity called *intelligence*. We scarcely entertain the notion that man may be equipped with highly specialized, biological propensities that favor and, indeed, shape the development of speech in the child and that roots of language may be as deeply grounded in our natural constitution as, for instance, our predisposition to use our hands. To demonstrate the logical possibility—if not probability—of such a situation is the purpose of this paper. It is maintained that clarity on the problem of the biological foundation of language is of utmost importance in formulating both questions and hypotheses regarding the function, mechanism, and history of language.

The heuristic method to be employed here will be analogous to procedures employed in studying processes too slow and inert to be amenable to laboratory experimentation, notably biological evolution. The reasoning of our argument may gain by a few general statements on this type of theory construction and by a review of the basic, modern principles evoked in current discussions of evolution.

In many scientific endeavors we are faced with the problem of reconstructing a sequence of events from scattered, static evidence. The writing of geological, phylogenetic, and cultural histories is alike in this respect. But our treatment of geological and phylogenetic history differs from cultural history when it comes to "explaining" the causal relationships that hold between the events.

*An extended version of an article, written while its author was Career Investigator, National Institute of Mental Health, and published under the title "Language, Evolution, and Purposive Behavior" in S. Diamond, ed., *Culture in History: Essays in Honor of Paul Radin* (New York: Columbia University Press, 1960), pp. 869–93. Revised and reprinted by permission.

In geology we may trace cycles of elevation of the continent: subsequent leveling by erosion, followed by sedimentation at the bottom of the sea, and then recurrent elevation of the once submerged land, far above the level of the sea, resulting again in erosion and so forth. We cannot *explain* these sequences in terms of purpose, for purpose assumes a planned action, a pre-established end. Erosion, for instance, serves no more the *purpose* of establishing a balance than the eruption of a volcano serves the purpose of making erosion possible. It is appropriate to speak about disturbed and re-established equilibria; but the use of the word *purpose* has the common connotation of striving toward a goal, and, therefore, ought to be reserved for pieces of behavior that do indeed aim at a pre-established end without, however, being bound by nature to reach such ends by pre-established means.

In our discussions of phylogeny we must be as careful to avoid teleological explanations as in the case of geological history. Yet, many a time we seem to have no small difficulty in living up to this ideal. It seems so reasonable to say that the *purpose* of man's increased cranial vault is to house a large brain; and that the *purpose* of a large brain is the perfection of intelligence. We must take exception to this formulation because it implies finality in evolution or, at least, the assumption of a pre-established direction and end.[1] The geneticist looks at evolution as the interplay between a *random* process and certain constraining factors. The random process is the blind generation of inheritable characteristics, i.e., mutations, while all the constraining factors have to do with viability of the individual or the species as a whole. Of the many new traits that may chance to appear, the great majority will have a lethal effect under given environmental conditions and are thus of no consequence for evolution. But occasionally there is one that *is* compatible with life and will thus result in perpetuation, at least over a limited period of time.

Attempts have been made to discover whether specific types of mutation could be regarded as adaptive responses of the germ plasm to environmental necessities, but I believe it is fair to say that so far results are not sufficient to conclude that there is a generally adaptive directionality in mutations. Dobzhansky states: "Genetics . . . asserts that the organism is not endowed with providential ability to respond to the requirements of the environment by producing mutations adapted to these requirements."[2]

If it is conceded that variability of inheritable traits due to mutation does not reflect direct responses to *needs*, it is quite conceivable that we may find characteristics that are compatible with life under prevailing conditions but that have no heightened adaptive value and can therefore not be explained in terms of utility to the organism.[3] The differentiating characteristics of human races may be cases in

---

[1]For a philosophical treatment of this point, see H. Feigl, "Notes on Causality" in H. Feigl and M. Brodbeck, eds., *Readings in the Philosophy of Science* (New York, Appleton-Century-Crofts, Inc. 1953), pp. 408–18, and E. Nagel, "Teleological Explanations and Teleological Systems," in S. Ratner, ed., *Vision and Action: Essays in Honor of Horace Kallen* (New Brunswick, N.J.: Rutgers Univ. Press, 1953). For a biotheoretical view see L. V. Bertalanffy, *Theoretische Biologie* (Berlin: Borntrager, 1932), vol. I. For the geneticist's position see J. B. S. Haldane, *Causes of Evolution* (New York: Harper & Row, Publishers, Inc., 1932).

[2]T. Dobzhansky, *Genetics and the Origin of Species* (3rd ed.; New York: Columbia Univ. Press, 1951) p. 51. See also the same author's broad survey of the entire field, *Evolution, Genetics, and Man* (New York: John Wiley and Sons, Inc., 1955).

[3]Cf. H. J. Muller, "Human Values in Relation to Evolution," *Science*, **127** (1958), 625f.

point. The shape of skulls or the textures of hair cannot be rated by usefulness; nor can those mutations that have resulted in new species without extermination of limitation of the older forms.

The problem is more complicated when we observe a long and linear evolutionary trend, for instance the more or less steady increase in the body size of a species. When such a linear development occurs, we say that the evolved trait is *useful* to the species. I would like to stress, however, that the word *useful* (or reference to utility) must be employed with great care in this context and not without careful definition lest it be confused with purposiveness. In case of gradually increasing body size (take for instance the history of the horse), an individual animal stays alive if it is of a certain size, whereas an individual may perish if it falls short of the size that is critical at the time it is born. Since the individual cannot alter its inherited size, it also cannot change its fate of starving or being killed before maturation. Thus, no matter how *useful* it may be to be large, this state of affairs cannot be reached by purposeful striving of individual animals. Much less can we conceive of a super-individual entity (such as the species as a whole), making *use* of this or that trait in order to "insure the continuation" of the species. Something can become useful after it has come into being by a random process; but to make systematic use of a trait, such as size, seems to imply foresight and providence not usually accorded to the driving forces of genetics.

The situation is quite different when we come to a discussion of cultural history. Here, explanations in terms of long-range purpose and utility often are in order because man, indeed, does have final ends in view which he strives to achieve by this or that means. Frequently there are even explicit criteria for usefulness in reaching a goal, such as reduction of physical effort, maximizing gratification, or introducing order and manageability into a certain situation. In the development of coin money, for instance, there may have been some trial and error in the course of history, but many changes were introduced by fiat with the explicit purpose of facilitating economic intercourse. In other words, the development of coin money is the direct result of a certain property of human behavior, namely purposiveness. Or, more generally, it may be said that the phenomenon of *culture per se* is the outgrowth of this characteristic trait. But this should not obscure the fact that man and his abilities are also the product of biological evolution and that many of his traits are genetically determined and as such their existence must not be explained in terms of purpose. For instance the alternations between sleep and wakefulness, the shedding of tears, the closure of the epiglottis in swallowing, or any other unconditioned responses cannot be considered as the outcome of rational invention, as the end product of a purposeful striving just as any other genetic phenomena must not be accounted for in this way.

It is well to remember that purposiveness is a trait that is itself the result of evolutionary history, of phylogenetic development. Rudimentary forms of short-term purpose are observable as far back as the invertebrates. It is the ability to strive toward a goal (say nest building) by more than a single rigid action pattern. It is an ability to take advantage of specific environmental conditions in the accomplishment of certain tasks. For instance, birds are not confined to one specific type of material in the construction of their nests; the use of tiny shreds of newspaper incorporated in these structures is not an uncommon finding. Purposiveness requires anticipation or expectancy together with a flexibility in the choice of routes that lead to the goal.[4]

The purposiveness displayed in man's activities differs from that seen in lower animals not so much in quality as in degree. No other animal seems capable of performing actions with such long-range purpose as is seen in our socio-cultural activities. Not even such activities as nest building in birds which may last for days and weeks are the result of long-range purpose. This has been described by Tinbergen and commented on by Thorpe.[5] The nest is merely the end result of a very long series of individual tasks where each accomplishment seems to trigger off a striving for the fulfillment of the next task, and there is evidence that purposiveness, as defined above, does not actually extend over the entire plan; each task has its own characteristic, short-term purposiveness.

Our objective now is to examine language and to decide in which of its aspects we must assume it to be a genetically determined trait and in which of its aspects it might be the result of cultural activity. Insofar as it is revealed to be a biologically determined affair, we cannot explain it as the result of a purposefully devised system; we may not claim that *the reason* a child learns it is the inherent possibility of providing pleasure, security, or usefulness; or that language has this or that property because this was found in pre-historic times to serve best the purpose of communication. Any hedonistic or utilitarian explanation of language is tantamount to claiming that speech as such is a cultural phenomenon or, at least, that it is the product of purposive behavior. Whereas, a demonstration that language is at least partly determined by innate predispositions would put serious constraints on utilitarian explanations of language and would instead focus our attention on physiological, anatomical, and genetic factors underlying verbal behavior.

Before embarking on the actual argument, a brief warning may be in place. The distinction between genetically determined and purposive behavior is *not* the same as the distinction between behavior that does or does not depend upon environmental conditions. The following example based on work by B. F. Riess will illustrate this point; the quotation is due to Beach.

> The maternal behavior of primiparous female rats reared in isolation is indistinguishable from that of multiparous individuals. Animals with no maternal experience build nests before the first litter is born. However, pregnant rats that have been reared in cages containing nothing that can be picked up and transported do not build nests when material is made available. They simply heap their young in a pile in a corner of the cage. Other females that have been reared under conditions preventing them from licking and grooming their own bodies fail to clean their young at the time of parturition.[6]

---

[4]W. H. Thorpe, *Learning and Instinct in Animals* (Cambridge, Mass.: Harvard Univ. Press, 1956). This is the most scholarly source on the subject of innate and acquired behavior. My entire article has been thoroughly influenced by this book.

[5]Thorpe, *op. cit.*, chap. 2; N. Tinbergen, "Specialists in Nest Building," *Country Life*, 30 (January 1953), 270–71.

[6]F. A. Beach, "The Descent of Instinct," *Psychological Review*, 62 (1955), 401–10. Since writing this article H. L. Teuber has drawn my attention to contrary evidence: I. Eibl-Eibesfeld, "Angeborenes und Erworbenes im Nestbauverhalten der Wanderratte," *Naturwissenschaft*, 42 (1955), 633:34.

From this example it is obvious that innate behavior may be intimately related to or dependent upon the organism's interaction with its environment, yet the action *sequence* as a whole (first carrying things in an unorganized way; then, when pregnant, carrying things in an organized way so that the end product is a nest) is innately given. In other words, it would not be reasonable to claim that the young female rat carries things around because she is planning to build a nest if she should be pregnant and that she is purposefully training herself in carrying around material to be better prepared for the eventualities in store for her.

On the other hand, *purposive* behavior may only be very indirectly related to environmental conditions and thus give the impression of completely spontaneous creation; the composition of the Jupiter Symphony is an example.

In our discussion of language, we shall proceed in the following way. We shall juxtapose two types of human activities, one of which we have good reasons to believe to be biologically given, i.e., walking, while the other one we can safely assume to be the result of cultural achievement and thus a product of purposiveness, namely, writing. By comparing these two types of activities, it will be shown that there are at least four good criteria which distinguish in man biologically determined from culturally determined behavior. When these criteria are applied to language, it will be seen that verbal behavior in many important respects resembles the biological type, while in other respects it bears the sign of cultural and purposive activity. Since the culturally determined features in language are widely noted, the discussion will emphasize innate factors more than cultural ones.

| *Bipedal Gait* | *Writing* |

CRITERION 1

No intraspecies variations: The species has only one type of locomotion; it is universal to all men. (This is a special case of the more general point that inherited traits have poor correlations—if any—with social groupings: cf. black hair or protruding zygoma.)

Intraspecies variations correlated with social organizations: A number of very different successful writing systems have co-existed. The geographical distribution of writing systems follows cultural and social lines of demarcation.

CRITERION 2

No history within species: We cannot trace the development of bipedal gait from a primitive to a complex stage throughout the history of human *cultures*. There are no geographical foci from which cultural diffusion of the trait seems to have emanated at earlier times. All human races have the same basic skeletal foot pattern. For significant variations in gait, we have to go back to fossil forms that represent a predecessor of modern man.

Only history within species: There are cultures where even the most primitive writing system is completely absent. We can follow the development of writing historically just as we can study the distribution of writing geographically. We can make good guesses as to the area of invention and development and trace the cultural diffusion over the surface of the globe and throughout the last few millenia of history. The emergence of writing is a relatively recent event.

CRITERION 3

Evidence for inherited predisposition: Permanent and customary gait cannot be taught or learned by practice if the animal is not biologically constituted for this type of locomotion.

No evidence for inherited predisposition: Illiteracy in nonWestern societies is not ordinarily a sign of mental deficiency but of deficiency in training. The condition can be quickly corrected by appropriate practice.

CRITERION 4

Presumption of specific organic correlates: In the case of gait, we do not have to *presume* organic correlates; we *know* them. However, behavioral traits that are regarded as the product of evolution (instincts) are also thought to be based on organic predispositions, in this case, on the grounds of circumstantial evidence and often in the absence of anatomical and physiological knowledge.

No assumption of specific organic correlates: We do, of course, assume a biological capacity for writing, but there is no evidence for innate predisposition for this activity.[7] A child's contact with written documents or with pencil and paper does not ordinarily result in automatic acquisition of the trait. Nor do we suppose that the people in a society that has evolved no writing system to be genetically different from those of a writing society. It is axiomatic in anthropology that any normal infant can acquire all cultural traits of any society given the specific cultural upbringing.

BIOLOGICAL AND SOCIO-CULTURAL FACTORS IN LANGUAGE

Let us now view language in the light of the four criteria discussed above in order to see to what extent language is part of our biological heritage.

1   First Criterion: Variation within species. One of the major contributions of modern linguistics was the dispelling of the eighteenth-century notion of a *universal grammar* which, at that time, was based on the assumption of a universal logic. In America it was particularly the descriptivist school initiated by Franz Boas that has been most active during the last thirty years in demonstrating the truly amazing variety of phonological, grammatical, and semantic systems in the languages of the world. These workers have shown how the traditional method of describing languages in terms of logic must be abandoned for more objective, formal, and unprejudiced analyses; they have shown that lexicons of different languages are never strictly comparable; in fact, they have made us aware of the difficulty inherent in such notions as *word, tense,* or *parts of speech.* Thus, today anyone interested in language and speech is keenly aware of the great diversification of linguistic form in the languages of the world, and it is commonly acknowledged that their histories cannot be traced back to a common "*ur-language.*" In the light of this realization,

---

[7]Cf. A. L. Drew, "A Neurological Appraisal of Familial Congenital Word-Blindness," *Brain,* **76** (1956), 440–60.

it is very remarkable to note that in some respects all languages are alike and that this similarity is by no means a *logical* necessity. Following are three points in which languages are identical; they are, however, not the only similarities.

1.1 *Phonology*. Speech is without exception a vocal affair, and, more important, the vocalizations heard in the languages of the world are always within fairly narrow limits of the total range of sounds that man can produce. For instance, we can faithfully imitate the noises of many mammals, the songs of a number of birds, the crying noises of an infant; yet, these direct imitations never seem to be incorporated in vocabularies. There is onomatopoeia, to be sure; but onomatopoetic words are never faithful imitations but phonemicized expressions. This is precisely the point: all languages have phonemic systems; that is, the morphemes of all languages can be further segmented into smaller, *meaningless*, components of functionally similar sounds. Words and morphemes are constituted in all languages by a sequence of phonemes. This is not a matter of definition or a methodological artifact. One can visualize a very complex language in which the symbol for *cat* is a perfect imitation of that animal's noise (and so on for other mammals), for *baby* the infant's characteristic cries, for a *shrew* scolding yells; the *size* of objects could be represented by sound intensity, *vertical direction* by pitch, *color* by vowel quality, *hunger* by roaring, *sex* by caressing whimpers, and so on. In such a language we would have morphemes or words that could not be segmented into common, concatenated sound elements. Most words and perhaps all morphemes would constitute a sound-Gestalt *sui generis* much the way pictograms and idiograms cannot be analyzed into a small set of letters.

It would be interesting to see whether parrots speak in phonemes or not; if they do not speak in phonemes (as I would assume), we would have an empirical demonstration that the phonemic phenomenon is neither a methodological artifact nor a logical necessity. One could, for instance, take a parrot who was raised in Brazil and who has acquired a good repertoire of Portuguese phrases and words, and suddenly transplant him to an English-speaking environment where he would add English bits to his stock of exclamations. If the first few words are pronounced with a heavy Portuguese accent, we would have evidence that the bird generalizes his Portuguese habits, that is, that he has actually learned Portuguese phonemes which he now uses in the production of English words. However, if his English acquisitions sound at once *native*, it would appear that the parrot merely has an ability for imitating sounds without deriving from it a generalized habit for the production of speech.

Whether this experiment is practically possible, I do not know. It is related here rather to highlight the problem at stake. It also suggests some empirical research on human subjects. If foreign accents are a proof for the existence of phonemes and if the child at three is said to speak phonemically (which every linguist would have to affirm), we would expect him to have an English accent if he is suddenly asked to pronounce say a simple German word—provided he has never heard German before. This is a project that could be done quite easily and objectively and which would be very revealing. (We are not speaking here of the young child's ability quickly to learn foreign languages, i.e., learn more than a single phonemic system. This is a different problem that will be discussed in greater detail.)

1.2 *Concatenation.* This term denotes the phenomenon of stringing up morphemes or words into a complex sequence called *phrases, sentences,* or *discourse.* No speech community has ever been described where communication is restricted to single-word discourse, where the customary utterance would be something like "water!" or "go," or "bird"; where it would be impossible, for example, to give geographical directions by means of concatenated, independent forms. Man everywhere talks in what appears to be a "blue streak."

1.3 *Syntactic structure.* We know of no language that concatenates randomly, that is, where any word may be followed by any other. There are contingencies between words (or, languages have typical statistical structures)[8] but this in itself does not constitute grammars.[9] We can program stochastic processes into machines such that they generate symbols (e.g., words) with the same statistical properties as that noted for languages; yet these machines will not "speak grammatically," at least not insofar as they generate new sentences. It is generally assumed by linguists —and there are compelling reasons for this—that there must be a finite set of rules that defines all grammatical operations for any given language. Any native speaker will generate sentences that conform to these grammatical rules, and any speaker of the speech community will recognize such sentences as grammatical. We are dealing here with an extremely complex mechanism and one that has never been fully described in purely formal terms for any language (if it had, we could program computers that can "speak" grammatically); and yet, we know that the mechanism must exist for the simple reason that every speaker knows and generally agrees with fellow speakers whether a sentence is grammatical or not. (This has nothing to do with familiarity or meaning of an utterance. One may easily demonstrate this by comparing Chomsky's two sentences, "colorless green ideas sleep furiously" and "furiously sleep ideas green colorless," where neither of the sentences are likely to have occurred prior to Chomsky's illustration, yet one is recognized as grammatical and the other not.) Note that types of sentence structures are as variable as speech sounds among languages of the world, but the phenomenon of grammar as such is absolutely universal.

1.4 *Conclusion.* The importance of the universality of phonematization (evidenced by the universality of small and finite phoneme stocks), of the universality of con-catenation, and of the ubiquitous presence of grammar cannot be overestimated. Consider the vast differences in the forms and semantics of languages (making a common and focal origin of language most unlikely); consider the geographical separation of some human societies that must have persisted for thousands of years; consider the physical differentiation into a number of different stocks and races. Yet, everywhere man communicates in a strikingly similar pattern. There are only two kinds of conclusion that can be drawn from this situation. Either the similarities

---

[8]G. A. Miller, *Language and Communication* (New York: McGraw-Hill Book Company, 1951), chap. 10.

[9]N. A. Chomsky, *Syntactic Structures* (The Hague: Mouton, 1957), and N. A. Chomsky, "Three Models for the Description of Language," *IRE Transactions on Information Theory,* IT-2, 3 (no date), 113–24. I am also indebted to Chomsky for reading an earlier version of this article and for making valuable suggestions. See also G. A. Miller, E. Galanter, K. H. Pribram, *Plans and the Structure of Behavior* (New York: Holt, Rinehart & Winston, Inc., 1960), pp. 139–58.

are due to the fact that, by happenstance, identical principles of communication have developed completely independently over and over, hundreds of times—an extremely improbable supposition, or the universal phenomena reflect some trait that is related to the genetic mutation that has constituted the speciation of *homo sapiens* and are, therefore, of a venerable age. I should like to take the latter view, and I feel strengthened in this position by the evidence that follows.

Perhaps someone would like to argue that a third explanation *is* possible, namely, that languages are alike because everywhere it was discovered that there is an "optimal way of oral communication" and that languages as we find them simply reflect optimization of conditions. This statement is either false or else it turns out to be simply a different formulation of my second alternative. It is objectively not true that languages are the most efficient communication systems possible. From an information-theoretical point of view, they are very redundant; as far as their grammars are concerned, they seem to be "unnecessarily complicated" (the simplicity of English grammar as against, say, Navaho is certain to be an illusion); in semantic efficiency they leave much to be desired. They can only be said to be ideally efficient if we add "given man's articulatory, perceptual, and intellectual capacity." But with this concession we have admitted that man's pattern of speech is determined by his biological equipment, a point that will be further expanded in connection with the fourth criterion.

2   Second Criterion: History within Species. Languages, like fashions, have histories, but nowhere does the historical evidence take us back to a stage where the phonemic mode of vocalization was in its infancy: we have no records testifying to an absence of grammar; we have no reason to believe that there are places or times where or when concatenation had not been developed. Perhaps this ought to be attributed to the rather recent development of written records. Yet, a lingering doubt remains: writing can be traced back some five thousand years, and, while the earliest written records give us few clues about the language they represent, some of our linguistic reconstructions reach back to about the same era. This is a time span that comprises about one tenth of the age of the earliest evidence of Levalloiso-Mousterian culture (some 50,000 years ago) and the appearance of fossil forms that may be considered to be the direct ancestors of modern man. Thus, the oldest documented history of languages may be short when compared with palaeontological history; but it would not be too short to demonstrate trends in the development of, for instance, phonematization if this phenomenon *did have a cultural history*. We might expect that historical phonemic changes follow a general pattern, namely, from a supposedly *primitive* stage to one that could be called *advanced*. But the phonemic changes that we actually find—and they occur rapidly (within periods of 10 to 15 generations), frequently, and continuously—seem to follow no universal line and have, by and large, a random directionality; we cannot make predictions as to the qualitative changes that will occur in English 300 years hence.

The concatenating phenomenon is, historically, completely static. Throughout the documented history there is evidence that concatenation must have existed in its present complex and universal form for at least some five thousand years and most likely considerably longer.

The history of syntax is the same as that of phonemes. Our oldest linguistic reconstructions are based on reliable evidence that there was *order* in the concatenation of forms, that there were rules and regularities governing the sequences of morphemes which from a formal point of view cannot have been much different from grammatical processes of modern languages. We are not speaking here of specific grammars, but merely of the grammatical phenomenon as such. Syntax changes as rapidly and widely as phonemic structures, but, again, we cannot discern any constant and linear direction. At the most, there is a certain cyclicity, one grammatical type perhaps alternating with another. The so-called "analytical languages," such as Chinese and English, were preceded by synthetic types; and there is reasonable evidence, at least for Indo-European, that the grammatical *synthesis* as seen in ancient Greek was preceded by a more analytic stage (inflectional endings having been derived from once independent words). We cannot be sure, however, whether synthesis *generally* alternates with analysis; indeed, the very polarity expressed by these two terms is not very well defined in grammatical theory. It is widely agreed today that no typology of modern grammars reflects stages of absolute, nonrecurring grammatical development. Nor do we have any means for judging one grammatical system as more primitive than another.

Contrast to this situation the forms found in the animal kingdom. Species *can* be ordered in terms of anatomical simplicity (which we equate with primitivity) so that an arrangement from low to high forms results; and since phylogenetic stages are assumed to be unique and nonrecurring, we can construct phylogenetic history merely from taxonomy. But this reasoning may not be extended to linguistics. No classification of languages in terms of structural type (such as *synthetic, analytic* or *agglutinative*) provides us with a theory for a universal development of language.

There can be no question today that we are unable to trace languages back to an ungrammatical, aphonemic, or simple imitative stage; and there is, indeed, no cogent reason to believe that such a stage has ever existed. This does not imply a nineteenth-century assumption of an instinct, particularly not an instinct for specific languages. Obviously, the child's acquisition of Chinese consists in the acquisition of certain culturally evolved traits. But a phenomenon such as phonematization *per se* need not be thought of as a cultural achievement, need not constitute the summation of inventions, need not have resulted from a long series of trial and error learning in communication.

To put my point more bluntly: the absolutely unexceptional universality of phonemes, concatenation, and syntax and the absence of historical evidence for the slow cultural evolvement of these phenomena lead me to suppose that we have here the reflection of a biological matrix or Anlage which forces speech to be of one and no other basic type. From the point of view of genetic theory we would not have to expect a *gradual* and *selective* process culminating in present-day languages. Mutations are thought of today as sudden intracellular reorganizations in germ plasm, resulting in changes of the gross anatomical structures and also in radical, innate, neuronal re-organization manifested by highly specific behavioral patterns.[10]

3 Third Criterion: Evidence for Inherited Predisposition. The obvious experiments

---

[10]See my article "Understanding Language without Ability to Speak: A Case Report" *Journal of Abnormal and Social Psychology*, **65** (1962), 419–25.

for testing the question, to what degree language is inherited, cannot be performed: we may not control the verbal stimulus input of the young child. However, pathology occasionally performs some quasi-experiments, and, while anomaly frequently introduces untoward nuisance variables, it gives us, nevertheless, some glimpses into the immensely intricate relation between man's nature and his verbal behavior.

Just as we can say with assurance that no man inherits a propensity for French, we can also and with equal confidence say that all men are endowed with an innate propensity for a type of behavior that develops automatically into language and that this propensity is so deeply ingrained that language-like behavior develops even under the most unfavorable conditions of peripheral and even central nervous system impairment.

Language development, or its substitute, is relatively independent of the infant's babbling, or of his ability to hear. The congenitally deaf who will usually fail to develop an intelligible vocal communication system, who either do not babble or to whom babbling is of no avail (the facts have not been reliably reported), will nevertheless learn the intricacies of language and learn to communicate efficiently through writing. Apparently, even under these reduced circumstances of stimulation the miracle of the development of a feeling for grammar takes place.

There is another important observation to be mentioned in connection with the deaf. Recently I had occasion to visit for half a year a public school for the congenitally deaf. At this school the children were not taught sign language on the theory that they must learn to make an adjustment to a speaking world and that absence of sign language would encourage the practice of lip-reading and attempts at vocalization. It was interesting to see that all children, without exception, communicated behind the teacher's back by means of "self-made" signs. I had the privilege of witnessing the admission of a new student, eight years old, who had recently been *discovered* by a social worker who was doing relief work in a slum area. This boy had never had any training and had, as far as I know, never met with other deaf children. This newcomer began to "talk" sign language with his contemporaries almost immediately upon arrival. The existence of an innate impulse for symbolic communication can hardly be questioned.

The case history of another handicapped child[11] gives an illustration that true organic muteness in the presence of good hearing is no hindrance for the development of a speech comprehension that is ever so much more detailed than, for instance, a dog's capacity to "understand" his master. This was a five-year-old boy who, as a consequence of fetal anoxia, had sustained moderate injury to the brain pre-natally, resulting in an inability to vocalize upon command. When completely relaxed and absorbed in play he was heard to make inarticulate sounds which at times appeared to express satisfaction, joy, or disappointment (when a tall tower of blocks would tumble to the floor). But the boy has never said a single word, nor has he ever used his voice to call someone's attention. I was once able, after considerable coaxing and promises of candy, to make him say "ah" into a microphone of a tape recorder. The tape recorder had a voltmeter with a large pointer that

---

[11]See E. Schroedinger, *What is Life* (Garden City, N.Y.: Doubleday & Company, Inc., 1956, chaps. III and IV; also Haldane, *op. cit.* and Dobzhansky, 1951 and 1955, *op. cit.*

would make excursions with each sound picked up by the microphone. The child had been fascinated by this and had learned to make the pointer go through an excursion by clapping his hands. After his first production of the sound "ah" he was able to repeat the sound immediately afterwards, but when he came back the next day, he tried in vain to say "ah," despite the fact that he seemed to be giving himself all the prompting that he could think of, like holding the microphone in both hands and approaching it with his mouth as if to say "ah." A series of examinations revealed that this boy had a remarkable understanding of spoken English; he could execute such complex commands as "take a pencil and cross out all A's in this book," "look behind the tape-recorder and find a surprise" (this was a tape-recorded instruction delivered in the absence of the experimenter), "point at all pictures of things to eat." He was able to distinguish pronouns ("touch my nose; touch your nose"), to show one, two three, four, or five fingers; he could distinguish between a question and a declarative statement by nodding a yes-or-no answer to the question but not to the declarative sentence. He would even nod yes or no correctly when asked about situations that were spatially and temporally removed. This is discrimination learning but on a plane that requires a much more intricate understanding and sensory organization than the simple association of an object and a sign.

These examples do not *prove* that language is an inherited phenomenon. But they do point to the degree of man's preparedness for speech, a preparedness which seems to be responsible for the universality of the speech phenomenon.

4 Fourth Criterion: Presumption of Specific Organic Correlates. From the title of this section it should not be inferred that we wish to draw a sharp line between behavior with and without organic basis. Thought and emotion have no less an organic basis than breathing or the tonic neck reflex. Yet there is a difference between the former and the latter types which can be described in empirical terms. In drawing the distinction we must not forget that we are dealing with a difference of degree, not quality.

4.1 *Onset and fixed developmental history.* Any innate reflex activity and sensory irritability appears at a characteristic moment in an individual's pre- or post-natal maturational process and follows a typical natural history throughout life. For instance, rudiments of the tonic neck reflex have been observed in a 20-week-old embryo; during the second half of fetal life this reflex seems to be well established, and it is strongest during the first eight post-natal weeks, with a peak of activity during the fourth week. At 12 weeks the reflex is less conspicuous and it is normally absent by the twentieth week. If the tonic neck reflex is observed at a later period, it is usually a sign of neurological disorder or pathognomonic retardation. Another example is manual dexterity: our hands become increasingly skillful throughout infancy, greatest control being achieved during young adulthood after which time there is a steady decrease which is accelerated about the fifth decade. Also the acuity of sensory perception follows characteristic age curves. Sensitivity to a number of acoustic stimuli is very low at birth, rapidly reaches a peak during the second decade and then steadily declines throughout the rest of life.[12]

---

[12]Cf. A. Gesell "The Ontogenesis of Infant Behavior" in L. Carmichael, ed., *Manual of Child Psychology* (New York: John Wiley and Sons, Inc., 1946). For data on hearing see J. Sataloff,

In the case of human behavior it is not always easy to rid ourselves of our pervasive and often quite irrational belief that all of our activities are the result of training. For instance, in the case of walking on two feet it is popularly believed that this is the result of the social environment. People who hold this view earnestly propose that the healthy child learns to walk between its 12th and 18th month because this is the time during which the mother is expected to teach her child this accomplishment. Speculation is often carried to the extreme where it is assumed that children brought up in social isolation would probably be seen with different modes of locomotion than is actually observed. That this need not even be regarded seriously as a possible hypothesis may be seen from the developmental events alone. Gesell and associates write:

> Although incipient stepping movements occur during the first week [after delivery!], they are more marked and appear with greater frequency at about 16 weeks. At this time also the infant pushes against pressure applied to the soles of the feet. At 28 weeks he makes dancing and bouncing reactions when held in the upright [N.B.] position. Flexion and extension of the legs are accompanied by raising the arms. At 48 weeks the infant cruises or walks, using support.[13]

We get a flavor here of how deeply walking is based on reflexes that must, under all circumstances, be called *innate*. Also, walking is not an isolated event in the child's developmental history. It is merely one aspect of his total development of motor activity and posture. Compare the same authors' description of the development of the upright position:

> [Stiffening of] the knees occurs before full extension of the legs at the hips. At 40 weeks the infant can pull himself to his knees. He can also stand, holding onto support. At 48 weeks he can lift one foot while he supports his weight on the other, an immature anticipation of a three-year-old ability to stand on one foot with momentary balance. At this age he can also pull himself to standing by holding onto the side rails of the crib. In standing he supports his weight on the entire sole surface.[14]

Anyone who has observed a child during the second half of his first year knows that there is continuous activity and exercise, so to speak, and that most accomplishments occur spontaneously and not as a response to specific training (for instance, climbing out of the playpen).

The most suggestive (even though not conclusive) evidence for this point comes from animal experiments. Thorpe[15] reports on an experiment by Grohmann in which young pigeons were reared in narrow tubes which prevented them from moving their wings. He writes:

> Thus they could not carry out the incipient flights which would naturally be regarded as in the nature of practice. When Grohmann's control birds, which were allowed free practice flights every day, had progressed to a certain point, both groups were

Industrial Deafness; Hearing Testing, and *Noise Measurement* (New York: McGraw-Hill Book Company, 1957), pp. 248ff.

---

[13]A. Gesell, *The First Five Years of Life; A Guide to the Study of the Preschool Child* (New York: Harper & Row, Inc., 1940), p. 70.

[14]Gesell, *op. cit.*, p. 68.

[15]Thorpe, *op. cit.*, p. 51.

tested for flying ability, but no difference was found between them. In other words, the instinctive behavior pattern of flight had been maturing at a steady rate, quite irrespective of the birds' opportunity of exercising it. Those that had been kept in tubes had reached just the same stage of development as those that had what appeared to be the advantage of practice. There is little reasonable doubt that at a later stage further skill in the fine adjustment of flight is acquired as a result of practice . . . ; [Grohmann's] work . . . suffices to show how cautious one must be in interpreting what appears to be the learning behavior of young birds.

Coghill[16] has shown how the primary neural mechanism of swimming and walking in Amblystoma is laid down before the animal can at all respond to its environment. Also, it is common knowledge that neonate colts or calves can stand immediately after birth and that most quadrupeds can either take a few steps or at least go through walking motions within the first few hours of life. If locomotion is innate in such a great variety of vertebrates, why should man be an exception?

The developmental history is not always perfectly synchronized with the advance of chronological age so that we often have the impression that individual maturational phenomena, such as control over equilibrium in stance or the onset of menstruation, occur more or less randomly within a given period. This is probably an erroneous notion arising from our lack of information on other concomitant developmental aspects. If we had complete and accurate longitudinal case histories (instead of dealing with data gathered in cross-sectional surveys), developmental histories would probably reveal fairly constant sequences of events.

Contrast now the appearance and history of acquired behavior. A child waves goodby when he is taught to do so. Some children may learn it before they can speak; some may learn it only in school; and in some cultures, it may never be practiced at all. Another characteristic of acquired habits or skills is that they may be lost at any time during the individual's life so that neither onset nor disappearance of the phenomenon fits into an established place of the life cycle.

When the development of speech is considered in this light, it appears to follow *maturational* development. Cultural differences seem to have no effect on the age of onset and mastery of speech. Unfortunately, completely reliable data on cross-cultural comparison of language development are still a desideratum, but a check through pertinent literature in anthropology and child development have revealed no contrary evidence. Nor have the author's personal experience with two North American Indian tribes (Zuni and Navaho) or his inquiries from natives of non-English speaking countries cast the slightest doubt on perfect chronological commensurability of language development throughout the world. This is also congruent with our present belief that a normal child will learn any language with the same degree of ease, whereas a child who has failed to learn the language of his native land by the time he is six, also could not learn a foreign *simpler* language without trouble. We have to conclude from this that natural languages differ little in terms of complexity when regarded from a developmental point of view.

Compare this situation with writing. Writing does not develop automatically at a specific age and it also seems that various cultures have developed writing systems

---

[16]G. E. Coghill, *Anatomy and the Problem of Behavior* (Cambridge, England: Cambridge University Press, 1929).

of varying degrees of difficulty. For instance, the *petroglyphs* left behind by the North American Indians of the South West can be roughly interpreted even today by the naïve observer. The picture of a woman, an infant, and two feet in a certain direction is most likely a message involving a mother, child, and walking. Narrowing down the meaning of this inscription is easier than one written in Runes. Knowledge of Chinese characters requires greater study than that of the Roman alphabet. I have also made some clinical observations that deserve mention in this connection.

Neuro-psychiatrists are familiar with a condition that is referred to in the American medical literature as *specific reading disability*. It consists of a marked congenital difficulty in learning to write. Intensive drill will sometimes correct this deficit but cases have been reported (see reference in 7*n* for bibliography) where writing was never acquired despite a normal IQ as measured by the usual tests. I have examined eight such cases (who were seen in a neuro-medical outpatient department) in order to find out whether these patients had learned some more primitive type of graphic representation. It appeared that none of them had the slightest difficulty in understanding such symbols as arrows pointing in certain directions, simple representations of stars, hearts, or crosses; nor was there any difficulty in interpreting simple action sequences represented by three very schematic stick-men designs:

("man walking   he enters a house   he is sitting down")

Figure 1

Each of these three pictures was understood when presented individually as well as in conjunction.

Presumably, these subjects have difficulty with some aspects of English orthography but not with visual pattern recognition or the interpretation of graphic symbols. The condition, therefore, is not actually a general *reading difficulty* but merely a difficulty with certain, at present unidentified, associative processes involved in *our* type of writing system. It would be interesting to know whether other countries have the same incidence and types of "specific reading disability" as encountered in England and the United States.

Let us now take a closer look at the longitudinal development of language acquisition. Unfortunately, we only have data gathered within our own culture; but even this much will be instructive, and there is, indeed, very little reason to believe that the main phenomena should differ significantly in nonEnglish speaking communities.

All children go through identical phases in the process of acquiring speech. First, they have a few words or phrases, never longer than three syllables, that refer to objects, persons, or complex situations. At this stage they may have a repertoire of fifty short utterances that are somewhat stereotyped and are never combined one with the other. All attempts to make the child string up the words that he is known to use singly will fail until he reaches a certain stage of maturation. When this is attained, the combining of words seems to be quite automatic, that is, he will surprise the parents by suddenly putting two words together that may not have been given him for repetition, in fact, that may often sound queer enough to make it quite unlikely that anyone in the child's environment has ever spoken these words in just that sequence. "Eat cup" may mean "the dog is eating out of the cup" or "is the dog eating the cup?" and so on. Whatever was meant by this utterance (which was actually heard), it is a sequence of words that nobody had used in the particular situation in which the words were spoken. As the child grows older, longer phrases are composed of individual vocabulary items which had been in the child's repertoire for many months, sometimes years.

Other aspects of language exhibit a similar developmental constancy. There are certain sentence structures that are virtually never heard during the first three years of life (for instance, conditionals or subjunctives). The frequency of occurrence of words shows certain characteristic constancies for child language, which, interestingly enough, are somewhat different from the frequency of occurrences of adult speech. In English, the most frequently occurring words are the articles *a* and *the*; yet, the child's first words never include these. (There is an active process of selection going on that must not be confused with mechanical parroting.) There is also a fairly constant semantic development. Children seem to begin speech with very characteristic semantic generalizations. The word *car* may be extended at first to all vehicles (a child of my acquaintance once pointed to a plane and said car); *dog* to all animals; *daddy* to all people or all men. But there is already an ordering activity apparent that is characteristic of speech as a whole.

Also, the usage of words have a characteristic history. All observers of longitudinal child-language development have reported a difficulty in naming colors correctly at an early stage.[17] The curriculum of many public Kindergartens includes special training in color naming. This characteristic difficulty for the child at $2\frac{1}{2}$ to $3\frac{1}{2}$ years of age is the more interesting as color words are among the most frequently occurring words in English, and it is hard to see that their correct use should have smaller reinforcement value than words such as *big* and *small*, *hot* and *cold*, or *heavy* and *light*, *wet* and *dry*, all of which are words used correctly before color words. Of course, we do not take this observation to mean that something like a special structure has to mature which is particularly involved in color naming. The point here is that naming is a complex process which presents varying degrees of difficulty or, in other words, which depends upon a number of skills that develop at a slow rate. All we can say at our present state of knowledge is that on his second birthday the child does not ordinarily have the capacity to learn to name four basic colors consistently and correctly, whereas he develops this capacity within the next two or three years. (To make a distinction between *concrete* and *abstract* names is of little help since we only have *post hoc* definitions of these terms.)

Another line of evidence that would support the thesis that language-learning follows a maturational course is the phenomenon of foreign accents; it seems as if

---

[17]For theory and experimental work on this problem, see my paper: "A Probabilistic Approach to Language Learning" *Behavioral Science*, 2 (1957) 1–13.

the degree of accent correlates fairly well with the age during which a second language is acquired. The following case will illustrate the point: Mr. R. W., whose major interest is the study of language, is a middle-aged graduate of one of this country's universities. He was born and lived in Germany until he was twelve years old when his family emigrated from Germany to a Portuguese-speaking country where he spent the next ten years. Within two years after his arrival in the new country he had such a perfect command over the second language that his foreign background was never suspected when he spoke to natives. At the age of 22 he came to the United States where he was at once obliged to speak English exclusively. From then on he had no further opportunity to speak Portuguese, and only occasionally (never more than a few hours at a time) has he spoken German since his arrival in this country. The result is interesting. His ability to speak English has completely displaced his facility in Portuguese and even the availability of his German vocabulary seems to have suffered in the course of the years. Yet, his pronunciation of English is marked by a gross and virtually insuperable foreign accent while his German continues to sound like that of a native and his Portuguese, as evidenced in the pronunciation of isolated words, continues to have the phonological characteristics of perfect Portuguese. (Yet, this person has heard and spoken more English during his life than either German or Portuguese.)

Here again it would be important to verify empirically the plasticity for the acquisition of languages throughout an individual's life history. Systematic research on immigrant families and their progress in learning English as a function of the age of the learner would seem to be a quite feasible and interesting study.

Before leaving the subject of fixed developmental histories in language learning, we must briefly consider those cases where language does not develop normally. Speech disturbances are among the most common complaints of the pediatric patient with neurologic disorders. It is precisely the area of speech disorders in childhood, which can shed the most light on the nature of language development; yet, despite a very prolific literature, the most elementary observations have either not yet been made or the reports cannot be used reliably. This is primarily due to the imprecise terminology common in these studies, to a predilection for subjective interpretation, to the complete absence of complete and accurate case reports of longitudinal descriptions (instead of the now fashionable cross-sectional studies of many hundreds of subjects), poor categories for classification, and similar other shortcomings. The only aspect in which little or no further spade-work needs to be done in this respect is the establishment of norms for speech development. We have little trouble today in deciding whether or not a patient's speech is normal for his age.

If speech disturbances were viewed as nature's own experiments on the development of speech, a wide variety of observational research projects could be formulated details of which need not be gone into here. Suffice it to point out that research could easily be conducted that would constitute direct verification of (or means for refining) the view that language development follows a characteristic, natural history. It would be very revealing, for instance, to know exactly under what circumstances the present practice of speech "therapy" (which is strictly speaking a training procedure) is successful. This would include detailed description of the patient's condition before and after treatment, perfectly objective evaluation of his improvement, and an accurate assessment of the role that specific speech therapy played in the course of the condition. In reporting on the patient's condition, it is not enough to mention one or another type of speech defect, but a complete inventory of the subject's speech facility ought to be given in addition to a complete and accurate report of his clinical and developmental status. Speech is so complicated a matter that we must not be surprised that a full case report is meaningful only after collecting most meticulous data on hours of patient testing and observations. A few scattered clinical notes, a random collection of psychological test results and a global statement of "improvement" is meaningless in this field. Among the most important objectives of a "log" of a long course of speech therapy is the determination whether language must be taught and learned in terms of a hierarchy of levels of complexity, whether it is essential that one set of skills precedes another, or whether almost anything can be taught and learned in a wide variety of orders. If there *is* a hierarchy of complexity, what are the linguistic correlates, what are the factors that make some linguistic aspects "easy," and what makes them "difficult"? Answers to these questions would be major contributions to our present state of knowledge.

In conclusion, I would like to suggest (subject to further verification) that the development of speech does not proceed randomly; there are certain regularities that characterize speech at certain stages of development, but empirical work still needs to be done on the individual differences that may also be observed. Moreover, we know that language development, viewed cross-culturally, has never been said to deviate essentially from development in Western cultures, and if we accept temporarily and subject to further work this indirect evidence, it would be more reasonable to assume that the acquisition of language is controlled by a biologically determined set of factors and not by intentional training, considering that cultures differ radically in their educational procedures.

4.2 *Dependence upon Environment.* Thorpe [18] describes the behavior of a hand-reared Tawny Owl "which, after being fed, would act as if pouncing upon living prey although it had never had the experience of dealing with a living mouse." This is not an isolated instance. Ethologists are familiar with this and similar types of action patterns that are usually triggered by so-called "innate releasing mechanisms." Thorpe[19] notes that for every action pattern there is an ideal training stimulus such that every time it acts upon the animal, the latter will go through the entire action pattern. However, it is said that if the animal has not encountered the ideal stimulus in his environment for some time, the threshold for the release of the action pattern is lowered so that a stimulus that ordinarily does not evoke the patterned response is now capable of so doing. In the complete and continuing absence of suitable stimuli for the release of the mechanical action pattern, the threshold is lowered to a zero point, that is, the action pattern will go off in the complete absence of any environmental stimulus. This is the significance of the behavior of Thorpe's hand-reared Tawny Owl. But the absence of environmental stimuli

---

[18]W. H. Thorpe, "The Modern Concept of Instinctive Behavior" *Bulletin Animal Behavior*, **1**, 7, (1948), 12f.

[19]Thorpe, *Learning and Instinct in Animals, op. cit.,* introductory chapters.

does not imply absence of stimulation. Just as there is no effect without a cause, so there is no biological activity without a stimulus. In the owl's case, the stimuli must be assumed to be within the organism, i.e., be reducible to chemico-physical events. Again, this is nothing that is peculiar to innate action patterns because the behavior of pigeons that learn to pick at certain spots is also the direct result of chemico-physical reactions that take place within the bird's body. But differences there are. Compare the owl's pouncing behavior with Skinner's rat that learned to "purchase" a token which it would drop into a food-dispensing machine.[20] In the case of the rat, various bits of spontaneous rat behavior have been artificially (from the rat's point of view, *randomly*) chained so that the *sequence* of rat-behavior-bits has a *perfect* correspondence to a sequence of environmental events. Or, in other words, every individual bit of behavior making up the food-purchasing sequence was at one time preceded by a distinct environmental stimulus or at least linked to a reinforcing event. The only reason the total food-purchasing behavior appears in the sequence that it does, is that environmental stimuli and reinforcements have been arbitrarily arranged in a particular order. But the owl's pouncing behavior, which may not be as complex an affair as the purchase of food but still is elaborate enough and may last for as long a time as it takes the rat to purchase food, cannot be decomposed into bits of individual behavior components that can be rearranged into any combination and sequence. The sequence is completely fixed. This is a very important point. These days of electronic computers have made it fashionable to use electronic metaphors. We may say that innate behavior, such as the owl's pouncing is *programmed* into the organism. Environmental conditions may trigger the sequence (or perhaps forcefully prevent it), but once it goes off it follows a prescribed course. It hardly needs to be pointed out that food purchasing is different.

If we were asked whether instinctive behavior, such as the predisposition for nest-building, or the pouncing of the owl, is primarily based on organic factors, we could hardly fail to answer in the affirmative. Since the environment alone is either insufficient for producing the behavior (dogs are not stimulated to build nests), or in some cases quite unnecessary, the action pattern must have an internal cause. This statement must be true even if we shall never discover the neuro-anatomical basis of the behavior.

Let us now consider how language development fits into this scheme. The purpose of the following discussion will be to show that the rat who learns to press a lever or to purchase food gives us no more insight into the process of language acquisition than, for instance, thorough observations on the nest building habit of the rat or the acquisition of flight in the bird.

The constancy in language developmental histories is merely an indirect cue for the deep-seated nature of language predispositions in the child. Much stronger arguments can be marshalled.

First of all, in the case of the food purchasing rat, the sequence of behavior is preplanned by the trainer and in that sense it has a rational aim. But language "training" and acquisition cannot possibly be the result of rational pre-planning because

---

[20]B. F. Skinner, *The Behavior of Organisms: An Experimental Analysis* (New York: Appleton-Century-Crofts, Inc., 1938).

no adult "knows" how he generates new grammatical sentences. This fact cannot be appreciated except by sophisticated analysis of the principles of language. In the current explanations of language-learning we hear a good deal of how the supposedly random babbling of the infant is gradually shaped into words by the trainer's waiting for the accidental appearance of certain sounds which can then be reinforced, and thereby elicited with greater frequency, and how from this procedure the infant learns to imitate in general. This conception of speech acquisition is unsatisfactory from many viewpoints; for the time being, we merely point out that *imitation* (whatever psychological processes this term might cover) may be part of language-learning but by no means its most important aspects. Speech activity is virtually never a mechanical play-back device. This is most readily seen on the morphological level, where children will automatically extend inflexional suffixes both to nonsense words[21] and to words that have irregular forms such as *good-gooder, go-goed, foot-foots*. Not quite so obvious, but in a sense much more striking, is the generalization that takes place in syntactic matters. Here it becomes quite clear that there must be a second process in addition to imitation, for the language of children is not confined to stereotyped sentences. Children ask questions that have never been asked before ("What does blue look like from in back?"), make statements that have never been stated before ("I buyed a fire dog for a grillion dollars!"), and in general apply grammatical rules that only few adults could make explicit ("I didn't hit Billy; Billy hit me!").

The phenomenon of morphological generalization puts great strains on a simple referent-symbol association theory of language. The -*s* suffix of the third person singular ("he go[e]*s*") has no demonstrable referent taking this word in its literal meaning; nor the *s* of plurality, the *ed* of the past tense, the -*er* of the comparative. The referent of the "small" words such as *the, is, will* is completely nebulous, and neither training nor learning can possibly be the result of any kind of referent-symbol contiguity, that is, the proximity of the words *the* and *man* welds them into a unit. As long as ten years ago, Lashley[22] thoroughly demonstrated the impossibility of explaining syntax on the grounds of temporal contiguity association, and he has pointed to the generality of his observations on language with respect to other motor behavior. Lashley's argument is so compelling that little can be added to it. More recently, Chomsky[23] has demonstrated from a purely formal approach that grammatical sentences cannot be the product of stochastic processes in which the probability of occurrence of an element (morpheme or word) is entirely determined by preceding elements, and Miller[24] and Chomsky[25] have discussed the psychological

[21]J. Berko, "The Child's Learning of English Morphology," *Word*, **14** (1958) 150–77. Compare also D. L. Wolfle, "The Relation between Linguistic Structure and Associative Interference in Artificial Linguistic Material," *Language Monograph*, **11** (1932) 1–55.

[22]K. S. Lashley, "The Problem of Serial Order in Behavior" in L. A. Jeffress, ed., *Cerebral Mechanisms in Behavior, The Hixon Symposium* (New York: John Wiley and Sons, Inc., 1951).

[23]Chomsky, Three Models for the Description of Language," *op. cit.*

[24]N. Chomsky, G. A. Miller, "Introduction to the Formal Analysis of Natural Languages" in R. D. Luce, R. R. Bush, E. Galanter, eds., *Handbook of Mathematical Psychology* (New York: John Wiley and Sons, Inc., 1963). N. Chomsky, G. A. Miller, "Finitary Models of Language Users," in R. D. Luce, R. R. Bush, E. Galanter, *op. cit.*

[25]J. S. Bruner, "Mechanisms Riding High," *Contemporary Psychology*, **2** (1957) 155–57.

implications of this observation. We have neither a good theoretical model nor any practical insights into how we could teach an organism to respond to plurality, third-person-ness, past-ness, let alone how we could train him to use these responses in the correct order and verbal contexts within original sentence constructions. Consequently, both the teaching and learning of language cannot simply be explained by extrapolating from rat and pigeon experiments where all learning follows an explicit program.

All that we have said about production of speech is equally valid for the understanding of speech. The baby can repeat new words with great ease and be satisfied with his own baby-talk replica of the adult prototype, because he seems to perceive adult words not like a tape recorder but like a "phoneme-analyzer." He recognizes the functional similarity between phones and between his own reproduction of the adult speech sounds, and this enables him to disregard the very marked, objective, physical differences between a baby's voice and a middle-aged man's voice. Chomsky and Miller regard the child at three as a machine that can make syntactic analysis of the input speech. Obviously, children are not given rules which they can apply. They are merely exposed to a great number of examples of how the syntax works, and from these examples they completely automatically acquire principles with which new sentences can be formed that will conform to the universally recognized rules of the game. (We must not be disturbed by the fact that a transcription of a child's speech—or adult's speech for that matter—would be quite unpolished stylistically. There might be incomplete sentences and every now and then ungrammatical constructions resulting primarily from beginning a sentence one way and finishing it another. The important point here is that words are neither randomly arranged nor confined to unchangeable, stereotyped sequences. At every stage there is a characteristic structure.)

A word on the problem of motivation is in place. Animals are not passive objects upon which the environment acts. Their peripheral sensitivities are centrally controlled to the extent that, for instance, a certain odor may at one time have an arousing effect upon an individual animal but at another time (say after consuming a satiating meal) leave it inert. Moreover, *ability to stimulate* is not an objective physical property such as weight or temperature. It can only be defined with reference to a given animal species. A tree might stimulate a monkey to do some acrobatics, a beaver to start gnawing, and a grandmother to rest in its shade (where the latter is merely a subspecies). Motivation for action resides in the physiological state of the organism and in some instances can be immediately correlated with clear-cut states of deprivation, say of food or sex. Ordinarily it is false to assume that the environment *produces* a given type of behavior; it merely triggers it. There are many ways of chasing and eating a rabbit, and even though all of its predators may be motivated by the same physiological drive, hunger, the mode of catching and consuming the rabbit will bear the characteristic stamp of the predator's species.

In view of this, it seems reasonable to assert that there are certain propensities built into animals and man to utilize the environment in a fairly species-specific way. Sometimes this is obscured (a) because of individual differences in behavior traits and (b) because behavior is also affected, within limits, by environmental variations (such as availability *either* of little sticks, *or* of leaves, *or* of rags for the building of nests; analogously, because a child may grow up *either* in a Chinese, *or* in a German, *or* in a Navaho speaking environment).

The appearance of language may be thought to be due to an innately mapped-in *program* for behavior, the exact realization of the program being dependent upon the peculiarities of the (speech) environment. As long as the child is surrounded at all by a speaking environment, speech will develop in an automatic way, with a rigid developmental history, a highly specific mode for generalization behavior, and a relative dependence upon the maturational history of the child.

It may seem as if we were begging the question here: If speech develops automatically provided a speech environment is given, how did the speech environment come about originally? Actually, we are in no greater logical trouble than is encountered by explanations of any social phenomenon in biology, for instance, communal life as the evolution of herds, flocks, or schools. Compare also the colonial life of ants, the family formation of badgers, the social stratification of chickens. Nor is human language the only form of communication that has evolved in the animal kingdom. Bees and many species of birds have communication systems, and in none of these cases do we find ourselves forced to argue either that these communication systems (or the social phenomena) are the result of purposeful invention or that an individual of the species undergoes a purposeful training program to acquire the trait. If in the case of lower animals we assume without compunction that the communicating trait is the result of an *innate predisposition elicited by environmental circumstances*, we have no reason to assume *a priori* that the language trait of man is purely acquired behavior (not pre-determined by innate predispositions). We are making no stronger a claim here than what is expressed by Dobzhansky's words:

> The genetic equipment of our species was molded by natural selection; it conferred upon our ancestors the capacity to develop language and culture. This capacity was decisive in the biological success of man as a species; . . . man . . . has become specialized to live in a man-made environment.[26]

CONSEQUENCES FOR THEORY AND RESEARCH

The great achievement of contemporary psychology was the replacement of mentalistic explanations by mechanistic ones and the simultaneous insistence upon empirical testability of hypothesized laws. In the search for laws of behavior it seemed at once desirable to discover the most universal laws since this alone, it was thought, could give our theoretical edifice insurance against *ad hoc* explanations. Many behaviorists have explicitly renounced interest in those aspects of behavior that are specific to one species and consequently, confine themselves, by program, to what is universal to the behavior of *all* organisms. This attitude has cost the science of behavior a price: it has made it difficult to recognize the very intimate connection between the behavior repertoire of a species and its biologically defined constitution, that is, its anatomy and physiology.

---

[26]T. Dobzhansky, "Evolution at Work," *Science*, **122** (1958) 1091–98.

The treatment of language by behaviorists is an excellent example of this situation. The literature, including experimental reports, in the area of verbal behavior is very voluminous and cannot be reviewed here. In general it may be characterized as a gigantic attempt to prove that general principles of association, reinforcement, and generalization are at work also in this type of behavior. The basic process of language acquisition is roughly pictured as follows: The child associates the sounds of the human voice with need-satisfying circumstances; when he hears his own random babbling, these sounds are recognized to be similar to those uttered by the adults so that the pleasure or anticipation of pleasure associated with mother's voice is now transferred to his own vocalizations. Thus, hearing his own sounds becomes a pleasurable experience in itself, the more so as mother tends to reinforce these sounds, particularly if they by chance resemble a word such as *Dada*. This induces a quantitative increase in the infant's vocal output. Soon he will learn that approximating adult speech patterns, i.e., imitating, is generally reinforced, and this is thought to put him on his way toward adult forms of language. Admittedly, this account is a gross simplification of what has been published on the subject, but the basic mechanisms postulated are not violated. Many psychologists have noted that the concept of imitation is not satisfactory in an explanation because it is precisely the process that needs to be accounted for. I am in agreement with this objection but would add to the current views on the problem of language acquisition that there is a host of other questions that have not even been recognized, let alone *answered*. A few illustrations follow.

(1) The perception of similarities is a general psychological problem closely related to the problem of generalization which, however, in the perception of speech sounds plays a particularly prominent role. Acoustically, the sounds of a two-month-old infant are totally different from those of the mother; how then can it become aware of similarities between his and his mother's voices? There is also great random variation in the acoustic nature of phonemes. The identical physical sound is in one context assignable to one phoneme and in another context to another phoneme. This is even true for the speech of one individual. Thus, phoneme identification is dependent upon analysis of larger language units thus calling for a sound-Gestalt perception which may well be based on highly specialized sensory skills. We cannot be sure, for instance, whether a dog that has learned to respond to some twenty spoken commands responds to these words phonemically or whether he responds to secondary extralinguistic cues such as its master's movements. (This is an empirical question and the evidence so far is in favor of the latter.)

(2) Even if we agree that we do not know how the process of imitation works, everyone has to admit that in some way the child learns to behave like those around him, that is, to imitate. Bracketing the problem of imitation *per se*, there is a still more primitive problem: why does the child begin to "imitate" in as highly characteristic a way as he does? His first goal does not appear to be a replication of the motor skill—he does not at first simply parrot—but his first accomplishment is to *name* objects; in fact, the motor skill lags significantly behind the naming. There is nothing necessary or obvious about this. Talking birds do the exact opposite—if they learn to name at all, for which there is, again, no good evidence. Reinforcement theory does not explain this; to the contrary, from the common psychological accounts of

the beginning of verbal behavior the perfection of the motor skill intuitively ought to have preference over the more abstract naming skill in the infant's learning agenda. The naming of objects, that is, to learn that there is a general class of objects called *cup* is notoriously difficult for animals.

(3) Most terrestial vertebrates make noises, and in mammals these are produced through the larynx and oro-pharyngeal cavity. Without exception these acoustic signals serve some biological function which, in their homologous form in man, would relate to emotions. Examples are courting, territoriality, warnings and danger signals, anger, care for the young. It is extremely difficult and, for many species, reportedly impossible to train animals to use these vocal signals for instrumental conditioning. It is not possible, to my knowledge, to teach a dog to howl in order to obtain a morsel of food; a tomcat to make courting noises to avoid shock; a rat to squeal in order to have doors opened in a maze. There are many indications that human vocalization is phylogenetically also related to the expression of emotions; yet, in the course of normal development a child begins to make use of his vocal apparatus independently from his emotions. Why is this so?

(4) The general problem of attention has haunted practically every research in psychology, and so we are not surprised to encounter it also in connection with language acquisition. The apes that were raised in human homes failed to develop speech partly, it was thought, because they could not be induced to pay attention to the relevant cues in their environment. But why do all children without any special training automatically attend to these cues?

(5) It is well known that there is a nearly perfect homology of muscles and bones in the head and neck of mammals and the geometry of the oral cavity of the great apes is sufficiently similar to that of man to make it potentially and physically possible to produce speech sounds. Except for a report on a single chimpanzee, who could whisper a few "words" in heavy and, to the outside, incomprehensible chimpanzee accent[27], no chimpanzee or other primate has been able to learn to co-ordinate respiration, laryngeal, and oral mechanism with the speed, precision, and endurance that every child displays. What is the extraordinary skill due to? Does it merely depend on practice, or are there physiological predispositions?

Many more questions of this kind could be asked. They are all essential to our understanding of language and speech yet we have no answers to any one of them. Present-day psychology tends to brush these problems aside by simply admitting that it is in the biological nature of man to behave in this way and not in that and that biological aspects of behavior may be disregarded in the psychological treatment of it. But such a position endangers the discovery value which a psychological description of behavior may have. It threatens many a conclusion to boil down to the triviality that children learn to speak because they are children and that all children learn to speak provided they are healthy and live in a normal environment.

If, on the other hand, the study of speech and language is from the outset seen as a study in biology (including the study of the interaction between heredity and

---

[27]K. J. Hayes and C. Hayes, "A Home-Raised Chimpanzee" in R. G. Kuhlen and G. G. Thompson, eds., *Psychological Studies of Human Development* (New York: Appleton-Century-Crofts, Inc., 1952), p. 117.

environment), we can hope to combine research on questions such as those posed above with those that are customarily asked in psychology and thus to obtain new insights into the nature of man. It is true that this approach will not allow us to generalize our findings to all species or to speak about "the organism" in general. But I see no reason why the difference between species and their behavior should be less interesting or pertinent to a general science than the similarities.

SUMMARY AND CONCLUSION

The behavior repertoire of many animals depends upon certain biological pre-dispositions. On the one hand, the animal may be constitutionally pre-destined or have an Anlage for the exercise of given behavior patterns, or, on the other hand, it is innately tuned to react to specific environmental stimuli in a species-characteristic fashion. In a sense, all of man's activities are a consequence of his inherited endowments including his capacity for culture and social structure. But some of his behavior patterns, for instance, bipedal gait, are based upon very specific anatomical and physiological predispositions, whereas other patterns, such as writing, are based on more general capacities of motor coordination, perception, and cognitive processes. In the present article, criteria were developed to distinguish behavior patterns based on specific predispositions from those based on general ones. When these criteria are applied to language, one discovers that it falls between these two poles, though considerably closer to the side of special predispositions than to its opposite.

Since it is proper to speak of language as species-specific behavior, we are implicitly postulating a biological matrix for the development of speech and language. This is tantamount to an assumption that the general morphology characteristic of the order *primates* and/or universal physiological processes such as *respiration* and *motor-coordination* have undergone specialized adaptations, making the exercise of this behavior possible. At present, there is scanty evidence for this because proper questions that might lead to decisive answers—either for or against the hypothesis—have not been asked. Let us hope that the present formulations help us to ask such novel questions.

23   Speech Recognition: A Model and a Program for Research*

Morris Halle
Kenneth N. Stevens

The fundamental problem in pattern recognition is the search for a *recognition function* that will appropriately pair *signals* and *messages*. The input to the recognizer generally consists of measured physical quantities characterizing each signal to be recognized, while at the output of the recognizer each input signal is assigned to one of a number of categories which constitute the messages. Thus, for instance, in machine translation, the signals are sentences in one language and the messages are sentences in another language. In the automatic recognition of handwriting, the signal is a two-dimensional curve and the message a sequence of letters in a standard alphabet. Similarly, research on automatic speech recognition aims at discovering a recognition function that relates acoustic signals produced by the human vocal tract in speaking to messages consisting of strings of symbols, the phonemes. Such a recognition function is the inverse of a function that describes the production of speech, *i.e.*, the transformation of a discrete phoneme sequence into an acoustic signal.

This paper proposes a recognition model in which mapping from signal to message space is accomplished largely through an active or feedback process. Patterns are generated internally in the analyzer according to a flexible or adaptable sequence of instructions until a best match with the input signal is obtained. Since the analysis is achieved through active internal synthesis of comparison signals, the procedure has been called *analysis by synthesis*.[1]

---

*This work was supported in part by the U.S. Army Signal Corps, the Air Force Office of Scientific Research, and the Office of Naval Research; in part by the National Science Foundation; and in part by the Air Force (Electronic Systems Division) under Contract AF 19(604)-6102.
[1]The relevance of such analysis procedures to more general perceptual processes has been suggested by several writers. See, for example, D. M. MacKay, "Mindlike Behavior in Artefacts," *Brit. J. for Philosophy of Science*, **2** (1951), 105–21; G. A. Miller, E. Galanter, and K. H. Pribram,

THE PROCESS OF SPEECH PRODUCTION

In line with the traditional account of speech production, we shall assume that the speaker has stored in his memory a table of all the phonemes and their actualizations. This table lists the different vocal-tract configurations or gestures that are associated with each phoneme and the conditions under which each is to be used. In producing an utterance the speaker looks up, as it were, in the table the individual phonemes and then instructs his vocal tract to assume in succession the configurations or gestures corresponding to the phonemes.

The shape of man's vocal tract is not controlled as a single unit; rather, separate control is exercised over various gross structures in the tract, *e.g.*, the lip opening, position of velum, tongue position, and vocal-cord vibration. The changing configurations of the vocal tract must, therefore, be specified in terms of parameters describing the behavior of these quasi-independent structures.[2] These parameters will be called *phonetic parameters*.[3]

Since the vocal tract does not utilize the same amount of time for actualizing each phoneme (*e.g.*, the vowel in *bit* is considerably shorter than that in *beat*), it must be assumed that stored in the speaker's memory there is also a schedule that determines the time at which the vocal tract moves from one configuaration to the next, *i.e.*, the time at which one or more phonetic parameters change in value. The timing will evidently differ depending on the speed of utterance—it will be slower for slower speech and faster for faster speech.

Because of the inertia of the structures that form the vocal tract and the limitations in the speed of neural and muscular control, a given phonetic parameter cannot change instantaneously from one value to another; the transitions from one target configuration to the next must be gradual, or smooth. Furthermore, when utterances are produced at any but the slowest rates, a given articulatory configuration may not be reached before motion toward the next must be initiated. Thus, the configuration at any given time may be the result of instructions from more than one phoneme. In other words, at this stage in the speech production process, discrete

---

"Plans and the Structure of Behavior," New York: Holt, Rinehart & Winston, Inc. (1960); M. Halle and K. N. Stevens, "Analysis by Synthesis," *Proc. of Senimar on Speech Compression and Processing*, W. Wathen-Dunn and L. E. Woods, eds., **2**, Paper D7: December, 1959.

[2]This view was well understood by the founder of modern phonetics, A. M. Bell, who described utterances by means of symbols ("Visible Speech and The Science of Universal Alphabetics," [London, Eng.: 1867] Simpkin, Marshall and Co.), from which the behavior of the quasi-independent structures could be read off directly. The subsequent replacement, for reasons of typographical economy, of Bell's special symbols by the Romic of the Internatl. Phonetic Assoc. has served to obscure the above facts and to suggest that phonemes are implemented by controlling the vocal tract as a single unit.

[3]We cannot discuss in detail at this point the nature of the phonetic parameters, and we do not take sides here in the present discussion between proponents of the Jakobsonian distinctive features (R. Jakobson and M. Halle, "Fundamentals of Language," The Hague, Netherlands: Moulton and Co., 1956) and those of more traditional views ("The Principles of the International Phonetic Association," University College, London, England; 1949). We insist however, that the control of the vocal-tract behavior must be described by specifying a set of quasi-independent phonetic parameters.

quantities found in the input have been replaced by continuous parameters. A given sequence of phonemes, moreover, may produce a variety of vocal-tract behaviors depending upon such factors as the past linguistic experience of the talker, his emotional state, and the rate of talking.

The continuous phonetic parameters that result from a given phoneme sequence give rise in turn to changes in the geometry and acoustic excitation of the cavities forming the vocal tract. The tract can be visualized as a time-varying linear acoustic system, excited by one or more sound sources, which radiates sound from the mouth opening (and/or from the nose). The acoustic performance of this linear system at a given time and for a given source of excitation can be characterized by the poles and zeros of the transfer function from the source to the output, together with a constant factor.[4] For voiced sounds the vocal tract is excited at the glottis by a quasi-periodic source with high acoustic impedance. Its fundamental frequency varies with time, but the waveform or spectrum of each glottal pulse does not change markedly from one speech sound to another. In addition the vocal tract may be excited in the vicinity of a constriction or obstruction by a broad-band noise source or by sound.

In the process of generating an acoustic output in response to a sequence of phonemes, a talker strives to produce the appropriate vocal-tract configurations together with the proper type of source, but he does not exert precise control over such factors as the detailed characteristics of the source or the damping of the vocal tract. Consequently, for a given vocal-tract configuration the shape of the source spectrum, the fundamental frequency of the glottal source, and the bandwidths of the poles and zeros can be expected to exhibit some variation for a given talker. Even greater variation is to be expected among different talkers, since the dimensions of the speech-production apparatus are different for different individuals. This variance is superimposed on the already-mentioned variance in articulatory gestures.

REDUCTION OF THE CONTINUOUS SIGNAL TO A MESSAGE CONSISTING OF DISCRETE SYMBOLS; THE SEGMENTATION PROBLEM

The analysis procedure that has enjoyed the widest acceptance postulates that the listener first segments the utterance and then identifies the individual segments with particular phonemes. No analysis scheme based on this principle has ever been successfully implemented. This failure is understandable in the light of the preceding account of speech production, where it was observed that segments of an utterance do not in general stand in a one-to-one relation with the phonemes. The problem, therefore, is to devise a procedure which will transform the continuously-changing speech signal into a discrete output without depending crucially on segmentation.

A simple procedure of this type restricts the input to stretches of sound separated from adjacent stretches by silence. The input signals could, for example, correspond to isolated words, or they could be longer utterances. Perhaps the crudest device

---

[4] G. Fant, "Acoustic Theory of Speech Production," (The Hague, Netherlands: Mouton and Co.), 1960.

capable of transforming such an input into phoneme sequences would be a "diction-ary" in which the inputs are entered as intensity-frequency-time patterns[5] and each entry is provided with its phonemic representation. The segment under analysis is compared with each entry in the dictionary, the one most closely resembling the input determined, and its phonemic transcription printed out.[6]

The size of the dictionary in such an analyzer increases very rapidly with the number of admissible outputs, since a given phoneme sequence can give rise to a large number of distinct acoustic outputs. In a device whose capabilities would even remotely approach those of a normal human listener, the size of the dictionary would, therefore, be so large as to rule out this approach.[7]

The need for a large dictionary can be overcome if the principles of construction of the dictionary entries are known. It is then possible to store in the "permanent memory" of the analyzer only the rules for speech production discussed in the previous section. In this model the dictionary is replaced by *generative rules* which can synthesize signals in response to instructions consisting of sequences of phonemes. Analysis is now accomplished by supplying the generative rules with all possible phoneme sequences, systematically running through all one-phoneme sequences, two-phoneme sequences, etc. The internally generated signal which provides the best match with the input signal then identifies the required phoneme sequence. While this model does not place excessive demands on the size of the memory, a very long time is required to achieve positive identification.

The necessity of synthesizing a large number of comparison signals can be elimin-ated by a *preliminary analysis* which excludes from consideration all but a very small subset of the items which can be produced by the generative rules. The preliminary analysis would no doubt include various transformations which have been found useful in speech analysis, such as segmentation within the utterance according to the type of vocal-tract excitation and tentative identification of segments by special attributes of the signal. Once a list of possible phoneme sequences is established from the preliminary analysis, then the internal signal synthesizer proceeds to gen-erate signals corresponding to each of these sequences.

---

[5]The initial step in processing a speech signal for automatic analysis usually consists of deriving from the time-varying pressure changes a sequence of short-time amplitude spectra. This trans-formation, which is commonly performed by sampling the rectified and smoothed outputs of a set of band-pass filters or by computing the Fourier transform of segments of the signal, is known to preserve intact the essential information in the signal, provided that suitable filter bandwidths and averaging times have been chosen.

[6]A model of this type was considered by F. S. Cooper *et al.*, "Some Experiments on the Percep-tion of Synthetic Speech Sounds," *J. Acoust. Soc. Am.*, **24** (November 1952), 605.

"The problem of speech perception is then to describe the decoding process either in terms of the decoding mechanism or—as we are trying to do—by compiling the code book, one in which there is one column for acoustic entries and another column for message units, whether these be phonemes, syllables, words, or whatever."

[7]This approach need not be ruled out, however, in specialized applications in which a greatly restricted vocabulary of short utterances, such as digits, is to be recognized. See, for example, H. Dudley and S. Balashek, "Automatic Recognition of Phonetic Patterns in Speech," *J. Acoust. Soc. Am.*, **30** (August, 1958), 721–32; P. Denes and M. V. Mathews, "Spoken Digit Recognition Using Time-frequency Pattern Matching," *J. Acoust. Soc. Am.*, **32** (November, 1960), 1450–55; G. S. Sebestyen, "Recognition of Membership in Classes," IRE TRANS. ON INFORMATION THEORY, **IT-6** (January, 1961), 44–50.

The analysis procedure can be refined still further by including a *control* component to dictate the order in which comparison signals are to be generated. This control is guided not only by the results of the preliminary analysis but also by quantitative measures of the goodness of fit achieved for comparison signals that have already been synthesized, statistical information concerning the admissible phoneme sequences, and other data that may have been obtained from preceding analyses. This information is utilized by the control component to formulate strategies that would achieve convergence to the required result with as small a number of trials as possible.

It seems to us that an automatic speech recognition scheme capable of processing any but the most trivial classes of utterances must incorporate all of the features discussed above—the input signal must be matched against a comparison signal; a set of generative rules must be stored within the machine; preliminary analysis must be performed; and a strategy must be included to control the order in which internal comparison signals are to be generated. The arrangement of these operations in the proposed recognition model is epitomized in Fig. 1.

PROCESSING OF THE SPEECH SIGNAL PRIOR TO PHONEME IDENTIFICATION

In the analysis-by-synthesis procedure just described, it is implied that the comparison between the input and the internally generated signal is made at the level of the time-varying acoustic spectrum. It is clear, however, that the input signal of Fig. 1 could equally well be the result of some transformation of the acoustic spec-

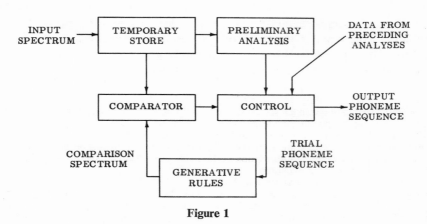

Figure 1

trum carried out at a previous stage of analysis. Indeed, in any practical speech recognizer, it is essential to subject the spectral pattern to a certain amount of preliminary processing before entering the phonemic analysis stage. The necessity for initial transformations or simplifications stems from the fact that many acoustic signals may correspond to a given sequence of phonemes. To account for all the sources of variance or redundancy in one stage of analysis is much too difficult an undertaking. Through a stepwise reduction procedure, on the other hand, variance due to irrelevant factors can be eliminated a small amount at a time.

The proposed procedure for speech processing contains two major steps. In the first stage, the spectral representation is reduced to a set of parameters which describe the pertinent motions and excitations of the vocal tract, *i.e.*, the phonetic parameters. In the second stage, transformation to a sequence of phonemes is achieved. These steps provide a natural division of the analysis procedure into one part concerned primarily with the physical and physiological processes of speech, and the other concerned with those aspects of speech primarily dependent on linguistic and social factors. In the first stage, variance in the signal due to differences in the speech mechanism of different talkers (or of a given talker in different situations) would be largely eliminated. The second stage would account for influences such as rate of talking, linguistic background or dialect of the talker, and contextual variants of phonemes.

Many of the problems involved in the first analysis stage are not unlike those encountered in reducing an utterance to a phoneme sequence. It is not feasible to store all possible spectra together with the corresponding articulatory descriptions. Since, however, rules for generating the spectrum from the articulatory description are known, it is possible to use an analysis-by-synthesis procedure[8] of the type shown in Fig. 1.

The output of this stage is a set of phonetic parameters (rather than the phoneme sequence shown in Fig. 1). The heart of this first-stage analyzer is a signal synthesizer that has the ability to compute comparison spectra when given the phonetic parameters, *i.e.*, an internal synthesizer in which are stored the generative rules for the construction of speech spectra from phonetic parameters. A strategy is required to reduce the time needed to match the input spectrum and the comparison spectrum. The strategy may again depend on the results of a preliminary approximate analysis of the input signal, and on the error that has been computed at the comparator on previous trials. It may also depend on the results that have been obtained for the analysis of signals in the vicinity of the one under direct study. Some of the instructions that are communicated by the control component to the generative rules remain relatively fixed for the matching of spectra generated by a given talker in a given situation. When signals generated by a different talker are presented, the strategy must be able to modify this group of instructions automatically after sufficient data on that talker's speech have been accumulated. The analysis-by-synthesis procedure has the property, therefore, that its strategy is potentially able to adapt to the characteristics of different talkers.

---

[8]Partial implementation (or models for implementation) of the analysis-by-synthesis procedure applied at this level, together with discussions of the advantages of the method, have been presented in K. N. Stevens, "Toward a Model for Speech Recognition," *J. Acoust. Soc. Am.*, 32 (January 1960), 47–51; L. A. Chistovich, "Classification of Rapidly Repeated Speech Sounds," *Sov. Phys. Acoustics*, 6 (January-March 1961), 393–98; (*Akust. Zhur.*, 6 [July 1960], 392–98); S. Inomata, "Computational Method for Speech Recognition," *Bull. Electro-Tech. Lab.* (Tokyo), 24, (June 1960), 597–611; M. V. Mathews, J. E. Miller, and E. E. David, Jr., "Pitch Synchronous Analysis of Voiced Sounds," *J. Acoust. Soc. Am.*, 33, (February 1961), 179–86; C. G. Bell, H. Fujisaki, J. M. Heinz, K. N. Stevens and A. S. House, "Reduction of Speech Spectra by Analysis-by-synthesis Techniques," *J. Acoust. Soc. Am.*, 33 (December 1961).

SUMMARY OF MODEL FOR
SPEECH RECOGNITION

The complete model for speech recognition discussed here takes the form shown in Fig 2. The input signal is first processed by a peripheral unit such as a spectrum analyzer. It then undergoes reduction in two analysis-by-synthesis loops, and the phoneme sequence appears at the right. In order to simplify the diagram, the group of components performing the functions of storage, preliminary analysis, comparison, and control have been combined in a single block labeled *strategy*.

The procedure depicted here is suitable only for the recognition of sequences of uncorrelated symbols, such as those that control the generation of nonsense syllables. If the speech material to be recognized consists of words, phrases, or continuous text, then the output of the present analysis scheme would have to be processed further to take account of the constraints imposed by the morphological and syntactic structure of the language.

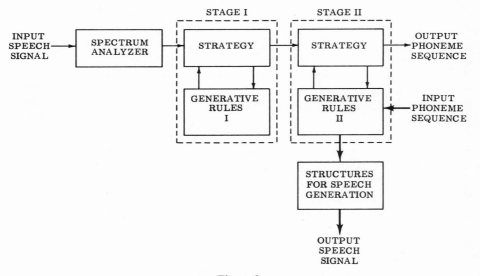

Figure 2

The final analysis stage of Fig. 2 includes, of course, the generative rules for transforming phoneme sequences into phonetic parameters. These are precisely the rules that must be invoked in the production of speech. During speech production the output from these stored rules can be connected directly to the speech mechanism, while the input to the rules is the phoneme sequence to be generated. Addition of peripheral speech-generating structures to Fig. 2 then creates a model that is capable of both speech recognition and speech production. The same calculations are made in the second set of generative rules (and in the generative rules at possible higher levels of analysis) whether speech is being received or generated. It is worthwhile observing that during the recognition process phonetic parameters are merely calculated by the "generative rules II" and direct activation of the speech structures is nowhere required.[9]

For the recognition of continuous speech it may not always be necessary to have recourse to analysis-by-synthesis procedures. A rough preliminary analysis at each of the stages in Fig. 2 may often be all that is required—ambiguities as a result of imprecise analysis at these early stages can be resolved in later stages on the basis of knowledge of the constraints at the morphological, syntactic, and semantic levels.[10]

IMPLEMENTATION OF THE MODEL: PROBLEMS FOR RESEARCH

While certain components in both major stages of analysis can be designed from present knowledge, further research is necessary before the remaining components can be realized and before the system can be designed to function as a whole.

In the first stage of analysis, one of the major problems is to devise a procedure for specifying in quantitative terms the "phonetic parameters." These must describe the behavior of structures that control the vocal-tract configuration as well as activities of the lungs and vocal cords. A great deal is known about some parameters, *e.g.*, parameters that relate to voicing, nasalization, interruptedness, and labialization. For others, such as tenseness or the so-called "point of articulation," our knowledge is still far from adequate.

A second task is to establish the generative rules describing the conversion of phonetic parameters to time-varying speech spectra. These rules involve a series of relations, namely, those between (1) the phonetic parameters and the vocal-tract geometry and excitation characteristics, (2) the transformation from vocal-tract geometry to the transfer function in terms of poles and zeros, and (3) the conversion from the pole-zero configurations and pertinent excitation characteristics to the speech spectra. The last two of these, which involve application of the theory of linear distributed systems, have been studied in some detail,[11] [12] whereas the first is less well understood.

The generative rules of the second stage are made up of several distinct parts. First, they embody the relation between what linguists have called a "narrow phonetic transcription of an utterance" and its "phonemic or morphophonemic

---

[9]This point was discussed by A. M. Liberman ("Results of Research on Speech Perception," *J. Acoust. Soc. Am.*, **29** [January 1957], 117–23), who suggested that speech is perceived with reference to articulation, but that "the reference to articulatory movements and their sensory consequences must somehow occur in the brain without getting out into the periphery."

[10]Knowledge of constraints imposed on phoneme sequences by the structure of the language has been incorporated in the design of an automatic speech recognizer described by Fry and Denes (D. B. Fry, "Theoretical Aspects of Mechanical Speech Recognition," and P. Denes, "The Design and Operation of the Mechanical Speech Recognizer at University College, London"), *J. Brit. IRE*, **19** (April 1959), 211–34.

[11]T. Chiba and M. Kajiyama, *The Vowel: Its Nature and Structure* (Tokyo, Jap.: Tokyo-Kaiseikan, 1941).

[12]H. K. Dunn, "The Calculation of Vowel Resonances, and an Electrical Vocal Tract," *J. Acoust. Soc. Am.*, **22** (November 1950), 740–53.

transcription." The nature of this relation has received a fair amount of attention in the last 30 years and a great deal of valuable information has been gathered. Of especial importance for the present problems are recent phonological studies in which this relation has been characterized by means of a set of ordered rules.[13] Secondly, the generative rules II must describe the utilization of those phonetic parameters that are not governed by the language in question, but are left to the discretion of the speaker. Thus, for instance, it is well known that in English speech, voiceless stops in word final position may or may not be aspirated. The precise way in which individual speakers utilize this freedom is, however, all but unknown. Thirdly, the generative rules II must specify the transformation from discrete to continuous signals that results from the inertia of the neural and muscular structures involved in speech production. There are wide variations in the delay with which different muscular movements can be executed, but the details of the movements are not understood. The study of these problems, which essentially are those of producing continuous speech from phonetic transcriptions, has just begun in earnest. We owe important information to the work of Haskins Laboratory on simplified rules for speech synthesis.[14] This work must now be extended to take physiological factors into consideration more directly, through the use of cineradiography,[15] electromyography, and other techniques. Contributions can also be expected from studies with dynamic analogs of the vocal tract.[16]

Finally, for both stages of analysis, the design of the strategy component is almost completely unknown territory. To get a clearer picture of the nature of the strategy component, it is useful to regard the generative rules as a set of axioms, and the outputs of the generative rules as the theorems that are consequences of these axioms. Viewed in this light the discovery of the phonemic representation of an utterance is equivalent to the discovery of the succession of axioms that was used in proving a particular theorem. The task of developing suitable strategies is related, therefore, to a general problem in mathematics—that of discovering the shortest proof of a theorem when a set of axioms is given. It should be clear, however, that the powerful tools of mathematics will be at our disposal only when we succeed in describing precisely and exhaustively the generative rules of speech. Until such time we can hope only for partially successful analyzers with strategies that can never be shown to be optimal.

[13]M. Halle, "The Sound Pattern of Russian," (Mouton and Co., The Hague, Netherlands: 1959). N. Chomsky and M. Halle, "The Sound Pattern of English," to be published.

[14]A. M. Liberman, F. Ingemann, L. Lisker, P. Delattre, and F. S. Cooper, "Minimum Rules for Synthesizing Speech," *J. Acoust. Soc. Am.*, **31** (November 1959), 1490–99.

[15]H. M. Truby, "Acoustico-cineradiographic Analysis Considerations," *Acta Radiologica,* (Stockholm), Supp. **182** (1959).

[16]G. Rosen, "Dynamic Analog Speech Synthesizer," Res. Lab. of Electronics, Mass. Inst. Tech., Cambridge, Tech. Rept. No. 353 (February 10, 1960).